Handbook of Restorative Justice

Handbook of Restorative Justice: A Global Perspective is a collection of original, cutting-edge essays that offer an insightful and critical assessment of the theory, principles, and practices of restorative justice around the globe. This much-awaited tome is a response to the cry of students, scholars, and practitioners of restorative justice for a comprehensive resource about a practice that is radically transforming the way the human community responds to loss, trauma, and harm.

Its diverse essays not only explore the various methods of responding nonviolently to harms-done by persons, groups, global corporations, and nation-states, but also examine the dimensions of restorative justice in relation to criminology, victimology, traumatology, and feminist studies. In addition they contain prescriptions for how communities might re-structure their family, school, and workplace life according to restorative values.

This handbook is an essential tool for every serious student of criminal, social, and restorative justice.

Dennis Sullivan is Adjunct Professor in the School of Criminal Justice at the University of Albany and is founder and director of the Institute for Economic and Restorative Justice.

Larry Tifft is Professor of Sociology in the Department of Sociology at Central Michigan University. His research interests are radical criminology and restorative justice.

Handbook of Restorative Justice

A Global Perspective

Edited by
Dennis Sullivan
and Larry Tifft

Routledge
Taylor & Francis Group

LONDON AND NEW YORK

First published 2006 by Routledge
2 Park Square, Milton Park, Abingdon, Oxon, OX14 4RN

Simultaneously published in the USA and Canada
by Routledge
270 Madison Avenue, New York, NY 10016

Reprinted 2007 (twice)

Routledge is an imprint of the Taylor & Francis Group, an informa business

© 2006 Dennis Sullivan and Larry Tifft for editorial matter and selection; individual chapters, the contributors

Typeset in Times by Taylor & Francis Books
Printed and bound in Great Britain by MPG Books Ltd, Bodmin

British Library Cataloguing in Publication Data
A catalogue record for this book is available from the British Library

Library of Congress Cataloging in Publication Data
Handbook of restorative justice : a global perspective / [edited by] Dennis Sullivan and Larry L. Tifft.
   p. cm.
  Includes bibliographical references and index.
  ISBN 0-415-35356-4 (hard cover)
1. Restorative justice. I. Sullivan, Dennis, 1940- II. Tifft, Larry.
  HV8688.H36 2006
  364.6'8–dc22

                                        2005022217

ISBN10: 0-415-35356-4 ISBN13: 978-0-415-35356-4

T&F informa

Taylor & Francis Group is the Academic Division of T&F Informa plc.

Contents

List of Illustrations

Tables

Figures

Acknowledgements

We would like to thank each of our colleagues who graciously agreed to write a chapter for this book. Their contributions are full of insight and inspiring. We would also like to thank our friend and colleague, Gerhardt Boomgaarden, editor extraordinaire at Taylor and Francis, who has been most supportive of this project from concept to publication.

We would also like to thank our many friends and colleagues who have encouraged us to continue our collaborative thinking and writing about justice matters and especially the perspective we bring to restorative justice. Harry Mika's and Doug Thomson's writings on community have provided a unique focus for understanding justice issues. David Gil's work and that of John Braithwaite, David Miller, Peter Kropotkin, Daniel Berrigan, and Noam Chomsky have inspired our thinking on structural issues.

There is a long list of persons whose friendship and openness to our ideas have sustained our writing over the past thirty years. We would like to offer especial thanks to: Hal Pepinsky, Richard Quinney, Harry Mika, Doug Thomson, Fred Boehrer, Walt Chura, Rich Allinson, Larry Siegel, Paul McCold, Howard Zehr, John Sullivan, Shadd Maruna, Pat Shields, Frank Faber, Peter Sanzen, Kathryn Sullivan, Richard Rudolph, Diane Schaefer, Tom Dexter, John Wozniak, Dragon Milovanovic, Stuart Henry, Mark Lanier, Dan Okada, Jim Acker, Lo Presser, Emily Gaarder, and Susan Caulfield.

For their unending patience and assistance editorially we thank as well Constance Sutherland and Jason Mitchell.

Our deepest gratitude goes out to Georgia Gray and Lyn Markham for being our partners, our day-to-day foundations for attempting to live as equals in a world where needs are largely unmet and injustice abounds.

Author biographical sketches

Mary Achilles has spent over twenty years in the field of victim services. She is serving her second six-year term as the Victim Advocate for the Commonwealth of Pennsylvania, having worked for over fourteen years as the Director for Victim Services in the Philadelphia District Attorney's Office.

James R. Acker is a Professor at the School of Criminal Justice, University at Albany, New York. He earned his JD at Duke University and his PhD in criminal justice at the University at Albany. He is co-editor, with Robert Bohm and Charles Lanier of *America's Experiment with Capital Punishment* (second edn 2003).

Bruce A. Arrigo, PhD, is Professor of Crime, Law, and Society in the Department of Criminal Justice at the University of North Carolina, Charlotte. He is a past recipient of the Critical Criminologist of the Year award and is a Fellow of the American Psychological Association.

Fred Boehrer, his wife Diana Conroy, and their three children have been living with homeless families at the Albany Catholic Worker Community at Emmaus House since 1996. Fred is a founding member of the Justice Studies Association and the Restorative Justice Council on Sexual Misconduct in Faith Communities.

Jim Bonta received his PhD in Clinical Psychology and began his career as a psychologist in a maximum security remand center. Dr Bonta's areas of interest are risk assessment and offender rehabilitation. One of his latest publications is *The Psychology of Criminal Conduct* (co-authored with D. A. Andrews, third edn 2003).

Judith Brink works for peace, justice, and a sustainable future. She lives in Albany, NY, where she facilitates Restorative Justice Conferences, produces an Indymedia radio program *Voices from the Prison Action Network*, and works with the Bill of Rights Defense Committee.

Todd R. Clear is Distinguished Professor, John Jay College of Criminal Justice, City University of New York. He has published three recent books on community justice: *Community Justice* (2003), *What is Community Justice?* (2002), and *The Community Justice Ideal* (2000). He is a founding editor of *Criminology & Public Policy*.

Robert B. Coates is currently part-time Senior Research Associate with the Center for Restorative Justice and Peacemaking. Dr Coates has also spent a dozen years serving churches as a pastor. He has authored numerous publications on deinstitutionalization, community-based services, system change, and restorative justice.

Peter Cordella is Professor and Chair in the Department of Criminal Justice at Saint Anselm College, Manchester, NH. He has edited (with Larry Siegel) *Readings in Contemporary Criminological Theory* (1996), is a former associate editor of *Contemporary Justice Review*, and has been a mediator and mediation trainer for more than twenty years.

Robert Cormier (PhD, McMaster University) began his career in 1974 with the Correctional Service of Canada at Kingston Penitentiary, and has occupied various positions in research, program development, and policy in the Department of the Solicitor General (now Public Safety and Emergency Preparedness) since moving to Ottawa in 1982.

Chris Cunneen is Professor of Criminology and Director of the Institute of Criminology, University of Sydney Law School. He has worked as a research consultant for the Australian Human Rights Commission and with various Aboriginal organizations, and has published widely on issues relating to restorative justice and human rights.

Kathleen Daly is Professor of Criminology and Criminal Justice, Griffith University (Brisbane). She received three major Australian Research Council grants to research restorative justice, race, and gender politics in Australia, New Zealand, and Canada. Her book, *Gender, Crime, and Punishment* (1994) received the Michael Hindelang award from the American Society of Criminology.

Yael Danieli is a clinical psychologist in private practice, a victimologist, traumatologist, co-founder and Director of the Group Project for Holocaust Survivors and their Children in the New York City area. She has done extensive psychotherapy, research/writing, and training with this and other massively traumatized populations.

Sinclair Dinnen is a Fellow on the State Society and Governance in Melanesia (SSGM) Project at the Australian National University. Recent works include *Law and Order in a Weak State: crime and politics in Papua New Guinea* (2001) and *A Kind of Mending: restorative justice in the Pacific Islands* (2003).

David Dyck is a restorative justice mediator, facilitator, trainer, and university instructor. He has been a consultant with Mediation Services of Winnipeg, the Nova Scotia Restorative Justice Program, and Correctional Service Canada's Circles of Support and Accountability. He holds a BA and MA in Conflict Resolution Studies. David lives in Winnipeg, Manitoba.

Robert D. Enright, PhD, is a licensed psychologist and Professor of Educational Psychology at the University of Wisconsin-Madison. He is the author of over a hundred publications, including such books as *Forgiveness is a Choice* (2001) and the children's book *Rising above the Storm Clouds* (2004).

Anna Eriksson is a graduate of Griffith University, Australia and the University of Cambridge. She is currently completing a PhD at the School of Law, Queen's University, Belfast, examining Restorative Justice in Community and State-Based Schemes in Northern Ireland. She is originally from Sweden.

David O. Friedrichs is Professor of Sociology and Criminal Justice at the University of Scranton. He is the author of *Trusted Criminals: White Collar Crime in Contemporary Society* (2004) and *Law in Our Lives* (2005) and has also authored some hundred journal articles, book chapters, and essays.

Emily Gaarder is a teacher, writer, and social justice activist. She has worked extensively with both victims of crime and young female offenders in the system. She is an Assistant Professor of Sociology/Anthropology at the University of Minnesota–Duluth.

David G. Gil earned a BA from Hebrew University, Jerusalem, a MA and DSW from the University of Pennsylvania. He joined the Brandeis faculty in 1964. He is active in the Socialist and War Resisters Movements. His widely published work includes *Violence Against Children* (1970) and *Unraveling Social Policy* (fifth edn 1992).

Michael L. Hadley, CD, PhD, FRSC, is Professor Emeritus at the University of Victoria (Canada), and Associate Fellow in the Centre for Studies in Religion and Society. He has published books and articles in three disciplines: Germanic Studies, Naval History, and Religious Studies.

M. Kay Harris is Associate Professor in the Department of Criminal Justice and Affiliated Professor of Women's Studies at Temple University. She has conducted research on community corrections for women, community corrections legislation, reducing prison crowding, and judicial intervention in corrections. She has published on feminism and justice and transformative justice.

Nathan Harris is a Research Fellow at the Regulatory Institutions Network at the Research School of Social Sciences, Australian National University. In 2001 he co-authored (with Eliza Ahmed, John Braithwaite, and Val Braithwaite) *Shame Management Through Reintegration*.

Hennessey Hayes is a Senior Lecturer in the School of Criminology and Criminal Justice, Griffith University, Brisbane, Australia. His current research focuses on the long-term behavioral impact of restorative justice conferencing in relation to re-offending and the ways young offenders understand restorative justice conferencing encounters.

Anthony C. Holter is an Educational Psychology doctoral student at the University of Wisconsin, Madison. His interest in the development and education of children led him to his current position as Project Coordinator for the Northern Ireland Forgiveness Education Initiative. He has worked with national and international peace and justice organizations.

Rebecca Jesseman has a MA in Criminology from the University of Ottawa. She began her research career in the field of illicit drugs with the Senate Committee on Illegal Drugs and Health Canada. She has been involved in the evaluation of various restorative justice initiatives with Corrections Research since 2003.

Jeffrey Kauffman is author of *Handbook on Helping Persons with Mental Retardation Mourn* (2004) and editor of *Awareness of Mortality* (1995) and *Loss of the Assumptive World* (2002). He maintains a psychotherapy practice in suburban Philadelphia, specializing in grief and trauma, and teaches at Bryn Mawr Graduate School of Social Work and Social Research.

Judith W. Kay is Associate Professor of Religious and Social Ethics at the University of Puget Sound. She received her PhD jointly from the Graduate Theological Union and University of California, Berkeley. Her book *Murdering Myths: The Real Story of the Death Penalty* appeared in the summer of 2005.

Dirk J. Louw is a Research Fellow of the Center for Applied Ethics at Stellenbosch University (South Africa) and former editor of the *South African Journal of Philosophy*. His publications include *Ubuntu and the Challenges of Multiculturalism in Post-apartheid South Africa* (2001) and *Religious Plurality and Truth* (forthcoming).

Anne-Marie McAlinden is a Lecturer in Law at Queen's University, Belfast. She has an LLB (1996) and an MSSc in Criminology and Criminal Justice from Queen's University. She has published widely on sex offender registration, the management of violent and sexual offenders, and responses to child sexual abuse.

Paul McCold received a PhD in criminal justice from the University at Albany in 1993. He was the principal investigator for the Bethlehem Experiment, the first randomized field trial of restorative conferencing in the US. He has published and lectured about restorative justice theory around the world.

Kieran McEvoy, Professor of Law and Transitional Justice at the School of Law, Queen's University, Belfast, was a Fulbright Distinguished Scholar at Harvard Law School 2001–2. He has worked with and written extensively about paramilitary groups in the jurisdiction on the monitoring of non-state actors, ex-prisoner, and community justice initiatives.

Edward J. Martin is Professor of Public Policy and Administration at California State University, Long Beach. He is the co-author of *Savage State: Welfare Capitalism and Inequality* (2004). Dr Martin received his BA from Loyola Marymount University (1980), MA University of San Francisco (1985), and PhD Arizona State University (2000).

Joseph Martin is an Educational Psychology graduate student at the University of Wisconsin-Madison. He is a project coordinator for the International Forgiveness Institute's Northern Ireland Initiative and specializes in behavioral observations. His work has included the study of temperament and emotion in young twins and cognition in infants.

Shadd Maruna is a Reader in Criminology at Queen's University, Belfast. His book *Making Good: How Ex-Convicts Reform and Rebuild Their Lives* was awarded the American Society of

Criminology's Hindelang Award in 2001. He is also the co-editor (with Russ Immarigeon) of *After Crime and Punishment* (2004).

Gabrielle Maxwell is an Associate of the Institute of Policy Studies in the School of Government at Victoria University of Wellington where she was previously Director of the Crime and Justice Research Centre. She has authored many books, chapters, and articles, most recently (with Allison Morris) *Restorative Justice for Juveniles*.

Allison Morris was Director as well as Professor of Criminology of the Institute of Criminology, Victoria University of Wellington. She was a Lecturer in Criminology at the University of Edinburgh and the Institute of Criminology, the University of Cambridge. She is a Fellow of the Royal Society of New Zealand.

Vesna Nikolic-Ristanovic is a Criminology Professor at Belgrade University, Serbia. She is also Founder and President of the Victimology Society of Serbia and Editor-in-Chief of the journal *Temida*. In addition to organizing international conferences she has published *Women, Violence and War* (2000) and *Social Change, Gender and Violence* (2002).

Christa Pelikan is a researcher at the Institute for the Sociology of Law and Criminology in Vienna. She has chaired the Committee of Experts on Mediation in Penal Matters within the European Committee on Crime Problems (CDPC) and been a member of the board of the European Forum for VOM and Restorative Justice.

Joan Pennell is Professor and Head, Department of Social Work, North Carolina State University. She is principal investigator of the North Carolina Family-Centered Meetings Project and previously directed the North Carolina Family Group Conferencing Project. She served as a principal investigator for a Newfoundland and Labrador demonstration of family group conferencing.

Hal Pepinsky teaches Criminal Justice at Indiana University, Bloomington.

Kay Pranis was the leader of an innovative restorative justice project in the Minnesota Department of Corrections for years. She has written and lectured widely on many issues of restorative justice.

Lois Presser is Assistant Professor of Sociology at the University of Tennessee. Her current research examines how offenders talk about their lives, their crimes, and their experiences of justice. In her pre-academic career, she worked with and on behalf of both offenders and victims of crime in New York City.

Tanya Rugge has a BA in Law, an MA in Psychology and is currently a Senior Research Officer focusing on restorative justice. Over the years she has interviewed numerous offenders and victims, worked clinically with female offenders, and conducted research on recidivism, high-risk offenders, young offenders and Aboriginal corrections.

Barry Stuart has worked extensively with First Nations in developing self-government laws, structures, and processes. As Chief Negotiator for the Yukon Land Claims, he negotiated the

Umbrella Land Claims Agreement that enabled eleven First Nations to conclude their Self-Government and Land Claims Agreements. For years he has been a judge and mediator.

Lorraine Stutzman-Amstutz is Director of the Mennonite Central Committee's Office on Crime and Justice. She has provided technical assistance and consulting in the victim offender field since 1984 when she began working in Elkhart, Indiana, the site of the first Victim Offender Reconciliation Program in the US.

Dennis Sullivan is a writer and teacher and a founder of the Justice Studies Association and the international journal *Contemporary Justice Review*. He lives with his wife, Georgia Gray, in Voorheesville, New York.

Larry Tifft has taught sociology at Central Michigan University for the past thirty years. His motive for writing has been to keep Peter Kropotkin's ideas and ideals alive for future generations. He lives in Mt Pleasant, Michigan, with his wife/partner, Lyn Markham, and their son, Skye.

Thomas Trenczek, Dr Juris, MA, is Professor of Law at the University of Applied Sciences in Jena, Germany. He holds a German Law degree PhD from the University in Tu«bingen. He has worked as a criminologist at the Institute for Criminology of Tu«bingen University and is an accredited mediator of the Queensland Supreme Court.

Mark Umbreit is a Professor and Founding Director of the Center for Restorative Justice and Peacemaking at the University of Minnesota in St Paul. In addition to numerous publications, Dr Umbreit has lectured and trained thousands of people throughout North America, Europe, China, Japan, and Israel/Palestine.

Charles Villa-Vicencio is Executive Director of the Institute for Justice and Reconciliation, based in Cape Town. He was formerly the National Research Director in the Truth and Reconciliation Commission, in which capacity he was responsible for the five-volume report of the Commission handed to President Mandela in October 1998.

Betty Vos, a social work practitioner for over thirty years, was an Assistant Professor of Social Work at Valparaiso University and the University of Utah before joining the Center for Restorative Justice and Peacemaking as a Senior Research Associate. Her recent research and publications have focused on restorative justice dialogue and peacemaking circles.

Lars Waldorf is Project Leader at the World Policy Institute and is completing a book on *gacaca*. He ran Human Rights Watch's field office in Rwanda from February 2002 to February 2004 and covered genocide trials at the UN's International Criminal Tribunal for Rwanda. He has taught at both Harvard and The New School.

Sandra Walklate is Professor of Sociology at Manchester Metropolitan University. She has written extensively on crime, victims, gender, and community and has worked as a volunteer with both victim support and feminist organizations. Her recent publications include *Understanding Criminology* (2003), *Gender, Crime and Criminal Justice* (2001) and *Criminology* (2005).

Robert Yazzie, JD, is a retired Chief Justice of the Navajo Nation Supreme Court, a member of the faculty of the University of New Mexico School of Law, and the Director of Legal Studies of the Crownpoint Institute of Technology in the New Mexico portion of the Navajo Nation.

James W. Zion, JD, is a practicing attorney in the Navajo Nation, a domestic abuse commissioner in the Crownpoint (Navajo Nation) Family Court, and a member of the faculties of the Department of Criminal Justice of Northern Arizona University and the National Judicial College.

Introduction: The healing dimension of restorative justice

A one-world body

Dennis Sullivan and Larry Tifft

The essence of restorative justice

When members of the Navajo Nation try to explain why people harm others, they say that a person who does harm to another 'acts as if he [sic] has no relatives' (Yazzie 1998: 126; see Kaplan and Johnson 1964: 216–17). That is, the offending person has become so disconnected from the world around him, so disengaged from the people he lives and works with each day, that his acts no longer have a personal foundation.

To remedy harm situations when they do occur, to help those affected by a harm to begin upon the path of healing, historically the Navajo have taken steps that are consistent with their views on the 'causes' of harm. They call upon the relatives of the person responsible for the harm (as well as those of the person harmed) to come forth and help their kin re-connect with the community they live in or, as happens in the case of some, become connected to that community for the very first time.

The Navajo call this process of connection and re-connection 'peacemaking'. It is a form of restorative justice an essential part of which is community members assembling to 'talk things out' so that harmony might be restored to relationships that have been set on end. It is the same kind of process that South Africans embraced with their Truth and Reconciliation Commission in 1995 in an effort to heal from the human rights violations that occurred during apartheid (Skelton and Frank 2001).

On the best of days these processes, and all other forms of restorative justice, enable those responsible for a harm-done to work through their twisted logic and excuses – what Robert Yazzie (1998), former Chief Justice of the Navaho Nation Court, used to refer to in good Navajo vernacular as 'fuzzy thinking' (125; see also Zion 1997). The hope is that those responsible for a harm will be able to acknowledge to the community and perhaps to the person(s) they harmed what they did and in some way make amends, to 'make things right.' As anyone who has begun to familiarize him- or herself with the meaning of restorative justice knows, those affected by the harm in question seek to reach an agreement whereby the needs of the person(s) harmed, the victims/survivors, are taken into account to the fullest extent possible.

The Navajo peacemaking process is a quintessential form of restorative justice because it involves the community in restoring people and groups to well-being in

1

a needs-meeting way: that is, the needs of everyone in the healing process are of paramount concern (Sullivan and Tifft 2005). Such a perspective or way of thinking derives from long-held indigenous customs in which kin, members of an immediate family, community, or nation seek to meet the needs of all involved in a harm situation. They know that, if a wrong is not righted in ways that take into account the needs of those who have been affected, the community will eat away at itself (Sather 2004).

Such an ethic is strange to so many of us in our post-modern world because it harkens back to a time when people saw their lives 'bound up together in . . . one common life. The members of one kindred looked on themselves as one living whole, a single animated mass of blood, flesh, and bones, of which no member could be touched without all the members suffering' (Smith 1907: 273–4). In other words, when one person suffers a harm, all suffer from the harm to one degree or other. And all are responsible for making things right in such situations because all are in some way responsible for that harm occurring in the first place, being a co-creator (whether actively or passively, directly or indirectly) of that 'single animated mass of blood, flesh, and bones.'

This is very powerful medicine and in part explains why restorative justice is at its core a form of insurgency and subversive in nature. That is, it is a process that competes with the state's way of doing business not only in ways to respond to harm (nonviolently, restoratively) but also in defining what harms we need to give attention to in the first place. Restorative justice sees the pain and suffering of all as worthy of our collective attention while the state discriminates between those worthy of the community's attention and those not. It is easy to see how such differing views contain the seeds of ideological and administrative dissension and why restorative justice is seen by the state as subversive, as an act of insurgency that must be put down, contained,

co-opted, or modified in some other way to meet the state's ideological and administrative requirements.

With respect to the process of 'making things right,' the greatest hope of restorative justice advocates is that those who have been traumatized by a harm will want to participate in the process by telling their story as well as by listening to the story of the person who has harmed them so as to gain a better sense of who that person is (Mika *et al.* 2003). In this way the person harmed and their kin are more likely to develop some degree of compassion and empathy for the harming person and those who care for her/him, and are more likely to set aside feelings of anger, vengeance, and loss. We know, however, that this cannot be anything other than a voluntary process for those who have been harmed (Achilles 2004: 72), for sometimes their greatest need and that of their family is to keep as much distance between themselves and those responsible for the harm. So victim needs/ wishes are paramount and must be respected at all times (Achilles 2004: 70; Amstutz 2004; Strang 2004).

While persons harmed may be receptive to participating in a victim–offender encounter and to accepting a genuine apology when offered, and occasionally come to forgive the person who harmed them, they should always receive, before deciding whether to participate in a restorative process, direct assurances from the community that they will not be re-victimized and that steps will be taken to ensure that other members of the community will be less likely to suffer as they have (McCold 2003: 96). Therefore, as members of this community, we must rally to support those harmed by providing the short- and long-term care they require even in cases when no one has been identified as the offending person (Achilles 2004: 71). Such support might come in the form of emergency medical, legal, counseling, victim compensation, and financial recovery services but it also might come in the form of challenge to the structural inequalities in our communities that prevent us from attending to the needs of those harmed in the way they expressed them (Thomson 2004).

What is distinctive about restorative justice as a response to harm, then, is that it is a process that belongs to relatives, to the community at large (Mika 2002) and that, when they become involved in the healing process, they develop greater competency not only in resolving community conflicts themselves but also in defining those acts they wish to pay especial attention to (Johnstone 2002; Bush and Folger 1994). As might be expected, the development of such competencies does not occur *sua sponte* but requires conscious and deliberate reflection on the part of people about what kind of restorative justice encounter – be it a conference or circle experience – will best meet the needs of all involved (Bush and Folger 1994: 81). By fostering such active participation, restorative justice empowers people in a world in which globalization increasingly excludes them from the definition and correction of what ails them (Garland 2001). And understandably so, for once community members commit themselves to developing competencies based in restorative principles, they are more likely to engage in effecting cultural and social change so as to prevent structural harms from occurring in the first place.

Barriers to restorative justice processes

As might be imagined, there are all sorts of ideological, political, social, and psychological barriers that can insert themselves into the restorative justice venture at any point (Zehr and Toews 2004). Indeed, one of the glaring ironies of restorative justice is that its wide array of programs are dependent upon the state for their funding, development, assessment, and continuation. As a result, many restorative programs quickly find themselves narrowed in focus and scope, soon evolving into little more than correctional alternatives such as probation and other forms of community supervision. Indeed, we see in such cases the restorative process become overwhelmingly 'offender-centered' with the 'offender's' liability becoming the event around which the justice system convenes to deliberate (Roche 2003: 143). Why, when this is the focus of justice, would anyone desire to work toward developing restorative, community competencies and toward fostering greater access to supportive 're-integrative' resources because the justice process is all about the state being harmed and state officials exacting retribution for the collective (Zehr and Mika 1998)?

But those who seek to encourage and/or regain interpersonal harmony restoratively know that it is not the state that has been physically harmed when interpersonal violence takes place, but persons; it is not the law that needs to be restored, but people's lives (Zehr 1990). We cannot call any correctional process restorative, therefore, if, in its defense of the state, it helps re-establish or reaffirms power-based, hierarchical, non-participatory, need-depriving relationships (Tifft and Sullivan 1980: 57). One of the competencies that restorative justice fosters is learning which questions to ask about the value or morality of social arrangements that manufacture and maintain structural inequities in societies, that are the root of most interpersonal crime, and that compete with restorative processes as an appropriate (healing) response to such crime (Lemonne 2003; Pavlich 2004).

When we look at the many ways that we might opt to relate to young people who grow up within non-participatory, needs-denying arrangements, restorative justice continually presents us with difficult moral choices (see Paul Goodman 1961; Sullivan 1982). For example, do we wish that young persons who harm others be deterred from

3

undertaking 'irrational,' unlawful actions and treated/rehabilitated so they might be adjusted to the exploited, development-thwarted life-positions in the social hierarchies they come from? Or perhaps we wish that these young persons be shamed and reintegrated into structurally and spiritually violent life conditions and strife-torn, dead neighborhoods and 'communities'? In other words, is it our wish that these young people become designated surrogates for the state's usurped responsibility for moral condemnation?

These are not rhetorical questions without consequence for, when we respond to them affirmatively, we insult those who have been harmed. We not only re-victimize them by not taking their suffering and needs into account but also lose an opportunity to commit ourselves to the restorative justice directive to create a more civil, participatory society (Braithwaite and Strang 2001), one with more competent individuals and communities. Lost is the opportunity that restorative justice offers as a philosophy of justice to facilitate a more inclusive society, one in which our prevailing concern is meeting everyone's needs (Sullivan and Tifft 2004, 2001, 2005; Tifft and Sullivan 2005), developing their talents and gifts, and thus greatly decreasing all forms of social harms and non-responsiveness (Pepinsky 1991). Also lost is 'the potential of restorative justice to transform entire legal systems, our family lives, our conduct in the workplace, our practice of politics' (Braithwaite 2003: 1; also see Sullivan and Tifft 2004 and the discussion in Johnstone 2004). When we set forth this larger, transformative vision of restorative justice, it is not surprising that many of its advocates come to see the restorative justice they practice (oftentimes begrudgingly) as the functional equivalent of an individual-offender-focused accountability process (see Bazemore 1996 regarding these paradigms). When we assess the needs of the young people we mentioned earlier within such a framework, restorative

justice processes become 'programs' that fail to take these young persons seriously and to provide them with an environment for positive moral growth, a vocation, a connection to their relatives (Bazemore 1996).

Restorative justice and community

The Navajo peacemaking process, though it might not meet all of the desired dimensions of the full restorative/transformative processes we alluded to, is a quintessential form of restorative justice because it involves the community in restoring persons and groups of people to well-being in a needs-meeting way. That is, the needs of everyone involved are of paramount concern (Sullivan and Tifft 2005). Such a perspective or way of thinking derives from long-held, pre-state, indigenous customs in which kin, members of an immediate family, community, or nation of people collaborate to meet the needs of all in daily life including in situations when someone was harmed. These relationships are of a continuous nature and, if not attended to, jeopardize the health and well-being of the community, even its collective survival. That is, if essential needs are not met, and if a 'wrong' is not righted in ways that take into account the needs of those who have been affected, the community loses its competencies to evolve successfully (Sather 2004; Piercy 1976; Kropotkin 1913).

In other forums and venues we have written extensively about the relationship between this needs-based perspective and personal and collective restoration (Sullivan and Tifft 2005). It is a perspective that repeatedly calls attention to our connectedness as relatives. In terms of needs it says that, when someone's essential needs are not met or when someone violates another's needs causing harm, all suffer from this harm to one degree or other (Gil 1999). And all have a responsibility to ensure that a restorative response is made, for all are additionally harmed when this situation is not addressed and things 'made right.' Again, 'made right,' especially in repetitive harm situations, requires social change, requires attention to how social life is organized, for clearly some persons' needs and freedoms have been thwarted. In such situations we recognize that we are all responsible for creating the contexts in which some persons' needs are (oftentimes with regularity) not met. And it is with this insight that we acknowledge that we are all responsible for making things right because we are all the co-creators of how we organize our collective social life and relate with one another. This perspective or re-conceptualization of restorative justice is one of immense human compassion and accountability. Making such a restorative response, a response that is simultaneously concerned with the personal empowerment and growth of each and the collective well-being of all, is powerful medicine. It explains why restorative justice is at its core subversive and a form of insurgency.

Restorative justice as insurgency

Restorative justice is a form of insurgency because it 'competes with' the state (and power-based social arrangements generally) in how it responds to interpersonal or inter-group conflicts and how it defines what harms the human community should give restorative attention to in the first place. But restorative justice is also subversive because it challenges, both conceptually and in practice, social arrangements and processes that thwart human development and prevent human needs from being met. As we mentioned earlier, it reflects a vision of social life that sees the pain and suffering of all as worthy of the community's attention while the state and power-based institutions discriminate between those worthy of attention and those not. In its transformative dimensions restorative justice exposes the nature of power-based orders (disorders) as

they manifest themselves in the home, the school, the workplace, and in societies throughout the world. And the measure restorative justice advocates use to assess the quality or value of social institutions in our globalizing world order is the extent to which they foster the full development of each and every person's human potential, meet each and every person's essential needs (Chomsky 2003). Are they organized to foster human development and meet the needs of all or of some at the expense and exclusion of others? Here we are introduced to the economics or political economy of restorative justice which many advocates of the process refuse to acknowledge as relevant to both its practices and theory (Sullivan and Tifft 1998).

But once we acknowledge the importance of understanding the political economy of restorative justice – how human relationships work and are enhanced or diminished – we find ourselves squarely situated in the realms of social and distributive justice, of visions of what kind of world we wish to live in, or must have, if we are to become a one-world (self-restoring) body. In puzzlement we have asked over and over how scholars and practitioners of restorative justice can speak of its various practices as responses to interpersonal harm without asking at the same time about the nature of the social conditions which the participants in a conference or circle come from and to which they return after the conference. Imagine for a moment holding a conference to address an instance or pattern of physical wife-battering. Would we call a restorative justice encounter successful that concluded with the persons involved returning home to resume a relationship in which one person was perceived as an object, an inferior, to be used in meeting the needs and desires of the other? That is, a relationship in which one person's life plan or existence is perceived as more important than the other's, in which the more powerful person relies on tyrannical decision-making patterns to uphold his power and his needs-meeting while the voice of his 'partner' was silenced? Clearly such an encounter would not be considered successful for these are not social conditions for relating as intimates (relatives). They not only stimulate harms such as battering but themselves constitute structural battering or violence (Tifft 1993).

Imagine as well holding a conference to address an instance of physical battery/ robbery between two strangers – a young man throwing an elderly man to the ground and taking his wallet and watch at a bus stop. Would we call a restorative justice conference successful that concluded with these persons returning to their neighborhoods that are without the resources to meet their respective needs? Of course not. Such 'killed neighborhoods,' as Nils Christie (1993) has described them, do not have the resources to help the elderly man ease his trauma or meet his need to have his trust in others revitalized, nor to help him physically recover from bodily injuries while paying his medical expenses. Such neighborhoods are without the resources to help the young man deal with his on-going trauma of being perceived as one of an economically produced 'army of superfluous workers,' with his need to belong to a real community where he is respected and acknowledged as being human: that is, viewed as worthy of attention in the first place going unrecognized. In such neighborhoods he will not be offered an opportunity to develop his human competencies and gifts, to channel his energy in ways that open him up to others, and to receive a livable wage. Yet these are the social conditions within which far too many young men and women grow up and suffer throughout their formative years and even later, the social conditions of having no 'relatives.'

Finally, imagine holding a series of truth and reconciliation hearings to acknowledge a pattern of gross human rights violations and attempting to make things right through a public airing and discussion of the impact of the harms on people's lives and the society as a whole (Walgrave 2003). Would such hearings be considered successful if they concluded with the persons involved returning home in largely segregated neighborhoods or in separate geographic regions of a nation-state to continue to relate as they had, with ethnic, tribal, or inter-nation-state hatred and gross stratification arrangements remaining intact, if only in less institutionalized and legal forms? Would such a series of processes be considered restorative if few acknowledgments were generated, if no reparations were forthcoming, or if a new nation-state administration instituted only slightly different modes of stratification and retribution? Restorative justice is a form of insurgency because it demands that we explore how the groups or nation-states involved are able to deny their responsibilities for such atrocities or, if they do acknowledge them, can go on without making things right, without reparation of a nature that supports those harmed recover their dignity and cultural autonomy (Friedrichs 2002; Friedrichs and Friedrichs 2002).

Public awareness of restorative justice

To many advocates of restorative justice it now seems strange that, despite restorative justice in its modern forms and contexts having been around for more than thirty years, only six, seven, or eight years ago very little was taught about restorative justice in colleges and universities everywhere but especially in the United States. You could have randomly polled a hundred students in any given criminology or criminal justice program in the US regarding the principles and practices of restorative justice and, on a good day, you might have found one person who had an inkling of what they were (Tifft 2000). Exceptions, of course, were likely to be found among students of religion, anthropology, and history – those who had familiarized themselves with the ways and customs of peoples in pre-modern societies – but the greatest irony (and disappointment) was to be found among those associated with criminology, criminal justice studies, and other disciplines dedicated to understanding the 'causes' of crimes and social harms and the ways societies choose to respond to 'make things right' after a harm has been done. They had all but walled themselves off from examining community-based responses to crime and harm that were of a restorative nature (Tifft 2002). Hence students in such programs would leave school without no or little understanding of the social and distributive justice arrangements within communities and societies (how benefits are structurally produced and distributed) and how responses to crime and social harms derive from such distributions and arrangements (Michalowski 1985; Kramer *et al.* 2002). Rarely did students grasp the connection between the distribution of healthcare, food, developmental and work opportunities and correctional measures such as restorative justice and victim support services: that is, the political economy of corrections (Sullivan 1980; Mika 1992). Therefore the role of law and the state in upholding certain distributions and corrective measures that limit people's opportunities to develop competencies to respond to harms restoratively remained below the curricular radar. We might conclude that the state – that is, all of us – shares responsibility for producing the killed neighborhoods we alluded to earlier and the loss of collective competencies that enable us to revive our life as relatives, as a one-world body.

Fortunately today, in 2006, we have begun to see some positive signs with regard to students being familiar with restorative justice. A growing number of criminology and criminal justice programs now offer undergraduate and graduate courses on restorative justice matters. The leading criminology and criminal justice texts contain a section, and some even a chapter, on restorative justice, so that those students who read course materials are aware of the development of the many diverse restorative justice modes and practices around the world (Siegel 2003). Indeed, as restorative justice programs and truth and reconciliation commissions continue to be implemented around the world, some scholars have asked whether restorative justice ought not to be considered a social movement (Daly and Immarigeon 1998; Hayner 2001). This is due in part to restorative justice initiatives nudging the state and communities to respond differently to interpersonal harms/crimes and, on a more ambitious level, nudging us all toward a more civil society (Braithwaite and Strang 2001), toward developing a needs-based economy of social life (Johnstone 2002; 2004; Sullivan and Tifft 2001; 2005; Braithwaite 2003).

But we must be prudent with our enthusiasm. The increased awareness of restorative justice on the part of some students in colleges and universities will certainly not be found among the citizenry of most societies. If you were to stop by your favorite pub in Chicago, London, Berlin, or Tokyo and ask patrons there about restorative justice, you would get the same kind of response you would have received from students and faculty in most colleges and universities only a few years ago. The same holds true if you were to ask people in your church, or teachers in the school your children attend, or your co-workers. Few in our communities – except perhaps in New Zealand and Australia – are aware of restorative practices, and so collectively we remain unaware of our role or position as relatives in the broadest and deepest sense of the term, family and community members helping others to connect and reconnect with each other when someone has suffered greatly at the hands of another (McCold 2004).

Again, this state of affairs should come as no surprise because nation-states and the corporate media almost universally project ideologically selected images of which specific harms the public should fear (e.g. robbery, drug dealing, and homicide – interpersonal street crimes largely committed by those in the dangerous class/caste) (Reiman 2001: Tifft and Sullivan 2001; 2005; Tifft 1994–5; 1982; Lanier and Henry 2004; Henry and Lanier 2001). They also present us with a skewed awareness of the 'right' ways to respond to these harms/crimes. Indeed, most state spokespersons and electronic and print media journalists seem incapable of or uninterested in covering existing restorative justice projects, designed to focus more on correctional responses of a deterrent, social defense, or punishment-violence nature. Thus most people in our communities and societies remain unacquainted with the existing range of restorative responses and lacking in everyday experiential familiarity for understanding and applying restorative responses to conflicts and harms in daily life – in our places of work, schools, and churches. And restorative principles are certainly not part of the tools we have available to us in our family lives. Thus at the beginning of the preface to the Second Edition of *Restorative Justice: Healing the Foundations of Our Everyday Lives* (Sullivan and Tifft 2005) we query:

What kind of mechanism or process existed, or now exists, for responding to harms or conflict in your family? Suppose you saw your younger sister, who had been teased and belittled for years by your older brother, reach her boiling point one day and haul off and smack him in the face? What if you had been terribly upset by this situation all along, but this was the last straw, and all the frustration and pain you had been feeling came to the surface? Did your family have a process which you could initiate so you could talk about your feelings and thoughts about this violence, and to which you could invite your brother and sister and the rest of the family to talk about their perspectives and feelings? And similarly, what if you saw your father mistreat your mother in a way that deeply affected you because you saw your mother close down emotionally for a fairly long period of time? Was there, is there, a forum in place wherein you might begin to tell your story of hurt feelings and ask everyone who was still smarting over this conflict, to talk about the underlying or precipitating issues so that your mother's and father's needs could be better met and their emotional and relational well-being restored?

This is strong medicine. It challenges our ignorance about handling conflicts and harms (and pain and suffering generally) through restorative measures and our failure to see that punishment, revenge, and making people pay are responses to harm that grow out of a limited subset of human emotions, those that rely on and reinforce a set of distributive principles that reflect the competitive compensatory ethic of the market and the corrective policies and practices of the state: that is, deserts-based and rights-based principles (Miller 1976: Sullivan and Tifft 2001, 2005). On a larger scale, the questions we raised in the preface to our book point to our continuing ignorance about the economy or political economy of 'person participation' in everyday life, about principles of need, participatory democracy, and human dignity. It was no surprise to some of us when US soldiers at the Abu Ghraib and Guantanamo Bay gulags treated prisoners with such ignominious disdain. Their vision of the freedom (and the retributive principles and emotions accompanying it) that the United States was exporting as liberators (occupiers) of Iraq and Afghanistan was/is a freedom of revenge, retribution, and non-reintegrative shaming. It certainly was/is not a vision of a one-world body of relatives.

With respect to restorative justice today, then, it may not be prudent to speak of it as a social movement. The signs of communal insurgency, of relatives-making, are too far and few between, notwithstanding our initial statements about the spread of such practices throughout the world. So what kind or level of insurgency or subversiveness are we talking about? What *is* the human community's current alternative to how the state conducts its justice business domestically and as export? Can a few scattered rumblings in the popular culture media in the past year or two provide a clue? That is, in the past year, several of the popular magazines that are sold at the check-out sections in supermarkets have carried articles on restorative justice, and the US television celebrity Oprah Winfrey has on several occasions dedicated full-hour programs to give voice to victims and offenders who have dealt with the loss and trauma from a harm-done in a restorative manner. What does the ordinary citizen make of such information, many having been introduced to non-retributive measures for the first time? It is hard to say but, at the very least, some community members in some societies are being introduced anew to our responsibility as relatives and to the healing competencies that are at our command if we choose to live a life of active participation, not only after a harm has been committed but also in creating the conditions that prevent such harm from occurring in the first place.

Restorative justice and the human community

Of course, one of the first questions that anyone asks when they become familiar with restorative justice is how the human community over time lost its sense of itself as healer and its indigenous competencies to help its members when disabled by pain and suffering. That is, how did this community become treasonous to its role as, or obligation to be, relatives? We can find one answer to this question in an often-read 1977 article written by the Norwegian criminologist Nils Christie for the *British Journal of Criminology* called 'Conflicts as

property.' Christie says that when we look at the history of the human community's responses to conflicts over time (and this includes crimes and other forms of social harm) we see that the state, as an agent of concentrated power, increasingly encroached upon indigenous communal processes (the commons), upon the community's competencies to behave as relatives when someone was in need, whether from a harm-done or otherwise. Of course, as Christie, and many other observers of human development have commented, the state's encroachment, domination, and control of communal competencies was not always the case, a fact that makes us interested in the origin, function, and development of the state.

While we will forego the history of the state here, we can point to how it gradually defined itself as the agent in charge of defining crime (Kennedy 1970; Kropotkin 1973): that is, of those acts worthy of corrective attention (Grotius 1926; Foucault 1977). We can also point to how the state began to define itself as the legitimate negotiator for resolving conflicts, crimes, and harms, and for responding to loss and trauma. These conflicts, crimes, and harms and the array of state-acceptable responses to them came to be treated as property, real estate that the state appropriated for itself. Little by little, the community gave up, or was forced to give up, its share in taking care of itself, and this includes how it chose to respond to harms, namely as kin, as relatives trying to connect and re-connect with each other (Kropotkin 1924; Gaster 1961). Backed by guns and muscle, the state called the shots, and since this administrative unit or entity is by nature a war machine, its response to crime has been in terms of war: deprivation of time and space, exclusion, punishment-violence, and execution (Kauzlarich *et al.* 2003). Not part of *a* or *the* community (by definition), the state has defined transgressions in terms of injury to itself, the symbolic citizen. In the face of loss

9

(crime, social injury, sickness, despair, dependency) community members have been increasingly forced to rely on the competencies of a professional class whose credentials have been certified by the state to deal with the management of communal affairs (Sullivan and Callaghan 1984). Hence, the human community in so many areas and venues has become more and more a passive observer of the 'care management' of the state and a cadre of professionals it has certified to handle such 'care' (Illich 1977; Sullivan 1980). And though there are multitudinous ways in which the human community has benefited from the actions and policies of this professional class over the years, such actions and policies are in effect acts of counter-insurgency for they compete with the indigenous processes and competencies associated with being relatives. It is not surprising that we have little choice but to submit to the professional who owns the processes of diagnosis and of health-restoring script-writing and script-filling.

The Navajo peacemaking process mentioned at the outset of this introduction serves as a good example of how the state destroyed indigenous, communal competencies. If we were to go back twenty-five years and ask members of the Navajo Nation about this indigenous practice of justice, only a few of the most elderly members of the community would have recalled it. This is because the United States Bureau of Indian Affairs imposed its Courts of Indian Offenses on the Navajo in 1892 so that the Navajo Nation became saddled with a US-style court system, a system of laws and procedures that was at odds with their culture and history. To retain some semblance of their earlier peacemaking principles, Navajo judges sought to render decisions according to Navajo customs and traditions and then dressed them up in the acceptable garments of imposed law.

In Rwanda we have seen the same mode of state invasiveness in that country's cus-tomary practices of justice. During a colonial period that began in 1897, first the Germans, and then the Belgians, introduced a formal state-centered legal system into Rwandan society (Hovsepian 2001: 9). The Belgian colonial project began to replace the traditional administrative system based on family elders with appointed administrative leaders by creating tribunals for each administrative unit. These tribunals 'slowly departed from customary law and began applying modern written legal texts imported by the colonial powers and whose logic regarding penalties differed from *gacaca*'s sole purpose of reconciliation' (Hovsepian 2001: 9). Consequently, a kind of legal pluralism evolved, with *gacaca*, on the one hand, reflecting an indigenous set of processes based largely on traditional values and standards of individual and community behavior, and state laws, on the other, reflecting the Belgian government's encroachment upon social life (Vandeginste 1999: 15; Tully 2003). In both instances of cultural repression, in the case of the Navajo and the people of Rwanda, we see communities of people wrestling for more than a century with the alienating and disempowering effects of imposed law, with conflict resolution practices alien to their cultures and histories. The indigenous values, practices, and social arrangements that embody the deep belief that 'people are relatives' were formally dismantled.

Searching for the embodiment of relativity

In the grand scheme of things, then, the restorative justice movement − if we can allow ourselves that phrase here − grew out of a desire on the part of justice activists and practitioners who were interested in helping the human community retain (or regain) its human dimensions, its relative status, specifically its needs-meeting competencies and the processes that foster both personal and collective development. Advocates of restorative justice have asserted that one way for the human community to regain its dignity was for us to hold a mirror up to ourselves so we might see, hear, and feel the effects of the harm we do to each other, understand the ways we fail to act as relatives by limiting 'the human' to the imposed realities and processes of the state and by failing to examine violence and justice at the social structural as well as personal level. We spoke about such issues of political economy earlier.

When we look at the first modern restorative justice program in Kitchener, Ontario, Canada, that began in the mid-1970s, we see that an effort was made to get two young men who had terrified people in a neighborhood and caused physical damage to their property to see, hear, and feel the effects of their actions so they might adjust their ethical compass, help those they harmed to heal, and perhaps patch up the cracks they had created in the community's infrastructure (Peachey 1989; Yantzi and Worth 1976). The Mennonites, who gave impetus to this first formal program, wanted to create new structures, new processes, new venues, new ways about speaking about problems that would help the human community progress in the relative-building business successful. Their efforts, and the efforts of so many others who followed, have been designed to help the human community regain its footing as kin, family, relatives, and so can be described, as we have, as acts of insurgency.

And there is a valid rationale for the emergence of restorative justice as a form of insurgency and it can be found in the insights of Marshall McLuhan, the mass media scholar. When McLuhan began to look at the history of the human community, he saw that a great change had taken place in its infrastructure with the invention of the telegraph, for with this invention 'Western man began a process of putting his nerves outside his body' (McLuhan 1985: 58). With respect to the development of previous technologies that the human community had invented for its well-being, McLuhan said these had been extensions of its physical organs: the wheel, for example, as an extension of the feet and the city's wall an 'outering' of the skin. But 'electronic media are, instead,' he asserted, 'extensions of the central nervous system, an inclusive and simultaneous field' (ibid.). Through television, radio, fax, telephone, cell phone, and Internet we now participate in each other's neurological lives as relatives, as one-world body relatives, but a central problem is that our existing political, economic, and social institutions, and systems of distribution (although they were modified by the electronic revolution) hearken to an earlier era, to an era of hierarchies and fiefdoms, operating as if the societal and global neural connection had never taken place. And globalization, as it is presently understood and implemented, can only be construed as an aggravated form of denial of the neurological revolution and of the steps the human community needs to take to retain (regain) – its human dimensions. It is our contention that restorative justice has emerged as one of a growing number of practices and social institutions that are designed to create a body politic, a political economy that is consistent with, a fit for, the neurological revolution that has been with us now for more than a century. But the media, for example, and state-certified education systems (though their processes are dialectically diverse) are structured to reify an earlier way of life, not the life of indigenous competencies but of dominating economic systems such as capitalism and state socialism.

When Herman and Chomsky (1988) began examining the political economic function of the media several decades ago, they observed that their (the media's) function had become one of manufacturing popular consent to social or political 'realities' of power rather than challenging these realities or by examining the extent to which they contribute to the meeting of our collective needs. Hence the role of the media has become one of pointing out the beneficence of existing political, economic, and social arrangements, lauding their cultural underpinnings, while neglecting to explore: (1) the many ways that these social arrangements and their cultural content foster and continue to produce disconnectedness, discontinuity, alienation, crass materialism, grave social inequities and injustices, and gross human rights violations; and (2) the restorative alternatives available to us globally, restorative justice for one (Judt 2005).

Media coverage on world matters rarely includes posing questions about why we are not creating a one-world body that is an appropriate fit for our global, everybody-already-connected nervous system, why we are not restoring ourselves to bodily wholeness. So when we talk about the function of the media within the current version of a globalizing world economy, we refuse to enter the debate about whether the media are 'liberal' or 'conservative.' This is an insidious diversionary tactic, one we ought not to fall for, because it fails to call attention to the media's failure to investigate the true costs of things, the genocidal cost of not taking steps to embody our already-in-place global neurological connections so as to make us one flesh, one bone, a one-world body (Sullivan 1986–7). It is not a question of the media failing to inform us about (most) genocides, gross human rights violations, mass hunger and malnutrition, and of the human community's continual destruction of natural processes and elements, but their failure (by economic design) to offer us a narrative as to why or how state officials, market moguls, and economic and political elites manage to exempt themselves from policies and practices to make us relatives to each other again: that is, to don the cloak of restorative justice and related healing alternatives.

McLuhan knew that 'The tribalizing power of the new electronic media, the way

in which they [can] return us to the unified fields of old oral cultures, to tribal cohesion and pre-individualist patterns of thought, is little understood' (McLuhan 1985: 60). He first wrote this in 1963, so since then we have begun to better understand and feel the tribal cohesion he alluded to, or at least to remind ourselves of our status as global relatives. Restorative justice has been instrumental in this because, especially through its commitment to narrative, it has called our attention to – though in many cases indirectly – the 'unified fields of old oral culture.' We see throughout the literature of restorative justice and throughout the literature of traumatology (recovery from pain, loss, and trauma), for example, great emphasis put on the life-giving potential of narrative, on telling our stories of what happened to us, of where 'we're at' presently, and of our dreams of a life of needs-met so we might live and grow and continue as healthy persons. Story-telling and narrative derive from 'pre-individualist patterns of thought' about relationship and social life, so here we see another reason why restorative justice is essentially subversive and the beginning of an insurgency movement. Its collective narrative questions our assumptions about power, social life, stability, change, and healing, assumptions that derive from, not pre-individualist, but individualistic patterns of thought. More positively it aims to design a new set of assumptions by which the human community might regain its 'tribal cohesion.' And the drive to redesign such a life milieu does not grow out of thin air nor is it based in wishful thinking. Rather, it derives from an awareness and an experience of our collective need to create a body that will fit an already existing, globally connected nervous system that will recognize or own up to our eternal consanguinity. And this includes owning up to our Cain and Abel heritage as well.

We spoke earlier of some of the barriers to our global adoption of restorative justice measures. One of these barriers derives from our refusal to acknowledge our Cain and Abel heritage, our continuing fratricide, sororicide, and genocide, directly, and by refusing to look at the global structural conditions that engender such death – all of which we are capable of modifying at any given time. Some of us refuse to take corrective action in this regard, having claimed that we live in a too complex, a too highly differentiated, and a too stratified world where we are too anonymous to one other to be able to incorporate restorative measures into our lives. Again, such assessments reflect ideological denials and camouflages, for we are already neurologically connected at a level that is far deeper than any of the current ways we have organized social life. As we cling to a logic that makes such denial statements possible, we deny the true task at hand, creating social arrangements, processes, and forums that are a managerial or administrative fit for our already existing neural connectedness: that is, engaging in restorative practices at all levels of social life.

Here, as we did earlier, we call attention to the first steps we need to take to achieve this, but in fact there is no one first step; there are many. One is to stop defining our social structural problems as personal failures and individual inadequacies rather than as matters of public policy. C. Wright Mills (1959) and Willard Waller (1936) informed us long ago that, when far too many persons experience similar personal troubles in their lives, these troubles can no longer be defined as personal in nature (though they have deeply personal consequences) but constitute a social structural problem. And this problem might be homelessness and poverty in the US, gross human rights violations in Rwanda, or displaced persons in Iraq and Afghanistan. Thus child/infant hunger has nothing to do with the personal failings of children but with how seeds are saved and food grown, harvested, and distributed in countries around the world. And the so-called 'drug problem' has more to do with the state's control of bodily enjoyment,

expansion of consciousness, and the regulation of pain reduction than it does with weakness of character.

So when it comes to responding to crime and social harms, we must recognize that expending our energies on intervention strategies and the processing of individuals is confusing the iceberg with its tip. Of course, we recognize the need to hold people accountable for their actions, but this means holding accountable as well those who have constructed the relational contexts within which 'troubled individuals' make their choices to harm others. This is why we subtitled our latest book on restorative justice 'Healing the foundations of our everyday lives' (Sullivan and Tifft 2005). We know that restorative justice conferencing and similar modes of restoration will be limited in what they can achieve if we do not work toward creating a social reality, that is, social institutions that reflect a one-world body of relatives. As relatives we will want to attend to the wounds of our brothers and sisters (restoratively) and we will want to hold accountable those responsible for causing those wounds (restoratively), but we will want as well to correct the conditions and social situations so that such pain and suffering are less likely to appear in our lives. This is, as we have said throughout, restorative justice in its most transformative dimension.

This *Handbook of Restorative Justice*

As we envisioned it from the beginning, this Handbook would be a forum, a restorative circle, in which all who come to read and all who have come to share their thoughts, beliefs, assessments, and research on restorative justice in the various chapters can explore the healing potential of restorative justice from the most personal to the most global level. This Handbook exists so we might begin to regain our status as relatives, look upon ourselves once again with pride and joy as we recognize that we are one living, whole, single, animated mass of blood, flesh, and bone. No one of us can be harmed or traumatized without all of us suffering and no one of us can prosper without all of us gaining in our common identity and well-being.

It is our hope that this Handbook will act as a catalyst for moving us to tell our stories, those of failure and those of success, to create a world in which it is easier for all of us to be good, to be kind and compassionate, to be welcoming of others. This is the kind of world in which we can enjoy each other's company and gifts, for we are a body that celebrates its every diverse and essential part – from the tiniest hair to the grandest thought.

References

Achilles, M. (2004) 'Will restorative justice live up to its promises to victims?' in H. Zehr and B. Toews (eds), *Critical Issues in Restorative Justice*, Monsey, NY: Criminal Justice Press; and Cullompton, Devon, UK: Willan Publishing.

Amstutz, L. (2004) 'What is the relationship between victim service organizations and restorative justice?' in H. Zehr and B. Toews (eds) *Critical Issues in Restorative Justice*, Monsey, NY: Criminal Justice Press; and Cullompton, Devon, UK: Willan Publishing.

Bazemore, G. (1996) 'Three paradigms for juvenile justice,' in B. Galaway and J. Hudson (eds) *Restorative Justice: international perspectives*, Monsey, NY: Criminal Justice Press; and Amsterdam: Kugler Publications.

Braithwaite, J. (2003) 'Principles of restorative justice,' in A. von Hirsch, J. Roberts, A. Bottoms, J. Roach and M. Schiff (eds) *Restorative Justice and Criminal Justice: competing or reconcilable paradigms*, Oxford: Hart.

Braithwaite, J. and Strang, H. (2001) 'Introduction: restorative justice and civil society,' in H. Strang and J. Braithwaite (eds) *Restorative Justice and Civil Society*, Cambridge: Cambridge University Press.

Bush, R. and Folger, J. (1994) *The Problem of Mediation: responding to conflict through empowerment and recognition*, San Francisco: Jossey-Bass.

Chomsky, N. (2003) *Hegemony or Survival: America's quest for global dominance*, New York: Henry Holt.

Christie, N. (1977). 'Conflicts as property,' *British Journal of Criminology*, 17: 1–14.

— (1993) *Crime Control as Industry: towards gulags western style?* New York: Routledge.

Daly, K. and Immarigeon, R. (1998) 'The past, present, and future of restorative justice: some critical reflections,' *Contemporary Justice Review*, 1(1): 21–45.

Foucault, M. (1977) *Discipline and Punish: the birth of the prison*, New York: Pantheon.

Friedrichs, D. (2002) 'State-corporate crime in a globalized world: myth or major challenge?' in G. Potter (ed.) *Controversies in White-Collar Crime*, Cincinnati, OH: Anderson.

Friedrichs, D. and Friedrichs J. (2002) 'The World Bank and crimes of globalization: a case study,' *Social Justice*, 29(1): 13–36.

Garland, D. (2001). *The Culture of Control: crime and social order in contemporary society*, Oxford: Oxford University Press.

Gaster, T. H. (1961) *Thespis: ritual, myth and drama in the ancient Near East*, New York: Anchor Books.

Gil, D. (1999) 'Understanding and overcoming social-structural violence,' *Contemporary Justice Review*, 2(1): 23–36.

Goodman, P. (1961) *Growing Up Absurd: problems of youth in the organized system*, New York: Random House.

Grotius, H. (1926) *The Jurisprudence of Holland*, trans. R. W. Lee, Oxford: Clarendon Press.

Hayner, P. (2001) *Unspeakable Truths: confronting state terror and atrocity*, New York: Routledge.

Henry, S. and Lanier, M. (eds) (2001) *What is Crime? controversies over the nature of crime and what to do about it*, Lanham, MD: Rowman and Littlefield.

Herman, E. and Chomsky, N. (1988) *Manufacturing Consent: the political economy of the mass media*, New York: Pantheon.

Hovsepian, G. (2001) 'The *gacaca* tribunals for trying genocide crimes and Rwanda's fair trial obligations under the international covenant on civil and political rights,' unpublished thesis, Institut Universitaire de Hautes Etudes Internationales, on file with *Boston College International and Comparative Law Review*.

Illich, I. (1977) *Toward a History of Needs*, New York: Pantheon.

Johnstone, G. (2002) *Restorative Justice: ideas, values, debates*, Cullompton, Devon, UK: Willan Publishing.

— (2004) 'How, and in what terms, should restorative justice be conceived?' in H. Zehr and B. Toews (eds) *Critical Issues in Restorative Justice*, Monsey, NY: Criminal Justice Press; and Cullompton, Devon, UK: Willan Publishing.

Judt, T. (2005) 'The new world order,' *The New York Review of Books*, 14 July, LII(12): 14–18.

Kaplan, B., and Johnson, D. (1964) 'The social meaning of Navajo psychopathology,' in A. Kiev (ed.) *Magic, Faith, and Healing: studies in primitive psychiatry today*, Glencoe: The Free Press.

Kauzlarich, D., Mullins, C., and Matthews, R. (2003) 'A complicity continuum of state crime,' *Contemporary Justice Review*, 6(3): 241–54.

Kennedy, M. (1970) 'Beyond incrimination: some neglected facets of the theory of punishment,' *Catalyst*, 5: 1–37.

Kramer, R., Michalowski, R. and Kauzlarich, D. (2002) 'The origins and development of the concept and theory of state-corporate crime,' *Crime & Delinquency*, 48(2): 263–82.

Kropotkin, P. (1913) *The Conquest of Bread*, New York: Benjamin Blom.

— (1924) *Ethics: origin and development*, New York: Mother Earth.

— (1973) *The State: its historic role*, originally published 1896, London: Freedom Press.

Lanier, M. and Henry, S. (2004) *Essential Criminology*, second edn, Boulder, CO: Westview Press.

Lemonne, A. (2003) 'Alternative conflict resolution and restorative justice: a discussion,' in L. Walgrave (ed.) *Repositioning Restorative Justice*, Cullompton, Devon, UK: Willan Publishing.

McCold, P. (2003) 'A survey of assessment research on mediation and conferencing,' in L. Walgrave (ed.) *Repositioning Restorative Justice*, Cullompton, Devon, UK: Willan Publishing.

— (2004) 'What is the role of community in restorative justice theory and practice?' in H. Zehr and B. Toews (eds) *Critical Issues in Restorative Justice*, Monsey, NY: Criminal Justice Press; and Cullompton, Devon, UK: Willan Publishing.

McLuhan, M. (1985). 'The agenbite of outwit,' *Tyuonyi*, 1: 58–61.

Michalowski, R. (1985) *Order, Law, and Crime: an introduction to criminology*, New York: Random House.

Mika, H. (1992) 'Mediation interventions and restorative justice: responding to the astructural bias,' in H. Messmer and H.-U. Otto. (eds) *Restorative Justice on Trial: pitfalls and potentials of victim–offender mediation: international research perspectives*, Dordrecht, Netherlands: Kluwer.

— (2002) 'Evaluation as peacebuilding? Transformative values, processes, and outcomes,' *Contemporary Justice Review*, 5(4): 339–50.

Mika, H., Achilles, M., Halbert, E., Amstutz, L. and Zehr, H. (2003) *Taking Victims and their Advocates Seriously: a listening project*, Akron, PA: Mennonite Central Committee.

Miller, D. (1976) *Social Justice*, Oxford: Oxford University Press.

Mills, C. W. (1959) *The Sociological Imagination*, Oxford: Oxford University Press.

Pavlich, G. (2004) 'What are the dangers as well as the promises of community involvement?' in H. Zehr and B. Toews (eds) *Critical Issues in Restorative Justice*, Monsey, NY: Criminal Justice Press; and Cullompton, Devon, UK: Willan Publishing.

Peachey, D. (1989) 'The Kitchener experiment,' in M. Wright and B. Galaway (eds) *Mediation and Criminal Justice*, London: Sage.

Pepinsky, H. (1991) *The Geometry of Violence and Democracy*, Bloomington, IN: Indiana University Press.

Piercy, M. (1976) *Woman on the Edge of Time*, New York: Fawcett Crest.

Reiman, J. (2001) *The Rich Get Richer and the Poor Get Prison: ideology, class, and criminal justice*, sixth edn, Boston: Allyn and Bacon.

Roche, D. (2003) *Accountability in Restorative Justice*, Oxford: Oxford University Press.

Sather, C. (2004) 'Keeping the peace in an island world: the Sama Dilaut of Southeast Asia,' in G. Kemp and D. Fry (eds) *Keeping the Peace: conflict resolution and peaceful societies around the world*, New York: Routledge.

Siegel, L. (2003) *Criminology*, eighth edn, Belmont, CA: Wadsworth/Thomson.

Skelton, A. and Frank, C. (2001) 'Conferencing in South Africa: returning to our future,' in A. Morris and G. Maxwell (eds) *Restorative Justice for Juveniles: conferencing, mediation and circles*, Oxford: Hart Publishing.

Smith, W. (1907) *Lectures on the Religion of the Semites*, London: Adam and Charles Black.

Strang, H. (2004) 'Is restorative justice imposing its agenda on victims?' in H. Zehr and B. Toews (eds) *Critical Issues in Restorative Justice*, Monsey, NY: Criminal Justice Press; and Cullompton, Devon, UK: Willan Publishing.

Sullivan, D. (1980) *The Mask of Love: corrections in America; toward a mutual aid alternative*, Port Washington, NY: Kennikat Press.

— (1982) 'Mutual aid: the social basis of justice and moral community,' *Humanity and Society*, 6: 294–302.

— (1986–7) 'The true cost of things, the loss of the commons and radical change,' *Social*

15

Anarchism: A Journal of Practice and Theory, 6(2): 20–6.

Sullivan, D. and Callaghan, K. (1984) 'The crime of certification: casting out what's no longer profitable to the corporate/state professional complex,' *The Community as Disciple Journal*, 1: 67–71.

Sullivan, D. and Tifft, L. (1998) 'A social structural alternative to the punishment response: toward a regrounding of the imagination in a needs-based economy,' paper presented at the annual meeting of the Academy of Criminal Justice Sciences, Albuquerque, NM.

— (2001) *Restorative Justice: healing the foundations of our everyday lives*, first edn, Monsey, NY: Willow Tree Press.

— (2004) 'What are the implications of restorative justice for society and our lives?,' in H. Zehr and B. Toews (eds) *Critical Issues in Restorative Justice*, Monsey, NY: Criminal Justice Press.

— (2005) *Restorative Justice: healing the foundations of our everyday lives*, second edn, Monsey, NY: Willow Tree Press.

Thomson, D. (2004) 'Can we heal ourselves? Transforming conflict in the restorative justice movement,' *Contemporary Justice Review*, 7(1): 107–16.

Tifft, L. (1982) 'Capital punishment research, policy, and ethics: defining murder and placing murders,' *Crime and Social Justice*, 17: 61–8.

— (1993) *Battering of Women: the failure of intervention and the case for prevention*, Boulder, CO: Westview Press.

— (1994–5) 'A social harms definition of crime,' *Critical Criminologist*, 6(3–4): 9–13.

— (2000) 'Social justice and criminologies: a commentary,' *Contemporary Justice Review*, 3(1): 45–54.

— (2002) 'Crime and peace: a walk with Richard Quinney,' *Crime & Delinquency* 48(2): 243–62.

Tifft, L. and Sullivan, D. (1980) *The Struggle to be Human: crime, criminology, and anarchism*, Over-the-Water, Sanday, Orkney, Scotland: Cienfuegos Press.

— (2001) 'A needs-based, social harms approach to defining crime,' in S. Henry and M. Lanier (eds) *What is Crime? Controversies over the nature of crime and what we should do about it*, New York: Rowman and Littlefield.

— (2005) 'Needs-based, anarchist criminology,' in S. Henry and M. Lanier (eds) *The Essential Criminology Reader*, Boulder, CO: Westview Press.

Tully, D. L. (2003) 'Note. Human rights compliance and the *gacaca* jurisdictions in Rwanda,' *Boston College International and Comparative Law Review*, 26: 385–414.

Vandeginste, S. (1999) 'Justice, reconciliation and reparation after genocide and crimes against humanity: the proposed establishment of popular *gacaca* tribunals in Rwanda,' paper presented at the All Africa Conference on African Principles of Conflict Resolution and Reconciliation, Addis Ababa, 8–12 November.

Walgrave, L. (ed.) (2003) *Repositioning Restorative Justice*, Cullompton, Devon, UK: Willan Publishing.

Waller, W. (1936) 'Social problems and the mores,' *American Sociological Review*, 1: 924–30.

Yantzi, M., and Worth, D. (1976) 'The developmental steps of the victim/offender reconciliation project,' unpublished paper, Kitchener, Ontario, on file with authors.

Yazzie, R, (1998) 'Navajo peacemaking: implications for adjudication-based systems of justice,' *Contemporary Justice Review*, 1(1): 123–31.

Zehr, H. (1990) *Changing Lenses*, Scottsdale, PA: Herald Press.

Zehr, H. and Mika, H. (1998) 'Fundamental concepts of restorative justice,' *Contemporary Justice Review*, 1(1): 47–56.

Zehr, H. and Toews, B. (2004) *Critical Issues in Restorative Justice*, Monsey, NY: Criminal Justice Press.

Zion, J. W. (1997) 'The dynamics of Navajo peacemaking,' paper presented at the 39th annual conference of the Western Social Science Association, Albuquerque, NM.

Section I

Restorative justice processes and practices

There is a rich diversity of understandings about the nature of restorative justice (Johnstone 2004; Sullivan and Tifft 2005). The parameters of this diversity range from providing a more humane, participatory, inclusive, need-meeting, and effective response to state-defined crime to proposing a new way of thinking, not merely about the nature of 'crime' (harm) and how to respond to its aftermath, but how to organize social life more justly. That is, how to organize social life to better meet our individual and collective needs and therefore to decrease the prevalence of harm in our communities and societies.

Corresponding to this diversity of understandings, there is controversy concerning what constitutes a restorative justice response to harm. That is, what are the essential components of a response that would lead one to conclude that it constituted a restorative one? Addressing this question, Paul McCold points out that the United Nations has adopted a working definition providing a minimum requirement for such programs. A restorative justice response creates a process within which all those affected by a harm come together to collaboratively decide how to respond to its aftermath and its implications for the future.

Following this working definition, McCold believes that only three models of 'restorative justice' practice – mediation, conferencing, and circles – meet these criteria. In Chapter 1 he reviews the evolution of these three process models over the past thirty years and places their development in a global chronological context, leaving the history of aggregative restorative processes (e.g. truth and reconciliation commissions) (Section V) and the cultural and spiritual foundations for the development of these models (Section II).

Following McCold's lead, we have organized the chapters in Section I to present detailed descriptions and analyses of these primary models. But, before discussing these models and the contributions of those who have written these chapters, we feel that it is necessary to more fully and explicitly describe the essential precepts that restorative justice response programs are built upon (Zehr and Mika 1998). The first precept is that when a harm or crime occurs, we should most centrally respond to the needs of the primary 'victims,' as they have been the persons most directly harmed. And yet, the family members of both those harmed and those who have harmed them, and members of the larger community, have been traumatized as well. A consequent second precept is that restorative processes should maximize the input and participation of these sets of persons in our search for healing, restoration, understanding, empathy, accountability, and prevention. A third precept is that the restorative justice process belongs to the community and that members of the communities affected should be involved in these justice processes and these processes should move beyond the individuals involved making a contribution to building and strengthening these communities. Restorative processes should not stop at addressing the present needs of all involved in this harm and its aftermath. They should act to address the social conditions that lead to harm and suffering, and as well, to safety and peace in these communities. A fourth precept is that the community, through this restorative process, has a responsibility to support victims' needs for information, validation, vindication, restitution, safety and empowerment – offering victims an opportunity to meet face to face with those who have harmed them and to collaborate in a dialogue with them to decide what actions should be taken to meet everyone's needs. Correspondingly, the community has a responsibility to provide an opportunity for those who have harmed others to tell their stories, to listen to the stories, the pain, and the life effects that this harm has led those they have harmed to suffer, and to participate in constructing a creative response to all the different issues raised in these processes. Furthermore, not only do those who have offended need to be treated respectfully and supported as persons, they need to be offered an opportunity to acknowledge their actions, to take responsibility for making things right, and to meet the challenge of undertaking personal change.

From these restorative justice precepts we can more clearly assess the degree to which ever-changing, differing modes of restorative justice processes are working toward embodying a full and extensive set of restorative justice components. The order of presentation of chapters in this section thus moves from an exploration of those models that are least extensively restorative to those that most fully embody our extensive definition of restorative justice principles. Hence, the order of chapters in this section moves from the consideration of various modes of mediation to modes of conferencing, and concludes with an assessment of circles.

Mark Umbreit, Robert Coates, and Betty Voss (Chapter 2) review the changes that have over time altered the scope of victim offender mediation processes in the United States. These processes have in name evolved from Victim Offender Reconciliation to Victim Offender Mediation to Victim Offender Conferencing, reflecting a shift from an emphasis on mediated settlements to dialogic conferring about the harm or conflict and how a resolution might be created and carried out by those involved, rather than by professionals or officials. The name changes also reflect the broadened scope of participation in the mediation process to include support persons (communities of care) and persons from the communities affected. Further, these name changes reflect use of mediation for a greater diversity of types of harms or crimes. Such changes appear to provide richer opportunities for those who have harmed others to see the ripple effects of their actions and for members of the communities affected to become more actively involved in helping 'offenders' to alter their behaviors and lives. They, as well, allow those who have been harmed and their supporters a greater opportunity to share their stories and suffering and place their experiences in a more understandable context.

Christian Pelikan and Thomas Trenczek (Chapter 3) extend this discussion on the evolution and implementation of mediation to Europe, where Victim Offender Mediation has become the most important model or practice of restorative justice. Here, the mediation model is spreading rapidly though unevenly, is marked by competing visions and a wide variety of practices, and is being implemented at different stages within the criminal justice system process, though most often as a diversionary process. And while mediation has met with considerable political resistance, it has been enshrined in legislation in many nations though its implementation is in its initial developmental stages.

Pelikan and Trenczek present the history of the development of Victim Offender Mediation processes among Europe's different nations and discuss how its development has been affected by two most recent Pan-European documents. Exemplary sketches of national developments are given for Albania, Austria, the Czech Republic, France, Germany, Finland, Italy, the Netherlands, Norway, Poland, Slovenia, and England and Wales. One of the most interesting comparisons given is between the community volunteer mediation scheme developed in Norway and the professional mediator scheme developed in Austria. Mediation in Norway is part of a program of community-based conflict resolution, where community action and self-help is vibrant. Here, volunteer work is seen as an expression of reliance on community and its potential. When harms occur and the conflict is referred to mediation services, people seem to be excited not to be confronted by professionals taking over; they are pleased to work with volunteers. In contrast, in Austria, where there is little sense of community or community trust, there is concomitantly a strong reliance on highly trained professional mediators who mediate far more serious harms than those coming to the community mediation services in Norway.

In Chapter 4 Gabrielle Maxwell, Allison Morris, and Hennessey Hayes describe restorative justice conferencing for juveniles with a particular focus on New Zealand and Australia. They also assess the extent to which conferencing reflects restorative justice values and results in restorative outcomes citing research chiefly drawn from Australasia and North America. Family Group Conferences were introduced in the New Zealand youth justice system in 1989 and since have been legislated for juvenile offenders in New Zealand, Australia, England and Wales, Canada, Ireland, and Singapore. Furthermore, differing versions of conferencing for young offenders have been introduced in nations as diverse as Belgium, Japan, the Netherlands, South Africa, Sweden, and the United States. Whatever the version, conferences are organized to engage all participants in collaboratively creating, a response to the harm caused by an offence and attempting to begin a process of healing or restoration in the relationships that have been harmed.

The reviewed research suggests that those who have been harmed who attend conferences often gain a better understanding of the reasons why they were harmed, often receive some kind of repair for the harm done (apology, reparation), are generally very satisfied with the negotiated agreements, and feel more safe. It also suggests that the quality of the conferencing experiences also has a positive impact on youthful 'offenders.' If years later the conference was viewed as a memorable experience, if it was seen as fair and not stigmatizing, if 'offenders' felt that they had had a say in, accepted, and complied with the agreements, and if they felt that they had had a chance to apologize to the person(s) they had harmed, the conference experience appears to make an important contribution to preventing further offending.

Importantly, however, participating in a conference is only *one* of the many life experiences that are involved in desistence from harm and crime or alternately in continuing one's involvement. No matter the quality of a conference and its psychological impact, a brief conference holds relatively little potential to alter or change the social conditions or circumstances of one's life. So, unless the conference agreement reaches out into the community and changes an 'offender's' access to resources or opportunities that have not been available to him/her and others in his/her community circumstances, even the best of all possible conferences is not likely to have a dramatic impact on the prevalence of harm and crime in a community. And, unfortunately, few conference programs make such life context extensions out into the community. They are, rather, more commonly individual interventions seeking to reduce the incidence of re-offending or recidivism.

In Chapter 5 James Bonta, Rebecca Jesseman, Tanya Rugge, and Robert Cormier provide us with an assessment of restorative justice processing and its impact on recidivism in comparison to the effects of deterrence and rehabilitation on recidivism. Their review of the effects of deterrent sanctions indicate that such sanctions have little impact on recidivism. And their review of the effects of treatment programs indicates that when treatment programs adhere to the principles of risk, need, and responsivity, they can have a significant impact on recidivism, especially if these appropriate treatments are administered in the community. Finally, their meta-analysis of the impact of restorative justice programs on recidivism indicates that such programs have a modest impact. However, there is a clear indication that the more recent programs that are more extensively restorative – those that attempt to involve victims and community members in a collaborative manner – produce larger effect size estimates of recidivism reduction.

This takes us to the reflections of Barry Stuart and Kay Pranis on peacemaking circles (Chapter 6). Peacemaking circles have greatly evolved from their initial 1982 construction as sentencing circles in Yukon. They draw heavily from the culturally steeped processes of First Nation circles and from the contemporary concepts of dialogue and consensus building, and are no longer centrally focused upon collaborative sentence construction. Peacemaking circles are flexible, continuing processes that may take on many differing circle forms such as healing, talking, and problem-solving in the process of making peace. As circles dig more deeply into the underlying 'causes' of conflict, the circle's flexibility enables new issues to be addressed, issues that often are far larger than the issues involved in an individual harm.

Peacemaking circles share many component features with other restorative modes, such as providing for the active participation of those most affected by a crime in resolving the incident, focusing on healing and repair, and respecting the dignity and worth of all persons. They also have unique features such as encouraging the full expression of emotions and deep listening so that deep truth-telling occurs. Circles feature thoughtful reflection and an unrushed pace; the use of keepers rather than facilitators; individual and collective responsibility for harm; and a concern for prevention as well as intervention. Peacemaking circles are most concerned with the development of understanding, respect and empowerment, and forging new relationships among the many participants.

To illustrate the heart and soul of the circle model, consider the following illustration. In a circle that was initiated to address domestic violence, the 'offender' refused to fully participate in the circle and failed to honor his commitment to the consensus-based sentence reached. However, the circle dialogue produced a remarkable change in community awareness of spousal abuse, a vast improvement in services for victims, and the forging of the partnerships needed to begin what became a very successful treatment program for spouses who abuse their partners. Circles connect criminal justice and social justice issues. To paraphrase these contributors: to focus solely on individual responsibility carries the risk of ignoring our social responsibility for the conditions that contribute to crime and harm. The vision of restorative justice that they see embodied in peacemaking circles is a social justice vision requiring both individual and community responsibility and requiring attention to the harms that 'caused' a crime, as well as those resulting from a crime.

Section I concludes with Kathleen Daly's cautionary reflections on the limits of restorative justice, those concerning its scope and practices (Chapter 7). Some limits, of course, can be seen as strengths. The diversity of conceptualizations of 'justice' and 'restorative' may lead to a hearty dialogue and the creation of diverse processes and programs – an expansion of the scope of restorative justice. It can lead, for example, to a consideration of the harmful or criminal community or societal conditions addressed by circles as discussed above, though this is not usual. The fact that most programs address the 'what should we do?' phase, rather than the fact-finding phase, of the criminal justice process opens this phase up, not only to collaborative participation in our response creating, but as well to serious consideration to the needs of those who have been harmed, a consideration that is generally absent in non-restorative modes of criminal justice. Daly points out that for those who have been harmed, fairness is easier to receive in conferences than is a sincere apology and recovery, and many 'victims' have needs that cannot be met through the limited scope of a brief conference experience. Finally, among other important insights, Daly points out that restorative justice programs are constrained by the abilities (e.g. empathy) and interests of 'offenders' and 'victims' (and, we might add, of program inventors and organizers) to think and act in restorative ways.

References

Johnstone, G. (2004) 'How, and in what terms, should restorative justice be conceived?' in H. Zehr and B. Toews (eds) *Critical Issues in Restorative Justice*, Monsey, NY: Criminal Justice Press; Collompton, Devon, UK: Willan Publishing.

Sullivan, D. and Tifft, L. (2005) *Restorative Justice: healing the foundations of our everyday lives*, second edn, Monsey, NY: Willow Tree Press.

Zehr, H. and Mika, H. (1998) 'Fundamental concepts of restorative justice,' *Contemporary Justice Review*, 1(1): 47–56.

The recent history of restorative justice
Mediation, circles, and conferencing

Paul McCold

This history addresses the rise of restorative justice practices in the US and Canada since the early 1970s. Too much has occurred to even briefly describe in a single chapter all the events leading to where we are.[1] To manage the task, this chapter employs two strategies. First, I use a circumscribed definition of restorative justice to focus on specific practices. Second, I provide an extended time-line of events to augment brief descriptions in the text.

Tony Marshall (1996) of the Restorative Justice Consortium (UK) proposed a working definition of restorative justice now adopted by the United Nations (McCold 1998; United Nations 2002; Van Ness 2003). He says that, 'Restorative justice is a process whereby all the parties with a stake in a particular offence come together to resolve collectively how to deal with the aftermath of the offence and its implications for the future' (Marshall 1996: 37). Marshall's 'process' definition provides a necessary but not sufficient theoretical definition of restorative justice (McCold 2000). But as a working definition, it provides a clear minimum requirement for restorative programs: (1) victims and their offenders in face-to-face meetings, where (2) they determine the outcome.

Only three models of restorative justice practice meet the Marshall criteria – mediation, circles, and conferencing. This paper reviews the evolution of these primary restorative justice practices since 1970 and then places developments in their chronological context. I leave to others to uncover the ancient seeds of restorative justice practices (Ross 1996; Van Ness and Heetderks-Strong 1997; Meyer 1998; Weitekamp 1999; Braithwaite 2002; also see Daly 1998, 2000, 2002; Delgado 2000; Sylvester 2003; Richards 2004).

Limiting the history of restorative justice to 'primary' practices (McCold 2003) omits various lesser restorative practices such as arbitration, financial restitution, victim compensation, community justice panels, victim impact panels, and community service sanctions (McCold 2000: 401). It also omits the unique history of aggregate restorative processes such as the South African Truth and Reconciliation Commission (Boraine 2000; Leebaw 2001) and other truth commissions (United States Institute for Peace (USIP) 2004; Hayner 1994). These histories are beyond the scope of this chapter.

Even with this restricted scope, space does not permit an exhaustive description of the significant historical events in the evolution of mediation, circles and conferencing. This chapter will document the initial and general pattern of developments in the field and provide literature references for fuller details. The sketchy historical accounts provided here are augmented by the more detailed chronology (below).

In the evolution of restorative justice, practice has preceded theory.[2] Mediation, circles, and conferencing were used to respond to criminal cases before there was an understanding that these practices were restorative justice. Each practice developed independently and each eventually influenced the others.

Mediation

In the beginning, mediation was restorative justice, and restorative justice was mediation. In mediation, a neutral third party (usually a trained community volunteer or social work specialist) facilitates a dialogue between victim and offender who (1) talk about how the crime affected them; (2) share information; (3) develop a mutually satisfactory written restitution agreement; and (4) develop a follow-up plan.

Perhaps the earliest systematic use of mediation as a restorative response to criminal behavior was in 1971. The Minnesota Restitution Center mediated restitution in direct meetings between offenders and their victims in a diversion program for adult male property offenders sentenced to prison (Fogel *et al.* 1972; Hudson and Galaway 1974). Also in 1971, the Night Prosecutor Program in Columbus, Ohio, used mediation backed up by arbitration to divert cases from the criminal justice system (Wright 1996: 67).

Except for these early independent examples, the practice of restorative mediation evolved into three general models: legal-based community mediation, faith-based victim offender reconciliation

(VORP), and social work-based victim offender mediation (VOM). Community mediation in the United States was the first generation mediation movement in the early 1970s. The VORP movement began a second wave of explicitly restorative mediation practices in the early 1980s, which morphed into the VOM movement of the 1990s.

Community mediation

The Institute for Mediation and Conflict Resolution, Inc. (IMCR) began in 1969 with a Ford Foundation grant to mediate interpersonal disputes and community conflicts, train others in negotiation skills and mediation, and design and develop dispute settlement systems. In 1970, the IMCR established mediator training and mediated disputes involving landlords and tenants, merchants and consumers, universities and students in New York City.

From 1972 to 1975, IMCR offered services to communities of color in conflict with established institutions or groups over issues with undertones of racism. In 1975, IMCR established the first Community Dispute Resolution Center in New York City to address interpersonal disputes outside of court. In 1977, IMCR opened the Brooklyn Dispute Center under contract with the Victim/Witness Assistance Project, a Vera program.

The IMCR established the standard for mediation practice in 1970, well before theoretical work on restorative justice (McGillis 1997). They began with fifty-three community volunteer mediators and received 1,657 referrals during their first ten months. By 1983, nearly 33,000 cases were referred and screened annually (Wright 1996; McGillis 1997). In 1994, many staff were laid off after IMCR lost the bid for services in Manhattan. Remaining staff relocated in South Bronx where they continue to mediate (Institute for Mediation and Conflict Resolution 2004).

Community mediation was encouraged by early theorizing about criminal restitution that directly foreshadowed restorative justice. In 1977, Randy Barnett of Harvard Law School proposed a paradigm of justice based on 'pure' restitution without punitive intent. 'Our goal is not the suppression of crime; it is doing justice to victims' (Barnett 1977: 296). Barnett recognized this would shift perspective in favor of the victim. The offense would be primarily against the individual victim, not the state, and the distinction between tort and crime would collapse (Wright 1996: 60).

In 1978, the US Department of Justice funded three experimental neighborhood justice centers. Eighty-eight per cent of complainants and respondents reported satisfaction with their overall experience (Cook *et al.* 1980). All four programs still operate. The Justice Center of Atlanta (http://www.justicecenter.org/) handled some 40,000 community, civil and criminal referrals by 1997, reporting a 70 per cent settlement rate. Dispute Resolution Services in Los Angeles (http://www.lacba.org/) handles civil, community cases and including peer mediation programs, now with an annual budget exceeding a million dollars. The Dispute Resolution Program in Kansas City, Missouri (http://www.kcmo.org/), handled some 15,000 community, civil, and criminal cases by 1997 (McGillis 1997).

The American Bar Association, American Arbitration Association, Institute for Mediation and Conflict Resolution, the Department of Justice Community Relations Service, and the National Institute of Justice provided national leadership in developing community mediation centers across the United States beginning in 1981 with funding from Law Enforcement Assistance Administration. As a result, community mediation programs and neighborhood dispute resolution centers began to proliferate. Mediation was so successful at diverting court cases in New York City that the state funded a network of community-based dispute resolution centers that now provide mediation services for all sixty-two counties (McGillis 1997; New York State Unified Court System 2003). The NYS Unified Court System's program of Community Dispute Resolution Centers (CDRCs) now operates the world's largest unified mediation program (McCold 2003).

In fiscal year 2002–2003, the CDRCs determined that 51,899 cases involving 118,690 individuals were appropriate for dispute resolution. Of those cases, the centers conducted 28,548 conciliations, mediations and arbitrations that served 66,070 people. Parties entered into voluntary agreements in 85 per cent of the cases that were mediated.

(New York State Unified Court System 2003: 1)

Other states would follow New York's example (see chronology). By 1982, a US survey reported 200 mediation services across the country, all accepting criminal cases primarily where there was a relationship between victim and the offender (Ray 1982, 1983). By 1985, that number had doubled, and it has remained fairly stable since. In 1990, just over 400 dispute resolution services in the US responded to an American Bar Association questionnaire (American Bar Association 1990). Currently, there are community mediation centers operating in every state and territory in the US (National Association for Community Mediation 2004).

In 1981 the community mediation model was also exported from the United States to several countries. Australia established three experimental community justice centers in New South Wales (Anderson 1982). The United Kingdom opened their first community mediation service, the Newham Conflict and Change Project (Wright 1996: 83), although they had experimented with mediation for juvenile court cases as part of a reparation scheme in Devon two years earlier (Marshall 1992: 16; also see Marshall

1999). Norway established their justice mediation program through the Child Welfare Conflict Councils, receiving 90 per cent of their referrals from police (Falck 1992).

International proliferation of community mediation continued in the early 1980s, especially in Europe. In 1982, Germany experimented with mediation to make criminal restitution more effective in Braunschweig (Kerner *et al.* 1992). In 1983, Finland established their youth justice mediation in Vantaa through the social welfare system using local volunteers as mediators (Iivari 1992: 137). In 1984, Germany experimented with mediation for both juveniles and adults (Kerner *et al.* 1992) and Austria used mediation to divert juvenile cases from court (Pelikan 2000). In 1985, Scotland began a reparation and mediation project in Edinburgh with juvenile cases using trained volunteer mediators (Warner 1992) and France began a paralegal community mediation project for juveniles in Valence and in Lyon the following year (Bonafé-Schmitt 1992: 182). Since 1985, most countries in western Europe have programs offering mediation for criminal cases and so, since the mid-1990s, do countries in eastern Europe (Miers 2001; Aertsen *et al.* 2004; Miers and Willemsens 2004).

Since its beginning, community mediation was largely professionalized – only half of the mediators and arbitrators are volunteers and lay people (American Bar Association 1990). With professionalization came a concern for quality control and qualifications for mediators (Bonafé-Schmitt 1992; Filner *et al.* 1995). Some bar associations sought to reserve certain classes of cases solely for lawyer mediators (McGillis 1997).

Community mediation programs have also specialized their services, offering family mediation, divorce mediation, custody mediation, landlord/tenant mediation, consumer mediation, court-annexed arbitration, labor mediation, victim offender mediation, school-based dispute resolution, inter-group dispute resolution, public policy dispute resolution mechanisms, peer mediation and other specialized efforts (American Bar Association 1990). Many programs also help institutions develop in-house dispute resolution mechanisms and provided training in conflict resolution skills and strategies for developing mediation programs (McGillis 1997: 14).

> The outcome of such mediation is quite unpredictable. Most times it is quite prosaic. Occasionally the right conditions occur at the right time between the right people for something quite considerable to occur. There have been sea-changes in attitudes on either side; some victims have been inspired to become volunteer mediators themselves, and long term friendships have been formed.
>
> (Marshall 1991: 9)

Mediation can transform victim offender relationships in a manner not predicted by alternative dispute resolution. This potential for transformation continues to attract volunteer mediators (McGillis 1997). This non-secular characteristic of the victim offender encounter attracted a faith-based effort in the latter 1970s to develop an alternative paradigm of justice.

Victim offender reconciliation programs (VORP)

The victim offender reconciliation movement began in Kitchener, Ontario, in 1974. In the 'Kitchener experiment' (Peachey 1989), two teenagers met directly with their victims following a vandalism spree in Elmira, Ontario, and agreed to restitution. The resulting restitution agreements became the impetus for the Kitchener Victim Offender Reconciliation Program (VORP). The Community Justice Initiatives Association began the first VORP in 1975 with support from the Mennonite Central Committee and collaboration with the local probation department (Peachey 1989; Victim Offender Reconciliation Resource Center 1984).

In 1978, the second VORP started with support from the Mennonite community in Elkhart, Indiana (Claassen and Zehr 1989; Gehm and Umbreit 1985), followed by the Mennonite Central Committee of Manitoba's VORP in 1979 (Perry *et al.* 1987). In 1982, two more Mennonite-sponsored VORPs were established in Langley, British Columbia (Gustafson and Smidstra 1989; Gustafson 2004), and in Fresno, California (Claassen 1999).

Out of these experiences, Mennonites in the US and Canada articulated the principles of restorative justice (Zehr 1980, 1985; Northey 1989; Cordella 1991; Wright 1996: 100–3), culminating in Howard Zehr's (1990) seminal book, *Changing Lenses: A New Focus on Crime and Justice*. In VORP, reconciliation – the healing of injuries and restoring right relationship – is the purpose. Direct mediation between victim and offender is the process wherever 'relationships have been broken' by the criminal act. VORP advocates believe that church-based restorative justice programs – operating from a Christian peacemaking perspective – are the best guard against program cooptation (Ruth-Heffelbower 1996).

During the 1990s, victim advocates raised concerns about crime victims participating in a process to reconcile with offenders and objected to advocating forgiveness of offenders (Young 1995, Van Ness and Heetderks-Strong 1997: 70). Some people were turned off by the Christian nature of VORPs. Those familiar with community mediation felt reconciliation was too high a goal and preferred a 'satisfactory mutual agreement rather than a complete reconciliation' (Kerner *et al.* 1992: 30).

Victim offender mediation (VOM)

The faith-based concepts underlying VORP were secularized by developing training techniques that encompassed both community mediation and VORP (Community Justice Initiatives Association 1983; Peachey *et al.* 1983) and in recognition of VORP's dependence on secular justice for cases. As the restorative justice movement reached out to the victims' movement, the Victim Offender Mediation (VOM) and its association (VOMA) picked up the mantle of restorative justice.

> VOMA developed out of an informal network of practitioners, researchers, and theorists in victim–offender mediation and restorative justice in the early 1980s. Originally called the US Association for Victim–Offender Mediation, the organization became VOMA in 1997. There are currently 350 VOMA members (individuals) and 30 agency members, in 40 states and 7 countries.
>
> (Victim Offender Mediation Association 2004)

VOM distinguishes itself from community mediation, which it sees as largely 'settlement driven.' VOM is primarily 'dialogue driven,' de-emphasizing reconciliation and emphasizing victim healing, offender accountability, and restoration of losses. Also VOM distinctively advocates a 'humanistic' model of mediation, a 'social work case development approach' (Umbreit 1978, 1996, 1997; Umbreit and Burns 2002).

The VOM model of mediation spread during the mid-1980s in the US. In 1985, Coventry and Leeds established the first British VOM programs (Liebmann 2000). Distinguishing between VOM and the older community mediation model is not always easy. That year, a survey by VOMA counted thirty-two VOM programs in the United States (Gehm and Umbreit 1985), compared to some 400 first generation community mediation programs identified by the American Bar Association (American Bar Association 1986; McGillis 1997).

Restorative circles

The circle is central to traditional aboriginal cultures and social processes. Circle processes for handling crime and wrongdoing originate from traditional concepts of freedom and individuality – one person cannot impose a decision upon another. Native cultures around the world have a variety of processes for responding to wrongdoing. Restorative justice circle models evolved along two paths: a healing paradigm (healing circles) to dispose of situations, and a co-judging paradigm (sentencing circles) limited to recommendations to judicial authority for case disposition (Ross 1994). Both circle models follow similar structural processes (Van Ness and Heetderks-Strong 1997).

> I think that when I describe what we call 'peacemaking' in English, I am describing the traditional justice of many aboriginal groups of people. I have been to the South Pacific, Norway and across the US and Canada to talk with aboriginal leaders. Others of the Navajo Nation court system have visited Australia, New Zealand, Bolivia, and South Africa to do the same. Often, when we describe peacemaking, other aboriginal leaders nod their heads with approval and tell us that it is the same as their traditional justice methods.
>
> (Yazzie 1998a: 129)

The re-emergence of tribal sovereignty on North American reservations spawned several circle models (Dickson-Gilmore 1992; La Prairie and Diamond 1992; La Prairie 1995). Circles differ in the purpose, who participates and the role of participants. Healing and talking circles focus on a particular concern common to all parties (men or women's healing circles, substance abuse groups) or are constituted to help someone with their healing journey (support groups for victims or for offenders). Such circles rarely involve justice professionals but may include professional counselors (Stuart 1996: 194). Perhaps the first acknowledged use of restorative circles in response to criminal cases began in 1982 among the largest nation of aboriginal Americans, the Navajo

in the desert southwest of the United States (Lewis 1998).

Peacemaking circles

Traditional Navajo conflict resolution involves *Hozhooji* – living in 'right relationship' (Yazzie 1994). If a person feels wronged by another they first demand the perpetrator to put things right. The term for the demand is *nalyeeh*, a demand for compensation. *Nalyeeh* is also a demand to readjust the relationship so that the proper thing is done (Yazzie and Zion 1996). If this fails, the wronged person may turn to a respected community leader to organize and facilitate a peacemaking process. In this non-confrontational process, family and clan members of victims and perpetrators talk through matters to arrive at a solution.

The Navajo Nation in southwestern US established the Navajo Peacemaker Courts in 1982 under the direction of tribal justice Robert Yazzie with assistance from attorney James Zion (Yazzie and Zion 1996; Yazzie 1998b; Zion 1998; Gross 1999).

> 'Anglos forced their court system on the Navajos back in 1892,' said Zion. In 1959, the Navajos formed their own court system and destroyed the family system of justice. Zion was first hired as head lawyer of the Navajo court system in 1981. At that point, the people in charge of the court felt that they had gone too far down the Anglo legal path. They asked Zion to write the court rules for Navajo peacemaking in 1982. 'They asked me to take them back to their Navajo roots. I had no idea how to do this,' said Zion. So he partnered with Navajo judges and rediscovered peacemaking.
>
> (Mirsky 2004b)

While the Navajo peacemaking predates the rise of modern restorative justice, the theory of restorative justice has influenced thinking about Navajo justice (Mirsky 2004b). Now fully asserting sovereignty on tribal lands and responding to many criminal offenses using peacemaking circles, the Navajo Nation is the largest restorative jurisdiction in the United States.

> In January 2000, the Navajo Nation Council decided to revamp the Navajo Nation Criminal Code. The Council eliminated jail time and fines for 79 offenses, required the use of peacemaking in criminal cases, and required that the courts see to the rights of victims. The Council also incorporated the traditional concept of nalyeeh into the criminal code.
>
> (Yazzie 2000)

Healing circles

The Hollow Water Healing Program in Manitoba began as a response to incest and sexual assault, seeking not only to heal intimate connections and human dignity but also addressing the social arrangements that enabled violence to flourish (Sivell-Ferri 1997; Taraschi 1998: 117). Like many aboriginal communities, Hollow Water had fallen into deep patterns of alcoholism and a culture of violence and was in danger of losing its culture entirely. Joyce Bushie (1997) describes how Hollow Water developed healing circles.

> The beginnings were in the community in the early eighties. Back then, what we were faced with was alcohol abuse at its highest point ... There was also violence against women, both physically, sexually, mentally and psychologically ... In the early eighties a few of us decided to sober up ... we did a lot of talking, did a lot of crying, and slowly, over time, more and more people came together ... At first we were saying alcoholism was the problem; suicide was the problem; child neglect was the problem; kids dropping out of school was the problem ... Then we started touching on sexual abuse. I always remember one workshop where there were sixty people ... It was there that we

couldn't ignore the problem any more because we were faced with actual numbers. For the first time we were able to talk about the sexual victimization of our past as children, and as young people in this community. It was not one incident. There were multiple incidents, multiple abusers. Many of us started off as victims, as children ... What happened here on a small scale was one person disclosed and gave courage to the next person, and to the next person, so that over time, you begin to share the burden ... That is how it works. That's how I see healing in the community – it's that web, making those connections. That's exactly what has happened amongst the women here.

> (Bushie 1997)

Unlike the other circle models, these healing circles were created by local tribal leaders, primarily the Ojibwa women (McCold 1999). Hollow Water has continued to use circles since 1986 to transform social dysfunction in their community. A recent study by the Native Counseling Services of Alberta (2001) confirmed that their approach is a highly cost-effective response to sexual offending.

Sentencing circles

A sentencing circle is a community-directed process that partners with the criminal justice system to find consensus on a sentencing plan (Griffiths and Hamilton 1996). Sentencing circles use traditional circle ritual and structure to create a respectful space. There, interested community members, victim, victim supporters, offender, offender supporters, judge, prosecutor, defense counsel, police, and court workers can speak from the heart in a shared search for understanding of the event. They identify steps for healing affected parties and to prevent future occurrences (Pranis 1997). Sentencing circles involve the players found in traditional court – and are often held in a courtroom.

Sentencing circles were begun in 1991 in the Yukon by Judge Barry Stuart (Plett

1999). At first, judges were the primary facilitator of circle hearings (Crnkovich 1995). Now most communities select one or two local people as keepers of the circle. The keepers ensure respect for the teachings of the circle, mediate differences and guide the circle towards a consensus. Everyone in the community has a stake in the outcome. All may not participate but are encouraged to do so (Stuart 1996; Pranis 1997).

> Circle sentencing was introduced to many of us by the Honorable Justice Barry Stuart of the Yukon Territorial Court in his decision in *R. v. Moses*, 11 C.R.(4th) 359 ... Since that decision, sentencing circles have been used in many aboriginal communities throughout Canada. These sentencing circles are attempting to incorporate what are identified as aboriginal traditions and values. It is important to be very clear on the point that the sentencing circle itself is not a 'traditional practice' of aboriginal peoples in Canada now being re-instituted. It is very much a creation growing out of the existing system introduced within aboriginal communities, for the most part by the judiciary serving these communities.
>
> (Crnkovich 1995: 2)

Unlike mediation and conferencing, circles have not followed a simple linear evolution. Many different reservations/reserves of First Nation people have experimented with peacemaking circles without much notice by the outside world. A serious attempt to bring circles off the reservation is underway in Minnesota. Kay Pranis led this effort by providing training for circle keepers in communities and schools. Peacemaking circles were introduced in South St Paul in 1998.

> Initially, several Council members were trained in Family Group Conferencing and this was the approach used in handling the Council's first case in early 1997. A lapse of time occurred after that first case during which a number of Council mem-bers were exposed to the idea of the circle as a way of promoting restorative justice ... The Council now uses restorative justice circles exclusively as its way of responding to cases.
>
> (Coates *et al.* 2000: 15)

It is too soon to tell how widely restorative circles will be tried in locations beyond Canadian and American aboriginal communities or how the practice might change in different cultural contexts. Circles are a more extensive intervention than mediations or conferences. Circles will not likely be cost-effective unless used in cases that save the cost of a prison sentence (Native Counseling Services of Alberta 2001).

Restorative conferencing

Restorative justice conferencing involves all direct stakeholders in determining how best to repair the harm of offending beha-vior (McCold and Wachtel 2002). Models vary in the involvement of the victim, victim supporters, and offender suppor-ters, including family members and sig-nificant others. Models also vary in who facilitates, whether the whole group or a family caucus negotiates outcomes, and who approves the agreements (Marsh and Crow 1998; Warner-Roberts and Masters 1999; McCold 2001).

Conferencing evolved in two arenas: child welfare conferencing and youth justice conferencing (McCold 2001). Conferences that respond to criminal behavior are obviously restorative. Those held in response to child abuse or neglect within families are less obviously restorative since they focus on developing a plan for the future, not redress for past harm. Child welfare conferencing is used for a variety of domestic and family abuse issues (American Humane Association 2004a). Youth justice conferencing is widely applied to adults. Both approaches are increasingly being used in school settings (for example, see van Pagee 2002, 2004; Henskens-Rejiman and van Pagee 2003).

Family group conferences (FGC)

Family decision-making approaches to social work share a common set of purposes: 'the participation of family in child protection, the strengthening of families and kinship networks, the connection or reconnection of children to their family and wider kinship group, and the continuity of care for children' (Connolly and McKenzie 1999: 15)

In 1986, the Children and Young Persons Bill in New Zealand proposed child protection multi-disciplinary teams of professionals requiring involvement of parents and family groups in developing solutions in care and protection cases (not proposed for youth justice) (Hassall 1996: 25). This legislation was criticized for creating more bureaucracy, not going far enough to empower families and failing to address Maori cultural concerns (Doolan 1999). The same year a Ministerial Advisory Committee on a Maori Perspective issued a committee report *PUAP-TE-ATA-TU (Daybreak)* calling for a bold new approach to child welfare by more directly involving families and clans in child protection decisions (Hardin 1996; Connolly and McKenzie 1999; Connolly 2004). The Department of Social Welfare responded by piloting two child protection teams who regularly invited families and their supporters to meetings to involve them in decision-making (Hassall 1996: 22). During one of these meetings, the private family caucus was born:

> At the end of the social worker's summary, there was a degree of uncertainty as everyone hesitated over what to do next. At that point, the cultural consultant suggested that he and the social worker could be available to help the family sort through the problems confronting them – or that they could withdraw and allow the family

some privacy to talk. One of the sisters exclaimed, 'Yous can go. We don't want you fellas around here!' And so it was, the cultural consultant and the social worker left the family to deliberate on their own ... the cultural consultant explained that this was how things were done in Maori: the family talking collectively to resolve family issues.

> (Connolly and McKenzie 1999: 20)

The draft legislation was substantially revised in response to the concerns raised during public hearings (Olsen *et al.* 1995; Hassall 1996; Maxwell 1996) resulting in the landmark Children, Young Persons and Their Families Act of 1989. Family group conferences (FGCs) both addressed the concerns of and bridged the gap between the competing paradigms of youth justice and child protection (Doolan 1991). The Act required that young people in serious cases of care-and-protection or young offenders charged with indictable offenses participate in a conference with their immediate and extended family members (Doolan 2004). The Act also established a new youth court where all serious juvenile offenses except homicide cases are now dealt with by FGCs (Maxwell and Morris 1993; Pratt 1996).

Family group decision-making (FGDM)

Practitioners in the US, Canada, England, and Australia widely replicated the New Zealand child welfare model (Marshall 1996; Dignan and Marsh 2001). Family group decision-making set a new standard for empowering, restorative social work. One of the first was the Canadian family group decision-making (FGDM) by Pennell and Burford (1994) in Newfoundland and Labrador in Canada, designed to test the efficacy of FGCs to address family violence more broadly than the care and protection of a child (Burford and Pennell 1994; Burford *et al.* 1995; Burford *et al.* 1996; Pennell and Burford 1996; Pennell 2003).

FGDM adopted the New Zealand child welfare model and incorporated aspects of an aboriginal response to domestic violence (Ma Mawi Nita Wi Iwewin Project 1987), feminist caring labor theory (Baines *et al.* 1991) and reintegrative shaming theory (Braithwaite 1989).

> Caring labour theory helps to clarify the structural context in which reintegrative shaming occurs and how this empowerment process spreads around the responsibility for caring. The family group conference makes it possible to listen to the voices of all participants and design culturally sound plans for meeting public standards.
>
> (Pennell and Burford 1996: 209)

The principles guiding the FGDM are that family violence requires intervention by mandated authorities and the best long-range solutions enable affected parties to develop a plan tailored to their family and cultural situation (Pennell and Burford 1996). The FGC and FGDM models continue to evolve as they are adopted into social welfare and child protection practices in a number of countries (Marsh and Crow 1998; also see chronology).

Family unity meeting (FUM)

While New Zealand developed the family group conference, the state of Oregon developed the Family Unity Meeting (FUM) (Keys and Rockhill 2000). In the Oregon FUM model, professional social workers and the extended family collaborate to plan for the care and protection of family members. Unlike New Zealand's FGC, parents can veto which family members are invited and professionals remain with the family throughout the process (North Carolina Department of Health and Human Services 2004).

In 1997, the Oregon Family Group Decision Meeting law required considera-

tion of an FUM whenever a child is placed out of home for longer than sixty days. By 1998, over 4,000 FUMs had been held in Oregon (Graber *et al.* 1996; Keys and Rockhill 2000). This model was tested in several US locations before the New Zealand model of FGCs was widely known. Some, for example the Family Unity Meeting Program in San Diego county, abandoned FUMs once they experimented with FGCs.

> The term 'family unity meeting' usually refers strictly to the Oregon model where the meeting is facilitated from beginning to end. In San Diego, this is how we began. We moved to family alone time and have not turned back. We retained the program name as it was well known in the County and it was not practical to change the name. It was the practice that seemed most significant, rather than the name.
>
> (Quinnett 2002)

It seems likely that the New Zealand model of conferencing will continue to eclipse the family unity model and limit its proliferation, absent empirical evidence to prefer it. Still, Oregon was the first state to pioneer family empowered social work in the United States.

Police conferencing (Wagga model)

Conferencing was revised and pioneered as a community policing technique in Wagga Wagga, New South Wales, Australia, in 1991 (Moore and McDonald 1995) by Terry O'Connell, based loosely on the idea of New Zealand's FGCs (O'Connell 1998; O'Connell *et al.* 1999).

> John McDonald, the New South Wales Police Commissioner's Youth Adviser, had visited New Zealand with a youth working party in 1990 and learned about their bold experiment with conferencing ... He attempted to promote debate and discussion on conferencing, but it was not until

he visited Wagga Wagga in early 1991 that he found any operational police who were interested in what was happening in New Zealand and willing to seriously consider the idea.

(O'Connell 1998: 1)

Police conferencing was a natural extension of the cautioning used in countries with British-style policing. It meets the tenets of problem-oriented policing (Goldstein 1990). Braithwaite's (1989) reintegrative shaming theory influenced O'Connell's view of conferencing. The police model later developed in Canberra was based on Braithwaite's theory. Conference protocols were eventually scripted – the key statements and questions written out for the convenience of the facilitator (O'Connell 1998: 8)

Wagga Wagga's conferencing model received widespread support from front-line police personnel and local community members (Graham 1993; Moore 1995; Moore and McDonald 1995; Moore and O'Connell 1994). The Wagga model led to script-based conferences in Queensland schools (Hyndman et al. 1995, Cameron and Thorsborne 1999). Several non-police models developed from the Wagga model, heavily influenced by David Moore's (1993, 1996, 1997, 2004) interest in Silvan Tomkins' 'affect theory' (Nathanson 1996) combined with Braithwaite's (1989) sociological theory. Together the theories explain why community conferences work, including that regularly occurring 'transformative moment' of interest to early mediation.

In 1994, Terry O'Connell received a Churchill Fellowship for a study tour of North America, England, and South Africa (O'Connell 1998), which has led to police conferences spreading to countries around the world. In Canada, the Royal Canadian Mounted Police train officers and community volunteers in conferencing (Chatterjee 2000; Chatterjee and Elliott 2003).

Real Justice was founded by Ted Wachtel (1998) in 1994 after he attended a presentation by O'Connell in Philadelphia. Real Justice is a private not-for-profit training and technical assistance program dedicated to the spread of community conferences and related restorative practices (www.realjustice.org). By 1998, Real Justice had trained more than 3,000 conference facilitators and nearly a hundred trainers in North America. More than 150 police departments in the US and Canada have officers trained by Real Justice.

Several restorative policing projects resulted from Real Justice training, including the first randomized research known as the 'Bethlehem Experiment' in Pennsylvania from 1995 to 1997 (McCold and Wachtel 1998). Also in 1995, the Woodbury, Minnesota, and the St Paul police began police conferencing projects (Umbreit and Fercello 1997). In 1996, the Hudson Institute provided Real Justice training for the Indianapolis police in the second US police experiment (McGarrell et al. 2000).

Following visits by O'Connell, the Thames Valley Police in England experimented with Wagga-style conferences as a form of police cautioning in 1995 in Aylesbury (O'Connell 1996, 1998; Warner-Roberts and Masters 1999; Nicholl 1998, Pollard 1999; Young and Goold 1999). A research evaluation was recently completed by Oxford University (Young 2001; Hoyle et al. 2002; Young and Hoyle 2003).

Community conferencing

Community conferencing (also known as Real Justice conferencing, community accountability conferencing, and restorative conferencing) provides forums for dealing with wrongdoing throughout society as well as peacemaking possibilities in schools, workplaces, communities, youth organizations, college campuses, and other settings (Wachtel 1998). Community conferences use a version of the original Wagga Wagga script developed by Terry O'Connell (1998). This revised Wagga model and script explicitly includes principles of restorative

33

justice and incorporates Braithwaite's (1989) reintegration shaming theory and Silvan Tomkin's affect theory (Nathanson 1996; Retzinger and Scheff 1996) to explain conference dynamics (O'Connell *et al.* 1999).

Community conferences evolved from a community policing model, to include a school and organizational model of discipline, and informal restorative practices in everyday interactions (Wachtel and McCold 2000). Because of the generic problem-solving nature of community conferences, the scripted process is used in several non-criminal contexts, including school misbehavior, and has implications for restorative responses to all forms and degrees of wrongdoing (Wachtel 1998; Wachtel and McCold 2000). Over 2,500 of the 8,400 conference facilitators trained by Real Justice since 1995 are school personnel.

Conclusions

The models reviewed here currently operate in both original and revised versions. The continued operation of restorative programs, some as long as thirty years, testifies to society's deep need for respectful, healing approaches to wrongdoing. The spread of these models around the world assures that many will be operating thirty years hence. The evolution of these three restorative models demonstrates some consistent trends in the role of community and the facilitator, and in the human conflicts addressed.

The concept 'community' evolved in the practice of restorative justice. Early models included only victim and offender, with the community represented by the volunteer mediator. Conference and circle models distinguish the role of the facilitator from representation of 'community' and explicitly recognize the families and personal supporters of victims and offenders as an important micro-community of concern. Circle models and some conferencing models encourage individuals to represent the wider community.

The role of the facilitator evolves in two directions. Some restorative justice programs, especially those with a 'humanistic social work' perspective, expect the facilitator to provide active counseling and place great emphasis on the interpersonal skills and training of the facilitator. These models seek to establish standards and minimum training requirements, creating an 'expert model' approach. Conferencing and circle models rely more on the micro-communities of care and existing local social programs to provide social work services for individual victims, offenders, and their families. In conferencing and circles, the facilitator determines who participates, prepares the parties, and organizes the restorative process. While facilitators do facilitate, they do not run the encounter, and therefore do not require special expertise beyond a clear understanding of the purpose of the process. Conferencing and circle models evolved from professional facilitation toward an 'everybody can do it' approach (O'Connell and McCold 2004).

The core restorative process has broad implications for resolving conflicts and restoring relationships. Conferencing models apply restorative processes and principles to internal organizational relations and to integrating ongoing formal and informal restorative practices in everyday relationships. Restorative practices evolved from a narrow focus on the amount of restitution in juvenile property cases to broadly applied practices that continuously engage affected micro-communities. The exploration of the potential of these practices is just beginning. From negotiating restitution agreements to transforming conflict into cooperation (McDonald and Moore 1999), restorative justice practice is in adolescence at the beginning of the twenty-first century.

It would be speculative, of course, to suggest which restorative practices will have historical significance. Likely, recent efforts to establish standards of practice will influence future developments (Home Office 2004). Probably, restorative practices will spread to more countries, given the consistency with developments in international human rights laws (Braithwaite 2000). The highest profile effort is underway at the United Nations.

On 24 July 2002, the United Nations Economic and Social Council adopted a resolution encouraging countries to apply Basic Principles on the Use of Restorative Justice Programs in Criminal Matters in developing and implementing restorative justice in their countries (Van Ness 2002; United Nations 2002). In April 2005, the Eleventh United Nations Congress on Crime Prevention and Criminal Justice held the first United Nations workshop on restorative justice to educate the delegations about its potential for criminal justice reform (United Nations 2004). These actions by the United Nations are likely to fuel greater adoption of restorative practices in many countries, making the 2000s the decade of international proliferation.

Chronology of restorative practice developments 1970–2004

1970

United States: The Institute for Mediation and Conflict Resolution dispute center established (McGillis 1997)

1971

United States: Minnesota Restitution Center mediation diversion project (Hudson and Galaway 1974)

United States: Night Prosecutor Program in Columbus, OH (McGillis 1997)

1973

United States: Rochester NY community mediation center opens (New York State Unified Court System 2003)

1974

Canada: the Kitchener experiment, Kitchener and Elmira, Ontario (Peachey 1989)

1975

Canada: first VORP started in Kitchener, Ontario (Gehm and Umbreit 1985)

United States: Community mediation centers opened in Dorchester, MA, Orange County, FL, and Bronx, NY (McGillis 1997)

1976

Canada: Community Diversion Centre of Victoria, British Columbia (Aubuchon 1978)

1977

Norway: Nils Christie *Conflict as Property*

United States: community mediation centers established in Brooklyn Rockland Suffolk and Long Island, NY, Venice, CA, Kansas City, MO, and Dade County, FL (McGillis 1997)

United States: community mediation centers established in Massachusetts (Davis 1986)

United States: Randy Barnett proposes restitution paradigm

1978

United States: DOJ neighborhood justice centers Atlanta, Los Angeles, and Kansas City (McGillis 1997)

United States: Elkhart, Indiana, begins VORP (Gehm and Umbreit 1985)

1979

Canada: VORP in Winnipeg established (Perry *et al.* 1987)

United Kingdom: reparation scheme in Exeter, Devon, juvenile court cases (Marshall 1992: 16)

United States: inauguration of the Makiki Neighborhood Justice Center, Hawaii (Barnes and Adler 1983)

1980

Australia: established three experimental community justice centers in New South Wales (Anderson 1982)

United States: funding from LEAA, American Bar Association, American Arbitration

Association, Institute for Mediation and Conflict Resolution, US DOJ's Community Relations Service and NIJ provided national leadership in developing community mediation centers (McGillis 1997)

1981

Netherlands: HALT program included mediation as one option (Miers 2001)

New Zealand: National Advisory Committee on the Prevention of Child Abuse by Minister of social welfare (Hardin 1996)

Norway: Child Welfare Conflict Councils establish juvenile mediation programs (Falck 1992; Paus 2000)

United States: New York State-funded network of community-based dispute resolution centers opened in Harlem, Manhattan, Syracuse and Ogdensburg, NY (New York State Unified Court System 2003)

1982

Canada: VORP for serious offenses established in Langley, BC (Gustafson and Smidstra 1989; Gustafson 2004)

Germany: Braunschweig pilot experiment in mediation for juveniles (Bilsky 1990; Trenczek 1990)

United Kingdom: first community mediation service in UK, Newham Conflict and Change Project (Wright 1996: 83)

United States: 200 mediation services in United States, all of which take criminal cases where there is a relationship between victim and the offender (Ray 1982, 1983)

United States: Brooklyn mediation experiment (Davis 1982)

United States: Fresno, California VORP begins (Claassen 1999)

United States: Navajo Nation established Navajo Peacemaker Courts (Yazzie and Zion 1996)

1983

Finland: youth justice mediation – social welfare approach using resident popula-

tion as mediators in Vantaa, Finland (Iivari 1992, 2000)

New Zealand: child protection teams – not uncommon for families to be a part of the decision-making meeting (Hassall 1996)

1984

Austria: begins using mediation to divert juvenile cases from court (Miers 2001; Pelikan 2000; Miers and Willemsens 2004: 19)

Germany: first generation of community mediation models began to implement criminal restitution more effectively (Kerner *et al.* 1992)

1985

France: paralegal community mediation Valence (Bonafé-Schmitt 1992)

New Zealand: Criminal Justice Act – reparation as preferred sentence for property offenders (Galaway 1992)

Scotland: reparation and mediation feasibility study Edinburgh using volunteer mediators (Warner 1992)

United Kingdom: Coventry and Leeds establish VOM programs (Wright 1996)

United States: more than 400 community mediation programs responded to ABA questionnaire (McGillis 1997)

United States: national survey located thirty-two victim offender mediation (VOM) programs (Gehm and Umbreit 1985)

United States: Zehr, 'Retributive justice, restorative justice,' Mennonite Central Committee

1986

Canada: healing circles initiated by Hollow Water First Nation (Ojibwa) in Manitoba (Bushie 1997)

France: Community mediation experiment, Lyon (Bonafé-Schmitt 1992)

New Zealand: Children and Young Persons Bill introduced (Connolly 2004)

New Zealand: Dept of Social Welfare pilots two child protection teams, regularly invite families and their supporters to meetings and involve them in decision-making (Hassall 1996)

New Zealand: *PUAP-TE-ATA-TU* ministerial committee report (Hardin 1996)

United States: twenty-eight community mediation programs in Massachusetts (Davis 1986)

1987

Belgium: Oikoten juvenile mediation pilot in Leuven (Claes 1998)

United Kingdom: VOM with adult offenders in Kettering, Northants (Marshall 1992)

1988

Canada: Daubney Report, House of Commons, *Taking Responsibility* (Cormier 2002)

New Zealand: VOM trialed by probation officers (Galaway 1995)

New Zealand: *Whakakpakiri Whanau! Family Decision Making*, report of Dept of Social Welfare on FGC pilots in child protection (Hardin 1996)

1989

New Zealand: Children, Young Persons, and Their Families Act requiring FGCs in care and protection and youth justice, both under Department of Social Welfare (Hardin 1996)

Norway: Conflict Councils extended to include adult mediation (Falck 1992; Paus 2000)

United States: US Association for Victim Offender Mediation created (Stutzman-Amstutz, 1996)

1990

Australia: McDonald visits New Zealand (O'Connell 1998)

United States: Oregon establishes Family Unity Meetings for child protection cases (Keys and Rockhill 2000)

1991

Australia: O'Connell pilots police-facilitated conferencing model in Wagga Wagga, NSW (O'Connell 1998)

Belgium: establishes adult penal mediation services (Miers 2001)

Canada: Yukon Territorial Court Judge Barry Stuart conducts first sentencing circle (Crnkovich 1995; Plett 1999)

Norway: establishes Municipal Mediation Service Act (Miers and Willemsens 2004)

1992

Austria: begins mediation program for adults (Miers and Willemsens 2004)

Canada: Provincial Court Judges Huculak and Fafard begin sentencing circles in Saskatchewan (Huculak 1997; Plett 1999)

Canada: Wet'suwet'en Unlocking Aboriginal Justice Program established in British Columbia (Mirsky 2003)

Israel: VORP introduced in juvenile probation (Grably 2003)

Spain: Law 4/92 authorizes mediation as part of judicial processing of juveniles (Miers 2001)

United Kingdom: Child Welfare FGCs piloted Family Rights Group, London (Marsh and Crow 1998)

1993

Australia: police facilitated conferencing started in ACT (Miers 2001)

Australia: state-wide conferencing for juveniles in South Australia (Daly 2001; Wundersitz and Hetzel 1996)

Canada: FGDM evaluation study begun in Newfoundland and Labrador (Pennell and Burford 1995)

New Zealand: mandatory training modules for social worker FGC facilitators (Hardin 1996)

South Africa: NICRO adopts restorative justice as model for justice reform and invites Gabrielle Maxwell (Skelton and Frank 2001)

United States: DOJ establishes national initiative the Balanced and Restorative Justice Project BARJ (Bazemore and Umbreit 1994; McCold 2004)

United States: Fresno VORP develops scripted Community Justice Conferences following visit by Fred McElrea and Matt Hakiaha (Claassen 1996)

1994

Australia: O'Connell Churchill Fellowship study tour of North America, England, and South Africa (O'Connell 1998)

Australia and New Zealand: Christian Ruth Morris presents transformative justice (Jantzi 2001)

Canada: Mohawk Nation of Akwesasne Justice Department organizes Council of Neh-Kanikonriio (Mirsky 2004c)

New Zealand: Zehr visits NZ as a 'prophet of justice' (Jantzi 2001)

United States: first US pilot of police conferencing in Anoka, MN (O'Connell 1998)

United States: national survey locates 123 VOM programs (Umbreit 1994)

United States: Real Justice standardized training of conference facilitators (Wachtel 1998)

1995

Albania: Albanian Foundation for Conflict Resolution and Reconciliation of Disputes offering VOM (Miers and Willemsens 2004)

Australia: Reintegrative Shaming Experiment (RISE) begins in Canberra (Sherman et al. 2004)

Canada: Sparwood (BC) Youth Assistance Program begins first conferencing program in Canada (Bouwman 1997)

Poland: juvenile mediation program begins (Czarnecka-Dzialuk and Wojcik 2000)

South Africa: Truth and Reconciliation Commission established (Boraine 2000)

Sweden: FGDM pilot programs established in ten localities (Sundell and Vinnerljung 2004)

United Kingdom: Milton Keynes restorative caution project started (Miers 2001)

United Kingdom: Thames Valley Police conferencing piloted in Aylesbury (Young and Goold 1999)

United States: experimental evaluation of police conferencing begins in Bethlehem, PA (McCold and Wachtel 1998)

United States: police conferencing in Woodbury, MN (Umbreit and Fercello 1997)

United States: states with the largest numbers of community mediation programs are New York, Michigan, North Carolina, Massachusetts, California, Florida, Ohio, Texas, and New Jersey (McGillis 1997)

1996

Canada: Criminal Code of Canada includes restorative purposes of sentencing (Plett 1999)

Scotland: Young Offenders' Mediation Project established by SACRO (Miers and Willemsens 2004)

United Nations: Working Party on Restorative Justice of the Alliance of NGOs on Crime Prevention and Criminal Justice (McCold 1998)

United States: Indianapolis Police experimental conferencing program (McGarrell et al. 2000)

United States: Mille Lacs Circle Sentencing Project initiated in central Minnesota (Pranis 1997)

United States: national survey locates 289 VOM programs (McKinney et al. 1996)

United States: Santa Clara County California pilots Family Conference Model by combining FGCs and family unity meetings (Wheeler and Johnson 2003)

1997

Belgium: Declaration of Leuven approved at first international conference of research on restorative justice (International Conference on Restorative Justice 1997)

Canada: Calgary conferencing program begun (Calhoun 2000)

Canada: Canadian Criminal Justice Association and the International Centre for Criminal Law Reform and Criminal Justice Policy national conference on restorative justice in Vancouver, BC (Cormier 2002)

Canada: RCMP begin conferencing program and facilitator trainings (Chatterjee 2000)

Netherlands: Ministry of Justice establishes mediation pilot in Hague (Miers and Willemsens 2004)

New Zealand: Crime Prevention Unit pilots adult conferencing projects (Jantzi 2001)

Russia: Bruce Shank visits Moscow, Public Center for Legal and Judicial Reform launches restorative justice in Russia (Fliamer and Maksudov 2001)

Singapore: Community Mediation Centres Act passed by Parliament (Wing-Cheong 2003) and peer mediation program begins in four secondary schools (Magnus *et al.* 2003: 209)

South Africa: Department of Welfare publishes White Paper calling for crime prevention through restorative justice (Skelton and Frank 2001)

United Kingdom: Home Office issues White Paper, *No More Excuses*

United States: Oregon passes the Family Group Decision-Making law (Keys and Rockhill 2000)

United States: South St Paul Restorative Justice Council begins circles (Coates *et al.* 2000)

United States: the US Association of Victim Offender Mediation becomes the Victim Offender Mediation Association (Victim Offender Mediation Association 2004)

United States: Washington State Division of Children and Family Services implements FGDM in child welfare statewide (Gunderson *et al.* 2003)

1998

Australia: New South Wales passes Young Offenders Act establishing Youth Justice Conferencing Directorate and prohibiting police from facilitating conferences (Miers 2001)

Canada: community conferencing begun in Calgary (Sharpe 2003)

Denmark: Ministry of Justice establishes mediation pilot for juvenile and adults (Miers and Willemsens 2004: 43)

Netherlands: establishes a number of FGDM pilots (Miers and Willemsens 2004: 89)

Netherlands: establishes Rotterdam housing mediation project (de Jong 2001)

Russia: Centre for Legal and Judicial Reform established mediation for juveniles in Moscow (Miers 2001: 60)

United Kingdom: Crime and Disorder Act establishes Youth Offending Teams (YOTS) (Dignan and Marsh 2001; Miers and Willemsens 2004: 49)

United Kingdom: Thames Valley Police begin restorative cautions and warnings (Young and Hoyle 2003)

United States: North Carolina FGC Project begins (Pennell 2003)

1999

Canada: Supreme Court supports sentencing circle in landmark case *R. v. Gladue* (Plett 1999)

Council of Europe: Committee of Ministers adopts Mediation in Penal Matters (Council of Europe Committee of Ministers 1999; Van Ness 2003)

European Union: EU-funded creation of European Forum for Victim Offender Mediation and Restorative Justice (Van Ness and Heetderks-Strong 2002: 35)

Hong Kong: mediation used for school bullying (Wong 2002)

Luxembourg: Code of Criminal Procedure amended to include mediation (Miers and Willemsens 2004: 83)

United Kingdom: Youth Justice Criminal Evidence Act (Miers and Willemsens 2004)

United States: American Humane Association established the National Center on Family Group Decision Making (American Humane Association 2004a)

United States: Arizona implements FGDM statewide beginning in two counties (Titcomb and LeCroy 2003)

United States: Miami-Dade Juvenile Court implements FGDM in three dependency divisions (Litchfield *et al.* 2003)

2000

Belgium: Flanders establishes pilot FGC projects using mediators trained by Allan MacRae (Vanfraechem 2003)

Hungary: Real Justice training established in Budapest (Negrea 2002; Mirsky 2004a)

Ireland: Mediation Bureau established (Miers 2001)

Israel: ASHALIM pilots NZ–style FGC in youth justice cases in two locations (Spak 2001; American Humane Association 2004b)

Netherlands: Echt Recht (Real Justice) established in Amsterdam (Henskens-Rejiman and van Pagee 2003)

Northern Ireland: Diamond House Family Group Conference Service establishes child welfare FGCs and Wagga–style conferences in schools (American Humane Association 2004c)

South Africa: Child Justice Bill calls for restorative response to youth crime (Skelton and Frank 2001)

United Kingdom: Powers of Criminal Courts (Sentencing) Act introduces referral orders and Youth Offender Panel (YOP) Youth Offending Teams (YOT) (Miers and Willemsens 2004)

United Nations: 10th Congress on the Prevention of Crime and the Treatment of Offenders in Vienna. Item 6, Offenders and Victims: Accountability and Fairness in the Justice Process (Van Ness 2003)

United States: California initiates two randomized trials of FGDM in child welfare in Fresno and Riverside counties (Thomas *et al.* 2003)

2001

Czech Republic: Probation and Mediation Act establishes adult and juvenile mediation services (Miers and Willemsens 2004)

Finland: begins experimental evaluation in six pilots of mediation for juveniles under fifteen years old (Miers and Willemsens 2004)

Israel: ASHALIM pilots NZ–style FGC in child welfare in eighteen locations (American Humane Association 2004b)

South Africa: NZ–style conferencing pilot in Wynberg, Cape Town (Skelton and Frank 2001)

United Kingdom: randomized controlled trials by Justice Research Consortium begins with adults CONNECT conferencing program and REMEDI mediation services for post-sentence cases in London, Northumbria, and Thames Valley (Shapland *et al.* 2004)

2002

Finland: begins experimental evaluation in four pilots of mediation in domestic violence (Miers and Willemsens 2004)

Thailand: Ministry of Justice broadcasts national seminar on restorative justice (Kittayarak 2004; Roujanavong and Utensute 2004)

United Kingdom: White Paper *Justice for All* (Miers and Willemsens 2004)

United Nations: ECOSOC experts committee adopts restorative justice basic principles (United Nations 2002; Van Ness 2002, 2003)

2003

Canada: Youth Criminal Justice Act calls for restorative basis for justice system (Huculak 2003)

Finland: begins experimental evaluation of mediation in refugee communities (Miers and Willemsens 2004)

Ukraine: Ukrainian Centre for Common Ground establishes pilot mediation project in Kiev (Miers and Willemsens 2004)

United Kingdom: Home Office consultation document, *Restorative Justice* (Home Office 2003)

2004

Australia: Australian Capital Territory's Crime Act allows the use of conferencing in all stages of the criminal justice process (Prison Fellowship International 2005)

Thailand: *Yutithum Samarn Chan* – justice for social harmony – basis for system-wide comprehensive reform (United Nations 2005: 11)

United Kingdom: conditional cautioning and restorative justice pilots begin as a diversion from court for serious offenses (Shapland *et al.* 2004)

United Kingdom: Home Office establishes best practice professional standards for restorative justice (Home Office 2004)

References

Aertsen, I., Mackay, R., Pelikan, C., Willemsens, J. and Wright, M. (2004) *Rebuilding Community Connections: mediation and restorative justice in Europe*, Strasbourg: Council of Europe Publishing/Editions du Conseil de l'Europe.

American Bar Association. (1986) *Dispute Resolution Program Directory 1986*, Washington, DC: American Bar Association Standing Committee on Dispute Resolution.

— (1990) *Dispute Resolution Program Directory 1990*, Washington, DC: American Bar Association Standing Committee on Dispute Resolution.

American Humane Association (2004a) *FGDM Programs Around the World*, National Center on Family Group Decision Making, online. Available at: http://www.americanhumane.org/site/PageServer?pagename=pc_fgdm_ programs [accessed 4 January 2005].

— (2004b) *Family Group Conference (FGC) in Israel*, National Center on Family Group Decision Making, online. Available at: http://www.americanhumane.org/site/PageServer?pagename=pc_fgdm_programs_israel [accessed 4 January 2005].

— (2004c) *Ulster Community and Hospitals Trust*, National Center on Family Group Decision Making, online. Available at: http://www.americanhumane.org/site/PageServer?pagename=pc_fgdm_programs_northern_ireland [accessed 4 January 2005].

Anderson, K. (1982) 'Community justice centres – alternatives to prosecution,' in P. Grabosky (ed.) *National Symposium on Victimology – Proceedings*, Canberra, Australia: Australian Institute of Criminology, pp. 57–74.

Aubuchon, J. (1978) 'Model for community diversion,' *Canadian Journal of Criminology*, 20(3): 296–300.

Baines, C., Evans, P. and Neysmith S. (eds) (1991) *Women's Caring: feminist perspectives on social welfare*, Toronto: McClelland and Stewart.

Barnes, B. and Adler, P. (1983) 'Mediation and lawyers – the Pacific way – a view from Hawaii,' *Hawaii Bar Journal*, 18(1): 37–52.

Barnett, R. (1977) 'Restitution: a new paradigm of criminal justice,' *Ethics: An International Journal of Social, Political and Legal Philosophy*, 87(4): 279–301.

Bazemore, G. and Umbreit, M. (1994) *Balanced and Restorative Justice*, Washington, DC: US Department of Justice, Office of Juvenile Justice and Delinquency Prevention.

Bilsky, W. (1990) 'Extrajudicial mediation and arbitration: evaluation of German victim–offender–reconciliation programs,' *International Journal of Conflict Management*, 1(4): 357–73.

Bonafé-Schmitt, J.-P. (1992) 'Penal and community mediation: the case of France,' in H. Messmer and H.-U. Otto (eds) *Restorative Justice on Trial: pitfalls and potentials of victim–offender mediation: international research perspectives*, Netherlands: Kluwer.

Boraine, A. (2000) *A Country Unmasked: the story of South Africa's Truth and Reconciliation Commission*, Oxford: Oxford University Press.

Bouwman, J. (1997) 'Sparwood Youth Assistance Programme,' paper presented to CIAJ national conference, Montreal, 24–6 April.

Braithwaite, J. (1989) *Crime, Shame and Reintegration*, New York: Cambridge University Press.

— (2000) 'Standards for restorative justice,' paper presented at the Ancillary Meetings of the Tenth United Nations Congress on the Prevention of Crime and Treatment of Offenders. Vienna, Austria, April, online. Available at: http://www.restorativejustice.org/rj3/UNBasicPrinciples/AncillaryMeetings/Papers/RJ_UN_JBraithwaite.htm [accessed 25 January 2005].

— (2002) *Restorative Justice and Responsive Regulation*, New York: Oxford University Press.

Burford, G. and Pennell, J. (1994) 'A Canadian innovation of family group decision making,' in *International Year of the Family Conference: strengthening families*, Wellington, NZ: New Zealand Social Welfare Department.

Burford, G., Pennell, J. and MacLeod, S. (1995) *Family Group Decision Making: manual for coordinators and communities*, School of Social Work, Memorial University of Newfoundland, St John's, Newfoundland, online. Available at: http://social.chass.ncsu.edu/

jpennell/fgdm/manual/TOC.htm [accessed 21 January 2005].

Burford, G., Pennell, J., MacLeod, S., Campbell, S. and Lyall, G. (1996) 'Reunification as an extended family matter,' *Community Alternatives*, 8(2): 33–55.

Bushie, B. (1999) 'Community holistic circle healing: a community approach,' paper presented at the Building Strong Partnerships for Restorative Practices conference, Burlington, Vermont, August, online. Available at: http://www.iirp.org/library/vt/vt_bushie.html [accessed 21 January 2005].

Bushie, J. (1997) 'CHCH reflections,' in Ministry of the Solicitor General of Canada (ed.), *The Four Circles of Hollow Water*, Aboriginal Peoples' Collection, Cat. No. JS5-1/15-1997E [CD ROM] Ottawa, Canada: Public Works and Government Services. Available at: http://www.sgc.gc.ca/epub/abocor/e199703/e199703.htm [accessed 4 January 2005].

Calhoun, A. (2000) *Calgary Community Conferencing: participant satisfaction: 1998– 2000*, Calgary: Calgary Community Conferencing, Youth Probation Services. Available at: http://www.calgary communityconferencing.com/rande/satisfaction.html [accessed 4 January 2005].

Cameron, L. and Thorsborne, M. (1999) 'Restorative justice and school discipline: mutually exclusive?' paper presented at the Restorative Justice and Civil Society. Australian National University, Canberra, February.

Chatterjee, J. (2000) 'RCMP's Restorative justice initiative,' *Forum on Corrections Research*, 12(1): 35–7, online. Available at: http://www.csc-scc.gc.ca/text/pblct/forum/v12n1/v12n1a11e.pdf [accessed 4 January 2005].

Chatterjee, J. and Elliott, L. (2003) 'Restorative policing in Canada: the Royal Canadian Mounted Police, community justice forums, and the Youth Criminal Justice Act,' *Police Practice and Research: An International Journal*, 4(4): 347–59.

Christie, N. (1977) 'Conflict as property,' *British Journal of Criminology*, 17(1): 1–14.

Claassen, R. (1996) '1995 conference brings restorative justice vision to Fresno community leaders,' *VORP News* (January), VORP of the Central Valley, Fresno, California, online. Available at: http://www.fresno.edu/pacs/vorpnews/9601.pdf [accessed 21 January 2005].

— (1999) '1998 review,' *VORP News* (February), VORP of the Central Valley, Fresno, CA, online. Available at: http://vorp.org/vorpnews/9902.pdf [accessed 21 January 2005].

Claassen, R. and Zehr, H. (1989) *VORP Organizing: a foundation in the church*, Elkhart, IN: Mennonite Central Committee, US Office of Criminal Justice.

Claes, M. (1998) 'The juvenile mediation project in Leuven (Belgium),' in L. Walgrave (ed.) *Restorative Justice for Juveniles: potentialities, risks and problems*, Leuven, Belgium: Leuven University Press.

Coates, R., Umbreit, M. and Vos, B. (2000) *Restorative Justice Circles in South Saint Paul, Minnesota*, Center for Restorative Justice and Peacemaking, School of Social Work, University of Minnesota, online. Available at: http://2ssw.che.umn.edu/rjp/Resources/Documents/Circles.Final.Revised.pdf [accessed 4 January 2005].

Community Justice Initiatives Association (1983) *Mediation Primer: a training guide for mediators in the criminal justice system*, Kitchener, Ontario: Community Justice Initiatives of Waterloo Region.

Connolly, M. (2004) 'A perspective on the origins of family group conferencing,' *American Humane FGDM Issues in Brief*, online. Available at: http://www.americanhumane.org/site/DocServer/fgdm_FGC_Origins_New_Zealand. pdf?docID=1901 [accessed 4 January 2005].

Connolly, M. and McKenzie, M. (1999) *Effective Participatory Practice. Family Group Conferencing in Child Protection*, New York: Aldine de Gruyter.

Cook, R., Roehl, J. and Sheppard, D. (1980) *Neighborhood Justice Centers Field Test: final evaluation report*, Washington, DC: US Government Printing Office.

Cordella, J. (1991) 'Reconciliation and the mutualist model of community,' in H. Pepinsky and R. Quinney (eds) *Criminology as Peacemaking*, Bloomington: Indiana University Press.

Cormier, R. (2002) *Restorative Justice: directions and principles – developments in Canada*, Ottawa: Solicitor General Canada, online. Available at: http://www.sgc.gc.ca/EPub/Corr/e200202/e200202.htm [accessed 4 January 2005].

Council of Europe Committee of Ministers (1999) *Mediation in Penal Matters Recommendation No. R(99)19*, Strasbourg, France: Council of Europe, online. Available at: http://www.victimology.nl/onlpub/other/R(99)19-e.pdf [accessed 4 January 2005]

Crnkovich, M. (1995) 'The role of the victim in the criminal justice system: circle sentencing in Inuit communities,' paper presented to the Canadian Institute for the Administration of Justice Conference, Banff, Alberta, October, online. Available at: http://www.casac.ca/issues/mary_crnkovich.htm [accessed 24 January 2005].

Czarnecka-Dzialuk, B. and Wojcik, D. (2000) 'Victim–offender mediation in Poland,' in European Forum for Victim Offender Mediation and Restorative Justice (ed.) *Victim–Offender Mediation in Europe: making restorative justice work*, Leuven: Leuven University Press.

Daly, K. (1998) 'Restorative justice: moving past the caricatures,' draft paper for Seminar on Restorative Justice, Institute of Criminology, University of Sydney Law School, online. Available at: http://www.gu.edu.au/school/ccj/kdaly_docs/kdpaper2.pdf [accessed 4 January 2005].

— (2000) 'Ideals meet reality: research results on youth justice conferences in South Australia,' paper presented to the Fourth International Conference on Restorative Justice for Juveniles, Tuebingen, Germany, October.

— (2001) 'Conferencing in Australia and New Zealand: variations, research findings, and prospects,' in A. Morris and G. Maxwell (eds) *Restorative Justice for Juveniles*, Portland, OR: Hart Publishing.

— (2002) 'Restorative justice: the real story,' *Punishment and Society*, 4: 55–79.

Davis, A. (1986) *Community Mediation in Massachusetts: a decade of development: 1975–1985*, Salem, MA: Administrative Office of the District Court, online. Available at: http://www.mediate.com/nafcm/docs/Fundingand Affiliation4.1.doc [accessed 4 January 2005].

Davis, R. (1982) 'Mediation: the Brooklyn experiment,' in R. Tomasic and M. Feeley (eds) *Neighborhood Justice: assessment of an emerging idea*. New York, NY: Longman.

de Jong, W. (2001) 'Neighborhood-centered conflict mediation in the Netherlands: an instrument for social cohesion – Part II,' *Contemporary Justice Review*, 4(1): 49–58.

Delgado, R. (2000) 'Goodbye to Hammurabi: analyzing the atavistic appeal of restorative justice,' *Stanford Law Review*, 52(4): 751–75.

Dickson-Gilmore, E. (1992) 'Finding the ways of the ancestors: cultural change and the invention of tradition in the development of separate legal systems,' *Canadian Journal of Criminology*, 34(3–4): 479–502.

Dignan, J. and Marsh, P. (2001) 'Restorative justice and family group conferences in England: current state and future prospects,' in A. Morris and G. Maxwell (eds) *Restorative Justice for Juveniles*, Portland, OR: Hart Publishing.

Doolan, M. (1991) 'Youth justice reform in New Zealand,' in J. Vernon and S. McKillop (eds) *Preventing Juvenile Crime*, AIC Conference Proceedings No. 9, Canberra: Australian Institute of Criminology, online. Available at: http://www.aic.gov.au/ publications/proceedings/09/doolan.pdf [accessed 4 January 2005].

— (1999) 'The family group conference – 10 years on,' paper presented at the Building Strong Partnerships for Restorative Practices conference, Burlington, August, online. Available at: http://www.iirp.org/library/vt/vt_doolan.html [accessed 21 January 2005].

— (2004) 'The family group conference: a mainstream approach in child welfare decision-making,' Family Group Decision Making, New Zealand, online. Available at: http://www.americanhumane.org/site/DocServer/fgdm_fgc0604.pdf?docID=1961 [accessed 4 January 2005].

Eglash, A. (1958) 'Creative restitution: a broader meaning for an old term,' *Journal of Criminal Law, Criminology and Police Science*, 48: 619–22. Reprinted in J. Hudson and B. Galaway (eds) (1975) *Considering the Victim: readings in restitution and victim compensation*, Springfield, IL: Charles C. Thomas.

Evarts, W. (1990) 'Compensation through mediation: a conceptual framework,' in B. Galaway and J. Hudson (eds) *Criminal Justice, Restitution and Reconciliation*, Monsey, NY: Criminal Justice Press.

Falck, S. (1992) 'The Norwegian community mediation centers at a crossroads,' in H. Messmer and H.-U. Otto (eds) *Restorative Justice on Trial: pitfalls and potentials of victim–offender mediation: international research perspectives*, Netherlands: Kluwer.

Filner, J., Ostermeyer, M. and Bethel, C. (1995) *Compendium of State Court Resource Materials*, Washington, DC: National Institute for Dispute Resolution.

Fliamer, M. and Maksudov, R. (2001) *Three and a Half Years of Restorative Justice in Russia*, Centre for Legal and Judicial Reform, online. Available at: http://www.sprc.ru/3hyears.html [accessed 4 January 2005].

Fogel, D., Galaway, B. and Hudson, J. (1972) 'Restitution in criminal justice: a Minnesota experiment,' *Criminal Law Bulletin*, 8(8): 681–91.

Galaway, B. (1977) 'Restitution as an integrative punishment,' in R. Barnett and J. Hagel (eds) *Assessing the Criminal: restitution, retribution and the legal process*, Cambridge, MA: Ballinger.

— (1992) 'The New Zealand experience implementing the reparation sentence,' in H. Messmer and H.-U. Otto (eds) *Restorative Justice on Trial: pitfalls and potentials of victim–offender mediation: international research perspectives*, Netherlands: Kluwer.

— (1995) 'Victim–offender mediation by New Zealand probation officers: the possibilities and the reality,' *Mediation Quarterly*, 12(3): 249–62.

Gehm, J. and Umbreit, M. (1985) *National VORP Directory*, Valparaiso, IN: National VORP Resource Center.

Goldstein, H. (1990) *Problem-Oriented Policing*, Philadelphia, PA: Temple University Press.

Graber, L., Keys, T. and White, J. (1996) 'Family group decision-making in the United States: the case of Oregon,' in J. Hudson, A. Morris, G. Maxwell, and B. Galaway (eds) *Family Group Conferences: perspectives on policy and practice*, Monsey, NY: Criminal Justice Press.

Grably, S. (2003) 'Restorative justice: victim offender mediation and circles in the youth probation service Southern and Jerusalem Districts of Israel,' paper presented at the Sixth International Conference on Restorative Justice, Vancouver, BC, June, online. Available at: http://www.sfu.ca/cfrj/fulltext/grabli.pdf [accessed 4 January 2005].

Graham, I. (1993) 'Juvenile justice in New South Wales,' in L. Atkinson and S.-A. Gerull (eds) *New Directions*, AIC Conference Proceedings No. 22, Canberra: Australian Institute of Criminology, pp. 149–66, online. Available at: http://www.aic.gov.au/publications/proceedings/22/graham.pdf [accessed 21 January 2005].

Griffiths, C. and Hamilton, R. (1996) 'Sanctioning and healing: restorative justice in Canadian aboriginal communities,' in B. Galaway and J. Hudson (eds) *Restorative Justice: international perspectives*, Monsey, NY: Criminal Justice Press.

Gross, E. K. (1999) *An Evaluation/Assessment of Navajo Peacemaking*, Flagstaff, AZ: Northern Arizona University.

Gunderson, K., Cahn, D. and Wirth, J. (2003) 'The Washington State long-term outcome study,' *Protecting Children*, 18 (1 and 2): 42–7.

Gustafson, D. (2004) 'Is restorative justice taking too few or too many risks?' in H. Zehr and B. Toews (eds) *Critical Issues in Restorative Justice*, Monsey, NY: Criminal Justice Press.

Gustafson, D. and Smidstra, H. (1989) *Victim Offender Reconciliation in Serious Crime: a report on the feasibility study undertaken for the Ministry of the Solicitor General*, Ottawa: Solicitor General of Canada.

Hardin, M. (1996) *Family Group Conferences in Child Abuse and Neglect Cases: learning from the experience of New Zealand*, Washington, DC: ABA Center on Children and the Law.

Hassall, I. (1996) 'Origin and development of family group conferences,' in J. Hudson, A. Morris, G. Maxwell, and B. Galaway (eds) *Family Group Conferences: perspectives on policy and practice*, Monsey, NY: Criminal Justice Press.

Hayner, P. (1994) 'Fifteen truth commissions – 1974 to 1994: a comparative study,' *Human Rights Quarterly*, 16(4): 597–655.

Henskens-Rejiman, J. and van Pagee, R. (2003) 'Restorative practices in a Dutch school,' paper presented at the Fourth International Conference on Conferencing, Circles and Other Restorative Practices, Veldhoven, Netherlands, August, online. Available at: http://www.iirp.org/library/nl03/nl03_henskens vanpagee.html [accessed 21 January 2005].

Home Office (2003) *Restorative Justice: the government's strategy*, London: HMSO, online. Available at: http://www.homeoffice.gov.uk/documents/rj_bestpractice.pdf?version=1 [accessed 21 January 2005].

— (2004) *Best Practice Guidance for Restorative Practitioners and their Case Supervisors and Line Managers*, London: HMSO, online. Available at: http://www.homeoffice.gov.uk/documents/rj_bestpractice.pdf?version=1 [accessed 24 January 2005].

Hoyle, C., Young, R. and Hill, R. (2002) *Proceed with Caution: an evaluation of the Thames Valley Police initiative in restorative cautioning*, York, UK: Joseph Rowntree Foundation.

Huculak, B. (1997) 'From the power to punish to the power to heal "restorative justice" the last hope,' *The ICCA Journal*, 3 (August): 34–5.

— (2003) 'Restorative justice and the Youth Criminal Justice Act,' *Justice as Healing*, 8(1): 4–6. A newsletter on Aboriginal concepts of justice, online. Available at: http://www.usask.ca/nativelaw/publications/jah/JAHvol8-no1.pdf [accessed 24 January 2005].

Hudson, J. and Galaway, B. (1974) 'Undoing the wrong,' *Social Work*, 19(3): 313–18.

Hyndman, M., Moore, D. and Thorsborne, M. (1995). 'Family and community conferences in schools,' in R. Homel (ed.) *Preventive Criminology*, Brisbane: Griffith University.

Iivari, J. (1992) 'The process of mediation in Finland: a special reference to the question "How to get cases for mediation?"' in H. Messmer and H.-U. Otto (eds) *Restorative Justice on Trial: pitfalls and potentials of victim–offender mediation: international research perspectives*, Netherlands: Kluwer.

Iivari, J. (2000) 'Victim–Offender mediation in Finland.' In the European Forum for Victim–Offender Mediation and Restorative Justice (ed.) *Victim–offender mediation in Europe: making restorative justice work*, 193–210. Belgium: Leuven University Press.

Institute for Mediation and Conflict Resolution (IMCR) (2004) website, November 2004. Available at: www.mediate.com/imcr/pg1.cfm [accessed 4 January 2005].

International Conference on Restorative Justice. (1997) 'The Leuven declaration on the advisability of promoting the restorative approach to juvenile crime,' in L. Walgrave (ed.) *Restorative Justice for Juveniles: potentialities, risks and problems*, Leuven, Belgium: Leuven University Press, online. Available at: http://www.sonoma.edu/cja/info/leuven.html [accessed 21 January 2005].

Jantzi, V. (2001) *Restorative Justice in New Zealand: current practice, future possibilities*, Auckland, New Zealand: Massey University, School of Social and Cultural Studies, Centre for Justice and Peace Development, online. Available at: http://www.massey.ac.nz/~wtie/Work/vern.htm [accessed 4 January 2005].

Kerner, H. J., Marks, E. and Schreckling, J. (1992) 'Implementation and acceptance of victim–offender mediation programs in the Federal Republic of Germany: a survey of criminal justice institutions,' in H. Messmer and H.-U. Otto (eds) *Restorative Justice on Trial: pitfalls and potentials of victim–offender mediation: international research perspectives*, Netherlands: Kluwer.

Keys, T. and Rockhill, A. (2000) 'Family group decision-making in Oregon,' in G. Burford and J. Hudson (eds) *Family Group Conferencing: new directions in community-centered child and family practice*, New York: Aldine de Gruyter.

Kittayarak, K. (2004) 'Restorative justice: the Thai experience,' paper presented to the Fifth International Conference on Conferencing, Circles and Other Restorative Practices, Vancouver, British Columbia, August, online. Available at: http://fp.enter.net/restorativepractices/bc04_kittayarak.pdf [accessed 12 January 2005].

Korn, R. (1971) 'Of crime, criminal justice and corrections,' *University of San Francisco Law Review*, 6(1): 27–75.

La Prairie, C. (1995) 'Altering course: new directions in criminal justice – sentencing circles and family group conferences,' *Australian and New Zealand Journal of Criminology* special supplementary issue, 'Crime, criminology and public policy': 78–99.

La Prairie, C. and Diamond, E. (1992) 'Aboriginal criminal justice in Canada,' *Canadian Journal of Criminology*, 34(3-4): 281–521.

Laster, R. (1970) 'Criminal restitution: a survey of its past history and an analysis of its present usefulness,' *University of Richmond Law Review*, 5(1): 71–98.

Leebaw, B. (2001) 'Restorative justice for political transitions: lessons from the South African Truth and Reconciliation Commission,' *Contemporary Justice Review*, 4(3–4): 267–89.

Lewis, D. (1998) 'Native Americans: the original westerners,' in R. Hurt (ed.) *The Rural West since World War II*, Lawrence, KS: University Press of Kansas.

Liebmann, M. (2000) 'History and overview of mediation in the UK,' in M. Liebmann (ed.) *Mediation in Context*, London: Jessica Kingsley, pp. 19–38.

Litchfield, M., Gatowski, S. and Dobbin, S. (2003) 'Improving outcomes for families: results from an evaluation of Miami's family decision making program,' *Protecting Children*, 18(1 and 2): 48–51.

McCold, P. (1998) 'Restorative justice handbook,' *Corrections Compendium*, 23(12): 1–4, 20–8.

— (1999, August) 'Restorative justice practice: the state of the field 1999,' paper presented to the Building Strong Partnerships for Restorative Practices Conference, Burlington, VT, online. Available at: http://www.iirp.org/library/vt/vt_mccold.html [accessed 21 January 2005].

— (2000) 'Toward a mid-range theory of restorative criminal justice: a reply to the maximalist model,' *Contemporary Justice Review*, 3(4): 357–414.

— (2001) 'Primary restorative justice practices,' in A. Morris and G. Maxwell (eds) *Restorative Justice for Juveniles*, Portland, OR: Hart Publishing.

— (2003) 'A survey of assessment research on mediation and conferencing,' in L. Walgrave (ed.) *Repositioning Restorative Justice*, Cullompton, Devon, UK: Willan Publishing.

— (2004) 'Paradigm muddle: the threat to restorative justice posed by the merger with community justice,' *Contemporary Justice Review*, 7(1): 13–35.

McCold, P. and Wachtel, B. (1998) *Restorative Policing Experiment: the Bethlehem Pennsylvania police family group conferencing project*, Washington: National Institute of Justice GPO.

McCold, P. and Wachtel, T. (2002) 'Restorative justice theory validation,' in E. Weitekamp and H.-J. Kerner (eds) *Restorative Justice: theoretical foundations*, Cullompton, Devon, UK: Willan Publishing, pp. 110–42.

McDonald, J. and Moore, D. (1999) 'Community conferencing as a special case of conflict transformation,' in H. Strang and J. Braithwaite (eds) *Restorative Justice and Society*, Cambridge: Cambridge University Press.

McGarrell, E., Olivares, K., Crawford, K. and Kroovand, N. (2000) *Returning Justice to the Community: the Indianapolis juvenile restorative justice experiment*, Indianapolis: Hudson Institute, online. Available at: http://www.hudson.org/files/publications/ Restoring_Justice_Report.pdf [accessed 4 January 2005].

McGillis, D. (1997) 'An overview of developments in the community mediation field,' in *Issues and Practices: community mediation programs: developments and Challenges*, Washington: National Institute of Justice GPO, pp 1–23, online. Available at: http://www.mediate.com/nafcm/docs/National%20Institute %20of%20Justice[1]. %20chapter%201.doc [accessed 4 January 2005].

McKinney, B., Kimsey, W. and Fuller, R. (1996) 'A nationwide survey of mediation centers,' *Mediation Quarterly*, 14(2): 155–66, online. Available at: http://www.mediate.com/nafcm/docs/A%20Nationwide%20Survey%20of %20 Mediation%20Centers.doc [accessed 4 January 2005].

Ma Mawi Nita Wi Iwewin Project. (1987) *Proposal for an Integrated Aboriginal Family Domestic Violence Program*, Winnipeg, Canada: Ma Mawi Wi Chi Itata Centre.

Magnus, R., Hui Min, L., Mesenas, M. L. and Thean, V. (eds) (2003) *Rebuilding Lives, Restoring Relationships: juvenile justice and the community*, London: Eastern Universities Press.

Marsh, P. and Crow, G. (1998) *Family Group Conferences in Child Welfare*, Oxford: Blackwell Sciences.

Marshall, T. (1991) 'Victim offender mediation,' *Home Office Research Bulletin*, 30: 9–15.

— (1992) 'Restorative justice on trial in Britain,' in H. Messmer and H.-U. Otto (eds) *Restorative Justice on Trial: pitfalls and potentials of victim–offender mediation: international research perspectives*, Netherlands: Kluwer.

— (1996) 'The evolution of restorative justice in Britain,' *European Journal on Criminal Policy and Research*, 4(4): 21–43.

— (1999) *Restorative Justice: an overview*, London: Home Office. Research Development and Statistics Directorate, online. Available at: http://www.homeoffice.gov.uk/rds/pdfs/occ-resjus.pdf [accessed 4 January 2005].

Maxwell, G. (1996) *Restorative Justice: a Maori perspective*, Wellington: The New Zealand Maori Council, Ministry of Justice.

Maxwell, G. and Morris, A. (1993) *Family, Victims and Culture: youth justice in New Zealand*, Wellington: Victoria University.

Meyer, J. F. (1998) 'History repeats itself: restorative justice in Native American communities,' *Journal of Contemporary Criminal Justice*, 14(1): 42–57.

Miers, D. (2001) *International Review of Restorative Justice*, London: Home Office Research, Development and Statistics Directorate, London, online. Available at: http://www.homeoffice.gov.uk/rds/prgpdfs/crrs10.pdf [accessed 4 January 2005].

Miers, D. and Willemsens, J. (2004) *Mapping Restorative Justice: developments in 25 European countries*, Leuven, Belgium: European Forum on Victim Offender Mediation and Restorative Justice.

Mirsky, L. (2003) 'The Wet'suwet'en unlocking aboriginal justice program. Restorative practices in British Columbia, Canada,' *Restorative Practices e-Forum*, International Institute of Restorative Practices, 21 October, online. Available at: http://fp.enter.net/restorativepractices/wuaj.pdf [accessed 4 January 2005].

— (2004a) 'A new reality for troubled youth in Hungary: an update,' *Restorative Practices e-Forum*, International Institute of Restorative Practices, 31 January, online. Available at: http://fp.enter.net/restorativepractices/csfhungary.pdf [accessed 4 January 2005].

— (2004b) 'Restorative justice practices of Native American, First Nation and other indigenous people of North America: Part I,' *Restorative Practices e-Forum*, International Institute of Restorative Practices, 27 April, online. Available at: http://fp.enter.net/restorativepractices/natjust1.pdf [accessed 4 January 2005].

— (2004c) 'Restorative justice practices of Native American, First Nation and other indigenous people of North America: Part II,' *Restorative Practices e-Forum*, International

Institute of Restorative Practices, 27 April, online. Available at: http://fp.enter.net/restorativepractices/natjust2.pdf [accessed 4 January 2005].

Moore, D. (1993) 'Shame, forgiveness, and juvenile justice,' *Criminal Justice Ethics*, 12(1): 3–25.

— (1995) *A New Approach to Juvenile Justice: an evaluation of family conferencing in Wagga Wagga. A Report to the Criminology Research Council*, Wagga Wagga, NSW: Centre for Rural Social Research, Charles Sturt University-Riverina, online. Available at: http://www.aic.gov.au/crc/reports/moore/ [accessed 4 January 2005].

— (1996) 'Criminal action – official reaction: affect theory, criminology, and criminal justice,' in D. Nathanson (ed.) *Knowing Feeling*, New York: W.W. Norton.

— (1997) 'Pride, shame and empathy in peer relations: new theory and practice in education and juvenile justice,' in K. Rigby, K. Slee and P. Slee (eds) *Children's Peer Relations*, London: Routledge.

— (2004) 'Managing social conflict: the evolution of a practical theory,' *Journal of Sociology and Social Welfare*, 31(1): 71–91.

Moore, D. and McDonald, J. (1995) 'Achieving the "good community": a local police initiative and its wider ramifications,' in K. Hazlehurst (ed.) *Perceptions of Justice. Issues in indigenous and community empowerment*, Brookfield, VT: Ashgate.

Moore, D. and O'Connell, T. (1994) 'Family conferencing in Wagga Wagga: a communitarian model of justice,' in C. Alder and J. Wundersitz (eds) *Family Conferencing and Juvenile Justice: the way forward or misplaced optimism?* Canberra: Australian Institute of Criminology, pp. 45–86.

Nathanson, D. (ed.) (1996) *Knowing Feeling*, New York: W. W. Norton

National Association for Community Mediation (2004) *Mediation Center Directory and Links*, online. Available at: http://www.nafcm.org/pg35.cfm [accessed 12 January 2005].

Native Counseling Services of Alberta (2001) *A Cost–Benefit Analysis of Hollow Water's Community Holistic Circle Healing Process*, Ottawa: Solicitor General of Canada, Aboriginal Corrections Policy Unit, online. Available at: http://www.sgc.gc.ca/publications/abor_corrections/apc2001_e.pdf [accessed 4 January 2005].

Negrea, V. (2002) 'Dreaming of a new reality for troubled youth in Hungary,' paper presented at the Third International Conference on Conferencing, Circles and Other Restorative Practices, Minneapolis, Minnesota, August, online. Available at: http://www.iirp.org/library/mn02/mn02_negrea.html [accessed 4 January 2005].

New York State Unified Court System (2003) *Dispute Resolution Centers Program. Annual report for the fiscal year 2002–2003*, Albany, NY: Office of Alternative Dispute Resolution, Division of Court Operations, New York State Unified Court System, online. Available at: http://www.nycourts.gov/ip/adr/publications.shtml [accessed 4 January 2005].

Nicholl, C. (1998) *Implementing Restorative Justice: a toolbox for the implementation of restorative justice and the advancement of community policing*, Washington, DC: Office of Community Oriented Policing Services, US Department of Justice, online. Available at: http://www.cops.usdoj.gov/default.asp?Open=-True&Ite m=578 [accessed 21 January 2005].

North Carolina Department of Health and Human Services (2004) *Chapter IV: 1201 Child Placement Services*, DHHS On-line Publications. Available at: http://info.dhhs.state.nc.us/olm/manuals/dss/csm-10/man/CSs120 1cYP-03.htm#P226_25315 [accessed 4 January 2005].

Northey, W. (1989) 'Biblical/theological works contributing to restorative justice: a bibliographic essay,' *New Perspectives on Crime and Justice* (Issue 8), Akron, PA: Mennonite Central Committee Office of Criminal Justice.

O'Connell, T. (1996) 'Community accountability conferences,' paper presented at ACPO Summer Conference in Manchester, England, July.

— (1998) 'From Wagga Wagga to Minnesota,' in *Conferencing: a new response to wrongdoing*, Proceedings of the First North American Conference on Conferencing, Bethlehem, PA: Real Justice, online. Available at: http://www.iirp.org/library/nacc/nacc_oco.html [accessed 21 January 2005].

O'Connell, T. and McCold, P. (2004). 'Beyond the journey, not much else matters: avoiding the expert model with explicit restorative practice,' paper presented at Massey University International Conference on Restorative Justice: Albany, Auckland, New Zealand, December.

O'Connell, T., Wachtel, B. and Wachtel, T. (1999) *Conferencing Handbook: the new real justice training manual*, Pipersville, PA: Piper's Press.

Olsen, T., Maxwell, G. and Morris, A. (1995) 'Maori and youth justice in New Zealand,' in

K. Hazlehurst (ed.) *Popular Justice and Community Regeneration*, London: Praeger.

Paus, K. (2000) 'Victim–offender mediation in Norway,' in European Forum for Victim Offender Mediation and Restorative Justice (ed.) *Victim–Offender Mediation in Europe: making restorative justice work*, Leuven, Belgium: Leuven University Press.

Peachey, D. (1989) 'The Kitchener experiment,' in M. Wright, and B. Galaway (eds) *Mediation and Criminal Justice; victims, offenders and community*, London: Sage.

Peachey, D., Snyder, B. and Teichroeb, A. (1983) *Mediation Primer: a training guide for mediators in the criminal justice system*, Kitchener, Canada: Community Justice Initiatives of Waterloo Region.

Pelikan, C. (2000) 'Victim–offender mediation in Austria,' in European Forum for Victim Offender Mediation and Restorative Justice (ed.) *Victim–Offender Mediation in Europe: making restorative justice work*, Leuven, Belgium: Leuven University Press.

Pennell, J. (2003) 'North Carolina family group conferencing project: research summary,' *Protecting Children*, 18(1 and 2): 70–3.

Pennell, J. and Burford, G. (1994) 'Widening the circle: family group decision making,' *Journal of Child and Youth Care*, 9(1): 1–11.

— (1995) 'Family group decision making: new roles for "old" partners in resolving family violence,' *Implementation Report (Vol. 1)*, Family Group Decision Making Project, School of Social Work, St John's, Newfoundland: Memorial University of Newfoundland, online. Available at: http://social.chass.ncsu.edu/jpennell/fgdm/ImpReport/index.htm [accessed 21 January 2005].

— (1996) 'Attending to context: family group decision making in Canada,' in J. Hudson, A. Morris, G. Maxwell and B. Galaway (eds) *Family Group Conferences: perspectives on policy and practice*, Monsey, NY: Criminal Justice Press.

Perry, L., Lajeunesse, T. and Woods, A. (1987) *Mediation Services: an evaluation*, Manitoba, Canada: Manitoba Attorney General.

Plett, I. (1999) *Restorative Justice in Urban Aboriginal Communities*, Alberta, Canada: Canadian Forum on Civil Justice.

Pollard, C. (1999) 'Scenarios for the future,' in *Community Safety, Citizenship and Social Inclusion*, Chilton, Buckinghamshire, UK: Thames Valley Partnership, online. Available at: http://www.thamesvalleypartnership.org.uk/visionjuly99.pdf [accessed 19 January 2005].

Pranis, K. (1997) 'Restoring community: the process of circle sentencing,' paper presented

at Justice Without Violence: Views from Peacemaking Criminology and Restorative Justice, Albany, New York, June.

Pratt, J. (1996) 'Colonization, power and silence: a history of indigenous justice in New Zealand society,' in B. Galaway and J. Hudson (eds) *Restorative Justice: international perspectives*, Monsey, NY: Criminal Justice Press.

Prison Fellowship International (2005) '2004 in review', *Restorative Justice online*, PFI Centre for Justice and Reconciliation, January, online. Available at: http://www.restorativejustice.org [accessed 18 January 2005].

Quinnett, E. (2002) 'The family unity meeting program in the county of San Diego child protection setting,' paper presented at the Third International Conference on Conferencing, Circles and other Restorative Practices, Minneapolis, Minnesota, August, online. Available at: http://iirp.org/library/mn02/mn02_quinnett.html [accessed 4 January 2005].

Ray, L. (1982) 'Alternative dispute resolution movement,' *Peace and Change*, 8(2/3): 117–28.

— (1983) *Dispute Resolution Program Directory 1983*, Washington, DC: ABA Special Committee on Dispute Resolution.

Retzinger, S. and Scheff, T. (1996) 'Strategy for community conferences: emotions and social bonds,' in B. Galaway and J. Hudson (eds) *Restorative Justice: international perspectives*, Monsey, NY: Criminal Justice Press.

Richards, K. (2004) 'Exploring the history of the restorative justice movement,' paper presented at the Fifth International Conference on Conferencing and Circles, Vancouver, Canada, August, online. Available at: http://fp.enter.net/restorativepractices/bc04_richards.pdf [accessed 4 January 2005].

Ross, R. (1994) 'Dueling paradigms? Western criminal justice versus aboriginal community healing,' in R. Gosse, J. Henderson and R. Carter (eds) *Continuing Poundmaker and Riel's Quest*, Saskatoon, Canada: Purich.

— (1996) *Returning to the Teachings: exploring aboriginal justice*, Toronto: Penguin Books.

Roujanavong, W. and Utensute, T. (2004) 'Family and community group conferencing in Thailand,' paper presented to the Fifth International Conference on Conferencing, Circles and other Restorative Practices, Vancouver, British Columbia, August.

Ruth-Heffelbower, D. (1996) 'Toward a Christian theology of church and society as it relates to restorative justice,' presentation to Fourth Annual Restorative Justice Conference, Fresno, CA, October.

Shapland, J., Dignan, J., Robinson, G., Atkinson, A., College, E., Howes, M., Johnstone, J., Pennant, R. and Sorsby, A. (2004) *Implementing Restorative Justice Schemes (Crime Reduction Programme): a report on the first year*, London: Home Office, online. Available at: http://www.homeoffice.gov.uk/rds/pdfs04/rdsolr3204.pdf [accessed 4 January 2005].

Sharpe, S. (2003) *Beyond the Comfort Zone: a guide to the practice of community conferencing*, Calgary: Calgary Community Conferences.

Sherman, L., Barnes, G., Strang, H., Woods, D., Inkpen, N., Newbury-Birch, D., Bennett, S. and Angel, C. (2004) 'Restorative justice: what we know and how we know it. Working Paper No. 1,' Jerry Lee Program on Randomized Controlled Trials in Restorative Justice. University of Pennsylvania and Centre for Restorative Justice Australian National University, online. Available at: http://www.sas.upenn.edu/jerrylee/rjWorkingPaper1.pdf [accessed 4 January 2005].

Sivell-Ferri, C. (1997) 'The Ojibwa circle: tradition and change,' in Ministry of the Solicitor General of Canada (ed.), *The Four Circles of Hollow Water*, Aboriginal Peoples' Collection, Cat. No. JS5-1/15-1997E. Ottawa, Canada: Public Works and Government Services, online. Available at: http://www.sgc.gc.ca/epub/abocor/e199703/e199703.htm [accessed 4 January 2005].

Skelton, A. and Frank, C. (2001) 'Conferencing in South Africa: returning to our future,' in A. Morris and G. Maxwell (eds) *Restorative Justice for Juveniles*, Portland, OR: Hart Publishing.

Spak, S. (2001) *Pilot Project for FGC for Child Protection in Israel*, Denver, CO: National Center on Family Group Decision Making.

Stuart, B. (1996) 'Circle sentencing: turning swords into ploughshares,' in B. Galaway and J. Hudson (eds) *Restorative Justice: international perspectives*, Monsey, NY: Criminal Justice Press.

Stutzman-Amstutz, L. (1996) 'From the board,' *VOMA Quarterly Conference Review* (Fall/Winter), online. Available at: http://voma.org/docs/vomaq96.html [accessed 4 January 2005].

Sundell, K. and Vinnerljung, B. (2004) 'Outcomes of family group conferencing in Sweden: a 3-year follow-up,' *Child Abuse and Neglect*, 28: 267–87.

Sylvester, D. (2003) 'Myth in restorative justice history,' *Utah Law Review*, 2003(1): 471–522, online. Available at: http://www.law.utah.edu/pdf/law_review_symposia/restorative_justice/16Sylvester.pdf [accessed 4 January 2005].

Taraschi, S. (1998) 'Peacemaking criminology and aboriginal justice initiatives as a revitalization of justice,' *Contemporary Justice Review*, 1(1): 103–21.

Thomas, K, Cohen, E. and Duerr Berrick, J. (2003) 'California's waiver evaluation of FGDM: a unique opportunity,' *Protecting Children*, 18(1 and 2): 52–6.

Titcomb, A. and LeCroy, C. (2003) 'Evaluation of Arizona's family group decision making program,' *Protecting Children*, 18(1 and 2): 58–64.

Trenczek, T. (1990) 'A review and assessment of victim–offender reconciliation programming in West Germany,' in B. Galaway and J. Hudson (eds) *Criminal Justice, Restitution, and Reconciliation*, Monsey, NY: Criminal Justice Press.

Umbreit, M. (1978) *Community Based Corrections in Indiana: a humanistic perspective*, Michigan City, IN: PACT Institute of Justice.

— (1994) *Victim Meets Offender: the impact of restorative justice and mediation*, Monsey, New York: Willow Tree Press.

— (1996) 'A humanistic mediation model: moving to a higher plane,' *VOMA Quarterly*, 7(3), (Fall/Winter), online. Available at: http://voma.org/docs/vomaq96.html#Humanistic

— (1997) 'Humanistic mediation: a transformative journey of peace-making,' *Mediation Quarterly*, 14(3): 201–13.

Umbreit, M. and Burns, H. (2002) *Humanistic Mediation: Peacemaking Grounded in Core Social Work Values*. St Paul, MN: Center for Restorative Justice and Peacemaking, School of Social Work, University of Minnesota. Available at http://2ssw.che.umn.edu/rjp/Resources/Documents/Final%20HumMed.pdf

Umbreit, M. and Fercello, C. (1997) *Woodbury Police Department's Restorative Justice Community Conferencing Program: an initial assessment of client satisfaction*, St Paul, MN: Center for Restorative Justice and Mediation, University of Minnesota.

United Nations, Economic and Social Council (2002) *Restorative Justice: report of the Secretary-General* (E/CN 15/2002/5/Add.1), Vienna, Austria: United Nations, online. Available at: http://www.unodc.org/pdf/crime/commissions/11comm/5e.pdf [accessed 4 January 2005].

— (2004) *Preparations for the Eleventh United Nations Congress on Crime Prevention and Criminal Justice – Report of the Secretary-General*, Vienna, Austria: United Nations, online. Available at: http://daccess-ods.un.org/access.nsf/Get?OpenAgentandDS=E/2004/90andLang=E [accessed 4 January 2005].

— (2005) *The Eleventh United Nations Congress on Crime Prevention and Criminal Justice – Background Paper for the Workshop on Enhancing Criminal Justice Reform including Restorative Justice*, Vienna, Austria: United Nations.

United States Institute for Peace. (2004) *Truth Commissions*, online. Available at: http://www.usip.org/library/truth.html [accessed 4 January 2005].

Vanfraechem, I. (2003) 'Conferencing for serious juvenile crimes,' paper presented at the Fourth International Conference on Conferencing, Circles and Other Restorative Practices, Veldhoven, Netherlands, August, online. Available at: http://fp.enter.net/restorative practices/ConfForSeriousJuvCrimes.pdf [accessed 21 January 2005].

Van Ness, D. (2002) *UN Economic and Social Council Endorses Basic Principles on Restorative Justice*, Washington, DC: Prison Fellowship International, online. Available at: http://www.restorativejustice.org/rj3/Feature/August02/ECOSOC%20Acts.htm [accessed 4 January 2005].

— (2003) 'Proposed basic principles on the use of restorative justice: recognising the aims and limits of restorative justice,' in A. Von Hirsch, J. Roberts, A. Bottoms, K. Roach and M. Schiff (eds) *Restorative Justice and Criminal Justice: competing or reconcilable paradigms?* Oxford: Hart Publishing.

Van Ness, D. and Heetderkstrong, K. (1997) *Restoring Justice*, Cincinnati, OH: Anderson Publishing.

— (2000) *Restoring Justice*, 2nd edition, Cincinnati, OH: Anderson Publishing.

van Pagee, R. (2002) 'Youth justice and child protection conferences in the Netherlands,' paper presented at the Third International Conference on Conferencing, Circles and Other Restorative Practices, Minneapolis, Minnesota, August.

— (2004) 'Family group conferencing as a first choice: empowerment versus intervention,' paper presented at the Fifth International Conference on Conferencing, Circles and Other Restorative Practices, August, Vancouver, BC, Canada, online. Available at: http://fp.enter.net/restorativepractices/bc04_vanpagee.pdf [accessed 21 January 2005].

Victim Offender Mediation Association (2004) *Learn about VOMA: history and development*, VOMA website. Available at: www.voma.org/abtvoma.shtml

Victim Offender Reconciliation Resource Center (1984) *The VORP Book: an organizational and operation manual*, Valparaiso, IN: PACT Institute of Justice.

Wachtel, T. (1998) *Real Justice*, Pipersville, PA: Piper's Press.

Wachtel, T. and McCold, P. (2000) 'Restorative justice in everyday life,' in J. Braithwaite and H. Strang (eds) *Restorative Justice in Civil Society*, New York: Cambridge University Press.

Warner, S. (1992) 'Reparation, mediation and Scottish criminal justice,' in H. Messmer and H.-U. Otto (eds) *Restorative Justice on Trial: pitfalls and potentials of victim–offender mediation: international research perspectives*, Netherlands: Kluwer.

Warner-Roberts, A. and Masters, G. (1999) *Group Conferencing: restorative justice in practice*, Minneapolis: University of Minnesota, Center for RJ and Mediation, School of Social Work, online. Available at: http://2ssw.che.umn.edu/rjp/Resources/Documents/B%20Ro b&Mas98a%20-Part%201.PDF [accessed 21 January 2005].

Weitekamp, E. (1999) 'The history of restorative justice,' in G. Bazemore and L. Walgrave (eds) *Restorative Juvenile Justice: repairing the harm of youth crime*, Monsey, NY: Criminal Justice Press.

Wheeler, C. and Johnson, S. (2003) 'Evaluating family group decision-making: the Santa Clara example,' *Protecting Children*, 18(1 and 2): 65–9.

Wing-Cheong, C. (2003) 'Victim–offender mediation, making amends and restorative justice in Singapore,' in T. Ota (ed.) *Victims and Criminal Justice: Asian perspective*, Tokyo: Hogaku-Kenkyu-Kai, Keio University.

Wong, D. (2002) 'Developing restorative justice for juvenile delinquents in Hong Kong,' paper presented at the Third International Conference on Conferencing, Circles and Other Restorative Practices, Minneapolis, Minnesota, August, online. Available at: http://www.iirp.org/library/mn02/mn02_wong.html [accessed 4 January 2005].

Wright, M. (1996) *Justice for Victims and Offenders: a restorative response to crime*, second edn, Winchester, UK: Waterside Press.

Wundersitz, J. and Hetzel, S. (1996) 'Family conferencing for young offenders: the South Australian experience,' in J. Hudson, A. Morris, G. Maxwell, and B. Galaway (eds) *Family Group Conferences: perspectives on policy and practice*, Monsey, NY: Criminal Justice Press.

Yazzie, R. (1994) 'Life comes from it: Navajo justice concepts,' *New Mexico Law Review*, 24:

175–90, online. Available at: http://www.context.org/ICLIB/IC38/Yazzie.htm [accessed 21 January 2005].

— (1998a) 'Navajo peacemaking: implications for adjudication-based systems of justice,' *Contemporary Justice Review*, 1(1): 123–31.

— (1998b) 'The healing and community justice policy of the judicial branch of the Navajo Nation,' remarks of the Honorable Robert Yazzie, Chief Justice of the Navajo Nation, presented at Northern Arizona University in Flagstaff, Arizona, online. Available at: http://spa.american.edu/justice/publications/navajosp.htm [accessed 21 January 2005].

— (2000) 'Navajo justice,' *Yes! Magazine*, 15, online. Available at: http://www.futurenet.org/15prisons/yazzie.htm [accessed 4 January 2005].

Yazzie, R. and Zion, J. (1996) 'Navajo restorative justice: the law of equity and harmony,' in B. Galaway and J. Hudson (eds) *Restorative Justice: international perspectives*, Monsey, NY: Criminal Justice Press.

Young, M. (1995) *Restorative Community Justice: a call to action*, Washington, DC: National Organization for Victim Assistance.

Young, R. (2001) 'Just cops doing "shameful" business? Police-led restorative justice and the lessons of research,' in A. Morris and G. Maxwell (eds) *Restorative Justice for Juveniles*, Portland, OR: Hart Publishing.

Young, R. and Goold, B. (1999) 'Restorative police cautioning in Aylesbury – from degrading to reintegrative shaming ceremonies?' in D. Roche (ed.) (2003) *The International Library of Essays in Law and Legal Theory*, Aldershot, Hants, England: Dartmouth/Ashgate.

Young, R. and Hoyle, C. (2003) 'New improved police-led restorative justice,' in A. Von Hirsch, J. Roberts, A. Bottoms, K. Roach, and M. Schiff (eds) *Restorative Justice and Criminal Justice: competing or reconcilable paradigms?* Oxford: Hart Publishing.

Zehr, H., (1980) 'Mediating the victim–offender conflict,' in *New Perspectives on Crime and Justice* (Issue 2), Akron, PA: Mennonite Central Committee and US Office of Criminal Justice.

— (1985) 'Retributive justice, restorative justice,' in *New Perspectives on Crime and Justice* (Issue 4). Akron, PA: Mennonite Central Committee and US Office of Criminal Justice.

— (1990) *Changing Lenses: a new focus for crime and justice*, Scottsdale, PA: Herald Press.

Zion, J. (1998) 'The use of custom and legal tradition in the modern justice setting,' *Contemporary Justice Review*, 1(1): 133–48.

Notes

1. I would like to acknowledge my appreciation for the most comprehensive annotated listing of the literature on restorative justice from Justice Fellowship International at Restorative Justice On-line http://www.restorative justice.org/asp/Advanced_search.asp [accessed 25 January 2005].

2. Theoretical work on restitution as a basis for justice may have encouraged mediation in criminal cases (Eglash 1958; Laster 1970; Korn 1971; Barnett 1977; Galaway 1977; Evarts 1990).

2

Victim offender mediation

An evolving evidence-based practice

Mark S. Umbreit, Robert B. Coates and Betty Vos

Introduction

Experimentation in the late 1970s and early 1980s with Victim Offender Reconciliation Programs is widely considered to be the core from which restorative justice theory emerged (Zehr 2002). These initial efforts brought victims and offenders together with a trained mediator/facilitator to talk through what happened and to decide together what yet might happen. Such experiments typically focused on youth and on misdemeanor cases, although even in those early days there were some exceptions, the most notable being in Genesee County, New York, where violent crime was the focus (Umbreit 1989b).

These efforts to humanize the justice process and find ways for offenders to help repair the harm done to victims appealed to many practitioners working in community-based programs and churches as well as to some within the justice system. Such experiments also raised fears and doubt among many victim advocates. And enthusiasm for these alternative forms of justice often cast a chill on criminal justice administrators. Yet there were courageous judges and administrators who welcomed an increase in dispositional options and there-

fore provided the necessary access to offenders and victims as well as to limited resources.

As with any innovation that lasts thirty-nine-plus years – including reform efforts – the initial experiments in bringing offenders and victims together to share their experience and work towards some repair of harm have gone through numerous evolutions. Change has often colored the look of the encounter, at times its focus, and even its name.

A fairly constant commitment to documentation and assessment has accompanied the development of this particular restorative justice approach. It is probably more documented and assessed that almost any attempt to impact the justice process. Thus it seems quite appropriate to refer to this approach as an 'evidence-based' practice (Umbreit *et al.* forthcoming).

Here, we will highlight some of the changes over time that have altered the scope of victim offender mediation. We will also point to some of the core elements of the process that have remained quite constant even during its evolution. We will summarize the empirical research conducted in numerous US jurisdictions and in other nations regarding its implementation. And we will underscore continuing issues that will likely affect its ongoing evolution.

The evolution of victim offender mediation

Selected changes

Naming the process. Like so many reform efforts, the process that brings together victim and offenders in face-to-face dialogue has undergone name changes. Victim Offender Reconciliation Program (VORP) was the initial banner, and there remain programs today that continue to claim that name. However, some practitioners and criminal justice personnel were uncomfortable with the word 'reconciliation', feeling that it was too religious-sounding or too mushy and that it did little to describe a process. Furthermore, victims often balked at the notion of seeking reconciliation with the offenders. Many practitioners shifted their way of talking about the process by describing it as Victim Offender Mediation (VOM), and there are many programs that continue to operate under that banner.

While this name was more descriptive of the process, critics worried that VOM would be regarded as simply one more form of mediation, or worse, that these important offender victim encounters would now follow the negotiation settlement guidelines of other mediation services. Concern was also voiced that the emphasis on using trained community volunteers might be replaced with that of using professional mediators. Hence, many program administrators began referring to the mediators as facilitators.

Currently, Victim Offender Conferencing (VOC) is the name in vogue. Whether it sticks or not only time will tell. Proponents of this banner believe that 'conferencing' blunts the potential threat posed by professional mediators and the standards they might impose. Further, it shifts the emphasis away from a mediated form of settlement and towards some form of conferring about

a conflict in which any subsequent resolution is largely identified and agreed to by the involved parties, rather than by their advocates and/or lawyers. It is believed that this name keeps the emphasis on the process rather than on potential outcomes.

Who is present for the face-to-face encounter? The early experiments with VORP and VOM brought together an offender and a victim or victims with a trained community volunteer. The volunteer also provided a community presence. Typically, if multiple offenders or multiple victims were involved, as in cases of slashing tires on several vehicles, each offender was expected to meet with each victim. Soon this became unwieldy and programs began to encourage all offenders involved to meet with a single victim. Gradually, notions regarding who should be present at the face-to-face encounter shifted, and the process began to include a support person for the victim and/or for the offender. Typically such support persons did not participate in the actual conversation. Eventually, support persons came to include parents of involved youths, and they often gained a voice in the process.. Under the conferencing banner, face-to-face encounters often involve an even larger number of persons. Not only are victims and offenders as well as their support persons invited to meet; additional persons may be invited from the community or neighborhood. Their presence and participation underscores the impact of crime beyond the primary victims upon the larger community as a whole. In addition, their presence may also be drawn upon to address the resources available to help meet the ongoing needs of victims and/or offenders.

The role of community. The role of the community in victim offender mediation has gradually increased over the three decades of its development (Umbreit *et al.* 2004). Initially, the community's voice in the process was typically limited to the presence of the mediator as a community representative. As support persons were added to the mix, they too came to represent the larger community, at least in part. More recently many programs have focused directly on making the community more visible in the process and expanding its role through the explicit inclusion of community representatives such as neighbors or other concerned citizens in the dialogue or conferencing sessions.

This does not mean that all such programs look alike in practice. Some still focus primarily on the victim offender relationship. Some include the possibility of multiple support persons. And some purposefully seek broader community involvement. Many program staff indicate that who is invited is largely determined by the nature of the case.

Types of cases. With rare exceptions, cases in the early developmental days focused on youth and on misdemeanors. Although it is difficult to determine the actual percentage of types of cases across the wide range of programs existing today, it is at least clear that contemporary VORP, VOM, and VOC programs are working with adults as well as with youth and are increasingly being relied upon in very serious cases (Umbreit *et al.* 2003).

Selected core elements

Interventions of any type typically vary considerably within type; however, in order to qualify as a 'type,' they also share much in common. Such is the case with the broad cluster of programs included under the victim offender mediation umbrella. While not every program will equally embrace all of the core elements described below, they characteristically adopt most of the core elements to at least some degree.

Establishing a safe environment. Program staff realize that victims have already been victimized and that many offenders have also been victimized. These facts make providing a safe environment for their encounter paramount. It is always hoped that something good will come out of the encounter but, at the very least, no participant should suffer further harm. Thus, mediator/facilitators will devote time to determining whether participants are able to meet without being subjected to verbal abuse or threat. To the extent possible, staff will determine if the participants are emotionally ready to meet and will ascertain what kinds of safeguards might be put in place. Ground rules for the conduct of the encounter are agreed upon ahead of time. Other safeguards have included the addition of support persons, the use of first names only, and mechanisms for requesting a break or a breather.

Preparation. Establishing a safe environment is greatly dependent upon adequate preparation of all participants: victims, offenders, support persons, and community representatives. Participants want to know what will be expected of them, how the dialogue typically unfolds, what the role of mediator/facilitator is, and what the role of support persons and community members will be. In addition, victims and offenders often desire to know what one another wants from the encounter, how threatening the other party might be or become, how remorseful the offender appears. Preparation will involve talking about the setting where the dialogue will take place; if necessary a dry-run visit to the setting is often arranged. This is particularly helpful if the setting is a jail or prison and the victim has never been inside such an institution. Preparation underscores yet another core element: the choice to participate.

Voluntary participation. A strong commitment held in common across most victim offender mediation programs is belief in a victim's right to choose whether or not to meet with an offender. A major value undergirding this commitment is prevention of re-victimization. Still, some staff and observers are aware of subtle pressures and sometimes not so subtle pressures that may be put on victims to participate or not participate by program staff, prosecutors, and judges (Achilles 2004).

Right of choice for the offender is more complex. Though many advocates would wish otherwise, it has been recognized since the early developmental days that offender choices to participate or not are frequently more constricted than those of victims. Choosing to meet the victim may be regarded as the lesser of two or three options, including possibly that of doing jail time. Or as is the case in a number of jurisdictions, the offender may simply be ordered by the court to participate. In an ideal world, all offenders and victims would voluntarily choose to participate. These programs, thus far, do not function in an ideal world.

Face-to-face encounter. At the core of VORP, VOM and VOC has been an emphasis upon bringing victims and offenders together in face-to-face dialogue. This remains a core element even while more variations are being accepted. Notably in England in particular, some programs practice a kind of 'shuttle diplomacy' whereby the mediator travels between victim and offender who are present in separate rooms. In other instances where the offender has not been apprehended or is unwilling to participate, or where the victim remains fearful of direct contact with the offender, surrogates are being relied upon. In such cases offenders who have committed similar crimes meet with victims or vice versa. Even with these caveats in mind, a core element in victim offender mediation is face-to-face encounter, and participants tend to be more satisfied with their experience if the meeting has been face to face.

Follow-up. There has long been an understanding in victim offender mediation work that the face-to-face encounter is not the sum total of what happens. Not only can preparatory work, in and of itself, be beneficial to participants but there is also an essential need for follow-up on the face-to-face encounter/s. Follow-up efforts may involve additional direct contact between staff and victims and offenders to determine how well they believe any agreed-upon plans are going. It may involve keeping track of agreed-upon restitution. It may involve making referrals to other services when requested. Some programs have experienced great difficulty with closing cases. Demarcating an end point for follow-up may be as important as taking the time to engage in follow-up in the first place.

What we have learned through assessment

As we indicated in the introductory paragraphs, victim offender mediation programs have received close scrutiny since their early days. Staff at the University of Minnesota Center for Restorative Justice and Peacemaking, in addition to conducting a number of studies over the past three decades on VORP, VOM, and VOC, are engaged in an ongoing process of collecting empirical studies assessing the victim offender encounter process. We make no claim to have discovered every piece of such research conducted but we are attempting to collect and summarize any that we can locate whether they exist in journals, on the world-wide web, or buried somewhere in the files of a program. Currently, we are aware of about sixty empirically based studies conducted on these programs. In addition there have been a few published meta-analyses, in which researchers assess findings across a number of studies that meet certain levels of rigor, usually the presence of a comparison or control group.

The following is an effort to convey in broad strokes the findings contained across these studies. Readers may pursue these findings further by considering the references appearing at the end of this chapter.

Participation rates and reasons

Who decides to participate in these kinds of programs? In a study of 555 eligible cases, 47 per cent of the victims were willing to participate (Gehm 1990). In that same study, victims (who were primarily white) were more likely to participate if the offender was white, if the offense was a misdemeanor, and if the victim was representing an institution. In a recent study that included a comparison group, persons who were victims of personal crimes were more likely to agree to meet with offenders than those who were victims of property crime (Coates *et al.* 2002).

Victims choose to meet offenders for a host of reasons. Numerous studies report that victims select into these kinds of programs because they wish: (1) to learn more about why the crime happened; (2) to share their pain with the offender; (3) to help the offender change; (4) to hold the offender accountable; (5) to receive restitution for losses; (6) to avoid court processing; (7) to see that offender is adequately punished. Likewise, offenders choosing to meet victims reported a desire (1) to take direct responsibility; (2) to apologize; (3) to pay back the victim; and (4) to get the whole experience behind them (Coates and Gehm 1985; Perry *et al.* 1987; Roberts 1995; Umbreit 1995; Niemeyer and Shichor 1996; Umbreit *et al.* 2001; Umbreit *et al.* 2003; Coates *et al.* 2002).

Across a number of studies, victims who refused to meet offenders reported that (1) they believed the crime was too trivial to be worth the time and trouble; (2) the matter had already been resolved; (3) they feared meeting the offender; or (4) the offender deserved more punishment (Coates and Gehm 1985; Umbreit 1995; Coates *et al.* 2002). Offenders who refused to participate were sometimes advised by lawyers to take that action (Schneider 1986) and others indicated that they didn't want 'to be bothered' (Coates and Gehm 1985).

These studies also provide a sense for what participants may find satisfying or helpful about such meetings. This is particularly borne out in secondary analysis of two studies in the United States and Canada (Bradshaw and Umbreit 1998). Three factors emerged from a step-wise multiple regression analysis depicting those variables most associated with victim satisfaction. Those factors were: (1) victim felt good about the mediator; (2) victim perceived the resulting restitution agreement as fair; and (3) victim, for whatever reason, had a strong initial desire to meet the offender.

Satisfaction

Not surprisingly, nearly all the studies we reviewed contained some measures of participant satisfaction with the process and outcomes. Across a variety of sites, cultures, and types of offenses, eight or nine out of ten victims and offenders participating in victim offender mediation indicated being satisfied with the process and with the resulting agreements (Coates and Gehm 1985; Perry *et al.* 1987; Marshall 1990; Umbreit and Coates 1992, Warner 1992; Roberts 1995; Carr 1998; Evje and Cushman 2000; Umbreit *et al.* 2001; Umbreit *et al.* 2003). In a large meta-analysis of restorative justice programs (including victim offender mediation programs), in all but one of the thirteen restorative programs studied that dealt with satisfaction, victims reported higher levels of satisfactions than those going through traditional justice processes (Latimer *et al.* 2001).

We believe it is worth highlighting that these levels of satisfaction were also attained in two programs working with victims of violent crimes (e.g. rape, attempted homicide, vehicular homicide, and homicide). Of forty victims in the study, all but one reported being very satisfied with their involvement in the program. This victim, who had participated in surrogate mediation because the offender in the case refused to meet, clarified that the offender's refusal was the only factor contributing to less than complete satisfaction. Among the thirty-eight offenders who rated their satisfaction levels, thirty-two reported being very satisfied, five were somewhat satisfied, and only one was somewhat dissatisfied (Umbreit et al. 2003).

From a qualitative perspective, victims interviewed regarding satisfaction often elaborated on their responses with comments about being able to share their stories and pain with the offender as well as gaining a better understanding of why they were victimized in the first place. Many offenders indicated being surprised that the meetings went so well. In one of the first studies of this sort, offenders said their greatest fear in this process was meeting the victim face to face, but the same youths reported after the meeting that what they liked most about the process was meeting the victim (Coates and Gehm 1985).

The criminal justice system as a whole also seems to benefit from its association with these kinds of programs. Victims expressing high levels of satisfaction with the victim offender mediation process were also likely to express fairly high levels of satisfaction with the criminal justice system in contrast to comparison groups who did not participate in victim offender mediation (Umbreit and Coates 1992; Umbreit 1995; Coates et al. 2002).

Fairness

Fairness is often perceived as the cornerstone upon which justice is built. Many studies of victim offender mediation asked participants about the fairness of the mediation process and of the resulting agreement (Collins 1984; Coates and Gehm 1985; Strode 1997; Umbreit 1989a; Umbreit 1995; Umbreit and Coates 1993; Umbreit

and Roberts 1996; Evje and Cushman 2000; Umbreit et al. 2001). Consistent with the high levels of satisfaction described above, the vast majority of VOM participants (typically over 80 per cent) across settings, cultures, and types of offenses reported believing that the process was fair to both sides and that the resulting agreement was fair. Again, these experiences led to feelings that the overall criminal justice system was fair. Where comparison groups were employed, those individuals exposed to mediation came away more likely to feel that they had been treated fairly than those going through the traditional court proceedings.

These positive satisfaction and fairness experiences have generated support for VOM as a criminal justice option. When asked, typically nine out of ten participants would recommend a VOM program to others (Coates and Gehm, 1985; Umbreit 1991; Evje and Cushman 2000; Umbreit et al. 2001).

Restitution

Although in the early developmental days of victim offender mediation restitution was frequently regarded as a by-product of the process, in many jurisdictions today restitution is inextricably linked with victim offender mediation. About half the studies under review looked at restitution as an outcome of mediation (Collins 1984; Coates and Gehm 1985, Perry et al. 1987; Galaway 1989; Umbreit and Coates 1992; Warner 1992; Roy 1993; Evje and Cushman 2000; Umbreit et al. 2001). Of those cases that reached a meeting, typically 90 per cent or more generated agreements. Restitution of one form or another (monetary, community service, or direct service to the victim) was part of the vast majority of these agreements. Looking across the studies reviewed here, between 80 and 90 per cent of the contracts are reported as having been completed. In some instances, the length of contract exceeded the length of the research study.

Most comparison group studies examining restitution report higher completion rates and/or greater total restitution for offenders participating in VOM than for those who do not (Umbreit and Coates 1992; Evje and Cushman 2000; Bradbury 2002), although there have been exceptions (Roy 1993). However Latimer *et al.* (2001) report in their meta-analysis that offenders participating in restorative justice programs had substantially higher rates of restitution compliance than did those who were processed through other avenues.

Diversion

Many VOM programs are nominally established to divert offenders into less costly, less time-consuming, and frequently thought less severe options. While diversion was a goal lauded by many, others expressed concern about the unintended consequence of widening the net – that is, ushering in youth and adults to experience a sanction more severe than they would have if VOM did not exist. While much talk continues on this topic, there is a dearth of study devoted to it. Only a handful of the studies reviewed here address this question.

One of the broadest studies examining the diversion question was that conducted over a three-year period in Kettering, Northamptonshire, England (Dignan 1990). Offenders participating in the VOM program were matched with similar non-participating offenders from a neighboring jurisdiction. The author concludes that at least 60 per cent of the offenders participating in the Kettering program were true diversions from court prosecution. Jurisdictional comparisons also led him to conclude that there was a 13 per cent widening the net effect – much less than local observers would have predicted.

In a Glasgow, Scotland, agency, where numbers were sufficiently large to allow random assignment of individuals between the VOM program and a comparison group

going through the traditional process, it was discovered that 43 per cent of the latter group were not prosecuted (Warner 1992). However, most of these pled guilty and were fined. This would suggest that VOM in this instance was a more severe sanction and indeed widened the net of government control.

In a sizeable three-county study of mediation in North Carolina, results on diversion were mixed (Clark *et al.* 1992). In two counties, mediation had no impact on diverting offenders from court. However in the third county the mediation programs appeared to have reduced trials by as much as two-thirds.

Mediation impact on incarceration was explored in an Indiana–Ohio study by comparing consequences for seventy-three youth and adults going through VOM programs with those for a matched sample of individuals who were processed in the traditional manner (Coates and Gehm 1985). VOM offenders spent less time incarcerated than did their counterparts. And when incarcerated, they did county jail time rather than state time. The length and place of incarceration also had substantial implications for costs.

Recidivism

While recidivism may be best regarded as an indicator of society's overall response to juvenile and adult offenders, it is a traditional measure used to evaluate the long-term impact of justice programs. Accordingly, a number of studies designed to assess VOM have incorporated measures of recidivism.

Results are somewhat mixed across studies. When comparison groups are examined, most studies have found some decrease in recidivism problems for VOM cases as compared to others (Schneider 1986; Dignan 1990; Umbreit and Coates 1992; Nugent and Paddock 1995; Miers *et al.* 2001). In these studies, participants in VOM tended to recidivate less than those in comparison groups, and when they did recidivate, they tended to do so with less serious offenses. A smaller set of studies found no difference (Roy 1993; Stone *et al.* 1998), and a study of six California programs (Evje and Cushman 2000) found mixed results, with five counties showing decreased recidivism rates and one county showing an increase.

Nugent *et al.* (1999) conducted a reanalysis of recidivism data reported in four previous studies involving a total sample of 1,298 juvenile offenders. Of these, 619 participated in VOM; 679 did not. The authors used ordinal logistical regression procedures for this meta-analysis. Youth processed through VOM recidivated at a statistically significant lower rate, 35 per cent, than did youth who did not participate in VOM. Furthermore VOM participants, when they did reoffend, did so for less serious offenses. This base study was expanded (Nugent *et al.* 2003) to include fourteen studies. The combined sample consisted of 9,037 juveniles. This vastly expanded data base yielded similar results to the base study: that is, VOM youth tended to reoffend less and tended to commit less serious reoffenses.

Another way of looking at recidivism is to consider before-program participation and after-program participation rates of recidivating. Wynne and Brown (1998) report on a longstanding study of the Leeds Victim Offender Unit that began in 1985. Of the ninety offenders who met in face-to-face mediation from 1985 through 1987, 87 per cent had had previous convictions before mediation. Sixty-eight per cent had no convictions during a two-year follow-up post mediation. Recidivism data were gathered on VOM programs in two Oregon counties in a study conducted by Umbreit *et al.* (2001). These data reflect one year before intervention comparisons of number of offenses with one year after. For the group of youth in the Deschutes County program there was a 77 per cent overall reduction in reoffending. Similarly, for the group of juveniles going through the victim offender program in Jackson County there was an overall 68 per cent reduction in recidivism.

A Lane County Oregon study (Nelson 2000) provides more detailed comparisons than do most of the studies. In that study, 150 youth referred to VOM from July of 1996 to November 1998 were followed for a year after referral. Comparing their referral frequencies during the year prior to being referred to VOM with the year after, all referred youth had 65 per cent fewer referrals to the system in the subsequent year. Those who actually met with their victims did better. Juveniles referred to VOM but refusing to participate had 32 per cent fewer referrals; youth who met with their victims had 81 per cent fewer referrals than the preceding year.

Continuing issues

The ongoing evolution of a practice

The evolution of a practice such as VORP, VOM, or VOC is natural. Change can be positive, strengthening the practice and grounding it in the experience of victims and offenders. Broadening the scope of victim offender mediation to include support persons and community representatives more directly has provided richer opportunities for offenders to see the ripple effect of their actions. It has also provided opportunities for citizens to be actively involved in a justice process through helping to hold offenders accountable and finding ways to help offenders alter their behaviors.

Change is not without risk; in fact, change can put at risk some of the very core elements of the victim offender encounter. These programs can be regarded as so beneficial by persons inside and outside the justice system that more offenders and more victims are encouraged to participate. Subtle and sometimes not so subtle pressures may be placed on victims as well as offenders – after all, the process will only help. It is that kind of thinking that puts at risk the voluntary nature of the program.

Safety, follow-up, and overall quality of the process can be jeopardized as these programs grow in size to meet the demands of a host system. If growth is not accompanied by adequate resources, then the program begins to cut back on what it does. Preparation becomes rote if it is carried out at all. Without adequate preparation the entire foundation for victim offender encounters is in danger of imploding. Thus, there is a tension that victim offender mediation practitioners and proponents must hold in balance between the desire to embrace ideas and opportunities that will enhance the practice and the desire to hold on to the core elements that define the practice.

The place of victim offender mediation in the context of restorative justice

Victim offender mediation is a practice that shares common values with other practices falling under the restorative justice umbrella. It is not the only such practice. It may not necessarily be the best practice. It is, however, a fairly well-established approach for bringing victims and offenders together, with an option of varying levels of community participation, to repair the harm done to victims and to help offenders move on. In our own work, we have moved toward talking about restorative justice dialogue as encompassing victim offender mediation, family group conferencing, and peacekeeping circles. We do this because these approaches, in varying degrees, emphasize getting persons engaged in conflict to listen to one another, to engage one another in some form of dialogue. Which approach is best in a particular instance will depend largely upon the characteristics of the case, the desires of the participants – particularly victims – and the resources available to the program.

These dialogue approaches are not the sum total of restorative justice practices. For example, some practices are designed to affect justice policies and system change (Coates et al. 2004).

Crimes of violence

As late as the mid-1990s, most victim offender mediation type programs in the United States typically excluded violent offenders (Hughes and Schneider 1990; Greenwood and Umbreit 1998). While it is unlikely that a huge shift to more serious kinds of cases will occur, program administrators indicated in a 1996–7 survey that they were being requested to work with crimes of increasing severity and complexity, and that these cases required additional resources, particularly more advanced training (Greenwood and Umbreit 1998).

Studies involving murder, vehicular homicide, manslaughter, armed robbery, and sexual assault in such far-reaching places as New York, Wisconsin, Alaska, Minnesota, Texas, Ohio, and British Columbia (Umbreit et al. 2003) document efforts at bringing together violent offenders and victims of violent crime. These very intense efforts have yielded promising, positive results. Victims who seek and choose this kind of encounter and dialogue with an individual who brought unspeakable tragedy to their lives report feelings of relief, an improved capacity for integrating what has happened to them, and gratefulness for not being forgotten and unheard. In several jurisdictions, lists of victims seeking to meet with violent offenders far exceed the resources available to accommodate them.

Commitment to accountability through program assessment

The process of bringing victim and offender together in face-to-face dialogue is a very human process that often draws upon and impacts emotions, spirituality, energy, thinking capacity, and the physical body. At their best, these encounters are a gestalt that is difficult to describe. For some practitioners, the notion of assessing this process threatens the very nature of the process.

We take a different position. We believe that while we will never be able to fully capture what takes place in this particular form of human interaction, it is critical to describe it and to obtain participant views of what has happened to them, in order to learn from their experiences and thereby be in a position to make informed choices about how this process ought to continue to evolve. Given that most of these programs function in relationship with criminal justice or social service system, it behooves us to be in the best position possible to address the long-run outcomes of victim offender mediation such as victim satisfaction, restitution compliance rates and recidivism.

Conclusion

Studies reviewed for this work include exploratory studies as well as studies with experimental designs. The reader is encouraged to consider studies of particular interest in their entirety. Generating and maintaining a database on the effectiveness of victim offender mediation approaches is an ongoing undertaking in which many around the world participate. At this point it seems reasonable to conclude that victim offender mediation does contribute to increased involvement of victims in the justice process and to their own sense of healing, to offenders taking responsibility for their behaviors and learning from their experiences, and to community members participating in a just response to law breaking.

References

Achilles, M. (2004) 'Will restorative justice live up to its promise to victims?' in H. Zehr and B. Toews (eds) *Critical Issues in Restorative Justice*, Monsey, NY: Criminal Justice Press.

Bradbury, B. (2002) *Deschutes County Delinquent Youth Demonstration Project. Secretary of State Audit Report # 2002–29*, Salem, OR: Office of the Secretary of State.

Bradshaw, W. and Umbreit, M. S. (1998) 'Crime victims meet juvenile offenders: contributing factors to victim satisfaction with mediated dialogue,' *Juvenile and Family Court Journal*, 49(3): 17–25.

Carr, C. (1998) *VORS Program Evaluation Report*, Inglewood, CA: Centenela Valley Juvenile Diversion Project.

Clarke, S., Valente, E. and Mace, R. (1992) *Mediation of Interpersonal Disputes: an evaluation of North Carolina's programs*, Chapel Hill, NC: Institute of Government, University of North Carolina.

Coates, R. B. and Gehm, J. (1985) *Victim Meets Offender: an evaluation of victim offender reconciliation programs*, Valparaiso: PACT Institute of Justice.

Coates, R. B., Burns, H. and Umbreit, M.S. (2002) *Victim Participation in Victim Offender Conferencing: Washington County, Minnesota Community Justice Program*, St Paul, MN: Center for Restorative Justice and Peacemaking.

Coates, R. B., Umbreit, M. S. and Vos, B. (2004) 'Systemic change toward restorative justice in Washington County, Minnesota,' *Federal Probation*, 68(3): 16–23.

Collins, J. P. (1984) *Final Evaluation Report on the Grande Prairie Community Reconciliation Project for Young Offenders*, Ottawa: Ministry of the Solicitor General of Canada, Consultation Centre Prairies.

Dignan, J. (1990) *Repairing the Damage: an evaluation of an experimental adult reparation scheme in Kettering, Northamptonshire*, Sheffield: Centre for Criminological Legal Research, Faculty of Law, University of Sheffield.

Evje, A. and Cushman, R. (2000) *A Summary of the Evaluations of Six California Victim Offender Rehabilitation Programs*, San Francisco, CA: Judicial Council of California, Administrative Office of the Courts.

Galaway, B. (1989) 'Informal justice: mediation between offenders and victims,' in P. Albrecht and O. Backes (eds) *Crime Prevention and Intervention: legal and ethical problems*. New York: Walter de Gruyter.

Gehm, J. (1990) 'Mediated victim offender restitution agreements: an exploratory analysis of factors related to victim participation,' in B. Galaway and J. Hudson. (eds) *Criminal Justice, Restitution, and Reconciliation*, Monsey, NY: Criminal Justice Press.

Greenwood, J. and Umbreit, M. S. (1998) 'National Survey of Victim Offender Mediation Programs in the US', *VOMA Connections*,

Winter. Available at: http://www.voma.org/docs/connect1/voma1.html

Hughes, S. and Schneider, A. (1990) *Victim Offender Mediation in the Juvenile Justice System,* Washington, DC: Office of Juvenile Justice and Delinquency Prevention.

Latimer, J., Dowden, C. and Muise, D. (2001) *The Effectiveness of Restorative Practice: a meta-analysis,* Ottawa: Department of Justice Research and Statistics Division Methodological Series.

Marshall, T. (1990) 'Results of research from British experiments in restorative justice,' in B. Galaway and J. Hudson (eds) *Criminal Justice, Restitution, and Reconciliation,* London: Sage.

Miers, D., Maguire, M., Goldie, S., Sharpe, K., Hale, C., Netten, A., Uglow, S., Doolin, K., Hallam, A., Enterkin, J. and Newburn, T. (2001) *An Exploratory Evaluation of Restorative Justice Schemes: executive summary,* Crime Reduction Research Series Paper 9, London: Home Office.

Nelson, S. (2000) *Evaluation of the Restorative Justice Program,* Eugene, OR: Lane County Department of Youth Services.

Niemeyer, M. and Shichor, D. (1996) 'A preliminary study of a large victim/offender reconciliation program,' *Federal Probation,* 60(3): 30–4.

Nugent, W. M. and Paddock, J. (1995) 'The effect of victim offender mediation on severity of reoffense,' *Mediation Quarterly,* 12: 353–67.

Nugent, W., Umbreit, M. S., Wiinamaki, L. and Paddock, J. (1999) 'Participation in victim offender mediation and severity of subsequent delinquent behavior: successful replications?' *Journal of Research in Social Work Practice,* 11(1): 5–23

Nugent, W. R, Williams, M., and Umbreit, M.S. (2003) 'Participation in victim offender mediation and the prevalence and severity of subsequent delinquent behavior: a meta-analysis,' *Utah Law Review,* 1: 137–65

Perry, L., Lajeunesse, T. and Woods, A. (1987) *Mediation Services: an evaluation,* Manitoba: Manitoba Attorney General, Research, Planning and Evaluation.

Roberts, T. (1995) *Evaluation of the Victim Offender Mediation Project, Langley, BC: final report,* Victoria, BC: Focus Consultants.

Roy, S. (1993) 'Two types of juvenile restitution programs in two midwestern counties: a comparative study', *Federal Probation,* 57(4): 48–53.

Schneider, A. (1986) 'Restitution and recidivism rates of juvenile offenders: results from four experimental studies,' *Criminology,* 24: 533–52.

Stone, S., Helms, W. and Edgeworth, P. (1998) *Cobb County Juvenile Court Mediation Program Evaluation,* Carrolton, GA: State University of West Georgia.

Strode, E. (1997) 'Victims of property crime meeting their juvenile offenders: victim participants' evaluation of the Dakota County MN Community Corrections victim offender meeting program,' unpublished thesis, Northampton, MA, Smith College School of Social Work.

Umbreit, M. S. (1989a) 'Crime victims seeking fairness, not revenge: toward restorative justice,' *Federal Probation,* 53(3): 52–7.

— (1989b) 'Violent offenders and their victims,' in M. Wright and B. Galaway (eds) *Mediation and Criminal Justice,* London: Sage.

— (1991) 'Minnesota mediation center produces positive results,' *Corrections Today,* August: 194–7.

— (1995) *Mediation of Criminal Conflict: an assessment of programs in four Canadian provinces,* St Paul, MN: Center for Restorative Justice and Peacemaking.

Umbreit, M. S. and Coates, R. B. (1992) *Victim Offender Mediation: an analysis of programs in four states of the US,* Minneapolis: Minnesota Citizens Council on Crime and Justice.

— (1993) 'Cross-site analysis of victim offender mediation in four states,' *Crime & Delinquency,* 39: 565–85.

Umbreit, M. S. and Roberts, A. (1996) *Mediation of Criminal Conflict in England: an assessment of services in Coventry and Leeds,* St Paul, MN: Center for Restorative Justice and Mediation.

Umbreit, M. S., Coates, R. B. and Vos, B. (2001) *Juvenile Victim Offender Mediation in Six Oregon Counties,* Salem, OR: Oregon Dispute Resolution Commission.

Umbreit, M. S., Vos, B., Coates, R. B. and Brown, K. A. (2003) *Facing Violence: the path of restorative justice and dialogue,* Monsey, NY: Criminal Justice Press.

Umbreit, M. S., Coates, R. B. and Vos, B. (2004) 'Restorative justice versus community justice: clarifying a muddle or generating confusion?' *Contemporary Justice Review,* 7(1): 81–9.

— (forthcoming) 'Victim offender mediation: evidence-based practice over three decades,' in M. Moffit and R. C. Bordone (eds) *Handbook of Dispute Resolution,* San Francisco, CA: Jossey-Bass.

Warner, S. (1992) *Making Amends: justice for victims and offenders,* Aldershot: Avebury.

Wynne, J. and Brown, I. (1998) 'Can mediation cut reoffending?' *Probation Journal,* 45(1): 21–6.

Zehr, H. (2002) *The Little Book of Restorative Justice,* Intercourse, PA: Good Books.

Victim offender mediation and restorative justice

The European landscape

Christa Pelikan and Thomas Trenczek

Introduction: VOM and Europe's diversity

Victim offender mediation (VOM) is spreading rapidly and continually in European countries. It is not easy though to draw a picture of VOM in Europe that has a clear profile. Tony Peters (2000: 14) spoke about 'a diversified landscape of competing visions.' However, although we do find considerable diversity with regard to the scope of VOM (i.e. the number of referrals or the range of offences to be included, the degree of its being grounded in legislation, its community or its professional orientation), there are some features of VOM in Europe that differ from the African, Anglo-American, or Asian approach. This pertains especially to:

- the extent of activities in setting up VOM-programs or pilot projects;
- the extent of legislative activity; and
- the extent of professional training programs for mediators.

In addition, we find two 'Pan-European' documents in the fields of VOM that provide overall guidelines for the countries of Europe. In September 1999 the European Committee of Ministers adopted the Recommendation No R (99) 19 'Mediation in Penal matters' (henceforth: CoE-R 99-19) which can be regarded as a milestone in the development of VOM in Europe. The CoE-R 99-19 and its 'Explanatory Memorandum' (EM) refers especially to the general principles of VOM, to its legal basis as well as practice and training standards. Even though the recommendations are generally not a binding legislation for the different member states, they give a firm orientation and address essential issues of victim offender mediation we will cover in this article.

The CoE-R 99-19 was followed by the Council Framework Decision (2001/220/ JHA) of 15 March 2001 on the 'Standing of victims in criminal proceedings' which refers to victim offender mediation, especially in Article 10.[1] Although this document is not as precise and detailed as the CoE-R 99-19, it obliges member states of the European Union to adapt their national laws. The CoE-R 99-19 even had a marked influence on the work and the final draft of the United Nations Basic Principles on Restorative Justice (UN 2002), although some provisions with regard to the training and qualification of mediators reflecting a typical Euro-centric perspective had to be changed as a result of intensive discussions.

The European Forum for Victim Offender Mediation and Restorative Justice founded in December 2000 regards the CoE-R 99-19 as one of its policy-guidelines and as a pivotal instrument for achieving its objectives. In some countries (especially Austria, France, Germany, Norway, England and Wales) the development of VOM practices and of VOM legislation has been taking place in the years – or even decades – prior to the issuing of the CoE-R 99-19. In Norway and in Austria, which can be regarded as the vanguards of VOM-development in Europe, the CoE-R 99-19 was of no importance; the same holds true for England and Wales (which represent a special case altogether). In other countries (e.g. in France, Germany, partly also in Spain), it has contributed to and enhanced a national policy establishing VOM. But we find also a number of countries (Belgium, Cyprus, Finland, Poland, and Slovenia) where the CoE-R 99-19 had a decisive influence on the drafting of national legislation regarding VOM. In other countries (e.g. Ireland, Italy, the Netherlands, Portugal, Spain, Sweden) the CoE-R 99-19 has at least contributed to the introduction of VOM, providing orientation and support, while in a few states (Albania, Bulgaria, Denmark, the Czech Republic, Russia) the CoE-R 99-19 has mainly been noticed and used by NGOs and individual professionals outside the criminal justice system and thus exerted only limited or (in the case of Greece) no influence, as yet.

Defining victim offender mediation and restorative justice

The mediation and restorative justice movement draws support from different ideological sources and strands of thought. Throughout Europe we can observe that different 'players' in the field of legal and

criminal policy emphasize different, sometimes contradictory aspects of VOM, and put forward different objectives to be achieved by way of VOM: i.e. to humanize the criminal justice process, to increase the offender's personal accountability, to provide meaningful roles and restitution for victims, to punish the offender, to provide an alternative to imprisonment, to ease the probation service's case load, to improve the community's understanding of crime and criminal justice and to provide an opportunity for reconciliation. VOM seems to offer something for everyone and can be very attractive to policy-makers of different political affiliation. While this may promote consensus about drafting legislation (for Norway cf. Kemeny 2000: 86) it also has its drawbacks: it makes programs vulnerable to those influences which tend to co-opt innovative processes to make them function smoothly within the traditional system (cf. Trenczek 2002, 2003a; Zehr 1985). Therefore it is necessary to clarify the definition and goals of VOM and RJ. According to the CoE-R 99-19 (Appendix I) we will define victim offender[2] mediation (VOM) as a process which is offered to the parties of a dispute arising from the commitment of a crime, to talk (ideally face to face) about and deal with the offending behavior. With the assistance of a neutral third party (the mediator) the parties identify the disputed issues, develop options, consider alternatives and endeavor to reach a (restitution) agreement. The mediator has *no* advisory or determinative role on the content of the dispute or the outcome of its resolution.

VOM is just one – but in the European context the most important – model, or practice of restorative justice (RJ).[3] RJ is seen as a broad approach oriented at repairing the harm caused by crime as far as possible (Wright 1996; Zehr 1990). In 'modern,' 'western' societies the criminal justice system defines crime in terms of violation of the state law. Therefore, the state alone becomes responsible for determining and executing punishment (as a manifestation of the *Gewaltmonopol*, the exclusive right to use force), implying that the accused is protected from the personal revenge or retribution which might be exacted upon him/her by a victim or victim supporters. The function of the criminal justice system is to protect rights, to determine guilt and to decide on the sentence of punishment accordingly. Therefore the focus is on the alleged perpetrator, on due process and a fair trial. It has been stated repeatedly that victims often feel that they are left out or even used by the system rather than listened to and cared for. This is one of the prime motivations for instigating an RJ approach which places the victim with the offender at the center of the process. Therefore three main, closely interrelated elements are constitutive for the European RJ approach:

- a specific sociological foundation: the so-called life-world (*Lebenswelt*) experience approach;
- active participation of the conflict parties involved, aiming at empowerment; and
- the reparative element, the notion of balance and equity (restoration in the narrow sense of the term) reaching beyond punishment, treatment and therapy.

Lifeworld element

Instead of defining crime in terms of breaking the law, RJ defines crime in terms of the harm done by one person to another. The focus of interest is not the abstract violation of the peace under the law, but rather the problems of the persons directly involved: victim and offender. This is a revival of the understanding of crime as a cause, expression, and consequence of a conflict, of difficulties and problems of and between victim and offender (Hanak *et al.* 1989;

Trenczek 1990: 110). In its theoretical foundation VOM in Europe stands very close to the heritage of Nils Christie who stated as early as 1977:

> Conflicts are ... taken away from the directly involved parties. Criminal Conflicts have either become other people's property – primarily the property of lawyers – or it has been in other people's interest to define conflicts away.
>
> (Christie 1977: 5)

> Lawyers are particularly good at stealing conflicts.
>
> (ibid.: 4)

> It is the conflict itself that represents the most interesting property taken away, not the goods originally taken away from the victim.
>
> (ibid.: 5)

Active participation

RJ goes beyond restitution or reparation and connotes a dynamic dimension and an interactive process of establishing justice and fairness. The German word *Ausgleich* (literally translated 'balancing') means both, the process of dispute resolution and problem-solving as well as the settlement. With its focus on conflict resolution, the central objective of RJ is to facilitate *participation* (Netzig and Trenczek 1996). In Europe the initiation and facilitation of a controlled forum for settling and resolving conflicts is at the center of the VOM philosophy. Active participation of the parties concerned forms a core element of RJ. Thanks to its participatory nature, mediation is likely to produce a more comprehensive solution to the problems arising from the offence or which have led to the offense than the criminal justice system can do alone (cf. CoE-R 99-19, EM p. 13). Hence, VOM processes are best characterized by a direct meeting of victim and offender. Victim and offender are given the chance to handle their own conflict, to represent their own interests. Mediation gives those involved the necessary freedom and space to cope with or make good both the emotional and material consequences of criminal acts, and thus actively participate in reducing and resolving conflicts. Consensus is inconceivable without the active participation of its addressees. Therefore, empowerment is related to mediation's essential element of active participation. It is based on the premise that full participation in the process of mediation requires the capacity of both victim and offender to stand up for oneself and one's interests, to speak out and to be able to 'agree and to disagree' (Pelikan 1993: 3). Where these capacities are lacking completely, mediation must not take place (cf. CoE-R 99-19, No. 13). Where they are impaired on one side, it is the task of the mediator to help the 'weaker' party towards a more firm perception and articulation of his/her standpoint and his/her interests. With VOM, this relates mostly (but not exclusively) to the position of the victim. Large power imbalances, such as a relationship of dependence of one party on another, implicit or explicit threats of violence, would prevent free participation and true consent to agreement. However, it should be recognized that many discrepancies in power and skills can be corrected by mediators who will seek to redress the balance in favor of disadvantaged parties (CoE-R 99-19, No. 15).

There was – and still is, to some degree – disagreement as to whether criminal justice officials should play an active role as mediators and/or facilitators in RJ processes. The CoE-R 99-19 clearly states that the autonomy of the VOM-services should be preserved, with criminal justice officials remaining in the role of gatekeepers. On the other hand there is strong *option* to involve representatives of the community, or of supportive networks of victim and offender in the RJ process. This holds especially with

the conference approach following traditions of indigenous people in New Zealand, Australia, Canada, and the US. Here the whole community (of tribes) meets together to resolve conflicts of crimes between its members. There are also very enthusiastic comments within the scientific community about these arrangements. However, very often it is neglected that these traditional models depend on very strong integrated communities and are therefore not generally applicable in modern societies. Therefore, 'community' is not a constituent part of RJ *a priori* but has to be defined (McCold 1996: 91; see below). The conferencing approach has been of interest in several European countries; however, conferencing schemes are used on a wider scope only in the United Kingdom and, on an experimental basis, in Belgium, the Netherlands, in Sweden, and Norway. The focus of RJ in Europe is on the individual victim and his/her relation to the perpetrator.

Reparative element

Instead of understanding justice simply in terms of guilt and punishment, justice needs to have a restorative element. RJ and mediation focus on equity and balance. Crime causes harm to victims, and offenders have an obligation to make things right. From the perspective of RJ, justice is achieved through offenders accepting responsibility for their actions and taking steps to make amends to balance the harm caused, by a material or symbolic action that is to benefit the victim. RJ and VOM, however, go far beyond restitution and compensation schemes (Trenczek 1996: 21). Even more important and implied by the element of active participation, the victim also gets the opportunity to contribute in a responsible way to his/her recovering from the consequences of the act, and to cope with the weakening, sometimes even traumatic, experience. Therefore, the victim needs support, sometimes but not always treatment and therapy. Active participation is the first and essential step to help the victim to leave the victim-role, to regain control and to overcome and prevent secondary victimization. The goal is for both the victim and offender, and, therefore, also the community, to be restored to well-being. This reflects an interactive, conflict-oriented perspective on crime, a move away from one-sided concern, towards an *integrative* approach which is sensitive to the needs and problems of both victims and offenders. VOM is neither predominantly about the victim nor is it first and foremost about the offender. By definition RJ is not a process that aims at penalization. It is not 'penal mediation' as it is wrongly called as a translation of the French 'mediation pénal',[4] but mediation in penal matters, which means conflicts that have become relevant within the criminal justice system.

Development of VOM programs in Europe

General view over a diverse landscape

The debate on how the consequences of an offence could be faced and resolved by those immediately involved, namely the victim and the offender, had already started in Europe in the early 1970s. This discussion took place at the same time as the first experiments with VOM were set up in Canada and the US in the middle of the 1970s. Moreover, some of the first North American initiatives were clearly influenced by the scientific work of European scholars like Nils Christie (1977), Herman Bianchi (1964) and Peter Noll (1962).

In European countries, the present forms of VOM came into existence in the 1980s. A first pilot project began in Norway in 1981 and Finland followed two years later. In Austria the first model (1985) was called 'conflict resolution' (*Konfliktregelung*), and then – as a term included in the new Juve-

nile Justice Act 1988 – 'out-of-court offence resolution' (*Außergerichtlicher Tatausgleich* – ATA). In England, after small-scale experiments from 1979 onwards, the Home Office funded and evaluated four projects between 1985 and 1987. But they have not expanded nearly as rapidly as in Germany, which started at about the same time (1985) but now has over 400 services which offer VOM, both in the juvenile as well as in the adult crime cases. In France, where work also began in the mid-1980s, VOM was linked from the outset with victim support.

Initially, in most countries (with Austria presenting an exception), VOM showed a rather slow development. Although experiments were deemed positive, not least by the victims and offenders involved, the movement did not immediately receive the influence and support that was hoped for, but was met with considerable resistance from the protagonists of the criminal justice system. The approach was very new within the culture of legal professionals and criminal justice policy-makers. In most countries more than a whole decade had to pass in order for them to develop a practice of noticeable scope and some significance. The creation of a legal framework sometimes provided an important impetus, but did not lead to the expected breakthrough everywhere. From a quantitative point of view the practice remained rather limited. From a qualitative point of view, however, many small-scale experiments and programs provided conclusive evidence that this way of responding to crime contained a strong innovative potential. During the 1990s, the number of mediation programs and the amount of cases dealt with on an annual basis increased steadily in European countries. VOM has now become a well-founded practice in some countries. In some of these countries, like Norway and Slovenia, volunteers play an important role in daily mediation practice, whereas in other countries, like Austria and Germany, the intervention is highly professionalized (see more below).

Although VOM started in Europe predominantly with juvenile offenders, its application in general criminal law is gaining more and more acceptance. While most European programs work within a diversion approach with pre-trial cases, experience of mediation in the successive stages of the criminal justice process, also after sentencing, is growing. The latter refers to the increasing trend of promoting restitution and redress as eminent principles of criminal justice in general.

Diversity also exists with regard to the type of cases dealt with by VOM programs. We find that the practice – contrary to common belief – does not in any way remain limited to property or less serious offences. Meanwhile in some countries, like Austria and Germany, the focus is on violent crime, especially cases of spouse and family violence. The same practice is still heavily opposed by parts of the shelter movements in the UK and in Scandinavian countries.

At the end of the 1990s, a new phase in the European development of VOM could be distinguished. While countries like Austria, Belgium, Germany, France and Norway already had legislation at their disposal at the beginning of the 1990s, at the end of the decade a legal framework was developed in several other countries (England and Wales, Finland, the Czech Republic, Poland, Slovenia, Spain) or the field of practice was enlarged legally and refined considerably (France, Germany, Austria). At this moment, still other countries, such as Sweden, are in the process of adopting new legislation, after a nation-wide experimentation period. Pilot projects on VOM are equally taking place in Denmark, the Netherlands, Ireland, Luxembourg, and Italy amongst others. Eastern European countries deserve to be mentioned separately. Apart from Poland, the Czech Republic and Slovenia, initiatives have been taken in Albania, Bulgaria, Hungary, Romania and Russia.

Exemplary sketches of national developments in European countries

In Europe one can find common law systems like England and Wales, but so-called statutory civil law systems prevail. A prominent feature within the civil law tradition is the principle of legality – as opposed to the principle of opportunity. Unlike common law jurisdiction, where prosecutors may choose whether or not to prosecute, and may take the result of VOM engagement into account if they wish, prosecutors in statutory systems can act only within the confines of their code provisions (cf. Miers and Willemsens 2004: 158). While Germany and Austria, as well as Italy, Spain and Portugal, adhere to the principle of legality, Scandinavian countries follow a prosecution practice that can be best understood as a mixture of both principles, with features of the opportunity principle being more pronounced. In the following paragraphs we will draw a rough picture of the main lines of VOM developments in some European countries (for a comprehensive mapping of the European landscape cf. Miers and Willemsens 2004).

VOM in Albania. In Albania, in March 1999, the 'Law on Mediation in Conflict Resolution and Reconciliation of Disputes' was issued which deals with mediation in criminal cases. It was followed up and expanded by a 'Law on Mediation in Dispute Resolution' (Law No. 9090 of 26 July 2003). Mediation is an optional procedure that can be started at the request of the injured party; referral is made by the police, the attorney's office and by the court. It is carried out by subjects or centers that are licensed by the Ministry of Justice, and which are registered with the court. The Albanian Foundation for Conflict Resolution and Reconciliation of Disputes

(AFCR) is the most important NGO applying VOM. It has been active since 1995 and it has established mediation centers that cooperate with the prosecutor's office and with the courts on district level. It has also set up training for mediators. The criminal cases that are handled by the AFCR amount to 500–550 cases per year and make up about 40–42 per cent of the total number of VOM cases per year in Albania.

VOM in Austria. After introducing the *Außergerichtlicher Tatausgleich* (ATA) in Juvenile Law in 1988, VOM for adults became a topic for legislation in 1991. A pilot project was started and gradually spread throughout the country. On 25 February 1999 the National Assembly passed an amending law to the Code of Criminal Procedure. This came into force on 1 January 2000, providing for various methods of diversion and, most importantly, giving victim offender mediation a legal basis. VOM is applicable to offences committed by juveniles and by adults. The provision of VOM for both adults and juvenile offenders is diversionary in nature and discretionary in its application; it is determined in any case by the public prosecutor, and only as a subsidiary measure by the trial judge. The prosecutor can make the determination conditional on the offender's agreement to accept responsibility and to make amends.[5] If the public prosecutor is the gatekeeper to mediation, responsibility for its implementation lies with the ATA unit of the association NEUSTART, the former Association for Probation Service and Social Work. NEUSTART is a private organization subsidized by the Ministry of Justice, but is functioning as an autonomous body with its own management and supervisory committees.[6]

Mediators must possess a professional qualification in social work. A degree in law or psychology is accepted if the applicant also has practical experience in social work. All newly recruited mediators are required to undergo initial as well as follow-up training. The training program consists of two parts: the first for 'beginners' to acquire basic qualifications and a second part to become a certified mediator in penal matters. Both parts comprise training at a theoretical and practical level; altogether training lasts three to four years. Once in practice, mediators' work is entirely to do with mediation. Only a very small number also work as probation officers. The association's national character, its standards of quality and the description of the entire VOM process ensure a relatively high degree of conformity to common standards and practices. NEUSTART works closely with prosecutors and judges, and pays particular attention to the need to induct new appointees into the ethos of a national policy on mediation.

Between 1995 and 1998, cases involving juvenile offenders (around 2,500–2,750 a year) represented about 10 per cent of all cases that came to the prosecutors' attention. This figure comprises about 50 per cent of all young offenders punished with a fine or imprisonment. Since the Procedural Law Amendment Act 1999 provides for a greater range of diversionary measures, nowadays prosecutors or judges resort more often to other diversionary instruments: for example, community service. While the numbers of juvenile cases are decreasing, referral of cases of adults remains relatively stable.

The majority (65 per cent) of referred cases (8,800 in 2002) comprises offences against the person (*Aggressionsdelikte*), in particular assault and battery. Other instances of personal violence include threats, coercion, harassment, and robbery. The remaining 35 per cent comprises mainly offences against property (*Vermögensdelikte*): for example, theft, burglary, vandalism. With regard to conflict types and their social context, a matter that is particularly important, 55 per cent of cases concern close and established social relations. These comprise conflicts between partners (domestic violence), family and friends, at the workplace, in school, and, the most difficult type to mediate, between neighbors.

VOM in the Czech Republic. The Czech Republic represents an example of one of those Eastern European countries where in the course of the 1990s the development of probation and mediation went hand in hand. The most important legislative activity in this regard was the issuing of the 'Law on Probation and Mediation Service' (PMS) that came into force on 1 January 2001. An amendment to the Criminal Procedural Law of 1 January 2002 opens the possibility to refer cases to mediation as early as the investigation phase. This legislation also deals in some detail with the procedure of mediation and especially its relation to the criminal justice system.

VOM is defined as out-of-court intervention for the purpose of resolving conflicts between the offender and the victim. It is used mainly as a means of diversion from criminal proceedings but also 'as a source of information' relevant to the decision-making about the sentence, and it can also be used as an addition to a non-custodial sentence, as a means of strengthening 'its rehabilitative purpose' (Miers and Willemsens 2004: 37).

The Probation and Mediation Service is a government agency within the Ministry of Justice and consists of independent probation and mediation centers in each of the seventy-four court districts. The present (2003) staff consists of 157 officers, sixty-one assistants, and twelve headquarter staff, in total 230 persons. The training of the mediators is organized by the Ministry of Justice in close cooperation with the Probation and Mediation Service. It can be characterized as professional service with a high standard set for the qualification of mediators (twelve three-day sessions of training required for so-called 'officers' and six three-day sessions for assistants).

Figures supplied by the Probation and Mediation Service show a remarkable increase of the caseload since 2001. They amounted to 6,323 cases in 2002: that is 21.5 per cent of all cases held at the pre-trial stage of criminal proceedings. However, one has to consider that handling these cases by the PMS also involves preparing conditions for 'conditional cessation of prosecution', with no mediation effort taking place.

VOM in France. In France significant developments have taken place since 1999 in the field of legislation which introduced an array of clearly defined diversionary measures; one of these is '*la mediation entre l'auteur des faits et la victime, avec l'accord des parties.*' These diversionary measures are to be realized '*directement ou par delegation*': delegation to special agencies (or individuals) is increasingly made use of. The '*décret d'application*' of 29 January 2001 provides for the placement of the mediators and mediation's relation to the state prosecutors; another decree defines the conditions under which legal aid can be provided for VOM and for other alternative measures (*la composition penal*). For juveniles the main text is Article 12-1 of the 1945 legislation governing the entire juvenile justice system. The measure is called 'reparation' and places particular emphasis on the educative benefits to the young person. In this case the measure can be used between charge and first appearance, during the pre-trial phase or after conviction. For adults the state prosecutors can propose mediation to both parties, before taking a decision on whether to prosecute or to choose some diversionary measure. The objectives of mediation are to repair the harm of the victim, to restore social harmony and to contribute to the offender's rehabilitation. The diversionary effect of mediation applies to the pre-prosecution stage only.

Many types of association may practice 'mediation penal' or 'reparation' and it is also possible to call on individual mediators. But in all cases the mediators must be accredited by the local prosecutor and by the president of the tribunal. Normally the associations or the individual mediators agree upon the working protocols that are to govern their relationship with their prosecutor's office. Many associations' mediators are highly professionalized. An important exception is the National Institute of Victim Assistance and Mediation (INA-VEM), where the majority of mediators are volunteers.

In general, offences of medium severity are regarded as suited for VOM. The offences included are theft, family conflicts (ranging from domestic violence to non-payment of maintenance), brawls and assault, insult, bodily injury, and environmental offences. The penal mediation program deals with some 30,000 adult offenders per year. The number of reparation interventions for young offenders is less developed; moreover, it is rather a 'traditional' social work intervention aiming at behavioral change and less of an interactive, truly 'restorative' event.

VOM in Germany. Victim offender mediation (in German: *Täter–Opfer-Ausgleich* – offender victim balance) was the first form of mediation to find substantial recognition in both theory and practice in Germany (cf. Alexander *et al.* 2003: 182). The first pilot programs began in 1985 in the juvenile sector. Today there are about 400 VOM programs across the country; about one third of the schemes work with juvenile as well as adult offenders. In Germany one can find mediation centers that only employ trained (professional) mediators as well as (juvenile) court services that use 'mediation' (sometimes with, sometimes without any training) as one among other additional tools. Most institutions supporting victim offender mediation are small, many of them employing only one (part-time) mediator dealing with fewer than fifty cases a year. However, there are some vanguard programs run by non-profit organizations. The largest VOM program is the Waage ('Scales') Conflict

Resolution Center in Hanover. Waage employs four (one full-time, three part-time) paid and ten to twelve volunteer mediators who handle more than 650 cases a year, involving approximately 600 adult offenders and even more victims.

VOM was integrated into the German criminal justice system as early as 1991 through a series of legislative reforms. Although in Germany the so-called legality principle asks for mandatory prosecution in general, there are specific exceptions to the requirement to prosecute. With respect to juveniles, the office of public prosecutions can refrain from a formal procedure if the juvenile makes a serious attempt at victim offender reconciliation (§ 45 (2) 2 JGG – Juvenile Criminal Code). With respect to adult offenders, German criminal law due to the legality principle does not – prima facie – allow extensive use of discretion. In the past decade, however, VOM has been established as a significant exception to this general rule; § 153a (1) No. 5 StPO (Code of Criminal Procedure) allows a prosecutor to defer and/or refrain from formally charging an accused person in a misdemeanor case if VOM is undertaken. In addition, § 46a StGB (German Criminal Code) was introduced in 1994 to permit a judge to mitigate or refrain from imposing a sentence in cases involving a maximum of one year's imprisonment if the offender has made honest attempts towards VOM. Further, in such cases the prosecutor can even drop the charge prior to sentencing (§ 153b StPO). Finally, several regulations relating to VOM were introduced into the Code of Criminal Procedure in 1999, the result of which is that prosecutors and judges must assess and continue to reassess the suitability of VOM at each stage of the criminal procedure and trial (§ 155a StPO). Where appropriate, cases may be referred to a VOM program (§ 155b StPO).

Although VOM cases are not recorded systematically and large gaps still exist with regard to the number of services cooperating in the nationwide compilation of data, there now exist at least reliable estimates of cases dealt with in the way of VOM in Germany. Based on the data of the National VOM-Statistics, roughly 25,000 cases were mediated in 2002 (cf. Kerner and Hartmann 2003). More than 80 per cent have been referred at a pre-charge diversion stage via the prosecutor's office. Nearly two-thirds of the caseload involves juvenile offenders and the offences include violent cases, mostly assaults, bodily injury, but also (juvenile) robbery (9 per cent). In property offenses, referral agencies only seldom seem to assume a conflict that needs to be resolved. In about 70 per cent of the cases there has been a prior relationship between the victim and the alleged offender; this number has increased steadily during recent years from about 50 per cent in the early 1990s.

Despite significant legislative reform and the growth in VOM programs throughout Germany, VOM today is utilized in less than 5 per cent of criminal matters, although studies have revealed that at least one quarter of all prosecutorial charges are eligible for VOM (cf. Hartmann 1995: 186). According to existing legislation, § 46a StGB/§ 153b StPO could potentially be used in over 90 per cent of criminal matters (Dölling and Hellinger 1998: 15; Kilchling 1996: 311). The gap between actual and potential use reflects the difference between legislative intentions and expectations and the limited understanding of many stakeholders in the criminal justice system of the role VOM can play (Trenczek 2002, 2003b). On the other hand, VOM programs are becoming increasingly successful in directly attracting disputants involved in criminal matters and other disputes, before the legal system becomes involved. In this context the boundaries between VOM and community mediation begin to blur – a reflection of the universal application of the mediation process.

Mediators in Germany are not subject to national regulation and, as a consequence, standards and mediation styles vary greatly. At postgraduate level, mediation accreditation programs are being designed and offered on an interdisciplinary basis (i.e. interdisciplinary instructors and participants). The vast majority of VOM is undertaken by professional mediators who have a basic university degree in social work/social science and have undertaken a specialized one-year training (120 hours) of the National VOM Service Bureau, which has also published standards of good practice since 1995 (TOA Service Buero 2003). Volunteer mediators play a limited role, yet community conflict resolution centers have integrated volunteer mediators in their professional teams with growing success.

The development of mediation accreditation and practice standards by mediation organizations in specific practice areas is a current trend in Germany. These standards are not legally binding; rather, they provide a performance benchmark for mediators in the relevant area. In terms of victim offender mediation, the National VOM Service Bureau together with the Federal Association of VOM has developed a quality certificate and accreditation procedure.

VOM in Finland. Finland has extensively used pilot projects for trying out VOM, and it will now have mediation services all over the country, organized by the municipalities, staffed with lay persons who have taken special training at general centers for adult training and education. The basic course takes thirty hours; additional specific 'advanced' courses may follow; some municipalities provide for supervision.

Legislation is pending for a 'Law on Mediation in Penal Matters'. The government proposal of the Ministry of Social Affairs and Health was submitted in August 2002. This would be the type of legislation that is also to be found in Norway – with the Social Policy Administration taking the lead and attributing the municipalities an important role.

Where VOM is practiced so far, it is either used as a diversionary measure at the police level (who refer about 80 per cent of all cases), at the recommendation of the prosecutor or at the trial phase, where the judge might take mediation into consideration when deciding on the sentence. To some small degree VOM is also practiced at the initiative of one or both of the parties affected. The scope of mediation according to the proposal pending will include all offences 'where compensation for damages is possible and where the parties voluntarily agree to participate in mediation.' There are no more recent figures concerning the number of VOM referrals in Finland; studies conducted in the 1990s suggested an average of 3,000 referrals per year.

In the absence of national guidelines, there is little uniformity in practice. In some municipalities mediation applies primarily to juveniles and children under the age of criminal responsibility (fifteen years). In these cases it is the social services who refer the case to mediation.

VOM in Italy. In Italy VOM is still in its initial stages, with a few projects scattered all around the country. At the beginning of 2002 a 'Law on Criminal Proceedings in Front of the Justice of the Peace' was introduced. The justice of the peace deals with minor offences only and – beyond imposing fines, house arrest or community service orders – may promote reconciliation between parties. For that purpose he/she suspends the hearing for a period not exceeding two months and may refer the case to mediation services. But he/she can also carry out mediation between the parties relying on his/her own skill. The justice of the peace may be any person with a legal education who has to pass an exam after a six months' training period. In juvenile justice there is the possibility for the judge to suspend criminal proceedings and to give probation time; within this probation time that is monitored by social services, reconciliation,

and reparation to the victim can be one of the requirements the offender has to comply with. And it is the social workers that act as mediators and write an assessment of the 'evolution of the offender's personality.' In line with this tradition is the fact that only a sizeable minority (40 per cent) of the cases dealing with young offenders apply direct mediation, while for the majority the intervention does not involve a direct meeting of the parties. Mediation practice in general is strongly inspired by the theories and the work of Jeanne Morineau in France, who trained the majority of Italian mediators. The absence of reliable statistics makes it very difficult to be precise about referrals. Over the period 1995–2001 the nine VOM centers dealt with a fewer than 1,000 referrals, resulting in about 560 successful mediations.

VOM in the Netherlands. Although in general the Netherlands is well known for its variety of creative pilot projects in the field of criminal justice, as well as in the conflict mediation field, in regard to VOM the Netherlands has been judged as a laggard within the European movement. There are still no statutory rules concerning VOM (or family group conferencing). In the past, the Dutch approach became manifest in the police-driven HALT (*het alternatief* = the alternative) projects that focus on material restitution. In addition, 'claims mediation' can take place in the context of the Directive for the Care of Victims 1995, amended in 1999. It is a diversionary measure, mainly concerned with the victim. It can take effect either at the investigation stage of the offence, where it is handled by the police, or at the prosecution stage, where it is handled by the public prosecutor. A successful mediation followed by payment to the victim will lead, in less serious cases, to the case being dismissed; in the more serious cases success can be taken into account in sentencing.

In 2002, the Board of Prosecutors General issued a statement articulating a positive attitude towards RJ programs. As a consequence, several initiatives and different programs became active in the Netherlands. One can find family conferencing with juvenile offenders, so-called 'restorative mediation' in juvenile and also in adult cases, experiments with restorative mediation in relation to very serious offences, and mediation is also taking place in the community justice context (*Justitie in de Buurt* = Justice in the neighborhood). 'Restorative Mediation,' one of the most exciting experiments, normally takes effect following sentence. It is both victim- and offender-oriented and it is concerned with non-material or symbolic reparation. The principal referral authorities are the Probation Service, Victim Support, and the prison spiritual welfare system. The aim is explicitly not to influence the criminal process, but to help victims and offenders to cope with the psychological burdens of crime and victimization. It aims to assist victims and offenders in coming to terms with the pain on the part of the victim and the guilt on the part of the perpetrator. It supplements but does not replace the criminal law track (and therefore constitutes an example of a 'dual track model,' see below). Within this project from January 2001 to September 2002, 168 case enrolments were registered, with 16 per cent of cases concerning lethal violence, 30 per cent violence leading to injury, 9 per cent lethal traffic accidents and 9 per cent robbery; the scheme needs a lot of preparation and careful preliminary talks – a variety of differentiated outcomes is possible. Due to budgetary restrictions the project was terminated in January 2004. Instead, a network of new mediation projects will be developed gradually, based on a model designed by Victim Support.

Although mediation as a methodology has received a lot of attention and – quite recently – more pronounced support by the Ministry of Justice, VOM is explicitly not to benefit from this favorable attitude. Despite the fact that a number of different RJ programs have been developed in the Nether-lands, the overall number of cases continues to be small, and in that sense restorative practices remain a marginal phenomenon. On the other hand, one has to mention that important contributions have been made by Dutch researchers and scientists, e.g. a special journal, *Tjidschrift voor herstelrecht*, which is published in Dutch by John Blad and others from the Erasmus University in Rotterdam, has gained international reputation.

VOM in Norway. Norway, the home of Nils Christie, is considered to be one of the vanguards in VOM development in Europe, using a unique volunteer approach and having a nationwide program boasting the highest number of VOM cases in Europe. The legislation authorizing VOM in Norway comprises the Municipal Mediation Service Act 1991, regulations made in 1992, a departmental circular, and a circular from the General Director of Public Prosecution, extending discretion to the prosecuting authority to refer suitable cases to mediation and to discontinue further action against the offender. On 1 January 2004 an amendment came into force stating that the mediation scheme should no longer be a municipal responsibility but instead a governmental service fully integrated in the justice system. (We might add that this amendment did not result in big changes concerning the practice of VOM in Norway.) The Mediation Act applies to both civil and criminal disputes and it opens the path of mediation for both juvenile and adult offenders. VOM is predominantly used as a diversionary measure, applied by the prosecutor at police level (80 per cent of all cases are referred by the police or by the prosecutor). But it can also be offered as a supplement to punishment either as a condition in a suspended sentence or as a part of a community sanction sentence. The mediation centers also deal with (small) numbers of self-referred cases.

There are now, after the reform of 2004, twenty-two mediation services all over the country, divided geographically in accordance with the police districts. A central secretariat located in Oslo is responsible for the management and development of the services. Mediators continue to be recruited from each municipality. Local mediation services typically comprise a paid coordinator and office staff, and volunteer mediators who receive a small hourly fee and expenses for each case. No specific professional background is required. A national team of trainers provides four days of basic mediation training. There are about 700 mediators in Norway.

The caseload consists mainly of acts of vandalism, minor violence and shoplifting. We are told that recently (2003) there has been more variation across the country in the profile of the cases referred. In Oslo they have become more serious and complex. On the other hand, VOM is applied to a large degree in cases involving children under the age of criminal responsibility (which is fifteen years). In 1998 the main group of offenders consisted of young boys between fifteen and seventeen years of age, but already the second largest group were children from twelve to fourteen years.

Between 5,000 and 6,000 cases are referred to mediation each year, of which approximately 3,000 are criminal cases. Of the civil cases, 65 per cent were police referrals of young offenders under fifteen years. The vast majority of cases in Norway end up with an agreement. An evaluation done in 1996 showed high rates of offender and victim satisfaction (98 and 95 per cent respectively; cf. Paus 2000).

VOM in Poland. In Poland changes in the Code of Criminal Law and the Criminal Procedural Law happened as early as 1997, with a special regulation mentioning mediation added in 1998. An amendment issued on 13 June 2003 has widened the scope of the mediation provisions. The new section 23a para. 5 deals with the conditions to be met by institutions and persons authorized to conduct mediation, the methods of appointing and dismissing them, the scope and terms under which they are given access to the case files, and the course of the mediation procedure.

Mediation in juvenile cases was regulated in May 2001. It is the family judge who refers cases in juvenile matters, while the state prosecutors are the referring agencies for adult offenders. Mediation services in Poland are run by private organizations (NGOs), the most important being the Polish Center of Mediation. In addition there are three mediation services led by another NGO: the Lower Silesian Mediation Center (DOM). Training is obligatory and regulated within the Juvenile Justice Law only; this law also contains quite detailed provisions concerning the way the mediation process is to be linked to the criminal procedure. The Ministry of Justice's regulations state that mediation services may only be provided by 'approved' bodies; these are the presidents of the provincial courts who are responsible for registration of mediators. Mediators may operate independently or as employees of an approved body. The regulations also require them to have no current professional or occupational relationship with the criminal justice system. Although the Treasury pays a fixed fee per case (about €40) mediators are, in essence, volunteers.

Referrals concerning adults are predominantly within the state prosecutor's discretion. Successful mediation may result in the discontinuation of the process or in affecting the decision of the court. It can react either by conditionally suspending the proceedings, refrain from passing a sentence, or mitigate the sentence. There is no clear limit as to the type of cases amenable to mediation. But Article 66 of the 1998 regulation provides that discontinuance of procedure can only apply to offences that do not attract sentences in excess of five years' imprisonment. Finally, the 'permissive nature' of the Polish Penal Executory Code has enabled the Prison Service to introduce mediation during the term of an adult offender's custodial sentence. More detailed information exists on the juvenile cases dealt with during the experimental phase. There the majority of cases were petty offences against property. However, there were also felonies and quite a significant number of offences involving violence. According to the data collected by the Ministry of Justice, the number of referrals of cases of adult offenders were, in the years 1999–2001, 395, 850 and 690 respectively. The number of young offenders cases remains very small indeed. While during the pilot phase about 200 mediations took place, only 212 cases were referred in 2001 and forty-two in 2002; however, the number rose to ninety-two during the first three months of 2003.

VOM in Slovenia. Slovenia has implemented a nation-wide program of VOM as introduced by Article 161a of the Code of Criminal Procedure, and, in the particular case of juveniles, Article 77(2) of the Penal Code. The revision of 2001 has considerably broadened possibilities for VOM at the later stages of the criminal proceedings. VOM in Slovenia follows the model of volunteer (lay) mediators who have to undergo a basic training of a few days. VOM is a diversionary measure, with the state prosecutors being the referring agency. Referrals can take place at all stages of the criminal procedure until a conviction has taken place ('a judgment has been passed'), but it is restricted to petty cases. The instigation of the VOM procedure that is to take place with the help of a 'neutral and independent' mediator needs the express written agreement of both parties. This might also be one reason why direct face-to-face mediation prevails in Slovenia.

In April 2004 an amendment of the Code of Criminal Procedure further broadened the possibilities for VOM. Up to this date, a case could be referred for mediation if the sanction prescribed for the criminal act in question was up to three years' imprisonment. According to the amendment of 2004, the state prosecutor may now refer a case for mediation if the case involves a juvenile offender and the sanction prescribed is up to five years' imprisonment. In addition, a case may be referred to mediation regardless of the age of the offender if the offence in question is grievous bodily harm, burglary, concealment of a property of an important value, or damaging another person's property of significant value (all mentioned offences may otherwise be punished with imprisonment of five years) or extremely grave bodily harm (the sanction prescribed is up to ten years' imprisonment).

The role of the state prosecutor's office as the referring agency is a strong one. However, the number of referrals is quite high and has remained fairly stable: 2,158 cases in 2002 (2,237 in 2000 and 2,071 in 2001). Considering that the total number of cases prosecuted in Slovenia in 2002 was around 13,000 and the total number of cases where an offender was convicted (regardless of the type of the sanction pronounced) in 2002 was around 7,000, this represents a substantial, even a stunningly high number of cases to take the VOM track. According to Alenka Meznar (2002), the Slovenian criminal justice system experienced substantial personnel savings because of VOM (in 2000, 837 fewer court hearings, which corresponds to the caseload of almost five judges in local courts).

VOM in England and Wales. England and Wales as 'common law' countries were early in launching a large number of VOM programs. They represented a wide array of different approaches. The latest count done by the umbrella organization Mediation UK lists 222 local mediation projects on its website and indicates that roughly 60 per cent of the UK is served by a local mediation service (Miers and Semenchuk 2002).

In 2001 the so-called Auld Report (*The Review of the Criminal Justice System*) recommended the 'development and implementation of a national strategy to ensure consistent, appropriate and effective use of RJ techniques across England and Wales' (Lord Chancellor's Department 2002). The review identifies six stages at which RJ might be applicable within the criminal justice system across all age groups and at all stages of the criminal process. In 2002 the Home Office confirmed that the UK is developing a national RJ strategy. It voiced the intention to consider the availability of RJ across all age groups and at all stages of the criminal process: pre-crime, especially with juveniles; pre-charge; post-conviction; pre-sentence; and post-sentence. Within this national RJ strategy, VOM, however, is only one of several practices outlined in the Crime and Disorder Act 1998, the Youth Justice and Criminal Evidence Act 1999, and the 'Guidance Documents' related to these statutory provisions. The array of measures introduced consists of final warnings, referral orders, of reparation, action plan, and supervision orders. At any of these stages a restorative element is to be considered, the arrangement of VOM being one means to realize this element of restoration.

The agencies to organize these new measures are the Youth Offending Teams (YOTs). They are multi-agency organizations which may co-opt others, for example from the voluntary sector. Statutory oversight is provided by the Youth Justice Board, a non-departmental body whose sponsoring department is the Home Office. When VOM is undertaken within the statutory framework for juveniles the activity is funded from the budget allocated to the local YOT, itself funded by the local authority. On the other hand, we have to state that no specific legal basis for the use of VOM and other RJ practices exists for adults.

VOM as a specific instrument of an RJ approach is not offered and carried out by any state agency. It has always been an activity provided by the voluntary sector and, in some areas commercial organizations. Mediation UK and the Restorative Justice Consortium are the most important umbrella organizations. They are funded by a variety of sources, both public and private. Mediation UK offers comprehensive and well-respected national training and accreditation programs for mediators. Both Mediation UK and the Restorative Justice Consortium publish statements of principle and practice standards for RJ mediation. They include a strong ethical dimension.

Practice in England and Wales is pragmatically rather than theoretically driven (Miers and Willemsens 2004: 50). There is no all-encompassing theoretical tradition. The interventions of the YOTs therefore include various forms of reparation: a letter of apology, a meeting or restorative conference at which the nature and consequences of the offence are discussed and the offender apologizes directly to the victim, or several hours per week of practical activity which benefits the victim or the community at large. Where possible the nature of the reparation should be linked to the offence or type of offence for which reparation is to be made. Due to the highly diversified landscape in England and Wales, no nationwide figures are available on the use made of VOM. On the other hand, one finds extensive documentation and evaluation of specific programs (Crawford and Newburn 2003, Dignan and Marsh 2001, Hoyle *et al.* 2002, Miers and Willemsens 2004).

Results of empirical research

Quantitative and qualitative use of VOM (within the Criminal Justice System)

According to the CoE-R 99-19 (II.4), RJ methods should be used at all stages of the criminal justice process without a limit in regard to the seriousness of the offense. The number and content of the legal provisions in the European countries therefore seems to be an ideal basis for a substantial use of VOM within the criminal justice system.

However, the practical use of VOM and other RJ practices in European countries does not exceed 5 per cent of all criminal law proceedings, Austria, France, Norway, and especially Slovenia representing remarkable exceptions. The practical development therefore stagnates in some countries on a low level. Although in most countries the existing legislation allows for a large scope of offences to be referred to VOM, the cases that are in fact referred to the VOM services are usually limited to trifles and bagatelles, simple misdemeanors and other minor offenses.

Agreements and compliance

The numbers of agreements reached in VOM programs is very high, in general over 80 per cent (Aertsen *et al.* 1994: 37; Kerner and Hartmann 2003: 74; Miers and Willemsens 2004). It is about 90 per cent in Norway (Paus 2000: 302), but only about 60 per cent in Slovenia (Meznar 2002). More agreements seem to be generated when there is a personal encounter between victim and offender (Hammerschick *et al.* 1994). The results of the mediation agreements are extremely varied: in some cases, a financial redress such as compensation for injury or damages has top priority. The parties often agree on a symbolic gesture, for example that the offender makes a donation to charity. Sometimes, after a successful settlement they decide on a joint activity and go for a coffee or meet in the evening for a drink. In domestic cases, the affected parties are very often concerned with laying down rules for future behavior, for example a strict ban on any form of contact. With disputes amongst neighbors, VOM usually ends in binding agreements which govern specific aspects of living next door to one another. Mediation agreements are usually fulfilled to a high percentage in all programs; compliance rates between 60 and 100 per cent have been reported (Aertsen *et al.* 1994: 37; Kerner and Hartmann

2003: 90; Paus 2000; Miers and Willemsens 2004).

In Germany some VOM programs manage so-called victim funds, out of which offenders without sufficient financial means may receive an interest-free loan in order to pay the compensation to the injured party. The offenders then either pay back the money by installments or do community or charity work. The rate of back repayments from the offender is over 90 per cent and thus exceeds the repayment of bank loans.

Effects on the criminal procedure – rates of dismissals and discontinuations

The effects of VOM with regard to the criminal procedure, its continuation or termination, vary according to the national laws and the stage of criminal procedure at which VOM is established. In those cases where a mediation agreement is reached (and fulfilled) the German prosecutors dismiss the case in more than 80 per cent. The rate is between 71 and 86 per cent in Austria (Hofinger and Pelikan 2004) and it is 100 per cent in Norway, where the report to the prosecutors suffices as a basis for the discharge.

Acceptance and satisfaction of participants

Overall, criminological research in Europe shows that informal dispute resolution (even) in criminal offenses is very well accepted by the parties involved as well as by the general public (Kilchling 1995; Mattinson and Mirlees-Black 2000; Sessar 1992, Strang 2002; Wright 1989). The preference for restorative solution is higher among victims of crime compared to persons who have not been victimized, and higher among non-lawyers compared to criminal justice officials. State prosecutors showed the most pronounced punitive attitudes.

European studies confirm that the willingness to participate in mediation schemes is extremely high on the part of victims (60–80 per cent) as well as offenders (80–90 per cent) (cf. Aertsen and Peters 1998; Kerner and Hartmann 2003: 54; Kilchling and Löschnig-Gspandl 1998). These figures are even higher in matters involving monetary claims and in conflicts involving youth offenders. Neither the seriousness of the offence nor the injury caused seems to be a significant factor in predicting the willingness of victims to participate. However, not all participants opt for a direct face-to-face meeting with the offender. According to various studies, 30–60 per cent of the victims want to meet their perpetrators personally (Aertsen *et al.* 2004, 36; Kerner and Hartmann 2003: 70).

Victims and offenders give a broad range of reasons for taking part in mediation (Dölling and Henninger 1998: 203; Netzig and Trenczek 1996: 255). One motive is very dominant: victims want to get more information and explanations about the offense and about the reasons it happened to them. In cases involving juvenile offenders victims often express educative motives. Another dominant motive, especially in cases involving adult offenders, seems to be the claim for compensation. However, during the course of the mediation process a surprising turnaround frequently occurs: financial demands take a back seat and non-material aspects gain importance. Victims of violent conflicts, in particular, express that even after initial skepticism, the mediation talks have helped them to overcome the excessive fears resulting from the incident and that, during mediation talks, they were able to overcome fear, anger, hate, and thoughts of revenge.

Victims who participated in RJ processes were significantly more satisfied than those participating in the traditional criminal justice procedure (cf. Aertsen *et al.* 2004: 35). The majority of participants in a VOM process experience a high level of satisfac-

tion in the process and outcome, with satisfaction rates up to more than 90 per cent also on the side of the victim (Altweger and Hitzl 2000; Lins 1998; Netzig and Trenczek 1996: 256; Paus 2000; Pelikan and Hoenisch 1999). Apart from the generally high satisfaction rate reported, studies that contained a wider range of differentiated questions and answers were also able to point out a program's strengths and weaknesses and the influence of mediator performance.

Research on recidivism rates

The type of evaluation which usually receives the most attention is the recidivism study. In England and Wales particularly, a more systematic and thorough evaluation effort was started when elements of RJ became part of the mainstream response to juvenile delinquency in 1997. Despite a host of criticisms[7] that were voiced regarding the use of recidivism as main or sole yardstick of the success of an intervention, it is still traded as a most important 'hard' and objective evidence of the effectiveness of any new type of intervention. There is empirical evidence from British, from Belgian, and from German studies showing that participation in a mediation procedure at least has no negative effect, but rather – compared to the conventional criminal procedure – produces better figures (Dölling and Hartmann 2003; Gerhard 2004; Geudens 1998; Miers *et al.* 2001; Schütz 1999).[8] According to the Home Office study by Miers *et al.* (2001) these effects are even more distinctive in cases of (severe) violent crime, as happened in the West Yorkshire scheme. David Miers remarks that

> the fact that West Yorkshire was the only scheme in which a statistically significant outcome was found in terms of reducing reconviction, raises the distinct possibility that mediation works more effectively – and cost effectively – with 'high tariff' cases than with more minor cases.
>
> (Miers 2004: 33)[9]

79

General – main issues

VOM – voluntary or mandatory?

The ideal of RJ requires that for both sides, victim and offender, participation in the mediation procedure is voluntary. However, apart from the difficulties in defining what voluntariness actually means within the context of criminal justice (Trenczek 1996: 227) the notion is broken down to the requirement that both victims and offenders are able to make an informed choice whether or not they want to participate. There should be no pressure, nor urging or persuasion on both sides, for the victim and offender to agree to mediation. The criminal justice authorities must make sure that no form of improper constraint influences the parties' agreement to mediation (CoE-R 99-19 No. 11; EM p. 17). Both victim and offender have a right to refuse and a right to go to court. This implies – with regard to the alleged offender – that the consequences of not having a mediation process (whether by choice of the offender or the victim) should not be more severe than those ensuing without the offer being made. In most European jurisdictions participation within a VOM-program requires an acknowledgement of involvement in the alleged offense on the side of the perpetrator; however, a legal admission of guilt is not required. According to the CoE-R 99-19 and in compliance with the principle of the presumption of innocence (Article 6.2 ECHR) participation in mediation should not be used as evidence of admission of guilt in subsequent legal proceedings (CoE-R 99-19, No. 14). Procedural safeguards have to be implemented. The right to legal counseling/assistance, translation/interpretation and parental assistance (or, if need be, assistance by other representatives) and special legal safeguards for minors should be explicitly regulated (CoE-R 99-19, No. 8 and No. 12). With regard to the outcome of mediation the requirement that the negotiated agreements should be completely voluntary is absolute. However, according to the CoE-R 99-19, with regard to the compensation agreed, proportionality should be observed, meaning that within rather wide limits there should be a proportionality between the burden of the offender and the seriousness of the offense (R (99) 19, No. 31).

Direct or indirect mediation?

In Germany face-to-face meetings occur in about 60–75 per cent of cases (in about 10–15 per cent an encounter of the parties even occurs without a mediator); the rate of direct mediation is a little higher in Austria. In Norway and in Slovenia almost all cases are dealt with by way of direct mediation. The programs in the UK show very different rates and quite often the vast majority of cases are dealt with by indirect or shuttle mediation, i.e. with the mediator transporting information, suggestions and offers between the parties.

The manner in which cases are mediated should be determined by the needs and interests of the victims and offenders concerned. Although a face-to-face meeting is supposed to be offered as an opportunity, there is nothing wrong if a mediation takes place indirectly, with the mediator talking to each of the affected parties individually. In cases where there is no ongoing relationship, where damage to property has been minor and the emotional problems caused negligible, participants often find proceedings involving face-to-face contact too time-consuming and unnecessary for settling financial compensation. On the other hand, we do have some empirical evidence lending support to the use of direct mediation. In Austria, the accompanying research (Hammerschick *et al.* 1994; Altweger and Hitzl 2000) and the study of Kilchling and Löschnig-Gspandl (1998) comparing the provinces of Styria (Austria) and Baden-Württemberg (Germany), have all pointed to the fact that direct mediation makes for more victim satisfaction and for the victim's perception of the perpetrator as having taken responsibility. In addition, compliance with agreements is also higher where direct mediation has taken place.

Volunteer or professional mediators?

According to the CoE-R 99-19, mediators should be recruited from all sectors of society and should generally possess good understanding of the local culture and community. Community involvement is often seen as an essential element of RJ. Therefore, the involvement of volunteers (as members of the community) in the mediation process can make it more restorative (Aertsen *et al.* 2004: 71). However, in any case mediators should receive initial training before taking up mediation duties as well as in-service training (CoE-R 99-19, No. 24).

In Europe one can find both types of mediation schemes, one based on professional mediators, the other mainly based on volunteer mediators. The two opposing models are represented by Austria and Norway respectively, with Norway relying on volunteers who get a very short basic training, Austria on professionals with lengthy training. In Norway, VOM is part of a community-based conflict resolution approach. There, the orientation towards community activity and self-help is quite alive. Doing volunteer work is seen as an expression of reliance on the community and its potential. And when conflicts that have come to be reported as criminal acts are referred to the mediation services, people seem to be glad for once not to be confronted with psychologists and social workers taking over. In Norway a general skepticism regarding professionals seems to prevail: 'some people find it easier to turn to the mediation service where they are met by volunteers and not some kind of expert that examines them with x-ray eyes

and a professional air,' says Siri Kemeny (Kemeny *et al.* 2003: 8). The opposite is true for Austria. There is a strong trust in professionals and little sense of community. To put it even more strongly, community in the Nordic or the Anglo-American sense does not exist. Further, one has to take into account that the case profile is quite different, with mainly acts of vandalism and shoplifting marking the caseload in Norway, while acts against the person – slight bodily injury, dangerous threat, and robbery – are dealt with in the Austrian VOM.

Norway and Austria are perceived as role models for other countries. While Slovenia copied the Norwegian approach, the Czech Republic has favored the professional approach. In most German VOM programs, cases are mediated by professional social workers who have undergone a special mediation training (minimum 120 hours) offered by the National VOM-Service Bureau. During the last two years, however, pilot programs like the Waage Conflict Resolution Center in Hanover have been established to integrate thoroughly trained (up to 200 hours) volunteers in a mixed, interdisciplinary mediator team. The goal is to foster a new conflict culture, giving the citizens the possibility of resolving their conflicts prior to making a charge within the court system.

A problematic development is taking place in countries (e.g. England, Wales, Germany) where due to limited resources mediation is conferred to professional services as an add-on job of social workers and jurists, police and criminal justice officers, probation and court assistants, whose main goals and tasks are typically not compatible with the impartial attitude of a mediator. Even if the pressure of routine work would allow for adequate training in individual cases, the lens through which cases and clients are assessed is different and is likely to prevent suitable conflicts being (impartially) mediated (cf. CoE-R 99-19, No. 26). Probation and juvenile court services often give priority to rehabilitation and educational goals, and this often leads to an abuse of mediation (and therefore the victim) and results in piling up several possible sanctions (so-called 'sanction-cocktails') or an educational measure in juvenile proceedings.

Confidentiality

Confidentiality is a prerequisite for a fruitful exchange and constructive outcome. It helps to create an environment where the parties can safely bring in more aspects of their 'story' than may be admissible in traditional court proceedings. Such additional information is often the basis for reaching an out-of-court settlement (CoE-R 99-19, No. 2, EM No. 2). Therefore, mediation sessions should be performed 'in camera' and not be open to the public (CoE-R 99-19, No. 29). Confidentiality applies not only vis-à-vis the general public but also in relation to the criminal justice system. However, according to the CoE-R 99-19, the principle of confidentiality does not extend strictly to imminent serious crime that may be revealed during mediation.

VOM and its relation to the criminal justice system

The diversion approach and its limits. Although mediation can be used at all stages of the criminal procedure, in most European countries VOM programs were established as diversion models. Therefore, prosecutors are the main source of case referrals in most programs. Because of VOM being closely connected to the idea and the policy of diversion, VOM is perceived as instrument to deal with petty crime only, to the exclusion of more serious offences. VOM services, therefore, have to argue with the public prosecutor's office about the appropriateness of a case for mediation without distinguishing between the two aspects of 'appropriateness': the suitability of conflict mediation and the judicial criteria for dis-

continuing the criminal procedure. On the other hand, in an effort to keep good relations with criminal law officials, representatives of VOM programs are often too ready to agree with the notion that VOM 'obviously' is not suitable for heavy crimes:

> In cases of aggravated assault with considerable physical and psychological damage, it is quite clear that measures like mediation or restitution do not work. Therefore it would be more sensible to concentrate on offences of minor and medium severity, because there we have the highest amount of cases.
>
> (U. Hartmann 1994: 6)

This contention flies in the face of some important empirical evidence gathered so far in the course of evaluating Anglo-American projects (Sherman *et al.* 2000; Marshall 1996), but there are also bits and pieces of evidence to be found in the accompanying research done in Austria (Hammerschick *et al.* 1994). It shows that the positive effect on victims is greater and more pronounced when it is used with more serious crime.

Dual track restorative justice. Beyond the diversion programs in some European countries (especially in Belgium) VOM is also applied to cases where prosecution and a criminal procedure are already on the way on a 'dual track' (Van Ness and Heetderks-Strong 2002). The mediation process runs alongside or parallel to the criminal process. With this type of program VOM is not a substitute for the criminal procedure but complementary to it and affects a criminal law response. The agreement as to material and/or non-material compensation is to influence the sentence of the court that has offered the restorative effort. There are some findings indicating that, more than the agreement itself, the proposal for mediation and the communication between the parties, i.e. the process, has a meaning and importance in its own right, especially for the victim (Aertsen 2000).

Add-on restorative justice programs. Restorative processes in the prison context (in the Netherlands, in Belgium, in Germany, in the UK) are also of the type that keeps different modes and different logics of reacting to crime apart. At the final stage of the criminal justice system the aspects of emotions and of social relations: the pain and the remorse felt, and the disruption of social bonds experienced in the course and in the aftermath of the act somebody has committed and was found guilty and sentenced for, are – at last – attended to. This happens depending on the willingness of both parties and/or the availability of a supporting network to establish a circle or a conference. The encounter and its potential effects pertain not only to the sphere of relations and emotions but also to concerns of and to care for the safety for the victim and the reintegration of the offender.

Autonomy of conflict resolution – danger of cooptation? The mediation process operates on the basis of a different rationale from the traditional criminal justice system. From the very beginning of VOM its relation to the criminal justice system was the focus of many policy discussions. In connection with the reformatory efforts in the criminal law system, Feeley (1979) and Zehr (1985) draw attention to the problem that good innovative ideas are not immune to being co-opted by powers within the system. The criminal justice system seems to be 'so impregnated with self-interests, so adaptive that it takes in any new idea, molds it, changes it until it suits the system's own purposes' (Zehr 1985: 3). From an organization-related sociological perspective, such a self-referencing cooptation seems to be necessary because the alternatives are supposed to be threatening to the system.. The CoE-R 99-19 has stated that mediation services should have sufficient autonomy to develop standards concerning qualifications of the personnel, codes of conduct and/or ethical codes for performing mediation (CoE-R 99-19, No

20). Therefore we have to take a closer look at the way autonomy is realized. Despite positive research outcomes, almost everywhere the use of mediation is severely restricted by the reluctance of criminal justice officers to refer cases to VOM. But considering not only the numbers but also the quality of cases, we have to notice that VOM is being used for the treatment of minor offences and other criminal justice marginalia. The directives stated in the CoE-R 99-19 are also neglected with regard to the voluntariness of the mediation outcome (cf. R (99)19, No. 31). Quite often criminal justice officials (want to) determine the result to be reached through the mediation process, or they insist on further penal sanctions as add-ons to the agreed mediation outcome.

A reliable assessment of the degree of autonomy or dependence in different countries is not possible. Legal provisions or soft law regulations might differ considerably from the practice observed (Aertsen 2000; Trenczek 2002). A hint can be derived though from the comparative research done by Kilchling and Löschnig-Gspandl (1998) in the mid-1990s. It points to a more favorable result concerning the agreements reached and concerning victim satisfaction for Austria, where directives of state prosecutors were fairly unknown while they happened quite often in the German programs (Kilchling and Löschnig-Gspandl 1998).

The mode of relation between VOM-programs and the criminal justice system that allows the potential of RJ to unfold but also preserves the achievements of positive criminal law, i.e. protection of the rights of the alleged perpetrator, is 'temporary autonomy' or, in the words of Leo van Garsse the 'semi-internal position' (Van Garsse 2002). What does this imply? Temporary autonomy means mediation work being carried out without interference from the criminal justice system-agencies that retain discretion as to the referral and also retain discretion as to continuation or discontinuation of the procedure (discharge). This temporary or 'conditional autonomy' should indeed leave space and time for handling the case according to the inner dynamics and the rationale of the mediation process, this process being guided by the principles of impartiality and of confidentiality and by the working principles of 'recognition' and 'empowerment' guiding the interventions of the mediator.

Where do we go from here? More diversity – some convergence

As stated in the introduction, the European landscape of VOM and RJ is marked by competing visions and by a wide variety of practices. In that respect not much has changed since the assessment of the CoE-R 99-19 (EXM p.10) The European development of mediation models is uneven across European countries and in the majority of countries it is still in its initial stages. On the other hand, it is a peculiarity of the continental European scene, and especially of those countries that are marked by a civil law jurisdiction, to have developed schemes and programs of VOM where the relationship to the criminal justice system is clearly defined. It is enshrined in legislation, most often as part of, or specific annexes to, the codes of Criminal Procedural Law (Austria, France, Germany, Poland, Slovenia). Another type of legislation-based mediation is to be found in Norway and in Finland (also to some degree in Sweden) where the practice of VOM is based on a special type of social welfare legislation. In any case legislation will guarantee a certain degree of similarity, if not uniformity – at least with regard to the rules and modes of referral of cases and the way mediation outcomes are dealt with by the agencies of the criminal justice system.

The diversionary mode is prevalent in countries that have a civil law jurisdiction,

and state prosecutors (in Norway, the prosecutor at police level) are by and large the most important gatekeepers. The influence of these gatekeepers on the process of mediation is stronger in some countries than in others. We think that in Germany, France and in Spain (probably also in Portugal where VOM is only at its initial stages), as well as in Slovenia, the state prosecutor and the court respectively put in considerable weight. In France this pertains to the type of mediation that is practiced in law courts or in *maisons de justice et du droit*. Norway's mediation services, by contrast, work with a high degree of independence from the referring agency (the police and the prosecutor). The Austrian nationwide ATA service and its relation to the state prosecutors might be positioned somewhere in the middle, coming close to the arrangements of a temporary autonomy. This arrangement, as set out in the chapter on VOM and its relation to the criminal justice system, could indeed serve as a guideline for establishing and following through good policies concerning the relation of the criminal justice system and RJ programs.

The diversionary mode of VOM and its grounding in legislation accounts for nationwide coverage and it has – in some countries – succeeded in leaving its mark on the face of the criminal justice system. This can be said for Slovenia, for Austria, also for France. But it also has severe drawbacks. The diversionary mode of inclusion restricts VOM and other RJ practices to the realm of petty offences. It becomes a kind of preliminary or introduction (*Vorspiel*) to the use of the traditional scale of sanctions to be applied where and when more serious offences are at stake. It is questionable if the criminal law perspective gives VOM a chance to be accepted as a real alternative to the punishment-oriented catalogue of measurements. Despite the growth and success of single programs until now, mediation in general has as yet had almost no chance to develop more than a marginal existence. In many European countries, VOM as an instrument within the criminal justice system still leads a shadowy existence, and its quantitative and qualitative importance is conversely proportional to the public and political interest displayed.

To counteract this tendency, the Belgian model 'Mediation for reparation' has been set up. It is a very well-designed example representing the 'dual track' mode of RJ and its position vis-à-vis the criminal justice system (Van Ness and Heetderks-Strong 2002). But despite a surge of interest displayed by practitioners in the field, there seems considerable reluctance (caused by indifference or fear?) on the side of the protagonists of the criminal justice system to think of constructing such dual track models as are also compatible with the more pronounced civil law jurisdictions. Concerning the models of introducing restorative elements into the prison system (the add-on model), where again Belgium but also Switzerland and the UK are vanguards, they are now considered more widely, albeit with caution, e.g. in Germany and in Poland. The fact that over the last few years Norway has started to consider the inclusion of more severe crimes can also be seen as an instance of 'European convergence,' and the same holds true for conferencing models that are slowly spreading – to England and Wales, to Belgium and the Netherlands, and again Norway is deliberating the idea.

Towards a general (community-oriented) mediation approach?

Finally there is one topic that constitutes a point of divergence – one of the most complicated, and confusing themes: the point about the community. We will build our final attempt at positioning Norway, the UK and also the Eastern European countries around the discussion of this topic. The mediation approach, as put forward by the CoE-R 99-19 has been criticized for being 'individualistic' and isolating the conflict at

stake from its social surroundings, thus again reducing the understanding of crime to aspects of personal behavior. The community, says Martin Wright, has to come into the picture, and it did so, at least in the Anglo-Saxon parts of Europe, at an early point in time (Aertsen *et al.* 2004: 14). However, in a modern society the definitions of community are not unchallenged (cf. McCold 1996). In our opinion there are three different strategies to realize community involvement:

- the use of lay mediators, of volunteers recruited from the local community as in Norway;
- VOM or RJ programs can be provided by independent organizations (NGO voluntary organizations, *Freie Träger, associations sans but lucrative*), that are rooted in the community, i.e. managed by a board of local citizens;
- inviting representatives of the local community insofar as they are affected by the crime.

Norway and the UK and their societies can rely on some sense of community that can be traced back in history, with various socio-economic factors contributing to its emergence and present prevalence. In most of the other European countries the individualistic approach prevails. Although we contend that much is to be said in favor of a professional VOM model (Pelikan 2000) – it clearly has its drawbacks. And moreover, the continental diversionary model appears to meet certain insurmountable limits that hamper its wider use. Its role as a mere preliminary to the 'real thing,' the scale of sanctions and therefore its remaining at the margins of the criminal justice system has not yet been overcome.

Is there a chance for a community-oriented approach in Europe? Mediation even without conference elements provides a chance to bring the community closer to the criminal justice system by the participation of those who are directly concerned with the crime, by the use of voluntary mediators from the local community, and by the possibility of programs run by community-based agencies. Community involvement may lead to a better public understanding of crime and consequently encourage community support for victims, rehabilitation of offenders, and the prevention of crime.

VOM in this perspective is perceived as only one step on a continuum of provisions for the treatment of conflicts. Conflicts can be mediated before they come to the notice of the agencies of the criminal justice system because they are experienced as disruptive behavior that hurts or harms others. A mediation or a so-called community or neighborhood justice center, where criminally relevant conflicts as well as civil law conflicts (for example, neighborhood, consumer, and family conflicts) can be mediated, seems to meet the needs of citizens for participation, justice, and security (Trenczek 2002).

Although the experience with community or neighborhood centers for conflict resolution, where civil disputes as well as those that have not yet come to the notice of the authorities are dealt with, have not been too successful in the past, we do observe some new and exciting tendencies presently. In Germany, an increasing number of parties turn to the TOA bureaus on their own initiative, prior to involving or even without any notice of the criminal justice system (so-called *Selbstmelder* [self-referrals]). And also in Germany, projects that involve volunteers working with professional management and supported by team supervision are thriving and seem attractive to the 'community' (Trenczek *et al.* 2004).

Even more surprising is that in some of the Eastern European countries (as we know from the Ukraine, from Russia, and from Estonia) RJ activities undertaken by various NGOs attract attention and support from their local communities. In general, however, we have to notice that the path seems very stony indeed. Only small pockets of

restorative practices have emerged and – which is more important – have kept going. But in spite of democratic traditions being weak and a passive attitude prevailing in vast segments of the society, there is simultaneously what we call *Aufbruchsstimmung*, a spirit of awakening in this part of Europe. It could be the case that exactly because of the fact that relevant traditions are missing, something completely new is sprouting, a new understanding of participation and of shared responsibility. The spirit of RJ seems to go very well with this movement. And it could point the way to a new community-oriented approach to reach for the unreachable start of justice.

References

Aertsen, I. (2000) 'Victim–offender mediation in Belgium,' in European Forum for Victim Offender Mediation and Restorative Justice (ed.) *Victim Offender Mediation in Europe: making restorative justice work*, Leuven: Leuven University Press.

Aertsen, I. and Peters, T. (1998) 'Mediation for reparation: the victim's perspective,' *European Journal of Crime, Criminal Law and Criminal Justice*, 6(2): 106–24.

Aertsen, I., Mackay, R., Pelikan, C., Willemsens, J. and Wright, M. (2004) *Rebuilding Community Connections – mediation and restorative justice in Europe*, Strasbourg: Council of Europe Publishing.

Alexander, N., Gottwald, W. and Trenczek, T. (2003) 'Mediation in Germany,' in N. Alexander (ed.) *Global Trends in Mediation*, Köln: Centrale for Mediation GmbH KG, pp. 179–212.

Altweger, A., and Hitzl E. (2000) *Kundenzufriedenheit der Geschädigten im ATA Innsbruck*, Innsbruck: Akademie für Sozialarbeit.

Bianchi, H. (1964) *Ethiek van het straffen*, Nijkerk: Callenbach.

Christie, N. (1977) 'Conflicts as property,' *British Journal of Criminology*, 13: 104–18.

Council of the European Union (1999) Recommendation No. R (99) 19 'Mediation in Penal matters.' Available at: https://wcd.coe.int/ViewDoc.jsp?id=420059andBackColor Internet=B9BDEEandBackColorIntranet=FFCD 4FandBackColorLogged=FFC679#Top (cited: CoE-R 99-19).

— (2001) 'Council Framework Decision of 15 March 2001 on the standing of victims in criminal proceedings' (2001/220/JHA). Available at: http://europa.eu.int/eur-lex/pri/en/oj/dat/2001/l_082/l_08220010322en00010004.pdf

Crawford, A. and Newburn, T. (2003) *Youth Offending and Restorative Justice*, Cullompton, Devon, UK: Willan Publishing.

Dignan, J. and Marsh, P. (2001) 'Restorative justice and family group conferencing in England: current state and future prospect,' in A. Morris and G. Maxwell (eds) *Restorative Justice for Juveniles*, Oxford: Hart Publishing.

Dölling, D. (ed.) (1998) *Täter–Opfer-Ausgleich in Deutschland*, Bonn: Forum Verlag.

Dölling, D. and Hartmann, A. (2003) 'Re-offending after victim–offender-mediation in juvenile court proceedings,' in E. Weitekamp and H.-J. Kerner (eds) *Restorative Justice in Context: international practice and direction*, Cullompton, Devon, UK: Willan Publishing.

Dölling, D. and Henninger, S. (1998) '*Sonstige empirische Untersuchungen zum TOA*,' in D. Dölling (ed.) *Täter–Opfer-Ausgleich in Deutschland*, Bonn: Forum Verlag.

Faget, J. (1997) *La Mediation. Essai de politique pénale*, Ramonville Saint Agne: Eres.

Feeley, M. (1979) *Court Reform on Trial: why simple solutions fail*, New York: Basic Books.

Gerhard, H. (2004) 'Rückfalluntersuchungen nach Restorative Justice-Programmen – ein kritischer Überblick,' Center for the Study of Law and Economics, Discussion Paper No. 2004–10 (unpublished).

Geudens, H. (1998) 'The recidivism rate of community service as a restitutive judicial sanction in comparison with the traditional juvenile justices measures,' in L. Walgrave (ed.) *Restorative Justice for Juveniles: potentialities, risks and problems for research*, Leuven: Leuven University Press.

Hammerschick, W., Pelikan, C. and Pilgram, A. (1994) 'Soziale Konflikte vor Gericht und im Außergerichtlichen Tatausgleich – eine Gegenüberstellung,' in W. Hammerschick, C. Pelikan and A. Pilgram (eds) *Ausweg aus dem Strafrecht – Der außergerichtliche Tatausgleich*, Jahrbuch für Rechts-und Kriminalsoziologie '94, Baden-Baden: Nomos, pp. 95–129.

Hanak, G., Stehr, J. and Steinert, H. (1989) *Ärgernisse und Lebenskatastrophen: über den alltäglichen Umgang mit Kriminalität* (Everyday Nuisances and Life-Catastrophes: on the every-day handling of crime), Bielefeld: AJZ-Verlag.

Hartmann, A. (1995) *Schlichten oder Richten. Der Täter-Opfer-Ausgleich und das (Jugend)Strafrecht*, München: Fink.

Hartmann, U. (1994) *Victim–Offender-Reconciliation with Adult Offenders in Germany*, Hanover: Institute of Criminology in Lower-Saxony, KFN-Forschungsberichte No. 27.

Hofinger, V. and Pelikan, C. (2004) 'Victim–offender mediation with juveniles in Austria,' paper presented at the Seminar of the GROTIUS II Project: 'Victim Offender Mediation: organization and practice in the juvenile justice systems,' Bologna, 19–20 September 2002.

Hoyle, C., Young, R. and Hill, R. (2002) *Proceed with Caution. an evaluation of the Thames Valley Police initiative in restorative cautioning*, London: Joseph Rowntree Foundation.

Kemeny, S. (2000) 'Policy developments and the concept of restorative justice through mediation,' in European Forum for Victim Offender Mediation and Restorative Justice (ed.) *Victim Offender Mediation in Europe: making restorative justice work*, Leuven: Leuven University Press, pp. 83–97.

Kemeny, S., Pelikan, C. and Willemsens, J. (eds) (2003) 'Restorative justice and its relation to the criminal justice system,' papers from the second conference of the European Forum for Victim Offender Mediation and Restorative Justice, Oostende (Belgium), 10–12 October 2002, online. Available at: http://www.euroforumrj.org/html

Kerner, H.-J., and Hartmann, A. (2003) *Auswertung der bundesweiten Täter-Opfer-Ausgleichs-Statistik für die Jahre 1993 bis 1999*, Bericht für das Bundesministerium der Justiz. Available at: http://www.bmj.bund.de/media/archive/517.pdf

Kilchling, M. (1995), *Opferinteressen und Strafverfolgung*, Freiburg: Max-Planck Institute.

— (1996) 'Aktuelle Perspektiven für Täter-Opfer-Ausgleich und Wiedergutmachung im Erwachsenenstrafrecht. Eine kritische Würdigung der bisherigen höchstrichterlichen Rechtsprechung zu § 46a StGB aus viktimologischer Sicht,' *Neue Zeitschrift für Strafrecht*, 16: 309–14.

Kilchling, M. and Löschnig-Gspandl, M. (1998), 'Vergleichende Perspektiven zum Täter-Opfer-Ausgleich in Baden-Württemberg und der Steiermark – Ausblick auf ein vergleichendes empirisches Forschungsprojekt,' in Friedrich-Ebert-Stiftung (ed.) *Der Täter-Opfer-Ausgleich (TOA) Moderner Beitrag zur Konfliktregulierung und zur Sicherung des sozialen Friedens*, Potsdam: Friedrich-Ebert-Stiftung.

Lins, J. (1998) *Out of Court Offence Compensation with Juvenile Offenders*, Linz: University of Linz.

Lord Chancellor's Department (2001) *The Review of the Criminal Justice System*, online. Chairman Sir Robin Auld. Available at: http://www.criminal-courts-review.org.uk

— (2002) *The Review of the Criminal Justice System*, online. Available at: http://www.criminal-courts-review.org.uk

McCold, P. (1996) 'Restorative justice and the role of the community,' in B. Galaway and J. Hudson (eds) *Restorative Justice: international perspectives*, Monsey, NY: Criminal Justice Press.

— (2004) 'Protocols for evaluating restorative justice programs in a European context,' unpublished paper for the COST 21 project.

McCold, P. and Wachtel, T. (2002) 'Restorative justice theory validation,' in E. Weitekamp and H. J. Kerner (eds) *Restorative Justice: theoretical foundations*, Cullompton, Devon, UK: Willan Publishing.

Marshall, T. (1996) 'The evolution of restorative justice in Britain,' *European Journal on Criminal Policy and Research*, 4: 21–43.

Mattinson, J., and Mirlees-Black, C. (2000) *Attitudes to Crime and Criminal Justice: findings from the 1998 British Crime Survey*, London: Home Office.

Meznar, A. (2002) 'Victim offender mediation in Slovenia,' *Newsletter of the European Forum for Victim Offender Mediation and Restorative Justice*, 3(1): 1–3.

Miers, D. (2004) 'Situation and researching restorative justice in Great Britain,' *Punishment and* Society, 6: 23–47.

Miers, D. and Semenchuk, M. (2002) 'Victim offender mediation with juveniles in England and Wales,' paper presented at the Seminar of the GROTIUS II Project, 'Victim Offender Mediation: organization and practice in the juvenile justice systems', Bologna, 19–20 September.

Miers, D., and Willemsens, J. (eds) (2004) *European Forum of Victim Offender Mediation and Restorative Justice*, Leuven: Leuven University Press.

Miers, D., Maguire, M., Goldie, S., Sharpe, K., Hale, C., Netten, A., Doolin, K., Uglow, S., Enterkin, J. and Newburn, T. (2001) *An Explanatory Evaluation of Restorative Justice Schemes*, Crime Reduction Research Series, Paper 9, London: Home Office.

Netzig, L., and Trenczek, T. (1996) 'Restorative justice as participation: theory, law, experience and research,' in B. Galaway and J. Hudson (eds) *Restorative Justice: international perspectives*, Monsey, NY: Criminal Justice Press.

Noll, Peter (1962) 'Die ethische Begründung der Strafe', *Recht und Staat*, Heft 244, Tübingen: np.

Paus, K.K. (2000) 'Victim offender mediation in Norway,' in European Forum for Victim Offender Mediation and Restorative Justice (ed.) *Victim Offender Mediation in Europe: making restorative justice work*, Leuven: Leuven University Press.

Pelikan, C. (1993) 'Who wants what kind of justice?,' paper presented at the 11th International Criminological Congress, 22–27 August, Budapest.

— (2000) 'Victim offender mediation in Austria,' in European Forum for Victim Offender Mediation and Restorative Justice (ed.) *Victim Offender Mediation in Europe: making restorative justice work*, Leuven: Leuven University Press, pp. 125-153.

— (2002) *Follow-up of the Recommendation No. R (99) 19 'Mediation in Penal Matters,'* Strasbourg: Council of Europe Criminological Scientific Council.

— (2004) 'A European overview of victim offender mediation: examples of good practice,' paper presented at the final meeting of the project 'M.E.D.I.A.Re: Verso il futuro', Rome, 18–19 June 2004, unpublished.

Pelikan, C. and Hoenisch, B. (1999) *Die Wirkungsweise strafrechtlicher Interventionen bei Gewaltstraftaten in Paarbeziehungen*, research report, Vienna: Institute for the Sociology of Law and Criminology.

Peters, T. (2000) 'Victim offender mediation: reality and challenges,' in European Forum for Victim Offender Mediation and Restorative Justice (ed.) *Victim Offender Mediation in Europe: making restorative justice work*, Leuven: Leuven University Press, pp. 9–18.

Schütz, H. (1999) 'Die Rückfallhäufigkeit nach einem Außergerichtlichen Tatausgleich bei Erwachsenen', *Österreichische Richterzeitung*, 77: 161–6.

Sessar, K. (1992) *Wiedergutmachung oder Strafen; Einstellung in der Bevölkerung und der Justiz*, Pfaffenweiler: Centaurus.

Sherman, L. W., Strang, H. and Woods, D. (2000) *Recidivism Patterns in the Canberra Reintegrative Shaming Experiment*, Canberra: Centre for Restorative Justice, Australian National University.

Strang, H. (2002) *Repair or Revenge: victims and restorative justice*, Oxford: Clarendon Press.

TOA Service Buero (2003) *TOA-Standards – ein Handbuch für die Praxis des Täter-Opfer-Ausgleichs*, Köln 1995, latest version available at: http://www.toa-servicebuero.de (accessed 4 January 2003).

Trenczek, T. (1990) 'A review and assessment of victim offender reconciliation programming in West Germany,' in B. Galaway and J. Hudson (eds) *Criminal Justice, Restitution, and Reconciliation*, Monsey, NY: Criminal Justice Press, pp. 109–24.

— (1996) *Restitution – Wiedergutmachung, Schadensersatz oder Strafe?* (Restitution – Making Good, Compensation or Punishment?), Baden-Baden: Nomos.

— (2002) 'Victim offender-reconciliation: the danger of cooptation and a useful reconsideration of law theory,' *Contemporary Justice Review*, 5: 23–34.

— (2003a) 'Within or outside the system? Restorative justice attempts and the penal system,' in E. Weitekamp and H.-J. Kerner (eds) *Restorative Justice in Context: international practice and directions*, Cullompton, Devon, UK: Willan Publishing, pp. 272–84.

— (2003b) 'Mediation im Strafrecht' (Mediation in criminal law), *Zeitschrift für Konfliktmanagement*, 3: 104–9.

Trenczek, T., Klenzner, J. and Netzig, L. (2004) 'Mediation durch Ehrenamtliche, Einbindung von ehrenamtlichen Mediatoren in professionelle Strukturen sozialraumnaher Schlichtung' (Mediation with volunteers), *Zeitschrift für Konfliktmanagement*, 7: 14–19.

United Nations Economic and Social Council (2002) *Basic Principles on the Use of Restorative Justice Programmes in Criminal Matters*, as of 12 August 2002. Available at: http://www.pficj-r.org/programs/un/ecosocresolution

Van Garsse, L. (2002) 'A place for restorative justice: motives behind a tentative conclusion based on practical experience,' in S. Kemeny, C. Pelikan and J. Willemsens (eds) *Restorative Justice and its Relation to the Criminal Justice System*, papers from the Second Conference of the European Forum for Victim Offender Mediation and Restorative Justice, Ostend (Belgium), 10–12 October 2002. Available at: www. euforumrj. org.readingroom.oestende conf.pdf

Van Ness, D. and Heetderks-Strong, K. (2002) *Restoring Justice*, second edn, Cincinnati: Anderson Publishing.

Wright, M. (1989) 'What the public wants,' in M. Wright and B. Galaway, *Mediation and Criminal Justice*, London: Sage, pp. 264–69.

— (1996) *Justice for Victims and Offenders: a restorative response to crime*, second edn, Winchester: Watergate Press.

Zehr, H. (1985) *Retributive Justice, Restorative Justice*, Elkhart: MCC US Office of Criminal Justice.

— (1990) *Changing Lenses: a new focus for crime and justice*, Scottsdale, PA: Herald Press.

Acknowledgment

This paper would not have been written without the support of friends. We would like to thank Johanna Pelikan-Lex for her thorough checking through regarding the English language and to acknowledge the long-standing exchange with our European colleagues and friends which helped us to get an insight in the European landscape of VOM and RJ.

Notes

1. Article 10: 1. Each Member State shall seek to promote mediation in criminal cases for offences which it considers appropriate for this sort of measure. 2. Each Member State shall ensure that any agreement between the victim and the offender reached in the course of such mediation in criminal cases can be taken into account. According to Article 17 each Member State shall bring into force laws, regulations and administrative provisions to comply with the said article 10 before 22 March 2006.

2. Because most European programs operate on a pre-charge and pre-trial phase, the term 'offender' is somewhat problematic as there was no judicial determination of guilt. Therefore the Austrian term 'out-of-court offence resolution' (*Außergerichtlicher Tatausgleich* – ATA) is most appropriate instead of victim (alleged)offender mediation.

3. Differences in terminology of the different European languages hint at differences in the genesis, objective and framework of mediation programs (CoE-R 99-19, EM p. 16). Other types of restorative justice devices are e.g. family/group conferencing schemes or sentencing circles; cf. UN basic principles (United Nations Economic and Social Council 2002).

4. Jacques Faget (1997: 6) has very pointedly addressed this problem, stating: 'the expression penal mediation juxtaposes two terms, mediation and punishment which raise antagonistic philosophies and can lead people to believe that mediation has a punitive character.'

5. Additional prerequisites for diverting a case are: no serious culpability on the part of the suspect; a maximum range of punishment for the offense of no more than five years (e.g. serious body injury, burglary); adequate clarification of the facts and circumstances; and no loss of life.

6. Its headquarters are based in Vienna with two chief executive officers responsible for the entire organization. There are fifteen regional offices. Each is managed by a director who is responsible for all aspects of contact with the prosecutor and the court, for personnel, and for supervision of the standards of quality to be met in casework.

7. These criticisms pertain to both sides of the 'causal' relationship. First of all there is the fact that criminal policy interventions, traditional court interventions as well as 'alternative measures', are by and large of less importance for people's behaviour and their interactions with others than the whole set of their personal and socio-economic resources, i.e. their prior experience and acquired attitudes and the social support the receive and the opportunities that are open to them. On the other hand the event of recidivism, the fact that the perpetrator is caught and being reported to the police again, is criticized as too narrow and arbitrary, not catching the complex nature of the perpetrator's failure to get on with his/her life and be fully integrated.

8. In an Austrian study Schütz (1999) compared the recidivism rates of cases dealt with by VOM and cases that had received the court sentence of a fine; the researcher restricted the comparison to cases of slight assault. The results point to a recidivism rate of 14 per cent for the VOM cases and 33 per cent for cases where a fine was been imposed. When looking at perpetrators with a previous conviction, the difference became less pronounced: 30 per cent for the VOM cases versus 47 per cent for the court cases (10 per cent for those without a previous conviction who had been at the ATA and 22 per cent for those having reoffended).

9. It is true, though, that most studies suffer from a 'system selection bias' (McCold 2004). Referrals by the criminal justice agencies take the appropriateness of a case, its positive prognosis, into account. This is the place to point to the fact that in the civil law systems, due to the principle of legality, there is no way to constitute control (comparison) groups by random assignment of cases! (See also Miers and Willemsens 2004: 158.)

4

Conferencing and restorative justice

*Gabrielle Maxwell, Allison Morris
and Hennessey Hayes*

Introduction

Family group conferences in the New Zealand youth justice system have been the centre of international interest since they were introduced there in 1989, and they have since been imitated by a number of countries (Hudson *et al.* 1996). Enabling legislation for juvenile offenders has been passed in New Zealand, Australia, England and Wales, Canada, Ireland, and Singapore. Also in New Zealand, legislation has been passed for adult offenders. Various versions of conferencing for young offenders have been introduced or trialed in countries as diverse as Belgium, Hong Kong, Japan, the Netherlands, South Africa, Sweden, and the United States. More recently, new initiatives have been taken to introduce restorative conferencing in Brazil and Argentina for both adults and young people. In this chapter, we describe restorative justice conferencing for juveniles with a particular emphasis on New Zealand and Australia and assess the extent to which it can be said to reflect restorative justice processes and to result in restorative justice outcomes using research chiefly drawn from Australasia and North America. In addition, we examine data on the extent to which conferencing

can reduce re-offending. But first, we discuss the development of restorative justice conferencing.

The development of restorative justice conferencing

The idea of a restorative approach to resolving issues for victims and offenders has been traced to a key paper by Christie in 1977 (1997). However, the first major publications that articulated and shaped the theory of restorative justice were: *Crime Shame and Reintegration* (Braithwaite 1989) and *Changing Lenses* (Zehr 1990). While the early theoretical writings articulated the view that meetings between victims, offenders, and communities were an essential feature of a restorative approach, they did not clearly articulate a format that could be integrated into a conventional justice system.

The Children, Young Persons and Their Families Act 1989 in New Zealand provided the first model of how this could occur through the use of the family group conference. The phrase 'restorative justice' did not feature in the New Zealand debates about family group conferences at this time, but conferencing in general is now commonly presented as an example of restorative justice in practice, since the values underlying conferencing are seen as reflecting restorative justice values (see, for example, NACRO 1997; Dignan 1999; McIlrea 1996; Maxwell and Morris 1993). For example, both conferencing and restorative justice give a say in how the offense should be resolved to those most affected – victims, offenders, and their supporters – and both give primacy to their interests. Both conferencing and restorative justice processes also emphasize addressing the offending and its consequences in meaningful ways, reconciling victims, offenders, and their communities through reaching agreements about how best to deal with the offending, and trying to reintegrate or reconnect both victims and offenders at the local community level through healing the harm and hurt caused by the offending and through taking steps to prevent its recurrence.

In many parts of the world, there are examples of meetings within extended families and communities to settle disputes and resolve conflict. Examples include the Inkundla or Makgotla in South Africa (Skelton and Frank 2001), the peace circles of the First Nations peoples in North America (Stuart 1996; Lilles 2001) and the Ufonga in Samoa. In New Zealand, the notion of arranging a conference involving all parties affected by an offence developed out of: (1) Maori *whanau* (extended family) meetings that were traditionally used to resolve conflict; and (2) the practice of arranging meetings of the family and others involved in the care of the child (the family group) through family therapy during the 1970s and 1980s. These two examples were combined in the 1989 legislation as the family group conference, to provide a way of making decisions about the care of children when there was child abuse or neglect, as well as a method that involved the child, the family and the victim in making decisions about how best to respond to offending.

Conferencing in practice

Not all examples of conferencing operate the same way. For example, in some jurisdictions, conferencing is managed by the police (as in parts of England), in some by the youth courts (as in South Australia), in some by social welfare (as in New Zealand) and in some by other organizations relying on facilitators or conveners recruited from the community (as in the Australian state of Queensland). In some jurisdictions, conferencing has a statutory basis (as in New Zealand and most Australian states and territories); in others, it does not (as in the Australian state of Victoria).[1] In some jurisdictions, conferencing deals with minor to medium serious and/or first offenders (as in Western Australia); in others, it deals with the most serious and repeat offenders (as in New Zealand). In some jurisdictions, conferencing is central to the operation of the youth justice system and acts as a barrier or aid to decision-making by criminal justice professionals (as in New Zealand);[2] in others, it is part of police diversion (as in parts of England). Similarly, not all types of conferences have the same theoretical underpinnings. Some systems of conferencing are based on values of restorative justice (though not necessarily explicitly or to the exclusion of other, even contradictory, objectives).[3] Other systems are more explicitly based on Braithwaite's (1989) notion of 'reintegrative shaming'.[4] Some forms of conferencing are 'scripted,' which means that the facilitator follows a prescribed pattern in guiding discussion by the participants (as in parts of England and some Australian jurisdictions). Other conferences take a variety of forms depending on the culture and wishes of the participants. Despite these differences, there are many commonalities and the following description focuses on these.

Conferencing intends to involve not only the victim and the offender but also their family members, friends and supporters (their communities of care). The conference facilitator is responsible for preparing the parties for the meeting, arranging the meeting and making sure that everyone present is able to participate fully, but is not meant to play an active role in the substantive discussions. In addition, in some examples of conferencing, the police, lawyers, probation officers and social workers participate.[5] Typically, after the welcome, introductions and reminders of the process, the offender begins the discussion by explaining what happened and how the offence has affected others. The victim then describes his or her experience and the harm that resulted. The victim's and offender's supporters may speak next. The group then decides what the offender needs to do to repair the harm, and what assistance the offender will need in doing so.[6] Common outcomes are apologies, reparation, and community work. The agreement reached is put into writing, signed, and sent to the appropriate criminal justice officials and to the participants. Conference recommendations (and plans), therefore, frequently reflect restorative values but also, at times, reflect rehabilitative, retributive, and crime-control values.

Meeting restorative justice values

Previous writers have identified several key goals of restorative justice (Van Ness *et al.* 2001). These include the importance of participation and consensual decision-making; healing what is broken; the accountability of offenders; and the restoration of relationships through the reintegration of both offender and victim into the community. In this section, we examine the extent to which conferencing meets the first three goals as these have been a principal focus of research.

Involving participants

Decision making in conventional justice systems is hierarchical in that the decisions are imposed, and they are imposed by 'others': they are not made by offenders, victims, and their families, and they do not have to be agreed to by them. In contrast, a key aim of the conference is to engage all participants in reaching a consensus about how to respond to the harm caused by an offence.

Involving young offenders

Research has shown that the participation and involvement of offenders is achievable through conferencing: offenders feel that they have been listened to and have a better understanding of the consequences of what they have done (Maxwell and Morris 1993; Sherman *et al.* 2000b; Maxwell *et al.* 2004). Young offenders are expected to actively participate in discussions about how best to deal with their offending, and they in turn can expect their views to be taken into account in the decisions. For example, Maxwell and Morris (1993) interviewed young offenders who attended a family group conference between 1990 and 1991 and found that most young people felt involved in the decision-making process, at least partially, and that most were satisfied with the outcomes reached. However, at that time, they also found that some young people remained uninvolved. They speculated that this was likely to be due to families' and professionals' unwillingness or inability to hear and value young people's views, especially when these young people were offenders.

More recent data (Maxwell *et al.* 2004), based on interviews with 520 young offenders who were involved in family group conferences in 1998 (the retrospective sample) and with just over a hundred young offenders who were involved in family group conferences in 2000–1 (the prospective sample), showed that around half of both groups said they felt involved in making decisions at the family group conference. Also, two-thirds of the retrospective sample and three-quarters of the prospective sample said they had the opportunity to say what they wanted to at the conference. Almost all the young offenders in both samples said that they understood the decision, and the majority (61 per cent of the retrospective sample and 73 per cent of the prospective sample) said that they agreed with it. The following two quotes provide some sense of the positive nature of most young offenders' experiences of family group conferences: 'It was good having my parents there and having support from them' and 'It was good – just saying my side and saying sorry and being able to have a say in the plan' (Maxwell *et al.* 2004: 125).

However, it is also clear that a significant proportion of these young offenders did not feel so positively: over two-fifths of the retrospective sample and more than a quarter of the prospective sample said that they did not feel involved in making decisions at the conference; a quarter of the retrospective sample (but less than a tenth of the prospective sample) also said that they did not have the opportunity to say what they wanted to at the conference. Just over two-fifths of the retrospective sample and almost a third of the prospective sample said that they felt too intimidated to say what they wanted to at the conference. More than a quarter of the retrospective sample and 15 per cent of the prospective sample did not agree with the decisions reached.

Although these figures have to give some cause for concern in terms of whether family group conferences are fully meeting their objects and principles and whether they are realizing their restorative potential, they should perhaps not be read too pessimistically. The overall picture is more positive than that which emerges in comparisons with how young offenders feel about their involvement and treatment in conventional youth and juvenile courts. Even in New Zealand, where efforts have been made to transform the youth court by encouraging offenders' participation and by simplifying language, only a third felt involved in the

decisions there, and only half felt able to say what they wanted to the judge (Maxwell *et al.* 2004).

Results from Australia also indicate that conferencing increases offenders' sense of involvement in decisions but there are differences in the extent of their reported involvement depending on the jurisdiction. In New South Wales, for example, Trimboli (2000) reports results from surveys with 391 young offenders conferenced in early to mid 1999. Her research showed that 89 per cent of these young offenders felt that the conference took account of what they said in deciding outcomes, and 91 per cent felt that the conference gave them the opportunity to express their views. In Queensland, Hayes *et al.* (1998) reported results from post-conference surveys with 116 young people referred to a conference. Almost all (99 per cent) reported that they felt they had had a say in the conference and were satisfied with outcomes.[7]

However, fewer young offenders in the Canberra RISE study felt they were involved (Strang *et al.* 1999). For example, between 56 per cent and 77 per cent of offenders in the juvenile property and youth violence experiments felt they had control over the conference outcomes. And only between 46 per cent and 54 per cent of these offenders felt that they had enough control over the way things were run. Nevertheless, larger proportions felt they were able to express their views (69 per cent of juvenile property offenders; 84 per cent of juvenile property security offenders; 77 per cent of youth violence offenders).

Variation in research results across Australian jurisdictions could be due in part to differences in the types of offences and offenders referred to conferences (for example, property versus violent offenders, young offenders versus adult offenders). However, results from RISE may largely stem from the conferencing format adopted in the ACT, where conferences were managed and convened by police officers. In all other Australian jurisdictions running legislated conferencing schemes, the 'New Zealand model' has been adopted, where conferences are led by community coordinators with special training as facilitators.

Involving families

Most families who participated in Maxwell and Morris's (1993) research felt that they had been involved in the decision-making process; only a fifth said that they had not felt involved. Almost half the parents said that they had decided how the offending should be dealt with and nearly two-thirds felt the family had been involved in the decision, at least in part; only a fifth identified the professionals alone as the decision makers. There also was little doubt that those families who had experienced both conferences and courts preferred family group conferences. Their comments highlighted the participatory nature of the family group conference and the greater degree of support available to them in contrast to the stress that often accompanied a court appearance. As well as feeling more comfortable at the family group conference, families also understood more of what had happened and believed that it provided a more realistic forum for decision-making. However, Maxwell and Morris (1993) found that some families were not well prepared for what was expected of them, and that families were not always provided with the information they needed to come up with good outcomes. In a few cases, professionals (particularly the police) took over the process and, in the families' views, dictated outcomes.

The families of Maxwell et al.'s (2004) prospective sample were asked for their views on family group conferences, and these again were mainly positive: almost all understood what was happening at the conference, 88 per cent felt treated with respect, 85 per cent agreed with the decisions made, and 80 per cent said that they were able to express their views and felt involved in the decisions made. In the words of one family member: 'It was a very open sharing. It dealt with the anger and hurt experienced by the victim but in a non-threatening manner and we [the young person and the family] were able to respond by apologising to her and her family' (Maxwell et al. 2004: 166).

However, one in ten families did not feel able to express their views at the conference, and one in ten did not feel involved in the decisions made. Indeed, 70 per cent of these said that they felt that they were treated like a 'bad person.' It is difficult to know just how to treat these more negative findings. While perhaps indicative of some failures in practice and failures to reach restorative ideals, these findings are probably more positive than the views of families involved in conventional juvenile or youth courts. Certainly, Maxwell and Morris's (1993) early research supports this claim. Maxwell et al. (2004) do not present more recent New Zealand data on families' views of courts.

Results from several studies carried out in Australia are consistent with what has been observed in New Zealand. Hayes et al. (1998) found that almost all of the parents/caregivers of young offenders in their study reported satisfaction with the agreements reached and with the fairness of the conference process. Similarly, Trimboli (2000) reported that 93 per cent of offenders' supporters felt that their views were taken into account in deciding outcomes, and nearly all (99 per cent) felt that they were able to express their views during conferences.

Involving victims

Generally speaking, research has consistently shown that conferencing can more fully involve victims than conventional criminal justice processes. First, victims have the right to be present. However, in most jurisdictions, conferences can continue despite the absence of the victim and attendance rates here vary quite considerably. Some studies reveal quite high attendance rates. For example, Wundersitz and Hetzel (1996) reported that 75 to 80 per cent of conferences in South Australia involving offences with victims had at least one victim present[8] and victims were present at 86 per cent of RISE conferences (Strang and Sherman 1997).[9] Also, Trimboli (2000) reported that victims attended in approximately three-quarters of all the conferences she observed. On the other hand, Maxwell and Morris's (1993) early research of family group conferences in New Zealand indicated that victims attended only around half of the family group conferences there, and more recent data (Maxwell et al. 2004) suggest that this figure has not changed much over this time period. According to Young (2001) the victim is not commonly present at restorative conferences in the Thames Valley area of England.

It is unclear why victims' participation rates are higher in some Australian jurisdictions, compared to New Zealand. It may be that victims are more willing to participate when offences are of a less serious nature. Alternatively, victims may be better prepared for conferences there and hence more likely to agree to attend and to know more what to expect. Elsewhere, however, offence type does not seem to influence victims' level of participation. Young (2001), for example, reports low levels of victims' attendance in the Thames Valley area despite the relatively low level of offending dealt with by conferences there.

Research conducted in New Zealand suggests that the degree to which victims are prepared for conferences influences participation rates. Maxwell and Morris (1993) suggested that the reasons for the low level of victims' attendance at family group conferences in New Zealand in 1990/1 were primarily poor practice.[10] This finding has clear policy and practice implications: it suggests that it is crucial to spend time informing victims about what a restorative justice process involves and the potential

benefits in it for them. The kinds of reasons victims themselves give for attending conferences include: feeling that this is a better way of resolving the situation, giving offenders another chance, not wanting the case to go to court, dislike of conventional court processes, knowing the offender, wanting to have a say and to confront the offender, wanting to see the offender, the effects of the meeting on him/her and the offender's remorse, and seeking reparation. The major reasons given by the fifty-eight victims who did attend the family group conferences observed by Maxwell et al. (2004) were to tell the young offender how they felt (this was said by more than half) and to express their views on what should happen (this was said by more than two-fifths). Almost a third wanted to find out more about the young offender, and more than a fifth wanted to obtain reparation.

All of these motivations reflect what we know about victims' interests (or what victims want out of meetings with offenders) and are embedded in restorative values. Indeed, most of the victims who attended these conferences said they were able to express their views at the conference and were given a chance to explain the impact of the offending on them. As one victim put it:

> I do think conferences are a good thing. They allow people to get things off their chest. A victim like myself finds out more and it gives you a better understanding to see the offending face to face. I saw the young person showing respect, listening and contributing.
>
> (Maxwell et al. 2004: 161)

However, not all victims will want to be involved in conferences and this takes us to the question of whether or not this really matters. The first point to make here is that the absence of the victim does not mean that the victim's views cannot be put forward in a conference. The police or the facilitator can put these forward on the victim's behalf, for example by reading a letter from the victim or by playing a recorded statement. Or the family, relatives, or friends of the victim can be invited to speak on behalf of the victim. Also, other participants who have experienced similar victimization in the past can speak about their experiences. All of these different ways can effectively and powerfully communicate to offenders the consequences of their offending. It also allows the focus on victims to shift to also involve a consideration of the consequences of offending on what can be called indirect victims: for example, the consequences of offending for the offender's family, for the community or even for offenders themselves.

The second point is that, while conferences certainly encourage the attendance of victims, they are not intended to be entirely victim-focused. Many of the victims' needs and interests can be addressed without their presence – offenders can still agree to make amends to them. And the goals of providing a forum for the involvement of communities of care in decision-making and/or of addressing offenders' needs and interests can also still be achieved. In addition, it could be argued that denying an offender access to a conference simply because the victim does not wish to take part is unjust.

Maxwell *et al.* (2004) asked the forty-two victims who had not attended the family group conferences that they observed in 2001–2 why they had not attended. By far the most common reason (given by 45 per cent) was that they did not want to meet the young offender or his or her family. The next most common reason (given by almost a third) was that they would have liked to attend but were unable to. Both of these reasons could still be linked to poor practice – for example, victims may not want to meet the offender if the process or potential benefits to them are not adequately explained, or if they do not feel well enough prepared for such a meeting. However, victims' unwillingness to meet offenders also

may strike more fundamentally at the ability of conferences to fully meet restorative justice aspirations and ideals.

Healing victims' hurt

Most people working in the field of restorative justice agree that preparation is a key to making conferences effective, and we mentioned above the importance of explaining to victims how the process potentially benefits them. What are these potential benefits? Research suggests that victims whose offenders are dealt with in conferences gain some understanding of reasons behind the offending, receive some kind of repair for the harm done (for example, through an apology, reparation, or community work), are more often satisfied with the agreements reached, feel better about the whole experience (for example, they feel less angry or more safe), and gain a sense of closure. For example, Maxwell and Morris (1993) found that about 60 per cent of the victims interviewed by them described the conference they attended as helpful and rewarding. They speculated that conferences were unhelpful for some victims because of poor practice: at that time, victims were not able to have support people with them, and they could feel quite isolated and vulnerable when confronted with the offender and his or her family and supporters; they also speculated that much of the dissatisfaction about agreements stemmed from the lack of knowledge about the completion of the agreed outcome rather than objections to the agreement itself.

There seem to have been some significant changes since the earlier study. Eighty-one per cent of the victims who attended the family group conferences observed by Maxwell *et al.* (2004) said that they felt better as a result of attending, and only 5 per cent said that they felt worse. Indeed, 90 per cent said that they felt treated with respect, and almost three-quarters said that their needs had been met at the conference. Also, most victims who attended the family group conference agreed with the decision, and more than two-thirds said that it had helped put matters behind them. In addition, more than two-thirds of the victims who had not attended had been told about the outcome reached, and more than half felt that the outcome was 'about right.'

These more recent outcomes in New Zealand are similar to what has been observed in several Australian jurisdictions. For example, 60 per cent of victims who attended conferences in the RISE experiment said they felt 'quite' or 'very' angry at the beginning of the conference, but only 30 per cent said so afterwards; and many said that the conference had made them feel safer: only 6 per cent of conference victims feared re-victimization compared with 19 per cent of the victims whose cases went to court (Strang and Sherman 1997). In Queensland, Palk et al. (1998) reported that 88 per cent of the victims they interviewed agreed that 'doing the conference means I can make a fresh start.' And in the US, nearly all (ranging from 92 per cent to 94 per cent) of the victims in McCold and Wachtel's (1998) research said that the meeting had been helpful, that they would choose to do the same again and that they would recommend participation to others.

However, Maxwell et al. (2004) did note some negative findings: for example, victims who attended the family group conference did not always feel involved in making the decision – only about half of them reported this.[11] Also, more than two-fifths of the victims who had not attended the family group conference thought that the decision reached was 'too soft.' Overall, however, the findings on victims' experiences of conferences are reasonably favorable, particularly when contrasted with their almost total lack of involvement in conventional youth or juvenile courts (other than as witnesses) or similar decision-making forums.

Obviously, conferences do not always 'work' for victims. Some angry or distressed victims remain so, and some victims find it difficult to cope with what happens in a conference and with the range of emotions – anger, hurt, sadness, fear, and so on – which they experience there. They may, therefore, leave the meeting feeling re-victimized and unsupported. For example, about a quarter of Maxwell and Morris's (1993) sample of conference victims said that they felt worse as a result of participating in a conference. There were a variety of reasons for this: the inability of the family and young person to make reparation, the victims' inability to express themselves adequately, their difficulty in communicating cross-culturally, the lack of support offered to them, the perceived failure of the offender to show remorse to the victim for the offending, feeling that their concerns had not been adequately listened to, and feeling that people were uninterested in or unsympathetic to them. Importantly, most of these concerns seem to be rooted in poor practice and hence can be addressed through good preparation of both victims and offenders, through encouraging victims to have realistic expectations of the process in terms of possible outcomes, and through providing support to them.

On the other hand, more recent findings from New Zealand suggest that most victims report feeling satisfied with the conference outcomes benefiting from the conference process. Maxwell et al. (2004) reported not only that 87 per cent of those attending agreed with the decisions but also that 81 per cent said that they felt better after the conference. Only 5 per cent said that they felt worse. Furthermore, 69 per cent said that the conference had helped them 'put matters behind me.' These findings again are similar to trends in several Australian jurisdictions. In Queensland, Hayes et al. (1998) reported that 78 per cent of victims said that 'what the offender did in the agreement helped to make up for the offence,' and most said that the conference helped them to cope with the offence (82 per cent) and to put the whole experience behind them (89 per cent). In Canberra, results from the RISE study show that 85 per cent of personal property victims and 65 per cent of youth violence victims said 'the conference took adequate account of the effects of the offence on them' (Strang *et al.* 1999). And, in NSW, 95 per cent of victims interviewed felt that the conference took account of the harms caused (Trimboli 2000).

However, Daly (2002) highlights that such positive outcomes should not always be expected. From observing a number of conferences in 1997 and interviewing the victims afterwards she found that 'restorativeness'[12] was 'solidly' evident in only about a third of cases. Despite this caveat, most (80 per cent) of the victims interviewed by Daly (2002) judged conferences as fair. And this finding seems consistent across several jurisdictions. Hayes and Daly (2003, 2004) report that all the published research up to 2004 on conferencing in Australia has indicated higher levels of victims' satisfaction compared to courts, and conferences are perceived as being more effective in delivering procedural justice (that is to say, they are seen as fairer). Similarly, Latimer *et al.* (2001) report higher levels of victims' satisfaction in Canada and for most of the offenders who were involved in restorative processes (conferences or victim offender mediation) compared to those who were not. They also reported more compliance with restitution agreements in restorative processes.

Holding offenders accountable

Research suggests that conferences can hold offenders accountable for their offences and give offenders constructive opportunities to make amends to their victims by apologizing, making reparation, or performing community work or services for victims (Maxwell and Morris 1993; Wundersitz and Hetzel 1996; Maxwell *et al.* 2004). Conferences also seem to achieve this 'better'

than courts. For example, in the Canberra RISE study, Sherman *et al.* (1998) found that offenders who participated in conferences were much more likely to apologize and to make restitution than those offenders who appeared in court. They also found that offenders who had experienced conferences were more likely to say that they felt that they had repaid their debt to society and to the victim. In Queensland, all of the young people interviewed by Palk *et al.* (1998) felt that the conference had helped them 'make up for the offence' (and three-quarters of the victims felt this too). Similar results have been obtained in New Zealand. Maxwell and Morris (1999) reported asking young people (some six years after they first attended a family group conference) whether or not they had been able to make good the damage they had done. More than half said that they felt that they had. More recently, information from the 520 young offenders in Maxwell *et al.*'s (2004) retrospective sample shows that around two-thirds said that they had completed at least part of the plan agreed to at the family group conference. However, the failure to monitor the plans agreed to at conferences (or at least the failure to record whether or not they were monitored and by whom) and the failure of young offenders to complete all elements of the plans remain a matter of concern. The remedy is, however, relatively simple. A good conference should identify who is to monitor the completion of the different elements of the conference's outcome and should also set a review date to check whether the agreements have been completed. Where there is a failure to complete the agreement, the conference should then be reconvened.

Reducing re-offending[13]

There will always be debate about the extent to which restorative conferences are 'just' for offenders and victims, given the different meanings and values attached to the notions of justice. Nevertheless, the weight of the empirical evidence amassed to date convincingly suggests that conferencing benefits the participants of the process. We consistently find that offenders and victims rate conferencing processes highly on fairness and they are largely satisfied with conference outcomes.

This said, there remains the persistent question about conferencing's ability to reduce crime. Unfortunately, this question is not easily answered, and the current empirical foundation upon which one might attempt an answer is rather weak. Two factors seem to have produced uncertainty around the re-offending question. First, the use of restorative conferencing to resolve issues around offending is a relatively new phenomenon and this has limited the opportunity to examine its long-term impact on future offending. Second, there are problems in defining re-offending and in determining how it should be assessed. Some researchers compare the effects of conferences with other legal interventions, such as the youth court (e.g. McCold and Wachtel 1998; Strang *et al.* 1999). Other research focuses attention on the variable effects of conferencing processes (e.g. Maxwell and Morris 1999, 2001; Hayes and Daly 2003, 2004). While comparison studies have been effective in telling us *if* conferences effect changes in future offending behavior, they have not been able to show *what it is* about conference processes that is associated with behavioral change. Variation analyses, on the other hand, have been able to identify the key features of conferencing processes which seem to be associated with reduced re-offending.

There also are important differences in how researchers have chosen to define re-offending. Some count post-conference arrests and some count re-convictions. There are also important differences in the periods of time researchers choose to follow offenders after a conference. Measuring re-

offending before and after a specific conference ignores the fact that with each new offence the probability of re-offending can change. A number of other questions prove problematic. Is a single re-offence a suitable criterion or should we be concerned with the amount and seriousness of offences? What is a suitable comparison group or criterion against which to assess re-offending? And how can the research take account of the other previous and post-offence life events that often impact on offending? Given these difficulties, it is hardly surprising that the outcomes from the studies on re-offending conducted over the past few years have been highly variable. Nevertheless, some important findings have emerged from the research to date.

Results of the studies

Comparison studies

Studies in North America that compare restorative justice conferences with other interventions, such as court or other court diversion, have produced mixed results. McCold and Wachtel compared re-offending among young offenders randomly assigned to a police-run restorative justice conference or to the youth court in the Bethlehem Pennsylvania Restorative Policing Experiment (McCold and Wachtel 1998). Findings suggested that re-offending was significantly less likely for certain types of offenders attending conference (e.g. violent offenders) compared to offenders who went to court. However, the researchers were not able to conclude that the effects of the conference led to reductions in re-offending because of problems around the random assignment of offenders to conference and court. Instead they state: 'It appears that any reductions in recidivism are the result of the voluntary program diverting from formal processing those juveniles who are least likely to re-offend in the first place' (McCold and Wachtel 1998: 4).

In another experiment, McGarrell *et al.* (2000) compared re-arrest rates for very young (fourteen years of age or younger) first-time offenders randomly assigned to restorative justice conferences or other court diversion program in Indianapolis, Indiana. Their results suggest that restorative justice conferences significantly reduced offenders' rates of re-arrest, compared to other court diversion programs, including victim offender mediation. At six months following initial arrest, there were nearly 14 per cent fewer recidivists among the restorative justice conferencing group compared to the control group. This difference was statistically significant and represented a 40 per cent reduction in re-offending. However, no statistically significant group differences were observed after twelve months (cf. 29 per cent re-offended in the control group and 23 per cent re-offended in the restorative justice group).

Finally, a recent meta-analysis conducted in Canada (Latimer *et al.* 2001) renders the issue of re-offending even more perplexing. Researchers analyzed thirty-two 'effect sizes' across twenty-two studies that compared a restorative justice intervention with other types of interventions on re-offending. The average effect size was 0.07, which means that restorative justice programs yielded an average 7 per cent reduction in re-offending, compared to other non-restorative programs. However, effect sizes ranged from −0.23 to 0.38, which means that some programs reduced re-offending by as much as 38 per cent, while other programs led to increases in re-offending by up to 23 per cent.

Results of comparison studies in Australia also produce variable results. In New South Wales, Luke and Lind (2002) conducted a retrospective analysis of several thousand first offenders (i.e. those with no prior proven court appearance) who went to a conference or a court from 6 April 1997 to 5 April 1999. They compared post-intervention offending for three groups of offenders: offenders in court during the twelve months before the introduction of conferencing; offenders in court during the first twelve months of conferencing; and offenders in conferences during the first twelve months of their operation. Records for first offenders were chosen to control for the effects of prior offending. After making several comparisons between the conference and court groups, Luke and Lind (2002) concluded that conferencing rendered a 15 to 20 per cent reduction in predicted risk of re-offending.

Data from RISE (Sherman *et al.* 2000a) also support the suggestion that restorative processes can make some differences: they showed that, for youth violence, conferences reduced offending rates by thirty-eight crimes per hundred offenders per year, compared with the effect of being sent to court. On the other hand, with respect to drink driving, conferences resulted in a very small increase in offences and, with respect to juvenile property offences involving personal victims, there was no difference in offending rates according to whether offenders were assigned to conferences or to courts. Sherman *et al.* (2000b: 18) stated that their next task was to explore the reasons for these differences. They inferred, however, that the difference was likely to be due to restorative processes impacting differently on different types of offences rather than to differences in the offenders' background. They also (Sherman *et al.* 2000b) raised the possibility that the skills of facilitators rather than their level of experience can impact on re-offending. If this is confirmed, this has important implications for practice.

Variability in conferences

In South Australia, Hayes and Daly (2003) examined how features of family conferences, as well as offenders' characteristics (such as age, gender, race and prior offending), related to future offending behavior. Drawing on observations of eighty-nine conferences and the offending history data for the primary offenders in these conferences, they found, as might be expected, prior offending, sex, and race to be highly predictive of post-conference offending.[14] However, they also found that when young offenders were observed to be remorseful and when conference decision-making about outcomes (agreements) was observed to be consensual, re-offending was less likely.

Hayes and Daly (2004) obtained similar results in Queensland, where they followed 200 young offenders for three to five years following their youth justice conference to assess the variable effects of youth justice conferencing and offender characteristics on re-offending. As in other studies, they too found that offenders' characteristics (such as age at first offence, age at conference, gender and prior offending) were highly predictive of future offending. However, unlike the findings of the research in South Australia, no features of conferences were associated with future offending: high proportions of both re-offenders and desisters (i.e. those with no further detected offences three to five years following their conference) agreed to statements such as 'People seemed to understand my side of things,' 'Doing the conference means I can now make a fresh start,' 'Overall, I thought the conference was fair,' 'I got to have my say at the conference.' This could indicate that the conferences had little effect on re-offending or that other key factors also need to be taken into account.

On the other hand, in New Zealand, Maxwell and Morris (2001) followed 108 young offenders attending a family group conference for six and a half years and found that, in addition to prior negative life experiences and what happened to offenders after their conference (e.g. unemployment), things that happened during the conferences were related to reductions in re-offending. These included offenders feeling remorseful, not being made to feel a bad person, conferences being memorable for offenders, offenders agreeing to and complying with conference agreements, and offenders meeting and apologizing to their victims.

A second and more recent study in New Zealand also suggests that attending an 'effective' family group conference is associated with reductions in future offending. In this study, Maxwell *et al.* (2004) gathered case file and adult offending history data for a 'retrospective' sample of 1,003 young offenders who were between fifteen and seventeen years of age at the time of their family group conference in 1998 as well as interviewing 520 of these young people in 2000–1. In this study, Maxwell *et al.* were able to hold constant not only traditional predictors of re-offending such as age, sex, and prior offending and the type of offences committed, but also prior family and school experiences and life events after the conference. They concluded that 'the family group conference can make an important contribution to preventing further offending despite the existence of negative background factors and irrespective of the nature of the offending' (p. 224). The key conference factors identified for offenders in this study were participation, avoidance of stigmatic shaming, forming the intention not to re-offend, a fair process, feeling forgiven and able to put matters behind them, and being able to make up for what they had done.

Summary

To summarize, studies of re-offending that compare the effects of restorative justice conferences to other interventions, such as court appearances or arrests, produce variable results: some show that restorative justice conferences may reduce crime, some report no effect on re-offending, and others actually report an increase in further offending. However, many questions remain about these studies including questions about the appropriateness of comparison samples, the way re-offending was measured and potential differences in offenders' characteristics and types of offences.

On the other hand, most of the studies that have examined the variable effects of restorative justice conferences on re-offending show that conferences have the potential to reduce offending. The actual nature of the critical process factors is not always the same in all studies, but it seems likely that when there is active participation, when decision-making about conference agreements is consensual, when there is no stigmatic shaming and when offenders are remorseful and feel forgiven, re-offending is less likely. However, what young offenders bring to their conferences (e.g. demographic, prior offence, and family background characteristics), as well as pre- and post-conference life events remain highly predictive of whether or not they offend afterwards. Further research will undoubtedly tease out the importance of these and other factors relating to conference practice and will add to our knowledge of how to ensure that the processes used in the delivery of restorative justice will optimize the chances of reducing re-offending and reintegrating offenders.

Conclusion

In New Zealand and Australia, restorative justice conferencing for juveniles seems now firmly established in both legislation and practice and its use is growing in many other countries. In this chapter, we have reviewed the development of restorative justice conferencing for juveniles and summarized results from empirical research. To a large extent, the data show that conferencing has achieved the key restorative aims of involving offenders, victims and supporters, achieving agreement about a cooperative and constructive response to offending, healing victims' hurt and holding offenders accountable. Results from research conducted in New Zealand, Australia and sev-

eral other jurisdictions supports the conclusion that offenders, their victims and their supporters generally have positive experiences in conferences. Compared to offenders and victims in youth or juvenile courts, those in restorative justice conferences perceive the process as fair and they are generally more satisfied with outcomes.

However, not all conferences go well. In some, ideal outcomes are not achieved (Daly 2002). Sometimes offenders are indignant and do not apologize; sometimes victims are indifferent and do not offer forgiveness; sometimes the process does not heal and restore. This should not surprise us but it is cause for some concern. Some of the research discussed here identifies key factors that are critical in ensuring that practice is effective and that restorative goals are reached. Much of what we have learned about the effects of conferencing on participants clearly indicates that practice standards are related to participants' experiences. Negative conference experiences often flow from offenders and victims not being adequately prepared and entering conferences with little or no understanding of the process and what to expect (Maxwell *et al.* 2004; Braithwaite 2002).

Thus, offenders and victims may form unrealistic expectations and feel genuinely dissatisfied with conference outcomes. But other factors such as not being treated with respect, not having an opportunity to 'have one's say' and professional domination of decision-making can undermine the essential restorativeness of the conferences and its effects on the participants. It is important that these lessons are learnt and that research continues to be undertaken so that it may constructively inform the practice of restorative justice conferencing.

Despite the minority of instances where offenders and victims come away from a restorative justice conference unhappy or dissatisfied, one thing seems clear: restorative justice conferencing is a more constructive way of responding to offending than traditional alternatives. The benefits to offenders and victims seem to outweigh the potential for negative outcomes. More often than not, offenders and victims in conferences report a better 'justice' experience compared to those appearing in court. There is now compelling evidence to suggest that restorative justice conferencing 'works' insofar as offenders are held accountable, victims' needs are met, and offenders and victims are restored. However, the key conditions for reducing crime are still insufficiently understood.

The literature makes clear that restorative justice processes were not established for the express purpose of reducing crime but instead were developed with other benefits in mind (e.g. addressing victim needs and holding offenders accountable) (Dignan 1992; Hassall 1996). While perhaps restorative justice initiatives should not be graded on their ability to effect reductions in recidivism because there are other, more salient, benefits for offenders and victims (see, for example, Miers 2001; Maxwell and Morris 2002), observers will undoubtedly continue to scrutinize conferencing processes to determine their ability to reduce further offending. We suggest that the more profitable focus of such research will be on linking the very complex nature of conference encounters with offenders' personal characteristics and experiences and future behavior.

The results to date make it clear that the restorative conference itself is only one of the many life events that are involved in desistence from crime (compare Maxwell and Morris 1999; Bushway *et al.* 2001). Early life events and offenders' characteristics will always have an important impact on re-offending. So too will future life circumstances. Nevertheless, some of the research reviewed here indicates that key factors in conferences, in particular those that are associated with achieving restorative aims and reintegrative outcomes, are likely to be associated with a lessened probability

of re-offending. Our aim in future research on restorative justice conferencing should perhaps be to understand more about *how* conferences work in reducing crime and creating conditions for life change for offenders through changing the psychological impact of the process of resolution of conflict and through ensuring that reintegrative options are made available for young offenders.

References

Braithwaite, J. (1989) *Crime, Shame and Reintegration*, Cambridge: Cambridge University Press.

— (2002) 'Setting standards for restorative justice,' *British Journal of Criminology*, 42: 563–77.

Bushway, S., Piquero, A., Briody, L., Cauffman, E. and Mazerolle, P. (2001) 'An empirical framework for studying desistance as a process,' *Criminology*, 39(2): 491–516.

Christie, N. ([1977]1997) 'Conflicts as property,' *British Journal of Criminology*, 17(1): 1–15.

Daly, K (2002). 'Restorative justice: the real story,' *Punishment and Society*, 4(1): 55–79.

Dignan, J. (1992) 'Repairing the damage: can reparation be made to work in the service of diversion?' *British Journal of Criminology*, 32: 453–72.

— (1999) 'The Crime and Disorder Act and the prospects for restorative justice,' *Criminal Law Review*, January: 48–60.

Hassall, I. (1996) 'Origin and development of family group conferences,' in J. Hudson, A. Morris, G. Maxwell and B. Galaway (eds) *Family Group Conferences: perspectives on policy and practice*, Annandale, Australia: Federation Press.

Hayes, H. (forthcoming 2005) 'Assessing re-offending in restorative justice conferences,' *The Australian and New Zealand Journal of Criminology*, 38(1).

Hayes, H. and Daly, K. (2003) 'Youth justice conferencing and re-offending,' *Justice Quarterly*, 20(4): 725–64.

— (2004) 'Conferencing and re-offending in Queensland,' *The Australian and New Zealand Journal of Criminology*, 37(2): 167–91.

Hayes, H., Prenzler, T. and Worley, R. (1998) *Making Amends: final evaluation of the Queensland Community Conferencing project*, Brisbane, Centre for Crime Policy and Public Safety, Griffith University.

Hudson, J., Morris, A., Maxwell, G. M. and Galaway, B. (1996) *Family Group Conferences:*

perspectives on policy and practice, Annandale, NSW, Australia: Federation Press.

Latimer. J. C., Dowden, C. and Muise, D. (2001) *The Effectiveness of Restorative Justice Practices: a meta-analysis,* Canada: Department of Justice.

Lilles, H. (2001) 'Circle sentencing: part of the restorative justice continuum,' in A. Morris and G. Maxwell (eds) *Restorative Justice for Juveniles: conferencing, mediation and Circles,* Oxford: Hart Publishing.

Luke, G. and Lind, B. (2002) 'Reducing juvenile crime: conferencing versus court,' *Crime and Justice Bulletin: Contemporary Issues in Crime and Justice.* 69: 1–20.

McCold, P. and Wachtel, B. (1998) *Restorative Policing Experiment: the Bethlehem Pennsylvania police family group conferencing project,* Pipersville, PA: Community Service Foundation.

McGarrell, E., Olivares, K., Crawford, K. and Kroovand, N. (2000) *Returning Justice to the Community: the Indianapolis juvenile restorative justice experiment,* Indianapolis, IN: The Hudson Institute.

McIlrea, F. (1996) 'The New Zealand youth court: a model for use with adults,' in B. Galaway and J. Hudson (eds) *Restorative Justice: international perspectives,* Monsey, NY: Criminal Justice Press.

Maxwell, G. and Morris, A. (1993) *Families, Victims and Culture: youth justice in New Zealand,* Wellington, New Zealand: Social Policy Agency and Institute of Criminology.

— (1999) *Understanding Reoffending. Final report to Social Policy Agency and the Ministry of Justice,* Wellington: Institute of Criminology, Victoria University of Wellington.

— (2001) 'Family group conferences and reoffending,' in A. Morris and G. M. Maxwell (eds) *Restorative Justice for Juveniles: conferencing, mediation and circles,* Oxford: Hart Publishing.

— (2002) 'Restorative justice and reconviction,' *Contemporary Justice Review,* 5(2): 133–46.

Maxwell, G., Kingi, V., Robertson, J. and Morris, A. (2004) *Achieving Effective Outcomes in Youth Justice Research: final report,* Wellington, New Zealand: Ministry of Social Development.

Miers, D. (2001) *An International Review of Restorative Justice,* London: Home Office.

Moore, D. and Forsythe, L. (1995) *A New Approach to Juvenile Justice: an evaluation of family conferencing in Wagga Wagga,* Canberra: Australian Institute of Justice.

Morris, A. and Maxwell, G. (1997) *Family Group Conferences and Convictions,* Occasional Paper 5, Wellington: Institute of Criminology, Victoria University of Wellington.

NACRO (National Association for the Care and Resettlement of Offenders) (1997) *A New Three Rs for Young Offenders,* London: NACRO.

Office of Crime Statistics and Research (1998) *Crime and Justice in South Australia, 1997: Juvenile Justice,* South Australia: South Australian Attorney-General's Department.

— (2000) *Crime and Justice in South Australia: Juvenile Justice 1999,* South Australia: South Australian Attorney-General's Department.

— (2001) *Crime and Justice in South Australia: Juvenile Justice 2000,* South Australia: South Australian Attorney-General's Department.

— (2002) *Crime and Justice in South Australia: Juvenile Justice 2001,* South Australia: South Australian Attorney-General's Department.

— (2003) *Crime and Justice in South Australia: Juvenile Justice 2002,* South Australia: South Australian Attorney-General's Department.

— (2004) *Crime and Justice in South Australia: Juvenile Justice 2003,* South Australia: South Australian Attorney-General's Department.

Palk, G., Hayes, H. and Prenzler, T. (1998) 'Restorative justice and community conferencing: summary findings from a pilot study', *Current Issues in Criminal Justice,* 10(2): 138–55.

Sherman, L. W., Strang, H., Barnes, G., Braithwaite, J., Inkpen, N. and Teh, M. (1998) *Experiments in Restorative Policy: a progress report on the Canberra Reintegrative Shaming Experiments (RISE),* Canberra: Australian Federal Police and Australian National University, online. Available at: http://www.aic.gov.au/rjustice/rise/progress/1988.html

Sherman, L. W., Strang, H. and Woods, D. (2000a) 'Captains of restorative justice: experience, legitimacy and recidivism,' paper presented at the Fourth International Conference on Restorative Justice for Juveniles, University of Tuebingen, 3 October.

— (2000b) *Recidivism Patterns in the Canberra Reintegrative Shaming Experiments (RISE),* Centre for Restorative Justice, Research School of Social Sciences, Australian National University.

Skelton, A. and Frank, C. (2001) 'Conferencing in South Africa: returning to our future,' in A. Morris and G. Maxwell (eds) *Restorative Justice for Juveniles: conferencing, mediation and circles,* Oxford: Hart Publishing.

Strang, H. and Sherman, L. W. (1997) *The Victim's Perspective,* RISE Working Paper 2, Law Program, RSSS, ANU, Canberra: Australian National University.

Strang, H., Barnes, G., Braithwaite, J. and Sherman, L. (1999) *Experiments in Restorative Policing: a progress report on the Canberra Reintegrative Shaming Experiments (RISE)*, Canberra: Law Program, Research School of Social Sciences, Institute for Advanced Studies, Australian National University.

Stuart, B. (1996) 'Circle sentencing: turning swords into ploughshares,' in B. Galaway and J. Hudson (eds) *Restorative Justice: international perspectives*, Monsey, NY: Criminal Justice Press.

Trimboli, L. (2000). *An Evaluation of the NSW Youth Justice Conferencing Scheme*, NSW: Bureau of Crime Statistics and Research.

Van Ness, D., Morris, A. and Maxwell, G. (2001) 'Introducing restorative justice,' in A. Morris and G Maxwell (eds) *Restorative Justice for Juveniles: conferencing, mediation and circles*, Oxford: Hart Publishing.

Wundersitz, J. and Hetzel, S. (1996) 'Family conferencing for young offenders: the South Australian experience,' in J. Hudson, A. Morris, G. Maxwell and B. Galaway (eds) *Family Group Conferences: perspectives on policy and practice*, Sydney: Federation Press.

Young, R. (2001) 'Just cops doing "shameful" business? Police-led restorative justice and the lessons of research,' in A. Morris and G. Maxwell (eds) *Restorative Justice for Juveniles: conferencing, mediation and circles*, Oxford: Hart Publishing.

Zehr, H. (1990) *Changing Lenses: a new focus for criminal justice*, Scottsdale, PA: Herald Press.

Notes

1. The Department of Human Services in Victoria is evaluating a trial of conferencing currently running in metropolitan Melbourne, Hume and Gippsland.

2. The family group conference in New Zealand operates at two distinct and key points: as an alternative to courts (for young people who have not been arrested), and as a mechanism for making recommendations to judges before sentencing (for young people who have been arrested). This means that the police can refer young offenders directly to a family conference without an arrest or appearance in the youth court; most of these conferences end in an agreement that does not involve a court appearance. It also means that judges cannot sentence young offenders who have been arrested without first referring them to a family group conference and taking into account its recommendations. This key positioning of family group conferences is consistent with the restorative justice value of empowering young people, families, and victims by giving them a role in the decisions about how best to respond to offending and thereby reducing the powers of professionals who must take these parties' views into account.

3. The Young Offenders Act 1993 in South Australia, for example, specifies deterrence, community protection, accountability and restitution among its objectives.

4. Stigmatic shaming is a recognized part of the criminal justice system; many of its rituals serve to signify the separation and segregation of defendants. In 'reintegrative shaming,' at least in theory, the offence rather than the offender is condemned and the offender is reintegrated with rather than rejected by society. Examples of conferencing based on reintegrative shaming are the system of conferencing first introduced in Wagga Wagga in New South Wales (Moore and Forsythe 1995) and subsequently developed in the Reintegrative Shaming Experiment (RISE) in Canberra, ACT (Sherman *et al.* 1998; Strang *et al.* 1999) and copied in some areas of the United States through Real Justice (McCold and Wachtel 1998).

5. In some, they are full participants; in others, as in some of the conferences for adult offenders in New Zealand, they are observers only.

6. One distinctive feature about conferencing in New Zealand is that the family and the young person are given the opportunity to discuss privately how they think the offending should be dealt with. When the conference reconvenes with all the participants present, this plan is then discussed and agreement is sought or amendments are made.

7. Hayes and Daly (2004) report similar outcomes for another group of young offenders referred to a conference between 1997 and 1999 and speculate that survey results in Queensland show higher levels of perceived involvement and satisfaction than other research because post-conference surveys were administered immediately after conferences were concluded, often a time when emotions are high.

8. This figure is not, however, supported by the Annual Statistical Report of the Office of Crime Statistics and Research (1998). It is stated there that only 47 per cent of conferences in 1997 had at least one victim present.

9. More recent data from South Australia shows that the proportion of conferences where victims are present has declined considerably. From 1999 through 2003, the percentage of conferences convened where no victims attended ranged from 56 per cent in 1999 to 67 per cent in 2003 (Office of Crime Statistics and Research 1998, 2000, 2001, 2002, 2003, 2004). This may suggest that maintaining high rates of victim attendance becomes more challenging as case numbers grow. In 1994, SA convened 1,110 conferences. This number has climbed to more than 1,600 referrals over the past five years.

10. Reasons include that the victim was not invited to the conference, the time arranged for the conference was unsuitable for them or they were given inadequate notice of the conference.

11. This finding is perhaps explained by the fact that families are allowed and encouraged to deliberate privately about possible outcomes to try to ensure that they take ownership of them. There is a tension here between empowering the family and the young offender and empowering victims.

12. Restorativeness was defined as 'the degree to which offenders and victims recognized the other and were affected by the other ... the degree to which there was positive movement between the offender and victim' (Daly 2002: 70).

13. A more developed discussion of issues surrounding restorative justice and recidivism research is provided by Hayes (forthcoming 2005), Morris and Maxwell (1997) and Maxwell and Morris (1999).

14. Re-offending was measured for eight to twelve months following the conference. Where there were multiple offenders, observers consulted conference convenors on who they thought was the 'primary offender' for the purpose of observation.

5

Restorative justice and recidivism

Promises made, promises kept?

James Bonta, Rebecca Jesseman,
Tanya Rugge and Robert Cormier

Without a doubt, restorative justice (RJ) has attracted widespread attention and it has challenged our traditional notions of justice and the application of justice. RJ offers an alternative to the traditional adversarial and mainly offender-centered system of justice by assigning a greater role in dealing with crime to victims and community members. Throughout the world many countries are not only experimenting with RJ but also enshrining RJ principles into law and policy. In short, RJ may represent the beginnings of a paradigm shift.

Fundamentally, restorative justice is an approach to justice that focuses on repairing the harm caused by crime while holding the offender responsible for his or her actions. Restorative justice programs, at their best, are designed to render a more satisfying sense of justice by engaging the parties directly affected by a crime – victims, offenders, and community – in a process where collectively they can identify and address their needs in the aftermath of a crime, and seek a resolution that affords reparation, healing, and prevents future harm. Enmeshed in this definition of restorative justice are a number of outcomes that restorative justice program evaluators need to address. These include, but are not limited to, the extent to which

harm was repaired, the nature and quality of the engagement, the level of satisfaction of the parties with the process and the outcomes, the extent to which needs were identified and addressed satisfactorily for each of the parties, the impact on the offender and, in this respect, most notably, whether the likelihood of recidivism is reduced.

The last of these intended outcomes, reducing recidivism, is one that restorative justice has in common with two other prominent approaches to addressing criminal behavior, i.e. deterrence, which is based on the premise that punishment can serve to reduce the likelihood that offenders will re-offend, and rehabilitation, which is based on the premise that appropriate treatment of offenders reduces recidivism. The focus of this chapter is an examination of the evidence regarding restorative justice and its impact on recidivism in the context of the more extensive literature on the effects of deterrence and rehabilitation on recidivism.

What do we know about recidivism reduction?

Before reviewing the RJ research specifically as it relates to recidivism, it is helpful to summarize the research on the effects of deterrence and rehabilitation on recidivism. We will deal first with deterrence, as the evidence is relatively straightforward and unequivocal.

There are a number of reasons why societies punish those who transgress laws and norms. First, punishing offenders demonstrates to the public that justice was served. For many, there is something inherently satisfying to have an element of offenders getting their 'just deserts' (von Hirsch 1976). The punishment of offenders also expresses society's disapproval of certain acts, thereby communicating cultural norms and values. Finally, punishment is intended to deter offenders and others from behaving in an antisocial manner. It is to this last reason for having criminal justice sanctions that we turn our attention.

Punishing offenders has become prevalent in many industrialized nations as evidenced by increasingly stringent laws and methods for dealing with offenders. This popularity is no better seen than in the United States. Fueled by 'three strikes (and even two strikes) and you're out' laws, America has the highest incarceration rate in the world, at least among countries that report their prison populations. It houses one-quarter of the world's prison population with nearly two million offenders incarcerated (Walmsley 2002). Add to this more than four million offenders under community supervision and it is little wonder that one of every thirty-two American citizens in 2003 was under some form of correctional control (Glaze and Palla 2004). And these are only the numbers for adults.

Not only have the laws become more stringent, leading to high incarceration rates, so have the conditions of correctional control. In terms of custody, the US has 'no-frill prisons' where even basic amenities such as radio, television and access to daily exercise are removed. Community correctional control is no longer limited to probation; there is now a wide range of intermediate sanctions that are *added* to probation and parole. Probation and parole in many jurisdictions includes electronic monitoring, urinalysis and sometimes even public humiliation. As Erwin (1986) wrote nearly twenty years ago, probation is under pressure to 'turn up the heat' and be as punishing as prison.

The popularity of the get-tough movement is not restricted to the US. Other countries have seen rising prison populations and the imposition of stricter controls over offenders. For example, in the UK the prison population grew 7 per cent between 2001 and 2002 (Councell 2003). The apparent insatiable appetite of the public to cause suffering upon offenders appears, however, to be subsiding. Legislators and policy-makers are beginning to realize that getting tough on criminals is extremely expensive. Concerns have been raised that getting tough on offenders comes at the expense of funding social programs such as health, education, and crime prevention (Austin *et al.* 1999; Greenwood 1998). Moreover, and quite simply, punishment does not appear to deter offenders from further crime.

The evidence for the ineffectiveness of criminal justice sanctions comes from both narrative and meta-analytic reviews of the research findings. A narrative literature review is a conventional approach to summarizing empirical studies on a particular topic. Studies are identified, read, and evaluated based on the reviewer's judgment of the findings. Andrew von Hirsch and his colleagues (von Hirsch *et al.* 1999) conducted such a review on the effects of punishment on offender recidivism and found limited support for deterrence. The problem with the narrative review is that it is dependent upon the qualitative assessment of findings by the reviewer(s) and final conclusions are limited to a simple 'vote count' (i.e. how many studies favor a certain conclusion and how many do not).

Meta-analysis has come to replace the traditional narrative literature review as the preferred approach to summarizing the findings from studies. The advantages offered by meta-analysis are many. First, this method is more rigorous in its approach to examining studies, as meta-analysis uses a structured and transparent methodology to examine the features of a study that relate to the issue of interest. Next, all study results, whether they are statistically significant or not, are coded. Counting only statistically significant results can be misleading, especially when sample size is small. Lastly, meta-analysis provides a *quantitative* summary of the findings. Assigning a quantitative weight to the findings, or what is commonly referred to as an 'effect size,' allows for an estimate of the magnitude of the findings, its relationship to various characteristics of the study, and by pooling the effect size with other studies it increases the power of the findings beyond that which a single study can provide.

Studies on the same topic often report their results in different ways. The problem is taking the different results and being able to compare them. The solution lies with the meta-analytic technique of statistically transforming the findings from individual studies to a standardized quantitative weight or an effect size. For example, if conducting a meta-analysis on the effects of a certain type of diet on weight loss then there may be a need to transform the weight losses that are reported in various studies as pounds or stones into kilograms. There are a number of effect sizes that can be chosen by the meta-analyst (e.g. Cohen's *d*, odds-ratio). However, in this chapter we describe studies that use either the Pearson correlation coefficient (*r*) or phi. The phi coefficient is the same as the Pearson correlation coefficient when used with dichotomous data.

To date, there have been two meta-analytic reviews that have addressed the question of whether sanctions impact on recidivism. Smith *et al.* (2002) conducted the first meta-analysis involving over a hundred studies with 442,471 offenders. Smith *et al.* (2002) found that serving a prison sentence, as

compared to a community sentence, was not associated with a reduction in recidivism (phi = 0.07; CI = 0.05–0.09). CI is the confidence interval that gives the range of values that are likely to occur around the mean effect size and is usually set at 95 per cent. Thus, the finding of a CI in the range of 0.05 to 0.09 means that there is a 95 per cent likelihood that the true population mean will fall within this range. It is important to note that the CI for this particular finding did not include zero, meaning that the result was not due to simple chance. If the confidence interval includes zero then the findings are not statistically significant using the conventional 0.05 probability level. Another advantage of reporting the CI associated with a mean effect size is that if we are examining two or more relationships and the CIs overlap then we cannot be certain that one relationship is greater than the other. Here, the mean phi coefficient was 0.07 and it was positive, indicating that incarceration was associated with an *increase* in recidivism (a negative phi would have indicated a decrease in recidivism).

Smith *et al.* (2002) also found that the length of time incarcerated was not associated with reductions in recidivism (phi = 0.03, CI = 0.02–0.04). On the contrary, longer periods of incarceration were associated with an increase in recidivism. To simplify the interpretation of phi, the value approximates percentages, and a phi of 0.03 suggests an increase in recidivism in the neighborhood of 3 per cent. Their second major set of analyses focused on the effects of intermediate sanctions (e.g. electronic monitoring programs, boot camp, drug testing, etc.). Once again, intermediate sanctions had no impact on recidivism (phi = -0.01, CI = -0.02–0.00).

The second meta-analysis comes from the larger review of the offender rehabilitation literature (Andrews and Bonta 2003). Within the Andrews and Bonta (2003) review there were 101 tests of the impact of sanctions on recidivism. The mean effect size (r in this case) was -0.03 with a 95 per cent confidence interval of -0.05 to -0.03. Because the coding direction was reversed from that in the Smith *et al.* (2002) review, the negative sign indicates that sanctions were associated with increases in recidivism. Specifically, it was rehabilitation programs that were associated with decreases in recidivism (r = 0.12, CI = 0.09–0.14). Thus, two independent meta-analyses confirmed the earlier findings from the von Hirsch *et al.* (1999) narrative review of the deterrence literature but this time with quantitative precision. The overall conclusion is that deterrence does not 'work.'

So, if deterrence does not reduce recidivism then what about the delivery of rehabilitation services to offenders? We turn now to the literature on offender rehabilitation and recidivism.

Offender rehabilitation and recidivism

In our discussion of the research on deterrence we noted the meta-analysis reported by Andrews and Bonta (2003). Although they found that deterrence, if anything, had a negative impact, the focus of their meta-analytic review was on the effectiveness of providing human service interventions to offenders. On this latter point, there was a significant relationship between human service delivery and reduced recidivism. Of 273 tests of the impact of human service programs (e.g. family therapy, skill-building, substance abuse interventions, etc.) on recidivism, the average r was 0.12 (CI = 0.09–0.14). In other words, for those offenders who receive treatment, the recidivism rate is 12 per cent lower than for offenders who do not receive treatment. This reduction in recidivism may not be dramatic but it is certainly more impressive than the findings with deterrence (note that the confidence intervals for deterrence and treatment do not overlap).

The review of offender treatment by Andrews and Bonta (2003) is consistent with the findings from other meta-analytic reviews focusing on different kinds of offenders and social contexts. For example, Lipsey (1989) reviewed the treatment literature for juvenile delinquents and reported an average effect size estimate of 0.10 based on 443 effect sizes. Redondo and his colleagues (Redondo *et al.* 1999) examined forty-nine European studies and found a mean effect size of 0.15. There have been more than a dozen meta-analytic reviews of the offender rehabilitation literature and their findings are remarkably consistent (McGuire 2001) in showing that treatment 'works.'

Most reviews of the treatment literature make only broad differentiations among the treatment programs. It has been recognized since the 1980s that not all offender treatment programs are equally effective (Andrews 1980; Palmer 1983). However, the principles of differential treatment were not clearly formulated and empirically demonstrated until 1990 (Andrews, Bonta and Hoge 1990; Andrews *et al.* 1990).

In 1990, Andrews, Bonta and Hoge presented three important principles for effective rehabilitation. They were the principles of Risk, Need, and Responsivity. The Risk principle states that the intensity of human service intervention should be proportional to the offender's risk to re-offend. That is, more intense levels of services should be directed to the higher-risk offender and minimal services directed to the low-risk offender. Many therapists like to treat low-risk clients who are cooperative, verbal, intelligent and motivated, but the research shows that treating low-risk offenders has minimal impact on recidivism (r = 0.03, ninety-six tests; Andrews and Bonta 2003). It is the higher-risk offender that shows the most benefit from treatment (r = 0.10, 278 tests).

The Need principle makes a distinction between criminogenic and *non*-criminogenic needs. Criminogenic needs are offender needs that are functionally related to criminal behavior. They are dynamic, changeable risk factors. Some examples are substance abuse, cognitions supportive of crime and social support for crime. Examples of non-criminogenic needs are vague feelings of emotional discomfort, self-esteem and increasing group cohesiveness. In order to reduce recidivism, treatment programs must target criminogenic needs ($r = 0.19$, 169 tests).

An offender may be high risk and with clearly defined criminogenic needs, but treatment may have little impact if it is not delivered in a way that the offender can understand and that motivates him/her. Many offenders have a concrete thinking style, are poorly educated, and have a restless, energetic temperament. Placing them in a treatment program that is dependent on 'talking it out' and discussing abstract ideas is unlikely to help. The Responsivity principle speaks to tailoring the treatment to the learning style of the individual. For most offenders, this means a structured, cognitive-behavioral style of intervention that is rich in concrete exercises and that shapes the desired behavior with the appropriate use of interpersonal rewards and punishments. Behavioral forms of intervention work best with offenders ($r = 0.23$, seventy-seven tests).

In the Andrews et al. study (1990), the presence of these principles was clearly associated with reductions of recidivism. When treatment programs adhered to all three principles (i.e. appropriate treatment) the mean phi coefficient was 0.32 (fifty-four tests). When none of the principles were followed (i.e. inappropriate), treatment actually made things worse with an increase in recidivism ($r = -0.07$, thirty-eight tests).

An updated analysis of the expanded treatment database reinforced the conclusion that rehabilitation programs adhering to the three principles led to reductions in recidivism ($r = 0.26$, sixty tests; Andrews

and Bonta 2003). The more recent findings also showed that treatment was more effective when delivered in the community. The mean effect size was 0.35 for appropriate programs delivered in the community and 0.17 for similar programs delivered in prison/residential settings. Moreover, the number of principles that are followed is associated with a step-wise reduction in recidivism. When only one principle was followed the mean r was 0.02 and for two principles, $r = 0.18$.

In summary, there is convincing evidence that treatment programs with certain characteristics can reduce recidivism. Those programs associated with reductions in re-offending are those that target the criminogenic needs of higher-risk offenders using behavioral intervention techniques. This, we do know. Can restorative justice programs have a similar effect and, if so, under what conditions? We turn to these questions next.

A meta-analysis of the impact of restorative justice on recidivism

In order to answer the question of whether or not restorative justice programs can impact offender recidivism, we undertook a meta-analytic review of the pertinent literature. The present review is an update and expansion of the meta-analyses conducted by Bonta and his colleagues (Bonta et al. 2002) and Latimer et al. (2001). These earlier reviews found a small relationship between restorative justice interventions and reductions in recidivism. Bonta et al. (2002) reported an average reduction of recidivism of 3 per cent and Latimer et al. (2001) found a 7 per cent reduction. Although the two reviews found different effect size estimates, the overlapping confidence intervals from the two studies suggest that the differences are not significant.

The reviews, however, were heavily weighted by studies that included court-imposed restitution and community service agreements. For many (e.g. Bazemore 2000; Zehr 2004), court-ordered reparation does not represent restorative justice because the parties are not engaged in a process that leads to a restorative agreement. With the recent publication of studies that better fit a more refined definition of restorative justice, it is time to re-examine the literature and explore the impacts from programs that more fully involve victims and the community.

As with earlier reviews (Bonta *et al.* 2002; Latimer *et al.* 2001), our net was cast widely in selecting studies to include in our meta-analysis. Restorative justice was broadly defined as 'any intervention that attempts to repair the harm caused by the offender to the victim or the community.' Consequently, court-imposed restitution and community service with limited victim involvement remained along with studies of victim offender mediation. Newer interventions such as family group conferencing and community forums were added to the database. We decided to keep court-imposed restoration schemes for two reasons. First, it would allow us to make comparisons of court-ordered reparation programs with non-coercive reparation programs. Second, many of the early studies of court-ordered restitution and community service provided restorative justice rationales involving offender accountability and repairing the harm.

To be included in the review, the study had to meet the following three criteria. First, there had to be a comparison group of some type (comparison groups were coded as to whether they were the result of random assignment, some type of matching, etc.). Second, post-program recidivism data had to be reported in a way that permitted the calculation of an effect size. As all the studies provided results that could be used to construct two-by-two tables (type of treatment and recidivism outcome), the phi coefficient was selected as our effect size measure. Finally, the assessment of recidivism had to be based on a longitudinal research design. Retrospective analysis of criminal histories and cross-sectional comparisons were omitted.

Over fifty variables were coded for each study. The variables could be grouped into three main categories. The first category dealt with evaluation methodology and measured such things as type of research design (e.g. random, quasi-experimental, etc.), the comparability of the control group to the RJ group (e.g. checks for group equivalence conducted) and length of follow-up. The second category assessed participant characteristics (e.g. adult or youth, race, age, etc.). The last category dealt with the characteristics of the program (e.g. was restitution required? was participation mandatory? did the program follow restorative justice principles? etc.). Given the strong evidence concerning the effectiveness of offender rehabilitation programs in reducing recidivism, we also coded for the presence of treatment programming and its appropriateness following the principles of effective rehabilitation.

Our review of the literature uncovered thirty-nine studies that met the criteria for inclusion. Most (72.1 per cent) of the programs were from the United States, and approximately half of the programs were situated within a court setting (see **Table 5.1** for a summary of program characteristics). Given that the studies dated back to 1976 when restorative justice was in its infancy, it is not surprising that 36.1 per cent of studies were categorized as having minimal adherence to today's standards of restorative justice. Only 31.1 per cent of the studies provided a detailed description of the restorative justice model. Not shown in the table, 52.7 per cent of cases involved face-to-face meetings between victims and offenders. The mean attrition rate (i.e. per cent who did not complete the program) was 21.5 per cent.

Perhaps because of our study selection criteria, we found that most evaluations used acceptable research designs. Random assignment was conducted in 29.5 per cent of the studies and another 54.1 per cent used quasi-experimental, matched designs, while the remaining studies used control groups selected for their convenience and availability or a pre-post design. Fully 83.3 per cent of studies made efforts to verify the equivalence of the experimental and control groups. Most (84.7 per cent) of the control groups were exposed to traditional criminal justice processing. The remaining control groups consisted of either an alternative restorative justice program or a treatment intervention.

As presented in **Table 5.2**, most of the offenders in the restorative justice programs were low-risk, male, Caucasian youth. Very few programs targeted serious cases such as violent offenders or those who committed crimes against the person. Although not a focus of our review, this highly select group also displayed very high rates of satisfaction with restorative justice. On average, 87.7 per cent of offenders expressed satisfaction with their experience. Victims expressed slightly lower rates of satisfaction (81.6 per cent).

The thirty-nine studies yielded sixty-seven effect size estimates for recidivism. The number of effect size estimates exceeds the number of studies because a study may report more than one comparison. For example, Umbreit and Coates' (1992) study yielded two effect sizes (one for a victim offender mediation program in Oakland, California, and another for a program in Minneapolis, Minnesota). The most common measure of recidivism was reconviction (50.8 per cent) followed by rearrest (44.1 per cent). The average follow-up interval was 17.7 months. The average phi coefficient for all programs was 0.07 and the CI did not include zero (**Table 5.3**). In other words, restorative justice interventions do have an impact on recidivism in the order of a 7 per cent reduction. Further inspection of Table 5.3 finds little variation in the mean effect size across sample (juvenile/adult) and type of RJ intervention (e.g.

Table 5.1. Characteristics of restorative justice interventions

Program characteristics

Age of program (per cent)	
Less than two years	42.6
Two years or more	57.4
Type of setting (per cent)	
Court	50.8
Police	16.4
Probation/parole	26.2
Institution/residential	6.6
Program ownership (per cent)	
Criminal justice agency	63.9
Private agency	26.2
Public, non-criminal justice agency	9.8
Participation mandatory (per cent)	35.0
Treatment provided (per cent)	15.0
Adherence to RJ principles (per cent)	
Minimal	36.1
Moderate	21.3
High	42.6
Staff trained in RJ (per cent)	74.5
Elements of ...	
Victim offender mediation or reconciliation (per cent)	62.3
Restitution	82.0
Community service	82.0
Family group conference	24.6
Community forum	8.2

Table 5.2. Characteristics of the participants

Characteristic

Sample (per cent)	
Juvenile	75.0
Adult	25.0
Gender (per cent)	
Male	97.7
Female	2.3
Race (per cent)	
Caucasian	79.2
Black	6.3
Other	14.5
Mean age (years)	18.7
Prior record (per cent)	46.1
Low risk (per cent)	72.0
Major offence type (per cent)	
Person	14.2
Property	67.3
Vandalism	8.2
Other	10.3

Table 5.3. Restorative justice interventions and recidivism (CI)

Type of sample/program	RJn	N	k	phi	CI
All programs	11,701	25,771	67	0.07	0.06–0.08
Juvenile	9,595	21,766	50	0.06	0.05–0.07
Adult	1,858	3,507	16	0.09	0.06–0.12
Victim offender mediation	3,440	6,949	40	0.08	0.06–0.10
Restitution	10,822	23,934	55	0.08	0.07–0.09
Community service	10,495	23,252	57	0.07	0.06–0.08
Family group conference	1,878	3,741	16	0.09	0.06–0.12
Community forum	705	1,435	5	0.11	0.06–0.16

Notes RJn = rj sample size; N = total sample size including control; k = number of effect sizes; CI = 95 per cent confidence interval.

victim offender mediation, restitution). The overlapping CIs indicate that there are no differences between programs with youthful offenders and adult offenders, nor does one particular RJ intervention perform better than another.

Exploring further what could possibly influence the magnitude of the phi coefficient, we examined the role of the evaluation methodology used in the studies. There were no differences in the mean effect size among the studies that used random assignment, quasi-experimental designs or even studies with poor methodologies (e.g. control with no checks for equivalence). However, the year of publication was related to phi ($r = 0.25$, $p < 0.05$) with studies after 1995 yielding larger effect size estimates than studies prior to 1996 (average phi of 0.12 and 0.04 respectively).

The positive effects found with recent evaluations may be due to the fact that these RJ programs have more developed and conceptually refined models of restorative justice. The restorative justice rationale/model underlying the programs was more clearly formulated in the recent studies. No study after 1995 was coded 'vague or poor' in their description of a restorative justice model. Most of the recent programs (65 per cent) were highly structured as evidenced by manuals or formalized routines. In the earlier programs, only 10 per cent were coded as highly structured. Furthermore, all the programs after 1995 described staff as being specifically trained in the delivery of restorative justice services. Finally, prior to 1996 only 18.4 per cent of the programs were coded as 'high adherence to RJ' whereas the rate jumps to 82.4 per cent for programs published in 1996 or later.

The recent studies could be characterized as not only being more true to restorative justice principles, but also these programs were not simply mere 'add-ons' to criminal justice sanctions. Many of the early RJ programs were closely tied to criminal justice sanctions, usually in the form of restitution and community service. Sometimes offenders met the victim or negotiated through a mediator the terms and conditions for repairing the harm. However, criminal justice officials administered most of the early interventions where the court assigned the amount of restitution or community service with minimal victim involvement. A closer analysis of the data shows that RJ interventions that were contextualized within criminal justice sanctions showed little effect on recidivism (phi = 0.01) whereas programs that were outside of the sanctioning process were more effective in reducing recidivism (phi = 0.10, $t = 2.26$, df = 49, $p < 0.05$).

Treatment, restorative justice and recidivism

As reviewed earlier, offender rehabilitation programs can have significant impacts on

115

reducing recidivism. Human service interventions, without differentiation according to risk, need and responsivity, produce a mean effect of 0.12. This effect size is of the same order as that found for RJ programs that operate outside of the criminal sanctioning process (0.10). RJ programs that are court-ordered reparation programs have an average effect size of 0.01, almost identical to that found with criminal justice sanctions.

Only eleven interventions had any evidence of treatment provided to offenders. There was no difference in the effect size for those who received treatment (0.09) and those who did not (0.07). The treatments provided were further coded as to their adherence to the principles of effective interventions. Three programs could not be evaluated because of a lack of information and six programs were coded as inappropriate. The six inappropriate programs produced a mean effect size of 0.01. The Bonta et al. (2002) study was the only one that was coded as appropriate and it had a mean effect size of 0.31.

In recent years, justice practices have been extended to offenders who have committed more serious crimes and to higher-risk offenders. We make a distinction between those who have committed serious, violent crimes and those who are at a high risk to re-offend. They are not necessarily the same. An offender with no prior record but who has committed a serious crime can be a low risk to re-offend (Rugge et al. 2005). Five RJ programs, all published after 1997, targeted mostly violent offenders. The mean phi coefficient was 0.15 but the range was high (0.02 to 0.26). Although this result appears promising, more studies are needed.

With respect to offender risk level, thus far our data suggests that RJ interventions have no impact on recidivism for the higher-risk offender (phi = -0.01, n = 17). Surprisingly, RJ programs targeting low-risk offenders showed a greater impact on recidivism (phi = 0.08 for low-risk offenders vs -0.01 for the higher-risk offenders; t = 2.14, df = 54,

p < 0.05). This finding raises two questions. Why would restorative justice work better, in terms of recidivism reduction, with lower-risk offenders than with higher-risk offenders and why does it have absolutely no impact on higher-risk offenders?

The effectiveness of RJ programs with low-risk offenders is contrary to the rehabilitation literature where treatment provided to low-risk offenders is largely ineffective. In trying to understand this finding it is helpful to be reminded that low-risk offenders, by definition, have very few criminogenic needs that require attention. Moreover, when considering only the offender, RJ targets increasing acceptance of responsibility for the harm caused, empathy for the victim and stimulating feelings of remorse and shame. None of these factors are established criminogenic needs that are functionally related to criminal behavior (Andrews and Bonta 2003). Yet, we see reductions in re-offending.

There are two possible explanations that account for the reduced recidivism. First, the control groups in the studies were exposed to traditional criminal justice processing. Labeling theorists would argue that official processing might actually increase offending because the offender assumes the criminal label given by the criminal justice system. There is some evidence that interventions with low-risk offenders can sometimes increase recidivism (Andrews et al. 1990; Bonta et al. 2000). In other words, the exposure to criminal justice processing experienced by comparison groups may not be without effect. Some offenders may have worsened, thereby accentuating differences with the restorative justice groups.

A second explanation may relate to the reintegrative shaming model forwarded by Braithwaite (1989, 1999). Reintegrative shaming with its non-stigmatizing approach to labeling (the traditional criminal justice system's approach) may be well suited for the low-risk offender. Low-risk offenders are individuals who still have relatively close ties to the norms and values of society. The harms that they have caused to victims and the communities can be addressed without the heavy-handed approach of criminal justice processing. In a sense, their deviation from the norm is not so great that it cannot be corrected with something as simple as meeting the victim or involving community volunteers in repairing the harm. Rebuilding relationships is not insurmountable for the low-risk offender and can form the basis for 'relational rehabilitation' (Bazemore 1999).

With the higher-risk offender, we have an individual with a variety of criminogenic needs who generally has weak bonds to society. In this case, restorative justice may well be deficient in reducing recidivism. As more and more restorative justice experimentation is extended to higher-risk offenders, the hazard of doing harm becomes a possibility. With the higher-risk offender, appropriate treatment interventions will be needed to reduce recidivism, and yet the evidence thus far suggests that restorative justice practitioners are ill equipped to deal with these offenders. The studies that we reviewed found that when treatment was given, the treatment was likely to be inappropriate. The very first principle for effective treatment intervention requires an assessment of offender risk, and this is almost absent in the literature on restorative justice. Only five studies used an actuarial, evidence-based measure of offender risk. It may not be the role of restorative justice facilitators to deliver treatment programming; yet it would be useful if they would recognize the need for treatment and the type of programming that would assist in reducing offender recidivism, and make the appropriate referrals for treatment.

Summary and implications

Our meta-analytic review of the literature on restorative justice and recidivism provides a number of observations about what we know and what we need to know. We can summarize them as follows:

1 RJ interventions, on average, are associated with reductions in recidivism. The effects are relatively small but they are significant. It is also clear that the more recent studies are producing larger effects.

2 There is evidence to indicate that court-ordered RJ programs have no impact on recidivism. Programs that operate in a non-coercive environment and that attempt to involve victims and community members in a collaborative manner produce the largest effect size estimates.

3 RJ interventions appear more effective with low-risk offenders. This may be because low-risk offenders are diverted from the potential harm caused from traditional criminal justice processing and they are easier to reintegrate into the mainstream culture.

4 For high-risk offenders, restorative justice may be insufficient to decrease recidivism. If restorative justice practitioners continue to deal with the higher-risk offenders, then careful consideration of delivering appropriate treatment programming to these offenders in conjunction with the restorative process will be required.

We saw from our restorative justice meta-analysis that considerable progress has been made, particularly since 1996. We anticipate that as new evaluations of restorative justice and its impact on recidivism are published we will reach a point where we can derive some basic principles of practice for restorative justice that are associated with a reduction in recidivism. The establishment of treatment principles in the offender rehabilitation field has contributed significantly to program development. Similar principles in the area of restorative justice would surely be a welcome addition to basic principles that relate to the underlying philosophy of restorative justice and safeguarding the rights and interests of the parties (see the United Nations Basic Principles on the Use of Restorative Justice Programs in Criminal Matters; United Nations 2002). The goal is to elucidate the elements of restorative justice interventions that will meet a range of objectives, including repairing harm, producing a satisfying sense of justice, meeting the needs of victims, and increasing the likelihood that offenders will adopt law-abiding lives.

Note

We would like to thank Jeff Latimer for kindly sharing studies that were used in his meta-analysis (Latimer *et al.* 2001). The opinions expressed are those of the authors and do not necessarily represent the views of Public Safety and Emergency Preparedness Canada.

References

Andrews, D. A. (1980) 'Some experimental investigations of the principles of differential association through deliberate manipulations of the structure of service systems,' *American Sociological Review*, 45: 448–62.

Andrews, D. A. and Bonta, J. (2003) *The Psychology of Criminal Conduct*, third edn, Cincinnati: Anderson.

Andrews, D. A., Bonta, J., and Hoge, R. D. (1990) 'Classification for effective rehabilitation: rediscovering psychology,' *Criminal Justice and Behavior*, 17: 19–52.

Andrews, D. A., Zinger, I., Hoge, R. D., Bonta, J., Gendreau, P., and Cullen, F. T. (1990) 'Does correctional treatment work? A psychologically informed metaanalysis,' *Criminology*, 28: 369–404.

Austin, J., Clark, J., Hardyman, P. and Henry, A. D. (1999) 'The impact of "three strikes and you're out,"' *Punishment and Society*, 1: 131–62.

Bazemore, G. (1999) 'After shaming, whither reintegration: restorative justice and relational rehabilitation', in G. Bazemore and L. Walgrave (eds) *Restorative Juvenile Justice:*

repairing the harm of youth crime, Monsey, NY: Criminal Justice Press.

— (2000) 'Rock and roll, restorative justice, and the continuum of the real world: a response to "purism" in operationalizing restorative justice,' *Contemporary Justice Review*, 3(4): 459–77.

Bishop, T. Y. (1981) 'The effects of the recorder's court restitution program on the inmate population, criminal recidivism, and educational and sociological status of offenders,' PhD thesis, Wayne State University.

Bonta, J., Boyle, J., Sonnichsen, P. and Motiuk, L. (1983) 'Restitution in correctional halfway houses: victim satisfaction, attitudes, and recidivism,' *Canadian Journal of Criminology*, 20: 277–92.

Bonta, J., Wallace-Capretta, S. and Rooney, J. (2000) 'A quasi-experimental evaluation of an intensive rehabilitation supervision program,' *Criminal Justice and Behavior*, 27: 312–29.

Bonta, J., Wallace-Capretta, S., Rooney, J. and McAnoy, K. (2002) 'An outcome evaluation of a restorative justice alternative to incarceration,' *Contemporary Justice Review*, 5(4): 319–38.

Braithwaite, J. (1989) *Crime, Shame and Reintegration*, Cambridge: Cambridge University Press.

— (1999) 'Restorative justice: assessing optimistic and pessimistic accounts,' in M. Tonry (ed.) *Crime and Justice: a review of research*, Chicago: University of Chicago Press.

Butts, G. and Snyder, H. N. (1992) *Restitution and Juvenile Recidivism* (NCJRS No. 137774), Washington, DC: US Department of Justice.

Cannon, A. and Stanford, R. M. (1981) *Evaluation of the Juvenile Alternative Services Project* (NCJRS No. 080633), Tallahassee: Office of Children, Youth and Families.

Compass Management Group (1978) *Snohomish County Superior Court Juvenile Court Division Program Evaluation of the Youth Community Service Project – Final Report* (NCJRS No. 46733), Everett, WA: Snohomish County Juvenile Court.

Councell, R. (2003) 'The prison population in 2002: a statistical review,' *Findings*, 228, London: Home Office.

Crotty, J. and Meier, R. D. (1980) *Evaluation of Juvenile Restitution Program Project: Detour*, East Lyme, CT: Behavioral Systems Associates.

Erwin, B. S. (1986) 'Turning up the heat on probationers in Georgia,' *Federal Probation*, 50: 17–24.

Evje, A., and Cushman, R. C. (2000) *A Summary of the Evaluations of Six California Victim*

Offender Reconciliation Programs, California: The Judicial Council of California.

Forsythe, L. (1995) 'An analysis of juvenile apprehension characteristics and reapprehension rates,' in D. Moore, L. Forsythe and T. O'Connell (eds) *A New Approach to Juvenile Justice: an evaluation of family conferencing in Wagga Wagga*, New South Wales: Charles Stuart University.

Fulkerson, A. (2001) 'The use of victim impact panels in domestic violence cases: a restorative justice approach,' *Contemporary Justice Review*, 4(3–4): 355–68.

Glaze, L. E., and Palla, S. (2004) 'Probation and Parole in the United States, 2003,' *Bureau of Justice Statistics Bulletin, July 2004* (NCJRS No. 205336), Washington, DC: US Department of Justice.

Greenwood, P. W. (1998) 'Investing in prisons or prevention: the state policy makers' dilemma,' *Crime and Delinquency*, 44: 136–42.

Griffith, W. R. (1983) *The Effect of Washington, DC's Restitution Program on the Recidivism Rates of the Disadvantaged, Serious Offender* (NCJRS No. 098581), Eugene, OR: Institute of Policy Analysis.

Heinz, J., Galaway, B. and Hudson, J. (1976) 'Restitution or parole: a follow-up study of adult offenders,' *Social Service Review*, March: 148–56.

Hudson, J. and Chesney, S. (1978) 'Research on restitution: a review and assessment,' in B. Galaway and J. Hudson (eds) *Offender Restitution in Theory and Action*, Lanham, MD: Lexington Books.

Krussink, M. (1990) 'The Halt program: diversion of juvenile vandals', in *Dutch Penal Law and Policy: notes on criminological research from the research and documentation centre, 1708(1)*, The Hague: Dutch Ministry of Justice, Research and Documentation Centre.

Lahners, R. and McMasters, E. A. (1981) *The Lancaster County Pretrial Diversion Program – 1978 Felony Diversions: an assessment of recidivism, system impact, and cost-effectiveness* (NCJRS No. 78358), Lincoln, NE: Lancaster County Pretrial Diversion Program.

Latimer, J., Dowden, C. and Muise, D. (2001) *The Effectiveness of Restorative Justice Practices: a meta-analysis*, Ottawa: Department of Justice, Canada.

Levi, K. (1982) 'Relative redemption: labeling in juvenile restitution,' *Juvenile and Family Court Journal*, February: 3–13.

Lipsey, M. W. (1989) 'The efficacy of intervention for juvenile delinquency: results from 400 studies,' paper presented at the 41st Annual Meeting of the American Society of Criminology, Reno, NV.

McCold, P. and Wachtel, B. (1998) *Restorative Policing Experiment: the Bethlehem Pennsylvania Police family group conferencing project*, Pipersville, PA: Community Service Foundation.

McGarrell, E. F. (2001) 'Restorative justice conferences as an early response to young offenders', *OJJDP Juvenile Justice Bulletin*, August. Available at: http://www.ncjrs.org/html/ojjdp/jjbul2001_8_2/contents.html [accessed 1 February 2005].

McGuire, J. (2001) 'Methods to reduce the risk of re-offending: international perspectives,' invited address to the 'What Works' seminar, Helsinki, Finland, October.

Marshall, T. F. and Merry, S. (1990) *Crime and Accountability: victim/offender mediation in practice*, London: Home Office.

Maxwell, G. and Morris, A. (2002) 'Restorative justice and reconviction,' *Contemporary Justice Review*, 5(2): 133–46.

Niemeyer, M. and Shichor, D. (1996) 'A preliminary study of a large victim/offender reconciliation program,' *Federal Probation*, 60(3): 30–4.

Nuffield, J. (1997) *Evaluation of the Adult Victim–Offender Mediation Program Saskatoon Community Mediation Services*, Regina: Saskatchewan Justice.

Nugent, W. R. and Paddock, J. B. (1995) 'The effect of victim–offender mediation on severity of re-offense,' *Mediation Quarterly*, 12(4): 353–67.

Onyskiw, M. F. N. (1984) 'An evaluation of the impact of community service on recidivism of adult first offenders,' MA thesis, University of Toronto.

Palmer, T. (1983) 'The effectiveness issue today: an overview,' *Federal Probation*, 46: 3–10.

Pearson, F. S. (1988) 'Evaluation of New Jersey's intensive supervision program,' *Crime and Delinquency*, 34(4): 437–88.

Redondo, S., Garrido, V. and Sánchez-Meca, J. (1999) 'The influence of treatment programs on the recidivism of juvenile and adult offenders: a European meta-analytic review,' *Psychology, Crime, and Law*, 5: 251–78.

Roy, S. (1993) 'Two types of juvenile restitution programs in two Midwestern counties: a comparative study,' *Federal Probation*, 57(4): 48–53.

Rugge, T., Bonta, J. and Wallace-Capretta, S. (2005) *Evaluation of the Collaborative Justice Project: a restorative justice program for serious crime*, User Report (2005-01), Ottawa: Public Safety and Emergency Preparedness Canada.

Schneider, A. L. (1986) 'Restitution and recidivism rates of juvenile offenders: results from four experimental studies,' *Criminology*, 24(3): 533–52.

Sherman, L. W., Strang, H. and Woods, D. J. (2000) *Recidivism Patterns in the Canberra Reintegrative Shaming Experiments (RISE)*, Canberra: Centre for Restorative Justice, Research School of Social Sciences, Australian National University. Available at: http://www.aic.gov.au/rjustice/rise/recidivism/ [accessed 1 February 2005].

Shichor, D. and Binder, A. (1982) 'Community restitution for juveniles: an approach and preliminary evaluation,' *Community Justice Review*, 7: 46–50.

Smith, P., Goggin, C. and Gendreau, P. (2002) *The Effects of Prison Sentences and Intermediate Sanctions on Recidivism: general effects and individual differences*, User Report 2002-01, Ottawa: Solicitor General Canada.

Umbreit, M. S. and Coates, R. C. (1992) *Victim–Offender Mediation: an analysis of programs in 4 states of the US*, Minneapolis, MN: Minnesota Citizens Council on Crime and Justice.

United Nations. (2002) *Resolutions and Decisions Adopted by the Economic and Social Council at its Substantive Session of 2002*, online. Available at: http://www.un.org/esa/coordination/ecosoc/doc2002.htm [accessed 16 February 2005].

von Hirsch, A. (1976) *Doing Justice: the choice of punishments*, New York: Hill and Wang.

von Hirsch, A., Bottoms, A. E., Burney, E. and Wikström, P.-O. (1999) *Criminal Deterrence and Sentence Severity: an analysis of recent research*, Oxford: Hart Publishing.

Walker, J. D. (2002) 'Conferencing – a new approach for juvenile justice in Honolulu,' *Federal Probation*, 66(1): 38–43.

Walmsley, R. (2002) 'World prison population list (third edition),' *Findings*, 166, London: Home Office.

Wax, M. L. (1977) 'The effects of symbolic restitution and presence of victim on delinquent shoplifters,' PhD thesis, Washington State University.

Wiebush, R. G. (1985) *Recidivism in the Juvenile Diversion Project of the Young Volunteers in Action Program*, Columbus, OH: US Department of Justice.

— (1993) 'Juvenile intensive supervision: the impact on felony offenders diverted from institutional placement,' *Crime and Delinquency*, 39(1): 68–89.

Wilson, R. J. and Picheca, J. E. (2005) 'Circles of support and accountability – engaging the community in sexual offender management,' in B. Schwartz (ed.) *The Sex Offender*, Vol. 5, New York: Civic Research Institute.

Zehr, H. (2004) 'Commentary: restorative justice: beyond victim–offender mediation,' *Conflict Resolution Quarterly*, 22(1–2): 305–15.

6

Peacemaking circles

Reflections on principal features and primary outcomes

Barry Stuart and Kay Pranis

We thank you for this opportunity to share our thoughts about peacemaking circles. We wish to honor the presence of you, the reader, and to invite you to engage with these thoughts through your own experience and wisdom. Please take what is useful and set gently aside what is not.

Introduction

Several features of peacemaking circles date back to a time in all cultures when everyone in the community was important, when survival depended upon resolving differences in ways that reinforced relationships and strengthened connections to the larger community. Unlike Western cultures, many indigenous cultures continue to rely on many aspects of these practices. Principles and practices of indigenous approaches to conflict in many locations, especially in Yukon, Papua New Guinea, Hawaii, and New Zealand, inspired and profoundly shaped the early development of peacemaking circles. While not designed to replicate the culturally steeped rituals of First Nation circles, peacemaking circles are profoundly indebted to First Nation teachings.

Peacemaking circles also draw heavily on contemporary concepts of dialogue and consensus building. Peacemaking circles, by melding the best of ancient and contemporary concepts, aspire to approach conflict in ways that achieve the same outcomes as the ancient sacred space of circles: respect for every voice, improved relationships, and stronger connections to the larger community.

Peacemaking circles have evolved significantly from the earlier version of sentencing circles that began in 1982 in Yukon. The change in name was prompted by two realizations. First, the sentence was not the central focus, nor the most important outcome of a circle. Second, the circle was adapted to use in many other conflicts within the justice system and for public and private matters in many different settings. The use of circles for many different purposes in communities in Manitoba, Saskatchewan, Yukon, and Minnesota and the work of ROCA in Boston have especially influenced its evolution. The longstanding use of circles to explore personal values and build relationships, especially within the feminist movement, is another stream shaping circles.

For some the struggle to find an appropriate name continues. Some note that circles do not make peace but rather give participants opportunities to find a way to peacefully interact, and therefore might best be called *peacegiving* circles. Circles have been adapted for many different settings, for resolving conflict, for developing new visions or new plans. Given the inordinately diverse uses of circles, perhaps any name other than merely 'circles' may be misleading. The name 'peacemaking circles' aspires to distinguish the process we describe here and in our book from other processes. We recognize that the name does not matter: the values, principles, and practices used throughout the process do matter.

This circle process has evolved a long way and continues to evolve. It belongs to no one. It belongs to everyone. Our description of peacemaking circles here, as in all of our writings and trainings, incorporates the teachings and experiences of many different people. We offer what we have learned to enhance the use of circles by people all over the world. We do so without claiming any one way is the only way to do circles. We thank our many teachers as we continue to learn more about the power of circle dialogues.

What is a circle?

Sharing stories is an essential source of the power of circles. What better way to begin describing peacemaking circles than to share a story about circle?

Background

Hector, fifteen, is accused of riding his bike into the back of Jamie, sixteen, and hitting Jamie several times in the face as Jamie struggled to get up. The incident took place after school in the school parking lot. Jamie suffered a broken ankle and bruises to his face. Hector is charged with assault causing bodily harm. Both boys attend the same school.

Hector has a criminal record for assault and for the possession of drugs. He has an older brother, nineteen (serving time in jail for trafficking in drugs), and two younger brothers, thirteen and eleven. His mother Maria is a single parent who works at the school as a teacher's assistant.

Jamie has two older brothers; one is serving time for assault and the other dropped out of school two years ago in grade 9 at sixteen. Their parents are struggling to run a small office-cleaning business.

Hector's mother has asked the community justice committee for help. The community justice committee has not been working in the school but has dealt with other young people charged with offences. They want to become more involved in the school and have offered to help. The committee asked two volunteers to serve as keepers.

Stage One: suitability. One keeper met with Hector and his mother. Hector knows he will likely go to jail this time and on the advice of his lawyer has pled not guilty. His lawyer believes Hector, younger and much smaller than Jamie, can claim Jamie tried to grab Hector off his bike since Jamie had been threatening Hector over the previous several days. His mother fears her son may join a gang and drop out of school. She feels he does not realize the serious nature of the trouble he faces.

The other keeper met with Jamie and his father, Frank. They were not interested in anything but going to court. His father believes Jamie's only hope for a future is ruined as he will not be able to play football due to his broken ankle.

The keepers met with the school principal and a teacher who has both boys in her class. The principal thinks the case must remain in the court to serve as an example of the harsh consequences befalling violations of the school policy of zero tolerance of violence.

The prosecutor believes Hector had his chance six months ago when he went to jail for only a week for fighting in the park as part of a large brawl with kids from another school. The prosecutor has no doubt this time Hector will go to jail for at least a year.

The justice committee holds a circle every week to assess whether any case is appropriate for the circle process. They decide to take one more step despite the only interest in the committee's involvement coming from Hector's mother and teacher. The committee proposes a circle for Hector and all of his family and a separate circle for Jamie and all of his family. They invite the principal and the teacher to the circles. The principal does not attend but the teacher attends both circles.

Stage Two: preparation. At both closed circles many new facts come out. Jamie had been asked to enforce a drug debt Hector owed to a gang Jamie was interested in joining. Jamie and his friends on several occasions had hurled racial taunts at Hector and his girlfriend. At school that day Jamie had roughed up Hector's girlfriend. Jamie was failing in school and was on the verge of being kicked out for numerous absences. His parents were in the middle of a divorce. He had already been kicked out of his mother's house and was in trouble with his dad for disobeying almost every rule set down to live with his dad. The teacher thought with extra tutoring Jamie could pass his school year. She remarked that in fifteen years of teaching she had never found any student with as much raw artistic talent as Jamie. He had a great future if he turned his energy to art. She talked about a wonderful art teacher at the school who was interested in helping Jamie.

Hector admitted in his closed circle that he had ridden his bike into Jamie. He was very angry after finding out about Jamie pushing his girlfriend to the ground. He also knew that Jamie was looking for him 'to lay on a beating.' As Jamie was much bigger he knew he would have to arm himself with a weapon to defend himself. He was riding to

a friend's to get a knife or gun when he saw Jamie walking in front of him. He saw a chance to knock him down and get the jump on him.

Hector was failing in school. He was bright but turned off. On intelligence tests his results clearly indicated he could excel at university. Hector had a significant addiction to drugs. His girlfriend had been trying for a year to get him off drugs.

One keeper visited Hector's older brother Rabbie in jail and explained what the community justice committee wanted to do. Rabbie sent Hector a letter and participated in part of the circle by speakerphone. He was very supportive of the circle process. With the full support of his family and his girlfriend, Hector decided to plead guilty and become involved in the community circle process. His lawyer disagreed, but when unable to convince Hector to change his mind, asked for time to cut a deal on sentencing with the prosecutor if Hector pled guilty.

The keepers met with the prosecutor and asked the prosecutor to support their request for the judge to participate in a circle sentencing process. The prosecutor was not interested and would oppose any application in court for a community process. He would not make any deals with Hector's lawyer. The community justice committee decided to proceed with the circle process. If the justice officials did not participate in the community process they would take the outcome of the circle process to the court

A preparation circle was held separately for Jamie and his family and for Hector and his family. Before each preparation circle, the keepers, by talking with both families as well as the teacher, began to identify other people who might play an instrumental role in the process. The keepers met with everyone who had participated in the first circle and with others identified as possible important contributors to explain the process.

In the separate preparation circles the issues for the larger circle were identified and several plans were formulated for immediate action. Both keepers met first with counsel and then with the court to once again invite their participation. The judge declined to participate due to the prosecutor's opposition but welcomed hearing a full report from the committee.

Stage Three: full circle gathering. The larger circle involved twenty-four people. In addition to the participants in the preparation circles the circle included: the art teacher from the school, friends of the different families, four volunteers from the justice committee, the local probation officer, a police officer dealing with youth programs, a businessman interested in helping youth in the community, a youth substance abuse councilor, Hector's uncle, Jamie's grandparents, and an aunt. The circle met for three hours followed by an informal sharing of refreshments. The circle generated a difficult and comprehensive dialogue around many crucial issues. Most of the time was spent on drug issues, racism, and the challenges Hector and Jamie and their families face every day. No consensus was reached on a sentence for Hector or in what was to be done to address the victim's needs. Many good ideas were contributed, and support for both Jamie and Hector came from all participants in the circle. Everyone agreed to meet again in circle in three weeks.

Before the next circle the keepers met with people who were important to building a consensus plan. The keepers also helped Hector act on some of the ideas raised in the circle.

At the next circle any information missing at the last circle was shared and the developments since the last circle were revealed by Hector and others. Within two hours a consensus was reached on the *recommendation* the circle would make in court. Hector and his family, Jamie and his family, as well as the support group formed for both Jamie and Hector, agreed no matter what the court decided they would carry out the commitments made to each other in the circle. The key people all agreed to attend court.

In court the community process and outcomes for both Hector and Jamie were explained. The judge asked many questions. He spoke highly of all the work achieved and of the agreements the parties reached but, unlike the consensus of the circle, he felt a term of incarceration was unavoidable. However, in view of what the community had achieved and the work that Hector had done to follow the community plan, the judge significantly reduced the term of incarceration and included in the sentence many of the circle plans. Hector and his family were disappointed but decided not to appeal.

Stage Four: follow-up. At the follow-up circle two months later, when Hector was out of the correctional facility, more support emerged for Hector due to his acceptance of what the court had imposed and his active commitment to the original plan of the circle. His support group kept in regular contact while he was incarcerated. Over the next year the support groups provided the support promised to both Hector and Jamie. At a final follow-up circle a year after Hector was released from the correctional facility, all the parties shared their experiences in a circle and gathered for a meal to celebrate what they had achieved. Both boys were back in school. Hector with the help of a tutor and a job in a local store progressed past two relapses with drugs and was turning to work with other kids abusing drugs. Jamie did not play football. He worked in an advertising company part-time, learning the trade and fully engaged in his art. He had a difficult time breaking free of the gang and finally decided to move in with an aunt living in another town. With the references and direct intervention of his employer, he snagged a similar work experience with another advertising company in his aunt's town.

124

Several salient features of a peacemaking circle are demonstrated by this example of a circle process:

1 *A process, not an event* The full power of a circle derives from engaging all stages of a circle process: assessing suitability, preparation, a full circle gathering, and follow-up circles.
2 *Different kinds of circles* In each stage of the process different kinds of circles are used. Healing, talking, problem solving, and small private confidential circles, as well as large public circles, can be used throughout the peacemaking circles process.
3 *Flexible process* The only features of the circle process that remain unchanged are the core values and principles, and the fundamental structural elements of circles. The circle process affords enormous scope for adapting the process to fit the particular circumstances of each case. As the circle process digs deeper into underlying causes of conflict, the innate flexibility of a circle process enables new issues to be addressed and all new interests to be included.
4 *Unique place of keepers* The most important mediator in a circle is the talking piece. Participants are as important as keepers in facilitating a circle. Keepers' contributions are vital, but are primarily made not in circles but in preparing all participants for the circle. Keepers are gardeners. They prepare and nurture the ground for participants to flower within the circle. They do so by sharing responsibility with all participants for creating and maintaining a safe space for a constructive dialogue about very difficult issues.

Uses of peacemaking circles

Peacemaking circles emerged in the criminal justice system in Canada and the US as an innovative way to involve all interested parties in key decisions regarding sentencing in criminal cases. In addition to the circle to determine an appropriate sentence the process includes healing circles for victims and circles of understanding with offenders to explore underlying causes of the criminal behavior and to prepare offenders for participation in sentencing circles.

Circles have been used for a wide range of offenses. Some communities use circles for lower-level offenses, while several communities use circles to deal with serious crimes. Peacemaking circles are used throughout all stages of the justice system. Some juvenile facilities use circles to resolve conflict in living units. Both adult and juvenile facilities use circles with family members to support the process of reintegration into the community. Circles of support for high-risk sex offenders returning to the community provide weekly check-in and daily contact with community volunteers to manage a safe re-entry into the community. A similar approach with chronic offenders on probation uses peacemaking circles to break cycles of destructive behavior.

Some neighborhoods use circles to support victims regardless of the status of the case in the criminal justice system. Circles provide a way to respond to victims in cases where offenders are not prosecuted.

Educators use circles to resolve and prevent conflict. Regular check-in circles in a classroom allow students to raise concerns at an early stage before they escalate into conflict. Circles are an effective tool for creating positive classroom climate and for engaging all students in dialog on any topic. In schools circles can be used to:

- uncover problems or concerns of students that might interfere with learning at an early stage;
- resolve conflicts by addressing the underlying causes;
- build relationships in the classroom;

125

- foster respect for differences and build cross-cultural communication;
- create spaces for students to share responsibility for their interactions with others;
- identify and act on shared personal values;
- promote dialogues that empower everyone to participate equally;
- develop shared responsibility to reach and implement agreements;
- build group problem-solving capacity;
- assess student level of understanding and engagement with a topic;
- enhance speaking and listening skills;
- provide a readily accessible process for students to use among friends, within their families and in the community to peacefully manage differences.

Staff in several prisons in Minnesota use peacemaking circles to resolve staff conflict and to heal emotionally toxic work environments. Staff at a juvenile correctional facility used circles to heal from the bitter affects of a state workers' strike. Other organizations use circles for team building, planning or dialog about difficult issues. The Minneapolis YWCA holds a regular circle about racism to provide an opportunity for staff to share experiences and views on the issue.

The Methodist Church uses circles to work through congregational conflict. Community organizations have used circles for dialog among gangs, between police and communities of color, between immigrant communities and local government, and between adults and youth.

Social workers use circles in child welfare cases and for transition of dependents of the state reaching the age of eighteen and moving toward independent living. Many people have used circles in their families to heal old wounds and to talk about topics that have been avoided for years because they are so uncomfortable.

Like strawberry runners in a garden, peacemaking circles have spread organically to the many places that humans need a better way to be in dialog and to express feelings, in order to be in a healthier relationship with one another and to work through the hurts that are inevitable in human interactions.

This discussion describes the development and use of circles in several communities in Canada and the US – the primary experience of the authors. That work has largely been nurtured by the indigenous justice movement and the restorative justice movement. Around the globe there are similar processes operating in small communities as they have for hundreds of years. They are often a part of the fabric of the community and would not be identified as a separate philosophy or activity. In those places circle-like processes are simply the way that people are in community with one another.

Unique qualities of circles

Peacemaking circles share many characteristics with other restorative practices and they have some qualities that are unique to the circle process. Like other restorative practices, they provide for active involvement of the people affected by a crime in resolving the incident; they focus on healing and repair of harm; they respect the dignity and worth of every person.

There are also several characteristics of the peacemaking circle process that are unique to circles:

- collective creation of safe, respectful space for dialog;
- relationship building before discussion of the core issue;
- an invitation to express oneself emotionally and spiritually as well as mentally and physically;
- use of the talking piece to create safety and freedom;
- intentional use of ceremony to create a protected space for truth telling;

■ usefulness as prevention as well as intervention;

■ capacity for dealing with muddy, confusing situations that may not have a clear victim and offender;

■ attention to underlying causes;

■ facilitator as a member of the group.

Peacemaking circles use a *self-governing process* in which all participants are a part of creating the behavioral expectations for the group interaction. Participants create the guidelines for their process by consensus. Collective creation of the guidelines shares the responsibility for protecting the quality of the collective space with all participants.

Peacemaking circles deliberately delay the dialog about the contentious issues until the group has done some work on *relationship building*. An introduction round with a question inviting people to share something about themselves, the creation of circle values and guidelines, and a story-telling round on a topic tangentially related to the key issue precede the discussion of the difficult issues that are the focus of the circle. These parts of the circle generate a deeper awareness within the circle of how their human journeys have generated similar experiences, expectations, fears, dreams, and hopes. These opening parts of the circle also present participants to one another in unexpected ways, gently challenging assumptions they may have made about one another. Creating guidelines together provides an opportunity for the group to experience finding common ground in spite of serious differences. A circle intentionally does *not* 'get right to the issues.' Taking time to create a sense of shared space and connection in the group increases the level of emotional safety which allows deeper truth telling. It also promotes awareness of the humanity of all participants.

One of the fundamental beliefs of the peacemaking circle process is that there are *four dimensions of human experience – the mental, physical, emotional, and spiritual*. All of these dimensions affect how humans behave and all of those dimensions need to be acknowledged to understand differences or harm and to promote healing. The circle invites participants to be present physically, emotionally, mentally, and spiritually. Each participant may speak his truth in each of those dimensions but may not assume that is the truth for anyone else. The circle can hold the complexity of the physical, emotional, mental, and spiritual aspects of each participant's reality.

Perhaps the most obvious characteristic of peacemaking circles is the use of a talking piece to regulate the dialog. The talking piece is an object with meaning to the group that is circulated around the group. Only the person holding the talking piece may speak. That person has the undivided attention of everyone else in the circle and can speak without interruption. The use of the talking piece allows for full expression of emotions, deeper listening, thoughtful reflection, and an unrushed pace. Additionally, the talking piece creates space for people who find it difficult to speak in a group but it never requires the holder to speak. The profound listening and respectful speaking promoted by the use of the talking piece *create safety for speaking difficult truth*.

Peacemaking circles use some form of *ceremony to mark the opening and closing of the special space of circle*. Within the space of the circle participants are asked to be more mindful of the core values that define the best in them and to act according to those values. For most people that requires dropping masks and protections – it feels vulnerable. It becomes safe to do so because everyone else in the circle is making the same commitment. Because that level of safety is not present in most collective spaces, it is important to clearly define when that safe space begins and when it ends. The opening ceremony helps participants to relax, to release anxieties not related to the circle, to focus on their inner state, to be mindful of interconnectedness and to open to positive possibilities. Closing ceremonies honor the contributions of the group and remind participants once again of their connectedness to one another and the larger universe. Opening and closing ceremonies are varied and are designed to fit the particular group. Some are simple, some elaborate. Inspirational readings, deep breathing, music, body movement, and silence are ways to open or close a circle.

The peacemaking circle work began in the justice system as an intervention to respond to harm after the harm happened. As that work spread to other settings, practitioners recognized the potential of the process for *prevention of harm*. Circles are a proactive tool as well as a reactive tool. Regular check-in circles in a school classroom prevent both behavior problems and learning problems by building a positive classroom climate. Because circles build connections and reduce social distance, they *strengthen community and mutual caretaking*.

Circles are useful in situations where there is mutual harm or general harm but not clearly defined victims and offenders. For instance, in a fight sometimes there is responsibility on both sides, or in a classroom there may be a climate of picking on one child. In both of those cases circles allow the group to work through the feelings and experiences of all involved and to create healthier connections that address the harm and change the dynamics among the group.

Circles are intentional in probing for *underlying causes* of behavior problems. The circle does not confine itself to the presenting behavior or incident. In a circle participants discuss related issues that they believe are important to developing long-term solutions to the problem. Consequently, plans developed in the circle may involve changes and responsibilities for other participants, not just the offender.

The role of the facilitator in a circle is distinctly different than in the common restorative processes of Western countries.

The circle facilitator, often called a keeper, is a *participant* in the group. The indigenous roots of the process bring a different perspective to the problem of potential bias. Rather than solving the problem of bias with the concept of neutrality as clinical distance or separation, an indigenous perspective requires that the facilitator care equally about everyone in the process. As a caring member of the community the facilitator's participation is important to the process. Because the talking piece regulates who will speak next, the facilitator has less control over the process than in other restorative practices. The collective creation of guidelines also reduces the responsibility of the facilitator and shares that with everyone in the circle. The facilitator is responsible for monitoring the quality of the interaction and bringing any process problems to the attention of the group when they are not self-correcting. The facilitator is not solely or principally responsible for determining how process problems might be solved.

Nature of outcomes

Energy of conflict

Conflicts generate energy, often enormous energy. This energy can be destructive or constructive. The process used to deal with conflict enormously influences whether the energy within conflict will be destructive or constructive. Usually this energy is engaged in ways that are destructive and expensive. The destructive wrath of this energy, like an insidious cancer, can adversely impact lives well beyond the immediate parties and undermine the morale and capacity of an organization. Understanding the nature of outcomes circles produce begins by appreciating that circles treat conflict as an opportunity to constructively engage this energy in ways that foster respect for differences and that improve relationships and connections to communities.

Accordingly, circles may not be ideally suited for many conflicts. While circles can be used to settle specific conflicts, mediation, conferencing, and arbitration are usually better suited when the outcome sought is to settle a specific issue. For instance, if the conflict can be settled by compensating a victim for property vandalized by the offender, a conference is better. If the conflict can be settled by a landlord agreeing to make repairs to the premises, mediation is a better alternative. Circles are more appropriate for complex conflicts where the underlying causes of conflict must be addressed and where significant changes in relationships and innovative solutions to seemingly intractable problems are needed to realize and sustain changes.

Primary building blocks of circle outcomes

The outcomes circles produce derive primarily not from removing or ignoring differences but from generating understanding and respect for differences; not from settling conflicts but from engaging the conflict as an opportunity to probe emotionally charged feelings and have the difficult conversations essential to redressing causes of chronic conflict. This work in circles may not produce an agreement but can lay the foundation for building relationships that make it possible for those involved to eventually find ways to prevent and resolve destructive aspects of their conflicts. Our experience suggests this is often the most important outcome of circles. Many circles are a success if participants have an opportunity to share personal stories, to base their interactions on shared values, to learn to actively listen, to speak from the heart, and to respectfully engage others. These experiences foster new capacities for participants to appreciate their differences and to engage each other.

For example, the first child protection circle in one community failed to reach a consensus plan and the case had to be referred back to the court. Was this circle a failure? The dialogue within the circle generated a new understanding and respect for key state officials and galvanized community involvement in a local support group for families in trouble. These outcomes laid the foundation for a new partnership among different agencies at the community level and ultimately produced a better working relationship between the community and local public officials responsible for the care and protection of children.

In a sentencing circle the offender failed to fully participate and later failed to honor his commitment to the consensus-based sentence reached in the circle. The circle dialogue and subsequent experience with the offender and victim in this spousal abuse case produced a remarkable change in community awareness of spousal abuse and of what they could do to help families to prevent spousal abuse. This circle contributed to vastly improving services for victims and to forging the partnerships needed to begin what became a very successful treatment program for spouses who abuse their partners.

In many circles the most important outcome is not what consensus agreements may be reached, but rather what new understandings, new respect, and new relationships are formed.

Surprise outcomes

Circle outcomes are often totally unexpected. Participants are surprised by the creative and 'outside the box' solutions that circle dialogues can produce.

> Who would have thought we would come up with this very different solution ... none of us going in and certainly not me if asked could have said we'd leave the circle agreeing to anything and certainly not this ... many people moved a long way to get to this point.
>
> (Prosecutor, Yukon, after a circle sentencing)

129

These 'very different solutions' usually involve dramatic changes in perspective, changes that stem from deep listening and from speaking from the heart. It can take time for the head to catch up to the heart, time to adjust to new perspectives, to outcomes not anticipated. Follow-up circles provide the time to test the foundations of new perspectives, time to enable all participants to act on their promises to the circle. Promises when honored are instrumental in reinforcing significant changes in perspective. *Follow-up circles enable participants to relate how they have walked their promises to the circle.* These circles are not just an opportunity for accountability but as well for celebrating individual and group accomplishments. Tangible results demonstrate the power of collective action and intensify belief in and commitment to working together in circles.

Fine tuning

Fine tuning is a crucial element in sustaining both new relationships and outcomes. Fine tuning (and at times substantial re-configuring) enables a circle consensus to survive the unexpected and sometimes expected challenges all agreements inevitably encounter in the real world.

Shared ownership of outcomes

Participants retain a greater stake in making an agreement work when they have genuinely participated in building the agreement. The circle process engages not just the parties and keepers but everyone in shaping the outcome of the circle. Shared ownership fosters shared accountability not just to the agreement but to all other participants.

Implementation of outcomes less reliant upon state sanctions

Decisions made by others are rarely fully understood or endorsed. They primarily depend upon the threat of or use of state sanctions to be enforced. Outcomes in circles depend principally upon the new relationships, new levels of understanding and trust that call on all participants to be accountable by doing their part to implement the agreement. Participants mutually develop safety nets around circle outcomes. These safety nets include a wide range of interventions from further circles, to monitoring and reporting requirements, to state sanctions.

Outcomes encompass all interests

Circle dialogues dig into underlying causes and thereby reveal other conflicts, other issues that extend beyond the issue that initiated the circle. Consequently circle outcomes often include measures that extend beyond the initial conflict and involve more participants than the immediate parties. For example, in a circle dealing with a vicious assault by a student on another student, racial tensions and drug trafficking emerged as primary factors in provoking the assault. Further, the dynamics in the homes of both offender and victim left both vulnerable to crime. The focus of the circle shifted to search for ways to deal with these factors. The outcomes of this circle in addition to plans that encompassed a sentence for the offender and measures to assist the victim also included several measures to redress racial tensions and drug use among students and to explore what might be done to improve or offset the conditions in their homes that rendered both offender and victim vulnerable to crime and to dropping out of school.

More circles

Finally, the most important outcome of a circle is more circles. For instance, in the case of the assault between students, that circle spawned other circles to bring together people who could work with the families of the victim and offender and another circle to deal with racial issues.

In many cases there is neither a clear beginning nor a clear end to a circle process. The crime or specific conflict that generated a circle may soon be revealed in the circle as merely a salient event in a complex web of interactions that take place within a history of festering socio-economic conditions. The end of a circle is not a sentence or agreement. Circles demonstrate the power of active listening, of speaking from the heart, of acting on values, and of dialogue. Circles introduce all participants to a means of and the importance of creating a safe place for difficult conversations – conversations that are essential for individual and community well-being. How participants carry their experiences in circles into their homes, workplace, and community is the most important outcome of circles.

Evaluating circle outcomes

The most important evaluation of circles flows from the most important outcome of a circle process. Have participants continued to act on the values and use the communication skills demonstrated in the circle? Have they continued to use circles to build relationships and deal with differences in their personal lives and in their various communities? Too much attention is focused on whether the circle reached an agreement on the specific conflict or issue that prompted the call for a circle. In evaluating all processes the focus is too concentrated on the immediate result. The richness and value of any process lies in whether the process built sustainable relationships and outcomes and whether the process contributed to changes in the behavior of participants within all the communities (family, social, work, and political) they inhabit.

For example, regular talking circles for men whose lives were principally defined by crime and substance abuse were started by an offender on his own initiative long after he had completed all his commitments to

the circle. This marked a more important outcome of his circle than fully carrying out his circle sentence. A woman from the community who participated in a support group for a parent in a child protection circle became actively involved as a volunteer in several community health projects. Before the circle she had never been involved in any community activities.

> I saw [in circle] I could make a difference and saw we had to get involved eh ... because leaving it all up to the professionals wasn't going to cut it.

After a circle within a company, employees and managers began using circles for several different matters: personal disputes, planning a company baseball team, and developing company polices. Offenders, victims, and volunteers after their involvement in a circle have helped other victims and offenders as well as people not before the court.

> Some of us did not wait to be asked or wait for a circle to get involved ... we knew who was headed for trouble either as a victim or offender and often could wind up as either one ... so I and others just stepped up and got involved ... you know sometimes we just did our own circles ... I know we prevented lots of stuff from going to court, lots of stuff from ending up as a crime ... you know we all can see it coming ... can tell shit is going to happen ... so we got the shit into a circle before it happens.

In places where circles have become integrated into all aspects of a community's decision-making processes, there are widespread changes in the culture and energy of that community.

> It has been difficult, but immensely worthwhile ... we are in a very different place ... we removed a lot stuff that kept getting in our way ... we are cleaner, clearer about what we do and much better connected to each other and to our values.
> (Molly Baldwin, Director ROCA)

131

We consider the capacity of circles to introduce ways to conduct constructive dialogues an essential feature of the circle process. The capacity for participants in circles to continue the dialogues started in circles and to use circles to create the space for dialogues on other issues lies at the core of the circle's most important objectives – building relationships and communities. These are the features of a circle that need to be evaluated. Our experiences suggest that, when a community takes time to build, through circle training, the networks, shared values, and comprehensive understanding of all parts of the circle process, the ability of circles to realize these objectives is immeasurably enhanced.

Dealing with systemic issues

One of the greatest challenges facing the restorative justice movement is making the connection between criminal justice issues and social justice issues. The focus on individual responsibility carries the risk of ignoring social responsibility for conditions that may contribute to crime. Our vision of restorative justice is a social justice vision requiring both individual and community responsibility and requiring attention to the harms that caused a crime as well as those resulting from a crime.

Circles are a powerful tool for assuring that the social justice issues are acknowledged and potentially addressed as well as the individual issues. Circles are organic in their approach. They do not try to confine the discussion or isolate a particular event from related experiences. The circle dialog is open to anything the participants feel is relevant to discuss in order to repair the harm and change conditions so it won't happen again. This approach leads to a holistic look at the situation and allows acknowledgement of forces that affect individual behavior that are not of their making. In a suburban community a circle for a

group of juveniles who vandalized an empty home led to a discussion about the lack of places for young people to gather.

Criminal justice circles are also open to anyone who cares enough to be involved. Since everyone has voice in the discussion and in making decisions, it means that no point of view can be systematically excluded. The wide variety of people involved in a circle increases the likelihood that someone in the group will recognize and speak to larger social justice issues related to the case. In a reintegration circle for a black juvenile who robbed someone at gunpoint, his adult brother talked about how difficult it is to grow up as a young black man.

The story-telling process of circles reveals the patterns of community life, making it possible to see beyond the individual case to larger contributing forces. In a circle about domestic violence many women told of their experience as victims of domestic violence. As participants listened to the many women who shared that experience, they realized that the issue was not just a problem for that family, but for the whole community. They began to ask what was wrong at a community level.

One of the most important ways that circles contribute to a vision of social justice is the experience of equality within a circle. An African-American woman who does a lot of work in circles states, 'The only place I feel truly equal in this culture is in circle.' The circle gently challenges the patterns of inequality by giving everyone voice and by requiring that decisions be made by consensus. The circle is a place where people practice genuine equality, gradually learning to take that experience to other settings. In a circle the judge is no more important than anyone else. In a circle in a Minnesota community, members firmly reminded the judge that he cannot make decisions without them. In court when a judge added a condition to the sentence decided by the circle, a community member spoke up and reminded him that the circle had not agreed to the extra provision.

The judge acknowledged that truth and withdrew his addition to the sentence. The equality of the circle empowered the community member to speak up in court and brought that equality to the courtroom.

For lay community members the practical hands-on experience of trying to help someone make changes increases awareness of the barriers faced by many people caught up in the criminal justice system. Community members then begin looking for ways to remove or reduce those barriers. In one case the offender in circle had fines in multiple counties because of driving offenses. As the circle worked with this person, they realized that it was impossible to pay those fines and support a family on a minimum wage. The offender was making progress on significant changes in his life, but the threat of jail for failure to pay the fines was undermining the progress. The group began to question the judge about the policy of imposing fines. In circles policy questions come alive as people struggle with the reality of the lives of those affected by a particular policy.

Conclusion

Like other restorative processes, circles reduce the social distance that allows indifference to the pain and struggles of others. Empathy is an ally of social justice. Circles nurture the capacity for empathy in individuals and communities by sharing stories in an atmosphere of respect. In addition, circles provide a forum for concerned community members to begin thinking about how to change the conditions that are revealed by the stories and experiences in circle. The circle creates awareness and empowers action based on that awareness. The sense of collective capacity to make a difference is a very important element of social justice action. Circles build a sense of capacity by engaging more resources and perspectives and by demonstrating that no one is alone in their desire to make things better. Knowing that others will share the work helps people offer their own gifts with confidence that the sum of all the gifts will make a difference.

7

The limits of restorative justice

Kathleen Daly[1]

Restorative justice (RJ) is a set of ideals about justice that assumes a generous, empathetic, supportive, and rational human spirit. It assumes that victims can be generous to those who have harmed them, that offenders can be apologetic and contrite for their behavior, that their respective 'communities of care' can take an active role of support and assistance, and that a facilitator can guide rational discussion and encourage consensual decision-making between parties with antagonistic interests. Any one of these elements may be missing and thus potentially weaken an RJ process. The ideals of RJ can also be in tension. For example, it may not be possible to have equity or proportionality across RJ outcomes, when outcomes are supposed to be fashioned from the particular sensibilities of those in an RJ encounter.

Achieving justice – whether RJ or any other form – is a fraught and incomplete enterprise. This is because justice cannot be achieved, although it is important to reach for it. Rather, drawing from Derrida, justice is an 'experience of the impossible' (Pavlich 1996: 37), 'an ideal, an aspiration, which is supremely important and worth striving for constantly and tirelessly' (Hudson 2003: 192).

This chapter addresses a selected set of limits of RJ, those concerning its scope and its practices. My discussion is selective and limited. I do not consider the discursive limits of liberal legality as these are viewed through a postmodern lens (Arrigo 2004), nor do I consider related problems when nation states or communities cannot imagine particular offences or understand 'ultra-Others' (see Hudson 2003: 212–13). My focus instead is on the limits of current RJ practices, when applied to youth justice cases in common law jurisdictions. There are other contexts where RJ can be applied, including adult criminal cases; non-criminal contexts (school disputes and conflicts, workplace disputes and conflicts, and child welfare); and responding to broader political conflict or as a form of transitional justice practice, among other potential sites (see Braithwaite 2002). I focus on RJ in youth justice cases because it currently has a large body of empirical evidence. However, as RJ is increasingly being applied in adult cases and in different contexts (pre- or post-sentence advice, for example, as is now the case in England and New Zealand), we might expect to see different kinds of limits emerging.

The scope of RJ

Limit (1): there is no agreed-upon definition of RJ

There is robust discussion on what RJ is or should be, and there is no consensus on what practices should be included within its reach. One axis of disagreement is whether RJ should be viewed as a process or an outcome (Crawford and Newburn 2003). A second is what kinds of practices are authentic forms of RJ, what kinds are not, and what is in between (McCold and Wachtel 2002; *Contemporary Justice Review* 2004). A third is whether RJ should be viewed principally as a set of justice values, rather than a process or set of practices (compare, e.g. Braithwaite 2003 and Johnstone 2002, with von Hirsch *et al.* 2003), or whether it should include both (Roche 2003). Finally, there is debate on how RJ can or should articulate with established criminal justice (CJ).

A lack of agreement on definition means that RJ has not one but many identities and referents; and this can create theoretical, empirical, and policy confusion. Commentators, both advocates and critics, are often not talking about or imagining the same thing. Although the lack of a common understanding of RJ creates confusion, especially for those new to RJ, it reflects a diversity of interests and ideologies that people bring to the table when ideas of justice are discussed. A similar problem occurred with the rise of informal justice in the late 1970s. Informal justice could not be defined except by what it was not, i.e. it was not established forms of criminal justice (Abel 1982). An inability to define RJ, or justice more generally, is not fatal. Indeed, it is a logical and defensible position: there can be no 'fixed definition of justice' because justice has 'no unchanging nature' and 'it is beyond definition' (Hudson 2003: 201, characterizing the ideas of Lyotard and Derrida).

Gerry Johnstone (2004) suggests that the RJ advocates have too narrowly focused their efforts on promoting RJ by claiming its positive effects in reducing re-offending and increasing victim satisfaction. Instead of taking this instrumental and technical tack, Johnstone argues that we should see RJ as a set of ideas that challenge established CJ in fundamental ways. There is much to commend in having this more expansive vision of RJ as a long-term political project for changing the ways we think about 'crime,' 'being a victim,' 'responding to offenders,' among other categories nominated by Johnstone. However, I restrict my use of the term to a set of core elements in RJ practices. I do so not to limit the potential applicability of RJ to other domains or as a political project for social change but rather to conceptualize justice practices in concrete terms, not as aspirations or values. As RJ takes shape and evolves, it is important that we have images of the social interactions being proposed. I identify these core elements of RJ:

- It deals with the penalty (or post-penalty) not fact-finding phase of the criminal process.
- It normally involves a face-to-face meeting with an admitted offender and victim and their supporters, although it may also take indirect forms.
- It envisions a more active role for victim participation in justice decisions.
- It is an informal process that draws on the knowledge and active participation of lay persons (typically those most affected by an offence), but there are rules circumscribing the behavior of meeting members and limits on what they can decide in setting a penalty.
- It aims to hold offenders accountable for their behavior, while at the same time not stigmatizing them, and in this way it is hoped that there will be a reduction in future offending.
- It aims to assist victims in recovering from crime.

As we shall see, some (or all) of these elements may not be realized in RJ practices. For example, an RJ process aims to assist victims in recovering from crime, but this may be possible for some victims more than others. And although it is hoped that an RJ process will shift admitted offenders toward a law-abiding future, this too may occur for some, but not others. It should be emphasized that victims are not forced to meet an admitted offender in an RJ process. There can be other ways in which victims may engage an RJ process, including through the use of victim representatives or material brought into the meeting itself. In fact, some have proposed that victims have access to RJ processes when a suspect has not been caught for (or admitted to) an offence.

Limit (2): RJ deals with the penalty not fact-finding phase of the criminal process

There is some debate over whether RJ processes could be used in fact-finding, but virtually all the examples cited are of dispute resolution mechanisms in pre-modern societies, which rely on particular sets of 'meso-social structures' that are tied to kinship, geography, and political power (see discussion below by Bottoms 2003; see also Johnstone 2002). When we consider the typical forms of RJ practices, such as family group conferences (in New Zealand), family or community conferences (in Australia), police restorative cautioning schemes (in selected jurisdictions in England and North America), circles and sentencing circles (North America), or enhanced forms of victim offender mediation (North America and some European countries), we see that all are concerned with what a justice practice should be *after* a person has admitted committing an offence. RJ does not address whether a 'crime' occurred or not, or whether a suspect is 'guilty' of a crime or not. Rather, it focuses on 'what shall we do?' after a person admits that s/he has committed an offence.

Ultimately, as I shall argue, we should view this limit as a strength of RJ. The reason is that it bypasses the many disabling features of the adversarial process, both for those accused of crime and for victim complainants. Without a fact-finding or investigating mechanism, however, RJ cannot replace established CJ. To do so, it must have a method of adjudication, and currently it does not. However, RJ can make inroads into methods of penalty setting (in the context of court diversion or pre-sentence advice to judicial officers), and it may be effective in providing assurances of safety to individual victims and communities when offenders complete their sentences (in the context of post-sentence uses of RJ), but all of these activities occur only after a person has admitted committing an offence.

Several commentators point out that RJ differs from established CJ in that it is participatory and consensually based, not adversarial. However, this muddles things greatly. The reason that established CJ is adversarial is that its adjudication process rests on a fundamental right of those accused to say they did not commit an offence[2] and to defend themselves against the state's allegations of wrong-doing. There may well be better methods of adjudicating crime, and a troubling feature of established CJ is how long it takes for cases to be adjudicated and disposed; but surely, no one would wish to dispense with the right of citizens to defend themselves against the state's power to prosecute and punish alleged crime.

The focus of RJ on the penalty (or post-penalty) phase can be viewed as a strength. It enables us to be more imaginative in conceptualizing what is the 'right response' to offending behavior, and it opens up potential lines of communication and understanding between offenders, victims, and those close to them, when this is desirable (and it may not always be desirable). Communication and interaction are especially important elements because many victims want answers to questions: for example, about why *their* car was stolen, and not another person's car. They may be concerned about their security and seek reassurances from an offender not to victimize them again (although this may not stop an offender from victimizing others). There can be positive sources of connection between the supporters of offenders (say, a mother or father) and victims or their supporters. All of this is possible because RJ processes seek a conversational and dialogic approach to responding to crime. Decisions are not made by a distant magistrate or judge and an overworked duty solicitor and prosecutor with many files to process. In established CJ processes, research shows that in the courtroom, a defendant is typically mute and a victim is not present. State actors do all the work of handling and processing crime. The actual parties to a crime (the persons charged and victim-complainants) are bystanders or absent.

Some victim advocates who are critical of RJ think that it is 'outside' or not part of established CJ. Although a common perception, it is inaccurate. In all jurisdictions where RJ has been legislated in response to crime, it is very much 'inside' the established CJ process, as the police or courts make a decision about how to handle a case.

RJ ideals and practices

There is a gap between the ideals or aspirations for RJ and actual practices. This gap should not surprise us because the ideals for RJ are set very high, and perhaps too high. Advocates have made astonishing claims for what RJ can achieve and what it can do for victims, offenders, their family members, and communities. Thus, a gap arises, in part from inflated expectations for what RJ can achieve. There are deeper reasons for the gap, however.

First, as Bottoms (2003: 109) argues, the 'social mechanisms of RJ' rest on an assumption that 'adequate meso-social

structures exist to support RJ-type approaches.' By 'meso-social structures,' Bottoms refers to ordered sets of relationships that are part of pre-modern societies (for example, residence, kinship, or lineage). These relationships embed elements of 'intra-societal power' and coercion, which make dispute settlement possible (see also Merry 1982). A second feature of relationships in pre-modern societies is that disputants are 'part of the same moral/social community.' They live in close proximity to one another or are related to one another, and typically wish to continue living in the community. These meso-social structures and 'thick' social ties, which are commonly associated with pre-modern (or *gemeinschaft*) societies,[3] are not present in modern urban contemporary societies. Thus, as Bottoms (2003: 110) suggests, 'a "blanket" delivery of RJ . . . is always likely to achieve modest or patchy results in contemporary societies.'

Second, as I suggest elsewhere (Daly 2003: 200), gaps emerge because those participating in an RJ process may not know what is supposed to happen, how they are supposed to act, nor what an optimal result could be. Participants may have an idea of what 'their day in court' might be like, but they have little idea of what 'their day in an RJ conference' would be like. Moreover, effective participation requires a degree of moral maturity and empathetic concern that many people, and especially young people, may not possess. Finally, we know from the history of established CJ that organizational routines, administrative efficiency, and professional interests often trump justice ideals (Daly 2003: 232). RJ is no exception. It takes time and great effort to create the appropriate contexts for RJ processes to work effectively, including a facilitator's contacting and preparing participants, identifying who should be present, coordinating the right time for everyone, running the meeting, and following up after it is over.

Some commentators argue that it is more appropriate to compare 'what restorative justice has achieved and may still achieve with what conventional justice systems have to offer' (Morris 2002: 601). This is a valid and important point. We know that substantial gaps exist between the ideals and practices of established CJ. Thus, for example, it would be relevant to compare the effects of the court's sentencing practices on victims, offenders, and others with their participation in penalty discussions in RJ meetings. Although court-conference comparative research can be illuminating and helpful, there is also a value to observing and understanding what happens in an RJ process itself, including the variable degree to which the aims of RJ are achieved. When we do that, several limits of RJ are apparent. It is important to bear in mind that these limits are not necessarily peculiar to RJ; they may have their analogy in established CJ as well. I draw from my research on youth justice conference in South Australia (the South Australia Juvenile Justice [SAJJ] project, Daly 2000, 2001a, 2002, 2003, 2005; see Daly *et al.* 1998, Daly 2001b for SAJJ technical reports), along with other research, to elucidate these limits.

Limit (3): it is easier to achieve fairness than restorativeness in an RJ process

Studies of RJ in Australia, New Zealand, and England often examine whether the observer-researcher, offender, and victim perceive the process and outcome as fair. All published studies find high levels of perceived fairness, or procedural justice, in the process and outcome (see review in Daly 2001a for Australian and New Zealand research; see also Hoyle *et al.* 2002; Crawford and Newburn 2003). For example, to questions such as 'Were you treated fairly?' 'Were you treated with respect?' 'Did people listen to you?' among other questions, a very high percentage of participants (80 per cent or more) say that they were. In addition, studies show that offenders and victims

are actively involved in fashioning the outcome, which is indicative that laypeople are exercising decision-making power. Overall, RJ practices in the jurisdictions studied definitely conform to the ideals of procedural justice.

Compared to these very high levels of procedural justice, there appears to be relatively less evidence of 'restorativeness.' The measures of restorativeness used in the SAJJ project include the degree to which the offender was remorseful, spontaneously apologized to the victim, and understood the impact of the crime on the victim; the degree to which victims understood the offender's situation; and the extent of positive movement between the offender, victim, or their supporters. Depending on the variable, restorativeness was present in 30 to 60 per cent of the youth justice conferences studied.[4] Thus, RJ conferences receive high marks for procedural fairness and victim and offender participation, but it may be more difficult for victims and offenders to resolve their differences or to find common ground in an RJ meeting (Daly 2001a, 2003).

Why is fairness easier to achieve than restorativeness? Fairness is largely, although not exclusively, a measure of the behavior of the professional(s) (the facilitator and, depending on the jurisdiction, a police officer). As the professionals, they are polite, they listen, and they establish ground rules of respect for others and civility in the conference process. Whereas fairness is established in the relationship between the professionals and participants, restorativeness emerges in the relationships between a victim, an offender, and their supporters. Being polite is easier to do than saying you are sorry; listening to someone tell their story of victimization is easier to do when you are not the offender. Indeed, understanding or taking the perspective of the other may be easier when you are not the actual victim or the offender in the justice encounter.

Restorativeness requires a degree of empathic concern and perspective-taking;

and as measured by psychologists' scales, these qualities are more frequently evinced for adults than adolescents. For example, from interviews with youthful offenders, the SAJJ project found that over half had not thought *at all* about what they would say to the victim. Most did not think in terms of what they might *offer victims*, but rather what they would be *made to do by others*. It is possible that many adolescents may not yet have the capacity to think empathetically, to take the role of the other (Frankenberger 2000); they may be expected to act as if they had the moral reasoning of adults when they do not (Van Voorhis 1985). And, at the same time, as we shall see in limits (4) and (5), victims may have high expectations for an offender's behavior in the conference process which cannot be realized, or victims' distress may be so great that the conference process can do little to aid in their recovery.

Limit (4): a 'sincere apology' is difficult to achieve

It is said that in the aftermath of crime, what victims want most is 'symbolic reparation, primarily an apology' (Strang 2002: 55, drawing from Marshall and Merry 1990). Perhaps for some offences and some victims this may be true, but I suspect that most victims want more than an apology. Fundamentally, victims want a sense of vindication for the wrong done to them and they want the offender to stop harming and hurting them or other people. A sincere apology may be a useful starting point,[5] but we might expect most victims to want more. In research on violent offences, for example, Cretney and Davis (1995: 178) suggest that a 'victim has an interest in punishment,' not just restitution or reparation, because punishment 'can reassure the victim that he or she has public recognition and support.'

Let us assume, for the sake of argument, that a sincere apology is what victims mainly desire. What are the elements of a sincere

apology and how often might we expect this to occur in an RJ process?

Drawing from Tavuchis' work on the sociology of apology (1991) Bottoms (2003: 94–8) distils the 'experiential dynamics' of an 'ideal-typical apology':[6]

> In the fully-accomplished apology ... we have first a *call* for an apology from the person(s) who regard themselves as wronged, or from someone speaking on their behalf; then the *apology* itself; and finally an expression of *forgiveness* from the wronged to the wrongdoer.
>
> (p. 94, emphasis in original)

Bottoms then says that 'each of these moves' in the fully accomplished (or ideal-typical) apology 'can be emotionally fraught' such that 'the whole apologetic discourse is (on both sides) "a delicate and precarious transaction"' (quoting Tavuchis 1991: vii).

It is important to distinguish between two types of apologies: an 'ideal-typical apology,' where there is an expression of forgiveness from a victim to an offender, and a 'sincere apology,' where there is a mutual understanding between the parties that the offender is really sorry but there is no assumption of forgiveness. I make this distinction because we might expect a 'sincere apology' to occur in an RJ process but we should not expect a victim to forgive an offender. In fact, I wonder if Tavuchis' formulation may be unrealistic in the context of a victim's response to crime. Tavuchis analyzes a range of harmful or hurtful behavior, not just crime; and I suspect that forgiveness may arise more often in non-criminal than in criminal contexts.

There is surprisingly little research on the character of apologies in RJ processes. From the RISE project, we learn that conference victims rated the offender's apology as 'sincere' (41 per cent), and a further 36 per cent rated it 'somewhat sincere' (Strang 2002: 115; 2004). Hayes's (2004) summary of RISE observational and interview data on the apology process concludes that 'the ideal of reconciliation and repair was achieved in less than half of all cases.'

The SAJJ project explored the apology process in detail (see Daly 2003: 224–5). When we asked the youth why they decided to say sorry to victims, 27 per cent said they did not feel sorry but thought they'd get off more easily, 39 per cent said to make their family feel better, and a similar per cent said they felt pushed into it. However, when asked what was the *main reason* for saying sorry, most (61 per cent) said they really were sorry. When we asked victims about the apology process, most believed that the youth's motives for apologizing were insincere. To the item, 'The youth wasn't sorry, but thought they would get off more easily if they said sorry,' 36 per cent of victims said 'Yes, definitely,' and another 36 per cent said 'Yes, a little.' A slim majority of victims believed that the youth said sorry either to get off more easily (30 per cent) or because they were pushed into it (25 per cent). Just 27 per cent of victims believed that the main reason that the youth apologized was because s/he really was sorry.[7]

This mismatch of perception between victims and offenders was explored further, by drawing on conference observations, interview material, and police incident reports to make inferences about the apology process for all eighty-nine conferences in the SAJJ sample (Daly 2005). The results reinforce the findings above: they reveal that communication failure and mixed signals are present when apologies are made and received. Such communication gaps are overlaid by the variable degree to which offenders are in fact sorry for what they have done. In 34 per cent of cases, the offenders and victims agreed (or were in partial agreement) that the offender was sorry,[8] and in 27 per cent, the offenders and victims definitely agreed that the offender was not sorry. For 30 per cent, there was a perceptual mismatch: the offenders were not sorry, but the victims thought they were (12 per cent); or the offenders were sorry, but the victims did not think so (18 per cent). For the remaining 9 per cent, it was not possible to determine. The findings show that a sincere apology may be difficult to achieve because offenders are not really sorry for what they have done, victims wish offenders would display more contrite behavior, and there are misreadings of what the other is saying.

Hayes (2004) proposes an added reason for why sincere apologies are difficult to achieve. He suggests that there are 'competing demands' placed on youthful offenders in the conference process: they are asked both to explain what happened (or provide an 'account') and to apologize for what they did. Hayes surmises that 'offenders' speech acts ... may drift from apologetic discourse to mitigating accounts and back again.' Victims may interpret what is said (and not said) as being insincere.

Limit (5): the conference process can help some victims recover from crime, but this is contingent on the degree of distress they experienced

One of the major aims of a RJ process is to assist victims in recovering from the disabling effects of crime. This central feature of RJ has not been explored in any systematic way. The SAJJ data offer insights on this complex process, and here I distil from a study of the impact of crime on victims for their likelihood of recovery a year later (see Daly 2005).

An important finding, although typically not discussed in the RJ literature, is that victims experience crime differently: some are only lightly touched, whereas others experience many disabling effects such as health problems, sleeplessness, loss of self-confidence, among others. To describe this variability, I created a measure of 'victim distress,' which was derived from a set of questions about the effects of crime.[9] Initially, I identified four categories of victims: no distress (28 per cent), low distress (12.5 per cent), moderate distress (36.5), and high distress (23 per cent). For ease of analysis, I then collapsed the four groups into two, combining the no/low distress (40.5 per cent) and the moderate/high distress (59.5 per cent), which, for convenience, I will refer to as the 'low' and 'high' distress victims, respectively.

Some important findings emerged. The high distress group was significantly more likely to be composed of female victims, personal crime victims (including those victimized in their occupational role or at their organizational workplace), violent offences, and victims and offenders who were family members or well known to each other. The offences most likely to cause victims distress were assaults on family members or teachers (89 per cent in the high distress group); adolescent punchups (76 per cent); and breaking into, stealing, or damaging personal property (75 per cent). By comparison, the offences least likely to cause victims distress were breaking into, stealing, or damaging organizational property (19 per cent) and stranger assault (33 per cent). Theft of bikes or cars was midway (55 per cent of victims were in the high distress group).

Victims' distress was significantly linked to their attitude toward offenders and their interest to find common ground during the conference. For example, while 43 per cent of high distress victims had negative attitudes toward the offender after the conference, this was the case for just 8 per cent of low distress victims. Most high distress victims said it was more important for them to be treated fairly (67 per cent) than to find common ground with the offender, whereas most low distress victims (71 per cent) said it was more important to find common ground. This is a key finding: what crime victims hope to achieve from an RJ process – that is, whether to seek mutual understanding with offenders (other-regarding victims) or to be treated well as individuals (self-regarding) – is related to the character and experience of the victimization. Organizational and stranger assault victims were most likely to be other-regarding – that is, to want to find common ground; personal property crime victims were least likely to be other-regarding; and adolescent, family, and teacher assault victims fell in between.

In general and in the context of youth justice, victims who are only lightly touched by a crime orient themselves more readily to restorative behaviors. Compared to high distress victims, it was easier for the low distress group to be other-regarding because the wrong had not affected them deeply. After a conference ended, the high distress victims were far more likely to remain angry and fearful of offenders, and to be negative toward them, than the low distress victims. This result anticipates findings on victim recovery a year later.

In 1999, the SAJJ researchers re-interviewed the victims and asked them, 'Which of the following two statements better describes how you're feeling about the incident today? Would you say that it is all behind you, you are fully recovered from it; or it is partly behind you, there are still some things that bother you, you are not fully recovered from it?' Two-thirds said that they had recovered from the offence and it was all behind them. Thus, most victims had recovered from the offence a year later, but which ones? And did the conference process assist in their recovery?

When comparing victim distress in 1998 with their recovery a year later, there were startling results. Whereas 63 per cent of the moderate, 78 per cent of the low, and 95 per cent of the no distress victims had recovered in 1999, 71 per cent of the high distress victims had *not* recovered. Thus, for the most highly distressed victims, an RJ process may be of little help in recovering from crime. In 1999, we also asked victims,

'Would you say that your ability to get the offence behind you was aided more by your participation in the justice process or things that only you could do for yourself?' Half (49 per cent) said their participation in the justice process, and 40 per cent, only things they could do for themselves; 11 per cent said both were of equal importance. The recovered victims were more likely to say participation in the justice process (72 per cent) than the non-recovered victims (38 per cent). Likewise, the low distress victims were more likely to say participation in the justice process (77 per cent) than the high distress victims (49 per cent).

Non- (or partly) recovered victims held more negative views of the offender and how their case was handled compared to the recovered victims. They were significantly more likely to see the offender as a 'bad' person rather than a 'good' person who had done a bad thing, less satisfied by how their case was handled, and more likely to say they wished their case had gone to court. When asked what was the most important thing hindering their recovery, 74 per cent of the non- (or partly) recovered victims cited financial losses, injuries, and emotional harms arising from the offence.

These findings on victim distress and recovery pose significant challenges to the RJ field. They invite reflection on the variable effects of victimization for the ways in which victims orient themselves to a restorative process. For the high distress victims, it was harder to act restoratively at the conference, and it was more difficult to be generous to offenders. The effects of victimization did not end with the conference but continued to linger for a long time. A process like RJ, and indeed any legal process (such as court), may do little to assist victims who have been deeply affected by crime. Improving practices by conference facilitators may help at the edges but this too is unlikely to have a major impact. Victims who are affected negatively and deeply by crime need more

than RJ (or court) to recover from their victimization.

Limit (6): we should expect modest results, not the nirvana story of RJ

The nirvana story of RJ is illustrated by Jim Consedine (1995: 9), who opens his book by excerpting from a 1993 New Zealand news story:

> The families of two South Auckland boys, killed by a car, welcomed the accused driver yesterday with open arms and forgiveness. The young man, who gave himself up to the police yesterday morning, apologised to the families and was ceremonially reunited with the Tongan and Samoan communities at a special service last night.

> The 20-year-old Samoan visited the Tongan families after his court appearance to apologise for the deaths of the two children ... The Tongan and Samoan communities ... later gathered at the Tongan Methodist Church in a service of reconciliation. The young man sat at the feast table flanked by the mothers of the dead boys.

Later, in discussing the case, Consedine sees it as

> ample evidence of the power that healing and forgiveness can play in our daily lives ... The grieving Tongan and Samoan communities simply embraced the young driver ... and forgave him. His deep shame, his fear, his sorrow, his alienation from the community was resolved.
> (Consedine 1995: 162)

This nirvana story of RJ contains elements that are not likely to be present in most RJ encounters: it was composed of members of racial-ethnic minority groups, who were drawn together with a shared experience of church, and there appeared to be 'meso-social structures' and 'thick' social ties between the families and kin of the offender and victims. These *gemeinschaft* qualities are atypical in modern urban life, and thus we should expect 'modest and patchy results' (Bottoms 2003: 110) to be the norm, not the exception. Much depends on the capacities and orientations of offenders and victims to be empathetic or to understand the other's situation, and on the degree to which offenders are genuinely sorry for what they have done and can communicate their remorse effectively. It also depends on the character of the victimization itself and how deeply it affects victims. All of these elements are largely outside the control of facilitators or other professionals, who are in a position only to coordinate, guide, or encourage such processes. We must also recognize the limits of time and resources that can be put to RJ processes. Some propose, for example, that with better preparation, RJ conferences will go more smoothly and achieve intended results. This may well be true, but it sets up a policy question: does one put a lot of resources (including more time in preparation) in a fewer number of RJ encounters, or does one attempt to apply RJ as widely and broadly as possible? We should not assume that the nirvana story of RJ is typical, nor that it can be achieved often.[10] This sets up RJ to fail with unrealistic and too high expectations.

Conclusion

That there exist limits on what RJ can achieve should not be grounds for dispensing with it, nor for being disillusioned, once again, with a new justice idea. My reading of the evidence is that face-to-face encounters between victims and offenders and their supporters *is* a practice worth maintaining, and perhaps enlarging, although we cannot expect it to deliver strong stories of repair and goodwill most of the time.

In the penalty phase of the criminal process, both RJ and the established court process have limits. RJ is limited by the abilities and interests of offenders and victims to think and act in ways we may define as restorative. Established CJ is limited by the inability of formal legality to listen to the accounts of crime and their effects by those most directly involved. Legal professionals do the talking, and what is legally or administratively relevant takes precedence.

By recognizing the limits of both RJ and established CJ in the penalty (or post-penalty) phase of the criminal process, we more effectively grasp the nettle of justice as a promise, as something that may be partly but never fully realized. As such, we see that all justice practices, including RJ, are limited.

References

Abel, R. (1982) 'Introduction,' in R. Abel (ed.) *The Politics of Informal Justice: the American experience*, Vol. 1, New York: Academic Press.

Acorn, A. (2004) *Compulsory Compassion: a critique of restorative justice*, Vancouver: University of British Columbia Press.

Arrigo, B. (2004) 'Rethinking restorative and community justice: a postmodern inquiry,' *Contemporary Justice Review*, 7 (1): 91–100.

Bottoms, A. E. (2003) 'Some sociological reflections on restorative justice,' in A. von Hirsch, J. Roberts, A. E. Bottoms, K. Roach, and M. Schiff (eds) *Restorative Justice and Criminal Justice: competing or reconcilable paradigms?* Oxford: Hart Publishing.

Braithwaite, J. (2002) *Restorative Justice and Responsive Regulation*, New York: Oxford University Press.

— (2003) 'Principles of restorative justice,' in A. von Hirsch, J. Roberts, A. E. Bottoms, K. Roach and M. Schiff (eds) *Restorative Justice and Criminal Justice: competing or reconcilable paradigms?* Oxford: Hart Publishing.

Consedine, J. (1995) *Restorative Justice: healing the effects of crime*, Lyttelton, NZ: Ploughshares Publications.

Contemporary Justice Review (2004) Special issue 7 (1) on 'Restorative Justice and Community Justice.'

Crawford, A. and Newburn, T. (2003) *Youth Offending and Restorative Justice: implementing reform in youth justice*, Cullompton, Devon, UK: Willan Publishing.

Cretney, A. and Davis, G. (1995) *Punishing Violence*, London: Routledge.

Daly, K. (2000) 'Revisiting the relationship between retributive and restorative justice,' in H. Strang and J. Braithwaite (eds) *Restorative Justice: philosophy to practice*, Aldershot: Dartmouth/Ashgate.

— (2001a) 'Conferencing in Australia and New Zealand: variations, research findings, and prospects,' in A. Morris and G. Maxwell (eds) *Restorative Justice for Juveniles: conferencing, mediation and circles*, Oxford: Hart Publishing.

— (2001b) *South Australia Juvenile Justice (SAJJ) research on conferencing, technical report No. 2: research instruments in year 2 (1999) and background notes*, Brisbane: School of Criminology and Criminal Justice, Griffith University. Available at: http://www.aic.gov.au/rjustice/sajj/

— (2002) 'Restorative Justice: the real story,' *Punishment & Society*, 4 (1): 55–79.

— (2003) 'Mind the gap: restorative justice in theory and practice,' in A. von Hirsch, J. Roberts, A. E. Bottoms, K. Roach, and M. Schiff (eds) *Restorative Justice and Criminal Justice: competing or reconcilable paradigms?* Oxford: Hart Publishing.

— (2005) 'A tale of two studies: restorative justice from a victim's perspective,' in E. Elliott and R. Gordon (eds) *Restorative Justice: emerging issues in practice and evaluation*, Cullompton, Devon, UK: Willan Publishing.

Daly, K., Venables, M., Mumford, L., McKenna, M. and Christie-Johnston, J. (1998) *SAJJ technical report No. 1: project overview and research instruments in year 1*, Brisbane: School of Criminology and Criminal Justice, Griffith University.

Frankenberger, K. D. (2000) 'Adolescent egocentrism: a comparison among adolescents and adults,' *Journal of Adolescence*, 23 (3): 343–54.

Hayes, H. (2004) 'Apologies and accounts in youth justice conferencing: reinterpreting research outcomes,' unpublished manuscript, Brisbane, School of Criminology and Criminal Justice, Griffith University.

Hoyle, C., Young, R. and Hill, R. (2002) *Proceed with Caution*, Layerthorpe, York: York Publishing.

Hudson, B. (2003) *Justice in the Risk Society*, London: Sage.

Johnstone, G. (2002) *Restorative Justice: ideas, values, debates*, Cullompton, Devon, UK: Willan Publishing.

— (2004) 'The idea of restorative justice,' inaugural professorial lecture, University of Hull, 11 October.

McCold, P. and Wachtel, T. (2002) 'Restorative justice theory validation,' in E. Weitekamp and H.-J. Kerner (eds) *Restorative Justice: theoretical foundations*, Cullompton, Devon, UK: Willan Publishing.

Marshall, T. and Merry, S. (1990) *Crime and Accountability: victim–offender mediation in practice*, London: HMSO.

Merry, S. (1982) 'The social organization of mediation in nonindustrial societies: implications for informal community justice in America,' in R. Abel (ed.) *The Politics of Information Justice: comparative studies*, Vol. 2, New York: Academic Press.

Morris, A. (2002) 'Critiquing the critics: a brief response to critics of restorative justice,' *British Journal of Criminology*, 42 (3): 596–615.

Pavlich, G. (1996) *Justice Fragmented: mediating community disputes under postmodern conditions*, New York: Routledge.

Roche, D. (2003) *Accountability and Restorative Justice*, Oxford: Clarendon Press.

Strang, H. (2002) *Repair or Revenge: victims and restorative justice*, Oxford: Clarendon Press.

— (2004) Email communication on RISE data, 24 November.

Tavuchis, N. (1991) *Mea Culpa: a sociology of apology and reconciliation*, Stanford: Stanford University Press.

Van Voorhis, P. (1985) 'Restitution outcome and probationers' assessments of restitution: the effects of moral development,' *Criminal Justice and Behavior*, 12(3): 259–87.

von Hirsch, A., Ashworth, A. and Shearing, C. (2003) 'Specifying aims and limits for restorative justice: a "making amends" model,' in A. von Hirsch, J. Roberts, A. E. Bottoms, K. Roach and M. Schiff (eds) *Restorative Justice and Criminal Justice: competing or reconcilable paradigms?* Oxford: Hart Publishing.

Notes

1. My thanks to Brigitte Bouhours for her assistance in preparing this chapter.
2. In inquisitorial criminal justice processes, a judge takes a more active role in gathering evidence and questioning witnesses and defendants; but in these systems as well, a defendant has a right to deny committing the offence.
3. Bottoms (2003: 91–2) takes care to discuss the varied expression of dispute resolution in premodern societies.
4. Researchers use different measures to tap restorativeness. For example, in the Re-Integrative Shaming Experiments (RISE),

restorative justice for offenders was defined as the opportunity to repair the harm they had caused, and for victims it was defined as recovery from anger and embarrassment. In the SAJJ project, restorativeness was measured by items that tapped the *degree and quality of interaction* between victims, offenders, and their supporters.

5. For some offences, it may be the wrong starting point. As Acorn (2004: 73) points out in the context of partner abuse, 'the skill of contrite apology is routinely practiced by abusers,' but it can serve to perpetuate a cycle of violence.

6. Parallel with the experiential dynamics (or interactional features), Bottoms (2003: 94–8) also considers the social structural context of an apology, which I do not address here.

7. The percentages are of a sub-set of forty-seven conference cases, in which victims were present at the conference and both the victim and offender were interviewed in 1999.

8. This group was evenly divided between those who agreed that the offender was really sorry (18 per cent) or was somewhat sorry (16 per cent).

9. This set of items, adapted from a RISE instrument, asked the victim to consider the period of time after the incident and before the conference, whether they had suffered from the following: fear of being alone, sleeplessness or nightmares, general health problems, worry about the security of their property, general increase in suspicion or distrust, sensitivity to particular sounds or noises, loss of self-confidence, loss of self-esteem, and other problems. Each of these items was asked separately for the conference victims, and in a more summary form for the victims who did not attend the conference (see Daly *et al.* 1998).

10. In fact, some argue that the 'utopian vision' of RJ ('where every story of violation and loss ends happily in right-relation') is itself misguided and wrong (Acorn 2004: 162).

Section II

The foundations of restorative justice

Throughout human history, in pre-state and pre-modern societies, and in parts of the world today among indigenous peoples, extended families, kin groups, and communities, people have created ways for those most affected by relationally disruptive conflicts, disputes, and harms to come together to discuss what is at issue and what should be done. The foundations for modern restorative justice processes can be located in these political-economic and cultural arrangements. In hunting-gathering, herding, and agricultural economies, indigenous dialogue tends to be based on affect or feelings, on the notion that there are many different ways to perceive a situation and that how people feel about a situation and others is more important than what has actually, factually, happened. Listening to others' points of view, their suffering, and their ideas for how the situation might be resolved requires empathy and understanding and, correspondingly, knowing that one's own feelings and perceptions will similarly be heard. Problem-solving must strike a balance, as the Zapotec tell us. Communicative processes keep alive the feelings of unity and relational continuity and growth that harms and conflict disrupt and threaten to sever. As Jim Zion and the Honorable Robert Yazzie (Chapter 8) point out, Navajo life ways embody these dialogic ways of healing and problem-solving for there is a common relational interest in what is decided. What is decided affects everyone's relationships and the solidarity of the group. Such life ways reinforce the Navajo values of mutuality, respect, equality, dignity, compassion, reparation, balance, and solidarity.

Many of the restorative justice processes and programs discussed in Section I have their foundations in indigenous cultural and spiritual practices and beliefs. In New Zealand the modern notion of arranging a conference involving all the persons affected was borrowed from Maori *whanau* – extended family meetings – that were traditionally organized to resolve conflicts, and the practice of arranging meetings of family members and others involved in the care of a child through family therapy during the 1970s and 1980s. Similarly, the South African Truth and Reconciliation Commission in part drew its healing process and form from the cultural and spiritual dynamic of *ubuntu*. As well, the modern notion of organizing sentencing circles, which have more recently evolved into peacemaking circles, was heavily influenced by the peace

147

circles of First Nations Peoples in North America and the contemporary concepts of dialogue and consensus building. Further, Victim Offender Reconciliation Programs and the use of circles in North America have been inspired and initiated by members of the Mennonite Church. As Michael Hadley explores in Chapter 10, the spiritual foundations for modern restorative justice processes are also found in communities of faith and in the theological reflections and teachings of the world's religions: Judaism, Christianity, Islam, Hinduism, Sikhism, Buddhism, Confucianism, and Taoism.

In Chapter 8, Zion and Yazzie present the philosophical and relational framework for Navajo peacemaking and discuss its history and the context for its development. Navajo peacemaking is a life way, not simply a restorative justice process. It reflects the Navajo view and practice of life, of relating with others where feelings are far more important than establishing 'facts.' The traditional natural community and *naat'aanii*-based justice arrangements used a talking-out procedure to temporarily 'resolve' conflict. And Navajo families had their own *naat'aanii*, wise relatives who guided family meeting discussions. When individuals give their different versions of reality, of what went on in a situation, choosing which version of reality or which truth is not as important as the feelings that flow from the statements of what each person believes is true and what is at the heart of the problem, harm, or conflict. When individuals discuss what happened, why, the effects of the events on them and their relationships with others in the group, *k'e* emerges – that is, empathy, understanding, compassion, and feelings of solidarity, respect, and mutuality. *K'e* prompts striking a balance, finding the 'main stalk,' articulating a temporary path for successful living and right relating ('a way out'). A commonality of shared interests develops for what needs to be done to repair or make up for the harm, to yield a reparative outcome, or *nalyeeh,* and to

attempt to insure that new and evolving relating does not lead to a repeat of this harmful experience. While Navajo peacemaking is a culturally unique life way, it serves as an example of the human capacity for people to solve their own problems in a non-violent and non-authoritarian way.

In Chapter 9 Dirk Louw discusses the African concept of *ubuntu*, a concept that inspired the South African Constitutional Court's abolition of the death penalty and its upholding of the constitutionality of the Truth and Reconciliation Commission's practice of granting amnesty to those who had committed gross human rights violations during apartheid in exchange for truthful accounts of these violations. It is also the concept that underpins current attempts to develop restorative practices in South Africa. *Ubuntu* is a social ethic that not only describes human being as 'being with others,' but prescribes how we should be with them. *Ubuntu* is the principle of caring for each other's well-being, a spirit of mutuality that posits the idea that each individual's humanity is expressed through his or her relationships with others, that we have a responsibility for promoting individual and societal well-being, for the restoration of community. The spirit of *ubuntu* is the healing of breaches, the redressing of imbalances, the restoration of broken relationships. It is a recognition of each person's connection to life, to a community of people that transcends the society of those presently living to those ancestors no longer alive. The person one is and is becoming is an ancestor, a relative, a member of an extended family. The person one is is always changing, united with and being through one's diverse relationships with others. The *ubuntu* perception of others is always open-ended, never reducing the other to a specific category or type. The other, like the self, is in flux, the reality of what one has experienced is in flux, how disputes and harms should be responded to and repaired is consequently to be decided collaboratively and with the realization that one's new relationships with others are likely to change. In Louw's view, *ubuntu* gives a distinctly African rationale for relating with others and self with compassion, warmth, understanding, and care.

That we should interact with one another with empathy, compassion, care, understanding, and warmth is also underscored by all the major worldviews, ideologies, and religions of the world. In Chapter 10 Michael Hadley points out that restorative justice experiences can foster a deeply spiritual process of transformation of persons, situations, and social conditions. Drawing on spiritual values, restorative justice finds a natural home in religious communities responding to human needs holistically in order to restore a moral bond. And faith traditions, in that they tend to be communal, have played a major role in the processes of restoration advocating the principles of accountability, forgiveness, compassion, empathy, and reconciliation. They have a spiritual affinity with *ubuntu* and Navajo life ways in that 'one is because one belongs' and in that 'no one is ever isolated.' It is understood that harm and joy impact everyone in a community, leaving no one untouched. Holistic patterns similar to those found in the oral traditions of indigenous cultures are as well witnessed in the world's religions, and Hadley takes us on the differing spiritual paths of Judaism, Christianity, Islam, Hinduism, Sikhism, Buddhism, Confucianism, and Taoism. All these spiritual paths run directly counter to the culture of conflict, the religion of state, and the worship of wealth and power. Faith traditions and values, like restorative justice values, envision a different, more just, and compassionate world.

As there are many different ways to perceive a situation and how people feel about a situation and others, talking things out is a core component of restorative justice practice. Listening to others' points of view, their suffering, their reasons for acting as they have, and their ideas for how the situation might be resolved and, correspondingly, knowing that one's own feelings and perceptions will similarly be heard, characterizes the notion of empathy. According to Hal Pepinsky (Chapter 11), a major challenge to successful peacemaking is fostering dialogue and relationships in which empathy is reciprocated and balanced, rather than one-sided. His personal narrative presents a seeming paradox: one cannot listen and hear where another is coming from without oneself having been heard. Nonviolence is not simply a matter of empathizing; it is a matter of allowing safe, respectful expression of its counterpart, narcissism. Trustworthiness and safety in relationships increase as empathy and narcissism are reciprocated, are balanced. Perhaps listening to one's self and to others about one's self allows one to listen and to hear others talk about themselves and their circumstances. This is certainly at the foundation of restorative interaction and a vibrant life.

In contrast to furthering the development of empathy, talking things out, and inclusion, contemporary state criminal justice processes are fundamentally exclusionary. According to Peter Cordella (Chapter 12), transgressors of the laws of the modern state and those who are harmed by these transgressions are typically excluded from the processes of criminal justice. Transgressors are excluded because they are perceived to be rationally deficient (the utilitarian model), morally deficient (the retributive model), or psychologically deficient (the therapeutic model). They are perceived as persons incapable of participating in determining what has happened and what should be done in response to what has happened. They are, as well, seen as incapable of mediating their full integration into their communities and society. Similarly, those who have been harmed ('victims') are absented as irrelevant to these processes, for the state defines itself as the citizen-victim, not the actual person(s) harmed. The needs of the human victim are deemed not relevant to these proceedings and are consequently ignored. Direct participation by either those who have transgressed or those transgressed upon poses a threat to the bureaucratic rationality of these proceedings and to the possibility that the legal fairness, reasonableness, substance, and consistency of state law could be called into question.

In contrast, Cordella points out that the social framework most conducive to empathy and communicative 'law' is sanctuary. The concept of modern sanctuary proposes a condition of suspended community membership for one who has transgressed pending his/her acknowledgement of the harm and its effects, an agreement to repair the harm, and a good faith effort to avoid future transgressions. In return, the community guarantees a removal of the suspended membership and full reinstatement. Trust and mutuality are essential to conciliation processes and communicative 'law,' which guides the concept of sanctuary and the processes of conciliation, implies indications, road signs, and invocations to discussions. It involves real assent generated through a continuous process of interaction and adjustment among members of the community.

Sanctuary is, according to Cordella, the most participatory and least punitive of dispute resolution models. Sanctuary requires direct participation by the disputants in an open and flexible conciliatory process, and as a conciliatory process, sanctuary justice creates an environment in which participants are solely responsible for the resolution of their conflict. A negotiated settlement balances the remediation of past harm with a blueprint for the future. For the transgressor this settlement means a full and complete reintegration into the community. For the community this settlement means that all the issues regarding equity and freedom have been addressed and resolved. For the victim this settlement means that the harm associated with the transgression has been acknowledged and reparation has been rendered. Sanctuary is the antithesis of state justice. Sanctuary exemplifies the participatory dynamic of restorative justice and underscores the necessity and sanctity of equitable human relationships.

8

Navajo peacemaking

Original dispute resolution and a life way

James W. Zion and Robert Yazzie

Navajo peacemaking, translated from the term *hozhooji naat'aanii*, is a form of traditional indigenous dispute resolution that was integrated into the western-styled judicial system of the Navajo Nation of Arizona, New Mexico and Utah in 1982 (Zion 1985). It is based upon traditional leadership arrangements that Navajos evolved in a high desert environment and a grazing and agricultural economy (Bailey 1998). This chapter reviews the philosophical and institutional framework of Navajo peacemaking to give an overview of how it evolved, what it is, how it works, and why it is relevant to the broader field of restorative justice.

The model for analysis is the concept that 'law' is norms that are applied by institutions (Bohannan 1967: 45). There are problems in defining what a 'norm' is, and indigenous 'institutions' are different from bodies we usually associate with that term. There are more subtle considerations of both concepts, such as viewing norms as feelings within a broader concept of a 'life way,' and institutions as relationships and not necessarily bodies that exercise authority.

The term 'norm' is usually defined as statements of 'ought' or 'ought not' (Bohannan 1967: 45). Norms are also discussed as values, moral principles, and other statements of shared perception. There are difficulties in understanding how they operate because of differences in the way western legal systems apply them, as contrasted with customary institutions (Zorn and Care 2002). Adjudication systems view norms as 'rules,' which are principles that vertical institutions elaborate and apply to given problems (Yazzie 1994 citing Barkun 1968: 16–17). A rule is a statement of what the law 'is,' defined by an institution, and a 'vertical' institution is one that has authority to develop a rule and apply it. The problem is that norms offer many choices in horizontal legal systems rather than a given rule to apply for a decision in a vertical one. Horizontal process is plastic and flexible. A horizontal legal system has individuals who are at least nominally equal who negotiate norms and compliance with a consensual decision is voluntary. Norms may be stated in terms of right and wrong, or they may be unstated but expressed as feelings about a given situation. We are used to a process where facts are developed and rules applied, and even when they are negotiated rather than applied by an authoritarian institution, norm statements do not necessarily say 'the law is . . . ' but rather 'the right thing to do is ... ' They are part of a fluid negotiation process.

A major difference between western adjudication and indigenous dialogue is that western thought tends to be rational and is based on Aristotelian logic, using inductive or deductive reasoning. Indigenous thought tends to be based on affect or feeling, where feelings are often more important than finding 'facts,' and both are expressed in languages that are more sophisticated than English (see Witherspoon 1977). Western adjudication is largely based on a third person, viewed as an impartial professional, who hears contested assertions of fact by parties in dispute, and decides the facts to which rules will be applied. That creates a separate and often artificial reality. Findings of fact may or may not coincide with what actually happened. Following a determination of fact, the adjudicator decides the appropriate rule to apply to drive a decision.

Horizontal systems use a different process. There too, individuals give their versions of the facts, but choosing truth or reality among them is not as important as feelings that flow from statements of what people believe is true. The determination of reality after the fact can be negotiated, and how people feel about the situation is more important than what actually happened. At end, relationships and acknowledged feelings may dispense with the facts of the dispute that initiated negotiation.

Adjudication is largely rationalistic and impersonal, while negotiation (an unsatisfactory term because it sounds too rational) is a relational process that actively engages people. As individuals discuss their perceptions of norms in an affective way, the exchange should lead from 'I' statements to 'we' statements as communication and empathy prompt an affect shift (Grohowski 1995). When individuals discuss what happened, why, the effects of events on them and their relationships with people in the group, feelings of solidarity, and respect,

recognized mutual dependence and the like can prompt consensus in a commonality of shared interests for a decision about what needs to be done.

Consensus is not simply the product of fact-clarification, exchanges of feelings and empathy. There are other processes that distinguish horizontal and indigenous process from adjudication. Navajo thought has a problem-solving concept of *nahat'a* or planning. Following an exchange of what people think happened, the facts, and expressions of feelings about what happened and its impact, Navajos then ask, 'Where do we go from here?' Planning prompts questions such as 'What needs to be done to repair or make up for the injury?' and 'What can be done to make sure this does not happen again?' The resolution of the conflict might not be a concrete one that finally concludes the dispute. Things are not absolute and continuing relationships are fluid. There are two applicable Navajo concepts: the 'main stalk' and 'the way out.' The 'main stalk' uses a simile of a stalk of corn (Farella 1984). The leaves are the opposites of 'good' and 'evil.' The stalk is a path in between that symbolizes the mid-way between good and evil, because excesses of either are harmful. Put another way, successful living and right relationships can be conceived as a path, and we know from experience that it is easy to veer off a path because life is unpredictable. The concept of 'a way out' recognizes that it is impossible to make a decision that will remain valid over time because of emergent events in the future (Schwarz 1997: 39). Decisions and relationships can be renegotiated and adjusted as new problems arise.

A more subtle idea of norms is that they are part of a larger 'life way.' That is an unconscious appreciation of the fact that there is something deeper to negotiated solutions. In Navajo, it is expressed in terms of *k'e*, an elusive word that cannot be defined concretely in English. It has to do with relationships, and terms such as 'solidarity,' 'interdependence,' and 'mutuality' help give it some content and context. It is an affective or emotional word that conveys feelings such as respect and compassion in sharing, caring and wisdom. Sharing illustrates another difference between adjudication and negotiation, distributive justice. When examining possible outcomes in peacemaking, individuals will speak of the need to share. Participants identify relationships in living, family, clan or other ongoing arrangements and interaction, and identify resources to be shared. One of the major concepts of a proper outcome in peacemaking is *nalyeeh*, another elusive Navajo term about compensation or reparation (to repair an injury rather than award its market value in restitution), that is measured by there being 'enough so that there are no hard feelings' (Yazzie 1994: 184–5). That also demonstrates the affective nature of the process.

There is no one norm, stated as a rule, that resolves conflicts in peacemaking. The emphasis is upon relation-based and affective process rather than the application of rules by a neutral third party. Outcomes are driven by relationships and needs. There is also a different perception of individualism. Navajos have evolved concepts of individual liberty and freedom that are broader than western concepts in the maxim, 'It's up to him' (Zion 2002: 525). Peacemaking recognizes individualism in a process where it is improper to judge individuals, but their actions are evaluated. Navajo justice, as a feeling, does not assume that people are evil or that they have 'bad souls' (Haile 1943: 83–4). The 'good' or 'evil' of an action caused by an individual, or the product of an individual's inaction, depends upon its effects. When they are recognized, in terms of the harm they caused others, appropriate *nalyeeh*, based upon the ability of the actor *and* supportive family members to pay or give, is negotiated, and it can be symbolic or nominal when empathy guides consensus on the amount. It is negotiated based on need and available resources.

Navajo 'institutions' include families, clans, elders, and civil leaders. Given an inability of colonial writers to accurately view and describe indigenous thought and life ways accurately, indigenous institutions are generally conceived as 'chiefs,' 'warrior societies,' and like unrealistic leadership terms. Perceptions of traditional Navajo leadership generally follow the same misconception, describing traditional Navajo leaders as 'war chiefs,' 'peace chiefs,' and 'head men.' During a phase of conflict between Navajos and settlers of the Defiance Plateau (a high desert area in northern Arizona and New Mexico, including parts of Colorado and Utah) that spanned from Spanish occupation in 1598 through American occupation in 1846 and the 1868 Navajo treaty with the United States, there was a great deal of emphasis on war and war leaders. Such leaders, *hashkeeji naat'aanii*, were largely self-selected and had a following based upon decisiveness in battle and personal charisma. The more important leaders, and the model for contemporary peacemakers, were *hozhooji naat'aanii*, usually translated as 'peace chiefs' or 'head men.'

Geographic and economic foundations of Navajo leadership are important. Navajos were hunter-gatherers who adopted and adapted a grazing culture that came from Spain. It had and has a transhumant grazing economy based upon moving cattle and sheep from low-lying areas during cold months to high areas in warm ones. The Colorado Plateau where aboriginal Navajo lands lie is similar to parts of Spain. The Plateau is a semi-arid region with mountains and valleys, expanses of desert, mesas, and canyons. The original Navajo land, Dinetah, centered on large rivers in northwest New Mexico, and through processes of contact and conflict with colonizers it became a land between four sacred mountains in southwest Colorado, north central New Mexico, north central Arizona, and southeast Utah – Dine Bikeyah ('the people, the land belongs to them' or 'Navajoland'). There was a process of cultural borrowing where Navajos adopted an economy based upon transhumant grazing, agriculture, weaving, and silversmithing. Navajos organized in groups based on families, marriage, and extended clan relations called a 'natural community.' It consisted of up to forty families that took livestock to high areas during warm months and returned to low areas during cold ones. Natural communities also grew corn, beans, and squash and gathered herbs and plants. There were watered areas where crops grew, and agriculture also depended upon shifts in prevailing winds in mid-to-late summer that brought thunderstorms for flood irrigation. Weaving developed, and Navajos became famous for their waterproof blankets and rugs during the Spanish colonial period. Silversmithing developed, and silver jewelry was a medium of exchange and a sign of wealth.

What kinds of institutions does such an economy generate? Natural communities evolved the *naat'aanii* system. Navajos also developed a system of ceremonies based upon concepts of spirit beings (*Diyin Dine'*) that could be moved by prayer and ceremonies using the expertise of medicine people (Reichard 1944). (There is a misconception that there are only 'medicine men' – there were and are medicine women.) Individuals were selected as leaders by consensus, often based upon their knowledge of ritual.

It is important to understand the leadership selection process in its own context, abandoning notions of elections or some kind of group meeting to make a choice. *Naat'aanii* were relatives and clan relations of members of natural communities, so individuals who distinguished themselves would have a following without formal group action. Those who were respected for their knowledge of ceremony, speaking ability, and uprightness in bearing were leaders. There was another component to recognized leadership ability, namely *nahat'a*

or planning, and the ability to plan. There is a story of a *naat'aanii* in the mid-nineteenth century who was said to be able to 'talk the goods in.' That referred to his success in leadership by planning and guiding that resulted in material wealth for the group that followed him. They say (as it is put in Navajo) that when a Hopi killed that *naat'aanii*, his Navajo women followers led a raid on a Hopi village that almost destroyed it (Preston 1954).

It is difficult to place Navajo leadership in a neat category of various kinds of authority. A *naat'aanii* was more than a persuasive leader whose only authority was to convince others to follow his or her suggestions, but not quite a chief, who led through authoritarian rule (Spicer 1976: 383–4). It was a form of leadership where the wisdom and planning ability of the leader usually guided members of the natural community without question. A *naat'aanii* used a discursive planning process, whereby an assistant 'runner' would summon interested individuals to discuss problems and solutions in an informal 'council.' There are accounts of large gatherings of *naat'aanii*, in twelve traditional groups, to discuss war – a *naachid*. There are stories of *naat'aanii* gathering members of the natural community early in the morning to discuss the work of the day and make assignments.

Another aspect of leadership was based upon the high value of wisdom and tradition among Navajos. One of the main carriers of Navajo wisdom is a journey and creation narrative that describes how Navajos evolved and how things came to be (Matthews 1994). It is an oral tradition that is preserved in narratives, stories, songs, and ceremonies. It is possessed by medicine people who know one or more ceremonies, and it is held by individuals who have that knowledge from years of experience. Knowledge is information, and the ability to interpret it successfully for application is wisdom. Individuals, both men and women, who are recognized to have knowledge and the ability to interpret it in a way that brings successful outcomes are recognized. They are usually older people, but age alone does not necessarily mean that an individual is knowledgeable or wise. They are elders, individuals who may or may not be *naat'aa-nii*, but who can be called 'the keepers of the tribal encyclopedia.'

Those are some of the approaches to Navajo concepts of norms and how they are applied in traditional institutions. Navajos developed a successful means for survival in a plateau region of high desert, mountains, valleys, and plains and it was impacted and changed forever by war and conquest.

Navajos waged war with Spanish and later Mexican settlers (Spain from 1598 through 1820 and Mexico from 1820 through 1848), and with the United States (1846–68), when it conquered Nuevo Mexico, which later became the New Mexico Territory and then the states of New Mexico and Arizona. The Spanish and Mexicans were never able to assert effective control over Navajos who, unlike the Pueblos of the Rio Grande Valley and outlying areas, were always able to resist domination. Spanish and Mexican territorial governors would dispatch soldiers for periodic raids, and Navajos could escape them using scatter-and-run tactics. There are many mountains, valleys, and canyons in Dine' Bekeyah that are suitable for hiding. In contrast, following initial attempts by the newly arrived United States forces and governors to resolve conflict in failed treaty-making (with treaties that usually fell apart because of the refusal to return captive Navajo women and children), the United States waged total war on Navajos during the US Civil War to subjugate them. A military force chased Navajos wherever they fled, in campaigns that lasted throughout the year, and implemented a plan to round up as many Navajos as possible to death-march about 400 miles away from their homeland to a sandy patch of land located on the alkali-filled waters of the Pecos River in eastern New Mexico. The plan was to turn Navajos into village-based agriculturalists, and it was so unrealistic that even enemies of Navajos in the capital of Santa Fe called for their return. The government of the United States negotiated one last treaty, imposed at gunpoint, and Navajos returned home in the latter part of 1868. The period of rounding Navajos up, terrorizing them, and confining them in a 'reservation' called Bosque Redondo changed Navajo life forever.

Given the foundations of the topography and nature of Dinetah and Dine' Bekeyah, and the cultural, economic, political, and legal arrangements that evolved from them, a new foundation for Navajo society developed after 1868. That was a 'reservation' period where the Navajo economy rebuilt and modern institutional relationships with the United States developed. 'Head men' negotiated with representatives of the United States, 'the agent to the Navajos,' and Navajo society continued much as before. However, new economic forces developed. Gas and oil were discovered near the Four Corners (of Colorado, New Mexico, Arizona, and Utah) in the 1920s, and the United States formed the Navajo Tribal Council to sign leases. Negotiations with head men broke down, and it was more convenient to have a council based upon a western corporate form to sign the leases. The United States undertook an initiative to take control of the West from Indians in a series of treaties immediately before, during, and just after the US Civil War, starting the 'reservation' period where Indians were confined to lands with boundaries and somewhat left alone. Given a record of mismanagement and corruption by non-Indians who controlled interaction with Indian societies, the United States recognized the failure of the 'reservation policy' by the late 1920s. When the Roosevelt administration took office in 1933 at the height of the American Depression, a reform administration evolved a new policy for Indian reservations. It was articulated in the Indian Reorganization Act of

1934, that imposed corporate self-government upon Indian nations.

At the same time the Roosevelt administration assumed power, Navajo population and herds grew, and there was a period of drought in the region. The Roosevelt administration planned and commenced a series of dams on the Colorado River to bring water and energy to the Southwest, and the administration's lead man for Indian policy, John Collier, coerced Navajos to reduce their numbers of livestock. He initiated another trauma on Navajo society in a brutal livestock reduction program (that is still remembered), and he carved the Navajo Nation into grazing districts where Navajos had to have grazing permits in limited grazing districts, with a limitation on the number of head of horses, cattle, sheep, and goats that could be grazed. One of the aspects of the brutality of the plan was that Collier particularly targeted horses and goats as unworthy animals, while men prized horses as an aspect of their identity and individuality, and goats were a favored women's animal (because of their meat and fine wool for weaving).

Given an increasing population and confinement to grazing districts, the Navajo transhumant grazing economy began to collapse. The United States policy of Indian self-government waned by the end of World War II, and erratic shifts in national Indian policy created two trends that bring us to modern times – the 'Termination Era' of the 1950s and 1960s, and the 'Self-Determination Era' that began in the 1970s and persists to the present.

The Termination Era was based upon a view that it was time for Indians to assimilate into American society. Reservation policies assumed that Indians would be assimilated individually and that, as they abandoned their traditional culture through boarding schools, employment programs, entrance into a wage economy, and other initiatives designed to 'destroy the Indian' in them, reservations and the need for them

would disappear. The policy of individual assimilation assumed that using weak treaties to bind Indian tribes to the national government, Indian leaders who could be controlled, and limited autonomy, would lead to transformation. The Termination Era policy was that individual assimilation took too long, was not successful, and that toleration of 'Indian-ness' had reached its limits. Instead, there was a policy to assimilate Indians as groups by terminating reservations, putting Indians under state control, and making them only another American 'minority,' subject to political manipulation and domination as such.

The Navajo Nation resisted a corporate form of government under the Indian Reorganization Act. In the meantime, another transforming event for Navajo society occurred – World War II. For the first time, Navajos left their nation in large numbers to serve in the military, engage in war work, and replace agricultural workers as far away as California. Navajos returned speaking English, and they brought with them an appreciation for things such as wages, alcohol, and non-Navajo forms of law and governance. That experience, coupled with a fear that Navajos would be subjected to state jurisdiction, prompted the evolution of Navajo political society from a tribal to a state system with a strong elected tribal council and a bureaucracy.

The Navajo Nation Council began enacting western-styled laws in the 1950s and in 1959 created a modern judicial system – the Courts of the Navajo Nation. It was modeled upon the justice of the peace system, and policies of adopting modern law codes, developing court rules, and training a judiciary on them were designed to stave off group assimilation and termination by demonstrating that Navajos could govern themselves and administer justice in a way that looked familiar to the dominant society.

Focusing now on legal institutions and norms expressed as rules of law, Navajos developed a successful modern western legal system that grew along with the population and the economy. There were two other cultural revolutions that impacted Navajo society. President Lyndon Johnson's 'War on Poverty' had an impact as monies went to the Navajo Nation to form community organizations, such as the Office of Navajo Economic Opportunity (ONEO), and the national Legal Services Program prompted the formation of DNA-People's Legal Services, Inc. ONEO was the training ground and political springboard for Peter MacDonald, Sr, a strong leader who dominated modern Navajo Nation politics, and DNA-People's Legal Services trained successive generations of Navajo advocates, judges, and lawyers on the rule of law concept. Additional reorganization, fueled by President Richard Nixon's 'Self-Determination Policy,' created a large, centralized governmental bureaucracy and a modern state system. The Indian Civil Rights Act of 1968, which depended upon strong Indian judicial systems as a check on arbitrary governmental action, caused the Navajo Nation judiciary to grow in strength and sophistication. All those changes in policy, economy, and society exploded in heightened levels of social disruption and violence in recent decades, and methods of suppression and control in the judicial system began to alienate Navajos, who felt that their courts were as oppressive as outside ones.

Second thoughts began to emerge about the role of the judiciary a decade after President Nixon announced his self-determination policy. Some monies began to flow to the Navajo Nation courts under the Indian Self-Determination and Education Assistance Act of 1975 (which gave monies to Indian nation governments to perform federal functions, including law enforcement and judicial programs), and as the court system grew, doubts about its role grew as well. There were conflicts between a chief justice with a strong personality and Peter MacDonald, Sr, who had an equally strong will, and following MacDonald's attempts to control the judiciary that were injurious to the rule of law concept, MacDonald, some Navajo judges, and political leaders in the Council began to question whether the court system had 'gone too far down the Anglo path' and called for a return to Navajo justice values by reintegrating traditional law into the judiciary.

The dilemma was – and is – how to do that. The most obvious approach is to utilize traditional Navajo values for decisions and to explain them in decisions written in English. Navajo judges who had training on the rule of law with DNA-People's Legal Services experimented with approaches to such a process, using judicial notice, methods to elicit traditional principles from indigenous 'experts,' literature, and linguistics. The last approach was and is important, because Navajo judges learned how to take Navajo words and phrases, articulate them as legal 'rules,' and put them in opinions written in English, using Navajo terminology and explaining how it applied in English. That used western adjudication process in a vertical system to articulate Navajo values as 'rules.'

In the meantime, something else was taking place. The United States first attempted to impose western adjudication upon Navajos in 1892 in the Navajo Court of Indian Offenses. It attempted to use Navajo police to enforce a misdemeanor code by arresting offenders and taking them before a justice of the peace-modeled judicial system with Navajo judges. The traditional natural community and *naat'aanii*-based justice system used a talking-out procedure to resolve conflict. Navajo families had their own *naat'aanii*, wise relatives who guided family meeting discussions, and there were community *naat'aanii* who resolved conflicts by talking things out. Adjudication took dispute resolution authority out of the hands of families and local groups, told Navajos that they were not competent to deal with things such as offending, and made them dependent upon western legal institutions. Studies

157

of what Navajos actually did with the imposed system done in the late 1930s and 1940s showed that Navajo judges still used a talking-out process in trials that were actually community meetings. That was destroyed in the reforms after the creation of a Navajo Nation-controlled judicial system in 1959.

Following the call of Peter MacDonald, Sr, to revive traditional Navajo justice and to reintegrate it in the judicial system, there was recognition of a custom under the former Navajo Court of Indian Offenses for judges to refer certain kinds of problems to community leaders that performed the functions of a *naat'aanii*. When Chief Justice Nelson McCabe identified it, he presented a plan to the Navajo Nation judges, meeting as a judicial conference, to revive the traditional justice method. The judges adopted the Rules of the Navajo Peacemaker Court in 1982 and institutionalized the traditional Navajo justice method, *hozhooji naat'aanii*, in the courts. The rules provided for the selection of peacemakers by chapters (110 local governments) and having peacemakers work with cases that were referred by the judges.

The Navajo Nation reformed its judicial system again in 1985 under the leadership of Chairman Peterson Zah, a DNA-People's Legal Services-trained leader and its former director. The reform created the Navajo Nation Supreme Court, a permanent three-justice court of last resort. There was an understanding by Council members when they adopted the reforms, not fully articulated but still a consideration today, that the Supreme Court would have as its members a trial court judge with extensive judicial experience, a traditionalist, and a law school-trained member. The Court installed after the reforms had the Honorable Tom Tso as its first chief justice, another DNA-People's Legal Services practitioner and a bar association president; the Honorable Homer Bluehouse, a trial judge who was widely recognized for his knowledge of tradition; and the Honorable Raymond D. Austin, a law school graduate who practiced in a legal

services program. All three endorsed the movement to return Navajo tradition to the law, and the Court announced that Navajo common law (the name used for 'traditional Navajo law') was the 'law of preference' of the Navajo Nation. The Court also evolved a discourse of Navajo common law in legal opinions that prevails today.

Peacemaking was dormant between its creation in 1982 and the reform of the judicial system in 1985. The judges who took action in 1982 chose to create peacemaking using their court rulemaking authority, something that was not popular with the political branch of government, and they chose to pay peacemakers with the contributions of users rather than rely on appropriations. That was done to distance peacemaking from political influence or interference. There was a great deal of discussion of federal financial support for Indian court systems following the Indian Civil Rights Act of 1968 and how to do that in a systematic way, and Congress authorized 'special tribal court funds' for innovative programs. Chief Justice Tom Tso was informed that since the funds flowed through each of the twelve Bureau of Indian Affairs area offices and there was a Navajo Area Office, so the Navajo Nation court system did not have to compete with other courts, there was a pot of money available to him. All he needed to do was present the Area Office with a plan on how he intended to spend the money.

Tso was committed to modern Navajo peacemaking as one of its founders, so the plan he submitted envisioned the creation of a peacemaking division of the court to oversee the development and growth of peacemaking, and peacemaker liaisons in each of seven judicial districts to give administrative support to judges and peacemakers. Tso hired Philmer Bluehouse as the first director of the division, and as he recruited peacemaker liaisons with knowledge of tradition and a commitment to it, the system we see today grew.

The Honorable Robert Yazzie, a law school graduate who served as a trial judge for eight years and who presided over sensational political trials during a period of governmental transition, assumed the office of Chief Justice in 1992. He shared the commitment of his predecessors to Navajo common law and peacemaking, guided peacemaking to be an essential part of Navajo Nation justice and gave it worldwide fame. He watched the restorative justice movement in its early beginnings and made certain that Navajo peacemaking was recognized as a model for the movement.

Modern peacemaking had its shortcomings. The 1982 rules are based upon a non-Navajo model of court-annexed mediation and arbitration. Yazzie recognized that peacemaking is not 'mediation' in the sense of a stranger to parties who is completely 'neutral' presiding, and said that peacemaking does not follow a non-Navajo model. He rejected the term 'alternative dispute resolution,' coining 'ODR' or 'original dispute resolution' to distinguish peacemaking. He noted that one of the major shortcomings in the process was having judges act as gatekeepers to control the flow of cases into it and to grant or withhold judgments based on decisions made in peacemaking. He attempted to get trial judges to commit to the process, and when most did not, he encouraged a policy of having peacemaker liaisons accept cases directly in 'walk-ins' where members of the public can select a peacemaking option. Today, most of the cases in peacemaking are voluntary walk-ins and not judicial referrals.

The rules have limited categories of cases that can be handled, but the walk-in procedure allows users to self-select the kinds of cases peacemaking can handle. They are largely 'family problem' cases, where individuals address separation and divorce, children's problems, reconciliation, and issues such as adultery, jealousy, and family abuse. There are other kinds of cases, and there have been some controversial ones involving modern tort litigation when judges who approve of peacemaking have used it. The Navajo Nation Council reformed the criminal code in 2000 to expand the range of criminal cases that are to go into peacemaking, but those reforms have not been fully implemented due to various factors, most notably judicial gatekeeping.

Is peacemaking 'restorative justice'? An academic from Florida once asked Chief Justice Yazzie that question over lunch as she began a study of Navajo peacemaking and domestic violence. She warned of connotation problems using that terminology, and while Yazzie uses it, he takes care to distinguish it from other forms. He insists upon what he calls 'Navajo thinking,' and continues to grow his own understanding of it. He published a major article on Navajo legal philosophy saying that when it comes to law, 'life comes from it' (1994), and he continues to equate traditional law with 'life,' describing it as a 'life way' to put it in a broader context.

This analysis of Navajo peacemaking attempts to describe how Navajos use concepts of norms and institutions in a traditional justice process. It shows that there are similarities and differences between restorative justice principles in general and 'Navajo restorative justice,' and identifies points of divergence. However, as the concept of restorative justice evolves, because it is a plastic term for many manifestations of problem-solving outside adjudication, Navajo peacemaking is an example of an indigenous approach and a potential model. There are some who say that peacemaking is so spiritually and culturally unique to Navajos that it cannot be replicated, but the authors of this chapter maintain that while it is unique, it is also an example of the human ability to solve problems in a nonviolent and non-authoritarian way. It allows, and encourages, people to solve their own problems, and over two decades of peacemaking in practice shows that the process works.

Navajos revived an ancient form of problem-solving for many of the same reasons that the restorative justice movement grew – from necessity. Modern adjudication did not satisfy lingering Navajo expectations about the right way to solve problems by utilizing relationships, and the forces that prompted modern 'reform' caused new problems of social disruption, violence and crime. Navajos are consciously using a 'back to the future' movement of revitalization based on tradition to deal with new problems using peacemaking. At end, however, it is not simply another kind of dispute resolution mechanism or ADR – it is a life way and a way of life that reflects centuries of Navajo customs and values.

References

Bailey, L. (1998) *Bosque Redondo: the Navajo internment at Fort Sumner, New Mexico, 1863–68*, Tucson, AZ: Westernlore Press.

Barkun, M. (1968) *Law without Sanctions: order in primitive societies and the world community*, New Haven, CT: Yale University Press.

Bohannan P. (1967) 'The differing realms of the law,' in P. Bohannan (ed.) *Law and Warfare: studies in the anthropology of conflict*, Garden City, NY: The Natural History Press.

Farella, J. (1984) *The Main Stalk: a synthesis of Navajo philosophy*, Tucson, AZ: University of Arizona Press.

Grohowski, L. (1995) 'Cognitive-affective model of reconciliation CMR,' unpublished thesis, Nova Southeastern University.

Haile, B. (1943) *Soul Concepts of the Navajo*, Vatican City: Tipografia Poliglotta Vaticana.

Matthews, W. (1994) *Navaho Legends*, Salt Lake City, UT: University of Utah Press.

Preston, S. (1954) 'The Oraibi massacre,' in R. W. Young and W. Morgan (eds) *Navajo Historical Selections: selected, edited and translated from the Navajo*, Phoenix, AZ: Phoenix Indian School Print Shop.

Reichard, G. (1944) *Prayer: the compulsive word*, Seattle, WA: University of Washington Press.

Schwartz, M. (1997) *Molded in the Image of Changing Woman: Navajo views on the human body and personhood*, Tucson, AZ: University of Arizona Press.

Spicer, E. (1976) *Cycles of Conquest: the impact of Spain, Mexico, and the United States on the Indians of the Southwest, 1533–1960*, Tucson, AZ: University of Arizona Press.

Witherspoon, G. (1977) *Language and Art in the Navajo Universe*, Ann Arbor, MI: University of Michigan Press.

Yazzie, R. (1994) '"Life comes from it": Navajo justice concepts,' *New Mexico Law Review*, 24(2): 175–90.

Zion, J. (1985) 'The Navajo peacemaker court: deference to the old and accommodation to the new,' *American Indian Law Review*, 11(2): 89–109.

— (2002) 'Civil rights in Navajo common law,' *University of Kansas Law Review*, 50(3): 523–44.

Zorn, J. and Care, J. (2002) '"Barava Tru": judicial approaches to the pleading and proof of custom in the South Pacific,' *International and Comparative Law Quarterly*, 51(3): 611–39.

9

The African concept of *ubuntu* and restorative justice

Dirk J. Louw

Introduction

Umuntu ngumuntu ngabantu. Motho ke motho ka batho. These are, respectively, the Zulu and Sotho versions of a traditional African aphorism, often translated as 'a person is a person through other persons' (Shutte 1993: 46; 2001: 12; Ramose 2002a: 42). Its central concept, *ubuntu*, means 'humanity,' 'humanness,' or even 'humaneness.' These translations involve a considerable loss of culture-specific meaning. But, be that as it may, generally speaking the maxim *umuntu ngumuntu ngabantu* articulates a basic respect and compassion for others. As such, it is both a factual description and a rule of conduct or social ethic. It not only describes human being as 'being-with-others,' but also prescribes how we should relate to others: that is, what 'being-with-others' should be all about. The 1997 South African Governmental White Paper for Social Welfare officially recognizes *ubuntu* as:

> The principle of caring for each other's well-being ... and a spirit of mutual support ... Each individual's humanity is ideally expressed through his or her relationship with others and theirs in turn through a recognition of the individual's humanity. *Ubuntu* means that people are people through other people. It also acknowledges both the rights and the responsibilities of every citizen in promoting individual and societal well-being.
>
> (http://www.welfare.gov.za/ Documents/1997/wp.htm)

Ubuntu also features in the postamble of the (interim) Constitution of the Republic of South Africa, which points out that 'there is a need for understanding but not for vengeance, a need for reparation but not for retaliation, a need for *ubuntu* but not for victimisation.' Hence the South African Constitutional Court's abolition of the death penalty (in 1995) and its upholding (in 1996) of the constitutionality of the Truth and Reconciliation Commission's practice of granting amnesty to perpetrators of gross human rights violations during apartheid in exchange for truthful accounts of these violations. These rulings and the values that underpin them resonate with what has come to be called 'restorative justice' (Anderson 2004: 11).

Restorative justice has been defined in a variety of ways to the extent that it would perhaps be more accurate to speak of restorative *approaches* to justice than of *the* restorative approach (Johnstone 2003: 1). However, for the purposes of this paper the following working definition will suffice:

> Restorative justice is a process whereby parties with a stake in a specific offence resolve collectively how to deal with the aftermath of the offence and its implications for the future. The aim is offender accountability, reparation to the victim and full participation by all those involved ... Restorative justice ... is based on the assumption that within society a certain balance and respect exists, which can be harmed by crime. The purpose of the justice system is then [not punishment, but rather] to restore this balance and to heal relationships [through the direct involvement of] all the parties to the crime (victim, offender and the community).
>
> (Anderson 2004: 7–8)

In short, the process of restorative justice involves the reaching of an agreement or consensus through dialogue and negotiation with a view to reintegrate a community violated by crime. In what follows, I shall argue that 'consensus through dialogue' is also indicative of the *ubuntu* approach to the restoration of community. That is, I shall use 'consensus through dialogue' as a point of departure (or, if you like, hermeneutical key or lens) for identifying connections or overlappings between restorative justice and *ubuntu*. More specifically, I aim to show how *ubuntu* both demonstrates and instructs us toward restorative justice, thereby vindicating Archbishop Desmond Tutu's claim that such justice is characteristic of traditional African jurisprudence in so far as its 'central concern is not retribution or punishment but, in the spirit of *ubuntu*, the healing of breaches, the redressing of imbalances, the restoration of broken relationships' (as cited by Roche 2003: 27).

Ubuntu and consensus

Agreement

A first important overlap between *ubuntu* and the process of restorative justice pertains to the extremely important role that agreement plays in this process. Restorative justice requires that the victim, offender, and community must find a common understanding of the offense and its resolution, including, among other things, how the offender will make amends for the harm caused by the crime to the victim and the community, and how the offender will be reintegrated into the community (Dzur and Wertheimer 2002: 4–8, 10–11). *Ubuntu* underscores the importance of agreement or consensus. African traditional culture, it seems, has an almost infinite capacity for the pursuit of consensus and reconciliation (Teffo 1994a: 4). Democracy the African way does not simply boil down to majority rule. Traditional African democracy operates in the form of a (sometimes extremely lengthy) discussion, whether it be an *indaba* (open discussion by a group of people with some or other common interest), a *lekgotla* (discussion at a secluded venue), or an *imbizo* (mass congregation for discussing issues of national concern) (Boele van Hensbroek 1998: 186f, 203f; Du Toit 2000: 25–6; Shutte 2001: 28–9; Broodryk 2002: 77). These discussions, in so far as they may also involve the settlement of criminal cases, overlap in varying degrees with what advocates of restorative justice call 'family group conferencing,' 'peacemaking circles,' and 'victim offender mediation' (Anderson 2004: 8).

Critics of restorative justice often point out that restorative dialogue is not held between equals, since victims are necessarily given the dominant voice (Dzur and Wertheimer 2002: 6, 10). A hierarchy of speakers may also apply to *ubuntu* dialogue in so far as some participants may be allowed to air their views first. But, whatever the case may be, every person (eventually) gets an equal chance to speak up until some kind of an agreement, consensus, or group cohesion is reached. This important aim is expressed by words like *simunye* ('we are one,' that is, 'unity is strength') and slogans like 'an injury to one is an injury to all' (Broodryk 1997a: 5, 7, 9).

However, the desire to agree, which – within the context of *ubuntu* – is supposed to safeguard the rights and opinions of individuals and minorities, is often exploited to enforce group solidarity. Because of its extreme emphasis on community, *ubuntu* democracy might be abused to legitimize what Themba Sono calls the 'constrictive nature' or 'tyrannical custom' of a derailed African culture, especially its 'totalitarian communalism' which 'frowns upon elevating one beyond the community' (1994: xiii, xv). The role of the group in African consciousness, says Sono, could be:

> overwhelming, totalistic, even totalitarian. Group psychology, though parochially and narrowly based ... nonetheless pretends universality. This mentality, this psychology is stronger on belief than on reason; on sameness than on difference. Discursive rationality is overwhelmed by emotional identity, by the obsession to identify with and by the longing to conform to. To agree is more important than to disagree; conformity is cherished more than innovation. Tradition is venerated, continuity revered, change feared and difference shunned. Heresies [i.e. the innovative creations of intellectual African individuals, or refusal to participate in communalism] are not tolerated in such communities.
> (1994: 7; cf. also Louw 1995)

In short, although it articulates such important values as respect, human dignity and compassion, the *ubuntu* desire for consensus also has a potential dark side in terms of which it demands an oppressive conformity and loyalty to the group. Failure to conform will be met by harsh punitive measures

(Mbigi and Maree 1995: 58; Sono 1994: 11, 17; Van Niekerk 1994: 4).

Avoiding such a derailment of *ubuntu* poses the challenge of affirming unity while valuing diversity. This challenge is at the center of the still raging debate amongst African philosophers concerning the appropriateness of Western style multi-party democracy in African societies. For example, in his plea for an African non-party polity, Kwasi Wiredu argues for a consensual democracy which draws on the strengths of traditional indigenous political institutions and which, as such, does not 'place any one group of persons consistently in the position of a minority' (1998: 375). Instead, it aims to accommodate the preferences of all participating individual citizens (note: not parties). In the same vein, Mogobe Ramose blames the 'adversarial multi-party systems of western democratic cultures' for undermining the principle of solidarity in traditional African political culture. Not that he undervalues the importance of opposition for a democratic dispensation. On the contrary, Ramose points out that 'traditional African political culture embodied and invited opposition in the very principle of consensus. Surely, one cannot speak of consensus where there is no opposition at all' (2002a: 113). In fact, one gets the idea that Ramose is not as much *against* multi-party democracy, as he is *for* the maintenance of the African solidarity principle, precisely because it safeguards the rights of individuals and minorities better than any majoritarian democracy could.

But how attainable and practicable is the solidarity or consensus at which *ubuntu* democracy aims? In this regard, Wiredu's reference to the importance of a 'willingness to compromise' and to the 'voluntary acquiescence of the momentary minority' (1998: 380) so as to allow the community to make a decision and follow a particular line of action, is significant. *Ubuntu* democracy allows for agreements to disagree, Wiredu seems to claim. Note that the minority does not simply have to put up with or passively tolerate the overriding decisions of a majority. No, the minority *agrees* to disagree, which means that their constructive input is still acknowledged or recognized in communal decisions. No wonder then that Mfuniselwa Bhengu (1996) dares to call *ubuntu* the 'essence' of democracy, in spite of its strong emphasis on solidarity and community (and therefore, seemingly, not on plurality). *Ubuntu* as an effort to reach agreement or consensus should thus not be confused with outmoded and suspect cravings for (an oppressive) universal hegemonic sameness, often associated with so-called teleological or 'modernistic' attempts at the final resolution of differences (cf. Van der Merwe 1996: 12; Van Tongeren 1998: 147; Ramose 2002a: 105, 106). True *ubuntu* takes plurality seriously. While it constitutes personhood *through other persons*, it appreciates the fact that '*other* persons' are so called precisely because we can ultimately never quite 'stand in their shoes' or completely 'see through their eyes.' When the *ubuntu*ist reads 'solidarity' and 'consensus,' s/he therefore also reads 'alterity,' 'autonomy,' and 'co-operation' (note: not 'co-optation').

Finally, in spite of all that was said in the foregoing about the *ubuntu*ist's seemingly endless pursuit of agreement and the capacity of *ubuntu* consensus to incorporate plurality, it would nevertheless be wrong to assume that a restorative, harmonious settlement of criminal cases could *always* be reached in traditional African indigenous communities. Moreover, when such settlements failed or when settlements were dishonored, restorative practices often made way for retributive measures, like blood feuds between kin groups or the 'taking up of spear' against the offender (that is, killing him/her) – which was deemed to be the victim's right amongst, for example, the Nuer of Sudan (Hoebel and Weaver 1979: 497). 'As a legal category,' claims the anthropologist and intercultural philosopher, Wim van Binsbergen, rightly, *ubuntu* 'is not

infinitely accommodating, not without boundaries' (2001: 55).

Community

Sono's warning against the derailment of *ubuntu* into totalitarian communalism (see above) is reminiscent of an important contention of postmodernist critics of restorative justice, namely that the 'community' which it aims to restore also and fundamentally involves *exclusion*. According to these critics, the restorative ideal of free and uncoerced collective association is being undermined by the tendency to fortify and preserve a given identity through limitation and segregation. As such, 'community' may easily depict xenophobia and racism; class, cultural or ethnic purity – at which point restorative justice becomes exactly 'what it opposes: a practice which closes, limits and excludes individuals, rather than reintegrating them' (Cunneen 2003: 186).

This sounds all too familiar for Africans, including (or perhaps especially) those in a traditional environment which poses the question: 'Just how inclusive is the community that *ubuntu* both describes and prescribes?' One sometimes wonders whether the *ubuntu* of traditional African societies really coincides with the 'universal law of love' it is claimed to be. At times – especially if one concentrates on the deeply religious significance of *ubuntu*, including the importance of initiation rites (more about these rites later) – one gets the impression that, in traditional societies, *ubuntu* functioned (and still functions) as a binding ethic *exclusively* within the boundaries of a specific tribe or clan. This negative impression is strengthened by *ubuntu*'s apparent potential to motivate ethnic clashes (Du Toit 2000: 30), and by the way in which some black South Africans sometimes refer to *ubuntu* as *the* definitive difference between themselves as Africans and non-Africans (including so-called 'coloreds,' Asians, and whites) (Shutte 2001: 15). Seemingly membership of the *ubuntu* community does not come easily for non-Africans or, at least, non-black Africans. As Van Binsbergen claims:

> in Africa,-*ntu* ['human,' as in *ubu-ntu* or 'human-ness' – DJL] invokes local, autochthonous humanity, by contrast to beings who somatically and historically clearly stand out as *not* autochthonous and whose very humanity therefore may be called into question, or even denied ... part of [the struggle of white persons who identified with blacks against the perceived, short-term interest of the white colonial presence] for an Africa-orientated self-definition was to be accepted, by African friends, as *muntu* ['a human'].
>
> (2001: 55–6)

Generally speaking, though, the advocates (including black African advocates) of *ubuntu* emphasize its inclusiveness. Ramose, for example, speaks of a 'family atmosphere,' that is, 'a kind of philosophical affinity and kinship among and between the different indigenous people of Africa' (2002a: 81). This claim rings true in view of one of Steve Biko's (somewhat puzzling) remarks about traditional African society. Biko claims: 'In almost all instances there was help between individuals, tribe and tribe, chief and chief, etc., even in spite of war' (1998: 28; cf. also Ramose 2002a: 119–22). These remarks underscore the fact that *ubuntu* does *not* exclusively apply within specific tribes or clans, though they may still create the impression that the *ubuntu* 'community' only refers to indigenous Africans, and therefore not to, as Van Binsbergen puts it, 'beings who somatically and historically clearly stand out as *not* autochthonous' (2001: 55). However, in his explanation of the *ubuntu* concept of 'extended family,' Johann Broodryk rectifies this impression by pointing out that 'the idea of extended family has the potential or seems to be capable of extension even beyond those related by blood, kinship or marriage to include

strangers. There is a sense in which ... humanity itself constitutes a kind of family' (2002: 98; cf. also 1997a: 14; 1997b: 70f; Shutte 2001: 29). Thus understood, *ubuntu* is on a par with the stipulations of the UN's *International Handbook on Justice for Victims* regarding the inclusivity of restorative justice. 'The framework for restorative justice,' it reads, 'involves ... the *entire* community' (as cited by Anderson 2004: 8 – italics mine).

However, *ubuntu* also moves beyond the UN's Handbook. In its fullest sense, the African concept of community transcends the society of the living. Ramose refers in this regard to the 'constant communication between the living and the living-dead ("ancestors"),' as well as to 'the triad of the living, the living-dead and the yet-to-be born' which 'forms an unbroken and infinite chain of relations' (2002a: 94). This 'indivisible whole-ness' constitutes 'the foundation of law' in *ubuntu* philosophy in so far as the authority of law depends on the approval thereof by the living-dead. The enhancement of harmony in human relations through law, so it is believed, is indicative of the fact that the living-dead gave their approval of the law in question. For Ramose, this understanding of the foundation and authority of law may mean 'that *ubuntu* philosophy of law is the continuation of religion – but not theology – by political means ... [which] ... is another way of saying that the political is always the arena of ongoing dialogue with the metaphysical' (2002a: 97; cf. also 2002b: 643).

The *ubuntu* conception of 'community' is thus more controversial than it may seem on face value. Be that as it may, it is important to note that indigenous restorative justice was traditionally applied in small, close-knit communities. This means that the victim knew the offender and thus probably still held him/her in some positive regard. The victim was therefore reluctant to take an adversarial stance towards him/her. One would expect victim offender reconciliation and mediation programs to be more effective in such a setting than in a 'faceless,' individualistic society (Sarnoff 2001: 35). Restorative practices, like the shaming of offenders (Moore and O'Connell 2003: 220–1), would also have an impact. For example, just pretending not to hear or understand an offender was often sufficient to shame his/her offence in a Khoisan community (Booyens 1980: 55–7).

Religion and the metaphysical

Ramose's reference to religion and the metaphysical (see above) resonates with the fact that, while the (European) proponents of restorative justice predominantly explains its values and virtues through a *secular* emphasis on our common humanity, the champions of *ubuntu* are not averse to religion or the metaphysical. *Ubuntu* philosophers, for example, explain the communal harmony, equilibrium or 'justice' at which *ubuntu* law aims in terms of the perpetual exchange and sharing of (invisible) forces of life:

> The altar gives something to a man [sic], and a part of what he received he passes on to others ... A small part of the sacrifice is for oneself, but the rest is for others. The forces released enter into the man, pass through him and out again, and so it is for all ... As each man gives to all the rest, so he also receives from all. A perpetual exchange goes on between men, an unceasing movement of invisible currents. And this must be so if the universal order is to endure ... for it's good to give and to receive the forces of life.
>
> (M. Griaule, as cited by Ramose 2002a: 93)

While many strands in Western Humanism tend to underestimate or even deny the importance of religious beliefs, *ubuntu* or African Humanism is resiliently religious (Prinsloo 1995: 4; 1998: 46). For the Westerner, the maxim, 'a person is a person through other persons,' has no obvious religious connotations. S/he will probably interpret it as nothing but a general appeal to treat others with respect and decency. However, in African tradition this maxim has a deeply religious meaning. The person one is to become 'through other persons' is, ultimately, an ancestor. And, by the same token, these 'other persons' include ancestors. Ancestors are extended family. Dying is an ultimate homecoming. Not only must the living therefore share with and care for each other but the living and the dead depend on each other (Ndaba 1994: 13–14; Van Niekerk 1994: 2).

This accords with the daily experience of many (traditional) Africans. For example, at a *calabash*, which is an African ritual that involves the drinking of beer (Broodryk 1997a: 16), a little bit of beer is often poured on the ground for consumption by ancestors. And, as is probably well known (yet often misunderstood), many Africans also believe in God through the mediation of ancestors (Broodryk 1997a: 15). In African society there seems to be an inextricable bond between man, ancestors and whatever is regarded as the Supreme Being. *Ubuntu* thus inevitably implies a deep respect and regard for religious beliefs and practices (Teffo 1994a: 9).

In fact, even the faintest attempt at an 'original' or indigenous understanding of *ubuntu* can hardly overlook the strong religious or quasi-religious connotations of this concept. According to traditional African thought, 'becoming a person through other persons' involves going through various community prescribed stages and being involved in certain ceremonies and initiation rituals. Before being incorporated into the body of persons through this route, one is regarded merely as an 'it,' that is, not yet a person. Not all human beings are therefore persons. Personhood is acquired (Shutte 2001: 24–5). Moreover, initiation does not only incorporate one into personhood within the community of the living but also establishes a link between the initiated and the community of the living-dead or ancestors (Ramose 2002a: 66, 71). Through circumcision and clitoridectomy blood is spilled onto the soil, a sacrifice is made which binds the initiated person

> to the land and consequently to the departed members of his [or her – DJL] society. It says that the individual is alive and that he or she now wishes to be tied to the community and people, among whom he or she has been born as a child. This circumcision blood is like making a covenant, or a solemn agreement, between the individual and his [her] people. Until the individual has gone through the operation, he [she] is still an outsider. Once he [she] has shed his [her] blood, he [she] joins the stream of his [her] people, he [she] becomes truly one with them.
>
> (J. S. Mbiti, as cited by Ramose 2002a: 71; cf. also Kimmerle 1995: 42)

However, claims regarding the religiousness of African society or, for that matter, any other claim regarding this society, are not uncontroversial, even if only because of the fact that there is not just one African society but many African societies. My claims regarding 'African society' are therefore generalizations – that is, at most, family resemblances between a plurality of (predominantly traditional sub-Saharan) African societies. Societies or cultures are in any event not monolithic, transparent, and neatly demarcated wholes. They overlap in a variety of ways. Important differences obtain inside and run across more or less discernable societies or cultures (Van der Merwe 1996: 8; 1999: 324).

Ubuntu and dialogue

This brings us to the process of dialogue as an important overlap between restorative justice and *ubuntu*. The importance of dialogue in the process of restorative justice can

hardly be overemphasized. Within this process dialogue is best understood as 'restorative communication': it fosters interpersonal reconciliation between victims and offenders, and social reconciliation between offenders and the community. It vents harmful emotions, repairs relationships, and, importantly, *challenges any stereotypes* that the partners in dialogue (that is, the victim, offender, and community) may harbor (Dzur and Wertheimer 2002: 3–7). Such dialogue epitomizes the conduct prescribed by *ubuntu*. *Ubuntu* inspires us to expose ourselves to others, to encounter the difference of their humanness so as to inform and enrich our own (Sidane 1994: 8–9). Thus understood, *umuntu ngumuntu ngabantu* translates as: 'To be human is to affirm one's humanity by recognizing the humanity of others in its infinite variety of content and form' (Van der Merwe 1996: 1). This translation of *ubuntu* attests to a respect for particularity, individuality, and historicity, without which the deconstruction of stereotypes and the healing of relationships will not materialize.

Particularity

The *ubuntu* respect for the *particularities* of the beliefs and practices of others is especially emphasized by a striking, yet (to my mind) lesser-known translation of *umuntu ngumuntu ngabantu*, namely, 'A human being is a human being through (*the otherness of*) other human beings' (Van der Merwe 1996: 1 – italics mine). For post-apartheid South Africans of all colors, creeds, and cultures, *ubuntu* dictates that, if we are to be human, we need to recognize the genuine otherness of our fellow citizens. That is, we need to acknowledge the diversity of languages, histories, values, and customs, all of which constitute South African society. For example, white South Africans tend to call all traditional African healing practices 'witchcraft,' and to label all such practitioners as 'witchdoctors.' However, close attention to

167

the particularities of these practices would have revealed that there are at least five types of doctors in traditional African societies. And of these five, witchdoctors are being singled out as possible causes of evil by Africans themselves. By contrast, the cooperation of the other traditional healers is vital in primary health care initiatives, such as AIDS education, family planning, and immunization programs (Broodryk 1997a: 15; 1997b: 74–5). In this sense, but also in a more political sense, the *ubuntu* emphasis on respect for particularity is vital for the survival of post-apartheid South Africa. In spite of our newly found democracy, civil or ethnic conflict cannot be ruled out. In fact, our multi-cultural democracy intensifies the various ethnic and socio-cultural differences. While democracy allows for legitimate claims to the institutionalization of these differences, these claims are easily exploited for selfish political gain (Van der Merwe 1996: 1).

Individuality

Ubuntu's respect for the particularity of the other links up closely to its respect for *individuality*. But note that the individuality that *ubuntu* respects is not of Cartesian making. On the contrary, *ubuntu* directly contradicts the Cartesian conception of individuality in terms of which the individual or self can be conceived without thereby necessarily conceiving the other. The Cartesian individual exists prior to, or separately and independently from the rest of the community or society. The rest of society is nothing but an added extra to a pre-existent and self-sufficient being. This 'modernistic' and 'atomistic' conception of individuality lies at the bottom of both individualism and collectivism (Macquarrie 1972: 104). Individualism exaggerates seemingly solitary aspects of human existence to the detriment of communal aspects. Collectivism makes the same mistake, only on a larger scale. For the collectivist, society is nothing but a bunch or collection of separately existing, solitary (that is, detached) individuals.

By contrast, *ubuntu* defines the individual in terms of his/her relationship with others (Shutte 1993: 46f). According to this definition, individuals only exist *in* their relationships with others, and as these relationships change, so do the characters of the individuals. Thus understood, the word 'individual' signifies a plurality of personalities corresponding to the multiplicity of relationships in which the individual in question stands. Being an individual by definition means 'being-with-others.' 'With-others,' as Macquarrie rightly observes, 'is not added on to a pre-existent and self-sufficient being; rather, both this being (the self) and the others find themselves in a whole wherein they are already related' (1972: 104). *Ubuntu* unites the self and the world in a peculiar web of reciprocal relations in which subject and object become indistinguishable, and in which 'I think, therefore I am,' is substituted for 'I participate, therefore I am' (Shutte 1993: 47). This is all somewhat boggling for the Cartesian mind, whose conception of individuality now has to move from solitary to solidarity, from independence to interdependence, from individuality vis-à-vis community to individuality à la community.

To be sure, the *ubuntu* conception of individuality does seem contradictory. *Ubuntu* claims that the self or individual is constituted by its relations with others. But if this is so, what are the relations between? Can persons and personal relations really be equally primordial (Shutte 1993: 56)? African thought addresses this (apparent) contradiction in the somewhat controversial (Kaphagawani 1998: 170–2) idea of *seriti* – that is, an energy, power or force which is claimed to both make us ourselves and unite us in personal interaction with others (Shutte 1993: 55; 1998: 434–5; 2001: 21–3). This idea allows us to see the self and others as equiprimordial or as aspects of the same universal field of force. However, as Shutte observes, this 'solution' of the contradiction posed by the *ubuntu* conception of individuality, comes at a price:

> in the perspective opened up by the African idea of the universe as a field of forces, it is difficult to see how the existing individual can have any enduring reality at all, much less how he [or she – DJL] can be possessed of the freedom and responsibility that is usually reckoned the most valuable mark of personhood.
>
> (1993: 56)

Furthermore, like the *ubuntu* desire for consensus, this inclusivist, collectivist, or communalist conception of individuality can easily derail into an oppressive collectivism or communalism. This fact has evoked various responses from African authors. For example, while he lauds the 'distinctive African' inclination towards collectivism and a collective sense of responsibility, Teffo (1994a: 7, 12) is quick to add that the African conception of man does not negate individuality. It merely discourages the view that the individual should take precedence over the community. In the same vein, Khoza (1994: 9; cf. also Prinsloo 1995: 4) challenges *ubuntu* to create a balance between complete individual autonomy and homonymy, that is, to broaden respect for the individual and purge collectivism of its negative elements. And Ndaba points out that:

> the collective consciousness evident in the African culture does not mean that the African subject wallows in a formless, shapeless or rudimentary collectivity ... [It] simply means that the African subjectivity develops and thrives in a relational setting provided by ongoing contact and interaction with others.
>
> (1994: 14)

I concur. An oppressive communalism constitutes a derailment, an abuse of *ubuntu*. By contrast, true *ubuntu* incorporates dialogue:

that is, it incorporates both relation and distance. It preserves the other in her otherness, in her uniqueness, without letting her slip into the distance (Macquarrie 1972: 110; Shutte 1993: 49, 51; Kimmerle 1995: 90–3).

Historicity

Ndaba's emphasis on the 'ongoing-ness' of the contact and interaction with others on which the African subjectivity feeds, points to a final important ingredient of the 'restorative communication' prescribed by *ubuntu*, namely respecting the *historicity* of the other. Respecting the historicity of the other means respecting his/her dynamic nature or process nature. The flexibility of the other is well noted by *ubuntu*. Or, as is sometimes claimed: 'For the [African] humanist, life is without absolutes' (Teffo 1994a: 11). An *ubuntu* perception of the other is never fixed or rigidly closed, but adjustable or open-ended. It allows the other to be, to become. It acknowledges the irreducibility of the other – that is, it never reduces the other to any specific characteristic, conduct or function. This accords with the grammar of the concept *ubuntu* which denotes both a state of being and one of becoming. As a process of self-realization *through* others, it enhances the self-realization *of* others (Broodryk 1997a: 5–7).

And again, to return briefly to the agreement or consensus that *ubuntu* both describes and prescribes, this consensus is not conceived of in fixed, ahistorical, or foundationalist terms. It is not expected to apply or remain the same always and everywhere. On the contrary, such an expectation fundamentally contradicts the African's pantareic conception of the universe – that is, his/her conception of being 'as a perpetual and universal movement of sharing and exchange of the forces of life' (Ramose 2002a: 47). When the *ubuntu*ist thus reads 'consensus,' s/he also reads 'open-endedness,' 'contingency,' and 'flux' (Louw 1999b: 401).

Concluding remarks

By highlighting the overlap between *ubuntu* and restorative justice, I meant to show exactly why *ubuntu* might be used to explain, motivate or underscore such justice, or why *ubuntu* could add a distinctly African flavor and momentum to it. However, my argument will hold water only if what has been described here as a distinctly African philosophy and way of life, does in fact exist as such. Do Africans in fact adhere to *ubuntu* or, at least, aspire to do so? And if so, is *ubuntu* uniquely or exclusively African?

These are controversial issues. For example, until recently, in the South African province of KwaZulu-Natal (where *ubuntu* is claimed to be part of every day life), violent ethnic and political clashes occurred frequently – and this is surely not the only example of such clashes on the continent of Africa! How can this be reconciled with *ubuntu* (cf. Broodryk 1997a: 10)?

The apparent anomaly posed by the occurrence of such violent conflicts significantly fades once one concentrates on the many counter examples. African examples of caring and sharing, and of forgiving and reconciliation abound (though you will seldom read about them in the papers or see them on cable news). The relatively nonviolent transition of the South African society from a totalitarian state to a multiparty democracy is not merely the result of the compromising negotiations of politicians. It is also – perhaps primarily – the result of the emergence of an ethos of solidarity, a commitment to peaceful coexistence amongst ordinary South Africans in spite of their differences (Van der Merwe 1996: 1). *Ubuntu*, argues Teffo (1994a) rightly (though he risks overstatement), pervasively serves as a cohesive moral value in the face of adversity. Although the policy of apartheid greatly damaged the overwhelming majority of black South Africans:

there is no lust for vengeance, no apocalyptic retribution ... A yearning for justice, yes, and for release from poverty and oppression, but no dream of themselves becoming the persecutors, of turning the tables of apartheid on white South Africans ... The ethos of *ubuntu* ... is one single gift that African philosophy can bequeath on other philosophies of the world.

> (Teffo 1994a: 5)

Maphisa agrees:

South Africans are slowly re-discovering their common humanity. Gone are the days when people were stripped of their dignity (*ubuntu*) through harsh laws. Gone are the days when people had to use *ubulwane* [that is, animal-like behaviour – DJL] to uphold or reinforce those laws ... the transformation of an apartheid South Africa into a democracy is a re-discovery of *ubuntu*.

> (1994: 8; cf. also Shutte 2001: 3, 33)

These observations would probably not make much sense to the bereaved families of the victims of political violence. I do not mean to insult those who suffer the growing pains of a new South African society. I respect their pain and share their anger and frustration. *Ubuntu* is a given, but clearly also *a task*. *Ubuntu* is part and parcel of Africa's cultural heritage. But it obviously needs to be revitalized in our hearts and minds (Teffo 1995: 2; Koka 1997: 15).

In fact, I have been speaking of *ubuntu* primarily as an ethical ideal – that is, something that still needs to be realized, although encouraging examples thereof already exist (Shutte 2001: 32–3). Moreover, my deliberations on *ubuntu* should not be viewed as an ahistorical ethical blueprint, nor as a precise reflection of the value orientations and practices of precolonial (Southern) African villages (Van Binsbergen 2001: 53). The conception of *ubuntu* that I have been developing is admittedly a provisional re-evaluation or reinterpretation of an inherited traditional notion. Some may even want to claim that I have been enslaving the African Other through Eurocentric, neo-colonialist (re)definition. If so, then it should be viewed as the, perhaps inevitable, off-spin of an honest effort to understand and effectively apply a pre-modern inheritance in a postmodern world deeply suspicious of the consensus principle and with very different notions of solidarity (Louw 2002: 20). It is, in any event, impossible to restore the so-called 'original' version of *ubuntu*. Our account of *ubuntu* can at best be an innovative reconstruction – that is, a narration or, in this peculiar sense, 'myth.' But, whatever the 'original' version of *ubuntu* might have been, surely the more important question has to be: given the current call and need for an African Renaissance, how should *ubuntu* be understood and utilized for the common good of *all* Africans, and of the world at large (Shutte 2001: 14; Ramose 2002a: 107–8)? The ideal of an African Renaissance calls for critical re-readings of existing narratives of reconciliation and reintegration, including the *ubuntu* narrative. It does *not* call for the romanticization of an indigenous past or socio-legal rituals (Shutte 2001: 33; Daly 2003: 367).

In what sense, if any, is *ubuntu* then uniquely African? Is *ubuntu* only part of the *African* cultural heritage? Just how distinctly African is the flavor and momentum that *ubuntu* could add to the decolonization of the other? Is the ethos of *ubuntu* in fact the 'one single gift that African philosophy can bequeath on other philosophies of the world' (Teffo 1994a: 5)?

It would be ethnocentric and, indeed, silly to suggest that the *ubuntu* ethic of caring and sharing is uniquely African. After all, the values which *ubuntu* seeks to promote can also be traced in various Eurasian philosophies (Van Binsbergen 2001: 65–6). This is not to deny the intensity with which these values are given expression by Africans. But the mere fact that they are intensely expres-

sed by Africans does not in itself make these values exclusively African.

However, although compassion, warmth, understanding, caring, sharing, humanness, etc., are underscored by all the major worldviews, ideologies and religions of the world, I would nevertheless like to suggest that *ubuntu* serves as a *distinctly African rationale* for these ways of relating to others. The concept of *ubuntu* gives a distinctly African meaning to, and a reason or motivation for, a restorative attitude towards the other. As such, it adds a crucial *African appeal* to the call for restorative justice – an appeal without which this call might well go unheeded by many Africans (Mphahlele, 1974: 36; Ndaba, 1994: 18–19; Prinsloo 1998: 48–9). In this, and only in this peculiar sense, the restorative justice that is *ubuntu* is of Africans, by Africans, and for Africans.

References

Anderson, A. M. (2004) '*Restorative justice, the African philosophy of "ubuntu" and the diversion of criminal prosecution,*' paper presented at the 17th International Conference of the International Society for the Reform of Criminal Law, The Hague, 24–28 August. Available at: http://www.isrcl.org [accessed 1 March 2005].

Bhengu, M. J. (1996) *Ubuntu: the essence of democracy*, Cape Town: Novalis Press.

Biko, S. (1998) 'Some African cultural concepts,' in P. H. Coetzee and A. P. J. Roux (eds) *Philosophy from Africa: a text with readings*, Johannesburg: International Thomson Publishing.

Boele van Hensbroek, P. (1998) 'African political philosophy, 1860–1995: an inquiry into three families of discourse,' unpublished dissertation, University of Groningen.

Booyens, J. H. (1980) *Die San en Khoisan vandag*, Potchefstroom: Pro Rege.

Broodryk, Johann (1995) 'Is Ubuntuism unique?,' in J. G. Malherbe (ed.) *Decolonizing the Mind*, Pretoria: Research Unit for African Philosophy, UNISA.

— (1997a) *Ubuntu Management and Motivation*, Johannesburg: Gauteng Department of Welfare/Pretoria: Ubuntu School of Philosophy.

— (1997b) 'Ubuntuism as a worldview to order society,' DLitt thesis, University of South Africa (UNISA).

— (2002) *Ubuntu: life lessons from Africa*, Pretoria: Ubuntu School of Philosophy.

Cunneen, C. (2003) 'Thinking critically about restorative justice,' in E. McLaughlin and R. Fergusson (eds) *Restorative Justice: critical issues*, London: Sage.

Daly, K. (2003) 'Restorative justice: the real story,' in G. Johnstone, *A Restorative Justice Reader: texts, sources, context*, Cullompton, Devon (UK): Willan Publishing.

Du Toit, C. W. (2000) 'Roots of violence: is a South African common good possible?' in C. W. du Toit (ed.) *Violence, Truth and Prophetic Silence*, UNISA, Pretoria: Research Institute for Theology and Religion.

Dzur, A. W. and Wertheimer, A. (2002) 'Forgiveness and public deliberation: the practice of restorative justice,' *Criminal Justice Ethics*, Winter/Spring: 3–20.

Goduka, M. I. and Swadener, B. B. (1999) *Affirming Unity in Diversity in Education: healing with Ubuntu*, Cape Town: Juta.

Hoebel, E. A. and Weaver, T. (1979) *Anthropology and the Human Experience*, fifth edn, New York: McGraw-Hill.

Johnstone, G. (2003) *A Restorative Justice Reader: texts, sources, context*, Cullompton, Devon, UK: Willan Publishing.

Kaphagawani, D. N. (1998) 'African conceptions of personhood and intellectual identities,' in P. H. Coetzee and A. P. J. Roux (eds.) *Philosophy from Africa: a text with readings*, Johannesburg: International Thomson Publishing.

Khoza, R. (1994) *African Humanism*, Soweto, Johannesburg: Ekhaya Promotions.

Kimmerle, H. (1995) *Mazungumzo: dialogen tussen Afrikaanse en Westerse filosofieën*, Amsterdam: Boom.

Koka, Kgalushi K. (1996) *Ubuntu: a peoples' humanness*, Midrand: The Afrikan Study Programme/Pretoria: Ubuntu School of Philosophy.

— (1997) *The Afrikan Renaissance*, Midrand: The Afrikan Study Programme/Pretoria: Ubuntu School of Philosophy.

Lenaka, J. (1995) *Some Misconceptions about Cultural Differences: intercultural communication*, Pretoria: Ubuntu School of Philosophy.

Louw, D. J. (1995) 'Decolonization as postmodernization,' in J. G. Malherbe (ed.) *Decolonizing the Mind*, Pretoria: Research Unit for African Philosophy, UNISA.

— (1999a) 'Ubuntu: an African assessment of the religious Other,' *Noesis: Philosophical Research Online*. Available at: http://noesis.evansville.edu/Author_Index/L/Louw,_-Dirk_J./ [accessed 1 March 2005].

— (1999b) 'Towards a decolonized assessment of the religious other,' *South African Journal of Philosophy*, 18(4): 390–407.

— (2001) 'Ubuntu and the challenges of multiculturalism in post-apartheid South Africa,' *Quest: An African Journal of Philosophy*, XV(1–2): 15–36.

— (2002) *Ubuntu and the Challenges of Multiculturalism in Post-Apartheid South Africa*, Utrecht: Center for Southern Africa, Utrecht University.

Macquarrie, J. (1972) *Existentialism*, London: Penguin Books.

Maphisa, S. (1994) *Man in Constant Search of Ubuntu: a dramatist's obsession*, Pretoria: Ubuntu School of Philosophy.

Mbigi, L. (1995) *Ubuntu: a rainbow celebration of cultural diversity*, Pretoria: Ubuntu School of Philosophy.

Mbigi, L. and Maree, J. (1995) *Ubuntu. the spirit of African transformation management*, Randburg: Knowledge Resources.

Mokgoro, Y. (1998) '*Ubuntu* and the law in South Africa', *Potchefstroom Electronic Law Journal (PER)* (1): 51–5. Available at: http://www.puk.ac.za/law/per/per.htm [accessed 1 March 2005].

Moore, D. B. and O'Connell, T. A. (2003) 'Family conferencing in Wagga Wagga: a communitarian model of justice,' in G. Johnstone, *A Restorative Justice Reader: texts, sources, context*, Cullompton, Devon (UK): Willan Publishing.

More, M. P. (1996) 'Philosophy for Africa,' *South African Journal of Philosophy*, 15(4): 152–4.

Mphahlele, E. (1974) *The African Image*, London: Faber and Faber.

Ndaba, W. J. (1994) *Ubuntu in Comparison to Western Philosophies*, Pretoria: Ubuntu School of Philosophy.

Pityana, N. B. (1999) 'The renewal of African moral values,' in M. W. Makgoba (ed.) *African Renaissance: the new struggle*, Sandton: Mafube; Cape Town: Tafelberg.

Prinsloo, E. D. (1994) *Ubuntu: in search of a definition*, Pretoria: Ubuntu School of Philosophy.

— (1995) *Ubuntu from a Eurocentric and Afrocentric Perspective and its Influence on Leadership*, Pretoria: Ubuntu School of Philosophy.

— (1998) 'Ubuntu culture and participatory management,' in P. H. Coetzee and A. P. J. Roux (eds) *Philosophy from Africa: a text with readings*, Johannesburg: International Thomson Publishing.

Ramose, M. B. (2002a) *African Philosophy Through Ubuntu*, revised edn, Harare: Mond Books.

— (2002b) 'Globalization and *ubuntu*,' in P. H. Coetzee and A. P. J. Roux (eds) *Philosophy from Africa: a text with readings*, second edn, Cape Town: Oxford University Press Southern Africa.

Roche, D. (2003) *Accountability in Restorative Justice*, Oxford: Oxford University Press.

Sarnoff, S. (2001) 'Restoring justice to the community: a realistic goal?' *Federal Probation*, 65(1): 33–9.

Shutte, A. (1993) *Philosophy for Africa*, Rondebosch, South Africa: UCT Press.

— (1998) 'African and European philosophising: Senghor's "Civilization of the Universal,"' in P. H. Coetzee and A. P. J. Roux (eds) *Philosophy from Africa: a text with readings*, Johannesburg: International Thomson Publishing.

— (2001) *Ubuntu: an ethic for a new South Africa*, Pietermaritzburg: Cluster Publications.

Sidane, J. (1994) *Ubuntu and Nation Building*, Pretoria: Ubuntu School of Philosophy.

— (1995) 'Democracy in African societies and *ubuntu*,' *In Focus* 3(3): 1–16.

Sono, T. (1994) *Dilemmas of African Intellectuals in South Africa*, Pretoria: UNISA.

South African Government (1997) 'White Paper for Social Welfare.' Available at: http://www.welfare.gov.za/Documents/1997/wp.htm [accessed 1 March 2005].

Teffo, L. J. (1994a) *The Concept of Ubuntu as a Cohesive Moral Value*, Pretoria: Ubuntu School of Philosophy.

— (1994b) *Towards a Conceptualization of Ubuntu*, Pretoria: Ubuntu School of Philosophy.

— (1995) *Resume of Ubuntu/Botho*, Pretoria: Ubuntu School of Philosophy.

Teffo, L. J. and Roux, Abraham P. J. (2002) 'Themes in African metaphysics,' in P. H. Coetzee and A. P. J. Roux (eds) *Philosophy from Africa: a text with readings*, second edn, Cape Town: Oxford University Press Southern Africa.

Van Binsbergen, W. (2001) 'Ubuntu and the globalisation of Southern African thought and society,' *Quest: An African Journal of Philosophy*, XV(1–2): 53–89.

Van der Merwe, W. L. (1996) 'Philosophy and the multi-cultural context of (post)apartheid South Africa,' *Ethical perspectives*, 3(2): 1–15.

— (1999) 'Cultural relativism and the recognition of cultural differences,' *South African Journal of Philosophy*, 18(3): 313–30.

Van Niekerk, A. (1994) *Ubuntu and Religion*, Pretoria: Ubuntu School of Philosophy.

Van Tongeren, P. (1998) 'Multiculturaliteit, identiteit en tolerantie,' in J. Gruppelaar and J.-P. Wils (eds) *Multiculturalisme*, CEKUN Boekenreeks 3, Best: DAMON.

Wiredu, K. (1998) 'Democracy and consensus in African traditional politics: a plea for a non-party polity,' in P. H. Coetzee and A. P. J. Roux (eds) *Philosophy from Africa*, Johannesburg: International Thomson Publishing.

10

Spiritual foundations of restorative justice

Michael L. Hadley

Restorative justice is at root a deeply spiritual process of transformation: of persons, situations, and even institutions. Drawing on spiritual values, it responds to human needs holistically in order to restore the moral bond of community. It involves recognizing justice not solely in terms of forensic and adversarial legal processes alone, but in terms of restoration, healing and peace. Militating against this approach is the fact that 'there is, unfortunately, no coherent understanding of justice in the modern world,' though indeed one finds practical agreement on enforceable concepts of Law and Order (De Gruchy 2002: 200). Exacerbating this lack of agreement are two global value-systems which themselves operate with religious force: consumerism and redemptive violence. Consumerism, the religion of the market-place, dehumanizes by promoting the commodification of all things, even human persons. According to this view, the value of everything is ultimately reducible to money (Loy 1997). Closely linked with this is what Wink (1998) regards as the most dominant religion today: redemptive violence. On both the interpersonal and international stages, its adherents live out the catechism that violence alone can solve human problems.

Both these value systems promote an aggressive and confrontational culture of winners and losers, and peace through conflict and strife (Wink 1998; Hadley 2004). They influence our understandings of justice and shape our responses to crime. But they run counter to the religious and spiritual foundations of restorative justice.

Historically, the relationship between law and religion has been very close. For example, we can speak of the Torah of the Hebrew Bible as 'the wedding or interweaving of religion and law, that is, religion understood primarily in the categories of law, or law understood as the epitome or summation of religion, its essential expression' (Freedman 1985: 316). By implication, the law (*halakhah*) translates 'the Torah's master narrative into the design for Israel's social order by articulating the implicit lessons that Scripture's stories yield and framing those lessons in terms of public policy and conduct' (Goldberg 1989: 232). In the case of both Hindu and Muslim traditions as well, every legal prescription has a religious dimension. Further, undergirding the evolution of the Western legal tradition – a fact largely ignored or unrecognized today – is the 'more fundamental belief in God as a God of judgment and of justice and of law'

(Berman 1983: 12). Writing on justice as sanctuary, Bianchi sheds light on the relevance of religion to justice issues.

> Crime control has generally been based on religious justifications of some kind; that being the case, it is much better to trace these religious concepts and use them for a better conception than to allow them to float in our unconscious, where they will do more harm than good.
>
> (Bianchi 1994: ix)

Of course, religious belief is in itself no guarantee of morality. Religious convictions can lead to ugly encounters and govern oppressive regimes and policies. For that reason scholars point out a critical corrective: 'the litmus test of any religiosity right across the board in all major religions is that it must result in practically expressed compassion' (Armstrong 2004: A6). Compassion is a common theme in the thought of those engaged in multifaith reflection on criminal justice. The critical test of the genuineness of religion or spirituality is the degree to which it commits itself to compassion and mercy, to peace with justice. In other words, 'the true function of religion is to evoke disclosures of love and wisdom,' and to 'transform the believer's life to make it a vehicle of that love and wisdom' (Ward 1991: 68).

This is the context in which faith traditions play a major role in restorative justice and in the process of restoration. More than any other spiritual culture, they have committed themselves to a covenant of justice, peace, and the integrity of Creation. This holds true no matter how far individual sects or denominations may have veered from original principles: accountability, repentance (or radical change of direction), forgiveness, compassion, and reconciliation. Too often, religious traditions themselves have undervalued – even undermined and distorted – their own transforming wisdom. Where they could have served as a means of grace, they have all too frequently sided with the dominant power-political interests of the political state. Where they might have promoted peace with a transformative and healing justice, they have insisted on Law and Order. Primarily because of this negative legacy, many observers tend to prefer the term 'spirituality' when discussing current religious experience or when seeking the life-enhancing truths of religious tradition (Hinnells 1998). As the Dalai Lama understands these distinctions, religion is 'concerned with faith in the claims to salvation of one faith tradition or another,' as well as with adherence to creeds and liturgies as a means to spiritual discipline (Dalai Lama 1999: 22). Spirituality he regards as 'concerned with those qualities of the human spirit – such as love and compassion, patience, tolerance, forgiveness, contentment, a sense of responsibility, a sense of harmony – which bring happiness to both self and others.' In short, as King explains,

> spirituality has become a universal code word to indicate the human search for direction and meaning, for wholeness and transcendence. In contemporary secular society spirituality is being rediscovered as a lost or at least hidden dimension in a largely materialistic world.
>
> (King 1997: 667)

The context for this re-discovery is both an immanent and transcendent reality, for our 'universe is a value-realizing emergent totality [and] within that totality human persons have their proper role to play in realizing such values' (Ward 1991: 147). This means that spiritual values are not random, but rather 'an intuition of the inner tendency of the whole physical system of the cosmos to move towards the realization of conscious value, self-knowledge and self-direction.' In this light, Ward insists, 'religion is the quest for the meaning and purpose of the whole cosmic process, and for the role we can play within it.'

One striking feature of recent multifaith reflection on crime and criminal justice systems has been the 're-appropriation' of traditions (Hadley 2000). This has meant digging back through the layers of custom, habit, and convention in order to find the spiritual roots of the faith. This has nothing to do with a back-to-the-basics mentality, with its largely ideological, retributive stance. Thus scholars of Islam and Christianity – religions widely regarded as ultra-conservative, judgmental, and unforgiving – are rediscovering and re-enunciating gospels of reconciliation and restoration. Likewise Chinese scholars, under the shadow of modern China's harsh justice system, have re-examined the classical traditions of Confucianism, Taoism, and Moism; by doing so they too have retraced new possibilities for criminal justice reform. Aboriginal thinkers as well are becoming articulate in sharing their rediscovered spirituality. Long on the periphery of mainstream Western thought, they are reminding us of a peace that heals. More importantly, representatives of these traditions are showing us how this actually works in the criminal justice system. Healing Circles, Sweat Lodges, Family Group Conferencing, Victim Offender Mediation are but some of the creative variations on this theme.

In short, multifaith interdisciplinary dialogue among scholars and justice officials, between former victims and offenders, is creating space for new dynamics and new ways of seeing old truths. Of course, sociological and psychological perspectives continue to provide valuable empirical insights into justice issues. But they necessarily omit from their reflections the diagnoses of the human condition which religious traditions claim to provide. As studies on the re-appropriation of religious traditions suggest, a 'return to the teachings,' to borrow the title of a study on Aboriginal spirituality and justice, promises a clear focus on the theme of order in cosmos, nature, and society (Ross 1996). Drawing on a system of related traditions, Murray's deeply meditated, analytical study reminds us:

> biblical religious thought enshrines supremely important ideas and ideals of *order*: the order of God's creation, displayed both in the whole cosmos and in nature on earth; peace and justice in the relationships of humankind, as between nations, parts of society and individuals, and again between humans and animals; right thinking (wisdom) and right worship.
>
> (Murray 1992: 172)

This 'cosmic covenant,' as he calls it, 'is not uniform but is a complex of models.' Here we must remind ourselves of the centrality of metaphor in our modes of thought and expression. The striking image of a cosmic covenant suggests, among other things, the dynamic reciprocity between rights and obligations, between individual and community. It suggests as well that genuine order is not a system imposed by political fiat but rather a 'just and harmonious relationship' between human beings, and by extension between everything in the created world. And this is so, as Tutu reminds us, because

> this universe has been constructed in such a way that unless we live in accordance with its moral laws we will pay a price. And one such law is that we are bound together in what the bible calls the 'bundle of life.' Our humanity is caught up in that of others. We are human because we belong. We are made for community, for togetherness, for family, to exist in a delicate network of interdependence.
>
> (Tutu 1999: 154)

In short, we live in a moral universe.

Central to theological reflection on crime is a critical principle: religious traditions continue to shape human reality and experience and are therefore central to social dialogue and social cohesion. The tremendous creative energy these traditions have released is a matter of historical record (Hinnells 1998: 3). Many who insist on the primacy of the secular state suggest that this role should be diminished. Religion, they argue, is really a purely private matter that must not be allowed to encroach on public policy debates. Religion deserves only a marginal role at best. For the sake of democratic processes and fairness to all sectors of the public, they insist, religion must be marginalized, simply because the body politic is both secular and pluralistic. Yet by arguing so, secular society forgets that secularism itself is in fact only one part of that plurality (Marshall 1991). Political states are shared by faith traditions and religious cultures as well; they are permeated by them. At the very least, we need reminding of the foundational role these traditions have played throughout history, and which they continue to play in envisioning the good life and civil society. The strict application of the principle of excluding religion from public life would have prohibited not only Martin Luther King Jr's dream from American politics; it would also have blocked the work of the Truth and Reconciliation Commission in South Africa. Moreover, it would have excluded the profound social revolutions these visions triggered (Forrester 1997: 30). Religion, in short, cannot be compartmentalized for political purposes, if only because each tradition

> shapes not only particular questions of right and wrong but also basic questions about the nature of reality – what human nature is, what sin is and how it is manifested, what the nature and direction of history is, what law is, what idolatry is, and what the root meaning of human life is.
> (Marshall 1991: 1–9)

These questions 'involve matters of epistemology, historical causality, jurisprudence, social structure, psychological variation' and are rooted in 'the core of culture, and also at the core of faith' (Marshall 1991: 1–9).

Culture and faith are intricately interwoven and express themselves outwardly in the experience of a community of 'ultimate concern.' This is one of the major characteristics of faith traditions that distinguish them from secular cultures and fraternal organizations. Spiritual cultures nurture a transcendental dimension and tend to be communal, whereas secular cultures tend to be individualistic and insist on the primacy of Self over society. This distinction proves crucial in dealing with justice issues. For where the retributive model of conventional justice depends on an adversarial approach that splits community, and does so for the express purpose of ascertaining guilt and assigning punishment, the restorative model relies on the communal approach with a view to healing the harms caused by crime and fostering the reintegration of the offender. Conventional justice is rights based; it provides legal justice, and is monocultural. Restorative justice, by contrast, is based on responsibilities; it provides moral justice and is multicultural. The restorative model, as we will see, finds its natural home in the holistic concepts of religious cultures. This is so despite their diversity; and even despite the diversity of emphases within the historical and cultural experience of any one faith tradition.

What sustains and nurtures the spiritual tradition is its plausibility and consistency in the face of human experience – a factor enhanced by encounter with conflict. In time, of course, the deeply experienced realities and profoundly contemplated notions of a few pioneers may become the unexamined axioms of a whole cultural tradition, and be in need of re-appropriation. Such rediscoveries of spiritual truths will themselves be expressed metaphorically, most importantly in new metaphors, for we embrace our values not according to dictionary definitions but in terms of whole realms or domains of experience (Lakoff and Johnson 1980: 117). Thus, whether we understand life as a journey or a trial will depend not only on how we experience life but also upon the values and experiences associated with journeys and trials. Likewise, whether we envision justice as the Blind-folded Goddess with a set of balances in her hand or as a healing circle of family members will depend upon the values and experiences associated with them.

In a real sense, 'every culture has to create its own idea of God' (Armstrong 1993: 118). That is, every culture must create the metaphors that best embody – and communicate – its experiences of ultimate concern. The metaphors we live by reveal our relationship to the truths of our experi-ence. In this process, revelation, prophecy, and inspiration claim their part, as does the existential experience of living in human society. Here, the key is relationships. Speaking of human rights abuses De Gruchy explains the significance of restorative or covenantal justice: these have to do 'with renewing God's covenant, and therefore the establishing of just power relations without which reconciliation remains elusive'(De Gruchy 2002: 204). Reflecting on South Africa's Truth and Reconciliation Com-mission, he points out that it is 'only as we seek to restore the power relationships that have been broken by human rights abuses that we really lay the necessary foundations for preventing further abuses and enabling healing.'

The holistic world of First Nations' tradi-tions in North America is a case in point. Through its myths, legends, ceremonies, and spiritual practices Aboriginal cosmology reveals a hierarchy of Creation with its inherent dependencies and interdependencies. Recognizing the interconnectedness of all things – the organic and inorganic, the human and non-human – Aboriginals experience their world in terms of relation-ships, or in terms of what Ross (1996) has called 'fluid reality.' For the Gitxsan people, for example, Creation consists of a spiritual continuum that pervades even everyday life. Thus humans participate in an ongoing cycle throughout history that includes non-human life-forms and the whole physical universe. All events, even crime itself, are a communal responsibility simply because they arise out of relationships (Napoleon 1997). In the words of Sakéj Youngblood Henderson, director of the Native Law Centre of the University of Saskatchewan, 'Indigenous people view reality as eternal, but in a continuous state of transformation ... It is consistent with the scientific view that all matter can be seen as energy, shaping itself to particular patterns' (Ross 1996: 115). The nature of Creation is fundamentally spiritual and can ultimately only be understood in spiritual terms. As will be seen, this point is crucial for under-standing the dynamics of the healing process when dealing with offences against both persons and community. Both as metaphor and symbol, the circle plays a central role in ritual; it serves to bind individuals in com-munity with time past, time present, and time future.

Typical of the close spiritual affinities within faith communities is the concept of *ubuntu* central to Aboriginal cultures of South Africa. Significantly, principal themes in African theology emphasize values such as community solidarity and inclusiveness that are frequently neglected by many practi-tioners of Westernized faith traditions (Stuart 1997: 697). African holistic views embrace conceptions of illness and health, good and evil. The social and spiritual dynamic of *ubuntu* proved a key to the healing process undertaken by the Truth and Reconciliation Commission in the aftermath of the apartheid crises (South Africa, Truth and Reconciliation Commis-sion 1999). With no exact equivalent in other languages, *ubuntu* describes the very essence of being human: compassion, gen-erosity, caring, interrelated to one another in community, affirming the dignity of others. It recognizes that each of us is 'a person through other people.' Where the Western tradition might insist on the Descartian 'I think therefore I am,' *ubuntu* insists that 'I am a human because I belong' (Tutu 1999: 35). Or, as another African theologian expressed it, 'I am related, therefore we are' (Dedji 2000). In the deepest existential context of *ubuntu*, no person is ever isolated. Of striking importance, *ubuntu* means that harms impact upon the whole social fabric of a culture, leaving no one untouched. In the case of apartheid, even the perpetrators of crimes were victims of the vicious system they spawned. By dehumanizing others, they dehumanized themselves as well.

Ubuntu accords strikingly with the Navajo of North America and the Maori of New Zealand. Maori justice, for example, is completely integrated into the communal life and does not constitute a separate authority which intrudes when needed for public order. It has always been 'a way of doing justice built on the belief that socially harmful behavior (*hara*) whether of a civil or criminal nature in Western terms, had been caused by an imbalance to the social equilibrium' (Pratt 1996: 138). Likewise, Navajo legal thinking teaches

> that law is not a process to punish or penalize people, but to teach them how to live a better life. It is a healing process that either restores good relationships among people or, if they do not have good relations to begin with, fosters and nourishes a healthy environment.
>
> (Yazzie and Zion 1996: 160)

Holistic patterns similar to those found in Aboriginal oral traditions are witnessed in mainstream religions. Judaism, for example, speaks of the sanctity of people in a universe where God places upon each individual the responsibility for working toward the completion of His Creation. God expects each one to be a prophet – that is, to speak God's Word. Unlike the oral traditions, it draws its strength from revealed scriptures that are mediated and interpreted by historical tradition. Through theological reflection in terms of life's experiences, as well as through the interplay between Sacred Scripture and oral traditions, Judaism is a vibrant and diverse faith that encompasses the whole of life. Reflection on these laws and traditions provides, among other things, a means of imposing a pattern of disciplined self-respect. Judaism sees a world in which no human being is a 'throw-away' person; it is a world in which no one is born 'in sin,' but rather 'with choice.' This is important for restorative justice initiatives, which seek healing and reconciliation. In this system, whoever is not involved in alleviating human need is not living a full life. The ultimate goal of Jewish law is to achieve a harmony among persons and with God. For many adherents in this tradition, justice is inseparable from spirituality; or, in the graphic expression of the eminent eleventh-century thinker Rashi, 'a court house should not be far from a synagogue' (Lerman 1998: 2).

This rich Judaic tradition forms the seedbed in which Christianity is rooted. Both here and in the Christian Gospels we encounter Christianity's original – but often forgotten – message of compassion, love, and liberation. Human beings, according to Christians, have been created 'in the image of God,' and set in an ultimately meaningful and purposeful universe. The spiritual and social community – the *ecclesia* – is understood as a living organic relationship with God through Jesus, the Christ. This means, in the metaphor of St Paul's letter to the Christians in Corinth, that each person functions like a specialized organ in a living body; and this body is the spiritual, redemptive community. The health of every member or organ is vital for the health of the whole body. Each individual human being has unique value; each individual is seen as endowed with special qualities and talents, all of which are necessary to the well-being of Creation. These concepts are central to principles of justice. Importantly, human beings are born with free will, and can therefore choose between good and evil. In free will lies the potential for causing moral evil. Significantly, however, the Christian way is pre-eminently restorative, for Jesus Himself preached the revolutionary ethic of repentance, forgiveness, non-violence, reconciliation, and love for each human individual. As we read in Jesus' Sermon on the Mount as recorded in St Matthew's gospel (Matthew 5: 1–48): 'Blessed are the merciful ... Blessed are the peacemakers.' The term 'gospel' means 'Good News.' Though much of what passes for Christianity appears to negate this 'Good News,' the message of peace and reconciliation is nonetheless clear and unequivocal.

Like Christianity and Judaism, Islam is rooted in the Abrahamic tradition. The term 'Islam' means submission: submission to the will of Allah, the 'Compassionate' and 'Merciful' Creator and Ruler of all. It is a holistic system of paths, the *shari'ah*; it is at root not so much a catechism of beliefs, as it is a way of living according to Divine precept as inspired by the revelations received by the Prophet Muhammed and recorded in the sacred Qur'an. Islam holds that God has a universal and generous plan for the salvation of all nations. Like the other spiritual traditions, Islam too has been subject to far-reaching self-criticism. Thus what passes in the public eye for a militant, harsh, unforgiving, and antifeminist religion is arguably not the Islam of the Qur'an but the un-Qur'anic result of historical, cultural, and political processes. Islamic law is a product of specific cultures in response to specific historical issues and conditions, and is therefore not a unified, monolithic body of legislation. For example, scholars have distinguished two principal versions of Islam: the one is the culturally determined, repressive social order that nurtures privilege and injustice, and which preoccupies the media; the other, lesser known in the West, is the authentic version – which envisions a humane, compassionate, and all-embracing social order (Ahmad 1997). For this

authentic version the nature of God forms the foundation. From Him human nature and human society ideally derive. As the Qur'an repeatedly proclaims, Allah Himself is the Compassionate, the Merciful. Like Christianity, Islam sees the potential for moral evil to lie in mankind's free will. Thus where Allah 'permits' the possibility of choosing evil, he may also 'restore' the harms that evil causes by redeeming the doer. 'If anyone does evil or wrongs his own soul, but afterwards seeks Allah's forgiveness, he will find Allah oft-Forgiving, most Merciful' (al-Nisa: 110). Or again: 'If you stretch your hand against me, to slay me, it is not for me to stretch my hand against thee: for I do fear Allah, God of the universe' (al-Maidah: 28). Keys to restorative processes lie not only in the Qur'an itself but in the complex relationships between individual and community. To this end, 'many Muslims are harkening back to their spiritual roots in search of identity, meaning and self-fulfillment' (Khan 2004). They are being supported by such reformers as the charismatic Egyptian Amr Khaled and his female counterpart in Pakistan, Farhat Hasmi. Khaled 'presents a face of Islamic piety rarely found in the Middle East' by teaching a faith both compassionate and relevant to daily life and asserting a Muslim spiritual identity in harmony with the modern world. Central for him are principles of humility and mercy. Likewise, Hashmi offers a message of personal spiritual reform that emphasizes the principles of God's mercy and forgiveness. In returning to their teachings, such voices underscore the unique spiritual foundation from which all other considerations and actions flow.

Hinduism as well claims a purposeful Creation, an objective universal order, of which spiritual and social realities are vital expressions. For Hindus the world is not a random product of diverse, fortuitous elements, and for precisely that reason the Hindu understanding of interrelationships is of critical importance. The concept of *dharma* – 'Sacred Law,' 'duty,' 'justice,' and 'religious or moral merit' – is key among them. Like *karma* – the objective law of moral cause and effect – *dharma* is one of the most comprehensive and wide-ranging terms in Sanskrit literature, and in religious ritual deals with issues of behavior, justice, repentance, and atonement (Narayanan 2001). In some contexts *dharma* is seen as co-extensive with – as sharing a spectrum of experience with – ultimate liberation (*moksha*). It is in the context of such principles as *karma*, *dharma*, and *moksha* that we are to understand the full range of spiritual and social obligations. These include the relationship between crime, punishment, penance, and grace. Significantly, penance has a function beyond repentance and making recompense in interpersonal relations. It is not merely a matter of 'making things right' again in the social context. Ultimately, penance is intended to re-harmonize the offender with the eternal order of being. Though sometimes violent and brutal, penances have the function of expiating for even the most heinous crimes. They have the potential for liberating and restoring individuals. In this light, penance is seen as an attempt at reparation and restoration. On one level it is an attempt to restore the social order while on another restoring the offender to his or her place in that order. Of central importance to the devotional traditions of Hinduism – traditions followed by the masses of Hindus – is the experience of grace, forgiveness, and compassion which these traditions encapsulate and embody. As in other theologies, grace here is a free gift from God. If classical Hinduism in all its variety seems more concerned with spiritual processes than charitable works, it has shown remarkable capacity for engagement in social activism through the example of such spiritual leaders as Swami Vivekananda (1863–1902) and Mahatma Gandhi (1868–1948). Their engagement in practical concerns grew out of their deeply meditated insights into the richness of Hindu tradition.

Like other theistic traditions, Sikhism too insists on Creation as an objective ultimate Reality. The God of the Sikhs is a merciful God. Thus, because of the moral and spiritual universe they experience and the profound witness of their founder, Guru Nanak, Sikhs assert divine justice and promote peaceful reconciliation. Significantly, in contrast to the retributive nature of the inexorable law of *karma* in Indian religious traditions, *karma* in Sikh doctrine undergoes a radical change. Sikhs acknowledge the primacy of divine grace over *karma*, and stress the values of mercy, forgiveness, compassion, and benevolence in the justice process. What separates individuals both from God and from one's fellow human beings is self-centeredness (*haumai*). This self-centeredness, in turn, is the source of the five primary vices (lust, anger, covetousness, attachment to worldly things, and pride), and is the principal obstacle to forgiveness. In the life and tradition of spirituality, forgiveness (*khima*) is a pre-eminent virtue. It is the basis for true happiness and contentment and is itself a spiritual source. In Sikh tradition, penance (*tanakhah*) is a practical means for achieving restoration. Whatever disturbs peace between one individual and another impairs relationships throughout the community. And by extension it is seen to harm the divine order as well.

Similarly, the Buddhist approach to life derives from the meditative insights into the nature of Reality and Being and the cultural traditions which give expression to them. As the Dalai Lama expresses it, all things are 'dependently originated,' thus creating a matrix or network of interrelationships and 'mutual dependence.' This is a key to the principles and practice of justice. The legal cosmology of pre-modern Tibet, for example, reveals the multivalent character of Reality. In consequence, any and every event or incident offers a number of 'appearance levels' (French 1995a). The way any incident (or crime) looks depends on a number of perspectives: karmic, phenomenological, and forensic among them. We see here a challenge similar to that faced by South Africa's Truth and Reconciliation Commission in addressing questions about the truth of the violence enacted under apartheid: for example, forensic truth (facts discovered by trained investigators), personal or narrative truth (the experience of victims or offenders), social or dialogue truth (the understandings emerging from victims and offenders when sharing their experience).

According to Mahayana Buddhist cosmology, all persons harbor within themselves the same ultimate authentic Self; this is the Buddha-nature. Thus in sharing this one being, all creatures are intimately related. Significantly, human pain and unhappiness are caused by craving and self-delusion. But by following the Noble Eightfold Path – which includes among its steps right understanding, right aspiration, right conduct and right concentration – reform and peace are possible for all. Hence our intentions are a key to enlightened living, for human beings are ultimately the result of their own deeds and thoughts. That there is such a thing as an inexorable result of moral choices derives from the concept of *karma*: the objective law of moral cause and effect. By contrast with the Jewish and Christian traditions, then, we are not so much punished *for* our sins, as *by* them. Liberation from them is a personal matter. Non-violence in all things is a central stance because of Buddhism's critical psychological insight that violence breeds further violence. Buddhism, therefore, rejects retribution and vengeance in favor of compassion. For Buddhism, justice grows out of mercy.

Ancient sources in classical Chinese philosophy and spirituality reveal important reconciliatory and transformative roots as well. Confucian, Taoist, and Moist theories of human nature and the human community offer illuminating insights into issues of responsibility, identity, harmony, and social obligation. Confucius (551–478 BCE) taught, for example, that love is the regulating principle in human relationships. His five Cardinal Virtues – benevolence, moral excellence, propriety, practical wisdom, and good faith – are perhaps best summarized as Reciprocity or Considerateness. (The latter is a precursor of the Categorical Imperative, or Golden Rule of Western philosophy.) The implications of this for restorative justice are clear for in this system human nature is essentially good, though evil and wrongdoing regularly occur. They arise not solely because of personal weakness, but because of improper social influences. Significantly, criminal behavior results from what may be regarded as a more fundamental cause: faulty moral cultivation. This lies at the very root of a person's inability to ward off temptation and to curb desires. It is in the Analects of Confucius that we find the twin social concepts governing human behavior: *Ren* and *Li*. The principle of *Ren* translates variously as 'benevolence,' 'humanity,' 'charity,' and 'altruism.' The person acting without *Ren* defiles his very nature. Thus the first victims in criminal offences are actually the offenders themselves. Closely linked to this concept is *Li* (propriety, virtue). Understood as the ideal for interpersonal relations in civil society, *Li* becomes the goal to which the wrong-doer is directed during the process of restoration. Thus when an offender is rehabilitated to values of *Li*, he finds himself identified with the dignity and value of his tradition and culture.

As distinct from this humanistic thought, Taoism bears witness to the metaphysical roots of justice and reconciliation. Taoism recognizes a fundamental principle operative in the cosmos: *Tao* ('the way,' 'the road,' or 'the road in which the Universe moves'). *Tao* is both transcendent existence, and its immanence in the world; it is both the ultimate Ground of Being, and its spontaneous expression. This all-permeating principle operates both in the cosmos and in society.

Taoism is a reasoned quietism. Taoist theory presupposes human nature as essentially reasonable, harmonious, and good. For that reason it regards the primary cause of crime as disobedience to *Tao*. But the social order itself may also cause crime. Indeed 'the world' itself – or any system that distorts the essential goodness of humankind – constitutes an ever-present threat to the moral life by triggering our desires and seducing us from 'the path.' In returning the offender to the 'path,' adherents of the tradition hearken to one of the many ethical maxims of our primary source of Taoism, the *Tao Te Ching* of Lao-tse (b. 604 BCE): 'Recompense injury with kindness.' This alone seems to anticipate restorative processes. Punishment can only make matters worse.

Of course, religious texts are meant to be experienced, rather than merely grasped by the intellect. The same is true for religious traditions. Only by living these texts and traditions in spirit and in truth can one actualize the wisdom they profess. Whatever grave disparities have often separated theory from practice, and however much political expediency has over-ridden a well-grounded faith, the essential wisdom of these traditions continues to shape human lives and inform human judgments. One thing is clear from our survey: 'devotional religion can open up patterns of forgiveness, endurance and compassion, that constitute a major contribution of the religions to the problem of coping with moral evil, enabling people to bear suffering, and inspiring them to relieve it' (Hebblethwaite 1976: 32).

Given the fact of escalating globalization and information technologies, one can in fact speak of our spiritual interdependence upon one another. This requires us to draw upon multiple ways of knowing. This is the meaning of Mahatma Gandhi's new understanding of *dharma* – 'Sacred Law,' 'duty,' 'justice': 'One's dharma is to seek for and practice the truth of all religions [and] this truth is non-violence and selfless service to all human-kind [for] we are all children of god.' We live, in other words, in an age of pluralism (Eck 1993: 190–9). This has nothing to do with moral relativism.

Ultimately, pluralism is rooted in a dialogue of real encounter with those of other persuasions. Just how we might go about this has been suggested as fostering a 'grounded openness' to our multi-cultural, pluralist world. Grounded openness is what Ingham terms 'a posture of discernment, of critical and discriminating participation in the possibility of grace within the unfamiliar' (Ingham 1997: 125). And here we might understand 'grace' within the broad context of the Perennial Philosophy, Leibniz's *philosophia perennis*. Grace 'originates in the Divine Ground of all being' (Huxley 1978: 168). Anticipating the possibility of convergent spirituality, Ward emphasizes the need for 'the moral commitment which is aroused by loyalty and total obedience … to supreme goodness itself' (Ward 1991: 197). This, Ward argues, involves 'the pursuit of an ideal joy, wisdom and compassion, not for oneself, but for the whole earth.'

Such spiritual formulations run directly counter to a value system that is effectively shaping our global culture: consumerism and market capitalism. This New Social Order, as critics call it, is of direct relevance to issues of criminal justice, for it too lays claims to ultimate concerns. Studies reveal consumerism as having all the theological underpinnings and vocabulary of a religious tradition (Loy 1997; Cox 1999). Sustained by faith in its truths, 'The Market' deals in matters of faith, heresy, orthodoxy, redemption, and even eschatology – the teaching of the final end and purpose of all things: wealth and power. The 'econologians,' as Cox calls the theologians of this value-system, even deal in theodicy by attempting to justify The Market's ways to man. The Market teaches that in the final analysis nothing is sacred; everything can be bought; indeed, it actively promotes the commodification of all things: the environment (real estate, clear-cut options); war ('defense' industries); the body (sperm banks, blood banks, organ banks); human sexuality (pornography and sex tourism); and the list goes on (Gorringe 2001). This commodification of life, particularly of individual persons, determines social values. The bottom line is ultimately a matter of money. Christie's critique *Crime Control as Industry* (1994) said as much by arguing that incarceration is now big business. Private business has recognized the opportunities. Wackenhut Corrections Corporation is a clear example. It has reportedly grown in recent years to be the world's largest commercial prison operator, with fifty-six institutions in the USA, Britain, and Australia. Listed on the New York Stock Exchange, its primary focus is on earnings for both the corporation and its shareholders. Pondering criminal justice in the context of commercial profit and prison business prompted one critic to ask whether the court-house had not become society's modern cathedral (Redekop 1993: 3). Or, as Auerbach said of American society: 'Law is our national religion; lawyers constitute our priesthood; the courtroom our cathedral, where contemporary passion plays are enacted' (Auerbach 1983: 9). The analogies are all the more appropriate when one considers the essentially theological vocabulary – guilt, atonement, retribution, for example – so often involved in jurisprudence, but which has been severed from its spiritual roots. This seeming intrusion of religious vocabulary into the secular world highlights often divisive tensions between religious conscience, the state, and the law (McLaren and Coward 1998).

Given the role of competition, of individualism, and of rights-based legal systems in modern Western culture, it is not surprising that the metaphors we use daily are metaphors of conflict. Thus the media speak with increasing fluency and frequency of price wars and turf wars, of legal battles and court battles, of fighting for market share and, of course, war on crime. No sphere of human activity is entirely free of metaphors of confrontation and conflict. Even when we account for the prevalence of expressions that are merely speech formulas or fixed-form expressions, we are left with the fact that the predominance of metaphors of conflict actually reflects the world as our culture sees it. In other words, the metaphor of conflict is actually 'built into the conceptual system of the culture' in which we live (Lakoff and Johnson 1980: 63). In an adversarial approach to life, metaphors of dialogue are strikingly rare. Redemptive violence is the rule (Wink 1998).

Most of the metaphors we use when speaking of justice are commodity metaphors (Zehr 1990). Thus we 'hand out' justice, 'deal' justice, 'get' justice and 'face' justice. This, Zehr confesses, is the vocabulary that best fits a capitalist society. An examination of figurative language demonstrates that 'we define our reality in terms of metaphors and then proceed to act on the basis of the metaphors' (Lakoff and Johnson 1980: 158). The predominance of the vocabulary of conflict and confrontation leads to social alienation and a distortion of reality.

> Our problem is finding a way to heal the cultural alienation that has disabled us from creating a loving and caring society ... we need to envision a new kind of legal culture that preserves individual liberty against group-sanctioned injustice but that also understands the legal arena as a moral environment within which to build greater empathy, trust and solidarity.
>
> (Gabel 1997: 8)

The spiritual foundations of restorative justice provide the answer (Hadley 2000). Their principles of accountability, forgiveness, repentance (or radical change of direction), and reconciliation require all the participants in the process to come to grips with fundamental issues: the nature and purpose of human life; the value of the human person; the nature of conflict; and one's responsibilities toward both society and the common good. Only through personal engagement can one begin to heal the wounds that crime causes. In the spirit of *ubuntu*, as Desmond Tutu explains, this faith-based justice focuses on 'the healing of breaches, the redressing of imbalances, the restoration of broken relationships' (Tutu 1999: 51). Restorative justice differs from conventional justice by viewing criminal acts more comprehensively and by involving more interest groups in dealing with the issues (Zehr and Mika 1997). Significantly, it measures success not in terms of numbers of cases solved or numbers of criminals imprisoned but by how much harm has been repaired or prevented (Van Ness and Strong 1997). As Brunk has explained: 'It is a mistake to defend Restorative Justice on the grounds that it chooses the values of mercy and forgiveness over justice, as many of its critics (and some of its defenders) argue.' Rather, he continues, it 'is much more accurate to say that forgiveness and reconciliation are critical aspects of restoration, and restoration is an important precondition, if not part of the very definition, of *justice*' (Brunk 2000: 48).

Like the proverbial leaven in the bread, spiritual principles of healing have risen from the human encounter with ultimacy. Whether or not the participants in restorative justice recognize the roots of these principles as the first fruits of faith traditions, these principles are nonetheless working through a number of initiatives, social movements, organizations, and programs. Some of these are overtly based on faith traditions, others are motivated by principles which the Dalai Lama regards as the outcome of a tacit spiritual revolution. Indeed, the restorative approach to promoting a justice that heals, forms the very foundation of civil society. This is emphasized by the Interfaith Committee on Chaplaincy in the Correctional Service of Canada:

Our goal is to seek Shalom, harmony and security for all, with reconciliation and healing replacing revenge and pain. We believe that the search for true and satisfying justice is forever linked to the spiritual growth of all concerned. The path of over-incarceration, of a vengeful spirit and a punitive mentality, can only dry up the soul of our country.

(CSC 1998)

Acknowledgement

For insights into the sources of major faith traditions I acknowledge the contributions of participants in the Spiritual Roots Project (Hadley 2000, 2001): Pierre Allard, Nawal A. Ammar, Arthur W. Blue, Meredith A. Rogers Blue, Conrad G. Brunk, Harold Coward, Kaijun Geng, Bria Huculak, Edwin C. Hui, David R. Loy, Ron Neufeldt, Wayne Northey, Eliezer Siegal, Pashaura Singh.

References

Ahmad, N. (1997) *Qur'anic and non-Qur'anic Islam*, second revised edn, Lahore: Vanguard Books.

Armstrong, K. (1993) *A History of God: the 4,000-year Quest of Judaism, Christianity and Islam*, New York: Ballantyne Books.

— (2004) 'US on dangerous course, expert warns,' *Globe and Mail*, 6 August: A6. Available at: www. couch.ca/

Auerbach, J. S. (1983) *Justice without Law?* New York: Oxford University Press.

Berman, H. J. (1983) 'Religious foundations of law in the West: an historical perspective,' *The Journal of Law and Religion*, 1(1): 3–43.

Bianchi, H. (1994) *Justice as Sanctuary: toward a new system of crime control*, Bloomington and Indianapolis: Indiana University Press.

Brunk, C. (2000) 'Restorative justice and the philosophical theories of criminal punishment,' in M. L. Hadley (ed.) *The Spiritual Roots of Restorative Justice*, Albany, NY: SUNY Press.

Christie, N. (1994) *Crime Control as Industry: toward Gulags western style*, London and New York: Routledge.

Cox, H. (1999) 'The market as God,' *The Atlantic Monthly*, 283(3): 18–23.

CSC (Correctional Service of Canada) (1998) 'A proclamation by the Interfaith Committee on Chaplaincy', *Restorative Justice Week*, Ottawa: CSC.

Dalai Lama (1999) *Ethics for the New Millennium*, New York: Riverhead Books.

Dedji, V. (2000) 'Embodying forgiveness and reconciliation: towards a theology of reconstruction for Africa,' unpublished seminar paper, the Systematic Theology Seminar, Faculty of Divinity, Cambridge, 8 March.

De Gruchy, J. W. (2002) *Reconciliation: restoring justice*, Minneapolis: Fortress Press.

Eck, D. L. (1993) *Encountering God: a spiritual journey from Bozeman to Benares*, Boston: Beacon Press.

Forrester, D. B. (1997) *Christian Justice and Public Policy*, Cambridge Studies in Religion and Ideology 10, Cambridge: Cambridge University Press.

Freedman, D. N. (1985) 'The formation of the canon of the Old Testament: the selection and identification of the Torah as the supreme authority of the post-exilic community,' in D. B. Firmage (ed.) *Religion and Law: biblical, Judaic and Islamic perspectives*, New York: Eisenbrauns.

French, R. R. (1995a) 'The cosmology of law in Buddhist Tibet,' *Journal of the International Association of Buddhist Studies*, 18(18): 97–116.

— (1995b) *The Golden Yoke: the legal cosmology of Buddhist Tibet*, Ithaca, NY: Cornell University Press.

Gabel, P. (1997) 'The moral obligation of defense lawyers,' *Tikkun: A Bimonthly Jewish Critique of Politics, Culture and Society*, 12 (July/August).

Goldberg, R. (1989) 'Law and spirit in the Talmudic tradition,' in A. Green (ed.) *Jewish Spirituality*, New York: Crossroad Publishing.

Gorringe, T. J. (2001) *The Education of Desire: toward a theology of the senses*, London: SCM Press.

Griffiths, C. T. and Hamilton R. (1996) 'Sanctioning and healing: restorative justice in Canadian aboriginal communities,' in B. Galaway and J. Hudson (eds) *Restorative Justice: international perspectives*, Monsey, NY: Criminal Justice Press.

Hadley, M. L. (ed.) (2000) *The Spiritual Roots of Restorative Justice*, Albany, NY: SUNY Press.

— (2001) *The Justice Tree: multifaith reflection on criminal justice*, Victoria, BC: Centre for Studies in Religion and Society.

— (2004) 'The ascension of Mars and the salvation of the world,' in D. J. Hawkin (ed.) *The Twenty-First Century Confronts its Gods: globalization, technology, and war*, Albany, NY: SUNY Press.

Hebblethwaite, B. (1976) *Evil, Suffering and Religion*, London: Sheldon Press.

Hinnells, J. R. (ed.) (1998) *A New Handbook of Living Religions*, London: Penguin Books.

Huxley, A. (1978) *The Perennial Philosophy*, New York: Harper and Row.

Ingham, M. (1997) *Mansions of the Spirit: the gospel in a multi-faith world*, Toronto: Anglican Book Centre.

Khan, S. (2004) 'A Muslim message more irresistible than hate,' *The Globe and Mail*, 7 September: A15.

King, U. (1997) 'Spirituality,' in J. R. Hinnells (ed.) *A New Handbook of Living Religions*, London: Penguin Books, 677–81.

Lakoff, G. and Johnson, M. (1980) *Metaphors We Live By*, Chicago and London: University of Chicago Press.

Lerman, D. (1998) 'Underlying principles: restorative justice and Jewish law,' *Full Circle: Newsletter of the Restorative Justice Institute*, 2(2): 2–3.

Loy, D. (1997) 'The religion of the market,' *Journal of the American Academy of Religion*, 65(2): 275–89.

McLaren, J. and Coward, H. (1998) *Religious Conscience, the State, and the Law: historical contexts and contemporary significance*. Albany NY: State University of New York Press.

Marshall, P. A. (1991) 'Overview of Christ and culture,' in R. E. VanderVennen (ed.) *Church and Canadian Culture*, Lanham, MD: University Press of America.

Murray, R. (1992) *The Cosmic Covenant: biblical themes of justice, peace and the integrity of creation*, London: Sheed and Ward.

Napoleon, Val (1997) 'Peace and justice plan: Gitxsan restorative justice,' unpublished plan submitted to the Gitxsan people (Canada).

Narayanan, Vasudha (2001) 'Hindu ethics and dharma,' in J. Runzo and M. Martin (eds) *Ethics in the World Religions*, Oxford: Oneworld.

Nasr, S. H. (2002) *Heart of Islam: enduring values for humanity*, San Francisco: HarperCollins.

Pratt, J. (1996) 'Colonization, power and silence: a history of indigenous justice in New Zealand society,' in B. Galaway and J. Hudson (eds) *Restorative Justice: international perspectives*, Monsey, NY: Criminal Justice Press.

Redekop, V. (1993) *Scapegoats, the Bible and Criminal Justice: interacting with René Girard*,

Occasional Papers of the MCC Canada Victim Offender Ministries Program and the US Office of Criminal Justice. Issue No. 13 (February), Akron and Clearbrook: MCC.

Ross, R. (1996) *Returning to the Teachings: exploring aboriginal justice*, London: Penguin Books.

South Africa, Truth and Reconciliation Commission (1999) '*Ubuntu*: promoting restorative justice,' in *Truth and Reconciliation Commission*, 5 vols, London: Macmillan, vol. 1, pp. 125–31.

Stuart, O. (1997) 'African diaspora religion,' in J. R. Hinnells (ed.) *A New Handbook of Living Religions*, London: Penguin Books.

Tutu, D. (1999) *No Future Without Forgiveness*, London, Sydney, Auckland, Johannesburg: Rider.

Van Ness, D. and Strong, K. H. (1997) *Restoring Justice*, Cincinnati: Anderson Publishing.

Ward, K. (1991) *A Vision to Pursue: beyond the crisis in Christianity*, London: SCM Press.

Wink, W. (1998) *The Powers That Be: theology for a new millennium*, New York, London, Toronto: Doubleday.

Yazzie, R. and Zion J. W. (1996) 'Navajo restorative justice: the law of equality and justice,' in B. Galaway and J. Hudson (eds) *Restorative Justice: international perspectives*, Monsey, NY. Criminal Justice Press.

Zehr, H. (1990) *Changing Lenses: a new focus for crime and justice*, Scottsdale, PA: Herald Press.

Zehr, H. and Mika, M. (1997) *Fundamental Concepts of Restorative Justice*, pamphlet published and distributed by Mennonite Central Committee, Akron and Clearbrook: MCC.

11

Empathy and restoration

Hal Pepinsky

Empathy is the feeling and awareness people have when they transform and transcend violence. Empathy is the emotional glue that binds people together in respect and dignity. I call the way we relate when we exchange empathy 'peacemaking.' The practice, the science, the art of peacemaking is essentially a matter of learning how to engender empathy in place of narcissism. To me, the process of peacemaking, of building empathy, works the same way all the way from one-on-one human encounters (and encounters with other life forms and eco-systems), to the course of national and trans-national relations, and, as members of First Nations worldwide add, to all our relations.

Empathy defined

I define empathy as trying to put oneself in another's place, so as to imagine that in the other person or group's place I would feel and act as they do. When we are empathic, we are open to the possibility that others are misunderstood, and want to be understood. In empathic moments, therefore, curiosity replaces passing of judgment or condemnation of others. Empathy expresses sensitivity to others' sensibilities.

Eliciting empathy depends on recognizing subtle, tentative cues and respecting personal privacy. When people seem on the verge of telling me something private and painful, I take my cue from their eyes, for instance. If they want to look at me, I look as openly and emptily back as I can, as though to say, 'This is your moment.' If they look away, I try not to invade their privacy by staring at them. It generally in my experience has taken less than half my attention to avoid further prompting, keep quiet, and get an openly and yet respectfully delivery of honest response. All I can do is convey the sincerity of my own curiosity – that I really think they know things I don't and want to learn. I try to convey comfort and safety for emotionally intense disputes to be aired. I have never found it necessary to do more than fail to bail out a friend overnight whose needs I felt unable to meet in my own home in wee morning hours. Otherwise, I have only gained confidence that emotional conflict can only and safely be expressed and addressed no matter how intense the underlying fears and anger. The earlier the fears and anger are expressed openly and respectfully addressed, the better.

In one victim offender 'reconciliation' session I co-mediated, a 'victim' was really, I thought, on the verge of cussing a young guy out, was at a loss for words. I interrupted his silence to ask, 'How are you feeling?' As he almost visibly steamed up inside, I followed up, as softly as I could muster, 'Take your time.' After a while he was able to look the 'offender' in the face while he spoke in firm voice without shouting. The quiet interlude, where the 'victim' was left safely to his own reflections, proved a crucial basis through which victim and offender came to agreement on a settlement, to be followed up, ending in relaxed handshakes.

An essential element of empathy is conveying that it is safe for parties to be honest with each other in the presence of others committed solely to keeping the conversation purely voluntary and safe. To this end, when I have introduced victims and offenders as mediator, I have made a personal point of looking everyone in the room (co-mediator and staff or trainee observer(s) included) in the eye as I deliver a message that for my part as a volunteer, even if we have to schedule another session, I am determined above all (whatever we do or don't accomplish) to remain here with you until everyone in this room has had a chance to say anything that hasn't been said, and still needs to be said. I add a personal invocation (some call the functional equivalent 'prayers'), that whatever form the result ('An agreement perhaps? My co-mediator will write it out in your words and read it back because the staff can't read my handwriting, but you don't have to agree to anything'), I volunteer the hope that everyone personally involved will leave the room at the end of the session feeling that the matter is settled, and fairly so.

As a volunteer victim offender mediator I have been through a number of training sessions. Although session contents vary considerably and inevitably in many cases of conflict, we mediators in training invariably practice the art of active listening. We learn to 'trust the process.' We trust that whatever surprise emerges from confrontation among opposing forces, with a little help at keeping dialogue open, we can help them work it out.

Techniques we role-play and practice in training range from nodding gentle encouragement for the speaker to continue, to paraphrasing back some part of what the speaker says when the speaker pauses, to reframing what the speaker has said. For example, if a victim were to tell a young offender how to get his or her act together, a mediator might want to reframe a moral sermon to capture an apparent feeling behind the moral sermon, as by saying, 'I see that you really have X's future at heart,' and allowing the speaker to agree or correct the mediator.

In mediation as everywhere, every day in life (especially for the demons that most haunt us when we are alone, if nowhere else when we are trying to sleep), empathy is communicated first and foremost by conveying that, no matter what happens as a consequence of what you want to tell me, I will not leave you or wrest control of your story from you. I don't have to be anywhere just now, or if I do, let's agree on a time we can meet where I am at your disposal. This is just a back-up possibility when I sense special urgency in a request for my whole-hearted attention. At less urgency, as with correspondence I do with prisoners over years at a time and with most student inquiries, it matters more that I get back seriously than that I get back instantly. Let's face it, giving one's time and personal attention is as precious an interpersonal gift as any gift one can give. In *Small is Beautiful: economics as if people mattered* in 1975, E. F. Schumacher observed the irony that in the nation that at the time was per capita richest in the world, the United States, was where people on average had the least leisure time. Leisure time is the time when you can decide to lay aside all those things you *have* to do, and get to do what you *want* to do. In my experience in this life and home of mine, it is harder and harder for people to find time to empathize, and all the more precious and valuable therefore when it happens.

Empathy as peacemaker

The crucial feature of empathy is that, by definition, in empathic moments the empath cannot persist in inflicting pain, fear, disrespect, or disregard on the other. By definition, if you see that you are hurting someone, to grit your teeth or become stimulated to persist entails turning empathy off, dissociating your own feelings and actions from awareness and from desire to put yourself in the other's place and let yourself share the other's feelings.

Dissociation and separation from others, and for that matter from one's own feelings, are survival mechanisms. I am with those who believe that we separate and dissociate in defense against those who persist in hurting or threatening us. There is no telling how much empathy it may take for a survivor to trust that it is now safe and potentially rewarding to open up and empathize back, rather than continuing to have openness and emotional transparency betrayed once again. For that matter, there is no telling how long a lag there may be between someone's offer of empathy and the other's opening to empathize in response, if ever. When empathy is requited, however, cooperation by definition supplants exploitation and violence.

We all reach limits where others simply exploit or ignore our offers of empathy long and hard enough that we reach our limits of unrequited compassion or being abused and threatened, and separate from or resist others. In self-defense, we withdraw into narcissism, and concentrate on meeting our own selfish needs. Persistently offering unrequited empathy can in fact feed others' narcissism rather than catalyzing their empathy. Part of the art and science of peacemaking is to work out when and how to draw a balance between offering empathy and resisting abuse and violence. This, for example, was what Mohandas Gandhi saw as the need for a twin commitment: to *satyagraha*, or refusal to cooperate with persistent violence on one hand, and to *ahimsa*, which I have heard translated as 'love' – a willingness at all moments to embrace one's adversary as a brother or sister when the violence stops. In the form of victim offender mediation I practice, we have a couple of ground rules to keep anyone from exploiting an empathic climate – that parties not interrupt each other or call each other names. I have mediated where these rules have been broken but I have never felt a need to interrupt and intervene to stop it instead of letting it pass. Narcissism including a measure of getting carried away by anger, fear or frustration has its place, and letting narcissism have its day instead of suppressing it helps clear the air for empathy to take its own turn.

The major challenge of institutionalizing peacemaking or mediation is to build relationships in which empathy is reciprocated and balanced rather than one-sided.

Verbalized empathy

On the surface, verbalization ought to be the most robust indicator of whether displays of empathy are genuine. Verbalization is also a source of ambiguity. Consider displays of remorse. On one hand, across cultures, it keeps turning out that people who feel victimized or aggrieved want sincere apologies from their offenders, promptly and without reservation. Sometimes the complainants are liberated into feeling more openly angry and less terrified of an offender, but even then, reports time and again are that apology means a lot to people worldwide.

The trouble is that expressions of remorse may be entirely narcissistic. Indeed, legal systems around the world, for millennia, have manifestly rewarded, encouraged, and even tortured people into accepting of blame and expressing remorse. I find myself listening to how long remorseful people spend talking about their own feelings and about what they will do to make it up and all; as against how readily they turn the conversation back to those they have hurt and offended, and listen to and talk about what they themselves are feeling and wanting (narcissism) rather than about what the offenders are feeling and wanting (empathy). The crucial issue is whether the remorseful party is spending more time talking and thinking about him/her/itself, or talking and apparently thinking about the other party's injuries and feelings. Concentrating on getting expressions of remorse is one of the failures of adjudication, of trying to put offenders in their place. By contrast, in victim–offender mediation as I have been trained to practice it, mediators never ask or advise those identified as offenders to say they're sorry. All we ask is that they acknowledge that they are the ones who have caused the harms that victims report having suffered. In restorative justice we focus on harms done rather than on rules broken to promote empathy rather than narcissism. While some advocates and practitioners of restorative justice favor trying to shame offenders for what they have done, as a prelude to 'reintegrating' offenders into communities, I join those who disagree. It is one thing for the shame or guilt that an 'offender' already feels to rise to the surface and be expressed. It is another thing for mediators to focus on making shame happen instead of concentrating on eliciting honesty and modeling active listening. Shaming centers the problem at hand inside the offender while, to make mediation work and encourage empathy, the focus needs to be on progress of the relationship among the parties. Empathy is manifest when parties are talking about other parties' circumstances and feelings rather than focusing on themselves.

Non-verbal empathy

Non-verbally, patience, calm, and relaxation are signs of empathy. Someone who is eagerly reassuring you is probably more concerned about how s/he is doing in the interaction than attending to how you are doing. I once accompanied a friend to her psychiatrist just after my friend had been discharged from a hospital unit where she had ridden out a manic episode. The psychiatrist asked how my friend was doing. I asked the psychiatrist whether she (the psychiatrist) knew what had triggered my friend's manic episode. I turned to my friend. 'Tell her,' I said. My friend described that ten years to the day before the onset of her latest manic attack, when she previously had just been released from hospitalization, her father tried to rape her. She began to cry softly. The psychiatrist pushed a box of tissues across the table toward my friend, leaned back in her chair, and responded, 'Perhaps we had better adjust your medication.' At that moment, as I saw it, the psychiatrist, who seemed genuinely to want to help my friend, also was incapable of hearing about, let alone empathizing with, my friend's world. That's a prime display of passive separation.

One illustration of active narcissism is the patter of the proverbial used-car salesman. Given my own preoccupation with criminal justice images, I think of active narcissism as junkie behavior. The person who is acting out narcissism can't stop talking. Oh yes, s/he may sound very sympathetic, but if you think about it, s/he never stops to ask how you feel. S/he may even tell you s/he knows just how you feel. I have heard judges in several sentencing situations over the years, including those of friends of mine, actually say, 'This hurts me more than it hurts you.' Who are they kidding? Themselves perhaps, a risk that narcissism carries. Alternative forms of fast talking include reassurance ('Everything will be all right,' 'I'll take care of it,' 'On the bright side') and

191

unsolicited advice ('You need to ... '). Reassurance and support has its place. One way that radical feminists talk about the difference between narcissism and empathy is quite literally by what proportion of time people take in conversation. For instance, in co-ed classes, it is well documented worldwide that schoolboys are more often called upon by teachers and more verbose when they talk, or that in a school gym for instance, where boys are sent to one end and girls to the other, the boys quickly occupy more than half the space.

These are instances of expressions of narcissism at the group level that follow the same pattern at the individual level. To paraphrase the theme song from the movie *Midnight Cowboy*, when somebody keeps talking at me, no matter how warmly and reassuringly, I infer that s/he probably scarcely hears a word I'm saying. Note too that 'speech' and 'talk' can mean any bodily action and what it communicates. I envision all social interaction as 'conversations.' In our conversations, then, differences in expression of empathy and of narcissism follow the same patterns across social levels, across media of human expression, and across social and cultural contexts.

Reacting to narcissism

There are a number of signs that displays of empathy are genuine. In this process of discernment (and by contrast focus on oneself) there are a number of signs that people are too preoccupied with their own problems or agendas to be empathizing. Whether this narcissism is threatening is another matter. For example, when people go off on me, they may just be tired and sense that I am the safest person at hand at whom to vent. They are not out to get me. They may not even consciously notice that they are being hostile or otherwise aggressive. I don't have to take hostile or antagonistic responses personally, which helps me keep my calm,

especially when I am in a power position, notably as professor or mediator. Even a threat, once voiced, is less likely to be carried out than violence suppressed behind a friendly, subservient, or remorseful exterior.

In the longer run, I think that by sharing stories we can build a body of knowledge of how to sort out threats to take personally from those to acknowledge and let pass. More generally, false positives abound. For all I can see, for everyone who has turned out to have hurt me and consciously to have betrayed my trust and compassion, there are many others 'matching the profile' who turn out just to have been so distracted that they hardly noticed what I was doing and saying, let alone feeling hostile or lying to me. I draw a lesson that I cannot know who my enemies are nearly as easily as I can discern those who at any moment are honest and empathic.

Whether my seemingly most empathic friends or I might at some point feel scared enough to 'roll over' on one another, as people are routinely threatened into in drug enforcement let alone by torture, is inherently unpredictable as far as I can see, not worth 'profiling' at all. In sum, I see less point in trying to identify false friends of mine than in celebrating signs of empathic friendship that I do not think can be faked.

Balancing narcissism and empathy

A seeming paradox is that you cannot give empathy without having received it. The psychiatrist I just described probably entered psychiatry out of a genuine desire to empathize with others. Her manner was soft and gentle. I infer that she was unable to empathize with my friend because the good doctor had been traumatized or betrayed enough in her own life that, to survive, she had set up defenses to wall off and become incapable of describing her own feelings, let alone of reaching out and touching my friend's trauma. It seems to me that she was in the same position as the classic narcissist who is full of him/herself and thinks others are to blame for their own problems, and ought to pick themselves up, get on with their lives, and make something of themselves. You might call the first form of narcissism compassionate narcissism and the second self-righteous narcissism. There is no room for empathy either way.

In my experience, the only way to break through walls of narcissism, ironically, is to indulge the narcissism. My strongest evidence of this comes from the classroom, particularly from that big class on alternative social control systems. Over the years, the way I respond to students who openly disagree with me has changed.

I call myself a recovering lawyer. I still get carried away arguing my position with students who openly disagree with me, but, I think, less so. My law school training was that true service to a client meant anticipating conflict and ensuring that my client's legal interests would prevail in all imaginable cases. In this law-school-perpetuated tradition, when an interpretation of law or fact was up for grabs, I got caught up in the ethos of anticipating opposition to one's claims and winning the ensuing legal argument. In law-school classes, we dealt primarily in the lofty and ethereal realm of formal opinions by appellate judges, on arguing who should have prevailed.

Given this training in what it meant to excel as a legal pro (which among other things helped me with a lot of friendly assistance to survive to get tenure and promotion myself at my third job), I entered teaching believing it was my duty to debate any student who disagreed with me. I would do it even one-on-one during an office hour. I thought I was doing my students a favor by debating them as best I could. That would get them thinking. I won a lot of debates, one-on-one and in front of the entire class. I seldom, then or now, got called to account for having

embarrassed or humiliated any student who spoke out. Then as now, when I did so, I felt it my obligation, first and foremost, to thank the complainant for opening up to me and apologize for the pain I had caused. I could also draw a more general idea of how I would guard against repeating the same offense. I would do so as publicly as the student who had complained. I see these as necessary elements of trust and spreading empathy then as now. But my propensity to argue my points has been replaced by honest curiosity about why people who challenge my conclusions reach their own conclusions, and to explore the possibility that we both agree and disagree on fundamental points.

I notice change in my own response to open disagreement. Often, as some students first dare to challenge my conclusions openly, I hear clichés, the kind of lines one might hear on nationwide talk radio. When I hear a cliché, I can bet that most times, I can throw out more information – history of an issue particularly – than my challenger.

I won a lot of cheap debates that way. Sometimes then as now, someone would present a slant on an issue that caught me by surprise. Then as now, I would acknowledge that the speaker had raised a good point that I hadn't considered and would think about further. Often especially at the beginning of a semester, I would hear a line of disagreement that I had confronted countless times before. What would I do with it?

When I debated and won, I found myself later lamenting what I called a 'rubber-band effect.' My opponent would concede that I was entirely right. Then, the next time s/he spoke or wrote, s/he would be back in her or his original position. It was almost as though I had redoubled the determination of my opponent to shut out my pearls of wisdom with more determination than ever. I could sense, and see in anonymous formal student evaluations, a considerable reservoir of student opinion remained that my commitment to respecting students' disagreements with me was phony. In the process, in political exchanges wherever they occurred, as at a party or family reunion, I began to notice on the spot how people's eyes would begin to glaze over as I worked to prove my own points.

I have not kept records or detailed memories of how the prevailing pattern of my response to open student disagreement has changed since I began teaching in January 1977. I am nonetheless conscious of a sea change in my reflex response to student challenge in and around the classroom. Notably, my stake in proving who between us is wrong or right has weakened dramatically.

I invite disagreement by laying out things I believe that run obviously counter to conventional wisdom, then ask the class for 'any reaction.' Over my decades at conferences and in classes, I have noticed how rarely any response but 'questions' is invited. I try to be brief but plain, as by saying, 'I know what I have said is unusual and almost surely crazy or dangerous to all kinds of people in this room. Tell me what you think of what I've said as well as asking me to explain myself.'

I offer thanks to anyone who takes a lead in saying or writing things I'm sure many other class members also feel and believe. If in lecture, I make sure I have repeated back the student's first name correctly and thereafter respond by name. Then I paraphrase the point made, and ask the person by name whether this is what s/he is really saying. I then look that person in the eye as I offer the best sound bite I can think of for what, if anything, I agree with. To those who say that they are conservative while I'm a liberal, I might reply that I'm in many ways a Goldwater/Buckley conservative Republican partisan, as in opposing the drug war and believing in small government. I follow this with another sound bite on respects in which I disagree and why. At that point I ask, 'Does that make sense?' Occasionally

we continue an exchange two or three times back and forth. If the student comes back I try to give the student the last word, and conclude the exchange by thanking the student, for instance for presenting a side of a disagreement I'm sure many others in class share, and go on to the next hand that has gone up. We all have other chances to write further responses on the university course web mail site. For my own part, for the most part, I am conscious of letting go of trying to prove points and of seeing that my 'antagonists' more and more do likewise, rather than bouncing back as though on ideological rubber bands. In writing and in the classroom, my students show a lot more often and concretely that they are learning from me these days as I learn to focus more on what I can learn from their challenges to my own conclusions.

I realize now that I could not afford to hear and respond empathically to students or anyone else unless I received a lot of personal validation of my own worldviews. Like the views of all of us, in some respects honest worldviews will be weird to people who otherwise are our closest family and friends. When for instance I was gently but essentially kicked out of my first two university jobs, I considered whether the kind of 'science' I was accused of not doing was something I could do or should do. It took a receipt of a whole lot of personal empathy for my own views and sentiments to sustain my will to make classroom confrontations meaningful to me, let alone to anyone else. I started learning more noticeably, more often, and being able to tell students when it happened. I switched from evaluations that my lectures were boring or naive to being asked by students to 'lecture' more. I have found that I get more of my own points across the less I monopolize the talking, let alone the dictating of who among us is wrong or right.

I could not have begun to refrain from having argued ad nauseam with students (and regrettably even with friends at parties and family at the dinner table) unless I had more and more readily accepted occasional reassurance that I was not just out there, crazy, nonsensical. I need to have people whose honesty I feel shows acceptance of me and belief in me, if only a moment at a time, to keep my empathy battery charged. I need moments of believing that my most vulnerable, most shameful sides can come out even in bits and pieces among a variety of friends, that I can be loved and appreciated for being the real me, warts and all, and not have to pretend to be what I am not or more than I am to earn acceptance. I have talked this issue over with a number of people; it rings true for them as well.

I infer these needs to be universal. Without these personal battery charges, all of us burn out on teaching and learning. We either keep trying to win arguments and prove what we already know, or keep trying to fit in and do, say and feel as we must. The harder I had pressed my own truths on students, the more discouraged I expect I would have become about whether I was teaching or learning anything meaningful. To stay alive and open to learning, I needed vitally to have my moments of sharing myself and being the center of other people's attention. Bottom line: I have to be convinced that my opinions and feelings matter before I can let go of my own preoccupations and let contrasting opinions and feelings grab my attention and imagination. Insofar as I can believe those who say they see beauty in me, I can stop looking in the mirror. My own narcissism needs to be fed in order to give way to empathy, and I imagine that my students and everyone else I encounter are in the same boat. I do not believe that anyone can hear where others are coming from without having been heard her/himself.

On the other hand, if we spend all our time being full of ourselves, we don't have a chance to hear the empathy others offer us because we are tuning them out of our awareness except perhaps for looking for

openings to bend them to our will. One real consequence, surely, is that people tend to give up on or become wary of being taken advantage of if they offer empathy. Another is that in this one-sided separation from others, there are only two ways to get by: retreating from and minimizing dependence on human contact, or becoming a control freak – making it so that others pay you or feed you or protect you or even adore you because you manipulate and control them. Command and obedience are the relevant parameters in this way of thinking about and practicing social control. I call this paradigm of control 'warmaking,' where the only remedy for conflicting human force is superior counterforce, also known as 'violence.'

Warmaking is a lonely, even desperate, self-defeating way to gain control of one's relations.

It was only this past year that I really faced what I now regard as plain fact: nonviolence isn't just a matter of empathizing, it is a matter of allowing safe, respectful expression for its counterpart, narcissism, in some sort of 'balance' across our relations. I have given increased lip service to 'balance' the last several years. I now recognize that 'balance' means more to peacemaking than 'empathy' itself.

A focus on balance is personally liberating. Once I accept that I need and deserve a balance of narcissism and empathy, I can arrange time to myself to figure out which of the two sides of myself is more needful at the moment, and if I'm lucky (as I happen to be), pick some moments and personal exchanges in which I indulge my narcissism, and others in which I invest empathy. I can go to a therapist who feeds me empathy, trusting that apart from our many moments of laughter and celebration together, she can empathize with my suffering and relieve her own in some other relationship. We have so many opportunities for contact. We can pick and choose among them where to unload and where we are emotionally and physically equipped to be empathic with others. A moment in one exchange may be worth as much as a lifetime of exposure to another pattern.

As I see it now, empathy has maximum growing room in my own life when in moments of reflection I can see a combination of narcissistic indulgence others have given me and significant things that I have learned from others' experience. Across languages and cultures, 'balance' and 'circles' are celebrated. This to me reflects the common finding that violence abates as give and take, listening, reflecting and talking, go up and down, round and round. The trustworthiness and safety of relationships increase as empathy and narcissism are reciprocated. In one's own life as in larger interpersonal and inter-group interaction, the empirical danger sign is that someone's side of a story or cause consistently prevails over others, yours or mine regardless.

As a would-be peacemaker, I seek to engender empathy in all our relations. To that end, I seek ample opportunity for all of us as individuals and as groups to indulge our pride, honor, and needs to apologize and excuse ourselves, and match this with our indulgence of others' narcissism, with our empathy. This has the potential of generating a positive feedback loop or synergy in our relations. Attention to balancing narcissism and empathy pays feeds the force of empathy into all our relations. This is how restorative justice processes such as victim offender mediation make peace.

Studying relationships

My interest in empathy and take on how empathy works stem from my unit of analysis. I am interested in understanding, predicting, and planning how relationships evolve. Most of my social science colleagues are interested in understanding, predicting and planning individual behavior. I use the term 'individual' loosely here. An individual could be a single person or a group of any size. In the United States, corporations are even legally defined as persons. Social scientists may study why individual corporations grow or violate the law. Others may study why 'societies' or nation states evolve this way or that. Still others may evaluate how humanity as a whole evolves. The point is that in this latter paradigm, actors are studied as separate and distinct entities.

Were I to follow social science's current mainstream, I might try to explain or predict who would become a bigger and better empath, and to distinguish individuals in that category from those who become the bigger and worse narcissists. There has been quite prominent work along those lines, like Lawrence Kohlberg's studies of who evolved to higher 'moral maturity' than whom. My definition of empathy sounds just like Kohlberg's definition of his highest level of moral maturity. The difference is that I don't consider empathy to be a defining character trait of individuals or organizations. I used to try to find examples of the good, the true, or the beautiful community to hold out as a role model. Now I might for instance point out that bringing interested parties together by law in circles or 'family group conferences' cut the juvenile detention rate in half in New Zealand, but that would not imply to me that anyone else including folks in my home state should adopt New Zealand's 1989 law in order to achieve the same result. It would simply be an indication that although there's no telling in advance, there is great potential to shift away from adjudication and separation of parties toward forging stronger community ties with victims and offenders alike and even together.

Instead, I am interested in what helps or hinders empathy from being shared so that people end up being either more together or more separated. As I look at the process, I even find that amplification of empathy across a group at one level entails sustained individuation and separation (or 'narcissism') at another. When levels of empathy build in relationships, each actor within the relationship takes turns being self- and other-centered. In balanced relationships, no actor has a monopoly on virtue or vice. It is how actors take turns and shift roles that counts, not what kind of actor or plan of action takes hold. Where empathy is established in human relationships, outcomes of interaction are unpredictable precisely because blending empathy and narcissism keeps opening new directions and possibilities for each and every actor, which makes evaluation of whether actors meet predetermined goals nonsensical within my paradigm.

As I see it, we are born with the universe of body memories of human experience within each of us. I think of this as the human soul. I infer that bodily existence is personally and socially enriched as people discover words and gestures others truly understand. As we build vocabularies of language for feelings and descriptions of contexts, we at once extend our capacities for empathy and enrich awareness of and capacity to describe our own feelings and account for them. As we enjoy opportunities to give and receive empathy, I believe that we become safer, more inclusive, and more genuine in our relations, and richer in personal life journeys and in being valued personally by others. Hence, when I'm being didactic, as I am as I write here, I'm celebrating the benefits of learning about evolution of relationships as against learning about evolution of separated individuals.

To me as a full-time state employee hired to teach criminal justice, I think of conventional criminal justice as designed to separate victims from offenders, and offenders from every other legitimate source of support. Identify the enemy, subdue or kill the enemy, is the focus of most criminological research around me.

As far as I can see, proponents of restorative justice agree on aiming toward forging and strengthening fair, open, accountable ties among people split apart by violence – aiming to resist separation and isolation. Why? Because on one hand separation and isolation are dangerous and explosive, while on the other hand empathic relations are what make life fulfilling and give life positive meaning in the face of suffering.

Empathic relations add to reservoirs of knowledge of varying responses people have made to conflict and suffering, and for that matter to being praised and celebrated. This is knowledge not of what people have to do but of options anyone can choose. Insofar as anyone makes and communicates a choice among options, s/he assumes responsibility for her/his actions. I find manifest exercise of choice free of threats like 'do this or else' a sign that relations are safe. This amounts to what in diplomatic talk is called 'trust-building.' I can think of no higher life's objective than building trust into my relations, not about what we will do, but about how we will share decision-making and accommodation as we go along.

12

Sanctuary as a refuge from state justice

Peter Cordella

How a given society will achieve and maintain social order is determined by the relative balance between willing conformity and mechanisms of social control. More inclusive societies are characterized by a high level of willing conformity and a modest use of the instruments of social control, while more exclusive societies are characterized by the inverse. The contemporary conception of criminal justice employed by the modern nation state is defined much more by its use of mechanisms of social control than its ability to generate willing conformity. Whether it is utilitarian, retributive or therapeutic the contemporary conception of justice focuses little or no attention on the process by which individuals come to obey because they believe it is the right thing to do (Michalowski 1985). Such willing conformity can be achieved only within the context of inclusiveness. Inclusiveness is the prerequisite for willing conformity. Without the assumption of inclusiveness, justice is defined primarily by whom it excludes from full membership as is the case with the modern nation state. Contemporary criminal justice in all its forms is fundamentally exclusionary. Transgressors of the norms and laws of the modern state are excluded in some form (either fully or partially, temporarily or permanently) because they are perceived to be rationally deficient (the utilitarian model), morally deficient (the retributive model) or psychologically deficient (the therapeutic model). In none of these models is the transgressor recognized and dealt with as a moral agent capable of mediating their full reintegration into society.

In the context of contemporary justice the rationally, morally or psychologically deficient transgressor is viewed as incapable and unworthy of the opportunity to negotiate their return to society. In each of these models the transgression is viewed not as an isolated act but as the symptom of a condition that renders the transgressor incapable of participating in the justice process. These are fixed models that transfer the resolution of the transgression to either legal or medical professionals. The ownership of conflict, and it is important to remember that crime is a form of conflict, has increasingly been transferred from the community to the bureaucratic state (Christie 1977). This shift of ownership has transformed the transgressor from a moral agent capable of carrying out a dialogue of justice with fellow members of the community to a passive participant whose future is determined by a prescriptive formula based on the criminality of the transgression and the deficiency that caused it. The prescriptive nature of contemporary criminal justice precludes participation by the community as well. In bureaucratic justice direct participation in the process by either the transgressor or the community is seen as potentially compromising the fairness, reasonableness, and consistency of the law. The legitimacy of criminal law in the modern state is believed to be dependent upon the presence of these three qualities in justice process. Contemporary criminal justice is defined by process rather than outcome. In order to create a more participatory system of justice, law must be conceived as a communicative act (Mathiesen 1990). Herman Bianchi (1994) in his discussion of justice as sanctuary suggests that such a communicative conception of law encourages people – law in hand – to discuss the main problems of their social lives. By engaging in such a discourse, members of a society keep alive the sense that law unites them rather than separates them. The social framework most conducive to the establishment and maintenance of communicative law is the sanctuary.

The sociology of sanctuary

The modern understanding of sanctuary is almost exclusively associated with refugee status (Bianchi 1994). The establishment of legal sanctuaries, however, can be traced to antiquity where the right to asylum was first extended to those accused of crime. Initially sanctuary was used effectively to preclude the possibility of vigilantism or blood feuds. The modern sanctuary as defined by Bianchi has become a place of community and refuge, where fugitives from prosecution by state authorities or revenge by victims can be secured against arrest or violence on the condition that they contribute to the negotiation of a resolution of their conflict. The

sanctuary creates a state of suspended community membership for transgressors. While they are protected from the coercion of the state they are at the same time prevented from fully participating in the life of the community. A dynamic tension characterizes the condition of sanctuary. Sanctuary creates a tension between the transgressor's desire to fully reintegrate and the community's desire for a genuine apology from the transgressor which would include recognition of the harm, agreement to compensate and good faith effort to avoid future transgressions. In return for a genuine apology by the transgressor, the community must guarantee their reintegration (Tavuchis 1991).

The factors and conditions associated with the effective use of sanctuary include an appropriate length of asylum status, open negotiations, and good faith bargaining (Bianchi 1994). Without the social structure of sanctuary communicative legal discourse is not possible.

Although the establishment of modern sanctuary as a response to crime is both intriguing and potentially restorative, it does not fully address the possibility of reestablishing a communicative system of law in contemporary society. Sociological evidence suggests that such a system is only possible within a larger communitarian or mutualist unity pattern (Bianchi 1994). The social context in which crime is defined and addressed is of critical importance in determining the communicative and restorative potential of sanctuary justice. Louk Hulsman (1986) has suggested that the failure to differentiate between the properties of a group or community and the properties of a society is the primary obstacle to reestablishing communicative law and restorative justice. Hulsman argues that groups and communities differ from societies in three fundamental ways: geographic location, interdependence and identity. A group or community has a sense of place, a relational interdependence and an identity of commitment while a society is characterized by

199

an absence of place, a functional inter-dependence, and a competitive identity.

In the societal context prescriptive law and bureaucratic justice are considered superior because they are believed to guar-antee fairness among a population that is perceived to be atomistic in its relations and contractual in its interactions (Macmurray 1974). Members of society view justice as protection against the violation of their individual rights by others. Law is seen as serving their individual needs rather than promoting the common good. The insis-tence on the preservation and protection of individual rights precludes the possibility of communicative law which requires a com-mitment to the common good as the start-ing point for legal discourse (Feinberg 1974). Communicative law assumes that most people are integrated into groups and communities. Unlike society these groups and communities are not geared toward marginalizing or excluding any member. In the context of groups and communities the opposite is true. Groups and communities are geared toward inclusion and harmony (Hulsman 1986). Their interest is in resol-ving conflict and reintegrating those mem-bers whose participation in the common life of the group or community has been tem-porarily restricted by their transgressions. The underlying assumption of commu-nitarian conflict resolution is that most members of a group are willing to come to an agreement to redress the transgression that has momentarily estranged the trans-gressor from the community. Because indi-viduals in a community (as opposed to individuals in a society) have a rootedness in their community, a mutual commitment to each other, and a sense of belonging to a common ethos, they are able to create what Herman Bianchi described as assensus. Unlike the consensus model which 'pre-sumes that there is a basic agreement among members with regard to the interpretation of norms and values' (Bianchi 1994) the assensus model 'recognizes that full agree-ment with regard to the interpretation of norms and values among members of society does not exist, has never existed and will not exist' (Bianchi 1994: 83). In the consensus model any deviation from the accepted interpretation of the norms and values is perceived as a serious threat to the order of society thereby triggering rigid rules (i.e. criminal law) and a prescribed response (i.e. punishment or treatment). Failure to engage the formal legal process represents a threat to the consensus. In the assensus model trans-gressions are transformed into dispute set-tlements between the parties involved.

Implicit in the assensus model is the recognition of the 'human incapacity to make final judgments in matters of right and wrong, interpretation of norms and values must be made in a never-ending, open pro-cess of discussion' (Bianchi 1994: 83). That never-ending open process is the foundation of communicative law. A communicative system of law is a life-affirming model of justice. Bianchi uses Martin Buber's descrip-tion of Tredeka justice, 'the incessant dili-gence to make people experience the genuine substantiation of confirmed truths, rights and duties' as the definition of a life-affirming system of law (Bianchi 1994: 22). The assensus that guides communicative law enables the system to combine the two pri-mary functions of justice (order main-tenance and conflict resolution) whereas the consensus that guides repressive law tends to separate them into criminal and civil realms. The combining of the two functions of jus-tice enables the community to view all transgressions as disputes among the mem-bers which interfere with their ability to fully experience the common life they share.

Communicative law is structured so as to allow people to participate in the experi-ence of rules. Such rules are specifically life-supporting. The presence of life-indicating rules characterizes what Herman Bianchi describes as eunomic communities. In eunomic communities members 'engaging in a system of rules experience the system as supporting their lives and their social interaction' (Bianchi 1994: 57). Conversely, the absence of life-indicating rules characterizes anomic societies. Bianchi, in contrast to Emile Durkheim (1933), argues that anomie is not a lack of norms but a lack of the supportive qualities of norms such as reconciliation, compensation, education, and reintegration. The rise of anomie as defined by Bianchi can be traced to the increasing bureaucratization of society. In the bureaucratic world legal participation is reserved for those who are formally trained in the practice of law. As a result, rank and file members of society no longer need to develop the social skills necessary to engage in legal discourse. The increasing disuse of one's normal abilities to deal with conflicts has led to an alienation from the process of dispute settlement. Increasingly members of society turn to the formal legal system both criminal and civil, to resolve conflicts that have in the past been addressed by less formal and more communicative processes (Cordella 1996). Whether a legal system is eunomic or anomic is determined by how a community or society defines crime.

The criminalization of behavior can be guided by consensus or assensus. The consensus perspective views norms as the embodiment of society's will. Any transgression of these norms is perceived as a threat to the general will and is therefore defined as a crime that requires a punitive or therapeutic response as a way of maintaining social order. By contrast the assensus perspective views norms as broad directives that inform the ever-changing interaction of everyday life. Any transgression of the norms is perceived as an opportunity for norm clarification and is therefore defined as a conflict that requires a conciliatory response as a way of maintaining harmony within the community. Conciliation as a means of conflict resolution requires law to be communicative.

Communicative law is a dyadic process that facilitates a conciliatory dialogue between the community and the transgressor. The conciliatory dialogue must include sentiments from the community articulating its affirmation of the general directives that guide community life and sentiments from the transgressor articulating their need for complete reintegration. The ensuing negotiation should address the extent of harm and nature of compensation, as well as the mutual understanding of normative expectations and the details pertaining to the process of reintegration. Conciliation requires full and direct negotiations among all relevant parties; the transgressor, the victim, and the larger community. The community is represented by deeply embedded members who possess a genuine sense of the normative sentiments of their fellow members rather than by a professionally trained bureaucratic functionary whose legitimacy is dependent on their personal detachment from the community. Conciliation as means of dispute settlement is only possible within a personal unity pattern which unlike a functionalist unity pattern is not based on a common purpose (Macmurray 1974). Rather it is constituted by a common life.

The common purposes that occur in the context of the personal express rather than constitute the unity of association. Common purposes may change or disappear but the association remains because its principle of unity is personal. Its unity is one of persons as persons (Macmurray 1961). Personal unity does not express itself in terms of status or functional differentiation. Unlike functional unities, personal unities do not and cannot involve the functional subordination of one person to another. Personal unity is predicated on two basic principles. The first principle is equality. Although natural and functional differences between individuals do exist and cannot be ignored, personal equality overrides them. 'It means that any two human beings whatever their individual differences can recognize and treat one another as equals' (Macmurray 1977: 33). The second principle

201

of personal unity is freedom. It cannot be imposed; it must be based on trust. Interaction begins with and remains a free activity between equal persons; it must be mutual and unconstrained. In the context of personal freedom an individual can express their whole self rather than a more limited functional identity (e.g. teacher–student, manager–employee, judge–criminal). Only in personal unity, because of its basis in trust, do the constitutive principles of freedom and equality come together (Macmurray 1974).

The trust and mutuality that characterize personal unity patterns are essential to the conciliation process and the sanctuary concept. Trust and mutuality are established through a communicative process. While all social institutions are characterized by interdependence only in the context of personal unity is this interdependence based on trust and mutual obligation (Braithwaite 1994). Personal unity is established and maintained through sustained interaction among the members of a social group, regardless of the material or functional differences among them. The sense of mutuality and trust is engendered in an extended series of communicative interactions. Such a communicative process creates a flexible and adaptive normative system. In the context of personal unity, law guided by the concepts of equity and freedom is a process of social interaction rather than a theoretical concept applied in a formal organizational context. According to Herman Bianchi, the communicative law that guides the concept of sanctuary and process of conciliation; 'does not allow final judgments, it implies rather general directives, indications, road signs and invocations to discussions' (1994: 85) Communicative law requires real assent generated through a continuous process of interaction and adjustment among all persons in the community. Because communicative law is dependent on direct personal involvement, it must remain in the hands of those directly involved in the conflict. In the context of communicative law and the conciliation process, perception and cognition of the normative expectations are always part of the interaction associated with dispute settlement. From the standpoint of the communicative conception of law, much of the failure of contemporary crime control can be traced to the shift from community-based conflict resolution to bureaucracy-based criminal processing. By redefining conflict as crime and shifting responsibility from the community to the state, the probability of stigmatizing and marginalizing the transgressor has increased thereby decreasing the prospects for reintegration (Braithwaite 1994; Pepinsky 1980).

Sanctuary as an alternative to state justice

An examination of the functional potential of various dispute resolution techniques reveals a continuum of coercion with criminal adjudication at one end and sanctuary at the other. Adjudication stands as the most coercive because it is the least participatory and most punitive of the possible dispute resolution techniques. Conversely, sanctuary stands as the most participatory and the least punitive of dispute resolution techniques. Between these ends of the continuum lie in order of their coerciveness: arbitration, fact-finding and mediation (Aubert 1963). The relative coerciveness of each of these techniques is determined by the level of participation afforded the actual disputants (the transgressor, the victim, and the community), the potential for normative dialogue, institutional autonomy, substantive focus, third-party intervention, and outcome parameters. In adjudication the level of disputant participation is minimal, normative dialogue is extremely prescribed, its institutional location is within the state apparatus, its focus is procedural, third-party intervention is central and potential outcomes are limited to legally determined punitive sanctions.

As a less coercive alternative, mediation allows direct participation by the disputants under the guidance of a mediator; normative dialogue is possible but within the context of legally allowable options such as restitution, community service or victim offender reconciliation. Its focus is a blending of the substantive and the procedural, its institutional locus is outside the legal apparatus but within the state bureaucracy, third-party intervention is informal and generally non-professional and potential outcomes are legally sanctioned but generally non-punitive.

As the least coercive approach, sanctuary requires direct participation by the disputants alone. The normative dialogue, while informed by general directives, is open and flexible, its focus is entirely substantive, its institutional location is purposely outside the state bureaucracy, third-party intervention is by invitation of the disputants and usually limited to mutually acceptable community members, and potential outcomes are socially rather than legally inspired. As a conciliatory process sanctuary justice creates an environment in which the participants are solely responsible for the resolution of their conflict. Their participation is bounded by time and space. The participants are channeled toward a settlement by the social structure of the sanctuary concept. The sanctuary is structured to allow only a limited amount of social interaction for the transgressor while the dispute is being settled. At the same time sanctuary temporarily protects the transgressor against state intervention and vigilante justice. Therefore, it is in the best interest of the transgressor, the community, and the victim to move forward toward a negotiated settlement.

For the transgressor a settlement means a full and complete reintegration into the community. For the community a settlement means that all issues regarding equity and freedom have been addressed and resolved. For the victim a settlement means that the harm associated with the transgression has been acknowledged and compensation has been rendered. Unlike criminal convictions and legal judgments which are focused almost exclusively on redressing past actions, a negotiated settlement balances the remediation of past harm with a blueprint of future action. The underlying forward focus of conciliation is the primary catalyst for moving the disputants toward a settlement (Susskind and Cruikshank 1987). While criminal and civil proceedings rely on state coercion to initially bring disputing parties together, the sanctuary structure and conciliation process provide an autonomous opportunity for constructing a settlement.

Conciliation begins with the assumption that the best settlement possible is one that is crafted by the disputants themselves. Not only is it assumed that the disputants can settle their own conflict but they must settle it with a minimum of outside influence or assistance. The conciliation process is informed by the belief that disputants own their own conflict (Christie 1977). Therefore, the disputants and the disputants alone are responsible for the resolution of their own conflict. The assumption of ownership creates a social expectation to settle. The disputants experience this expectation not as a coercive force but as a life-affirming connection to community. The intentionality of community creates a feeling of attachment that is stronger and more permanent than the commitment that characterizes a person's connection to less intentional and more functional institutions such as school or work. The personal, mutual nature of attachment prevents the community from reducing the whole person to a narrowly defined negative label as is the case with state justice. Persons bonded by attachment are perceived as moral agents who are capable of moral growth and deserving of moral guidance (Morris 1981). As is the case in mutually supportive families, transgressions are viewed by the community as opportunities to advance the moral development of individual members.

The long-term objective of mutualist moral development is the internalization of the central virtues of the community by each individual member. The primary objective of state justice is the improvement of society. The measure of success for state justice is the relative rate of crime and degree of social order. When crime rates fall state justice is assumed to be more efficient and when crime rates rise state justice is assumed to be less efficient. Within the context of state justice the recidivism of an individual is of interest only in the way it impacts crime control and social order. The individual transgressor is viewed not as a moral agent capable of personal transformation but as a mechanical being susceptible to behavioral manipulation through punishment or treatment. By contrast, the moral development of the individual is the primary objective of the mutualist model of justice. Moral agency demands that actions directed toward the transgressors must be for their own good rather than for the good of society (Morris 1981). The moral transformation of transgressors will ultimately contribute to the good of the community. When the community engages the transgressor for their own sake it suggests to the transgressor that participation in the conciliatory process is in their best interest. Without the underlying mutualism of conciliation the process would revert to an adversarial relationship in which the participants assume positions of demand and denial.

In an adversarial system, society acting through the state makes punitive or therapeutic demands of the transgressor. In response the transgressor denies or minimizes responsibility in an attempt to limit his or her exposure to state intervention. The demands of the state generally take the form of correctional or rehabilitative supervision. The denial of the transgressor is usually expressed in terms of excuse or justification (Tavuchis 1991). When the transgressor 'resorts to excuse or justification they attempt to distance themselves from their actions and unique personal identities . . . They appeal variously, to impaired self or external forces to exonerate their doings and their consequences' (Tavuchis 1991: 19).

The cycle of demand and denial precludes the possibility of life-affirming processes such as conciliation because it profoundly constrains the settlement discourse. The rigidity of demand and denial does not allow for the open and full discussion of normative standards. Without normative discourse communicative law and conciliation are impossible. Among all the alternatives to state justice: arbitration, mediation, fact finding, and conciliation, only conciliation can fully neutralize the tendency toward demand and denial that characterizes contemporary conflict.

Of all the alternatives to state justice conciliation is the least procedural. It is conceived as a free form discussion among equal members of a shared community. The only expectation of the discussion is a mutually satisfactory agreement. While participants in conciliation may reference broad normative directives to guide their discussion, they cannot refer to either specific legal statutes or procedural rules to structure their dialogue. The parameters for their discussion are established by the concept of sanctuary which channels the disputants toward conciliation by providing a communicative framework that is characterized by a community context, limited time frame, open negotiations and good faith bargaining. Together these three features move the disputants toward conciliation. The limited time frame creates an urgency to initiate and complete the conciliation process, the open negotiations reinforce the ownership of the dispute by the three relevant parties (the transgressor, the victim, and the community), and the good faith bargaining insures that the participants can proceed with the conciliation process knowing that their interests will be central to any settlement. Given its conciliatory potential sanctuary stands as the antithesis of state justice.

As the antithesis of state justice sanctuary effectively solves the three major problems associated with the contemporary system of criminal law: the power imbalance between the individual accused and the agents of the state making the accusations; the normative rigidity that drastically limits potential solutions; and the marginalization of the transgressor which increases rather than decreases the chances of recidivism. The power imbalance between the individual and the state in any criminal case creates 'downward law' which is overwhelmingly decided in favor of the party with more power (Black 1976). The predominance of downward law in contemporary criminal proceedings contributes to the alienation of the accused and their supporters and leads directly to a decline in the legitimacy of law. Downward law creates a sense of powerlessness among the weakest members of society which further alienates them from the life of their community. Their reduced stake in the common life makes it more likely that they will transgress in the future (Hulsman 1986). The application of rigid normative standards in contemporary criminal processing creates a context of absolute justice, where a guilty verdict is viewed as a win for society and a loss for the transgressor and a not guilty verdict is viewed as a win for the transgressor and a loss for society. In either event the root cause of the transgression remains unaddressed. The marginalization of the transgressor that occurs as a byproduct of a successful state prosecution makes it exceedingly difficult for the transgressor to reintegrate into society. The further a person is from the center of social life the more difficult it is to participate in the legitimate activities that immunize them from the temptation to transgress.

Sanctuary justice is able to overcome each of these problems because it is based on the principles of equality, assensus, and mutualism. The invitation to participate in sanctuary justice is predicated on the assumption that only equals are capable of negotiating for themselves. Because it is a truly voluntary process from its outset to its conclusion, the participants always possesses the power to exit the process if they feel it is in their best interest and the best interest of the community. Once the conciliation process has commenced, the negotiation of a resolution is enhanced by a legal discourse that is informed by assensus. In a context of assensus, law is conceived as a discussion that is cohesive rather than as an edict that is disruptive. Assensus keeps alive the sense that law unites members of community rather than separates them. Finally, the potential for use of sanctuary as an alternative to state justice rests with its mutualist capacity. The participants in a conflict, the transgressor, the victim, and the community will only embark on the conciliation process if they perceive a sense of mutual support. The trust engendered by the concept of sanctuary is the source of its legitimacy. Persons have used and will use sanctuary as a means of resolution, reintegration, and restoration because they believe that it supports the interests of the community and all its members and they trust that the conciliation process will yield settlements that contribute to the common life and the common good.

References

Aubert, V. (1963) 'Competition and dissensus: two types of conflict resolution,' *Journal of Conflict Resolution*, 7: 26–42.

Bianchi, H. (1994) *Justice as Sanctuary*, Bloomington: Indiana University Press.

Black, D. (1976) *The Behavior of Law*, New York: Academic Press.

Braithwaite, J. (1994) *Crime, Shame and Reintegration*, New York: Cambridge University Press.

Christie, N. (1977) 'Conflict as property,' *British Journal of Criminology*, 17: 1–15.

Cordella, Peter (1996) 'A communitarian theory of social order', in P. Cordella and L. Siegel (eds) *Readings in Contemporary Criminological Theory*, Boston: Northeastern University Press.

Durkheim, E. (1933) *The Division of Labor in Society*, New York: Free Press.

Feinberg, J. (1974) *Doing and Deserving*, Princeton: Princeton University.

Hulsman, L. (1986) 'Critical criminology and the concept of crime,' *Contemporary Crises*, 10: 63–80.

Macmurray, J. (1961) *Persons in Relations*, New York: Harper and Brothers.

— (1974) *Freedom in the Modern World*, London: Faber and Faber.

— (1977) *Conditions of Freedom*, Toronto: Mission Press.

Mathiesen, T. (1990) 'General prevention as communication,' in T. Mathiesen, *Prison on Trial: a critical assessment*, Newbury Park: Sage.

Michalowski, R. (1985) *Order, Law and Crime*, New York: Random House.

Morris, H. (1981) 'A paternalistic theory of punishment,' *American Philosophical Quarterly*, 18: 263–71.

Nonet, P. and Selznick, P. (2001) *Law and Society in Transition*, New Brunswick: Transaction Press.

Pepinsky, H. (1980) *Crime Control Strategies: an introduction to the study of crime*, New York: Oxford University Press.

Susskind, L. and Cruikshank, J. (1987) *Breaking the Impasse: consensual approaches to resolving public disputes*, Boston: Basic Books.

Tavuchis, N. (1991) *Mea culpa: a sociology of apology and reconciliation*, Stanford: Stanford University Press.

Section III

The needs of victims and the healing process

Restorative justice processes follow the precept that when a harm occurs, we should most centrally be concerned with responding to the needs of those harmed. And, while it is true that a person who harms another harms him/herself and likely those who love him/her, the focus of the chapters in this section concern responding to the needs of those who have been directly victimized or traumatized by this person's actions. Over the past thirty years there have been significant advances in meeting the needs of victims of crime to be heard, informed, and compensated. But, there is a long distance to be traveled on the path of listening to victims' stories, acknowledging and understanding the nature of their harm experiences, and fully grasping the evolution of their processes of healing or the degree to which they remain frozen in the rupture of self and processes that hinder their healing. Healing, the integration of harm or trauma in one's life, cannot, however, be individually accomplished. Trauma is a socio-political experience that disrupts not only the assumptive world of the person victimized, but their relatives and members of their communities. They, too, need to experience acknowledgement, voice, participation, and social reparation in order to heal. And, while social reparation, shared mourning, and shared memory are critical components of healing in the wake of massive collective trauma such as that experienced by survivors of the Holocaust and gross human rights violations throughout the world (Section IV), such components are also critical in the healing process for 'individually' traumatized persons.

The social construction of self is ever-evolving; therefore it is critical that we understand disruptions of the assumptive world of self in their social context. This is why many restorative justice models welcome the families of those directly victimized and members of the larger community. However, in state-criminal justice processes, there are whole sets of victims who are denied voice. Victims and their families who are opposed to the nature of the sentences advocated by prosecutors are often denied voice, as are murder victims' families for reconciliation who are against the death penalty. Furthermore, family members of those sanctioned, imprisoned, or put to death are rarely considered real victims and given respect, consideration, dignity, and voice in matters of sentencing and prison policy.

Mary Achilles and Lorraine Stutzman-Amstutz (Chapter 13) discuss the increased participation of victims in state criminal justice systems and in our recognition of victims' need for support services and compensation. Yet, the rights of victims are systemically placed in the hands of prosecutors whose interests can conflict with the implementation of these rights and with meeting the needs these victims express. This issue is most clearly seen in the situation where the state is seeking the death penalty and the victims' family, or some members of the victims' family, are against the death penalty.

While we have learned to respect victims' capacities to know what they need, we also have learned that we need to attend to what they say they need to reconstruct their lives. We need to recognize that healing is a complex and dynamic process that evolves over time as an individual struggles to reconstruct his/her sense of self, relations with others, and life views. This is the context within which we must help victims listen to themselves and help them in their healing and restoration processes. Our efforts and services must be far more extensive than those needs that simply relate to offender processing. They must be available to victims even when those who have harmed them have not been named. The experience of victims in reconstructing their lives requires a wide variety of options. The more options, the more victims can empower themselves by making choices to meet their individual needs and senses of justice.

The grief and trauma that often follow victimization are disruptions of the assumptions of everyday life and the deep values, beliefs, and concepts that compose the self. The meaningfulness of self, one's place in the world, the nature of life and of one's relationship to others, and the predictability of the future is in varying degrees damaged or shattered by trauma. In other words, one's identity is reflectively called into question. Such processes are explored by both Jeffrey Kauffman (Chapter 14) and

Judith W. Kay (Chapter 15). What is to be restored in restorative justice is the wound that occurs because of the loss of the assumptive world. Kauffman's main concern is to explore the nature of this wound. Traumatic injustice stimulates both generative and deconstructive energies. It leaves a person prone to become disconnected from her/himself and others, from the past, as well as the future. It simultaneously stimulates a self-conscious struggle to reconstruct a new self-being, one of worth, constancy, and meaningfulness. The role of restorative justice in this process is that of helping victims to create new connections with themselves and others; to help them transcend their self-accusing, self-blaming, self-diminishing, and self-defeating identity feelings.

Those who have lost loved ones to murder face a set of daunting questions similar to those faced by those less seriously physically harmed: 'Why has this happened to us?' 'What kind of person will she/he, and I, become?' and 'How will this experience and its aftermath shape the way each of us thinks of ourselves, others, and the world?' Murder shatters the self and the stories we tell ourselves. It shatters the family we once knew. Healing is, of course, a difficult and turbulent process, but for many relatives of homicide victims there are added impediments to addressing these issues. They are often ignored and silenced by the state creating a major obstacle to their benefiting from the healing potential of telling their stories. They are often shunned by friends and associates who find their stories too troubling to listen to. And yet, as Kay insightfully relates, for murder victims' family members who oppose the death penalty, telling their stories can be both psychologically healing and politically necessary.

Describing narrative as the heart and soul of restorative justice, Kay explains that the act of telling one's personal story rescues the narrator from the realm of silence, isolation, and despair about self and helps to restore his/her faith in the possibility of deeply connecting with others and self. It rescues one from the personal space of having no assurance that one will ever be able to re-integrate one's life, to abandon one's self-fears. Reciprocally, deep listening to a wound narrative opens oneself to self-change, signaled by integrating this narrative into one's own biography. However, when no one listens or the story-telling's reciprocity of telling and listening is lost, telling one's story can become wooden and rote, a fixture of degeneration, and can leave the story-teller feeling worse. In contrast, when survivors find or create a network of listeners who affirm their common humanity, relaying their stories is more likely to be beneficial and move the teller from passive, alienated victim to active survivor and/or passionate witness.

Murder victims' families opposed to the death penalty challenge the social premise that the world is just and that harsh punishment violence is necessary to restore moral order and the current distributions of benefits and burdens in our societies. Instead, they testify to a broken world in which humans who are in pain harm others. They call for a pedagogy of suffering in which responsiveness to each other's humanness and to each other's suffering are the chief norms. What telling their stories can communicate is not how to get over being a murder victim's relative and return to 'normality' by securing the ultimate punishment, but rather, how to live a healthy life that has had an experience of violent tragedy within it.

Jim Acker (Chapter 16) continues this discussion by critically examining the justification for capital punishment offered in the name of murder victims and their survivors. He concludes that this argument lacks credibility as executions are rare; survivors' vulnerability is increased because the death-penalty process is unusually protracted, and there is no guarantee that an execution will bring healing even for those who advocate its undertaking. For those family members who oppose the death penalty, the whole process often leads to feelings of isolation, rejection, and betrayal by the very system upon which they must rely for justice following the violent death of a loved one.

Acker also explores the legal history of victim impact evidence and the assertion that victim impact evidence affords murder victims' survivors meaningful input and voice in the criminal justice process. Following this analysis, he presents some possibilities for how restorative justice precepts might be creatively activated and inserted into capital case processes. Nevertheless, he concludes that the death penalty signals a society's uncompromising rejection of the offender and precludes any prospect of redemption or reconciliation. And, it causes profound new trauma, including suffering to be endured by the offender's family. In these and other respects, capital punishment is anathema to many murder victims' survivors and is at odds with the basic precepts of restorative justice.

In accord with this conclusion, Judith Brink (Chapter 17) tells her story asserting that the families and other loved ones of incarcerated men and women are not only victims of this crime, but, as well, victims of the state's punishment violence. Rarely is it publicly acknowledged that the mothers and fathers, the close friends and relatives, the husbands, wives, and especially the children of the incarcerated are victims. They constitute an invisible and voiceless set of victims.

Until you experience it first hand, she says, the victimization of those who maintain contact with a person in prison is not obvious. They are often subject to demeaning and insulting actions by prison officials, judgments placed upon them by their neighbors, and the disruption of their family life, especially their economic situation which is greatly affected by the financial cost and stress of maintaining the relationship. The effects of this victimization are particularly disturbing for the children of those incarcerated, whose stories are strikingly filled with feelings of abandonment, anger, unworthiness, and shame. They are often left on their own to comprehend what is happening and they are often traumatized by their visits or by not being allowed to visit. Furthermore, as they frequently face social conditions similar to those that their incarcerated parent faced, they feel that they are themselves at risk for making similar choices to those made by this parent. Here, Brink reminds us that social responsibility is a two-way street. If the way society is organized reasonably meets the needs of children through adolescence and young adulthood so that they have an opportunity to become active, positive members of a community, a person who harms others needs our support with restorative reconstruction and healing. And, correspondingly, if the society's institutional structures provide little support for the nurturance of a child and young person, and in fact does the opposite by fostering and legalizing social conditions that lead to counter-violence, delinquency, dysfunctionality, and crime, then the society needs our support with restorative reconstruction.

13

Responding to the needs of victims

What was promised, what has been delivered

Mary Achilles and Lorraine Stutzman-Amstutz

The Victim Rights Movement has over the last thirty years achieved great advances on behalf of crime victims. These advances can be seen in the increased participation of victims in our systems of justice and in our societal recognition of victims' need for compensation. In all fifty states we have seen the passage of legislation that established crime victims' bills of rights and crime victims' compensation programs. These advances address the needs of victims to be included in the process and in assessing the financial impact that the crime had on them. The more salient elements of victim participation in the system can be summarized as the right to be notified, to be present, and to be heard. These advancements can be seen in the legislative histories of the individual states and are paralleled at the national level. Let's take a look at an illustration of the overall movement.

Pennsylvania has a strong history of advocacy on behalf of crime victims. We would certainly claim that, like our counterparts in other states and at the national level, we have been, and continue to be, successful in our efforts to advance the rights and interests of crime victims. We certainly have seen an increased awareness of crime victims by the system and would say that many of the hopes and dreams of the victims' rights movement have been achieved. A review of our history indicates that the rights of victims have been evolutionary in their identification and implementation and that, as each new initiative is implemented, we evolve in our understanding of the needs of victims.

Pennsylvania has one of the first statewide rape crisis coalitions and the first domestic violence coalition in the nation. Its first Crime Victims' Bill of Rights was passed in 1984. This list consisted of three rights.

1 the right to be treated with dignity and respect;
2 the right to provide a victim impact statement should a pre-sentence investigation be ordered; and
3 the right to receive notification from the prosecutor's office when a prisoner convicted of a feloniously assaultive crime is released from prison.

This was Pennsylvania's first exercise in the inclusion of victims in the criminal justice system. Along with the establishment of these rights, the enabling legislation established a mandatory penalty assessment on

211

criminal offenders. This money was used to fund the crime victims' compensation program and the implementation of these new rights.

This new funding stream dedicated to victim rights spawned the hiring of victim witness coordinators, primarily in prosecutor's offices, to ensure these functions. Between 1984 and 1992 it became evident that these rights, although originally well intended, fell short of the needs of crime victims. Many issues arose as these rights were reviewed and implemented. Some of the questions needing to be addressed included:

1 How can the treatment of victims be legislated?
2 Why is the right to a victim impact statement, detailing the impact of the crime on the victims, dependent upon whether or not the court orders a pre-sentence report on the offender?
3 How can the prosecutor's office provide notice of the offender's release from prison when they do not have that information?

This statute and these resulting questions became the starting point for a cascade of legislation that would be enacted over the next twenty years. This first Crime Victims' Bill of Rights was quickly followed by a statute in 1986 that required victim input into parole decisions made on state sentenced offenders. This was in turn followed by a statute that required notice to the victim of their right to have input into the parole decision of state sentenced prisoners at each and every parole review.

The most sweeping changes came in 1995 when, in addition to expanding the existing rights of victims in the criminal justice process, then Governor Tom Ridge signed into legislation a bill that created the Office of the Victim Advocate. Governor Ridge stated that in signing this and other victim-related legislation he was 'elevating the voices of victims.' The Victim Advocate position,

which requires nomination by the Governor and confirmation by the Senate, brought the voices of victims into the highest levels of government. The status of the position was a clear statement of the commitment and importance of victim input into decisions being made about particular offenders (the Victim Advocate represents the rights and interest of crime victims before the Board of Probation and Parole and the Department of Corrections) and on how the state justice system operates.

Between 1995 and 2001 there were significant additions made to the Pennsylvania Crime Victims' Bill of Rights. Pennsylvania parallels other states in this search for enhanced rights for victims of crime. This illustrates the evolving recognition of the needs of victims as we began to include them in the process. It is also reflective of the attitudes of those implementing the rights. Some legislation was clearly enacted to force parts of the system to be more inclusive of the victim. The second statute mentioned previously on victim input into parole decisions seems to be a case in point, forcing the Parole Board into ensuring that victims get the opportunity for input at each and every parole hearing, not just the first hearing. In the process of including victims the inevitable view of the rights from their perspective came to shape ours. Victims could tell us whether or not the right was on point, whether or not it addressed a need for them, and whether or not it was being implemented in a manner that addressed their needs.

According to the National Center for Victims of Crime there are currently thirty-two states that have passed state constitutional amendments. The three results sought by the amendments are:

1 Crime victims' rights are protected in the way that the defendants' rights are protected.
2 Crime victims' rights are a permanent part of the criminal justice system.

212

3 Courts would have the power to enforce crime victim rights if they were violated.

The federal constitutional amendment which has been proposed by Representative Diane Feinstein (D California) and Senator Jon Kyl (R Arizona) has sought to achieve the same results as the state constitutional amendments. However, the federal amendment includes the additional result of ensuring that no matter where a crime occurs within the United States there would be a uniform set of rights that would include the right to be informed, be present, and be heard in the criminal justice process.

Overall, we believe that the victim rights movement in Pennsylvania and nation has been a success. This is particularly evident simply looking at our increased attention to the rights of victims. While there are some who believe that victims hold too much power, we would argue that this is not true. First, when you look at the statutes and case law both in Pennsylvania and at the federal level, the rights of offenders continue to have stronger protections under our system of justice than do those of victims. Second, despite our great advancements in victim rights, crime victims have no legal standing and are dependent on other stakeholders in the system providing them with access. For example, under current Pennsylvania law the following prevails when it comes to notification for victims:

1 Local police are responsible for providing victims with a comprehensive brochure detailing rights and services available to them.
2 County prosecutors are responsible for providing notice of all pre-trial hearings.
3 State prisons are responsible for notification to victims of any pre-release consideration (in Pennsylvania, that means prior to completion of the minimum sentence).

The rights of victims in Pennsylvania are not enforceable. In fact, the Pennsylvania Crime Victims' Bill of Rights contains a clause that states that nothing in the statute creates no cause of action or defense in favor of any person arising out of the failure to comply.

This lack of enforcement ability places victim rights at the discretion of those mandated to implement them. Including victims through police and prosecutor channels began as a good faith attempt to include victims in the process but, as time has gone on and we have gained more insight into the operations of the system, we are left with some very daunting questions about the true status of victims' rights in our system. For example:

1 What happens when the wants, needs and interests of the victim do not coincide with those of the prosecutor?
2 How does this conflict affect victim rights implementation?

What is often not talked about in the search for justice for victims is that sometimes the interest of the victim conflicts with that of the prosecutors. Sometimes what victims want and need may not fit into the broader responsibility of the prosecutor. The responsibility of a prosecutor is often articulated in terms of community safety. Community safety is a more comprehensive mission than representing the rights and interests of an individual crime victim. What do we do when that occurs? There are countless undocumented tales of situations that illustrate this point, but the most acute situation is slowly creeping up on us. This issue of conflict is most clearly seen in cases where the state is seeking the death penalty and the victim's family are against the death penalty.

The organization Murder Victims' Families for Reconciliation (MVFR) has published a booklet which discusses this issue and documents experiences of their members from across the nation. There

213

seems to be a somewhat natural, albeit atrocious, conflict that appears when the family member of the murder victim does not believe in execution and the state is seeking an execution for the murder of their loved one. Members of this organization have recounted stories of family members who oppose the death penalty and are thus silenced, marginalized, and abandoned by the people who are theoretically charged with assisting them through this legal process.

We would agree that all victims should be treated with dignity and respect no matter what their race, color, creed, and belief system. However, when you have actors within the system who are responsible for including victims but who struggle with what to do when including the victim will derail, destroy or stand in opposition to the actors' agenda, how do we reconcile this? No family member of a murder victim should be excluded from the prosecution of the case. However, no prosecutor should be required to provide information to those that seek to derail the agenda. Should victims have the right to have input into whether or not the state seeks the death penalty? In Pennsylvania this has only just begun to surface. Where it tends to come into play is at sentencing, where victims have the right to submit an oral and/or written victim impact statement during the penalty phase. The law is clear that the testimony should be directed to the impact that the crime has had on the victim.

In non-death penalty cases, should the victims wander from the impact of their crime to what they would like to see happen in terms of sentencing, no one really takes notice. But the stakes are much higher in a death penalty case where a human life is on the line. This creates a situation where the prosecutor will ask the court to direct the victim to keep their comments focused on the impact that the crime has had on them and other details allowed by law. Often prosecutors are reluctant to present victim

impact testimony during the penalty phase for fear of appellate issues arising from the testimony. In these situations the victims either have no opinion on the death penalty or are in agreement with the state seeking the death penalty. They will agree to waive their right to provide a victim impact statement if they believe that their testimony will provide grounds for appeal. This leaves those victims who oppose the death penalty, and who wish to exercise their right to find a place where their thoughts about the defendant's punishment can be heard, out in the cold.

In light of dilemmas such as these and the issues raised earlier, can we conclude that the victim rights movement is a success or a failure? With due consideration to what still remains to be done we would suggest that it falls somewhere in the middle of a continuum between success and failure. Success can be seen in the vast amount of the victims' rights legislation passed and an overall greater awareness of victims' need to be included in the process. We now have a system in which victims are required to be included at various significant stages in the process. One of the greatest critiques of the victim rights movement is that many of the needs of victims are not addressed with the advances made to date. But we suggest that the identification of victims' needs has been dynamic and has evolved over time. And the advances have kept pace. Early in the victim rights movement the focus was on rights in the criminal and juvenile justice system. The future of the movement will be defined by our ability to continue to listen to what victims really want and need from our systems of justice and the community.

The question becomes, first, how do we define success, and second, how do we measure it? This might be a starting point for the future of the victims' movement. What does success really look like for a victim? Is success measured in the framework of the system? Is it measured in the framework of the overall experience of crime victims? Can the system address all of the needs of victims? These are questions with no particular answers at this time but which provide us guidelines about where we should go from here.

Elsewhere we have written about personal experiences having to do with our listening to victims that have changed the way in which we now listen. This is a greater challenge than most of us know. We think we listen to victims but we hear them within a framework of the lessons we have learned. We need to recognize that, as we advanced over the last thirty years to ensure the rights of victims, we now need to take a long hard look at ourselves and see that victims have taught us not only what they need in terms of rights in the current system but what they need to reconstruct their lives. We need to pay attention to victims so that we can recognize and respect their capacity to know what they need. After our initial success we often settle into a way of thinking that includes an assumed knowledge base on what victims want and need. This precludes us from seeing the experiences of victims as dynamic and as something that evolves over time as an individual victim attempts to move forward in life after the experience of victimization.

We participated in 'The Listening Project' conducted from 1999 to 2002, which provided us with a range of opinions and observations from victims and their advocates about their needs and how they can be met. This project was completed largely to hear what victims had to say about restorative justice practices pertaining to victims and the impact for victims. There are those victims who said,

> I think this is one of the best tools we have had to get offenders to be accountable and to take a good hard look at themselves and their lives, and how crime affects their families, affects the victim and the community. This is the important part of what restorative justice has to be.

On the other hand, a participant commented

> there are people in my field who when they hear the term 'restorative justice' they think of a very offender-based system that is not informed by knowledge of victim issues. And that is a lot of the fear about restorative justice.

Another victim commented that,

> I want to give up on this version of restorative justice, the one that we have. It gets a bad grade. It is not good. What version would I like? Somehow it would have to include the tough piece of having equal power shared by the victim community. And I mean decision making, money and power, from the start.

Victims have taught us to hear with curiosity, not judgment. We must respond to their voices with an attitude of 'How can we make that happen for you?' This is hard for those of us who work in the system. The structure, size, volume, and history of the system seem to force our thinking into a box. We are then unconsciously trying to get the next victim to fit into it. I have previously described this as asking victims if they want what is behind door number one, door number two, or door number three. In fact, what they want may be behind door number four and it is more tailored to their specific needs. This often appears challenging to many of us. It takes time, patience, and the ability to listen to ensure that we are creating arenas in which victims can voice their unique needs. It makes us wonder if we are actually trying to find a standardization of needs across the board as we listen to victims. We must hear what victims say they need.

The challenge of listening openly to victims also lies in our willingness to be open to change. For example, when we first introduced the victim impact statement, did we mean to limit the ability of victims to comment on the sentence of the offender?

The victim impact statement is probably one of the most significant rights that has been legislated. When victims choose to exercise this right to give an oral or written statement they also get the opportunity to make their statement before the offender. More often than not this is an empowering moment for them. But did we really mean to limit their testimony to the impact that the crime had on them, as outlined in Pennsylvania statute and in similar statutes across the nation? Experience has taught me that victims often have something to say about the sentence, what it should be, how it should be served and, more important, what it may take for them to feel a sense of justice and accountability. Staying open to this evolutionary process is important in addressing the needs of victims.

Listening to victims is not always that easy. Sometimes when we think that we are listening, we find by their response that we are missing the boat. As one example, Lorraine's experience while working in Elkhart, Indiana, in 1984 illustrates the way we often allow our agenda to supersede the needs of victims:

> I was two years out of college and had my social work degree with an interest in women's issues. I was working for a victim offender mediation program at the time and decided to volunteer at the local YWCA which ran a program for victims of domestic violence. Following our training and after gaining experience I began co-facilitating a support group for women in abusive relationships. This was exciting. There was no curriculum available to us so my co-facilitator and I developed some goals of where we wanted to take this group. We wanted to empower them to want something better for themselves including a non-abusive relationship. We believed that one goal for these women should be to leave the abusive relationship. Although we thought the group should be self-determinate, as facilitators we believed that it was our job

> to get them to that point. We believed that we could do this through sessions on self-esteem, employment issues, managing finances, etc. The group met each week and each week we would establish goals for the following meeting. Each week the goals would not be met. After several weeks of the goals not being met it occurred to me that these were not the goals of the group but our goals as facilitators. We went into our next meeting and asked them what they wanted the goal to be for the next week. Without hesitation one of the women responded that by next week she wanted to buy a pair of slacks. She knew what she wanted. Since her spouse (as in many battering relationships) controlled the money she just wanted to take some control back. Not enough to leave, or at least leave at this point, but enough to exercise some control over herself while at the same time attending to her need to look good. She was much more aware of what would lift her self-esteem than any presentation or discussion that we could have conducted. The group's support in this seemingly small step was essential to her success. She bought those pants that week.

Listening is always a challenge but listening must be our top priority with victims. Empowering people is more important than our need to fix or lead the way. Victims need us to walk with them and assist them, not lead them. Listening is most important because the experience of victims is ever evolving. It is a dynamic process.

Victims of violent crime are victims of trauma. The trauma of victimization has both short- and long-term impacts. Not all victims will experience all of the elements of trauma. Since crime does not occur in a vacuum it is important to remember that when victimization occurs, who the victim was prior to the experience and what was going on in their life will affect their response to the trauma. One of the best descriptions of the psychological trauma of victimization can be found in *Victim Assistance: Frontiers and*

Fundamentals by Marlene Young (1993). Young breaks the experience into short- and long-term impacts of the crisis reaction. The short-term crisis reaction can be defined by both its physical and emotions dimensions. The physical response is the shock, disorientation, and numbness where the adrenaline increases and causes the release of a variety of danger hormones. These hormones create a physical response to the trauma which can be seen in the often identified fight-or-flight experience. The emotional component of the short-term crisis reaction parallels the physical response with shock, denial and disbelief. This is often followed over a period of time with a cataclysm of emotions including anger/rage, confusion/frustration, fear or terror, guilt or self-blame, shame or humiliation, and grief and sorrow.

The long-term responses to the trauma can manifest into post traumatic stress disorder and other depressive disorders, though not all victims experience post traumatic stress disorder. Many victims will suffer a re-experience of the crisis reaction for long periods of time after the event as they attempt to reconstruct their lives. These re-experiences are often cued by events that contain some reminder of the original experience of victimization. There are many systems, such as the medical system and the justice system, that are riddled with cues for a crisis response. For example, the physical exam for victims of sexual assault, police and other justice system interviews during the investigation, or the anniversary of the event are just a few of the cues.

The victim's attempt to reconstruct their life is often both interrupted and supported by their participation in the justice system. The victim's experience in the justice system, although often criticized, provides a needed recognition that the system as the symbol of the community acts to validate the victimization and provide the official effort to extract accountability from the offender. Our experience is that although there may be needs that go unaddressed, most victims would not trade the overall experience. They frequently feel a sense of justice or at least elements of justice. They are provided with an opportunity to participate in the system, and overall the system does acknowledge that they exist. However, they are not fundamentally a legal stakeholder and, although no longer viewed as only a witness for the prosecution, they still have not achieved a status equal to that of the offender.

Restorative justice has promised significant standing to victims as they advocate that placing the harm done to them should be the starting point of justice. This centrality of harm is in stark contrast to our current justice system which places the violation of the law as the centerpiece of our legal process. The promise of restorative justice is:

1 an elevation of the victim's status;
2 identification of the victim as the person that the offender is first and foremost accountable to;
3 greater and more meaningful participation in the legal process;
4 a focus on the harm to provide a necessary identification of victim needs as the starting point of justice;
5 the creation of a space where victims in the aftermath of trauma can control the process of justice.

Restorative justice theory parallels the standard crisis and trauma intervention techniques for victims (Achilles and Zehr 2001). Listed below are the standard crisis and trauma intervention techniques for victims and the application promise of restorative justice (Young 1993: 13–24).

Crisis intervention techniques – Restorative justice promise
Safety and security – Elevation of the status
Ventilation and validation – Recognition of the harm as the starting point of justice

Preparation and prediction – Identification of harms and corresponding needs

Information and education – Participation based on victim needs

Restorative justice theory surpasses the current system in its ability to address the crisis and trauma of victimization, because the process would be defined with the needs of the victims and the offender as the starting point. Our current system was not designed that way. Its focus is on the violation of the law and the protection of the rights of the accused. The rule of law prevails in our current system over the needs of the victim. The basic tenet of restorative justice is that crime is a violation of relationships and as such creates obligation and responsibilities (Stutzman Amstutz and Zehr 1998). It creates an arena where victims can be heard, empowered, and assisted in the reconstruction of their lives.

Restorative justice has clearly delivered for victims through the creation and expansion of mediation programs and other programs where, either directly or indirectly, the victim has an opportunity to engage in contact with the offender. As a result of our exposure to the theory of restorative justice, we were both part of the establishment of the Pennsylvania Office of the Victim Advocate Mediation Program for Victims of Violent Crime. The planning of this program began in 1995 with its implementation effective in 1998. Designed to provide victims of violent crime with an opportunity to meet and/or exchange communications with each other, over thirty mediations have occurred since implementation. Most of the cases involve victims of sexual assault and/or homicide. The existence of this mediation program provides a new option for victims which can address needs that the current system had failed to do. Many within the victim community had failed to hear this need in victims. Our exposure to restorative justice theory created an opportunity for advocates

in Pennsylvania to hear victims and their need to talk with their offender.

One of the most significant ways in which restorative justice has delivered for crime victims in Pennsylvania has been the incorporation of restorative justice principles into the mission of the Pennsylvania juvenile justice system. Act 33 of Special Session No. 1, 1995, of the Pennsylvania legislature established a new mission for Pennsylvania's juvenile justice system that has its roots in the concepts of restorative justice, which gives priority to repairing the harm done to victims and communities, and defines offender accountability in terms of assuming responsibility and taking action to repair harm. The new purpose clause is premised on the concept that clients of the juvenile justice system include the victim, community, and the offender, and that each should receive 'balanced attention' and gain tangible benefits from their interactions with the system (Stutzman Amstutz and Zehr 1998).

Since this change in mission, the juvenile justice system in Pennsylvania and its leadership have advanced the issue of the rights and needs of crime victims. In fact it was the juvenile justice system leadership that went to then Governor Tom Ridge and expressed concern about the lack of legislative rights for victims of juvenile offenders. This was viewed as a welcome initiative from the view of the victim service community, and within a short time the legislature created those rights and the Governor's office provided the necessary budget to implement those rights. What is of equal importance is the continued efforts of the juvenile justice system to hold true to the values of restorative justice. Constant re-evaluation of police and procedures, training of system and non-system staff on issues related to victims and restorative justice, and inclusion of crime victims and victim advocates on planning committees, are some ways that an entire system is constantly striving to achieve balanced attention for the victim and the community.

218

To really look at whether or not restorative justice has delivered for victims at the national level, we would like to focus on the signposts that we developed to guide program development in including victims in the process of restorative justice. These signposts, written primarily for restorative justice advocates, still hold the fundamental elements for including victims appropriately in a restorative justice process.

We are working toward appropriate victim involvement in restorative justice programs when:

1 victims and victim advocates are represented on governing bodies and initial planning committees;
2 efforts to involve victims grow out of a desire to assist them, not offenders. Victims are not responsible to rehabilitate or assist offenders unless they choose to do so;
3 victims' safety is a fundamental element of program design;
4 victims clearly understand their roles in the program including potential benefits and risks to themselves and offenders;
5 confidentiality is provided within clear guidelines;
6 victims have as much information as possible about their case, the offense, and the offender;
7 victims can identify and articulate their needs and are given choices;
8 victims' opportunity for involvement is maximized;
9 program design provides referrals for support and assistance;
10 services are available to victims even when their offenders have not been arrested or are unwilling or unable to participate.

(Achilles and Zehr 2001)

We have made progress on many of the above but our progress has been limited. There are still many programs that do not include victims and victim advocates at the point of design. This may in fact be a result of not understanding what it is they do not know. Most programs believe they know what victims need and want, but are they truly listening if victims' and victim advocates' voices are not included? Often mediation programs will tell us that they cannot get victims involved despite their outreach efforts. It often does not occur to them that including the local victim service program in the design and development of the mediation program might lead to increased participation from victims. The victim service programs have some expertise in victim rights and the crisis and trauma of victimization which could be useful to the design of a program. Restorative justice advocates as a whole have failed to include victim advocates in their planning process. This creates a situation where the vision for the victim service community is that someone is developing a program and now they want to get victims involved. This creates tension and mistrust and a perception that including victims is an afterthought. Including victim advocates early in the process will eliminate all of these unintended consequences. It will not eliminate the need to build trust and create alliances but it will eliminate the creation of more reasons to mistrust.

Many restorative justice programs are designed with the primary focus being on the offender or at least attached to the existing system which provides this perception. The attachment of programs of mediation within departments of correction, although well intended, still provides a natural lean to the offender in the eyes of victim advocates. How can the wants and needs of the offender or the system in which the offender is being processed not take precedence over the needs of the victim? Safety and security concerns for departments of correction will always have the potential to overshadow the wants and needs of offenders. The subtle coercion that the system provides over the offender in mediation

219

cases is offset by the offender-oriented nature of the system. It is a system where the offender gets most of the attention, albeit negative attention but attention nevertheless. In these settings centrality of harm to the victim is seen as the starting point of justice. It is challenging to keep the focus on including victims based on a desire to assist them. Efforts to rehabilitate the offender are extremely important in these settings. The desire to assist victims could get lost. Restorative justice has not yet delivered a program totally designed from the standpoint of the desire to assist victims. While there have been programs developed that address the needs of victims, it has only been the needs of victims that relate to offenders.

The inclusion of victim service programs, or at least an alliance, increases the possibility of the needs of victims getting addressed. Victim service programs and others who provide assistance to victims have noted resources and expertise that would be beneficial to program development and to program staff once the program is implemented.

The presentation of the promise of restorative justice is most often framed in contrast to the current system of justice. This presentation negates the good that the current system has to offer victims. Most victims that we have encountered are clearly interested in the new opportunities that restorative justice theory has to offer. However, that does not mean that they would trade off the existing opportunities that the current system has to offer them. This is important in that it reflects a narrow view of the needs of victims. The experience of victims in reconstructing their lives is circuitous. It is not a linear process. The needs of victims are ever evolving and require a variety of options to address them. The more options that exist, the more victims can be empowered to make the choices that will address their individual needs, making the experience of justice unique to them.

Our hope is that constructive dialogue between restorative justice and victim advocates continues, which means restorative justice advocates must continue to demonstrate their understanding that:

1 the safety of the victims, both physical and emotional, is a fundamental element of any program design;
2 the courage of the victim to participate in any restorative justice process is appreciated and understood;
3 any services provided are designed to further empower victims;
4 victim experiences and reactions will not be judged;
5 victims are not to be used to benefit the offender or any other person.

References

Achilles, M., and Zehr, H. (2001) 'Restorative justice for crime victims: the promise and the challenge,' in G. Bazemore and M. Schiff (eds) *Restorative Community Justice: repairing harm and transforming communities*, Cincinnati, OH: Anderson Publishing.

Stutzman Amstutz, L. and Zehr, H. (1998) *Victim Offender Conferencing in Pennsylvania's Juvenile Justice System*, Harrisburg, PA: Commonwealth of Pennsylvania.

Young, M. A. (1993) *Victim Assistance: frontiers and fundamentals*, Washington, DC: National Organization for Victim Assistance.

14

Restoration of the assumptive world as an act of justice[1]

Jeffrey Kauffman

But the canoe is made of stone.
This is a sign that my words are true.
(Deganaweda, founder and lawgiver
of the League of the Iroquois)

Assumptive world theory and its relation to restorative justice

The assumptive world concept has a history that is rooted in a broad modern tradition of constructivism in psychology and sociology, and expresses a modern way of thinking about reality and experience that philosophers trace back to Kant. The idea and ascendancy of constructivist thinking is associated with the origin and unfolding of modernity. Modernity is the epoch in which constructivist ideologies, beliefs, or assumptions replaced *traditional* norms, while the ancient, sacred powers of God, which gave meaning, were weakening. Modernity, defined as the decline of traditional sociocultural order, is replaced by a belief that humans construct the human world, the belief that humans construct themselves as beliefs or assumptions, including the belief in justice as a fundamental organizing norm of assumptive worlds.

The 'assumptive world concept' is introduced by Parkes (1971, 1988) as a *psychological*, and a *cognitive* theory of construction. The concept has proved useful in understanding both grief and trauma and could be a common language of the theories of grief and trauma. Grief and trauma are disruptions of the constancy of the familiar, expected and idealized constructs or assumptions of everyday life and of the deep values and reflexivities that hold the assumptive world together, or resist fragmentation. Also important to Parkes' conception of the assumptive world is that it is preoccupied with constancy on an epistemic level, in which expectations about the future must maintain predictability, the very knowledge disrupted by a loss of the assumptive world.

Parkes' concept has been broadened, first by Janoff-Bulman (1992), who pointed out that constant internal constructs are constructs that have to do with the *valuation and meaningfulness of oneself and the world, shattered by traumatization.* In Janoff-Bulman's account of the loss of the assumptive world, the self's valuations of itself, its relationship with itself as an idealized object, can be recognized as the core meaning of the assumptive world, which is damaged by trauma. Parkes' picture of the griever does not suggest this important reflexive dimension. Recent thanatological constructivists, such as Neimeyer (2001) and Attig (1996), have been constructing more reflexive mourners – that is, conceptually a mourner who is a self-conscious human being.

Parkes thinks the assumptive world constructs are cognitions; the act of constructing is taken to be a cognitive act. This opinion is very widely accepted. Constructionist theory usually constructs itself as being cognitive. Attig (1996), however, demonstrates that the assumptive world could be an existential, practical world of normative relationship and everyday being. Attig's *self* is a reflexive self, of Heidegerian origins, of being fully in the world.

Kauffman (2002a, 2002b) argues that the assumptive world is a 'belief' construct – that is, that what is assumed is the believed world, and that *believing* is not an act of thinking, even when it does take a cognitive form. Believing is an act of identifying, valuing, and *trusting* to be true, while a cognitive act is a thought construct. At the root of the word 'belief,' the *OED* cites 'to hold estimable, valuable, to satisfactory, to be satisfied with,' and ' to hold dear, to like when also to Love' (*OED* 1971). Believing is an act of *holding and valuing*. Believing is taking upon oneself, and involves a certain committing of oneself to, the belief held and valued. Believing vests human reality; cognition beholds, with ability to disbelieve and to look upon, for example, with compassion, scorn, amusement, etc. As an act of constructing the assumptive world, the cognitive is subordinated to, and at the service of, belief. The 'cognitive narrative' is not the story. The story of the assumptive world, which includes justice, is not occurring on the level of thought but on the level of identity, even as cognition is part of a matrix of reflexive identities.

The choice of the word 'assumption' to name the self-power which constructs human reality of self and world has some very significant implications – most of all, that constructions of the human self and world are, ultimately, *groundless*. It implies that human reality, as the believed world we live in, has no ground beyond being taken for granted. The act of assuming is constructing an object which is *taken* as granted – that is, in holding and valuing, dissociated from its being 'merely' an assumption. It is not based on any authority beyond its own assumptive powers. The assumptive world is presumed, and as such raises questions about the ontologic and epistemic status of the self and world, or the reality of human consciousness and cultural constructs.

The desire, power and solidity of the self to basically believe in goodness and justice, to take a normative assumptive world as given, is inherently vulnerable to being shattered, to losing its normative constructive power and solidity, by traumatic injustice. Assumptions about oneself and the world are degraded and lost hold of by traumatic violation of the self. The *ideality* of assumptive world constructs and the constancy or cohesion of human reality are as *acts of assuming* which are subject to disruption, corruption, dissolution, decay, annihilation, etc. The world, in that case, is the lived illusion of constant idealized objects (in conjunction with a mixture of deviations from the norm), the lived illusion of idealities of the self which are inherently disposed to be vulnerable to violation and disruption by acts of injustice.

Between constancy and disruption, with the complex interactions between this pair, there has arisen in modernity what appears to be an enormous and increasing tension. The assumptive world of modernity is in *a state of rapid change*. And, as constancy tries to secure its mooring, a tension builds, and the assumptive world appears to be having a more difficult time holding things together.

This extreme disintegration of the assumptive world is unimaginable but it is an extreme that has occurred in some trauma victims, and defines a *tendency* in the contemporary world. Justice, in such a world, is the restoration of the assumptive world's normative constructive powers. And just persons mourn the losses suffered by the rapidity of change in modern times, and help establish a much deepened social tolerance for trauma, and death, and such. How do we construct new norms of deepened social tolerance for loss and a sociocultural way of holding grief and suffering?

Restorative justice is a shift of concern from the retributive justice of the state, focused on the criminal and the debt he or she is due to pay, to a focus upon the victim, marginalized by retributive judicial passion inherent to the organization of modern political states, a view that also involves concern for the wound of the offender. It is also a shift of concern to the *wound* inflicted upon the victim, the offender, and the society. It appears that what is to be restored in restorative justice is the wound inflicted by injustice. This concern about the *wound* of injustice brings the fields of law and justice, on the one hand, and the field of psychology, on the other, in very close proximity, or even melds them.

A primary concern in restorative justice has been on instituting a healing social exchange system between the victim and the offender, both of whom are stigmatized by the injustice. In this brief article we are focusing on the loss of the assumptive world wound of the victim independent of restorative possibilities that may exist by social exchange with the offender. Here, the main concern is *understanding the wound of injustice* inflicted on the victim.

The assumptive world, as a principle of constancy, is the psychological site of injustice

In his discussion of the assumptive world theory, Parkes is primarily concerned with psychosocial change, and notes that psychosocial change involves, at the core of the grief, a loss of the assumptive world, by which he means, to a significant degree, the predictability of the future, or the *constancy,* over time, of 'constant internal constructs' that are basic to the human sense of order and reality. In his theory of the assumptive world, Parkes was interested in a psychological epistemology of change: that is, how knowledge grounds our being in the world, constructs, and maintains, and organizes psychosocial reality. This organization is *constancy*; its disruption is change, or grief over the lost 'constant internal construct.' Parkes writes,

> the assumptive world is the only world we know and it includes everything we know or think we know. It includes our interpretation of the past and our expectations of the future, our plans and our prejudices. Any or all of these may need to change as a result of changes in the life space.
>
> (1988: 53)

Parkes' assumptive world principle is, in effect, a basic organizing principle of human experience, beliefs, and temporality. The assumptive world is the ordering principle for the psychological or psychosocial construction of oneself and the human world.

The basic function of the assumptive world is to resist change, or maintain constancy, in a world thereby constituted as a tension between change and constancy. The temporal/constitutive function of the assumptive world is constancy. The basic assumptions by which we live and organize our sense of existence, reality, identity, value, meaning, and the security that our world is sufficiently predictable (knowable), are *beliefs* which maintain the constancy of both individual and sociocultural reality.

The presumption of the assumptive world

The assumptive self and world is a simultaneous occurrence of active presuming *and* receptive believing. The simultaneity of these is a paradox that assumptive world theory does *not* presume to make sense out of. The paradox is in part the paradox that the beginning prepossess itself. This is a very knotty philosophical problem. But our main concern here is with another paradoxical aspect of assumptive world presumption. This paradox has to do with psychology's identification of the object of its study: that is, who is the subject of psychology? What I am saying is that the psychological subject is the subject generating assumptive world constructs, including the construct(s) of itself. This theory has two difficulties: (1) a disjointedness within the subject in being both subject and object; and (2) antagonism with Otherness that is recalcitrant to totalizing inclinations of this subject in reflexive exchanges. But the shattering of the assumptive world by traumatic injustice breaks down the relationship of subject and object self, and self tends to become peculiarly lost in Otherness, losing assumptive world generating powers.

The assumptive world theory, as it is developed here, is that this generative-believing self is vulnerable to violent injustice which disrupts the bond within self between generative and believing self. This theory also tends to assume that in the background there is an injustice of which the construction of the assumptive world is a restorative response. Part of the condition for the possibility of the reflexive act of constructing oneself is that there has been a prior trauma. Traumatic injustice, then, beyond being a disruptive event, would be a *source* of the reflexive psychological subject of modernity. Becker (1973; Caruth 2002) saw the generativity of death, which is restorative justice; the theory of the assumptive world as originally a generative or restorative response to death is a variation on the concept of generative death.

The relationship of generation and destruction

The act of assuming a world is an act of constructing an ideal reality in which to be.

The act of assuming is an act of generating and maintaining idealized normative structures of consciousness and culture, including justice. The idealized nature of assumptive world constructs, is, however, really inseparable from its opposite, the dense, primordial, destructive, nihilistic loss of an adequately intact assumptive world constructive power. Generation and destruction are opposites sides of the same normative nature of the subject. Like cover and exposure, assumptive constancy and destruction of constancy are covariates. This 'covariancy,' established by the normative nature of the subject, demarcates a domain of the self who experiences him/herself or else is dead to him/herself, or somewhere in between.

The relationship between an ideal and a reviled self-construction is intricate, as the *constancy* of the assumptive world operates to differentiate ideality and its opposite, which is *death*. Justice and injustice is a similar distinction, as is the distinction between good and bad, and health and illness. They articulate normative distinctions of human existence. The construction of a normative assumptive world is the boundary that differentiates norm and deviance. Traumatic violation disrupts assumptive world boundaries that secure idealized normative structures, and tend to confuse generation and destruction, such as in addiction, and in post traumatic stress disorder.

The victim of injustice needs, first of all, to be accorded social norms in which the victim is empathically identified with, validated, treated with dignity, destigmatized, and, on the level of being victimized, reintegrated into social order. The sociocultural world, however, has conflicting tendencies, which include an urge to invalidate, stigmatize, and blame the victim. The victim is very prone to have these same feelings self-generated, as an aspect of the violation of self that is experienced in injustice. The impediments to restorative justice are formidable.

The constancy of constructs

Traumatic loss prompts an urge to conserve, or maintain constancy, and for an assumptive world to reassert itself. The assumptive world concept is, in the broadest sense,

> a principle of the normative constancy of experience and belief, a constancy principle of the psychological organization of the human world and one's experience of oneself and of the world. The assumptive world is the principle of the conservation of psychosocial reality.
>
> (Kauffman 2002b: 206–7)

This 'normative constancy' is, psychologically, *self* or *identity*, or some other psychological name for the human being, particularly in his/her reflexivity. It also applies to other reflexive phenomena, such as sociocultural history. The assumptive world holds together by beliefs, which are present exclusively in the reflexivity of assumption.

Psychologically, traumatic injustice shatters the *conservancy* of assumptive world beliefs, and leaves the victim exposed to a flux of meaninglessness, purposelessness, worthlessness, shame, and helplessness. It leaves the victim prone to be disconnected from him or herself and others, from past, and future, absent in the present, and the flow of time; with retributive desires raging. Parkes argues that the assumptive world is a world of 'constant internal constructs.' By 'internal' he means internal to the psychological self, or the internality of the psychological self, or simply the psychological self, who is his/her internality; as noted, an assumptive world is organized in every reflexive system. The internality of any reflexive system of norms is an assumptive world. The concept works well with social, cultural, historical, political, artistic, and metaphysical constructs.

Constancy means *not changing*, but also suggests that one can depend upon the steadfastness, endurance, firmness, fortitude, and persistence of the assumption. Constancy is a temporal continuity that is similar to the physical idea of solidness, or the metaphysical idea of substance. The steadfast, enduring, rudimentary, constant internal constructs of a system of reflexive order is *disrupted* by traumatic injustice. The loss of constancy is often difficult for the traumatized victim to name, or even to put his or her finger on, but it is normally omnipresent in traumatic loss of an assumptive world in which justice ceases to exist. There are many aspects of traumatic victimization that are elusive but the voices of victims of traumatic injustice are beginning to be recognized as an historic force to contend with.

Shame, the assumptive world, and the restoration of justice

If money is stolen, restoration of the money *may* satisfy the victim. But the experience of being robbed may also inflict a psychological injury. And the victim's need for restoration often has to do with this secondary 'injury of the self,' which, in terms of the experience of the victim, may be primary. And in some acts of injustice, especially intrusive or violent acts, the self injury may be the primary injustice. The injustice is experienced in the violation of the reflexive self.

The name for the diverse disturbances of self-consciousness inflicted by the violation of the self is *shame*. And the injustice in the loss of the assumptive world, shame, is key to what needs to be restored.

In my experience as a psychotherapist I have observed that the injury that is inflicted by having an unjust act committed against oneself involves two basic elements: (1) the disruption of the constancy of assumptions; and (2) the wound of being *exposed* to a violation of self, inflicting wounds for which there is not a language. These wounds involve stigmatization that contaminates the self's relationship with

225

itself. The crux of what needs restoration is the shame, in which the self is exposed to a primitive violence against itself. This psychological phenomena is inwardly generated, often in concert with, or in response to social cues.

Shame means discretion and modesty, and this is called 'cover shame,' as well as its more familiar and opposite meaning, embarrassment and humiliation, which is called 'exposure shame' (Schneider 1977; Erwin Straus 1966; Kauffman 2002b, 2002a). 'Shame' is a special type of word which contains opposite meanings, even though somewhere in the twentieth century we lost the ear, and an appreciation, for 'cover shame.' When the word 'shame' is spoken today it normally means 'exposure shame', and usage in which 'cover shame' is meant is rare, except, perhaps, when we remember the history of the word and call upon the now archaic fullness of it having opposite meanings.

When self is understood reflexively, we may speak of it in terms of its relationship with itself (and the world). This reflexivity of the self, or generative boundary on which the self experiences itself, is a boundary that is regulated, in a normative function, by shame. This defines the self by its normative idealization of itself, especially *violated* in traumatic loss. The self relates to itself, experiences itself, values itself, etc., on a boundary on which injustice registers as a disruption in the relation of the self to itself, as well as to the world. The relation of the self with itself, like the norms of social order, is regulated by shame. Shame is the basic boundary regulator of all reflexive, or self-conscious identity systems. Exposure shame interferes with a sense of integration into the social fabric, and to a sense of being present in time. The loss of the assumptive world in traumatic violations that shatter the self is the wound that the sense of injustice is based upon.

A potent energy engendered in traumatic injustice is forcefully internalized through the violation inflicted on the primary protective cover of the assumptive self, which gives being, value, meaning, belonging, identity, and hope. The traumatized self loses the power to hold itself together, to be whole, to be a self, to be (in his or her reflexivity) sure whether he or she is real or not. The self has a tendency in traumatic injustice towards a collapse of coherence, cohesion, and constancy of the self. The psychological wound of injustice which calls for restoration is this exposure that opens up when the assumptive world is shattered. The safe cover of generative shame provides the self with restorative powers. However this may be achieved, the wound of exposure can only be partially mitigated and dissociated.

Restoration of the assumptive world, damaged in traumatic loss, pivots on the restoration of *the shame that regulates the assumptive construction of self and world*. Injustice leaves a shame wound that *lives, dies, rages, and collapses* based on a stubborn hope of restoration, even as it relives being violated. To be victimized tends to induce an implicit stigmatization, humiliation, degradation of the self – that is, *exposure shame*.

Self-annihilation: the recalcitrant core of traumatic grief

I think that the violence that constitutes injustice is very difficult to name. We have here been calling the violation of traumatic injustice 'exposure'. Loss of social cover burrows in the most private contingencies of the self and takes over the power to construct. Loss of the cover through which the self comes to be (Straus 1966), the aperture (Vattimo 1991) of Being, exposes the soul to a force that turns it against itself, that uses the victim's own self, in traumatic loss, as a reflexive agent of self-loathing or self-annihilation.

Shame is the regulative emotion of all reflexive systems, inter- and intra-personal.

The regulative power of shame, in such a psychology as this, functions in a role analogous to the way God functions in theology. The primary power of the religions of the Book (Judaism, Christianity and Islam) is the impelling, compelling, indwelling power of shame in human beings. Shame operates by regulating and defining a realm of sacred constructs, which have to do with value, meaning and purpose in human life, and the presence of transcendent powers, all endangered by traumatic exposure injustice.

Traumatic injustice induces a very heightened dissociative functioning so that connections to oneself are obliterated. This can affect any reflexive 'system' from a private individual to global politics and stability. It appears to me that this dissociative trend has been gaining momentum, and fragmentation is a dominant sociocultural trend, despite diverse efforts made to restore justice. The turtle upon whose back our world rests collapses, not being substantial enough to bear the injustice in the world.

The assumptive world power of shame as an analogue of theology

Suppose the destructive (exposure), as well as the constructive powers (generative protective cover) of shame were analogous to the subject of theology. Perhaps, due to all the praise He demands, and the powers He has, believing persons will shun, or disregard, or be puzzled by, or circumvent, or justify the disturbing, and embarrassing situation about His destructive powers. The Covenant of Abraham and Yahweh is based on a test of willingness to overrule morality and to murder one's own son, in a sacrificial act to seal your side of a deal and establish a sociocultural exchange system with this God (Kierkegaard 1954). This is a deep mystery about the power of God: in assumptive world theory God is a construct of the human powers of assumption, in which case the assumptive world could also be taken to be an enactment of God. In any case, the narrow point here is that a power associated with religion since the beginning of human shame, reflexivity, or self-consciousness has been appropriated by psychology, as by other humanities, in *the assumptive world concept*, by the belief that the self is an assuming agent, who constructs himself by beliefs. The modern self is left with the responsibility of constructing itself to be a just self, while recognizing clearly that, at its origin, destruction and construction may be undifferentiated. We do not seem to have a word for undifferentiated destruction and construction, though 'omnipotence' might be the word.

Restorative shame

The just soul is ordered by (restorative) cover shame, which provides *safety* for the self to exist, and to experience itself. The soul wounded by injustice is fragmented and disordered in exposure shame anxiety. Restorative shame – that is, restoration of the protective cover of self's relation with itself, or (self-) reflexivity – is the *justice* in healing recalcitrant shame wounds of injustice. Restorative shame establishes and maintains human dignity, normative for the restoration of a just assumptive world in the soul of the victim. While exposure shame threatens the sense of safety and self-worth, the victim of injustice longs for a restoration of the cover of safety, self-worth, meaningfulness, and constancy. Justice is then taken to be restorative when it provides a protective cover of shame from exposure to the violence of stigmatizing degradation and annihilation of self.

Shame is the emotional expression, Darwin argues, of human self-consciousness. The boundary on which the self experiences itself is shame. Self, conscious of itself, is the reflexivity of consciousness. In Darwin's ethnology (Darwin 1965), he distinguishes shame as the only uniquely human emotion, the *emotion* of self-consciousness. The self-consciousness of shame as an emotion usually implies exposure anxiety, but in Darwin's time the ambivalent meaning of shame was more alive, and the meaning of self-consciousness as cover is in the *discretion, humility, dignity, and pride of the human animal* which would have been recognized as covariates of exposure anxiety.

Self-consciousness, as exposure anxiety, emotionally expressed by a blush, marks the difference between the emotional expression of our species and all other animal species, by Darwin's reckoning the only difference. While a diversity of implications may be drawn from this, I will limit myself to saying that *the need for justice* emerges, in the language of the biblical myth about the origin of mortality and self-consciousness, as an inevitable post-lapsarian human construction. The assumptive world constructs itself as a *covering of the shame of the self-consciousness of death*. Justice, as restoration from exposure, is the uniquely and expressly human restoration of the reflexivity traumatically ruptured injustice.

Traumatization

This article is focused on traumatic injustice for a number of reasons: (1) it is the extreme case and so aspects that may be more subtle in other instances of injustice may be more evident; (2) in recent years, a decline in the normative power of the sociocultural assumptive world to sustain a sense of global justice among humans has gained momentum, and there is much concern about a disintegration of assumptive world constancy; and, (3) the generative presumption of the assumptive world hypothesis may be understood as itself the fundamental human response to mortality and traumatic anxieties associated with death.

Reflexivity disturbances in traumatic dynamics

A disturbing and revealing psychological occurrence in acts of injustice is the self-blame of the victim. This is a very significant part of the psychology of injustice: the guilt and shame of the victim. The violation of self by another wounds the victim in a way that arouses self-blame, with an intense, often hidden, shame. This is not an incidental aspect of the psychological woundedness of injustice; injustice has a powerful tendency to fault the victim, perhaps based in a belief that I am responsible for what happens to me. Even where there is a clear conscious awareness that blame is unequivocally assigned to the offender, there is likely to be an undertow trend of self-blame. This self-blaming involves guilt, but more deep and recalcitrant is a self-blaming shame that can make one into nothing. A case may be made for seeing the self-blame assigned socially and by oneself to be guilt. But a closer look suggests that it is not the guilty deeds but the shameful self that is most recalcitrant to the restoration of justice within the victim and within the offender. This type of guilt may be called shame–guilt, in which the primary object of attack is oneself, more than one's deeds. A persistent wound, self-shaming accusations and humiliation are very much in need of restorative justice.

Justice

In the year 1400 or a little later, a 600–year war had become a way of life among the different tribes of the Iroquois. Deganaweda (also spelled Dekanawida) went forth in his stone canoe from tribe to tribe to bring mourning and a new meaning of justice. Mourning replaced retribution. Called 'the peace giver,' Deganaweda led the five tribes of the Iroquois to cease blaming each other for every death and to live in peace. The starting place of Deganaweda's Law is in replacing avenging with mourning (Morgan 1984). The institution of justice is established and maintained by mourning. Ideally, mourning is communal as it was in each of the Iroquois tribes, but this is not so in the developed West today, nor is mourning usually able to sustain a restoration of justice, as appears to have been the case in premodern social organization. Modern mourning is more sequestered and more private (Jackson 1977; Farrell 1980; Walter 1994). And here in America, as no doubt in other places too, revenge has more popular appeal than restoration.

References

Attig, T. (1996) *How We Grieve: relearning the world*, New York: Oxford University Press.

Becker, E. (1973) *The Denial of Death*, New York: The Free Press.

Caruth, C. (2002) 'Parting words,' in J. Kauffman (ed.) *Loss of the Assumptive World*, New York: Brunner-Routledge.

Darwin, C. (1965) *The Expression of Emotions in Man and Animal*, Chicago: University of Chicago Press.

Farrell, J. J. (1980) *Inventing the American Way of Death, 1830–1920*, Philadelphia: Temple University Press.

Jackson, C. O. (ed.) (1977) *Passing, The Vision of Death in America*, Westport: Greenwood Press.

Janoff-Bulman, R. (1992) *Shattered Assumptions: towards a new psychology of trauma*, New York: The Free Press.

Kauffman, Jeffrey (2001a) 'Shame,' in G. Howarth and O. Leaman (eds) *Encyclopedia of Death and Dying*, London: Routledge.

— (2001b) 'The psychology of disenfranchised grief,' in K. Doka (ed.) *Disenfranchised Grief: new directions, challenges and strategies for practice*, Champagne, IL: Research Press.

— (2002a) 'Safety and the assumptive world: a theory of traumatic loss,' in J. Kauffman (ed.) *Loss of the Assumptive World*, New York: Brunner-Routledge.

— (2002b) 'Introduction,' in J. Kauffman (ed.) *Loss of the Assumptive World*, New York: Brunner-Routledge.

Kierkegaard, S. (1954) *Fear and Trembling*, W. Lowrie (trans.), New York: Doubleday Anchor Books.

Morgan H. L. (1984) *League of the Iroquois*, New York: Citadel Press.

Neimeyer, R. A. (2001) *Meaning Reconstruction and the Experience of Loss*, Washington, DC: American Psychological Association.

OED (1971) *Oxford English Dictionary*, Oxford: Oxford University Press.

Parkes, C. M. (1971) 'Psycho-social transition: a field of study,' *Social Science and Medicine*, 5: 101–15.

— (1988) 'Bereavement as a psychosocial transition: processes of adaptation to change,' *Journal of Social Issue*, 44(3): 53–65.

Schneider, C. (1977) *Shame, Exposure and Privacy*, Boston: Beacon Press.

Straus, Erwin (1966) 'Shame as a historiological problem,' in *Phenomenological Psychology*, New York: Basic Books.

Vattimo, G. (1991) *The End of Modernity*, J. R. Snyder (trans.) Baltimore: The Johns Hopkins University Press.

Walter, T. (1994) *The Revival of Death*, London: Routledge.

Note

1. I wish to thank David Balk and Robert Neimeyer for reading an earlier version of this paper and offering helpful comments.

15

Murder victims' families for reconciliation

Story-telling for healing, as witness, and in public policy

Judith W. Kay

People who have lost loved ones to murder face daunting questions, such as 'How will I integrate this ordeal into my life story?' 'What kind of person will I become?' and 'How will the story I tell eventually inform the way I view the world?' The crucial test of any sustaining narrative is the sort of community and person it shapes (Hauerwas 1981). However, many relatives of homicide victims encounter serious impediments to addressing such questions and thus are hindered from crafting efficacious stories. Being ignored and silenced are major obstacles to benefiting from the healing potential of telling their stories. Relatives of murder victims may be shunned by friends and associates, who appear to regard murder as so far outside normal human experience that they cannot listen to their friends' travails. Those family members who oppose the death penalty may also find themselves silenced by the state.

In 1980, Randy Reeves killed Janet Mesner and her visiting friend Vicki Zessin, who left behind a two-year-old daughter, Audrey, and husband Gus Lamm. Nineteen years after Reeves received the death sentence, the Nebraska Board of Pardons met to consider a hearing about possible commutation. Gus and Audrey Lamm, who

oppose the death penalty, requested to speak to the Board and were denied; Vicki's sister, who supports the death penalty, was permitted to speak (King 2003). Nebraska had amended its state constitution to grant victims the right to 'be informed of, present at, and make an oral or written statement at sentencing, parole, pardon, commutation, and conditional release proceedings.' The Lamms filed suit against the Board of Pardons but the District Court ruled against them. The Court declared Gus and Audrey not victims but rather 'agents of Randy Reeves,' despite being husband and daughter of the deceased. The only true victims, the judge's ruling implied, are those who support the state's efforts to secure a sentence of death (Cushing and Sheffer 2002). Being denied the status of victim is only one way in which relatives of the murdered[1] who oppose the death penalty are prevented from telling their stories.[2]

This chapter explains why telling stories can be both psychologically healing and politically necessary for murder victims' family members who oppose the death penalty. After introducing a survivor group committed to death penalty abolition, it shows how reframed narratives about the deceased and/or the perpetrator inform some survivors' opposition to the death penalty. The chapter examines the contested role of personal narratives in the community, the victim rights movement, the criminal justice system, and public policy, and how certain contexts can deprive narrative of most of its transformative power.

Murder Victims' Families for Reconciliation (MVFR)

Cushing and Sheffer (2004) write that MVFR was founded not only as part of the emerging victim movement but also in response to the green light given to individual states by the US Supreme Court in *Gregg v. Georgia* (1976) to reinstate the death penalty. They recount that when members of Amnesty International's Death Penalty Committee met to determine their abolitionist strategy, one member, Marie Dean, asked about the role of victims in that effort. Dean's mother-in-law had been shot and killed in 1972. Her family opposed the death penalty but discovered that friends reacted to their stance with surprise and some horror – as if pursuing the death penalty were a way to show that they loved this woman. The Amnesty committee responded to Dean's call to incorporate a victim's perspective by collecting a small group of people who were willing to speak to the media and be identified with a new organization, Murder Victims' Families Against the Death Penalty (Cushing and Sheffer 2004).[3]

In the early 1990s, the group changed its name to Murder Victims' Families for Reconciliation, indicating what they stood for rather than against. Although members shared the experience of loss, they differed in how they understood reconciliation. Some sought forgiveness while others formed bonds with the perpetrator. Others aimed at being reconciled to the murder by not letting it control the rest of their lives. One member, Teresa Mathis, whose

brother was beaten to death with a baseball bat, paraphrases Vietnamese Zen master Thich Nhat Hanh: 'Reconciliation is to understand both sides, to go to one side and describe the suffering being endured by the other side; then to go to the other side and describe the suffering endured by the first side' (Bosco 2001: 83). MVFR members seek to address the suffering that murder and the death penalty cause the whole society.

MVFR, like other victim groups, has been built around first-person narratives by relatives of murder victims. Preserving the memory of the deceased, unveiling a culture of violence, wanting to prevent further deaths, and naming the injustices endured by families of both victims and perpetrators – these powerful motivations propel relatives of the dead to speak. Their story-telling has taken the form of bearing witness and influencing criminal justice policy as well as personal healing.

Survivors' narratives and healing

Narrative is the heart and soul of restorative justice. Notwithstanding the different conceptions of restorative justice, narrative remains its quintessential feature. Why is story-telling so powerful?

Restorative justice practitioners know that sitting in a private room with a victim and an offender who open themselves to each other by telling their stories offers the potential for truly human communication and transformation. When a person tells her story to another who hears, both the teller and listener can be changed for the better. The act of telling a personal story to a listener rescues the narrator from a realm of silence, isolation, and despair about human connection. Such a moment revives the teller, restoring her faith in the possibility of deeply satisfying connection with other humans. If the listener is the offender, his willing listening ignites her hope that he may truly come to understand the harm he

231

caused, be moved by her story, and be able to treat others better in the future. When a listener is open to the story and the person telling it, he opens himself to change, signaled by integrating the story into his own biography. His story needs to be reconstructed in order to include the reality of having harmed this precious human, the effects of that harm on her, and the respect she has shown in communicating with him her pain and struggle. The victim and offender exhibit deep mutual respect by entrusting their stories to each other. This attempt by each to reach the other begins the process of unraveling the legacy of disregard and blindness that has disconnected them. In a world where few people listen deeply to one another, even a brief session of mutual telling and listening may be enough to re-ignite a spark of hope in humankind and begin the healing process.

Although such powerful moments do not always occur, practitioners of restorative justice have experienced them often enough to be committed to pursuing story-telling's emancipatory possibilities (Morris and Young 2000). Why can telling one's story be so healing and liberatory?

Stories are the primary way humans shape identities and form bonds with others (Bruner 1987; Coles 1989). Stories are relational; they need listeners. Babies do not obtain a sense of themselves in isolation but through interaction with attentive humans. Without such relational contact, they feel lost and unimportant with no way to define themselves. (Stern 1973; Sroufe 1995). With the acquisition of verbal skills, stories become a major locus of children's contact with others. Telling their stories to avid listeners builds their world and sense of self (Sarbin 1986). Being listened to without interruption confers reality to the teller and her experience. Events only become historical when they can be told, when they 'implicate others' (Caruth 1996: 18).

Humans use personal life narratives to interpret the past, meet the present, and anticipate the future. Because of their capacities for memory and imagination, humans (with intact brains) do not experience life as a string of random events. Instead, people use stories to explain causes, anticipate consequences, and make sense of what has occurred. With the use of stories, people interpret new events while they are happening by comparing and contrasting the new situation with past experiences. In light of this interpreted information, a person can formulate a creative and original response to the unique moment. Afterwards, she can tell a story to provide an account of her thinking and judgments to explain why she acted as she did. It takes little effort to integrate most daily experiences into a person's ongoing life narrative.

Humans rely not only on individual life stories but also on communal narratives for these interpretive and interactive endeavors (Felman and Laub 1992). Communities have traditions through which they interpret their legacy and vision for the future (Shils 1981). Such traditions shape their participants but do not determine them, since individuals can alter the stories of their communities. People interpret events in their lives in terms of a narrative's metaphors, so that a Christian survivor might refer to the 'dark night of the soul' and a Jew to 'wandering in the desert.' Traditions are not like musty books but rather ongoing lively debates about what it means to be a Palestinian or a Maori (Bellah *et al.* 1985). All humans draw on competing narratives with which they forge their own life stories, creating order out of chaos (Goldberg 1991). Sometimes new narratives can 'bring on disintegration and indeterminacy,' according to Mitchell (1981), leading to 'unpredictable transformations in a culture or individual' (p. viii). Narrative has value, therefore, in either 'imposing order on reality or as a way of unleashing a healthy disorder' (Mitchell 1981: ix). Not any personal or communal story will do. Some are more adequate than others, connecting many events, elucidating those events fully, and leading to fruitful engagements with others (Redmond 1989; Monk *et al.* 1996; Spungen 1997).

Hurtful experiences disrupt this normally uncomplicated story-formation process (Culbertson 1995). This is not to say that surviving family members do not remember when they were first told about their loved ones' murders. But the events and interactions of the subsequent weeks may become a blur, expressed by phrases, such as 'I was in a fog after my son's death,' or 'I was blind with rage.' Such shocks temporarily suspend people's ability to analyze the loss, think it through, and evaluate how it modifies their view of the world. Yet even while they are unable to incorporate the crime into their life story just yet, the brain and body continue to record incoming information. People in emotional shock form literal recordings of such events, available later when they have recovered their senses (Kauffman and New 2004). For some, these recordings of the trauma may contain immediate reactions, such as 'I wish he had killed me instead of my son,' 'It's God's will,' or 'I want to kill the guy who did this.' Such initial interpretations may later become obstacles to integrating the tragedy into a life narrative (Rose *et al.* 1998).

The shock of learning that a beloved has been taken willfully at the hands of another is something that cannot be understood in the moment. As Caruth (1996) says, 'What returns to haunt the victim ... is not only the reality of the violent event but also the reality of the way that its violence has not yet been fully known' (p. 6). This shock and dissolution of the world the family once knew can lead to silence. Murder shatters the self and its stories. People who have lost someone to murder may initially find themselves telling what Frank (1995) calls 'chaos stories' (p. 97), with neither coherence nor a sense of progression; rather, they are strings of events that the teller is unable to connect and put into context. The inability to tell a coherent narrative is a major hindrance because it prevents events from entering the 'world of meaning,' White (1981) writes. Antoinette Bosco (2001), whose son and daughter-in-law were murdered, worried, 'Who was I going to become as a result of this radical alteration of my being? Who was I now that this calamity struck with such force?' (p. 48). With their stories in chaos, survivors have no assurance that they will ever be able to re-integrate their lives.

Ironically, outliving the deceased becomes problematic. This *crisis of death* has a 'correlative *crisis of life*: between the story of the unbearable nature of an event and the story of the unbearable nature of its survival' (Caruth 1996: 7). When not healed enough to transition out of a chaos narrative and when overwhelmed by present reminders of past events, individuals are tempted to replay their initial interpretations of violent incidents, instead of enlarging or reformulating their interpretative framework (Kauffman and New 2004). One father, whose daughter was murdered, was so enraged when the murderer received a light sentence that he pursued the man by having him followed by a private detective. 'Then he gradually understood that he was becoming obsessed with this injustice, spending so much of his time reading reports, stuck in his pain.' He had worked with a group calling itself the National Victims Center. '"So many of them were living lives of revenge," he said.' He concluded that he did not want to 'live this way' (Bosco 2001: 49). Survivors whose stories are enmeshed in narratives of revenge and hatred find that their story-telling causes them to re-experience the wound repetitively rather than being able to heal their emotional pain and craft a transformational narrative (Gasker 2002).

Family members of victims fight hard to find narratives that allow them to continue to live in a world that includes murderers, refuse to let this wound erode their humanity, and find a way to make a positive contribution to their community (Magee 1983; Cleary 2004). Survivors have transformed their lives by abandoning scripts of revenge, releasing the emotional pain that makes vengeful worldviews plausible, changing their behavior and interpretations, re-evaluating the past, and living from a revised story, often of forgiveness or transcendence (Hankiss 1981; McAdams 1993; Morgan 2000; Bosco 2001; Zehr 2001).

Telling one's story may not be sufficient for survivors to abandon revenge for a path of healing and transformation. Since the suffering of relatives of murder victims is not identical, neither is their healing (Wessel 2004). For example, some of what passes for help actually makes it harder to move beyond bitterness. When nobody listens and story-telling's essential reciprocity of telling and listening is lost, then a person's retelling may become rote and wooden. Without open-hearted and high-minded listeners, such narrations are likely to leave the teller feeling worse rather than better. In contrast, when survivors find or create a network of listeners who affirm their common humanity, then relaying their stories is more likely to be beneficial (Shay 1994).

Furthermore, listening by itself, however attentive, may not be sufficient to permit the healing of painful emotions that bind together people's feelings to their initial interpretations of the murder. Asking survivors to tell their stories repetitively without listening for and welcoming the release of such emotion can reinforce feelings of victimization rather than transform the telling into a gift of human connection. Repetitive talking with no emotional affect is not useful to survivors. Some members of MVFR were in support groups run by Parents of Murdered Children, in which they retold their stories over and over but without reaching for a larger perspective beyond rage and revenge. They eventually left because they could see that such retelling stoked negative affects and solidified narrow perspectives (Bosco 2001; Kay 2005a).

In contrast, narrating the event with the release of painful emotions allows initial perspectives to be reinterpreted by the victim (Jackins 1994; Parry and Doan 1994). This re-evaluation often places the trauma in a different framework and allows the person to move from passive victim to active survivor or passionate witness (Eron and Lund 1996). The following example of someone who was initially focused on revenge but came to oppose the death penalty illustrates the power of emotional release and reframed narratives to unleash powerful moral action.

Bill Pelke lost his beloved seventy-eight year old grandmother, Ruth, to murder in her own dining room. She taught Bible lessons to neighborhood children. On 14 May 1985, some ninth-grade girls came to her door about lessons. After she had let them in, one hit her over the head with a vase and another pulled a knife and stabbed her over thirty times. One of the girls, Paula Cooper, received the death sentence, which Pelke originally supported. Pelke struggled with his anger and despair about ever feeling anything but total rage toward Paula. Pelke's 'story' about his grandmother became reduced to her final moments; all he could think about was the scarred floorboards of the dining room where Ruth had been stabbed. One day on his job at Bethlehem Steel, working in the cab of a crane sixty feet over the plant floor, he broke down sobbing, praying to God for the courage to have compassion. With a rush, his story of his grandmother was enlarged and reframed; he was now able to remember her as a complete person whose life story included helping others and affirming their humanness. Once he regained a fuller story about his grandmother, he was able to extend this narrative to the perpetrator, Paula. She, too, must be a human being with a past and hopes for the future. Seeing Paula freshly in this new way, he could no longer want her future to include execution. Armed with a new narrative about the perpetrator – that she had a story that transcended the categories of victim or perpetrator – Pelke became an outspoken opponent of the death penalty and a board member of MVFR (Pelke 2003). Thus, the new story Pelke told about the deceased transformed the story he told about the perpetrator, demonstrating the liberating potential of narrative.

Other survivors are also able to use the life narrative of their beloved as a basis to oppose the death penalty. For example, Renny Cushing's father was shot in his home by a policeman with a grudge against the family (Hood and King 1999). Cushing cites his father's life-long opposition to the death penalty and practice of forgiveness as a basis for his own opposition to capital punishment. Similarly, when Marietta Jaeger's seven-year-old daughter was kidnapped and murdered, Marietta appealed to her little girl's loving and generous character as a model for how all humans should act (Jaeger 1998). Other times, survivors may appeal not to a story about the victim but to their own narrative of being a parent or family member. Using their own experience of grief, they want to minimize the suffering that other families have to endure. This means that they oppose capital punishment in an effort to prevent such harm to the offender's family. MVFR is unique among victims' groups in the United States by incorporating in its membership family members whose loved ones have been executed. These members were able to do this because of the compassion released by telling a story about the humanness of all the parties affected by crime and violent punishment.

Thus, telling one's story to caring others can permit tears to flow, hearts to open, and new perspectives to emerge. This healing helps survivors transform their narratives about the deceased, the perpetrator, and the perpetrator's family. Such healing has the power to motivate surviving relatives to embrace alternatives to the death penalty.

Survivors' narratives and bearing witness

Many surviving relatives feel the moral call to bear witness. When forced to face the degree to which humans can harm other humans, many survivors have a need to sound the alarm and warn others. The unnecessary waste of human life gives rise to the desire to communicate the preciousness of existence. A community's silence and denial about the reality of murder compound murder's dual trauma of being both a death and a crime. The community's silence resembles the realm of the dead, who will never speak again. The 'primary source of the will to bear witness [is that] the survivor allows the dead their voice; he makes the silence heard' (Des Pres 1976: 36). Bearing witness wards off oblivion in the hopes that the truth will prevail. What is a witness?

Becoming a witness entails 'moral responsibility' and 'implies a social ethic' (Frank 1995). Members of MVFR are witnesses – not in the legal sense of seeing the crime (although some have) – but in the sense of having *experienced* the loss, of *being* (Marcel 1960). They *live* the story that others merely hear; the witness that matters is not only what one says but what one *is* (Garro 1992). They are witnesses in the moral sense of 'assuming a responsibility for telling what happened,' offering 'testimony to a truth that is generally unrecognized or suppressed' (Frank 1995: 137). They witness both by becoming a person who has been privileged enough to integrate the murder into their life stories without losing their moral compass, and by their actions in the community.

Some prominent members of MVFR, such as Bud Welch, whose daughter, Julie Marie, was murdered in the 1995 Oklahoma City bombing, found their voice in the public arena. Welch had to do a lot of raging and grieving before he could become a witness, a shift that has undoubtedly taken him further along his journey of transformation. Welch was able to tell his story and express some of his painful emotions in a way that moved audiences, while opening his own heart and mind to such an extent that he opposed McVeigh's execution and met with McVeigh's family. Welch's witness alone inspired people to see beyond hatred and fear toward a possibility of remaining human with one another (Welch 2001).

But bearing witness by itself does not always lead to healing. Some other members of MVFR found it taxing to bear witness. They discovered that telling their stories over and over without adequate listening by others kept their attention on their loss in unhelpful ways. One member, whose granddaughter was raped and murdered, feels that her later near-fatal physical collapse was a result of 'all those talks I did for MVFR' (Kay 2005b). Some family members found bearing witness eventually was incompatible with their personal needs. Too much activism around murder risked making the past more important than the present. Thus, bearing witness may or may not promote healing.

Other family members withdrew from public speaking because their stories no longer matched cultural expectations. TV interviewers were not interested in the hard-wrought positive changes secured by some relatives, such as discovering that they felt healed, not by demands for vengeance and capital punishment but by 'owning our common humanity with each person' and 'seeing ourselves as a piece in the whole human family who have the capacity to hurt and heal' (Mathis 2005). Some family members found that the stories they wanted to tell no longer served the needs of the abolition movement. For example, if a family member spoke in a cool and intellectual fashion, listeners wrongly inferred that the relative no longer cared about the victim and dismissed the testimony.

MVFR wants its members to counter the use of stories by the community to stoke fear and revenge. MVFR hopes, of course, that its members' stories will move bystanders, inviting them to change their worldview and to become engaged. In the best-case scenario, listeners' own biographies are transformed, as their life-narrative now includes the story of the witness.

Survivor narratives in the community

The witness of murder victims' families who oppose the death penalty makes a witness of the rest of the community. Frank (1995) writes, 'Testimony is distinct from other reports because it does not simply affect those who receive it; testimony implicates others in what they witness' (p. 143). Herman (1997) observes that those who hear victims' testimonies are caught in the conflict between victim and perpetrator. 'It is morally impossible to remain neutral in this conflict. The bystander is forced to take sides' (p. 7). The side that bystanders take depends, initially, on available cultural narratives.

One dominant discourse used in many communities is that the world is just. Lerner (1980) describes this as a belief that people may avoid negative events if they have 'met the appropriate preconditions to avoid the undesirable' (p. 11). According to this just-world perspective, people who look or act in certain ways (or fail to do so) deserve whatever bad things happen (Sher 1987). If a person has behaved, worked hard, lived in the right part of town, and avoided bad places and people, then according to this worldview, he or she has met the preconditions for avoiding undesirable events such as murder.

In the face of counterevidence to the belief in a just world, such as innocent suffering or bad luck, bystanders may employ several tactics to guard against threats to their preferred perspective (Lerner 1980). Bystanders may willfully filter out incongruent data, not distorting reality so much as ignoring it (Milburn and Conrad 1998). Another tactic used in communities is reinterpreting the outcome so that the suffering is seen to have a greater benefit or some compensating reward if not now, then certainly in heaven. 'The murder of her sister made her a better person.' Other times, subscribers to this script reinterpret the cause of the violence or the character of the victim, which results in blaming the victim for some failure (Lerner 1980: 20–1). A murder victim was at the wrong place at the wrong time or with the wrong people. Even if such bystanders encounter someone who did not bring violence upon herself, they may rearrange events to make the victim appear as if she deserved her fate.

Bystanders, when faced with murder in their community and in an effort to sustain the narrative that the world is just, may employ an additional strategy: a belief in two worlds. One world is occupied by privileged, white, respectable, and decent citizens who can expect to get what they deserve. The other world is occupied by losers, who 'are doomed to live in a world where they cannot affect their fates in any appreciable way. They appear destined to live in a state of chronic suffering or deprivation in terms of goals that we value and expect' (Lerner 1980: 25). Murder victims must come from the second world, such bystanders persist in believing.

Ironically, some family members of murder victims may have once employed such a life narrative (Harris 1987). Murder shatters the illusion of two worlds that some relatives may have held before the crime. The outrage and grief facing any homicide survivor will be enormous; but for those who had initially believed in two worlds, the encroachment of the world of the losers into the world that allegedly shields from violence, causes special rage. Family members with a narrative of a just world may have a more difficult time incorporating a murder into their life narrative than do those whose narrative had recognized injustice and the randomness of bad luck prior to the murder (Janoff-Bulman 1992; Flanigan 1998).

Another tactic employed by bystanders to sustain their just-world perspective is to silence the stories about murder victims provided by their devastated families (Huyssen 1995; Milburn and Conrad 1998; Northey 1999). Preventing traumatic events from becoming part of an individual's or community's narrative portends nonexistence. A Holocaust survivor, Nadezhda Mandelstam (1970) writes, 'It is a man's way of leaving a trace, of telling people how he lived and died . . . If nothing else is left, one must scream. Silence is the real crime against humanity' (pp. 42–3). Silencing of stories is achieved in a myriad of ways and has several damaging effects on relatives of homicide victims.

Bystanders may be reluctant to face the reality of human violence, and if overburdened and undersupported, look away (Staub 2003). 'As a witness the survivor is both sought and shunned; the desire to hear his truth is countered by the need to ignore him' (Des Pres 1976: 41). Bystanders are often complicit in subtly glorifying murderers while ignoring victims and silencing their survivors. Herman (1997) observes that even when victims have high status, such as decorated soldiers, few people can listen attentively to their experiences. Those of low status find their losses relegated to oblivion. The stories survivors need to tell, for example, may be silenced through threatened violence, denial and accusations of lying, indifference, or non-responsiveness. If silence and secrecy fail, then the credibility of the survivors is attacked. If victims cannot be silenced, then some bystanders try to ensure that no one listens. Herman (1997) observes,

> After every atrocity one can expect to hear the same predictable apologies: it never happened; the victim lies; the victim exaggerates; the victim brought it upon herself; and in any case it is time to forget the past and move on.
>
> (p. 8)

237

Suppression of stories prevents alternative views of reality to be told, inhibits correction or revision of dominant discourses, and renders sufferers and suffering invisible.

Against such silencing, being heard confers reality on the experience, brings the narrator to life, and through memory assures the continuity of the deceased beyond the grave. These are additional reasons why story-telling can be healing for victims and transformative for bystanders.

The witness is almost always a source of social disruption. Therefore, surviving family members have been best able to bear witness when their story-telling has been linked to movements for political change.

The backlash against this silencing has been the victim movement (although the word 'movement' is contestable [Elias 1990; Frank and Fuentes 1990]). Its emergence worldwide since the 1970s suggests how widespread silencing has been (Strang 2002). As Geis (1990) observes: victims' 'condition for centuries aroused little comment or interest. Suddenly, they were "discovered" and afterwards it was unclear how their obvious neglect could have so long gone without attention and remedy' (p. 255). Now there is more political and public permission for some family members to tell their stories (O'Brien 1996), although this permission is often denied those who oppose capital punishment.

Survivors' narratives within the victims' rights movement

In the United States, the victims' rights movement began when the use of victim surveys 'gave an insight into the low regard for the justice system felt by crime victims' (Skogan 1978; Strang 2002: 27–8). Simultaneously the women's movement exposed how female victims of rape and domestic violence were maltreated by the criminal justice system, while male perpetrators received light sentences. This social movement was influential in linking the fears, concerns, and needs of victims with demands for stiffer sentences (Schlosser 1997).

The victim movement from its earliest days in the United States involved radical feminists and conservative Republicans whose narratives and goals differed. This unlikely coalition focused on the rights of victims within the criminal justice system, legislative changes to that system, and a concern for harsher punishments (Mosteller 1998). The movement became dominated by a concern for increased use of the death penalty with a narrow focus on survivors' rights to be present, to be informed, and to be used by the prosecution to influence sentencing (Maguire and Shapland 1990).

The dominant paradigm of the victims' rights movement within which murder victims' families sought to be seen and heard has been called 'revenge, retribution, and closure through execution' (Kay 2005a). This model of justice about the necessity and importance of capital punishment makes particular claims about the role of murder victims' family members' stories to achieve a death sentence.

The paradigm posits that legal retribution does not aim at satisfying victims by letting them (or their relatives) take personal vengeance. Instead, with the state as the victim on whose behalf the prosecution proceeds, victims are to derive satisfaction from having certain rights met. These rights include using their stories to contribute to the success of the prosecution in winning a conviction and the death penalty.

This concern for rights additionally offers families execution as a means of closure. Increasingly, since the 1980s, the public has come to believe that capital punishment is done as a sort of therapy for survivors, enabling them to reach closure (Zimring 2003; Gross and Ellsworth 2003). The state as avenging angel kills in the name of victims' families. Scant research has been done about what closure means, how it is allegedly secured, and how it benefits family members (Zimring 2003). Using the concept of rights, closure seems to mean that the victims are to tell their tale to benefit the prosecution, reassure the community after the execution that justice was served, and then go silent. Families who subscribe to this paradigm may find that it works for them – that is, they relish exercising their right to tell their story in court, witness the execution, and tell the community that they feel satisfied that the execution occurred (Turow 2003: 52).

Yet some believers in victims' rights find them deficient when the reality of murder and execution enter their own lives. 'Jay Stratton, who lost his mother in the Oklahoma City bombing ... reportedly said, "I thought I would feel satisfied, but I don't"' (Turow 2003: 52). The victims' rights movement neglects consideration of human needs related to the crime, needs that persist for fifteen and twenty years after the murder.

Cushing and Sheffer (2004) observe that MVFR benefited from the emergence of the victims' rights movement but also 'maintained a healthy skepticism about what "paying attention to victims" really means,' since too often it focused on sentencing rather than compensation, counseling, or other forms of genuine help. For example, funds made available from the Victims of Crime Act sometimes were 'contingent upon' a family's 'cooperating with prosecutors and sharing their agenda' (Cushing and Sheffer 2004).

The victims' rights movement attempts to end the silencing of murder victims' families but from within a paradigm of retribution. Within a context that seeks harsh sentences, often the only murder victims' family members permitted to tell their stories in the courtroom are those who want the state to commit violence on their behalf.

Survivors' narratives in the criminal justice system

Victims (of non-lethal crimes) repeatedly express dismay if they are not made part of the criminal justice proceedings. Studies conducted in the 1980s and 1990s showed that victim dissatisfaction focused on the process, not the outcome (Hagan 1982; Forst and Hernon 1985; Shapland *et al.* 1985; Umbreit 1989; Shapland 2000). A resulting strategy to improve victim satisfaction in the criminal justice system in the United States, Canada, Australia, and the United Kingdom has been the victim impact statement (Erez 2000). Victim impact statements are intended to portray murder's aftermath and affirm the worth of the victim. Although victim impact statements were designed to increase victims' feelings of participation in a trial, several studies show that this has not occurred (Erez 1991; Davis and Smith 1994).

Not all survivors are equal in their willingness and/or ability to tell their story in the context of a victim impact statement. Some may lack the confidence or suffer from too much humiliation. Many simply find language ineffective to convey the magnitude of their loss, feeling the futility of speaking (Langer 1995). Others may try to talk but their need to cry overtakes them. Trauma 'can obliterate one's former emotional repertoire ... [leaving] the survivor not only numbed, but also without the motivation to carry out the task of constructing an ongoing narrative' (Brison 2002: 50). A request to tell a coherent story for the court in terms of a victim impact statement eludes some. Others find their stories are used to support the prosecution.

Within murder proceedings, the prosecution hopes that the family's statement will evoke the jury's sympathy so that a tougher sentence will be imposed. Many observers believe that this use of narrative smuggles revenge back into the courtroom (Sarat 2001). Zimring (2003) contends that with the defense presenting its report of mitigating circumstances, which reveals the defendant's often substantial and gruesome past victimization, family members are forced into a sort of 'status competition' over whose suffering is worse. If the court does not impose the death penalty, relatives of the victim may feel unheard, as if their statement had no affect on the outcome (pp. 55; Erez and Roeger 1995). Being heard becomes equated with a particular outcome – the harshest sentence possible.

The cooptation of the victims' rights movement by political conservatives in the United States has resulted in privileging only certain survivors in the courtroom (Elias 1990). Even direct victims of attempted murder who have opposed the death penalty have been barred from speaking in court, such as SueZann Bosler. She and her father, the Reverend Billy Bosler, were attacked by James Campbell. Her father died from his injuries; SueZann barely survived hers. The judge forbade her to say anything about the death penalty during her testimony (as a witness to the murder of her father), saying, 'SueZann, you are not to mention anything about the death penalty or your feelings toward the defendant. If you violate my order, you will be in criminal contempt and face six months in jail.' SueZann later reported, 'I felt like a criminal instead of a victim' (King 2003: 158). Victims do have rights. However, these are often denied to those who oppose the death penalty (Cushing and Sheffer 2002).

Because the court exploits victims' stories by using them for vengeful and retributive purposes, some survivors oppose the use of victim impact statements. Bosco (2001) argues, 'I would oppose any law that would give us, murder victims' survivors, the right to address the jury in a death penalty case telling them of the impact of the crime on us. Such an emotional account could wrongly influence a jury' (p. 227). MVFR agrees. In a Washington State death penalty case, MVFR issued a statement opposing the use of victim impact statements in capital cases. A responsible victims' movement should not, in its opinion, set up a contest about which victims are worth more.

Narrative and public policy

With respect to justice, many people believe that murder victim families occupy the moral high ground with unassailable credibility. Since no one can fully understand the trauma of murder unless one has been through it, there is a primacy given to the experience of families of homicide victims not accorded other victims.

Telling stories has been an activist tool for MVFR. Having a network behind them enabled many members to speak publicly about their loss and their stance against the death penalty. Telling their stories had a powerful effect on audiences, who wondered, 'How would I react if someone I loved were murdered?' Members' accounts of rage and despair, fantasies of revenge, and inability to forgive dispel the audience's illusion that they are saint-like or do not share the same feelings as other crime victims. First-person narratives were also 'harder for audiences to argue with ... than with other anti-death-penalty statements' (Cushing and Sheffer 2004). Stories communicate a message in a unique way. MVFR members gathered personal testimonies into a booklet with photos, Not in Our Name, that became a tool to influence public policy.

> For example, when the New Hampshire legislature was considering a death penalty abolition bill in 2000, we sent copies of Not in Our Name to all the lawmakers and one of them quoted from it in his testimony on the day of the Senate vote.
> (Cushing and Sheffer 2004)

Unlike in the courtroom, family members use their stories to touch legislators' hearts, to challenge their preconceptions, and to prompt changes in their votes.

But the use of personal narrative as a basis for changing public policy has been subject to several criticisms.

The first criticism is the status given to experience. Some theorists are cautious about the use of personal narratives, because while appearing uncontestable, they may fail to honor different experiences, perpetuating cultural, class, gender, or race exclusion (Scott 1992). The most vocal family members opposed to capital punishment have generally been white and middle class, and the different experiences of murder within various ethnic groups of varying economic means still have not been heard.

Most relatives of murder victims who bear witness against the death penalty in the United States grew up in communities with assumptions of civic trust, with a sense of belonging and being important, which made it easier for them to tell their stories publicly and be heard. However, people who have never experienced civic trust may never become witnesses. Their stories will not be told. For example, children who have experienced prolonged sexual abuse or who grew up in violent communities may never have developed civic trust. When encountering murder, such persons battle cynicism, despair, or powerlessness as one more death seems to be a continuation of a nightmarish script with no happy endings. As the work of Athens (1992) shows, some family narratives may themselves be so violentized that they perceive early death as the normal course of events. The absence of stories from diverse constituencies can inhibit the formation of sound public policy.

Although the relative speaks as a member of at least one group, she cannot speak for all members of her group, much less for people of other groups. These two problems can be mitigated somewhat, Brison (2002) suggests, by making clear the background from which one speaks and avoiding over-generalizing. Particular survivors, she says, 'need not speak *for* other survivors of trauma in order to speak *with* them' (p. 30). The fact that personal narratives will always be partial does not lessen their power. Frank (1995) argues,

no analysis can ever 'settle the hash' of testimony. Any analysis is always left gazing at what remains in excess of the analyzable. What is testified to remains the really real, and in the end what counts are duties toward it.

(p. 138)

A second criticism is the tendency to take personal narratives at face value while forgetting the inevitable gap between events and the survivors' interpretations of them (Brison 2002). Trauma is not known intelligently until its accompanying painful emotions can be accessed and released, freeing up the information in frozen images that had been stored for later evaluation (Nathanson 1992; Jackins 1994; Kauffman and New 2004). The rigid thoughts trapped in a recording about a crime include the initial categorization of the event, such as Bud Welch's fevered desire to kill McVeigh for the first few months after the bombing. This initial interpretation is cemented by painful emotions. Unless and until these are discharged and healed, allowing for re-categorization of the experience, survivors are likely to call for revenge.

A third danger is that bystanders feel the need to honor the emotions of family survivors. Because the traumatized feel strongly, those around them often feel prompted to respect that emotion by giving the traumatized what they want. For those who have been disempowered or discredited in the public square, 'emotional conviction may seem like the only weapon available for fighting back' (Haaken 1998: 181). Strang (2002) observes, 'there is a reluctance by citizens everywhere to engage in debate with people who have suffered so much, which in itself can be a serious impediment in moderating victims' demands' (p. 31). The emotional intensity of survivors' wants and preferences should never be taken naively as a guide to public policy, without critically examining how wants, desires, needs are molded by culturally available scripts and previous life experiences (Elias 1986).

241

A fourth criticism is that because narration is a reciprocal act, telling is vulnerable to abuse. Because everyone has a history of not being listened to and has a backlog of untold stories of pain, many feel compelled to replay their hurts in a bid for attention. For some people, this unaware clamor for attention takes the form of telling their stories, without having secured the listener's interest or permission. There is, as Aristotle said, a right person, a right time, and a right manner in which to express anger, shed tears, or relay one's woes. Trauma and the brutality of silencing often leave victims without the flexibility to discern the appropriateness of who to trust with their story and how to reciprocate with active listening. However, asking permission and waiting for a positive response are often enough to create the conditions for recounting a story and the spontaneous healing of painful emotions. Just as good parents learn to separate the wheat from the chaff, the irrational from the human, the genuine need from the whiny demand, practitioners of restorative justice can learn how to listen with discernment to personal narratives.

A fifth criticism is that listeners tend to accept the story of the trauma at face value rather than understanding it as experience that is interpreted through personal and communal narratives (Brison 2002). Individual experiences and emotions are expressed in metaphors from available worldviews. Such dominant scripts, such as 'revenge is natural,' 'the more he loved the deceased, the angrier he should be,' and 'a harsh punishment will make him feel better' are taken as truths, not choices. When hurts become scripted as reality, they set up expectations, such as 'people should feel vengeful,' 'relatives who opposed the death penalty must not have loved the deceased very much,' or 'harsh punishment makes a victim feel better.' Policy-makers are not likely to question the retributive paradigm in which victims' stories are told because that paradigm serves their interests.

The sixth pitfall of using narratives is identified by Scheingold et al. (1994) who observe that victims tend to be incident-driven in their activities. Their narratives of horrible suffering can terrify a community, resulting in outcomes that are strongly punitive even though not all victims were 'unremittingly punitive and short-term in their concerns and were interested in policies directed to crime prevention and the treatment of offenders' (Strang 2002: 31). In Strang's words, Scheingold et al. (1994) concluded that the narratives of survivors can 'leave their communities vulnerable to manipulation by forces specifically concerned to introduce more punitive policies, even if retribution is only half of what victims say they want' (p. 31). Even MVFR has felt the pressure from the media who wanted the most sensational stories involving a high-profile case in which the perpetrator was a stranger and the victim a helpless female. Relatives who lost family members to murder in which no perpetrator was apprehended, no conviction secured, or no death penalty imposed were ignored by the media as not important.

Members of MVFR have sought to use their stories in socially responsible ways. Their social ethic identifies the fundamental moral problem as 'man's inhumanity to man' and the cycles of suffering this spawns. Administrative systems of criminal justice do not in general see it as part of their mission to bring about healing from violence. They treat victims and victimizers as if they fall into two neat categories, without dealing with the complexity of how hurtful treatment sets people up to mistreat others. If they were to place human suffering into the foreground by listening to people's stories, they would have to question how harming one human (through capital punishment) helps the victim. Murder victims' families opposed to the death penalty tell stories that disrupt received categories and dominant discourses. They challenge a social ethic based on the premises that the world at present is just and that harsh punishment is needed to restore moral order. Instead, they testify to a broken world in which humans who are in pain harm other humans, in which the death penalty plays a small but horrific part. They call for a pedagogy of suffering in which responsiveness to each other's humanness and to each other's suffering are the chief norms.

Responsiveness to the humanity of the other is the antidote for harming others and the heart of a new social ethic that takes stories as foundational. What stories can teach is not how to get over murder by securing the ultimate punishment but how to live a good life that has had violent tragedy in it (Tedeschi and Calhoun 1995; Zehr 2001).

References

Athens, L. (1992) *The Creation of Dangerous Violent Criminals*, Chicago: University of Illinois Press.

Bellah, R., Madsen, R., Sullivan, W., Swidler, A. and Tipton, S. (1985) *Habits of the Heart*, Berkeley: University of California Press.

Bosco, A. (2001) *Choosing Mercy: a mother of murder victims pleads to end the death penalty*, Maryknoll, NY: Orbis.

Brison, S. J. (2002) *Aftermath: violence and remaking of the self*, Princeton: Princeton University Press.

Bruner, J. S. (1987) 'Life as narrative,' *Social Research*, 54: 11–32.

Caruth, C. (1996) *Unclaimed Experience: trauma, narrative, and history*, Baltimore: Johns Hopkins University Press.

Cleary, C. (2004) *Life Sentence: murder victims and their families*, Dublin: O'Brien.

Coles, R. (1989) *The Call of Stories*, Boston: Houghton Mifflin.

Culbertson, R. (1995) 'Embodied memory, transcendence, and telling: recounting trauma, re-establishing the self,' *New Literary History*, 26: 169–95.

Cushing, R. and Sheffer, S. (2002) *Dignity Denied: the experience of murder victims' family members who oppose the death penalty*, Cambridge, MA: Murder Victims' Families for Reconciliation.

— (2004) *Twenty-five years of MVFR: a brief history*, Murder Victims' Families for Reconciliation [Internet]. Available at: http://www.mvfr.org/ShowObject.jsp?object_id=7 [accessed 25 November 2004].

Davis, R. and Smith, B. (1994) 'Victim impact statements and victim satisfaction: an unfulfilled promise?' *Journal of Criminal Justice*, 22(1): 1–12.

Des Pres, T. (1976) *The Survivor: an anatomy of life in the death camps*, New York: Oxford University Press.

Elias, R. (1986) *The Politics of Victimisation: victims, victimology and human rights*, New York: Oxford University Press.

— (1990) 'Which victim movement? the politics of victim policy,' in A. Lurigio, W. Skogan and R. David (eds) *Victims of Crime: problems, policies and programs*, Newbury Park, CA: Sage.

Erez, E. (1991) 'Victim impact statements,' in P. Grabosky (ed.) *Trends and Issues in Crime and Criminal Justice*, No. 33, Canberra: Australian Institute of Criminology.

— (2000) 'Integrating a victim perspective in criminal justice through victim impact statements,' in A. Crawford and J. Goodey (eds) *Integrating a Victim Perspective within Criminal Justice*, Aldershot: Ashgate.

Erez, E. and Roeger, L. (1995) 'The effects of victim impact statements on sentencing patterns and outcomes: the Australian experience,' *Journal of Criminal Justice*, 23(4): 363–75.

Eron, J. and Lund, T. (1996) *Narrative Solutions in Brief Therapy*, New York: Guilford Press.

Felman, S. and Laub, D. (eds) (1992) *Testimony: crises of witnessing in literature, psychoanalysis, and history*, New York: Routledge.

Flanigan, B. (1998) 'Forgivers and the unforgivable,' in R. Enright and J. North (eds) *Exploring Forgiveness*, Madison: University of Wisconsin Press.

Forst, B. and Hernon, J. (1985) *The Criminal Justice Response to Victim Harm*, N.I.J. Research in Brief (June), Washington, DC: US Department of Justice.

Frank, A. (1995) *The Wounded Storyteller: body, illness, and ethics*, Chicago: University of Chicago Press.

Frank, A. and Fuentes, M. (1990) 'Social movements,' in School of Justice Studies, Arizona State University, Temple, Arizona (ed.) *New Directions in the Study of Justice, Law and Social Control*, New York: Plenum Press.

Garro, L. (1992) 'Chronic illness and the construction of narratives,' in M. Good, P. E. Brodwin and B. J. Good (eds) *Pain as Human Experience: an anthropological perspective*, Berkeley: University of California Press.

Gasker, J. (2002) *Incorporating Sexual Trauma into the Functional Life Narrative*, Lewiston, NY: The Edwin Mellen Press.

Geis, G. (1990) 'Crime victims: practices and prospects,' in A. Lurigio, W. Skogan and R. David (eds) *Victims of Crime: problems, policies and programs*, Newbury Park, CA: Sage.

Goldberg, M. (1991) *Jews and Christians: getting our stories straight*, Philadelphia: Trinity Press.

Gregg v. Georgia (1976) 428 US 153.

Gross, S. and Ellsworth, P. (2003) 'Second thoughts: Americans' views on the death penalty at the turn of the century,' in S. Garvey (ed.) *Beyond Repair? America's death penalty*, Durham, NC: Duke University Press.

Haaken, J. (1998) *Pillar of Salt: gender, memory, and the perils of looking back*, New Brunswick, NJ: Rutgers University Press.

Hagan. J. (1982) 'Victims before the law: a study of victim involvement in the criminal justice process,' *The Journal of Criminal Law and Criminology*, 73(1): 317–30.

Hankiss, A. (1981) 'On the mythological rear-ranging of one's life history,' in D. Bertaux (ed.) *Biography and Society: the life history approach in the social sciences*, Beverly Hills, CA: Sage.

Harris, J. (1987) *This Could Never Happen to Me: a handbook for families of murder victims and people who assist them*, Fort Worth, TX: Mental Health Association of Tarrant County.

Hauerwas, S. (1981) *The Character of Our Communities*, Notre Dame: University of Notre Dame Press.

Herman, J. R. (1997) *Trauma and Recovery*, New York: Basic Books.

Hood, B. and King, R. (1999) *Not in Our Name: murder victims' families speak out against the death penalty*, third edn, Cambridge, MA: Murder Victims' Families for Reconciliation.

Huyssen, A. (1995) *Twilight Memories: marking time in a culture of amnesia*, New York: Routledge.

Jackins, H. (1994) *The Human Side of Human Beings*, revised edn, Seattle: Rational Island Publishers.

Jaeger, M, (1998) 'The power and reality of forgiveness: forgiving the murderer of one's child,' in R. Enright and J. North (eds) *Exploring Forgiveness*, Madison: University of Wisconsin Press.

Janoff-Bulman, R. (1992) *Shattered Assumptions: towards a new psychology of trauma*, New York: Free Press.

Kauffman, K. and New, C. (2004) *Co-Counselling: the theory and practice of re-evaluation counseling*, New York: Routledge.

Kay, J. (2005a) *Murdering Myths: the story behind the death penalty*, Lanham, MD: Rowman and Littlefield.

— (2005b) 'Is restitution possible for murder? Family members speak,' in J. Acker and D. Karp (eds) *Wounds that do not Bind: victim-based perspectives on the death penalty*, Durham, NC: Carolina Academic Press.

King, R. (2003) *Don't Kill in Our Names: families of murder victims speak out against the death penalty*, New Brunswick, NJ: Rutgers University Press.

Langer, L. (1995) *Art from the Ashes*, New York: Oxford University Press.

Lerner, M. (1980) *The Belief in a Just World: a fundamental delusion*, New York: Plenum.

McAdams, D. P. (1993) *The Stories We Live By: personal myths and the making of the self*, New York: W. Morrow.

Magee, D. (1983) *What Murder Leaves Behind: the victim's family*, New York: Dodd Mead.

Maguire, M. and Shapland, J. (1990) 'The "victims movement" in Europe,' in A. Lurigio, W. Skogan and R. David (eds) *Victims of Crime: problems, policies and programs*, Newbury Park, CA: Sage.

Mandelstam, N. (1970) *Hope Against Hope*, Max Hayward (trans.), New York: Atheneum.

Marcel, G. (1960). *The Mystery of Being, vol. 2, Faith and reality*, Rene Hague (trans.), Chicago: Henry Regnery.

Mathis, T. (2005) Personal communication, 26 January, Seattle, WA.

Milburn, M. and Conrad, S. (1998) *The Politics of Denial*, reprint edn, Boston: MIT Press.

Mitchell, W. J. T. (1981) 'Foreword,' in W. J. T. Mitchell (ed.) *On Narrative*, Chicago: University of Chicago Press.

Monk, G., Winslade, J., Crocket, K. and Epston, D. (1996) *Narrative Therapy in Practice: the archaeology of hope*, Hoboken: John Wiley and Sons.

Morgan, A. (2000) *What is Narrative Therapy?* Adelaide, South Australia: Dulwich Centre.

Morris, A. and Young, W. (2000) 'Reforming criminal justice: the potential of restorative justice,' in H. Strang and J. Braithwaite (eds) *Restorative Justice: philosophy to practice*, Burlington, VT: Ashgate.

Mosteller, R. (1998) 'Victims' rights and the United States' constitution: moving from guaranteeing participatory rights to benefiting the prosecution,' *St. Mary's Law Journal*, 29: 1053–65.

Nathanson, D. (1992) *Shame and Pride: affect, sex, and the birth of the self*, New York: W. W. Norton.

Northey, W. F. (1999) 'The politics of denial: a postmodern critique,' *Offender Programs Report*, 3: 17–18 and 30–32.

O'Brien, Bill (1996) *Shattered Dreams: families of New Zealand murder victims speak out*, Auckland, NZ: David Ling Publishing.

Parry, A. and Doan, R. E. (1994) *Story Revisions: narrative therapy in the postmodern world*, New York: Guilford Press.

Pelke, B. (2003) *Journey of Hope*, Philadelphia: Xlibris Corporation.

Redmond, L. (1989) *Surviving: when someone you love was murdered: a professional's guide to group grief therapy for families and friends of murder victims*, Clearwater, FL: Psychological Consultation and Education Service.

Rose, N., Ash, M. and Woodward, W. (1998) *Inventing Our Selves: psychology, power and personhood*, reprint edn, New York: Cambridge University Press.

Sarat, A. (2001) *When the State Kills: capital punishment and the American condition*, Princeton: Princeton University Press.

Sarbin, T. (1986) 'The narrative as a root metaphor for psychology,' in T. Sarbin (ed.) *Narrative Psychology: the storied nature of human conduct*, New York: Praeger.

Scheingold, S., Olson, T. and Pershing, J. (1994) 'Sexual violence, victim advocacy and republican criminology: Washington State's community protection act,' *Law and Society Review*, 2(4): 729–63.

Schlosser, E. (1997) 'A grief like no other,' *The Atlantic Monthly*, 280(3): 37–76.

Scott, J. (1992) 'Experience,' in J. Butler and J. Scott (eds) *Feminists Theorize the Political*, New York: Routledge.

Shapland, J. (2000) 'Victims and criminal justice: creating responsible criminal justice agencies,' in A. Crawford and J, Goodey. (eds) *Integrating a Victim Perspective within Criminal Justice*, Aldershot: Ashgate.

Shapland, J., Willmore, J. and Duff, P. (1985) *Victims in the Criminal Justice System*, Cambridge Studies in Criminology, Aldershot: Gower.

Shay, J. (1994) *Achilles in Vietnam: combat trauma and the undoing of character*, New York: Atheneum.

Sher, G. (1987) *Desert*, Princeton: Princeton University Press.

Shils, E. (1981) *Tradition*, Chicago: University of Chicago Press.

Skogan, W. (1978) *Victimization Survey and Criminal Justice Planning*, Washington, DC: US National Institute of Law Enforcement and Criminal Justice.

Spungen, D. (1997) *Homicide: the hidden victims: a resource for professionals*, Newbury Park, CA: Sage.

Sroufe, A. (1995) *Emotional Development*, New York: Cambridge University Press.

Staub, E. (2003) *The Psychology of Good and Evil*, New York: Cambridge University Press.

Stern, D. (1973) *The Interpersonal World of the Infant*, New York: Basic Books.

Strang, H. (2002) *Repair or Revenge: victims and restorative justice*, Oxford: Clarendon Press.

Tedeschi, R. and Calhoun, L. (1995) *Trauma and Transformation: growing in the aftermath of suffering*, Thousand Oaks, CA: Sage.

Turow, S. (2003) *Ultimate Punishment: a lawyer's reflections on dealing with the death penalty*, New York: Farrar, Straus and Giroux.

Umbreit, M. (1989) 'Crime victims seeking fairness not revenge: towards restorative justice,' *Federal Probation*, 53(3): 52–57.

Welch, B. (2001) *Bud Welch Statement about Timothy McVeigh*, Coloradans Against the Death Penalty [Internet]. Available at: http://www.coadp.org/thepublications/pub-2001-Welch OnMcVeigh.html [accessed 11 May 2004].

Wessel, I. (2004) *Families of murder victims*, On Good Authority [Internet]. Available at: http://www.ongoodauthority.com/product_detail.cfm?Item=35 [accessed 12 July 2004].

White, H. (1981) 'The value of narrativity in the representation of reality,' in W. J. T. Mitchell (ed.) *On Narrative*, Chicago: University of Chicago Press.

Zehr, H. (2001) *Transcending: reflections on crime victims*, Intercourse, PA: Good Books.

Zimring, F. E. (2003) *The Contradictions of American Capital Punishment*, New York: Oxford University Press.

Notes

1. I call the relatives of the deceased *victims* because they have to live with the trauma. I also call such relatives *survivors*.
2. Many thanks to Teresa Mathis, Jerry Saltzman, Ronnie Friedman-Barone, Sharon Russell, and Joshua Kay for helpful comments on this chapter.
3. MVFR is distinctive among victims' groups because members are attracted to prison work 'by our desire to understand the sources of violence – what drives someone to commit a murder – and by our interest in violence prevention.' As a result, many members 'have supported Victim–Offender Reconciliation Projects and other restorative justice programs' (Cushing and Sheffer 2004).

16

Hearing the victim's voice amidst the cry for capital punishment

James R. Acker

Introduction

Neither murder nor capital punishment allows for reconciliation. Each act is violent, final, and unforgiving. Still, the seductive lure of 'eye-for-an-eye' symmetry between crime and punishment regularly causes the death penalty to be demanded in the name of murder victims and their survivors, or co-victims. Capital trials and executions are promoted as offering benefits to murder victims' loved ones. The use of victim impact evidence in capital sentencing hearings is defended in part to allow murder victims' survivors an active voice in the justice process. Executions bring a crime to final resolution, and although incapable of undoing murder's awful consequences, they are said to hold the promise of closure for co-victims.

This chapter critically examines the justifications for capital punishment offered in the name of murder victims and their survivors. It begins with a brief overview of death-penalty laws and practice in the United States, with a particular focus on whether capital punishment is likely to promote the interests of murder co-victims. It then explores the premise that victim impact evidence affords murder victims' survivors meaningful input into the criminal justice

process, a process that in capital cases has been activated to secure the offender's death. Initiatives designed to infuse restorative justice into death-penalty systems then are reviewed. The chapter concludes by arguing that capital punishment offers false promises to murder victims' survivors, embodying a regime that ultimately is far more likely to be destructive and work new injustices than promoting principles faithful to restorative justice.

Murder victims and the death penalty

With a homicide rate nearly four times higher than average among industrialized nations, the United States is a 'world leader' in murder (Hoskin 2001: 569; Leonard and Leonard 2003). The United States also is one of the world's foremost executioners, making it an anomaly among its neighbors in North America, South America, and Europe, which have almost universally abandoned the death penalty (Hood 2002). Despite comparatively high numbers of murders and executions, only a small percentage of criminal homicides in this country result in capital punishment. For example, while approximately 16,000 to 24,000 murders and non-negligent manslaughters were committed annually in the United States over the twentieth century's last decade, no year saw the number of executions top one hundred (Pastore and Maguire 2002: 530). Even allowing for the considerable time lag between murders and executions, these discrepancies suggest that the death penalty is carried out no more than five to ten times for every 1,000 intentional killings committed (Bedau 1997: 31–2).

There are many reasons for this low ratio of executions to intentional criminal homicides. In the first place, not all states authorize capital punishment. Although most of the populous states, where the vast majority of killings occur, and the federal government have enacted death-penalty laws, twelve states and the District of Columbia make life imprisonment the maximum punishment for murder (Bonczar and Snell 2003). In addition, most killings are not capital crimes even where the death penalty is recognized. Only aggravated forms of murder are punishable by death (Acker and Lanier 1993; *Zant v. Stephens* 1983) and the Constitution also forbids the execution of some classes of murderers, including mentally retarded offenders (*Atkins v. Virginia* 2002) and offenders younger than sixteen (*Stanford v.* Kentucky 1989; *Thompson v. Oklahoma* 1988).[1]

Even in potentially capital cases, the discretionary decisions made by prosecutors and juries rule out death sentences for the vast majority of murderers. Capital trials are expensive and time consuming. District attorneys must carefully assess the strength of the evidence, the heinousness of the crime, and a host of other factors before deciding whether to mount a capital prosecution (Pokorak 1998: 1813–15). When capital prosecutions go forward, juries frequently reject death sentences in favor of life imprisonment (Baldus *et al.* 1990). Moreover, appellate courts vacate many of the capital sentences that are imposed. Approximately

two-thirds of the death sentences entered throughout the country between 1973 and 1995 were invalidated by later court action, with more than 80 per cent of those cases ultimately resulting in non-capital dispositions ranging from life sentences to exoneration (Liebman *et al.* 2000).

Capital punishment can scarcely be sustained because of its presumed importance to murder victims' survivors when intentional killings culminate so infrequently in executions. Such an argument not only lacks credibility but also is disrespectful to the co-victims in 99 per cent of criminal homicides who are denied whatever satisfaction the death penalty promises. The death penalty not only fails to help most co-victims, it can work new hardships. The disruptive nature of the capital punishment process risks subjecting survivors to further victimization (Hoffmann 2003: 541–2; Amick-McMullan *et al.* 1989) and some co-victims want no part of the death penalty under any circumstances.

Co-victims may find their privacy shattered by the intense and relentless publicity surrounding capital trials, appeals, and the scheduling, postponement, and carrying out of executions (Danto 1982: 92; Gross and Matheson 2003: 493–4). Survivors' vulnerability is increased because the death-penalty process is unusually protracted. Trials can last for weeks and more than a decade typically ensues between trial and execution (Bonczar and Snell 2003: 11). Co-victims also must endure the roller-coaster emotions accompanying the frequent reversals and retrials (Burr 2003: 527; Vandiver 2003: 615–24) and there are no guarantees that if executions occur they will bring co-victims relief. Although survivors' reactions differ, the pain of losing a loved one can even intensify following an execution, as anticipation gives way to undiluted emptiness and sorrow (Henderson 1998: 601–2; Prejean 1993: 226).

Justifying capital punishment in the name of victims rests on the unwarranted assumption that all murder victims and their survivors necessarily would support the death penalty. Yet crime victims are not monolithic. They have diverse perspectives about crime, punishment, and justice. Although homicide victims have been silenced in voicing an opinion about their killer's punishment, their views would certainly differ. For instance, thousands of Americans have signed documents known as a 'declaration of life.' These expressions affirm 'that should I die as a result of a violent crime, I request that the person or persons found guilty of homicide for my killing not be subject to or put in jeopardy of the death penalty under any circumstances' (Logan 1999a: 42). Such statements are not binding on prosecutors, and almost certainly would be inadmissible in a trial.

> The fact that a declaration has been completed by a murder victim ... in no way negates the reality that the state's moral order and laws have been transgressed. At the same time, however, the victim's unequivocal and stated aversion to maximum punishment raises serious concerns over the moral legitimacy of the death penalty under such circumstances.
>
> (Logan 1999a: 42)

Murder victims' survivors also hold disparate views about the propriety of capital punishment. Some fervently support the death penalty while others stand in steadfast opposition. Coretta Scott King, widow of the murdered Martin Luther King, Jr, and Senator Edward Kennedy, whose brothers John and Bobby were slain by assassins' bullets, are among the family members of murder victims who have not wavered in their opposition to capital punishment (Schwartzchild 1982: 367). There are many others like them (Cushing 2002; King 2003; Pelke 2003; Welch 2002).

A district attorney's decision to seek a death sentence has dramatic implications for co-victims. Family members who favor capital punishment, or who at least are willing to accept it, are quickly aligned with the prosecution's efforts to achieve that outcome. Conversely, survivors who oppose the death penalty can feel isolated, rejected, and betrayed by the very system on which they must rely for justice following the violent death of a loved one (Beck et al. 2003: 393–4; Cushing and Sheffer 2002). Owing to their dependence on the justice system and their unique vulnerability, co-victims have even reported that 'in some ways, the second injury [they suffer at the hands of the criminal justice process] is even worse than the murder itself' (Spungen 1998: 10).

One unfortunate example of the criminal justice system making outcasts of co-victims because of their failure to support the death penalty occurred in Nebraska, where Randy Reeves was sentenced to death for murdering Victoria Zessin. At the clemency hearing held shortly before Reeves' scheduled execution, the Pardons Board considered a statement offered by the victim's sister urging the Board to deny clemency. However, the Board refused to recognize the victim's husband and daughter, Gus and Audrey Lamm, both of whom were present and had planned to speak in favor of sparing Reeves. The Lamms were convinced that Ms Zessin also would have been opposed to Reeves' execution. A Nebraska trial court upheld the Board's action after a temporary reprieve gave the Lamms a chance to contest their inability to be heard at the clemency hearing. The court reasoned that the Lamms' opposition to the death penalty had robbed them of victim status; that although they were husband and daughter of a murdered woman whom they both dearly loved, they 'are not victims as that term is commonly understood.' Rather, their anti-death penalty sentiments were said to have aligned them with the murderer, transforming them into 'agents of Randy Reeves' (Cushing and Sheffer 2002: 9; King 2003: 189–220).[2]

SueZann Bosler, whose father was murdered during an attack that also left her critically injured, was threatened with being jailed for contempt of court when she attempted to express opposition to capital punishment at the offender's sentencing hearing. She broke down in tears on the witness stand, later explaining that 'I felt like a criminal instead of a victim. I felt that if I said one wrong word I would go to jail' (King 2003: 158; see also Cushing and Sheffer 2002: 11). Not all co-victims who object to the death penalty suffer such unsympathetic responses from criminal justice officials (King 2003: 9–28; Logan 1999a: 51, n. 53), although many other regrettable instances unfortunately exist (Coyne 2003: 103–5; Cushing and Sheffer 2002).

Even when official actors are respectful of murder victims' survivors, a prosecutor's decision to pursue the death penalty can cause further turmoil in families when co-victims disagree about the propriety of capital punishment. Already distraught about their loved one's murder, family members with divided views about the death penalty may find themselves pitted against each other in legal proceedings and embroiled in emotionally devastating interpersonal disputes (Johnson 2003; King 2003: 55–6, 206–7). Survivors frequently must cope with the tragedy of intrafamilial homicides. Their grief and trauma can be compounded by guilt and a sense of divided loyalties between offender and victim, and the stakes are much higher when capital punishment is a part of the mix (Coyne 2003: 109; Spungen 1998: 83–4; Vandiver 2003: 619).

Several states have enacted laws giving murder victims' family members the right to witness the offender's execution (Goodwin 1997–8; Janick 2000). Lawmakers and victims' assistance offices typically assume that survivors who avail themselves of this option support the death sentence and hope for a measure of closure from the execution (Barnes 1996; Kanwar 2001–2). Although sometimes accurate, these assumptions are not universally true. Murder co-victims'

reasons for attending executions differ, as do reactions to an execution. Some survivors may oppose capital punishment yet attend an execution in an attempt to offer the offender comfort or forgiveness, or for other personal reasons. Officials may be unwelcoming of and unprepared for such witnesses, which can make an already traumatic experience even more difficult (Coyne 2003: 105–10; Cushing and Sheffer 2002: 14–17).

Considerable rhetoric promotes the death penalty as bringing closure to murder victims' survivors but whether it is capable of doing so involves complex issues that have not yet been adequately researched (Vandiver 2003: 622–3). A relative newcomer to discourse about capital punishment, closure first surfaced in newspaper stories in 1989 as a justification for the death penalty (Zimring 2003: 58). The term has since saturated the media (Gross and Matheson 2003) while eluding systematic scrutiny. Skeptics question whether bringing closure to grieving co-victims is a legitimate objective of a system of law (Bandes 2000; Kanwar 2001–2). Others speculate that the protracted and uncertain capital punishment process, which only sporadically produces executions, simply prolongs and intensifies survivors' suffering in most cases (Lifton and Mitchell 2000: 202–4).

The prospect of achieving full closure for co-victims is of course illusory, since nothing can expunge or reverse a loved one's murder (King 2003: 7; Spungen 1998: 239). The real question is whether the capital punishment process provides net benefits to murder victims' survivors. The most likely answer is that it does not. The death penalty is irrelevant to almost all homicides; is unpredictable, divisive, and unwelcome in the aftermath of others; and ultimately is incapable of eradicating the root cause of co-victims' suffering. Only an argument strained to the breaking point is capable of justifying capital punishment based on its presumed benefits to murder's co-victims.

249

Giving victims a voice? Victim impact evidence in capital trials

Spurred by rising crime rates, the strides made by women's rights activists and other advocacy groups, and years of neglect and indifference by policymakers and criminal justice officials, reform efforts on behalf of the victims of crime gained rapid momentum in the early 1970s (Beck *et al.* 2003: 386–9; Carrington 1978; Roland 1989; Tobolowsky 2001). Coincidentally, an assault on capital punishment was peaking at the same time in the federal courts (Meltsner 1973). The legal campaign against capital punishment crested in 1972 when the Supreme Court nullified death-penalty laws nationwide in its landmark decision in *Furman v. Georgia*. The sharply divided ruling focused primarily on the arbitrariness of capital punishment administered under laws that gave juries unfettered sentencing discretion. The justices were concerned that the resulting death sentences were 'freakishly imposed' and 'pregnant with discrimination' (*Furman v. Georgia* 1972: 310, 257). The four dissenting justices found many reasons to rue the decision. Justice Blackmun pointedly noted that none of the opinions in support of striking the capital punishment laws 'makes reference to the misery the [offenders'] crimes occasioned to the victims, to the families of the victims, and to the communities where the offenses took place' (pp. 413–14, dissenting opinion).

Adverse reaction to *Furman* was immediate and widespread. President Nixon, California Governor Ronald Reagan, and several other political leaders who were intent on waging a war on crime and upholding states' rights quickly pledged to restore capital punishment (Epstein and Kobylka 1992: 84–90; McFeely 2000: 48–50; Zimring and Hawkins 1986: 38–45). Public opinion spiked in support of the death penalty (Bohm 2003: 31; Ellsworth and Gross 1994). By 1976, just four years

after *Furman*, thirty-five states had enacted revised death-penalty legislation and the Supreme Court gave its stamp of approval to statutes that constrained sentencing discretion in capital cases without altogether eliminating it (Acker 1996; *Gregg v. Georgia* 1976; *Woodson v. North Carolina* 1976). Barely a decade later, the Court was called on to review whether victim impact evidence should be admissible in capital sentencing proceedings.

In *Booth v. Maryland* (1987), a probation officer called as a prosecution witness during the penalty phase of a capital murder trial read from an extensive report describing how relatives of Irvin and Rose Bronstein had been affected by their murder. The victim impact evidence also included family members' opinions relevant to the offenders' punishment.

> The [victims'] son, for example said that he suffers from lack of sleep and depression, and is 'fearful for the first time in his life.' He said that in his opinion his parents were 'butchered like animals.' The daughter said she also suffers from lack of sleep, and that since the murders she has become withdrawn and distrustful. She stated that she can no longer watch violent movies or look at kitchen knives without being reminded of the murders. The daughter concluded that she could not forgive the murderer and that such a person could '[n]ever be rehabilitated.' Finally, the granddaughter described how the deaths had ruined the wedding of another close family member that took place a few days after the bodies were discovered.
>
> (pp. 499–500)

Justice Powell's majority opinion in *Booth* ruled that victim impact evidence 'is irrelevant to a capital sentencing decision, and that its admission creates a constitutionally unacceptable risk that the jury may impose the death penalty in an arbitrary and capricious manner' (pp. 502–3). Such evidence focuses 'not on the defendant, but on the character and reputation of the victim and the effect on his family. These factors may be wholly unrelated to the [defendant's] blameworthiness' (p. 504). Victim impact evidence invites arbitrariness because 'in some cases the victim will not leave behind a family, or the family members may be less articulate in describing their feelings even though their sense of loss is equally severe' (p. 505). Justice Powell's opinion warned that '[w]e are troubled by the implication that defendants whose victims were assets to their community are more deserving of punishment than those whose victims are perceived to be less worthy' (p. 506, n. 8). The family members' statements that alluded to an appropriate punishment for the murders 'can serve no other purpose than to inflame the jury and divert it from deciding the case on the relevant evidence concerning the crime and the defendant' (p. 508).

Four justices dissented in *Booth*. Justice White argued that victim impact evidence is relevant to alert jurors to the full magnitude of the harm caused by murder. He additionally asserted that such testimony is necessary to help counterbalance evidence offered by the offender in mitigation of punishment. Victim impact evidence reminds 'the sentencer that just as the murderer should be considered as an individual, so too the victim is an individual whose death represents a unique loss to society and in particular to his family' (p. 517). Justice Scalia's dissent expanded on this theme.

> Recent years have seen an outpouring of popular concern for what has come to be known as 'victims' rights' – a phrase that describes what its proponents feel is the failure of courts of justice to take into account in their sentencing decisions not only the factors mitigating the defendant's moral guilt, but also the amount of harm he has caused to innocent members of society. Many citizens have found one-sided and hence unjust the criminal trial in which a parade of witnesses comes forth to

> testify to the pressures beyond normal human experience that drove the defendant to commit his crime, with no one to lay before the sentencing authority the full reality of human suffering the defendant has produced – which (and *not* moral guilt alone) is one of the reasons society deems his act worthy of the prescribed penalty.
>
> (p. 520)

Although *Booth's* proscription against admitting victim impact evidence applied only to the unique context of capital sentencing rather than criminal cases generally (p. 509, n. 12), the Court's ruling angered and 'bitterly disappointed' crime victims' advocates (Gest and Ellis-Simmons 1989: 17). The enactment of legislation and state constitutional amendments guaranteeing crime victims rights within the criminal justice system accelerated during the latter part of the 1980s (Anderson and Woodard 1985; Polito 1990; Roland 1989). At the conclusion of the decade the Supreme Court narrowly reaffirmed its controversial ruling in *Booth* in *South Carolina v. Gathers* (1989). In another 5–4 decision, the justices invalidated the death sentence imposed in *Gathers* because the prosecutor's argument during the trial's penalty phase had improperly highlighted the murder victim's personal characteristics. However, *Booth's* vitality, which was tenuous from the outset, was increasingly in doubt following the retirement of Justices Powell and Brennan, the respective authors of the majority opinions in *Booth* and *Gathers*.

The Court wasted little time at the dawn of the 1990s revisiting the admissibility of victim impact evidence in capital trials. It did so in *Payne v. Tennessee* (1991), a case involving the murder of twenty-eight-year-old Charisse Christopher and her two-year-old daughter Lacie. Although three-year-old Nicholas was critically wounded during the same rampage that had left his mother and sister dead, he was rushed to a hospital and survived. Pervis Payne was convicted and sentenced to death for the double murder following a sentencing hearing in which the prosecutor elicited the testimony of Nicholas's grandmother describing the impact of the slayings on the young child.

> He cries for his mom. He doesn't seem to understand why she doesn't come home. And he cries for his sister Lacie. He comes to me many times during the week and asks me, Grandmama, do you miss my Lacie. And I tell him yes. He says, I'm worried about my Lacie.
>
> (*Payne v. Tennessee* 1991: 814–15)

The prosecutor's penalty-phase argument echoed this theme and implored the jury to return a death sentence in recognition of Nicholas and the murder victims.

> Somewhere down the road Nicholas is going to grow up, hopefully. He's going to want to know what happened. And he is going to know what happened to his baby sister and his mother. He is going to want to know what type of justice was done. He is going to want to know what happened. With your verdict, you will provide the answer ...

> No one will ever know about Lacie Jo because she never had the chance to grow up. Her life was taken from her at the age of two years old. So, no there won't be a high school principal to talk about Lacie Jo Christopher, and there won't be anybody to take her to her high school prom. And there won't be anybody there – there won't be her mother there or Nicholas' mother there to kiss him at night. His mother will never kiss him good night or pat him as he goes off to bed, or hold him and sing him a lullaby.

> (pp. 815–16)

By vote of 6–3, the Supreme Court affirmed Payne's death sentence, overruling *Booth* and *Gathers* in the process.[3] Chief Justice Rehnquist's majority opinion reasoned that

victim impact evidence helps document the full extent of harm caused by a murder and consequently is relevant to a punishment decision (pp. 819–21). It also sanctioned victim impact evidence as counterbalancing the offender's open-ended opportunity to present evidence in mitigation of a capital sentence.

> *Booth* ... unfairly weighted the scales in a capital trial; while virtually no limits are placed on the relevant mitigating evidence a capital defendant may introduce concerning his own circumstances, the State is barred from either offering 'a quick glimpse of the life' which a defendant 'chose to extinguish,' or demonstrating the loss to the victim's family and to society which has resulted from the defendant's homicide.
>
> (p. 822)

Justice Marshall's angry dissent charged that 'Power, not reason, is the new currency of this Court's decisionmaking ... Neither the law nor the facts supporting *Booth* and *Gathers* underwent any change in the last four years. Only the personnel of this Court did' (p. 844).

In the wake of *Payne*, victim impact evidence is admissible in capital trials in all but a handful of jurisdictions. Such evidence is regularly introduced. The federal trial resulting in Timothy McVeigh's death sentence for his deadly bombing of the Alfred P. Murrah Building in Oklahoma City was awash with the intensely moving testimony of victims' family members. The jury even heard from rescue workers who recounted their traumatic experiences in the bombing's aftermath (Burr 2003; *United States v. McVeigh* 1998). At least thirty-three of the thirty-eight states with death-penalty laws currently allow sentencing juries to consider victim impact evidence (Blume 2003: 267–9; Mosteller 2003: 544–6). A few state statutes place limits on the type and number of witnesses who can offer testimony, and some require victim impact evidence to be presented in writing instead of orally (Nadler and Rose 2003: 453). Nevertheless, such legislative restrictions frequently are honored in the breach (Logan 1999b, 2000).

Many have expressed concern that the highly emotional testimony of murder victims' survivors will overwhelm jurors and prejudicially tip the scales toward death in capital trials (Bandes 2000; Burr 2003; Donahoe 1999; Luginbuhl and Burkhead 1995; Nadler and Rose 2003). Although such fears cannot be discounted, research studies suggest that victim impact testimony has limited effect on judges' sentencing decisions in non-capital trials (Erez 1990; Erez and Tontodonato 1990). Surprisingly, it may also be the case that survivor testimony does not figure prominently in jury decisions involving capital punishment. Studies relying on interviews with former jurors in death-penalty cases have reported that neither victim impact evidence nor jurors' perceptions about whether murder victims were admirable or 'worthy' significantly influenced sentencing decisions (Eisenberg *et al.* 2003; Sundby 2003).

The assumption that victim impact testimony benefits murder victims' survivors by offering them a voice in the capital sentencing process merits close scrutiny. Although talking about the grievous loss of a loved one is potentially therapeutic (Hoffmann 2003: 537–8; Mosteller 2003: 548–53), scant evidence supports the proposition that offering victim impact testimony in a capital trial entails such benefits (Arrigo and Williams 2003: 609; Davis and Smith 1994; Henderson 1999: 408). Justifying victim impact evidence as benefiting murder victims' survivors also portends disastrous boomerang effects in cases in which juries reject death sentences. Co-victims are apt to interpret selection of a life sentence as a slight against both themselves and their deceased family members (Beck *et al.* 2003: 393, n. 57; Henderson 1985: 1006; Spungen 1998: 96). Additionally, as the Court recognized in *Booth* (1987: 506–7) as well as *Payne* (1991: 823), evidence reflecting favorably on a murder victim is subject to rebuttal. Although tactically unlikely, in principle defense lawyers have free rein to attempt to sully a murder victim's character following testimony extolling the victim's virtues (Berger 1992: 55–9).

The presentation of victim impact evidence can add strain to intrafamilial relations when murder victims' survivors disagree about capital punishment (Johnson 2003). Moreover, individual survivors who disfavor the death penalty may nevertheless experience conflict about whether to offer victim impact evidence (Blume 2003: 280). For example, Charisse Coleman appeared as a prosecution witness at the penalty phase of the trial that resulted in a death sentence for her brother's killer even though she firmly opposed capital punishment. She explained the Hobson's choice she confronted.

> To the degree that I spoke eloquently or movingly of my loss, or made vivid for the jury even a sliver of the brightness that was Russell, I would be helping them make a decision I find morally, politically, economically and spiritually insupportable. I was jammed into a miserable position. Either I kept silent in order to preserve the integrity of my beliefs, or I swallowed my discomfort and took the stand. If my bearing witness to my love for Russell brought another human being closer to death, then it felt like a terribly selfish thing to do. Even so, I could not surrender my chance to speak. My need to be a witness – to Russell's life, to his appalling absence from all these proceedings, to the lasting grief Bobby Lee Hampton had brought – that need drove me onto the stand.
>
> (Coleman 2000)

Susan Hirsch, whose husband was killed in the 1998 bombing of the US embassy in Kenya, faced a similar conflict. She disagreed with the government's decision to pursue death sentences in the offenders' ensuing trial, yet ultimately acquiesced to federal prosecutors' request for a photograph of her husband so he could be 'humanized' before the jury. She later reflected on issues likely to confront murder co-victims as the prosecution readies for a capital sentencing hearing.

> Whether they testify or not, victims hold many different understandings of the penalty phase and a variety of motivations for participating. Some hope to confront the convicted defendant with the horror of his crime. Other victims, through telling tragic stories in court, seek public acknowledgment of their pain or loss. Still others feel a solemn obligation to make a public representation of a dead loved one, to make sure that the dead victim is 'present' in the legal proceeding.
>
> (Hirsch 2002)

Some co-victims experience more than conflict, and feel devalued or betrayed when their voice in opposition to the death penalty is stifled as prosecutors make their case for a capital sentence. SueZann Bosler's threatened citation for contempt in a Florida courtroom when she wanted to speak in opposition to the death penalty for her father's killer is an extreme example (King 2003: 138–62). Other survivors have felt rejected and alienated because of their resistance to capital punishment (Cushing and Sheffer 2002). For example, some co-victims of the Oklahoma City federal building bombings who opposed the death penalty felt ostracized during the government's efforts to secure Timothy McVeigh's execution (Coyne 2003: 97–9; Henderson 1998: 590–1). In another notorious case, Rusty Yates opposed the prosecution's ultimately unsuccessful attempt to have his wife Andrea sentenced to death. Mrs Yates had drowned the couple's children in a bathtub. As the father of the slain children, Rusty Yates clearly qualified as a 'victim' under Texas law and thus had a right to attend the murder trial. However, his failure to support the prosecutor's quest for his wife's capital punishment resulted in his not being reserved a seat in the courtroom.

> 'Can you imagine the family of the victims having to worry about getting a seat at a huge trial like this?' [Mr Yates] asked. 'That's the last thing we need to worry about. I can't help but think that if we supported the prosecution we'd have a front-row center seat.'
>
> (Coyne 2003: 105)

Worse yet is the prospect that using victim impact evidence in capital cases is exploitative of murder victims' survivors. Critics have charged that the victims' rights movement is only nominally concerned with individual victims of crime and instead masquerades to promote a punitive 'law and order' crime control agenda (Dubber 2002; Henderson 1985; White 1998). A similar theme of co-optation and exploitation has been advanced with specific reference to the death penalty. In this context, it has been suggested that 'victim impact statements work to prompt a return of revenge' (Sarat 2001: 38).

> The symbolism of . . . victim impact presentation is of extraordinary importance in the transformation of the image of capital punishment in the United States . . . [T]he penalty phase is remade into what sociologists call a 'status competition' between the offender (whose claims to sympathy and understanding are the subject of his penalty phase presentation) and those who were directly or derivatively injured by the crime.
>
> (Zimring 2003: 55)

[M]any citizens feel uncomfortable watching governments kill to achieve solely governmental purposes. It is far more comfortable to imagine the executioner as the personal servant of homicide survivors than to accept the legitimacy of a government killing for its own purposes.

> (ibid.: 63)

Capital punishment and restorative justice

Although sometimes justified by the utilitarian objectives of general deterrence and incapacitation, the death penalty most fundamentally promises retribution (Berns 1979; *Gregg v. Georgia* 1976; van den Haag 2003). It is separated from other punishments by its absolute repudiation of the offender's continuing entitlement to life. In the words of nineteenth-century English legal historian Sir James Fitzjames Stephen, 'When a man is hung, there is an end of our relations with him. His execution is a way of saying, "You are not fit for this world, take your chance elsewhere"' (*Furman v. Georgia* 1972: 290, quoting Stephen 1864: 763).

Because its ultimate objective is the offender's execution, the death penalty is difficult if not impossible to square with principles of restorative justice. Although retribution is not inherently incompatible with models of restorative justice (Daly 2000; Duff 2003), capital punishment takes retribution to an extreme. It preempts any possibility of the offender's reintegration into the community. It inflicts unmitigated pain. Its unequivocal rejection of the offender essentially disavows any societal responsibility for harmful conditions that may have helped spawn the criminal behavior. In these fundamentals, the death penalty is flatly inconsistent with a restorative outlook (Long 1999; Radelet and Borg 2000; Sullivan and Tifft 2001: 30–7).

Nevertheless, reformers have attempted to temper the death-penalty process with restorative justice initiatives directed toward murder co-victims. For example, attorneys representing defendants charged with capital crimes have utilized a strategy of defense-based victim outreach, employing victim liaisons who make contact with and try to be responsive to survivors' case-related needs. Defense lawyers may assume that co-victims will support a prosecutor's decision to seek a death sentence and necessarily will

be hostile to defense-initiated overtures. In fact, just the opposite might be true. Co-victims' priorities may have little to do with capital punishment, and survivors can welcome respectful offers of assistance, even if by a member of the defense team. In meeting the somewhat daunting challenge of being supportive of the murder victim's family while not losing sight of the best interests of the accused, a victim liaison performs various functions. One role could be to help shape a plea agreement that spares the offender death and simultaneously insulates the co-victims from the travails of a lengthy trial and its potentially harrowing aftermath. The liaison also helps ensure that co-victims are afforded such rudimentary yet crucially important courtesies as being provided with timely information about the case, an explanation of the criminal justice process, and a chance to have their questions answered (Burr 2003; Grunewald and Nath 2003).

Restorative justice techniques might also embrace offenders' family members, who can be the forgotten victims of capital punishment. The defendant's family must cope with intense pain, grief, shame, anxiety, and guilt stemming from their loved one's criminal conduct and scheduled execution, as well as the stigmatization and hostility that inevitably spill over from the crime, trial, and death sentence (Ingle 1990: 206–9; Vandiver 2003: 624–9). Notwithstanding their considerable trauma, offenders' relatives typically receive no support or offers of assistance from criminal justice agencies. To the contrary, their interactions with the criminal justice system tend to be negative, which compounds their distress. 'These families are in need of healing . . . Restorative justice is the only approach that focuses on healing offenders and their family members, victims and their family members, and the community' (Eschholz *et al.* 2003: 175–6).

Perhaps the most ambitious attempt to apply restorative justice within the shadow of capital punishment involves carefully monitored mediation sessions that offer co-victims the chance to meet and talk with the offenders who have been sentenced to death for murdering their loved ones. Although once rare, at least fifteen states now sponsor or are developing programs encompassing mediated encounters between offenders and victims of violent crimes (Umbreit *et al.* 2003: 1). Victims who choose to participate in such programs have diverse motivations, including 'to express the full impact of the crime upon their life, to get answers to many questions they have and to gain a greater sense of closure so that they can move on with their lives' (ibid.: 13). For their part, offenders typically participate to acknowledge responsibility for the harm they have caused, to apologize, and help victims in their recovery process (ibid.: 24–5). Victim–offender mediation sessions have included death row encounters between murder victims' survivors and offenders who are awaiting execution.

Such face-to-face meetings between co-victims and murderers clearly will not be appropriate in all cases. They are feasible only when all parties are willing to participate. Intensive preparations involving the parties and a skilled mediator are a prerequisite for such interactions. Interviews conducted with participants in a small number of death row victim–offender mediation sessions have revealed that both co-victims and offenders benefited from the chance to meet, share information, and express their feelings (Umbreit *et al.* 2003; Umbreit and Vos 2000). All participants comprising this select sample described being 'moved beyond their expectations, all were relieved, and all reported significant impact on their healing' (Umbreit *et al.* 2003: 369).

Interventions based on restorative justice, including defense-based victim outreach, healing circles that include offenders' families, and even mediated victim–offender dialogues, need not be foreign to the capital punishment process. Still, those same efforts would be equally appropriate and salutary in non-capital cases. The looming presence of the death penalty can intensify and be an additional source of the pain and suffering that inevitably accompany criminal homicide. In short, restorative justice efforts in this context can do little more than serve as a form of damage control. They must respond not only to the harm caused by the crime of murder but as well to the consequential hardships springing from the punishment of death.

Conclusion

Capital punishment is a statistically rare response to murder. Just as a solution to a housing, educational, or medical crisis would be impossible to justify if it benefited only one in a hundred needy individuals, the death penalty cannot be supported as a service to murder victims when ninety-nine out of a hundred are excluded from its reach. Such a calculus not only fails to support capital punishment in the name of murder victims, it borders on being insulting.

> The creation of an expectation that will satisfy the relatives of victims in fewer than one in every fifty killings would be problematic no matter what the priorities of the sentencing system. But to create such a formula for certainty of disappointment in the name of victim's rights is particularly ironic.
> (Zimring 2003: 56)

Even when death-penalty cases go forward, the rewards that murder victims' survivors realize are uncertain and dubious. In the first place, some co-victims want no part of the death penalty. Survivors' sentiments about capital punishment range from passionate support to ardent opposition. These divisions sometimes surface in the same grieving family, causing emotions to spiral from anguish into destructive anger. Victim impact evidence has limited therapeutic value and risks co-victims' experiencing a sense of rejection when jurors choose to sentence their loved one's murderer 'only' to life imprisonment, as occurs in many capital trials. Death sentences are frequently vacated at some point during the decade or more that cases ordinarily remain under judicial review. Retrials and renewed rounds of appeals delay finality in the legal proceedings and bring survivors unwanted publicity and further disruption. The quest for closure in capital cases can be self-defeating. When executions do occur, they can provide surprisingly little satisfaction or relief. In general, capital punishment is far more likely to promote the political rhetoric of the victims' rights movement than the best interests of individual murder victims or their survivors.

While the death penalty simply represents failed policy for most murder victims and their families, it affirmatively misrepresents and distorts the voices of others. Many co-victims feel betrayed and re-victimized by a system of criminal justice that would purposefully compound the tragedy of one senseless killing with another. These survivors reject the extreme retributivism of capital punishment, finding such a philosophy irreconcilable with their own values or those of their deceased loved ones. The death penalty signals the community's uncompromising rejection of the offender. It precludes any prospect of redemption or reconciliation. It causes profound new harm, including suffering to be endured by the offender's family (Radelet and Borg 2000: 88–9). In these and other respects, capital punishment is anathema to many murder victims' survivors and is at odds with basic precepts of restorative justice.

References

Acker, J. R. (1996) 'The death penalty: a 25-year retrospective and a perspective on the future,' *Criminal Justice Review,* 21(2): 139–60.

Acker, J. R. and Lanier, C. S. (1993) 'The dimensions of capital murder,' *Criminal Law Bulletin,* 29(5): 379–417.

Amick-McMullan, A., Kilpatrick, D. G., Veronen, L. J. and Smith, S. (1989) 'Family survivors of homicide victims: theoretical perspectives and an exploratory study,' *Journal of Traumatic Stress,* 2(1): 21–35.

Anderson, J. R. and Woodard, P. L. (1985) 'Victim and witness assistance: new state laws and the system's response,' *Judicature,* 68(6): 220–44.

Arrigo, B. A. and Williams, C. R. (2003) 'Victim vices, victim voices, and impact statements: on the place of emotion and the role of restorative justice in capital sentencing,' *Crime and Delinquency,* 49(4): 603–26.

Atkins v. Virginia (2002) 536 US 304.

Baldus, D. C., Woodworth, G. G. and Pulaski, C. A., Jr (1990) *Equal justice and the death penalty: a legal and empirical analysis,* Boston: Northeastern University Press.

Bandes, S. (2000) 'When victims seek closure: forgiveness, vengeance, and the role of government,' *Fordham Urban Law Journal,* 27(5): 1599–1606.

Barnes, P. G. (1996) 'Final reckoning: states allow victims' families to watch executions,' *ABA Journal,* March: 36–7.

Beck, E., Blackwell, B. S., Leonard, P. B. and Mears, M. (2003) 'Seeking sanctuary: interviews with family members of capital defendants,' *Cornell Law Review,* 88(2): 382–418.

Bedau, H. A. (1997) 'The laws, the crimes, and the executions,' in H. A. Bedau (ed.) *The Death Penalty in America: current controversies,* New York: Oxford University Press.

Berger, V. (1992) '*Payne* and suffering – a personal reflection and a victim-centered critique,' *Florida State University Law Review,* 20(1): 21–65.

Berns, W. (1979) *For Capital Punishment: crime and the morality of the death penalty,* New York: Basic Books.

Blume, J. H. (2003) 'Ten years of *Payne*: victim impact evidence in capital cases,' *Cornell Law Review,* 88(2): 257–81.

Bohm, R. M. (2003) 'American death penalty opinion: past, present, and future,' in J. R. Acker, R. M. Bohm and C. S. Lanier (eds) *America's Experiment with Capital Punishment: reflections on the past, present, and future of the ultimate penal sanction,* Durham, NC: Carolina Academic Press.

Bonczar, T. P. and Snell, T. L. (2003) *Bureau of Justice Statistics Bulletin: capital punishment, 2002,* Washington, DC: US Department of Justice.

Booth v. Maryland (1987) 482 US 496.

Burr, R. (2003) 'Litigating with victim impact testimony: the serendipity that has come from *Payne v. Tennessee,' Cornell Law Review*, 88(2): 517–29.

Carrington, F. G. (1978) *Neither Cruel nor Unusual*, New Rochelle, NY: Arlington House.

Coleman, C. (2000) 'Life or death: a death-penalty opponent remembers the trial of her brother's murderer,' *The Independent Weekly*, 8 November, online. Available at http://www.indyweek.com/durham/2000-11-08/news2.html

Coyne, R. T. (2003) 'Shooting the wounded: first degree murder and second class victims,' *Oklahoma City University Law Review*, 28(1): 93–107.

Cushing, R. (2002) 'Amazing grace: reflections on justice, survival, and healing,' in D. R. Dow and M. Dow (eds) *Machinery of Death: the reality of America's death penalty regime*, New York: Routledge.

Cushing, R. and Scheffer, S. (2002) *Dignity Denied: the experience of murder victims' family members who oppose the death penalty*, Cambridge, MA: Murder Victims' Families for Reconciliation.

Daly, K. (2000) 'Revisiting the relationship between retributive and restorative justice,' in H. Strang and J. Braithwaite (eds) *Restorative Justice: from philosophy to practice*, Burlington, VT: Ashgate Publishing.

Danto, B. L. (1982) 'Survivors of homicide: the unseen victims,' in B. L. Danto, J. Bruhns and A. H. Kutscher (eds) *The Human Side of Homicide*, New York: Columbia University Press.

Davis, R. C. and Smith, B. E. (1994) 'Victim impact statements and victim satisfaction: an unfulfilled promise,' *Journal of Criminal Justice*, 22(1): 1–12.

Donahoe, J. F. (1999) 'The changing role of victim impact evidence in capital cases,' *Western Criminology Review*, 2(1), online. Available at: http://wcr.sonoma.edu/v2n1/donahoe.html

Dubber, M. D. (2002) *Victims in the War on Crime: the use and abuse of victims' rights*, New York: New York University Press.

Duff, R. A. (2003) 'Restoration and retribution,' in A. von Hirsch, J. V. Roberts, A. E. Bottoms, K. Roach and M. Schiff (eds) *Restorative Justice and Criminal Justice: competing or reconcilable paradigms?* Portland, OR: Hart Publishing.

Eisenberg, T., Garvey, S. P. and Wells, M. T. (2003) 'Victim characteristics and victim impact evidence in South Carolina capital cases,' *Cornell Law Review*, 88(2): 306–42.

Ellsworth, P. C. and Gross, S. R. (1994) 'Hardening of the attitudes: Americans' views on the death penalty,' *Journal of Social Issues*, 50(2): 19–52.

Epstein, L. and Kobylka, J. F. (1992) *The Supreme Court and Legal Change: abortion and the death penalty*, Chapel Hill, NC: University of North Carolina Press.

Erez, E. (1990) 'Victim participation in sentencing: rhetoric and reality,' *Journal of Criminal Justice*, 18(1): 19–31.

Erez, E. and Tontodonato, P. (1990) 'The effect of victim participation in sentencing on sentence outcome,' *Criminology*, 28(3): 451–74.

Eschholz, S., Reed, M. D., Beck, E. and Leonard, P. B. (2003) 'Offenders' family members' responses to capital crimes: the need for restorative justice initiatives,' *Homicide Studies*, 7(2): 154–81.

Furman v. Georgia (1972) 408 US 238.

Gest, T. and Ellis-Simons, P. (1989) 'Victims of crime,' *US News and World Reports*, 107(5) (31 July): 16–19.

Goodwin, M. L. (1997–8) 'An eyeful for an eye – an argument against allowing the families of murder victims to witness executions,' *Brandeis Journal of Family Law*, 36(4): 585–608.

Gregg v. Georgia (1976) 428 US 153.

Gross, S. R. and Matheson, D. J. (2003) 'What they say at the end: capital victims' families and the press,' *Cornell Law Review*, 88(2): 486–516.

Grunewald, K. R. and Nath, P. (2003) 'Defense-based victim outreach: restorative justice in capital cases,' *Capital Defense Journal*, 15(Spring): 315–52.

Henderson, L. N. (1985) 'The wrongs of victim's rights,' *Stanford Law Review*, 37(4): 937–1021.

— (1998) 'Co-opting compassion: the federal victim's rights amendment,' *St Thomas Law Review*, 10(3): 579–606.

— (1999) 'Revisiting victim's rights,' *Utah Law Review*, 1999(2): 383–442.

Hirsch, S. F. (2002) 'Victims for the prosecution,' *Boston Review*, October/November, online. Available at: http://bostonreview.net/BR27.5/hirsch.html

Hoffmann, J. L. (2003) 'Revenge or mercy? Some thoughts about survivor opinion evidence in death penalty cases,' *Cornell Law Review*, 88(2): 530–42.

Hood, R. (2002) *The Death Penalty: a worldwide perspective*, third edn, New York: Oxford University Press.

Hoskin, A. W. (2001) 'Armed Americans: the impact of firearm availability on national homicide rates,' *Justice Quarterly*, 18(3): 569–92.

Ingle, J. B. (1990) *Last Rights: 13 fatal encounters with the state's justice*, Nashville: Abingdon Press.

Janick, D. (2000) 'Allowing victims' families to view executions: the eighth amendment and society's justifications for punishment,' *Ohio State Law Journal*, 61(2): 935–77.

Johnson, S. L. (2003) 'Speeding in reverse: an anecdotal view of why victim impact testimony should not be driving capital prosecutions,' *Cornell Law Review*, 88(2): 555–68.

Kanwar, V. (2001–2) 'Capital punishment as "closure": the limits of a victim-centered jurisprudence,' *New York University Review of Law and Social Change*, 27(2–3): 215–55.

King, R. (2003) *Don't Kill in Our Names: families of murder victims speak out against the death penalty*, New Brunswick, NJ: Rutgers University Press.

Leonard, I. M. and Leonard, C. C. (2003) 'The historiography of American violence,' *Homicide Studies*, 7(2): 99–153.

Liebman, J. S., Fagan, J. and West, V. (2000) *A Broken System: error rates in capital cases, 1973–1995*, online. Available at: http://www2.law.columbia.edu/instructionalservices/liebman/liebman1.pdf [accessed 8 July 2004].

Lifton, R. J. and Mitchell, G. (2000) *Who Owns Death? Capital punishment, the American conscience, and the end of executions*, New York: William Morrow.

Logan, W. A. (1999a) 'Declaring life at the crossroads of death: victims' anti-death penalty views and prosecutors' charging decisions,' *Criminal Justice Ethics*, 18(2): 41–57.

— (1999b) 'Through the past darkly: a survey of the uses and abuses of victim impact evidence in capital trials,' *Arizona Law Review*, 41(1): 143–92.

— (2000) 'Opining on death: witness sentence recommendations in capital trials,' *Boston College Law Review*, 41(3): 517–47.

Long, W. C. (1999) 'Karla Faye Tucker: a case for restorative justice,' *American Journal of Criminal Law*, 27(1): 117–27.

Luginbuhl, J. and Burkhead, M. (1995) 'Victim impact evidence in a capital trial: encouraging votes for death,' *American Journal of Criminal Justice*, 20(1): 1–16.

McFeely, W. S. (2000) *Proximity to Death*, New York: W.W. Norton.

Meltsner, M. (1973) *Cruel and Unusual: the Supreme Court and capital punishment*, Boston: Northeastern University Press.

Mosteller, R. P. (2003) 'Victim impact evidence: hard to find the real rules,' *Cornell Law Review*, 88(2): 543–54.

Nadler, J. and Rose, M. R. (2003) 'Victim impact testimony and the psychology of punishment,' *Cornell Law Review*, 88(2): 419–56.

Pastore, A. L. and Maguire, K. (eds) (2002) *Bureau of Justice Statistics Sourcebook of Criminal Justice Statistics – 2001*, Washington, DC: US Department of Justice.

Payne v. Tennessee (1991) 501 US 808.

Pelke, B. (2003) *Journey of Hope … From Violence to Healing*, No location: Xlibris Corporation.

Pokorak, J. J. (1998) 'Probing the capital prosecutor's perspective: race of the discretionary actors,' *Cornell Law Review*, 83(6): 1811–20.

Polito, K. E. (1990) 'The rights of crime victims in the criminal justice system: is justice blind to the victims of crime?' *New England Journal on Criminal and Civil Confinement*, 16(2): 241–70.

Prejean, H. (1993) *Dead Man Walking: an eyewitness account of the death penalty in the United States*, New York: Vintage Books.

Radelet, M. L. and Borg, M. J. (2000) 'Comment on Umbreit and Vos: retributive versus restorative justice,' *Homicide Studies*, 4(1): 88–92.

Roland, D. L. (1989) 'Progress in the victim reform movement: no longer the "forgotten victim"', *Pepperdine Law Review*, 17(1): 35–58.

Roper v. Simmons (2004) 124 S. Ct. 1171.

Sarat, A. (2001) *When the State Kills: capital punishment and the American condition*, Princeton, NJ: Princeton University Press.

Schwartzchild, H. (1982) 'In opposition to death penalty legislation,' in H. A. Bedau (ed.) *The Death Penalty in America*, third edn, New York: Oxford University Press.

South Carolina v. Gathers (1989) 490 US 805.

Spungen, D. (1998) *Homicide: the Hidden Victims – a guide for professionals*, Thousand Oaks, CA: Sage.

Stanford v. Kentucky (1989) 492 US 361.

State ex rel. Lamm v. Nebraska Board of Pardons (2001) 620 N.W. 2d 763.

Stephen, J. F. (1864) 'Capital punishments,' *Fraser's Magazine*, 69: 753–72.

Sullivan, D. and Tifft, L. (2001) *Restorative Justice: healing the foundations of our everyday lives*, Monsey, NY: Willow Tree Press.

Sundby, S. E. (2003) 'The capital jury and empathy: the problem of worthy and unworthy victims,' *Cornell Law Review*, 88(2): 343–81.

Thompson v. Oklahoma (1988) 487 US 815.

Tobolowsky, P. M. (2001) *Crime Victim Rights and Remedies*, Durham, NC: Carolina Academic Press.

Umbreit, M. S. and Vos, B. (2000) 'Homicide survivors meet the offender prior to execution:

restorative justice through dialogue,' *Homicide Studies*, 4(1): 63–87.

Umbreit, M. S., Vos, B., Coates, R. B. and Brown, K. A. (2003) *Facing Violence: the path of restorative justice dialogue*, Monsey, NY: Criminal Justice Press.

United States v. McVeigh (1998) 153 F. 3d 1166 (10th Cir.).

Van den Haag, E. (2003) 'Justice, deterrence and the death penalty,' in J. R. Acker, R. M Bohm and C. S. Lanier (eds) *America's Experiment with Capital Punishment: reflections on the past, present, and future of the ultimate penal sanction*, Durham, NC: Carolina Academic Press.

Vandiver, M. (2003) 'The impact of the death penalty on the families of homicide victims and of condemned prisoners,' in J. R. Acker, R. M. Bohm and C. S. Lanier (eds) *America's Experiment with Capital Punishment: reflections on the past, present, and future of the ultimate penal sanction*, Durham, NC: Carolina Academic Press.

Welch, B. (2002) 'Speaking out against the execution of Timothy McVeigh,' in D. R. Dow and M. Dow (eds) *Machinery of Death: the reality of America's death penalty regime*, New York: Routledge.

White, A. A. (1998) 'Victims' rights, rule of law, and the threat to liberal jurisprudence,' *Kentucky Law Journal*, 87(2): 357–415.

Woodson v. North Carolina (1976) 428 US 280.

Zant v. Stephens (1983) 462 US 862.

Zimring, F. E. (2003) *The Contradictions of American Capital Punishment*, New York: Oxford University Press.

Zimring, F. E. and Hawkins, G. (1986) *Capital Punishment and the American Agenda*, New York: Cambridge University Press.

Notes

1. Several states and the federal government have enacted statutes making eighteen the minimum age for death-penalty eligibility. The Supreme Court has granted certiorari in *Roper v. Simmons* (2004) to consider whether the constitutional threshold for death-penalty eligibility should be fixed at age eighteen.

2. The Nebraska Supreme Court later invalidated Reeves' death sentence and Reeves ultimately was re-sentenced to life imprisonment. The court did not directly address the Lamms' claim that their rights as 'victims' had been denied under the Nebraska Constitution's victims' rights amendment, instead ruling that their claim was moot and that no enabling legislation had been enacted to give effect to the state constitutional amendment (King 2003: 215–18; *State ex rel. Lamm v. Nebraska Board of Pardons* 2001).

3. *Booth's* prohibition against admitting surviving family members' opinions about an appropriate punishment for the offender was not disturbed (*Payne v. Tennessee* 1991: 830, n. 2).

17

The other victims

The families of those punished by the state

Judith Brink

The very first man I met in the hospital's secure unit, to which I was called in the wee hours of the night as the chaplain-on-call, was in the seventh year of a twelve-and-a-half to twenty-five-year prison sentence. He was twenty-five years old. My continuing relationship with him led to meeting his mother and sister, who traveled between New York City and the Albany, NY hospital after not visiting him for the several years that he had been incarcerated in a prison close to the Canadian border. Our conversations often focused on his eight-year-old daughter who was only a year old when he began his sentence and now lived in another state.

Since then I have met many other incarcerated people and their loved ones. In hearing their stories I have concluded that the families and other loved ones of incarcerated men and women are not only other victims of the crime but are also victims of punishment violence. And I would suggest that children are the primary victims. It is the purpose of this article to share some of the experiences which led me to these conclusions.

In restorative justice practice, and in its literature, we give a lot of attention to the needs of victims. It's one of the defining

elements of restorative justice theory and practice. Courts give victims an insignificant, if any, role in the legal process. Restorative justice 'conferences' include not only the direct victims but also the families and friends of both the person who harmed and the person who was harmed, making a significant step toward identifying the full impact of a crime. Restorative justice recognizes that those people who are close to the victim *or* to the offender can also be classified as victims.

Nevertheless, in the literature, in the media, and in most people's consciousness this is not a widely recognized concept. Convicted men and women have been the subject of much media attention, from newspaper articles to books and movies. Many of these stories are sympathetic and point out the injustices of prison conditions. Victims get their moment of exposure in the media immediately after the crime (particularly if the crime was especially vicious or they or the offender are famous) and in scholarly articles about victim services or restorative justice. Rarely are the mothers and fathers of prisoners, the husbands, wives, and especially the children of the incarcerated, other relatives or close friends, given any notice by the public.

261

They remain an invisible and voiceless set of victims.

A pioneer in addressing the needs of these victims, Alison Coleman formed Prison Families of New York (PFNY) over twenty years ago when her husband had just received a twenty-five-to-life prison sentence. She found herself with no one who understood the sentence she was serving on the other side of his bars. At first a support group for families of prisoners, with a child care component for the children, it has grown into a state-wide network of people who support one another through meetings, holiday get-togethers, information sharing, and activism. One of PFNY's goals is to eliminate the stigma attached to their relationships. Her organization is surely one of the reasons that more attention is finally being given to the plight of 'prison families.'

My eyes were opened as a result of that first spiritual support given to the young prisoner. Richard's family is made up of some of those invisible and voiceless victims. In time I would meet many more. They inform my thinking here and I'm very grateful for their willingness to share their stories with me.

The criminal justice system, by focusing primarily on guilt or innocence, has put almost total attention on the accused person who, to avoid punishment, denies responsibility, leaving the other people who were affected with nowhere to get their needs met unless the accused is convicted, when perhaps victim services will include a recommendation from the victim to the sentencing judge.

Richard's family was not invited to participate in the trial or sentencing process. His mother and sister and their extended family were totally unfamiliar with the system, and didn't know what to do. Lacking funds and not realizing how important it could be to hire a private lawyer, they relied on an overburdened public defender who didn't have time to advise them as thoroughly as they needed. As a result Richard got a much stiffer sentence than most of the other youth

with whom he was charged. He was sent to a prison about as far away from his home in Queens as one can get in New York State, essentially the distance between Liverpool and Brussels. His family visited him once; they were offended by the treatment they received, and angry at him for requiring it, so they didn't visit again until he called them from the hospital to tell them his diagnosis of terminal lung cancer. At that point they began to visit as often as possible, at considerable expense and inconvenience, to try to assist his recovery with prayer and food packages.

When a mother learns her only son is seriously ill, the normal reaction is to want to go to him, stay with him, take care of him. She may want a family conference with the medical team. Richard's mother did not have access to any of these things. Her visits consisted mostly of waiting in a hospital corridor, where there was no seating, until the correctional officers allowed her into the locked unit for two hours. She had no place to stay in Albany, not having funds for a hotel, so she and her daughter could only visit once or twice a week at most. Her son, who was too sick to do anyone any harm, was forced to remain in prison despite his application for medical parole. Her family, who had done no harm to anyone, continued to be treated with the same lack of respect as is every other family of a prisoner. It is a time when a mother and father, or husband, wife, child, sister, brother need support. Not only do these families fail to get it from the institutions where their loved ones are held, but often they don't get it from family and friends either. Because of the stigma our society attaches to people with relatives in prison, families often hide the fact from more distant members of their family as well as from friends and co-workers. It is a lonely and helpless time for them. Imagine how the children feel in the middle of such a family crisis.

I was married to an incarcerated man. Telling someone that makes me a target of possible misunderstanding and judgment, but if the reader notices such a response in him or herself it will illustrate the point that people who love prisoners are often looked at with similar attitudes and assumptions as are the people in prison. Somehow we are lessened by this association with a person who made a serious mistake and is paying for it. I attended PFNY support groups. We complained about our victimization. The others in the group were sometimes the only ones to whom we ever revealed the whereabouts of our loved one. Many people make up stories for the outside world: she's in the service, he has an important job across the country, she's in the hospital, he's overseas taking care of a relative. With so many people incarcerated in this country, United States readers are very likely to know someone who is hiding his or her relationship with a jailed person.

Many spouses, like me, married after the prison sentence began. In one sense it is difficult to call ourselves victims. We knowingly signed up for the conditions of incarceration. In fact, we sometimes signed up in order to get around some of the harsher conditions. In many prisons next of kin have privileges and influence not accorded to other relationships. The next of kin can be the prisoner's health care proxy, can talk to his or her counselor, or in some facilities may have a forty-eight-hour private visitation in housing provided for 'family reunification.' Being my husband's health care proxy was a great privilege since he did die in prison and because I could advocate for his treatment. When he was ready to die he received hospice care and died with dignity and grace. In general, however, the restrictions of a prison relationship far outweigh the privileges.

Until you experience it first hand, the victimization of innocent people who maintain connection with a person in prison is not obvious. But out of sight to the general public they are subject to demeaning and insulting assaults to their autonomy by prison officers; judgments placed upon them

by their neighbors; the disruption of their family; and financial stress created from maintaining the relationship. Most people in prison come from families who are not affluent. Wealth is a good deterrent to incarceration, though not necessarily to crime. The extra expenses involved in having a family member in prison can be overwhelming to a family who was already just barely surviving. With one breadwinner missing, the burden falls on the family's remaining members. Prison does not promote family values! It puts an unnecessarily heavy burden on a family. I have been amazed to see so many families survive a prison sentence intact.

Some of these burdens are relevant to all prisoner relationships:

Letters

Very soon after a loved one is incarcerated, most people become letter writers. I don't know a prisoner or a family member who doesn't write letters. Letters are the least expensive and least restricted way to keep in touch. They also are the least immediate but they are the lifeline for most prisoners. I've been told by prisoners that a letter every day is almost a requirement for their sanity. Yet some do not get them. Although the cheapest, letters are not always possible. Some prisoners are illiterate, and some family members are also. Those that do write letters know that their letters are opened by the prison staff who are ostensibly checking for contraband. They know that on a slow day a bored guard may read the letter first. That can lessen the ease of writing. Prisoners seal their letters before mailing, but whether there is any truth to this or not, many suspect that their mail can be opened and read if a staff member wants to. So one is always on guard about putting anything into writing that could in any way be used against the prisoner. And because there is no way of knowing what that is, spontaneity is lost.

Packages

Prisoners are given the bare necessities of life and some manage to exist on state issue. But most who have families ask to be sent things like warm blankets, warm clothing, toiletries, and food. If you love someone, you want them to have at least the basic comforts of warmth and good hygiene. So most families try to squeeze out of their budgets enough money to keep their loved one warm, adequately clean, and nourished. It's not just the money that creates a hardship. The arbitrary nature of the rules dictating what is allowed is impossibly complicated. Colors and styles are regulated and make shopping difficult. Try purchasing a pair of men's shoes without metal shanks, for instance. Food items may be allowed one time and not the next, thus wasting the money spent on them. There are printed food regulations but they fill scores of pages, so you tend to rely on the receiving officer's judgment. Some items that can't be brought or sent in can be purchased in the prison's commissary. In many prisons there are no jobs and therefore no way for a prisoner to earn money. In order to pay for these things families must send them money. I am not affluent but I live comfortably on a fixed income. I was not able to afford the added expense of my husband's needs. We had to make a decision whether to talk on the phone, have visits, or send/receive packages. We opted for visits and the very rare (and small) package. I refused to go into debt. Many families are more generous and accumulate large debts to ease the situation of their loved one. Imagine what the children have to give up.

Phone calls

Phone calls and visits are the two other ways to maintain contact. It's a toss-up which is more expensive, phone calls or visits. The cost of phone calls from a person in prison is always more expensive than for the average consumer. In some states, and in federal prisons, the incarcerated person pays for the calls with a calling card purchased in commissary. In others, including New York where I live, prisoners can only make collect calls using a carrier that has a contract with the prison in return for which the company pays a commission on each call. The cost of that commission comes out of the families' pockets. The people paying for these calls, remember, have committed no crime. A family trying to keep an incarcerated member involved in family affairs often pays over $100 per month for phone calls just from prison. Also keep in mind that many already live below the poverty level.

People new to the system often learn a quick lesson when they receive a month's bill for several hundred dollars from just this one caller. Even if the recipient can pay the bill, MCI in New York will sometimes put a block on the phone without informing anyone. This sets up a distressing situation. Making his or her next call, the caller from prison is told there is a block on the phone, and wonders why the family no longer wants his calls. In an already stressful environment, this can be extremely worrisome. The family, not knowing about the block, wonders why the caller did not call at the usual time. They begin to worry that he or she is ill, hurt, or in some kind of trouble which has caused denial of phone privileges. For as long as it takes a letter to be sent and a response to be received, the two parties are left to worry. The anxiety is prolonged by the process of having the block removed. First one has to find out why the block was put on, and then pay the current charges before the block will be removed. For people living from paycheck to paycheck, which is true of many families these days, it can take as much as a week to obtain the money and then more time before it can be taken to the nearest payment office. In the meantime, family communications are at a standstill. Imagine a child waiting to talk to his or her incarcerated parent about an upcoming event.

Beyond the expense of phone calls, there is also a lack of privacy. All calls can be monitored and recorded. The speakers never know if this is happening. In the case of a friend who is fighting his conviction, he cannot reveal strategies or give instructions over the phone for fear his strategy will be supplied to his adversary. The safest place to exchange such information is on a visit, which is less convenient and usually more expensive. A last fact about phone calls: in prison, a person is assigned a certain time frame in which he can make calls. This requires the recipient to arrange his or her schedule to accommodate the prison's rules. For people working two jobs, this can be difficult to arrange.

Visits

I still visit prisons as a spiritual advisor and prisoner advocate. Most that I visit are one and a half to two hours away. These are very short trips compared to most, yet they cost at least $20 not counting the food I may buy for us from the visiting room vending machines. A large majority of people in NYS prisons come from one of the boroughs of New York City and many are incarcerated in prisons that are a six- to ten-hour drive away. For those having a loved one in federal prison, the trip can be thousands of miles. Lacking a car, there are four options that I know of: (1) car-pooling, which requires you be part of a network by which you can find another person traveling to the same prison; (2) private or non-profit van services that have pick-up locations which may require additional time and expense to get to; (3) public transportation: bus, train, plane; and (4) in NYS there is a free bus, provided by DOCS, which travels to each prison hub (a location where six to twelve prisons are grouped within a short distance from one another) once every few

weeks. Depending on where the visitor lives and how often they are able to make the trip, these trips can be made in a day or require one or more overnight stays. The visitor must be there by a certain time in order to be allowed a visit. If more visitors show up than there are seats, some prisons shorten the time of each visit. People may have traveled twelve hours, stayed overnight in a hotel, waited three hours to be processed, and then be allowed less than three hours to visit their loved one. I've heard of people being turned away altogether. This could be a family with very young children. We're all familiar with the cry, 'Are we there yet?!' Imagine children on the way to see their mom or dad who then have to sit patiently for more hours once they do get there. It doesn't have to be this way. In a state that truly supported 'family values' visiting rooms could be larger, more staff could be assigned to process visitors, and a more efficient processing system could easily be designed by any business consultant, or a prison visitor for that matter.

I just got off the phone with a woman who described her situation. Her son is incarcerated in a prison which is a five-hour drive from where she lives. Four phone calls a month from him cost her $50. She had to request a block be put on her phone, restricting him to four calls a month, because without it he had run her bill up to over $400 in one month. Because it is a five-hour trip one-way to visit him, and because she works twelve-hour shifts starting at 7.00 p.m., she can only visit on her one day off. She departs at 4.00 a.m. to get there by 9.00 a.m. when visiting hours begin. She has to leave the prison at 1.00 p.m., two hours before visiting hours end, in order to get home in time to go to work at 7.00 p.m. A restorative system, a system that valued family integrity, would, at the very least, incarcerate people closer to home.

My experiences are easier than most; I travel alone, I drive, and I don't accept phone calls, so visits are my only expense besides stamps. A typical visit, in the winter (which lasts a long time here in the north-east), takes place on a cold day, with gusting wind. From the visitors' parking lot I walk to a trailer which provides warmth while I wait to be called into the prison itself. I often have to wait for an hour. When my number is called, I walk to an outdoor shelter, which is not entirely enclosed, so the cold wind gushes through. There I wait for up to half an hour until I hear a loud-speaker calling the next visitor to come to the gate. I walk to the gate, stand there for a few minutes, now thoroughly chilled, until the gate clicks. I open it, walk to another iron door, wait until it clicks open, and then walk up some stairs to the last door, which clicks open. Inside I am faced by usually bored and hostile-looking guards. If it had been my first visit, and I have experienced this every time I've visited a prison for the first time, I would not be told what the procedure is, and would be treated as if I was stupid and disobedient when I didn't do it properly. I have to fill out a form, provide photo ID, and get in line behind all the other waiting visitors. Finally reaching the processing desk I have to remove all metal objects, including an underwire bra if I am wearing one, and my shoes, in order to pass successfully through the metal detector. (Women with underwire bras can trigger the metal detector, requiring them to go into the bathroom with a paper bag, remove their bra, place it in the bag, return bare breasted under often revealing blouses, suf-fer the stares of the correctional officers, take back the bag and redress.) Once I am through the metal detector my wrist is stamped with invisible, and hopefully non-toxic, ink and I'm given a pass to proceed. I'm told, although I've never experienced this, that some prisons now have an ion scanner which detects small amounts of drugs. Apparently it makes a lot of noise and is scary, particularly to children, who are randomly scanned just like the adults. This scanner detects quantities so minute, I am told, that a person could have acquired them simply from passing someone smoking mar-ijuana on the street. Persons who trigger the device are denied visiting privileges, with no immediate means of appeal. Imagine being a child visiting a parent in the company of that adult.

But on my typical visit this does not hap-pen. Automatically locking doors open and clang shut behind me as I progress to the visiting room. At one point my invisible stamp is scanned by an ultraviolet light monitored by a correctional officer (CO). With gray hair and white skin, the identifi-cation marks of the privileged class, I am for the most part treated courteously, but I have seen other people treated with flagrant dis-respect. In the waiting room, I hand in my pass, am told exactly which seat to take, and sit there for another fourteen to forty min-utes waiting for my friend to appear. I use this time to buy food and drinks at the vending machines, which are serviced by an outside vender who has the contract with this particular prison. It is usually a local business, and this increase of business makes them happy to have a prison in their area. The machines often malfunction and there is no immediate source of redress. Finally the friend whom I came to see arrives. He must report to the desk officer and be told where to sit. If we were close family we would be allowed a hug and a kiss, after which we would sit on opposite sides of the counter or the table, allowed to hold hands, and occasionally to exchange a brief kiss, but if a guard felt we went beyond what is allowed, we might be yelled at, and possibly the visit terminated. Imagine children observing this. What goes on in their minds and souls?

Richard's mother and sister had resumed visiting and his daughter and her mother were in frequent telephone contact. Until he died he was once again part of his family. Tragically, his family did not get to be with him at the end. I lived closer to the regional medical unit where he had been transferred and so he did not die alone. I was able to be with him and he died in my arms. But it took such a long time for his family to find a way to get there that when they arrived his body had already been put in a bag and moved into storage. They were overwhelmed with pain and grief. Why weren't they notified sooner? Why doesn't the prison have a viewing room for situations like this, which must be common? Why wasn't he granted medical parole in time to go home to die? What did his daughter learn from all of this?

Not counting Richard himself, who essentially got a death sentence for a childish prank, four other people who had nothing to do with his act suffered lasting pain and grief. His daughter was left with minimal memories of her father. From the time he left home when she was one year old she had seen very little of him. Her memories of her father, a very intelligent and caring person who made a stupid mistake when he was seventeen, consist of phone calls, a few prison visits and a letter he wrote her shortly after he learned his prognosis. At his wake she stared down at a body barely recognizable.

Yes, it is the children of prisoners who appear to me to be the most severely punished amongst the other victims. And there are a lot of them! According to a report by the Bureau of Justice Statistics (Mumola 2000), in the USA there were 1,498,800 children under eighteen who had a parent in prison in 1999. Almost a quarter of those children (22 per cent) were under five (Women in Prison Project of the Correctional Association of New York 2001). Ninety per cent of children whose fathers are in prison live with their mothers (Mumola 2000) in what has now become a single-parent household, but with the same – actually more – expenses and demands as before he left. Eighty-seven per cent of children with incarcerated mothers do not live with their fathers (Mumola 2000); they

are sent to live with other relatives or neighbors or are put into foster care situations. One in five of those children watched their mother being arrested (Women in Prison Project of the Correctional Association of New York 2001).

Personally I find arrest scenes disturbing. A young child watching his or her mother being handcuffed and dragged out of the house must find it more than disturbing. The arrested mother is not given time to arrange temporary child care so the children are left to the mercy of whoever finds them. It may take weeks for the child and the mother to regain contact. Mothers in prison can literally lose their children in the foster care system as the child is shifted from family to family, even if the child is living with kin. The Women in Prison Project writes that the Federal Adoption and Safe Families Act (ASFA) of 1997 stipulates that

> if a child is in foster care for 15 of the last 22 months, the state can begin legal proceedings to terminate parental rights. After parental rights are terminated, parents have no legal relationship with their children. This means that they are legally considered a stranger to their children and are not permitted to have any contact with them.
> (Women in Prison Project of the Correctional Association of New York 2002: 2)

The state has the right to prohibit a child from any contact with his or her parent, if that parent has been incarcerated for more than twenty-two months! Children are not only taken from their parents and homes but also from their schools and their communities as well. Removed from parents and siblings, they are left on their own to comprehend what is happening and how to adjust to it. I have spoken to such children, and to their teachers and their social workers (in situations where these professionals are educated about the issues faced by the children of the incarcerated). The stories are sadly the same: failure at school; feeling abandoned, angry, unworthy, and ashamed. Many children begin to repeat the behaviors that led their parent to prison. 'The lifetime risk that children of incarcerated parents will end up in prison has been estimated to be between two and six times the average risk of their peers' (Brenner 1998: 2).

One daughter I know, whose parents worked hard to provide her with understanding and support, told of feeling compelled to become the caretaker, not only of her siblings but of her mother, who was struggling to keep the family together, and also of her incarcerated father, who was needing reassurance of her continued love and respect. If nothing else, these children lose their sense of innocence very early on. There needs to be another way to deal with crime. One that does not harm innocent children, perhaps irreparably.

In closing I will quote from a letter to me from George Baba Eng, a prisoner who has spent the past twenty-seven years behind bars. He suggests a restorative approach to crime and incarceration that addresses the needs of the invisible victims I've been describing, as well as the needs of all the rest of society:

> I believe imprisonment should be about treatment. I also believe in the idea of social contract. If the needs of a person *from birth through adolescence and adulthood* are provided for by society so that the person can become a contributing as well as receiving member of that society and if that person then violates that contract there is obviously something wrong with the person. Thus, the need for treatment. However, if the society does nothing to nurture the person and in fact does the opposite in creating conditions that lead to delinquency, dysfunctionality and crime then the society also needs treatment! Social responsibility is a two-way street. Unfortunately, for Black, Latino, poor White and other people marginalized in our society there is no two-way street to responsibility. The conditions are created to make these people fail in their lives; the system then imprisons those people and refuses to take any responsibility. Vengeance (for God knows what) and punishment are the orientation and whole generations are demonized in order to justify our treatment of prisoners so that we can keep them imprisoned, continue to destroy families and whole communities, and make an enormous profit from doing it, as the prison industrial complex does!

References

Brenner, E. (1998) *Fathers in Prison: a review of the data*, National Center on Fathers and Families, online. Available at: http://fatherfamily-link.gsc.upenn.edu/org/ncoff/briefs/breener-brief.pdf [accessed 29 January 2005].

Child Welfare League of America (1996–2005) *Children of Incarcerated Parents: what happens to children?* online. Available at: http://www.cwla.org/programming/incarceration/whathappens.htm [accessed 28 January 2005].

Mumola, C. J. (2000) *Incarcerated Parents and their Children*, Bureau of Justice Statistics Special Report, August 2000, online. Available at: http://www.ojp.usdoj.gov [accessed 21 January 2005].

Women in Prison Project of the Correctional Association of New York (2005) *The Effects of Imprisonment on Families Fact Sheet*, 21 January, online. Available at: http://www.correctionalassociation.org

Section IV

Making things right

Extending restorative justice

The chapters in this section continue to expand our thinking about differing kinds of victims, and the construction of innovative models of restorative justice designed to meet the differing needs of these victims for healing and restoration. Restorative justice is often characterized as victim-centered justice. But, as we have seen, sometimes 'restorative' programs lose sight of this desired focus and become 'offender-focused,' paying little attention to the needs of 'victims' beyond those met in a restorative encounter. Just as critically, the use of the term 'victim' belies the reality that those who have been harmed are involved in a symbolic process engaging the construction and deconstruction of self and one's self-categories. To varying degrees and at varying times, those who have been traumatized move back and forth in rupture-resilience processes between being locked into victimhood, being actively healing survivors, and integrating their harm experiences into their personhoods. Co-victims (e.g. victims' family members) and 'offenders' are, of course, engaged in similar self-interactive processes as discussed in prior sections.

Sandra Walklate (Chapter 18) cogently informs us that the meaning of 'victim' is enmeshed in a political economy of victi-mization images that greatly affects all our lives. In fact, she reminds us that our lives are immersed in a culture of fear, a culture of compensation/consumption, a culture of exclusivity, and a culture of control. We are all potential 'victims.' We are the victims of power relations – intimate, economic, or political. The culture of fear, of power and control, images whole nations as victims, demonizing 'others' as 'enemies' to legitimate imperialist initiatives. It images a nation's population as potential victims, designating 'others' as out of control, to widen the net and criminalize youth. It images 'others' as just like us, ignoring the worlds of stratification, able to participate as equals in restorative justice mediations, conferences, and circles.

To some degree we have to this point in the book largely confined our discussion to 'neutral victims,' as Walklate images them, and to the relatively circumscribed programs of healing and reintegration being initiated within or alongside state criminal justice processes. Restorative justice responses have until recently only sparingly been extended to respond to serious interpersonal crimes/ harms and especially to serious crimes/harms among intimates – to battering and child sexual abuse. Joan Pennell (Chapter 19) and

Anne-Marie McAlinden (Chapter 20) rectify this slight of attention and discuss these specific extensions giving testimony to the creative applicability that restorative ideas can inspire.

Pennell examines the impact of widening the circle of those committed to stopping family violence by creating a coordinated response within a North Carolina, USA, community. The mission of the North Carolina Family Group Conferencing Project is to advance the use of family group conferencing in child welfare in order to build partnerships with and around families to safeguard child and adult family members. This forum was created to encourage: joint planning, rather than assigning fault as in court proceedings; family leadership, rather than professional deliberations as in case conferencing; decision making, rather than treatment as in family therapy; and group responsibility, rather than the reconciliation of different persons, as in mediation. From this innovative program she concludes that such a restorative justice forum has considerable potential to reshaping visions and practices, to coordinate informal and formal support networks, and to build a local community dedicated to both child safety protection and women's safety.

Anne-Marie McAlinden believes that there is a need to extend the work of restorative justice in the area of domestic violence and adult sexual offences to child sexual abuse, especially abuse by those in positions of trust. This is one of the most abhorrent yet ubiquitous of crimes in contemporary society. And since most of this abuse remains undisclosed and beyond the reach of formal criminal justice responses, there is considerable room for exploring alternative models, especially circles of support and accountability. Such extensions must, of course, address our fears that restorative responses would trivialize these harms, allow a denial of responsibility, maintain relations of power and control, thus keeping victims in a situation that is abusive and likely to reoccur, and encourage local vigilantism. McAlinden addresses these fears or criticisms and proposes that carefully devised diversionary and additive custody and release programs like those instituted in Canada would be far more effective for everyone involved.

But extensions of restorative justice are not limited to the interpersonal harm sphere. Restorative justice precepts as well form the foundation for some national processes of healing and reconciliation in societies undergoing transition and reconstruction in the wake of war and gross human rights violations (e.g. South Africa, Rwanda, and Northern Ireland). Victimization in these settings is collective as well as interpersonal. Restorative reconstruction requires change at the national political level and, just as importantly, at the community grassroots, and personal-relational levels of societal organization.

One inspiring extension of restorative justice is found in work of Anthony Holter, Joseph Martin, and Robert Enright (Chapter 21) who have been doing forgiveness education work in elementary school classrooms in war-torn communities in Belfast, Northern Ireland. In areas of the world where community violence has been common, psychological and emotional distress is frequent among those who have experienced, participated in, and witnessed such trauma. These persons and their children are at risk for perpetuating the cultures of fear, violence, and inter-group conflict to which they have been exposed. In areas such as Belfast there is a great need for forgiveness education, for helping children grasp and practice the five foundations of this restorative program: inherent worth, moral love, kindness, respect, and generosity. In this way children are provided an opportunity to learn and practice the social skills and understandings that hold the potential to break the cycle of systemic violence and injustice, and to promote personal well-being.

Northern Ireland is also the setting for the ambitious, controversial, highly innovative, and successful community-based programs discussed by Kieran McEvoy and Anna Eriksson (Chapter 22). These community-based programs, Community Justice Ireland and Northern Ireland Alternatives, were established to persuade members of the Irish Republican Army and the Ulster Volunteer Force to forego their paramilitary punishment shootings and beatings in favor of direct dialogue and community-based programs of restorative justice. Seven years since the inception of these programs, they have been assessed by our colleague, Harry Mika, as having made a significant contribution to decreasing punishment violence, to changing attitudes towards violence, and to enhancing the capacity of local communities not only to take responsibility for local justice issues, but to develop the self-confidence to form a partnership with statutory agencies on a more balanced footing. McEvoy and Eriksson argue that the interactive effect between three special features of these programs has offered the potential for personal and communal transformation of the cultures of violence. These special features are: (1) the strong sense of grassroots community ownership and participation in the programs; (2) the prominent transformative and moral leadership which ex-prisoners and ex-combatants have played in the establishment and development of the programs, in the process of community building, and in efforts to transform attitudes toward violence in communities and paramilitary groups; and (3) the prominence of human rights discourse as an embedded feature of restorative practice which has been a defining characteristic of these programs.

It is clear from these chapters that restorative justice processes are uniquely suited for the challenges we face in responding to our most serious intimate crimes and for those challenges which we face in societies in transition, especially in relation to reintegration, community capacity building, and for embedding a bottom-up culture of human rights.

18

Changing boundaries of the 'victim' in restorative justice

So who is the victim now?

Sandra Walklate

Introduction

In the context of a world post–September 11th 2001 (9/11) and the events that have ensued, including those of Madrid in March 2004 (3/11), the impact of the tsunami in Asia, December 2004, alongside ongoing instability in Iraq, bloody ethnic conflict in the Sudan and organized brutality in Zimbabwe, we are all reminded that simply avoiding aggression, violence, and natural disaster is a way of life for some. In Western cultures, alongside the seemingly ceaseless fixation with domestic crime, such world-wide considerations feature in the twenty-first century primarily in terms of the international potential of 'new terrorism.' Some would argue that this latter pre-occupation has provoked political uncertainty and public anxiety in equal measures.

Moreover, recent events in Asia serve to remind us that nature can never be under control, with the aftermath of those events provoking worldwide emotional and practical responses. All of these events conjure different images of the 'victim' and 'victimization' and all of them provide different ways of thinking about how victims might be restored, made whole again. Given the global nature of the restorative justice movement, whether that be in the form of peace and reconciliation in South Africa or Northern Ireland, or the more circumscribed policies of 'reintegration' being introduced in criminal justice systems within the Anglo-American axis, the purpose of this chapter is to explore how different images of victimization might, or might not, inform how we might respond to the victim of restorative justice. In order to engage in this exploration, this chapter will first offer an overview of how the risk society thesis might help us to make sense of the impact of some of the events outlined above; second, it will consider the relevance of this thesis in the context of understanding victimization; third, it will explore some of the questions that this consideration raises for restorative justice; and finally it will consider, in light of these developments, whether or not the concept of victim per se has any continuing value. In all of this there is an overriding concern to connect images of the victim in victimology and restorative justice to questions of wider sociological concern.

Victims and the risk society thesis

In the context of a world suggested by the events with which this chapter began, it is possible to argue that an understanding of the nature and impact of the 'risk society' (Giddens 1991; Beck 1992) is ever more pertinent. Growing awareness of the ways in which 'risk' transcends national boundaries and filters through international experiences has led, for example, the United Nations to form its own Commission on Human Security. As that Commission justly notes, the demand for 'freedom from fear' has ascended the global political agenda (UN Commission on Human Security 2003: 4). Such 'freedom from fear,' the search for 'human security,' is one concern that connects all of the events listed above. This is despite the analytical commitment made by both Beck and Giddens that current risk pre-occupations reflect 'manufactured insecurities': a pre-occupation with what it is that we have done to nature rather than what it is that nature can do to us, a commitment that in 2005 is clearly subject to criticism. However, from this point of view, in 2005, anxieties are high indeed given the global focus on the potential impact of terrorist activity alongside the global focus on natural disaster. Both raise the stakes for an understanding of victims and victimization so it is perhaps worth exploring the risk society thesis in this context just a little more fully.

What the risk society thesis presents is a vision of macro social conditions that are permeated with doubt and uncertainty. One place at which to embark upon an understanding of how these macro conditions might impact upon local and individual experience is with the victim of crime. Furedi (2002) is one commentator who has made much of the risk society thesis and the concomitant cultural changes that have occurred in the United Kingdom over the last twenty-five years. Furedi posits that there has been a shift away from risk-taking as a positive emblem of societal progress toward a more negative 'morality of low expectation' in which we have become fixated with the negative impacts of theoretical

risks (though again some would raise the question as to how theoretical these risks might be). A 'culture of fear' has taken hold in which individuals are encouraged – most notably by sound-bite politics and an uncritical mass media – to transform every human experience into a safety situation (Furedi 2002: 5). Everything from the food we eat, to the nature of our workplace, to the utensils we might use in our homes, is classified as a potential site of danger. Guided by health and safety legislation and the threat of litigation, workers in all kinds of settings are required to conduct their business in the light of the 'what if?' question. Moreover, the proliferation of 'no win, no fee' law firms has facilitated the endorsement of a compensation culture. Such increasingly widespread processes and practices result in what might be termed the paralysis of a culture of fear: 'I am a victim therefore I am.' The increasing importance of these practices, and what they signify, is indeed one way in which the risk society theorists would argue that the late modern world is pre-occupied with safety: with the desire to control what we have done to nature (see Giddens 1998).

Not too far removed from this kind of analysis has been Garland's (2001) articulation of the 'culture of control.' Targeted more precisely at the processes that have occurred within the criminal justice system, Garland's analysis draws attention not only to the extent to which there is an increasing convergence between the United States and the United Kingdom in their respective responses to the crime problem, but also to the extent to which the victim of crime (in various guises) has been harnessed symbolically and practically in order to manage crime. This analysis has not been without its critics (see, for example, Braithwaite 2003; Feeley 2003; Walklate 2005; and Young 2003a) but what is beyond question is the current significance given to the victim of crime both in criminal justice policy and in the political rhetoric in support of criminal justice policy. Young (1999, 2003b) argues that this significance in the UK reflects the move from the inclusive to the exclusive society that is particularly characterized contemporarily by vindictiveness. Garland's analysis is much more concerned to document the embedded nature of the risk society in criminal justice policy and its manifestation as a 'culture of control' in which we are all implicated.

Whichever of these theses appeals more, they are both concerned to articulate how victimization has become an important cultural device. How and why this has happened is still open to debate, but what is clearly important is the need to understand the cultural context in which the notion of the victim in general, but the crime victim in particular, is being constructed and reconstructed. To be sure, both of these analysts amongst others are endeavoring to do just this. There are, however, several issues that are glossed over by assigning too much significance to cultural articulations of risk alone. Those questions, especially in a world post 9/11 and post 3/11, address the issue of what it is that is defined as criminal and how it is that events are understood and articulated as criminal. The horrors of 9/11 and 3/11 might arguably supersede such niceties of intellectual argument. Nevertheless, the failure to embrace their relevance for how people might understand, and be encouraged to understand, the problem of their criminal victimization should not be disregarded.

Mixed in with Furedi and Garland's broadly cultural considerations is a second set of harder-edged political issues about the social construction of criminality/victimhood. Following Hudson (2003), it is important that we recognize the ways in which the categories of perpetrator and victim are politically as well as culturally manufactured. Hudson (2003) notes that law and order institutions in the UK have recursively sought to separate out victims and villains through processes of assessment, classifica-tion and surveillance. In so far as such techniques of risk management are unremarkable in themselves, their input into the broader construction of the criminal 'other' has exacerbated the divide between right-thinking citizens and lawless offenders. Moreover, in practice, as has been borne out by 'stop and search' measures implemented under anti-terrorist legislation in the UK, it is not just individuals but entire communities that are scrutinized and surveyed. As Hudson points out 'suspect people do not have (actually) to commit crimes to be identified as criminal, nor do respectable people have to experience crime to identify themselves as (potential) victims' (Hudson 2003: 65).

We can see then how subjects are constructed through risk discourses, socially designated according to whether they fit the profile of offenders or innocents, in a range of different domestic contexts but arguably primarily the UK and the USA. However, it is not only domestically that victim communities are being set against offender groups. On a wider geopolitical plain, countries in North Africa and South Asia are denominated as 'good' or 'bad' on the basis of their willingness to submit to the demands of dominant Western countries. The discursive construction of a morally decent 'us' and a volatile and unruly 'them' fuels religious, economic, and cultural tensions. As Soyinka (2004) reasons, the debilitating return to a counter-modern either/or-ism is typified in the doctrinal pronouncements of George Bush: 'You are either with us and against the terrorists, or you are on the side of the terrorists.' There is little need to unpack the crude underlying logic at play here, but it is worth making two further observations about the political construction of offender and victim communities.

First, neo-liberal politicians are actively generating and harnessing fear as a tool to reinforce political strategy and to legitimate law and order policies. Second, domestic

275

and international conflicts are increasingly being fused, both in terms of political discourse and methods of crime control. As Steinert observes 'regulating the consequences of crime and fighting an enemy have now become indistinguishable' (Steinert 2003: 266). For those interested in issues of justice, political horse-trading with the currency of fear, coupled to the binary construction of 'deviant' offenders and 'normal' victims, has eased the way for the introduction of authoritarian governance and oppressive legislation:

> The fearfulness of risk society is leading western societies to respond to dangers in ways that undermine the basic values of liberal societies, values honed to guard against the dangers of repression and inhumanity as well as to express commitment to democratic governance.
>
> (Hudson 2003: 225)

Much of this discussion implies the potential for dramatically changing boundaries to understandings of the victim and victimization. This is also the backcloth against which restorative justice initiatives of various kinds have been in the ascendancy. The question is, how, if at all, are these two processes connected?

The victim of victimology

The origins of victimology are often located in the work of Von Hentig and Mendelsohn. They were two émigré lawyers cum criminologists who worked in the United States in the late 1940s. Like many other like-minded intellectuals of the late 1940s and the 1950s who found themselves in the United States as a consequence of the Second World War, they were perplexed by the events that had happened in Germany during that time. That perplexity led Von Hentig and Mendelsohn to think about the dynamics of victimization, though being

lawyers how they understood those dynamics was very much at the level of the individual and very much informed by their legal training. However, in addition to the influence of their legal training, it is also possible to see the influence of early criminological thought in their ideas.

Both of these theorists were concerned to develop ways of thinking about the victim that would enable the victim to be differentiated from the non-victim. In other words, both were clearly suggesting that there is a 'normal person' and that, when the victim is measured against them, the victim somehow falls short. In order to develop this kind of understanding they each developed victim typologies. Von Hentig's typology worked with a notion of 'victim proneness.' He argued that there were some people, by virtue of their socio-economic characteristics, who were much more likely to be victims (in this case of crime) than other people. These he identified as being women, children, the elderly, the mentally subnormal, etc. (He had thirteen categories in all.) Thinking about this categorization critically, it is possible to see that Von Hentig thought the normal person against whom the victim was to be measured was the white heterosexual male. Von Hentig does not suggest that there is a 'born victim'; however, there are clear parallels with the ideas of Lombroso, especially with respect to the concern to mark out the differences between victims and non-victims as Lombroso did with offenders, understood as the principle of differentiation. Von Hentig's work has been very influential in the development of victimological thinking and is perhaps most keenly identified in the concept of 'lifestyle' that has informed much criminal victimization survey work.

Mendelsohn adopted a more legalistic framework in developing his typology. His underlying concept was the notion of 'victim culpability.' Using this concept he developed a six-fold typology from the victim who could be shown to be completely innocent, to the victim who started as a perpetrator and during the course of an incident ended as the victim. Arguably, his typology is guided by what might be considered a reasonable or rational way of making sense of any particular incident given the nature of the law. Moreover, given this as the starting point from which these ideas are derived, it is possible to suggest that his understanding of reasonable also equates with that which the white heterosexual male would consider reasonable. This is especially demonstrated in the later work that was generated from Mendelsohn's ideas, in which victim culpability is translated into 'victim precipitation.'

From these beginnings the concepts of lifestyle and victim precipitation have formed the core of much traditional victimological work and illustrate what Miers (1989: 3) has called a positivist victimology. Moreover, despite a brief incursion into the discipline by the work of people like Quinney (1972) who wanted to make a claim for a radical victimology that included notions of the victim of state oppression (a way of thinking about victimization that has been continued by Elias 1986, 1993), the parallels with criminology are clear. Within positivistic victimology there is an emphasis on measuring differences, seeing those differences as being somehow abnormal, and looking for explanations of those differences that lie outside individual choice. The point of reiterating these ideas is to suggest that within them are to be found parallels with the thinking of more contemporary times. In this early work people were either more likely to be victims or not dependent upon their different personal characteristics or experiences and it was certainly assumed that they were different from offenders; you are either with us or against us. Moreover, there is another either/or dichotomy stitched into much early victimological work. That dichotomy is to do with gender and raised particular problems for the feminist movement.

When the word 'victim' is gendered, as in French for example, being la victime, it is denoted as female. If the genealogy of the word 'victim' is examined, it is connected to processes of sacrifice in which again the victim was more often than not female. The links between this word and being female imply that the passivity and powerlessness associated with being a victim are also associated with being female. It is this link that is problematic for those working within the feminist movement, who prefer to use the term 'survivor' to try to capture women's resistance to victimization. At the same time the tensions between being a victim or being a survivor are also problematic for others interested in criminal victimization, since this either/or distinction fails to capture the *processes* of victimization. In other words, it is possible that an individual at different points in time in relation to different events could be an active victim, a passive victim, an active survivor, a passive survivor, or at a point on a whole range of experiences in between. The label 'victim,' as a consequence, seems quite sterile when considered in this way.

There is, however, another problem associated with the word 'victim' that is derived from appreciating the process whereby an individual becomes identified as a victim. This problem is connected with what Nils Christie (1986), a Norwegian criminologist, has called the 'ideal victim.' In other words, there are certain assumptions attached to the label 'victim' that mean not everyone actually acquires the label of victim. For Christie the 'ideal victim' is the Little Red Riding Hood fairy-story victim: a young, innocent female out doing good deeds who is attacked by an unknown stranger. Indeed this 'ideal victim' fits all the common sense stereotypes of the 'legitimate' victim of rape. In other words, some people are 'deserving' victims – that is, acquire the label of victim very readily and easily – and other people are 'undeserving' victims and may never acquire the label of

277

'victim' at all. Awareness of this problem has led Carrabine and others (2004: 117) to talk of a 'hierarchy of victimization.' This hierarchy is most readily identified in the media construction of the elderly female as the victim of violent crime and the readiness with which such events are given full and graphic coverage in the media. This is despite the evidence from the most commonly used data source on criminal victimization, the criminal victimization survey, that the group of people most likely to be the victim of violent crime are young males who go out drinking two or three times a week. Such dichotomous thinking not only pictures the female more easily as the victim and the male less visibly so (both processes resulting in different consequences that need not concern us here), but they also fail to capture the reality of people's lives: how do people deal with the political and cultural imagery alongside their own experiences of victimization? There has been some, though limited, effort to answer this question within victimology.

Some years ago now, Miers (1990) made a plea for the development of what he called a 'critical victimology.' His understanding of this kind of victimological work placed itself very much within the tradition of interactional sociology. Moreover, whilst the tradition of symbolic interactionism has been subjected to detailed and thorough critique, there are gains to be had in developing a detailed appreciation of what Rock (2002: 19) calls 'crime as an embedded transaction unfolding in space and time . . . as a process involving people in interaction, constituting themselves and one another, and deploying situated gestures, emergent meanings, and changing identities.' Or as Rock (2002: 19) puts it, 'when and with what consequences does a person understand himself or herself to have become some existential entity called a victim?' An understanding of crime and criminal victimization 'in the round,' as Rock suggests, may well be a valuable addition to our understanding of the pro-

cesses that heighten or lessen the impact of crime through embellishing our appreciation of the social processes that underpin victimization. However, such an 'in the round' approach needs also to appreciate the impact of those processes that we may not be able to observe or articulate that effectively. What about those processes that go on behind our backs (*qua* Mawby and Walklate 1994)? The central question for the Mawby and Walklate version of critical victimology as it was then conceived, and now by implication, draws attention on how the current circumstances of structural doubt and uncertainty might impact upon who we take the victim to be and why.

In both of these versions of critical victimology the explicit intention is to disrupt the dichotomies that have so far been identified in this discussion. For the interactionist approach, that disruption challenges the categories of victim and survivor in favor of appreciating process. A process whereby an individual might succeed in transcendence (Zehr 2001), may end up locked into victimhood, or may find themselves at any point on this scale of experience. For those interested in the ways in which victimization may be structured by the things that 'go on behind our backs' – that is, events over which we have no control nor in which are we implicated – the categories of victim and offender are disrupted in favor of treating each as parties to an often not dissimilar human condition: searching for a sense of well-being or as Giddens (1991) would have it 'ontological security.' Each of these versions of critical victimology embraces the current climate of doubt and uncertainty (the risk society) in different ways in their analyses of the nature of victimhood, and each differently challenges whether there is any value in the concept of victim at all. (This is a point that will be returned to.) However, what yet remains to be considered is how, if at all, the potential of these challenging conceptualizations of the victim are connected with, or reflected in, the restorative justice movement.

The victim of restorative justice

As Goodey (2005) has observed, restorative justice (RJ) is more often than not represented as victim-centered justice. Indeed, some proponents of this way of doing business would point to United Nations resolutions and those passed by the Council of Europe as indications of a paradigm shift towards this way of conducting criminal justice work. Given the huge amount of activity that interest in restorative justice has generated over the last twenty years worldwide, my comments here will inevitably reflect how that activity has played itself out in the United Kingdom, and what, if anything, that rather circumscribed knowledge can reveal about the more general question of the potential for changing boundaries of the victim.

As Miers (1978) commented and Garland (2001) has embellished, the victim (of crime) is deeply embedded in political rhetoric about crime in the UK and the associated imagery is of significant symbolic importance. No Home Secretary in the UK would now propose policy initiatives without referring to the victim of crime either symbolically or in terms of concrete policy. The use of the victim in this way has become an increasingly important device in seeking support for and justifying criminal justice policy developments in the UK, including those concerned with RJ. In a recent essay Miers (2004) documents and analyses some of the research conducted in the UK on restorative justice since the implementation of the legislation in 1998 and 1999. Proponents of RJ heralded this legislation as constituting a sea change in criminal justice policy, especially in relation to responding to the criminal behavior of young people. RJ was seen as the means not only by which the victim might participate in the criminal justice system but also through which, in their participation, young people in particular could be made aware of the impact of their behavior and take responsibility for it.

As Miers (2004) observes, in the UK the importance of the victim of crime to the criminal justice system has been variously described as a supplier of information, a beneficiary of compensation, a partner in crime prevention, and a consumer of services. In his words, 'Restorative justice purports to take this relationship and these changes a step further – to one of victim participation in the system' (2004: 24) and 'has at its core the bringing together of victims and offenders' (Hudson 2003: 178). In the light of these efforts to shift criminal justice policy in the direction of such participation, much time and effort has been spent in the UK establishing whether or not this works and who it works for, without – and this is the nub of Miers' analysis – there being any consensus on what the question of what works actually means. Such issues notwithstanding, the focus of concern here is: who is the victim in all of these developments, and how, if at all, does this victim mirror or challenge the victim of victimology or connect with the wider concerns with which this chapter began?

As Dignan (2005) has observed, many practitioners and advocates of RJ have implicitly worked with the 'ideal type' victim that was identified by Christie in 1986. Moreover, Dignan goes on to comment that questions on the concept of the victim rarely appear in the RJ literature, perhaps with the notable exception of the observations made by Young (2002), who suggests that RJ works with a highly undifferentiated view of the victim. So exploring concepts of the victim within RJ is relatively uncharted territory. Arguably, it is possible to trace three differently constructed images of the victim within RJ in the UK: (1) the structurally neutral individual victim; (2) the image of the socially inclusive community as victim; and (3) the offender as victim. I shall say something about each of these and their relationship with victimology in turn.

From a point of view for most people in the UK, their experience of crime is, as Goodey (2005: 229) suggests, home grown, conventional and local. In other words, the global changes with which this chapter began notwithstanding, the experience that people are likely to have of criminal victimization is more often than not the result of some petty act of vandalism or more serious burglary that has been committed by someone in their locality who is likely to have access to the same kinds of personal and social resources that they do. If we take this kind of experience as given, then it is not surprising that the victim of RJ initiatives directed towards these kinds of offences, which for the most part reflect a desire to bring an individual victim face to face with their offender, would also take as given a structurally neutral image of the victim. This is the victim of positivist victimology discussed earlier: the victim who, through lifestyle choices, proneness or their own precipitating behavior, had a part to play in what happened to them. So, in restoring the harm done and reintegrating the behavior of the offender, the focus of attention is on bringing the two parties to the event together, in the sense of an equal relationship, to make repairs for what has happened. This depiction captures some of Marshall's (1999) interpretation of RJ's role in dealing with the aftermath of an event that may have much to commend it. However, what if we take another interpretation of people's routine experiences of criminal victimization that may also be characterized as home grown, conventional and local? What if we take that experience to be domestic violence, child abuse, or elder abuse? Here the victim imagery is not the structurally neutral victim of positivist victimology but implicated and embedded in the power relationships of a critical victimology and/or radical feminism. There are serious concerns about

the efficacy of RJ in this context, some of which have been documented by Stubbs (1997), Gelsthorpe and Morris (2000) and Strang and Braithwaite (2002). These concerns point up the difficulty of how such individuals might be brought together face to face, resolve their differences and in that process assume an equality where none may exist. This view, by implication, raises the importance of these questions more generally. Whose agenda is being met by RJ, whose is being lost, how do RJ initiatives connect with other aspects of people's lives, where do those people fit whose starting point is from a structurally less powerful position? As Goodey (2005) points out, it should not be assumed that the inequalities of the adversarial system cannot, or are not, reproduced in RJ.

The second depiction of the victim of RJ to be discussed here is that of the socially inclusive community. In this depiction of the victim, the offender is required to make amends not to their victim but to a rather more diffuse imagery of their community. As Goodey (2005) observes, community is frequently invoked as the third element that underpins successful RJ. However, as Crawford (2000) has cogently argued, there is a good deal of slippage between the political and policy rhetoric on which some RJ initiatives are built and the lived reality of communities. Parallel work on the role of informal justice in communities (see, for example, Walklate and Evans 1999; Feenan 2002; Newburn and McEvoy 2003) offers quite a different take on what restorative justice might look like in socially included communities whose dynamics are rooted in law-breaking behavior rather than law-abiding behavior. Nevertheless, some aspects of the RJ movement reflect a commitment to the idea of reintegrating the offender into their community and look to community-based options to facilitate this. Such a socially inclusive view of the relationship between the victim and the offender sees both categories as being 'just like us.' In other words, they challenge the either/or-ism of either the victim or the offender that can be found in positivist victimology.

Sanders (2002), however, suggests that RJ used in this way is untenable since it assumes that the interests of both victims and offenders are always reconcilable. This, indeed, may not always be the case, or may only be possible where community and community relationships pre-existed in some meaningful, normative way. Moreover, the normative invocation of some 'ideal' community that often permeates RJ discourse clearly elides question of the role of the locally powerful on the one hand and the relevance of such normative imagery on the other, especially in the current social and political context of either/or-ism. In some respects it could be argued that both of the depictions of the victim discussed so far and found in RJ within the criminal justice system in the UK, taken together contribute to a view that RJ policy contrives to render the offender as victim. This is a view that can be discerned within the use of RJ for young offenders in the UK in particular. This returns us to some dimensions of the radical victimology proposed by Quinney (1972) and the process of politicization with which this paper began.

Pitts (2001) has argued that the 'new correctionalism' of New Labour is drawing more and less problematic young people into the criminal justice system, leading Muncie (2002) to talk about the 'repenalization' of youth offending. No wonder, if this is the case, that the Home Office can declare a 26.4 per cent reduction in the reconviction rate for juvenile offenders (Jennings 2003). Indeed, a careful examination of these findings could lead one to conclude that the 'more serious' offenders have been excluded from this statistical picture to fit the political story. Further examination of the data by offence type shows considerable variation in reconviction rates with both males and females having the highest rates for the 'other' category (motor vehicle-related offences) and (whilst the numbers were small) there was no overall reduction in reconviction rates for offences of robbery, fraud and forgery. Moreover, as Bennett and Appleton (2004: 48) observe, with respect to the claims made by the Youth Justice Board 2000–1 Annual Review *Building on Success* (2002):

> it was reported that predicted reconviction rates for youth crime had been cut by nearly 15%. In making such claims it has been highly selective in utilizing the findings of independent evaluations that the Youth Justice Board itself commissioned, thus conveniently drawing a veil over less encouraging findings.

So the question of which young people are being targeted and what aspects of their behavior may be being changed by recent policy interventions, especially restorative justice interventions, appears to be very much a matter of conjecture and debate (echoing some of the observations also made by Miers 2004). According to Muncie (1999), in giving a prominent position to restorative justice, New Labour have established not only a 'new correctionalism' but also an 'institutionalized intolerance' of the young, that has been exacerbated by the anti-social behavior legislation in which if an individual breaches an anti-social behavior order they can find themselves incarcerated for what was not a substantive criminal offence!

Pitts argues that ' the prime target of New Labour's youth justice strategy is not about the criminal behavior of a handful of young offenders, but the voting habits of a far larger and much older constituency' (ibid.: 189). However, in the space provided by these political processes RJ has developed an unprecedented swagger in the UK:

> Far from wilting in the face of controversy and resistance as so many other justice innovations of recent vintage have, restorative justice appears to be trading the temerity of cautious reform for a kind of

swagger. Whether such self-confidence is justified, time will tell. It will however be very difficult to ignore.

(McEvoy *et al.* 2002: 475, my emphasis)

This swagger is sustaining this policy for a range of different reasons, few of which connect with the victim of crime but which do connect with the socio-cultural processes emergent within the UK from the early 1990s that were commented on earlier and that are especially focused on young people.

The first of these Young (2001) has called the 'dynamic of essentialism': the repeated recreation of 'the Other,' those problematic outsiders who are not 'us.' The second connected process is characterized by Garland (2001) as the 'culture of control': the increasingly expressed need in cultural and policy terms to control those who are not 'us.' In the culture of control, of course, our collective response to 'the Other' is not about tolerance but intolerance. Manifestations of intolerance can be observed at a number of different levels in contemporary UK society, not the least of which has been the targeting of young offenders in recent legislation. It is in this latter context that restorative justice initiatives have proved to be increasingly popular within contemporary criminal justice policy. It is within this context that they have a swagger. From this point of view the victim is the offender inexorably pushed upwards on the criminal justice ladder for offences that may have not previously received a formal sanction. This depiction of the changing boundary of the victim in RJ also usefully returns us to some of the more macro-sociological concerns and global events with which this chapter began.

Re-imagining the victim of restorative justice

In many ways the previous discussion implies that whilst RJ initiatives have as their intent the desire to repair the harm done to the victim of crime through either face-to-face contact with their offender or through the offender making amends to their community in some way, RJ as a movement has reflected little on how it has imagined the victim. This does not mean that some RJ initiatives do not work well at a local level, or that some victims who participate in such initiatives do not feel better about their participation, or that some proponents of RJ are not aware of the problematic status that results for the victim consequent to a commitment to RJ. However, in a socio-cultural process characterized by global doubt and uncertainty and a domestic pre-occupation with control, the potential for sensitivity that the previous questions of RJ demand is lost. So is the potential for unpicking the imagery of the victim that is being employed and exploring the potential of thinking differently about that imagery. Moreover, whilst people may not necessarily experience global uncertainty as part of their individual response to their criminal victimization, it is nevertheless the case that such processes form the backcloth against which spaces and opportunities are made available for the development of policies in different directions. RJ has been one such policy development which, as this chapter has suggested, because of the imagery of the victim that it invokes, has had both intended and unintended consequences in the current socio-political climate within the UK. The question remains: in a climate in which we are all potentially victims, are different imaginings of the victim in RJ possible?

It is evident that some efforts have been made to extend the use of RJ to those victims of crime that were imagined in the critical victimology of Mawby and Walklate (1994). Young (2002), for example, makes a convincing case for the use of restorative justice between business corporations. Moreover, there are clear implications for the possibilities of RJ to be derived from

Goodey's (2005) expansive victimological agenda that includes such activities as Internet crime, environmental crime, sex trafficking, and genocide, some of which takes victimology into the realm of human rights (an agenda not far from that proposed by Elias in 1986). Moreover, in the same collection of papers in which Young (2002) is to be found, there is clear support for an extended victimological agenda that takes the critical victimology of Miers (1990) a stage further, introducing us, as it does, to the male victim of domestic violence (Grady 2002), the male victim of rape (Allen 2002), or indeed the male victim of paramilitary violence (Hamill 2002). All of these share in similar opportunities for RJ intervention including, in the case of the latter, peace and reconciliation work. So it would seem that different imaginings of the crime victim are possible and, indeed, are being tried. However, despite these imaginings, there are structural, cultural, and political limitations to their realization. Elsewhere I have called this the rhetoric of victimhood as a source of oppression (Walklate 2005) in which both RJ and victimology are implicated in being vehicles for contemporary state policy.

It is difficult to deny the increasing importance of victimhood, not just as a cultural process (Furedi 2002) but also as a claim to status. In this sense victimhood, whilst not a state to be recommended experientially, is nevertheless the status whereby the state through increasingly subtle and not so subtle global and local processes is reasserting its power over citizenship. In this sense, victimhood is harnessed as a source of oppression in the interests of the increasingly diverse and hegemonic (capitalist) state (Jessop 2002). These processes may not play themselves out in exactly the same way either globally or locally (though it would be of huge value to explore how such processes resemble or fail to resemble each other), but how they play themselves out does cumulatively contribute not only to the culture of control but

also to the maintenance of economic relationships. In the contemporary political and policy setting there are real divisions of inequality that have a real impact (*qua* Young 2003a). As Hutton (2002: 84) has observed:

> It is not just a matter of accepting how the state can and should act to build an infrastructure of justice that diminishes inequality, equalises opportunity and tries to enlarge individual's capacity for self-respect. It is as the German philosopher Hannah Arendt argues about needing a public realm to allow the full flowering of our human sensibilities. For taken to its limits, a society peopled only by conservative 'unencumbered selves' jealously guarding their individual liberties and privacy, is a denial of the human urge for association and meaning.

It is within these processes that the real nature of oppression lies and the possibilities for change lie. For me, the key concept in the quote above is respect.

Treating people with respect – that is, as individuals with personal resources – is key for ensuring that, traumatic circumstances notwithstanding, they are enabled to make use of their resources in order to make sense of what has happened in their lives. A number of implications can be derived from this position. But first and importantly, it challenges any presumed 'special' status associated with being a victim of crime. Victims are, after all, complainants in the criminal justice system as offenders are defendants. To use any other terminology prejudges the outcome of a case. Moreover, victims are not necessarily the 'good' in opposition to the offender's 'bad.' Second, this position serves to remind us that whilst crime does impact upon people's lives, victims of crime are people too. So by implication, in this regard, it makes little sense to talk of people as victims or offenders, or indeed victims or survivors. They are people, and people need to feel OK about themselves and sometimes need some help and support to achieve that. And what makes people feel OK? Respect. Whether male or female, whether a member of an ethnic minority, whether old or young, the maintenance of respect and the avoidance of contempt sustains a sense of well-being and contributes to people feeling OK. So as Harre (1979: 405) said, 'The task of the reconstruction of society can be begun by anyone at any time in any face to face encounter.' Indeed, it is this process of reconstruction that is the most powerful message to be derived from Zehr's (2001) *Transcending*.

Conclusion

Victimhood is not a condition to be recommended. Nevertheless, in the face of an increasingly diverse society in which difference is to be valued, there may also be some value in working with, exploring, and learning from, the commonalities of the human condition: of doing away with the label of 'victim'. This may be the real lesson for both victimology and restorative justice in the current global climate of doubt and uncertainty. From a point of view this is especially the case for people who have least resources, either personally or financially, to help themselves, whatever part of the world they may be in.

References

Allen, S. (2002) 'Male victims of rape: responses to perceived threat to masculinity,' in C. Hoyle and R. Young (eds) *New Visions of Crime Victims*, Portland, OR: Hart Publishing.

Beck, U. (1992) *The Risk Society*, London: Sage.

Bennett, R. and Appleton, C. (2004) 'Joined up services to tackle youth crime: a case study in England,' *British Journal of Criminology*, 44(1): 34–54.

Braithwaite, J. (2003) 'What's wrong with the sociology of punishment?,' *Theoretical Criminology*, 7(1): 5–28.

Carrabine, E., Iganski, P., Lee, M., Plummer, K. and South, N. (2004) *Criminology: a sociological introduction*, London: Routledge.

Christie, N. (1986) 'The ideal victim,' in E. A. Fattah (ed.) *From Crime Policy to Victim Policy*, London: Macmillan.

Crawford, A. (2000) 'Salient themes and the limitations of restorative justice,' in A. Crawford and J. Goodey (eds) *Integrating a Victim Perspective within Criminal Justice*, Aldershot: Ashgate.

Dignan, J. (2005) *Understanding Victims and Restorative Justice*, Maidenhead: Open University Press.

Elias, R. (1986) *The Politics of Victimisation*, Oxford: Oxford University Press.

— (1993) *Victims Still*, London: Sage.

Feeley, M. (2003) 'Crime, social order and the rise of the neo-Conservative politics,' *Theoretical Criminology*, 7(1): 111–30.

Feenan, D. (ed.) (2002) *Informal Justice*, Aldershot: Ashgate.

Furedi, F. (2002) *The Culture of Fear*, London: Cassell.

Garland, D. (2001) *The Culture of Control*, Oxford: Oxford University Press.

Gelsthorpe, L. and Morris, A. (2000) 'Re-visioning men's violence against female partners,' *Howard Journal*, 39(4): 412–28.

Giddens, A. (1991) *Modernity and Self-Identity*, Oxford: Polity.

— (1998) *The Third Way*, Oxford: Polity.

Goodey, J. (2005) *Victims and Victimology*, London: Longman.

Grady, A. (2002) 'Female on male domestic violence: uncommon or ignored?' in C. Hoyle and R. Young (eds) *New Visions of Crime Victims*, Portland, OR: Hart Publishing.

Hamill, H. (2002) 'Victims of paramilitary punishment attacks in Belfast,' in C. Hoyle and R. Young (eds) *New Visions of Crime Victims*, Portland, OR: Hart Publishing.

Harre, R. (1979) *Social Being*, London: Basil Blackwell.

Hudson, B. (2003) *Justice in the Risk Society*, London: Sage.

Hutton, W. (2002) *The World We're In*, London: Little, Brown.

Jennings, D. (2003) 'One-year juvenile reconviction rates: first quarter of 2001 cohort,' *Home Office Online Report 18/03*, London: Home Office.

Jessop, R. (2002) *The Future of the Capitalist State*, Cambridge: Polity.

McEvoy, K., Mika, H. and Hudson, B. (2002) 'Introduction: practice, performance and prospects for restorative justice,' *British Journal of Criminology*, 42(3): 469–75.

Marshall, T. (1999) *Restorative Justice: an overview*, London: HMSO.

Mawby, R. and Walklate, S. (1994) *Critical Victimology*, London: Sage.

Miers, D. (1978) *Responses to Victimisation*, Abingdon: Professional Books.

— (1989) 'Positivist victimology: a critique, part 1,' *International Review of Victimology*, 1(1): 1–29.

— (1990) 'Positivist victimology: a critique, part 2,' *International Review of Victimology*, 1(3): 219–30.

— (2004) 'Situating and researching restorative justice in Great Britain,' *Punishment and Society*, 6(1): 23–46.

Muncie, J. (1999) *Youth and Crime*, Buckingham: Open University Press.

— (2002) 'Policy transfers and "what works": some reflections on comparative youth justice,' *Criminal Justice*, 1(3):27–35.

Newburn, T. and McEvoy, K. (eds) (2003) *Criminology, Conflict Resolution and Restorative Justice*, London: Macmillan.

Pitts, J. (2001) *New Politics of Youth Crime*, Basingstoke: Macmillan.

Quinney, R. (1972) 'Who is the victim?' *Criminology*, November: 309–29.

Rock, P. (2002) 'On becoming a victim,' in C. Hoyle and R. Young (eds) *New Visions of Crime Victims*, Portland, OR: Hart Publishing.

Sanders, A. (2002) 'Victim participation in an exclusionary criminal justice system,' in C. Hoyle and R. Young (eds) *New Visions of Crime Victims*, Portland, OR: Hart Publishing.

Soyinka, W. (2004) *Reith Lecture 1: the changing mask of fear*, online. Available at: http://www.bbc.co.uk/radio4/reith2004/lectures.shtml

Steinert, H. (2003) 'The indispensable metaphor of war: on populist politics and the contra-dictions of the state's monopoly of force,' *Theoretical Criminology*, 7(3): 265–91.

Strang, H. and Braithwaite, J. (2002) *Restorative Justice and Family Violence*, Cambridge: Cambridge University Press.

Stubbs, J. (1997) 'Shame, defiance and violence against women,' in S. Cook and J. Bessant (eds) *Women's Encounters with Violence; Australian Experiences*, London: Sage.

UN Commission on Human Security (2003) Final Report, United Nations: New York.

Walklate, S (2005) 'Victimhood as a source of oppression,' *Social Justice*, special edition, T. Kearon and R. Lippens (eds), 32(1): 88–99.

Walklate, S. and Evans, K. (1999) *Zero Tolerance or Community Tolerance: managing crime in high crime areas*, Aldershot: Ashgate.

Young, Jock. (1999) *The Exclusive Society*, London: Sage.

— (2001) 'Identity, community and social exclusion,' in R. Matthews and J. Pitts (eds) *Crime, Disorder and Community Safety*, London: Routledge.

— (2003a) 'Searching for a new criminology of everyday life: a review of the Culture of Control by D. Garland,' *British Journal of Criminology*, 43(1): 228–43.

— (2003b) 'Merton with energy Katz with structure: the sociology of vindictiveness and the criminology of transgression,' *Theoretical Criminology*, 7(3): 389–414.

Young, R. (2002) 'Testing the limits of restorative justice: the case of corporate victims,' in C. Hoyle and R. Young (eds) *New Visions of Crime Victims*, Portland, OR: Hart Publishing.

Youth Justice Board (2002) *Building on Success*, Youth Justice Board 2000–1 Annual Review, London: Youth Justice Board.

Zehr, H. (2001) *Transcending: reflections of crime victims*, Intercourse, PA: Good Books.

19

Stopping domestic violence or protecting children?

Contributions from restorative justice

Joan Pennell

Child welfare services and domestic violence programs are potential allies – they both seek to create safe homes. Their differences of vision and mandate in the United States, however, generate strong tensions. Here, unlike in some European countries, child welfare emphasizes legally mandated interventions to protect children from parental maltreatment rather than voluntary services to support families (Hetherington 2002; Hill *et al.* 2002). From a domestic violence perspective, forensic investigations and child placements blame abused mothers for failing to protect their children and, worse yet, punish them by removing their children. To counter such mother blaming, domestic violence advocates have urged a redesign of child welfare services that takes into account children's varying responses to adult domestic violence, avoids automatically ruling that such exposure is child maltreatment, and encourages supportive and voluntary interventions for many families (Edleson 2004).

For their part, child welfare systems in the United States have become increasingly dissatisfied with adversarial approaches that alienate families from workers and incur extensive costs for investigations, court, and foster care. They are calling for a more balanced approach between child protection and family support (Pecora *et al.* 2000). As a result, states are legislating differential response systems that permit workers to retain legal interventions for the most troubling situations and to assign the majority of cases to more collaborative approaches (National Child Welfare Resource Center for Family-Centered Practice 2001). One aspect of differential response is to involve families, community organizations, and other public agencies in service planning.

To carry out this joint planning, US states are employing some form of family meeting that brings together family members, community groups, and child welfare workers to negotiate agreements (Center for the Study of Social Policy 2002). These face-to-face forums resonate well with restorative justice principles of repairing harm, including key stakeholders, and transforming government–community relations (Bazemore and Schiff 2004). Domestic violence advocates welcome giving mothers a greater voice in child welfare decisions and building in more community supports; however, many object to convening family meetings in situations of domestic violence because of the possibility of re-victimizing abused partners (Stubbs 2002). They hold legitimate fears about offending partners dominating the meeting or child welfare workers holding mothers accountable for their partner's failure to implement the service agreement (Francis 2002).

A possible option is screening out domestic violence referrals to family meetings, but this raises many questions. Will this limit the say of family members over their own affairs? Will children and other family members be denied a potentially beneficial intervention? Given the extensive co-occurrence of both child maltreatment and domestic violence (Edleson 1999), how many families would be rejected? Because families often conceal the violence from their child welfare worker and from the community at large, how will referrals be screened?

Another option is to hold the meeting but to exclude known abusive partners and their side of the family from attending. Batterers should be excluded if there is a restraining order against their being in contact with the survivor and if their attendance poses undue risk for the women and children. Even if the abusers are excluded, does this mean that their families should also not attend? Child welfare often wishes to include the children's parents at a meeting because of child custody issues and to invite all sides of the family in order to increase the likelihood of kinship care for children requiring placement. Likewise women, young persons, and children may want the support of the father's side of the family (Pennell and Burford 1995; Pennell and Francis, 2005).

This chapter examines the impact of including more than one side of the family in meetings to reach child welfare agreements. The type of family meeting studied here is one approach to restorative practice – the family group conference (FGC) (Galaway and Hudson 1996) – and this study examines its use with African American and white families that received child welfare services in a southeastern state. The data are from the North Carolina Family Group

Conferencing Project (Pennell 2002). The project had a series of nine guiding principles, each with associated practices. Carrying out these practices was defined as meeting the FGC objectives. One guiding principle of the project was to 'foster understanding of the family and creativity in planning,' and an associated conference objective was 'inviting different sides of the family' (Pennell 2003: 17). Results are presented from a canonical correlation analysis examining family views on satisfaction with their conference against achievement of its objectives. This makes it possible to see what other objectives are associated with 'inviting different sides of the family' and how these objectives relate to conference satisfaction. The analysis includes responses from families with and without known histories of domestic violence.

This chapter begins by reviewing the development of the child protection and domestic violence movements since the middle of the twentieth century and their divergences in visions, convergences on legal interventions, and resulting conflicts in strategies. Then described are the North Carolina Family Group Conferencing Project and its model of conferencing, the study method, and the findings on including different sides of the family. The conclusion discusses the potential contributions of restorative justice to reshaping visions and practices and forming a coordinated response of informal and formal support networks to safeguard women and children.

Evolving positions of the child protection and domestic violence movements

Efforts to protect children and stop domestic violence in the United States re-emerged in the mid-twentieth century from different social movements (Breines and Gordon 1983). The child protection movement was galvanized in the 1960s by physicians and to a lesser extent by legal advocates advancing the 'battered-child syndrome' (Pleck 1987: 169). They departed from the earlier progressive approaches of charity volunteers and social workers who addressed a range of environmental conditions generating child neglect and abuse (Schene 1998). The campaign to raise awareness of violence against women in the 1970s had quite different origins coming out of the second-wave feminist movement (Schechter 1982). Unlike the child protection initiative, the battered-women's movement did not rely on professionals to advance their cause and instead created a series of networks of women's advocates.

Child welfare services and domestic violence organizations in the United States continued to reflect these disparate roots over the rest of the twentieth century. This led to divergences in their primary strategies for addressing family violence and creating safe homes. Child welfare agencies sought to protect children from their parents even to the extent of removing them from their homes. They focused on the parent–child relationship, with poverty, discrimination, and other threats to safety sidelined, and their dominant metaphor was maternal failure to care for and protect children (Schorr 1997). Conversely, domestic violence programs sought to advance safety for women by offering shelter, counseling, and other supports. Distancing themselves from mainstream services, they created an alternative child welfare system to which mothers with their children could seek refuge (Callahan 1993). They were primarily concerned about the relationship between intimate partners, and their overarching metaphor was male violence against women, redirecting attention away from other forms of family violence, including in same-sex couples (Ristock and Pennell 1996).

Despite these divergences, both groups converged over the 1980s and 1990s in turning increasingly to legal interventions to address their respective areas of concern. In doing so, they conformed to the general trend in the United States to respond punitively to social problems (Coker 2004). Over this period, reports to child protection escalated as government reduced its social welfare programs, and, as a result, child welfare services narrowed from a broad range of family services down to forensic investigations and child placements (Kamerman and Kahn 1997). Although the battered-women's movement was initially suspicious of courts and law enforcement which they saw as upholding patriarchy, domestic violence advocates had generally accepted the necessity of legal interventions such as mandatory arrests and protective (no-contact) orders by the 1980s (Pleck 1987).

The relationship of both child welfare and domestic violence groups to legal interventions remained uneasy. Child welfare systems in the United States were overwhelmed by high levels of referrals, investigations, court time, and paperwork; these heavy workloads combined with low salaries, inadequate supervision and training, and threats of violence from clientele and led to an annual worker turnover estimated at between 30 to 40 per cent (US GAO 2003). Given these conditions, not surprisingly, federal reviews concluded that all assessed state child welfare systems were failing to meet national standards for child outcomes and service delivery (US DHHS 2004).

Likewise, domestic violence programs were troubled by the results of relying on legal interventions. Abused women were charged for resisting orders to testify against their abusers, and mandatory arrest policies of abusers greatly elevated the number of women arrested for fighting back (Martin 1997). Discriminatory policing practices heightened these risks for poor women, women of color, immigrant women, and native women; and state control escalated all the more for these groups when legal interventions for battering intersected with other government interventions including child welfare (Coker 2004). The *Nicholson v. Williams* (203 F. Supp. 2d 153) case in New York has directed public attention to the impact of their intersection. This federal civil rights class suit was brought on behalf of abused women whose children were removed because of their exposure to domestic violence (Schwartz 2004). Although the mothers won in court, city child welfare officials maintained that it would have little impact on daily practices (Kaufman 2004).

With such fallout from state interventions, both child welfare and domestic violence proponents called for a greater emphasis on community-based responses. In child welfare circles this is phrased as 'family supports' that are voluntary and comprehensive (Parton 1997; Pecora *et al.* 2001) or 'family-centered practice' that encourages the participation of family members and community groups in child welfare service planning and implementation (Walton *et al.* 2001). The push for such family-friendly approaches was fostered by states' adopting differential response systems permitting them to intervene less intrusively in many families. For their part, domestic violence advocates were less sanguine about the 'family' and referred to a 'coordinated response' that helps the criminal justice system and batterer-intervention groups to work in concert with programs for women and children (Shepard and Pence 1999).

Such partnerships between the state and community, though, pose dilemmas: Can we retain the state's role in protecting victims as long as its legitimacy is derived from a system that privileges certain groups over others? Can women and children advocates collaborate with state institutions without becoming co-opted to goals contrary to their own beliefs (Stark 2004: 1304)? In answer, some women's advocates are calling for divestment from state intervention and proposing community-based solutions, including restorative practices. This might take the form of 'intimate abuse circles' in which the couple meet with their supporters to tell their stories and reconstruct their relationships (Mills 2003) or increased activism to urge government supports for women and children's economic and cultural needs and instituting alternative systems of accountability by using restorative justice processes (Das Dasgupta 2003). Such disengagement from state intervention is far less appealing to child welfare reformists given children's dependence on adult caregivers and the closer ties historically between child protection and government in the United States.

Moreover, divestment is not the solution according to the recipients of service. Parents involved with child welfare, although often angered and intimidated, want their workers to exert 'power with' rather than 'over' them and apply the agency's authority on their and their children's behalf (Dumbrill 2003: 113). Abused women, including those from marginalized populations, want police intervention for good reason (McGillivray and Comaskey 1999) – arresting perpetrators lessens the danger that abused women will be killed in the future (Campbell *et al.* 2003).

Turning to alternatives found in restorative justice does not necessarily mean divestment from the legal system (Strang and Braithwaite 2002). Indigenous people may want restorative programs under their leadership but they also want support from the criminal justice system to safeguard participants (Kelly 2002) and serve as an alternative recourse as needed (Bushie 1997). Restorative processes such as family group conferencing to address youthful offending often divert cases from the court. These, however, are not typically situations where the perpetrator and victim have an on-going and close relationship. For this reason, some restorative justice proponents are cautious about applying their practices in domestic violence situations (Zehr 2002). Advisedly, if restorative processes are employed with family violence, they should include careful safety assessments and interface with the legal system (Busch 2002). Family violence studies in Canada (Pennell and Burford 2000) and England (SSRIU 2003) report positive results from family group conferencing that combined leverage over offending family members from both informal networks and public authorities. These forums made it possible to advance both child protection and women's safety.

In summary, over the twentieth century, the positions of child welfare and domestic violence on stopping family violence have diverged in terms of their foci – child protection versus women's safety – and converged in terms of their investment in legal interventions. Today, both movements are questioning their over-reliance on the law and looking for alternatives, including from restorative justice. Restorative practices do not require disengagement from state intervention. Instead, 'widening the circle' of those committed to stopping family violence is a way to create a coordinated response of informal and formal resources (Pennell and Anderson 2005). This was the intent of the family group conferencing project in North Carolina.

North Carolina Family Group Conferencing Project

The mission of the North Carolina Family Group Conferencing Project was to advance the use of family group conferencing (FGC) in child welfare in order to build 'partnerships with and around families' that safeguard child and adult family members (Pennell 2002). These partnerships were to include extended family, friends, community organizations, and public agencies. The four-year project provided training and evaluation to the thirteen participating North Carolinian counties and developed practice guidance with the state Division of Social Services. Each county department of

social services was responsible for delivery of FGC with their clientele.

The project adapted the New Zealand model of FGC as applied in child welfare (Connolly and McKenzie 1999) to the policy and cultural context of North Carolina. Planning sessions were held to gain input from a wide spectrum of community representatives on how they wanted the project to be conducted in their county and state (Pennell and Weil 2000). FGC was defined as a forum that brings together the family members with their relatives and other close supports to form the 'family group' and make a plan for addressing the areas of concern. Providing a system of checks and balances, the child welfare worker was to approve the plan before its going into effect. In trainings, FGC was distinguished from a number of other strategies in order to highlight the model's particular contributions. The aim was to encourage joint planning rather than assigning fault as in court proceedings, family leadership rather than professional deliberations as in case conferencing or staffings, decision making rather than treatment as in family therapy, and group responsibility rather than reconciliation of different parties as in mediation.

Families were referred by their child welfare worker to a conference coordinator who prepared the family group and service providers for taking part. Because the coordinator did not carry the case, this helped the family and coordinator to focus on organizing the conferences rather than negotiating child welfare decisions. Preparations included explaining the purpose and process of the meeting and checking that the family wanted to proceed with the FGC; figuring out with the family who was their family group and inviting participants; conducting an assessment of safety issues and building in supports and protections for participants; making logistical arrangements such as on travel and food; and asking the family if they wanted a particular beginning or ending ceremony at their conference.

According to a checklist completed by FGC coordinators, for the most part these preparations were carried out with families; and coordinators averaged thirty hours in preparatory time per conference.

The conferences had five phases. First, to highlight from the outset that the conference belonged to the family, meetings started with an opening of the family's selection such as passing around photos of the children or saying a prayer. Second, information was shared on the purpose and process of the meeting, the relevant family history, and available resources for possible inclusion in the plan. Third, once the family group had the opportunity to comment or ask questions, all service providers including the FGC coordinator left the room, and during this private time the family group often shared a meal and then developed their plan for resolving the issues. Fourth, once the family group had formulated a plan, they invited back the FGC coordinator, child welfare worker, and other remaining service providers to review the plan. Often at this time action steps were clarified further and workers approved the plan or deferred its approval until checking with supervisory staff. Fifth, at the meeting, the coordinator distributed FGC Evaluation forms to be completed by participants and thanked them for taking part in the deliberations; and according to the family's wishes, a closing might take place such as joining in song. From beginning to end, the conferences averaged four hours, and the mean attendance was eight family group members and four service providers.

After the FGC was the work of carrying out the plan. Copies of the plan were mailed to participants to assist with follow-through. The child welfare worker remained responsible for the case but plans might include a monitor from the family group or community, and this individual checked that everyone was fulfilling their tasks as stated in the FGC plan. At times, FGCs were reconvened to evaluate progress and reformulate the plan in light of new developments in the family.

For the project evaluation, counties were asked to refer families. Participation of the families was voluntary, and they could choose to take part or not without this affecting their having a conference. As noted above, a FGC Evaluation form was administered at the end of the conference. Overwhelmingly participants reported being satisfied with the proceedings and its resulting plan. Nevertheless, there were pockets of discontent regarding who was missing from the conference (Pennell, in press). In their comments, participants frequently wished that a key family member such as a father or just more family group members had been present for the deliberations, but rarely urged the exclusion of a family group member (cf. Pennell and Burford 1995). The project interviewed family group participants at various points to gain their perspectives on the conference and post-conference work.

The interviews held shortly after the conference provided an opportunity to gain their perspectives on the conference and complete the Achievement of FGC Objectives instrument. This was a way to check whether in their view twenty-five key FGC objectives had been met and, thus, whether practice was faithful to the FGC model. In addition, the FGC coordinators and research observers completed the Achievement of FGC Objectives. As reported elsewhere (Pennell 2003), for the most part the respondents agreed that the objectives had been achieved, but with some exceptions. One of these was the earlier noted objective 'inviting different sides of the family' to the FGC; here, 18 per cent disagreed or strongly disagreed. A separate analysis of the objectives found that fourteen of the twenty-five formed three factors; however, omitted from these factors was 'inviting different sides of the family' (Pennell 2004). Because including the father and his family is of particular relevance to FGC when there is a history of domestic violence, further analysis of the FGC objectives was carried out, and its findings are reported in this chapter. Next the method of this further study is presented.

Method

Two main questions were addressed in this study. From the perspective of family group members: (1) how does the objective 'inviting different sides of the family' relate to the achievement of other FGC objectives? and (2) how does achievement of the FGC objectives relate to satisfaction at the conference? To answer these questions, data from two instruments were used: the 'Achievement of FGC Objectives' and the 'FGC Evaluation.'

The Achievement of FGC Objectives questionnaire asks to what extent key FGC practices were carried out before and during the conference. These include clarifying the conference purpose and the roles of FGC coordinator, service providers, and family group; arranging the conference in a way that supported family group members taking part and set them at ease; and finalizing a plan that incorporated the contributions of family group and service providers. The specific items are listed below in **Table 19.1**. The twenty-five Likert items were scored on a four-point scale of 'strongly disagree,' 'disagree,' 'agree,' and 'strongly agree' with space for 'don't know' and 'not applicable.' The last two along with no response were coded as missing datum. During the course of the project, the instrument was completed by 151 participants from thirty conferences. Of these participants, 60.3 per cent were family group members. On average about one month after the conferences, consenting family group members (twelve years and above) scored the questionnaire during an interview, usually by telephone.

The FGC Evaluation form was distributed at the end of the conferences to all partici-

pants twelve years and older in order to assess their satisfaction with the FGC preparations, process, decision making, and resulting plan. They were asked to score sixteen Likert items on the same scale as used with the Achievement of Objectives (see Table 19.1) and could comment further on their views. It was completed by 278 participants from thirty-three conferences of whom 59.4 per cent were family group. The number of respondents was greater on the FGC Evaluation than on the Achievement of Objectives because the latter was administered by interview only with key family group members (and completed separately by FGC coordinators and research observers) rather than being handed out to FGC participants.

Participants' responses could be linked on both instruments because they were asked to provide the last four digits of their social security number. Matches between the two instruments were only sought for those participants identifying themselves as family group. The rationale was that their feedback was of greatest interest and they were the respondents with the least number of missing responses on either instrument. The number of matches for family group was seventy-three out of a possible ninety-one Achievement of Objectives and 165 FGC Evaluations. These respondents included seven young persons for whom the conference was held, thirteen parents, thirty-five relatives, six friends, four foster parents, five religious leaders, and three others. The matched group had some missing data on both instruments: 5.48 per cent for the FGC Evaluation and 5.92 per cent for the Achievement of Objectives. In order to carry out the analysis, missing data were imputed by taking the median family group response on an item. Imputing minimizes bias but increases random error.

The matched group came from twenty-one conferences, of which four had a known history of domestic violence. For extended descriptions of these FGCs with

Table 19.1. Canonical correlation analysis of FGC Evaluations and Achievement of Objectives ($N = 73$)

	FGC Evaluations	*Correlation*
1	Preparation for the conference was adequate.	**0.4447**
2	I liked where the conference was held.	**0.5719**
3	The right people were at the conference.	0.2542
4	At the conference, I got the information that I needed.	0.2134
5	I was satisfied with the way that the conference was run.	0.2284
6	The group used effective decision-making techniques.	0.2297
7	I believe that I had a lot of influence on the group's decision making.	0.1855
8	I contributed important information during the group's decision-making process.	0.2716
9	During the group meeting, I got to participate whenever I wanted to.	**0.5124**
10	Other members of the group really listened to what I had to say.	0.2767
11	I felt that I was a genuine member of the group.	**0.4830**
12	The group reached the right decision.	**0.5529**
13	I support the final group decision.	**0.4144**
14	I would be willing to put my best effort into carrying out the group's final decision.	**0.6160**
15	I think that the right people were involved in reaching the decisions.	0.3573
16	I am satisfied with the plan that was agreed upon at the conference.	**0.5519**

	Achievement of Objectives	
1	A number of service providers contributed to the FGC (e.g. information, funding, services).	0.1443
2	Each service provider was clear about their roles (e.g. child protection, counseling).	−0.0714
3	The FGC coordinator was respectful of the family group.	0.0540
4	The only job of the FGC coordinator was to organize the conference. He/she did *not* have other jobs to do with the family.	−0.2236
5	The FGC coordinator got any needed advice on how to organize the conference (e.g. on the family's culture, community services).	−0.1336
6	The family group understood the reasons for holding the conference.	−0.0601
7	The family group agreed with the reasons for holding the conference.	−0.1006
8	The service providers understood the reasons for holding the conference.	−0.1362
9	The service providers agreed with the reasons for holding the conference.	0.2130
10	The conference was held in a place that felt right to the family group.	0.0112
11	The conference was held in a way that felt right to the family group (e.g. the right food, right time of day).	−0.0346
12	More family group members than service providers were invited to the conference.	0.1069
13	Different sides of the family were invited to the conference (e.g. father and mother's sides of the family).	**−0.3915**
14	People at the conference were relatives and also people who feel 'like family' (e.g. old friends, good neighbors).	0.1139
15	The family group was prepared for the conference (e.g. got enough information on what happens at a conference).	−0.1133
16	The service providers were prepared for the conference (e.g. got enough information on what happens at a conference).	−0.1290
17	The conference had enough supports and protections (e.g. support persons).	−0.2284
18	Arrangements were made for special needs that the family had (e.g. transportation, child care, interpretation).	−0.1304
19	Service providers shared their knowledge but they did not tell the family group how to solve the problems.	0.0585
20	The family group had private time to make their plan.	0.1546
21	The plan included ways that the family group will help out.	**−0.3745**
22	The plan included ways that service providers will help out.	−0.1205
23	The plan included a monitor to keep an eye on whether the plan is being carried out.	−0.2235
24	The plan included steps to evaluate if the plan is working and to get the family group back together again if needed.	**−0.3210**
25	Social services approved the plan without unnecessary delays.	**−0.3972**

Notes: Canonical correlation of 0.8989, Wilks' Lambda: F = 1.22, df = (400, 490.24), $p = 0.0172$.
Source: The FGC Evaluation was adapted from Pennell and Burford (1995) and DeStephen and Hirokawa (1988), used with kind permission of Sage Publications

family violence, see Pennell and Anderson (2005). Because these were child welfare referrals, the reason for holding the conferences did not center on domestic violence but instead on matters such as where the children would live. As the coordinators prepared for the conference, they learned about the domestic violence. It is likely that in some families the domestic violence was not disclosed because of legitimate fears that witnessing the mother's victimization could lead to removal of the children.

Including different sides of the family

To compare the scores on the two forms, a canonical correlation analysis was used. A canonical correlation analysis permits examining the patterns of interrelationships between sets of variables, in this case the FGC objectives and the FGC evaluation variables. The canonical correlation analysis showed that one set of interrelationships between the Achievement of FGC Objectives and FGC Evaluation was at a significant level ($p = 0.0172$) and had a strong correlation of 0.899 between the two sets of variables. No other canonical correlations were significant. For the significant correlation, Table 19.1 displays the correlations between the individual items and its canonical variate or linear combination of the set of variables, first for the FGC Evaluation and then for the Achievement of FGC Objectives. Following the norm of treating structure coefficients at or above 0.30 as meaningful (Pedhazur 1982: 732), correlations meeting this criterion are highlighted for both instruments. These highlighted correlations are unipolar, meaning that the direction of the sign is the same within each set of correlations; as the level of agreement increases on an evaluation item or decreases on an objective, so it does on the other items in the set. The positive sign on the FGC Evaluation and the negative sign on

the Achievement of FGC Objectives indicate that the values for the former are increasing as the values for the latter are decreasing.

For the Achievement of FGC Objectives, item 13 on inviting different sides of the family is highlighted along with three other items (21, 24, and 25) that all related to the plan. This set of negative correlations indicates that having different sides of the family present and meeting objectives regarding the plan are in an inverse relationship to their canonical variate. As agreement fell that different sides of the family attended the FGC, likewise agreement fell that the plan included steps on how the family group members would assist, that the plan stipulated how they would evaluate the plan and reconvene as needed, and that Social Services approved the plan in a timely manner. In other words, the canonical variate can be defined as exclusive planning attended by only one side of the family and failing to establish ways of supporting on-going family involvement. The obverse of this canonical variate or dimension to which the four objectives contribute can be conceptualized as:

■ Inclusive planning – a decision-making process that involves different sides of the family in making a plan, incorporates means of sustaining the family group's participation, and is authorized and supported by the protective authority.

The FGC Evaluation has nine bolded items: two on preparations (items 1 and 2), three on the decision process (9, 11 and 15), and four on the resulting plan (12, 13, 14, and 16). Notably, the bolded item with the highest correlation with the FGC Evaluation canonical variate was number 14 regarding willingness to put a best effort into carrying out the plan, and the highlighted item with the lowest level was number 15 on thinking that the right people were involved in making the plan. These correlations indicate both the family group's commitment to the plan and an unease about who took part or did not take part in the making the plan. This unease on attendance was probably offset by satisfaction with the conference preparations, decision process, and resulting plan. Combined these variables point to the canonical variate or dimension:

■ Effective planning – a decision-making process for which participants are prepared, in which they are encouraged to participate, and from which they produce a plan with strong support.

According to this analysis, the dimension 'effective planning' is apparent at the conclusion of the conference, although there was some disquiet even at the time as to whether or not the right people were present at the conference. Over the next month, the family group members became more cognizant of the impact of omitting certain participants on what was happening or not happening in the aftermath of the conference. Because some plans did not include a number of ways more family groups could have contributed to the plan and means for monitoring and evaluating the plan, the capacity to carry out the plan was reduced. These problems were aggravated if Social Services delayed approving the plan.

Contributions of restorative justice

The child protection and domestic violence movements re-emerging during the mid-twentieth century in the United States both sought to create safe homes and stop family violence. Their respective guiding metaphors – protecting children from their parents and liberating women from their male batterers –

divided two potential allies. Child protection agencies sought to save children often from the very women whom domestic violence programs perceived as survivors deserving support, not blame. By the last part of the century, child welfare agencies and domestic violence programs, following a general trend in the country, turned increasingly to legal measures. Although both child welfare clients and domestic violence survivors welcomed and required firm action on their behalf, there were also troubling consequences. Over-reliance on the law meant that child welfare clients were more likely to receive forensic investigations than family supports, domestic violence victims could be charged for defending themselves against their abusers, and abused women might lose their children for exposure to their mother's victimization. As a result, some within child welfare and domestic violence circles considered alternatives already applied within restorative justice.

For their part, proponents of restorative justice hold mixed views on whether practices such as family group conferencing (FGC) are safe with domestic violence. If applied, a number caution that restorative practices should not serve as a diversion from the court system and that safeguards must be built in order to exert both formal and informal leverage to stop family violence. One possible safeguard is excluding the batterer and his family from deliberations. The reality in child welfare, however, is that such exclusions would be difficult to put into effect because of child custody issues and because workers are often unaware of the extent of domestic violence on their caseloads. Another counter-indication to such a solution concerns the dynamics of conferencing as found in an analysis of data from the North Carolina Family Group Conferencing Project.

If only one side of the family was present at the FGC, then family group members were more likely to express at the end of the conference higher satisfaction with the effectiveness of their decision making. On further consideration of the FGC composition a month or so later, though, family group participants reported achieving some key FGC objectives if more than one side of the family had been in attendance. Where conferences included multiple sides of the family, they tended to build more family contributions into the plan, establish clearer systems of evaluating and revising plans, and receive more timely approvals by Social Services.

Inclusive decision making must be accompanied with safeguards for participants before, during, and after the conference. This means following good restorative processes: involving women and child advocates in planning an FGC program, carefully preparing family group and service providers prior to conferencing and putting in place safety measures, creatively formulating and thoughtfully authorizing FGC plans that keep child and adult family members safe, and coordinating follow through by informal and formal support network in carrying out and revising the FGC plan. Inclusive decision making makes it possible to go beyond the question of either legal intervention or divestment and to build a community dedicated to both child protection and women's safety.

References

Bazemore, G. and Schiff, M. (2004) *Juvenile Justice Reform and Restorative Justice: building theory and policy from practice*, Cullompton, Devon, UK: Willan Publishing.

Breines, W., and Gordon, L. (1983) 'The new scholarship on family violence,' *Signs: Journal of Women in Culture and Society*, 8(3), Spring: 490–531.

Busch, R. (2002) 'Domestic violence and restorative justice initiatives: who pays if we get it wrong?' in H. Strang and J. Braithwaite (eds) *Restorative Justice and Family Violence Restorative Justice and Family Violence*, Cambridge, UK: Cambridge University Press.

Bushie, B. (1997) 'A personal journey,' in *The Four Circles of Hollow Water*, Hull, Quebec: Aboriginal Peoples' Collection, Aboriginal Corrections Policy Unit, Supply and Services Canada, JS5-1/15-1997E.

Callahan, M. (1993) 'Feminist approaches: women recreate child welfare,' in B. Wharf (ed.) *Rethinking Child Welfare in Canada*, Toronto: McClelland and Stewart.

Campbell, J. C., Webster, D., Koziol-McLain, J., Block, C., Campbell, D. and Curry, M. (2003) 'Risk factors for feminicide in abusive relationships: results from a multisite case control study,' *American Journal of Public Health*, 93(7): 1089–97.

Center for the Study of Social Policy, Center for Community Partnerships in Child Welfare (2002) *Bringing Families to the Table: a comparative guide to family meetings in child welfare*, Washington, DC: CSSP/CCPCW.

Coker, D. (2004) 'Race, poverty, and the crime-centered response to domestic violence,' *Violence Against Women*, 10(11): 1331–53.

Connolly, M., and McKenzie, M. (1999) *Effective Participatory Practice: family group conferencing in child protection*, Modern Applications of Social Work Series, New York: Aldine de Gruyter.

Das Dasgupta, S. (2003) *Safety and Justice for All: examining the relationship between the women's anti-violence movement and the criminal legal system*, New York: Ms Foundation, online. Available at: http://www.ms.foundation.org/user-assets/PDF/Program/safety_justice.pdf [accessed 17 January 2005].

DeStephen, R. S. and Hirokawa, R. Y. (1988) 'Small group consensus: stability of group support of the decision, task process, and group relationships,' *Small Group Behaviour*, 19(2): 227–39.

Dumbrill, G. C. (2003) 'Child welfare: AOP's nemesis?' in W. Shera (ed.) *Emerging Perspectives on Anti-Oppressive Practice*, Toronto: Canadian Scholars' Press.

Edleson, J. L. (1999) 'The overlap between child maltreatment and woman battering,' *Violence Against Women*, 5(2): 134–54.

— (2004) 'Should childhood exposure to adult domestic violence be defined as child maltreatment under the law?' in P. G. Jaffe, L. L. Baker and A. Cunningham (eds) *Protecting Children from Domestic Violence: strategies for community intervention*, New York: Guilford Press.

Francis, S. (2002) 'Results of focus groups with domestic-violence advocates,' unpublished paper, Raleigh, North Carolina Family

Group Conferencing Project, North Carolina State University.

Galaway, B., and Hudson, J. (eds) (1996) *Restorative Justice: international perspectives*, Monsey, NY: Criminal Justice Press.

Hetherington, R. (2002) 'Learning from difference: comparing child welfare systems,' Waterloo, Ontario, Canada: Wilfrid Laurier University, Faculty of Social Work, Partnerships for Children and Families Project, online. Available at: http://info.wlu.ca/pcfproject [accessed 9 January 2005].

Hill, M., Stafford, A. and Lister, P. G. (2002) *International Perspectives on Child Protection*, report on seminar held on 20 March 2002. Part of the Scottish Executive Child Protection Review, *Protecting Children Today and Tomorrow*, Glasgow: Centre for the Child and Society, University of Glasgow, online. Available at: http://www.scotland.gov.uk/about/ED/CnF/00017834/page1979535343.pdf [accessed 15 January 2005].

Kamerman, S. B. and Kahn, A. J. (eds) (1997) *Children and their Families in Big Cities: strategies for service reform*, New York: Columbia University Press.

Kaufman, L. (2004) 'Court limits removing child when mother is abuse victim,' *New York Times*, 27 October: A-1.

Kelly, L. (2002) 'Using restorative justice principles to address violence in aboriginal communities,' in H. Strang and J. Braithwaite (eds) *Restorative Justice and Family Violence*, Cambridge, UK: Cambridge University Press.

McGillivray, A. and Comaskey, B. (1999) *Black Eyes All of the Time: intimate violence, aboriginal women, and the justice system*, Toronto: University of Toronto Press.

Martin, M. E. (1997) 'Policy promise: community policing and domestic violence victims satisfaction,' *Policing: An International Journal of Police Strategies and Management*, 20(3): 519–31.

Mills, L. G. (2003) *Insult to Injury: rethinking our responses to intimate abuse*, Princeton, NJ: Princeton University Press.

National Child Welfare Resource Center for Family-Centered Practice (2001) 'Meeting each family's needs: using differential response in reports of child abuse and neglect,' *Best Practice/Next Practice*, 2(1), Spring: 1–14.

Parton, N. (1997) 'Child protection and family support: current debates and future prospects,' in N. Parton (ed.) *Child Protection and Family Support: tensions, contradictions and possibilities*, London and New York: Routledge.

Pecora, P. J., Whittaker, J. K., Maluccio, A. N. and Barth, R. P. (2000) *The Child Welfare Challenge: police, practice, and research*, Modern Applications of Social Work Series, second edn, New York: Aldine de Gruyter.

Pecora, P. J., Reed-Ashcraft, K. and Kirk, R. S. (2001) 'Family-centered services: a typology, brief history, and overview of current program implementation and evaluation challenges,' in E. Walton, P. Sandau-Beckler and M. Mannes (eds) *Balancing Family-Centered Services and Child Well-Being*, New York: Columbia University Press.

Pedhazur, E. J. (1982) *Multiple Regression in Behavioral Research: explanation and prediction*, second edn, New York: CBS College Publishing.

Pennell, J. (with Turner, T. and Hardison, J.) (2002) *North Carolina Family Group Conferencing Project: building partnerships with and around families: final report to the North Carolina Division of Social Services, fiscal year 2001–2002*, Raleigh, North Carolina State University, Social Work Program, North Carolina Family Group Conferencing Project. Online executive summary at http://social.chass.ncsu.edu/jpennell/ncfgcp/NCFGCPExecSummary

Pennell, J. (2003) 'Are we following key FGC practice? Views of conference participants,' in L. Merkel-Holguin (ed.) 'Promising results, potential new directions: international FGDM research and evaluation in child welfare', special issue of *Protecting Children*, 18(1–2): 16–21.

— (2004) 'Family group conferencing in child welfare: responsive and regulatory interfaces,' in P. Adams (ed.) 'Restorative justice, responsive regulation, and social welfare', special issue of *Journal of Sociology and Social Welfare*, 31(1), March: 117–35.

— (in press) 'Restorative practices and child welfare: toward an inclusive civil society,' in B. Morrison, and E. Ahmed (eds), 'Restorative justice and civil society', special issue of *Journal of Social Issues*.

Pennell, J. and Anderson, G. (2005) *Widening the Circle: the practice and evaluation of family group conferencing with children, young persons, and their families*, Washington, DC: NASW Press.

Pennell, J. and Burford, G. (1995) *Family Group Decision Making: new roles for old partners in resolving family violence: implementation report*, vol. I, St John's, NF: Memorial University of Newfoundland, School of Social Work.

— (2000) 'Family group decision making: protecting children and women,' *Child Welfare*, 79(2), March/April: 131–58.

Pennell, J. and Francis, S. (2005) 'Safety conferencing: toward a coordinated and inclusive response to safeguard women and children,' in J. Ptacek (ed.), special issue of *Violence Against Women* 11(5), 666–692.

Pennell, J. and Weil, M. (2000) 'Initiating conferencing: community practice issues,' in G. Burford and J. Hudson (eds) *Family Group Conferences: new directions in community-centered child and family practice*, Modern Applications of Social Work Series, Hawthorne, NY: Aldine de Gruyter.

Pleck, E. (1987) *Domestic Tyranny: the making of social policy against family violence from colonial times to the present*, New York: Oxford University Press.

Ristock, J. L. and Pennell, J. (1996) *Community Research as Empowerment: feminist links, postmodern interruptions*, Don Mills, Ontario: Canada, Oxford University Press.

Schechter, S. (1982) *Women and Male Violence: the visions and struggles of the battered women's movement*, Boston: South End Press.

Schene, P. A. (1998) 'Past, present, and future roles of child protective services,' *The Future of Children: Protecting Children from Abuse and Neglect*, 8(1) Spring: 23–38.

Schorr, L. B. (1997) *Common Purpose: strengthening families and neighbourhoods to rebuild America*, New York: Anchor Books/Doubleday.

Schwartz, A. (2004) 'Court of appeals to rule on child witnessing of domestic violence as neglect,' *Legal Services Journal*, Greater Upstate Law Project, Albany, NY, June, online. Available at: http://www.gulpny.org/Domestic %20Violence/childwitnessdvneglect.htm [accessed 31 July 2004].

Shepard, M. F. and Pence, E. L. (eds) (1999) *Coordinating Community Responses to Domestic Violence: lessons from Duluth and beyond*, Thousand Oaks, CA: Sage.

SSRIU (Social Services and Research Information Unit) (2003) 'The Dove Project: the Basingstoke domestic violence family group conference project,' unpublished manuscript, University of Portsmouth, Hampshire, UK, June.

Stark, E. (2004) 'Insults, injury, and injustice,' *Violence Against Women*, 10(11): 1302–30.

Strang, H., and Braithwaite, J. (eds) (2002) *Restorative Justice and Family Violence*, Cambridge, UK: Cambridge University Press.

Stubbs, J. (2002) 'Domestic violence and women's safety: feminist challenges to restorative justice,' in H. Strang and J. Braithwaite (eds) *Restorative Justice and Family Violence Restorative Justice and Family Violence*, Cambridge, UK: Cambridge University Press.

US DHHS (Department of Health and Human Services), Administration for Children and Families, Children's Bureau (2004) *General findings from the Federal Child and Family Services Review*, online. Available at: http://www.acf.hhs.gov/programs/cb/cwrp/results/statefindings/genfindings04/index.htm [updated 9 September 2004].

US GAO (General Accounting Office) (2003) *Child Welfare: HHS could play a greater role in helping child welfare agencies recruit and retain staff*, Washington, DC: US GAO.

Walton, E., Sandau-Beckler, P. and Mannes, M. (eds) (2001) *Balancing Family-Centered Services and Child Well-Being: exploring issues in policy, practice, theory, and research*, New York: Columbia University Press.

Zehr, H. (2002) *The Little Book of Restorative Justice*, Intercourse, PA: Good Books.

Notes

1. The author wishes to acknowledge the funding provided by the North Carolina Division of Social Services, research coordination of Jennifer Hardison, consultation of Dr. Tom Gerig, and research assistance of Alvin van Orden and Seong-Tae Kim.

20

Are there limits to restorative justice?

The case of child sexual abuse

Anne-Marie McAlinden

Introduction

The sexual abuse of children, particularly by those in a position of trust, is one of the most abhorrent yet ubiquitous of crimes in contemporary society. One of the underlying facets of child sexual abuse is its hidden nature and the fact that it is often allowed to remain a secret. Contrary to popular belief, a high proportion of child victims – figures suggest between 80 (Grubin 1998: 15) and 98 per cent (Leggett 2000: 7) – are abused by someone known to them rather than predatory strangers. Children or their carers often feel a sense of shame or embarrassment in coming forward to report the abuse, let alone confront their abuser. This problem is even more manifest when the abuser is a trusted intimate of the child or their family.

These difficulties are compounded by the fact that the criminal justice system is often limited in its response to these types of offences. In tandem with significant increases in levels of recorded sexual offending, there is a parallel disillusionment with the ability of the justice system to curb it.[1] Research shows that while overall levels of sexual offending are increasing, re-conviction rates for sexual offenders have declined (Friendship and Thornton 2001). More

recent research shows that fewer than 5 per cent of sex offenders are ever apprehended (Salter 2003). Moreover, evidence from self-report studies also suggests that those convicted of sexual offences often reveal the commission of many more offences than are reported to authorities by their victims (Groth *et al.* 1982; Abel *et al.* 1987). In this respect, Home Office research reveals that actual recidivism rates for sexual offenders are 5.3 times the official reconviction rate (Falshaw *et al.* 2003). The very nature of the system means that, at best, it can only ever hope to deal effectively with those offenders who have come to the attention of law enforcement authorities. In practice, this actually covers very few offenders since, as I have already said, the majority of abuse remains hidden and undisclosed.

Indeed, child sexual abuse is a small component of the broader category of 'gendered and sexualized violence' (Hudson 2002), including domestic violence, which causes significant trauma for victims (Herman 1997) yet continues to evade conventional approaches to justice. Writers such as Finstad (1990) and Braithwaite and Daly (Braithwaite and Daly 1994; Daly 2000, 2002) underline the need to devise more constructive ways of responding to sexualized violence, precisely because of its damaging, domineering, and harmful nature. The failure of formal criminal justice thus far with respect to these types of offences means there is considerable scope for exploring alternative forms of justice and their potential for improving the outcome for victims, offenders, families, and communities affected by sexual offences.

At the same time, however, sex offenders, particularly those who offend against children, and how best to deal with them, are issues which feature prominently in the law and order debate (Silverman and Wilson 2002). The central importance of risk to social and political theory generally (Beck 1992; Ericson and Haggerty 1997) has been reflected in mainstream criminal justice debates (Feeley and Simon 1992, 1994; Braithwaite 2000; Shearing 2000) and has been particularly evident in relation to concerns over the risk posed by released sex offenders living in the community (Kemshall and Maguire 2003; Matravers 2003). Indeed, it has been argued that the concepts of risk management (Parton *et al.* 1997: 232–40) and, more recently, governance (Ashenden 2002, 2004) have become the key signifiers for the regulation of child (sexual) abuse and managing sexual offenders in the community generally, both in terms of policy development and practical decision-making. However, given the failure of traditional approaches, it is contended that criminal justice policy and practice need to recognize the opportunities offered by restorative justice in order to better manage risk and protect the public more effectively.

This essay hopes to show that, in carefully managed contexts, the restorative paradigm could be extended beyond the traditional and generally accepted domain of less serious forms of offending. In effect, contrary to the major arguments put forward by the critics, it is contended that restorative justice may represent a wider and more holistic response to child sexual abuse. In the main, it will be argued that unlike traditional

retributive measures which make up the current criminal justice response to sexual offences, the theory and practice of restorative justice may offer a more meaningful, progressive, and ultimately more effective response to the problem. It will further argue that those affected by child sexual abuse could gain significant benefits from the widespread adoption of such an approach.

To put these arguments in perspective, it is necessary to begin by providing an outline of the broad principles of restorative justice as well as some examples of restorative practice with sex offenders.

The principles and practices of restorative justice

In modern thinking about restorative justice, such approaches routinely comprise the three central actors of the victim, the offender, and the community (Zehr 1990). It views crime not as a violation of a general legal category but as harm to individual people and relationships and, as the term suggests, seeks to redress or restore that harm. Essentially, as Hudson has said, it focuses on 'changing the normative orientation of law from retribution to restoration' (Hudson 1998: 238).

Restorative justice approaches in various jurisdictions may differ but are often based on the following common aims: engaging with offenders to help them appreciate the consequences of their actions and the impact they have had on their victims; encouraging appropriate forms of reparation by offenders towards their victim, if they agree, or the wider community; seeking reconciliation between the victim and offender where possible, and the reintegration of the offender within the community. It is these broad aims of restorative justice which could effect considerable advantages for victims, offenders, and the wider community affected by sexual abuse which will be discussed further below.

Indeed, the term 'restorative justice' has been used to cover a variety of practices that seek to respond to crime in what is seen to be a more constructive way than through the use of conventional criminal justice approaches. The main variants include victim–offender mediation in the USA, UK, Germany, and Austria (Marshall 1991; Davis 1992; Umbreit 1994), family group conferencing in New Zealand and Australia (McElrea 1994; Retzinger and Scheff 1996; Morris and Maxwell 2000) and circles of support and accountability in Canada (Cesaroni 2001; Petrunik 2002; Silverman and Wilson 2002: 167–84; Wilson *et al.* 2002).

The first two of these measures, discussed elsewhere in this volume, bear some of the principal hallmarks of restorative justice practices. They offer an opportunity for all parties to meet on a voluntary basis supported by family, friends, and even the wider community; the victim is able to relate how their life has been impacted by the acts of the offender; in turn, the offender is able to reflect on what they hear, acknowledge the harm and pain they have caused, apologize for their actions and ultimately offer restitution. These measures, routinely confined to young offenders and less serious offences at present, could perhaps be employed within local communities where child sexual abuse has occurred. It is the third measure – circles of support and accountability – however, which is of particular relevance to reintegrative efforts with sex offenders and which arguably offers the greatest possibility for developing effective responses to child sexual abuse.

Circles of support and accountability

Although restorative schemes for sex offenders are in short supply, a few have been developed in Canada and parts of the United States which emphasize both treatment and reintegrative principles. In the United States, several states have developed dynamic ways of treating and supporting sexual offenders in the community (Knopp 1991: 191; Zehr 1995: 208). These include most notably 'The Safer Society Program' (Knopp 1991), and 'The Stop It Now Program.'

One of the most notable schemes is the 'Community Reintegration Project' provided by the Correctional Service of Canada which operates circles of support and accountability with selected sexual offenders who are considered at high risk of re-offending and who are re-entering the community on release from prison (Cesaroni 2001; Petrunik 2002: 503–5; Silverman and Wilson 2002: 167–84; Wilson *et al.* 2002).[2]

The scheme, which had its origins in the restorative work of the Canadian Mennonite Church, is based on the twin philosophies of safety and support – it operates as a means of addressing public concerns surrounding the reintegration of offenders and also the offender's needs in terms of rehabilitation. The scheme provides intensive support, guidance, and supervision for the offender, mediating between the police, media, and the general community to minimize risk and assist in reintegration.

The circle is focused on the development of a network of informal support and treatment built around the offender, the core member, involving the wider community in tandem with state and voluntary agencies. The circles consist of four to seven core members drawn from the local community, usually members of a church or religious faith group (Petrunik 2002: 504). This inner circle may also be supplemented by an outer circle consisting of police, social workers, and significant others such as family and friends who sit in occasionally as needed (Petrunik 2002: 504).

Once the circle is established, members are involved in assisting the offender with reintegration in a number of ways, from helping them find housing and employment to helping them change their attitudes and behavior and avoid situations that might lead to re-offending (Petrunik 2002: 504). In this respect, the offender and other members of the circle enter into a signed covenant which operates as a reintegrative plan of action and specifies each member's area of assistance. The circle confronts offenders about their deviant attitudes and behavior and holds them accountable to the community and their commitment not to re-offend. The offender in turn agrees to relate to the circle of support and accept its help and advice, to pursue a pre-determined course of treatment and to act responsibly in the community. The offender has contact with someone from the circle each day in the high-risk phase just after release. All members meet weekly to discuss any issues which may have arisen and need to be addressed. The life of a circle extends as long as the risk to the community and the offender are above average.

The research evidence available suggests that circles have used successfully with high-risk sex offenders. A recent evaluation of circles in Ontario found offenders receiving assistance via a circle re-offended at a lower rate incrementally in comparison with a matched control sample. In comparing the expected recidivism rate with the observed rate, recidivism was reduced by more than 50 per cent (Wilson *et al.* 2002: 378). Furthermore, from a harm reduction perspective, each incident of sexual recidivism was categorically less invasive and severe than the offence for which the offender had most recently been imprisoned (Wilson *et al.* 2002: 378).

Before outlining the possible benefits which such schemes could have in terms of constituting an effective response to child sexual abuse, there are a number of obvious caveats. First, as yet there are no long-itudinal studies available to establish with any certainty how effective these treatments are in terms of recidivism rates following participation in a program. Second, there are the logistical problems of ensuring suffi-

cient availability of programs with suitably qualified staff, and the monitoring and evaluation of programs which ensure genuine engagement on the part of the offender. The overwhelming positive aspect of these schemes, however, is the fact that they encourage and facilitate the treatment and reintegration of the offender and provide some level of engagement and truth for the parties about what has happened.

Restorative justice and child sexual abuse: addressing the critics

While differences and debates continue among proponents and practitioners of restorative justice, its general principles of providing restitution to victims and communities, promoting offender reintegration and repairing relationships between victims, offenders, and communities are well understood and increasingly accepted (Johnstone 2001; Sullivan and Tifft 2001; Braithwaite 2002; McEvoy *et al.* 2002).

However, the framework of restorative justice has not been without its critics. Many commentators are willing to accept its usefulness and viability for particular types of offences, usually low-level crime, and for particular classes of offenders, most notably first-time and young offenders (Johnstone 2003). However, these writers are usually less willing to extend the restorative paradigm to serious and persistent forms of offending. Moreover, these fears may seem even more compelling when we are concerned with the sexual abuse of children by intimates or others in a position of trust.

Proponents such as Barbara Hudson (1998, 2002), Allison Morris and Lorraine Gelsthorpe (Morris and Gelsthorpe 2000; Morris 2002), and Kathleen Daly (2000, 2002), among others, have significantly advanced the case for the application of restorative justice to sexual and violent (and racial) crime. These writers have addressed some of the traditional critiques concerning restorative justice as applied to 'hard' cases and how they can be overcome. They highlight what they perceive as the failings and inadequacies of the formal criminal justice system in responding to these types of offences and the greater potential of restorative justice for providing satisfactory outcomes for victims, offenders, and the community in more cases (Hudson 2002: 621).

This essay represents an attempt to extend this formative work in the area of domestic violence and adult sexual offences to child sexual abuse. It seeks to underline these supporting arguments, and address the key concerns put forward by the critics of restorative justice as applied to sexual offences. It ultimately argues that in fact child sexual abuse may be particularly apposite for a restorative approach.[3]

Indeed, Morris and Gelsthorpe have summarized the particular set of characteristics which underlie family violence which, they argue, seem to be perpetuated by the use of conventional criminal justice processes and which make it particularly suitable for a restorative approach. Although these comments were made in the context of domestic abuse, it is argued here that these could apply equally to victims of child sexual abuse:

> the existence of a prior relationship between the parties; the fact that the parties have lived together and may wish to continue living together; the likelihood of repeat victimisation; the context of emotional abuse and ongoing power imbalances in the relationship; the victim's fear of the offender; the secrecy of the violence; the isolation of the victim; and the offender's minimising of the seriousness of the violence.
>
> (2000: 421)

It is proposed to further discuss several of these elements as they apply to child sexual abuse and the potential difficulties which they pose for restorative approaches.

First, one of the major criticisms put forward against the use of restorative justice with sexual offences is that it may minimize or trivialize what are very serious criminal offences, particularly where children are concerned (Hudson 1998: 253; Morris and Gelsthorpe 2000: 417–8; Morris 2002: 603). Critics suggest that such offences are too grave or sensitive to be dealt with by means other than the traditional criminal justice system and that nothing should be done which might return them to the status of a 'private' matter.

The use of the restorative process, however, does not signify the decriminalization of sexual offences. The criminal law remains as a signifier and a denouncer but the belief within restorative processes is that the abuser's family, friends, and community are far more potent agents to achieve this objective of denunciation and of mobilizing censure (Morris and Gelsthorpe 2000: 418; Morris 2002: 603). In this way, restorative approaches also have the potential to engage the wider community and challenge community norms and values about what is acceptable behavior and to make sure that deviant sexual behavior is something which is strongly disapproved of (Hudson 1998: 250, 254; Morris and Gelsthorpe 2000: 418). In addition, as will be discussed further below, a system which makes provision for state intervention as the formal backdrop for more informal processes is clearly workable within the restorative framework.

A second concern is that restorative justice allows the offender to reject responsibility for the offence and is powerless to challenge the offender's attitudes (Morris and Gelsthorpe 2000: 417). However, most offenders are not made accountable for acts of abuse or rape against intimates (Braithwaite and Daly 1994: 191–2; Morris and Gelsthorpe 2000: 415). Research suggests that for every pedophile known to the police there are ten more not identified (Leggett 2000: 7). In addition, as mentioned at the outset, a high proportion of child victims –

figures suggest between 80 (Grubin 1998: 15) and 98 per cent (Leggett 2000: 7) – are abused by someone known to them rather than predatory strangers.[4] The possibility of a parent or other relative being labeled and singled out for public harassment and rejection may impede the sexually abused victim, particularly children, from coming forward in the first place and reporting the incident.

Restorative or reintegrative programs may ultimately help break cycles of abuse and help the offender to desist. If an offender knows that they may not face the possibility of a criminal prosecution or ultimately a prison sentence if they come forward, then more offenders may be willing to come out in the open, admit to their crimes and seek treatment. The availability of a restorative option may encourage more victims to come forward and report the offence. Increasing numbers of offenders, therefore, would be made accountable for their offences. This in turn could have the net result of reducing the incidence of child sexual abuse.

Moreover, those offenders who are arrested and prosecuted for sexual abuse against children may have ingrained patterns of abusing and assaulting the vulnerable which the criminal justice system does little to address (Braithwaite and Daly 1994: 191–2). The restorative process, however, provides an opportunity for early intervention and offers a way to engage the abuser and confront them about both the factors underlying their offending behavior and the consequences of offending, for the victim in particular (Morris 2002: 603). The offender is expected to accept responsibility for the abuse and techniques of neutralization can be challenged (Morris and Gelsthorpe 2000: 417). Contrition and apology, key elements in the restorative approach, may be part of the cycle of abuse. The difference in restorative processes is that the 'public' nature of that contrition and apology and the shared monitoring of subsequent events help

to ensure that it is 'real' (Morris and Gelsthorpe 2000: 417).

A third major criticism which is often put forward in this context is that many forms of sexual assault such as rape or child sexual abuse are about power and control. To confront the victim of a sexual offence with their offender may serve to reproduce and reinforce the imbalance of power entrenched in abusive relationships and lead to possible re-victimization (Hudson 1998: 247; Morris and Gelsthorpe 2000: 416–17). With children in particular there is the risk that the unequal power relationships between child victims and adult perpetrators of sexual offences may be further increased.

One could argue, however, that there is always a power imbalance between offenders and victims as offenders have 'taken' from victims (Morris and Gelsthorpe 2000: 424, n.18) and that it is the conventions of present formal criminal law and punishment which reproduce the power relations that produce violent and sexual crime (Hudson 1998: 249). Restorative justice processes and practices, however, routinely work towards removing this imbalance by focusing on the empowerment of victims.

Furthermore, with restorative justice the victim's perspective is made central to the proceedings whereas it is only a source of evidence in criminal cases (Hulsman 1991: 681; Hudson 1998: 248). Restorative processes could provide a forum in which the victim can make clear to the offender and their families and friends the affects of the abuse on them (Morris 2002: 608). Families and friends can also help to reduce the victim's feeling of isolation by providing a supportive basis for that voice to be heard. (Morris and Gelsthorpe 2000: 417). Offenders can also give victims some insight into the reasons for their offending. The personal experience of seeing that the offender is affected by a genuine feeling of remorse and shame should have a healing and restorative effect for the victim (Walgrave and Aersten 1996: 77).

A fourth and related criticism leveled against restorative justice in this context is that it may encourage victims to remain in abusive situations and cause repeat victimization. An implicit or underlying assumption when parties seek legal remedies is that where there was a relationship, it has broken down and contact is not desired (Morris and Gelsthorpe 2000: 419). However, as will be discussed below, this is not necessarily so when women are assaulted by their partners or children are abused by their parents. Indeed, a principal argument presented in support of the use of restorative processes with respect to child sexual abuse is that many children, for a range of reasons, wish to remain in or return to the family home and it is often desirable for them to do so (Hudson 2002: 622). By offering constructive rather than penal solutions, restorative processes may also be opted for at an earlier stage in children's experience of sexual abuse (Morris and Gelsthorpe 2000: 422).

Moreover, restorative justice may actually increase the safety of child victims (Morris and Gelsthorpe 2000: 422). As mentioned at the outset of this article, in debates about social ordering, the concept of risk increasingly furnishes a discursive framework within which 'responses-to-problems' are being considered (Beck 1992; Parton et al. 1997). The criminal justice system, however, at best protects children from sexual abuse by known offenders. Due to the hidden nature of child sexual abuse, it can do little to increase general victim safety and control the risk presented by unknown sex offenders in the community. Friends and families of the offender are equally well if not better placed than professionals to prevent the recurrence of abuse and to play a role in monitoring the offender's behavior and the victim's safety. Restorative justice processes directly involve them, in contrast to the exclusion intrinsic to criminal justice interventions.

This 'opening up' of knowledge and awareness on the part of the community is especially important when one considers that many sexual offenders are manipulative and devious by nature and will seek to infiltrate unsuspecting families. Many sexual offenders seek to 'groom' children for sexual purposes. Criminal justice interventions can do little to prevent this risk unless the offender has already come to their attention. Communities can, however, by arranging networks of support and control where necessary.

A fifth concern which has arisen is that restorative justice encourages vigilantism (Morris and Gelsthorpe 2000: 420) because of its association with community or popular justice. As Ashenden puts it '[t]he underside ... is the "danger" of ... vigilance turning into vigilante action' (2002: 203). As recent popular responses to sexual offending in the form of 'name and shame' campaigns clearly demonstrate, community justice can be repressive, retributive, and vengeful (Morris 2002: 609).[5] These values, however, are fundamentally at odds with the defining values of restorative justice and cannot, therefore, be part of it (Morris and Gelsthorpe 2000: 420).

On the other hand, the schemes which have developed thus far, albeit on an ad hoc basis, should inspire confidence that the community is capable of responding to delicate issues surrounding the reintegration of sexual offenders in the community in a responsible and constructive manner. Operating programs on the basis of a referral by statutory agencies will ensure the provision of adequate safeguards and standards (Ashworth 2002; Hudson 2002; Wright 2002), and that individuals who claim that their human rights have been infringed may be able to seek a direct remedy against a public authority under human rights principles. Formal law could stand behind restorative justice procedures as a guarantor of rights which cannot be overridden by decisions arrived at by consensus or majority (Hudson 1998: 256). As such, if there were concerns about communities taking over this process for non-restorative processes, checks could be introduced.

Furthermore, if properly operated and applied, restorative justice schemes may also provide a process of education and engagement for vigilante groups, as well as an opportunity for the wider community to approach the problem of managing sexual offenders in the community in a more considered way. Vengeful community attitudes often make the work of statutory and voluntary agencies in the resettlement of the offender extremely difficult. Restorative approaches, in this way, may serve to facilitate an effective partnership approach between the statutory, voluntary, and community sector in responding to contentious sexual offender issues.

From theory to practice: applying restorative justice to child sexual abuse

In relation to how such a system would work with respect to the present regulatory framework, some criminologists continue to emphasize the difference of the restorative justice vision as a paradigm shift in criminal law (Zehr 1990, 1995; Bazemore 1996; Barnett 2003; Walgrave 2003). Others, however, call for recognition of alternative forms of justice and highlight the compatibility of restoration and retribution. These two concepts may in fact be integrated as part of the same system of justice where they would complement and work in tandem with each other rather than operate as opposing or alternative systems (Zedner 1994; Levrant et al. 1999; Daly 2000; Duff 2002; Hudson 2002).[6]

There are two main possibilities as to how such a system could actually operate in practice. One is as an avenue to diversionary treatment. As an alternative to the traditional criminal justice system, sexual offenders would forego criminal prosecution in exchange for undergoing a treatment and

support program. The other main possibility is to prosecute all but the most minor sexual offences and then put this new system into operational effect after the convicted offender is released from prison. In this instance, it would operate as an addition rather than as an alternative to custody.

As outlined at the outset of this chapter, restorative approaches advocate that the opinion of victims and their families should be taken into account. There are two competing views which victims may have, however, which are difficult to reconcile in any system of justice. On the one hand, some victims of intra-familial abuse in common with domestic abuse victims may want to see the offender punished or vilified, but more commonly they simply want the abuse to stop (Carbonatto 1995, 1998; Hoyle 1998). On the other hand, for many other victims, particularly those who have been abused or assaulted by strangers, the victims of extra-familial abuse, the expressive functions of punishment in public and state condemnation of the offence are an important part of the healing and vindication process (Morris and Gelsthorpe 2000: 412; Hudson 2002: 622; Wright 2002: 664). In the latter instance, a diversionary scheme may unjustly release the offender from criminal prosecution. In the former instance, it may act as a powerful incentive to offenders coming forward to seek help.

In this respect, it is contended that the better approach would be one where restorative schemes were integrated within the current retributive framework and where they operated as an addition rather than as an alternative to custody (Hudson 2002). The offender would be prosecuted in the normal way and, if convicted, informal networks of treatment and support in the community would then be available on release from custody on the basis of a referral by a statutory criminal justice agency. Perhaps such schemes could be integrated into existing inter-agency risk assessment procedures where recommendations could be made about how to process the case and where the various agencies would agree a restorative response. Schemes could also be developed as part of the offender's program of supervision or treatment in the community and, in common with current arrangements, would address all aspects of the offender's life necessary for successful reintegration including finding suitable accommodation and employment, and not just their abusive behavior.

The participation of victims and offenders, however, must be voluntary and either party should have the right to opt out of the process at any stage. To force victims to participate would lead to further victimization and disempowerment. To force offenders to participate in programs may be futile, since the research evidence suggests that the effectiveness of interventions is often increased when offenders become involved voluntarily (McIvor 1992; McGuire 1995).[7]

Conclusion

It seems appropriate to conclude this piece by returning to the initial question posed at the outset – are there limits to restorative justice in the case of child sexual abuse? I have argued here that there is nothing in principle that would appear to limit restorative justice to less serious forms of offending and deliberately prohibit it from being applied to more serious and persistent forms of offending, like child sexual abuse. In fact, there is a growing recognition that a purely punitive response, as represented by the current traditional criminal justice system, is no longer sufficient for these types of offences. There is a real need, therefore, to examine other forms of justice in order to develop a more progressive and holistic response to the problem. Such a response would address not just the punishment and control of the offender but also their rehabilitation and reintegration, while at the same time safeguarding the welfare of chil-

dren and addressing the concerns of the wider community.

Some may feel that child sexual abuse is inappropriate, unsuitable, or too delicate an area within which to use a restorative response and may criticize these arguments as naive and somewhat utopian. Restorative programs may not be appropriate for all abusers but they may provide an effective alternative for low-to-middle risk offenders when operated on a voluntary basis. Restorative justice does not have all the answers. However, in the absence of workable alternatives there is a need to extend the use of restorative justice to the most difficult of society's problems. It has been used, for instance, in the Truth and Reconciliation Commissions of South Africa (Villa Vincenzo 1999) and Rwanda (Drumbl 2000) with respect to genocide, mass torture, and rape. Surely, despite the concerns of critics, the fuller extension of this paradigm to child sexual abuse at least merits careful consideration.

References

Abel, G. G, Becker, J. V., Mittleman, M. S., Rouleau, J. L. and Murphy, W. (1987) 'Self-reported sex crimes of non-incarcerated paraphiliacs,' *Journal of Interpersonal Violence*, 2(1): 3–25.

Ashenden, S. (2002) 'Policing perversion: the contemporary governance of paedophilia,' *Cultural Values*, 6(1): 197–122.

— (2004) *Governing Child Sexual Abuse: negotiating the boundaries of public and private, law and science*, London: Routledge.

Ashworth, A. (2002) 'Responsibilities, rights and restorative justice,' *British Journal of Criminology*, 42(3): 578–95.

Barnett, R. E. (2003) 'Restitution: a new paradigm of criminal justice' in G. Johnstone (ed.) *A Restorative Justice Reader: texts, sources, context*, Cullompton, Devon: Willan Publishing.

Bazemore, G. (1996) 'Three paradigms for juvenile justice,' in B. Galaway and J. Hudson (eds) *Restorative Justice: international perspectives*, Monsey, NY: Criminal Justice Press.

Beck, U. (1992) *Risk Society: towards a new modernity*, London: Sage.

Boyes-Watson, C. (1999) 'In the belly of the beast? Exploring the dilemmas of state-sponsored restorative justice,' *Contemporary Justice Review*, 2(3): 261–81.

Braithwaite, J. (2000) 'The new regulatory state and the transformation of criminology,' *British Journal of Criminology*, 40(2): 222–38.

— (2002) *Restorative Justice and Response Regulation*, Oxford: Oxford University Press.

Braithwaite, J. and Daly, K. (1994) 'Masculinities, violence and communitarian control,' in T. Newburn and E. Stanko (eds) *Just Boys Doing Business? Men, masculinity and crime*, London: Routledge.

Carbonatto, H. (1995) *Expanding Intervention Options for Spousal Abuse: the use of restorative justice*, Occasional Papers in Criminology New Series No. 4, Wellington, New Zealand: Institute of Criminology, Victoria University of Wellington.

— (1998) 'The criminal justice response to domestic violence in New Zealand,' *Criminology New Zealand* (a newsletter from the Institute of Criminology, Victoria University of Wellington), 10: 7–8.

Cesaroni, C. (2001) 'Releasing sex offenders into the community through "circles of support" – a means of reintegrating the "worst of the worst",' *Journal of Offender Rehabilitation*, 34(2): 85–98.

Daly, K. (2000) 'Revisiting the relationship between retributive and restorative justice,' in J. Braithwaite and H. Strang (eds) *Restorative Justice: philosophy to practice*, Aldershot: Ashgate.

— (2002) 'Sexual assault and restorative justice,' in H. Strang and J. Braithwaite (eds) *Restorative Justice and Family Violence*, Melbourne: Cambridge University Press.

Davis, G. (1992) *Making Amends: mediation and reparation in criminal justice*, London and New York: Routledge.

Drumbl, M. (2000) 'Sclerosis: retributive justice and the Rwandan genocide,' *Punishment and Society*, 2(3): 287–308.

Duff, A. (2002) 'Restorative punishment and punitive restoration,' in L. Walgrave (ed.) *Restorative Justice and the Law*, Cullompton, Devon: Willan Publishing.

Ericson, R. V. and Haggerty, K. D. (1997) *Policing the Risk Society*, Oxford: Clarendon Press.

Falshaw, L., Friendship, C. and Bates, A. (2003) *Sexual Offenders – Measuring Reconviction, Reoffending and Recidivism*, Home Office Research Findings No. 183, London: Home Office.

Feeley, M. and Simon, J. (1992) 'The new penology: notes on the emerging strategy of corrections and its implications,' *Criminology*, 30(4): 449–74.

— (1994) 'Actuarial justice: the emerging new criminal law,' in D. Nelken (ed.) *The Futures of Criminology*, London: Sage.

Finstad, L. (1990) 'Sexual offenders out of prison: principles for a realistic utopia,' *International Journal of the Sociology*, 18(2): 157–77.

Friendship, C. and Thornton, D. (2001) 'Sexual reconvictions for sexual offenders discharged from prison in England and Wales: implications for evaluating treatment,' *British Journal of Criminology*, 41(2): 285–92.

Groth, A. N., Longo, R. E. and McFadin, J. B. (1982) 'Undetected recidivism among rapists and child molesters,' *Crime and Delinquency*, 28(3): 450–8.

Grubin, D. (1998) *Sex Offending Against Children: understanding the risk*, Police Research Series Paper 99, London: Home Office, Policing and Reducing Crime Unit, RDS Directorate.

Herman, J. (1997) *Trauma and Recovery*, New York: Basic Books.

Hoyle, C. (1998) *Negotiating Domestic Violence: police, criminal justice and victims*, Oxford: Oxford University Press.

Hudson, B. (1998) 'Restorative justice: the challenge of sexual and racial violence,' *Journal of Law and Society*, 25(2): 237–56.

— (2002) 'Restorative justice and gendered violence: diversion or effective justice?' *British Journal of Criminology*, 42(3): 616–34.

Hulsman, L. (1991) 'The abolitionist case: alternative crime policies,' *Israeli Law Review*, 25(3–4): 681–709.

Jackson, S. and Scott, S. (1999) 'Risk anxiety and the social construction of childhood,' in D. Lupton (ed.) *Risk and Sociocultural Theory: new directions and perspectives*, Cambridge: Cambridge University Press.

Johnstone, G. (2001) *Restorative Justice: ideas, values, debates*, Cullompton, Devon: Willan Publishing.

— (2003) *A Restorative Justice Reader: texts, sources, context*, Cullompton, Devon: Willan Publishing.

Kemshall, H., and Maguire, M. (2003) 'Sex offenders, risk penality and the problem of disclosure,' in A. Matravers (ed.) *Sex Offenders in the Community: managing and reducing the risks*, Cambridge Criminal Justice Series, Cullompton, Devon: Willan Publishing.

Knopp, F. H. (1991) 'Community solutions to sexual violence,' in H. E. Pepinsky and R. Quinney (eds) *Criminology as Peacemaking*, Bloomington: Indiana University Press.

Leggett, S. (2000) 'Paedophiles and other child abusers,' *The Ulster Humanist*, 5(11): 7–8.

Levrant, S., Cullen, F. T., Fulton, B. and Wozniak, J. F. (1999) 'Reconsidering restorative justice: the corruption of benevolence revisited?' *Crime and Delinquency*, 45(1): 3–27.

McAlinden, A. (2005) 'The use of shame with sexual offenders,' *British Journal of Criminology*, 45(3): 373–94.

McElrea, F. W. M. (1994) 'Justice in the community: the New Zealand experience,' in J. Burnside and N. Baker (eds) *Relational Justice: repairing the breach*, Winchester: Waterside Press.

McEvoy, K., Mika, H. and Hudson, B. (2002) 'Introduction: practice, performance and prospects for restorative justice,' *British Journal of Criminology*, 42(3): 469–75.

McGuire, J. (1995) *What Works: reducing re-offending?* Chichester: John Wiley.

McIvor, G. (1992) *Sentenced to Serve?* Aldershot: Gower.

Marshall, T. (1991) *Victim–Offender Mediation*, Home Office Research Bulletin No. 30, London: HMSO.

Matravers, A. (ed.) (2003) *Sex Offenders in the Community: managing and reducing the risks*, Cambridge Criminal Justice Series, Cullompton, Devon: Willan Publishing.

Mills, L. (2003) *Insult to Injury: rethinking our responses to intimate abuse*, Princeton, NJ: Princeton University Press.

Morris, A. (2002) 'Critiquing the critics: a brief response to critics of restorative justice,' *British Journal of Criminology*, 42(3): 596–615.

Morris, A. and Gelsthorpe, L. (2000) 'Re-visioning men's violence against female partners,' *The Howard Journal*, 39(4): 412–28.

Morris, A. and Maxwell, G. (2000) 'The practice of family group conferences in New Zealand: assessing the place, potential and pitfalls of restorative justice,' in A. Crawford and J. Goodey (eds) *Integrating a Victim Perspective in Criminal Justice*, Aldershot: Ashgate.

Parton, N., Thorpe, D. and Wattam, C. (1997) *Child Protection: risk and the moral order*, Hampshire: Macmillan.

Petrunik, M. G. (2002) 'Managing unacceptable risk: sex offenders, community response, and social policy in the United States and Canada,' *International Journal of Offender Therapy and Comparative Criminology*, 46(4): 483–511.

Retzinger, S. M. and Scheff, T. J. (1996) 'Strategy for community conferences: emotions and social bonds,' in J. Hudson and B. Galaway (eds) *Restorative Justice: international perspectives*, Monsey, NY: Criminal Justice Press.

Salter, A. (2003) *Predators, Pedophiles, Rapists, and Other Sex Offenders: who they are, how they operate, and how we can protect ourselves and our children*, New York: Basic Books.

Shearing, C. (2000) 'Punishment and the changing face of governance,' *Punishment and Society*, 3(2): 203–20.

Silverman, J. and Wilson, D. (2002) *Innocence Betrayed: paedophilia, the media and society*, Cambridge: Polity Press.

Sullivan, D. and Tifft, L. (2001) *Restorative Justice: healing the foundations of our everyday lives*, Monsey, NY: Willow Tree Press.

Umbreit, M. (1994) *Victim Meets the Offender: the impact of restorative justice and mediation*, Monsey, NY: Criminal Justice Press.

Villa Vincenzo, C. (1999) 'A different kind of justice: the South African Truth and Reconciliation Commission,' *Contemporary Justice Review*, 1(4): 403–28.

Walgrave, L. (2003) 'Imposing restoration instead of inflicting pain,' in A. Von Hirsch, J. V. Roberts, A. E. Bottoms, K. Roach and M. Schiff (eds) *Restorative Justice and Criminal Justice: competing or reconcilable paradigms?* Oxford: Hart Publishing.

Walgrave, L. and Aersten, A. (1996) 'Reintegrative shaming and restorative justice: interchangeable, complementary or different?' *European Journal of Criminal Policy and Research*, 4(4): 67–85.

Wilson, R. J., Huculak, B. and McWhinnie, A. (2002) 'Restorative justice innovations in Canada,' *Behavioural Sciences and the Law*, 20(4): 363–80.

Wright, M. (2002) 'The court as last resort,' *British Journal of Criminology*, 42(3): 654–67.

Zedner, L. (1994) 'Reparation and retribution: are they reconcilable?' *Modern Law Review*, 57(2): 228–50.

Zehr, H. (1990) *Changing Lenses: a new focus for crime and justice*, Scottdale, PA: Herald Press.

—— (1995) 'Justice paradigm shift? values and vision in the reform process,' *Mediation Quarterly*, 12(3): 207–16.

Notes

1. Recorded crime statistics show that the total number of recorded sexual offences has increased by 9.6 per cent in the period 1999/ 2000 to 2001/2002 and by 94.4 per cent in the last twenty-five years (*Recorded Crime Statistics: 1898–2001/02*, available at: http://www. homeoffice.gov.uk/rds/pdfs/100years.xls).

2. Similar arrangements, in the form of 'intimate abuse circles' have recently been proposed in relation to domestic violence (Mills 2003).

3. For a recent discussion of these arguments in the context of reintegrative shaming in particular, see McAlinden (2005).

4. As Jackson and Scott (1999: 92–3) point out, media coverage of the risks posed by adults to children tends to 'reverse the order of danger' in that so-called 'stranger danger' is given more media coverage than cases of assault upon children by intimates.

5. These campaigns have been particularly evident in England and Wales where local communities have protested at the presence of pedophiles living in their community and the failure of the authorities to notify them of their whereabouts.

6. Some restorative justice commentators, however, have argued that in fact restorative justice systems are corroded by their partnership with a retributive framework within the criminal justice system (Boyes-Watson 1999).

7. Although non-coercive practice is often cited as one of the key principles which underpin restorative practices, there is an increasing honesty within restorative thinking that coercion is never truly absent from restorative processes. If an individual is given the choice between a sentence of imprisonment or engagement in a restorative program, it is a fallacy to say that this does not involve at least some element of latent coercion.

21

Restoring justice through forgiveness

The case of children in Northern Ireland

*Anthony C. Holter, Joseph Martin
and Robert D. Enright*

Ten years ago, we were chatting with an attorney who was interested in both ideas of forgiveness, as they were emerging in the social sciences, and the ideas surrounding the restorative justice movement, as they were emerging in the study of law. In his enthusiasm, the attorney presented a paper on the interplay of forgiveness and social justice at a national conference. He came back from that conference stoop-shouldered and embarrassed. His talk did not go well. A prominent lawyer came up to him after that talk and said, 'Forgiveness? Don't you know that the "f" in that word stands for "folly"? Forgiveness has no place in the field of restorative justice.' Surely, that harsh opinion was not the only one extant in the field but it was a view not isolated to a few. Perhaps times have changed.

A decade is a long time in the scholarly world. Perhaps times, indeed, have changed in that forgiveness is more acceptable in the fields of social science and law. In our view, there is no reason why forgiveness should not be accepted as a viable part of the healing process for victims and even offenders. Aristotle, in his wisdom, suggested that no virtue should be practiced in isolation. In other words, justice and forgiveness need each other to keep one another, shall we

say, honest. Justice without mercy and forgiveness can be cold and distant. Forgiveness without justice may be weak and misunderstood. Together, they may offer a warm-hearted justice and a mercy that does not become a doormat.

In our studies of forgiveness, going back to 1985, we have come to understand the following: (a) forgiveness is an internal process by the one wronged in that he or she reduces resentment and offers beneficence to the wrongdoer; (b) in doing so, the forgiver is neither condoning nor excusing the behavior, but instead is offering a gift of mercy to that wrongdoer; (c) when one forgives, one can and should seek justice; (d) a person who forgives need not reconcile with an offender who insists on continuing with abusive ways. This latter point diffuses many criticisms of forgiveness (see Enright and Fitzgibbons 2000).

We further have come to two impressions that have guided our work. First, when people are faced with horrendous wrongdoing, true justice and genuine reconciliation are rarely if ever possible without forgiveness being a part of the healing process. This is so because underlying anger can thwart the best peace plans. Reduced anger makes the glimmer of hope possible and can play a part over time in the restoration of trust. Forgiveness when taught well can reduce anger (Enright *et al.* 2001). So, while forgiveness by itself does not restore justice, it is a valuable player in the process because it targets anger, one underlying cause of keeping people apart and fighting.

Second, when a *community*, not just a small group of individuals within that community, is faced with entrenched and deep injustices, we think that the promise of a restored justice is more probable when forgiveness is taught to children in particular. We say this because adults who have grown up with violence and injustice are more difficult to change than are children. After all, adults on different sides of violent conflicts in such historically violent communities as Kosovo, Belfast, and Jerusalem grow up with decidedly different histories of what happened to create the societal divide. Prejudice and hatred, we find, are rather easily learned but difficult to ameliorate. Prejudice and hatred together make civil interaction difficult. Yet, forgiveness can reduce such caustic emotions as resentment, hatred, and anger. If we start when children are quite young, we have a better chance of reducing the intensity of the prejudice and anger and of giving the children a tool, forgiveness, for combating these emotions later in life. Armed with the tool of forgiveness, these children, when it is their turn to lead and navigate through the community, may do so with greater mercy and civility than their forebears. It is for these reasons that we have turned our attention in our forgiveness studies to children within violent communities.

The purpose of this article is to introduce the reader to our recent work in Belfast, Northern Ireland, where we have been doing forgiveness education work in elementary school classrooms since the fall of 2002. We will first briefly review the published literature on the psychology of forgiveness, then turn to a brief discussion of how violence impacts children's emotional health. We next turn to a discussion of the

Northern Ireland problem and the place of forgiveness within the Belfast community in particular. We end with a call to action centered on forgiveness education, alongside a quest for justice, in war-torn communities.

Research on forgiveness and mental health

In the early 1990s we began to offer forgiveness education programs to people who have experienced considerable injustice. For example, we worked with elderly women hurt in a variety of ways by family members (Hebl and Enright 1993), incest survivors (Freedman and Enright 1996), men hurt by the abortion decision of the partner (Coyle and Enright 1997), adolescents whose parent was emotionally distant (Al-Mabuk *et al.* 1995), adolescents at-risk for academic failure because of excessive anger (Gambaro 2002), and people in drug rehabilitation (Lin *et al.* 2004). In each of these cases, we used a randomized, experimental and control group design with follow-up testing once the program was over. In each case, forgiveness successfully lowered unhealthy levels of negative emotions such as anger, anxiety, and/or depression.

For our work with children in Northern Ireland, critical among the reported findings is that forgiveness reduces anger. Evidence suggests that anger interferes with adequate solutions of the two main developmental tasks of childhood: establishing positive peer relationships (Sullivan 1953; Price and Dodge 1989) and achieving academically (Gambaro 2002; Pekrun *et al.* 2002). Anger is also linked to aggression in general and in particular to 'reactive' aggression (Price and Dodge 1989; Zeman *et al.* 2002). 'Reactive' aggression involves responding with hostility and defensiveness to another's behavior. It can be contrasted with 'proactive' aggression, which is unprovoked. The data show that children who demonstrate 'reactive' aggression are at-risk for poor peer relationships and a variety of other social and psychological problems (Price and Dodge 1989). Of course, if such patterns of reactive aggression follow the child into adulthood, then he or she is at-risk for being a perpetrator of injustice, especially if the community already is at war. Although less well documented, some evidence suggests that anger may be negatively related to learning and academic achievement (Gambaro 2002; Pekrun *et al.* 2002), which is associated with quality of life as an adult.

Our review of the literature and our subsequent theory suggest that forgiveness reduces anger, and that a decrease in anger will lead to more positive social behavior and academic achievement and to less depression and anxiety. This chain of events is proposed based on several sources of evidence. First, Enright and Fitzgibbons (2000) reviewed the empirical and clinical data on forgiveness and mental health and concluded that anger reduction was the key component of forgiveness' beneficial impact on mental health. Second, some correlational data show that children's problems with anger regulation in particular predict negative internalizing symptoms. In fact, *anger regulation* better predicts internal psychological health than difficulties with regulating sadness, suggesting that when a person experiences co-morbid negative emotional states, anger may be the primary one (Zeman *et al.* 2002). These various strands of evidence suggest that a reduction in anger in particular could be a key to the successful navigation of appropriate developmental tasks in childhood and better adjustment in adulthood. As we will see next, and not surprisingly, children who live in violent communities do not fare well from an emotional standpoint.

Terrorism, community violence and mental health

In areas of the world where terrorism and community violence are common, psycho-logical and emotional distress are often outcomes for those who experience such trauma. Children are especially at risk because trauma experienced at a young age may affect developing neurological systems. This may create neuropsychological vulnerability for children exposed to trauma that adults may not experience (Perry and Pollard 1998). Untreated, this damage can impact a child's development throughout the life course. Unfortunately, psychological vulnerability is not the only outcome of living in a violent community. In Northern Ireland (NI) alone, children who experienced 'The Troubles' during the most violent period, in the 1970s and 1980s, experienced increased psychosomatic and behavioral problems, such as asthma, sleep problems, and stuttering. These problems are linked to anxiety from exposure to violence (Fraser 1974). Curran and Miller (2001) found that in NI, children's exposure to conflict and violence increased levels of post traumatic stress disorder (PTSD) symptomology, mood disorders, behavioral problems, and academic struggles. Children who were exposed to the community violence, or had even just heard about it were found to have increased levels of depression, PTSD symptoms, anger, anxiety, and sleep problems (Fletcher 1996).

Experiencing the conflict firsthand is not the only way children can be impacted by the violence. In Oklahoma City, children who were exposed to media attention of the federal building bombing and did not know a victim reported comparable levels of PTSD symptomology as did those who lost a parent or sibling (Pfefferbaum *et al.* 1999). Back in NI, children have been shown to absorb trauma-related vulnerability from parents who experienced violence (Harkness 1993; Baranowsky *et al.* 1998).

The relationship between the exposure to terrorism and community violence and adverse psychological outcomes is moderated by other variables closer to the child, such as family and school. Research suggests that children from supportive families are less likely to show the negative effects of violence than those children who do not have supportive families (Gorman-Smith and Tolan 1998; Kliewer *et al.* 1998). Another moderating factor, school-related variables, has been shown to be effective in the resiliency literature and empirical studies (Roeser *et al.* 1998; Botcheva *et al.* 2002). School-based programs, caring adults, and stable environments are all factors from schools that can help children overcome tragedies.

The specific case of Northern Ireland

In Northern Ireland, the conflicting political and religious differences between Protestant and Catholic groups have existed for hundreds of years, yet the ramifications of this centuries-old conflict are palpable today (Kee 1995; Connolly *et al.* 2002). These political and religious tensions in Northern Ireland have become known as The Troubles, and reached a pinnacle in the 1970s and early 1980s. Although often referred to in terms of religious differences, The Troubles are in actuality a complex combination of idyllic and pragmatic differences. At the center of these differences are issues of self-governance, political representation, economic independence, and freedom. Each of these components is deeply connected to a history of war and conflict.

The multi-faceted conflict known as The Troubles is made even more stark by the physical, sectarian separation of the two groups throughout the city. Some Protestant and Catholic neighborhoods are demarked with brightly colored flags and political paintings known as murals, which can divide communities located within blocks of each other on the same street (Rolston 1991; 1994; 1998). In some areas, these divergent communities are further divided by what is known as 'the peace wall,' a large

wall designed and built to separate Catholic and Protestant communities and keep at least a tentative peace.

These divided neighborhoods effectively became war-zones, patrolled by clandestine soldiers of political and religious armies such as the IRA (Irish Republican Army), the UDA (Ulster Defence Association) and several other paramilitary groupings. At the height of The Troubles, car bombs, kidnapping, and random shootings were the military-like tactics employed to express power and instill fear (Kee 1995; Geraghty 1998; Power and Duffy 2001). These tactics are what Gurwitch *et al.* define as terrorism – violent strategies designed to kill and intimidate (2002).

Since this centuries-old conflict is often simplified into a war-like conflict between two divergent groups – Catholic and Protestant – it is not at all surprising that deep inter-group conflict, prejudice, and bias have developed. Such group bias and inter-group conflict is especially evident in Belfast during the Marching Season, a time during the summer in which participants parade through neighborhood streets to display and celebrate sectarian colors, flags, and heritage. Enright *et al.* (2003) report that incidents of disorder at these parades have increased significantly from 2000 to 2001 which is indicative of a trend toward increased expression of and exposure to violence.

Research regarding the inter-group conflict between Catholics and Protestants in Northern Ireland indicates that attitudes and habits of prejudice and bias based on religious affiliation are evident in children as young as three years old (Connolly *et al.* 2002). Furthermore, the children's ability to identify and make judgments based upon religiously significant items such as colors and names sharply increases with their age (Connolly *et al.* 2002). Clearly these three-year-old children are not developing an acute sense of out-group bias without some influence from their immediate surroundings such as their parents, siblings, relatives, and other community members. These prejudiced and biased expressions tend to increase and escalate, sometimes to physical violence, when groups with intense outgroup bias encounter members of the other group.

One of the most disturbing expressions of this inter-group conflict and out-group bias happened only a few years ago at Holy Cross Girls' School. Located in what the local community calls an 'interface' or a 'flashpoint' area (a neighborhood of intense sectarian conflict due in part to the close proximity of the groups), Holy Cross Girls' School and its students were the target of a prolonged protest and severe expressions of violence. Primary school girls were met with verbal abuse and obscenities, taunted with whistle blowing and banging of trash lids, and attacked with rocks and bags of urine (Doyle 2004; Walker 2001). As Protestant children and parents lined the streets, even barricading the entrance of the school, the Catholic schoolgirls 'wept with fear while clinging on to their parents' (Walker 2001: 5). These young girls were terrorized over a period of days and weeks as they walked to and from school each day; not because of something they had done, but because of their religious identity. What lessons are these precious children learning about justice and its restoration before they even enter a classroom? We should note that because the two sides in this conflict have two decidedly different histories, the description above is likely to be disputed by some who were there and have created their own version of the incident.

Unfortunately, such intense expressions of sectarian prejudice and out-group bias are not uncommon. Furthermore, such incidents are not exclusively associated with one group or another. Both Protestant and Catholic groups alike have participated in such disturbing violations of human rights and social justice.

Enright et al. (2003) report that although terrorist threats and attacks such as those described above are not as common today as they once were in Northern Ireland, violence associated with The Troubles persists. Citing a report from the Police Service of Northern Ireland, Enright et al. state that incidents of bombing, personal attacks, and kidnappings have all increased significantly in the last decade (2003). Direct exposure to such violence, even the threat or potentiality of violence, can have a profound and long-lasting impact on a child's mental health and personal well-being. Enright et al. (2003) also note that, although some studies claim adults have successfully coped with their experience of The Troubles, 'people directly exposed to violence were clearly at risk for PTSD' (Loughrey et al. 1993).

Therefore, it is not surprising that an experience of terrorism and violence stemming from, but not limited to, The Troubles would negatively impact an individual's psychological, emotional, and relational well-being. Furthermore, individuals who suffer from emotional and psychological difficulties as a result of direct experience with violence and other social injustices are at risk of perpetuating the very system of fear, inter-group conflict, and violence that has so unfairly afflicted them. Unless these beleaguered people are afforded an opportunity to confront the harm done to them, and empowered to work through their pain toward hope and a new vision of justice, there is danger that fear and terror will deny future generations of peace and reconciliation.

Centuries of conflict, violence, and social injustice have created a pressing need for healing, peace and justice: a restoration and rebuilding of relationships. The Troubles have affected and continue to affect people in significant ways. Therefore, in areas such as Belfast, Northern Ireland, where centuries of conflict have created systems of injustice that tear at the integrity and well-being of its

315

community members, any discussion of restorative justice must *begin* with the individual.

Forgiveness education is a journey whereby individuals begin the process of emotional and psychological wellness that is necessary if community restorative justice efforts are to be fruitful. Identifying and managing anger, developing a new understanding of the future by reframing the past, and preparing hearts for compassion instead of hate are just some of the fundamental steps of forgiveness that prepare and empower individuals to proactively seek answers to the difficult questions of restorative justice.

The place of forgiveness education in Northern Ireland

Because violence and the threat of violence have existed in Northern Ireland for centuries, with a particular psychological danger for youth, forgiveness education may be one antidote to the anger and resentment that often follow the violence. Introducing forgiveness to the school children of Belfast may combat anger, anxiety, and depression that can emerge when children are exposed to war. By starting with the young generation just beginning school, forgiveness education can help to end the cycle of further violence that continues to be an issue in the area. If these children grow up with the tools to forgive and better understand those who hurt them, they may be able to pass on these tools to the generation that follows them.

Forgiveness takes time to learn because it is filled with subtleties (it is not the same as excusing, condoning, forgetting, or reconciling). Curricula geared to children must be carefully written with an eye toward developmental changes as the students mature through the grade levels. Parents and teachers must start slowly with young children and introduce only those concepts that the children can understand at a given age level.

Forgiveness education was first offered to schools in Belfast, NI, in the fall of 2002. The ten schools involved in the intervention were situated in areas made up almost entirely of either Catholics or Protestants only. Some of the schools were targets of violence in past years and in the present year.

Beginning in first grade (Primary 3 in NI) children are exposed to the ideas of forgiveness in a manner complicit with their cognitive development (Knutson *et al.* 2002). Through a manualized intervention for primary school children, a particular aspect of social-cognitive development is targeted: reframing (through role-taking, learning about the wrongdoer by viewing him or her in context). This is done to help the child learn and understand that all people, even those that hurt others, have worth. Children are taught about inherent worth of all people and to act on this insight by displaying the ethical qualities of moral love (acting more out of concern for the well-being of another), kindness, respect, and/or generosity to those around them, including the ones who have hurt them. These five foundations (reframing for inherent worth, moral love, kindness, respect, and generosity) are the focus of the first-grade program.

The first-grade forgiveness curriculum has three parts. In Part 1, we do not yet mention forgiveness but only introduce the children to the five foundations (see above paragraph) that will underlie forgiveness. For example, the teacher reads the Dr Seuss story *Horton Hears a Who*, in which the kindly elephant, Horton, tries to save an entire world of Whos, existing on a small flower. The other jungle animals, unable to see or hear the Whos, want to destroy them. Horton gently protests with his moral lesson that 'a person's a person, no matter how small.' The children then begin to learn the inherent worth of all people, even the small, or disabled, or poor, or even those with different religious affiliations. It should be noted that the first-grade curriculum never asks the children to confront The Troubles because, from a developmental framework, they are not yet ready for this type of complex thinking.

In Part 2 of the curriculum, the children again learn the five foundations (inherent worth, moral love, kindness, respect, and generosity) by examining how *story characters* have appropriated each foundation in forgiving a wrongdoer. Finally, in Part 3, the children apply their learning by trying, if they choose, to forgive someone while using the moral tools of inherent worth, moral love, kindness, respect, and generosity.

Throughout the curriculum, the teachers make the important distinction between learning *about* forgiveness and choosing *to practice it* in certain contexts. Children are always free to try or not try forgiveness in response to their own personal hurts. The child's own classroom teacher delivers the curriculum, to insure cultural and religious sensitivity regarding the nuances of forgiveness.

The forgiveness curriculum asks the teachers to balance the learning of forgiveness with the learning of fairness. For example, the children are taught that they might consider forgiving a bully but then not reconcile if that bully remains entrenched in aggressive behavior. The children are taught that when they forgive, they still must protect themselves and seek help from adults when there is danger. The curriculum asks the children to become sophisticated enough to think of forgiveness and justice existing side by side. Too often we find that adults erroneously think in either–or terms about these moral virtues: either I can forgive and let fairness go, or I must be tough and seek justice without offering forgiveness. The curriculum corrects this.

Each year, the effectiveness of the program is evaluated with psychometrically sound instruments given to the children and teachers as well as with direct observation of the children's interactions.

Impact of forgiveness in Belfast, Northern Ireland

At the end of the first year of the intervention, children who participated in the forgiveness education showed greater decreases in anger than did the children who did not participate. The angriest children who had the forgiveness curriculum decreased the most in anger. The participating children were less depressed than were the children who did not participate in the program. Finally, children who received the forgiveness curriculum ignored one another less and participated in more friendly behavior than did the children who did not receive the curriculum.

In the following years, the curriculum was offered to the children who did not receive it the first year. The first-grade curriculum was also given to more schools, and a second-grade and third-grade curriculum were designed and used in the schools.

Vision for the future

Communities that emphasize and exacerbate interpersonal and inter-group conflict necessarily dispose children within those systems to developmental difficulties. These developmental difficulties have the potential of diminishing the child's quality of life and of perpetuating systems of injustice, intolerance, and violence. We are hopeful that communities dedicated to peace and justice can have an equally powerful, pervasive, and positive influence on the healthy development of young children. Our vision and mission is to equip the youngest members of society with the necessary skills and processes to break the cycle of systemic injustice, and to promote personal well-being, peace, and justice.

Of course, we do not expect six- and seven-year-old primary school students to be perfect forgivers. Surely, forgiveness is difficult enough for adults to comprehend and express. However, we begin forgiveness education at an early age so that the students may begin practicing and refining those fundamental skills necessary for future expressions of forgiveness. We challenge them to practice compassion and forgiveness within the school and family contexts. We help them see that people have value and worth no matter how big or popular or Catholic or Protestant they may be. We assist them as they seek to identify and manage their emotions. The forgiveness education curriculum begins with the five foundations of forgiveness and builds incrementally toward a mature understanding and practice of forgiveness.

As these children progress through primary and secondary school, they will be encouraged to put their forgiveness knowledge into practice, to incorporate what they know about forgiveness into their relationships with friends, family, and throughout their communities. These same children who use forgiveness in their daily lives to overcome feelings of anger after deep hurt or injustice, and as a lens to better understand the world around them, will be better equipped to stand up for peace and to demand justice than if they were to succumb to the fear and violence that permeates their communities now.

What then is the goal of forgiveness education; what is the vision? The forgiveness education initiative in Belfast, Northern Ireland, aims to 'improve the mental health of the youngest generation of Belfast … targeting those reactions to interpersonal hurt that contribute to less-than-optimal mental health and probably are also proximal causes of interpersonal violence' (Enright *et al.* 2003: 51). Simply put, forgiveness is a tool of justice in that it provides children an opportunity to experience healthy development and to live well together with others. Forgiveness is more than an isolated event or series of actions. It is an outlook on the world, a framework for understanding human interaction. A student

of forgiveness is a person who is able to identify those thoughts and emotions of anger and resentment naturally associated with experiences of deep hurt and injustice, and to transform them into kindness, compassion, and love.

In our view, the concept of restorative justice is one of the most important paradigm shifts ever to happen for any society. This is so because the model challenges all of us to create a justice system that is 'warmer' than before. It challenges us to pay attention to the people who are personally wounded, not only to those who wound and to the state that has a claim against them. Because restorative justice asks much of a society in terms of new thinking and new acting within the justice system, then much will be demanded of those who work for restorative justice. Those seeking to plant restorative justice within societies must now be challenged themselves. The folly of forgiveness must be brought into the light and examined. If the restorative justice seeker truly is interested in the wounded, then how will the wounds of resentment and hatred be mended without forgiveness? How can forgiveness work alongside justice if we keep hiding it in the basement's corner? Is it not time to give forgiveness its due, together with the new forms of justice-seeking? A fuller, more satisfying justice is likely to emerge.

Our own case in point of how justice and forgiveness can be partners is Belfast and its children. These pioneer students of forgiveness, these young primary school children, will one day become parents, teachers, business owners, and community leaders. They will be equipped with skills and tools that will help them navigate the hurt and disappointment inseparable from our human condition, and they will know that it is a symbol of strength to respond to such situations not with anger and violence, but with kindness, compassion, and love. It is with and through these children, perhaps some of whom have been assaulted with rocks or taunted with obscenities on their way to school, that we will one day break the violent and fear-driven cycle of injustice. These littlest ones will one day change their community for the good. Their example might change the world.

References

Al-Mabuk, R. H., Enright, R. D. and Cardis, P. (1995) 'Forgiveness education with parentally love-deprived late adolescents,' *Journal of Moral Education*, 24: 427–43.

Baranowsky, A. B., Young, M. Johnson-Douglas, S. Williams-Keller, L. and McCarrey, M. (1998) 'PTSD transmission: a review of secondary traumatization in Holocaust survivor families,' *Canadian Psychology*, 39: 247–56.

Botcheva, L. B., Feldman, S. S. and Leiderman, P. H. (2002) 'Can stability in school processes offset the negative effects of socio-political upheaval on adolescent adaptation?' *Youth and Society*, 34: 55–88.

Connolly, P., Smith, A. and Kelly, B. (2002) *Too Young to Notice: the cultural and political awareness of 3–6 year olds in Northern Ireland*, Belfast, Northern Ireland: Community Relations Council.

Coyle, C. T. and Enright, R. D. (1997) 'Forgiveness intervention with postabortion men,' *Journal of Counseling and Clinical Psychology*, 65: 1042–46.

Curran, P. S. and Miller, P. W. (2001) 'Psychiatric implications of chronic civilian strife or war: Northern Ireland,' *Advances in Psychiatric Treatment*, 7: 73–80.

Doyle, S. (2004). 'History of violence at our schools,' *The Irish News*, 4 June: 5.

Enright, R. D. and Fitzgibbons, R. P. (2000) *Helping Clients Forgive: an empirical guide for resolving anger and restoring hope*, Washington, DC: American Psychological Association.

Enright, R. D., Mullet, E. and Fitzgibbons, R. P. (2001) 'Forgiveness as a means of emotional regulation,' *Journal de Therapie Comportementale et Cognitive*, 11: 123–35.

Enright, R. D., Gassin. L and Knutson, J. (2003) 'Waging peace through forgiveness education in Belfast, Northern Ireland: a review and proposal for mental health improvement of children,' *Journal of Research in Education*, 13: 51–61.

Fletcher, K. E. (1996) 'Childhood posttraumatic stress disorder,' in E. J. Mash and R. A. Barkley (eds) *Child Psychopathology*, New York: Guilford.

Fraser, M. (1974) *Children in Conflict*, Middlesex, England: Penguin Books.

Freedman, S. R. and Enright, R. D. (1996) 'Forgiveness as an intervention goal with incest survivors,' *Journal of Counseling and Clinical Psychology*, 64: 983–92.

Gambaro, M. E. (2002) 'School-based forgiveness education in the management of trait anger in early adolescents,' unpublished doctoral dissertation, University of Wisconsin–Madison.

Geraghty, T. (1998) *The Irish War*, London: HarperCollins.

Gorman-Smith, D. and Tolan, P. (1998) 'The role of exposure to community violence and developmental problems among inner-city youth,' *Development and Psychopathology*, 10: 101–16.

Gurwitch, R. H., Sitterle, K. A. Young, B. H. and Pfefferbaum, B. (2002) 'The aftermath of terrorism,' in A. M. LaGreca, W. K. Silverman, E. Vernberg and M. C. Roberts (eds) *Helping Children Cope with Disasters and Terrorism*, Washington, DC: American Psychological Association.

Harkness, L. L. (1993) 'Transgenerational transmission of war-related trauma,' in J. P. Wilson and B. Raphael (eds) *International Handbook of Traumatic Stress Syndromes*, New York: Penguin Books.

Hebl, J. H. and Enright, R. D. (1993) 'Forgiveness as a psychotherapeutic goal with elderly females,' *Psychotherapy*, 30: 658–67.

Kee, R. (1995) *Ireland: a history*, London: Abacus.

Kliewer, W., Lepore, S. J., Oskin, D. and Johnson, P. D. (1998) 'The role of social and cognitive processes in children's adjustment to community violence,' *Journal of Consulting and Clinical Psychology*, 66: 199–209.

Knutson, J. and Enright, R. D. (2002) 'The adventure of forgiveness', unpublished curriculum, University of Wisconsin – Madison.

Leichty, J. and Clegg, C. (2001) *Moving Beyond Sectarianism: religion conflict, and reconciliation in Northern Ireland*, Blackrock, Co. Dublin: Columbia Press.

Lin, W., Mack, D., Enright, R. D., Krahn, D. and Baskin, T. (2004) 'Effects of forgiveness therapy on anger, mood, and vulnerability to substance use among inpatient substance-dependant clients,' *Journal of Consulting and Clinical Psychology*, 72(6): 1114–21.

Loughrey, G. C., Curran, P. S. and Bell, P. (1993) 'Posttraumatic stress disorder and civil violence in Northern Ireland,' in J. P. Wilson and B. Raphael (eds) *International Handbook of Traumatic Stress Syndromes*, New York: Plenum.

Pekrun, R., Goetz, T., Titz, W. and Perry, R. P. (2002) 'Academic emotions in students' self-regulated learning and achievement: a program of qualitative and quantitative research,' *Educational Psychology*, 37: 91–105.

Perry, B. D. and Pollard, R. (1998) 'Homeostasis, stress, trauma, and adaptation: a neurodevelopmental view of childhood trauma,' *Child and Adolescent Psychiatric Clinics of North America*, 7: 33–51.

Pfefferbaum, B., Nixon, S. J., Tucker, P. M., Tivis, R. D., Moore, V. L. and Gurwitch, R. H. (1999) 'Posttraumatic stress responses in bereaved children after the Oklahoma City bombing,' *Journal of the American Academy of Child and Adolescent Psychiatry*, 38: 1372–79.

Power, P. C. and Duffy, S. (2001) *Timetables of Irish History*, London: Worth Press.

Price, J. M. and Dodge, K. A. (1989) 'Reactive and proactive aggression in childhood: Relations to peer status and social context dimensions,' *Journal of Abnormal Child Psychology*, 17(4): 455–71.

Roeser, R. W., Eccles, J. S. and Stobel, K. R. (1998) 'Linking the study of schooling and mental health: selected issues and empirical illustrations at the level of the individual,' *Educational Psychologist*, 33: 153–76.

Rolston, B. (1991) *Politics and Painting: murals and conflict in Northern Ireland*, Cranbury, NJ: Associated University Presses.

— (1994) *Drawing Support: murals in the north of Ireland*, Belfast, Northern Ireland: Beyond the Pale Publications.

— (1998) *Drawing Support 2: murals of war and peace*, Belfast, Northern Ireland: Beyond the Pale Publications.

Sullivan, H. S. (1953) *The Interpersonal Theory of Psychiatry*, New York: Norton.

Walker, K. (2001) 'Youngsters handed whistles to intimidate Holy Cross girls,' *The Express*, 7 September: 6.

Zeman, J., Shipman, K. and Suveng, C. (2002) 'Anger and sadness regulation: predictions to internalizing and externalizing symptoms in children,' *Journal of Clinical and Adolescent Psychology*, 31: 393–8.

22

Restorative justice in transition

Ownership, leadership and 'bottom-up' human rights

Kieran McEvoy and Anna Eriksson[1]

Introduction

Restorative justice (RJ) is widely under-stood as a series of theoretical and practical discourses which attempt to facilitate dialogue and reconciliation among victims, offenders, and community (Braithwaite 2002a; Dzur and Olson 2004). The goals include the acceptance of responsibility by offenders, reparation of harm, strengthening the connections of victims and offenders to their community, and the promotion of more stable and peaceful communities (Thomson 2004). Such principles resonate strongly with the needs of political transitions where values such as reconstruction and reintegration are pursued and occasionally run into conflict with notions of justice and indeed justice reconstruction (Minow 1998; Teitel 2000; Leebaw 2001).

In more settled societies, the claims of RJ advocates are substantial. They include reduced recidivism, greater satisfaction for victims, more involved and regenerated communities, even a new way of living our daily lives (Sullivan and Tifft 2005). In different transitional contexts, the ambitions of restorative justice have been no less expansive. Thus RJ has been suggested as the key theoretical and practical base for a national process of healing and reconciliation through the Truth and Reconciliation Commission in South Africa (Villa Vincenzio 1999). In Rwanda, the adaptation of the *gacaca* system of tribal justice to deal with the after-effects of genocide is commonly viewed as being firmly located within a RJ framework (Drumbl 2002). Even at the supra-national level within the traditionally retribution-focused realm of international criminal justice, important scholars have begun to suggest that restorative justice too must play a role in dealing with the after-effects of war in legal settings such as the ad hoc tribunals established to deal with Rwanda, the former Yugoslavia, and of course the nascent International Criminal Court (Roberts 2003). In all of these instances what Harry Mika (2002) has referred to as the 'swagger' of RJ has become one of its pronounced features.

The community-based RJ programs in Northern Ireland arguably set themselves a similarly ambitious program of work. As has been detailed extensively elsewhere (McEvoy and Mika 2001, 2002; Mika and McEvoy 2001, 2002) Community Restorative Justice Ireland (CRJI) and Northern Ireland Alternatives were established as part of broader peacemaking efforts to persuade

Republican and Loyalist paramilitaries – specifically the Irish Republican Army (IRA) and Ulster Volunteer Force (UVF) – to forego violent systems of paramilitary punishment shootings and beatings in certain areas in favor of community-based systems of restorative justice. On both sides the programs began with direct dialogue with Republican and Loyalist activists. That dialogue was designed to persuade them to 'responsibly disengage' from such activities and instead hand the cases over to locally trained and recruited volunteers and staff to be dealt with in a lawful and non-violent fashion, using restorative justice techniques such as shuttle diplomacy, mediation, and family group conferencing. Seven years on from their original inception the programs have been evaluated as having made a significant contribution to lowering levels of punishment violence in communities where they operate in Northern Ireland, having contributed to changing attitudes towards violence in such communities (and indeed inside some of the paramilitary groups who operate there) and contributing to an enhanced capacity for local communities not only to take ownership over local justice issues but also to develop the self-confidence for a partnership with statutory agencies (including the police) within a more balanced set of power relationships than is often the case (Mika 2004).

In this chapter we wish to draw out the significance of a number of features of these programs which have not been fully developed elsewhere. In particular we have chosen to focus upon three themes of distinct significance. These are: the strong sense of grassroots community ownership and participation in the programs; the prominent leadership roles which ex-prisoners and ex-combatants have played in the establishment and development of the programs and related efforts at transforming attitudes towards violence in communities and paramilitary groups; and the prominence of human rights

discourses as an embedded feature of RJ practice which has been a defining characteristic of the programs. We will argue that the intersections among these three elements offer the potential for personal and communal transformation of cultures of violence.

Restorative justice, grassroots ownership, and transition

Restorative justice in transitional societies faces a number of additional difficulties to those traditionally associated with more stable jurisdictions. For example, state-based initiatives may be regarded with some cynicism by affected communities where the state justice system has been contorted during the conflict (e.g. through emergency legislation) or where the police or state security forces have been guilty of human rights abuses in their war against the non-state forces (Roche 2002). Adherence to legal formalism, due process, proportionality and related benchmarks for ensuring good RJ practice in state-based programs are not easily divorced from such violent histories when government and politics have been so closely related (Chayes and Chayes 1998; Ruth-Heffelbower 2000). Indeed, as has been the case in Northern Ireland (O'Mahony et al. 2002), programs which have been led by police or other criminal justice agencies may struggle to develop partnerships with precisely those local communities most directly affected by the conflict, thus severely limited the transformative potential of RJ in the areas where it is arguably most obviously needed.

In such a context, it makes sense that communities themselves should take primary ownership over the establishment of programs, deciding what type of intervention might be suitable, who is going to be involved, which values will guide their work and devise their own benchmarks as part of a broader 'legitimation process' (Mika and McEvoy 2001). Those with the greatest stake in justice reconstruction – often those who have been on the receiving end of violence and criminality from the state, paramilitary actors, and indeed local 'ordinary' offenders – should themselves be direct participants in the process as innovators, planners and implementers (Ratuva 2002). Community participation in decision-making processes regarding the rebuilding of a society adds transparency, accountability, legitimacy, and, importantly, minimizes the risk of renewed conflict (Candio and Bleiker 2001; Roche 2003). Top-down initiatives need to be accompanied by culturally appropriate grassroots programs such as the efforts in East Timor (Candio and Bleiker 2001; Babo-Soares 2004); Rwanda, (Verwimp and Verpoorten 2004); South Africa (Leebaw 2001; Roche 2002; Cartwright *et al.* 2004); Indonesia (Ruth-Heffelbower 2000); and Northern Ireland have illustrated.

By way of illustration, in South Africa in 1997, Clifford Shearing and his colleagues initiated the Community Peace Programme in the Western Cape province. This was an experiment in trying to build a model which, drawing upon local skills, knowledge and capacities, could help the local communities to help themselves, especially in areas such as safety and security. After the end of apartheid, there was a deficit in poor neighborhoods regarding all areas of public service, including policing. There was, and still is, 'a serious "governance deficit" in poor communities, not only in relation to security but also in matters such as health and the provision of services such as garbage removal, water and electricity' (Cartwright *et al.* 2004: 5–6). The restorative justice work in local communities in Northern Ireland closely mirrors the initiatives in South Africa which build on local capacity, knowledge, and experience for devising appropriate solutions to conflict within their own communities. The affirmation and development of social norms through participatory practices such as RJ is an especially important feature in a transitional society, where the social norms are not only changing rapidly, but expected to do so (Dzur and Olson 2004). Moving away from violent conflict, where severe punitiveness characterized people's response to norm transgression, towards a strong, peaceful, inclusive, and democratic community requires an enormous mind shift for many people.

As mentioned, in Northern Ireland, the community-based RJ programs in both Republican and Loyalist communities had as their aim to replace the use of so-called punishment violence as practiced by the different paramilitary groups (Feenan 2002). However, since their inception, the scope of these programs has become much broader, in particular the projects in the Republican communities. They deal with neighborhood disputes, often very serious ones, children and families who are at risk of coming to the attention of the paramilitaries, and more general anti-social behaviors, often in connection with drugs and alcohol. Consequently, preventative work is a large component of their practice.

How does one judge, then, whether the local communities, in which these RJ programs operate, actually feel and posses ownership over these informal justice alternatives? Keeping in mind that widespread community ownership is the result of a successful legitimation process, grassroots ownership could perhaps be gauged in three ways: (1) the number of cases dealt with each year; (2) the range of sources who refer to the RJ programs; and (3) the number and representativeness of local community and statutory agencies which take referrals from the programs.[2]

On the Republican side, CRJI dealt with just over 1,500 cases in 2004, the majority of which were neighborhood disputes and youth-related. Between 5 and 30 per cent (depending on area) dealt with people under threat from or excluded by the armed groups. The majority of referrals to CRJI came from the people directly involved in any particular dispute, the rest were a mix from the different paramilitary groups, Social Services, the Housing Executive, individual police officers, the local Sinn Fein office, neighborhood associations, and quite a large number from neighborhood initiatives such as Community Watch. On the Loyalist side where the project is considerably smaller, targeted exclusively at young people under paramilitary threat and involves intensive work with clients including a one-to-one mentoring system (McEvoy and Mika 2001), a total of 132 cases were processed between 1999 and 2004 (Mika 2004). Again the vast majority of the referrals came from community sources, self-referrals and paramilitary groups, with some also coming from statutory sources, including the police. As the British government-appointed Justice Oversight Commissioner suggested in his review of the work of CRJI and Alternatives:

> These organizations are engaged in valuable and effective work in their respective communities. Their growth gives evidence of the value they have. They share a common intention and a motivation to make a positive and peaceful contribution to the welfare of the communities which they serve. The differences between them may be far less significant than the positive steps which they take to find solutions to actual or potential local problems. If these organizations did not exist it might be difficult as matters stand to provide a similar service. Indeed the void might have undesirable consequences.
>
> (Clyde 2004: 101)

A second way to judge levels of local ownership – that is, the extent to which practice has become embedded in the local community – is to see what and how many local resources are used when drawing up and implementing outcome agreements. The absolute majority of cases extensively use local resources in their outcome agreements. Obviously, not all cases need to

make use of another agency. CRJI is very much a needs-based practice, and hence the individual and family needs of the participants in any one conference will dictate the content of the outcome agreement that is decided in any one conference. Most of the resources used are voluntary organizations which deal with such things as alcohol and drug problems; offender awareness programs (specifically in relation to car crime which is a significant and serious problem in many of these communities); counseling, not just for offender and victims, but often for the whole family; vocational programs; and programs which help prepare children and young people who are trying to get back into school.

Of course, one of the traditional arguments put forward by those who are cautious of grassroots involvement in the ownership of justice is the risk that the notion of community becomes idealized, which may in turn obscure the reification of exclusionary or authoritarian practices (e.g. Dignan 2000; Pavlich 2001). Certainly we would not wish to suggest that the establishment of community ownership in these projects was a smooth linear process. For example, it took some time initially for people to accept not just the existence of these programs, but also the nature of their practice.[3] Particularly in the early days, some people in local communities presumed that because well-known former combatants were involved, punishment violence would be on offer as part of the range of possible disposals. Time after time the staff had to explain that:

> no, if you want someone shot then you have come to the wrong place, and no, we do not know of anyone who can provide that service for you in this community.[4]

In fact, given their absolute commitment to non-violence, the principal similarity the programs share with 'the old way' of dealing with conflict in these communities is the speed with which they deal with complaints.[5] This alacrity was viewed as crucial to the success of these programs. People in these communities were so used to a certain type of response to norm transgression that anything resembling the slow-moving response by the formal criminal justice system would have seriously undermined the program's legitimacy.[6] But the real big change for many people is not necessarily the speed or the visibility of the response: it is the fact that, maybe for the first time, they have to *own* their own problems and take responsibility for the solution of them:

> It is difficult to convince people on the ground that a quick fix is not the answer. That is probably where we encounter the changing of mindsets here in this community. It's our hardest job. For thirty years people put their problems on someone else, to get someone beaten up, to get it sorted, to get it resolved. And the resolution was often to put the person out. To punish them ... Now we say 'you own it.' We will support you to reach a resolution, but we can't make it go away for you.[7]

Such an educative process speaks directly to the transformation of cultures of violence discussed below. Indeed, it is precisely the kind of intervention that is required to guard against the legitimate concerns associated with authoritarian communitarianism and the related resort to what Maureen Cain (1985) has termed 'defensive formalism': that is, falling back on the flawed capacity of the formal justice system to deliver because of a failure of imagination regarding the potential of local communities. It is our view that the involvement of ex-prisoners and former combatants has been absolutely crucial in providing leadership in that process.

Ex-combatants, leadership, and transition

The fate of ex-prisoners and former combatants in the process of transition from conflict has been widely recognized as central to attempts at peacemaking. In some of the most lengthy and complex armed conflicts, the failures in planning and delivery in finding new roles for former armed actors has been viewed as highly destabilizing for nascent transitional processes. A number of reports on the issue have been produced by the World Bank and other agencies concerning a range of African states (e.g. Colletta *et al.* 1996; Gear 2002). Traditionally much of the focus has been upon breaking up armed groups as quickly as possible and removing their weapons in order to better stabilize the security situation. However, more recently, the emphasis of the international community has shifted in emphasis somewhat. As Kofi Annan argued in a speech in Derry, Northern Ireland, peace cannot be secured without:

> providing the fighters with an alternative, peaceful means of earning their living. Nowadays we no longer contemplate demobilization and disarmament – the two 'Ds' – without adding an 'R,' which stands for reintegration into the civilian economy. Without this, it is a virtual certainty that new weapons will be acquired and violence will resume.
>
> (Annan 2004)

It is our contention that many former combatants and ex-prisoners have been at the forefront in providing leadership in the Northern Ireland transition in seeking to prevent the resumption of organized political and communal violence. In making this claim, it is important to stress that we are not postulating some form of naive post-conflict eulogizing of all of those who once took up arms. Certainly it is possible to argue cogently that at least one of the paramilitary organizations whose members benefited from early release from prison under the Good Friday Agreement (the Ulster Defence Association) has largely morphed into a criminal gang involved in drug dealing, racketeering, and prostitution (McDonald and Cusack 2004). The Ulster Volunteer Force (which supports the Loyalist restorative justice programs) has also been heavily involved in drugs and ordinary criminality (McDonald and Cusack 2000). While the IRA has not been credibly linked to drug dealing or distribution, its long tradition of robberies, smuggling, and related criminality to fund the Republican 'cause' has apparently survived well beyond the ceasefires of 'military' operations in the mid-1990s (O'Leary 2005). Indeed, recent Republican concerns at the 'fraying' of individual IRA members into ordinary criminality are apparently one of the motivating factors for intense ongoing debates within the organization that it should formally 'stand down'.

Notwithstanding those tendencies, and indeed contradictory trends have been a constant feature of the Northern Ireland transition, namely political, military, and moral leadership, we believe that it is possible to identify at least three overlapping styles of leadership by ex-combatants in the Northern Ireland transition.

Political leadership

There is a considerable literature on leadership in general and the notion of political leadership in particular (e.g. Burns 1978; Blondel 1987; Gardner 1995; Elcock 2001). Of particular relevance for current purposes is that work which focuses upon the way that political leaders prepare, cajole, and sometimes bully their constituencies in national and international peacemaking processes (Sheffer 1993; Westlake 2000). Much of that work also considers the intersection between agency and structure, the ways in which individual actors transform themselves from armed actors to negotiators often as a result of changed political circumstances (McGarry 1998; Gormley-Heenan 2001). At a general level, the political leadership provided by ex-combatants in Northern Ireland has been obvious. Most of

those who negotiated the Good Friday Agreement from the Republican and Loyalist parties were ex-prisoners who had been convicted of politically motivated offences committed during the conflict (Mitchell 2000). Indeed, many are quite candid that the negotiation skills employed were actually learned in their dealing with the prison authorities when incarcerated (Sinnerton 2003). In addition, both sets of protagonists have demonstrated finely honed antennae as to the potential for 'stretching' their political base and considerable dexterity at overcoming seemingly insurmountable political difficulties. Such skills have also been evidenced at the micro-level through the community RJ programs.

In the working-class Republican and Loyalist communities in which these programs are based, ex-combatants are largely regarded as having 'done their bit' on behalf of their communities. While there are subtle differences between the attitudes of the two communities (Shirlow et al. 2005), the ex-combatants involved in RJ bring a considerable degree of credibility, respect, and legitimacy to the programs. Individually a number of the most prominent RJ activists are highly skilled and charismatic practitioners, but it is also clear that over the years there has been considerable 'routinization of charismatic leadership' (Weber 1946) institutionalized into the working practices of the organizations. As well as their previous organizational and often 'jail time' experience, many have also been involved in community work for years. As was noted above, by working with and subscribing to values of non-violence, human rights, inclusiveness, respect and tolerance for differences, they are providing small 'p' political leadership in transforming community attitudes to violence. In addition, and in particular in the Republican communities where it is considerably more politically sensitive, they are also providing leadership towards the building of relations between the state agencies such as the police and other aspects of the criminal justice system, and communities which have traditionally been estranged from them. As one of the RJ program co-coordinators said:

> When people see us as community leaders actively using those resources [statutory agencies], then they are more comfortable using them themselves. Historically, working with the state was something you did not do in this community for a long, long time. But I think that now people see someone who they perceive as community leaders doing that, then it filters down.[8]

Military leadership

> Leadership is holistic. Leadership means leading laterally or collaboratively, and not just from upper echelons. Leadership entails leading the people, the structure, the process ... Leadership is symbolic. Leadership is about the influence of meanings and interpretations that important constituencies give to the organization's function.
>
> (Paparone 2004: 9)[9]

Within military studies generally, there is an increased recognition that the notion of leadership is much more complex than rigid hierarchical structures which give orders and expect them to be carried out (e.g. Mathews 2002). Certainly the more sophisticated literature on how volunteer paramilitary organizations 'think' would suggest that the exercise of leadership in a process of change is much more likely to be based on internal discourses, relationships, organizational cultures, and mythologies than simply instructions being issued from senior management and obeyed by the rank and file (Crenshaw 1990; Irvin 1999). Central to this behavioral rather than instrument approach to military leadership is again the notion of *credibility*. Put simply, unless those who bring the peacemaking message have credibility amongst paramilitary activists and can frame it appropriately within the organization's way of thinking, the message will not be heeded.

As mentioned earlier, the active role of ex-combatants and former prisoners in community-based restorative justice in Northern Ireland has been key to its success. As well as working and volunteering in the restorative justice programs, ex-combatants and former prisoners have been central to efforts at persuading paramilitary organizations to desist from punishment violence, to refer 'complainants' from the community to the programs and to consider their own internal organizational attitudes towards violence. The Director of Alternatives, a former UVF life-sentenced prisoner, himself conducted the original research and interviews with the UVF which led to the establishment of the program (Winston 1997). Similarly, the Director of CRJI, a former Republican internee, was one of four individuals involved in direct dialogue with the IRA and other Republicans which led to the establishment of the programs on the Republican side (Auld *et al. 1997*). Many others working on the programs have served lengthy sentences for their respective organizations. Hence, no one within the respective constituency can question their past commitment. Together with other ex-combatants, and again precisely because of their collective credibility with the respective paramilitary groupings, they have been involved in countless peacemaking efforts with such groups.

Again, such a process of persuasion or leadership in trying to move paramilitary organizations should not be understood as either smooth or easy. For example, in agreeing to cooperate with the establishment of Alternatives, the UVF inserted a number of caveats where they would reserve the right to shoot or beat particular individuals (McEvoy and Mika 2002). Similarly, while the IRA has cooperated with the CRJI programs in the areas where such programs are established, they have continued beatings and shootings in other areas. In Derry where CRJI had received considerable plaudits for their peacemaking efforts after there had been no punishment attacks for almost a year, the sheen was somewhat taken off those efforts when the IRA conducted a punishment shooting on a bus driver for alleged anti-social activities in front of terrified pensioners who he was driving on an excursion.[10] Both sets of paramilitary groups have continued to recruit younger members since the cease-fires. Older former combatants may at times struggle with inter-generational tensions and face accusations that they have 'gone soft' through their involvement in restorative justice, and must at times rely on leaders their own age who are still inside the organizational structures to counsel against the tried and failed methods of the past.[11]

Despite these difficulties, it is through the leadership and persuasion efforts of former combatants involved in restorative justice that we have seen significant reductions in punishment violence in the areas where the projects are operational as well as changes (for the better) in the ways in which local paramilitary organizations conduct their policing activities, such as referring cases to one of the schemes rather than punishing alleged anti-social offenders (Mika 2004). If, as appears possible at time of writing, the current internal debate within the IRA leads to the organization 'standing down,' that result too will have been achieved through the stewardship of former Republican combatants. Indeed, the RJ programs are a living example of the kind of progressive outlets of community capacity building that such individuals could apply their political energies.

Moral leadership and community building

The third overlapping style of leadership provided by former combatants and ex-prisoners is this notion of transformative or moral leadership in the process of community building. As Burns has argued: 'transforming leadership ultimately becomes moral in that it raises the level of human conduct and ethical aspirations of both lea-

der and led, and thus has a transforming effect on both' (1978: 20).

Bazemore and Schiff (2002) have argued that community building is facilitated by connecting people more closely to existing relationships and to new ones based on trust and reciprocity which are then connected to networks of social capital (Putnam 2000) and by skill building within those networks. The issues of community building and the attention paid to the needs of former combatants are strongly connected (Babo-Soares 2004; Knight and Özerdem 2004; Verwimp and Verpoorten 2004). Indeed, the process of being involved in community development work also guards against elitist tendencies which are sometimes identified with those who have been involved directly in armed struggle (e.g. Irvin 1999). Although the reality of the twenty-five-year conflict in Northern Ireland which saw thousands of people imprisoned from relatively small geographical working-class areas is that, as one seasoned community worker told one of the authors, 'everyone has a history here.' Nonetheless, involvement by ex-combatants in strong and independent community organizations – utilizing their existing organizational and political skills as well as demonstrating a willingness to learn new ones – is an appropriately balanced organic relationship between such individuals and the communities from which they come.

It is often ex-combatants who are taking the lead within Republicanism and Loyalism on how these respective constituencies should deal with the legacy of violence, discussions on whether or not Northern Ireland should have a truth process, victim offender reconciliation work, cross-community projects designed to lessen tensions at interface areas as well as the restorative justice programs under discussion here (Shirlow et al. 2005). Indeed, it could be argued that community building around issues such as the ongoing dialogue about the injustices of the past and its legacy is a goal that represents the central potential of restorative principles in the context of political transitions (Leebaw 2001: 286–7). Transitional contexts such as Northern Ireland demonstrate that the potential of RJ is not limited to addressing the issues surrounding individual criminal acts but rather also makes a contribution towards addressing elements of larger social problems which intersect with the criminal act under discussion.

As was noted above, in the working-class communities which suffered the brunt of violence, it is often the best of the ex-prisoners and former combatants who are showing leadership in moving communities away from such cultures of violence. As individuals who have been directly involved in committing acts of political violence, and whose organizations have been guilty of punishing alleged anti-social criminals, ex-combatants are perfectly placed to make the arguments to local communities about the failings of such exclusionary practices directed against the 'hoods.' For those RJ practitioners who have both inflicted and been on the receiving end of extreme violence, it holds little allure. Their rejection of the efficacy of punishment violence is itself a powerful exercise in both moral leadership and community capacity building.

'Bottom-up' human rights and transition

There has been increasing interest in recent years concerning the intersection between restorative justice and human rights discourses. Given that the origins of the modern human rights movement lie in the prosecutions of Nazi and Japanese war criminals in the wake of the Second World War, it is perhaps little wonder that human rights discourses have largely made retribution synonymous with accountability (Ignatieff 2001). Although RJ scholars have recently highlighted the richness of the notion of accountability beyond legal form-

alism (e.g. Roche 2003), the fact remains that many human rights advocates remain suspicious of RJ and its intentions. The application of RJ theory and practice to reconciliation initiatives in places like South Africa, Rwanda or more recently Colombia has done little to assuage the suspicion that it is a politically fashionable framework to afford de facto impunity to those who have been guilty of the most egregious human rights abuses (Wilson 2001; Human Rights Watch 2003).

Even in more settled societies, human rights discourses are often portrayed as being at odds with RJ, albeit from a rather different angle. Thus, for example, some of the most prominent critics of RJ in the United Kingdom frame their criticisms of restorative justice as potentially impinging upon the right to fair trial guaranteed under Article 6 of the European Convention on Human Rights (e.g. Ashworth 2002). Thus questions concerning the proportionality of outcomes agreed at an RJ conference, the right to have access to a lawyer, the right to appeal, the principle of double jeopardy and a range of other offender-focused fair trial concerns have been raised in recent discussions on restorative justice (Brown 1994; Skelton and Frank 2004). Similarly with regard to the 'rights' of victims (which are admittedly less well protected under international human rights law), issues such as coercion to participate in RJ programs, proceedings which are offender-dominated, failure to monitor outcomes and imbalances in power relations between victims and offenders have all been discussed as potentially undermining the rights of victims (Crawford 2000; Lewis et al. 2000). In both instances, human rights discourses are again perceived as being to varying degrees in conflict with RJ theory and practice.

In the Northern Ireland context, in the absence of a formal state-run truth and reconciliation process, the debates concerning RJ and human rights have largely been focused on these perceived fair trial and victims' rights tensions. Indeed, in the persistent efforts by state agencies to deny breathing room to the community-based restorative justice programs (McEvoy *et al.* 2001), the desire to protect the human rights of perpetrators and victims has been one of the most oft-stated rationales for state domination of the programs (Dignan 2000; Criminal Justice Review 2000). As the government-directed review of the criminal justice in Northern Ireland stated:

> We think it is important that only statutory criminal justice agencies should be able to refer offenders to the community base schemes, so that the state retains ultimate responsibility for criminal justice. This will mean that individuals who claim their human rights have been denied may be able to seek a direct remedy against a public authority under the Human Rights Act 1998. We cannot, therefore, endorse schemes that act outside the criminal justice system, which are without links to the criminal justice system, and yet which purport to deal with criminal activity.
>
> (Criminal Justice Review 2000: 216)

At first glance this argument concerning the state's responsibility to protect the human rights of those going through an RJ program may appear unproblematic. Of course, the rights of those going through a RJ scheme (particularly one which has as close a relationship with the state justice system as that envisaged by the Criminal Justice Review) should be protected. However, as Skelton and Frank (2004: 209) have argued, there are dangers in RJ practitioners becoming fixated upon the confined parameters of providing the same due process rules as the courts, rules which were after all designed to deal with specific dangers inherent in the criminal justice trial. They go on to argue for a broadening of the discourse around human rights. We strongly agree with both views. We would argue that the Northern Ireland experience offers illustrative examples of both the negative and positive potential of human rights and RJ discourses.

First with regard to the negative, the quote above from the Criminal Justice Review is illustrative. Although in recent years there have been attempts to argue that human rights norms may be binding on non-state actors (McEvoy 2003), the usual focus with regard to RJ is as stated by the Review to bring programs within the exclusive remit of the state so that there can be no ambiguities as to whether or not human rights law is binding. At its worst, this is simply a reframing of the desire on the part of some state agencies for exclusive control and ownership over justice under the convenient guise of human rights concerns. CRJI and Alternatives have made it clear that, subject to agreed protocols as to how they should be conducted, both organizations are amenable to inspection by the Independent Criminal Justice Inspectorate which could indeed test their practice against relevant international standards.[12] However, both are determined that their grassroots legitimacy depends upon their ability to take referrals from the community they serve rather than solely from statutory agencies. The explicit linkage of sources of referrals to human rights protections is essentially a negative one: it is a statecentric, top-down perspective on human rights discourses as a mechanism to 'rein in' and control potentially unruly community programs.

On a more positive note, however, it is important to remember that international human rights standards have always been intended as a floor rather than a ceiling in seeking to maximize rights protections. While state-based justice institutions have tended to view them as placing a cap on the 'maximum one can get away with' (Galligan and Sandler 2004), community-based programs such as those in Northern Ireland have the potential for a more expansive view. John Braithwaite (2002b) has argued persuasively for a 'bottom-up' approach to setting standards for restorative justice practice wherein local practitioners don't have to 'wait for the United Nations' but rather can take existing international standards and develop them based on local experience. This is precisely what has happened in the Northern Ireland context. From their inception both Community Restorative Justice Ireland and Alternatives have placed human rights standards at the core of their training and published standards of practice. In both instances, what would normally be framed as due process rights concerning fair trial in the formal justice system have been substantially 'filled in' with RJ values concerning fairness, impartiality, quality, non-violence and so forth. The 'Blue Book' contained a draft 'community charter' which articulated these human rights in clear and accessible language. Indeed as Braithwaite contended in the same article (2002b: 572), perhaps precisely because of the acutely political nature of the debate here, Northern Ireland has a more sophisticated debate on standards for RJ practice than many other jurisdictions.

At its best, the Northern Ireland example provides concrete evidence that human rights can become embedded in grassroots RJ practice. Northern Ireland has community projects which are properly linked and networked within local communities, which are led and staffed by individuals with credibility in those communities and which have the capacity to translate occasionally complex human rights standards into shared and understood standards of practice. Such projects offer the potential for a rich human rights culture beyond the state (Mamdani 2000). As the former UN High Commissioner for Human Rights, Sergio Vieira de Mello, argued the year before he was killed in an attack on the UN building in Baghdad:

Responsibility for the protection of human rights lies with states ... but the understanding, respect and expectation of human rights by each individual person is what gives human rights its daily texture, its day to day resilience.

(Viera De Mello 2003)

Conclusion

In this chapter we have argued that RJ principles can be uniquely suited for the challenges which face a society in transition, especially in relation to reintegration, community capacity building, and for embedding a bottom-up culture of human rights. In many countries which have undergone, or are currently undergoing, a transition from violent political conflict, it has in later years become obvious that top-down approaches to conflict resolution are often not enough. They must be complemented by well-designed bottom-up initiatives where the needs of the local communities are at centre stage. Grassroots ownership of justice can empower local communities to take responsibility for the peaceful resolution of their own conflicts, and transparent, inclusive and consensual practices such as RJ can be an invaluable tool in such a period of change. In Republican and Loyalist areas in Northern Ireland where RJ programs are in operation, they have helped to add transparency, accountability, and legitimacy to a vital transformation of deeply ingrained cultures of violence, which in turn reduces the risk of renewed conflict.

The social norms of what is an acceptable response to conflict are changing in Northern Ireland, and, as we have argued, ex-prisoners and ex-combatants are providing crucial political, military, and moral leadership in this slow and difficult process. Importantly, this leadership does not only affect the 'ordinary' community members, it also has an impact on changing cultures of violence within the armed groups with whom they come into contact, especially the mainstream Republican movement. When the very people who took up arms to defend or advance their own communities (and who have often served lengthy prison sentences for such actions) are: (a) openly arguing for non-violent approaches to conflict; (b) encouraging respect for human rights; and (c) slowly leading their communities towards cooperation with statutory agencies – then the ripple effect on communal attitudes should not be underestimated. Together with the other community activists and workers who are involved from across the community spectrum in RJ, these ex-prisoners and former combatants are leading their communities through the transition in the areas in which they operate.

Finally the truism that human rights must be a key organizing framework around justice reconstruction in the aftermath of conflict has been given a particular prominence by the Northern Ireland experience. The Good Friday Agreement placed human rights at the very core of the conflict resolution process here. The introduction of the Human Rights Act into domestic law, the creation of a Human Rights Commission, Equality Commission, the drafting of a local Bill of Rights specific to the jurisdiction and the myriad of oversight bodies which have been created around different parts of the criminal justice system – all of these developments have had the impact of 'mainstreaming' human rights issues within the administrative structures of the state (see generally Harvey 2001). The community-based RJ programs have provided an additional 'bottom-up' dimension which has taken that mainstreaming process beyond the confines of the state structures into the communities which were most affected by the conflict.

The Northern Ireland context, of course, has its own peculiarities and the dangers concerning 'off the shelf' superimpositions of models of practice are well known. However, with a sensible and sensitive approach to local circumstances, we would argue that, cumulatively, the dimensions of ownership, leadership, and grassroots human rights entrenchment offer a template for RJ in transition which may be of considerably broader applicability.

References

Annan, K. (2004) 'Learning the lessons of peace building,' The Tip O'Neill Lecture, Magee Campus, University of Ulster, 18 October 2004.

Ashworth, A. (2002) 'Responsibilities, rights and restorative justice,' British Journal of Criminology, 42(3): 578–95.

Auld, J., Gormally, B., McEvoy, K. and Ritchie, M. (1997) 'The Blue Book': designing a system of restorative justice in Northern Ireland, Belfast: The authors.

Babo-Soares, D. (2004) 'Nahe Biti: the philosophy and process of grassroots reconciliation (and Justice) in East Timor,' The Asia Pacific Journal of Anthropology, 5(1): 15–33.

Bazemore, G. and Schiff, M. (2002) Understanding Restorative Justice Conferencing: a case study in informal decision making in the response to youth crime (draft report), Washington, DC: National Institute of Justice, US Department of Justice.

Blondel, J. (1987) Political Leadership: towards a general analysis, London: Sage.

Braithwaite, J. (2002a) Restorative Justice and Responsive Regulation, Oxford: Oxford University Press.

— (2002b) 'Setting standards for restorative justice,' British Journal of Criminology, 42: 563–77.

Brown, J. G. (1994) 'The use of mediation to resolve criminal cases: a procedural critique,' Emory Law Journal, 43: 1247–1309.

Burns, J. M. (1978) Leadership, New York: Harper and Row.

Cain, M. (1985) 'Beyond informal justice,' Contemporary Crisis, (9): 335–73.

Candio, P. and Bleiker, R. (2001) 'Peace building in East Timor,' The Pacific Review, 14(1): 63–84.

Cartwright, J., Jenneker, M. and Shearing, C. (2004) 'Local capacity governance in South Africa: a model for peaceful coexistence,' paper originally presented at the 'In Search of Security' Conference in Montreal hosted by the Law Commission of Canada, February 2003. Updated March 2004.

Chayes, A. H. and Chayes, A. (1998) 'Mobilizing international and regional organizations for managing ethnic conflict,' in E. Weiner (ed.) *The Handbook of Interethnic Coexistence*, New York: Continuum.

Clyde, Lord (2004) *Second Report of the Justice Oversight Commissioner*, Belfast: HMSO.

Colleta, N., Kostner, M. and Wiederhofer, I. (1996) *Case Studies in War-to-Peace Transitions: the demobilization of ex-combatants in Ethiopia, Namibia and Uganda*, Washington, DC: The World Bank.

Crawford, A. (2000) 'Salient themes towards a victim perspective and the limitations of restorative justice,' in A. Crawford and J. Goodey (eds) *Integrating a Victim Perspective within Criminal Justice*, Aldershot: Ashgate.

Crenshaw, M. (1990) *Theories of Terrorism: instrumental and organizational approaches*, University Park, PA: Pennsylvania State Press.

Criminal Justice Review (2000) *Review of the Criminal Justice System of Northern Ireland*, Belfast: HMSO.

Dignan, J. (2000) *Restorative Justice Options for Northern Ireland: a comparative review*, Belfast: HMSO.

Drumbl, M. (2002) 'Sclerosis: retributive justice and the Rwandan genocide,' *Punishment and Society*, 2(3): 287–309

Dzur, A. W. and Olson, S. M. (2004) 'The value of community participation in restorative justice,' *Journal of Social Philosophy*, 35(1): 91–107.

Elcock, H. (2001) *Political Leadership*, Northampton, MA: Edward Elgar.

Feenan, D. (2002) 'Justice in conflict: paramilitary punishment in Ireland (North),' *International Journal of the Sociology of Law*, 30: 151–72.

Galligan, D. and Sandler, D. (2004) 'Implementing human rights,' in S. Halliday and P. Schmidt (eds) *Human Rights Brought Home: socio-legal perspectives on human rights*, Oxford: Hart Publishing.

Gardner, H. (1995). *Leading Minds: an anatomy of leadership*, New York, NY: Basic Books.

Gear, S. (2002) *Wishing Us Away: challenges facing ex-combatants in the New South Africa*, Braamfontein: Centre for the Study of Violence and Reconciliation.

Gormley-Heenan, C. (2001) *From Protagonist to Pragmatist: political leadership in societies in transition*, Derry: Incore.

Harvey, C. (ed) (2001) *Human Rights, Equality and Democratic Renewal in Northern Ireland*, Oxford: Hart Publishing.

Human Rights Watch (2003) *Colombia's Checkbook Impunity: a Human Rights Watch briefing paper*, 22 September 2003. Available at: http://hrw.org/backgrounder/americas/checkbook-impunity.htm

Ignatieff, M. (2001) *Human Rights as Politics and Idolatry*, Princeton: Princeton University Press.

Irvin, C. (1999) *Militant Nationalism: between movement and party in Ireland and the Basque Country*, Minnesota: University of Minnesota Press.

Knight, M. and Özerdem, A. (2004) 'Guns, camps and cash: disarmament, demobilization and reinsertion of former combatants in transitions from war to peace,' *Journal of Peace Research*, 41(45): 499–516.

Leebaw, B. (2001). 'Restorative justice for political transitions: lessons from the South African truth and reconciliation commission,' *Contemporary Justice Review*, 4(3–4): 267–89.

Lewis, R., Dobash, R. P., Dobash, R. E. and Cavanagh, K. (2000) 'Protection, prevention, rehabilitation or justice? Women's experience of the justice system to challenge domestic violence,' *International Review of Victimology*, 7(1/2/3): 179–205.

McDonald, H. and Cusack, J. (2000) *UVF*, Dublin: Poolbeg.

— (2004) *The UDA: inside the heart of loyalist terror*, Dublin: Penguin Books.

McEvoy, K. (2003) 'Beyond the metaphor: human rights, humanitarian law and new peacemaking criminology,' *Theoretical Criminology*, 7(3): 319–46.

McEvoy, K. and Mika, H. (2001) 'Policing, punishment and praxis: restorative justice and non-violent alternatives to paramilitary punishments in Northern Ireland,' *Policing and Society*, 11(3/4): 259–382.

— (2002) 'Restorative justice and the critique of informalism in Northern Ireland,' *British Journal of Criminology*, 43(3): 534–63.

McEvoy, K., Gormally B. and Mika, H. (2001) 'Conflict, crime control and the "re" construction of state/community relations in Northern Ireland,' in G. Hughes (ed.) *Crime Prevention and Community*, Buckingham: Open University Press.

McGarry, J. (1998) 'Political settlements in Northern Ireland and South Africa,' *Political Studies*, XLVI: 853–70.

Mamdani, M. (ed.) (2000) *Beyond Rights Talk and Culture Talk: comparative essays on the politics of rights and culture*, London: Macmillan.

Mathews, J. (ed.) (2002) *The Future of the Army Profession*, Boston: McGraw Hill Primis.

Mika, H. (2002) 'Introduction: practice, performance and prospects in restorative justice,' special issue, *British Journal of Criminology*, 42(3).

— (2004) 'Unpublished evaluation of Community Restorative Justice Ireland and Northern Ireland Alternatives' (author's copy).

Mika, H. and McEvoy, K. (2001) 'Restorative justice in conflict: paramilitarism, community and the construction of legitimacy in Northern Ireland,' *Contemporary Justice Review*, 3/4: 291–319.

Minow, M. (1998) *Between Vengeance and Forgiveness: facing history after genocide and mass violence*, Boston: Beacon Press.

Mitchell, G. (2000) *Making Peace: the inside story of the making of the Good Friday Agreement*, London: Heinemann.

O'Leary, B. (2005) 'Mission accomplished? Looking back at the IRA,' *Field Day Review*, 217–46.

O'Mahony, D., Chapman, T. and Doak, J. (2002) *Restorative Cautioning: a study of police based restorative cautioning pilots in Northern Ireland* (4), Belfast: Northern Ireland Statistics and Research Agency.

Paparone, C. (2004) 'Deconstructing army leadership,' *Military Review*, January–February: 2–10.

Pavlich, G. (2001) 'The force of community,' in H. Strang and J. Braithwaite (eds) *Restorative Justice and Civil Society*, Cambridge: Cambridge University Press.

Putnam. R. D. (2000) *Bowling Alone: the collapse and revival of American community*, New York: Touchstone.

— (ed.) (2002) *Democracies in Flux the evolution of social capital in contemporary society*, New York: Oxford University Press.

Ratuva, S. (2002) 'Restorative justice and conflict management: potential for Fiji and Pacific communities,' paper presented at the 2002 Pacific Research Development Symposium.

Roberts, P. (2003) 'Restoration and retribution in international criminal justice: a exploratory analysis,' in A. von Hirsch, J. Roberts, A. E. Bottoms, K. Roach and M. Schiff (eds) *Restorative Justice and Criminal Justice: competing or reconcilable paradigms?* Oxford: Hart Publishing.

Roche, D. (2002) 'Restorative justice and the regulatory state in South African townships,' *British Journal of Criminology*, 42: 514–33.

— (2003) *Accountability in Restorative Justice*, Oxford: Oxford University Press.

Ruth-Heffelbower, D. (2000) 'Indonesia: restorative justice for healing a divided society,' paper presented at the April 2000 'Just Peace?' conference in Auckland, New Zealand.

Sheffer, G. (ed.) (1993) *Innovative Leaders in International Politics*, Albany: SUNY Press.

Shirlow, P., Graham B., O'Hamaill, F., Purvis, D. and McEvoy, K. (2005) *Ex-Prisoners and Conflict Transformation in Northern Ireland*, Belfast: Community Relations Council.

Sinnerton, H. (2003) *David Irvine: uncharted waters*, Cork: Brandon.

Skelton, A. and Frank, C. (2004) 'How does restorative justice address human rights and due process issues?' in H. Zehr and B. Toews (eds) *Critical Issues in Restorative Justice*, Monsey, NY: Criminal Justice Press.

Sullivan, D. and Tifft, L. (2005) *Restorative Justice: healing the foundations of our everyday lives*, second edn, Monsey, NY: Willow Tree Press.

Teitel, R. G. (2000) *Transitional Justice*, New York: Oxford University Press.

Thomson, D. (2004) 'Can we heal ourselves? Transforming conflict in the restorative justice movement,' *Contemporary Justice Review*, 7(1): 107–16.

Verwimp, P. and Verpoorten, M. (2004) 'What are all the soldiers going to do? Demobilization, reintegration and employment in Rwanda,' *Conflict, Security and Development*, 4(1): 39–57.

Viera De Mello, S. (2003) 'Statement to the Opening of the Fifty-Ninth Session of the Commission on Human Rights by Sergio Vieira De Mello,' Geneva, 17 March 2003. Available at: http://www.unhchr.ch/huricane/huricane.nsf/0/90EDF4CFB1A078B3C1256CEC003B6C13?opendocument

Villa Vincenzio, C. (1999) 'A different kind of justice: the South African Truth and Reconciliation Commission,' *Contemporary Justice Review*, 1: 407–29.

Weber, M. (1946) 'The sociology of charismatic authority,' in H. Mills and C. W. Mills (eds) *From Max Weber: essays in sociology*, New York: Oxford University Press.

Westlake, M. (2000) *Leaders of Transition,* New York: St Martin's Press.

Wilson, R. (2001) *The Politics of Truth and Reconciliation in South Africa: legitimizing the post-apartheid state*, Cambridge: Cambridge University Press.

Winston, T. (1997) 'Alternatives to punishment beatings and shootings in a loyalist community in Belfast,' *Critical Criminology*, 8(1): 122–8.

Notes

1. Institute of Criminology and Criminal Justice, School of Law, Queen's University, Belfast. Parts of this chapter are drawn from a paper delivered by Kieran McEvoy at the Police Service of Northern Ireland Conference 'Restorative Justice: From the Mechanics to the Dynamics' in February 2005 and ongoing PhD fieldwork conducted by Anna Eriksson. We are grateful for the comments from a number of people who attended that conference and from the restorative justice practitioners at both Community Restorative Justice Ireland and Northern Ireland Alternatives for their assistance with our ongoing research.

2. In relation to Northern Ireland, this analysis can be applied to initiatives in both Republican and Loyalist areas; however, this chapter will deal mainly with the RJ programs in Republican areas for the reason that the fieldwork in Loyalist communities had just started when this chapter was written, hence the data is incomplete.

3. Interview with CRJ Director, 9 November 2004.

4. Interview with CRJI office co-ordinator, 16 November 2004.

5. On average, each new case is dealt with within a day or two. Time spent on a case varies depending on complexity and the needs of the participants, but on average a case takes about ten hours to resolve. However, it can vary between one and forty hours, and some cases are ongoing for several years whereas others are closed that same day. (Based on qualitative and quantitative data from five different CRJI offices).

6. Interview with CRJI office co-ordinator, 16 November 2004.

7. Ibid.

8. Interview with CRJI office co-ordinator, 16 November 2004.

9. Colonel Paparone is an instructor at the US Army War College.

10. 'Provos shot bus driver says Durkan,' *Belfast Telegraph*, 2 October 2002.

11. Interview with CRJI practitioner, 2 December 2004.

12. The Independent Criminal Justice Inspectorate was created in the wake of the Good Friday Agreement to improve public confidence in the administration of justice.

Section V

Gross human rights violations and transitional justice

The chapters in this section focus on the processes of healing and reconciliation in nations undergoing transition and reconstruction in the wake of war and gross human rights violations. Collective restorative reconstruction requires change at the national, political level of the society undergoing transition and these transitions are filled with great tension in establishing co-existence and building public trust. In South Africa, the Truth and Reconciliation Commission was established to acknowledge the truth and affix responsibility for the past conditions of privilege, oppression and massive harm. It was an attempt to strike a middle ground between retributive trials and national amnesia. It was an attempt to end social divisiveness and oppression, and to form a positive base for a new South African society. The end of apartheid was a stalemate and victors' tribunals could not have been imposed, nor could a cleansing of the state apparatus and civil service. South Africa could not afford the wounds and divisiveness of such trials, though some have argued that the Truth and Reconciliation Commission hearings opened these wounds and as well failed to provide reparations. Nevertheless, the new South Africa has created an institutional basis for unity.

A far more complex and fragile political circumstance has been faced in Serbia. Racked by long-standing ethnic and religious conflicts in the former Yugoslavia, the dictatorship of Milosevic, international pressures for retributive accountability for past atrocities committed by Serbs, political dissensus, stark economic conditions and transitions, the entrenchment of former administration officials in state institutions, and the effects of the NATO bombings, the people of Serbia have struggled, and the state has failed to find the will to create a politically practical path for truth and reconciliation. Yet, members of Serbian society have initiated innovative programs designed to disclose the whole truth and begin the process of healing.

Just how to meet the needs of survivors of massive collective trauma is an equally complex problem intertwined with that of political transition. The question of who are the victims who require social reparation, shared mourning, and shared memory is often not as clear as it was/is with regard to the Holocaust survivors and other victims of the Nazi regime, those subjected to apartheid in South Africa, those indigenous/ aboriginal peoples subjected to historical injustices, and those subjected to state terrorism in some US-client states in Central and South America. The notion of 'victim' is challenged in the Serbian context as the whole region has a history of past and present atrocities and wars of liberation. People from different ethnic groups living in differing parts of the former Yugoslavia have constructed multiple truths that they have passed on from generation to generation. Serbs have exploited other Serbs, and the UN, through its economic sanctions, has impoverished and criminalized the whole of Serbia, making all Serbs 'victims,' and designating them collectively responsible for gross human rights violations.

Healing in the aftermath of massive trauma and establishing truth and reconciliation in a society in transition from such trauma experiences are very complex and fragile processes. The contributions in this section present critical insights into these processes.

In Chapter 23, Yael Danieli sets out the necessary, complementary components for healing in the wake of massive trauma and points out that these components must be applied in different weights, in different situations and cultures, and at different points in time, in accord with the participation and choices of victims/survivors. These components, as both she and Chris Cunneen (Chapter 24) point out, are recognized and informed by the United Nations Declaration of Basic Principles of Justice for Victims of Crime and Abuse of Power, the recently adopted (April 2005) Basic Principles and Guidelines on the Right to a Remedy and Reparation for Victims of Gross Violations of International Human Rights Law and Serious Violations of International Humanitarian Law, and the recently revised Set of Principles for Protection and Promotion of Human Rights Through Action to Combat Impunity. There is widespread agreement on these components: the right to dignity and equality under law; the right to know and have the truth acknowledged; the right to combat impunity; the right to reparation and a guarantee of non-recurrence, and compliance with internationally accepted human rights norms.

Victims/survivors tell us that in order to combat personal mistrust and loneliness, they need to have the conspiracy of silence ended, to know what occurred. They also tell us that their personal healing requires shared mourning and a shared sense that this memory is preserved as a part of human consciousness. Thus, building monuments may give survivors a physical place to go to remember and mourn, to commemorate, document, and educate – to bear witness to our children and to our collective commitment to NEVER AGAIN. Further, victims/survivors tell us that the experience of seeking and receiving reparation must not revictimize them, and that while they can never be compensated, that compensation can for some signify vindication – an acknowledgement of responsibility and apology. However, different victim groups vary in their acceptance of, for example, receiving a continuous monetary compensation. Some accept this form of compensation and others reject it, feeling that in the context of their victimization such compensation is an insult and a continued denial that those who were subjected to crimes of state were political opponents.

In Chapter 24 Chris Cunneen points out that those writing about restorative justice have largely failed to discuss crimes of the modern political state, especially when the state has been the perpetrator of large-scale violations of human rights. He explores how recent and not so recent systematic and large-scale abuse of human rights has been perpetrated and legitimated by law within modern states, and what the role of restorative justice might be in responding to these atrocities. Such a discussion is critical, for some of these crimes are still on-going and when they subside, the state will play a pivotal role in the process of providing or failing to provide collective reparations for the harms which a prior administration has inflicted. Cunneen examines the relationship of reparation and restorative justice, focusing on illustrations from Canada, South Africa, and Australia and notes that reparations are highly dependent on differing socio-political–economic–historical contexts. To illustrate, the Canadian government has recently offered a statement of reconciliation for the long-term inter-generational effects of its removals of children through the residential school system and has provided a relatively modest fund to support initiatives for indigenous peoples affected by this removal. Acknowledgement, apology, and commemoration are key components of this reconciliation offer.

Vesna Nikolic-Ristanovic (Chapter 25) gives a detailed exploration of the very complex historical, ethnic, religious, and political-economic context for the failure of the Serbian state to develop a national program of truth and reconciliation or to initiate such a commission on a regional basis. We have mentioned many of the contextual factors involved in this failure, but want to add that many people in the former Yugoslavia have been victims in more than one war/conflict, that there are ethnic divisions that cross borders between areas, now states, that continue to prevent the establishment of peaceful co-existent relationships within ethnically mixed communities. Further, some people who were victimized were, as well, victimizers, and many have been victimized by different perpetrators who belong to different communities and ethnic groups. This means that among the population of Serbia there are both victims and perpetrators of crimes/gross violations of human rights, with these groups overlapping. Furthermore, there has been insistent international pressure on the government of Serbia to comply with a retributive prosecutorial response. Such an initiative, of course, serves to hide and deny the role of the international community in immiserating and bombing the peoples of Serbia.

Nikolic-Ristanovic argues that in the Serbian context restorative reconstruction must confront both violence among Serbs themselves and violence between Serbian citizens/Serbs from other parts of the former Yugoslavia and other ethnic groups/nations, including both those from the former Yugoslavia and those from Western nations in relation to the NATO bombings. Truth and reconciliation processes in Serbia need to deal with victimhood and truth in a holistic and inclusive way, allowing for healing through making the victimization of all visible. But, just because the state has found itself tentative and/or unwilling to initiate such politically 'risky' activities and initiatives, this has not meant that other restorative programs have not been initiated. She presents a brief description of these holistic and creative initiatives.

Charles Villa-Vicencio (Chapter 26) continues this discussion regarding the tension between retributive and restorative justice in societies in transition, though, as Daly (Chapter 7) has pointed out, this tension is ever-present in our responses to 'ordinary' conflict and crimes. The political costs of sustained political prosecutions and a comprehensive program of retribution is not a viable option for societies in transition from repressive regimes or from internal wars or genocide. However, a restorative justice policy that allows impunity is also not viable, for this jeopardizes the legal rights and material well-being of victims and the development of the civic responsibility of perpetrators, enabling them to be reintegrated into society and to play a positive role in rebuilding a new future society.

Pursuing justice in a transitional society requires a set of ethical values and a political-legal initiative that is flexible enough to meet the needs associated with nation-building, all of which have the capacity to derail the fragile initiative for peaceful coexistence and national reconciliation between former enemies. According to Villa-Vicencio, a genuine non-malicious retributive justice involves more than the punishment of offenders. It is necessary to achieving a society built on the rule of law.

In his view, building a restored society involves four interrelated imperatives: to affirm moral decency and human dignity by condemning past wrongs; to affirm the dignity of victims/survivors by offering reparations; to acknowledge the humanity of those who have harmed others by requiring them to accept responsibility for their actions; and to make mercy and forgiveness possible, allowing those who have harmed to at some time contribute to the new society. Restorative justice is putting energy into peacebuilding and the future.

Peacebuilding imperatives are further examined in Chapter 27. Here, Sinclair Dinnen explores the historical and current transitional political-economic contexts of the Melanesian nations of the Southwest Pacific, in particular the nations of Papua New Guinea, Solomon Islands, Vanuatu, and to a lesser extent Fiji. In these differing post-colonial contexts of pluralism, transition, the disruption of traditional authority, rapid social and economic change, and an ever-encroaching global materialistic culture, the institutions of governance are pressed to meet the dual demands for the rule of law and the needs of differing peoples. As in other cultural and community contexts there is congruence between the approaches to conflict and harm in many Melanesian communities and the processes of restorative justice. And, here as elsewhere, the institutions of the nation-state and its retributive-oriented justice systems have been to varying degrees superimposed on to a patchwork of numerous small-scale local polities with their traditions of self-regulation and custom-driven modes of conflict resolution. In Papua New Guinea (PNG) for minor offenses and juvenile offenders the adoption of restorative justice programs and a Village Court system have been developed with the recognition that retributive policing and custodial punishments are counter-productive to the needs for crime prevention, rehabilitation, and community mobilization. However, there is also the recognition that local initiatives and courts must be monitored because of their susceptibility to capture by local elites and their potentiality to become oppressive and discriminatory. On the positive side, Sinclair notes that the weakness and limited reach of the state in these societies has provided a context for the growth of civil society and a rich repertoire of restorative experience and innovation, such as the programs for the surrender of criminal gangs in PNG, the community-driven peace process on the island of Bougainville, the work of the Kup Women for Peace, and the Saraga Peace Committees.

In his view, the way forward is neither a single reliance on community or state justice, but a creative configuration of governance that integrates the best of both, while reaching out to address the larger issues of social justice.

In Chapter 28 Lars Waldorf explores the historical and political context within which Rwanda experienced genocide and has attempted to respond to its aftermath. Eight years after the genocide in Rwanda, the Rwandan government launched *gacaca* as a pilot project, expanding it nationwide earlier this year (2005). But prior to turning to this traditional method of dispute resolution, where respected male elders adjudicated disputes over property, inheritance, personal injury and marital relations, the RPF rejected the idea of a South African-style truth and reconciliation commission, insisting that only retributive prosecution could end a culture of impunity. But, as Gacaca Courts have been reconstructed there is little tradition remaining. *Gacaca* had been characterized by accessibility, informality, economy, public participation, restitution, reconciliation, and social pressure. In contrast, the new *gacaca* system has become a formal institution, intimately linked to the state apparatus of prosecutions and incarceration, applying codified rather than customary law. Gacaca Courts are now judging genocide with participation being almost exclusively that of Tutsi survivors telling their stories. Increasingly, participation has become state-coerced, and Hutu have little incentive to participate because they fear being accused as either perpetrators or bystanders and because they are offered no opportunity to talk about the crimes committed by the RFP forces. The success of speeding up the prosecution of accused defendants has relied on confessions for which sentence reductions are received. In addition, after eleven years, the Rwandan government has not created the long-promised compensation fund for survivors, though an assistance fund for the neediest survivors has been implemented. Taking all of this in, Waldorf concludes that the new *gacaca* cannot produce reconciliation and peace as long as it is largely one-sided, discouraging Hutu participation, and potentially ascribing collective guilt to most Hutu.

There are enormous difficulties in achieving acknowledgement and truth, providing reparation, and establishing reconciliation in societies rebounding from mass atrocity and trauma. Peacebuilding requires tremendous collective and institutional will and energy, a commitment to meeting the essential reparative needs of victims/survivors, and the changed consciousness on the part of all of us relatives in the human community to support initiatives of social justice.

23

Essential elements of healing after massive trauma

Complex needs voiced by victims/survivors

Yael Danieli

Previously I summarized what victims/ survivors themselves stated as the necessary components for healing in the wake of massive trauma.[1] These components emerged from interviews with survivors of the Nazi Holocaust, Japanese- and Armenian-Americans, victims from Argentina and Chile, and professionals working with them, both in and outside their countries. Presented below as goals and recommendations, they are organized from the: (1) individual, (2) societal, (3) national; and (4) international perspectives.

1 the reestablishment of the victim's equality of value, power, esteem (dignity), the basis of reparation in a society or nation. This is accomplished by: compensation, both real and symbolic; restitution; rehabilitation; and commemoration;
2 relieving the victim's stigmatization and separation from society. This is accomplished by: commemoration; memorials to heroism; empowerment; and education;
3 repairing the nation's ability to provide and maintain equal value under law and the provisions of justice. This is accomplished by: prosecution;

apology; securing public records; education; creating national mechanisms for monitoring, conflict resolution; and preventive interventions;
4 asserting the commitment of the international community to combat impunity and provide and maintain equal value under law and the provisions of justice and redress. This is accomplished by: creating ad hoc and permanent mechanisms for prosecution (e.g. ad hoc tribunals and ultimately an International Criminal Court); securing public records; education; and creating international mechanisms for monitoring, conflict resolution, and preventive interventions.

It is important to emphasize that this comprehensive framework, rather than presenting *alternative* means of reparation, sets out necessary *complementary* elements, to be applied in different weights, in different situations and cultures, and at different points in time. It is also crucial that victims/ survivors participate in the choice of the reparation measures adopted for them.[2]

Some of these elements had already been recognized among the measures recommended in the United Nations Declaration

343

of Basic Principles of Justice for Victims of Crime and Abuse of Power (A/RES 40/34), the so-called Magna Carta for victims, to improve access to justice and fair treatment, restitution, compensation, and necessary material, medical, psychological, and social assistance and support for such victims.

This framework partly informed the Basic Principles and Guidelines on the Right to a Remedy and Reparation for Victims of Gross Violations of International Human Rights Law and Serious Violations of International Humanitarian Law (Resolution E/CV.4/2005/L.48) which were adopted on 13 April 2005. During its same session, in April 2005, the United Nations Human Rights Commission also took note, with appreciation, of the recently revised Set of Principles for the Protection and Promotion of Human Rights Through Action to Combat Impunity, updated by Professor Diane Orentlicher (E/CN.4/2005/102/ADD.1). This set of principles includes the right to know, the right to justice, and the right to reparation/guarantees of non-recurrence.

Based theoretically on the above Declaration and Basic Principles, and practically upon both the positive as well as negative practical experiences of the ad hoc tribunals for the former Yugoslavia and Rwanda, the sections relevant to victims in the Statute and Rules of the International Criminal Court (ICC) make for the most progressive provisions for victims in any international court, in fact, in international law. Moreover, it is the provisions for and the role of victims in the ICC that makes the ICC unique.

In its Resolution 1566 adopted 8 October 2004 (S.RES/1566 [2004]), the Security Council has also acknowledged the need to fill the gap in international deliberations about combating terrorism regarding the neglect of the aftermath to the victims and their families of their experiences of terrorism and their subsequent role in it.

This chapter will convey how victims and professionals who have worked with them view some of the psychological aspects of these measures and what the *victims themselves* feel is helpful or not. After describing and conceptualizing the aftermath of the victims' experiences, the chapter will examine some of the meanings of compensation and will also draw attention to the often neglected aspect of commemoration.

The experience of the victim

The aftermath of the experience

After liberation, as during World War II, survivors were victims of a pervasive societal reaction comprised of obtuseness, indifference, avoidance, repression, and denial of their Holocaust experiences. Like other victims, survivors' war accounts were too horrifying for most people to listen to or believe. Similar to other victims who are blamed for their victimization ('You are stupid to live near the Bhopal plant'), survivors were faced with the pervasively held myth that they had actively or passively participated in their own destiny by 'going like sheep to the slaughter.' Additionally, bystanders' guilt led many to regard the survivors as pointing an accusing finger at them and projecting on to the survivors the suspicion that they had performed immoral acts in order to survive. Like other victims, they were also told to 'let bygones be bygones' and get on with their lives.

Such reactions have ensured the survivors' silence about their Holocaust experiences. They were forced to conclude that nobody cared to listen and that 'nobody could really understand' unless they had gone through the same experiences. The resulting *conspiracy of silence* (Danieli 1982, 1988a) between Holocaust survivors and society in general, and survivors and mental health and other professionals in particular, has proven detrimental to the survivors' familial and socio-cultural reintegration by intensifying their already profound sense of isolation, loneliness, and mistrust of society. This has further impeded the possibility of their intrapsychic integration and healing, and made their task of mourning their massive losses impossible (Danieli 1989; Eitinger and Krell 1985).

Children of survivors seem to have consciously and unconsciously absorbed their parents' Holocaust experiences into their lives (Bergman and Jucovy 1982; Danieli 1985, 1992, 1998; Dasberg, 1987; Sigal and Weinfeld 1989; Rubenstein *et al.* 1990). As Bettelheim observed, 'What cannot be talked about can also not be put to rest; and if it is not, the wounds continue to fester from generation to generation' (1984: 166). Families of survivors are extremely small. The Holocaust deprived them of the normal cycle of the generations and ages, and of natural death (Eitinger 1980). Survivors of the Holocaust age early and have higher than average rates of early death from all causes. Old age, in itself, is a trauma for them (Danieli 1981). Each survivor's family tree is steeped in murder, death, and losses; yet its offspring are expected to reroot that tree and reestablish the extended family and to start anew a healthy generational cycle. Edelman *et al* similarly reports that in Argentina 'a remarkably high number of fathers of missing people had major physical disorders and substantial increase of deaths, whereas mothers did not present the same symptoms' (1992: 1–2), and provides related speculations.

The healing process

Cognitive recovery involves the ability to develop a realistic perspective of what happened, by whom, to whom, and to accept the reality that it had happened the way it did – for example, what was and was not under the victim's control, what could not be, and why. Accepting the impersonality of the events also removes the need to attribute personal causality and consequently guilt and false responsibility. An educated and contained image of the events of victimization is potentially freeing from constructing one's view of oneself and of humanity solely on the basis of those events. For example, having been helpless does not mean that one is a helpless person; having witnessed or experienced evil does not mean that the world as a whole is evil; having been betrayed does not mean that betrayal is an overriding human behavior; having been victimized does not necessarily mean that one has to live one's life in constant readiness for its reenactment; having been treated as dispensable vermin does not mean that one is worthless; and taking the painful risk of bearing witness does not mean that the world will listen, learn, change, and become a better place (Danieli 1988b).

The Latin American Institute of Mental Health and Human Rights in Santiago, Chile, stated that,

> The victims know that individual therapeutic intervention is not enough. They need to know that their society as a whole acknowledges what has happened to them ... Truth means the end of denial and silence ... Truth will be achieved only when literally everyone knows and acknowledges what happened during the military regime ... [They concluded:] Social reparation is thus ... simultaneously a sociopolitical and a psychological process. It aims to establish the truth of political repression and demands justice for the victims ... both through the judicial process and through the availability of health and mental health services ... The new democracy that now offers the possibility of reparation will deteriorate into a frail bureaucratic system if the process of social mourning is not realized fully.
>
> (Becker *et al.* 1990: 147–8)

(For related programs see Kordon *et al.* 1988; Genefke 1992.)

Thus, you need to heal the sociopolitical context for the full healing of the individuals and their families, as you need to heal the individuals to heal the sociopolitical context. This is a mutually reinforcing context of shared mourning, shared memory, a sense that the memory is preserved, that the nation transformed it into a part of its global consciousness. The nation shares the horrible pain. The survivors are not lonely in their pain.

The conceptualization of the experience

Trauma and the continuity of self: a multidimensional, multidisciplinary integrative (TCMI) framework. To conceptualize the consequences of massive trauma, I proposed the multidimensional, multi-disciplinary integrative framework (Danieli 1998). It posits that an individual's identity involves a complex interplay of multiple systems, including: biological and intrapsychic; interpersonal, including the familial, social, and communal; ethnic, cultural, ethical, religious, spiritual, and natural; educational/ occupational; material/economic, legal, environmental, political, national, and international. These systems coexist along the time dimension, creating a sense of life continuous from past through present to the future. Ideally, one should have free psychological access to and movement within all these identity systems. Each system is the focus of one or more disciplines that may overlap and interact, such as biology, psychology, sociology, economics, law, anthropology, religious studies, and philosophy.[3] Each discipline has its own views of human nature and it is those that inform what the professional thinks and does.

Trauma exposure and 'fixity'. Trauma exposure can cause a rupture, a possible regression, and a state of being 'stuck' in this free flow, which I have called 'fixity' (Danieli 1998). The intent, place, time, frequency, duration, intensity, extent, and meaning of the trauma for the individual, and the survival strategies used to adapt to it, will determine the degree of rupture and the severity of the *fixity*.

Fixity can be intensified in particular by the aforementioned *conspiracy of silence*, the survivors' reaction to the societal (including healthcare and other professionals) indifference, avoidance, repression, and denial of the survivors' trauma experiences (see also Symonds 1980). Society's initial emotional outburst yet its demand for rapid return to apparent normality is an important example. This *conspiracy of silence* is detrimental to the survivors' familial and sociocultural (re)integration by intensifying their already profound sense of isolation and mistrust of society. It further impedes the possibility of their intrapsychic integration and healing, and makes the task of mourning their losses impossible. Fixity may increase vulnerability to further trauma. It also may render *chronic* the immediate reactions to trauma (e.g. acute stress disorder), and, in the extreme, become life-long (Danieli 1997) *post-trauma/victimization adaptational styles* (Danieli 1985). This occurs when survival strategies generalize to a way of life and become an integral part of one's personality, repertoire of defense, or character armor.

Recognition of the possible long-term impact of trauma on one's personality and adaptation and the *intergenerational* transmission of victimization-related pathology still await explicit inclusion in future editions of the diagnostic nomenclature. Until they are included, the behavior of some survivors, and some children of survivors, may be misdiagnosed, its etiology misunderstood, and its treatment, at best, incomplete. This framework allows evaluation of each system's degree of rupture or resilience, and thus informs the choice and development of optimal multilevel intervention. Repairing the rupture and thereby freeing the flow rarely means 'going back to normal.' Clinging to the possibility of 'returning to normal' may indicate denial of the survivors' experiences and thereby fixity.

346

Immediately after 11 September, I suggested (Danieli 2001) that, more than ever, issues related to the time dimension emerged as paramount. *First* was the imperative to resist the culturally prevalent (American) impulse to do something, to find a quick fix, to focus on outcome rather than process, to look all too swiftly for closure, and to flee 'back to normal.' *Second*, knowing that there will be long-term effects not only of the disaster itself but also of the immediate interventions, we must recognize the necessity for and importance of long-term commitment, and systematically examine every short-term decision from a long-term perspective. Since the urge to act and help others and oneself in the immediate aftermath is near universal, it should be harnessed and incorporated into long-term planning. I also noted (Danieli 2001) the necessity of considering *at-risk times* (e.g. family holidays, anniversaries) as well as *at-risk groups*.

Integration of the trauma must take place in *all* of life's relevant (ruptured) systems and cannot be accomplished by the individual alone. Systems can change and recover independently of other systems. Rupture repair may be needed in all systems of the survivor, in his or her community and nation, and in their place in the international community. To fulfill the reparative and preventive goals of trauma recovery, perspective and integration through awareness and containment must be established so that one's sense of continuity and belongingness is restored. To be healing and even self-actualizing, the integration of traumatic experiences must be examined from the perspective of the *totality* of the trauma survivors' and family and community members' lives.

What victims tell us about reparation

In order to understand more fully the experience of receiving reparation, compensation, and how it can be helpful to individuals and to their society, as well as to gain a long-term perspective, I interviewed victims/survivors of the Nazi Holocaust survivors and then newer populations, such as Japanese-Americans, Argentineans, and Chileans, and professionals working with them, both in and outside their countries. Following a description of the process of claiming redress are some quotations of statements, discussions and conclusions from these interviews.

Claiming redress

The process of applying for German *Wiedergutmachung* (literally means 'to make something good again', to make amends for their suffering during the Nazi regime) was experienced by survivors as yet an additional series of hardships. The Allied Powers after World War II issued laws restricted to restoring to the original owners property confiscated by the Nazis. The laws did not take into account personal damage to victims of Nazi persecution – those who had suffered in mind and body, or had been deprived unjustly of their freedom, or whose professional or economic prospects had been summarily cut short. Nor did these laws consider assistance to the widows and orphans of those who had died as a result of Hitler's policies. The Western Allies placed the responsibility for the reparation of such damages in the hands of the newly constituted German Federal States. Following a few stages, the Federal Republic of Germany enacted the 'Final Federal Compensation Law' on 14 September 1965. Thus, indemnification for persecution of persons was differentiated from restitution for lost property. The implementation of the compensation law was traumatic in itself.

Kestenberg (1980), a reparation lawyer, states:

> Even when most German officials showed concern and willingness to compensate Jews for the wrong done to them, their

so-called *Wiedergutmachung*[4] ... was only concerned with monetary matters. A moral *Wiedergutmachung* was not planned and did not exist. No one bothered to restore the survivor's dignity. On the contrary, the procedures inherent in some of the paragraphs of the Restitution Laws, inflict indignities upon the claimants while at the same time German authorities are elevated to the status of superior beings who adjudge the claimants' veracity and honesty and classify them in accordance with the degree of their damage.

(pp. 2–3)

[Even if] the applicant had indeed been confined in a concentration camp ... they behaved as if he were trying to extort money from the German government under false pretenses.

(p. 4)

The survivors had to prove that they had been damaged. Their attempts at self-cure were destroyed once they had to admit that their damage was permanent, sealed, and signed by the authorities. To receive payments, often sorely needed, the applicants had to subject themselves to the most humiliating and degrading, seemingly very correct legal type of investigation (p. 5).

Bureaucratic deadlines are used for the unfair and prejudicial practice of rejecting claims ... The German treasury enriches itself when a claimant dies before his case is concluded. At this time 50 per cent of claims are denied, 25 per cent are still pending, and only 25 per cent have been resolved in favor of the claimants. A case in the highest court alone takes eight years for determination while many of the elderly claimants are not only humiliated but also suffer from lack of economic necessities and moneys for treatment of ailments which exacerbate in old age (p. 9). The victimization of the once persecuted continues (p. 12).[5]

Crucial to having a claim processed was undergoing a psychiatric examination. To be an examiner, the only requirement was

that the psychiatrist be able to speak and write German, not Yiddish or Polish, which were the languages spoken by many survivors. The psychiatric examiner had to determine, and try to express in numbers, how much, or what fraction of the patient's emotional illness is, in his opinion, due to the persecution he suffered. The law required a minimum of 25 per cent damage in order for the applicant to receive a pension.

Examiners had intense emotional and moral reactions to this process. These reactions motivated much of their writings and were poignantly expressed in most of them (Danieli 1982). Eissler (1967) speculates that one major reason for the experts' (and the courts') 'open or concealed hostility against those who have had to bear great sufferings' has to do with the 'universal,' archaic, pagan 'contempt that man still tends to feel for the [weak and] humiliated, for those who have had to submit to physical punishment, suffering, and torture' (p. 1357). He concludes:

The minimum one may demand, under such circumstances, is that the responsible authorities recognize those who cannot control this archaic feeling and exclude them from the position of experts in matters of compensation for suffering. When a physician refers to concentration camp experiences as 'disagreeable' he has given away his secret contempt ... He has thrown away the right to be called an 'expert'; if he continues to avail himself of that privilege, he must share the blame with those who continue to use his services.

(p. 1358)

Krystal and Niederland (1968) add, 'Even the hearing of the tales of the concentration camp survivors is so disturbing and traumatic, so abusive to the examiner that some are compelled to avoid obtaining the details of the traumatization.[6] They then arrive at a meaninglessly brief summary of the experiences' (p. 341), and Hocking (1965) reports cases 'where patients have been told not to describe their experiences, only their symptoms' (p. 481).

FT, a Czech Jew of Viennese origins and the sole survivor of a well-to-do family, whose total possessions in Prague were taken over by the Germans, and then by the Communists ... left, via France to the United States and began pursuing compensation in the 1950s. He describes his ordeal as follows:

> The fact that I was three and a half years in concentration camps didn't count. At that time unless you were literally disabled – such as missing a hand – they recognized nothing. I always found it distasteful to spend days fighting a bureaucracy that tried to tell me that I am not entitled to that money, providing documents, writing letters, having to prove that I was indeed worthy of compensation. When I tried to get payment for some medical bills they wanted copies of the bills from 1946 to 1956. I had no way of finding them so they figured out an 'average' and offered me $200 if I waive claims against medical bills and I said that that is an insult and told them to keep the money and leave me alone. Fighting for these things absorbs so much emotional energy ... It is bad enough that I have to live with memories, but to have to stir them up and to also face one's persecutors. I don't have to face Nazis anymore, but I still have to deal with German bureaucracy. I got disgusted and wanted to quit. But I knew that if I didn't claim it, the money will remain in Germany. They won't give more to someone else.

Restitution and compensation

Of course, everybody says that money is not enough. There is a disagreement over whether we should take money or not. Some people don't need it at all financially, yet insist on getting reparations; for others the check is practically necessary, especially the elderly. Compensation is a symbolic act because you can never be compensated. It is

minor in amount but major in significance. Many people are desperate and need the support; they are living on a pension and $200 a month is critical. For a family in Bhopal even $15 a month may make a difference even though it's a pittance.

How does one compensate for three and a half years in concentration camps? For the loss of a child? It is impossible. How do you pay for a dead person? For a Korean woman sexually abused by the Japanese in World War II? It's not the money but what the money signifies – vindication. It signifies the government's own admission of guilt, and an apology. The actual value, especially in cases of loss of life is, of course, merely symbolic, and should be acknowledged as such.

The money *concretizes* for the victim the confirmation of responsibility, wrongfulness: he is not guilty, and somebody cares about it. It is at least a token. It does have a meaning. Just a letter of apology doesn't have the same meaning, and even if it is a token it adds. In our system of justice, of government, when damage has occurred, money is paid.

We have demonstrated that people can be damaged. There must be an acknowledgment that wrong was done. Then those who were damaged are entitled to compensation for their damages and a program of rehabilitation. The acknowledgment is necessary because without an admission of guilt people are still angry. Rehabilitation programs must be available on a long-term basis.

In Israel, idealists fought against [taking money]:

> I refused. Today I am sorry, because I concluded that I did not succeed to change anything by refusing and the truth is that here and in Israel there are aging survivors who don't have an extended family. The steady sum enables them to go on. The fact that I gave up only left the money in the hands of the Germans. We were wrong.

Should there be one payment? No. The monthly check in some ways weakens the trauma. When it becomes routine, it transforms into something permanent that somehow enables overcoming survivor guilt. The routine swallows the guilt.

For the Argentinean and Chilean parents it was a matter of the state admitting that a horrible crime was done to them and that it was done without any justification or reason and was purely an expression of political harm and abuse of power and violation of their freedoms and human lives. Not only was there a crime of taking lives – suddenly they are without their children. They were also robbed of the chance of their children helping and supporting them and standing by them in their old age. Thus at least they should have compensation for the rest of their lives, not a single lump-sum. There is no place for a single payment. A house is a house, but when it is human life you compensate for something that could have accompanied them throughout their lives. Therefore there is logic in receiving regular compensation. This should be legalized.

In Argentina, responses of different victim groups seem to vary. The Madres de Plaza de Mayo organization officially refused economic reparations as the government's attempt to buy their silence and in the absence of social and historical recognition that their children had been political or social opponents and not criminals. The former political prisoners, especially if they had been in prison for a long time, consider economic compensation as their rightful reparation. Mostly young people, their imprisonment deprived them of finishing their studies, progressing in a job, or establishing their own home and families. In married cases, the long period in jail caused great economic difficulties to their families. Many of them feel that this is a partial moral recognition of the damage they suffered and that, albeit in a small way, they can at least win something from the state. For people who are ambivalent, their ambivalence

increases when compensation is experienced as an offense, yet is very necessary economically.

Perhaps the most crucial aspect is that of *impunidad*: that traitors, collaborators, torturers are not punished. As long as persons who have violated human rights or exerted torture can go free, there can never be a true democracy in a society. A democratic constitution is no guarantee against torture. Impunity under a democratic constitution is a continuous repression. Impunity stops democratic processes. Torturers for example should have absolute maximum punishment. To practice torture is equal to committing murder.

Most Japanese-Americans felt finally vindicated after fifty years, having spent ten years fighting the system, not as a Japanese-American issue, but as an American constitutional one. So many of our people could now talk about it and express deep-seated feelings for the first time in fifty years. That was the positive, therapeutic side. It was only a token compensation; $20,000 won't cover what was lost: jobs, names, all properties, horrible living conditions, dignity, citizenship. It's not the money but what the money signifies. Psychologically it lifted a big burden off the Japanese-Americans who always feel that the system couldn't trust us but viewed us as potential enemies, as second-class citizens. At least we now feel not accepted but vindicated for what happened fifty years ago. The apology was more important than the amount of money. After fifty years of maintaining that they were right, the government did acknowledge that they were constitutionally wrong (for intergenerational effects, see Nagata 1998).

Economic compensation given to torture victims should be very substantial. The torturers should compensate for their crime by having all of their property confiscated in order to pay back to those they have tortured. Whether members of governments, police officers, and doctors who have parti-

350

cipated in torture, *all* property should be confiscated from them – this is the most important aspect of restitution – and used for compensation to the victim. Furthermore, there should be general awareness in the whole population about this aspect and the situation as such. It might be very effective preventively if this principle was generally known.

Before anything else the victim wants an acknowledgement of a debt that somehow, sometime a government writes laws and one of them is 'Mr— deserves the praise of the country.' The first step of a government such as Argentina is 'the state of Argentina has woefully wronged those people who were persecuted by the military and we feel contrite and wish to apologize.' The full sense of it is that it *should* be a *law*, nothing else. And put it on the books. We have done wrong, we acknowledge it. It is *very* important. As a *political* matter I would absolutely have the books open ... open the files and let the facts speak for themselves.

Let us find a way and make a general statement. Clearly victims of governmental wrong should be compensated and this is the way we should go about it. As we had established norms of international minimal behaviors, crimes against humanity, we need parallel legislation for compensation for the victims.

Legal procedures against the victimizers and financial arrangements compensating the victims are necessary steps in the aftermath of man-made calamities. However, they are not sufficient steps for societies to recover. In societies which moved out of totalitarian regimes, into quasi-democratic ones (Argentina, Chile, Eastern Europe), victims and victimizers of the former regime go on living in the same society. As they do not have any social and psychological mechanisms to repair these past relations, these may just penetrate deeper inside, and thereby be transmitted to the next generations. Therefore, along legal and financial steps, in each of these countries, a socio-

psychological institute should be established to work on the after-effects of the traumata with children of both victims and victimizers. The end result of this process should be to try to bring them together, to think about the overall social responsibility: What can they do together so that detrimental tensions will not burst out again and again within those societies?

I am still concerned that it makes it easier to just assign monetary value, and not address the profound emotional and moral breach.[7]

Because of the long-term and/or intergenerational transmission of victimization there should be no statute of limitation. If the victim, for moral reasons, refuses the meaning of the reparation payment, the money should, nonetheless, not remain in the hands of the perpetrators or the silently acquiescing proceeding socio-political system but it, or its equivalent sum, should be put in a special long-term fund whose purpose should be future-oriented, both in terms of education, prevention, and later care as provisions for the future – for themselves and/or their offspring's care, if needed and necessary.

Commemoration and education

The need for commemoration is for the victims and for society. Rituals are very important; there is no organized society, religion or culture that does not have rituals of memory. Commemorations can fill the vacuum with creative responses and may help heal the rupture, not only internally but also the rupture the victimization created between the survivors and their society.

It is a shared context, shared mourning, shared memory. The memory is preserved; the nation has transformed it into part of its consciousness. The nation shares the horrible pain. What may be an obligatory one-day-a-year ritual to others the victims experience as a gesture of support, of sharing the pain. They are not lonely in their pain.

351

There should be general awareness on a high level: information and education about the situation, how it arose, and what are the consequences. Statues of heroes/martyrs, paintings. Streets should be named after them, as could rooms in colleges and museums. There should be memorial services, scholarship funds, concerts and theatre performances, and educational books.

Commemoration should be done with great dignity and with a feeling that, while it honors those who suffered, those who have died, it is also done for preventive purposes, in the spirit of the knowledge that compensation for loss of lives, health, hopes, can never be fulfilled. Yet maintain the commitment to NEVER AGAIN! and the possibility for intergenerational dialogue, which may include dialogues between children of survivors and of perpetrators.

In Elie Wiesel's (1985) words, 'they have no cemetery; we are their cemetery.' Building monuments serves some important functions in the reestablishment of a sense of continuity for the survivors, and for the world. Much of the chronic grief, the holding on to the guilt, shame, and pain of the past have to do with these internally carried graveyards. Survivors fear that successful mourning may lead to letting go, thereby to forgetting the dead and committing them to oblivion. The attempt to make these graveyards external creates the need for building monuments so that the survivors might have a place to go to remember and mourn in a somewhat traditional way. Visiting Yad Vashem seems to provide such an opportunity for some survivors.

Building monuments also has the significant functions of commemoration, documentation, and education – an extension of bearing witness – and of leaving a legacy so that the victims, the survivors, and the Holocaust, and other examples of gross human rights violations, will not be forgotten. The latter are comforting to some of the essential components of the aging survivor's preoccupation: 'Who cares if I live?'

'Who loves me?' 'Who will remember me?' 'Will the memory of my people and of the Holocaust perish?' and, 'Did/Will the world learn anything from it?'

Clearly this whole area calls for further comprehensive, systematic cross-cultural, and interdisciplinary research.

References

Becker, D., Lira E., Castillo, M. I., Gomez, E. and Kovalskys, J. (1990) 'Therapy with victims of political repression in Chile: the challenge of social reparation,' *Journal of Social Issues*, 40(3): 133–49.

Bergman M. S., and Jucovy, M. E. (eds) (1982) *Generations of the Holocaust*, New York: Basic Books.

Bettelheim, B. (1984) Afterword to C. Vegh, *I Didn't Say Goodbye*, R. Schwartz (trans.), New York: E. P. Dutton.

Danieli, Y. (1981) 'On the achievement of integration in aging survivors of the Nazi Holocaust,' *Journal of Geriatric Psychiatry*, 14(2): 191–210.

— (1982) 'Therapists' difficulties in treating survivors of the Nazi Holocaust and their children,' unpublished doctoral dissertation, New York University (1981), University Microfilms International, #949-904.

— (1985) 'The treatment and prevention of long-term effects and intergenerational transmission of victimization: a lesson from Holocaust survivors and their children,' in C. R. Figley (ed.) *Trauma and Its Wake*, New York: Brunner/Mazel.

— (1988a) 'Confronting the unimaginable: psychotherapists' reactions to victims of the Nazi Holocaust,' in J. P. Wilson, Z. Harel and B. Kahana (eds) *Human Adaptation to Extreme Stress*, New York: Plenum.

— (1988b) 'Treating survivors and children of survivors of the Nazi Holocaust,' in F. M. Ochberg (ed.) *Post-traumatic Therapy and Victims of Violence*, New York: Brunner/Mazel.

— (1989) 'Mourning in survivors and children of survivors of the Nazi Holocaust: the role of group and community modalities,' in D. R. Dietrich and P. C. Shabad (eds) *The Problem of Loss and Mourning: psychoanalytic perspectives*, Madison: International Universities Press.

— (1992) 'The diagnostic and therapeutic use of the multi-generational family tree in working with survivors and children of survivors of the

Nazi Holocaust,' in J. P. Wilson and B. Raphael (eds) *The International Handbook of Traumatic Stress Syndromes,* Stress and Coping Series (Donald Meichenbaum, Series Editor), New York: Plenum Publishing.

— (1997) 'As survivors age: an overview,' *Journal of Geriatric Psychiatry,* 30(1): 9–26.

— (ed.) (1998) *International Handbook of Multigenerational Legacies of Trauma,* New York: Kluwer Academic/Plenum Publishing Corporation.

— (2001) 'ISTSS members participate in recovery efforts in New York and Washington, DC,' *Traumatic Stress Points,* 15(4): 4.

— (ed.) (2002) *Sharing the Front Line and the Back Hills: international protectors and providers, peacekeepers, humanitarian aid workers and the media in the midst of crisis,* Amityville, NY: Baywood Publishing.

Dasberg, H. (1987). 'Psychological distress of Holocaust survivors and offspring in Israel, forty years later: a review,' *Israel Journal of Psychiatry and Related Sciences,* 23(4): 243–56.

Edelman, L., Kordon, D. and Lagos, D. (1992) 'Argentina: physical disease and bereavement in a social context of human rights violations and impunity,' in L. H. M. van Willigen (Chair), 'The limitations of current concepts of post traumatic stress disorders regarding the consequences of organized violence,' session presented at the World Conference of the International Society for Traumatic Stress Studies, Amsterdam, The Netherlands.

Eissler, K. R. (1967) 'Perverted psychiatry?,' *American Journal of Psychiatry,* 123: 1352–8.

Eitinger, L. (1980) 'The concentration camp syndrome and its late sequelae,' in J. E. Dimsdale (ed.) *Survivors, Victims, and Perpetrators: essays on the Nazi Holocaust,* New York: Hemisphere.

Eitinger, L. and Krell, R. (eds) (1985) *The Psychological and Medical Effects of Concentration Camps and Related Persecutions on Survivors of the Holocaust: a research bibliography,* Vancouver: University of British Columbia Press.

Genefke, I. (1992) 'The most effective weapon against democracy: torture – it concerns us all,' testimony to the Subcommittee on Foreign Operations, Export Financing and Related Expenses for the Rehabilitation Centre for Torture Victims, Copenhagen, Denmark, 1 May 1992.

Hocking, F. (1965) 'Human reactions to extreme environmental stress,' *Medical Journal of Australia,* 2(12): 477–83.

Kestenberg, M. (1980) 'Discriminatory aspects of the German restitution law and practice,' in Y. Danieli (Chair), 'Nazi Holocaust effects,' session presented at the meeting of the First World Congress of Victimology, Washington, DC, August 1980.

— (1985) 'Legal aspects of child persecution during the Holocaust,' *Journal of the American Academy of Child Psychiatry,* 24(4): 381–4.

Kordon, D. K., Edelman, L. I., Lagos, D. M., Nicoletti, E. and Bozzolo, R. C. (1988) *Psychological Effects of Political Repression,* Buenos Aires: Sudamericana/Planeta.

Krystal, H. and Niederland, W. G. (1968) 'Clinical observations on the survivor syndrome,' in H. Krystal (ed.) *Massive Psychic Trauma,* New York: International Universities Press.

Nagata, D. K. (1998) 'Intergenerational effects of the Japanese American internment,' in Y. Danieli (ed.) *International Handbook of Multigenerational Legacies of Trauma,* New York: Kluwer Academic/Plenum Publishing Corporation.

Roht-Arriaza, N. (2004) 'Reparations in the aftermath of repression and mass violence,' in E. Stover and H. M. Weinstein (eds) *My Neighbor, My Enemy: justice and community in the aftermath of mass atrocity,* Cambridge, UK: Cambridge University Press.

Rubenstein, I., Cutter, R. and Templer, D. I. (1990) 'Multigenerational occurrence of survivors syndrome symptoms in families of Holocaust survivors,' *Omega Journal of Death and Dying,* 20(3): 239–44.

Sigal, J. J. and Weinfeld, M. (1989) *Trauma and Rebirth: intergenerational effects of the Holocaust,* New York: Praeger.

Stover, E. and Weinstein H. M. (eds) (2004) *My Neighbor, My Enemy: justice and community in the aftermath of mass atrocity,* Cambridge, UK: Cambridge University Press.

Symonds, M. (1980) 'The "second injury" to victims (special issue),' *Evaluation and Change,* 36–8.

United Nations (1985) Declaration of Basic Principles of Justice for Victims of Crime and Abuse of Power (A/RES 40/34).

Wiesel, E. (1985) 'Listen to the wind,' in I. Abrahamson (ed.) *Against Silence: the voice and vision of Elie Wiesel,* Vol. I, New York: Schockens.

Notes

1. Originally published in 1992 in T. C. van Boven, C. Flinterman, F. Grunfeld and I. Westendorp (eds) *The Right to Restitution, Compensation and Rehabilitation for Victims of*

Gross Violations of Human Rights and Fundamental Freedoms, Netherlands Institute of Human Rights, Special Issue No. 12, pp. 196–213. Also published in N. J. Kritz (ed.) (1995) *Transitional Justice: How Emerging Democracies Reckon with Former Regimes*, Washington, DC: United States Institute of Peace, Vol. 1, pp. 572–82. An updated version, 'Justice and reparation: steps in the process of healing,' appeared in 1998 in C. C. Joyner (ed.) 'Reining in impunity for international crimes and serious violations of fundamental human rights: proceedings of the Siracusa Conference 17–21 September 1998,' *International Review of Penal Law*, 14: 303–12.

2. See also Roht-Arriaza (2004): 'A constant under all these approaches is the need to involve the victims and their organizations in discussions about what reparations, like other post-conflict strategies, should look like' (p. 136).

3. More recently, Stover and Weinstein (2004) also utilize an ecological model of social reconstruction.

4. Facts and figures on restitution in Germany, New York: German Information Center,

November 1977. (Available from German Information Center, 410 Park Avenue, New York, NY 10022.)

5. Elsewhere, Kestenberg (1985) elaborated on the difficulties particular to child survivors, a population whose special needs deserves special attention.

6. See the section 'In search for justice' in Danieli (2002) describing the toll paid by human rights and justice defenders in their work, particularly with victims.

7. See also the study carried out by the Chilean human rights organization CODEPU under the auspices of the Association for the Prevention of Torture, that interviewed about a hundred individuals and groups of family members of disappeared and summarily executed victims in Chile, Argentina, El Salvador, and Guatemala. Findings emphasized that, for the victims, 'moral and legal measures of reparation are fundamental, while monetary compensation is controversial and problematic' (Roht-Arriaza, 2004: 127). Of note is the emphasis survivors placed on education for the children of those killed.

24

Exploring the relationship between reparations, the gross violation of human rights, and restorative justice

Chris Cunneen

Introduction[1]

The relationship between reparations, responses to the gross violation of human rights, and restorative justice is only recently finding a place in the broad and expanding literature on restorative justice. This chapter explores the relationship through a consideration of the international movement to provide reparations for the victims of human rights abuses.

The linking of discussions on reparations for human rights abuses with discussions about restorative justice provides an important opportunity for rethinking a number of fundamental processes, relationships, and functions such as the role of the state, the relationship between victims and offenders, and the broader political and historical processes which shape how we define and respond to crime.

The restorative justice literature has been slow to think through the implications of situations where the modern political state has been the perpetrator of crime. For example, the view that crime is a conflict that must be returned to the community may be misplaced in certain situations. Communities may still play a fundamental role in identifying the crimes of the state and

may well play a role in forcing the state to acknowledge and respond to its own wrongdoing. Yet where there have been large-scale abuses of human rights, it is also the case that the state through the allocation of its own resources will play a pivotal role in the process of reparations for the harm which has been caused. In these cases, the state has a responsibility to repair the harm it has caused or allowed to occur. An additional player in these processes may be the international community to the extent that special tribunals may be created to deal with prosecutions in post-conflict situations. Thus in the Rwandan example there is the international criminal tribunal, the national justice system, and localized community-justice processes (*gacaca*), all operating simultaneously to deal with crimes arising from the genocide.

Working through the issues associated with reparations for the gross violation of human rights enables us to broaden our vision of restorative justice beyond a concern with individualized concepts of crime and criminal responsibility. There has been more than a decade of developing jurisprudence on the question of reparations for gross violations of human rights, particularly through a number of reports to the

United Nations by Van Boven and, more recently, Bassiouni. An understanding of these developments can work to deepen the theoretical underpinning of restorative justice. In addition there has been a developing reparations practice across a broad range of post-conflict situations from Africa to Southeast Asia, to South and Central America, where reparations have often been associated with the concept of 'transitional justice.' Finally, in liberal democracies in Australia, New Zealand, Scandinavia, and North America there have been various discussions of reparations (and sometimes restorative justice) as a process for dealing with historical injustices against Indigenous peoples. A connected but distinct question for reparations is slavery. A common theme then is: how do we respond to both recent (and not so recent) systematic, fundamental and large-scale abuses of human rights perpetrated and often legitimated by modern states?

The existing restorative justice literature which analyses potential connections between human rights abuses and restorative justice is sparse and not well developed. Van Ness (1996: 29–30) is one of the few writers in the field of restorative justice who has looked for links with international human rights norms. He finds that in five areas there is substantial consistency between international standards relating to criminal justice and restorative justice theory. These include the requirement that states must balance the interests of victims, offenders, and the public; the requirement that victims and offenders must have access to formal and informal dispute resolution mechanisms; the requirement for comprehensive action in regard to crime prevention; the requirement that governments provide impartial, formal judicial mechanisms for victims and offenders; and the requirement that there must be help for community reintegration of victims and offenders.

The problem with this approach is that it narrowly restricts the discussion on human

rights to particular issues relating to criminal justice norms and standards. Human rights are clearly far broader than this and relate to such areas as rights of particular groups including women, children, and minorities, and as freedom from and protection against a range of behaviors, including discrimination, arbitrary and unlawful treatment, torture, and genocide. The unnecessarily narrow discussion means that one of the thorniest issues which restorative justice proponents must tackle is avoided: how to consider the relationship between restorative justice as a remedy for the gross violation of human rights when the offender is the state and its agents.

A similar problem can be seen in discussions of the application of restorative justice approaches to criminal justice process. Galaway and Hudson (1996) have argued that there are three elements which are fundamental to restorative justice definition and practice.

> First, crime is viewed primarily as a conflict between individuals that results in injuries to victims, communities and the offenders themselves and only secondarily as a violation against the state. Second, the aim of the criminal justice process should be to create peace in communities by reconciling the parties and repairing the injuries caused by the dispute. Third, the criminal justice process should facilitate active participation by victims, offenders and their communities to find solutions to the conflict.
>
> (Galaway and Hudson 1996: 2)

The relationship between restorative justice remedies and the relative role of victims, offenders, community and the state in the Galaway and Hudson formulation become far more complex when it is the state which is responsible for criminal harm. This is clearly not merely a side issue when we consider the widespread role of the institutions of the state, often sanctioned by law, as the perpetrators of some of the greatest crimes against humanity. One estimate is that modern political states have been responsible for the murder of over 169 million people between 1900 and 1987, excluding deaths in wars, judicial executions and the killing of armed opponents and criminals (Green and Ward 2004: 1). The modern political state has been integral to the commission of genocide and other human rights abuses. Genocide and modernity have gone hand in hand (Bauman 1989). Indeed, the specific modernity of genocide is that the vastness and totality of 'final solutions' could only be pursued by the modern state (Gellately and Kiernan 2003: 4).

Reports of genocide, 'ethnic cleansing,' and mass crime continue in places like Rwanda, East Timor, the former Yugoslavia, and the Darfur region of western Sudan. Criminology has been largely silent on the issue of genocide, and restorative justice proponents have had little to say in the area. The extensive literature on genocide and the Holocaust has made little impact 'on the individuating tendencies of criminological thought' (Jamieson 1999: 132). That genocide, the 'crime of all crimes,' should be absent from criminology deserves full explanation in itself (Morrison 2004). However, the problem has not only been with criminology. Social sciences generally have been slow to develop the sustained study of genocide and mass murder until the 1990s (Bauman 1989; Gellately and Kiernan 2003: 4).

And of course, state crime is not restricted to genocide, mass murder, and torture. There is both petty corruption such as bribery and the large-scale corruption of political elites. There is also the intersection between state crime and corporate crime resulting in 'massive human rights and environmental violations' (Green and Ward 2004: 28). Perhaps the quintessential example of this intersection between business and state was the role of corporations in Nazi Germany in facilitating the Holocaust. As both Matthews and Kauzlarich (2000) and

Green and Ward (2004) note, the state may facilitate corporate abuses of human rights in a number of ways. It may include facilitating the takeover of land for exploitation, the relaxing of regulatory processes that allows environmental degradation to proceed unchecked, or facilitating the repression of resistance. Repression of local populations on the behalf of corporations may occur either directly through the use of state forces, or by allowing private forces employed by the corporate sector to operate freely. A current and well-researched example of this interconnection between the state and powerful corporate bodies in the abuse of human rights has been the relationship between the Nigerian state and US and European corporations (such as Shell) in the oil industry (Human Rights Watch 1999).

Often the law has played a constitutive role in crimes of the state. As Balint (1994: 13) has noted, the law was crucial to the Holocaust. 'It was law which provided the genocide with its order, it was law which legitimated it . . . Legislation defined the Jew and removed the Jew from the common world.' In South Africa it was the laws of apartheid which defined 'colored' groups along territorial, residential, political, social, and economic lines (Boraine 1999: 469). In liberal democracies like Australia, Canada and the US, it was the law which defined the 'Native' and the 'Aborigine' and which drew the boundaries around those people defined as 'half-caste,' 'quarter-caste,' 'quadroon,' or 'octoroon.' It was the law that was to provide the operational framework for policies founded in racist hierarchies of human worth (see, for example, NISATSIC 1997).

International law, reparations and restorative justice

The principles of restorative justice are not foreign to public international law. Brownlie (1998: 460) notes that reparation is a broad term covering a variety of measures which might be expected of a defendant state including restitution, compensation, an apology, punishment of the individuals responsible for the actions, steps undertaken to prevent a recurrence of the offence, and other forms of satisfaction. Satisfaction can involve any measure undertaken as part of reparation and may include an acknowledgment of wrongdoing.

The process of developing principles and guidelines on the right to reparation for victims of violations of international human rights law has been in motion for more than a decade and a half. It is uncontroversial, in international or domestic law, to state that where a right has been violated it should be remedied. However, the questions of 'who' and 'how' with respect to violations of international human rights law have always been difficult and are now being addressed systematically in the international arena. The Van Boven/Bassiouni principles have developed in response to these important questions of how to provide remedy and repair to victims of gross abuses of human rights. It is expected that these principles will be adopted eventually by the United Nations General Assembly.

The principles have gradually evolved since the then United Nations Sub-Commission on the Prevention of Discrimination and the Protection of Minorities first commissioned Special Rapporteur Van Boven to report on the issue in 1989. In 1998 the Commission on Human Rights appointed Cherif Bassiouni to further revise the principles developed by Van Boven on the right to reparations for victims of gross violations of human rights.

The Basic Principles and Guidelines on the Right to Remedy and Reparation for Victims of Violations of International Human Rights and Violations of Humanitarian Law contains twenty-nine principles. Broadly, the principles state the obligation to respect, ensure respect for and enforce international human rights, and firmly locate the right to afford remedies to victims within the scope of this obligation. The principles aim to identify and provide mechanisms, modalities, and procedures to implement existing obligations to victims, and in this sense also aim to rationalize a consistent approach to the means by which victims' needs can be addressed. For example, Principle 7 states that statutes of limitations should not unduly restrict the ability of a victim to pursue a claim against a perpetrator – a particular problem which victims of historical injustices such as Indigenous peoples have faced.

The Basic Principles set out an inclusive 'victim-centered' definition of victim, where the victim's harm and suffering (as opposed to the acts of, or relationship to, the perpetrator) is placed at the centre. A victim is 'a person or a collective group of persons who suffered harm, including physical or mental injury, emotional suffering, economic loss, or impairment of their fundamental legal rights' (Principle 8). A victim may also be a dependant or a member of the immediate family or household of the direct victim. In regard to the treatment of victims, it is set out that the state should afford special consideration to victims who have suffered violence and trauma, taking care to avoid re-traumatization in the course of legal or administrative procedures designed to provide justice and reparation.

The Basic Principles conceptualize the victim's right to remedy along four axes: access to justice, reparation, access to information and non-discrimination among victims. Principles 12–14 seek to ensure a victim's right of access to all judicial, administrative, and other public processes under both domestic and international law. To this end states should disseminate information regarding all available remedies, take measures to minimize inconvenience to victims and their representatives during proceedings that affect their interests, facilitate assistance to victims seeking to access justice, and make available diplomatic and legal means to ensure that victims can exercise their rights to remedies. Provision should be made for collective claims from groups of victims and the ability to receive reparations collectively.

Principles 16–25 address the right to adequate, effective, and prompt reparation. The issue of reparation is dealt with in detail; it is in these principles that vital questions about responsibility are addressed. Who is responsible? What is the extent of that responsibility? What forms should this responsibility take? The basic purpose of reparations – to promote justice – is stated in the first principle in this section, as well as the basic principle underpinning the quantum of reparations – a proportional response to the gravity of the violations and the harms caused.

Ultimate responsibility for reparations lies with states: a state is to provide reparation for its own violations and, in the event that another party is responsible and unwilling or unable to meet their obligations to repair, the state should endeavor to provide assistance, including reparations. Successor states shall provide reparations for violations of previous governments.

Questions of *how* to repair are given extensive attention under the headings: restitution, compensation, rehabilitation, and satisfaction and guarantees of non-repetition.

- Restitution should, whenever possible, restore the victim to the original situation. Restitution can include the restoration of social status, identity, return to one's place of residence, restoration of employment and return of property (Principle 22).
- Compensation should be provided for any economically assessable damage: physical or mental harm, including pain, suffering and emotional distress; lost opportunities, including employment, education and social benefits; material damages and loss of earnings; harm to reputation or dignity; and costs required for legal or expert assistance, medicines and medical services, and psychological and social services (Principle 23).
- Rehabilitation should include, as appropriate, medical and psychological care as well as legal and social services (Principle 24).
- Satisfaction and guarantees of non-repetition includes cessation of continuing violations, verification of the facts and full public disclosure of the truth (to the extent that such disclosure does not cause further unnecessary harm to the victim), the search for the whereabouts of the disappeared and for the bodies of those killed, and assistance in the recovery, identification and reburial of the bodies in accordance with the cultural practices of the families and communities; apology, including public acknowledgement of the facts and acceptance of responsibility; commemorations and tributes to the victims; inclusion of an accurate account of the violations that occurred in educational material at all levels (Principle 25).

International acceptance of reparations

Internationally there has been growing acceptance that governments acknowledge and make reparations for the victims of human rights abuses. There has been widespread agreement on the principle of reparations, including a variety of methods of redress; the importance of public acknowledgment of wrongdoing and apology for harm; the importance of participation of victims in the process of acknowledgment; and the acceptance of internationally accepted human rights norms as a basis for reparations (HREOC 2000: iv). The Van Boven/Bassiouni principles outlined above provide a broad principled framework for reparations.

What can restorative justice offer in the development of responses to the systematic abuse of human rights? In the first instance, it is worth recognizing that the rebuilding of societies torn apart by systematic human rights abuses has involved processes of truth, justice, and reconciliation. In some cases there have been ad hoc international criminal tribunals; however, there has also been a reliance on various types of truth commissions in South Africa and South America. In other countries there have been processes for reparations and reconciliation put in place.

One of the central differences in approaches to responding to the gross violation of human rights is between those who advocate for retribution and punishment arising from criminal proceedings and those who argue that alternatives, often described as restorative justice, are more desirable (Garkawe 2003a: 339).

For example, Orentlicher (1994) argues strongly for the criminal prosecution of alleged perpetrators, arguing that there is a duty on states to prosecute offenders, that prosecution will strengthen democratic institutions and that punishment of offenders will ensure deterrence. Criminal prosecution as a strategy is often portrayed as 'victor's justice.' The Nuremberg and Tokyo International Military Tribunals, or the International Criminal Tribunals in Rwanda and the former Yugoslavia, are perhaps less politically achievable in transitional states where political forces are more precariously balanced. For example, Archbishop Desmond Tutu has argued that South Africa was unable to follow the 'Nuremburg' option of trials. The end of apartheid had been a stalemate and a 'victor's justice' could not have been imposed. South Africa could not afford long trials, nor would the judicial system have coped (Tutu 2004: 2).

An important point, however, is that irrespective of whether a restorative/reparations model or a criminal proceedings model

is followed, there are still obligations for certain conditions to be met. Garkawe (2003a) argues that where a restorative justice approach is used, and prosecution is not an essential element of the response, there are still obligations on the state to gather the truth behind the abuses, to ensure that there is no repetition of abuse, and to provide reparations for victims.

Conversely, there have been important restorative justice elements in contemporary international criminal proceedings such as the International Criminal Tribunal for the former Yugoslavia (ICTY), the International Criminal Tribunal for Rwanda (ICTR) and the International Criminal Court (ICC). The special tribunals have developed victims and witness units to assist and support victims, the tribunals were given powers to develop special procedural rules and measures for the protection of victims and witnesses, and vulnerable victims (particularly women and children) were given special consideration. As Garkawe (2003b: 349) notes, 'the final innovation was that for the first time an international criminal court made an attempt to facilitate victim reparation or compensation.'

The ICC built upon the earlier developments of the ICTY and the ICTR in terms of protecting the interests of victims. Of particular interest in the context of the current discussion is the creation of a reparations scheme for victims. The ICC provides that the Court shall establish principles relating to reparation, including restitution, compensation and rehabilitation (Article 75(1)). The Court is also empowered to order reparations directly against convicted offenders, and to order payments be made through a trust fund established for victims and their families.

Reparations and restorative justice in specific contexts

There are many examples where victims of human rights abuses and historical injustices have received public acknowledgment and reparations, including Romany children forcibly removed in Switzerland, institutional child abuse victims in Ireland, Holocaust survivors and other victims of the Nazi regime, and victims of repression in Chile, Argentina, Peru, Honduras, and Guatemala (Orentlichter 1994; Brooks 1999; Barkan 2000; Cunneen 2003). In the United States, President Clinton apologized to African Americans who had been victims of medical experimentation in Tuskegee. There have also been apologies and reparations in some US states for events arising from the Jim Crow and segregation periods including racist lynchings, property destruction, and riots. There have also been reparations for Japanese Americans interned during the Second World War. By way of contrast, there has been little movement in providing reparations for slavery.

Internationally there has been growing recognition of the need to respond to the historical injustices imposed upon Indigenous peoples. In September 1999 the Danish prime minister apologized to Inuit people who had been relocated in northern Greenland during the 1950s. A new agreement was signed between the prime minister and the premier of Greenland strengthening the provisions of the Greenland Home Rule Act (1978) which provides a political and legislative framework for self-rule and reconciliation.

In October 1997 the king of Norway publicly apologized to the Sami people for the injustices brought about by the Norwegian state particularly through the policies of assimilation. In December 1999 the Norwegian prime minister apologized to the Sami people and in early January 2000 announced a fund to be established to promote Sami languages and cultures as a form of collective reparation and compensation.

In New Zealand the Treaty of Waitangi provides the framework for the recognition of Indigenous rights and reparation for past harms. From the early 1990s the New Zealand government began to negotiate settlements of Maori treaty claims. Settlements are implemented through acts of parliament and may include land, compensation, and a formal apology for past abuses and wrongful acts.

The list of responses to historical injustices could go on. It is not my purpose here to discuss whether these specific responses have been adequate – rather, I wish to indicate the important contextual similarities in process and values. To do this I provide a brief discussion of several examples in slightly greater detail: Canada, Australia, and South Africa.

Canada

In 1996 the Canadian Royal Commission on Aboriginal Peoples (1996) released its five-volume final report. Two years later the Canadian government (1998) responded to the Commission's findings with a report *Gathering Strength*. The government report has a statement of reconciliation which acknowledges past injustice and includes an apology to Indigenous peoples, particularly in relation to the effects of the residential school system. The Canadian government has acknowledged the long-term inter-generational effects of removals through the residential school system and has provided a $350 million fund to support initiatives for Indigenous people affected by removal.

Also in Canada, the federal Law Commission of Canada (2000) has recently released a report which deals with the means of responding to the harm caused through the institutionalization of children, including Indigenous children. In terms of our discussion of the needs of people who have been the victims of systematic human rights abuse and criminal injury, the report discusses the needs of survivors.

The Commission was able to identify certain recurring themes in the manner these needs were expressed. Survivors seek: an

361

acknowledgment of the harm done and accountability for that harm; an apology; access to therapy and to education; financial compensation; some means of memorializing the experiences of children in institutions; and a commitment to raising public awareness of institutional child abuse and preventing its recurrence.

(cited in HREOC 2000: 62)

South Africa

In October 1998 the South African Truth and Reconciliation Commission (1998) published its five-volume report. In its approach to reparations the Commission noted that:

if we are to transcend the past and build national unity and reconciliation we must ensure that those whose rights have been violated are acknowledged through access to reparation and rehabilitation ... without adequate reparation and rehabilitation measures, there can be no healing and reconciliation, either at an individual or a community level.

(cited in HREOC 2000: 68–9)

The South African Truth and Reconciliation Commission was established to uncover the truth about past violations of human rights to enable the process of reconciliation and national unity to progress (Lyster 2000). The Commission had six purposes including the generation of a detailed record of the extent, nature and causes of human rights violations in South Africa, to name those responsible for the violations, to provide a public forum for the victims to express themselves, to make recommendations to prevent future abuses, to make reparations to victims, and to grant amnesty to those who made full disclosure of their involvement in such violations. Indeed, Bishop Desmond Tutu has characterized the Truth and Reconciliation Commission as working within the paradigm of restorative justice, in

contrast to approaches that rely on the prosecution of war criminals through special tribunals (*Sydney Morning Herald*, 27 November 1999: 7).

Australia

From the late-nineteenth century until at least the mid-1960s, large numbers of Indigenous children throughout Australia were removed from their families to be raised in institutions and by foster parents. The justifications and policy motives behind the practice varied but were broadly the result of theories such as eugenics and assimilation which assumed the biological and cultural inferiority of Indigenous peoples. The ultimate goal of these policies of removal was the 'absorption' of 'mixed race' children into the European community.

In May 1997 the Australian government tabled the report of the National Inquiry into the Separation of Aboriginal and Torres Strait Islander Children from Their Families (the Stolen Generations Inquiry). The Inquiry found that basic safeguards which protected non-Indigenous families were cast aside when it came to Indigenous children. The main components of the forced removal of Indigenous children were deprivation of liberty, deprivation of parental rights, abuses of power, and breach of guardianship duties. In relation to international human rights the main obligations imposed on Australia and breached by a policy of forced removals were the prohibitions on racial discrimination and genocide. The policy continued to be practiced after Australia had voluntarily subscribed to treaties outlawing both racial discrimination and genocide. The legislative regimes created for the removal of Indigenous children were different and inferior to those established for non-Indigenous children. They were racially discriminatory and remained in place until the 1960s in some states.

The Inquiry made a range of recommendations consistent with international remedies for human rights abuses and centered around the principle of reparation. Reparations were to include five components: acknowledgment and apology; guarantees against repetition; measures of restitution; measures of rehabilitation; and monetary compensation. The Inquiry also recommended that reparation be available for all who suffered because of forcible removal including individuals removed, family members who suffered, communities that suffered cultural and community disintegration, and the descendants of those forcibly removed. In other words, the harm arising from the forced removal of Aboriginal children is seen as affecting communities and it is communities that need to be healed.

Reparations for the gross violation of human rights

There is a consistency in approach to reparations across different jurisdictions. Further, we can see a consistency between reparations principles and the principles that are usually seen to underpin restorative justice. Some important similarities include the need for acknowledgment and apology, guarantees against repetition, processes for restitution and rehabilitation, and compensation. The examples of Canada, Australia, and South Africa further highlight these points.

Acknowledgment and apology. The importance placed on acknowledgment and apology is consistent with the principles of restorative justice as well as the recommendations and processes of inquiries and commissions into human rights abuses. For example, the Stolen Generations Inquiry recognized the need to establish the truth about the past as an essential measure of reparation for people who have been victims of gross violations of human rights. The Inquiry was told of the need for acknowledgment of responsibility and apology in many of the submissions from Indigenous

organizations and the personal testimonies of individuals.

The South African Truth and Reconciliation Commission placed a great deal of importance on the process of acknowledgment. Acknowledgment provides a type of 'healing' truth where there is a full and public record of the victim's pain. As one of the Commissioners has noted, the process is 'central to the restoration of the dignity of the victim' (Lyster 2000). In the South African context, a public record and public acknowledgment of the past abuses is central to the process of reconciliation. Similarly in Canada, acknowledgment, apology, and commemoration are seen as key components of reconciliation with Indigenous peoples.

Like victims of other crimes, people who have been subjected to the gross violation of their human rights want public recognition of the harm they have suffered – they are not necessarily vengeful. Further, it is recognized that commemoration is an important part of the reparation process. Commemoration allows both mourning and the memory to be shared and to be transformed into part of the national consciousness.

Guarantee against repetition. It is widely recognized that guarantees against repetition are an important part of the reparation process and there are usually recommendations which deal specifically with this issue. These include such things as democratization, political reforms, law reform, and the need for compulsory educational modules in schools and universities on the particular issue. The Australian, Canadian, and South African reports all had various recommendations specific to their context which were aimed at ensuring a guarantee against repetition.

Some form of guarantee against repetition is a necessary component of international redress for human rights abuses. It is necessary before the process of healing for all parties can begin and the reintegration of the offender back into the community can occur. The concept of a 'guarantee against repetition' also can be seen within the values of restorative justice. Such a notion is basically a reassurance to the community that future harmful acts will not occur.

Clearly, such a reassurance is more difficult in cases where the state has been the perpetrator rather than an individual offender. The process is made even more complex and more imperative when there are multiple victims and offenders and the offending behavior has at some time received legitimacy and support from state institutions.

Measures of restitution and rehabilitation. 'The purpose of restitution is to re-establish, to the extent possible, the situation that existed prior to the perpetration of gross violations of human rights' (NISATSIC 1997: 296). Truth commissions and inquiries have typically strongly supported measures of this type. The South African Truth and Reconciliation Commission (1998) recommended five components to a reparations and rehabilitation policy which include: urgent interim reparation for those in urgent need; individual reparation grants for individual victims; symbolic reparation measures (national remembrance days, memorials, monuments, museums, etc.); community rehabilitation programs to establish community-based services; and institutional reform to prevent the reoccurrence of human rights abuses. In Canada the government has responded to the findings of the Royal Commission on Aboriginal Peoples with a fund to support Indigenous people who were forcibly removed.

The Australian Stolen Generation's Inquiry recognized that 'children who were removed have typically lost the use of their languages, been denied cultural knowledge and inclusion, been deprived of opportunities to take on cultural responsibilities and are often unable to assert their native title rights' (NISATSIC 1997: 296). As a result the Inquiry made a number of recommendations concerning support for people returning to their land and the communities receiving them, the expansion of funding to language, culture, and history centers to ensure national coverage, and funding for the recording and teaching of local Indigenous languages where the community determines this to be appropriate. The Inquiry also made recommendations to assist in re-establishing Indigenous identity and funding for Indigenous community-based family tracing and reunion services, as well as the preservation of, and Indigenous access to, records. Measures for rehabilitation were also an important component of the reparations package. The Inquiry was made very aware of the long-term problems caused by forcible separation. It made significant recommendations in relation to mental health care and assistance in parenting and family programs.

Restitution and rehabilitation for victims have been considered an important component of restorative justice. In general terms the principle has been identified as repairing the harm caused to victims through some form of recompense, involving where possible restitution, compensation, and reparation (Petit and Braithwaite 1993).

Monetary compensation. Typically, commissions inquiring into human rights abuses recognize that the loss, grief, and trauma experienced by those who were abused can never be adequately compensated. However, typically such inquiries also recommend some form of monetary compensation for the harm that has been suffered – particularly as a form of recognition of the responsibility for the causes of that harm. It is common for such commissions to advocate for simple and relaxed procedural principles to be applied in dealing with applications for compensation.

Thus there is a consistent view expressed in commissions of inquiry into gross violations of human rights that victims should be entitled to monetary compensation. Such a view is also consistent with international law. The South African Truth and Reconciliation Commission recognized that many people wanted financial compensation for their losses and felt that this was an appropriate and just response. The Commission recommended that the South African government not take a narrow and legalistic approach to the question of compensation. International obligations for adequate compensation for people who have been subjected to human rights violations arise from Article 8 of the Universal Declaration of Human Rights, Section 3 of the International Covenant on Civil and Political Rights and the Convention against Torture and Other Cruel, Inhuman and Degrading Treatment. The Canadian government also recognized that compensation is an important part of the process of reparation and reconciliation and that contemporary governments must shoulder the responsibility of the actions of previous governments.

By way of contrast, despite the Stolen Generation's Inquiry recommending compensation, the Australian government had ruled out compensation even before the Inquiry had finished its deliberations and presented its final report. The Inquiry recommended that a National Compensation Fund be established to provide an alternative to civil litigation. The Australian government has continued to refuse compensation.

Conclusion

At a basic level we can see similarities between reparations and restorative justice, particularly in the broad emphasis on establishing truth as a way of resolving conflict, of providing the opportunity for reintegration of victim and offender, and on developing the principles of reintegration, restitution, and compensation. Both restorative justice and reparations emphasize an approach which breaks down the divisions between civil and criminal wrongs, and instead prefers to consider the broader issue of individual and community harm. Restorative justice and reparations for human rights abuses are clearly identified as both a process and a set of values.

As a process both bring together those affected to establish truth and provide the framework for reconciliation. As a set of values or principles both are concerned with healing and reconciliation between parties. As Alex Boraine has noted, the South African Truth and Reconciliation Commission was established in the context of 'the compelling need to restore the moral order which was put in jeopardy by the abdication of the rule of law and gross violations of fundamental human rights' (Boraine 1999: 469). More recently the International Centre for Transitional Justice (ICTJ) (2002) has noted that the objectives of reparative programs are recognition, civic trust, and social solidarity.

There are also a number of insights that restorative justice proponents might take from the movement for reparations. One insight is the importance of understanding the values that are embodied in internationally accepted human rights. Both restorative justice and the demands for reparations for past abuses are about responding to the claims of injustice. An obvious issue is how we define 'injustice.' For those seeking redress for historical injustice, internationally accepted human rights norms provide the basis on which claims can be developed (Brooks 1999: 7). They provide a framework through which the demands for specific types of reparations can be made. Perhaps more importantly, the core international human rights provide a moral framework through which we can assess and evaluate the behavior of governments. This moral framework is not an arbitrary collection of disparate behaviors which are disapproved. International human rights law provides us with the means to place content into fundamental notions of human injustice.

A second insight revolves around the question of responsibility. Reparations for human rights abuses involve a fundamental move beyond individual responsibility to collective responsibility for wrongdoing. Thus thinking about reparations for the gross violation of human rights enables us to broaden the concept of restorative justice. It is important to acknowledge Blagg's (1998) point that restorative justice must not be narrowly defined to simple notions of individual crime. As noted above, perhaps the greatest crimes in the twentieth century have been committed by governments. Again, this poses a challenge for the development of restorative justice because the state as perpetrator is also ultimately responsible for ensuring reparations. This raises a further issue that requires some rethinking for restorative justice advocates. How can civil society through social movements force the state to take responsibility for its harms?

Connected to this point is the question of responsibility for the actions of others in cases of historical injustices. There is a considerable literature on the question of why 'we' should be responsible for actions of previous generations. Generally, the justification is based on a conception of society 'as an intergenerational community. Its institutions and moral relationships persist over time and through a succession of generations, and it depends for its moral and political integrity on its members accepting transgenerational obligations and honoring historical entitlements' (Thompson 2002: xviii). Perhaps these insights into collective responsibility might broaden the way restorative justice proponents understand responsibility in relation to individual offenders of everyday crimes, and challenge us to think beyond the simple dyad of victim and offender.

A third insight revolves around the importance of social, political, and historical *context*. In general terms, the reparations

packages that have been advocated for victims of human rights abuses are consistent with the values and processes of restorative justice. The Van Boven/Bassiouni principles use a language familiar to restorative justice: acknowledgment and apology, restitution, rehabilitation, compensation, and reassurance against future acts. Indeed, this is the approach which has been adopted in South Africa and Canada, and recommended in Australia. In South Africa, the Truth and Reconciliation Commission consciously referred to the notions of restorative justice as characterizing their approach.

However, one of the important lessons that also can be drawn from a review of international reparations processes is that *they are highly dependent on context*. In particular, whether and how reparations develop will be affected by factors external to the principles of either restorative justice or reparations. External factors will include:

- legal context (e.g. successful civil litigation by Indigenous people in Canada, and unsuccessful civil litigation in Australia have had differing political influences on governments' willingness to engage in a reparative and restorative approach);
- historical context (e.g. the 1840 New Zealand Treaty of Waitangi is fundamental to the legitimacy of the contemporary Waitangi Tribunal. Similarly, historical treaties in Canada have influenced contemporary approaches to the recognition of rights);
- political context (e.g. the ongoing political and economic power of former apartheid supporters after the collapse of the apartheid regime in South Africa has influenced the development of reparations);
- non-state institutional power (e.g. the role of the church in Ireland and Canada in institutional child abuse has influenced the approach to reparations in those countries).

The ICTJ (2002) has also noted a range of other factors which will influence the course of the reparations process including scope of the reparations program, its funding, and its institutional context.

Finally there is the question of social and political reconciliation. Perhaps restorative justice advocates and the advocates of human rights can both learn from their potentially differing interpretations of this concept. In broad terms, reconciliation is about healing, about bringing together warring parties, about ending conflict. Yet reconciliation cannot be achieved without justice to the aggrieved party. Reconciliation is a fundamental principle of restorative justice: reconciliation between the offender and victim, between offender and community. Yet reconciliation is also a much broader collective and political process. For restorative justice to have resonance in the political process of reconciliation in the aftermath of gross violations of human rights, the broader political processes need to be clearly articulated.

References

Balint, J. (1994) 'Towards the anti-genocide community: the role of law,' *Australian Journal of Human Rights*, 1(1): 12–42.

Barkan, E. (2000) *The Guilt of Nations*, New York: W. W. Norton.

Bauman, Z. (1989) *Modernity and the Holocaust*, Cambridge: Polity Press.

Blagg, H. (1998) 'Restorative visions and restorative justice practices: conferencing, ceremony and reconciliation in Australia,' *Current Issues in Criminal Justice*, 10(1): 5–14.

Boraine, A. (1999) 'Alternatives and adjuncts to criminal prosecutions,' in R. L. Brooks (ed.) *When Sorry Isn't Enough*, New York: New York University Press.

Braithwaite, J. (1989) *Crime, Shame and Reintegration*, Melbourne: Cambridge University Press.

Brooks, R. L. (ed.) (1999) *When Sorry Isn't Enough*, New York: New York University Press.

Brownlie, I. (1998) *Principles of Public International Law*, fifth edn, Oxford: Clarendon Press.

Canadian Government (1998) *Gathering Strength*, Ottawa, online. Available at: http://www.ainc-inac.gc.ca/gs/index_e.html [accessed 21 March 2005].

Cunneen, C. (2003) 'Legal and political responses to the stolen generations: lessons from Ireland,' *Indigenous Law Bulletin*, 5(27): 14–19.

Galaway, B. and Hudson, J. (eds) (1996) *Restorative Justice: international perspectives,* Monsey, NY: Criminal Justice Press.

Garkawe, S. (2003a) 'The South African Truth and Reconciliation Commission: a suitable model to enhance the role and rights of victims of gross violations of human rights?' *Melbourne University Law Review*, 27(2): 334–80.

— (2003b) 'Victims and the international criminal court: three major issues,' *International Criminal Law Review*, 3: 345–67.

Gellately, R. and Kiernan, B. (eds) (2003) *The Spectre of Genocide. mass murder in historical perspective*, Cambridge: Cambridge University Press.

Green, P. and Ward, T. (2004) *State Crime: governments, violence and corruption*, London: Pluto Press.

HREOC (Human Rights and Equal Opportunity Commission) (2000) *Submission to the Senate Legal and Constitutional References Committee's Inquiry into the Stolen Generations*, Sydney: HREOC, online. Available at: www.hreoc.gov.au/ [accessed 21 March 2005].

Human Rights Watch (1999) *The Price of Oil: corporate responsibility and human rights violations in Nigeria's oil producing communities*, online. Available at: http://www.hrw.org/reports/1999/nigeria/ [accessed 21 March 2005].

International Centre for Transitional Justice (ICTJ) (2002) *Parameters for Designing a Reparations Program in Peru*, New York: International Centre for Transitional Justice, online. Available at: http://www.ictj.org/default.asp [accessed 21 March 2005].

Jamieson, R. (1999) 'Genocide and the social production of immorality,' *Theoretical Criminology*, 3(2): 131–46.

Law Commission of Canada (2000) *Restoring Dignity: responding to child abuse in Canadian institutions*, Ottawa: Minister of Public Works and Government Services.

Lyster, R. (2000) 'Why a Truth and Reconciliation Commission?' *Current Issues in Criminal Justice*, 12(1): 114–22.

Matthews, R. A. and Kauzlarich, D. (2000) 'The crash of Valujet Flight 592: a case study in state-corporate crime,' *Sociological Focus*, 3: 281–98.

Morrison, W. (2004) 'Criminology, genocide and modernity: remarks on the companion that criminology ignored,' in C. Sumner (ed.) *The Blackwell Companion to Criminology*, Oxford: Blackwell.

NISATSIC (National Inquiry into the Separation of Aboriginal and Torres Strait Island Children from their Families) (1997) *Bringing Them Home*, Sydney: HREOC.

Orentlicher, D. (1994) 'Addressing gross human rights abuses: punishment and victim compensation,' in L. Henkin and L. Hargrave (eds) *Human Rights: an agenda for the next century*, Washington: American Society of International Law.

Petit, P. and Braithwaite, J. (1993) 'Not just deserts, even in sentencing,' *Current Issues in Criminal Justice*, 4(3): 225–39.

Royal Commission on Aboriginal Peoples (Canada) (1996) *Report of the Royal Commission on Aboriginal Peoples*, Ottawa, online. Available at: http://www.ainc-inac.gc.ca/ch/rcap/ [accessed 21 March 2005].

Thompson, J. (2002) *Taking Responsibility for the Past: reparation and historical injustice*, Cambridge: Polity Press.

Truth and Reconciliation Commission of South Africa (1998) *Truth and Reconciliation Commission of South Africa Report*, online. Available at: www.info.gov.za/otherdocs/2003/trc [accessed 15 November 2005].

Tutu, Archbishop Desmond (2004) 'The Truth and Reconciliation process – restorative justice', *The Third Longford Lecture*, The Prison Reform Trust and the Frank Longford Charitable Trust, 16 February 2004. Available at: www.prisonreformtrust.org.uk

Van Ness, D. (1996) 'Restorative justice and international human rights,' in B. Galaway and J. Hudson (eds) *Restorative Justice: international perspectives*, Monsey, NY: Criminal Justice Press.

Notes

1. The author acknowledges the research assistance of Julia Grix and Jocelyn Luff. This article is part of a broader research project funded by the Australian Research Council.

25

Truth and reconciliation in Serbia

Vesna Nikolic-Ristanovic

Ethnic conflicts in the former Yugoslavia, the dictatorship of Slobodan Milosevic, as well as NATO bombing of Serbia, have produced enormous suffering for people of different ethnic and religious groups. At the same time, these conflicts had negative consequences for the daily lives of people in terms of extreme poverty, the decrease of trustful relationships between people, and the constant increase and emergence of new divisions within society.

After experiencing changes in 2000, Serbia found herself in an extremely difficult and complicated economic situation as she went through a painful and politically risky transition toward a market economy and democratization. Since the changes, the new government found itself under severe pressure from the international community to face the past atrocities committed by Serbs quickly and energetically. However, at the same time, the government was confronted with the opposition and obstructions of Milosevic supporters and nationalists, a large number of whom are deeply embedded into state institutions. In addition, immediately after the changes occurred, different views toward the past emerged within the ruling coalition as well.

The efforts toward facing the past atrocities committed by the Serbian state since 2000 have been shaped very much by the above-mentioned political divisions. As a consequence, positive initiatives were often minimized by obstructions of the opposing side, which prevented the new Serbian authorities from coming to a consensus about the past. More efforts toward uncovering past atrocities were, however, made by the civil society, though not in a very coordinated, comprehensive, and inclusive way. Thus, there is an obvious lack of a well-defined government policy and a clear aim for the activities of civil society organizations. Moreover, so far, the truth and reconciliation activities of both governmental and non-governmental organizations have been mainly unconnected so that there has been hardly any substantial cooperation in that regard.

At the same time, the specificity of the socio-historical context, the very nature of conflicts in the former Yugoslavia, as well as the high level of complexity of both victimization and contemporary political context (national, regional, and international), made the applicability of existing models of truth and reconciliation difficult in Serbia. All specificities are also strongly embedded in the social context of the region: that is, in the heritage of a similar cultural context and historical relationships with other newly established countries out of the former common country – Yugoslavia. All these specificities had a strong impact on both victimization and the acknowledgement/denial of such during and after the wars. Thus, all these specificities have to be taken into account in a search for an appropriate model of truth and reconciliation in Serbia (Nikolic-Ristanovic 2003a).

However, in spite of such obvious obstacles and difficulties, since 2000 civil society has undertaken a number of truth and reconciliation activities in Serbia. Looking at these initiatives together, and in connection with state initiatives, the socio-historical and current political (internal and international) context, seems to be a good way to assess their potential for producing an appropriate restorative justice model for healing the wounds of the past. Thus, the main aim of this chapter is to review and analyze these activities and initiatives and to evaluate the truth and reconciliation process in Serbia in terms of its importance for healing both individuals and the society as a whole, and thus, for breaking the cycle of violence and preventing future victimization in the former Yugoslavia. My aim as well is to suggest, on the basis of up-to-date developments in Serbia and experiences from other countries, a possible restorative justice model for Serbia. Bearing that in mind, this chapter is structured in a way which enables me to present both truth and reconciliation initiatives as well as the characteristics of the historical, social, and political contexts in which they developed.

The historical and socio-political context

As in any other post-conflict society (Fletcher and Weinstein 2002; Vanspauwen et al. 2003), it is difficult to understand the trends and problems related to the truth and reconciliation process in Serbia without understanding the historical and socio-political context. Thus, in this chapter I will review the features of these contexts that are most important for understanding the problems confronted by those trying to initiate a restorative process in Serbia.

In the first place, it is necessary to stress the historical background. The whole region has a history of wars for national liberation, with people from different ethnic groups waging wars against each other. Moreover, the region also has a history of denials and multiple truths (e.g. each ethnic group passing its own truth from generation to generation) as well as a history of exploiting (their own people's) victimization for feeding the cycle of violence. The implications of the lack of any attempt at getting a single (common) truth and reconciliation were so obvious in recent wars when past and present 'truths' were so interlaced that it was often difficult to know whether people were speaking about past or present atrocities and victims. In Serbia itself, Milosevic's regime misused the fact that Serbs, who have being living in different parts (now countries) of the former Yugoslavia, experienced severe victimization during the Second World War at the hands of Nazi collaborators belonging to other ethnic groups in order to reawaken old fears and create the project of Greater Serbia, promising all Serbs that they would live in one country.

Although Serbia was not directly affected by the wars in Croatia and Bosnia and Herzegovina, her citizens suffered in different ways. UN economic sanctions led to quick impoverishment and criminalization of the society (Nikolic-Ristanovic 1998). The enormous influx of refugees, mainly Serbs from other parts of the former Yugoslavia, caused the life of indigenous people to deteriorate further. At the same time, refugees found themselves in completely inappropriate conditions and were often further victimized by the local people. In addition, many men from Serbia were forced to go to fight, either as part of the police or as army recruits. Some of the men also went to fight voluntarily, mainly seduced by state war propaganda, strongly believing that they were obliged to protect their 'brothers.' Finally, the Kosovo conflict had a direct impact on the citizens of Serbia. This included gross human rights violations of both Albanians and Serbs, a new wave of (Serbian and Roma) refugees/internally displaced people,[1] and the large involvement of the Serbian police and army in violations of human rights, as well as the seventy-nine-day NATO war against the Federal Republic of Yugoslavia (Serbia and Montenegro).[2]

The end of the Kosovo conflict brought peace neither to Kosovo nor to the surrounding countries. On the contrary, NATO's intervention and the peacekeeping mission were proven to be inefficient in preventing further hostilities, and even allowed them to spread out of Kosovo to both the southern part of Serbia and Macedonia. As a result, six years after the NATO interventions, the conflicts are still not solved, while Serbia remains full of refugees whose prospects of returning to their homes (which they were forced to leave) are not very optimistic. The international government in Kosovo, which was established to prevent violations of human rights and ethnic cleansing of Albanians, allowed the gettoization and continuous ethnic cleansing of Serbs.

During the 1990s and especially after the NATO war, the repression of Milosevic's regime against those who opposed it was increasing. Many people were arrested and tortured while some were killed. Most of these politically motivated murders are still not cleared up.

When, in October 2000, the new government came to power, it was faced with a difficult economic situation as well as with a multiply-divided society and an extremely complex victimization situation. The gov-

ernment was established by the coalition of nineteen political parties which were very different but which came together to defeat Milosevic and bring the country through the transitional period. However, differences among the ruling coalition itself led to many conflicts, including the conflicts regarding dealing with the war crimes and past in general.

Kostunica, who was the president of Serbia immediately after the 2000 changes, was not willing to take any radical step while, at the same time, Prime Minister Djindjic was committed to working very energetically toward uncovering past atrocities and the prosecution of perpetrators. The situation became even more complicated after the assassination of Prime Minister Djindjic in 2003, leading to a deepening of existing, and the creation of new, political divisions, including new divisions and conflicts among democratic parties (Milosevic's former opposition). As a result of the governmental change and presidential elections in 2004, Serbia once again had a government and president whose opposing political views have been most striking just in relation to the crimes committed during the 1990s.[3]

In March 2003, when members of organized crime and former war criminals assassinated Serbian prime minister Zoran Djindjic, it became especially obvious how fragile the new Serbian democracy was. The assassination was part of an attempted *coup d'etat* and was experienced as a serious challenge to the new government. The prime minister was the symbol of the new Serbia and was very committed to cooperation with the Hague Tribunal, and to otherwise meeting the requirements of the international communities. This brought him under severe attack by both moderate and extreme nationalists, some of them situated within the police and judicial system and cooperating with organized crime.

However, it is worth mentioning that the police campaign, which followed the assassination, brought to light the connection between war crimes and crimes committed against Milosevic's opponents in Serbia (Nikolic-Ristanovic 2004; Nikolic-Ristanovic and Simeunovic-Patic forthcoming), which to some degree contributed to lessening the denial of war crimes committed by Serbs. But, at the same time, the reaction of the state had the form of 'war against organized crime' and 'moral panic.' As a consequence, it prioritized selective repression over uncovering the entire truth and, in this way, missed a unique opportunity to establish grounds for political consensus about the past (Nikolic-Ristanovic 2004).

Thus, since 2000, the new authorities mainly reflected, in all societal aspects, the great gaps and divisions in Serbia, with respect to both to the past and present. The political scene in Serbia was transformed into a long political conflict which turned from one conflict between the democratic opposition and Milosevic's regime into one between the nationalist anti-Hague forces, on the one hand, and pro-Hague-oriented groups and individuals, on the other.

It is clear that since 2000 the government has been sending contradictory messages and instead of contributing to the deconstruction of nationalism, stereotypes, and the divisions within the society, it has contributed to the creation of new divisions, prejudice and animosity. One of the important obstacles to a successful confrontation of the past is the absence of the rule of law, and widespread lack of differentiation between what is allowed and what is not, as well as the incorporation of criminals in the state apparatus itself, especially in the police and justice systems, which block attempts to determine the truth and render the process of lustration extremely hard and complicated.

An additional problem is the international community, which in general is not very interested in restorative ways of dealing with crimes in the former Yugoslavia. Moreover, it is not even allowing the possibility that people from these countries could decide for themselves about the possible use of amnesty (Nikolic-Ristanovic 2003a; Simonovic 2002). Unlike in other post-conflict countries, such as South Africa for example, in the former Yugoslavia in general, and in Serbia in particular, the international community insists on the traditional retribution model combined with suspicion toward the ideas related to initiatives of restorative justice, including those that relate to the Commission for Truth and Reconciliation (Kritz 2002). In addition, since the changes in 2000, international economic support has been rather modest and insufficient to help with the recovery of the Serbian economy and for drawing the attention and motivation of the population substantially from (irrational) political to economic interests. Also, the pressure from the international community for the extraditions of indicted war criminals often coincided with important political events in the country and, thus, was counterproductive for the domestic politics and truth and reconciliation process, because this produced negative consequences in terms of reinforcing nationalism and resistance towards discovering the truth.

Victimization, divisions, and denial

All individual victimizations were strongly embedded in a wider social and historical context so that their understanding is difficult if taken out of context. Some Serbian citizens were victims of ethnic conflicts and all, regardless of ethnic, religious, or political belonging, were victims of the NATO war: the entire population of Serbia (Serbs but also other ethnic groups such as Roma, Albanians, Muslims, Hungarians, and Croats) were victims of both immediate and long-term consequences of NATO air strikes. Also, a large part of the Serbian population feel victimized by Milosevic's regime. In addition, throughout the past fifteen years all Serbian citizens have been victims of severe structural victimization due to UN sanctions, ethnic conflicts, and destructions caused by NATO. Presently, they suffer further from transitional unemployment and other consequences of economic and social transformation, as well as from economic sanctions because of the government's lack of cooperation with the International Criminal Tribunal for the Former Yugoslavia (ICTY).

Moreover, many people were victims in more than one war/conflict (including the four different wars of the 1990s[4] and earlier wars and conflicts). There is not a clear division within society, as is the case in South Africa. Instead, there are many divisions within the same society (e.g. political, ethnic, in relation to belonging to different social groups etc.), and divisions along ethnic lines which cross borders and prevent establishment of normal relationships within ethnically mixed communities (e.g. conflicts between Serbs and Albanians in parts of Serbia close to Kosovo and Serbs and Muslims in parts close to Bosnia).

Thus, the features of victimization of Serbian citizens which need to be taken into consideration for understanding of the truth and reconciliation process in Serbia (Nikolic-Ristanovic 2002 and 2003a) are as follows:

- Many people were victimized by different perpetrators, who belong to different communities and ethnic groups (e.g. Serbian refugees from Croatia, who were later living in Bosnia and then Kosovo).
- Many people are multiple victims, even with memory of victimization in previous wars, or with war trauma passed to them by their parents or other relatives (e.g. Serbs from Croatia and Bosnia, now living in Serbia whose family members were killed by members of other ethnic groups during the Second World War, or Serbs whose family members were killed during and after the Second World War by other Serbs who belonged to different political/military groups).[5]
- There are conflicts and divisions among Serbs themselves which are connected to their belonging to different political and other social groups, differences in their war victimization and other factors (for example, between Communists and anti-Communists, between supporters of Milosevic/other nationalist leaders and their opponents, between Serbs from Serbia and Serbs from other parts of the former Yugoslavia, between refugees and the local population, war participants and those who did not participate in war, etc.).
- A large number of men were forced to participate in war as soldiers, or their national sentiments and their families' traumatic experiences from earlier wars were abused and manipulated to convince them to fight, and they were also often victims in more direct ways, so that it is important to consider the victimization of this part of the population in truth and reconciliation processes as well.[6]
- There was wide structural victimization.

Having in mind the above-mentioned, I argue that one of the main differences in the situation in Serbia, in comparison to other present-day societies faced with collective violence, is that it should confront the violence among Serbs themselves (see also Djokic 2002) as well as the violence between Serbian citizens/Serbs from other parts of the former Yugoslavia and other ethnic groups/nations (including both those from the former Yugoslavia and those from Western countries, in relation to NATO bombing). This means that among the population of Serbia there are both victims and perpetrators of crimes/gross violations of human rights, with these groups also overlapping.

Therefore, in any restorative process it is necessary to address two apparently opposite problems:

1 the denial of crimes committed by Serbs (from Serbia and from outside of Serbia) and other citizens of Serbia; and
2 the denial of crimes committed against Serbs from all parts of the former Yugoslavia and of crimes committed against all citizens of Serbia.[7]

Thus it seems that the truth and reconciliation process in Serbia needs to deal with victimhood and truth in a holistic and inclusive way, allowing for healing through making the victimization of all visible.[8] As observed by Blagojevic and further elaborated by myself elsewhere, it is a paradox that, in order to acknowledge the suffering of others, it is necessary first that people have their own suffering acknowledged (Blagojevic 2000; Nikolic-Ristanovic 2000). Or, as Rombouts stresses, victims all want a piece of the '*gâteau de la souffrance*,' so gaining recognition is crucially important to them (Rombouts 2002a: 225).

The way the recognition of victimhood and suffering is done in post-conflict society seems to have a strong impact on the direction and success of the restorative process. On the other hand, the up-to-date development of truth and reconciliation in Serbia confirms, as I will show later, that doing that in an exclusive way may not only slow down the whole process but may even be counterproductive in terms of the production of new conflicts.

Public discourse about the past

The public discourse which prevailed in Serbia from the end of the 1980s until 2000 was largely based on partial 'truth' about past and present conflicts, on the narrow and exclusive notion of victim, as well as on the hierarchy of victimization and victim competition. As such, this discourse could easily be used to feed the cycle of violence, and this is exactly what happened in the ethnic conflicts in the former Yugoslavia in the 1990s (Nikolic-Ristanovic 2003a). This was achieved in all parts of the former Yugoslavia in an almost identical way – through public discourse, used by the media. However, Western media adopted a very similar discourse as well, leading to the construction of a hierarchy of victimization as well as to notions of the ultimately innocent and those who deserved to be victims, and thus completely forgotten victims. As a consequence, for a very long time some victims, mostly those of Serbian origin, have been treated as non-existent by the Western media and aid organizations (Nikolic-Ristanovic 2003b).

Since the changes in 2000, two extreme discourses regarding the past have prevailed in the media, civil society, and politics.[9] Both of them had a significant negative influence on the development of truth and reconciliation in Serbia. Since both are highly visible, completely opposite, but similarly negative, they almost paralyzed it.[10] This is not unusual, keeping in mind that these two discourses have in common at least several features which are mostly counterproductive for restorative processes: (1) they do not listen to those who do not agree with them; (2) they accept accusations as their main communication tool; (3) they accept a hierarchy of victimization and an exclusive notion of victim and perpetrators; (4) they depersonalize victims: that is, deal with them in abstract ways; and (5) they accept partial and simplified (black and white) truth.

While the extreme nationalistic discourse recognizes the victimhood only of Serbs and considers war criminals national heroes, the extreme anti-nationalist discourse recognizes exclusively non-Serbs as victims and Serbs as war criminals. After the assassination of the Serbian prime minister, these two opposites reflected even more dramatically the 'the pro-Hague' and 'anti-Hague' stances, coupled with the demands for punishing the responsible ones for the crimes committed in Serbia on the one hand, and, on the other, accusing the victims and extolling the accused as national heroes. This way there is a merger of discourses on war crimes and discourses about (political) organized crime which accentuates the relationship between these crimes more than ever. As a consequence, the denial of the crimes that are committed against other ethnic groups is extended to the denial of crimes committed among Serbs themselves, i.e. within Serbia itself.

The third discourse emerged as well, but it became more visible only recently. This approach tends to deconstruct the victimization narrative used in war propaganda and to define victimhood and perpetrators in an inclusive yet not universalistic way. The third discourse acknowledges all victims without creating a hierarchy among them. This discourse became especially visible in media coverage of the international conference 'Truth and Reconciliation in the Former Yugoslavia: where are we now, and where to go?' organized by the Victimology Society of Serbia in 2004. In media presentations of the conference the prevailing messages were of the following kind: 'every country/ethnic group should clean its own yard' as well as that the initiatives and problems related to dealing with the past exist not only in Serbia but in other parts of the former Yugoslavia as well.

Truth and reconciliation initiatives in Serbia (2000–4)

The two opposed discourses presented above represent very well the main and most dangerous source of polarization within Serbian society. This polarization had a significant, if not decisive, impact on the way truth and reconciliation is perceived and dealt with in Serbia – by the state authorities, civil

society, and the larger population. However, both poles (extremes) have in common that they see prosecution and punishment as the only or the most efficient way of dealing with the past. As in other transitional societies, the repressive measures are widely seen as a 'magic' solution for crime in general and for the post-war dealing with war crime in particular. But, along with this, there is also a growing interest in restorative justice – primarily as a solution to the long-lasting litigations and juvenile crime.

The restorative justice initiatives in general, and in relation to dealing with past atrocities in particular, emerged as a spontaneous grassroots activism or responses to international pressure and donor policy rather than as deliberate, theoretically founded, restorative justice projects. The main initiatives for alternative ways of dealing with the past in Serbia are: the Truth and Reconciliation Commission; apologies and unsuccessful attempt of lustration, on the state level; and a range of civil society activities. So far there has not been any real dialogue about or co-ordination of efforts regarding the truth and reconciliation between authorities and civil society.

The state approach toward the past and truth and reconciliation initiatives

The divisions among the authorities which are simultaneously a constant 'generator' of new divisions are the biggest obstacle on the road to truth and reconciliation in Serbia. In a situation of this type, it is not unusual that the government has not been capable of reaching any consensus regarding its policy toward the past, and that the good actions and initiatives of certain state organs remained less efficient or their effects simply remained blocked.

The government's reluctance to position itself more clearly in relation to dealing with the past – in the same way as in other countries of the former Yugoslavia and as in other transitional countries – is often explained by the threat it could impose to the political stability of new democracy. As Bjelakovic put it, the priorities of core Yugoslav successor states' governments are more pragmatic than visionary and 'one should not blame them for that' (Bjelakovic 2002: 164).

However, this was an acceptable justification for only short time after the change, while in the long run the government's reluctance to deal more energetically with the past turned out to be risky for the new democracy itself. Finally, the overall impression is that the alleged inability of Serbian citizens to swallow the 'bitter pill' of acknowledging the crimes committed in their name is used by the authorities as an excuse for not dealing with the past. As Petrovic said in an interview in the radio program *Katarza* (Catharsis) on Radio B92 on 25 December 2004: 'If politicians in power oppose the reconciliation, they have a great opportunity to avoid saying it explicitly, by referring to a supposed will of the people, against which they allegedly cannot do anything.' Statements of the participants of panel discussions organized by the Victimology Society of Serbia in different parts of Serbia during 2003 and 2004 offer further arguments for the thesis about the authorities' manipulations of the alleged unreadiness of Serbian people to face the past. Participants noticed that neither the former nor the current government showed a clear political will to find out the truth about the past and to reconcile with neighbors, as well as that citizens expected the authorities to develop initiatives in that process. However, the new government never came out with a clear position/strategy about facing the past atrocities. Its policy all along has been rather reluctant and contradictory, representing somehow its own contradictions, i.e. contradictions among different political parties and their interests and attitudes in relation to facing the past.

The polarization was further increased by the pressure imposed by the international community on the new Serbian government to send war criminals to the Hague Tribunal. This was actually the source of one of the first disagreements[11] among the ruling coalition, leading to many others later. In addition, it led to the unnecessarily quick establishment of the Truth and Reconciliation Commission, motivated by gaining political points abroad and maybe by an attempt at preventing/postponing extradition of Milosevic to the Hague Tribunal (Simonovic 2002) rather than by making real change within society.[12]

The Truth and Reconciliation Commission (TRC) was established by Vojislav Kostunica, at that time the president of Federal Republic of Yugoslavia, in March 2001. Nineteen members of the TRC were appointed and their main tasks were as follows:

- to organize research work on recovering the records about social, international, and political conflicts which led to the war as well as clearing up causal links between events;
- to inform the domestic and international public about its work and results;
- to cooperate and exchange experiences with similar commissions and bodies in neighboring and other countries.

The Commission was established without serious public discussion and without consensus about its work. The president left it to the Commission to determine the conception and program of its activities, which actually was never done. The Commission had neither members from non-governmental organizations nor a clear concept of cooperation – that is, of the exchange of information and experiences with them. The Commission spent almost three years without undertaking any substantial activity.

In the meantime, it became the political tool of only one political party and person (President Kostunica and his party). Therefore, the message which was sent to the public about the role of the Truth and Reconciliation Commission was mainly confusing, and basically discredited the very idea of the Truth and Reconciliation Commission as a useful way of dealing with the past in Serbia (Rankovic 2002). Keeping in mind the above-mentioned reasons, it is not surprising that the Commission formally ceased to exist during the process of the country's transformation from federation to loose state unit between Serbia and Montenegro in 2002.

In addition to the Truth and Reconciliation Commission, it is worth mentioning the apologies of the president of Serbia and Montenegro, Svetozar Marovic, and of the Serbian president, Tadic, for war crimes committed by citizens of Serbia (and Montenegro).These apologies as well as the sporadic attempts of lustration basically had a similar goal as that of the Truth and Reconciliation Commission. They were not based on any kind of consensus and thus did not have a significant impact, either abroad or within Serbian society.

Civil society initiatives

Recent studies identified sixty-two non-governmental organizations (NGOs) in Serbia which are engaged in significant activities for facing the past. However, the same study also found that a small part of them implement activities directly dealing with it (Blagojevic and Milenkovic 2004). This means that there are not a lot of organizations which deal with truth and reconciliation in terms of restorative justice. Most of the organizations actually situate their activities on confronting the past in a broader context of their work or create indirect educational program-projects that benefit young people.

The precise ways of tackling the problems of the past include: collecting documentation; research; education; culture and art (films, exhibitions, literature); direct assistance to victims and combatants; advocacy; public debates; small group discussions; cross-border and cross-community dialogue/cooperation; and different publications (journals, translated studies on truth and reconciliation, etc.).

According to the above-mentioned studies, conferences, panels, round tables and similar events, as well as publications (mostly documentation about past atrocities and translations of foreign works on truth and reconciliation) seem to be the most frequent activities engaged in by these NGOs. The topics they cover are usually broader but useful as preparation for opening up discussions about truth and reconciliation (e.g. tolerance, differences, stereotypes, prejudice, human rights, conflict resolution, non-violent communication, etc.). Also, the role of panels and small group discussions was devoted to looking for the best way of dealing with the past in Serbia as well as of allowing war participants to speak about their experiences and reasons for going to fight. Recently, meetings and workshops which were part of cross-community and cross-border cooperation projects, often including young people, have become especially widespread.

We can assume that public discussion about truth and reconciliation has been going on in Serbia since 2001 through a number of fragmented, uncoordinated, and often counterproductive public events organized by NGOs. Public discussion about dealing with the past in Serbia started two months after establishment of the Truth and Reconciliation Commission. The discussion was initiated by independent media and the civil society at the international conference 'Truth, Reconciliation and Responsibility' in Belgrade in May 2001, when the Truth and Reconciliation Commission was promoted publicly.

After the conference, during 2001 and 2002, on a more or less regular basis, different panels and debates about war crimes in the former Yugoslavia – addressing in an exclusive way mostly crimes committed by Serbs against other ethnic groups, and mainly based on materials collected by Western authors – were held in Belgrade and other towns in Serbia. Consequently, until the end of 2002, it seemed that the exclusive notion of victimhood prevailed in non-governmental projects as well. Attempts at dealing with victimization in a more inclusive way, as well as using materials collected and produced by Serbian authors, were only sporadic. The consequence was that, until recently, dealing with the past mostly led toward the strengthening of the guilt complex within the Serbian population and feelings that the suffering of the Serbian population is not recognized, all with the negative consequences (e.g. anger, aggression, etc.) which these feelings produce.

This is not unusual, keeping in mind that the most visible, publicly, are the activities and views of the largest NGOs, who have the biggest funding and consequently a significant impact on the creation of an extreme anti-nationalistic discourse, which is not well accepted by the larger society. Moreover, this has contributed to the creation of public resistance toward the very notion of truth and reconciliation as it became widely understood in a very narrow sense – that is, as dealing exclusively with accusations of the Serbs as a nation for atrocities against non-Serbian victims. Moreover, the activities of the most influential NGOs are oriented toward mostly retributive ways of dealing with a past, such as prosecution, lustration and opening of secret files, while, on the other side, the activities of the mid to small NGOs, which are less visible publicly, are often much more restorative and, thus, inclusive.

The best example of the negative consequences of the acceptance of the exclusive notion of victimhood, and the attempts at imposing the truth in a rather aggressive way and without proper preparation and the

respect of the agency for the citizens (as potential stakeholders,[13] i.e. victims, perpetrators, bystanders, etc.), was the series of exhibitions of war photographs of American photographer Ron Haviv, 'Blood and Honey,' during 2002. Because of the insensitive way in which it was publicized, the exhibition produced conflicts between extremes on both sides even before it was shown. This occurred in all towns except Novi Sad, where efforts had been made for the inclusion of the sufferings of all and also enabling everyone, regardless of political and national allegiance, to participate in the dialogue and expose their own views, frustrations, dilemmas, etc. In Novi Sad the titles of the photographs suggesting the ethnic affiliations of victims and perpetrators were not displayed and the space was given to visitors to offer their own titles and comments.

This is how a new, inclusive approach toward the past was born within Serbian civil society. The exhibition in Novi Sad and the related panel were recorded and a documentary film, *VIVISECT*, was produced. All the later truth and reconciliation activities of the NGO Vojvodjanka are named after this film. Almost at the same time (October 2002), the Victimology Society's project 'From Remembering the Past toward a Positive Future' started. In addition to VIVISECT and From Remembering the Past toward a Positive Future, there have recently been other important activities which deal with the past in an inclusive and reconciliatory way. The photographs of the Serbian war photographer Milos Cvetkovic, showing victims and perpetrators from different ethnic groups, have been seen by many people throughout Serbia without a single incident. Also, there is the increasing production and broadcasting of films and TV programs which deal with the past in an inclusive way, while novels and short stories with a similar approach are published and even given awards by the government. In addition, the Serbian government has funded several NGO projects which tended toward the inclusion and cooperation of all stakeholders, including the above-mentioned exhibitions of Milos Cvetkovic and the Victimology Society project.

A third way: VIVISECT and From Remembering the Past toward a Positive Future

Keeping in mind the events that followed the exhibitions of Ron Haviv's photographs, the organizers in Novi Sad devised a new concept of exhibitions and supporting programs whose goals were: (1) to encourage public discussion of the wars in former Yugoslavia; (2) to present the truth about the wars as a mosaic comprised of different elements, which only when put together can offer a relatively complete picture of the tragedy that a part of Yugoslavia went through; (3) to point to the necessity of knowing the facts about war in every society; and (4) to provide the chance for everyone to deliver her or his opinion with respect for other people's views of the events from our recent past. So as to prevent incidents that took place in other towns, it was decided that the photographs would be shown for eight days without the name of the photographer. The intention was to enable visitors to write their commentaries or give their own titles to photographs on the basis of what they have seen. Every photo had blank sheets and pencils beside it. The 'book of impressions' and a special space within the exhibition, a 10-meter-long wall, were to offer alternatives for the visitors, who could display their own photos or documents there related to the 1991–9 conflict. Within the program of the exhibition in Novi Sad, two panel discussions were held and four documentary films were screened.

Through this concept the organizers enabled visitors to the exhibition to be not only passive observers but also active participants in the process of confrontation with the truth about the wars in the former Yugoslavia. It's very important to highlight that the exhibition was organized in cooperation with the institutions of the provincial and city administration in Novi Sad and in cooperation with the regional and city representatives of the Ministry of Internal Affairs. The visitors to the exhibition 'Blood and Honey' and the follow-up programs in Novi Sad belonged to all ages and all social, national and religious groups that live in this city. For the screenings of the documentaries there were mostly young people, whereas middle-aged and older people tended to visit the panel discussions. There were those who visited the exhibition several times as well as people who visited the exhibition every day for some time. Since the organizers of the exhibition offered the visitors an opportunity to bring photos and documents that refer to the war period in the former Yugoslavia, the exhibition gained new elements every day. The written messages that people left beside the photos of Ron Haviv attracted special attention and were read as 'a novel on sequels.' A special form of communication was established during the ten days of the exhibition, which managed to channel a wide range of emotions and impressions (from the extremist and aggressive attitudes to reasonable and objective attitudes) when it comes to the question of facing the truth and consequences of wars in the territory of the former Yugoslavia (Gajicki forthcoming).

The exhibition was seen by 5,000 people, and the material that was collected during the exhibition was transformed into a short documentary entitled *VIVISECT*; the commentaries that the visitors left beside the photographs of Ron Haviv were published in the book of the documents. In the book of the documents, Vivisect analyses the written messages of the visitors in Novi Sad, the social-historical context and the problem of victimization, as well as the results so far achieved in the process of truth and reconciliation in Serbia. Both the documentary and the book were used as a basis for discussions about the past within Serbian society. In addition to the NGO Vojvodjanka, the Victimology Society of Serbia used the book of the documents and the movie *VIVISECT* in its panel discussions within its project 'From Remembering the Past toward a Positive Future.' Also, the book is used at the University of Novi Sad as the basis for student discussions on the subject. The documentary *VIVISECT* was also broadcast during 2003 and 2004 on several TV channels in Serbia and Croatia.

The Victimology Society's project 'From Remembering the Past toward a Positive Future' is the only long-term and comprehensive truth and reconciliation project in Serbia which has been carefully planned and elaborated, using different experiences, and in particular Northern Ireland's experiences (Healing Through Remembering 2002; Hamber forthcoming) and the recent evaluation of the South African and other truth and reconciliation commissions (Chapman and Ball 2001; Vanspauwen *et al.* 2003; Borer 2003). The project was actually launched at the international conference entitled 'Which Model of Truth and Reconciliation is the Most Appropriate for the Former Yugoslavia?' held in Belgrade in October 2002. The main objective of the conference was the exchange of experiences concerning truth and reconciliation in different parts of the world, including different parts of the former Yugoslavia, as well as the launching of a broader public discussion on these issues on the level of the local community in Serbia. The very atmosphere of the conference was completely different in comparison to most other similar public events. Every session was followed by a lively yet highly constructive and positive discussion, with a high degree of tolerance. A film about the truth and reconciliation process in South Africa was also shown. Throughout the conference, the idea about ways of searching for a model of truth and reconciliation was very well developed and was especially

improved during the final panel discussion. On the basis of this, conclusions regarding future activities were made.

The main goals of the future activities regarding truth and reconciliation that were defined in the conference were (1) the continuation of discussions at the local level in order to provide as broad a public discussion as possible about these issues so as (2) to find a model of truth and reconciliation appropriate for the former Yugoslavia. While the first goal was short term in nature, the latter was long term, and the conference was understood as one step closer to it. Following these goals, the Victimology Society of Serbia, with the financial support of the Friedrich Ebert Foundation (Germany) and the Serbian Ministry of Culture and Media, have been working on a project entitled 'From Remembering the Past toward a Positive Future: what type of truth and trust/reconciliation is the most suitable for Serbia?' The project was devised on the basis of the 2002 conference discussion and the experiences of the Northern Ireland civil society project 'Healing through Remembering' (Healing Through Remembering 2002).

The major part of the project was a series of small group discussions organized during 2003 and 2004 in twelve towns in Serbia. The discussions were recorded and the transcripts were thoroughly analyzed. In addition, the Victimology Society published and distributed a leaflet consisting of two parts: basic information about truth and reconciliation, and an invitation to citizens to send their ideas, opinions, etc., about dealing with the past in a way which would lead to the narrowing of existing divisions and to positive peace within Serbia and the former Yugoslavia. In addition, there were two articles published in printed media with calls to citizens to deliver their proposals. The call for proposals was open to every citizen of Serbia, regardless of his/her ethnic, religious, political, or any other orientation. The distribution of this is still in progress. Ideas and proposals that were received from the citizens through brochures and responses to public calls were also analyzed in conjunction with the materials from the panel discussions. They reflected, to a great extent, views, dilemmas, and problems that citizens encounter in relation to truth and reconciliation (Hanak forthcoming).

The total number of participants thus far is 149. The participants were: members of NGOs and humanitarian organizations; representatives of the associations of prisoners of war, refugees, displaced people from Kosovo, and the associations of kidnapped and disappeared persons; the combatants; journalists; members of political parties; representatives of local authorities; individuals of different professional backgrounds, students and unemployed individuals.

The panels usually started with some introductory speeches from experts, followed by a showing of a Vivisect film, and then a discussion among participants. The discussion was moderated so as to enable the presentation of positive and negative personal experiences and reflections on the topic of truth, remembrance of the past, ability to establish trust, a model of reconciliation, problems that go with reconciliation, etc. The format of the small group discussions provided a relaxed atmosphere, with emotions being put in the background. Participants were encouraged to listen to each other, bring out their personal experiences, and be constructive in the discussions. Moderators pointed at similarities of experiences and the richness and importance of the ideas that were put forward, and then summarized them at the end of every panel discussion.

The analysis of the collected material was focused on the search for ideas and responses to several important questions: how people understand notions such as truth, reconciliation, and guilt; why a process of reconciliation is needed at all; what it should look like; what methods should be used in order for it to be successful; who should be included in the process; who should take the

initiative; how to reach the truth and make it visible and inevitable. A lot of ideas were collected about all the above-mentioned topics, and were systematized and analyzed. Results of the analyses were published in the book *From Remembering the Past toward a Positive Future: views and opinions of citizens of Serbia* (Nikolic-Ristanovic and Hanak 2004).

One of the main ideas of the project is that truth and reconciliation in Serbia needs to be developed in accordance with the will of the majority of its people, as well as that the attitudes expressed publicly so far were mainly attitudes of nationalists and anti-nationalist extremists and elites, while ordinary people, including victims, did not have opportunities to express their views. Also, the project presumed that thus far safe and relaxing spaces for discussions about the past and listening to others with patience, trust, and empathy did not exist on any level of society. Therefore, this is exactly what the project itself sought to achieve. In other words, similar to the South African TRC, the project is offering a gentle way toward facing the past (Borain and Livi 2000)

The most prominent conclusions thus far refer to: (1) the most important actors in the truth and reconciliation process; (2) the means of discovering the truth; and (3) the means for making the truth inevitable, solving conflict, and establishing trust.

As the most important actors in the process, the participants pointed to state organs, victims, and NGOs. According to them, state organs should take the responsibility for the initiation of the process of truth and reconciliation. The lack of political will to reveal facts, punish the perpetrators, and reconcile neighbors was pointed to as one of the major obstacles towards truth and reconciliation. However, citizens should be interested in the process as well. This is how the apposite cooperation was envisaged between the 'top' and the 'base'; however, it all depends on whether citizens trust the authorities.

The question of which nation from the former Yugoslavia should take the initiative in the process of truth and reconciliation emerged as well. Despite the prevailing attitude that all sides should contribute to the initiation of these activities, there was some obvious frustration due to the lack of information on initiatives in other parts of Yugoslavia, hence the prevailing opinion that only Serbia is assuming actions in the field of reconciliation.

Besides the state organs, the media are considered to be a key factor in the process. So far, they have played a negative role, with a few rare exceptions. It is necessary that the media become promoters of the acknowledgment of truth and reconciliation. Very similar attitudes were expressed regarding religious communities. The participants described NGOs as the initiators of essential topics and important activities but at the same time as insufficiently connected and coordinated, thus without major effect.

The inclusion of victims of war in the process presented an important topic in almost all the discussions. It was suggested that the process should begin by finding the whole truth about the victims, crimes, and criminals as well as about positive examples. Also, participants stressed that it is very important to acknowledge that it is necessary to find out the truth about the crimes in the recent and more distant past, since the history of denial and the lack of reconciliation is typical of this region. It is very important to insist on the significance of discovering the truth on crimes committed by all sides and connecting them into 'one truth' in order to understand what happened and thereby overcome denial. It is not possible to forgive if there is not understanding of the cause of the wars, the reasons for crimes, and why people supported the politics that led to the war. The opinion that every side should, before anything else, make efforts in discovering the truth about the crimes of its own compatriots was very often heard. Regarding the question of

where the process of reconciliation should start, there is a clear proposal that it should start from discovering the truth about what took place in Serbia itself over the last years. Closely related to this is the proposal that we should start by solving divisions and conflicts within the Serbian society itself, and only after these problems have been solved start solving related problems with others.

Participants proposed trials as the best way of discovering truth about the crimes as well as different forms of discussions, hearings, and collecting other reliable documents. They perceived problems and obstacles that follow the proceedings before domestic tribunals in Serbia as well as in other countries of the former Yugoslavia. It is because of such problems that primacy is often given to international courts, although it was believed that, from the standpoint of reaching the truth about the past, trials before domestic courts would be far more effective.

Discussions and hearings were held regarding ways for reaching the truth about negative as well as positive experiences, and about the initiatives regarding truth and reconciliation that exist in other countries of the former Yugoslavia. It was often pointed out that the model for the discussions organized by the Victimology Society is effective for reaching truth and trust/reconciliation between ideological and political opponents. It was suggested that these discussions receive some media attention so that they might have a greater effect.

Participants also mentioned specific forms of reaching the truth which were based on the public testimonies of victims and war participants/crime perpetrators, such as:

- the commission of truth and reconciliation as a state initiative;
- informal citizen tribunals, as initiatives of civil society at a local level.

Finding out a truth was seen as just the first phase of the process; it must then become visible to a wider public. The following ways were recommended in order to make the truth available and inevitable:

- production of films/series about crimes as well as about positive examples of people's solidarity, which would then be shown in all parts of the former Yugoslavia;
- establishment of a memorial museum with a live exhibition;
- establishment of a Day of Remembrance and Reflection and/or Day of Reconciliation;
- publication of the names of victims and perpetrators;
- campaigns;
- school programs and textbooks – deconstruction of ideology and the use of reliable information and verified facts.

It was also suggested that, in addition to discovering the truth, efforts be made to solve current conflicts as well as prevent potential conflicts.

These conclusions as well as other ideas from the small group discussions were presented in the conference 'Truth and Reconciliation in the Former Yugoslavia: where are we now and where to go?' organized by the Victimology Society in October 2004 in Belgrade, together with activities of other civil society projects from Serbia, other countries of the former Yugoslavia, South Africa, and Northern Ireland.

The main aims of this conference were to exchange ideas between different organizations and to present to the Serbian public up-to-date civil society initiatives from both Serbia and other countries of the former Yugoslavia. The conference gathered most mid- and small-sized NGOs from Serbia. The prevailing idea of the conference, shared by most of the participating NGOs from different parts of the former Yugoslavia (and confirmed by South African and Northern Ireland experiences), was the idea of inclusion and cooperation/coordination

of different truth and reconciliation initiatives (in particular countries and in the entire former Yugoslavia). Thus, it is not surprising that the main proposals that came out of the conference also became the platform for further development of the project as a whole. The main proposals include:

- the formalized cooperation between NGOs, organizations of victims and war participants, experts, journalists, and other citizens, regardless of their political beliefs, who are willing and able to work together on development of the truth and reconciliation model;
- the formalized cooperation between civil society and state initiatives in the form of a governmental body for developing a state strategy related to truth and reconciliation in Serbia; and
- the formalized cooperation between NGOs and other organizations and individuals in the former Yugoslavia.

In addition, by publishing the proposals from the conference in the printed media, an active involvement of individuals and organizations interested in the process of truth and reconciliation will further be promoted and developed.

Conclusion

An overview of the situation that exists in Serbia related to truth and reconciliation that was presented in this chapter points to a deep political division within Serbia (as reflected in the media as well as in the public space in a broader sense) as one of the most serious obstacles on the road to a constructive dealing with the past. The unsolved status of Kosovo, the inadequate approach of the international community, the unsystematic and uncoordinated activities of NGOs, as well as the lack of empirical research, have contributed to the slow progress of this process in Serbia as well.

It can be concluded from this overview that a clear strategy on the part of both state organs and NGOs, and coordinated action from governmental and non-governmental organizations, experts, and other citizens, are essential for the process of truth and reconciliation. The same principle applies to a broader inclusion of citizens in the process and the narrowing of the gap between NGOs and Serbian citizens, as well as to the transformation of, and a proactive role for, the media.

Telling what, why, and how things happened in a holistic way – that is, the deconstruction of narratives of victimization which led to violent conflicts (as opposed to the fragmented representation of reality which prevailed in the late-twentieth century) – may be a good way for the development of an understanding of the sufferings of others. It would also help in narrowing social distance between people who were affected in different ways, at different times, and in different measure, although sharing a similar context. Consequently, dealing with victimhood in an inclusive way, and by developing tools for active and empathetic listening of everyone's experience, may establish grounds for the healing of individuals and the society as a whole. These are exactly the ideas on which the third way of dealing with the past in Serbia recently emerged. Similarly, as in South Africa, this third way in Serbia is trying to fill the dangerous gap between two extremes in a polarized society, i.e. to find compromise between trials and blanket amnesty or national amnesia (Chapman and Ball 2001). Thus, it has a potential for developing an approach toward the past which may contribute toward ending social divisions and cycles of violence.

This approach has to be created on both the state and civil society level, with the state 1 strategy may have a form of truth and reconciliation commission (TRC) but it is not necessary. It may also be some decentralized yet coordinated body, based on the partnership between state and civil society, which may begin by analyzing the existing, already large, amount of collected material. However, restorative processes in Serbia have to be part of the regional process as well, which means that truth and reconciliation commissions or similar bodies should be established in all countries of the former Yugoslavia. Each needs to cooperate in terms of exchange of victims' and perpetrators' testimonies, research, publications, and other materials. Governments of the countries of the former Yugoslavia should allow for the free flow of TRC information so that all people in all parts can learn about crimes committed both against and by their own compatriots.

In addition to the TRC, other forms of restorative justice, as both state and civil society initiatives, should be used as well, such as: truth and reconciliation tribunals/small group discussions; reparation; recording the names of the victims and offenders; education; campaigns; museums and memorials; conflict management; and a Day of Reflection/Reconciliation.

References

Bjelakovic, N. (2002) 'Reconciliation, truth, and justice in the post-Yugoslav states,' *Southeast European Politics*, 2–3: 163–76.

Blagojevic, M. (2000) 'Prebrojavanje mrtvih tela: viktimizacija kao samoostvarujuce prorocanstvo' (Counting dead bodies: victimization as a self-fulfilling prophecy), *Temida*, 2: 5–11.

Blagojevic, M. and Milenkovic, N. (2004) *Suočavanje s prošlošću: Izveštaj za Srbiju i Crnu Goru* (Facing the Past: the report for Serbia and Montenegro), Beograd: Quaker Peace and Social Witness.

Borain, A. and Livi, D. (eds) (2000) *Zalecenje nacije?* (The Healing of a Nation), Beograd: SamizdatafreeB92.

Borer, T. (2003) 'A taxonomy of victims and perpetrators: human rights and reconciliation in South Africa', *Human Rights Quarterly*, 25: 1088–116.

Chapman, A. and Ball, P. (2001) 'The truth of truth commissions: comparative lessons from Haiti, South Africa, and Guatemala,' *Human Rights Quarterly*, 23: 1–43.

Dinkic, M. (1999) *Zavrsni Racun* (Final Account), Beograd: Stubovi kulture.

Djokic, D. (2002) 'The Second World War II: discourses of reconciliation in Serbia and Croatia in the late 1980s and early 1990s,' *Journal of Southern Europe and the Balkans*, 4(2): 127–40

Fletcher, L. and Weinstein, H. (2001) 'Violence and social repair: rethinking the contribution of justice to reconciliation,' *Human Rights Quarterly*, 3: 573–639.

Gajicki, M. (forthcoming) 'Novo iskustvo u suocavanju s prosloscu' (New experience in dealing with past), *Temida*, 4.

Hamber, B. (forthcoming) 'Coming to terms with the conflict in and about Northern Ireland: lessons from the healing through remembering project,' *Temida*, 4.

Hanak, N. (forthcoming) 'Projekat Od sečanja na proslost ka pozitivnoj buducnosti: kakav model istine i poverenja/pomirenja je potreban Srbiji?' (Project From Remembering the Past toward a Positive Future: what kind of model of truth and trust/reconciliation does Serbia need?), *Temida*, 4.

Healing Through Remembering (2002) *Report of the Healing Through Remembering Project*, Belfast: Healing Through Remembering.

Helsinki Committee for Human Rights in Serbia (2002) *Tacka razlaza* (The Point of Divergence), Belgrade: Helsinki Committee for Human Rights in Serbia.

Kritz, N. (2002) 'Progress and humanity: the ongoing search for post-conflict justice' in M. C. Bassiouni (ed.) *Post-Conflict Justice*, Ardsley, NY: Transnational Publishing.

Morrissey, M. and Smyth, M. (2002) *Northern Ireland after the Good Friday Agreement: victims, grievance and blame*, London: Pluto Press.

Nikolic-Ristanovic, V. (1998) 'War and crime in the former Yugoslavia' in V. Ruggiero. N. South and I. Taylor (eds) *The New European Criminology*, London: Routledge.

— (2000) 'Zrtve ratova u bivsoj Jugoslaviji: obim, struktura i obrasci viktimizacije,' (Victims of wars in the former Yugoslavia: scope, structure and patterns of victimization), *Temida*, 2: 11–21.

— (2002) 'Specifičnosti društveno-istorijskog konteksta i viktimizacije u Srbiji i njihov značaj za koncipiranje modela istine i pomirenja' (Specificities of socio-historical context and victimization in Serbia and their impact for the creation of the model of truth and reconciliation), *Temida*, 4: 56–66.

— (2003a) 'Possibilities for restorative justice in Serbia,' in L. Woldgrave (ed.) *Positioning Restorative Justice*, Cullompton, Devon: Willan Publishers.

— (2003b) 'Refugee women in Serbia – invisible victims of war in the former Yugoslavia,' *Feminist Review*, 73: 104–14

— (2004) 'Organized crime in Serbia – media construction and social reaction,' in G. Mesko, M. Pagon and B. Dobovsek (eds) *Dilemmas of Contemporary Criminal Justice*, Ljubljana: Faculty of Criminal Justice.

Nikolic-Ristanovic, V. and Hanak, N. (2004) *Od secanja na proslost ka pozitivnoj buducnosti – misljenja i ideje gradjana* (From Remembering the Past toward a Positive Future), Beograd: VDS and Prometej.

Nikolic-Ristanovic, V. and Simeunovic-Patic, B. (forthcoming) 'Researching war victimization through the deconstruction of organized crime,' *European Journal of Crime, Criminal Law and Criminal Justice*.

Rakic, D. (forthcoming) 'Neka razmatranja o položaju i perspektivi interno raseljenih lica na prostoru bivše SFRJ' (Some considerations on the status and perspectives of internally displaced people on the territory of the former Yugoslavia), *Temida*, 4.

Rankovic, V. (2002) *Jugoslovenska komisija za istinu i pomirenja* (Yugoslavian Truth and Reconciliation Commission), online. Available at: www.komisija.org [accessed 6 July 2003].

Rombouts, H. (2002a) 'Istina i pomirenje: da li je potrebno preispitati osnovne postavke? Iskustva Juzne Afrike i Ruande' (Truth and reconciliation: should the key notions be revised? Experiences from South Africa and Rwanda), *Temida*, 4: 33–45.

— (2002b) 'Importance and difficulties of victim-based research in post-conflict societies', *European Journal of Crime, Criminal Law and Criminal Justice*, 2–3: 216–33.

Simonovic, S. (2002) *Zasto je jugoslovenska komisija za istinu i pomirenje zapala u stanje poduze hibernacije?* (Why has the Yugoslavian Truth and Reconciliation Commission been so long in a State of Hibernation?), online. Available at: www.komisija.org [accessed 6 July 2003].

Vanspauwen, C., Parmentier, S. and Weitekamp, E. (2003) 'Collective victimization in post-conflict situations: in search of a restorative justice approach for countries in transition,' paper presented at 11th International Symposium on Victimology, Stellenbosch, South Africa.

Notes

1. At the end of 1999 Serbia had almost 1 million refugees and internally displaced people which made it the country with the highest number of refugees in Europe. In 2004, five years after the end of war in Kosovo, there were still 206,789 internally displaced people (Serbs, Roma and other non-Albanians) (Rakic forthcoming).

2. In the NATO war, several thousand people were killed and injured, and a lot of buildings, infrastructure, and many factories were destroyed, while the use of depleted uranium bombs and the destruction of chemical plants led to the short- and long-term pollution of the water and the ground. It is estimated that total economic damage as a consequence of the NATO bombing, was $29,608.5 millions and that the GDP drop was 44.4 per cent from the previous year (Dinkic 1999: 9).

3. This time, however, Kostunica became prime minister, while the president is from the Djindjic Democratic party.

4. For example, refugees now living in Serbia were often victims of the war in Croatia, Bosnia, and Kosovo/Serbia since they were forced to move from one part of the former Yugoslavia to another, always experiencing a new war.

5. Two opposed interethnic sides from the Second World War in Serbia (partisans and cetniks) were never reconciled. As noted by Djokic, although nationalist, Milosevic never called for national reconciliation so this division became even more striking during his regime (Djokic 2002).

6. For the importance of the overlapping of victims and perpetrators, and the failure of South African TRC to acknowledge it in a proper way, see Borer (2003).

7. This denial exists in other parts of the former Yugoslavia and internationally, but in Serbia as well.

8. For similar approach in Northern Ireland, see Morrissey and Smyth (2002).

9. This is basically the continuation of an earlier prevailing discourse now accompanied by the other one, which has been developed as a reaction to it.

10. These features of the public discourse were especially evident in the events surrounding the exhibition of American war photographer Ron Haviv during the year 2002, as well as in the discussion within the correspondence rubric of the magazine *Vreme* (Helsinki Committee for Human Rights in Serbia 2002).

11. The first split between late prime minister Djindjic and the then president Kostunica occurred after Slobodan Milosevic was sent to The Hague.

12. The Truth and Reconciliation Commission was established shortly before the expected extradition of Slobodan Milosevic to the Hague Tribunal.

13. According to the restorative justice typology developed by McCold and Wachel, 'the extent to which all the stakeholders are involved in a meaningful emotional exchange and decision-making determines the extent of restorativness' (quoted by Vanspauwen *et al.* 2003: 6).

26

Transitional justice, restoration, and prosecution

Charles Villa-Vicencio

Restorative justice can be broadly defined as a process that seeks to redefine crime: it shifts the primary focus of crime from the breaking of laws, or offences against a faceless state, to a perception of crime as violations against human beings ... Based on reparation, it aims at the healing and the restoration of all concerned – victims in the first place, but also of offenders, their families and the larger community. [It] encourages victims, offenders and the community to be directly involved in resolving conflicts.

(Truth and Reconciliation Commission of South Africa Report 1998, Vol. 1: 126)

Restorative justice seeks to recover dimensions of justice often lost within the institutional retributive justice process. It does not necessarily reject all punitive measures associated with the retribution justice. It seeks rather to be more inclusive in the promotion of justice. It is an immodest theory – sometimes a reach beyond our immediate grasp, located between vengeance and forgiveness.[1] At best, it is a process whereby the parties to a conflict resolve to deal with the consequences of the conflict and its implications for the future in a collective and mutually acceptable manner. Recognizing that space exists within the retributive process for this to happen, there can be more common ground between retributive and restorative justice than is often acknowledged. Restorative justice at the same time prioritizes the need to salvage and affirm the moral worth and dignity of everyone involved – victims, perpetrators, and society as a whole – in pursuit of a minimally decent society.

Applied in different ways in different applications of justice, restorative justice has recently emerged as an important ingredient of *transitional justice*, which effectively seeks to find a way beyond *de facto* impunity within which most perpetrators of an oppressive regime are unlikely to be prosecuted and there is no obvious program of restoration in place. In most transitional societies, the existing justice system is not able to sustain a comprehensive program of retribution and the political cost of sustained prosecutions is not a viable option. Perpetrators are simply not prepared to surrender their arms if they face the possibility of prosecution. In this situation transitional justice offers an alternative with which to counter crass impunity through conditional amnesty and reparations. It is here that this essay is located.[2] It is grounded primarily in the South African political and legal transition from apartheid rule to the beginning of democratic rule. The particularities of this process suggest nuances and insights relevant to the more general debate on justice – not least regarding the tension between retributive and restorative justice.

The pursuit of justice

Prison was traditionally conceived of as a place of detention, not explicitly a place of punishment. In most societies, however, the vindictive side of prosecution and detention has taken priority, often becoming an end in itself – without adequate attention being given to either the need for deterrence or rehabilitation.

Recidivism rates world-wide indicate that criminal justice, focusing primarily on punishment, has not been an adequate means of deterrence or rehabilitation. In politically driven conflicts, whether national or international, it seems even less likely that the threat of punishment is sufficient to curtail human rights abuses. Historically fixed mind-sets, entrenched prejudice and the kind of ideological bloody-mindedness that drives militant perpetrators of political crime are forces simply too powerful to be prevented by the possibility of prosecution alone. To argue that the threat of punishment will deter those who violate international conventions is a bit like arguing that the threat of capital punishment deters murder and related crimes.

Moreover, the prosecution of political offenders, if not carefully carried out, can turn villains into martyrs. It can stir others to go and do likewise. And yet trials and prosecution are an important part of the rule of law that needs to be established in the wake of the autocratic rule from which transitional societies need to recover. It is this tension that is central to the balance required to ensure that transitional societies lapse neither back into war nor into impunity. Suffice it to say that prosecution, while

necessary, is insufficient on its own. *More* is required. The more involves the neglected dimensions of a holistic theory of justice. In transitional societies it prioritizes the coexistence and restoration of relationships between former enemies as a basis for the prevention of the reoccurrence of human rights abuses and the restoration of the dignity and material well-being of victims.

The celebrated debate between Lon Fuller and H. L. A. Hart on legal positivism in the 1950s is pertinent to the debate on restorative justice – that has implications for societies seeking to recover from authoritarian rule.[3] Fuller asked what it is that gives legitimacy to 'a constitution for a country that has just emerged from a period of violence and disorder in which any thread of legal continuity with previous governments has broken' (see Hart 1958: 593; Fuller 1958: 630). It involves, he argues, acceptance by the people concerned of a set of moral qualities grounded in what is politically possible. It has to do with what Ronald Dworkin, speaking in a different context, refers to when he speaks of the 'law beyond law' which inspires us to discern 'the best route to a better future' (1986: 413). Effectively it concerns 'the people we want to be and the community we aim to have' (Dworkin 1986: 413).[4] The best possible route in this regard, envisaged by South Africans in their transition from apartheid to democracy, is captured in the postamble of the South African Interim Constitution (Act No. 200 of 1993). It involves the promotion of:

a secure foundation for the people of South Africa to transcend the divisions and strife of the past which generated gross violations of human rights, the transgression of humanitarian principles in violent conflicts and the legacy of hatred, fear, guilt and revenge. These can now be addressed on the basis that there is a need for understanding but not vengeance, a need for reparation but not for retaliation, a need for *ubuntu* but not victimization.

The complexity of pursuing justice in a transitional society is, of course, immense. It requires a set of ethical values and a political-legal initiative that is flexible enough to meet the different needs associated with nation-building – all of which have the capacity to derail the fragile initiative for peaceful coexistence and national reconciliation between former enemies.

There is a place, in this milieu for:

- *retributive justice,* as an alternative to unbridled revenge;
- *deterrent justice,* as a means of limiting future atrocities;
- *compensatory justice,* as a way of seeking to restore the losses of victims and survivors;
- *distributive justice,* as a means of correcting past imbalances;
- *rehabilitative justice,* aimed at the needs of victims and survivors, as well as the requirements of perpetrators – recognizing that no nation can afford the presence of unrehabilitated torturers and killers;
- *justice as the affirmation of human dignity,* as a basis for establishing a culture of human rights;
- *justice as exoneration,* restoring the records of persons falsely accused by the state and/or within their own communities.
- *restorative justice,* seeking to find a way forward with which all parties to the conflict can live. This requires a commitment to transformation that extends beyond any one judicial procedure or political initiative, recognizing that the level of transformation required for this to happen takes time. It must be progressive and it needs, necessarily, to be sustainable.

A priority in transitional societies is for former enemies to learn to live together on the basis of respect for human rights and common decency. The acid test of restorative justice within such contexts is whether it can succeed where retribution has failed – whether it can reduce recidivism and facilitate the emergence of a more just social order. Restorative justice must address the human dignity, the legal rights and the material well-being of victims, while seeking to restore the civic responsibility of perpetrators, enabling them to be reintegrated into society, there to play a positive role in rebuilding society. Chief Justice Ismael Mahomed (writing at the time as Deputy President of the Constitutional Court in response to a legal challenge to the South African Truth and Reconciliation Commission (TRC)) stressed the need to enable perpetrators, through the amnesty process, not merely to escape a jail sentence but 'to become active, full and creative members of the new order.' Victims and perpetrators need to cross the 'historic bridge' from the past to the future. This, suggests Mahomed, should *not* be 'with heavy dragged steps delaying and impeding a rapid and enthusiastic transition to the new society at the end of the bridge.'[5]

It is essentially this journey that is explored in the following proposal of a viable theory of restorative justice.

Retributive and restorative justice

Howard Zehr provides contrasting definitions of retributive and restorative justice. He argues that retributive justice views crime as 'a violation of the state, defined by lawbreaking and guilt'. It 'determines blame and administers pain in a context between the offender and the state directed by systematic rules.' For restorative justice, crime is essentially 'a violation of people and relationships. It creates obligations to make things right.' It 'involves the victim, the offender and the community in a search for solutions which promote repair, reconciliation and reassurance' (1995: 181).[6]

In a transitional society the integrity of the state and the efficacy of the rule of law is a process invariably still under threat. For justice to be respected in an emerging democracy where the memory of illegitimate rule and lawlessness is still an agonizing reality, the re-establishment of the rule of law is essential to the establishment of a partnership between victim, offender and community given to the building of a qualitatively different kind of society. The establishment of sustainable peace and the rule of law is, at the same time, impossible to attain without a reasonable level of co-operation between victims, offenders and others in pursuit of this goal.

Both retributive and restorative justice, as defined by Zehr, are necessary for democracy, the rule of law and the establishment of a culture of human rights to be realized in the wake of abusive rule. The one depends on the other. Justice is both a set of *judicial* (often constitutional) ideals to which a society aspires, and a *political* concept that requires democratic participation in a structure of authority and set of laws by which people agree to be governed. Differently put, political, economic, and other contextualities that shape transitional societies often produce a social contract between former enemies that results in principles of transition and law that are less than perfect when measured against the judicial and constitutional ideals espoused by human rights purists. It is at the same time a contract that could offer the only possible opportunity for sustainable peace and progress towards a better society.

A transitional society is by definition located between an illegitimate past and a future shaped by a set of ideals to which it aspires – without all such aspirations necessarily being immediately realizable. Established democracies acquire practices, values, and behavioral trends over time that make for the legitimacy and sustainability of the state. New democracies need to establish their legitimacy by demonstrating a willingness to be governed by such laws that made a political settlement possible. This requires them to live with the continuing negative impact of past realities, at least for the short- to medium-term future, without losing the capacity to reach towards the higher ideals that society has set for itself.

The question is how to create realistically, at the level of governance, a situation that promotes the fullest participation by citizens in a process that is driven by high constitutional ideals, while needing to be sustained by a process that persuades conflicting parties that such ideals are productive of the common good. The question is fundamental to transitional politics, especially in a situation where the principles that produced the settlement, although crucial to the ending of the earlier conflict, do not enjoy the unquestioned support of all citizens. Important in such situations is the need to ensure that the emotions, demands and expectations of those most alienated by the settlement are addressed with sufficient vigor to keep them within the agreed social contract.

Advocates of retributive justice essentially argue that this can best be achieved where the rights of victims are vindicated through legal processes in the courts of the land. This, it is argued, can produce a level of emotional appeasement and the re-establishment of the dignity for victims, made possible because the state is seen to have acknowledged and responded to their abuse and suffering. Proponents of restorative justice convincingly argue that the anger and loss of dignity of victims can also, perhaps more effectively, be redressed through the implementation of substitute measures that offset retributive demands. The ruling of the South African Constitutional Court in response to the application brought by AZAPO and others concerning the validity of the Promotion of National Unity and Reconciliation Act is a case in point.[7] Briefly stated, the court upheld both the criminal and civil clauses of the Act, while presenting reparations as a *quid pro quo* for victims and survivors being required to surrender their right to prosecution. It further ruled that parliament was justified in adopting a wide concept of reparations, which needs to be communally balanced against other state obligations for reconstruction.[8] A survey conducted by James Gibson, in collaboration with the Institute for Justice and Reconciliation in the wake of the South African TRC, shows that the vast majority of black South Africans, being the primary victims of apartheid rule, were ready to accept that the suffering and abuse they endured could be compensated for in ways other than through prosecution and imprisonment (Gibson 2002). Even the payment of compensation was not seen as the *only* such palliative. Truth, acknowledgment of past wrongs, and a sincere apology, plus the opportunity for victims to relate the stories of their suffering were cited as important alternatives to normative forms of retribution.

Genuine, non-malicious retributive justice involves, of course, more than the punishment of offenders as an end in itself. It is seen as a necessary means to achieving a society built on justice and rule of law. Restorative justice, in turn, recognizes the need to both condemn and transcend evil as a basis for restoring/rehabilitating those victims of past abuse as well as those responsible for their suffering. It is here that the conversation between the advocates of retributive and restorative justice needs to happen, recognizing that 'retributive emotions' (Murphy and Hampton 1994: 2)[9] brood understandably beneath the surface of perhaps most victims. Donald Shriver argues that there is nothing more natural in human relations than revenge. He also suggests that there is nothing less political (Shriver 1995: 13). These emotions need to be procedurally controlled and creatively directed to ensure that they are not reduced to naked revenge. As such, retributive justice is defended as a viable and appropriate alternative to what Susan Jacoby has called 'wild justice' or the revenge of vigilante groups (Jacoby 1998: 10). Restorative justice, in explicitly seeking to rehabilitate victims and perpetrators, restoring relations between them, and promoting social cohesion and justice will inevitably be unsuccessful if it fails to address the anger of victims, their instinctive demand for justice and the moral outrage of society that results (in a society undergoing political transition) from political and other forms of perpetration. As such it is required to promote initiatives of restoration that include the redress of this anger, a desire for vindication and moral outrage, noting that anger and resentment, even moral hatred, are both understandable and appropriate in certain circumstances. These sentiments often give expression to the struggle for self-respect and self-worth on the part of the victim concerned. They affirm the dignity of others when the anger is in response to the suffering of others. They constitute a refusal to turn the other cheek in the face of the bully and the perpetrator of evil.

Building a restored society

Within the context of transitional justice, the conversation on retribution and restoration is necessarily related to four pertinent inter-related imperatives: the condemnation of evil; the restoration of victims; the rehabilitation of perpetrators; and the restoration of the social order.

The condemnation of evil

Restoration and reconciliation are not possible without the pursuit of constructive ways to deal with retributive emotions. To expect the victims of gross violations of human rights simply to absorb and/or suppress their resentment and hatred is to entrench and perpetuate victimhood and defeat. The willingness of victims and survivors, on the other hand, to suspend or

391

foreswear revenge in response to an alternative way of dealing with their emotions, can offer a way of moving on in anticipation of the beginning of a restorative process (see Gibson 2002, the survey already referred to that was conducted in the wake of the South African TRC). Obviously, moving on rarely results in the resolution of all anger. The survey does, however, suggest that through the victims' hearings at the TRC and related initiatives, both within and outside of the Commission, many were able to deal constructively with the trauma of suffering – creating a channel for some victims to deal with unspent emotions. It also enabled the nation to seek ways to redress past wrongs in a viable restorative manner. Importantly, it further projected the possibility of a society within which victims and survivors, as well as perpetrators and others, could feel safe against the recurrence of gross violations of human rights. It is here, of course, where argument on whether retribution is an adequate deterrent and moral persuader against violence is located, provoking the question whether alternative restorative measures are not better able to produce the level of rehabilitation and restitution needed for former enemies to learn to live together.

Jean Hampton's affirmation of the retributive idea at the same time goes beyond the need to counter revengeful emotions (Murphy and Hampton 1994: 130). It involves the affirmation of *moral decency*, something in and of itself worth defending, which is presented as a deontological principle that provides moral order and human protection in a world threatened by radical evil. Carlos Nino, in turn, reminds the perpetrator that there is a price to be paid for violating the agreed rules of coexistence. He does so on the basis of *human autonomy* (which affirms the right of the individual to defend him- or herself against attack) and *social responsibility* (which involves the obligation of society to uphold moral decency). These, he suggests, are values entrenched

within a morally defensible theory of retributive justice (Nino 1996: 143, 160). He predicates his argument on a social contract that he sees as implicit to societal coexistence, arguing that we must either contribute to the common good or accept the consequences for failing to do so.

Nino suggests four essential principles that need to be addressed. They form the basis of the following discussion.

The vindication of moral consensus. This involves a corporate or communal responsibility to uphold and promote those values that a society comes to accept as the basis of its existence. It is a common good that every member of society has a moral and political responsibility to uphold as a basis for maximizing the possibility of peaceful coexistence. A society still tortured by the memory of the past, which is at the same time in pursuit of peaceful coexistence, is compelled to address the question how best to live with those responsible for massive human rights violations. Nino concludes that in this situation '*some* measure of retroactive justice for massive human rights violations helps protect democratic values' (ibid.: vii). The question is: what is meant by 'some measure of retroactive justice'? Alex Boraine argues that while 'there are those who argue that in order to protect democratic values no restorative justice should be attempted, particularly in states undergoing transition to democracy', transition is often simply not possible where retribution stares the perpetrator in the face.[10]

It is here that restorative justice contributes pertinently to the transitional justice process, seeing justice not primarily as the infliction of pain and revenge through the incarceration of the wrongdoer, but essentially the restoration of good order and the promotion of the common good. Ronald Dworkin speaks of 'law beyond law' that needs to inspire us to continually discern the 'best route to a better future' (1986: 413). In essence, he suggests that the mere application of a law in all situations, whatever the circumstances, could undermine the very *purpose* law is expected to serve. The deconstruction of law by critical legal scholars emphasizes the importance of uncovering the values implicit in law. Their concern is to ensure that the good of society be the adjudicator of how best to respond to a violation of the law, an exercise that lies at the heart of restorative justice efforts.

The dignity of victims and survivors. Inherent to the notion of moral consensus and the affirmation of ethical values is the human worth of all people. It involves the recognition that the disregard or playing down of the suffering of victims and survivors suggests that society is not particularly concerned about those who have suffered most – dismissing them as ciphers to be expended in pursuit of a cause. Punitive action against those responsible for the suffering of others is defended as being a necessary corrective to any suggestion that people can be abused in criminal violence or sacrificed with impunity in pursuit of a cause of one kind or another, whether ideological, class-driven or grounded in one or other ethnic prejudice. Restorative justice contends that this worth can be affirmed in non-retributive ways. It does not necessarily require the incarceration or criminal punishment of the perpetrator. It does require society and the perpetrator to contribute, to the extent that it is possible, to the emotional restoration and repair of the physical and material wellbeing of the victim.

The moral responsibility of perpetrators. If retribution reminds the perpetrator of his or her equal moral and social standing with his or her victims, it also elevates the level of moral responsibility expected of the perpetrator. Differently put, it refuses to allow that the perpetrator (except in the case of insanity or some other extraordinary situations) is incapable of better behavior, requiring the perpetrator to take responsi-

bility for failing to act in a responsible and moral way. It is to affirm the autonomy of the perpetrator as a potential agent of the common good, which involves a double-edged sword – involving acceptance and responsibility. It is to say to the perpetrator: precisely because we acknowledge your humanity, we require that you take responsibility for your behavior. On this premise, retribution is not punishment in order to satisfy some basic need for revenge. Restorative justice constantly asks how best to involve perpetrator, victim and society as a whole in the restorative process, which may well involve perpetrators being subjected to some form of community service and/or an income tax surcharge. What the South African experiment in restorative justice since 1994 shows, however, is that, unless legally imposed, restorative measures are not likely to be either commonplace or extensive enough to meet the demands of most victims and survivors of gross violations of human rights. Few perpetrators (or benefactors) seek to voluntarily restore the damage of the past. Restorative measures seek to persuade the perpetrator to recover his or her capacity for agency. The process is complex, requiring a remarkable kind of moral and political leadership that cajoles, challenges, invites and rewards participation. It seeks to persuade citizens of different opinions that there is more to be gained at the level of security, peace and long-term prosperity through contributing to a nation-building process that includes former perpetrators, rather than risking the exclusion and intensified anger of a group of people whose leaders and cadres languish in jail. If at all possible, it is often politically expedient to have potential troublemakers inside the camp rather than outside mobilizing for its downfall.

A space for mercy and forgiveness. The non-malicious retributionist does not accept the *lex talionis* principle in its entirety. The genuine (non-malicious) retributionist often settles for less than an eye for an eye – provided there is some indication of the primary objective, which is the restoration of the moral order and the common good, being served. This potentially includes the showing of mercy and understanding to the perpetrator. Alternatively, pardon or the imposition of a lesser penalty may be the price that needs to be paid for peace – as a first step towards the creation of a better society. It is here again that retribution and restoration meet.

The restoration of victims

Empathy and understanding, even moral outrage and condemnation of evil, are not enough to restore victims. In societies emerging from a period of exploitation and gross violations of human rights, appropriate action aimed at redressing the resentment and legitimate claims of victims and survivors is essential – which point has already been made. Few are ready to deny the *moral* right of victims to receive reparations, while a survey of international human rights instruments provides the *legal* case for reparations. The International Covenant on Civil and Political Rights declares the right of victims to reparations.[11] The right of victims to receive compensation is reiterated in the 1985 UN Declaration of Basic Principles of Justice for Victims of Crime and Abuse of Power, and the final report of the Special Rapporteur, Mr M. Cherif Bassiouni, to the UN Economic and Social Council affirms 'the right to restitution, compensation and rehabilitation for victims of gross violations of human rights and fundamental freedoms.'[12]

The shape, form and extent of reparations remain a matter of concern in any restorative justice program. The recommendations of Truth Commissions in South Africa, Peru, and Sierra Leone are extensive in this regard – ranging from individual monetary payment and personal counseling to institutional reform and demoralization.[13] The manner in which such recommendations are responded to by government and the process of prioritizing state expenditure towards this end is, at the same time, as important as the decisions themselves. Faced with a range of restorative challenges victims, survivors, perpetrators, ordinary citizens and the state are invariably obliged to find one another in compromise, through democratic debate and structured decision-making. Differently put, relationship-building constitutes a priority in any restorative justice program. This involves the victim, the offender and the community in a search for solutions that promote repair, reconciliation and reassurance. A difficult process, the debate needs to be taken beyond a narrow focus on victims of gross violations of human rights to a more systematic view of how to access who is worthy of reparation and how this can best happen. Above all, it involves participation in the restorative process by all citizens in what has been called a 'multiplicity of variables in terms of which equality can be judged' (Sen 1995: 1). The formula and practice of reparations with which a nation and, more especially, victims themselves are prepared to live can only be realized through a process of participation by victims, survivors and citizens in facing the socio-political as well as the social-psychological realties that impact on restoration.

It would be presumptuous to suggest that reparations can ever be adequate. The death of a child, the rape of a spouse, the destruction of a family home, a business, a community is irreparable. The restoration of human dignity at the same time comes in different ways. In a country seeking to recover from the ravages of war the simple termination of hostilities is a priority that cannot be sacrificed in pursuit of higher forms of reparation which is, of course, an essential base from which sustainable and incremental manifestations of psychological, material and other forms of restoration are possible.

The inter-relationship between sustainable peace and economic transformation is central to any successful restorative justice process. There can be no lasting peace without economic justice. There can, in turn, be neither economic justice nor lasting peace without broad-based economic growth. For this to happen there must necessarily be a state governed by the rule of law and able to formulate and execute long-term policies.

A seldom specified prerequisite for economic regeneration is the ability of ordinary citizens to look beyond immediate survival in order to plan future activity. Few are going to build, save, or put extra work into anything but self-preservation or defense if they have no reason to expect that they can retain the benefits of their hard work. As farmers will not plant if they cannot anticipate harvest, citizens cannot be expected to help build a new social framework if they cannot imagine a future without poverty and the eternal struggle for mere survival. Compounding the dynamic, it is also true that the more predictable the social framework, the livelier the economy that is able to develop.

The United Nations' *New Agenda for the Development of Africa* (Annual Report 1990 Preamble para 8 at http://www.un.org/documents/ga/res/46/a46r151.htm) concludes that:

> Peace is an indispensable prerequisite for development ... Peace initiatives by African countries should be encouraged and pursued in order to bring an end to war, destabilization and internal conflicts so as to facilitate the creation of optimal conditions for development. The international community as a whole should endeavour to co-operate with and support the efforts of African countries for a rapid restoration of peace, normalisation of life for uprooted populations and national socio-economic reconstruction.

Democracy, good governance, peace, security, stability and justice are necessary to create socio-economic development. The United Nations Secretary-General, in his 1998 *Report on Causes of Conflict and Promotion of Durable Peace and Sustainable Development in Africa*, recognized that conflicts and development should not be dealt with separately; rather, they need to be addressed though a comprehensive framework of governance that takes stock of the root causes of conflict and charts the potential for sustainable development.

This is not to suggest that a growing economy will necessarily heal or restore the victims of past abuse. It is to suggest that the adequate provision of psychological services, skills training, job creation and the restoration of human dignity is dependent on the availability of economic resources that enable a society to deliver such services and resources on a long-term basis. Support from international donors for this to happen is never adequate and rarely sustainable beyond emergency relief in the short term.

The rehabilitation of perpetrators

For the kind of sustainable peace to be achieved that makes the restoration of victims possible, it is crucial for perpetrators to be incorporated into the emerging new society. Of the more than thirty peace settlements signed in Africa during the past decade, over half have collapsed. The vast majority of Disarmament, Demobilization, Rehabilitation and Reintegration Programs (DDRR) on the continent have failed because of a focus on the two Ds to the neglect of the two Rs. Cease-fire agreements address demilitarization and demobilization. Where there is an opportunity to stop the war, the international community is often involved and the urgency of the moment compels the leadership of the parties to the cease-fire to control if not fully demobilize combatants. Peace treaties are more difficult to make operational. The process of drawing former combatants into rehabilitation programs and motivating them to be reintegrated into civilian society – from which some have never gainfully benefited – is more difficult. It is a situation often aggravated by post-treaty skirmishes, an economy unable to provide sufficient jobs, and a milieu that suffers from the eventual withdrawal of international and regional peacekeepers.

The magnitude of the extent and repetition of violence by perpetrators at the same time persuades many victims and those directly involved in building the new society that they are beyond rehabilitation. Truth Commissions are important as a means of uncovering the nature and extent of past atrocities. And yet, by drawing attention to the nation's worst perpetrators, they reinforce the common perception that they are not only unworthy of being reintegrated into society but that it is impossible to do so. The South African TRC left the nation horrified by its focus on the premeditated murder of apartheid's opponents as well as the extent of the brutalities committed in the detention camps of the African National Congress. South Africans across the political divide were outraged by the poisoning exploits and drug industry which emerged from the government's experiments in chemical and biological warfare. The chain of shallow graves across the country – containing the remains of abducted activists who were brutalized, tortured and ultimately killed – left many horrified. The media has understandably focused on these events, labeling Eugene de Kock, the infamous Vlakplaas commander in the security police, 'prime evil.' Jeffrey Benzien, a Western Cape Security Branch policeman who demonstrated his notorious wet bag method of torture before the amnesty committee, was seen on television screens and captured on the front page of most newspapers in the country. Such killers and torturers have been represented as psychopaths,

aberrations and misfits. Former state president De Klerk called them 'rotten eggs' – among the other disciplined, professional security force members. Steven Robins argues that all too often the public representation of the perpetrator before the TRC conformed to the Hollywood notion of a white South African policeman, portrayed as 'evil-looking Nazis with thick Afrikaans accents.' The outcome has been the undermining of the ability of ordinary South Africans to see themselves as represented by those who the TRC defines as perpetrators.

This focus on the outrageous often draws the nation's attention away from what Hannah Arendt has called the 'banality of evil.' We fail to recognize the pervasiveness of human capacity for evil. Perhaps there is a 'little perpetrator' in each one of us. Indeed, the size of the perpetrator, and its capacity to do harm, is arguably a matter of the circumstances in which we find ourselves. Jean-Paul Sartre, at the same time, reminds us that each one of us is 'condemned to be wholly responsible' for our own actions. To understand the source of evil does not mean to condone it. To recognize the possibility of evil in each of us is to claim the importance of taking responsibility to ensure that the past evil does not reoccur in the future.

Against this background, Pumla Gobodo-Madikizela interviewed and found levels of understanding and humanness in Eugene de Kock – the most visible and notorious of apartheid killers – opening up a range of perspectives on perpetrators that reach beyond the more popular perception of apartheid killers to the structures of society that gave them birth. She acknowledges the difficult terrain within which she works. 'No language should be created to understand evil,' she writes, fearing that it will distract from an appropriate focus on victims (Gobodo-Madikizela 2003: 17). Don Foster, the principal author of *A Theatre of Violence*, a study emanating from a study on perpetrators in the South African situation undertaken by the Institute for Justice and

Reconciliation, in turn argues that to understand perpetrators may not only 'reduce the attention given to victims', but may 'diminish our outrage towards their acts, shift the deeds out of focus and potentially draw our sympathies' (2000: 13). This said, to the extent that the restoration of peace and social stability in society is a prerequisite for victim restitution, the failure to understand the causes, motives and perspectives of perpetrators as a basis for seeking to rehabilitate and restore them to society is ultimately *in the interests of victims*.

The task is not easy. Suffice it to say, recidivism rates indicate that criminal justice that focuses primarily on punishment offers neither an adequate means of rehabilitation nor a form of effect deterrence. In *politically* driven conflicts, whether national or international, it seems even less likely that the threat of punishment is sufficient to curtail human rights abuses. Historically fixed mind-sets, entrenched prejudice and the kind of ideological bloody-mindedness that drives militant perpetrators of political crime, are forces simply too powerful to be curbed by the possibility of future prosecution. Trials, the removal of habitual perpetrators from society and appropriate punishment, are often necessary but essentially insufficient to deal effectively with crime. *More is required.*

The 'more' includes the need of perpetrators to unpack and talk about the layers of motivation and contradictions that drove them to do what they did. Interviews with perpetrators of gross violations of human rights at times reveal a sense of disillusionment with ideologies that no longer motivate. Looking back, Eugene de Kock says, 'Now, at the end of the day, I realize that I am actually a veteran of lost ideologies ... We killed a lot of people, they killed some of ours. We fought for nothing, we fought each other basically eventually for nothing' (*Cape Times*, 7 August 1997). Some are angry with their former masters. 'I will hate de Klerk for as long as I live,' a senior mili-

tary general said of the former state president. Some other perpetrators seek refuge in silence. Some show remorse. Some seek to make amends. 'Our capacity for empathy is a profound gift in this brutal world,' suggests Gobodo-Madikizela (2003: 77–8). The empathy, where it occurs, usually comes in a confused, sometimes a conflictual manner. It is often discrete acknowledgement rather than an apology. It does, at the same time, open a space between the extreme guises that appear in both academic and popular perceptions of *depraved monsters* or *legitimate defenders* of the people (whether as guardians of the state or liberators of the oppressed) making it possible for former enemies to explore options for learning to live together. It is this level of coexistence that constitutes the essence of restorative justice in the context of transitional politics – central to which is the breaking of the brutal silence that often optimizes the suspected and convicted perpetrator.

I have sought elsewhere to define the modest ingredients of former enemies learning to live together in coexistence or political reconciliation – as opposed to the more intimate forms of individual reconciliation that characterize religious notions of reconciliation and forgiveness (Villa-Vicencio 2004). This more modest process of social engagement does not necessarily involve forgiveness. It does, however, involve the interruption of an established pattern of events. It involves the possibility of a new future based on coexistence and building of civic trust. It is about memory, requiring a recognition and willingness to deal with the past. It means that perpetrators of gross violations of human rights, together with the benefactors of the past, need to acknowledge past privilege and responsibility as a basis for committing themselves to join victims in building a new and different kind of society. This includes the affirmation of a culture of common decency, broad-based human rights and a willingness at least to understand the motives that drove enemies to commit the deeds they did. This is a process that takes time to unfold, including time and space for the expression of mourning, anger and hurt, as well as healing. It involves individual and communal reparations and the affirmation of the human dignity of victims and perpetrators alike. It emphasizes a commitment to deal with conflict in a humane and civil manner. A Dinka elder, participating in a reconciliation forum for Sudanese civil society leaders, recently noted: 'Restoration and healing begins by being willing to sit under the same tree as your enemy and talk about ways for dealing peacefully with the issues that have hitherto driven us to war. That is where the possibility of reconciliation begins' (Gobodo-Madikizela 2003: 139).

The restoration of the social order

Restorative justice is necessarily a modest and inexact exercise – above all in a situation of political transition. Angry human-rights purists who demand radical repentance, punitive action and stringent legally imposed restitution by perpetrators make understandable moral sense. In reality, however, the rehabilitation of perpetrators is a complex process – especially in ideologically laden situations where the most hideous deeds are done in the name of what was believed to be decent and worth dying for.

The alternative approach of restorative justice sometimes produces the intended goal more readily than the more vindictive approach of the zealot whose demands often escalate conflict and war. The recalcitrant perpetrator needs to be persuaded and enabled as well as coerced through retribution and restoration to make the kind of shift in attitude and behavior that is required. This delicate balance requires a level of statecraft that sustains a number of internal contradictions with which ideological or moral purists find it difficult to live.

That's okay if peaceful coexistence and the possibility of national reconciliation replaces war. A little political indigestion has never done a purist too much harm!

The reward for political realism is dubious. Not all who are invited to share a soft transition from perpetration to restoration respond adequately or graciously. Many do, however, in a contradictory and often less than gracious manner, contribute to the rebuilding of a society based on coexistence and the beginning of civic trust. Comparisons are always tenuous; the contrast between the manner within which South Africa chose to deal with past military, police and civil-service personnel and the response of the United States to the officials of Saddam Hussein's regime is, however, both stark and informative. By incorporating apartheid generals and other state officials into post-apartheid structures, the country achieved a level of infrastructural stability infinitely different from that of the prevailing situation in Iraq. The long hours of negotiation, the sunset clauses incorporated into the settlement and the willingness of the new leaders (such as Nelson Mandela) to draw former enemies into a new alliance was criticized by many. At the same time this contributed to a level of political stability that few predicted at the height of apartheid. It enabled South Africans to sit under the same tree to explore ways of addressing the stubborn and entrenched heritage of racism and oppression that reached into the institutions of state.

Many social and economic contradictions remain despite the political transition that South Africans experienced ten years ago. An alternative approach involving the systematic imposition of retribution would have escalated the war; the imposition of lustration that expelled state officials from office could have crippled the civil service; the search for uncompromising change could have put sustainable transformation back by decades. It is partly this that distinguishes the South African transition from that of most other transitional societies in Africa and many other third world situations. Institutional reform is a slow and costly process. It is also essential for adequate restoration to take place. The point has been made: for a country seeking to recover from the ravages of war, to overcome the effects of decades of institutional oppression and the consequences of entrenched inequality, the *only* option for sustainable renewal is peace. This alone provides a base for realistic change. The long journey to freedom begins here, recognizing that there can be no ultimate peace without meaningful institutional change. Restoration is never a one-off exercise.

A postscript

The city of Thebes is afflicted and deeply troubled. The people of that city turn to *Oedipus the Tyrant*, pleading that he restore the city. They lament that there is:

> an unclean thing,
> Born and nursed on our soil, polluting our soil,
> Which must be driven away, not kept destroying us.

The people demand that those responsible be brought to justice and the blind Teiresias in exasperation confronts Oedipus saying, 'Your enemy is yourself.' Threatened with death, the blind man concludes:

> Fearful of nothing you can do to me:
> The man for whom you have ordered hue and cry,
> The killer . . . – that man is here.
> Go in, think on this
> When you can prove me wrong then call me blind.

In the ancient Greek theatre the truth slowly surfaces. Oedipus eventually tears his eyes out, perhaps in order that he, like Teiresias, may 'see.' More common is the persistence of denial. To demand that perpetrators *see* is perhaps to demand too much. Some suggest it is only the next generation, or perhaps the third generation, that is able to face up to the reality of past evil. Reflecting on the South African TRC at the time it was in session, a journalist wrote 'The TRC must fail.' She saw the demand for truth as simply too demanding, while going on to quote Emily Dickinson as saying 'the truth must dazzle gradually . . . or all the world would be blind.'

Truth recovery and restoration take time. The problem is that it is again victims who are required to face the pain of the non-disclosure of truth, the delay in reparations and the diffidence associated with reconstruction.

Restorative justice is about putting energy into the future. For this to happen the past needs to be dealt with. Silence, denial, and suppressed anger are the enemies of restoration. They limit the possibility of the level of change that has the potential to persuade victims to suspend their demands for retribution in the hope of restoration. Restorative justice is about restoration of victim and perpetrator. It is also about *justice*.

References

AZAPO and Others v. the President of the RSA and Others (1996) (8) BCLR 1015 (CC).

Doxtader, E. and Villa-Vicencio (eds.) (2004) *To Repair the Irreparable*, Cape Town: David Philip.

Dworkin, R. (1986) *Law's Empire*, Cambridge: Harvard University Press.

Foster, D. (2000) 'Entitlement as explanation for perpetrators' action,' *South African Journal of Psychology*, 30(1): 10–13.

Fuller, F. (1958) 'Positivism and the fidelity to law: a reply to Professor Hart,' *Harvard Law Review*, 71: 630–72.

Gibson, J. L. (2002) 'Truth, justice and reconciliation: judging amnesty in South Africa,' *American Journal of Political Science*, 46(3): 540–56.

Gobodo-Madikizela, P. (2003) *A Human Being Died That Night: a story of forgiveness*, Cape Town: David Philip.

Hart, H. L. A. (1958) 'Positivism and the separation of law and morals,' *Harvard Law Review*, 71: 593–29.

Jacoby, S. (1998) *Wild Justice: the evolution of revenge*, New York: Harper and Row.

Mackie, J. L. (1985) 'Morality and the retributive emotions,' in *Persons and Values*, Oxford: Clarendon Press.

Minow, M. (1998) *Between Vengeance and Forgiveness*, Boston: Beacon Press.

Murphy, J. G. and Hampton, J. (1994) *Forgiveness and Mercy*, Cambridge: Cambridge University Press.

Nino, C. (1996) *Radical Evil on Trial*, New Haven: Yale University Press.

Sen, A. (1995) *Inequality Reexamined*, Cambridge, MA: Harvard University Press.

Shriver, D. (1995) *An Ethic for Enemies*, Oxford, New York: Oxford University Press.

Truth and Reconciliation Commission (1998) *Truth and Reconciliation Commission Report of South Africa*, Cape Town: Truth and Reconciliation Commission.

Vandenginste, S. (2002) 'Victims of genocide, crimes against humanity, and war crimes in Rwanda: the legal and situational framework of their right to reparation,' in J. Torpey (ed.) *Politics and the Past: on repairing historical injustices*, Lanham, MD: Rowman and Littlefield.

Villa-Vicencio, C. (2003) 'Restorative justice: ambiguities and limitations of a theory,' in C. Villa-Vicencio and E. Doxtader (eds), *The Provocations of Amnesty: memory, justice and impunity*, Cape Town: David Philip, pp. 30–50.

— (2004) 'The politics of reconciliation,' in Tristan Borer (ed.) *Telling the Truths: truth telling and peacebuilding in post-conflict situations*, South Bend, IN: University of Notre Dame Press.

Zehr, H. (1995) *Changing Lenses*, Scottdale, PA: Herald Press.

— (2002) *Little Book of Restorative Justice*, Intercourse, PA: Good Books.

Notes

1. See Minow (1998: 12). Minow contends that vengeance needs to be 'tamed,' 'balanced' and 'recast' into a form of judicial retribution. Forgiveness is an ideal that few achieve, making coexistence and reconciliation more attainable goals.
2. See also C. Villa-Vicencio (2003).
3. See Hart (1958); see also Fuller (1958).
4. In his celebrated debate with H. L. A. Hart, Lon Fuller had similarly focused on the concept of 'purpose' in law, suggesting the need to show judicial flexibility in moving beyond a positivistic application of law. See Fuller (1958).
5. Judgment, *AZAPO and Others v. The President of the RSA and Others*, 1996 (8) BCLR 1015 (CC), para 18.
6. See also H. Zehr (2002).
7. *AZAPO and Others v. The President of the RSA and Others*, 1996 (8) BCLR 1015 (CC).
8. Section 2, 32 (4) of the Interim Constitution allows that no section of the Constitution, including the postscript on amnesty, should be regarded as having less validity than any other part of the Constitution. Of the nine judges, J. Didcott provided a separate concurring judgment, suggesting there is no way for the court to assess the cost involved or whether it is impossible to compensate all victims of apartheid. Arguing that the Act allows for 'some *quid pro quo* for the loss' suffered as a result of gross human rights violations, he concedes that nothing 'more definite, detailed and efficacious could feasibly have been promised at this stage.' His substantial argument is, however, that Section 33 (2) of the Interim Constitution allows for amnesty for vicarious liability.
9. See also Mackie (1985).
10. See Professor Alex Boraine (2000) 'Transitional justice in times of transition' (L05–3536), course outline, Fall semester, New York University.
11. See General Assembly Resolution 2200 A (XX1), 16 December 1966. For a discussion on the legal right to reparations, see S. Vandenginste (2002.
12. See Final Report of the Special Rapporteur, Mr M. Cherif Bassiouni, pursuant of Commission Resolution 1999/33. E/CN.4/2000/62, 18 January 2000. See also E/CN.4/RES/2000/41, 20 April 2000.
13. See Doxtader and Villa-Vicencio (eds) (2004).

27

Restorative justice and the governance of security in the Southwest Pacific

Sinclair Dinnen

Introduction

This chapter examines the social and historical foundations of restorative justice practices in the Melanesian[1] countries of the Southwest Pacific and, in particular, in the independent states of Papua New Guinea, Solomon Islands, Vanuatu, and, to a lesser extent, Fiji.[2] There are a number of reasons for considering restorative justice in what for many readers is likely to be an unfamiliar part of the world. In the first place, this region is distinguished by its extraordinary high levels of socio-linguistic diversity and legal pluralism. Consequently, there is a richness of regulatory traditions and practices, reflecting the complex entanglement of different social and political orders to be found within the national borders of each of these 'imagined communities' (Anderson 1983). This diversity is particularly marked in Papua New Guinea, Solomon Islands, and Vanuatu.[3] Large numbers of relatively autonomous and self-regulating tribal and clan-based associations continue to exert a significant influence at local levels alongside generally weak introduced national justice systems. While the former have evolved over thousands of years, the latter are the product of a relatively short and recent colonial past.

There appears to be significant congruence between the approaches to dispute resolution in many Melanesian communities and some of the qualities attributed to modern restorative justice practice. This similarity is often pitted against the apparent lack of congruence between these restorative-oriented local systems and the retributive-oriented criminal justice system operating at the national level. It is, of course, unwise to draw overly oppositional contrasts between restorative and retributive justice (Daly 2003). Elements of both are to be found in both traditional and modern approaches. Likewise, so-called traditional justice practices are neither uniform nor static and have adapted to the exigencies of introduced change, including the advent of modern criminal justice. Qualifications aside, there remains a strongly restorative flavor to many aspects of local dispute resolution as currently practiced in the Southwest Pacific. Indeed, while the term 'restorative justice' continues to be unfamiliar to most Pacific Islanders, a brief explanation is usually enough to elicit recognition as the familiar way of managing disputes in the village. Broad similarities include their inclusive and participatory character; acknowledgement of the social context of disputes and their impacts on a variety of parties; the emphasis on reparation for harm done; the importance of dialogue (story-telling) and negotiated decision-making; as well as attempts to reach consensus solutions.

Another reason for examining restorative justice in these countries is the increasing focus on 'law and order' and security issues in the region. An important aspect of this relates to the perceived inadequacies of introduced justice systems in preventing and deterring crime, as well as in resolving disputes and conflict. These shortcomings have, in turn, provoked a range of official and unofficial responses at local, regional, and national levels. Escalating lawlessness and violence, particularly in Papua New Guinea, and the incidence of serious conflicts in the PNG Highlands, Bougainville, Fiji, and Solomon Islands, has increased the urgency of efforts to improve the prevention and management of crime and conflict. The dramatically changed international security environment since the attacks on the US in September 2001 has added to this. International donors, with Australia at the fore, have embarked on a policy of intensified engagement with the Pacific island countries and have prioritized the task of improving the security and law and justice capacity of the countries concerned.

This renewed emphasis on the management of crime and conflict in the Southwest Pacific provides a timely opportunity to review existing approaches and to consider alternative policy options for the governance of security in these emerging states. Domestic governments and international donors have traditionally opted for strategies aimed at strengthening state justice institutions, notably the police, courts, and prisons. Until relatively recently, little attention was paid to the role of non-state and sub-national institutions in conflict prevention and resolution. The fact remains, however, that informal and often restorative-oriented approaches play a cri-

tical role in the maintenance of peace and good order at local levels throughout Melanesia. In addition to their routine use in the management of minor disputes, they have also made a significant, if often unacknowledged, contribution to the resolution of larger conflicts such as has been the case in the Bougainville peace process. This chapter argues that improving the articulation between different regulatory traditions and practices is an essential part of building an effective and integrated national system appropriate to the needs and circumstances of the Melanesian countries. It also provides an important way of addressing some of the shortcomings that have been attributed to both state and non-state approaches to crime and conflict.

The apparent deficit of order and fragility of the rule of law in parts of Melanesia, notably Papua New Guinea, has become a central strand in external framings of the region and the challenges it faces. However, given the degree of regulatory pluralism evident in these countries, it might be more accurate to view them as suffering from a surfeit or excess of order, rather than a lack of it. Attempting to reconcile the diversity of local regulatory practices within the unitary frameworks of national systems remains a formidable task. As Scaglion has noted, the 'great challenge in legal reform for Pacific peoples' lies in trying to reconcile the principle of the rule of law with the need to develop justice systems attuned to the particular circumstances of these countries (2004: 88). These systems have to 'meet both the demands of the modern state in a contemporary world and the needs of ordinary people increasingly affected by global processes' (ibid.). It is within this broader context of pluralism, transition and reform that we can consider the role – actual and potential – of restorative justice in the Melanesian context.

State-centered notions of order and security

The modern state has conventionally been attributed a central role in ensuring the maintenance of peace and order within its territorial borders. Indeed, the capacity to maintain domestic order and provide defense against external threats provides the basis of most classical definitions of the state. According to these, coercive powers are concentrated in the state in order to ensure order in the society at large. In Max Weber's well-known dictum, the state is said to exercise a monopoly over the legitimate use of violence (Weber 1972). Violence emanating from non-state sources that is not sanctioned by state authority is by definition illegitimate. To enable it to fulfill its role, the modern state has established an elaborate coercive and juridical apparatus dedicated to the task of maintaining peace, security and order. In addition to military forces for defense against external threats, the maintenance of domestic order is provided for through an elaborate law and justice system comprising, among other things, laws, police, courts, and prisons. This system is represented as separate from other domains of state activity, such as politics, and this differentiation is enshrined in the well-known constitutional doctrine of the separation of powers.

Criminal laws define and proscribe certain behavior and provide for the punishment of convicted offenders. While there may be subsidiary aims such as the rehabilitation of offenders, the principal rationale of state-sanctioned punishments is deterrence. Infractions of the criminal law are dealt with as offences against the state with the prosecution of alleged offenders being conducted in the name of the state. The victims are largely passive bystanders in this process. Laws are enacted, enforced, and interpreted by separate institutions, each staffed by personnel dedicated to particular aspects of the law and justice process. They are impersonal and universal in scope, applying, in theory at any rate, to every individual irrespective of his or her personal or official status. Criminal law has an obvious public quality. Suspected offenders are prosecuted by the state and, if found guilty, will be punished irrespective of whether any member of society claims to have been wronged or not. Given its concern with relationships between the state and individuals, criminal law is classified as a form of public law. Private law, on the other hand, concerns itself more with the regulation of relationships between individuals.

The Weberian depiction of states' exercising a monopoly over the legitimate use of violence is, of course, an ideal type and in practice there are many states that patently lack such a capacity. There has also been a powerful ideological critique of the centrality of the state as a vehicle of service delivery associated with broader international transformations including the liberalization of trade, mobility of capital, migration, and growth of supra-national bodies. Weber's idealized construct is best understood in the light of the distinctive historical processes of state formation that occurred among the proto-national states of Europe. These processes entailed a lengthy and often turbulent struggle to wrest power away from numerous relatively autonomous local and regional groups, and the gradual accumulation and concentration of this power in a unitary and centralized state for purposes of territorial domination (Cohen *et al.* 1981). In today's era of privatization and globalization, the monopoly over coercive powers of even the strongest states has been eroded as a result of rising levels of private sector involvement in areas previously dominated by the state. This is evident in, among other things, the massive growth of private policing and security, including the controversial expansion of private military services (Singer 2003).

While strong states have relinquished voluntarily or otherwise outsourced selected coercive powers, vulnerable states continue to struggle to assert their authority. Many of the latter never established control or domination of their designated territories in the first place. There are many reasons why some states are weaker than others. In some post-colonial environments, this weakness is often a consequence of the relatively short history of the state, its origins as a colonial imposition, and the manner of its poor articulation with indigenous non-state polities. While international thinking about states continues to be dominated by the particular histories and experiences of a relatively small number of European states, processes of state creation and consolidation throughout much of the post-colonial world have followed a radically different pattern (Herbst 2000). In the Melanesian countries, the institutions of the nation-state were superimposed on to a patchwork of small-scale local polities, each with its own conceptions of sovereignty and traditions of self-regulation (Strathern and Stewart 1997). These polities have not disappeared under the cumulative weight of external change. On the contrary, they have proven to be remarkably resilient and adaptable. The difficulties experienced by the Melanesian states in asserting their territorial domination today derive, in large part, from the continued dispersal of authority and power within the national society and the relative weakness of centralized authority. Primary identities and allegiances remain implanted in local languages and kin-based associations rather than in abstract concepts of nation and citizenship.

Order without state – 'traditional' Melanesian approaches to conflict and dispute resolution

Melanesian societies had ways of dealing with disputes and infractions of social norms long before their encounter with the modern world and the imposition of the first colonial states. Methods varied from society to society, as well as over time. There were no written laws in these oral cultures nor were there any discrete systems of justice comprising specialized institutions and personnel dedicated to the enforcement of rules and adjudication of disputes. Methods for managing disputes tended to be 'directly embedded in everyday life, unsupported by a differentiated legal system' (Roberts 1976: 667). Disputes were handled 'on a case-by-case basis, sometimes through consensus solutions based on notions of fairness or "equity", and sometimes by various forms of political maneuverings' (Scaglion 2004: 88).

Melanesian societies were typically small-scale, self-regulating, and relatively egalitarian. They were also stateless – that is, without the highly centralized political and administrative structures associated with modern states. Legitimacy tended to be dispersed widely, at least among all adult men. Political units were often led by 'big-men' (Strathern 1971) who acquired their prominence through individual prowess in areas such as warfare, trade, or the organization of ceremonial exchanges.[4] Women generally had a subordinate status. Disputes were understood and addressed within an elaborate complex of kinship, status and social relations. There was no concept of crime *per se*. Rather than being treated as impersonal 'citizen-units' vested with equal standing, as under modern law, the status, gender, kinship affiliations and social relationships of a person were critical to the determination of his or her rights and obligations in respect of others (Lawrence 1969). Given the importance of these social considerations and the case-by-case approach, there was little role for precedents. Disputes were resolved by settlement rather than adjudication, and in practice this was often the outcome of protracted negotiation, mediation, and compromise. Settlements between clan groups were rarely final and seemingly settled disputes might be revived at a later date (Strathern and Stewart 1997).

Given the high levels of social and economic inter-dependence in small-scale societies, the restoration of stable relationships ruptured by disputation was an important objective of resolution. Notions of reciprocity and equivalence were crucial to the redress of wrongs. Settlement of larger disputes might involve elaborate peace and reconciliation ceremonies with payment of compensation or exchange of gifts. Whereas restorative solutions were appropriate where parties to a dispute were bound together through kinship or other forms of continuing social or economic inter-dependency, retributive responses, including 'payback' killings, were more likely in the absence of such ties. Ostracism, exclusion from rituals and, occasionally, outright expulsion from the group provided other options. Raids and warfare were also common in many places and indicate the existence of asymmetrical encounters, alongside relationships determined by long-term conceptions of balance.

Colonial administration and justice

Colonial incursions by European powers in the late-nineteenth century constituted the first attempts to establish systems of centralized administration, or states, in the Melanesian territories. Initial encounters between these different ways of doing justice generated new sources of tension. They also gave rise to new synergies and the possibility for creative interplay between introduced and indigenous regulatory systems.

Colonization in Melanesia, as in many other places, involved the arbitrary partitioning of territories with little concession to existing social and political groupings and boundaries. While it inevitably had a profound effect on indigenous peoples and societies, its impacts were neither uniform nor wholly disintegrative. Lack of resources, the considerable challenges of local topography,

the relative modesty of colonial objectives, and the significant role of indigenous agency, ensured the survival and adaptation of many local institutions. Christian missions and commercial plantations often had a more profound impact on the daily lives of Pacific islanders than did colonial officials. In Fiji, where chiefly patterns of leadership existed alongside Melanesian 'big-man' models, attempts were made to co-opt indigenous power structures into the maintenance of colonial order. However, in the relatively egalitarian and decentralized societies found in other Melanesian territories, colonial authorities found it more difficult to identify suitable local structures to work through.

Colonial justice entailed the introduction of selected Western laws and specially adapted tribunals and processes for dealing with offences and disputes among 'natives.' Native courts dealt with alleged breaches of specially designated native regulations. These were presided over by European district officials who would draw on their own limited knowledge of local *kastom*, often as explained by an indigenous policeman. Colonial justice involved the subordination of many of the formal attributes of legal justice to the imperatives of native administration. Individual officers typically combined 'law jobs', serving simultaneously as magistrates, police and jailers. In the larger territories, such as Papua New Guinea, colonial authorities were more concerned with establishing a semblance of order and administrative control rather than building a sophisticated system of justice. This was colonial lite rather than monolithic domination. In Papua New Guinea, government by patrol often meant little more than a couple of visits a year for villages close to administrative centers, a single visit every one or two years for more distant villages, and even rarer visits in less accessible areas (Dinnen 2001: 16–24).

Colonial justice was different in its aims and organization to the modern justice

405

system that would eventually replace it, and had an extremely limited reach in practice. Indigenous institutions were only interfered with when it was considered absolutely necessary, as when they were perceived as a direct threat to colonial authority. Raiding and inter-group warfare were successfully suppressed. However, most communities continued to deal with disputes and conflicts according to local *kastom* as it adapted to externally induced change. While official thinking maintained the fiction that indigenous institutions were inadequate to the task, colonial authorities were, in fact, largely dependent on these very institutions for the successful maintenance of peace at local levels given the limited capacities of weak colonial states. In practice, informal interactions between isolated district officials and indigenous groups were often conducive to the resolution of disputes in a manner that satisfied local litigants. District officials were not bound by procedural formality or legal niceties and could draw on a range of agency powers extending well beyond their role as magistrates. The resolution of disputes in these circumstances contained a significant element of negotiation and could be linked to the provision or withdrawal of various government services, thereby allowing district officials to persuade and reward, as well as to punish. This allowed a more holistic, context-sensitive, and problem-solving approach than was possible under more formal justice practices.

Decolonization, modern criminal justice, and growing law and order problems

As the prospect of political independence loomed in the Melanesian territories, the old colonial systems were gradually dismantled in a process of institutional modernization aimed at establishing the institutional framework of the modern nation-state. This included modern criminal justice systems. The legal dualism underlying colonial approaches and the subordination of justice to administrative objectives were to be abandoned in favor of a unitary legal system with a clear division of labor between the principal agencies. Modern courts staffed by trained magistrates and judges were to take the place of native courts. Police forces created originally as instruments for extending colonial authority were to be transformed into impartial and professional law enforcement bodies.

The transition from colonial to modern justice system has been a difficult one. This is particularly so in Papua New Guinea, Solomon Islands, and Vanuatu, which share a much higher degree of social and political fragmentation than Fiji and had a shorter and more uneven experience of centralized administration. Vanuatu had the additional legacy of having been subject to two separate systems of colonial law under the administration of the British and French Condominium. In each case, local systems of self-regulation or *kastom* continued to exert a more direct influence on the daily lives of their predominantly rural inhabitants than did the realm of modern law and justice. There were obvious points of difference between the approaches adopted by local and modern justice systems (Lawrence 1969; Powles 1988). In the area of dispute resolution, these included:

- the individual-oriented focus of modern criminal justice and relative neglect of relationships and the social and historical context of disputes;
- emphasis in modern criminal justice on the punishment of individual offenders and neglect of victims and other aggrieved parties;
- the procedural formality and exclusionary character of criminal justice as opposed to the relatively informal and participatory character of local approaches to dispute resolution;

▓ the adversarial and 'winner takes all' character of criminal justice as opposed to the more negotiated and consensual dimension of local approaches.

The resurgence of tribal fighting in the Papua New Guinea Highlands shortly before independence was attributed by some to growing dissatisfaction with the approach to dispute resolution in modern justice. According to a committee established to investigate this phenomenon, formal courts were unable to process disputes quickly and were also encumbered by complex procedural requirements (Papua New Guinea 1973). There appeared to be little cooperation between the various law enforcement bodies. The committee argued that Western law with its focus on the interests of the individual was often inappropriate in Melanesian contexts and proposed that traditional local groups be recognized as legal entities.

Several of the independence constitutions acknowledged the legitimacy of both modern and traditional authority. Notions of *kastom* and 'tradition' were prominent in the rhetoric of decolonization, providing symbols of national identity and the break with the colonial past (Narakobi 1983). In Papua New Guinea, Solomon Islands, and Vanuatu, *kastom* was recognized as a source of law and was expected to play an important role in the development of the post-colonial legal order, although details of how exactly this was to be achieved remained elusive. The Papua New Guinea Constitution urged the courts to forge an 'indigenous jurisprudence' (S.21) and highlighted the continuing importance of villages and local communities 'as viable units of Papua New Guinea society' (S.5(4)). Early reports of the Papua New Guinea Law Reform Commission drew attention to the importance of restorative approaches to dispute resolution at community levels (Papua New Guinea 1977).

A number of courts and tribunals were designed specifically to handle local disputes and minor infractions and to be accessible and responsive to rural communities. Local Courts were established in Solomon Islands to deal with a range of local disputes including offences provided under legislation, local by-laws, and, in certain cases, *kastom*. These courts were also given unlimited jurisdiction in customary land matters subject to appeals to Customary Land Appeals Courts. Vanuatu's Island Courts consist of three or more justices knowledgeable in *kastom*, at least one of who should be a *kastom* chief residing in the court area (Bulu 1988). These courts are supposed to administer *kastom* prevailing in their area insofar as it is not in conflict with any written law or otherwise contrary to justice, morality, or good order. Papua New Guinea established a system of Village Courts shortly after independence with jurisdiction to settle minor disputes through the regulated application of local *kastom* (see p. 000).

Alongside courts and tribunals established by the state, numerous community-based mechanisms with no formal connection to the state play a significant role in dealing with local disputes. Some of these have a continuing existence, while others are more ephemeral and emerge in response to particular local problems. The gradual expansion of the formal justice system has not supplanted these community-based approaches. Indeed, in some places unofficial mechanisms and responses have increased as the inadequacies of state justice have become more pronounced, or as state presence has retreated in many areas. Local approaches provide an important source of continuity linking the post-colonial present to the colonial and pre-colonial pasts. Chiefs, elders, and other local structures, such as *komitis*,[5] continue to play a role in the settlement of disputes and maintenance of order in many rural and urban communities. Missions and church groups have also contributed to the mediation and settlement of disputes in many areas as well as in the management of young offenders.

The effectiveness of community-based processes of dispute resolution is to a large extent dependent on the degree of social cohesion at local levels. In practice, this varies considerably between different communities. Rapid social and economic change has had a seriously corrosive impact in many places, accentuating older divisions and generating new sources of tension. Conflict and crime have tended to follow larger patterns of developments. Large-scale extractive projects have contributed to local conflicts over the ownership and distribution of resources. This was illustrated dramatically on the island province of Bougainville, where landowner grievances over levels of compensation for mining development provided the catalyst for nine years of civil war (May and Spriggs 1990; Spriggs and Denoon 1992). In Papua New Guinea, robberies and violent crime have been concentrated along major highways and in urban and peri-urban areas where criminal opportunities are greatest. Migration to urban centers and regions with better development prospects, essential services, and infrastructure has contributed to growing ethnic tensions between local landowners and settlers. The recent conflict in Solomon Islands arose from growing tensions between the indigenous peoples of Guadalcanal and settlers from neighboring Malaita province (Fraenkel 2004). Declining levels of respect for village leaders and traditional authority are particularly evident among young people exposed to an urban-oriented education system and the hedonistic values of an ever-encroaching global culture. Increasing alcohol and drug abuse, and, in Papua New Guinea in particular, the availability of illegal firearms (Alpers 2004), have also contributed to the weakening of social cohesion in many rural and urban communities.

While traditional authority has been seriously eroded, the weak penetration of the state has meant that access to modern justice remains severely restricted for many citizens. Institutional resources, including police and courts, tend to be predominantly urban-based, while approximately 85 per cent of the populations of Papua New Guinea, Solomon Islands, and Vanuatu, continue to live in rural areas. From the vantage point of the ordinary villager, accessing the nearest police post, magistrate or, indeed, telephone,[6] might involve a lengthy and difficult journey by foot, truck, or canoe. In such cases, reliance on community-based approaches is often the only option for addressing outstanding grievances. The difficulties of local topography, limited coverage and poor quality of road networks, and prolonged government neglect of agencies like the police have compounded the problem of access to modern justice in these countries. Fragile criminal justice systems have also been progressively overwhelmed by the demands of rapidly growing populations and escalating law and order problems.

The limited reach and capacity of state justice has been most obvious in Papua New Guinea (PNG), by far the largest of the independent Melanesian countries. In 1975, the coverage provided by the national police was estimated to extend to only 10 per cent of Papua New Guinea's total land area and 40 per cent of the population (Dorney 1990: 296). An institution of just over 5,000 sworn officers has not grown significantly since independence despite the population having more than doubled to over 5 million people in the intervening years. The current police to population ratio in Papua New Guinea is estimated at 1:1,121, substantially less than the police/population ratio at independence, which was approximately 1:380 (Papua New Guinea 2002: 63). Police in PNG appear to be incapable of undertaking routine criminal investigations and apprehending suspects, prosecutions fail for lack of adequate evidence and preparation, lengthy delays in the processing of court cases have resulted in large numbers of detainees on remand awaiting their hearings, and mass escapes from the country's underresourced prison system occur regularly.

Reflecting their para-military origins, police continue to live in barracks and remain physically separated from the communities they are supposed to serve. A militaristic institutional culture contributes to an aggressive and confrontational style of policing and high levels of fear and distrust among ordinary citizens. The conclusion of a recent review commissioned by the Papua New Guinea government echoed a widely held view, namely that 'policing was close to total collapse' (Papua New Guinea 2004: 40) in many parts of the country. This alarming state of affairs was attributed to a lack of government support and direction; ineffective police leadership; inadequate and unreliable provision of resources to do the job; unpaid allowances and entitlements; barely adequate salaries; system-wide lack of discipline, accountability and self-respect; almost total absence of community trust and respect; and political interference in police operations (ibid.).

While the sheer size of Papua New Guinea has contributed to the scale of its law and order problems, many of the same underlying factors are evident in its smaller Melanesian neighbors. These include high population growth unmatched by economic growth, poor governance, corruption, deteriorating government services and essential infrastructure, pressures on customary land, internal migration, urbanization, and highly uneven patterns of development between different regions. The weakness of state controls, an evolving gun culture in some places, and the alarming spread of HIV/AIDS, have accentuated the growing problems of human security facing Melanesian peoples.

As the former colonial administrator with continuing strategic and trade interests in its former colony, Australia has provided substantial development assistance to Papua New Guinea, including assistance to the law and justice sector. Since 1975, Papua New Guinea has received A$540 million from Australia for the purposes of institutional

strengthening, capacity building, economic reform, and strengthening the rule of law (AusAID 2003: xii–xiii). In addition to significant support to the police, assistance has also been provided to the courts, prisons, the Ombudsman, and the public legal services to make their operations more transparent and accountable to the community. Australia's aid program is also aimed at improving public access to legal information and encouraging the effective operation of village courts.

Despite high levels of donor assistance, criminal justice systems in the Melanesian countries have continued to experience recurring crises and have manifestly failed to deter rising levels of crime and social disorder. Since mid-2003, there has been a significant change in Australia's engagement with the Pacific Islands region. In place of a formerly low-key approach to issues of internal security, Australia has adopted a distinctly more robust and interventionist approach. This increasingly involves the deployment – with the consent of the host government – of Australian personnel, including police officers and other law and justice specialists, to assist in restoring order and strengthening the rule of law in neighboring countries experiencing security problems.

The new approach was demonstrated most dramatically in Australia's agreement in mid-2003 to lead a regional intervention mission to help restore order in the troubled Solomon Islands. A police contingent of some 330 police, mainly from Australia but with participation from other Pacific Islands police forces, has successfully disarmed former militants and helped restore order. The mission has now moved into its post-stabilization phase. Longer-term objectives include assisting to rebuild the Solomon Islands police – that had effectively collapsed during the recent conflict – and strengthening the capacity of other law and justice agencies. The Australia and Papua New Guinea governments have also recently agreed to a five-year Enhanced

Cooperation Program (ECP) costing approximately A$800 million. The ECP comprises an expansive package of assistance measures including the deployment of approximately 220 Australian police officers, as well as up to eighteen Australian specialists working in various law and justice agencies.

The need for properly functioning state justice – including criminal justice – systems is not in contention and the external assistance has generally been welcomed in the countries concerned. Questions can nevertheless be raised about the narrow focus on the formal justice sector evident in the current flurry of external assistance. Less attention has been given to the issue of the appropriateness of existing institutions to the specific circumstances and requirements of the Melanesian countries. This issue, as we have seen, was at the forefront of nationalist thinking at the time of independence but has attracted little consideration by either domestic governments or international donors since. The fact is that the modern justice systems introduced during the twilight years of colonial administration have never worked particularly well in the diffuse and highly localized Melanesian environment. To what extent is the current weakness of criminal justice institutions in these countries a consequence of their failure to adapt to the particular circumstances found in these national settings? Are there ways in which they can actively build on, rather than simply ignore, the substantial restorative resources that exist at community levels throughout the region?

Restorative justice in modern Papua New Guinea

Extending the reach and effectiveness of Papua New Guinea's fragile criminal justice system is not just a matter of institutional strengthening at the center, important though that may be. The institutions and processes of formal justice need to be made more accessible and relevant to the everyday needs of the bulk of Papua New Guinea's citizens living in rural areas. This entails building appropriate linkages between formal and informal justice sectors in a way that promotes complementarity between them and that is ultimately consistent with respect for human rights and the rule of law. The challenge here is, in part, about making better use of existing community resources capable of enhancing the prevention and resolution of crime and conflict at local levels. It is also about reviewing and, where necessary, redesigning justice institutions so that they better meet the needs of the communities they are supposed to serve.

Papua New Guinea's National Law and Justice Policy – toward restorative justice

In mid–2000, Papua New Guinea's National Executive Council (Cabinet) endorsed a new National Law and Justice Policy. While in the past different agencies had their own corporate policies and plans, attempts to develop a unified policy for the whole sector had met with little success. The new policy – subtitled 'Toward restorative justice' – provides a broad vision for the future development of the sector. It was prepared by a small working group of senior law and justice officials. Previous reviews and reports were drawn upon and extensive consultations occurred with a range of local stakeholders from both government and non-government sectors. While the policy continues to advocate measures to strengthen the capacities of the various criminal justice agencies, as well as coordination between them, it places considerable emphasis on the need to mobilize community-based resources to assist in crime prevention, dispute resolution, and the rehabilitation of offenders. In proposing the adoption of restorative justice programs in relation to minor offences and juvenile offenders, the policy acknowledges the counter-productive consequences of over-reliance on retributive policing and custodial punishments. Significantly, it recognizes the congruence between modern restorative justice and longstanding indigenous practices for dealing with disputes at local levels:

> The concept of restorative justice is not new to Papua New Guinea. It embodies many of the values and practices familiar in our traditional societies. As such, it provides a framework for building a more responsive and socially appropriate system of justice and one that is capable of meeting the challenges that lie ahead.
>
> (Papua New Guinea 2000: 2)

As envisaged in the national policy, restorative justice in Papua New Guinea is essentially about connecting with communities and coordinating justice service delivery. The policy identifies the need to build the restorative capacity of both the formal justice system and that of community and other non-state organizations involved in crime prevention, dispute resolution, and rehabilitation of offenders. In particular, facilitating partnerships between state and non-state entities involved in 'justice work' is viewed as an important way of reducing the heavy demands on, and costs of, formal justice to manageable proportions. It is also seen as a way of contributing to broader community development objectives and, thereby, offer the prospect of a more holistic and sustainable approach to the prevention and management of crime and conflict. The Papua New Guinea policy characterizes restorative justice as:

- integrative of different justice forms and stakeholders;
- transformative of the intentions for justice, away from blame and towards problem solving;
- complementary of the operation of other justice forms such as deterrence,

while at the same time offering diversion and alternatives to the formal justice system;

- community based and inclusive of stakeholders interests, where the provision of restorative justice is situationally relevant and supportive of social bonding;
- directed to the goals of dispute resolution, order maintenance and peace making, while maintaining crime control, community safety, and rehabilitation of offenders;
- compatible with custom and sourced in constitutional legality;
- cooperative and reliant on partnerships;
- rationalizing formal resources to deal primarily with serious offenders; and
- coordinated across the formal justice sector and articulation between civil society and the professional justice agencies.

Tentative steps toward restorative justice in the formal justice system

While it remains early, some tentative first steps have been taken toward developing the restorative justice capacity of parts of the formal justice system. This has primarily involved attempts to develop a clearer role for Papua New Guinea's Community-Based Corrections (CBC) service and implementing juvenile justice reform.

CBC continues to face considerable challenges in practice but is a key agency for progressing the national policy's goal of reducing the prison population and developing community-based alternatives to imprisonment. Probation, the forerunner of CBC, was established in the late 1970s to provide assessment and reports to the courts and supervision of offenders serving community-based sentences such as probation or community work. A parole service was established under the 1991 Parole Act. The probation and parole services were later combined as Community-Based Corrections and now constitute a section within the Department of Justice and Attorney General. CBC has acquired a number of additional responsibilities over the past decade but has simultaneously been faced by a dramatic drop in staff levels and other available resources. Another significant problem has been that CBC has been viewed primarily as a vehicle for servicing the courts through the provision of additional sentencing options, rather than as a critical linking structure between the formal sector and community-based resources as envisaged in the policy. While it will take time and resources to address these outstanding issues, some CBC officers have already made significant progress in forging productive linkages and partnerships with community organizations, as well as in educating their more hidebound law and justice colleagues about the advantages of this approach.

After over a decade of inaction, steps have finally been taken to implement the Juvenile Courts Act 1991. The reforms are being phased in progressively, starting with the largest urban centers and a number of pilot exercises in selected provinces. A Juvenile Court Restorative Justice Program draws from existing restorative practices in Papua New Guinea including the work of Village Courts, Peace Foundation Melanesia and the Saraga Peace and Good Order Committees (see below), as well as from similar programs in New Zealand, Australia, and South Africa. Options for diverting juvenile offenders away from the formal criminal process will be available at various stages, including at the point of arrest, post-charging, and pre-hearing. Community-based mediation involving community panels will be developed as an alternative way of dealing with juveniles. Community panels will comprise a trained mediator, the offender, members of his/her family, the victim and a support person, community leaders, and representatives from the police and welfare department. Mediation facilities have already

been provided at the Juvenile Court in downtown Port Moresby. The goal of the mediation is to agree on a plan for dealing with the offending. Its purpose is to reintegrate the young person back into the community and redress the grievance of the victim. An advisory committee will be established to coordinate and develop the restorative justice program. While it is too early to assess this program, initial signs are positive and a high level of commitment has been demonstrated across the sector.

Village Courts

The most significant institutional innovation in Papua New Guinea's law and justice sector since independence has been the establishment of the Village Courts. These courts are hybrid institutions and provide an important link between formal and non-formal justice sectors. While their establishment and jurisdiction is provided by an Act of Parliament, they are empowered to settle disputes according to local *kastom*. Although not part of the National Judicial System (comprising the formal courts), they are connected to it through review and appeal provisions. These courts play a critical, if often under-valued, role in preventing conflict escalation and providing accessible and cost-effective dispute resolution. Without them, the workload of the more formal courts and the police would be considerably greater than at present.

Village Courts are also the most restorative-oriented court in Papua New Guinea. Their primary function is to 'ensure peace and harmony' and endeavour to obtain 'amicable settlement of disputes' and apply custom 'as determined in accordance with the Native Customs (Recognition) Act of 1963'. Under the enabling legislation, they should attempt to reach a settlement through mediation prior to exercising their formal jurisdiction. Magistrates can impose fines, issue community work orders, or order that compensation be paid to an aggrieved party. District Court magistrates are responsible for supervising Village Courts and ensuring that they stay within their jurisdictional powers.

While designed primarily for rural areas, Village Courts can now be found in most urban centers. They are presided over by local leaders appointed as magistrates after consultation with the community. Magistrates are assisted by Peace Officers and Court Clerks. Currently, there are approximately 1,082 Village Courts, with around 12,656 local officials, and they cover about 84 percent of the country. Over 603,000 disputes are heard by these courts every year, making them by far the busiest court in terms of caseload. Their restorative qualities are evident in the emphasis on preliminary mediation, the bringing together of victims and offenders, the focus on reparation, and the resolution of disputes within the community according to community norms and values.

Although their potential is enormous, there have also been a number of criticisms leveled at these courts. Most of these appear to relate more to failures on the part of the formal government sector rather than to any inherent design fault with Village Courts. For example, there have been significant delays in paying, and sometimes failure to pay, officials' allowances. This has resulted in some magistrates refusing to hear cases, while others have been asking parties to pay up-front fees before hearing their cases. The source of this problem lies in the ill-conceived transfer of responsibility for the administration of Village Courts from national to provincial governments that occurred in the mid-1990s. This transfer – enacted through the Organic Law on Provincial and Local Level Government of 1995 – was followed by a serious deterioration in the efficiency of Village Courts nationwide. In addition to problems with allowances, it contributed to lack of appropriate supervision and inspection, and lack of support from police and District Courts

if disputants refused to cooperate with court decisions.

Another complaint has been that Village Courts regularly exceed their jurisdictions under the Village Courts Act by, for example, processing serious cases that should only be heard by the formal courts, or by unlawfully imprisoning alleged wrongdoers. This, however, is also a reflection of inadequate training for magistrates and lack of supervision as required under the Village Courts Act.

A more substantive criticism of Village Courts, and one raised in relation to other forms of community or 'traditional' justice, is that they are susceptible to capture by local elites. As a result, they can become instruments for abusing the human rights of the most vulnerable groups, such as women and children. There have, for example, been reports of women accused of adultery being treated harshly by these courts, while their male partners go unpunished. Likewise, children have allegedly been locked up for minor offences. Some have claimed that magistrates and disputants use appeals to *kastom* and tradition to reinforce the subordinate status of women (Garap 2000). While this is a real problem in parts of the country, particularly the Highlands, where discrimination against women is endemic, evidence from other areas suggests that women are confident and reasonably successful disputants before these courts (Goddard 2004). These variations are, in part, a reflection of how well Village Courts have adapted to local circumstances, as intended originally.

The solution to these problems, however, is not simply to abandon Village Courts. That would be to ignore the enormous contribution they already make to the maintenance of peace and good order at local levels. In practice, it is lack of state support, notably resources and supervision, which has contributed to these difficulties. The remedy lies in strengthening the linkages between these courts and the formal

413

court system, principally through the provision of adequate levels of funding and training, as well as more effective processes of review and supervision. It should also be noted that the complaints of gender discrimination leveled at Village Courts and other community-based mechanisms are also raised regularly in relation to more formal justice agencies. Indeed, women often complain that they are discriminated against in both state and non-state justice processes.

Examples of community-driven restorative justice initiatives

There are many examples of community-drive restorative justice practices in Papua New Guinea and the other Melanesian countries. Some of these operate entirely independently of the state, reflecting either the absence of state in some rural areas or local dissatisfaction with the dispute resolution services offered by the formal justice sector. Others entail informal linkages with individual officials or agencies, such as the community police or a Community-Based Corrections officer. Some entail linkages between community groups and local business organizations. NGOs and church groups have also played important roles in the area of law awareness, violence reduction, peacemaking, and dispute resolution. These various initiatives constitute attempts to devise solutions to local problems and invariably draw on community-based cultural resources and knowledge. While some have succeeded, others manifest familiar problems associated with lack of capacity and inadequate regulation and support from the formal sector. Moreover, as many are taking place in rural areas, they are often invisible to the policy makers located in central government offices or provincial capitals. On a more positive note, they illustrate how the weakness of state can simultaneously be a catalyst for the growth of civil society, and despite their own manifest shortcomings they provide a rich

repertoire of restorative experience and innovation with much to offer the current reform process. Some examples from Papua New Guinea follow.

Criminal gang surrenders. An incipient restorative practice that is in many ways unique to Papua New Guinea is the phenomenon of criminal gang surrenders. Surrenders of self-proclaimed criminals have occurred regularly in different parts of Papua New Guinea in recent years (Dinnen 1995). Unusually, they are a potential resolution to crime proposed and executed by the criminals themselves. Community and church groups often act as brokers, engaging in protracted negotiations with leaders of the surrendering group and local law enforcement officials. The self-professed criminals attempt to negotiate their surrender and abandonment of crime. These are likely to include a plea for leniency in respect of any subsequent court proceedings, as well as requests for access to vocational training or legitimate income-generating opportunities. A formal surrender agreement is often drawn up and signed by gang members, community representatives, local government officials and, sometimes, the police. This is usually done at a public ceremony where the gang will formally surrender and hand over their weapons to authorities. Most surrenders involve less serious offenders who are looking for support to engage in a variety of small economic projects. Fear of police violence is often given as part of the explanation for surrenders. In practice, the level of support provided to surrendering gangs by community-based groups and government agencies varies widely and anecdotal evidence suggests that many individuals revert to crime when support is not forthcoming or sustained. Despite the obvious issues of moral hazard involved in these surrenders, they are potentially restorative and can, in theory, assist in breaking the reinforcing cycle of retributive violence that characterizes relations between police and criminal youth in Papua New Guinea. They also offer the prospect of sustainable solutions by linking abandonment of crime to economic and training opportunities.

Bougainville peace process. Community-driven restorative justice initiatives have also played a critical role in local peacemaking and reconciliation efforts on the island of Bougainville in the wake of the nine-year long conflict. While much of the initial violence occurred between armed secessionists and the Papua New Guinea security forces and their local allies, the conflict evolved into a series of sub-conflicts between and within Bougainvillean communities. The total collapse of state authority left the way open for the revival and, in some cases, creation of local structures and processes of governance in different parts of the island province. Operating on restorative justice principles, neo-traditional systems of chiefs have become a significant force in reconciliation activities between former enemies, as well as in the maintenance of peace and good order at local levels (Regan 2000).

Chiefs or elders have been brokers in the complex negotiations, including the payment of compensation, involved in attempts to reconcile divided communities. Compensation payments often comprise pigs, food, and traditional shell money. Reconciliation ceremonies are community affairs conducted with much ritual and symbolism, including 'the dividing up and sharing of food, the breaking of spears and arrows, the chewing of betelnut, exchanges of gifts, and singing, dancing, and feasting' (Boge and Garasu 2004: 572).

In addition to chiefs and elders, women's organizations and NGOs have also played a major role in peacemaking and reconciliation. There is a long history of women as peacemakers in Bougainville's predominantly matrilineal societies, as in some other parts of Melanesia (Saovana-Spriggs 2003; Rumsey

2000). Activities include organizing prayer meetings, reconciliation ceremonies, and petitions, as well as raising international awareness about the recent conflict (Garasu 2002).

The Peace Foundation Melanesia, a Port Moresby-based NGO, has been actively engaged in Bougainville since the mid-1990s, providing training in mediation, conflict resolution, and restorative justice skills to traditional leaders, women's groups, and others, (Howley 2002). Mediations have become the most common way of addressing a whole range of disputes and offences. For example, one traditional leader trained by the Foundation claims to have conducted over 300 mediations since 1997 covering a range of disputes, including many cases of homicide, which occurred during the conflict (Tombot 2003). According to that individual, restorative justice practices that accord closely with traditional methods are much more successful than formal adjudication in achieving sustainable resolutions.

The challenge of reconciling formal and informal justice systems is presented in a particularly stark manner in post-conflict Bougainville as the institutions of formal governance, including the criminal justice system, are re-introduced after an absence of more than a decade. There appears to be broad agreement among Bougainvilleans that there is a role for both modern and traditional approaches. The chiefly system is viewed by many as the appropriate mechanism for managing disputes and minor offences in the villages, while the police and courts should concentrate on the most serious offences and disputes including those arising in the more ethnically heterogenous urban context.[7]

The Report of the Bougainville Constitutional Commission – the product of extensive consultations and the first step in the drafting of the Constitution for the newly autonomous province of Bougainville – makes a strong case for building on the strengths of *kastom* approaches to dispute

415

resolution while rejecting 'an over-reliance upon aggressive policing and a penalty based justice system.'[8] The shortcomings of formal approaches to dispute resolution and advantages of *kastom* approaches are elaborated upon as follows:

> Often colonial administrators and later the Papua New Guinea policing and justice system failed to see that traditional problem resolution based upon kastom and the authority of traditional chiefs and other traditional leaders provided a more complete and suitable resolution of problems than western style justice ever could. Particularly, traditional reconciliation (often – but not always – involving compensation) provides effective means not only of resolving the particular problem involved in what modern society might regard as a criminal offence, but also of dealing with the problems in damaged relationships (between individuals and groups) that often result from crime. These problems are often left unresolved by a system that relies mainly on punishment of the 'offender'.[9]

Rather than simply returning to the policies and institutions for managing crime and disputes that existed prior to the conflict, the Report calls for an 'integrated approach' of meeting the particular needs of the Bougainville situation.[10]

As well as providing for the establishment a range of formal courts and the equivalent of a Village Court, the Draft Constitution provides that a Bougainville law

> shall utilize and encourage the utilization of –
>
> (a) customary dispute resolution and reconciliation practices; and
> (b) the role of traditional chiefs and other traditional chiefs and other traditional leaders in such dispute resolution and reconciliation practices.[11]

Kup Women for Peace. Another recent example of community-driven peacemaking is the work of the Kup Women for Peace in the Kup sub-district of Simbu Province in the Papua New Guinea Highlands. This volatile and relatively undeveloped sub-district comprises approximately 25,000 people divided into twelve distinct tribal groupings. People survive through a combination of subsistence agriculture and cash cropping. Coffee is the major cash crop, though average incomes tend to be low owing to a combination of poor road conditions, lack of market infrastructure, and law and order problems. Intermittent fighting has occurred between different tribal, clan, and sub-clan groups since the early 1970s and the area has acquired considerable notoriety for lawlessness. Fights have often been triggered by relatively minor disputes including adultery and drunken brawls but also by rapes, murders, and election-related disputes. Fighting has also increasingly involved the use of high-powered firearms and has resulted in many deaths and serious injuries, as well as extensive damage to property, gardens, and livestock. Government services are withdrawn when major fighting erupts and this has deprived many of basic services such as health and education. As elsewhere in the Highlands, women and children have suffered disproportionately from high levels of violence and insecurity

Kup Women for Peace (KWP) was established by a group of local activists in March 2000 with the aim of restoring peace and promoting sustainable livelihoods. They have received support from traditional leaders and others tired of living with constant violence, insecurity, and lack of development. Some leaders formed the Kup Restoration and Development Authority to help direct the rebuilding work and ensure a sustainable peace. While many problems remain, people are now able to travel beyond their own tribal boundaries without fear of attack. Communities have reconciled and are slowly beginning to regenerate. Displaced families are returning. Government officials have also started visiting the area again after many years of absence to prepare for the restoration of basic services. As peace has returned, Kup Women for Peace has shifted its focus to working with women on health issues, food production and marketing, education, and human rights. In August 2003, KWP organized the first of a planned series of surrender ceremonies where local criminals are to surrender themselves and their weapons before a large audience including representatives from the provincial government, police, and magistracy. There has been no major resurgence of fighting since KWP began their campaign (Garap 2004).

Saraga Peace Committees. Problems of violence and insecurity have also given rise to numerous informal responses in many of the sprawling multi-ethnic settlements to be found in Papua New Guinea's fast-growing towns. The work of the Saraga Peace and Good Order and Community Development Committees is a case in point. Saraga is a large settlement in Port Moresby with a population of approximately 18,000 people from around thirty-four different ethnic groups. Over the years it has acquired an unsavory reputation as a violent neighborhood and home to many criminals. Police have conducted periodic raids in search of criminals, prison escapees, and stolen property. Most residents are unemployed and survive precariously on the margins of the informal urban economy. Those in employment tend to work as security guards, domestic servants, and in other low-income occupations in Port Moresby. There is an absence of basic services such as water, power, health, sanitation, drainage, and education and the quality of house construction is extremely low. As well as tensions between different resident ethnic groups, there have also been tensions between many residents and the traditional owners of the land on which Saraga has developed.

The Peace and Good Order Committee was established in 2001 after the murder of a young girl by local criminals and subsequent conflict between different ethnic groups in the community. The initial aim was to provide a local mechanism for managing ethnic tensions in a non-violent way, but broader community development goals were subsequently added as a way of addressing some of the underlying issues contributing to social breakdown and violence.

Good working relations have been established between the Committee and a group of nearby companies with regular meetings. Assistance has been provided by the latter to support community sporting activities, as well as with some income-generating activities. The Committee has also established a good relationship with community police officers based at the nearest suburban police station.

Among the current objectives of the Peace and Good Order Committee are:

- efficiently managing land and tenancy agreements;
- responding rapidly to problems and reducing opportunities for crime and violence;
- improving access to basic services;
- improving relations with government agencies and civil society organizations;
- encouraging social development and income generating activities.

Peace Foundation Melanesia has been active in the community at various times and has provided training to local leaders in life skills, mediation and restorative justice techniques.

The Peace and Good Order Committee has representatives from the various ethnic groups in the community, and through the agency of a number of impressive and energetic community leaders has developed into an important vehicle of local governance. It has also established a number of sub-committees in the areas of sport, youth, women, community development, and justice.

417

In addition, each ethnic group has its own management committee and most have established sets of residential rules for their members. These rules address such matters as:

- anti-social behavior;
- disorderly conduct associated with alcohol or drug abuse;
- gambling and black market alcohol outlets;
- unhealthy and unsanitary living conditions;
- registration of cases for mediation;
- conduct of mediations;
- compulsory clean-up days.

While many problems remain, evidence suggests that the formerly prevalent sense of insecurity experienced by law-abiding residents of Saraga has diminished as a result of the activities of this initiative. The mediation work of the Peace and Good Order Committee has been recognized recently with its selection by the Port Moresby Family and Children's Court to take part in the national Juvenile Justice Pilot Project. Under this project, selected juvenile offenders will be diverted away from the formal criminal justice system and sent back to the community for mediation and supervision.

Conclusions

Improving the governance of security in the Melanesian countries presents a formidable challenge. There is no denying the fragility of the introduced justice systems, including criminal justice, and the need to improve their effectiveness and reach in the face of increasing problems of lawlessness and conflict. This task, as we have seen, is already the subject of considerable work being done by domestic governments and international donors.

It is equally clear that there needs to be much more emphasis on preventive strategies that address the hidden social and eco-nomic processes that give rise to crime and violence in the first place (Emmett and Butchart 2000). A potential strength of many of the restorative initiatives outlined above is the prospect they hold of more direct engagement with the underlying causes of conflict, including the structural conditions contributing to Papua New Guinea's escalating law and order problems, through, for example, providing pathways back to legitimate economic activities. A major source of the weakness of formal criminal justice lies in its inability to address broader issues of social justice. Indeed, many local critics view the operations of the formal justice system as reinforcing underlying injustices.

A major concern with the high levels of external assistance currently being deployed, particularly in Solomon Islands and Papua New Guinea, is the issue of long-term sustainability. What happens once these funds stop flowing and foreign personnel are withdrawn? Will improvements achieved be sustained? As we have seen, a significant, though by no means the sole, source of the Papua New Guinea police's problems has been a lack of adequate resources. With population growth outstripping economic growth in Papua New Guinea, Solomon Islands, and Vanuatu, there are real questions to be asked about whether these countries will ever be in a position to provide the support required to operate – let alone expand – these expensive and cumbersome justice systems without continuous external assistance. Given this situation, it is important to consider what other resources might be productively mobilized to assist in the task of building security and justice in these countries. This is where the existing wealth of community-based restorative justice resources needs to be recognized and engaged with.

It is important to move away from polarized conceptions of the realms of community and state justice. They are better viewed as different ends of the same continuum of justice practices. Restorative justice capacity needs to be built throughout this continuum. Enhancing restorative capacity in the state sector can increase its legitimacy in the Melanesian context, as well as being used to develop more enduring connections with community justice. Lack of state capacity is often viewed as a technical problem to be remedied by strategic inputs targeted exclusively at state institutions. The question of a state's relations to its wider society and the extent to which these might themselves be a source of its limited effectiveness is rarely raised. At the same time, it is clear that a large part of the fragility of state in Melanesia is as much a consequence of its limited legitimacy in an environment where authority remains widely dispersed at local levels, as it is a result of limited technical capacity.

It is also important to avoid romanticizing community justice in Melanesia, as elsewhere. For all those responses and initiatives to crime and conflict that appear to work, there are many others that do not. *Kastom* can be oppressive and discriminatory, just as it can be respectful and empowering. The risks are well known. Local initiatives are susceptible to capture by big-men and other local elites and can be used to perpetuate injustice against the weakest groups in the community. Traditional practices can also be corrupted, as in the case of the abuse of compensation during the recent crisis in Solomon Islands (Fraenkel 2004). Likewise, an offender might use appeals to *kastom* as a way of avoiding responsibility for his actions, as when a rapist claims that the matter has been settled through the payment of compensation. Of course, similar accusations of discrimination against women and other vulnerable groups, and charges of corruption, are leveled regularly against the police, courts, and prisons. Tackling unjust and illegal practices in the community justice sector requires engagement through training programs aimed at infusing knowledge and respect for human rights, and the establishment of accountability and regulation through appropriate links with the formal sector. Ultimately the object is to transform both state and community justice sectors, rendering the former more accessible, responsive, and accountable, while bringing the latter into a human rights and rule of law regulatory framework. The way forward is not a single reliance on either community or state justice but a creative reconfiguration of the governance of security that integrates the best of both.

References

Alpers, P. (2004) *Gunrunning in Papua New Guinea: from arrows to assault weapons*, special report prepared for AusAid and the Small Arms Survey, Geneva: Small Arms Survey.

Anderson, B. (1983) *Imagined Communities – reflections on the origin and spread of nationalism*, London and New York: Verso.

AusAID (Australian Agency for International Development) (2003) *The Contribution of Australian Aid to Papua New Guinea's Development 1975–2000. provisional conclusions from a rapid assessment*, Evaluation and Review Series No. 34, June, Canberra: AusAID.

Boge, V. and Garasu, L. (2004) 'Papua New Guinea: a success story of postconflict peacebuilding in Bougainville,' in A. Heijmans, N. Simmonds, and H. van de Veen (eds) *Searching for Peace in Asia Pacific – an overview of conflict prevention and peacebuilding activities*, Boulder, CO: Lynne Rienner Publishers.

Bulu, H. (1988) 'The judiciary and the court system in Vanuatu,' in G. Powles and M. Pulea (eds) *Pacific Courts and Legal Systems*, Suva: Institute of Pacific Studies, University of the South Pacific.

Cohen, Y., Brown, B. R. and Organski, A. F. K. (1981) 'The paradoxical nature of state making: the violent creation of order,' *American Political Science Review*, 75: 901–10.

Daly, K. (2003) 'Restorative justice: the real story,' in E. McLaughlin, R. Fergusson, G. Hughes and L. Westmarland (eds) *Restorative justice: critical issues*, London: Sage in association with The Open University.

Dinnen, S. (1995) 'Praise the Lord and pass the ammunition: criminal group surrenders in Papua New Guinea,' *Oceania*, 66(2): 103–18.

— (2001) *Law and Order in a Weak State: crime and politics in Papua New Guinea*, Honolulu: University of Hawai'i Press.

Dorney, S. (1990) *Papua New Guinea: people, politics and history since 1975*, Sydney: Random House.

Emmett, T. and Butchart, A. (eds) (2000) *Behind the Mask – getting to grips with crime and violence in South Africa*, Pretoria: Human Sciences Research Council (HRSC) Publishers.

Fraenkel, J. (2004) *The Manipulation of Custom: from uprising to intervention in the Solomon Islands*, Wellington: Victoria University Press.

Garap, S. (2000) 'Struggles of women and girls – Simbu Province, Papua New Guinea,' in S. Dinnen and A. Ley (eds) *Reflections on Violence in Melanesia*, Sydney: Hawkins Press and Asia Pacific Press.

— (2004) *Kup Women for Peace: women taking action to build peace and influence community decision-making*, State Society and Governance in Melanesia Discussion Paper 2004/4, 1–16, Canberra: Australian National University. Available at: http://rspas.anu.edu.au/melanesia

Garasu, L. (2002) 'The role of women in promoting peace and reconciliation,' in *Weaving Consensus: the Papua New Guinea–Bougainville peace process*, *Accord*, 12: 28–31.

Goddard, M. (2004) 'Women in Papua New Guinea's Village Courts,' State Society and Governance in Melanesia Discussion Paper 3/2004, 1–9, Canberra: Australian National University.

Herbst, J. (2000) *States and Power in Africa: comparative lessons in authority and control*, New Jersey: Princeton University Press.

Howley, P. (2002) *Breaking Spears and Mending Hearts*, Sydney: Zed Books and Federation Press.

Lawrence, P. (1969) 'The state versus stateless societies in Papua New Guinea,' in B. J. Brown (ed.) *Fashion of Law in New Guinea*, Sydney: Butterworths.

May, R. J. and Spriggs, M. (eds) (1990) *The Bougainville Crisis*, Bathurst: Crawford House Press.

Narakobi, B. M. (1983) *The Melanesian Way*, Suva: Institute of Pacific Studies, University of the South Pacific.

Papua New Guinea (1973) *Report of Committee Investigating Tribal Fighting in the Highlands*, Port Moresby: Government of Papua New Guinea.

— (1977) *The Role of Customary Law in the Legal System*, Law Reform Commission of PNG, Report No. 7, Port Moresby: Government of Papua New Guinea.

— (2000) *The National Law and Justice Policy and Plan of Action – Toward Restorative Justice 2000–2005*, Port Moresby: Department of National Planning and Monitoring, Government of Papua New Guinea.

— (2002) *A Review of the Law and Justice Sector Agencies in Papua New Guinea: opportunities to improve efficiency, effectiveness, coordination and accountability*, Report prepared by Public Sector Reform Management Unit, Department of Prime Minister and National Executive Council, Port Moresby: Government of Papua New Guinea, pp. 1–129.

— (2004) *Royal Papua New Guinea Constabulary*, Draft Report of Administrative Review Committee, September, Port Moresby: Government of Papua New Guinea, pp. 1–107.

Powles, G. (1988) 'Law, courts and legal services in Pacific societies,' in G. Powles and M. Pulea, *Pacific Courts and Legal Systems*, Suva: Institute of Pacific Studies, University of the South Pacific.

Regan, A. J. (2000) '"Traditional" leaders and conflict resolution in Bougainville: reforming the present by rewriting the past?' in S. Dinnen and A. Ley (eds) *Reflections on Violence in Melanesia*, Sydney: Hawkins Press and Asia Pacific Press.

Roberts, Simon (1976) 'Law and the study of social control in small-scale societies,' *Modern Law Review*, 39: 663–79.

Rumsey, Alan (2000) 'Women as peacemakers – a case from the Nebilyer Valley, Western Highlands, Papua New Guinea,' in S. Dinnen and A. Ley (eds) *Reflections on Violence in Melanesia*, Sydney: Hawkins Press and Asia Pacific Press.

Sahlins, Marshall (1963) 'Poor man, rich man, big-man, chief: political types in Melanesia and Polynesia,' *Comparative Studies in Society and History*, 5(3): 285–303.

Saovana-Spriggs, R. (2003) 'Bougainville women's role in conflict resolution in the Bougainville peace process,' in S. Dinnen, A. Jowitt and T. Newton Cain (eds) *A Kind of Mending: restorative justice in the Pacific Islands*, Canberra: Pandanus Books, pp. 195–213.

Scaglion, R. (2004) 'Legal pluralism in Pacific Island societies,' in V. S. Lockwood (ed.) *Globalization and Culture Change in the Pacific Islands*, New Jersey: Pearson Prentice Hall.

Singer, P. W. (2003) *Corporate Warriors: the rise of the privatized military industry*, Ithaca, NY, and London: Cornell University Press.

Spriggs, M. and Denoon, D. (eds) (1992) *The Bougainville Crisis: 1991 Update*, Canberra: Department of Political and Social Change,

Research School of Pacific and Asian Studies, Australian National University in association with Crawford House Press.

Strathern, A. J. (1971) *The Rope of Moka: big-men and ceremonial exchange in Mount Hagen, New Guinea*, Cambridge: Cambridge University Press.

Strathern, A. J. and Stewart, P. J. (1997) 'The problems of peace-makers in Papua New Guinea: modalities of negotiation and settlement,' *Cornell International Law Journal*, 30(3): 681–99.

Tombot, J. (2003) 'A marriage of custom and introduced skills: restorative justice, Bougainville style,' in S. Dinnen, A. Jowitt and T. Newton Cain (eds) *A Kind of Mending: restorative justice in the Pacific Islands*, Canberra: Pandanus Books.

Weber, M. (1972) 'Politics as a vocation,' in H. H. Gerth and C. W. Mills (eds) *Max Weber*, New York: Oxford University Press.

Notes

1. The term 'Melanesia' is used loosely here to denote the broad culture area extending from the Indonesian province of Papua (or Irian Jaya) in the west through to Fiji in the east.
2. Fiji is seen as the point where Melanesia and Polynesia meet and, as a result, is viewed as either Melanesia or Polynesia according to one's vantage point. Fiji became independent in 1970, Papua New Guinea in 1975, Solomon Islands in 1978, and Vanuatu in 1980.
3. While there is also diversity among indigenous Fijian societies, these are often obscured by the more obvious divisions between indigenous Fijians and Indo-Fijians – a legacy of Fiji's distinctive colonial experience under the British.
4. 'Big-man' status was more usually achieved than inherited. While the concept of 'big-man' has been increasingly questioned in recent writings, the Melanesian 'big-man' is often contrasted with the systems of hereditary leadership – chiefly systems – found in, for example, Polynesia (Sahlins 1963).
5. E.g. local committees.
6. In Papua New Guinea there is just one telephone subscriber for every hundred residents (*Post-Courier*, 17 March 2005).
7. The author visited Buka and Arawa in May 2004 and interviewed a range of community leaders and groups on issues of law and justice.
8. Report of the Bougainville Constitutional Commission. Arawa and Buka, Bougainville, July 2004, p. 182.
9. Ibid.
10. Ibid.
11. S.113 (2) of the Constitution of the Autonomous Region of Bougainville, Third Draft of 8 July 2004.

28

Rwanda's failing experiment in restorative justice

Lars Waldorf[1]

As for saying that you will not forgive him or that you will not do this or that, that is very bad. Whether you like it or not, the law is the law.

> (Rwandan prosecutor addressing a community; Penal Reform International 2002a: 23)

Where the violations are brutal, severe, and intimate, it can be a new assault to expect the victims to forgive ... Fundamentally, forgiveness must remain a choice by individuals; the power to forgive must be inextricable from the power to choose not to do so. It cannot be ordered or pressured.

> (Minow 2002: 18)

Introduction

Eight years after the 1994 genocide, the Rwandan government launched *gacaca* to speed justice and promote reconciliation.[2] As grassroots justice, *gacaca* is appropriately named for the 'lawn' where traditional dispute resolution took place. After almost three years as a pilot project, *gacaca* was expanded nationwide in early 2005: some 111,000 elected lay judges are now holding open-air genocide hearings in over 10,000 localities. In March 2005, the first *gacaca* trials commenced with *génocidaires* pleading guilty and receiving reduced sentences.

Several commentators have argued that restorative justice is better suited for post-genocide Rwanda than retributive justice, given the intermingling and interdependence of the majority Hutu and minority Tutsi, as well as the high levels of Hutu participation in the genocide. Generally, they have lauded *gacaca* for promoting a restorative justice model rooted in local, customary practices (Cobban 2002a, 2002b; Drumbl 2002; Harrell 2003; Power 2003; Uvin and Mironko 2003). In fact, *gacaca* has always been an uneasy mix of restorative and retributive justice: confessions *and* accusations, plea-bargains *and* trials, forgiveness *and* punishment, community service *and* incarceration. Early on, Penal Reform International warned that the implementation of *gacaca* was emphasizing legalistic retribution over socio-political reconciliation (Penal Reform International 2002a: 47–8). Since then, *gacaca* has become increasingly retributive, both in design and in practice.

Although *gacaca* has attracted a great deal of attention and commentary, there are relatively few empirical, local-level studies of whether *gacaca* is achieving its ambitious aims of justice, truth, and reconciliation.[3] While it is still too early to gauge *gacaca*'s success, the initial indications from those studies are not encouraging. Public confessions do not seem to lead to 'reintegrative shaming.' So far, confessions have been largely limited to the detainee population and have contained little in the way of either apology or shame. Over time, *gacaca* has become less participatory and more coercive. There is little prospect of Tutsi genocide survivors receiving reparations through *gacaca*. At the same time, the government has prohibited *gacaca* from providing accountability for war crimes committed by its forces against Hutu civilians. Finally, *gacaca* is likely to impose collective guilt on most Hutu.

Historical background

Ethnic violence in Rwanda is a modern, sporadic, and mostly state-initiated phenomenon: Hutu political elites whipped up violence against the Tutsi minority in the face of intra-Hutu and Tutsi political challenges in four distinct periods (1959–64, 1973, 1990–93, and the 1994 genocide). Despite the well-documented role of the state and political elites in the genocide (Des Forges 1999), some commentators persist in portraying the genocide as irrational mob violence. For example, Helena Cobban (2002a) describes it as 'the blood orgy of those terrifyingly irrational weeks.' Such rhetoric obscures the political rationality of genocide and mass atrocity.

In Rwanda, Hutu and Tutsi are complicated, socially constructed ethnic identities: both groups speak the same language, share the same culture, practice the same religion, live in integrated communities, and often intermarry. In pre-colonial times, Hutu and Tutsi were somewhat fluid ethnic and socio-economic categories. The German and Belgian colonialists, however, treated Hutu and Tutsi as fixed, racial identities and viewed the Tutsi as racially superior

'Hamites' from Ethiopia (Mamdani 2001). The Belgians imposed a system of ethnic identity cards and favored the Tutsi elite who had governed the pre-colonial kingdom. In 1959, Belgian colonialists switched allegiance from the Tutsi elite to the Hutu majority and condoned the ensuing anti-Tutsi violence. Tens of thousands of Tutsi fled the violence and became refugees in neighboring countries. Under the First Republic (1962–73), the Hutu government engaged in periodic pogroms against Tutsi, often in response to incursions from Tutsi guerrillas who sought to reinstate the Tutsi monarchy.

President Juvenal Habyarimana came to power in a 1973 military coup, promising to end the violence against Tutsi. Indeed, there was no anti-Tutsi violence from 1974 until October 1990, when the Rwandan Patriotic Front (RPF), a predominantly Anglophone Tutsi rebel movement from Uganda, attacked the country, setting off a civil war. In the early 1990s, President Habyarimana also came under donor pressure to allow multi-party democracy just as the Rwandan economy, built on coffee and tea exports, declined sharply as a result of falling commodity prices and structural adjustment. Facing demands for power sharing from the RPF and Hutu opposition parties, President Habyarimana and Hutu extremists sought to unify a Hutu population riven by regional and political differences under the banner of Hutu Power.

On 6 April 1994, as President Habyarimana returned from a regional peace summit in Tanzania, unknown assailants shot down his plane over Kigali, killing all on board. Within a few hours, Hutu extremists seized control of the Rwandan government and military and launched a planned extermination campaign against Tutsi. The extremists incited genocide by deploying racist stereotypes of Tutsi as 'Ethiopians' who wanted to re-impose a feudal monarchy and dispossess the Hutu majority. Using hate media, they also portrayed Tutsi civilians as a 'fifth column' of the RPF. By

423

the time the genocide ended in July 1994, with the RPF's military victory, an estimated 800,000 Tutsi, as well as thousands of Hutu, had been killed. The Rwandan genocide was marked by its speed, low-tech brutality, and large-scale participation.

The defeated genocidal government, army, and militias led a mass exodus of some two million Hutu into neighboring countries (principally Zaire and Tanzania), creating a refugee crisis of unprecedented proportions. Those forces subsequently used refugee camps on the Zaire–Rwanda border to stage attacks against the new RPF government, as well as genocide survivors. The Rwandan government invaded Zaire in 1996, dismantled the refugee camps, and repatriated most of the Hutu refugees back to Rwanda. Meanwhile, hundreds of thousands of Tutsi refugees, whose families had fled earlier ethnic violence, returned to the country after the genocide. Currently, Hutu make up approximately 85 per cent of Rwanda's 8.2 million people, while Tutsi comprise about 14 per cent – the same percentages that existed before the genocide.

The RPF's leadership is dominated by Anglophone Tutsi who grew up in exile in Uganda and returned to Rwanda following the genocide. With roots in Uganda's non-party system, the RPF is ideologically wedded to a de facto one-party state and democratic centralism, though under the guise of multi-party democratization. As the post-genocide government has achieved security, stability, and economic growth, and largely defeated the former genocidal forces inside the former Zaire, it has grown increasingly intolerant of political dissent, independent media, and civil society (Human Rights Watch 2000, 2003; Reyntjens 2004). Since 1994, the RPF has accused Hutu political opponents of being '*génocidaires*' or ethnic 'divisionists' and Tutsi opponents of being 'monarchists,' causing many to flee (International Crisis Group 2002). The RPF banned three opposition parties and co-opted the remaining ones. Not surprisingly,

then, President Paul Kagame won 95 per cent of the vote (the RPF 76 per cent) in the 2003 elections, which were marred by fraud and intimidation.

The RPF promotes a policy of 'national unity and reconciliation' through the media and *ingando* (re-education camps) which hearkens back to an imagined, Rwandan unity before colonizers introduced ethnicity (Pottier 2002; Penal Reform International 2004). Under that policy, discussions of ethnicity, including use of the terms 'Hutu' and 'Tutsi', have become politically taboo. Yet, it is difficult to erase perceptions of ethnic differences that were inevitably re-inscribed by the genocide, and nearly impossible to try genocide suspects without discussing ethnicity.

In part, the RPF's emphasis on 'national unity and reconciliation' reflects the legitimating needs of a minority government dominated by Anglophone Tutsi. Any criticism of the RPF is defined as an attack on 'national unity and reconciliation' and hence 'divisionist' or even genocidal. Thus, the government's declarations of reconciliation are undercut by its instrumentalization of the genocide to bolster its political legitimacy and to attack perceived opponents. For example, in mid-2004, the government accused a wide range of civil society and media organizations – including CARE International, the BBC, and VOA – of promoting a 'genocidal ideology' (Front Line 2005). The RPF also winds up re-essentializing and re-inscribing ethnic differences by denying victim status to Hutu civilians who suffered during the genocide and war and by portraying Hutu as collectively guilty for the genocide (Mamdani 2001; Eltringham 2004).

Gacaca

Re-inventing traditional gacaca

Following the genocide, the RPF rejected the idea of a South African-style truth commission, insisting that only retributive justice could end a culture of impunity. Soldiers, police, and officials arrested thousands of genocide suspects, often on the basis of vague denunciations. By 2001, approximately 120,000 genocide suspects were crammed into Rwanda's prisons and communal lock-ups under life-threatening conditions. From December 1996 to December 2003, Rwanda's courts managed to try about 9,700 people. The quality of justice has been poor due to political interference and a lack of resources (Des Forges and Longman 2004).

In an effort to speed up genocide trials and reduce the numbers of detainees, Rwandan officials turned for inspiration to *gacaca*, a traditional method of dispute resolution, where respected male elders (*inyangamugayo*, literally 'those who detest disgrace') adjudicated disputes over property, inheritance, personal injury, and marital relations. Traditional *gacaca* did not treat cattle theft, murder, or other serious crimes. *Inyangamugayo* could impose a range of sanctions to achieve restitution and compensation. Punishment was not individualized; rather, family and clan members were also obligated to repay any assessed judgment. The losing party typically had to provide beer to the community as a form of reconciliation (Karekezi 2001). By the late 1980s, *gacaca* had been transformed into a 'semi-official and "neo-traditional"' institution used by local authorities to resolve minor conflicts outside the official judicial system (Reyntjens 1990: 39). In a study of one local *gacaca*, Reyntjens concluded that it was 'quick justice, a good bargain (for the public authorities as well as for those being judged), extremely accessible, understood and accepted by all, and involving a large popular participation' (1990: 41).

In the aftermath of the 1994 genocide, several Rwandan scholars rejected the idea of using *gacaca* to try genocide cases because it had never even been used to judge homicide cases (UNHCHR 1996). Instead, they proposed that *gacaca* function as local truth commissions. The government did not adopt that suggestion. Beginning in 1998, prison officials encouraged detainees to start *gacaca* to hear confessions from their fellow inmates (Karekezi 2001).[4] The government decided to modernize *gacaca* for use with genocide cases in 1999 and passed a law establishing *gacaca* courts in 2001. The law has been subsequently amended, most recently in June 2004.

There is little tradition left in the modernized *gacaca* courts. Traditional justice systems are typically characterized by accessibility, informality, economy, public participation, restitution, reconciliation, and social pressure. By contrast, the new *gacaca* system is a formal institution, intimately linked to the state apparatus of prosecutions and incarceration, and applying codified, rather than customary, law. *Gacaca* courts are judging genocide, 'the crime of crimes,' and meting out prison sentences. Finally, *gacaca* court judges are elected (often after being nominated by local officials). In a wide-ranging study of 'traditional' justice systems, Stevens (1998: 44) concluded that attempts to marry the benefits of formal and informal justice systems have generally failed:

> Linking the two systems tends to undermine the positive attributes of the informal system. The process becomes no longer voluntary and is backed up by state coercion. As a result, the court need no longer rely on social sanctions, and public participation loses its primary importance ... Procedural requirements invariably become greater and public participation is curtailed.

As detailed below, *gacaca* has become increasingly coerced by the state as public participation has dropped.

Modernized gacaca *courts*[5]

While the national courts retain jurisdiction over the most serious cases (involving

425

planners, leaders, notorious killers, and rapists), *gacaca* courts will try lower-level perpetrators, as well as property offenses committed during the genocide. Murder, manslaughter, and assault cases are tried by the 1,545 sector-level *gacaca* courts and appeals from those cases will be heard by separate sector-level *gacaca* appeals courts.[6] The 9,201 cell-level *gacaca* courts are responsible for pre-trial fact-finding and for trying property offenses (except where the parties have reached an amicable settlement). Each *gacaca* bench consists of nine elected judges (with seven constituting a quorum). Procedurally, *gacaca* begins with a lengthy pre-trial phase at the cell level, where judges compile a local history of the genocide and establish several lists: (1) people who lived in the cell just before the genocide; (2) people killed in the cell during the genocide; (3) cell residents killed outside the cell during the genocide; (4) the victims (i.e. those eligible to be compensated for property damage or bodily injury); and (5) the accused. The pre-trial phase ends when the judges 'categorize' the accused, placing them in the criminal category that corresponds to evidence of their worst crimes. The files of the accused are then sent to the appropriate jurisdictions for trial (*Gacaca* Law 2004).

Both the 1996 genocide law and *gacaca* law adopted the common law practice of plea-bargaining but the *gacaca* law introduced community service. For example, defendants who confess to killings before their names appear on the list of perpetrators compiled by the cell-level *gacaca* court will receive sentences ranging from seven to twelve years, while those who confess after their names are on the list will get twelve to fifteen-year sentences. Regardless of the timing of their confessions, killers who confess will serve half their sentences doing community service. By contrast, defendants who refuse to confess and are found guilty of killing will be sentenced to prison for twenty-five to thirty years. In addition, all

killers, confessed or not, will be permanently deprived of the right to vote (*Gacaca* Law 2004).

Persons who plead guilty are eligible to serve half their sentences outside prison doing non-remunerated labor three days a week in public or private enterprises. In other countries, by contrast, community service is generally reserved for those who committed minor offenses. Community service has several advantages for Rwanda: it reduces the prison population, reintegrates convicted *génocidaires* back into their communities, provides a method for indigent *génocidaires* to make reparations to society, and contributes to national development. However, community service is not without drawbacks. A massive and expensive bureaucracy will be needed to manage the program. If not carefully monitored, community service could wind up benefiting political and economic elites more than the local communities.

The debate over restorative justice for Rwanda

As *gacaca* began in mid-2002, a public debate arose between Helena Cobban, a proponent of restorative justice, and Alison Des Forges and Kenneth Roth, senior advisor and executive director of Human Rights Watch, over the applicability of restorative justice to post-genocide Rwanda. Cobban (2002a) charged that the Western model of retributive justice 'simplistically divides humankind into victims and perpetrators.' Yet, she then made the same mistake by depicting 'the great mass of Hutu people' ('probably millions') as collectively responsible for the genocide. In so doing, she unwittingly underscored how 'reconciliation discourse relies on unproblematized identities of victims and perpetrators and on received and unchallenged constructions of "race" and identity' (Grunebaum 2002: 307). In the context of the Rwandan genocide, it is too simplistic to label Hutu as perpetrators and Tutsi as victims. There are numerous accounts of Hutu who saved Tutsi and of Hutu victimized by the *génocidaires*. Some Hutu took advantage of the genocide, and the political and economic opportunities it created, to settle local, private, intra-Hutu conflicts that often bore little relation to the genocide itself (Umutesi 2004). Sometimes Tutsi survivors participated in revenge killings against suspected Hutu perpetrators.

Equally problematic, Cobban lumped all 'grassroots participants' together as perpetrators, including those who 'simply moved into the homes of dead Tutsis or stole their cows or other belongings.' By failing to make moral distinctions among participants (i.e. those who killed willingly, those who killed under duress, those who looted, etc.), she put the probable number of perpetrators in the millions. However, based on empirical research in Rwanda, Straus (2004) estimated that approximately 200,000 perpetrators were responsible for most of the killing – an enormous number, to be sure, but not one that justifies collective blame.

Cobban (2002a) also argued that irrational, mass participation in the genocide makes individual accountability impossible:

> How can anyone start to assign a specific amount of responsibility to each one of the hundreds of thousands – probably millions – of people who took part ... Moreover, how does one identify the role of rationality and intention in the behavior of most of the grassroots participants in the blood orgy of those terrifyingly irrational weeks?

Taking this a step further, Drumbl (2002: 11) actually advocated collective responsibility: 'But are there not times and places where collective wrongdoing needs to be exposed and not hidden by the criminal trial's preference for individual fault?' However, collective responsibility corrodes the possibilities for peaceful coexistence. As Minow reminds us, 'The emphasis on individual responsibility offers an avenue away from the cycles of blame that lead to revenge, recrimination, and ethnic and national comments' (2002: 40). Andre Sibomana (1999: 113), a priest and human rights activist, denounced the idea of releasing genocide suspects without individualized determinations of guilt and innocence:

> The guilty would not have paid their dues. The innocent would not have been washed of their shame. The Hutu as a whole would have to bear responsibility for crimes committed by a minority [of them]. And those who ensured that innocent people were imprisoned would not be made to answer for their lies. It would all be too easy.

Cobban's diagnosis of the genocide as a 'social psychosis' led her to prescribe swift retribution ('decapitation') for the genocidal leadership and a mix of amnesties and community healing for everyone else. In a spirited response, Roth and Des Forges (2002) criticized Cobban for privileging therapy over justice at the expense of individual accountability, deterrence, and genocide victims. Cobban (2002b) subsequently countered:

> By dismissing restorative-justice approaches as mere 'therapy,' Roth and Des Forges obscure the demanding requirements that many such systems – including Rwanda's *gacaca* courts – place on suspected perpetrators of violent acts: that they make a full confession of their deeds, express apologies directly to victims and their kin, and undertake some concrete form of reparation. Taken together, such requirements can constitute a demanding form of personal accountability, far deeper, perhaps, than that required by conventional criminal proceedings.

Preliminary research from Rwanda, however, undermines Cobban's claim: *génocidaires* are not demonstrating personal accountability or making reparations to their victims in *gacaca* proceedings.[7]

Gacaca in practice

Accusations, confessions, and 'reintegrative shaming'

Gacaca gives survivors an official forum to tell their stories, relate their suffering, and level accusations. Yet, eyewitness testimony is notoriously unreliable, all the more so eleven years after a highly traumatizing event. In addition, most survivors were hiding or fleeing, and thus they are usually not the best witnesses to the crimes committed in their communities. Survivors, no less than perpetrators, have incentives to lie by making either false accusations or false exculpations. As Alice Karekezi, a prominent Rwandan academic, stated: 'There are survivors who visibly lie and other survivors say so ... Family members denounce their own kith and kin over land – the demographic pressures come into play.'[8]

Gacaca's success largely depends on confessions, rather than accusations: guilty pleas will speed up the proceedings, enable other perpetrators to be identified, persuade other perpetrators to confess, and hopefully repair relations between perpetrators and victims' families (Penal Reform International 2003a). Under the 2004 *gacaca* law, *génocidaires* who plead guilty must now make public apologies and reveal the whereabouts of their victims' remains.

At first glance, *gacaca*'s confessions and apologies appear to be the type of community-based 'reintegrative shaming' that could reconcile survivors with perpetrators (Drumbl 2002). However, as Minow points out, the concept of reintegrative shaming assumes 'a sufficiently coherent and engaged community' capable of reintegrating wrongdoers – exactly what is so often missing after mass violence (2002: 75, n. 53). Rwanda's local communities have changed dramatically since April 1994 as a result of the genocide, civil war, massive population displacements, and administrative reorganization of the country. Tutsi survivors are a small minority in most local communities. Not surprisingly, Hutu and Tutsi have differing perceptions of *gacaca*. Hutu generally view it as a way to release family members wrongly imprisoned, while Tutsi survivors often see it as a disguised amnesty for those who killed their family members (Penal Reform International 2002a; Longman and Rutagengwa 2004). Thus, perpetrators are unlikely to encounter much reintegrative shaming from their predominantly Hutu communities.

Although *gacaca* will result in a large number of confessions, the truthfulness and sincerity of those confessions is open to question. Surveying confessions in a range of countries undergoing transitional justice, Payne found 'perpetrators rarely make remorseful confessions. Even when they do, their expression of remorse is often undermined by the language of justification, excuse, and victimhood' (2004: 116). During *gacaca*, most confessions of serious crimes have come from prisoners, not the local population (Karekezi *et al.* 2004). Detainees have an obvious interest in minimizing their crimes and diminishing their responsibility so they can receive lighter sentences. In their confessions, killers often evaded taking personal responsibility and failed to explain how they became killers (Penal Reform International 2002b, 2003b). As Klaas de Jonge, an anthropologist who has been monitoring *gacaca* for several years with Penal Reform International, told this author: 'The accused think because they ask for forgiveness, they are entitled to forgiveness. You hear these people confessing as if they are describing a movie. There's absolutely no compassion.' Even full confessions may not necessarily lead to healing. A Rwandan psychologist noted, 'Confessions and seeking forgiveness do not remove fears and anger – they can even increase them.'[9] As the experience of the South African

Truth and Reconciliation Commission showed, public narratives from perpetrators and victims are just as likely to renew anger and conflict as to lead to catharsis and healing (Kiss 2000).

While restorative justice is commonly viewed as victim-centered, its emphasis on forgiveness runs the risk of demanding more from victims than from perpetrators (Grunebaum 2002). After all, apologizing is easier than forgiving, especially when the former brings a lighter sentence. To the extent that confessions and apologies are perceived as formulaic, insincere, untruthful or callous, they only serve to reinforce the bitterness of survivors, particularly when coupled with the public expectation that survivors should offer forgiveness (Penal Reform International 2002b, 2003b).

In pre-trial *gacaca* sessions, Tutsi survivors have done most of the talking, while their Hutu neighbors remained silent or defended the accused – a dynamic that only reinforced mistrust between the two groups (Penal Reform International 2002b, 2003a, 2003b; Karekezi *et al*. 2004; Molenaar 2004). In several communities, pre-trial *gacaca* proceedings have caused a worsening of inter-ethnic social relations (Penal Reform International 2003b; Molenaar 2004). This author also observed survivors sitting apart from their Hutu neighbors during some *gacaca* sessions. Survivors and perpetrators often fear retaliation, one from the other. A few survivors have been killed, and others have been intimidated to prevent them from testifying in *gacaca* (PAPG 2004; Penal Reform International 2004).

Gacaca's weaknesses

From a restorative justice perspective, *gacaca* has four major weaknesses: (1) it is not truly participatory; (2) it provides no compensation to victims; (3) it is 'victor's justice;' and (4) it risks imposing collective blame on Hutu. In addition, *gacaca*'s community service component, a crucial restorative jus-

tice element, remains stalled in the development phase.

Participation. *Gacaca* was initially hailed as participatory justice despite the fact that it was imposed on local communities in a top-down fashion by a highly centralized and authoritarian regime. Although early public opinion surveys indicated a high level of popular support for *gacaca* (Liprodhor 2000; Ballabola 2001; Gasibirege 2002; NURC 2003; Longman *et al.* 2004), it quickly became clear during the pilot phase that many Rwandans did not want to participate. Cell-level *gacaca*s often had to be cancelled for failing to meet the quorum of participants (one hundred adults) or even the quorum of judges (who receive no compensation for their work) (PAPG 2003; Penal Reform International 2003b; Karekezi *et al.* 2004; Molenaar 2004). There were several reasons for such poor attendance by the population. Ninety per cent of Rwandans are subsistence farmers who must spend most of their days working their fields or doing itinerant labor to survive (Liprodhor 2002). In some communities, people already devote one day a week to mandatory community labor (*umuganda*) and they do not want to sacrifice another day for *gacaca*. More crucially, Hutu have little incentive to participate in *gacaca* because they fear being accused as either perpetrators or bystanders and because they have no opportunity to discuss crimes committed by the RPF forces. In a study of pre-trial *gacaca* proceedings in one sector, Karekezi *et al.* concluded, 'the lack of popular participation that is due in part to a divided social climate may limit the ability of the *gacaca* process to rebuild social ties' (2004: 82).

During the pilot phase, local officials sometimes coerced attendance. They ordered the local paramilitary forces to close down shops, round up people for *gacaca*, and prevent people from leaving *gacaca* sessions. They also fined, or threatened to fine, people who were absent (Penal Reform International 2003b). The 2004 *gacaca* law reinforced the coercive element by making participation mandatory. Proclaiming that '[e]very Rwandan citizen has the duty to participate in the *Gacaca* courts [sic] activities,' the law imposes prison sentences (from three months to one year) on any witness who remains silent or refuses to testify (*Gacaca* Law 2004: 39). As a high-level *gacaca* official stated, a person who does not participate in *gacaca* risks being 'mistaken for a *génocidaire*.'[10] While initial reports suggest that public turnout is higher for *gacaca* where actual trials have begun, it is difficult to know whether that is due to greater interest or increased coercion.

Victim compensation. Restorative justice is impossible without reparations for survivors of mass atrocities. Eleven years after the genocide, the Rwandan government still has not created the long-promised compensation fund for survivors. That underscores the political marginalization of the Francophone Tutsi survivors, who have an uneasy relationship with the Anglophone, Ugandan-born Tutsi who lead the RPF. Until they were largely silenced in 2000, Tutsi survivors voiced disagreement with the RPF over several issues. First, they opposed the reintegration of suspected *génocidaires* into the government and military. In 1999, IBUKA ('Remember'), the collective of genocide survivor associations, opposed the RPF's appointment of a parliamentarian accused of having participated in the genocide. The RPF accused IBUKA of slander and arrested survivors who had made those accusations. Second, several survivor associations objected to the government's policy of publicly displaying skulls, bones, and corpses at genocide memorial sites, in violation of Rwandan religious and cultural traditions. Third, survivors' organizations publicly disagreed with the government over how to commemorate the genocide (Vidal 2001; Rombouts 2004).

In 2000, the RPF accused prominent Tutsi politicians of corruption or plotting the return of the Tutsi king from exile. Some fled, others were arrested, and one was assassinated under mysterious circumstances. That same year, the RPF installed one of its central committee members as the new president of IBUKA (Human Rights Watch 2000). Since then, IBUKA has been largely supportive of government policies. During the 2003 parliamentary election campaigns, the RPF (with backing from IBUKA) accused the Liberal Party of promoting ethnic 'divisionism' for advocating on behalf of Tutsi genocide survivors.

In 1998, the government established an assistance fund for the most needy survivors called the FARG (Fonds d'Assistance aux Rescapes du Genocide). Currently, the government gives 5 per cent of tax revenues (approximately US $3.5 million) each year to the fund, with 60 per cent of the FARG allocated to education and health care. The fund is not, properly speaking, a compensation fund, and it has been criticized for corruption. In mid-2002, IBUKA proposed draft legislation that would have replaced the FARG with a compensation fund and increased the government contribution to 8 per cent of tax revenues. The new compensation bill was highly problematic and has made no headway. First, the IBUKA leadership did not consult its member organizations or other survivors' organizations before offering the legislation. Second, the bill was fiscally unrealistic: it broadened the categories of potential beneficiaries and would have awarded each beneficiary approximately $23,000 (Rombouts 2004).

In the past two years, top government officials have stated that Rwanda cannot afford a compensation fund for survivors. Yet, government officials have shown no interest in expanding the FARG's in-kind benefits (education, health care, and housing) to all survivors. That leaves *gacaca*'s community service component as the only remaining mechanism for compensating survivors. Survivors strongly desire reparations (Longman and Rutagengwa 2004), and some widows would welcome free labor from released *génocidaires* (Aghion 2004). Yet, such a policy could exacerbate ethnic tensions because it could be seen as a return to the colonial-era forced labor system where Hutu clients worked for Tutsi patrons (Newbury 1988).

Victor's justice and RPF war crimes. Gacaca cannot produce restorative justice as long as it proceeds as victor's justice. The 2004 amendments expressly prohibited *gacaca* courts from trying war crimes and crimes against humanity committed by the RPF's predominantly Tutsi soldiers against Hutu civilians in the period 1990 to 1994. The RPF engaged in widespread and systematic killings of an estimated 25,000 to 45,000 Hutu civilians during and immediately after the genocide (Des Forges 1999: 728). Rwanda's military courts have tried only a few RPF soldiers, and most received light sentences (FIDH 2002). The RPF also has successfully blocked the United Nations International Criminal Tribunal for Rwanda (ICTR) from investigating RPF crimes. In July 2002, the Prosecutor informed the Security Council that the Rwandan government had prevented Rwandan witnesses from traveling to the Tribunal as a way of pressuring her to halt investigations of RPF war crimes. As of January 2005, the deadline for the completion of investigations, the ICTR had not indicted any RPF soldiers.

Obviously, the RPF's war crimes cannot be equated to the genocide, either in scope or intent. But if the Rwandan government is serious about ending impunity and achieving long-term peaceful coexistence in Rwanda, it should provide some accountability for RPF killings. Other transitional justice mechanisms have shown that it is possible to chart a middle course between victor's justice and revisionism. For example, the South African Truth and Reconciliation Commission heard testimony about crimes committed by the African National Congress without relativizing the crimes committed by the apartheid regime. Also, the International Criminal Tribunal for the Former Yugoslavia has prosecuted high-ranking Bosnian Muslim generals, without diminishing the responsibility of the Serbs for much of the ethnic cleansing that occurred in the former Yugoslavia.

Hutu are more likely to desire accountability for crimes committed by the RPF (Longman *et al.* 2004). In several pre-trial *gacaca* proceedings, people have raised RPF war crimes, only to be told not to confuse those with genocide and to take their allegations to the local political authorities or military courts. *Gacaca*'s one-sided focus does little to encourage Hutu participation.

Imposing collective guilt. The real danger of *gacaca* is that it will wind up ascribing collective guilt to most Hutu. The inclusion of property offenses in the genocide and *gacaca* laws is legally dubious, trivializes genocide, and risks criminalizing many Hutu who engaged in opportunistic looting. Given large-scale participation in roadblocks and patrols during the genocide, a broad interpretation of accomplice liability could lead to mass inculpation. An accomplice – defined as someone who, 'by any means, provided assistance to commit offences' (*Gacaca* Law 2004) – can be placed in the same category as the actual perpetrators. Thus, it is unclear whether a person who was at a roadblock where Tutsi were killed will be considered an accomplice to intentional homicide, even if he was there under duress and did not participate in the killings.

Although *gacaca* was designed to speed genocide trials and reduce the detainee population (approximately 55,000 in September 2005), it is likely to have just the opposite effect: government officials estimate that new confessions and accusations may result in up to a million new suspects.

That would overwhelm an already taxed judicial and prison system and undermine ongoing efforts at peaceful coexistence.

Conclusion

The preliminary empirical data collected during *gacaca*'s pilot phase suggests that its restorative justice goals are unlikely to be met. In part, this reflects the enormous difficulty of achieving truth-telling, reintegrative shaming, and reconciliation in any society recovering from mass atrocity. However, it also reflects the deliberate choices of an authoritarian government whose commitment to justice and reconciliation for all Rwandans remains half-hearted at best.

References

Aghion, A. (2004) *In Rwanda We Say . . . the Family that Doesn't Speak Dies*, documentary film, New York and Paris: Gacaca Productions/Dominant 7.

Ballabola, S. (2001) 'Perceptions about the *gacaca* law in Rwanda: evidence from a multi-method study,' *Cahiers du Centre de Gestion des Conflits*, 3: 97–120.

Cobban, H. (2002a) 'The legacies of collective violence: the Rwandan genocide and the limits of the law,' *Boston Review*, 27(2), online. Available at: http://www.bostonreview.net/BR27.2/cobban.html

— (2002b) 'Helena Cobban Replies,' *Boston Review*, 27(3–4), online. Available at: http://www.bostonreview.net/BR27.3/cobbanreplies.html

Des Forges, A. (1999) *Leave None to Tell the Story: genocide in Rwanda*, New York: Human Rights.

Des Forges, A. and Longman, T. (2004) 'Legal responses to genocide in Rwanda,' in E. Stover and H. Weinstein (eds) *My Neighbor, My Enemy: justice and community in the aftermath of mass atrocity*, New York: Cambridge University Press.

Drumbl, M. (2002) 'Restorative justice and collective responsibility: lessons for and from the Rwandan genocide,' *Contemporary Justice Reviews*, 5(1), 5–22.

Eltringham, N. (2004) *Accounting for Horror: postgenocide debates in Rwanda*, Sterling, VA: Pluto Press.

FIDH (Federation internationale des ligues des droits de l'homme) (2002) *Entre illusions et desillusions: les victimes devant le Tribunal Penal International pour le Rwanda*, Paris: FIDH.

Front Line (2005) *Front Line Rwanda: disappearances, arrests, threats, intimidation and co-option of human rights defenders, 2001–4*, Dublin: Front Line.

Gacaca Law (2004) Organic Law No. 16/2004 of 19/6/2004, *Journal Officiel*, 19 June 2004.

Gasibirege, S. (2002) 'Resultats definitifs de l'enquete quantitative sur les attitudes des Rwandais vis-à-vis des jurisdictions *Gacaca*,' *Cahiers du Centre de Gestion des Conflits*, 6: 38–92.

Grunebaum, H. (2002) 'Talking to ourselves "among the innocent dead": on reconciliation, forgiveness, and mourning,' *PMLA*, 117(2): 306–10.

Harrell, P. (2003) *Rwanda's Gamble: gacaca and a new model of transitional justice*, Lincoln, NE: Writer's Club Press.

Human Rights Watch. (2000) *The Search for Security and Human Rights Abuses*, New York: Human Rights Watch.

— (2003) *Preparing for Elections: tightening control in the name of unity*, New York: Human Rights Watch.

International Crisis Group. (2002) *Rwanda at the End of the Transition: a necessary political liberalization*, Brussels: International Crisis Group.

Karekezi, U. A. (2001) 'Juridictions *Gacaca*: lutte contre l'impunitie et promotion de la reconciliation nationale,' *Cahiers du Centre de Gestion des Conflits*, 3: 9–96.

Karekezi, U. A., Nshimiyiman, A. and Mutamba, B. (2004) 'Localizing justice: *gacaca* courts in post-genocide Rwanda,' in E. Stover and H. Weinstein (eds) *My Neighbor, My Enemy: justice and community in the aftermath of mass atrocity*, New York: Cambridge University Press.

Kiss, E. (2000) 'Moral ambition within and beyond political constraints: reflections on restorative justice,' in R. Rotberg and D. Thompson (eds) *Truth v. Justice: the morality of truth commissions*, Princeton, NJ: Princeton University Press.

Liprodhor (2000) *Juridictions Gacaca au Rwanda: resultats de la recherche sur les attitudes et opinions de la population rwandaise*, Kigali: Liprodhor.

— (2002) *Rapport d'observations sur les activites des assemblees des juridictions gacaca de cellule*, Kigali: Liprodhor.

Longman, T. and Rutagengwa, T. (2004) 'Memory, identity and community,' in E.

Stover and H. Weinstein (eds) *My Neighbor, My Enemy: justice and community in the aftermath of mass atrocity*, New York: Cambridge University Press.

Longman, T., Pham, P. and Weinstein, H. (2004) 'Connecting justice to human experience: attitudes toward accountability and reconciliation in Rwanda,' in E. Stover and H. Weinstein (eds) *My Neighbor, My Enemy: justice and community in the aftermath of mass atrocity*, New York: Cambridge University Press.

Mamdani, M. (2001) *When Victims Become Killers: colonialism, nativism, and the genocide in Rwanda*, Princeton, NJ: Princeton University Press.

Minow, M. (2002) 'Memory and hate: are there lessons from around the world?' in M. Minow (ed.) *Breaking the Cycle of Hatred*, Princeton, NJ: Princeton University Press.

Molenaar, A. (2004) '*Gacaca*: grassroots justice after genocide. The key to reconciliation in Rwanda?' graduation thesis, University of Amsterdam.

Newbury, C. 1988. *The Cohesion of Oppression: clientship and ethnicity in Rwanda 1860–1960*, New York: Columbia University Press.

NURC (National Unity and Reconciliation Commission) (2003) *Opinion Survey on Participation in Gacaca and National Reconciliation*, Kigali: NURC.

PAPG (Projet d'appui de la societe civile au processus *gacaca* au Rwanda) (2003) *Rapport de synthese de l'etat d'avancement des travaux des juridictions gacaca au cours des mois de mars-juin (2003)*, Kigali: PAPG.

— (2004) *Les cas d'insecurite des temoins et des rescapes du genocide dans les juridictions gacaca*, Kigali: PAPG.

Payne, L. (2004) 'In search of remorse: confessions by perpetrators of past state violence,' *Brown Journal of World Affairs*, XI(1): 115–25.

Penal Reform International. (2002a) *Interim Report on Research on Gacaca Jurisdictions and its Preparation (July–December (2001)*, Paris/Kigali: Penal Reform International.

— (2002b) *Report III, April–June (2002)*, Paris/Kigali: Penal Reform International.

— (2003a) *Research on Gacaca (Report IV): the guilty plea procedure, cornerstone of the Rwandan justice*, Paris/Kigali: Penal Reform International.

— (2003b) *Research on the Gacaca (Report V)*, Paris/Kigali: Penal Reform International.

— (2004) *Research Report on the Gacaca (Report VI): from camp to hill, the reintegration of released prisoners*, Paris/Kigali: Penal Reform International.

Pottier, J. (2002) *Re-imagining Rwanda: conflict, survival and disinformation in the late twentieth century*, New York: Cambridge University Press.

Power, S. (2003) 'Rwanda: the two faces of justice,' *The New York Review of Books*, 16 January: 1647–50.

Reyntjens, F. (1990) 'Le *gacaca* ou la justice du gazon au Rwanda,' *Politique Africaine*, 40: 31–41.

— (2004) 'Rwanda, ten years on: from genocide to dictatorship,' *African Affairs*, 103: 177–210.

Rombouts, H. (2004) 'Victim organisations and the politics of reparation: a case study on Rwanda,' unpublished dissertation, University of Antwerp.

Roth, K. and Des Forges, A. (2002) 'Justice or therapy?' *Boston Review*, 27(3–4), online. Available at: http://www.bostonreview.net/BR27.3/rothdesForges.html

Sibomana, A. (1999) *Hope for Rwanda: conversations with Laure Guilbert and Herve Deguine*, Sterling, VA: Pluto Press.

Stevens, J. (1998) *Traditional and Informal Justice Systems in Africa, South Asia, and the Caribbean*, Paris: Penal Reform International.

Straus, S. (2004) 'How many perpetrators were there in the Rwandan genocide? An estimate,' *Journal of Genocide Research*, 6(1): 85–98.

Umetesi, M. B. (2004) *Surviving the Slaughter: the ordeal of a Rwandan refugee in Zaire*, Madison, WI: University of Wisconsin Press.

UNHCHR (United Nations High Commission for Human Rights) (1996) *Gacaca: le droit coutumier au Rwanda*, Kigali: UNHCR.

Uvin, P. and Mironko, C. (2003) 'Western and local approaches to justice in Rwanda,' *Global Governance*, 9: 219–31.

Vandeginste, S. (2001) 'Rwanda: dealing with genocide and crimes against humanity in the context of armed conflict and failed political transition,' in N. Biggar (ed.) *Burying the Past: making peace and doing justice after civil conflict*, Washington, DC: Georgetown University Press.

Vidal, C. (2001) 'Les commemorations du genocide au Rwanda,' *Les Temps Modernes*, 1–46.

Weinstein, H. and Stover, E. (2004) 'Introduction: conflict, justice and reclamation,' in E. Stover and H. Weinstein (eds) *My Neighbor, My Enemy: justice and community in the aftermath of mass atrocity*, New York: Cambridge University Press.

Notes

1. This paper has been inspired by the impressive ethnographic work of Alison Des Forges on the Rwandan genocide and that of Klaas de Jonge and Anne Aghion on *gacaca*. They

bear no responsibility for the contents or conclusions of this paper.

2. Reconciliation is a highly ambiguous and problematic term (see Weinstein and Stover 2004) and seems too much to ask from Rwandans a mere eleven years after the genocide. Rather, a more appropriate goal at this stage is peaceful coexistence.

3. Using local observers and focus groups, Penal Reform International is conducting action research in pilot *gacaca* communities throughout Rwanda and producing an invaluable series of reports. The filmmaker Anne Aghion has made two remarkable documentaries illustrating how pre-*gacaca* hearings and the reintegration of confessed genocidaires have affected one particular community. The Center for Conflict Management at the National University of Rwanda (Butare) has been monitoring *gacaca* in a pilot sector in Butare province (Karekezi *et al.* 2004). Sadly, the Rwandan human rights NGO, LIPRODHOR, and its monthly publication, *Le Verdict*, were forced to suspend their monitoring and documentation of *gacaca* proceedings after being criticized and then co-opted by the government in mid-2004.

4. For a depiction of prison *gacaca*, see Anne Aghion's documentary film *Gacaca, Living Together Again in Rwanda?* (Gacaca Productions/Dominant 7, 2002).

5. This description is based on the amended 2004 law, which, among other things, reduced the levels of *gacaca* courts, the categories of offenses, and the quorum for judges. For an overview of *gacaca* before the 2004 amendments, see Vandeginste (2001).

6. In 2001, Rwanda's administration was reorganized into the following hierarchy: eleven provinces (formerly prefectures) plus the city of Kigali, 106 districts (formerly communes), 1,545 sectors, and 9,201 cells. The cell, the smallest administrative unit, averages 830 people, though there are considerable variations (Vandeginste 2001). In addition, cells are sub-divided into groupings of ten households called *nyumbakumbi*.

7. Cobban also overstated (and idealized) the restorative aspect of gacaca:

The final passage of the *Gacaca* Law, in early 2001, signalled not only a government consensus that the previous stress on prosecutions was no longer desirable for Rwanda, but also a willingness to try to incorporate elements of a very different, 'restorative' approach to issues of justice and wrongdoing into its policy.

(Cobban 2002a)

In fact, there has never been a government 'consensus' on post-genocide justice (including *gacaca*), with important differences apparent among government policy makers. More fundamentally, *gacaca* does not represent a departure from the government's emphasis on prosecutions.

8. Alice Karekezi, Director of the Center for Conflict Management, National University of Rwanda (Butare), CLADHO Conference on Gacaca, 14 February 2003.

9. Professor Simon Gasibirege, CLADHO Conference on Gacaca, 14 February 2003.

10. Reported to this author in a personal communication from a participant at the 22 June 2004 meeting.

Section VI

Critical commentaries on restorative justice

The chapters in this section place the development of restorative justice theory and practice within the history of criminological thought and critically explore some of its key concepts and processes. In addition, the problems and possibilities of restorative justice are assessed from a feminist, postmodern, and community justice perspective.

In Chapter 29 David Friedrichs, in placing the development of restorative justice in the context of criminological thought, notes that mainstream criminology has been positivistic in form and has privileged discovery, explanation, and prediction over a concern with developing the concept of justice. It has, as well, been primarily focused on street offenders, not victims, communities, or the organization of social life. In this regard, criminology has generally disregarded the political-economic context within which crime has been defined and largely accepted a state-legalistic definition. Restorative justice has challenged this definition, desiring to broaden the scope of inquiry to activity that is demonstrably harmful to people, relationships, other life forms, and the environment. Socially injurious harms by individuals, corporations, states, or suprastate organizations injure whole groups of persons, communities, and our planet.

In as much as restorative justice emerged from 'critical' criminologies (e.g. feminist, postmodern, Marxist, anarchist, constitutive, peacemaking) and radical victimology, it has a central concern for victims' needs, whether they have suffered from youth delinquencies, nursing home health and safety violations, violations of health and safety regulations in the workplace, harmful consumer product production for reasons of profit, or gross violations of human rights for reasons of state. It has, as well, a central concern for changing the structural conditions or arrangements that led to these harms – restorative justice is concerned with prevention and the future. Restorative justice may be regarded as extending too much power to communities unconstrained by due process and human rights concerns. It may be challenged for 'shaming' and reintegrating those affected by a harm into harmful, criminogenic community environments. It may be accused of extending the tentacles of the state even more invasively by widening the 'net.' But, these are challenges that can be reasonably met. The greater thicket that restorative justice faces is exposing the fact that the way many of our societies are organized fosters a world of pervasive harm and injustice. Restorative justice is ultimately about transforming our societies.

In Chapter 30, Nathan Harris and Shadd Maruna critically examine the key concepts of 'shame' and 'shaming' and their place in restorative justice theory and practice. They differentiate shaming that is reintegrative and that which is stigmatic. They, as well, carefully distinguish between processes that raise the consciousness of the effects of the wound/harm, and those that lead to self-threat and self-disapproval. In essence, shame means exposure. This leads us to the following questions: What exactly do different restorative justice processes expose? And, in reaction, what do those participating in these processes expose themselves to by simply being there and in response to these processes? Harris and Maruna suggest that shame can take the form of social threat, personal failure, or ethical threat and, as the labeling school has long informed us, the form that one being 'processed' selects has significance for self-concept and for future actions. Restorative justice processes must be carefully scrutinized for the type of shaming experience offered and the degree to which they encourage 'offenders' to manage feelings of shame constructively. They must encourage the constructive management of these feelings through the future relations encouraged between the 'offender' and his/her community of care and the degree to which positive, reintegrative life opportunities are programmatically offered following the restorative encounter. Such attention must correlatively be given to the exposure experiences of 'victims.'

In Chapter 31 Todd Clear asserts that both restorative justice and community justice are deeply penetrating critiques of formal criminal justice processes and provide profound challenges to the adversarial, due process model of criminal justice. Community justice advocates claim that the tremendous growth of the criminal justice system in the USA in the past thirty years has done more damage than good and that its strategies need to be recalibrated to address what communities need, rather than what those who commit harms deserve. After all, from the view of these advocates, the essential justification for the criminal justice system is to make communities better places for people to live, work, and raise families! This purpose assertion is, however, radically different from the critical criminological base out of which restorative justice emerged, which asserts that the essential purpose of the criminal justice system is to preserve the structures of privilege and stratification as codified in state law.

In further contrasting restorative justice and community justice concerns, Clear points out that they have different starting points: Restorative justice starts with a concern for the needs of the victims of crime, while community justice starts with a concern for the lives of people who live in impoverished communities and ends with a concern as to whether or not various community-wide strategies have made life in the community any better. These views are not necessarily in conflict, however, for an essential precept of restorative justice is that neither victims nor offenders of crime and harm can sensibly be reintegrated into a community that lacks the resources to meet their needs. On the other hand, the conflict is not without a base, as there are many restorative justice programs that are so wrapped up in the dynamics of interpersonal harm that they do not address the larger issues of the nature of the community into which these disputants are being placed. In these instances restorative justice programs need to change, for trying to restore victims and offenders of crime to pre-crime lives when they live in areas devoid of basic social infrastructure makes little sense. In conclusion, Clear believes that restorative justice gives the rationale and strategy that community justice initiatives can use to deliver its community improvement agenda without scapegoating 'offenders' and 'victims.'

Bruce Arrigo (Chapter 32) explores postmodernism's assessment of restorative justice both in theory and practice delineating its affirmative challenges. Beyond the critique that the most wooden, scripted models of restorative justice are largely non-voluntary for the 'offender,' refuse to make fully thematic the actual violence perpetrated against those harmed, embody exclusively individualist responsibility themes, serve the interests of the state and those who benefit from the current social distributions in society, discipline and regulate those who participate, and stress a commitment to prevailing cultural values and norms, postmodernism poses five challenges to restorative justice: (1) affirmative postmodern social theory questions whether and to what extent those who participate in, for example, a Victim Offender Mediation, freely and sensitively discuss their roles in mediation, for without this discussion the prospects for genuine power sharing and authentic healing are compromised; (2) in staged and unwittingly scripted discourse stability trumps conflict, predictability is privileged over unpredictability, and control rather than freedom and spontaneity underscores the reconciliation dialogue; (3) conventional, scripted restorative practices contain or sanitize conflict, regarding conflict as an altogether destructive and unhealthy feature of human interaction. Restorative discourse should resist routinized thinking, custom-driven practices, and conventional, polite dialogue so as to advance a deeper, more complete, sense of justice for all participants; (4) when the tools of legal discourse are at work in mediation, personal story-telling, incomplete knowledge, and local histories that signify our evolving identities are silenced. Scripted, normalized, formal processes conceal and discount different cultural images, perceptual differences, and divergent truth claims, yielding a largely hollow 'settlement;' (5)

conventional restorative justice models fail to recognize how social structure is a contributing factor in the manifestation of conflict. Recognition of the role of conflict, ambiguity, and disequilibrium could better make restorative practice deeper experiences and structural reform more realizable. A transformative praxis recognizes the link between conflict and change.

In the last chapter, Emily Gaarder and Lois Presser (Chapter 33) grapple with the question of whether or not restorative justice can become an important component of a feminist vision of justice, safeguarding women's rights and ensuring a peaceful, just, and non-violent society. Several features of restorative justice hold out the possibility that this may be possible. First, narrative offers a supportive stage for public acknowledgement, respect, vindication, responsive listening, and an opportunity for change. But such processes, as well, contain the potential that dialogic discourse is likely to replicate existing inequalities and that participatory choice may be neither voluntary nor one of many choices that women would have for restoration. Second, an involvement of those who care offers the potentiality that concrete help and need-meeting will be forthcoming. However, the most obvious problems here are that custom may reify existing power structures, that communities of care do not always exist, and that many such communities do not have the emotional or material resources to garner support for women whether 'offenders' or 'victims,' or to sanction the violence of men. Third, while circles and other restorative models hold out a promise of encouraging self-respect and empowerment, they also pose the challenge to ensure that violence is effectively confronted and that women are able to live safe lives.

Gaarder and Presser suggest that restorative justice proponents should embrace the language of rights, but detach these rights from the state and instead apply them to ethical principles that guide community

437

organization. A communitarian ecofeminist basis for rights would affirm the connectedness of all beings and acts, while inspiring a grounded ethical basis for organizing life. Doing justice in an unjust society forces us to consider the complexities of our problems and responses. Peacemaking and community building strategies are only part of a holistic package that includes structural and personal change with the goal of creating, maintaining, and repairing healthy, peaceful, and equitable relationships among all people. They conclude that although the distinct problems of gendered harms demand caution, dialogue, and self-reflexivity, there is reason to be encouraged and energized by the hope that the best possibilities offered by restorative justice might someday be realized.

29

Restorative justice and the criminological enterprise

David O. Friedrichs

The invention of criminology and the pursuit of justice

Criminology as an intellectual enterprise has had a problematic relationship with the pursuit of justice. Students of criminology are typically taught that a treatise by an Italian nobleman and economist, Cesare Beccaria, entitled *Of Crimes and Punishments,* published in 1764, was the earliest systematic attempt to address the subject matter of criminology and criminal justice (Rafter 2004; Vold *et al.* 2002). Beccaria's work is designated as the key contribution to a 'classical' school of criminological theory. It is associated with promoting a voluntarist conception of human nature, which has largely been adopted by the criminal law, and which also provides a fundamental point of departure for contemporary neo-classical or 'rational choice' theory (Vold *et al.* 2002: 196–7). This theoretical approach focuses on criminal offenders, their free will, and the choices made by such offenders.

Beccaria's essay has also been viewed as providing a basis for subsequent attention to the formulation of criminal justice policies. His essay is typically viewed as having called for humane, utilitarian reforms: famously, 'let the punishment fit the crime,' and

opposition to capital punishment. In this view Beccaria set forth a humanitarian response to the arbitrary, cruel punishments still inflicted in the eighteenth century. But some critics have claimed that Beccaria's essay was more ambiguous and contradictory than is typically suggested, with deterministic elements and a retributivist argument at its core. In this interpretation, Beccaria 'was responsible for introducing a nightmarish and ever-expanding system in which more and more of the population are even now incarcerated' (Beirne 1994: 2). If this is so, Beccaria's contribution set the stage for a criminological tradition focused on offenders, and on the aggressive prosecution and incarceration of such offenders. In this interpretation, then, criminology from the outset has been wittingly or unwittingly complicit in the expansion of an essentially retributive justice system.

For some practitioners, the goal of criminology has no necessary relationship to the pursuit of justice, however defined. The goal of criminology, in this view, is the pure pursuit of 'truth,' based upon empiricism (Gibbons 1979). Criminologists are considered scientists, objective and dispassionate students in search of verifiable explanations for observable phenomena. A positivistic

439

approach quite specifically applies the methods of the natural sciences to the subject matter of crime and criminal justice. The positivist approach can be viewed as emerging from eighteenth-century Enlightenment thought (Rafter 2004). Some students of the history of criminology trace the seminal origins of criminological positivism to the late-eighteenth and early-nineteenth century, when studies of moral derangement and moral insanity, the contours of the skull (phrenology), and statistics relating to the 'dangerous classes,' attempted to explain or predict criminality (Beirne 1987; Rafter 2004; Savitz *et al.* 1977). But a major step in the promotion of a positivistic approach to criminology occurred in the latter part of the nineteenth century, with the Italian physician Cesare Lombroso often cited as its most influential promoter (Gibson 2002). Lombroso is especially associated with the notion of the 'born' criminal or the criminal as an atavistic (not fully evolved) type. Positivistic criminology also directed attention to offenders and their control, although with some different premises than those of the classical school.

During the course of the twentieth century, as criminology evolved as a major field of scholarly inquiry, it gave rise to an especially broad array of underlying assumptions, theories, methods, and substantive topics of interest (Vold *et al.* 2002). Underlying assumptions have ranged from quite purely voluntarist to quite purely determinist; theories have encompassed biological, psychological, economic, political, and sociological dimensions; methods have ranged from highly quantitative and mathematical to thoroughly qualitative and interpretive; substantive topics of interest have ranged from petty theft to crimes of the nuclear state. The specific type of theory, methodology, and data that has been dominant during any period of the twentieth century has varied, at least in part as a function of what was happening in the larger society as criminologists came of age, and the influ-

ence of criminological peers during different periods (Savelsberg and Flood 2004). But early in the twenty-first century it seems reasonable to argue that the mainstream of criminology during this history has been positivistic in some form, and has privileged discovery, explanation, and prediction over the specific advancement of justice. In one interpretation, classical and positivist criminology are not incompatible, but differ mainly in the variables they focus upon in their mutual attempt to explain criminal behavior (Vold *et al.* 2002: 29). Both schools of thought – and the criminological traditions they gave rise to – have been focused principally upon offenders, not victims or communities. And the mainstream of criminology has continued to focus disproportionately on those encompassed by the label of conventional offenders.

Early in the twenty-first century Gottfredson and Hirschi's general theory of crime, focusing on low self-control as the critically important factor, was quite widely identified as among the most popular and widely cited and tested criminological theories (Marcus 2004). This theory was consistent with a long-standing tradition of focusing attention on the offender, and not the community or the victim. It was also consistent with a tradition treating the criminal offender as fundamentally different from non-offenders, and the explanation for crime as simple, not complex. On all these points one could make the case that 'low self-control' theory is fundamentally at odds with the tenets of the restorative justice movement. To the extent that criminologists (and policy-makers) embrace this theory and similar theoretical perspectives, they are likely to be resistant to adopting a restorative justice approach.

The core assumption of a positivistic criminology, that it is possible (and desirable) to 'explain' crime objectively, has been questioned (Rafter 2004). Indeed, especially from the late 1960s on, a variety of criminological perspectives and approaches emerged that challenged this assumption, and many other dimensions of mainstream criminology. The restorative justice approach was importantly rooted in these alternative criminological approaches, which are considered more fully further on.

The challenges of defining crime

Many criminologists who have studied crime have glossed over or largely disregarded the issue of how crime should be best defined, often incorporating a taken-for-granted legalistic definition of crime. At least some criminologists become impatient with definitional discussions. But the familiar term 'crime' can be defined in quite different ways, and the particular definitions or conceptions of crime that we adopt can influence our policy preferences for responding to crime in fundamental ways (Henry and Lanier 2001). It is perhaps true that people think of crime most readily in terms of state law, and its violation. This conception has inevitably drawn attention to the offender and the offense to the state's laws, as opposed to other dimensions of the broader class of harmful activity or behavior.

While legalistic definitions of crime are intrinsically political – i.e. both the legislative bodies that produce statutory law and the judicial bodies that adjudicate criminal cases are political institutions – it should be recognized that some conceptions of crime are more directly political: e.g. in totalitarian societies, where any actions deemed offensive to those in power are treated as crimes, regardless of legislative actions or court findings. A moralistic conception of crime is exemplified by the pro-life movement's characterization of abortion as a crime – and a very serious crime – independent of its status under state law. In this conception crime is an offense against the moral order of a particular group.

For progressive criminologists, a humanistic conception of crime is called for.

Rather than ceding to the state monopolistic control over the historically potent term, 'crime' in a humanistic approach is best defined as activity that is demonstrably harmful to human beings and their environment, regardless of the status of these activities under law. In a widely cited article Herman Schwendinger and Julia Schwendinger (1970) called for a humanistic definition of crime that would focus on objectively identifiable harm to human beings and violations of human rights as the criteria for labeling an activity a crime. By such criteria imperialism, racism, sexism, and other such oppressive conditions should be viewed as crimes. The Schwendingers argued that criminologists should not defer to elite groups in society the exclusive right to define crime. Crime should be defined in accordance with harm experienced by ordinary citizens, not simply those acts defined as crime by the propertied class (Schwendinger and Schwendinger 1977). In a similar vein, Dennis Sullivan and Larry Tifft (2001) have long argued that we should define crime in terms of needs-based social harms inflicted by the powerful on less powerful people, independent of formal legal institutions. Accordingly, actions that contribute to the denial of food, clothing, and shelter – and the realization of human potential – should be recognized as crime. How we choose to define crime, in this view, says something important about our own priorities and commitments in life.

The definition of crime that is adopted influences in important ways the types of activities we focus upon as crime, the types of individuals we focus upon as criminals, and the types of procedures and penalties we adopt in response to crime and criminals.

The restorative justice movement, then, has challenged traditional conceptions of crime. Howard Zehr (2002: 21) contrasts a restorative justice conception of crime – as 'a violation of people and relationships' – with the conventional conception of crime – as 'a violation of the law and the state.'

441

What is especially interesting about the restorative justice conception of crime is that it synthesizes, in certain respects, concerns of both conservative and progressive constituencies. On the one hand, the traditional criminological conceptions of crime are regarded as too centered on offenders as opposed to victims, often by those with a conservative outlook; on the other hand, traditional criminological conceptions of crime are regarded as too focused on identifying (and penalizing) individuals, as opposed to doing justice and reducing harm, by those with a progressive outlook. The term 'crime' itself might be regarded as having so much 'baggage' that any attempt to foster a fundamentally new approach to addressing what has traditionally been defined as crime must begin by abandoning the term 'crime' itself and replacing it with a new term. This seems to be one of the premises of those committed to a restorative justice approach, who promote the term 'harm' in place of crime.

Criminological orthodoxy and criminological heresy: the legitimate scope of criminological inquiry

If the concept of crime can be defined in many different ways, criminologists have historically chosen to focus on some kinds of activities defined as crime but to neglect others that have been so defined, or could be so defined. In a parallel vein, criminologists have embraced some forms of policy and practice in response to crime, but have chosen to disregard others.

The criminological orthodoxy, throughout the history of the field, has indisputably been characterized by a focus on conventional or 'street' crime. The relative neglect of white-collar crime (and especially corporate crime) in the criminological literature as well as the criminal justice/criminology curriculum has been documented (Cullen

and Benson 1993; Wright and Friedrichs 1991). More specifically, a recent study has established that juvenile crime, despite causing far less harm by any credible measure than corporate crime, received twice as much attention in the criminological literature as did corporate crime (Lynch *et al.* 2004). Indeed, a case can be made that criminological concern has traditionally taken the form of what amounts to an inverse relationship between levels of criminological concern and measures of objectively identifiable harm.

The legitimate scope of criminological concerns seems to expand only gradually. When Edwin Sutherland (1940) first introduced the concept of white-collar crime, in 1939, criminology as an emerging discipline was almost entirely focused on conventional forms of crime. For several decades following Sutherland's famous speech, relatively little white-collar crime scholarship was produced (with the work of Sutherland and some of his students as especially notable exceptions) (Friedrichs 2004). Only in the 1970s did attention to white-collar crime within the discipline begin to expand significantly. Early in the twenty-first century over a hundred criminologists were registered as members of the White-Collar Crime Research Consortium. During this period of time the scope of concerns addressed by white-collar crime scholars expanded as well. The principal forms of white-collar crime remained corporate crimes – or illegal, unethical, and harmful actions committed on behalf of corporations – and occupational crimes – or illegal, unethical, and harmful actions committed by individuals, partnerships and small enterprises, in the context of a legitimate occupation. But some attention was also increasingly focused on state-corporate crime (crimes carried out as cooperative ventures between state entities and corporations), finance crime (large-scale illegality that occurs in the world of finance and financial institutions), enterprise crime (cooperative ventures between syndicated crime and legitimate businesses), contrepreneurial crime (scams masquerading as legitimate businesses), and technocrime crime (crimes carried out through the use of computers and other forms of sophisticated technology) (Friedrichs 2004). Each of these cognate, hybrid or marginal forms of white-collar crime generates special challenges. There have been many practical constraints on applying traditional forms of adversarial and retributive justice to such crimes, and to other types of white-collar crime as well.

Crimes of globalization

One hybrid form of white-collar crime deserving of more attention has been designated as 'crimes of globalization,' or crimes perpetrated as a consequence of the policies of international financial institutions, such as the World Bank (Friedrichs and Friedrichs 2002). The World Bank has been characterized as paternalistic, secretive, and counterproductive, in terms of its claimed goals of improving people's lives. It has been charged with complicity in policies with genocidal consequences, with exacerbating ethnic conflict, with increasing the gap between rich and poor, with fostering immense ecological and environmental damage, and with the callous displacement of vast numbers of indigenous people in developing countries from their original homes and communities (Rich 1994). The World Bank does not set out to do harm but its mode of operation is intrinsically criminogenic and it functions undemocratically. Its key deliberations are carried out secretly, and it is insufficiently accountable to any independent entity.

Altogether, crimes of globalization exemplify forms of 'harm' not well-captured by conventional conceptions of crime. In this sense the restorative justice movement's focus on harm is especially applicable to crimes of globalization. Specifically, in response to crimes of globalization, we have witnessed in the current era the emergence of an anti-globalization movement, or global justice movement. This movement achieved high visibility following its massive protests against the World Trade Organization meeting in Seattle in 1999, and subsequent meetings of international financial institutions in Washington, DC, Genoa, and elsewhere (Graeber 2003; Starr 2000). The global justice movement is made up of a diversity of constituencies, with different agendas, united principally in their opposition to globalization driven by corporate and other elite interests, with a wide range of perceived harms to the global environment, and to workers, people of color, women, indigenous peoples, and other non-elite segments of the population. At least a significant proportion of those involved recognize the inevitability of globalization but want it to be 'globalization from below,' or globalization taking direction from those most affected, not elite institutions or individuals, or 'globalization from above' (Kellner 2002; Starr 2000). This movement recognizes that the supranational entities now dominating globalization are not democratic, and accordingly it calls for democratizing the globalization process (Hardt and Negri 2003). The movement is focused mainly on exposing, delegitimizing, and dismantling the mechanisms of rule of the global powers, rather than on seizing state power.

The global justice movement in important respects parallels the restorative justice movement: both are concerned with focusing on harms and their repair, rather than on punishing crime; both put much emphasis on the suffering of victims; both attempt to mobilize and engage communities in response to the identified forms of harm; and both have in identifiable ways attempted to foster dialogue between the affected parties. Accordingly, the global justice movement and the restorative justice movement can learn from each other.

Crimes of states

The claim that there is an inverse relationship between the level of attention directed by criminologists to different forms of crime, and the extent of harm caused by such crime, seems especially applicable to the realm of crimes of the state. For example, criminologists have produced a measurable literature on such relatively inconsequential activities as vandalism, petty theft, and marijuana use, but the specifically criminological literature on crimes of states, of war, of genocide, and of human rights, is remarkably thin (Barak 1991; Friedrichs 1998; Green and Ward 2004; Ross 2000). In his book *States of Denial: Knowing about Atrocities and Suffering*, Stanley Cohen (2001) provides arguably the most persuasive and fully realized account of the criminological neglect of large-scale crimes. Criminologists tend to share a more broadly diffused resistance to confronting monumental crimes and atrocities. Cohen explores in some depth both the foundations of this aversion and some of its consequences.

In 1988, in his presidential address to the American Society of Criminology, William Chambliss (1989) drew attention to 'state-organized' crime. Stanley Cohen (1993) has called for more criminological attention to human rights violations. In the 1990s, and into the early years of the twenty-first century, a relatively small number of criminologists began to focus on crimes of states. In the twenty-first century one could argue that the single most extreme threat is that relating to the use of nuclear weapons, or nuclear power, and with some isolated exceptions this issue has been almost wholly neglected by criminologists (with David Kauzlarich and Ronald C. Kramer's (1998) *Crimes of the American Nuclear State: At Home and Abroad,* as one noteworthy exception to this proposition).

Early in the twenty-first century, following the trauma of 11 September 2001, an exponential increase occurred in the perception of the threat of terrorism (Denzin and Lincoln 2003). The events of '9/11' and its aftermath also brought into especially sharp relief a range of complex issues relating to crimes of states, including: the complicity of states in the 9/11 attacks, and terrorism more generally; the status of pre-emptive invasions (e.g. on Iraq) in international law; the application of international treaties on treatment of war criminals to those taken into custody in the 'war on terrorism' (e.g. those held at Guantanamo Bay); and the viability of the newly established permanent International Criminal Court in responding to war crimes. It remained to be seen whether criminologists collectively would become significantly more engaged with such issues over time. It seems extremely likely that both the nature of and the perception of harm during the course of the twenty-first century will undergo a significant transformation. If criminology as a discipline is to maintain its credibility and currency, it will have to respond effectively to such changes. On the one hand, there is the question of how conventional forms of criminological methodology and knowledge can be applied to a deeper, richer understanding of crimes of states. On the other hand, there is the question of what we have learned about justice system responses to conventional forms of crime that can be appropriately applied to the response to crimes of states. The restorative justice movement suggests some novel and promising responses to large-scale crimes.

The emergence of victimology

The emergence of victimology must be regarded as one of the developments within the broader field of criminology that ultimately helped give rise to the restorative justice movement. Through the 1960s criminology as a discipline had been focused principally upon explaining offenders. Although attention to the criminal justice system, and its principal actors (e.g. the police), had preoccupied at least some criminologists from the earliest stages of the discipline's history, an identifiable field of criminal justice only really emerged following the President's Commission Report on Crime in the late 1960s. But victims of crime were the most neglected element in the crime drama, attracting little attention from criminologists until the emergence of a subfield, principally from the early 1970s on, of victimology (Karmen 2004; Shichor and Tibbetts 2002). In a related but not identical development, a victims' rights movement also emerged during this period of time. Both of these developments were in important ways responses to the dramatic increase in the conventional crime rate in the United States from the mid-1960s on. Although victimology evolved as a world-wide phenomena, with international conferences and journals, its focus was and remains primarily on victims of conventional forms of crime (Karmen 2004). The victims' rights movement has also been viewed as primarily driven by a conservative agenda, advocating a broader range of rights of victims, which in at least some cases is viewed as inevitably compromising the rights of the accused. Since offenders are disproportionately inner-city men of color, and victims include a somewhat higher proportion of privileged white people, questions arose about some victims' rights as introducing yet another form of bias into the criminal justice system. For example, victim impact statements have been criticized on the grounds that articulate, middle-class white people are likely to be able to inspire an even harsher response against a less articulate, lower-class person of color (Johnson and Morgan 2003). Achieving an appropriate balance between rights of the accused and of victims is an on-going challenge for the restorative justice model generally.

Despite the historical focus of victimology and the victims' rights movement, a concern with victims and victims' rights is hardly by definition an exclusively conservative preoccupation. A critical, progressive, or radical approach to victimization has long called for adoption of a more expansive conception of victimization, and the recognition that the most substantial victimization occurs at the hands of the state, or major corporations (Elias 1986; Friedrichs 1983; Kauzlarich *et al.* 2001). Restorative justice offers the possibility of exploring and attending more fully to concerns about victims that emerge both from conservative and from progressive movements (Kapstein and Malsch 2004; Strang 2002). And restorative justice approaches are now incorporated as a standard element of victimology texts and readings (Balboni 2003; Karmen 2004; Meyer 2003; Van Ness and Strong 2000). Victimology as a subfield of criminology, then, has a range of concerns that are especially interconnected with the central concerns of the restorative justice movement.

Transcending orthodox criminology and restorative justice

The mainstream of criminology has not been a principal source for the emergence of a restorative justice movement. Indeed, this movement has adopted premises and policy positions at odds with those either implicitly or explicitly embraced by mainstream criminology. Accordingly, it can more accurately be described as reflecting the influence of unorthodox criminological perspectives. The radical, neo-Marxist and 'new' criminology that emerged in the 1970s, and generated considerable controversy in the field, challenged some of the fundamental tenets of mainstream criminology (e.g. Inciardi 1980; Lynch *et al.* 2000; Taylor *et al.* 1973). Of particular relevance to the emergence of a restorative justice approach, this unorthodox criminology challenged the dependence on state-based, legalistic definitions of crime, and highlighted the need to understand crime and criminal justice within the context of the existing political economy, the focus on conventional offenders and the range of 'pathological' conditions giving rise to such offenders, and the true objectives of the conventional criminal justice response to crime. In this sense radical criminology contributed to opening the way to the heretical elements of a restorative justice movement. This criminological tradition gave rise, in the 1980s and 1990s, to a variety of critical criminological approaches, including: left realism; postmodern criminology; constitutive criminology; feminist criminology; and peacemaking criminology (Arrigo 1999; MacLean and Milovanovic 1997; Schwartz and Hatty 2003). Some commentators contend that these critical criminologies have not attended sufficiently to broader forms of harm in an increasingly globalized world (Hil and Robertson 2003). But at least some dimensions of a number of these strains of critical criminology intersect with the concerns of the restorative justice movement (Sarre 2003). For example, Bruce Arrigo (2003: 54) contends that postmodern criminology's deconstruction of traditional conceptions of 'truth,' and its promotion of 'reconstructive' approaches to the problem of crime, is compatible with restorative justice. But of all the different strains of critical criminology, peacemaking criminology has contributed most directly to the emergence of a restorative justice movement. Peacemaking criminology emerged at a time when the 'war on crime' in America was in full bloom. In the words of a leading commentator on peacemaking criminology, John Fuller (2003: 85), it takes issue with 'the separation of individuals and citizens ... the relegation of law violators into the "enemy" ... The war-like mentality [of conventional responses to crime] ... [and] the contribution that society's institutional arrangements make in the production of crime.' Peacemaking criminology, then, has promoted a range of responses to what is conventionally labeled as crime that have been compatible with or parallel to the objectives of restorative justice programs.

It follows from the predominance of a focus on conventional (and individual) offenders that the criminological orthodoxy has also privileged attention to retributive, incapacitation, and rehabilitative policies, over other types of responses to crime. The restorative justice approach, in calling for attention to a broader range of harms in a more even-handed manner, and for a fundamentally different response to these harms, challenges the criminological orthodoxy. It has obviously called for the adoption of a new framework and new premises for understanding 'crime' and 'punishment.'

Criminological engagement with restorative justice: the cases of Richard Quinney and John Braithwaite

The careers and work of two remarkable criminologists, active during the latter part of the twentieth century, and into the early years of the twenty-first century, provide us with models for criminological engagement with restorative justice. These criminologists are quite different from each other in the nature of the projects they chose to address, the style of their work, and the character of their contributions to restorative justice. They are separated, as well, by almost two decades in terms of age. But each of these criminologists, in his own way, has refused to be confined by the conventional or traditional parameters of what it means to be a criminologist, or by conventional understandings of the legitimate parameters for criminological research. Both of them have soundly rejected the role of the criminologist as dispassionate scientist, and both of them have in the course of their work promoted heretical forms of responses to the on-going problem of crime. While very few criminologists can hope to match these two individuals in terms of creative insights, breadth of knowledge, and sheer productivity, they do hold out to criminologists the liberating possibility of transcending the parameters of a conventional career in criminology. The restorative justice approach at this stage is still best characterized as unorthodox in relation to both current criminal justice policy and criminology itself.

The case of Richard Quinney

Richard Quinney has been a thoroughly unique figure within contemporary criminology (e.g. see Trevino 1989; Wozniak 2002). For his PhD at the University of Wisconsin, Quinney chose to address a form of white-collar crime, an unusual topic for criminology doctoral students of this era (the late 1950s and early 1960s). In the 1960s much of his work fit within the broad parameters of mainstream criminology, with the development of an influential criminological typology (Clinard and Quinney 1967) as one especially noteworthy contribution during this period. The late 1960s were a period of much turmoil and conflict in American society, and Richard Quinney was certainly affected by these developments. In 1970 he published his landmark work, *The Social Reality of Crime*. Quinney here produced a politically informed approach to understanding crime, defining it as a construct. He formulated a series of propositions designed to demonstrate how law is created and applied by authorized agents in a politically organized society, reflecting and advancing the interests of the powerful and privileged. This book came to be regarded as a seminal articulation of a conflict approach to understanding crime and criminal law.

Richard Quinney's (2000) subsequent work went through many distinctive stages in his on-going search for a way of making sense of human existence and some of the conditions of that existence. Following his work within the conflict criminology fra-

mework, these included neo-Marxist criminology, peacemaking criminology, and prophetic criminology. Quinney's work also addressed philosophical, aesthetic, and reflective questions not directly pertinent to the concerns of students of crime. Despite his 'heretical' status in the field, Richard Quinney received the American Society of Criminology's most prestigious award, the Sutherland Award, in 1984. And in his professional work, and as a person, Quinney served as an important source of inspiration for at least some criminologists who subsequently became involved with the restorative justice movement (Tifft 2002). In 1991, with Harold Pepinsky, he published an influential collection of readings, *Criminology as Peacemaking*. Peacemaking criminology calls for a repudiation of the 'war on crime' approach, to be replaced by a response to crime as a form of suffering, and a reconciliative approach to the offender and the problem of crime (Wozniak 2002). The inseparable character of our personal and public lives is one recurrent theme of Quinney's (1998) work during this period. We must be at peace with ourselves if we want to contribute effectively to a more peaceful world. Peacemaking criminology in particular is interrelated with the concerns of restorative justice, but Quinney's influence in this regard would appear to transcend his involvement in promoting peacemaking criminology.

The case of John Braithwaite

John Braithwaite of Australian National University is arguably the most versatile, accomplished, and prolific criminologist presently active. Other candidates might be put forth for such a characterization, but he would certainly be a serious contender. In 2004 he was presented with the Sutherland Award, and he has been the recipient of many other such honors as well. In light of the originality and sophistication of his work, Braithwaite would seem to merit

447

recognition as the closest thing we have to a criminological genius. Within the realm of those studying and promoting restorative justice Braithwaite has been a leading figure, and perhaps the best-known (and best-connected) of those identified with this approach. In one sense, Braithwaite can be put forth as an idealized model for a twenty-first century criminologist, because he has been equally active in the development of innovative theory, outstanding empirical research, and policy initiatives (Yeager 2004). Although John Braithwaite has made major contributions to the study of white-collar crime, especially in its corporate form, he has also made important contributions to the study of other, more conventional forms of crime, such as juvenile delinquency.

Braithwaite's current project to expand the parameters of criminological concern can be best understood by a consideration of his magisterial *Restorative Justice and Responsive Regulation* (2002). This book not only draws upon many years' work on a wide range of criminological issues, but also explores a large literature addressing matters beyond the traditional confines of criminology. He opens this book by noting the 'explosion' of interest in restorative justice in the recent era. He also contends that there should be no meaningful separation between criminology and business regulation. Indeed, he claims that crime is best regarded as representing a regulatory challenge, and accordingly regulatory theory may be superior to criminological theory in addressing crime. For Braithwaite, the regulatory focus on fixing a problem is superior to a criminal justice focus on imposing punishment on wrong-doers. Braithwaite here draws upon many years of experience with research on issues involved in the regulation of corporations and other forms of enterprise, and he has played an active role as well as a consultant on regulatory policy. He came to his broad interest in restorative justice at least in part out of the realization that this model had in fact been widely applied to the harmful conduct of corporations.

Braithwaite has not been content to promote restorative justice on principled grounds. He has also sought to demonstrate that it is consistent both with a wide range of criminological theories and with empirical evidence from a wide range of criminological studies. Braithwaite (1999) has addressed quite comprehensively the many reservations that have been raised in connection with restorative justice. Most impressively, he has sought to show how a restorative justice approach can be applied to the broadest range imaginable of humanly generated sources of harm, from juvenile delinquency and nursing home violations to crimes of states and threats to world peace, and everything in between. In this context he has demonstrated how lessons learned from addressing one form of harm can be applied to responding to very different forms of harm. In an increasingly globalized, complex world, it seems especially important to explore such connections and interconnections. For Braithwaite, cultural shifts currently taking place are seen as not inconsistent with a shift in a restorative and responsive direction. A synthesis of responsive regulation with restorative justice has the potential to have profound consequences across many realms of human harm and its control.

On Quinney and Braithwaite

Richard Quinney and John Braithwaite are both unique figures within criminology, and extraordinarily gifted. It may be neither realistic nor entirely desirable for criminologists to attempt to emulate the unique paths pursued by these two criminologists. But both of them have promoted important visions of alternatives to conventional approaches to the scope and style of criminological inquiry, and the possibility of alternatives to the 'war on crime' approach.

Restorative justice and the criminological enterprise

It is now commonly noted that restorative justice is rooted in the most ancient and enduring practices of indigenous peoples in responding to what in the modern world has come to be defined as crime. The imposition of 'reintegrative shaming' as one key element of restorative justice programs is also rooted in the ancient notion of shame and shaming, largely unfashionable within the framework of twentieth-century ('modern') criminology (Harris *et al.* 2004). The restorative justice movement has been importantly inspired by disenchantment with the costs and the failures of adversarial justice and retributive justice.

As criminology has in certain respects contributed to the legitimation of the existing forms of justice, it may have some moral responsibility to explore and support alternative models of justice. In the most cynical and pessimistic interpretation, an alternative model such as restorative justice is no more than a 'trendy' but ultimately doomed endeavor in the endless search for the 'holy grail' of criminal justice: a model that is truly effective in all respects. Perhaps inevitably, restorative justice is viewed by some criminologists as fundamentally utopian, and unrealistic, in its aspirations. On the other hand, those who embrace the restorative justice approach with various degrees of enthusiasm are more focused on the demonstrable limitations, and injustices, of the current criminal justice system approach, and put forth various arguments in support of the proposition that a restorative justice approach is demonstrably viable, and advantageous on various levels relative to what currently exists.

Criminologists of different ideological persuasions share some of the concerns that have been expressed about restorative justice (e.g. McLaughlin *et al.* 2003; von Hirsch *et al.* 2003). On the conservative or mainstream side, restorative justice might be regarded as inappropriately emphasizing rehabilitation, restitution, and reconciliation, at the expense of appropriate forms of punishment, incapacitation, and deterrence. On the progressive or critical side, restorative justice might be regarded as extending too much power to communities unconstrained by due process standards, empowering privileged victims over disadvantaged accused parties, imposing excessive forms of 'shame' on offenders, and widening the 'net' of those swept up in the criminal justice process. Accordingly, at least some criminologists may be leery of being perceived as endorsing or supporting an approach that ultimately reinforces aspects of ineffective or inequitable justice as currently practiced. A criminological approach to evaluating restorative justice must explore it both theoretically and empirically. It seems likely, however, that criminology will be contending with the restorative justice movement for some time to come.

References

Arrigo, B. (1999) *Social Justice/Criminal Justice: the maturation of critical theory in law, crime, and deviance*, Belmont, CA: West/Wadsworth.

— (2003) 'Postmodern justice and critical criminology: positional, relational, and provisional science,' in M. D. Schwartz and S. E. Hatty (eds) *Controversies in Critical Criminology*, Cincinnati, OH: Anderson Publishing.

Balboni, J. M. (2003) 'Balanced and restorative justice: reengaging the victim in the justice process,' in J. Scarzi and J. McDevitt (eds) *Victimology: a study of crime victims and their rules*, Upper Saddle River, NJ: Prentice Hall.

Barak, G. (1991) *Crimes by the Capitalist State: an introduction to state criminality*, New York: SUNY Press.

Beirne, P. (1987) 'Adolphe Quetelet and the origins of positivist criminology,' *American Journal of Sociology*, 92: 1140–69.

— (ed.) (1994) *The Origins and Growth of Criminology: essays on intellectual history, 1760–1945*, Aldershot, UK: Dartmouth.

Braithwaite, J. (1999) 'Restorative justice: assessing optimistic and pessimistic account,' in M. Tonry (ed.) *Crime and Justice: a review of research*, Chicago: University of Chicago Press.

— (2002) *Restorative Justice and Responsive Regulation*, New York: Oxford University Press.

Chambliss, W. J. (1989) 'State-organized crime,' *Criminology*, 27: 183–208.

Clinard, M. B. and Quinney, R. (1967) *Criminal Behavior Systems: a typology*, New York: Holt, Rinehart and Winston.

Cohen, S. (1993) 'Human rights and crimes of the state: the culture of denial,' *Australian and New Zealand Journal of Criminology*, 26: 97–115.

— (2001) *States of Denial: knowing about atrocities and suffering*, Cambridge, UK: Polity Press.

Cullen, F. T. and. Benson, M. L. (1993) 'White collar crime: holding a mirror to the core,' *Journal of Criminal Justice Education*, 4: 325–48.

Denzin, N. E and Lincoln, Y. S. (eds) (2003) *9/11 in American culture*, Walnut Creek, CA: Altamira Press.

Elias, R. (1986) *The Politics of Victimization: victims, victimology, and human rights*, New York: Oxford University Press.

Friedrichs, D. O. (1983) 'Victimology: a consideration of the radical critique,' *Crime & Delinquency*, 29: 280–90.

— (ed.) (1998) *State Crime. Volumes I and II*, Aldershot, UK: Ashgate.

— (2004) *Trusted Criminals: white collar crime in contemporary society*, Belmont, CA: Thomson/Wadsworth.

Friedrichs, D. O. and Friedrichs, J. (2002) 'The World Bank and crimes of globalization: a case study,' *Social Justice*, 29: 13–39.

Fuller, J. R. (2003) 'Peacemaking criminology,' in M. D. Schwartz and S. E. Hatty (eds) *Controversies in Critical Criminology*, Cincinnati, OH: Anderson Publishing.

Gibbons, D. C. (1979) *The Criminological Enterprise: theories and perspectives*, Englewood Cliffs, NJ: Prentice Hall.

Gibson, M. (2002) *Born to Crime: Cesare Lombroso and the origins of biological criminology*, Westport, CT: Praeger.

Graeber, D. (2003) 'The globalization movement and the new new left,' in S. Aronowitz and H. Gautney (eds) *Implicating Empire: globalization and resistance in the 21st century world order*, New York: Basic Books.

Green, P. and Ward, T. (2004) *State Crime: governments, violence and corruption*, London: Pluto Press.

Hardt, M. and Negri, A. (2003) 'Globalization and democracy,' in S. Aronowitz and H. Gautney (eds) *Implicating Empire: globalization and resistance in the 21st century world order*, New York: Basic Books.

Harris, N., Walgrave, L. and Braithwaite, J. (2004) 'Emotional dynamics in restorative conferences,' *Theoretical Criminology*, 8(2): 191–210.

Henry, S. and Lanier, M. (eds) (2001) *What is Crime? Controversies over the nature of crime and what to do about it*, Lanham, MD: Rowman and Littlefield.

Hil, R. and Robertson, R. (2003) 'What sort of future for critical criminology?' *Crime, Law & Social Change*, 39: 91–115.

Inciardi, J. (ed.) (1980) *Radical Criminology: the coming crises*, Beverly Hills, CA: Sage.

Johnson, I. M. and Morgan, E. (2003) 'Victim impact statements: fairness to defendants?' in L. J. Moriarty (ed.) *Controversies in Victimology*, Cincinnati, OH: Anderson Publishing.

Johnstone, G. (2002) *Restorative Justice: ideas, values, debates*, Portland, OR: Willan Publishing.

Kapstein, H. and Malsch, M. (2004) *Crime, Victims and Justice: essays on principles and practices*, Aldershot, UK: Ashgate.

Karmen, A. (2004) *Crime victims: an introduction to victimology*, Belmont, CA: Wadsworth Publishing.

Kauzlarich, D. and Kramer, R. C. (1998) *Crimes of the American Nuclear State: at home and abroad*, Boston: Northeastern University Press.

Kauzlarich, D., Matthews, R. A. and Miller, W. J. (2001) 'Towards a victimology of state crime,' *Critical Criminology*, 10: 173–94.

Kellner, D. (2002) 'Theorizing globalization,' *Sociological Theory*, 20: 285–305.

Lynch, M., Michalowski, R. and Groves, W. B. (2000) *Critical Perspectives on Crime, Power, and Identity*, Monsey, NY: Criminal Justice Press.

Lynch, M., McGurrin, D. and Fenwick, M. (2004) 'Disappearing act: the representation of corporate crime in criminological literature,' *Journal of Criminal Justice*, 32: 389–98.

McLauglin, E., Fergusson, R., Hughes, G. and Westmarland, L. (eds) (2003) *Restorative Justice: critical issues*, London: Sage.

MacLean, B. and Milovanovic, D. (eds) (1997) *Thinking Critically about Crime*, Vancouver, BC: Collective Press.

Marcus, B. (2004) 'Self-control in the general theory of crime: theoretical implications of a measurement problem,' *Theoretical Criminology*, 8: 33–55.

Meyer, J. (2003) 'Restoration and the criminal justice system,' in L. J. Moriarty (ed.) *Controversies in Victimology*, Cincinnati, OH: Anderson Publishing.

Pepinsky, H. E. and Quinney, R. (eds) (1991) *Criminology as peacemaking*, Bloomington, IN: Indiana University Press.

Quinney, R. (1970) *The Social Reality of Crime*, Boston: Little, Brown.

— (1998) 'A life of crime: criminology and public policy as peace-making,' *Journal of Crime & Justice*, 16 (2): 3–9.

— (2000) *Bearing Witness to Crime and Social Justice*, Albany, NY: State University of New York Press.

Rafter, N. (2004) 'The unrepentant horse-slasher: moral insanity and the origins of criminological thought,' *Criminology*, 42: 979–1008.

Rich, B. (1994) *Mortgaging the Earth: the World Bank, environmental impoverishment, and the crisis of development*, Boston: Beacon Press.

Ross, J. I. (ed.) (2000) *Varieties of State Crime and its Control*, Monsey, NY: Criminal Justice Press.

Sarre, R. (2003) 'Restorative justice: a paradigm of possibility,' in M. D. Schwartz and S. E. Hatty (eds) *Controversies in Critical Criminology*, Cincinnati, OH: Anderson Publishing.

Savelsberg, J. J. and Flood, S. M. (2004) 'Criminological knowledge: period and cohort effects in scholarship,' *Criminology*, 42: 1009–41.

Savitz, L., Turner, S. H. and Dickman, T. (1977) 'The origin of scientific criminology: Franz Joseph Gall as the first criminologist,' in R. F. Meier (ed.) *Theory in Criminology: contemporary views*, Beverly Hills, CA: Sage.

Schwartz, M. D. and Hatty, S. E. (eds) (2003) *Controversies in Critical Criminology*, Cincinnati, OH: Anderson Publishing.

Schwendinger, H. and Schwendinger, J. (1970) 'Defenders of order or guardians of human rights?' *Issues in Criminology*, 5: 113–46.

— (1977) 'Social class and the definition of crime,' *Crime & Social Justice*, 7: 4–13.

Shichor, D. and Tibbetts, S. G. (2002) *Victims and Victimization*, Prospect Heights, IL: Waveland Press.

Starr, A. (2000) *Naming the Enemy: anti-corporate movements confront globalization*, London: Zed Books.

Strang, H. (2002) *Repair or Revenge: victims and restorative justice*, Oxford: Clarendon Press.

Sullivan, D. and Tifft, L. (2001) *Restorative Justice: healing the foundations of our everyday lives*, Monsey, NY: Willow Tree Press.

Sutherland, E. H. (1940) 'White-collar criminality,' *American Sociological Review*, 5: 1–12.

Taylor, I., Walton, P. and Young, J. (1973) *The New Criminology: for a social theory of deviance*, New York: Harper and Row.

Tifft, L. (2002) 'Crime and peace: a walk with Richard Quinney,' *Crime & Delinquency*, 48 (2): 243–63.

Trevino, A. J. (1989) 'Richard Quinney: a Wisconsin sociologist,' *Wisconsin Sociologist*, 26(4): 126–34.

Van Ness, D. and Strong, K. H. (2000) 'Restorative justice: justice that promotes healing,' in P. M. Tobolonsky (ed.) *Understanding Victimology*, Cincinnati, OH: Anderson Publishing.

Vold, G. B., Bernard, T. J. and Snipes, J. B. (2002) *Theoretical Criminology*, fifth edn, New York: Oxford University Press.

Von Hirsch, A., Roberts, J., Bottoms, A. E., Roach, K. and Schiff, M. (eds) (2003) *Restorative Justice and Criminal Justice: competing or reconcilable paradigms*, Oxford: Hart Publishing.

Wozniak, J. F. (2002) 'Toward a theoretical model of peacemaking criminology: an essay in honor of Richard Quinney,' *Crime & Delinquency*, 48(2): 204–31.

Wright, R. A. and Friedrichs, D. O. (1991) 'White collar crime in the criminal justice curriculum,' *Journal of Criminal Justice Education*, 2: 95–119.

Yeager, P. C. (2004) 'Law versus justice: from adversarialism to communitarianism,' *Law & Social Inquiry*, 29: 891–915.

Zehr, H. (2002) *The Little Book of Restorative Justice*, Intercourse, PA: Good Books.

30

Shame, shaming and restorative justice

A critical appraisal

Nathan Harris and Shadd Maruna

The concepts of shame and shaming occupy a central, if controversial, position within the theoretical understanding of restorative justice, largely as a result of the formulation of reintegrative shaming theory (RST) (Braithwaite 1989). Although the normative theory of restorative justice should in no way be understood as being synonymous with the theory of reintegrative shaming (Walgrave and Aertsen 1996), the links between the two perspectives are undeniable. Braithwaite's RST has been widely used to explain the procedures used in restorative justice conferences and has been used in the development of conferencing techniques (see, e.g., Hyndman *et al.* 1996; McDonald *et al.* 1994; Moore and Forsythe 1995; O'Connell and Thorsbourne 1995; Retzinger and Scheff 1996; Van Ness and Strong 1997).

In this chapter, we will critically analyze the role of shame within restorative justice. We begin by reviewing the basics of RST. Surprisingly the original formulation of the theory (Braithwaite 1989) includes only a cursory discussion of what the emotion of shame even is. We turn next to the issue of defining shame, drawing on the psychological, sociological, and philosophical writing on the nature of shame, and attempting to distinguish it from related emotions such as guilt, humiliation, and embarrassment. Next, we look at the criticisms of RST, in particular those arguing that shame and shaming do not belong in restorative justice work. Finally, we conclude by seeking to salvage the notion of shaming within restorative justice, in particular, by drawing on the newer notion of 'shame management' (Ahmed *et al.* 2001). We argue that the concept of shame is indeed a dangerous emotion, but rather than trying to avoid it (which is probably impossible), restorative justice interventions are well suited to the task of managing and working constructively with the shame that all parties experience in situations of crime and conflict.

The reintegrative shaming thesis

The theory of reintegrative shaming argues that the importance of social disapproval has generally been underestimated by institutions of criminal justice as well as criminological theory. It argues that to understand crime rates we need to look at the degree to which offending is shamed and whether that shaming is reintegrative or stigmatic.

Braithwaite (1989) defines reintegrative shaming as disapproval that is respectful of the person, is terminated by forgiveness, does not label the person as evil, nor allows condemnation to result in a master status trait. The theory predicts that the practice of reintegrative shaming will result in less offending. Conversely, stigmatizing shaming is not respectful of the person, is not terminated by forgiveness, labels the person as evil and allows them to attain a master status trait. RST predicts that this latter type of shaming results in greater levels of offending (Braithwaite 1989; Makkai and Braithwaite 1994).

Although an important feature of the theory is that it integrates the predictions of several theoretical perspectives into a single framework, its focus upon shaming is probably its most distinctive contribution. The theory defines shaming as:

> all societal processes of expressing social disapproval which have the intention or effect of invoking remorse in the person being shamed and/or condemnation by others who become aware of the shaming.
> (Braithwaite 1989: 100)

This conception of shaming is distinctively broad, such that shaming is not necessarily public, humiliating or even defined as a special type of behavior. It might, for example, involve a discussion between parents and a child of how an act impacted upon others. Equally, a fine handed down by a court might be evaluated on the extent to which it is shaming: the extent to which it is an expression of disapproval towards the offender's behavior.

Use of the term 'shaming,' rather than simply 'disapproval,' implies the expectation that the process will result in a shame-related emotion and that this emotion is an important quality of the interaction. In arguing for the positive effects of reintegrative shaming, Braithwaite (1989: 69–75) highlights two mechanisms at work here.

One of these is that reintegrative shaming is an effective deterrent, particularly when it comes from those who the individual is close to, because it poses a threat to relationships that are valued. Yet, reintegrative shaming is meant to transcend the rational actor model of deterrence. The second mechanism, which Braithwaite suggests is more important, is that reintegrative shaming communicates that certain behaviors are morally wrong and thus builds internalized controls or conscience. Braithwaite (1989: 72) argues:

> Shaming is more pregnant with symbolic content than punishment. Punishment is a denial of confidence in the morality of the offender by reducing norm compliance to a crude cost–benefit calculation; shaming can be a reaffirmation of the morality of the offender by expressing personal disappointment that the offender should do something so out of character.

Although the specific emotion is not clearly identified, both of these mechanisms, fear of disapproval and bad conscience, allude to shame-related emotions. The implication, which has not yet been empirically tested, is that the effect of disapproval on behavior is mediated by the emotions that disapproval causes or what Braithwaite labels 'shame.' Still, despite the central role assigned to shame in his theory, Braithwaite (1989) provided almost no analysis of what the concept is and how it works.

What is shame?

Shame is a mysterious emotion. As illustrated by James Gilligan (1996: 64) and others, the etymological origins of the word 'shame' can help to provide some insight into the word's intended meaning. The word 'shame' derives from Old Germanic roots meaning to clothe or cover oneself, and in Greek the same word (*pudenda*) is used to refer to both shame and human genitalia. Shame, then, refers to an experience of exposure – as in the proverb 'shame dwells in the eyes' (Gilligan 1996: 71).

Save, perhaps, for a few brief moments in the Garden of Eden, these shame-related emotions appear to be universally experienced among humans. Yet, they are not well understood in academic work. Frankly, if one wants to understand shame and related emotions, one would learn more by turning to poetry, literature, and art than, for example, neuropsychology. This is not, however, from a lack of trying. Shame has been a central focus of clinicians (e.g. Lindsay-Hartz 1984), psychologists (Tomkins 1987; Nathanson 1992), anthropologists (Mead 1937; Benedict 1946), moral philosophers (Williams 1993; Taylor 1985), sociologists (Goffman 1959; Scheff and Retzinger 1991), legal scholars (Kahan 1996) and criminologists (Grasmick and Bursik 1990), to name just a few. The problem is that as this theoretical work on shame has occurred across so many disciplines and in rather a haphazard manner, well-defined schools of thought have not been systematically reviewed on the subject and there is no one obvious way to build a coherent typology to guide research. The three conceptions of shame described below (see also Harris 2001) are intended to provide an organizing framework rather than a neat typology.

Shame as a social threat

The first conception that can be identified characterizes shame as a result of the individual's perception of social rejection or disapproval. We will call it the social threat conception. Scheff and Retzinger (1991) and Leary (2000) both describe this as the perception that one's relationships or social bonds with others have been damaged or destroyed. Gilbert (1997) hypothesizes that shame is related to the perception of being unattractive to others, while Gibbons (1990)

discusses it as the result of not receiving approval. The anthropological perspectives of Benedict (1946) and Mead (1937) describe the emotion as a product of perceived disapproval. While these theories vary in their explanations of why people are sensitive to social evaluation, they all emphasize the need to be accepted by others. Leary (2000) argues that the need to have strong personal ties is a basic human motive, while Gilbert (1997) suggests that there is an evolutionary need to maintain status. Scheff (1996a) argues that shame is related to the person's perception of his or her own self-worth. An important characteristic of this conception is that it describes shame, in the words of Scheff, as exterior and constraining. The individual feels shame as a result of others' decisions to reject. As a result shame, or the fear of shame, is described as a powerful motivation for individuals to continually monitor and work on personal relationships and to comply with social expectations at a broader level. This perspective can be summarized as the *social threat conception*.

Shame as personal failure

The second conception that can be identified – the personal failure conception – is based upon the proposition that shame occurs when an individual perceives that they have failed to live up to their standards and this leads to the perception that the whole self is a failure. For H. B. Lewis (1971) and Wurmser (1994) failure is defined by the perception that the ego is not as good as the ego-ideal. M. Lewis (1992) defines shame as the attribution that the whole self has failed, while Lindsay-Hartz (1984) focuses not on failure to live up to an ideal but on failure to meet a minimum standard. Finally, affect theorists, Kaufman (1996) and Nathanson (1997) describe the feelings associated with shame as perceived inferiority and failure. The feature common to the second conception of shame is a feeling of failure attributed to the whole self. Unlike other emotions, such as guilt, the focus of attention is the self rather than, for example, a transgression or rule that might have been broken. Significantly, this conception does not suggest that the perception of failure results necessarily from social interaction but rather that it can occur in any context. This perspective can be summarized as the *personal failure conception*.

Shame as ethical threat

The third conception cuts across these two literatures and offers a conception that incorporates the notion of wrongdoing that is recognized by the individual and society. For Harré (1990) shame is connected with serious transgression as well as the idea of fault. The individual feels shame for having intentionally committed a wrong. This is implicit in Williams' (1993) description of shame as resulting from the perception that an abstract respected other, defined in ethical terms, would think badly of us. Taylor (1985) also emphasizes the ethical nature of shame. Shame is tied to the loss of self-respect, which defines what the individual feels is tolerable and what is not. These theories take on board the personal failure conception through recognizing the violation of internalized standards as a cause of shame. At the same time, they recognize the standards as incorporating wrongdoing and the transgression of social norms. As such, this *ethical conception* of shame recognizes the significance of social context. In summary, the ethical conception of shame acknowledges the importance that others play in feelings of shame, recognizes a shared moral code across individuals, and suggests that it is moral influence rather than rejection that is significant.

Central to all three of these accounts of shame are assumptions about how shame is distinct from related emotions (such as guilt, embarrassment, envy, low self-esteem, etc.), and it has been by testing these proposed distinctions that researchers have sought to empirically explore the emotion. This has been done primarily by asking participants to recall incidents in which they have felt shame, guilt, and/or embarrassment, and to describe their experiences of these emotions. Such studies confirm that people recall shame as involving concern at others' disapproval, negative evaluation of the self, and feelings of having done wrong (Lindsay-Hartz 1984). They also find that people report differences among experiences of shame, guilt, and embarrassment. For example, Wicker *et al.* (1983) found that when describing experiences of shame, participants reported feeling more helpless, self-conscious, and alienated from others (among other things) than they did when describing experiences of guilt. Similar results were found by Tangney, Miller *et al.* (1996), who also reported that embarrassment was perceived as less negative and as having fewer moral implications than either shame or guilt.

Although participants distinguish between the shame-related emotions, differences between their reported characteristics tend to be small in comparison to the similarities found (Wicker *et al.* 1983: 38). These studies have also provided only equivocal support for differentiating shame and guilt on the theoretical dimensions discussed above. Research has not found strong support for the proposition that shame is associated with greater evaluation by others than guilt (Tangney, Miller *et al.* 1996; Wicker *et al.* 1983) and evidence as to whether shame involves greater evaluation of the self than guilt is also equivocal (Tangney, Miller *et al.* 1996; Wicker *et al.* 1983; but see Niedenthal *et al.* 1994). A growing body of research (Harder 1995; Tangney 1991; Tangney, Wagner *et al.* 1992) has found these distinctions useful in measuring the disposition to feel either emotion (shame- and guilt-proneness). However, these studies impose a distinction between the emotions rather than testing for differences. As a

455

result, it can be concluded that there is still uncertainty about whether there is a distinction between shame and guilt and, if so, the basis of that distinction (Harris 2003; Sabini and Silver 1997). Studies into the nature of these emotions have also examined them in very general contexts. These emotions may occur differently within criminal justice, where someone's actions are clearly sanctioned as being against the law.

Can shame be restorative?

Notions of shaming, along with the implication that offenders should feel shame, are not uncontroversial within the restorative justice community and there are several reasons for legitimate suspicion of utilizing this concept as an organizing framework. First and most obviously, the emotion of shame has been linked to numerous explanations for violent behavior. The eminent prison psychologist James Gilligan (1996: 110) argues that the emotion of shame is 'the primary or ultimate cause of all violence' and claims 'I have yet to see a serious act of violence that was not provoked by the experience of feeling shamed and humiliated, disrespected and ridiculed.' Likewise, Thomas Scheff (1996b) argues that the 'purpose' of violence is to diminish the intensity of personal shame by discharging it in the form of violence toward others. Both Gilligan and Scheff account for the appeal of leaders such as Hitler by their ability to transform the shame of a humiliated people into righteous indignation against a scapegoat 'other.' To promote shame and shaming, then, in the name of peace-making and violence reduction appears on the surface to be an absurdity.

In response to the growing use of shaming punishments in American criminal courts Massaro (1997) urged greater caution in applying notions of shame and shaming to criminal justice because the emotion is a complex, context-dependent response that is potentially harmful to offenders and criminogenic. So-called 'shaming punishments' that became popular as alternative sanctions with some US judges in the 1990s included orders for offenders to carry signs or attach stickers to their cars that indicated their offence, or else engage in unpaid work during which they were publicly identified as offenders being punished. Massaro argues that this 'modern' kind of shaming is one that outcasts certain segments of society in a way that does not protect the individuals' dignity and ultimately undermines the dignity of the whole community. In addition to arguing against the decency of following this stigmatizing approach she argues that the complexity of shame emotions is such that courts are ill-equipped to handle the emotion and that the effect of shaming on offenders will be difficult to predict.

While Massaro's critique is not directed at restorative justice, which most commentators think is inherently more capable than courts of handling the complex emotions provoked by an offence (Harris et al. 2004), a number of scholars have also expressed concern at the use of shaming within restorative practices. Maxwell and Morris (2002; Morris 2002) disagree with the idea that shaming (disapproval) within family group conferences is the mechanism that results in remorse. They argue that 'There is certainly nothing in the processes or practices of family group conferences of family group conferences in New Zealand that is explicitly geared towards expressing disapproval in order to invoke shame or remorse in the offender' (Maxwell and Morris 2002: 279). Morris (2002) argues that shaming is a dangerous proposition in restorative conferences because even with the best of intentions shaming might be interpreted by offenders as stigmatizing. This concern is shared by Van Stokkom (2002), who argues that planned shaming efforts may block communication with offenders and consequently risk generating counter disapproval rather than restoration.

Divided by a common language

In part, these concerns and criticisms of shaming reflect different understandings of what is meant by the word 'shame.' Unlike Braithwaite, Gilligan (1996: 71) explicitly equates shaming with 'mocking,' 'despising' and 'scorning' and uses the term 'shame' to refer to a deep-rooted sense of personal worthlessness. Likewise, the concerns raised by Massaro (1997) and Maxwell and Morris (2002) are directed towards types of shaming (e.g. those advocated by Kahan 1996, and others) that Braithwaite's (1989) theory would classify as highly stigmatizing and non-reintegrative. This is most clearly evident in Massaro's concern regarding the use of shaming punishments in American criminal court cases. Forcing offenders to publicly humiliate themselves by means such as holding placards which announce their crimes is directly opposite to what RST advocates. While completely rejecting the use of this type of shaming, RST suggests that disapproval which is reintegrative is constructive in reducing re-offending.

While it is easy to see the difference between these overtly stigmatizing forms of shaming and what Braithwaite proposes, Maxwell and Morris also express concern at shaming within restorative justice conferences. They argue that direct expressions of disapproval are not a common feature of family group conferences, which focus more clearly on emphasizing the consequences that an offence had on its victims (Maxwell and Morris 2002: 278). Morris (2002), furthermore, worries that even if direct disapproval is intended to reintegrate it may not be interpreted as such by the offender. The degree to which disapproval can be expressed directly and yet also be perceived as reintegrative (or non-stigmatizing) is an empirical question that is yet to be fully explored. However, this also highlights an important difference in how the term is understood. Whereas Maxwell and Morris understand shaming as the verbal expression of disapproval, Braithwaite argues that shaming includes all social processes which express disapproval. Simply convening a family group conference expresses the community's concern or disapproval of an offence, as does discussion of the consequences of an offence. Indeed Braithwaite and Braithwaite (2001: 33) argue that it is these indirect forms of shaming that are most likely to be reintegrative:

> Finally, we hypothesize that the genius of well-constructed restorative justice processes is that they only confront wrongdoing indirectly, implicitly inviting the wrongdoer themselves to be the one who directly confronts it, apologizes and seeks to right the wrong. This indirectness is mostly accomplished by proceeding simply to invite the stakeholders affected by the crime, especially the victim, victim supporters and loved ones of the offender, to describe how the crime has affected them.

As Maxwell and Morris (2002) argue, these differences in how shaming is interpreted are not simply a semantic quibble as they are critical to how the theory is understood and may represent a significant obstacle to its translation into restorative practices. The implication of this critique is that where restorative practice seeks to apply the implications of reintegrative shaming theory it needs to be done in such a way that it is sensitive to the cultural sensitivities as to how disapproval can be indicated without it also being perceived as stigmatizing. In a recent revision of reintegrative shaming theory Braithwaite and Braithwaite (2001) acknowledge that additional shaming in contexts that are already highly shaming is unnecessary and may even be interpreted as stigmatizing.

Shame, guilt or remorse?

Although some scholars (Maxwell and Morris 2002, Van Stokkom 2002) have questioned whether the word 'shaming' is appropriate to describe the reintegrative forms of disapproval envisaged by RST, Braithwaite is clear in his use of the word to signify actions that result in a shame-related emotion (Braithwaite and Braithwaite 2001). A more substantial criticism of shaming is the challenge to whether shame is a good emotion for an offender to feel at all. Indeed, Morris (2002) argues that the reintegrative shaming perspective is mistaken in placing an emphasis on the emotion of shame. She argues that the more important mechanisms in restorative justice are the eliciting of remorse in offenders as a result of empathy. Empathy, she argues, results from discussing the consequences that an offence has for the victims.

Taylor (2002) also views shame as a dangerous emotion to invoke in offenders because it is a threat to the offender's sense of self-worth and is hence potentially destructive. Such concerns are provided some support by research which suggests that the propensity to feel shame, rather than guilt, as a result of transgressions is associated with less constructive responses, such as feelings of anger and hostility (Tangney 1991). Remorse is described by Taylor as a better central concept than shame, or guilt, because it is directed towards the behavior, as opposed to the self, and does not involve any negative self-directed feelings. Maxwell and Morris (2000) have found some support for the importance of remorse in a study that examined recidivism among a sample of offenders who had attended a restorative conference ten years previously. This research found that, among other variables, not being made to feel bad about oneself during the conference (which can be interpreted as a measure of not being stigmatized) and feelings of remorse, as measured through offender self-reports, predicted lower recidivism.

While accepting the importance of remorse, Harris et al. (2004) have since argued that it may not be possible to quarantine offenders from feelings of shame. This is because feelings of shame or guilt will often occur following apprehension for an offence due to the inevitable social strains caused by that event regardless of what criminal justice interventions do. Perceptions of having done the wrong thing, of having disappointed others, and fear that one will be rejected are likely in the aftermath of being caught. Furthermore, it is argued that any kind of social censure for the offence, such as a restorative conference, which causes offenders to feel remorse is likely to spill over into feelings of shame. It does not seem likely that the moral emotion that offenders feel can be chosen in the way implied by Taylor (2002), particularly in those contexts where a community wants to show that it does not support a particular type of behavior.

Some empirical evidence supports this proposition. In a study which examines the shame-related emotions experienced by offenders in family group conferences and court cases in Australia, Harris (2003) found that feelings of shame and guilt were not differentiated by participants. This suggests that those individuals who reported feeling bad because others had been hurt – feelings which are associate with guilt (Baumeister et al. 1995) or remorse (Taylor 2002) – also reported feelings of anger and shame at the self. Analyses also show that this emotion of shame-guilt was not a response to stigmatization but actually predicted by reintegration (having been treated with respect and forgiveness) which seems to confirm that it is difficult for justice interventions to avoid provoking shame-related emotions no matter how careful they attempt to be. (Indeed, if the justice system really wants offenders to avoid feeling ashamed, the best thing it could do might be to treat them so harshly and unjustly that offenders feel as if they are the victims themselves and hence have nothing to feel guilty about.) It is equally significant that self-reported feelings of shame in this sample seemed to be constructive rather than dysfunctional. That is, the emotion was found to be associated with observed expressions of remorse during conference cases (Harris 2001) as well as being positively correlated with self-reported empathy for those hurt and negatively correlated with feelings of anger and hostility.

From shaming to shame management

While the research just discussed suggests that shame appears to be a fairly constructive emotion, research also suggests that shame can have strongly negative consequences in some circumstances (Ahmed 2001; Lewis 1971; Nathanson 1992; Scheff and Retzinger 1991; Tangney 1991). Indeed, this was evident in the research project discussed above. Harris (2001) found evidence of an 'unresolved' form of shame, which was associated with having been stigmatized and with feelings of anger and hostility towards other people present at the case conference. While the self-reported experience of shame-guilt involved feeling bad during the conference, unresolved shame involved ongoing feelings that one might have been unfairly treated and that issues from the case were unresolved.

These findings are consistent with the research of Scheff and Retzinger (1991; Retzinger 1991), Lewis (1971) and Ahmed (2001) who found that when feelings of shame are not acknowledged and resolved by individuals, the emotion can become maladaptive. Lewis (1971), in particular, identifies a 'by-passed' form of shame that involves 'back and forth ideation about guilt' (p. 234) which continues to 'plague' the person over a period of time. She argues that in by-passed shame the person does not acknowledge or resolve their negative feelings and that this results in repetitive and obsessive thoughts about the event. Such unresolved shame is associated with feelings of anger and hostility towards others (see

also Nathanson 1992; Retzinger 1991). This is also consistent with research by Tangney and her colleagues (Tangney et al. 1992; Tangney, Wagner et al. 1996) who have found that a disposition to internalize negative feeling about the self ('shame-proneness') is linked to the disposition to feel hostility towards others.

These findings suggest that there is a more complicated relationship between shaming and the emotions it produces than initially outlined by Braithwaite (1989) (see Ahmed et al. 2001). It has generally been expected that shaming, and specifically reintegrative shaming, results in feelings of shame and that this emotion is significant in the reduction of offending. These findings suggest that a significant function of different types of shaming (reintegrative v. stigmatic) is not whether they produce shame but the effect they have on how individuals respond to that shame. While the experience of shame can involve the acknowledgment of wrongdoing and is associated with empathy for those hurt, unresolved (or unacknowledged) forms of shame would seem to result in an inability to resolve issues arising from the event and feelings of hostility towards others.

This suggests that what may be important about the types of shaming proposed in RST is the degree to which they encourage or discourage these different forms of shame. Reintegrative shaming may produce a positive effect by assisting individuals to cope with feelings of shame in more constructive ways, whereas the risk of stigmatization (or even no shaming at all) may be that it prevents individuals from resolving important issues and results in ongoing feelings of unresolved shame. Shaming maybe important for reducing offending not because it results in shame but because it provides a mechanism that assists offenders to manage their feeling of shame in more constructive ways (see Ahmed et al. 2001).

As such, in a recent revision to the RST, Braithwaite and Braithwaite (2001) argue that the focus of RST should shift from 'shaming' to 'shame management.' Braithwaite and Braithwaite's (2001) revision of reintegrative shaming theory does not alter the theory's primary prediction that reintegrative shaming reduces offending (while stigmatic shaming increases offending). Instead, it proposes that the reason for this is because individuals are more likely to manage any feelings of shame that occur more constructively if they are reintegrated rather than stigmatized. Questions about the individual's identity and their relationship to others, which are raised by the offence, are more easily managed if it is communicated to them that they are basically a good person and that they are accepted by those they care about (see Maruna 2001; Maruna and Copes 2005).

Conclusions: restorative justice as shame management

One claim of restorative justice has been that it is more reintegrative than the traditional court system. This was supported by research which demonstrates that participants assigned to conferences perceived others to be more disapproving, yet more reintegrative and less stigmatizing, than did participants who attended court cases (Harris 2001). Random allocation of participants to court and conference cases suggests that we can be somewhat more confident that these differences are caused by characteristics of the interventions themselves. As discussed, these differences in the way that disapproval was perceived corresponded to differences in the emotions reported by participants, with more shame or guilt freely reported following conferences and more unresolved shame and embarrassment-exposure reported following court cases. If emerging research on the shame-related emotions (Ahmed 2001, Harris 2003; Tangney et al. 1992; Tangney, Wagner et al. 1996) is correct, then the way in which offenders man-

age these feelings has an important impact on how they react to the event. Although more research is needed to verify the significance of these emotions (particularly in relation to offending), an implication of this work is that an important characteristic of criminal justice interventions is the degree to which they encourage offenders to manage feelings of shame constructively.

In short, it appears that 'shame will always be with us,' to coin a phrase. Those persons caught up in the criminal justice system are a long way from the Garden of Eden and the combination of their tasting of forbidden fruits and their exposure through criminal detection probably means that avoiding shame altogether is an impossibility. This is not altogether a bad thing. The complex emotion seems to have both very good and very bad consequences. Yet, shame is most problematic when it is unacknowledged, unresolved, and hence becomes projected on to others in a scapegoat fashion. Restorative justice interventions that allow all participants in an event to tell their stories (Zehr 1990) seem well suited to the difficult work of helping victims, offenders, and their supporters acknowledge, work through, and ultimately resolve the shame they are experiencing.

References

Ahmed, E. (2001) 'Part III. Shame management: regulating bullying,' in E. Ahmed, N. Harris, J. Braithwaite, and V. Braithwaite (2001) *Shame Management Through Reintegration*, Melbourne: Cambridge University Press.

Ahmed, E., Harris, N., Braithwaite, J. and Braithwaite, V. (2001) *Shame Management Through Reintegration*, Melbourne: Cambridge University Press.

Baumeister, R. F., Stillwell, A. M. and Heatherton, T. F. (1995) 'Interpersonal aspects of guilt: evidence from narrative studies,' in J. P. Tangney and K. W. Fischer (eds) *Self Conscious Emotions: the psychology of shame, guilt, embarrassment, and pride*, New York: Guilford Press.

Benedict, R. (1946) *The Chrysanthemum and the Sword: patterns of Japanese culture*, Boston: Houghton Mifflin.

Braithwaite, J. (1989) *Crime, Shame and Reintegration*, Cambridge: Cambridge University Press.

Braithwaite, J. and Braithwaite, V. (2001) 'Part I. Shame, shame management and regulation,' in E. Ahmed, N. Harris, J. Braithwaite and V. Braithwaite (2001) *Shame Management Through Reintegration*, Melbourne: Cambridge University Press.

Gibbons, F. X. (1990) 'The impact of focus of attention and affect on social behaviour,' in W. R. Crozier (ed.) *Shyness and Embarrassment: perspectives from social psychology*, Cambridge: Cambridge University Press.

Gilbert, P. (1997) 'The evolution of social attractiveness and its role in shame, humiliation, guilt and therapy,' *British Journal of Medical Psychology*, 70: 113–47.

Gilligan, J. (1996) *Violence: our deadly epidemic and its causes*, New York: A Grosset/Putnam Books.

Goffman, E. (1959) *The Presentation of the Self in Everyday Life*, Garden City, NJ: Doubleday-Anchor Books.

Grasmick, H. G. and Bursik, R. J. (1990) 'Conscience, significant others, and rational choice: extending the deterrence model,' *Law and Society Review*, 24(3): 837–61.

Harder, D. W. (1995) 'Shame and guilt assessment, and relationships of shame- and guilt-proneness to psychopathology,' in J. P. Tangney and K. W. Fischer (eds) *Self Conscious Emotions: the psychology of shame, guilt, embarrassment, and pride*, New York: Guilford Press.

Harré, R. (1990) 'Embarrassment: a conceptual analysis,' in W. R. Crozier (ed.) *Shyness and Embarrassment: perspectives from social psychology*, Cambridge: Cambridge University Press.

Harris, N. (2001) 'Part II. shaming and shame: regulating drink driving,' in E. Ahmed, N. Harris, J. Braithwaite and V. Braithwaite (2001) *Shame Management Through Reintegration*, Melbourne: Cambridge University Press.

— (2003) 'Reassessing the dimensionality of the moral emotions,' *British Journal of Psychology*, 94(4): 457–73.

Harris, N., Walgrave, L. and Braithwaite, J. (2004) 'Emotional dynamics in restorative conferences,' *Theoretical Criminology*, 8(2): 191–210.

Hyndman, M., Thorsborne, M. and Wood, S. (1996) *Community Accountability Conferencing: trial report*, Brisbane: Department of Education, Queensland.

Kahan, D. M. (1996) 'What do alternative sanctions mean?' *University of Chicago Law Review*, 63: 591–653.

Kaufman, G. (1996) *The Psychology of Shame: theory and treatment of shame-based syndromes*, second edn, New York: Springer Publishing.

Leary, M. R. (2000) 'Affect, cognition, and the social emotions: a theory of relational devaluation,' in J. P. Forgas (ed.) *Feeling and Thinking: the role of affect in social cognition*, Cambridge: Cambridge University Press.

Lewis, H. B. (1971) *Shame and Guilt in Neurosis*, New York: International Universities Press.

Lewis, M. (1992) *Shame: the exposed self*, New York: Free Press.

Lindsay-Hartz, J. (1984) 'Contrasting experiences of shame and guilt,' *American Behavioral Scientist*, 27: 689–704.

McDonald, J. M., O'Connell, T. A., Moore, D. B. and Bransbury, E. (1994) *Convening Family Conferences: training manual*, New South Wales: New South Wales Police Academy.

Makkai, T. and Braithwaite, J. (1994) 'Reintegrative shaming and compliance with regulatory standards,' *Criminology*, 32: 361–85.

Maruna, S. (2001) *Making Good: how ex-convicts reform and rebuild their lives*, Washington, DC: American Psychological Association.

Maruna, S. and Copes, H. (2005) 'Excuses, excuses: what have we learned in five decades of neutralization research?' *Crime and Justice: A Review of Research*, 32: 221–320.

Massaro, T. M. (1997) 'The meanings of shame: Implications for legal reform,' *Psychology, Public Policy, and Law*, 3(4): 645–704.

Maxwell, G. and Morris, A. (2000) *Understanding Reoffending*, Wellington, NZ: Institute of Criminology, Victoria University.

— (2002) 'The role of shame, guilt, and remorse in restorative justice processes for young people,' in E. Weitekamp and H.-J. Kerner (eds) *Restorative Justice: theoretical foundations*, Cullompton, Devon, UK: Willan Publishing.

Mead, M. (1937) *Cooperation and Competition among Primitive Peoples*, New York: McGraw-Hill.

Moore, D. and Forsythe, L. (1995) *A New Approach to Juvenile Justice: an evaluation of family conferencing in Wagga Wagga*, Wagga Wagga: Juvenile Justice, The Centre for Rural Research.

Morris, A. (2002) 'Shame, guilt and remorse: experiences from family group conferences in New Zealand,' in I. Weijers and A. Duff (eds) *Punishing Juveniles: Principles and critique*, Oxford: Hart Publishing.

Nathanson, D. L. (1992) *Shame and Pride: affect, sex and the birth of the self*, New York: W. W. Norton.

— (1997) 'Affect theory and the compass of shame,' in Melvin R. Lansky (ed.) *The Widening Scope of Shame*, Hillsdale, NJ: Analytic Press, pp. 339–54.

Niedenthal, P. M., Tangney, J. P. and Gavanski, I. (1994) '"If only I weren't" versus "If only I hadn't": distinguishing shame and guilt in counterfactual thinking,' *Journal of Personality and Social Psychology*, 67(4): 585–95.

O'Connell, T. and Thorsborne, M. (1995) 'Student behaviour outcomes: choosing appropriate paths,' paper presented at the conference 'A Restorative Approach to Interventions for Serious Incidents of Harm in the School Setting'.

Retzinger, S. M. (1991) *Violent Emotions: shame and rage in marital quarrels*, Newbury Park: Sage.

Retzinger, S. M. and Scheff, T. J. (1996) 'Strategy for community conferences: emotions and social bonds,' in B. Galaway and J. Hudson (eds) *Restorative Justice: international perspectives*, Monsey, NY: Criminal Justice Press.

Sabini, J. and Silver, M. (1997) 'In defense of shame: shame in the context of guilt and embarrassment,' *Journal for the Theory of Social Behaviour*, 27(1): 1–15.

Scheff, T. J. (1996a) 'Self-esteem and shame: unlocking the puzzle,' in R. Kwan (ed.) *Individuality and Social Control: essays in honour of Tamotsu Shibutani*, Greenwich: JAI Press.

— (1996b) 'Shame and the origins of World War II: Hitler's appeal to German people,' in D. Parker and R. Dalziel (eds) *Shame and the Modern Self*, Victoria: Australian Scholarly Publishing.

Scheff, T. J. and Retzinger, S. M. (1991) *Emotions and Violence: shame and rage in destructive conflicts*, Lexington, MA: Lexington Books/D. C. Heath.

Tangney, J. P. (1991) 'Moral affect: the good, the bad, and the ugly,' *Journal of Personality and Social Psychology*, 61(4): 598–607.

Tangney, J. P., Wagner, P., Fletcher, C. and Gramzow, R. (1992) 'Shamed into anger? The relation of shame and guilt to anger and self-reported aggression,' *Journal of Personality and Social Psychology*, 62(4): 669–75.

Tangney, J. P., Miller, R. S., Flicker, L. and Barlow, D. H. (1996) 'Are shame, guilt, and embarrassment distinct emotions?' *Journal of Personality and Social Psychology*, 70(6): 1256–69.

Tangney, J. P., Wagner, P. E., Hill-Barlow, D., Marschall, D. E. and Gramzow, R. (1996) 'Relation of shame and guilt to constructive versus destructive responses to anger across the lifespan,' *Journal of Personality and Social Psychology*, 70(4): 797–809.

Taylor, G. (1985) *Pride, Shame and Guilt: emotions of self-assessment*, Oxford: Oxford University Press.

— (2002) 'Guilt, shame and shaming,' in I. Weijers and A. Duff (eds) *Punishing Juveniles: principle and critique*, Oxford: Hart Publishing.

Tomkins, S. S. (1987) 'Shame,' in D. L. Nathanson (ed.) *The Many Faces of Shame*, New York: Guilford Press.

Van Ness, D. and Strong, K. (1997) *Restoring Justice*, Cincinnati: Anderson Publishing.

Van Stokkom, B. (2002) 'Moral emotions in restorative justice conferences: managing shame, designing empathy,' *Theoretical Criminology*, 6(3): 339–60.

Walgrave, L. and Aertsen, I. (1996) 'Reintegrative shaming and restorative justice: interchangeable, complementary or different?,' *European Journal on Criminal Policy and Research*, 4(4): 6785.

Wicker, F. W., Payne, G. C. and Morgan, R. D. (1983) 'Participant descriptions of guilt and shame,' *Motivation and Emotion*, 7: 25–39.

Williams, B. (1993) *Shame and Necessity*, Berkeley: University of California Press.

Wurmser, Leon (1994) *The Mask of Shame*, Northvale, NJ: Jason Aronson.

Zehr, H. (1990) *Changing Lenses: a new focus for criminal justice*, Scottsdale, PA: Herald Press.

31

Community justice versus restorative justice

Contrasts in family of value

Todd R. Clear

Introduction

I think of community justice and restorative justice as second cousins. They share a common ancestry, though they derive from different progenitors. Their common ancestry explains the distinct family resemblance. Despite their likeness, they have differing direct lineages, making their distinctions easy to discern. Like second cousins, they may be married when they mutually attract. In a good marriage, they can be extremely compatible.

Common ancestry

Both of these ideas have their genesis in deeply rooted dissatisfactions with the traditional criminal justice system.

Restorative justice

Most analysts trace the roots of restorative justice back to aboriginal practices that predate colonization by the West. This version of restorative justice portrays itself as an age-old prescription for crime that comes out of the sensitive and sensible practices of pre-democratic societies. While the idea of an ancient restorative justice paradigm is appealing as a critique of contemporary US criminal justice, the restorative justice strategies practiced today are not much more than a generation old. Their early days coincide with the early years of rising prison populations. At the time when the dominant ideology of justice policy makers was 'getting tough' with criminals, restorative justice reformers offered a different idea of what was needed. They called for a version of justice that sought more than 'getting tough' with crime, seeking instead to create sensible outcomes from criminal events.

In the 1970s, the country was lodged in a pattern of spiraling crime rates and hardening political rhetoric about criminals. A new political center was developing around a consensus that crime was out of hand and the criminal justice system needed to be made capable of treating crime with the kind of severe measures that many felt were called for by the extremity of the times. In the 'law 'n' order' ideal, the criminal justice system was asked to take the perspective of the victim of crime. 'What about the victim?' became one of the catch phrases capturing the dominant ethos of the times. A victims' rights movement arose which became associated with increasingly harsh judicial and legislative treatment of crime.

This newly articulated victim-focused idea portrayed victims in a unidimensional fashion. They were more or less innocent targets of unprovoked wrongdoing, and the only way the criminal justice system could give them the respect they needed was to let them speak up at the time of sentencing, describing the extent and painfulness of their losses. The criminal justice system would show its 'respect' for them by imposing the harshest possible sentence on the person convicted of the crime. To accommodate this new orientation, prosecutors opened up 'victim support' offices that worked with victims of crime to ensure active participation in the adversary process and to help document their losses in ways that would influence judges at the time of sentencing. The victims' movement which asserted itself during this time claimed the authority to speak for victims of crime, and almost always pressed for two reforms: financial support to help victims cope with the consequences of their victimization and harsher penalties for those convicted of crimes. Working within an adversarial model, the victims' movement was a main force in a complex of political alignments which ended up fueling a round of adversarial methods and outcomes ever harsher to the defendant.

The irony, of course, was that for all of the victim-centric rhetoric, victims themselves have maintained a back-seat role in court processes. Their testimony at sentencing has become more influential in court outcomes but prosecutors dominate the courtroom scene, speaking for the state, the community, and the victim alike. They call upon victims merely to describe their injuries and ask for the most severe penalties. After these rituals of suffering, victims often recede back into the courtroom woodwork.

Against this wildly popular but clearly ambivalent system of concern for the victim, restorative justice emerged as an alternative victim-oriented ethic with a dramatically different vision of who the victim is and what the victim's needs are. The restorative justice movement recognized the existence of many, many situations in which victims and offenders are connected by their lives' circumstances (and will continue to be connected by virtue of the crime itself). In many of these circumstances, harsh punishments are felt not just by the person convicted of the crime but by the victim of the crime as well. Moreover, the harsh punishment often felt good at the time of sentencing but left the victim of the crime with an abiding sense of emptiness in the weeks and months that followed the imposition of the sentence. Restorative justice advocates said that what victims *really* needed was not tougher penalties on offenders but: (1) a chance to speak face to face to the wrongdoer about the crime and spell out how it had affected the victim; and (2) concrete restitution compensating for the losses incurred as a victim. Restorative justice enthusiasts claimed that the adversarial practices of the criminal justice system, instead of helping these two outcomes to happen, impeded them from taking place. People convicted of crimes who are sent to prison are hardly in a position to make recompense for their crimes, and an adversarial system that emphasizes procedure and technical rules over facts and sentiment cannot lead to emotional closure.

Restorative justice proponents differed from traditional justice reformers in another respect. Rather than seeing victims as simplistically interested in 'getting back at the criminal,' they saw victims in a more complex light. They were people who were injured by crime but, at the same time, capable of seeing the wrongdoer as a human being who could be dealt with in other than draconian ways – if only the adjudication and penalty processes could be designed to allow these sorts of sentiments to emerge.

To create these restorative justice victim-oriented resolutions of criminal events, a variety of interactive strategies have been employed, from mediation meetings to sentencing circles, and more. All of these strategies give victims of crime a more prominent role in the process of deciding what penalty ought to be constructed, in order to meet the aims of restorative justice, and how it ought to be carried out. They also offer a ritual of interaction that gives both the accused and the victimized a chance to express thoughts and feelings. *In this way, restorative justice is a deeply penetrating critique of formal justice processes and a profound challenge to the adversarial due process model of criminal justice.* Today's restorative justice movement was born from a sense of dismay at the way the criminal justice system transformed the emotional appeal of a victim's suffering into a crass call for punitive suffering.

Thus, for the entire duration of the growth of criminal justice – since the early 1970s – restorative justice has stood as a critique of the criminal justice perception of the victim and strategy for holding the wrongdoer accountable in the victim's behalf. For most of the last thirty years, it has been a relatively quiet voice in the background, heard by few and spoken by few; it is only within the last decade or so that the ideas of restorative justice have begun to resonate with the general public.

Community justice

Community justice proponents are no less dissatisfied with traditional criminal justice, but what bothers them is different.

Community justice arises as an idea not at the outset of the get-tough movement but in its latter days, a good decade or more into the heights of the mass incarceration movement. It is not a reaction to what the justice juggernaut claimed about victims of crime and those who afflicted them but is a reaction to the very juggernaut itself.

Community justice advocates typically begin their public claims with a description of the stunning growth of criminal justice

since the 1970s (especially the prison). The numbers themselves are always stupefying in their recitation, because even the thick-skinned are taken aback when they hear that prisons have grown six-fold, or people of color are locked up at unconscionable rates. The stark description of the growth of the penal apparatus loosens the audience up for the community justice narrative. Advocates point to the enormous sense in which the growth of the justice system has not resulted in better, safer, more livable communities.

In this way, they do not dispute the traditional claims of criminal justice about how to deal with victims of crime, so much as they dispute the traditional claims of what the justice system ought to be accomplishing in the first place. For the last thirty years, justice advocates have said that the criminal justice system should apprehend as many offenders as it can prosecute and punish them with the fullness of the law. Under this scenario, the larger and tougher system is its own evaluation – it is doing what it ought to with more and more felons. Community justice advocates say that this is a mistaken aim. The prosecution of felons and their punishment is not an end in itself, it is a means to an end: to make communities better places for people to live, work, and raise families. *The claim is that the growing criminal justice system has, in the end, done more damage than good, and that its strategies need to be recalibrated to take account of what communities need rather than merely what wrongdoers deserve.* The community justice reformer argues that the adversarial model of catch 'em and jail 'em is at best largely irrelevant to the quality of a community's life, and sometimes even antithetical. What we need is not strategies to deal with individuals who engage in misdeeds but those that target places where these misdeeds concentrate. Arrests, charges, and punishments will, of necessity, occur, but their existence should not deflect attention from the main objective: to make places afflicted by crime and

465

disorder better places for the people who spend time there.

To achieve this vision, community justice proponents have developed a wide array of strategies that increase the prominence of community-level concerns and community members in the justice system. Some of these programs involved partnerships with criminal justice agencies, others have been much more local. All of them have in common the way they give prominence to the communities that are hardest hit by crime and have the most criminal justice involvement. All of them justify their strategies in promises of better communities.

Differing parents

In this way, the restorative justice movement begins with a concern about the victims of crime, and the community justice movement starts with a concern about impoverished communities. This difference explains why the restorative justice movement predates the community justice movement, for community justice could not have arisen as an appealing voice at the same time as restorative justice. While they both develop their strengths as counterpoints to a harsh, burgeoning justice system, community justice bases its case on an undeniable dissatisfaction with the feeble fruits of thirty years of growing criminal justice. It thus could not emerge as a new voice until the growth had reached a point where its poor consequences were undeniable. By contrast, restorative justice begins with alarm about the manipulative use of victims of crime for punitive purposes, and this alarm arises as soon as the victims' movement became aligned with the prosecution function.

Nonetheless, the great grandparents of both restorative justice and community justice are the various inadequacies of the adversarial system that gave rise to the rapidly growing penal justice system. Claims that society needs a harsh justice system and that ever-tougher punishments of those who are apprehended for crime will resolve the problems of society are directly disputed by restorative and community justice rhetoric. Thus, restorative justice and community justice both hail from a family of ideas that seek to soften the adversarial model and humanize its practice. That is the family resemblance. Restorative justice comes to life as a reconceptualization of the nature of the relationship between victims and wrongdoers, asserting the possibility that a restorative connection between them is possible (even necessary). Community justice shifts the object to be proven criminal justice from the punishment of wrongdoers to strengthening of community life.

Differing family of values

Neither community justice nor restorative justice could have come about without an ailing criminal justice system. That said, they arise from different proximate interests, as indicated in the description above. These differences go deeper, however, and they explain some of the tensions between the two ideas.

Restorative justice

Restorative justice is a theory of justice that asserts 'a right.' It comes from a class of theories that answer the questions 'why should we punish, and how should we punish' by describing the rights and duties of those involved in punitive activity. It bears a family resemblance, then, to retribution (or desert).

It may seem a bit surprising to say that restorative justice is best conceived as a variant of desert theory because it seems to have so little in common with that theory. They are estranged siblings. Desert is a theory that requires guilty people to be punished simply because they deserve it. (It is worth mentioning that there are many variants of this justification, emphasizing different lines of reasoning to arrive at the basic idea of punishment being deserved, and the differences are worth noting in the contexts of some discussions of punishment theory, but not so much here.) Desert sets the severity of punishment to be directly related to the seriousness of the criminal behavior. Restorative justice, of course, cares little about punishments and sets little store in any idea of a 'requirement' to punish. How, then, is it that retribution and restorative justice share a common forebear?

The answer lies in the fact that both are theories of what is 'right.' Desert claims to be correct as a theory because it compares a world in which the guilty are punished as they deserve to a world in which they are not punished, and sees an obvious preference for the former. Desert theorists vary in the degree to which they will entertain the value of rehabilitating or incapacitating those who have broken the law, but they will never give these ideas preference over the more basic requirement that the guilty must be punished according to their deeds. This is obviously not an empirical claim, it is a moral one, and desert theory is first and foremost a theory of what is moral.

The same may be said with regard to restorative justice. Comparing a world in which victims and their wrongdoers are, by virtue of the intervention they experience, restored (as much as possible) to the status and level they occupied before the crime, is simply seen as preferable to any other alternative. According to restorative justice theorists, to restore those afflicted by crime (actor and target alike) to full citizenship and wholeness of mind and body is the highest aspiration we might ask of the justice system, and it is the criterion against which all actions of the justice system ought to be measured. This assertion, like its desert counterpart, is not empirical, it is moral. Under restorative justice, the people who are involved in a criminal event are treated as ends in themselves, and not a means to another end. The integrity of their claim to

be 'whole' is seen as having a priority in the scheme of aims because no other set of outcomes gives them the same level of regard.

That restorative justice is a member of the class of moral theories of 'the right' is illustrated by the easy way in which restorative justice advocates accept 'accountability' (and inconvenience of a sanction) as not only an inevitable aspect of restoration but also typically a desirable one. The restorative justice worker will not allow a sanction to interfere with the aim of restoration because sanctions themselves are not a right. But what a sanction communicates to the victim and the offender about taking responsibility for the crime and providing some evidence of a desire and willingness to forego future criminality is often central to the possibility of restoration. Restoration may make the world a better place but that is not why it is the right aim to seek. It is sought because crime 'breaks things' and responses to crime should therefore repair them. A world in which the equilibrium which existed prior to the crime is restored by the response to crime is seen as superior to a world in which people are punished as they deserve.

Community justice

Community justice comes from a family of values which give important standing to the desire for public safety. It is, thus, a theory of 'the good' rather than the right. Its intellectual ancestors are earlier beliefs that penalties should be designed in ways such that they reform, restrain, or reeducate. Again, it may seem a bit odd to place community justice in this family of utilitarian ideals. The concepts of incapacitation and deterrence do not seem easily to fit the community justice mold, seen at first blush. Public safety is a demanding parent, and the often indirect strategies of community justice can seem a bit immaterial to the hard standard of safe places. But even a cursory

467

look into the heart of community justice will reveal its utilitarian roots.

The test of a community justice strategy is not whether it is 'deserved' by a community (to suggest such a phrase seems curious, in fact). The test of community justice is whether, after the various strategies are put into place, the community is in fact better off. It is a theory built upon the promise of an outcome. In this way, it resembles theories of incapacitation, deterrence, and reform, which are equally outcome-based theories of penal sanctions.

Community justice is not unmindful of moral claims. As for all utilitarian theories, it operates within constraints. For example, it cannot suspend civil rights, nor can it pretend that the distinction between those accused of crimes and those victimized by them can be passed over. Vigilantism is not a legitimate community justice strategy, any more than form-letter apologies are a legitimate restorative justice strategy. Still, it must be recognized that the constraints operating on community justice strategies are not aims in themselves (as they may be for desert theorists) but are rather limitations on action accepted as boundaries on the acceptable.

As often happens with utilitarian strategies, however, there is a tension between the desire for community justice outcomes and the limits we expect the state to accept in doing anything about crime. 'Weed & Seed' programs, arguably community justice in origin, provide an example, as do street sweeps. These strategies can mobilize community sentiment in ways that strengthen intra-group hostility and seem to advantage one sub-group in the community at the expense of another. Even supporters of community justice ideals can find themselves uncomfortable with some of the broader implications of these community mobilization models, not because of what they might accomplish, but because of how they might affect some people who live in these troubled communities.

Family squabbles

Even though restorative justice and community justice share a common heritage of distaste for the traditional criminal justice system, it should be clear from their closer lineage that this shared distrust of criminal justice can be matched by internecine antagonisms.

Most of the disagreements stem, in some way, from the way restorative justice hails from a background of 'right' while community justice upholds an ethic of 'good.' Where restorative justice enthusiasts find little room for negotiation of a central point regarding some principle or another of restoration, community justice advocates will readily discard the idea if it seems inconvenient to the aim of community well-being. While community justice advocates will negotiate all manner of action and strategy as an aspect of building community consensus – and will easily accept compromise, often enthusiastically seek compromise as community-building in its own right – restorative justice leaders often have stronger commitments to bedrock ideas that cannot be displaced.

Thus, when community justice workers create coalitions of police, civic groups, businesses, and faith communities, and develop plans to improve infrastructure or clean filthy streets or provide lighting (or build a park or form a youth group or . . . on and on), their restorative justice second cousins worry about the victim in all this activity. They worry that the victim's voice, already muted by crime and powerlessness, will dissipate entirely in the onslaught of the community (public) agenda. Restorative justice workers do not fully trust the instincts of law enforcement. They do not think that cleaning a park is the same as restoring the specific victim of a crime.

Here is a central difficulty. Community justice advances the interests of an aggregate – a community affected by crime (and justice reactions to crime). Restorative justice reserves its attention for the interests of the individuals caught up in the crime event itself. Where community justice theorists may see a recovering community as a metaphor for restoration following crime, many restorative justice workers feel alarm that the community's agenda is raised above that of the victim or the wrongdoer. Where one reformer sees the overarching need to advance community life, the other sees a danger that community desires will trump individuals' needs. Where one reformer sees too much concern for a process of sanctioning, leaving the problems of community intact, the other sees an appropriate priority being placed on the individual case.

The understandable strain between these belief systems can be increased by the differences in history. As indicated, restorative justice is an older idea. It stayed alive during very difficult times, when the entire energy of the criminal justice constellation – even the supposedly liberal types – was obsessed with 'getting tough.' In those dark days, when it seemed the softest idea around was a craving for intensive supervision with random and periodic drug testing or home confinement with electronic monitoring, restorative justice advocates stayed true to their core principles. In doing so, they suffered frequent taunts from a system interested in tougher stuff. Now that restorative justice has achieved a certain popularity among intellectuals and practitioners alike, we should not be surprised to feel among its earliest proponents a certain sense that restorative justice leaders have stayed honorable through very tough times for this kind of thinking.

Community justice is, by comparison, a johnny-come-lately. While serious writing and thinking about restorative justice is at least a generation old, such thinking about community justice has not yet reached the teenage years. While restorative justice has to stand tough to its principles in the worst of the onslaught of the get-tough years, community justice has benefited from a

growing uneasiness with the underlying ideas of get-toughism and its consequences. In some ways, restorative justice blazed a trail that community justice now enjoys traveling. A certain familial resentment would be understandable.

There is another matter that makes getting along difficult. Because restorative justice is at its core a theory of 'right,' it has trouble accepting as legitimate any theory that is disinterested in that right. To the extent that community justice gives priority to matters other than the final restoration of victims and wrongdoers, it is at odds with restorative justice in ways that a theory of the 'right' cannot easily abide. Community justice is a strategic theory, oriented to projects and compacts. If processes of restoration result in improved community, the community justice proponent is willing to adopt them as all well and good, but such processes are a means to an end for community justice practitioners. This kind of priority is, to restorative justice thinkers, fraught with risk. What if something else comes along that does a better job of building community? Will community justice leaders reject restorative justice principles? After all, the troubled approach used in 'Weed & Seed' is arguably a community justice strategy (one that may seem not to work as well as most of its advocates hope) but it is decidedly not a restorative justice one.

Solid marriages

Increasingly, some writers have argued that restorative justice and community justice need one another. They say that the two ideas pass the 'compatibility' test and that, to the extent they are based on divergent foundations, it may be that 'opposites attract.'

It is easy to see how this can be so. Seen from a macro level, the ideal of community justice, that the community be improved, is a variant of the restorative justice agenda. Indeed, community justice writers sometimes refer to the aims of community justice as 'restoring the community.' In this way, community justice is a higher order (not of quality, but of magnitude) restorative justice idea. It seeks not to restore a person so much as to restore a people. In high-volume criminal justice areas, community justice workers recognize that the distinction between victims and offenders, while often important, is just as often illusory. Trying to restore victims of crime or people who have committed crimes to pre-crime levels when they live in areas devoid of basic social infrastructure sometimes makes little sense.

Restorative justice workers recognize this dilemma when they search for strategies of restoration in individual cases in extremely disadvantaged communities, and see little foundation upon which to build. In fact, one of the abiding criticism of restorative justice is that it is a middle-class theory better suited for people of means than for the destitute. Yet without question, those who practice restorative justice are interested in the lives of people who lose terribly as a consequence of crime, and this is most often true for the poor who cannot afford to restore themselves from criminal losses. In these places, one day's offender is another day's victim. In these places, restoring a person to a prior level is not nearly as important as restoring a person to a new and better level that is higher than before.

It is precisely this intersection of poor places and troubled people, damaged by crime, that offers the best opportunity for restorative justice and community justice to serve each other's interests. In the poorest places, where large numbers of young men are missing on any given day because they are locked up, and most men will be locked up at some time in their adult lives, it makes no sense to avoid talking about the place as a criminogenic environment that needs to be changed. Restorative justice workers who would treat their subjects as ends whose

interests matter must, of necessity, take an interest in the places where they live. Changing those places – restoring them – is a natural way to restore those who live there and are afflicted by crime.

Restorative justice offers the best way to temper the excesses of community justice. By proposing a set of proven techniques that bring the victim and the wrongdoer together, restorative justice gives community justice advocates a place to start in their quest to rebuild communities hard hit by crime and criminal justice. If community justice is vulnerable to a certain proneness for stereotypes about criminals, restorative justice strategies hold the promise of defeating those stereotypes. Community justice reformers who begin their work by employing restorative justice methods will be less likely to find themselves faced with calls for 'Weed & Seed'. For community justice, if disregard is the seduction, restorative theory is the antidote.

Community justice workers need restorative justice, as well. It is not only that restorative justice provides a moral theory that buttresses the ability of community justice to withstand critique, but it is also that restorative justice provides the ceremonies and methods that enable community justice to close cases in ways that give permission to act. If community justice is about reclaiming communities hit hard by crime, then it has no way to deal with criminal cases. As well, it has no way to resist the call for tough dealing with the people who live in these places. Restorative justice gives the rationale and the strategy for justice that community justice can use to deliver its community agenda without scapegoating criminals and victims.

Final thought

This paper opened with a family metaphor for community justice and restorative justice. All metaphors are misleading when taken to an extreme. I chose a family metaphor because it fits the arguments I have made but also because it gives the feeling I want to convey. Restorative justice and community justice writers have been debating one another of late. This book is a tangible example of the developing debate. In general, debate is healthy for ideas, necessary for them to develop and mature into a more full blossoming of their value. I think this is true for the debates now underway between restorative and community justice thinkers.

But there is a danger in this debate. I use the family metaphor to call attention to the danger. It is this: when family members dispute one another, they can cause a rift that may be hard to repair. I fear the self-importance of some community justice writers will make it hard for restorative justice advocates to hear what is valuable in what they have to say about the needs of the communities they serve. I fear that the self-righteousness of restorative justice advocates will make it unlikely that community justice writers will take the time to learn what they need to know about the proven value of restorative justice.

If we begin with the recognition that we are family, perhaps we can build this conversation as a way to grow closer.

Suggested readings

In this essay, I have forgone the general fashion of citations because all the citations would have been quite general in nature. To get a sense of the sources on which I relied for my ideas, you may read below.

To read basic works about community justice, see:

Clear, T. R. and Cadora, E. (2003) *Community Justice*, Series on Contemporary Issues in Crime and Justice, Belmont, CA: Wadsworth Press.

Karp, D. R. and Clear, T. R. (2002) *What is Community Justice?* Thousand Oaks, CA: Pine Forge Press.

To read basic and analytical texts about restorative justice, see:

Sullivan, D. and Tifft, L. (2005) *Restorative Justice: healing the foundations of our everyday lives*, second edn, Monsey, NY: Willow Tree Press.

Van Ness, D. and Strong, K. (2002) *Restoring Justice*, second edn, Cincinnati: Anderson Publishing.

To read texts on desert theory and retribution, see:

Ashworth, A. (1983) *Sentencing and Penal Policy*, London: Weidenfeld and Nicholson.

Morris, N. *The Future of Imprisonment*, Chicago: University of Chicago.

von Hirsch, A. (1976) *Doing Justice: The Choice of Punishments*, New York: Hill and Wang.

For treatments of communication and sanctions, see:

Braithwaite, J. (2002) *Restorative Justice and Responsive Regulation*, New York: Oxford University Press.

Duff, A. (2000) *Punishment, Communication and Community*, New York: Oxford University Press.

von Hirsch, A., Roberts, R., Bottoms, A. E., Roach, K. and Schiff, M. (eds) (2003) *Restorative Justice and Criminal Justice: competing or reconcilable paradigms?* Portland, OR: Hart Publishing.

32

Postmodernism's challenges to restorative justice

Bruce A. Arrigo

Introduction

This article explores postmodernism's assessment of restorative justice (RJ) both in theory and in practice. In particular, the conceptual underpinnings of RJ and its procedural extension, victim offender mediation (VOM), are critically examined. At issue are the limits to justice, humanism, and change that unwittingly are legitimized and reproduced through the VOM dialogical exchange (Arrigo 2004; Schehr and Milovanovic 1999) This is a pivotal interaction involving the offender, victim, and mediator (e.g. Perry 2002; Strang and Braithwaite 2002; Weitekamp and Kerner 2002). The undoing of a more complete experience of justice is problematic, especially given RJ's genuine commitment to promoting redemption, mercy, forgiveness, and compassion (Sullivan and Tifft 2001). These are dimensions of a healing process that intend to foster a transformative experience for all parties concerned (Bazemore and Umbreit 1994; Weitekamp and Kerner 2002; Zehr 1990).

To address the issues identified above, this article is divided into three substantive sections. First, some summary observations on postmodern social theory, as appropriated in criminology, are outlined. These comments are particularly salient as the vagaries of the theory are often misinterpreted as nothing more than nihilistic, fatalistic, and anti-foundational criticism, devoid of a compelling agenda for sustainable reform or wholesale change (e.g. Handler 1992; Schwartz and Friedrichs 1994; Weinberg 1996). Missing from these interpretations are the affirmative dimensions of the theory that advance positional truths, relational knowledge, and provisional realities: the necessary conditions for advancing a fuller expression of justice (Arrigo 1995, 2003, forthcoming). Second, the contributions of a 'critical' approach to restorative justice are delineated. These remarks are significant in that they help situate and ground the more postmodern challenge that follows this analysis. Third, postmodernism's critiques of RJ and VOM are presented. These observations are designed to reorient the philosophy underpinning both so that a more humane and inclusive experience is realizable in practice for all restorative justice participants.

Postmodernism: outline of an affirmative social theory

The insights of postmodern social theory are derived from those 'first wave' luminaries responsible for crafting this heterodox tradition, and they are well documented in the extant literature (e.g. Arrigo *et al.* 2005; Best and Kellner 1997; Rosenau 1992). Within the realm of crime, law, and justice studies, the theory is principally traced to the work of Milovanovic (1992, 1997, 2003), Henry and Milovanovic (1996, 1999), and Arrigo (1993, 1996, 2002; see also Williams and Arrigo 2004). Although a number of scholarly texts now exist employing various conceptual and methodological strains of inquiry based on postmodern logic, the significance of this multifaceted theory is based on several assumptions about the overall knowledge process. In what follows, a number of these more salient presuppositions are succinctly described. The ensuing comments draw attention to the positive aspects of the theory. These are features that promote greater prospects for justice in society and in our lives through a deliberately engaged rethinking of human social interaction and dialogue.

Embracing the affirmative postmodern attitude in criminology

The affirmative postmodern attitude in criminology begins with an openness to and inclusiveness for how people speak about crime, law, and justice. This receptiveness to alternative ways of communicating and knowing is important, especially since the theory maintains that what we say/read or how we communicate/interpret are not neutral or objective endeavors. Indeed, the thoughts we think, the words we use to interact with others, the ideas we read about in books and magazines, and the images we encounter from movies and the Internet all convey multiple meanings. However, in instances such as these, certain interpretations get preferential treatment. In short, particular versions of reality are privileged while equally worthwhile others are simply discounted or dismissed. This is what is meant by the notion that language (i.e.

thoughts, words, ideas, and images) is not neutral or objective. It always and already is steeped in implicit values and concealed assumptions about social life and human subjects. Thus, to embrace the affirmative postmodern attitude is to admit that knowledge claims are themselves subjective and circumscribed renderings of the world that we make and that shapes us. What this signifies, then, is that the unspoken values and assumptions lurking within crime, law, and justice (especially those 'messages' that are privileged) need to be teased out, identified, dissected, and discussed.

Describing the different narratives on crime, law, and justice

When individuals (e.g. students, teachers, practitioners, offenders) adopt the affirmative postmodern attitude in criminology, then knowledge itself represents an opportunity for constructing multiple narratives about such matters as victimization, punishment, responsibility, and restitution. Truth, then, is much more a departure in meaning than an ultimate or final destination. Thus, for example, knowledge about criminal wrongdoing represents a living, though incomplete and fragmented, 'text' involving actors, events, and experiences. Describing, through ongoing dialogue, how all participants interpret, in their own words, the harm that has occurred means that different versions of reality will get articulated. In some instances, these stories may produce competing and conflicting interpretations for what transpired and for how individuals were impacted. However, this is not an occasion for manufacturing half-truths or for engaging in outright deceit. In addition, the aim in this story-telling process is not to privilege certain views while dismissing others. Rather, to describe the manifold narratives about shared crime and justice phenomena is to recognize that, as a composite, these multiple and divergent accounts represent an evolving stock of knowledge. This is a partial, though unfolding, script that symbolizes the nuanced and subtle ways in which different people uniquely assign meaning to their lives, to those of others, and to the experiences they confront.

Locating the 'desire' of subjects who speak about crime, law, and justice

It is not enough for participants involved in or interpreting a criminal justice event to fashion their own narratives based on their particular understanding of what transpired or their individual assessment of who was injured. Further, it is inadequate to simply examine, *ad infinitum*, the embedded meanings in each of the articulated renderings of reality (especially those that get preferred treatment), such as in a police–citizen interaction, a criminal trial, a criminological text, or in a juvenile waiver hearing. This strategy could easily disintegrate into some form of relativism or subjectivism and neither is consistent with affirmative postmodern sensibilities.

When people talk about crime, law, and justice there is typically something under, in back of, around, or through the very words they use to construct these narratives. What is intended here is not necessarily a deliberate attempt to conceal one's 'true words.' Certainly, this does occur in social interaction; however, this experience is not a part of affirmative postmodern criminological inquiry. Instead, in speech what is often not communicated, what is often dormant or repressed, is the self. This is a reference to the subject's intimate and felt sense of personal identity in relation to the topic about which the individual speaks. Thus, there are really two, distinct but related, languages that require careful attention in the knowledge or sense-making process. One is a discourse that publicly cultivates shared meanings about the crime, law, or justice phenomenon under consideration; the other is a discourse that privately embodies the person's being (e.g. fears, joys, uncertainties)

about the criminological topic under review. According to affirmative postmodernists, this is the realm of one's *desire* (Lacan 1977).

For example, distinguishing between the concepts 'mental state at the time a crime occurred' and 'mental fitness (i.e. competency) to stand trial' represents a collection of values and assumptions that teachers, practitioners, students, and others can articulate with some degree of facility. However, getting participants to speak about their relationship to the identified meanings that attach to these concepts (e.g. how does one understand the nature of mental illness versus mental wellness? in what contexts might one's culture relate to legal and clinical interpretations of similar behavior? to what extent are one's attitudes towards psychiatric disorder informed by media-manufactured and other representations of the same?) is more difficult. These more concealed values and implicit assumptions need to be expressed and made manifest. They (unknowingly) inform (or could inform) the meanings assigned to the criminological themes in question.

Constituting crime, law, and justice as languages of possibility

When all parties are encouraged to articulate, in their own words, their unique desire in relation to the criminological issue in dispute or under review, then prospects for discovering new, previously unspoken, meanings emerge. To illustrate: when criminal justice educators facilitate a dialogue of learning in which students' desires are announced, they can then more profoundly evaluate how such concepts as punishment, policing, crime, and victimization are routinely spoken, legitimized, and re-enacted. Perhaps more importantly, they can also assess what is left out in such discussions, identifying the limits (and possibilities) to reality construction. This is significant because the subject-in-speech – that is, the person whose desiring voice is now activated and at work – can invoke new and different ways by which to construct his/her criminological narrative. We see something of this vital process operating when juvenile gang members communicate their reality to police officers, when the argot of the inmate culture is invoked during a parole hearing, or when the magical thinking of psychiatric patients is uttered before confinement tribunals. The salient point for affirmative postmodern criminology is that unencumbered desire – when voiced and validated in a classroom or elsewhere – represents the potential for establishing replacement, more inclusive knowledge claims relevant to the constitution of criminological actors, agencies, and decisions.

Reconstructing justice

In the process of disassembling and reassembling criminological stories as languages of possibility, both collective meaning and individual being are validated. This, then, is an occasion for reconstructing how justice, humanism, and change could be embodied, articulated, lived, and affirmed in society. As such, articulating the positional truths, relational knowledge, and provisional realities about justice is a goal of affirmative postmodern criminology. In this context, that which is spoken is locally verifiable, intersubjectively knowable, and contingently universal. These are expressions of justice that locate and value the often excluded voices in criminological discourse not because they are better than the prevailing conceptions but because they contribute to, enhance, or otherwise deepen our knowledge about those that already exist or those that could be.

The critical approach to restorative justice

Although restorative justice and victim offender mediation represent well-intended

efforts at healing harm for all parties concerned, several critically inspired challenges have questioned their fundamental efficacy. Four such challenges are briefly discussed in this section. These include the insights of Harris (1989), Cobb (1997), Pavlich (1996, 1998), and Schehr (2000).

Following the logic of critical criminology, Harris (1989) argued that there are three principal areas that limit or erode the redemptive agenda pursued by RJ and VOM proponents. These include: (1) individualizing criminal activity both in terms of allocating responsibility and recommending remedies; (2) failing to recognize how factors beyond the scope or control of the offender (e.g. cultural, economic, political) profoundly impact human behavior; and (3) neglecting to examine how the VOM experience, in some significant respects, is built around coercive discourse.

Harris's (1989) position was a direct assault on the 'status quo' assumptions embedded within VOM practices. In particular, she explicitly challenged the notion that individual offenders alone were blameworthy for the injuries caused to victims, drawing attention to the role that culture, politics, the economy, and other external forces play in the constitution of one's choice making. Moreover, Harris took exception to the logic that VOM was a less intimidating practice than conventional adjudication interventions, processes, or remedies. As she noted, 'a far worse imbalance will emerge with the offender finding himself or herself not only lined up in defense against the state but also against the victim and perhaps some new entity or presence put there to represent the "community"' (Harris 1989: 34).

Linked to her concern for the coercive aspects of VOM, its normalizing practices, and the assignment of individual responsibility, Harris (1989) pointedly questioned whether offenders would genuinely benefit from their exposure to victim offender mediation. Interestingly, her critique anticipated

Braithwaite's (1989, 2002) position on reintegrative shaming. Harris viewed expectations of offender contrition with misgivings, especially when evaluating the likely gains that would befall either the offender or the community.

Harris's observations represented a well-reasoned critical criminological perspective designed to encourage RJ and VOM adherents to rethink the theory and practice of both. Following her analysis, several additional criticisms emerged, calling into question the mediation process itself. Among these, the observations of Cobb (1997) are particularly noteworthy.

The thrust of Cobb's (1997) challenge to VOM focused on the re-victimization experience for those already injured, especially when the discourse and logic of victim offender mediation are employed in reconciliation sessions. Relying on the insights of Foucault (1977), Cobb asserted that VOM discourse establishes a dichotomy: some cases require attention in the court system (i.e. criminal matters); and some others qualify for mediation through VOM (i.e. relational cases). The problem that Cobb identified was that VOM dialogue displaces (indeed, cleanses) the experience of one's violence by substituting the rights-based discourse typical of the adjudication process with a needs-based discourse characteristic of relational cases. Cobb referred to this as a 'domestication process,' one that de-legitimized the voice (the unarticulated pain, suffering, and injury) of the victim. Thus, in the more scripted and conventional narrative of victim offender mediation, the domestication of violence perpetuates and reinforces the felt oppression of those harmed because the process refuses to make fully thematic the actual violence perpetrated against those persons harmed.

In addition, Cobb explained how the VOM dialogical process represents the guise of moral neutrality where session participants presumably can speak freely without fear of reprisal, concern for judgment, or apprehension about perceived legitimacy. However, by avoiding the denunciation of violent acts enacted against victims through an assumed *laissez-faire* morality, those harmed experience marginal recognition for the suffering they endured (or are enduring). As Cobb (1997) observed, this phenomenon is akin to Foucault's (1977) notion on the 'micro politics of power.' In short, VOM discourse signifies the maintenance of violence against, and the oppression of, those injured.

Pavlich (1996, 1998) extended the insights of Cobb (1997). His assessment of victim offender mediation also utilized the logic of Foucault (1965, 1977), particularly with respect to the unspoken but felt control operating through the micro-physics of power. As Pavlich (1996) argued, VOM processes serve the aims of the state (e.g. reproducing the status quo, maintaining existing hierarchies) by disciplining and regulating subjects.

This critique also resonates in Schehr's (2000) interpretation. As he noted, VOM is an example of legal formalism – that is, a system-sustaining steering mechanism (Habermas 1984). In short, the state, through RJ and VOM, assists unstable sectors of society (e.g. the criminal justice apparatus) toward equilibrium conditions. Indeed, consistent with Pavlich (1998), Schehr (2000) indicated how mediators direct restitution agreements toward activities compatible with dominant cultural interests and values (e.g. youthful offenders are persuaded to participate in ancillary labor market activities); for an example to the community justice literature, see Maloney and Holcomb 2001. Moreover, similar to Pavlich (1996, 1998), Schehr (2000) emphasized how the rhetoric adopted by VOM practitioners stresses a commitment to prevailing cultural norms and beliefs (especially those relating to respect for authority, hard work, property, merit, and nationalism). Admittedly, such restitution activities can and do result in lower recidivism rates for offenders as borne out in the extant literature (e.g. Braithwaite 2002); however, these outcomes are based on the advancement of system-stabilizing discourse, practices, and conduct. As such, prospects for replacement, and more diverse (perhaps more meaningful), types of recompense, healing, forgiveness, and reclamation fail to find expression within the existing dialogical forum of VOM.

The contributions of Harris (1989), Cobb (1997), Pavlich (1996, 1998), and Schehr (2000) emphasized the system maintaining and reinforcing dimensions of VOM discourse and processes presumed to be *de facto* legitimate. Although certainly instructive, these critiques do not include the affirmative postmodern challenges to restorative justice and victim offender mediation. Accordingly, in the remaining portion of this chapter, selected contributions from this evolving intellectual approach are briefly reviewed. At issue here is how postmodern social theory can help promote greater prospects for justice, humanism, and change, given the limits of existing RJ dialogical strategies.

Postmodern challenges to restorative justice

There are five challenges to restorative justice and its procedural extension (i.e. VOM), based on selected insights from postmodern social theory. Other researchers have described or examined these criticisms in relation to (inter)national dispute resolution (Schehr and Milovanovic 1999), victim impact statements proffered during the sentencing phase of a capital case (Arrigo and Williams 2003), and community justice's link to restorative justice (Arrigo 2004). As Schehr and Milovanovic (1999: 208–9) succinctly noted, these limitations include

> the privileging of hierarchical representations, the supposition of order, the celebration of the ideal speech act and consensus dynamics, the continuous

encroachment of legal discourse at the expense of alternative discourses, and ... the lack of connected strategies between the macro and micro domains.

A summary of these shortcomings is presented below.

The privileging of hierarchical representations

According to postmodern social theory, the formation of individual and group identities is contingent upon political, economic, and cultural variables that often remain repressed, veiled, and unspoken in the dialogical exchange. When the mediation session includes genuine and open statements about these dynamics, their intersections, and the unique connections they portend for all participants (including the mediator), then VOM discourse is informed by power sharing. When these forces are not articulated or when they are not affirmed, particular views regarding victim interests, offender concerns, and reconciliation beliefs will govern the mediation process (i.e. some truths, experiences, meanings, etc., will be valued and legitimized over others). This is what is meant by the privileging of hierarchical representations. Thus, before any efforts at reparative dialogue are pursued, frank and revealing communication about one's sense of self and one's standing in the mediation group must be articulated.

As a practical matter, then, affirmative postmodern social theory questions whether and to what extent all of the parties in a VOM session freely and sensitively discuss their roles in mediation. Again, what is at issue here is how participants organize their thoughts; understand the harmful events in contention; and speak about injury, forgiveness, and reparation, mindful of the political, economic, and cultural dynamics that underscore that which is communicated. Without this preliminary and subtle focus on self, standpoint, and group, prospects for more genuine power sharing are neutralized and occasions for more authentic healing are compromised. Restorative justice neglects, underestimates, or dismisses the value of this important pre-narrative in the VOM dialogical exchange.

The assumption of order

VOM and RJ proponents assume that communicative order among participants is a crucial dimension informing the mediation session. Examples of order include the use of syllogistic reasoning and deductive logic, the reliance on cause and effect when describing conduct, the conviction that individuals are purposeful, rational and volitional in their decision making, and the presupposition that 'Truth' is knowable and identifiable (e.g. Arrigo *et al.* 2005; Best and Kellner 1997). In this approach to RJ and VOM discourse, stability trumps conflict, predictability is privileged over unpredictability, and control rather than freedom underscores the reconciliation dialogue. Indeed, in the conventional processes operating within VOM, the second term in each of these binaries (i.e. conflict, unpredictability, and freedom) is rendered 'anomalous and uncharacteristic of human behavior' (Schehr and Milovanovic 1999: 209).

Thus, fundamental to restorative justice is a commitment to order, homeostasis, and equilibrium. Both VOM's customary dialogue and RJ's overall efforts to establish a dispute resolution acceptable to all participants are examples of this. However, that which is spoken in the mediation session often is unwittingly scripted. For example, in their review of the staged discourse inherent in victim offender reconciliation, Arrigo and Schehr (1998: 647–8) observed the following, particularly in regard to the involvement of adolescents:

> Juveniles who engage in the VOM process are made to conform to procedural and organizational strictures that already

represent certain values about how to interact with others (i.e. their victims). Although these rules are not spoken, they are unconsciously organized to produce limited outcomes consistent with the linguistic coordinates of meaning representing the discourse of victim–offender reconciliation. In other words, the flow of communication is preconfigured: It is designed to result in definable, self-referential outcomes. These outcomes are to be consistent with the language of restoration and reconciliation as ensured, as far as possible, by the mediator who (by definition) speaks only to clarify, moderate, and reconcile.

Affirmative postmodern social theory takes exception to this approach. A healthier and more organic assessment of ongoing human interaction recognizes that absurdities, contradictions, spontaneities, and inconsistencies are also enduring features of social life. Admittedly, such randomness may engender frustration and uncertainty for some; however, these organic human tendencies are the source of considerable 'experimentation, creativity, and possibility' (Giroux 1992: 34). This is why affirmative postmodern theorists embrace such notions as orderly disorder or predictable unpredictability (Milovanovic 2003; Williams and Arrigo 2004). These more fully, although never completely, integrated realities are consistent with the fluid and natural rhythms of complex, adaptive, and chaotic systems like humans (Williams and Arrigo 2002). As such, these activities should be encouraged in the process of mediation and reconciliation.

The celebration of the ideal speech act and consensus dynamics

The first two affirmative postmodern critiques of restorative justice lead to a third challenge. Proponents of VOM assume that ideal types of communicative action or ideal speech acts (Habermas 1984) are possible, especially if rational, organized, purposeful, coherent, and unified discourse prevails. As the logic goes, in instances such as these, consensus dynamics and mutual agreement will most likely be assured. Stated differently, the processes that constitute the mediation – including the manner, flow, and intensity of the verbal, non-verbal, and extra-verbal discourse – are pivotal to the reconciliation experience.

However, affirmative postmodernism takes exception to the efficacy and legitimacy of this mostly linear, circumscribed, and limiting logic. Conventional VOM practices contain or sanitize conflict in the reconciliation discourse, regarding it as an altogether destructive and unhealthy feature of human conduct (Arrigo 2004). As such, occasions for investigating the fluid, variable, and mutable dimensions (i.e. far-from-equilibrium or unstable tendencies) of our identities, of our interpersonal encounters, and of our changing definitions of situations remain concealed and repressed amidst the (spoken and unspoken) pressure to domesticate violence (Cobb 1997) and to discipline (and normalize) the self (Pavlich 1996).

The victim offender mediation process is a site in which 'stability, continuity, coherence, order, and closure' are re-enacted and, thus, re-affirmed (Arrigo and Schehr 1998: 649). A commitment to ideal speech acts and consensus dynamics guarantees this. These activities, undertaken unreflectively, are assumed to be legitimate eroding prospects for a fuller articulation of redemption, mercy, and forgiveness for all parties involved in the dialogical exchange. However, by appropriating the insights of affirmative postmodern social theory, a replacement form of knowledge and experience is discernible in restorative justice practice. This is a VOM process that more completely embraces the anomalies, contradictions, absurdities, and inconsistencies of interpersonal communication and human interaction.

For example, because positional truths, relational knowledge, and provisional realities underscore the mediation dialogue, contingent universalities (Butler 1992) or conditional standpoints (Arrigo 1995) more fully and organically account for how people come to experience and speak about such things as harm, forgiveness, violence, and redemption. This mediation approach validates that mutable and fluid (i.e. orderly disorder) nature of the human condition. Thus, following the postmodern vision of RJ and VOM, routinized thinking, customary practices, and conventional dialogue are resisted. To do so would, unwittingly, limit or thwart greater opportunities for discovering new vocabularies of meaning that advance a deeper, more complete, sense of justice for all participants. In this model, there is no master reconciliation plan or grand mediation scheme. Participants are encouraged to speak their own 'true words' as a way to empower and liberate them through the dialogical exchange (Freire 1972). This orientation supports a minimalist morality in which difference is celebrated.

The encroachment of legal discourse at the expense of alternative discourses

One facet of agreement-driven reconciliation and consensus dynamics is the specific discourse that informs, indeed saturates, the mediation session. According to several affirmative postmodernists, legal language (i.e. legalese) often textures the VOM communication (e.g. Arrigo et al. 2005; Arrigo and Williams 2003; Schehr 2000). Examples of legal discourse in mediation include '[l]inear logic (syllogistic reasoning), deductive logic, legal abstractions (e.g. the juridic subject), formalism (e.g. formal rationality), and the law of equivalence (e.g. capital logic)' (Schehr and Milovanovic 1999: 209–10). Steady reliance on these dialogical strategies is reductionistic: difference is

479

reconstituted as sameness; fluid and changing identities are homogenized; and divergent interpretations of shared experiences are sanitized (Arrigo *et al.* 2005).

When the tools of legal discourse are at work in the mediation session, the personal story-telling, the incomplete knowledge, and the local histories that signify our evolving identities are silenced. Stated differently, the more formalized process conceals and discounts the cultural images, the perceptual differences, and the divergent truth claims of our orderly disordered selves. This is a postmodern condition in which a host of 'languages, experiences, and voices' are affirmed (Giroux 1992: 34). To the extent that the practice of restorative justice neglects these particularized accounts, the intrusion of legal discourse will prevail, and it will function as a master narrative (Lacan 1977). In the context of VOM discourse what this means for justice, then, is that 'the language of the possible [must be] free to circulate in narrative creativity through the vehicle of folklore, critical memory, nostalgia, tales, and myth' (Schehr and Milovanovic 1999: 217).

The lack of connected strategies between the micro and macro domains

Given the affirmative postmodern critique of restorative justice and victim offender mediation as enumerated above, a final shortcoming is now discernible. On a more integrative level, the question is whether the dialogical exchange is structured to bridge the divide between situations of reconciliation (i.e. local action) and large-scale reform (i.e. global transformation) (Arrigo *et al.* 2005). Proponents of existing RJ and VOM practices (e.g. Braithwaite 2002; Sullivan and Tifft 2001) have raised similar concerns. However, for affirmative postmodernists, what is at issue is the mostly confessional quality of the dialogical exchange in which the offender's identity is normalized,

homogenized, and fashioned into a non-conflictual self (Pavlich 1996: 728–30; see also Foucault 1977 on 'docile bodies' and 'bodies of utility').

As affirmative postmodernists have observed, when the language employed in VOM sessions endeavors 'to produce individual selves' based on the confessional strategy of disciplining identity, disagreements are resolved by promoting 'a civic society and legal "rights",' absent a consideration for their normalizing effects (Arrigo and Schehr 1998: 641). What makes this occurrence so (potentially) devastating is that the link between conflict and change is undone. In short, conventional RJ and VOM practices fail to recognize how social structure is 'a contributing factor in the manifestation of conflict' (Schehr and Milovanovic 1999: 210; Umbreit 1999). Reliance on third-party experts, hierarchical decision making, and consensus dynamics denies what could occur in the mediation session. Indeed, 'unanticipated outcomes, nonlinear modes of interaction, contingency-based conflict resolution strategies, fragmented and local knowledges, and mutable identities must be squarely positioned within the reconciliation process' (Arrigo 2004: 97). These affirmative postmodern strategies celebrate difference as articulated through the VOM discourse, thereby affirming the role of conflict, ambiguity, and disequilibrium. These are conditions that shatter ossified (and assumed) knowledge about harm, victimization, punishment, and redemption, making large-scale change and structural reform that much more realizable in restorative justice theory and practice (Umbreit 1999).

Conclusions

The theory and practice of restorative justice, as well as its procedural extension (i.e. victim offender mediation), strive to advance an agenda for meaningful reform. This well-intended strategy for change endeavors to assist victims, offenders, and the community to which both belong. However, as this chapter made evident, there are serious limits to the vision of justice adherents of RJ and VOM pursue. For example, hierarchies are privileged, order and stasis are presumed, consensus dynamics are extolled, legal discourse displaces replacement forms of communicating, and the path to structural change (i.e. conflict) is displaced in speech and action. In short, the knowledge process mostly is circumscribed while identities are unwittingly disciplined.

A more liberating blueprint for reform in restorative justice and the dialogical exchange that occurs in VOM, finds expression in affirmative postmodern social theory. By appropriating selected insights from this heterodox orientation, a new, more emancipating direction in reconciliation discourse was mapped. Future researchers would do well to examine more closely how the tools of affirmative postmodernism could significantly extend and deepen this commitment to humanism and inclusivity for all mediation participants. This, then, is the agenda of structural, sustainable change. In the final analysis, restorative justice, both in theory and in practice, necessitates this very call for transformative praxis.

References

Arrigo, B. A. (1993) *Madness, Language, and the Law*, Albany, NY: Harrow and Heston.
— (1995) 'The peripheral core of law and criminology: on postmodern social theory and conceptual integration,' *Justice Quarterly*, 12(3): 447–72.
— (1996) *The Contours of Psychiatric Justice: a postmodern critique of mental illness, criminal insanity, and the law*, New York: Garland.
— (2002) *Punishing the Mentally Ill: a critical analysis of law and psychiatry*, Albany, NY: State University of New York Press.
— (2003) 'Postmodern justice and critical criminology: positional, relational, and provisional science,' in M. D. Schwartz and S. Hatty (eds) *Controversies in Crime and Justice: critical criminology*, Cincinnati, OH: Anderson.
— (2004) 'Rethinking restorative and community justice: a postmodern inquiry,' *Contemporary Justice Review*, 7(1): 91–100.
— (forthcoming) 'Postmodern theory and criminology,' in S. D. Henry and M. Lanier (eds) *The Essential Criminology Reader*, second edn, Boulder, CO: Westview Press.
Arrigo, B. A. and Schehr, R. C. (1998) 'Restoring justice for juveniles: a critical analysis of victim offender mediation,' *Justice Quarterly*, 15(4): 629–66.
Arrigo, B. A. and Williams, C. R. (2003) 'Victim vices, victim voices, and impact statements: on the place of emotion and the role of restorative justice in capital sentencing,' *Crime and Delinquency*, 49(4): 603–26.
Arrigo, B. A., Milovanovic, D. and Schehr, R. (2005) *The French Connection in Criminology: rediscovering crime, law, and social change*, Albany, NY: State University of New York Press.
Bazemore, G. and Umbreit, M. (1994) *Balanced and Restorative Justice*, Washington, DC: US Department of Justice and Delinquency Prevention.
Best, S. and Kellner, D. (1997) *The Postmodern Turn*, New York: Guilford.
Braithwaite, J. (1989) *Crime, Shame and Reintegration*, New York: Cambridge University Press.
— (2002) *Restorative Justice and Responsive Regulation*, New York: Oxford University Press.
Butler, Judith (1992) 'Contingent foundations: feminism and the question of "postmodernism",' in J. Butler and J. W. Scott (eds) *Feminists Theorize the Political*, London: Routledge.
Cobb, S. (1997) 'The domestication of violence in mediation,' *Law and Society Review*, 31(3): 397–440.
Foucault, M. (1965) *Madness and Civilization*, New York: Vintage.
— (1977) *Discipline and Punish*, New York: Pantheon.
Freire, P. (1972) *Pedagogy of the Oppressed*, New York: Seabury Press.
Giroux, H. (1992) *Border Pedagogy*, New York: Routledge.
Habermas, J. (1984) *Theory of Communicative Action*, Volume 1, Boston: Beacon Press.
Handler, J. (1992) 'Postmodernism, protest, and the new social movement,' *Law and Society Review*, 26(4): 697–731.

Harris, M. K. (1989) 'Alternative visions in the context of contemporary realities,' in *New Perspectives on Crime and Justice: occasional papers of the MCC Canada.*

Victim Offender Ministries Program and the MCC US Office of Criminal Justice, Issue 7, Elkhart, IN: Mennonite Central Committee/US Office of Criminal Justice.

Henry, S. D. and Milovanovic, D. (1996) *Constitutive Criminology: beyond postmodernism*, London: Sage.

— (1999) *Constitutive Criminology at Work: applications in crime and justice*, Albany, NY: State University of New York Press.

Lacan, J. (1977) *Ecrits: a selection*, A. Sheridan (trans.), New York: W. W. Norton.

Maloney, D. and Holcomb, D. (2001) 'In pursuit of community justice,' *Youth and Society*, 33(3): 296–313.

Milovanovic, D. (1992) *Postmodern Law and Disorder: psychoanalytic semiotics, chaos theory and juridic exegeses*, Merseyside, UK: Deborah Charles.

— (1997) *Postmodern Criminology*, New York: Garland.

— (2003) *Critical Criminology at the Edge: postmodern perspectives, integration, and applications*, Westport, CT: Praeger.

Pavlich, G. (1996) 'The power of community mediation: government and formation of self-identity,' *Law and Society Review*, 30(5): 707–33.

— (1998) 'Justice in fragments: the political logic of mediation in "New Times,"' *Critical Criminologist*, 8: 20–23.

Perry, J. (ed.) (2002) *Repairing Communities through Restorative Justice*, Lanham, MD: American Correctional Association.

Rosenau, P. M. (1992) *Post-modernism and the Social Sciences: insights, inroads, and intrusions*, Princeton, NJ: Princeton University Press.

Schehr, R. (2000) 'From restoration to transformation: victim offender mediation as transformative justice,' *Mediation Quarterly*, 18(2): 151–69.

Schehr, R. and Milovanovic, D. (1999) 'Conflict mediation and the postmodern,' *Social Justice*, 25(2): 208–32.

Schwartz, M. D. and Friedrichs, D. (1994) 'Postmodern thought and critical discontent: new metaphors for understanding violence,' *Criminology*, 32(3): 281–95.

Strang, H. and Braithwaite, J. (2002) *Restorative Justice: philosophy to practice*, Aldershot, UK: Dartmouth/Ashgate Publishing.

Sullivan, D. and Tifft, L. (2001) *Restorative Justice: healing the foundations of our everyday lives*, Monsey, NY: Willow Tree Press.

Umbreit, M. (1999) 'Avoiding the marginalization and "McDonaldization" of victim–offender mediation: a case study moving toward the mainstream,' in G. Bazemore and L. Walgrave (eds) *Restoring Juvenile Justice: repairing the harm of youth crime*, Monsey, NY: Criminal Justice Press.

Weinberg, S. (1996) 'Sokal's Hoax,' *The New York Review of Books*, 8 August: 11–15.

Weitekamp, E. and Kerner, H.-J. (2002) *Restorative Justice: theoretical foundations*, Cullompton, Devon, UK: Willan Publishing.

Williams, C. R. and Arrigo, B. A. (2002) *Law, Psychology, and Justice: chaos theory and the new (dis)order*, Albany, NY: State University of New York Press.

— (2004) *Theory, Justice, and Social Change: theoretical integrations and critical applications*, Norwell, MA: Kluwer Academic/Plenum Publishers.

Zehr, H. (1990) *Changing Lenses: a new focus on crime and justice*, Scottsdale, PA: Herald Press.

33

A feminist vision of justice?

The problems and possibilities of restorative justice for girls and women

Emily Gaarder and Lois Presser

Feminists in the fields of law and criminology have contemplated the limits of state intervention into gendered crimes against women such as battering, rape, and sexual harassment (Smart 1995; Websdale and Johnson 1997). Despite legal innovations targeting these crimes, justice still eludes many women, especially those of low social status (Schafran 2004; Wriggins 1983) and those supposedly complicit in their own victimization (LaFree 1989; Miller and Schwartz 1995). Legal remedies very often lead to worse, even punitive outcomes for women, such as when rape victims are humiliated in court (United States Senate 1993), battering victims are arrested as a result of mandatory arrest policies (Women's Justice Center 2005), or immigrant battering victims are deported (Das Dasgupta 1998). If the law is no panacea for female victims, it is equally damaging for female offenders, as their sky-rocketing rates of incarceration demonstrate (Owen 1999). Female pathways to offending frequently involve sexual and/or physical abuse, racism and poverty, engendering survival strategies (e.g. running away, substance abuse, prostitution) that are criminalized (Chesney-Lind 1997). The 'blurred boundaries' of victimization and offending (Gilfus 1992) are largely ignored in the court process.

Clearly, a transformative justice is needed, one that will eliminate the structural inequalities that promote offending (Coker 2002; Sullivan and Tifft 2001). But after a crime has been perpetrated, a justice *intervention* is needed. As Daly (2002) remarks, 'criminal acts themselves create inequality which must be redressed in some way, even as we may recognize that those criminal acts may have come about because of, or be linked to, relations of inequality and oppression in the larger society' (p. 73). Restorative justice, a philosophy and movement focused on repairing harms rather than simply punishing the doers of harm, is gaining ground as an alternative or at least an important supplement to the current system of criminal justice (Van Ness and Heetderkstrong 2002). While some feminists have developed and endorsed restorative justice ideas and practices *as* feminist (Harris 1991; Pranis 1998), others have responded cautiously to their potential in creating justice for women (Daly 2002; Stubbs 2002).

This chapter grapples with the question of whether restorative justice is or can achieve a 'feminist vision of justice,' as M. Kay Harris (1991) forecast. First, we consider the problems that feminists have identified with the criminal justice system. Second, we analyze the unique promises and problems of restorative justice in addressing the needs of girls and women as both victims and offenders. We do so by considering three key features of ideal restorative justice practice: that it provide a forum for narrative; depend upon and build community; and address cultural concerns. The ideological connections between feminist ethics and the restorative justice philosophy are explored alongside a grounded consideration of restorative features in practice.

Questioning the law and the criminal justice system

Feminists have fought and continue to fight hard for laws outlawing battering, rape, sexual harassment, and other gendered crimes against girls and women. They do so not only because laws might offer relief to female victims but also because (if enforced) they communicate unequivocally that misogynist crimes are wrong (Daly 2002). Laws – and arrests, convictions, trials, and sentences – pronounce societal disapproval (Minow 1998a). Of course, like other institutions of the state, the law also plays a key role in maintaining the ruling relations of society (Snider 1998). This basic truth only begins to suggest how problematic the law can be and has been for girls and women.

The law reduces power relations to those between victim and offender at the moment of the offense, which is usually understood as a single event. Likewise, the agency/ responsibility and subjugation of these parties are reduced to those evident – by legal standards – in that moment. The law has no ready terminology for a harmful agency that is bounded by oppression. To entertain 'oppression' would be to consider various levels of aggregate responsibility for crime. But the law individualizes crime. It makes sense, then, that the decrees of law typically do not extend to the multiple agents and

social institutions that *facilitate* harm, both structurally and culturally (Braithwaite 2002; Crelinsten 2003; Minow 1998a). For example, torture of political prisoners requires 'silent acquiescence' (Crelinsten 2003: 303) by domestic and international bystanders. Mass atrocities rely, at the very least, on a concerted ignorance. And yet legal institutions do not as a rule 'crack down' on passivity.

The 'toughest' tools that the criminal justice system brings to bear on crime very often make matters worse. These tools were crafted to punish first, and not to help victims. At best, they leave unmet victims' needs. When victim and offender are acquaintances or intimates, as they most often are in cases of battering, rape, and sexual harassment, victims suffer various collateral consequences of the offender's punishment. These consequences include reduced income, loss of child custody, stigmatization, and even retaliation by the offender and/or his supporters, and arrest or deportation of the victim when her own status is criminalized. More indirectly, women suffer from the incarceration of men as money is diverted from social welfare programs to finance the prison-industrial complex (Owen 1999).

It is an unfortunate irony that criminal justice control, while seeming to signal female emancipation, tends to reify race, class, and gender oppression. A growing number of feminist scholars and activists recognize the effects of harsher penalties on the most marginalized members of society. Dianne Martin, for instance, suggests that we not view 'the recent innovations in criminal law' as 'a triumph for feminism, despite appearances' (1998: 157). There is no victory for feminists, she suggests, in equating judicial 'recognition of harm with the length of a prison term' (p. 170). Feminist reliance on the criminal justice system helps to legitimize the expansion of the prison-industrial complex, including, of late, rising numbers of criminalized and incarcerated girls and women.

Recognizing this, the question remains: if not the law, what will safeguard women's rights and ensure peaceful, non-violent communities? DeKeseredy and Schwartz's (1991) remarks apply to all of us for whom the 'policing' strategies of the state fail ideologically and practically:

> The problems for these dissenters is that while they are sure that increased intervention is a problem, many cannot locate an alternative to policing which can provide at least some protection to women from the predatory hordes of men who populate society.
>
> (p. 163)

Restorative justice proposes just such an alternative – by offering a forum for narrative; by emphasizing community involvement; and by addressing structural injustices, including cultural denigration associated with crime.

A forum for narrative

Story-telling is recognized as a crucial practice of restorative justice (Coker 1999; Presser 2004). The priority given to story-telling is quite contrary to the intended protocol of court proceedings. In a court of law, only certain elements of an event are considered pertinent to decide a question of justice. At best, the court works to uncover 'facts' and establish a linear timeframe of 'the event.' Such non-facts as emotional consequences of the crime are deemed irrelevant insofar as they do not help legal professionals figure out 'who did it' and what punishment they should receive (Zehr 1995). In rape trials, the complexities of power and coercion are reduced to the binary logic of consent or non-consent. Smart (1989) writes:

> There is also no room for the context of submission in the dichotomy of consent/ non-consent which dominates the rape trial. Yet submission may be what the majority of raped and sexually abused women have endured. In other words, in fear of future violence or in fear of losing a job, women may submit unwillingly to sex. Yet in legal terms, submission fits on the consent side of the dichotomy. Having submitted, but failing to meet the legal criterion of non-consent, women are deemed to have consented to their violation.
>
> (p. 34)

In effect, the rape victim is blamed for the nature of oppression itself, that it defines and narrows choices for the oppressed.

Actually, the most typical process by which a criminal court case is 'disposed of' – plea bargaining – precludes any story-telling at all. A supportive stage for public narrative, such as restorative justice would create, can therefore be a unique and powerful experience for crime victims. According to victimologist Judith Herman, the 'ultimate resolution of the trauma' of violence requires public acknowledgement (Herman 1997: 70). She states that 'recovery can take place only within the context of relationships; it cannot occur in isolation' (ibid.: 133). Alienation of self from community is a basic aspect of the trauma of victimization (Clear 1994: 130; see also Norris et al. 1997). Victims' emotional recovery requires social reintegration.

Truth-telling and responsive, supportive listening are the ideals. Yet, we should not be surprised if: (1) victims have difficulty telling truths due to shame or fear of retaliation; (2) victims tailor their truths for the sake of drawing empathy; and (3) participants are unsupportive.

The first possibility concerns the psychosocial dynamic that surrounds many women's experience of ongoing victimization. Lori Girshick (1999) writes: 'Women who survive (trauma) through suppression and isolation find expressing their real selves very threatening' (p. 152). No doubt, facing one's offender would heighten the threat.

485

Further, feelings of shame and 'deserved-ness' haunt the minds of many victims of sexual and domestic violence. The 'comfort women' who were sexually victimized by the Japanese Army during World War II, for instance, have been reluctant to come forward and even give their names, much less tell their stories. Many felt that a public proclamation of their forced prostitution would bring shame upon them and their immediate families (Barkan 2000).

The second possibility takes for granted a truism of social interaction. Victims, like everyone else, tailor their stories to the immediate context of story-telling. Persons whose victimization is structurally supported – as in the case of gendered crimes against women – have especially powerful reasons for deemphasizing agency in their stories. Such victims may be judged for their actions or inactions.

In this regard, Elizabeth Spelman (1997) cites the example of Harriet Jacobs, a nine-teenth-century black female slave who wrote about her experiences of white men's sexual violence in her 1861 work, *Incidents in the Life of a Slave Girl, Written by Herself.*

> Many if not most slave girls and women were raped or otherwise sexually assaulted or harassed by white boys and men ... (It was) painful and risky for slave women to talk about such experiences to white women they implored for help, on account of that cruel logic according to which being subject to sexual assault is first and foremost an indication of the victim's immorality.
>
> (Spelman 1997: 73)

Jacobs, who wrote under the pseudonym Linda Brent, faced what Spelman (1997) terms the 'dilemma of compassion':

> She could keep to a minimum the infor-mation necessary to invoke compassion, relying on stock images of trembling fugi-tives and kindly rescuers, and hence risk playing into the master–slave relationship she deplored; or she could reveal herself much further, in hopes of presenting her-self as more than a mere victim, but at the risk of incurring hard questions about her behavior.
>
> (pp. 73–4)

The agency of subordinated persons is scru-tinized. If the victim is too agentive in her account, listeners may blame her for her ordeal. Jacobs' experience reveals the harsh alternative – a kind of self-stereotyping and self-denigration.

The third possibility, that participants in a restorative justice encounter will be unsup-portive, is especially strong with crimes that derive from power differentials between victim and offender and, too, widely held ideologies supporting these. Structural injustice cannot be kept out of the restora-tive justice conference. The social statuses and acculturated expectations of the inter-locutors are always 'there.' Without purpo-seful interference, the conference is likely to be shaped along the lines of existing power relations. Daly (2002) puts it well: 'When one attempts to bring into conversation parties who are unequal, it is likely that the more powerful person will have his or her way' (p. 65). Consequently, harms may be re-experienced by victims in the 'truth-telling' process, no less than in court.

What is to be done? Much careful pre-paration is required in advance of a con-ference. During the conference, story-telling must be a process that allows a victim to fully express her narrative without being subject to a cross-examination of her perso-nal history, the model that persists in today's criminal courts. Finally, face-to-face encounter with one's offender must not be the only option for restoration – a recommendation we return to presently.

Thus far, we have discussed narrative as a resource for women as victims. Christine Alder (2000) sees numerous advantages of restora-tive justice for female and specifically girl *offenders.* Among other things, the narrative aspect of restorative justice provides an opportunity for these offenders to express their feelings, to be treated with dignity, and to participate meaningfully in decision-making processes – experiences of which young female offenders have been deprived in their encounters with the criminal justice system and more generally (Belknap *et al.* 1997; Gaarder and Belknap 2004).

Many restorative justice proceedings require not only that offenders acknowledge the harms they cause but also that they hear shaming messages about these behaviors (Braithwaite and Mugford 1994). Yet historically, shame has been used to control women. It has kept them from speaking out about rape and other violence. Rather than shame-desistance connections, some stipulate a shame–*self*-harm connection for girls and women with histories of victimization (e.g. Noll *et al.* 2003). We should therefore approach the shame–reintegration relation very carefully.

In their study of girls transferred to adult court and serving time in women's prison, Gaarder and Belknap (2002) spoke with many girls who had intense feelings of shame about themselves and what they had done. They did not minimize their actions. In fact, they sometimes maximized their responsibility and said that their difficult past was 'no excuse' for what they had done. Other girls did not acknowledge the harm they had caused others. Dialogue offers a possible way out of both these patterns. It offers opportunities for redemption and thus a way out of shame. It reconnects girls to their sense of compassion for others by putting them in direct contact with the people whom they have harmed. Restorative justice dialogue can also empower, as in one South Australian girl's experience, reported by Alder (2000: 106):

> Yes my family came to it and all the people that my family are involved in came too, to talk about the stuff that was going to happen and I was able to help decide

what was going to happen with me. They didn't just say, well, you're going to [detention] for 12 months for property damage. They said 'What do you think should happen?' and I told them what I thought should happen and my mum and they said they think that's fair and I thought that was really good. They respected your opinion like what you thought should happen. And what I said happened, which I thought was really good.

The challenges of using restorative justice practices with female offenders parallel those previously discussed in regard to female victims. Subjugating expectations and power hierarchies may shape the process. Community expectations of girls and women are often laden with strict standards of 'proper' behavior, such as repression of sexuality (Robinson 2005), as well as stereotypes based on race, class, and sexual orientation. Alder (2000) believes that conferencing in which a range of supportive figures participates 'could by its very nature begin to address negative community attitudes toward young women offenders' (p. 109).

Community involvement

As Alder (2000 suggests, many of the pitfalls and promises of restorative justice lead us back to the central role it assigns to *community* in solving crime problems and administering consequences. In the restorative justice literature, community is defined relationally more than geographically (Van Ness and Heetderkstrong 2002). Communities of care, it is argued, provide both support and control; both are deemed necessary to stop harm-doing and to repair harms. Friends, families, and neighbors support the victim by acknowledging the violation and by offering concrete help in the future. The community also regulates the behavior of offenders through social disapproval of offending and positive reinforcement for reform (Braithwaite 1989).

Perhaps the most obvious danger of greater communal control of justice, from a feminist perspective, is that community norms reify existing power structures and support criminal behaviors. Relatedly, restorative justice must not assume that 'communities of care' have enough resources – emotional, material, or other – to either support women or adequately sanction men's violence. Stubbs (1997) argues that some women have turned to the courts precisely because their family and friends were not supportive, could not offer support that was effective, or because such assistance had resulted in violence directed at the woman's supporters. Stubbs (2002) also points out that the work of the 'community' might and often does fall mainly on women. 'Community involvement must be more than a euphemism for the unpaid work of women' (Stubbs 2002: 14). Handing the responsibility of crime control over to communities that suffer from deficient resources in the first place could be disastrous. Restorative justice planners must take care to use conferencing and other practices as a way to mobilize resources and/ or draw on them equitably.

Gendered crimes against women are rooted in unjust ideologies and structures. Of domestic violence, Coker (1999) states:

> The batterer does not, indeed could not, act alone. Social supports for battering include widespread denial of its frequency or harm, economic structures that render women vulnerable, and sexist ideology that holds women accountable for male violence and for the emotional lives of families, and that fosters deference to male familial control.
>
> (p. 39)

Restorative justice advocates believe that most, if not all, participants will condemn violence if the encounter is adequately planned. With regard to woman battering, Tifft (1993) notes: 'Community-coordinated interventions embody exceptional vision in

their programs for the empowerment of women and the reorientation of men' (p. 133). Preliminary evaluation of various programs finds that even conferences dominated by multi-problem families and communities rarely end up condoning violent behavior and other harms (Braithwaite 1999). But participants need not condone violence against women in the abstract to tolerate some of the problematic ideas (e.g. that women are stewards of the family's emotional well-being) that Coker identifies as less obvious grounds for violence. Future research on restorative programming should seek to gain a better sense of when – under what conditions and in which contexts – *all* sorts of injustice are condemned and *all* those harmed are supported. Such research can help us better understand how to intervene.

The necessity of intervening actually highlights the unique promise of restorative justice practices. Communities may be changed in progressive ways through restorative justice dialogue. First, communities come together *to do something* about a problem; they grow that way. Second and relatedly, community problems require community solutions. Community solutions begin with communication, obviously so when the problem is one of condoning norms that support the denigration of some within the community. Hudson (1998) states: 'A narrative style of proceedings can therefore not only perform the norm-affirming expressive role of adversarial criminal justice; it can also perform an additional, norm-creating role' (p. 250). Here we see the possibility of restorative justice practices challenging racism and sexism by acknowledging their presence and harms, and modeling egalitarian methods of communicating and meeting needs.

Notwithstanding the promise of restorative justice to reproach attitudes that conduce to violence and to cultivate new (individual and group) attitudes, victim safety must be a paramount concern (Presser and Lowenkamp

1999; Umbreit *et al.* 2003). As such, victim–offender encounters may not be appropriate in certain cases, such as with offenders who (at least currently) deny wrongdoing or express little willingness to change. Encounters need not involve the offender or the victim to be useful in addressing the crime. Some victims may not wish to participate in restorative justice programming that involves their direct offender(s); they must have other options to choose from. Having real choices to make is itself a kind of justice.

Feminists have pointed to the lack of successful therapeutic interventions for girl and women offenders in the system (Chesney-Lind 1997; Gaarder and Belknap 2004; Owen 1999). Girls and women who become caught up in the criminal justice system typically present a complex web of issues, including being victims of prior abuse and deeply embedded structures of social inequality. Successful interventions for female offenders would include individual, relational, and community components (Greene, Peters and Associates 1998; Owen and Bloom 1998). Addressing victimization histories as well as offending behaviors is key. The importance of relationship and reintegration necessitates family and community involvement.

Circles and conferences have the capacity to deal with issues beyond the immediate harm caused by a crime. They invite dialogue on victimization experiences as well as offending of the so-called offender. Restorative justice engages with key figures in the lives of offenders, such as family members, friends, teachers, and other community members. Problems *of* these groups – for example, family dynamics – may be confronted. The observation that girls and women in the criminal system have numerous issues requiring attention could be addressed in a restorative framework that tends to multiple relationships, multiple identities (victim *and* offender), individual behaviors and structural strains. We urge more evaluations of restorative justice programming to help us better understand whether the promises of restorative justice translate into helpful processes for female offenders.

Attention to cultural concerns

Generally speaking, we believe that restorative justice does a better job than formal justice of addressing race, class and cultural concerns. We mentioned previously that the criminal justice system captures the most marginalized members of society. In the United States, African-American women have seen the largest increase in criminal justice processing: for instance, a 78 per cent increase from 1989 to 1994 (Mauer 1995). Beth Richie's (1996) study of incarcerated battered African-American women calls for critical attention to the dynamics of race, class, and gender oppression in the lives of women of color, whose low social status puts them at high risk of repeated cycles of victimization and offending. Restorative justice seeks alternatives to mass incarceration, coupled with attention to the root causes of crime. It concerns itself with intersections of victimization and offending, as well as the effects of structural inequality on individual agency.

Police and court officials may not understand the relevance of cultural traditions and norms in the lives of victims and offenders, or may misinterpret what a particular 'culture' represents. In a study by Gaarder *et al.* (2004), probation officers tended to ignore the impact of racism and poverty on girls and their families, or inadvertently blundered in efforts to be sensitive to race, class, and gender. Processes in which members of one's own community participate are more likely to address race, ethnicity, and culture without stereotyping. Minority and oppressed groups often have poor relations with the state, but in restorative justice processes members of the community are (or should be) active participants (Clear and Karp 1999). Simply having restorative justice options may increase victims' likelihood of reporting crime, providing alternatives to sanctions that 'get tough' on offenders from their communities.

Note that we ought not assume that women of color – however much their communities distrust the criminal justice system – do *not* wish to use that system in cases of domestic violence or sexual assault (Stubbs 2002). We must not leave women at the mercy of 'culture,' an ambiguous term that too often reflects male cultural preferences and practices (Coker 1999; McGillivray and Comaskey 1999; Razack 1994). Some cultural practices can and do work to sustain power imbalances within the group.

In her study of violence against Inuit women in the Canadian eastern Arctic, Zellerer (1999) concludes that community-based justice processes hold great promise but also pose specific challenges to ensuring that violence is effectively confronted and women are protected. For example, the strengths of extended families become weaknesses when family members conspire to hide violence. Zellerer (1999) observes that respect for elders is an important cultural value in Inuit communities but this respect may also lead to overlooking or excusing violence committed by older individuals. Elders are often considered a cornerstone of community-based justice programs in Native communities may not understand the nature, extent, and context of contemporary violence, and will not always support abused women. The older generation may feel that the family unit needs to stay together no matter what, and/or that women should obey their husbands. Some elders may instigate the violence, as was also seen in studies conducted by Das Dasgupta and Warrier (1996) and Fernandez (1997).

Like Zellerer, Coker (1999) reports on benefits (promised and realized) and pitfalls of indigenous forms of peacemaking for domestic violence. The use of traditional Navajo stories with gender anti-subordination themes 'may change the way in which the batterer and his family understand battering' (Coker 1999: 14). Peacemaking is less focused on separation than are formal agencies: 'The value Peacemaking places on relationships does not prevent divorce, but it does allow women to feel that they have explored all avenues for help' (Coker 1999: 73). The problem of battering is seen and dealt with more holistically. Women's material resources may be improved through connections to social services, community support, and reparations from the abuser's family. Reparations are especially important in the context of gendered harms, since intangible indications of changed behavior – namely, apology – may be elements in the cycle of abuse (Coker 1999; Stubbs 2002). Reparations made by the abuser's family – the Navajo tradition of *nalyeeh* – send an important message about collective responsibility for the abuse (Coker 1999: 46).

Yet Coker also notes the following problems in the peacemaking process. In her study peacemakers did not receive adequate training on issues of domestic violence. Offenders often failed to abide by agreements. *Nalyeeh*, though stressed in theory, was not generally provided in practice (Coker 1999: note 217). Within the session, batterers sometimes behaved in a bullying fashion toward victims. Some victims were encouraged to participate without being offered other options. Peacemaker liaisons did not consistently ask respondents whether they would feel safe attending sessions. Again, both formal and informal strategies should be available to victims, and they should not be coerced into participating in any particular one (Presser and Gaarder 2000). The importance of planning cannot be overstated.

Conclusions

The current model of law in the United States has failed to effectively prevent, address, or repair the harms of injustice toward women. In this chapter we have considered the potential of restorative justice to increase the well-being of women and to empower them. M. Kay Harris (1991) has called restorative justice a 'feminist vision of justice,' thus implying that restorative justice is essentially and conceptually compatible with feminism. Harris names three principles of a feminist vision of justice: 'that all people have equal value as human beings, that harmony and felicity are more important than power and possession, and that the personal is political' (p. 88). Harris writes that 'feminists stress the themes of caring, sharing, nurturing, and loving. This contrasts sharply with an orientation that values power and control above all else' (ibid.). Citing Carol Gilligan, Harris associates the care/response orientation to moral issues with females. Gilligan (1982) concluded in her pioneering book, *In A Different Voice*, that girls and women were more relationship-oriented than males due to early relations within the family. Consequently, according to Gilligan, females typically make moral decisions based on considerations of interpersonal connection rather than rights and rules.

Yet some critics theorize that oppression is the cause of the observed gender difference, and thus that the ethic Gilligan calls, simply, 'different' is actually problematic for them. Women may focus on care and relationship at least partially because of their exclusion from the rights granted to men (Hare-Mustin and Marecek 1988). Arguably, low social status conveys a need to constantly evaluate the relationship one is in, particularly if the ties to that partner include economic necessity or fear of violence. In short, an ethic of care may be decidedly unhealthy for women and girls. An anecdote from legal scholar Martha

Minow (1998b) suggests the problem. Minow recalls a horrific event that occurred in 1989, when a self-proclaimed anti-feminist man gunned down fourteen women at a university in Quebec. 'At the Women's Centre, shortly thereafter, there appeared a sign that read, "We are Gentle, Not Really Angry People." Later, an occupant of the Centre changed the sign to read, "We are Gentle, Not Nearly Angry Enough People"' Minow (1998b: 981) concludes: 'Both responses to violence are worth our attention; and thus we must also attend to how to make both avenues of responses viable, and when to pick between them.'

Harris acknowledges these difficulties, stating: 'Especially at present, when there are such vast differences in power among people, we are not in a position to trust that the interests of the less powerful will be protected in the absence of rules designed to insure that protection' (p. 89). Harris' use of the word 'response' in 'care/response orientation' (ibid.) reminds us that a feminist ethic calls not only for nurturing but also for responding. This is entirely consistent with the regulation pyramid Braithwaite (2002) endorses and the 'retributive censure' that Daly (2002: 86) calls for (see also Hampton 1998). Finally, Harris' vision suggests only that care be the guiding light of justice efforts. It does *not* suggest that women should be the primary providers of care.

Restorative justice theory does indeed sound many of the same themes as Harris does. First, it stresses human needs and human relationships. Zehr (1995) writes: 'Crime is first an offense against people, and it is here that we should start' (p. 182). For Sullivan and Tifft (2001), 'a restorative response to a harm grows out of a needs-based conception of justice' (p. 33). That is, people and not abstract standards of what is right are the ultimate concern. Second, when restorative justice advocates and scholars theorize interpersonal harm, they tend to posit structural injustice as a key exogenous cause (Braithwaite 2002; Coker

491

2002; Sullivan and Tifft 2001). Hence the personal (victimization) is political. For example, Braithwaite and Mugford (1994) state that 'in no sense is intervention to deal with individual offences the most important thing we can do to respond constructively to the crime problem: attacking deeper structures of inequality is more important' (p. 156).

We have argued that restorative justice may better address both the call for women's safety and the call for a reduction in formal punishments that reify structural inequities along race, class and gender lines. Throughout, we have called for planners to take care, at every step, that social injustices are not perpetuated by restorative justice practices.

The challenge, in a word, is one of 'doing' justice in an unjust society. Peacemaking initiatives are only useful as part of a package that includes structural change in society. As a social movement, restorative justice must continually expand to address wide concerns of inequity and wrongdoing. This does not mean that 'individual' restorative justice measures, such as repairing the harm between one victim and one offender, do not affect society as a whole. It *does* mean that restorative justice should concern itself with an agenda for structural change as well as individual change – with the goal of creating, maintaining, and repairing healthy, peaceful, and equitable relationships among people and between people and other creatures on the planet.

It will likely take years before we come to any general conclusions on whether restorative justice prevents, reduces, and repairs gendered harms. In the spirit of the restorative justice philosophy, we need to allow time for processes of peace-building to occur. Immediately calculable changes may not be the most important ones, from the perspective of social justice.

The essence of restorative justice lies in redress of harms and repair of relationships. Ultimately, the essence of restorative justice is compatible with feminism's chief aims.

Although the distinct problems of gendered harms demand caution and dialogue among restorative justice workers and scholars, there is reason to be encouraged and energized by the hope that the best possibilities offered by restorative justice might someday be realized.

References

Alder, C. (2000) 'Young women offenders and the challenge for restorative justice,' in H. Strang and J. Braithwaite (eds) *Restorative Justice: philosophy to practice*, Burlington, VT: Ashgate.

Barkan, E. (2000) *The Guilt of Nations: restitution and negotiating historical injustices*, New York: W.W. Norton.

Belknap, J., Holsinger, K. and Dunn, M. (1997) 'Understanding incarcerated girls: the results of a focus group study,' *Prison Journal*, 77(4): 381–404.

Braithwaite, J. (1989) *Crime, Shame and Reintegration*, Cambridge: Cambridge University Press.

— (1999) 'Restorative justice: assessing optimistic and pessimistic accounts,' in M. Tonry and N. Morris (eds) *Crime and Justice: a review of research*, Chicago: University of Chicago Press.

— (2002) *Restorative Justice and Responsive Regulation*, New York: Oxford University Press.

Braithwaite, J. and Mugford, S. (1994) 'Conditions of successful reintegration ceremonies,' *British Journal of Criminology*, 34: 139–71.

Chesney-Lind, M. (1997) *The Female Offender: Girls, women, and crime*, Thousand Oaks, CA: Sage.

Clear, T. R. (1994) *Harm in American Penology: offenders, victims, and their communities*, Albany: State University of New York Press.

Clear, T. and Karp, D. (1999) *The Community Justice Ideal: preventing crime and achieving justice*, Boulder, CO: Westview Press.

Coker, D. (1999) 'Enhancing autonomy for battered women: lessons from Navajo peacemaking,' *UCLA Law Review*, 47: 1–111.

— (2002) 'Transformative justice: anti-subordination processes in cases of domestic violence,' in H. Strang and J. Braithwaite (eds) *Restorative Justice and Family Violence*, Cambridge: Cambridge University Press.

Crelinsten, R. D. (2003) 'The world of torture: a constructed reality,' *Theoretical Criminology*, 7(3): 293–318.

Daly, K. (2002) 'Sexual assault and restorative justice,' in H. Strang and J. Braithwaite (eds) *Restorative Justice and Family Violence*, Cambridge: Cambridge University Press.

Das Dasgupta, S. (1998) 'Women's realities: defining violence against women by immigration, race and class,' in R. K. Bergen (ed.) *Issues in Intimate Violence*, Thousand Oaks, CA: Sage.

Das Dasgupta, S. and Warrier, S. (1996) 'In the footsteps of "Arundhati,"' *Violence Against Women*, 2(3): 238–59.

DeKeseredy, W. S. and Schwartz, M. D. (1991) 'British left realism on the abuse of women: a critical appraisal,' in H. E. Pepinsky and R. Quinney (eds) *Criminology as Peacemaking*, Bloomington, IN: Indiana University Press.

Fernandez, M. (1997) 'Domestic violence by extended family members in India: interplay of gender and generation,' *Journal of Interpersonal Violence*, 12(3): 433–55.

Gaarder, E. and Belknap, J. (2002) 'Tenuous borders: girls transferred to adult court,' *Criminology*, 40(3): 481–517.

— (2004) 'Little women: girls in adult prison,' *Women and Criminal Justice*, 15(2): 51–80.

Gaarder, E., Rodriguez, N. and Zatz, M. (2004) 'Criers, liars, and manipulators: probation officers' views of girls,' *Justice Quarterly*, 21(3): 547–78.

Gilfus, M. E. (1992) 'From victims to survivors to offenders: women's routes of entry and immersion into street crime,' *Women and Criminal Justice*, 4: 63–90.

Gilligan, C. (1982) *In a Different Voice: psychological theory and women's development*, Cambridge, MA: Harvard University Press.

Girshick, L. B. (1999) *No Safe Haven: stories of women in prison*, Boston: Northeastern University Press.

Greene, Peters and Associates (GPA) (1998) *Guiding Principles for Promising Female Programming: an inventory of best practices*, Washington, DC: Office of Juvenile Justice and Delinquency Prevention.

Hampton, J. (1998) 'Punishment, feminism, and political identity: a case study in the expressive meaning of the law,' *Canadian Journal of Law and Jurisprudence*, 11(1): 23–45.

Hare-Mustin, R. T. and Marecek, J. (1988) 'The meaning of difference: gender theory, postmodernism and psychology,' *American Psychologist*, 43(6): 455–64.

Harris, M. K. (1991) 'Moving into the new millennium: toward a feminist vision of justice,' in H. E. Pepinsky and R. Quinney (eds) *Criminology as Peacemaking*, Bloomington, IN: Indiana University Press.

Herman, J. L. (1997) *Trauma and Recovery*, New York: Basic Books.

Hudson, B. (1998) 'Restorative justice: the challenge of sexual and racial violence,' *Journal of Law and Society*, 25(2): 237–56.

Human Rights Watch (1996) 'All too familiar: sexual abuse of women in US state prisons,' online. Available at: http://hrw.org/reports/1996/Us1.htm

LaFree, G. D. (1989) *Rape and Criminal Justice*, Belmont, CA: Wadsworth.

McClellan, D. S. (1994) 'Disparity in the discipline of male and female inmates in Texas prisons,' *Women and Criminal Justice*, 5(2): 71–97.

McGillivray, A. and Comaskey, B. (1999) *Black Eyes All of the Time*, Toronto: University of Toronto Press.

MacKinnon, C. (1989) *Towards a Feminist Theory of the State*, Cambridge, MA: Harvard University Press.

Martin, D. L. (1998) 'Retribution revisited: a reconsideration of feminist criminal law reform strategies,' *Osgoode Hall Law Journal*, 36(1): 151–88.

Mauer, M. (1995) 'Disparate justice imperils a community,' *Legal Times*, 16 October.

Messerschmidt, J. W. (1993) *Masculinities and Crime: critique and reconceptualization of theory*, Lanham, MD: Rowan and Littlefield.

Miller, J. and Schwartz, M. D. (1995) 'Rape myths and violence against street prostitutes,' *Deviant Behavior*, 16(1): 1–23.

Minow, M. (1998a) *Between Vengeance and Forgiveness: facing history after genocide and mass violence*, Boston: Beacon Press.

— (1998b) 'Between vengeance and forgiveness: feminist responses to violent injustice,' *New England Law Review*, 32: 967–81.

Noll, J. G., Horowitz, L. A., Bonanno, G. A., Trickett, P. K. and Putnam, F. W. (2003) 'Revictimization and self-harm in females who experienced childhood sexual abuse,' *Journal of Interpersonal Violence*, 18(12): 1452–71.

Norris, F. H., Kaniasty, K. and Thompson, M. P. (1997) 'The psychological consequences of crime: findings from a longitudinal population-based study,' in R. C. Davis, A. J. Lurigio and W. G. Skogan (eds) *Victims of Crime*, second edn, Thousand Oaks, CA: Sage.

Owen, B. (1999) 'Women and imprisonment in the United States: the gendered consequences of the US imprisonment binge,' in S. Cook and S. Davies (eds) *Harsh Punishment: international experiences of women's imprisonment*, Boston: Northeastern University Press.

Owen, B. and Bloom, B. (1998) 'Modeling gender-specific services in juvenile justice:

493

policy and program recommendations,' final report submitted to the Office of Criminal Justice Planning of the State of California.

Pranis, K. (1998) 'Restorative justice and feminism: common themes,' paper presented at the Second Annual International Conference on Restorative Justice for Juveniles, Fort Lauderdale, FL.

Presser, L. (2004) 'Justice here and now: a personal reflection on the restorative and community justice paradigms,' *Contemporary Justice Review*, 7(1): 101–6.

Presser, L. and Gaarder, E. (2000) 'Can restorative justice reduce battering? Some preliminary considerations,' *Social Justice*, 27(1): 175–95.

Presser, L. and Lowenkamp, C. T. (1999) 'Restorative justice and offender screening,' *Journal of Criminal Justice*, 27(4): 333–43.

Razack, S. (1994) 'What is to be gained from looking white people in the eye? Culture, race, and gender in cases of sexual violence,' *Signs*, 19(4): 894–923.

Richie, B. (1996) *Compelled to Crime: the gender entrapment of battered black women*, New York: Routledge.

Robinson, R. A. (2005) '"Crystal virtues": seeking reconciliation between ideals and violations of girlhood,' *Contemporary Justice Review*, 8(1): 59–73.

Schafran, L. H. (2004) 'Overwhelming evidence: gender and race bias in the courts,' in B. R. Price and N. J. Sokoloff (eds) *The Criminal Justice System and Women: offenders, prisoners, victims, and workers*, third edn, New York: McGraw Hill.

Smart, C. (1989) *Feminism and the Power of the Law*, New York: Routledge.

— (1995) *Law, Crime and Sexuality*, London: Sage.

Snider, L. (1998) 'Feminism, punishment, and the potential of empowerment,' in K. Daly and L. Maher (eds) *Criminology at the Crossroads: feminist readings in crime and justice*, New York: Oxford Press.

Spelman, E. V. (1997) *Fruits of Sorrow: framing our attention to suffering*, Boston: Beacon Press.

Stuart, B. (1997) 'Building community justice partnerships: community peacemaking circles,' Report of the Ministry of Justice, Ottawa, Canada.

Stubbs, J. (1997) 'Shame, defiance, and violence against women: a critical analysis of "communitarian" conferencing,' in S. Cook and J. Bessant (eds) *Women's Encounters with Violence: Australian experiments*, Thousand Oaks, CA: Sage.

— (2002) 'Domestic violence and women's safety: feminist challenges to restorative justice,' in H. Strang and J. Braithwaite (eds) *Restorative Justice and Family Violence*, Cambridge: Cambridge University Press.

Sullivan, D. and Tifft, L. (2001) *Restorative Justice: healing the foundations of our everyday lives*, Monsey, NY: Willow Tree Press.

Tifft, L. (1993) *The Battering of Women: the failure of intervention and the case for prevention*, Boulder, CO: Westview Press.

Umbreit, M. S., Vos, B., Coates, R. B. and Brown, K. A. (2003) *Facing Violence: the path of restorative justice and dialogue*, Monsey, NY: Criminal Justice Press.

United States Senate, Committee on the Judiciary (1993) 'The response to rape: detours on the road to equal justice,' May.

Van Ness, D. and Heetderkstrong, K. (2002) *Restoring Justice*, second edn, Cincinnati, OH: Anderson Publishing.

Websdale, N. and Johnson, B. (1997) 'Structural approaches to reducing woman battering,' *Social Justice*, 24(1): 54–81.

Women's Justice Center (2005) 'Advocating for domestic violence victims who have been arrested for domestic violence,' online. Available at: http://www.justicewomen.com/tips_dv_victims.html [accessed April 2005].

Wriggins, J. (1983) 'Rape, racism, and the law,' *Harvard Women's Law Journal*, 6: 103–41.

Zehr, H. (1995) *Changing Lenses: a new focus for crime and justice*, Scottdale, PA: Herald Press.

Zellerer, E. (1999) 'Restorative justice in indigenous communities: critical issues in confronting violence against women,' *International Review of Victimology*, 6(4): 345–58.

Section VII

Transformative justice and structural change

The chapters in this section address the nature of the relationship between restorative justice and transformative justice. Although there are numerous different conceptualizations of these concepts and differing views on how they are related, both concepts imply change – the movement or transition from one personal circumstance to another, or from one structural circumstance to another, or both. The questions 'Restored to what?' and 'Transformed to what?' are critical substantive issues that must be explored. Earlier chapters discussed the transitions involved in the healing-of-the-self and one's relationships with others in the face of traumatizing interpersonal harm for both those who have harmed others and those subjected to these harms. Earlier chapters, as well, explored the transition processes involved in healing those subjected to gross violations of human rights and the relationship of these processes to the construction of the societies emerging from these harms. The chapters in this section respond to the critique that neither criminological nor restorative justice scholarship and practice has paid much attention to the meaning of justice. Furthermore, they respond to the criticism that this scholarship has paid little attention to assessing and

exploring various visions of how a just society might be organized and how we might move from our present life contexts to those imagined to be more just.

David Gil (Chapter 34) points out that most restorative justice practice and scholarship rarely confronts social-institutional violence, injustice, and privilege, the sources of counter-violent acts by individuals and groups. Like conventional criminal justice processes, restorative justice practice usually follows, rather than precedes, traumatic harms. It responds to the consequences of structural violence and injustice, but not the sources, and in its desire to help heal and reconcile those who are trapped in vicious cycles of structural violence and counter-violence, it unfortunately reintegrates them into structurally violent, 'killed communities,' and highly stratified, unjust societies. Like repressive social-structural violence it often tends to obscure rather than to reveal the real sources and dynamics of violence and denies the need for fundamental change in values and social institutions aimed at transforming structurally violent, unjust societies. Structurally violent and unjust societies are organized in ways that to a considerable degree prevent people from fulfilling their inherent needs and interfere with the development of individuals', groups', and entire peoples' full potential. A socially just society would to a high degree be organized to meet these needs and foster these full potentialities. People would have equal rights, equal responsibilities, and equal opportunities in all spheres of life, including governance, control of resources, organization of work and production, and the distribution of goods and services. Life would have to be organized in harmony with nature.

To move social life in greater congruence with this vision of a socially just society, restorative justice professionals, in the process of helping people affected by counter-violence and conflict, must act as change agents, confronting social-structural violence, oppression, and injustice. Radical or transformative practice implies devising and implementing strategies aimed at facilitating the emergence and spreading critical consciousness and engaging people in reflection and dialogue concerning the consequences of prevailing social, economic, political and cultural realities for the quality of their lives and their behaviors. It implies encouraging conference or circle participants and members of our communities to examine destructive events in relation to personal, family, and community history, social structural realities, and prevailing values. It implies becoming an advocate of social-structural justice, nonviolence, and real democracy.

Edward Martin's contribution (Chapter 35) builds on the transformative justice theme of organizing social life in greater harmony with the environment by exploring environmental and economic development policies as they have been developed in Costa Rica. Costa Rica has been at the forefront of the development of participative democratic models which attempt to promote civil discourse and insulate sustainable environmental policies from the negative externalities of postmodern capitalism. As such, they attempt to incorporate the basic features of an envisioned 'just society' by simultaneously prioritizing generational resource equity and their habitat's carrying capacity in order to secure an environmentally sustainable planet for future generations. Since 1996, Costa Rica has promoted development which respects the balances provided by political stability, social equity, economic stability, and development in harmony with nature. The development of an eco-economy has meant the furtherance of: the promotion of deliberative or participatory democracy; biodiversity prospecting and preservation; market-based and public policy mechanisms for constraining greenhouse gas emissions; autonomous energy and territorial agricultural development; environmental education; and the development of eco-tourism.

David Dyck's contribution (Chapter 36) builds on the transformative justice theme of developing a structurally more responsive practice of restorative justice. In a sense Dyck proposes a transformation of the scope of restorative practice that, in turn, leads to the transformation of society. Taking concrete illustrations from the work of Marie Dugan and Harry Mika, he explores how many interpersonal harms and conflicts are embedded in or nested in social-structural and historical conflicts, and that a restorative practice that ignores these facts unwittingly perpetuates the conditions that give rise to these harms, and provides only a very temporary and surface intervention. Restorative justice practice must be anchored in a future worldview or vision of just relations. It must seek a broader framework for peacebuilding and social change, a framework that adds consciousness raising, an analysis of power relations, educational programming, advocacy and networking for social change, and acting and relating with others in accord with one's vision of justice, in effect becoming a visible, human 'demonstration project.'

To illustrate this last dimension, we turn to Fred Boeher and Diana Conroy's struggle to incorporate restorative justice principles into their everyday lives. Fred and Diana are not restorative justice practitioners in the sense that they do not facilitate circles or conferences; nevertheless, they are, as Catholic Workers, restorative justice practitioners attempting to live a restorative lifestyle within the social structural violence we encounter in our everyday lives in the USA. They are living their lives in accord with their vision of justice rooted in the Christian gospels. They have committed their lives to voluntary poverty, vulnerability, an openness to others, nonviolence, and a personalist approach to offering works of mercy. While offering a home to families who are temporarily homeless, especially immigrant families, Fred and Diana share their home life. Fred's inspiring narrative story and reflections give us a personal example of living a life of being with others and confronting the social structural violence that pervades the fabric of USA culture. His is a view from the Good Samaritan *and* the person in the ditch.

Finally, Kay Harris (Chapter 38) explores the meanings of the concept of transformative justice, paying particular attention to questions about the connections or linkages between restorative justice and transformative justice. She explores four different linkages. If one takes the position that restorative justice and transformative justice should be considered distinct concepts, a sharp critique of restorative justice emerges: restorative justice does not address the structural injustices that underlie conflict and harm; it takes interpersonal harms out of their structural contexts and may serve to reify race, age, sex, and class stratification. On the other hand, this position recognizes transformative justice as extending the scope

of inquiry and practice, challenging the assumptions of corrective healing and seeks social change and a more just future. A dialogue on what social arrangements are desirable or 'just' social arrangements becomes critical.

If one takes the position that restorative processes contribute to personal transformations – self and relational changes – or even conflict transformations, but leaves a conception of transformative justice unformulated, there are also insights. For example, if restorative justice processes can help individuals change themselves, heal, relate more positively, and desist from harm, then there is positive hope that larger, more structural changes are possible. A third position is that both restorative justice and transformative justice represent movement away from conventional criminal justice practices, with transformative justice lying at a greater distance from repressive justice than restorative justice in both its scope and the level of its aspirations. The two orientations share common values and desired social arrangements. The final linkage position is that restorative justice should be conceptualized as encompassing the characteristics and goals identified for transformative justice to such an extent that there is nothing to be gained by treating transformative justice as a distinct concept. In this linkage, restorative justice carries the potential for prevention as well as repair at all the nested levels of impact and in all the spheres and levels of social life.

In our view, restorative justice must become transformative, leading to a structural and interpersonal everyday life that meets our essential needs, fosters our individual and collective potential, and is in harmony with the environment.

34

Toward a 'radical' paradigm of restorative justice

David G. Gil

Introduction

'Restorative justice' evolved as a humane alternative to conventional, adversary models of criminal justice that pursue punishment and retribution for 'deviant' behaviors and are meant to deter such behaviors in the future. However, in spite of its humane orientation, restorative justice practice and scholarship usually do not confront social-structural violence, injustice, and privilege, the sources of counter-violent acts by individuals and groups. Like conventional criminal justice processes, restorative justice practice follows, rather than precedes, destructive events. It deals with consequences of structural violence and injustice but not with their sources. It aims to rehabilitate people trapped in vicious cycles of structural violence and counter-violence; to change their deviant tendencies and behaviors into conformity with social expectations; and to re-integrate them into the status quo of structurally violent, unjust societies.

With few notable exceptions, practitioners and students of restorative justice do not aim to transform structurally violent, unjust societies into structurally nonviolent, just ones (Sullivan and Tifft 2005). How-ever, to fully realize the philosophical principles of restorative justice, its practitioners and students would have to move beyond rehabilitation and reintegration of offenders and victims toward prevention of counter-violent tendencies and behaviors. To do so, they would have to include a 'radical' dimension in their practice and scholarship aimed at transforming structurally violent, unjust societies. Such an expansion of the mission of restorative justice requires insights into the following aspects of human existence:

- inherent human needs and human development;
- social organization;
- social values;
- social justice;
- oppression, domination, exploitation, privilege and deprivation;
- social-structural violence, counter-violence, and repressive violence.

Based on these insights, to be sketched below, this essay suggests in its final section institutional patterns of structurally non-violent, just societies and a radical paradigm of restorative justice aimed at confronting social-structural violence and injustice.

Inherent human needs and human development

Humans share with all forms of life an innate drive to survive and develop. This drive has propelled people throughout history to establish ways of life suited to fulfillment of their needs. In this sense, the evolution of societies has always been motivated by human needs (Gil 1992).

While knowledge concerning inherent human needs is imperfect, fulfillment of the following interrelated needs seems necessary for healthy human development (Fromm 1955; Gil 1992; Maslow 1970):

- *biological-material needs:* provision of biological necessities; sexual satisfaction; and regular access to life-sustaining goods and services;
- *social-psychological needs:* meaningful social relations and a sense of belonging to a community, involving mutual respect, acceptance, affirmation, care and love, and opportunities for self-discovery and emergence of a positive sense of identity;
- *productive-creative needs:* meaningful participation in the work of one's community, in accordance with one's capacities and developmental stage;
- *security needs:* a sense of trust and security derived from the experience of steady fulfillment of biological-material, social-psychological, and productive-creative needs;
- *self-actualization needs:* becoming what one is innately capable of becoming; and
- *spiritual needs:* discovering meaning in one's existence in relation to people, nature, and the universe.

These interrelated inherent human needs tend to change their mode of expression over time, in different social realities. Their substance and dynamics seem, however, constant and universal. Human survival and development, and physical, mental, emotional, and social health depend always on adequate fulfillment of these needs. Such fulfillment can, therefore, be understood as the real interest of people, anywhere and anytime, regardless of their subjective perceptions of needs and interests, which may or may not include fulfillment of these inherent needs.

People's perceptions of needs and interests result not only from becoming conscious of their inherent needs but also from socialization in particular societies with unique ways of life and socially constructed definitions of needs and interests. People's actual perceptions of needs and interests may, therefore, correspond to, overlap with, substitute for, or conflict with their inherent needs and real interests. When perceived needs and interests do not overlap sufficiently with people's inherent needs and real interests, they may pursue and realize socially and culturally constructed substitutes (e.g. material wealth), while their inherent needs (e.g. meaningful human relations and security) remain unfulfilled. Some social scientists have referred to perceptions of needs and interests that do not include people's inherent needs and real interests as 'false consciousness' (Mannheim 1936).

When people can meet their inherent needs in their natural and socially shaped realities, they tend to develop spontaneously, normally, and healthily in accordance with their innate capacities. On the other hand, when people cannot meet their inherent needs in their societies at adequate levels, their physical, mental, emotional, and social health and development are likely to be stunted. Since efforts to satisfy needs have always been the motivating force behind the evolution and transformations of ways of life, *an appropriate criterion for evaluating and comparing ways of life and policy systems of different societies is the extent to which people can actually fulfill their inherent needs.*

From human needs to social organization

Since the earliest stages of human evolution, driven by their inherent and perceived needs, people have pursued survival in different locations on earth, by interacting with each other and with particular natural environments. This drive to survive has led gradually to the emergence of different ways of life, i.e. different forms of social organization, social institutions, and systems of social policies and social values.

In spite of significant differences in the ways of life of different human groups, and in the extent to which their ways of life are actually compatible with the fulfillment of human needs, the policy systems of all societies, anywhere and anytime, had to deal with, and to shape in particular ways, the following inter-related, universal dimensions of human existence (Gil 1992):

- development, control, and conservation of natural and human-created resources;
- organization of work and production of goods and services;
- exchange and distribution of goods and services and of social, civil, and political rights and responsibilities;
- governance; and
- biological and cultural reproduction, socialization, and social control.

The combined effects of these universal dimensions of social life, regardless of their modes of operation in different societies, shape the following related outcome variables of policy systems, and influence, therefore, the extent to which people are actually able to meet their inherent needs:

- circumstances of living of individuals and social groups;
- relative power of individuals and social groups;
- quality of human relations among individuals and social groups; and
- overall quality of life in society.

Social values and ways of life

Social values are guiding principles for human behavior and social relations. Values were evolved by every human society throughout history, based on judgments of behavioral outcomes. Outcomes judged desirable and worthy of repetition were valued positively while outcomes judged undesirable, and to be avoided, were valued negatively. Important issues concerning these judgments were who were the judges, and whose perceived interests were served by beliefs, attitudes, and behaviors shaped by the resulting values.

The history of values reveals that dominant groups and classes judged behavioral outcomes in internally divided societies, and that behaviors guided by the resulting values tended to serve the perceived interests of these dominant groups and classes. Values, once established in a society, tend to be internalized into the consciousness of most people and to shape their behavior, even when actions shaped by the values do not fit their real interests. An apt illustration of this tendency is the value that men are more worthy than women, which is often internalized, not only by men whose perceived interests are served by it but also by women whose real interests are hurt. Another apt illustration is the value of the 'sanctity of property' which tends to be internalized not only by property-owning classes but also by expropriated, propertyless classes, and which protects mainly the interests of owners of property.

The power of values to influence behavior is enhanced by teachings of religions and by sanctions imposed by religious systems on attitudes and behaviors that do not conform to the values. The notion of 'hell'

501

can be understood in this way. Over time, the human origin of values was projected on to super-human sources by many religions, and the role of humans in generating and changing their values was forgotten and denied.

Dominant values of societies tend to limit the scope of possible changes in their organization and policies. Significant changes in social policies and in social institutions are, therefore, unlikely to occur without prior changes in a society's dominant values.

Social justice

Insights concerning inherent human needs in relation to human development, social organization, and social values, can serve as frames of reference for clarifying the meaning of social justice on three related levels: individual relations; social institutions and values; and global relations (Gil 2004).

The distinction the philosopher Martin Buber (1937) made between 'I–thou' and 'I–it' relations is, perhaps, the most pithy conceptualization of social justice on the level of human relations. 'I–thou' relations mean that everyone acknowledges and treats everyone else as an autonomous, authentic subject with equal rights and responsibilities rather than as an object to be used, as is typically done in 'I–it' relations. Expansion of genuine 'I–thou' relations, from local to global levels, could eventually phase out all types of domination and exploitation among people and peoples.

On the level of social institutions and values, social justice means ways of life conducive to the fulfillment of everyone's inherent needs, and to the realization of everyone's innate potential. At different times, some human groups have actually created value and policy systems conducive to meeting everyone's needs, facilitating thus everyone's development. Societies that created such institutional systems did practice 'social justice' in accordance with the perspective suggested here.

Just societies, whenever they existed, have been egalitarian, structurally nonviolent, and genuinely democratic (Kanter 1972; Kropotkin 1956). 'Egalitarian' is used here as a social-philosophical, rather than a mathematical, notion (Tawney 1964). *It means that people have equal rights, equal responsibilities, and equal opportunities in all spheres of life, including control of resources, organization of work and production, distribution of goods and services and rights, governance, and reproduction.* Equality does not mean that everything is distributed in identical shares but that distributions are geared thoughtfully to individual differences and everyone's needs are acknowledged equally.

Just societies do not require 'social-structural violence,' as unjust societies do. Inequalities of rights, responsibilities, and opportunities are unlikely to be ever established and maintained voluntarily. Rather, their establishment requires social-structural violence in the form of physical coercion that is gradually complemented by a 'consciousness of submission' resulting from ideological indoctrination.

Just societies also tend to practice real, rather than merely ritualistic, democracy. In the context of social, economic, and political equality, no individuals, groups, or classes can exercise power over other people and the state, by using accumulated wealth to influence the outcomes of elections, as tends to be done in unjust, non-egalitarian societies.

The following value sets differentiate just from unjust societies:

just societies	unjust societies
equality	inequality
liberty	domination and exploitation
individuality	selfishness and individualism
collectivity-orientation and mutualism	disregard for community
cooperation	competition

Social justice on a global scale implies a vision of over six billion developed people living in developed communities and societies. This vision involves extending 'I–thou' relations to all the world's people, and extending the institutional context of social justice from local to global levels. Since living conditions shaped by social justice principles tend to prevent violence at its sources, the vision implies also a peaceful world without structural violence by states, and without counter-violence by individuals and groups, including the kind of counter-violence referred to as 'terrorism.'

The institutional requirements of global justice could be met by sharing the aggregate of the resources, knowledge, work, and goods and services of the global community in ways conducive to meeting everyone's needs, and realizing everyone's innate capacities. People everywhere would thus have equal social, economic, and political rights, responsibilities, opportunities, and constraints, and no one would be dominated and exploited by others.

Contrary to intuitive assumptions and fears, redistribution of resources, knowledge, work, and goods and services in accordance with principles of global justice need not cause major declines in the quality of life of privileged people and nations. Global wealth is not a fixed, zero-sum quantity and quality but is enhanced quantitatively and qualitatively as the productive potential of underdeveloped people and countries is liberated. Redistribution would have to be implemented gradually, thoughtfully, and non-coercively, as more and more people come to discover that social justice would serve their inherent needs and real interests and would, therefore, enrich everyone.

The quality of life for all would actually be enriched immensely when people everywhere are free to develop their innate capacities and are entitled to use necessary resources and accumulated knowledge and skills in meaningful, productive endeavors.

The 'real' wealth of humankind is, after all, not the aggregate of privately controlled concentrations of capital but the aggregate of realized human potential, the globe's natural and human created resources, and the aggregate of knowledge and skills generated since the early stages of social evolution.

Oppression, domination, exploitation, privilege, and deprivation

The dependence of human development on the fulfillment of inherent human needs is also a fitting frame of reference for understanding the nature of oppression (Gil 1998).

Oppression means social structures and human relations that obstruct fulfillment of inherent human needs and, consequently, interfere with individual and social development. Oppression involves domination and exploitation of individuals, communities, and classes within societies, and of peoples beyond a society's territory. Domination serves to institute and maintain economic, social, psychological, and cultural exploitation of its victims and to establish conditions of privilege for dominant classes and peoples and conditions of deprivation as for dominated classes and peoples. Oppression achieves its goals by expropriating resources and products of dominated classes and peoples and by controlling their work and productivity.

Oppression has usually been initiated by coercive force, followed by socialization and ideological indoctrination. Over time, these processes, backed by systems of social control and 'criminal justice,' tend to result in the internalization of the perspectives and culture of dominant classes and peoples into the consciousness of their victims, and in submission of the latter to the expectations of the former.

The consequences of oppression for its victims are 'social injustice,' i.e. multi-dimensional inequalities and development-obstructing and dehumanizing conditions of living. These coercively maintained conditions include: slavery, serfdom, and wage labor; unemployment, poverty, hunger, and homelessness; discrimination by race, ethnicity, age, gender, sexual orientation, disabilities and so forth; and inadequate healthcare and inferior education. The consequences of oppression for its perpetrators, on the other hand, are privileged conditions of living along with a sense of insecurity.

Oppression and injustice within and beyond societies have always been results of human choices rather than inevitable expressions of human nature. Being results of human choices, oppression and injustice are never inevitable.

Societies that evolved internal relations of oppression tended to extend these relations beyond their populations and territories. Colonialism, genocide of native peoples, and slavery, as well as contemporary economic and cultural imperialism illustrate this tendency. Such oppressive practices intensified over time as a result of resistance by victims and reactive repression by perpetrators, as well as competition for dominance among colonial and imperialistic nations. By now, relations of domination and conditions of injustice have penetrated most branches of humankind in the name of 'globalization' and 'free market' capitalism.

Relations of domination and exploitation from local to global levels have come gradually to be reflected not only in social, economic, political, legal, and cultural institutions but also in the consciousness, values, attitudes, and actions of most people, including victims of oppression. Overcoming oppression and injustice would, therefore, require not only transformations of the institutions that maintain them but also transformations of people's consciousness, values, attitudes, and actions.

Societies whose human relations are shaped by oppressive tendencies are usually not divided simply into perpetrators and victims of oppression. Rather, people in such societies, regardless of their social class position, tend to be oppressed in some contexts and oppressors in others. Dynamics of oppression can, therefore, be understood as chains of mutual 'I–it' relations reaching from local to global levels (Freire 1970).

People who are not engaging in oppressive processes and relations consciously and intentionally may nevertheless be indirectly involved in such processes and relations, and may benefit from privileged existential circumstances as a result of historic and contemporary, local and global patterns of domination and exploitation. Anyone purchasing and consuming food, clothing, and other goods and services, especially in 'developed' countries, benefits indirectly from long chains of exploitation of peasants and workers extending to many parts of the globe. This is, perhaps, the most challenging and painful insight to be gained from a study of oppression.

Social-structural violence, counter-violence, and repressive violence

> The more the drive toward life is thwarted, the stronger is the drive toward destruction.
> The more life is realized, the less is the strength of destructiveness.
> Destructiveness is the outcome of unlived life.
>
> (Fromm 1941)

Violence is often defined descriptively, rather than analytically as in Fromm's (1973) study of human destructiveness. An analytic definition that would reveal the sources and dynamics of violence could be derived from the above sketch of oppression and from insights concerning dependence of human development on fulfillment of inherent human needs. Accordingly, violence may be understood as: *Acts or inactions, by individuals and groups, as well as, socially established, perpetuated, and legitimated conditions, that interfere with fulfillment of inherent human needs, and inhibit the development of individuals, social groups, and entire peoples.*

Manifestations of violence tend to be perceived as discrete events, rather than as moments of historical, multi-dimensional (social, economic, political, cultural, and psychological) processes of vicious circles, involving the following interacting phases (Gil 1996):

- *social-structural violence* within and among human groups, establishing domination over, and exploitation of, individuals, social groups, and peoples;
- *counter-violence* by dominated and exploited people, social groups, and peoples, generating chain reactions of violent feelings, attitudes, relations, and interactions; and
- *repressive social-structural violence* in response to counter-violence, aimed at controlling, punishing, and 'correcting' perpetrators of counter-violence, and deterring further counter-violence.

Some comments on violence and human nature seem necessary here before examining the phases of circles of violence. Humans are widely assumed to be, by nature, a violent species. Violence in human relations is, therefore, considered inevitable and unpreventable. While these assumptions may seem reasonable in view of the history of the human species, they involve a logical fallacy. The capacity for violence is indeed inherent in human nature. However, being inherent in human nature does not mean that manifestations of violence are inevitable rather than merely possible.

While people frequently act violently, they also act often nonviolently, caringly, lovingly, peacefully, and cooperatively. These latter tendencies are also inherent in human nature. Violent and nonviolent expressions of human nature tend to occur in different situations and social conditions when they fit the dynamics, policies, and values of different ways of life.

Social-structural violence

This concept refers to coercive initiation and perpetuation of relations of oppression, domination, and exploitation within and among societies. It involves the establishment and maintenance of multi-dimensional inequalities, i.e. conditions of social injustice that inhibit the development of individuals, social groups, and peoples by interfering with fulfillment of their inherent human needs. Manifestations of social-structural violence include colonialism and genocide; slavery, serfdom and wage labor; unemployment, poverty, homelessness and hunger; inferior health care and education; concentration of wealth and privilege among dominant classes, and concentration of deprivation among dominated classes; etc.

Counter-violence

When conditions generated by social-structural violence consistently interfere with fulfillment of human needs and block developmental energy from unfolding spontaneously and constructively, that energy tends to be expressed destructively as *counter-violence*. Counter-violence is usually not directed against the sources, agents, and beneficiaries of social-structural violence but is displaced on to other targets and becomes manifest as crime, rape, domestic violence, physical and mental ills, suicide, substance abuse, addictions, 'terrorism,' etc. It also tends to generate chain reactions of violent feelings, attitudes, relations, and interactions among individuals, social groups, and peoples, resulting in circles of counter-violence and wars.

Though all manifestations of counter-violence have common roots in social-structural violence, they differ in form, substance, targets, intensity, and consequences as they are shaped by the unique circum-

505

stances and developmental histories of the people involved, and by the unique social contexts in which they occur.

Displacement of counter-violence from the sources, agents, and beneficiaries of social-structural violence is usually accomplished through processes of socialization and social control. These processes aim to promote conformity and to prevent challenges to established ways of life, by facilitating internalization of a society's dominant values and policies into people's consciousness.

Acts of counter-violence tend to be perceived and dealt with as discrete events rather than as moments in historical processes of violent interactions. Further, they tend to be interpreted in public discourse as results of personal defects of 'violent' individuals, rather than as consequences of social-structural violence and chains of reactive counter-violence.

Repressive social-structural violence

Public measures for dealing with counter-violence involve usually repressive social-structural violence. These measures, referred to euphemistically as 'criminal justice,' are designed to control, punish, and correct individuals and groups involved in counter-violence. They are also intended to deter others from engaging in acts of counter-violence, and to reinforce conformity to the social status quo. They focus on the counter-violence of individuals and groups, while disregarding the social-structural violations of their inherent needs.

Repressive social-structural violence tends to obscure rather than reveal the real sources and dynamics of violence. It denies, by implication, the social-structural sources of counter-violence and the need for fundamental changes in values and social institutions aimed at reversing the vicious circles of violence.

Institutional patterns of structurally nonviolent, just societies

Insights sketched in this essay suggest that societies and cultures are just and structurally nonviolent:

- when they practice 'I–thou' human relations;
- when their institutions enable people to meet their inherent needs and to unfold their innate capacities;
- when people have equal rights, responsibilities, opportunities, and constraints concerning the universal dimensions of human life, i.e. resources, work, goods and services, civil and political rights, governance, and reproduction;
- when their values stress equality, liberty, individuality, community, mutualism, and cooperation;
- when they are free of social-structural violence, counter-violence and terrorism, repressive structural violence, and wars from local to global levels;
- when they practice genuine democracy; and
- when their relations and interactions with people and nations all over the globe conform to the principles of social justice and 'I–thou' human relations.

Implicit in these attributes of structurally nonviolent, just societies are the following patterns for their key institutions:

Resources

Natural and human-created, concrete and non-concrete, productive resources would have to be considered and administered as 'public trust,' or 'commons,' available to all on equal terms, as individual producers or producer collectives, for use in productive, life-sustaining, and life-enhancing pursuits.

Stewardship of the public trust would have to be carried out through decentralized, horizontally coordinated, democratic processes, from local to global levels. The public trust would replace private and corporate ownership and control of productive resources, i.e. 'capital.' Goods for consumption could, however, be owned by individuals, groups, households, and consumer cooperatives.

Work and production

Work and production would have to be reorganized, redefined, and redesigned to meet the biological-material needs of all people anywhere on earth, as well as their social-psychological and productive-creative needs. Education for, and participation in, work and production, in accordance with individual capacities, would be assured to all throughout life. All people would have the rights, responsibilities, and opportunities to become self-directing 'masters of production,' using their faculties in an integrated manner rather than being forced to labor as 'hired hands,' or 'factors of production,' under alienating conditions in the perceived interest and at the discretion of individual or corporate employers.

Furthermore, all people would have equal rights, responsibilities, and constraints, to choose and change their occupations, to design, direct, and carry out their work, and to share by rotation in socially necessary work, not chosen voluntarily by enough people. Work would be redefined to include all activities conducive to the maintenance and enrichment of life and would exclude life-impeding activities. Thus, caring for one's children and dependent relatives would be considered and rewarded as socially necessary work while weapons manufacture – to use an extreme example – might be considered 'counter-work' and phased out. All socially necessary work would be deemed to be of equal worth and rewarded accordingly.

Finally, work would have to be in harmony with nature, with requirements of conservation, and with global demographic developments. It would, therefore, have to produce high-quality, long-lasting goods, use renewable resources when possible, and avoid waste.

Rights

Concrete and non-concrete goods and services would have to be exchanged and distributed on fair, non-exploitative terms. All people engaging in socially necessary work would have equal rights to have their needs acknowledged and met by obtaining goods and services in adequate quantity and quality. Social, civil, cultural, and political rights, responsibilities, and constraints would also be assured to all on equal terms.

Governance

Structures and processes of governance, on local and trans-local levels, would have to be truly democratic, non-hierarchical, decentralized, horizontally coordinated, and geared to assuring equal rights, responsibilities, and constraints, and to serving the real needs and interests of everyone living now and in the future. Government service would not entitle elected and appointed officials to privileged living conditions relative to the conditions of the people they represent and serve.

Socialization

Socialization during all stages of life would have to be shaped by egalitarian and democratic values so all children and adults would have equal rights, responsibilities, and opportunities to develop in accordance with their innate potential, with due regard for individual differences in needs, capacities, and limitations.

When people encounter visions for structural social change like the one sketched

507

here, they tend to doubt that such visions could actually be realized. This skepticism is understandable, given people's lifelong experiences with prevailing social, economic, political, and cultural realities, and their adaptation to and identification with these realities.

People living many centuries ago would have been similarly skeptical concerning the possibility of realizing long-range visions, involving comprehensive structural transformations toward contemporary ways of life. Yet such transformations did come about, not quickly, to be sure, and not spontaneously, but through lengthy political processes involving efforts and struggles by critical thinkers, social activists, and popular movements. By analogy, one may assume that visions of just and structurally nonviolent societies, which seem to most people 'utopian,' could eventually be realized, through persistent political efforts and struggles over long periods of time, by contemporary and future thinkers, activists, and social movements.

Toward a 'radical' paradigm of restorative justice

Can restorative justice professionals, in the process of helping people deal with particular conflicts, also act as agents of social change, confronting social-structural violence, oppression and injustice? Growing numbers of practitioners and educators in the human services think that a social change, or 'radical,' dimension can be integrated into professional practice, and many are actually practicing in this way. Doing so enables them to overcome contradictions between conventional practice tendencies to help people adjust to the status quo of structural injustice, and the ethical imperative to confront injustice and oppression.

To transcend conventional practice models of restorative justice and to function as

agents of fundamental social change, professionals would have to integrate into their work the insights discussed above concerning human needs and human development; social organization, social values, and social justice; and oppression and violence. They would also require insights into social change strategies.

History of recent revolutions reveals that fundamental transformations toward structurally nonviolent, just societies are unlikely to come about spontaneously through brief, revolutionary events. Rather, such transformations seem to require lengthy processes aimed at overcoming the forces that maintain and reproduce established, unjust and oppressive societies and cultures.

Societies and their institutional systems have always been shaped and reproduced by the consciousness, actions, and social relations of their members. Hence the forces that social change movements and activists must target for transformation include:

- patterns of consciousness that underlie, motivate, and facilitate existing patterns of action, interactions, and social relations; and
- established patterns of action, interactions, and social relations.

Accordingly, activists pursuing social justice ought to devise and implement strategies aimed at facilitating the emergence and spreading of 'critical consciousness' that could gradually induce appropriate changes in people's actions, interactions, and social relations, and in the resulting institutional systems of their societies (Freire 1970).

Moving toward structurally just societies by nonviolent, rather than violent means – the only strategic mode likely to be effective – requires transformation of status quo-reproducing consciousness into status quo-challenging critical consciousness. Radical restorative justice professionals would, therefore, have to facilitate the spreading of such critical consciousness by dialogical, counter-educational processes aimed at examining and revising:

- images of social reality that most people now hold;
- ideas, beliefs, and assumptions people tend to take for granted;
- perceptions of needs and interests that underlie actions, thoughts, and social relations;
- values and ideologies that derive from the perceptions of needs and interests and affect the thoughts, attitudes, choices, actions, and social relations of individuals, groups, and classes.

Expanding critical consciousness in everyday social encounters, as well as in professional service settings, involves political discourse. When people interact socially and professionally, their actions and communications can either conform to, or challenge, the social status quo and prevailing patterns of human relations. When people speak and act in accordance with 'normal' expectations, they reinforce, by implication, the existing social order and its 'common sense' consciousness. On the other hand, when people's words and actions 'transgress' the ranges of 'normal' communications and behaviors, by questioning and challenging the status quo, they create opportunities for reflection and for the emergence of critical consciousness on the part of others with whom they interact (bell hooks 1994).

Based on these considerations, the strategy suggested here involves efforts by 'radical' restorative justice professionals to 'deviate' in their professional encounters from system-reinforcing messages and behaviors, to pose challenging questions, and to engage people in reflection and dialogue concerning the consequences of prevailing social, economic, political, and cultural realities for the quality of their lives and their behaviors.

As such dialogues evolve, radical activists and professionals ought to identify themselves as advocates of social-structural justice, non-violence, and real democracy – feasible alternatives to capitalism and plutocracy. They should not engage in self-censorship concerning their political views, as people tend to do in unjust, oppressive realities, nor should they pretend to be politically 'neutral,' as many professionals do. One cannot help others to extricate themselves from the dominant ideology and culture unless one is no longer afraid to acknowledge one's alternative perspective.

In pursuing a strategy focused on inducing critical consciousness, one should be sensitive to the thoughts, feelings, and circumstances of people with whom one engages in dialogue. As the goal of such encounters is to stimulate reflection, one needs to be sure that people are ready to communicate. Also, one should respect people and be tolerant of their positions and values, even when these conflict with one's own. For, whatever positions and values people hold do make sense to them at the time in terms of their life experiences and resulting frames of reference.

There are many opportunities to act in accordance with this strategy in everyday social and professional encounters. Were many activists and radical professionals to use these opportunities routinely, many people might become involved in political discussions and the taboo against discourse that challenges capitalism and social-structural violence might be overcome. Gradually, growing numbers of people might undergo transformations of consciousness, join transformation movements, and carry on this strategy.

The foregoing comments on social change strategy have dealt mainly with an element of special relevance to radical restorative justice practice – advancing critical consciousness. Other essential, related elements of the strategy – changing individual and collective behavior, social relations, and societal institutions – are less relevant to direct restorative justice practice, and were not discussed here due to limits of space (Gil 2002).

In conventional models of restorative justice practitioners tend to share the 'common sense' consciousness of most people, according to which prevailing social realities are valid, legitimate, and essentially just. These practitioners pursue, therefore, the rehabilitation and reintegration of offenders and victims into these very realities, in spite of the social-structural violence and injustice that inhere in them, and that are likely to cause recidivism of acts of counter-violence.

Radical practitioners, on the other hand, could use the settings and processes of restorative justice as arenas for dialogue, conducive to the emergence of critical consciousness, concerning the circles of social-structural violence, deprivation of human needs, injustice, and counter-violence, in which people in our society, including offenders and victims, are now trapped. This would be a significant departure from the conventional models of restorative justice.

Radical dialogue in restorative justice settings concerning specific harm-causing encounters is intended to encourage offenders, victims, members of their families and community, and other participants to examine specific destructive events in relation to personal, family, and community history, social structural realities, and prevailing values. The aim is to gain insight into the causal dynamics of specific encounters, and to discern individual and societal sources underlying them. Understanding the causes of destructive encounters does not imply condoning and justifying counter-violent acts and disregarding individual responsibility. Rather, the purpose of pursuing understanding is to learn what could and should be done to reverse the vicious circles of destructive interactions.

Another focus of radical restorative justice conversation is to help participants discover that social realities are never constant, although they may feel that way, and that people, coming together in social movements, have the capacity to change ways of life that are incompatible with meeting their inherent developmental needs and interests. Once people discover their collective capacity and responsibility to change unjust social realities that underlie counter-violent encounters, the prevention of future destructive events may no longer seem an unattainable goal.

In ending this brief sketch of a radical paradigm of restorative justice, I should note that practicing in this way involves personal difficulties and institutional obstacles. For individual professionals, it can involve doubts and feelings of insecurity, loneliness, and alienation. Institutional settings may use overt and covert sanctions to discourage implementation of a radical paradigm. Radical professionals who opt to practice in this way are likely to benefit by forming or joining support groups of likeminded colleagues whose members can help one another to study critical philosophy and to examine and improve their social change practice (Gil 1998).

For individuals, radical restorative justice could provide constructive experiences of learning and maturing, and of finding new meanings for future roles out of a conflict.

References

Buber, M. (1937) *I and Thou*, New York: Charles Scribner's Sons.

Freire, P. (1970) *Pedagogy of the Oppressed*, New York: Herder and Herder.

Fromm, E. (1941) *Escape from Freedom*, New York: Holt, Reinhart and Winston.

— (1955) *The Sane Society*, New York: Holt, Reinhart and Winston.

— (1973) *The Anatomy of Human Destructiveness*, New York: Holt, Reinhart and Winston.

Gil, D. G. (1992) *Unravelling Social Policy*, fifth edn, Rochester, VT: Schenkman.

— (1996) 'Preventing violence in a structurally violent society: mission impossible,' *American Journal of Orthopsychiatry*, 66(1): 77–84.

— (1998) *Confronting Injustice and Oppression*, New York: Columbia University Press.

— (2002) 'Challenging injustice and oppression,' in M. O'Melia and M. K. Krogsrud (eds) *Pathways to Power*, Boston: Allyn and Bacon.

— (2004) 'Perspectives on social justice,' *Reflections*, 10(3), Fall.

Hooks, B. (1994) *Teaching to Transgress*, New York: Routledge.

Kanter, Rosabeth Moss (1972) *Communes: creating and managing the collective life*, New York: Harper and Row.

Kropotkin, P. (1956) *Mutual Aid*, Boston: Porter Sargent.

Mannheim, K. (1936) *Ideology and Utopia*, New York: Harcourt, Brace and World.

Maslow, A. H. (1970) *Motivation and Personality*, New York: Harper and Row.

Sullivan, D. and Tifft, L. (2005). *Restorative Justice: healing the foundations of our everyday lives*, second edn, Monsey, NY: Willow Tree Press.

Tawney, R. H. (1964) *Equality*, London: Allen and Unwin.

35

Environmental policy and management in Costa Rica
Sustainable development and deliberative democracy

Edward J. Martin

Introduction

The environmental doctrine of 'sustainable development' argues that economic expansion and natural resource depletion must maintain, within the broadest sense of the term, ecological limits on the utilization of natural resources (Merchant 1992). Based on the World Conservation Strategy Report (IUCN 1980), and the Brundtland Commission Report (World Commission on the Environment and Development 1987), the popular notion of sustainable development was developed. Though the concept is not entirely new, it is nevertheless the latest expression of a long-standing ethic involving the human community's interrelationship with the environment and the current generation's responsibilities to future ones. As such, the basic notion of sustainable development focuses on resource equity divided into two conceptual frameworks: *intergenerational equity* (fairness to posterity), and *intragenerational equity* (fairness to contemporary persons). As a result, both expressions signify a moral obligation and duty to assure future generations the capacity to maintain a secure level of well-being approximate to the current one. This means that the current generation possesses a moral

obligation not to over-utilize resources at the expense of future generations.

The principles of sustainable development establish guidelines for implementing 'green policies' fundamental to environmental justice. This is also related to principles of economic justice in which justice manifests itself in a 'fair' allocation of resources prioritized for majority populations with the intent of promoting a relatively humane standard of living. Furthermore, the Earth Summits in Rio de Janeiro (1992) and Johannesburg (2002) called on local populations, indigenous persons, and international organizations to inform others on the importance of the long-term benefits of sustainable environmental policies, domestic and global. Consequently, education regarding the principles of sustainable development becomes significant since knowledge and support of these policies have direct implications for communities. This also means that communities will invariably need to reevaluate their attitudes toward patterns of resource allocation and consumption.

The national prioritization of Costa Rica's green policies has captivated the interest of environmentalists around the world. As a case in point, Costa Rica has been at the forefront of implementing sustainable development policies based on Agenda 21.[1] In fact, Costa Rica's sustainable development policies provide a postmodern public administrative model specifically because the public sector in Costa Rica is becoming increasingly dependent on non-profit organizations to carry out public policies. Suffice it to say, sustainable development policies are a unique mechanism for implementing postmodern policies. Notwithstanding, sustainable environmental policies face unique challenges from what has become known as 'late' or 'postmodern capitalism.' In response to this challenge Costa Rica has adapted participative democratic models which attempt to promote civil discourse and insulate its environmental policies from the negative externalities of postmodern capitalism.

Sustainable development

One of the major concepts associated with sustainable development is that of *carrying capacity* (Brown 1995). While theorists have questioned this notion based on empirical analysis, it still signifies an important dynamic regarding ecology and the implications that it carries for social change (Ehrlich *et al.* 1995; Ehrlich and Ehrlich 1992). Carrying capacity is best understood as the maximum number of people that a given habitat can sustain for an indefinite period of time (Catton and Dunlap 1993). This does not exclude the fact that carrying capacity, in the short run, can also be understood based on the same definition, or the point at which environmental capacity is exceeded by human demand. The critical point is that a carrying capacity implies that if a particular population is to be sustained, the carrying capacity must perpetually utilize resources for 'the maximum population equipped with a given technology and a given type of social organization that a particular environment can

support *indefinitely*' (Catton and Dunlap 1993: 206).

In all, sustainable development which in effect promotes generational resource equity attempts to remedy the policy conundrum that exists between resource scarcity and the policy compromises that result. This very dilemma has continually broached numerous debates among policy analysts with respect to the equitable allocation and reallocation of resources. While it has been argued that sustainable resource allocation can be distributed with equity given the per-capita consumption, it may nonetheless be impossible to implement. Furthermore, to simply stabilize growth through limiting the depletion of resources may never be realized since a lack of consensus regarding sustainable priorities may never be reached (Baber 2004; Daly 1990, 1996). This problem is compounded since dependence on basic needs and access to natural resources is predicated upon a finite resource base (Schnailberg and Gould 1994), and the carrying capacity of the planet – which equals the resource base of ten Earths – continues at the current rate of 'resource overshoot.' If this results, then ecological disaster on an exponential level appears inevitable and any effort to correct this trend through generational resource equity could be fruitless (Brown 1981, 1982, 1996; Catton 1980).

Developing countries

One of the more significant issues among sustainable development advocates is the issue of developing countries and the application of neo-liberal development strategies. This includes but is not limited to the privatization of public institutions, introduction of market strategies in the public sector, deregulation of industries, financial institutions, environmental policies, and labor law. According to environmentalists, this implementation further perpetuates 'ecological disorder' (Boff 1995; Magyar 1995). Such policies are designed to aggressively penetrate global markets and expand investments and maximize profits. Elites have argued that neo-liberal trade arrangements have improved the living standard of host countries while simultaneously reducing poverty. On the other hand, others have argued that neo-liberal arrangements through its 'globalization of capital,' have achieved financial profitability at the expense of the world's poor and environment (Cornelius *et al.* 2002; Lash *et al.* 1984; Schumacher 1973).

The point of sustainable development policies is to nurture a deeper sense of community life while fostering a consensus among all stakeholders (Cairncross 1991). As such, these policies seek to incorporate the basic features of a 'just society' by simultaneously prioritizing generational resource equity and a particular habitat's carrying capacity (Broham 1995). Nonetheless, by rejecting short-term neo-liberal policies, sustainable development addresses on a long-term basis social justice and environmental concerns. In this way such policies attempt to secure a standard of justice and equity, grounded in cultural values while prioritizing the democratic utilization of natural resources (Rich 1994; Brown 1991). In effect, sustainable development policies place a greater priority on justice and equity than on economic efficiency (Clark 1989).

Recent study

At the present rate, individuals, communities, and societies now consume an increasing amount of the Earth's irreplaceable natural resources according to a study from the Proceedings of the National Academy of Sciences (PNAS) (Wackernagel *et al.* 2002). The PNAS study was intended for civic leaders and the business community in order to educate them on the ecological impact that government and business was having on the environment. PNAS's study (based on a method of accounting which assesses the cost incurred on the planet's resources in light of global economic expansion) indicated that over the last twenty years resource depletion has been occurring at a dangerously fast rate. Specifically, this deals directly with arable land, fisheries, and forests. Moreover, this is exacerbated by the fact that 5.75 acres of arable land is used to sustain each person on the planet. The ratio in Europe is nearly twice this acreage, while in the United States it amounts to four times. Arguably, this has been the result of global economic expansion which has: (1) increased the demand for scarce resources; and (2) simultaneously undermined the planet's capacity to regenerate scarce resources by approximately 20 per cent. As a result, the planet's resource depletion rate corresponded to 70 per cent of the capacity of the global biosphere in 1961. In 1999 this increased to 120 per cent.

According to research by PNAS, consumer demand in the 1980s outstripped the earth's ability to renew its resource base. PNAS discovered that no sustainable development policies had been implemented in order to regenerate depleted natural resources and guard against the despoliation of the environment. This carried over into agribusiness ventures such as crop production for human consumption and animal consumption, particularly for grazing animals, the meat industry, and industries related to milk, wool, logging, fishing, housing development, highways, energy industries including hydroelectric and nuclear power, and fossil fuel burning. With respect to fossil fuel, this is significant since five times the amount of land to produce and absorb both fossil fuel and carbon-based emissions is expended. What distinguishes PNAS's report from other environmental impact reports indicating potential environmental disasters is that increased carbon is being produced and emitted which the planet cannot absorb. In effect the pace of global warming has escalated.

This report nevertheless demonstrated a trend that requires serious policy remedies, even though the PNAS in the report has disavowed any inevitable conclusion based on their research. Yet a criticism of the PNAS report is that it does not address technological advances and land-use innovations which make farms, factories, and power plants more efficient with the use of resources. The problem is that the study fails to analyze the large holdings of natural resources kept in reserve on a national level. While these criticisms regarding replacement capacity may prove to be valid, the larger question of resource depletion and environmental pollution still poses the very serious question as to whether or not communities and nations can resist having their resources overdrawn (Fukuyama 2002; Daly and Cobb 1994; Rich 1994; Stone 1993; Berry 1987; Tolman 1981; Rifkin 1980; Lee 1982). As a result, securing an environmentally sustainable planet for future generations has become increasingly difficult (Brzezinski 1993; Rifkin 1991).

This may be increasingly difficult to envision within the context of a globalized consumer culture according to Illich, because this very phenomenon perpetuates its own environmental and socio-economic destruction (Illich 1989). Faced with increasing international poverty, transnational pollution, resource depletion, and ecological spoil, global technological sophistication finds itself confronted with attempting to restore ecological balance (Stern and Common 1996). While some undervalue the seriousness of this threat, it nevertheless becomes increasingly difficult to strategically address increased global poverty and ecological destruction (Moore 1998; Moore 1997; Beckerman 1996; Easterbrook 1995; Brzezinski 1993; Meadows *et al.* 1992). Indeed, the phenomenon of postmodern capitalism signifies a threat to market strategies aimed at attempting to resolve environmental and social justice issues (Commoner 1990).

Postmodern capitalism

Under the previous colonial-imperialist order, capitalism simply had to control the various forms of production. In typical European colonies enclaves of subsistence agriculture were well established. In order to increase productivity and profits, colonizers simply pushed workers (and in many cases slaves and indentured servants) to increase productivity. Yet with each new development within capitalism certain enclaves were assimilated, adapted, or destroyed. Generally this has been the result of new technologies such as the steam engine, electricity, etc. Today, capitalist innovations have taken place with atomic energy, cybernetics, chemical products, and information technologies (Aronowitz 1996; Conca 1995; Sale 1993, 1994; Aronowitz 1990; Elster 1983). In short, older, more traditional methods of production such as skilled labor have been replaced by advancements in science and technology. The development of capitalism, however, should not be understood simply as advancements in technology. Rather, the driving force of capitalism (profits) can better be understood by identifying the conduit for this transaction: media marketing aimed at mass consumption on a global scale. Under the guise of neo-liberal policies the media-marketing-capitalist strategy is designed to condition the subconscious of individuals to habitual consumption without which capitalism itself tends toward dysfunction. This phenomenon is described by Bauman as 'postmodern capitalism' (Bauman 1998, 1999, 2000).

Under postmodern capitalism economic arrangements are organized around the media's ability to habituate an entire culture to consumption. Since the lives of individuals and cultures are so thoroughly integrated into the workings of the media-marketing system, critical distance from this phenomenon is difficult to achieve. This is because postmodern capital is simply an accepted part of people's lives in which there is no substantial critique of the system (Baudrillard 1997; Jameson 1991). In fact, the consideration of any other form of economic organization or serious variation on postmodern capital accumulation is generally met with ideological resistance. The reason for this unconditional acceptance of, and simultaneous resistance to, capitalism is that the entire system itself has developed more subtle yet ubiquitous dimensions within the human psyche. Superfluous consumption in this context is marketed in the form of basic needs and with this the development of self-esteem and class identification of individuals and culture (Jameson 1991; Rifkin 1995; Marcuse 1967). According to Jameson,

> consumer capitalism constitutes the purest form of capitalism yet to have emerged, a prodigious expansion of capital into hitherto uncommodified areas. This purer capitalism of our own time thus eliminates the enclaves of precapitalist organizations it had hitherto tolerated and exploited in a tributary way. One is tempted to speak in this connection of a new and historically original penetration and colonization of Nature and the Unconscious: that is, the destruction of precapitalist Third World agriculture by the Green Revolution, and the rise of the media and the advertising industry.
>
> (p. 36)

While identifying the subtle tactics of postmodern capitalism is important, the more critical point of contemporary postmodern capitalist ethos is that the trivial productions of culture – its television shows, movies, fashionable clothing, stylish automobiles, and sexual nuance – are its very driving force not only for profits and increased market shares but also for the simultaneous exploitation of low-wage workers both domestic and global. The consumption of commodities, driven by media lore, has become a powerful symbolic force that gives expression to both a contemporary moral

code and social hierarchy. For postmodern social critics such as Baudrillard, this form of consumerism is now the axis of modern culture (Baudrillard 1997; Marcuse 1964). Conformity to this unwritten but powerful code within postmodern capitalism – in which people no longer consume goods and services based upon utility but rather upon a conformity to the code of consumption – is for Baudrillard the new embedded psychological mechanism that drives consumer culture. Baudrillard notes that this form of 'conspicuous consumption,' as Veblen has described it in *The Theory of the Leisure Class* (1924), becomes for the capitalist class a form of play or recreation. For the middle class and poor, Baudrillard argues that this becomes a form of Nietzschean 'slave morality.' In this sense certain poorer classes are 'consigned to finding their salvation in objects, consecrated to a social destiny of consumption' (Baudrillard 1981: 37).

What is at issue here is an unspoken code of conformity inherent to postmodern capitalism which diverts attention away from the systemic causes of hunger, oppression, and environmental exploitation. Baudrillard describes this as a form of 'simulation' or 'hyper-reality' (Baudrillard 1983: 25). The development of any socio-economic strategy for social justice and sustainable development becomes irrelevant and even hostile to the logic and ideology of commodity consumption. The very nature of postmodern capitalism in its global form thus threatens to undermine the well-being of the poor and the environmental sustainability of the planet through the depletion of natural resources and the increasingly rapid destruction of the environment (Routley 1981; Lee 1980; Habermas 1973; Horkheimer 1947).

Postmodern capitalism has also had a negative influence on debt in developing countries. Approximately fifty years ago the World Bank and International Monetary Fund (IMF) were founded, initially to finance Europe's reconstruction after World War II. These institutions also implement lending and financing policies to questionable development projects around the world. As a result of these projects, developing countries in particular were given little choice by the IMF and World Bank to accept stringent financial conditions for debt and payment structures. Indeed, some argue that the cause of the international debt crisis and draconian 'austerity programs' can be traced to the lending policies of First World financial institutions (Carter and Barham 1996; Cavanagh *et al.* 1994). These austerity programs, which have been insisted upon by the World Bank and IMF in order for developing countries to obtain funding, have led to what are called Structural Adjustment Programs (SAPs), whose purpose is to assure the lending countries that interest payments on debts are met. George points out that those countries borrowing money often spend funds on weapons and nonessentials (1992). Others such as Danaher argue that 'despite all the rhetoric about development and alleviation of poverty, the central function of these multilateral lending institutions has been to draw the rulers and governments of weaker states more tightly into a world economy dominated by large, transnational corporations' (Danaher 1994: 2). Consequently, developing countries in order to service their debt are forced to prioritize the export of cheap consumer goods over the logic of meeting basic needs. This strategy thus serves the needs of a postmodern capitalist structure at the expense of the poor and the environment.

The World Bank and the IMF are not without self-criticism. They admit a growing number of projects are unsatisfactory by their own standards, approximately 40 per cent. In fact, the World Bank and IMF argue that their administrators are socially isolated from the people who pay the real costs of austerity programs which negatively impact land, air, water, health care, and education (Cheney 1989). Nevertheless, no matter how hard the World Bank and IMF

try to construct a solution to the debt problem in developing countries, their policies of structural adjustment, according to David Abdullah, tend to promote 'debt servicing, capital flight, and profits from transnational corporations and the privatization of state-owned companies. In fact, the countries of the South are subsidizing the countries of the North. We are helping to subsidize the United States deficit' (as cited in Gerster 1994: 145). Consequently, the wealthiest nations (G8) dominate World Bank and the IMF policies primarily to their benefit.

Scholars who focus on neo-liberal development policy argue that it is debt itself which prevents the South from competing in the global market. This is especially important with respect to the viability of long-term economic development within debtor nations. The point of neo-liberal development policy is not only to 'privatize' and 'deregulate' government in order to stimulate investment in the private sector but also to pressure debtor nations into servicing international loans that the World Bank and IMF know can never be repaid (Cavanagh *et al.* 2000; Ruthrauff 1994; McAfee 1991; Berry 1987; Payer 1974). Thus developing countries encounter what is known as the 'boomerang effect' in higher taxes on the poor, chronic underemployment, prioritization on export trade rather than infrastructure development, and black market and drug trafficking problems (Danaher 1987, 1994; Bello 1994; George 1988, 1992).

Environmental policy in Costa Rica

The Earth Summits of Rio de Janeiro and Johannesburg encouraged cross-national strategic environmental policies based upon principles of socio-economic justice that protected both the environment and the needs of the poor. One country that has prioritized sustainable development policies is Costa Rica. Since 1996, Costa Rica's implementation of sustainable development policies has provided a new vision for maintaining the environment and the economic well-being of its people. It has promoted 'development which respects the balances provided by political stability, social equity, economic stability, and development in harmony with nature' (Figueres Olsen 1996: 1). Thus Costa Rica has supported a 'balanced development' mitigating the effects of poverty, advancing education, reorienting populations to new levels of social awareness and political attitudes, and ensuring high performance measurements in the public sector. Moreover, democratic deliberation has become a central focus in policy debates in order to ensure democratic consensus and insulate Costa Rican policy from the effects of excessive special interests. This means that public administrators have had to take on a new role of facilitator in public discourse regarding participation in local decision-making, implementing new methods of economic production and consumption, and ensuring equity in cross-national relations (Collinson 1996).

Promotion of deliberative democracy

One essential feature of a sustainable society and the policy-making process is the phenomenon known as deliberative democracy (Prugh *et al.* 2000). In attempting to formulate a consensus on key policy issues, Costa Rica has encouraged dialogue and debate on major policy issues. By promoting civil discourse as citizen participation, stakeholders from various sectors of society were solicited for their input on policy issues. Though the process has been cumbersome, it has nevertheless resulted in policies that have enjoyed popular support; it has energized once alienated persons –

specifically indigenous persons – to become active in local and national policy. This is because Costa Rica has placed a high value on greater environmental democracy by soliciting diverse perspectives.

Typically, the process of soliciting, collecting, and processing policy input from the people of Costa Rica is carried out through local governments and elected representatives. The strategic framework to promote participative democracy and expand citizen participation in the policy-making process is to strengthen and adapt the use of existing mechanisms and institutions while leaving open the possibility of incorporating new ones in response to changing situations. At the heart of this framework is the mandate for transparency and accountability within democratic institutions. Citizens must be able to have direct access to public officials. Moreover,

> channels of communication between citizens and their representatives in the periods between elections is required ... This covers the entire range of public policies, both in the phase of elaboration and in their implementation. Citizen participation is essential because nobody knows better the needs than those who are nearer to them.
>
> (United Nations Development Program
> Bureau for Latin America and the
> Caribbean 1999: 4)

The following examples are sustainable development Agenda 21 policies which Costa Rica has implemented as national priorities, derived from the Rio Summit and updated at the Johannesburg Summit. Through the participative or deliberative democracy model, Costa Rica and its citizens were able to dialogue on the need for Agenda 21 strategies. In addition to implementing sustainable development policies, Costa Rica has also ratified the Kyoto Protocol and its goal of eliminating greenhouse gas emissions (Medio Ambiente y Desarrollo en America Latina 1999).

Biodiversity

Fundamental to sustainable development is the notion of biodiversity and maintenance of the biosphere itself. Biodiversity ensures environmental resilience and a variety of other stabilizing factors for regional ecosystems (Daily 1997; Tilman 1999; Walker *et al.* 1999). This means that certain natural habitats are designated for human utilization while others are reserved for animal populations and plant species. What is implied here is careful management of human interaction with both animal and plant life in Costa Rica. Thus to ensure a sustainable level of management, Costa Rica has voluntarily agreed to protect 12 per cent of its biosphere in accordance with both the Brundtland Report commissioned by the United Nations and the Rio and Johannesburg Summits in 1992 (see World Commission on the Environment and Development 1987).

Costa Rica is also aggressively promoting 'biodiversity prospecting.' This is the collection and identification of genetic samples in its high-biodiversity tropical rain forest (Larson 2003; Hunter 1997). Environmentalists argued that this can be an economically viable alternative to tropical forest harvesting. In fact, bio-prospecting was introduced in 1991 through an agreement between Costa Rica's National Biodiversity Institute (INBio), and Merck & Co., Ltd, a pharmaceutical firm based in the United States. As early as 1991, INBio has been cooperating with Merck in the area of chemical extracts from indigenous vegetation, insects, and micro-organisms obtained from conservation lands in Merck's drug-screening research. On its behalf, Merck has allocated a generous research and sampling stipend for Costa Rica. This relationship has also included future royalties on any resulting percentage of commercial products. In turn, funds received from Merck are being reinvested in further research and protection of numerous conservation lands. In fact, INBio is currently negotiating other agreements of this nature with other pharmaceutical and chemical companies. This demonstrates Costa Rica's willingness to work with multinational corporations while still attempting to maintain the integrity of Costa Rica's environmental policies.

Climate change

Costa Rica has taken seriously the international scientific community's warnings regarding the looming threat of global warming (Figueres Olsen 1996). Negative social and economic impacts for Costa Rica could potentially result from a temperature change, even by a few degrees. In attempting to insulate itself for this threat, Costa Rica has ratified the United Nations Framework Convention on Climate Change (FCCC), and has become the first country in Central American to provide an inventory of the sources and sinks for greenhouse gases. In order to ameliorate this effect, Costa Rica has implemented precise goals and timetables for reducing dependence on fossil fuel consumption. Hence, Costa Rica's new policy on climate change has focused more on increasing dependence on renewable sources of energy, especially in the area of electric powered vehicles (Salazar-Cambronero 1993). Under the 'Rational Use of Energy' law, Costa Rica is promoting reductions in greenhouse gas emissions while working simultaneously to improve the transportation sector's use of cleaner and more efficient fuel systems. This clearly translates into greater incentives to purchase unleaded fuel and electric powered vehicles.

Costa Rica is also cooperating with industrialized countries in order to offset greenhouse gas emissions (GHG) through a policy known as 'joint implementation' (JI), and in other venues 'activities implementation jointly' (AIJ). JI, presently under an international trial phase directed by the United Nations FCCC, encourages arrangements based on international associations in

519

which private businesses, government agencies, and/or non-governmental organizations (NGOs) undertake joint mitigation or sequestration activities in another host country such as Costa Rica. These JI strategies generally fall within two categories: *land use*, which is inclusive of carbon sequestration by way of increasing a given area's potential to fix carbon (such as planting trees) or preserving natural carbon stocks (forests, soils, etc.) threatened by destruction; and, *energy projects*, which includes alternate fuel sources or use of renewable energy that decreases the use of carbon-based fuels. JI also represents a viable market strategy to aid countries in meeting FCCC objectives, while giving participants an opportunity to advance reductions in global emissions of greenhouse gasses in a mutually beneficial and cost-effective manner (Tattenbach and Petricone 1995).

Costa Rica is also exploring other market-based mechanisms for decreasing global greenhouse emissions. Currently, efforts are underway to provide titles that give the bearer permission to legally emit small amounts of carbon emissions in the parks and restricted lands within Costa Rica. Under this provision, funds generated through the sale of the titles will be secured to manage and purchase threatened and privately held lands. Additional funding will be issued to smaller landholders for the purpose of reforestation in buffer zones within protected areas. The titles are to be bought through a national fund, identical to a trust fund. Costa Rica will then transfer prior certified carbon rights to offset emitters and investors who could potentially present the titles regulators when declaring emissions. Trading these titles through a commodity exchange is also an available option. This initiative is important in that it provides the creation of a 'titles market' for global greenhouse gas emissions. As a result, Costa Rica has attempted to provide in part a market measure that has the potential to help limit negative externalities such as pollution.

Macroeconomic policies

In order for Costa Rica to establish a comprehensive framework in which meaningful sustainable development policies can be fostered, a more balanced approach to macroeconomic policies has been established (Carter and Barham 1996). Costa Rica seeks equitable market arrangements in order to promote further economic growth within its borders by making its natural resources available in a sustainable manner. The goal within this context is to promote greater economic independence for local people (Mitchell 1997). In order to develop a more comprehensive economic plan, and to provide the necessary implements and resources to promote a sustainable environment and economy, restructuring of the economy has become the single most important task facing Costa Rica. As a result, Costa Rica is committed to an open and balanced economy that promotes both short- and long-term sustainability (Daily 1997).

To realize this goal, Costa Rica intends to reduce both its fiscal and external deficit: (1) to provide incentives for increased internal savings (sustainable development in this case translates into fiscal incentives in order to ease taxation on income, savings, and work, while implementing a progressive consumptive tax inclusive of natural resource depletion); (2) remove unnecessary quotas and subsidies; and (3) increase entrepreneurial initiatives. By creating sustainable business enterprises at the local level, Costa Rica hopes to minimize poverty and unemployment by introducing marginalized communities to sustainable business practices (Broham 1995; Salazar-Cambronero 1993). Indeed, the Inter-American Development Bank has praised Costa Rica for its efforts at implementing effective sustainable market measures (Inter-American Development Bank 2000). In the attempt to introduce rural people to sustainable business enterprises, Costa Rica hopes to raise the awareness in its citizens that the market can be used to help promote greater independence from state support.

Energy policies

Principles of sustainable development can also be applied to various energy policies. One of Costa Rica's goals is to minimize its dependence on fossil fuel consumption in an attempt to preserve air quality in accordance with prudent market strategies (Daily and Ellison 2002). Costa Rica has also attempted to lessen its dependence on costly and expensive hydroelectric power while simultaneously increasing its emphasis on utilizing renewable energy sources such as geothermal, solar, and wind power. Moreover, Costa Rica is undergoing cutting edge research with respect to some of the latest developments in 'hydrogen power' (Rifkin 2002). This new technology development is based on a non-fossil fuel power source: *water*. The aim is to 'split water' (not atoms) into hydrogen and oxygen for the production of hydrogen as an energy source. Scientists such as Rifkin argue that this adaptation can be cheaply produced, accessed, and consumed by the poor on a global scale. The process involves absorbing sunlight on a titanium-based window with photoactive properties. Photo reactors then generate power that in turn splits water, thus producing hydrogen as a viable energy source (Rifkin 2002).

Agricultural policies

In Costa Rica a strong emphasis has been placed on promoting a sound productive agricultural sector. This involves soil conservation through the use of wind barriers and contour planting in order to establish financial incentives for the use of more efficient irrigation systems (Tilman 1999). The use of integrated pest management instead of chemical pesticides is a high priority for Costa Rica. In addition, farmers are being encouraged to utilize new integrated methods of cattle ranching and marketing of organic beef, while fishermen are being provided with economic incentives to reduce fishing in overly depleted fisheries. This includes the integration of tree planting and the regeneration of forests within those environmentally sensitive areas that experienced reckless deforestation. With respect to producing Costa Rica's two largest crops, coffee and bananas, incentives are provided to reward farmers with cleaner production and more efficient recycling alternatives to waste disposal.

Environmental education

The educational system in Costa Rica is attempting to nurture a population that is 'bio-literate,' in addition to its already high literacy rate of 94 per cent. 'Bio-literacy' is an educational approach that emphasizes the importance regarding the sensitive management of natural resources. Curricula have been implemented in all educational environments throughout Costa Rica to include sustainable development concepts and environmental policy issues (World Commission on the Environment and Development 1987). The goal of bio-literacy is to assist present and future generations in attempting to comprehensively understand the priority of the environment and how sustainable development methods can aid rational strategies for securing a balanced environment. Moreover, as a significant part of bio-literacy, Costa Rica is attempting to develop indigenous bilingual curricula in order to introduce sustainable development concepts to native populations. The overall program is to be extended throughout Costa Rica and include continued input from all sectors of Costa Rican society.

Territorial ordainment

Costa Rica until recently had one of the highest rates of tropical deforestation in Latin America, even though prior governments had secured unused land as protected parks and reserves (Tattenbach and Petricone 1995). Costa Rica has categorized its territory into distinct areas of usage and integrating agriculture into sustainable development strategies. The goal is to benefit from the protected regions instead of competing with them. As a result, Costa Rica has created a National System of Conservation Areas that consolidates the protected areas under a new democratic management system (Walker *et al.* 1999; Tilman 1999). The central features of this new policy are: (1) restructured and more democratic National Park Foundation; (2) decentralized management that links responsibility for the management of the areas to the communities in the local areas; (3) increased entrance fees to parks, helping individually protected areas to maintain self-sufficiency and improved services; and (4) retraining of Conservation Area staff in local biodiversity management and ecosystem maintenance.

Increasing national parks

In further efforts to promote a sustainable society, Costa Rica is increasing the size and number of its national parks and reserves, not simply for purposes of conservation, but as sources of income generation. These parks, known as 'biodiversity factories,' are storehouses for future income if wisely managed. Such biodiversity factories are significant to Costa Rica's popular form of nature-based tourism which is one of the major sources of foreign currency exchange for the country. Costa Rica is prioritizing the development of lower-impact 'eco-tourism' that values its ecological national treasures as opposed to mass tourism which

failed to prioritize a sustainable environment (Honey 1999). By increasing national parks and reserves, combined with planned access and eco-tourism in the private sector buffer zones, Costa Rica plans to facilitate increased tourism demands. In fact the tourism industry is attempting to implement an enlightened management policy in which the Ministry of Tourism is establishing a 'green classification' that will categorically rate hotel environment performance. When deciding on a hotel for lodging, tourists and guests will be freely able to assess the hotel's use of energy efficiency, solid waste disposal, and other environmental measures based on a set of established environmental factors rooted in Costa Rica's sustainable development priorities. While the '9/11' event has hampered tourism to some degree in Costa Rica, these factors when aggregated enhance sustainable development performance and other forms of responsible environmental stewardship.

Conclusion

One of the most significant challenges facing a sustainable development policy and the promotion of both social and natural capital is the phenomenon of postmodern capitalism. By enticing and even captivating consumers through sophisticated marketing techniques, postmodern capitalism has developed strategies in which individuals and cultures habitually and uncritically purchase and consume, based not on need per se, but rather on trend and status. Postmodern social critics argue that this phenomenon signifies increased demand for consumption while simultaneously exploiting environmental resources. This follows the logic of mass-marketing in the effort to create market demand and consumption in accord with capitalist interests. The ever-expanding markets within capitalist designs thus pose the greatest threat to undermining a sustainable world community since unlimited wants invariably conflict with limited resources.

Most developed countries, such as the United States, the British Commonwealth, Germany, and Japan, are capable of producing economic goods in excess of their patterns of consumption. These countries are then forced, by the logic of the free market, to aggressively seek newer and more profitable markets to sell their surplus goods. Other countries, such as China, Brazil, India, Thailand, and South Korea, are able to provide for basic domestic needs while simultaneously emerging as exporters of manufactured and agricultural goods. However, for a third group of countries in Africa, Latin America, and the Caribbean, economic production remains at, or below, a subsistence level. In fact, while birthrates increase, populations are kept at bay through civil strife, disease, and illnesses and deaths related to hunger. Typically, the natural resources of these countries are exploited based on leveraged economic arrangements that favor wealthy countries and international investors. However, in order to remedy these continuing global problems, both economic and environmental, Brown has argued that an 'eco-economy' must be at the heart of any sustainable development policy. This agenda will help prevent, in the long run, resource degradation that threatens more widespread food shortages.

The Costa Rican model provides a context for ongoing dialogue and civil discourse in promoting greater democratic control over environmental resource allocation and economic development through sustainable development policies. This form of civil discourse provides an important context for increased dialogue on the priority of securing environmental integrity and local indigenous economic needs over and above the strategies of global and postmodern capital ventures. It is precisely in sustainable policies that zero-sum effects within a global market can be mitigated. Working within the structures of limiting the use of natural resources

and the need to secure the integrity of local domestic needs is fundamental to a sustainable planet. Arguably the Costa Rican model on environmental policy and administration best supports the development of natural and social capital based on the Earth Summit's sustainable development principles and policies which have emerged from Rio de Janeiro (1992) and Johannesburg (2002). These environmental policies and management strategies could prove to be of great benefit to the populations of the North. In future planning strategies, the inclusive dimension of capacity building through civil discourse holds promise for a more democratic environment and economy.

References

Aronowitz, S. (1990) *The Crisis in Historical Materialism: class, politics and culture in Marxist theory*, second edn, New York: Macmillan.
— (1996) *Technoscience and Cyberculture*, New York: Routledge.
Baber, W. (2004) 'Ecology and democratic governance: toward a deliberative model of environmental politics,' *The Social Science Journal*, 41: 331–46.
Baudrillard, J. (1981) *For a Critique of the Political Economy of the Sign*, St Louis: Telos Press.
— (1983) *Simulations*, New York: Semiotext.
— (1997) *The Consumer Society: myths and structures*, Thousand Oaks, CA: Sage.
Bauman, Z. (1998) *Globalization: the human consequences*, New York: Columbia University Press.
— (1999) *In Search of Politics*, Stanford, CA: Stanford University Press.
— (2000) *Liquid Modernity*, Malden, MA: Blackwell.
Beckerman, W. (1996) *Green-Colored Glasses: environmentalism reconsidered*, Washington, DC: The Cato Institute.
Bello, W. (1994) *Dark Victory: the United States, structural adjustment, and global poverty*, Oakland, CA: Institute for Food and Development Policy.
Berry, W. (1987) *Home Economics*, San Francisco: North Point Press.
Boff, L. (1995) *Ecology and Liberation: a new paradigm*, Maryknoll, NY: Orbis Books.

Broham, J. (1995) 'Economism and critical silence in development studies: a theoretical critique of neoliberalism,' *Third World Quarterly*, 16(2): 297–319.

Brown, L. (1981) *Building a Sustainable Society*, New York: W. W. Norton.

— (1982) *Six Steps to a Sustainable Society*, Washington, DC: Worldwatch Institute.

— (ed.) (1991). *State of the World 1990*, New York: W. W. Norton.

— (1995) *Full House: reassessing the earth's population carrying capacity*, London: Earthscan.

— (1996) *Tough Choices: facing the challenge of food scarcity*, New York: W. W. Norton.

Brzezinski, Z. (1993) *Out of Control: global turmoil on the eve of the twenty-first century*, New York: Charles Scribner's Sons.

Cairncross, F. (1991) *Costing the Earth*, Boston: Harvard Business School Press.

Carter, M. and Barham, B. (1996) 'Level playing fields and laissez faire: postliberal development strategy in inegalitarian economics,' *World Development*, 24(7): 1133–278.

Catton, W. (1980) *Overshoot: the ecological basis of revolutionary change*, Urbana, IL: University of Illinois Press.

Catton, W. and Dunlap, R. (1993) 'Carrying capacity and the death of a culture: a tale of two autopsies,' *Sociological Inquiry*, 63(2): 202–23.

Cavanagh, J., Arruda, M. and Wysham, D. (1994) *Beyond Bretton Woods: alternatives to the global economic order*, Washington, DC: Institute for Policy Studies.

Cavanagh, J., Anderson, S. and Lee, T. (2000) *Field Guide to the Global Economy*, Washington, DC: The Institute for Policy Studies.

Cheney, J. (1989) 'Postmodern environmental ethics: ethics as bioregional narrative,' *Environmental Ethics*, 11(2): 117–34.

Clark, J. (1989) 'Marx's inorganic body', *Environmental Ethics*, 11(3): 243–58.

Collinson, H. (ed.) (1996) *Environmental Conflicts and Initiatives in Latin America and the Caribbean*, New York: Russell Press.

Commoner, B. (1990) *Making Peace with the Planet*, New York: Pantheon Books.

Conca, K. (1995) 'Greening the United Nations: environmental organizations and the UN system,' *Third World Quarterly*, 16(3): 441–57.

Cornelius, P., McArthur, J., Schwab, K., Porter, M. and Sachs, J. (2002) *The Global Competitiveness Report 2001–2002*, Geneva: World Economic Forum.

Daily, G. (ed.) (1997) *Nature's Services: societal dependence on natural ecosystems*, Washington, DC: Island Press.

Daily, G. and Ellison, K. (2002) *The New Economy of Nature: the quest to make conservation profitable*, Washington, DC: Shearwater Books.

Daly, H. (1990) 'Toward some operational principles of sustainable development,' *Ecological Economics*, 2: 1–6.

— (1996) *Beyond Growth: the economics of sustainable development*, Boston: Beacon Press.

Daly, H. and Cobb, J. (1994) *For the Common Good: redirecting the economy toward community, the environment, and a sustainable future*, second edn, Boston: Beacon Press.

Danaher, K. (ed.) (1987) *Help or Hindrance? United States economic aid*, San Francisco, CA: Institute for Food and Development Policy.

— (ed.) (1994) *Fifty Years is Enough: the case against the World Bank and the International Monetary Fund*, Boston, MA: South End Press.

Easterbrook, G. (1995) *A Moment on Earth*, New York: Viking, Penguin.

Ehrlich, P. and Ehrlich, A. (1992) 'The most overpopulated nation,' *The Egg: An Eco-Justice Quarterly*, Fall: 4–5.

Ehrlich, P., Ehrlich, A. and Daly, C. (1995) *The Stork and the Plow: the equity answer to the human dilemma*, New York: G. P. Putman's Sons.

Elster, J. (1983) *Explaining Technical Change: studies in rationality and social change*, New York: Cambridge University Press.

Figueres Olsen, J. (1996) 'Sustainable development: a new challenge for Costa Rica,' *SAIS Review*, 16(1): 187–202.

Fukuyama, F. (2002) 'Social capital and development: the coming agenda', *SAIS Review*, 22(1): 23–37.

George, S. (1988) *A Fate Worse than Debt*, New York: Grove Weidenfeld.

— (1992) *The Debt Boomerang: how Third World debt harms us all*, London: Pluto Press.

Gerster, R. (1994) 'The World Bank after the Wapenhans Report – what now?' in K. Danaher (ed.) *Fifty Years is Enough: the case against the World Bank and the International Monetary Fund*, Boston: South End Press.

Habermas, J. (1973) *Theory and Practice*, Boston: Beacon Press.

Honey, M. (1999) *Ecotourism and Sustainable Development: who owns paradise?* Washington, DC: Island Press.

Horkheimer, M. (1947) *Eclipse of Reason*, New York: Seabury Press.

Hunter, C. (1997) 'Sustainable bio-prospecting: using private contracts and international legal principles and policies to conserve raw medicinal materials,' *Environmental Affairs Review*, 25(1): 129–74.

Illich, I. (1989) 'The shadow of our future throws,' *New Perspectives Quarterly*, 6: 20–5.

Inter-American Development Bank (2000) *Citizen Participation in the Activities of the Inter-American Bank*, Argentina, Peru, Costa Rica, Columbia: Bank Information Center, 27 October, pp. 1–11.

IUCN (1980) *The World Conservation Strategy*, Gland, Switzerland: IUCN.

Jameson, F. (1991) *Postmodernism, or the Cultural Logic of Late Capitalism*, Durham, NC: Duke University Press.

Larson, A. (2003) 'Decentralization and forest management in Latin America: towards a working model,' *Public Administration and Development*, 23(3): 211–26, online. Available at: http://www.interscience.wiley.com

Lash, J., Gillman, K. and Sheridan, D. (1984) *A Season of Spoils: the Reagan administration's attack on the environment*, New York: Pantheon Books.

Lee, D. (1980) 'On the Marxian view of the relationship between man and nature,' *Environmental Ethics*, 2(1): 3–16.

— (1982) 'Toward a Marxian ecological ethic: a response to two critics,' *Environmental Ethics*, 4(4): 339–44.

McAfee, K. (1991) *Storm Signals: structural adjustment and development alternatives in the Caribbean*, Boston, MA: South End Press.

Magyar, K. (1995) 'Classifying the international political economy: a third world proto-theory,' *Third World Quarterly*, 16(4): 703–16.

Marcuse, H. (1964) *One-Dimensional Man*, Boston: Beacon Press.

— (1967) *Counterrevolution and Revolt*, Boston: Beacon Press.

Meadows, D., Meadows, D. and Randers, J. (1992) *Beyond the Limits*, Post Mills, VT: Chelsea Green Publishing.

Medio Ambiente y Desarrollo en America Latina (1999) *Consejo superior investigaciones cientificas, espana. Subdesarrollo y Medio Ambiente en America Latina*, Seville, Spain: Escuela de Estudios Hispano-Americanos.

Merchant, C. (1992) *Radical Ecology: the search for a living world*, New York: Routledge.

Mitchell, B. (1997) *Resources and Environmental Management*, London: Longman.

Moore, C. (1997) *Haunted Housing: how toxic scare stories are spooking the public out of house and home*, Washington, DC: The Cato Institute.

Moore, T. (1998) *Climate of Fear: why we shouldn't worry about global warming*, Washington, DC: The Cato Institute.

Payer, C. (1974) *The Debt Trap: the international monetary fund and the Third World*, New York and Harmondsworth: Penguin Books.

Prugh, T., Costanza, R. and Daly, H. (2000) *The Local Politics of Global Sustainability*, Washington, DC: Island Press.

Rich, B. (1994) *Mortgaging the Earth: the World Bank, environmental impoverishment, and the crisis of development*, Boston: Beacon Press.

Rifkin, J. (1980) *Entropy: a new world view*, New York: Bantam Books.

— (1991) *Biosphere Politics*, San Francisco, CA: HarperCollins.

— (1995) *The End of Work: the decline of the global labor force and the dawn of the post-market era*, New York: G. P. Putnam's Sons.

— (2002) *The Hydrogen Economy: the creation of the world wide energy web and the redistribution of power on earth*, New York: Tarcher/Putnam.

Routley, V. (1981) 'On Karl Marx as an environmental hero,' *Environmental Ethics*, 3(3): 237–44.

Ruthrauff, J. (1994) *A Layperson's Introduction to the Inter-American Development Bank, World Bank, and International Monetary Fund*, Washington, DC: Center for Democratic Education.

Salazar-Cambronero, R. (1993) *El Derecho a un Ambiente Sano: Ecologia y desarrollo sostenible*, San Jose, Costa Rica: Libro Libre.

Sale, K. (1993) *The Green Revolution: the American environmental movement: 1962–1992*, New York: Hill and Wang.

— (1994) *Dwellers in the Land: bioregional vision*, San Francisco: Sierra Club Books.

Schnailberg, A. and Gould, K. (1994) *Environment and Society: the enduring conflict*, New York: St Martin's Press.

Schumacher, E. F. (1973) *Small is Beautiful: economics as if peopled mattered*, New York: Harper Colophone Books.

Stern, D. and Common, M. (1996) 'Economic growth and environmental degradation: the environmental kuznets curve and sustainable development,' *World Development*, 24(7): 1151–60.

Stone, C. (1993) *The Gnat is Older than Man: global environmental and human agenda*, Princeton: Princeton University Press.

Tattenbach, F. and Petricone, S. (1995) *A Costa Rican–United States Certifiable Transferable Gas Offset*, San Jose, Costa Rica: Costa Rican Office for Joint Implementation, November.

Tilman, G. (ed.) (1999) *Benefits of Biodiversity*, Ames, IW: Council of Agricultural Science and Technology Task Force Report 133.

Tolman, C. (1981) 'Karl Marx, alienation, and the mystery of nature,' *Environmental Ethics*, 3(1): 63–74.

United Nations Development Program Bureau for Latin America and the Caribbean (1999)

Civil Society: participation and transparency in Central America, 25–28 May, 1–11.

United Nations Division for Sustainable Development (2000) *Agenda 21*, 29 June: 1–2. online. Available at: http://www.un.org/esa/sustdev/agenda21 text.htm

Veblen, T. (1924) *The Theory of the Leisure Class*, New York: Penguin Books.

Wackernagel, M. *et al.* (2002) 'Tracking the ecological overshoot of the human economy,' *Proceedings of the National Academy of Sciences of the United States of America*, 99(4): 9, 1–16.

Walker, B., Steffen, W. L., Canadell, J. and Ingram, J. S. I. (eds) (1999) *The Terrestrial Biosphere and Global Change: implications for natural and managed ecosystems*, Cambridge, MA: Cambridge University Press.

World Commission on the Environment and Development (The Brundtland Report) (1987) *Our Common Future*, Oxford: Oxford University Press.

Note

1. See Agenda 21 policies, United Nations Division for Sustainable Development, http://www.un.org/esa/sustdev/agenda21 text.htm, 29 June 2000: 1–2.

36

Reaching toward a structurally responsive training and practice of restorative justice

David Dyck

Introduction

One of the most persistent critiques of the field of restorative justice as it is manifested in the practical activities of community programs around the world is that it still fundamentally fails to address the structural dimensions of criminal conflict. Its critics argue that current restorative programming focuses too much energy on the interpersonal dimensions of crime and ignores the deeper roots of the trouble as found in class, race/ethnicity, and gender-based systemic conflict (Mika 1989).

Informal justice models, for all their rapid proliferation, essentially still serve to cover up deeply rooted divisions in favor of an 'ideology of harmony' wherein mediators and facilitators naively assume that 'shared feelings' bring empowerment (Abdennur 1987; Nader 1993: 402; Yngvesson 1993). Furthermore, restorative justice practice continues to be dominated by white, middle- to upper-class professionals with destructive, simplistic notions of neutrality that continue to serve the interests of the powerful and undergird the status quo (Lederach 2000; Yngvesson 1993). This is in keeping with the principle of political theory that states that those who most directly benefit from any system, if not 'conscientized' to their role within that system, will generally act in such a way as to maintain homeostasis – that is, to keep that system functioning as it is (Freire 1970; Friedman 1985: 23; Parenti 1993).[1] Since most practitioners of restorative justice have not been trained to think of their work within a systemic, structural frames of reference, by default they tend to carry out their role as if 'peace and conflict in one's life (were a purely) personal responsibility and prerogative' and not a function of contextual forces (Mika 1989: 4).

While few, if any, critics claim that the practitioners of restorative justice intend these grave effects or consciously plot to divert attention away from systemic sources of the conflict, the net result, they conclude, is the same. By embracing an almost exclusive focus on affective strategies, practitioners limit their focus to interpersonal concerns. The result is they become anesthetized to larger questions of consciousness and action (Mika 1989; Sullivan and Tifft 2001).

Since the criticism of restorative justice programs along the above lines has been fairly fully articulated elsewhere (see sources cited above), in this chapter I will focus on two less discussed areas. First, I will draw on two writers who offer specific, concrete examples of the shortcomings of restorative justice practices that fail to grapple with the structural conflicts that give rise to crime. Second, I will argue that it is possible, indeed critical, for restorative justice practitioner programs to design models and concrete approaches to intervention which reflect a structural consciousness. More specifically, I will demonstrate why it is important for program administrators to more consciously and consistently train their staff and volunteers to think in systemic/structural terms. To this end, I will review a number of specific educational components that I believe will be helpful in moving us toward a teaching of restorative justice that is more structurally transformative in nature.

The problem with current restorative justice practice

The problem according to Maire Dugan

In presenting her 'nested' theory of conflict, conflict resolution theorist and intervener Maire Dugan (1996) tells the story of how the Institute for the Analysis and Resolution of Conflict (ICAR) at George Mason University asked her to respond to a conflict situation on its behalf. A professor at the institute, Dugan was asked to contact the principal of a high school in northern Virginia to discuss the institute's possible involvement in a situation in which a fight had occurred on school grounds between two groups of white and African-American male students. The violence had erupted when the white boys had arrived on campus with jackets emblazoned with the Confederate flag (Dugan 1996).

Detailing the deep emotional impact of this event not only on the boys involved but on the school and community as a whole, Dugan then describes the approach the typical practitioner of conflict resolution is likely to take in such a situation. She (1996:

13) says the typical conflict resolver is likely to opt for some form of mediation or facilitated conversation between the main protagonists suggesting that 'The aim of such a conversation would be to help the boys in reaching understanding and agreement on the concerns that prompted the fight and the ways in which such disagreements could be better handled in the future.' Additional goals might include the creation of an environment in which all the boys could speak and listen openly about their feelings regarding the symbolism of the Confederate flag. In this way, the mediator might begin to cultivate a better understanding among all parties regarding their differences and common ground. Dugan concludes that the mediator might even dare to hope that the boys might leave the room feeling less belligerent toward one another, with the white boys more committed to expressing their identity in ways that were not offensive to the African-American boys. In the best of situations, having experienced a watershed event in their young lives, some of the boys might even be affected to the point of becoming active in the work of improving race relations (Dugan 1996).

Having, in my assessment, fairly described the typical actions and goals of the average mediator/facilitator, Dugan concludes that they are 'not enough' (1996: 13). They are not enough, she says, because they do not address the deeper sources of the conflict embedded in the structures of the broader society of which the boys are a part. The Confederate flag, for example, as a symbol of the South's right to maintain the institution of slavery of African Americans and, more broadly, the South's right to self-determination, preceded the births of all of the boys involved and the births of anyone in their social or familial circles. Thus the flag, as with similar symbols, suggested that this conflict had deep structural and historical roots that went well beyond the boys. Indeed, the reasons for this fight were embedded in more fundamental conflicts, both historical and current, within the boys' school, community, and nation. We can see why, therefore, the efforts of the typical mediator in responding to this incident are laudable and noble in intent but, ultimately, insufficient. It might even be argued that such efforts are actually destructive to the extent that they mislead the community into thinking that the problem is one of personal failing on the part of the boys (Dugan 1996; Mika 1989).

Dugan's analysis clearly illustrates the shortcomings of the present approaches to conflict that continue to predominate in the sphere of informal justice. Although the case Dugan describes does not appear to have been processed in the criminal justice system or a restorative justice program, it does illustrate how the typical professional or volunteer intervener acts within a restorative justice program on a day-to-day basis. Indeed, if criminal charges were not made in this case, they easily could have been and are in hundreds of similar conflicts every day across North America.

The case Dugan offers points to the need for a new understanding of the practice of conflict resolution and restorative justice that takes us beyond the surface and helps us to reach toward the structural roots of trouble. Dugan herself goes on to provide one of the critical elements of a more structurally aware approach to the practice of restorative justice. We will return to her valuable insights shortly.

The problem according to Harry Mika

Before we explore the possibilities of what a transformative approach to restorative justice training might look like, it is useful to review another example. Like Dugan, Harry Mika draws on a real-life case study to illustrate how the current practice of informal justice can serve to cover up more deeply rooted structural problems. And he, too, concludes that this practice may unwittingly contribute to the perpetuation of the con-

ditions that give rise to violence in the first place. Mika's illustration, however, involves a matter in which criminal charges were formally brought forth and the principal combatants were ordered to participate in a restorative justice mediation program. A second difference is that, whereas as Dugan endeavors to describe a typical mediator's response to her case, Mika recounts the details of his case as it was actually handled by a justice agency.

The precipitating incident in the case concerned a protracted conflict over street parking concerning who 'was "allowed" to park in front of whose house' (Mika 1989: 6). Although a wide range of neighborhood residents had been deeply affected by this ongoing dispute, one person, whom Mika refers to as 'Rio,' appeared to be central. The heart of the problem was that Rio refused to allow a certain African-American man to park in front of his home. Mediators brought together Rio and other players judged central to the dispute for facilitated deliberations, although some showed great reluctance to participate.

In summarizing the actions of the mediators in responding to this case, the author describes actions similar to those taken by the conflict resolver in Dugan's case. Here too, lengthy and multiple sessions were conducted which focused on allowing participants to express their feelings. And, in the same way, the peacebuilding process was principally focused around the interpersonal relations of Rio and his main antagonist. And, like the case of the school brawl, detailed agreements were pursued which stipulated specific expectations for the various individuals at the meeting, which implied that the conflict was primarily, if not exclusively, an interpersonal matter. Unlike the response of the conflict resolver in Dugan's case, however, the mediators in Mika's case focused heavily on 'technical issues, such as who would park where, how late and how loud parties would be, and the like' (Mika 1989: 7). While Dugan does not

529

specifically point out the tendency of informal justice facilitators to focus primarily on the most immediate, surface-level issues in this way, I agree with Mika that it is another common characteristic of many victim–offender processes (1989).

Having described the case and the mediators' attempts to respond, the author goes on to clearly illustrate the problem's deep-seated connections to much broader societal patterns of racism, sexism, classism, addiction, homophobia, violence, repression/control, and dependence. By enumerating the many ways in which this fight over parking had roots in a far more complicated web of community and socioeconomic forces, he thus powerfully demonstrates the shortcomings of the mediators' approach (1989). Since many mediators/facilitators lack the conceptual tools to view the conflicts they are responding to from Mika's 'longer and deeper' vantage point, there is a tendency to define problems in shallow, simplistic, linear, cause-and-effect terms. This, in turn, leads us to 'pathologize' particular individuals, usually those in trouble with the law, as *the* problem to be fixed.

What remains missing, then, is an ability to recognize or address the way in which 'problem people' reflect larger systemic problems. As Mika says, Rio may be sexist, racist, homophobic, and violent but 'he draws his definitions of masculinity and his license for the macho prerogatives he holds dear from a shared culture that tolerates intolerance and invidious distinctions between human beings' (1989: 8). Furthermore, Rio's attempts to deal with his own insecurity, fears, and personal failings by focusing on the perceived failings of other ethnic groups, sexual minorities, and women is not unique to him or his neighborhood, but is 'rather an enduring characteristic of the larger community' (1989: 8). Like Dugan, then, Mika concludes that although the mediators' efforts in the parking dispute were undoubtedly well intentioned and 'better than nothing,' their short-sighted focus on affective, interpersonal, individual accommodations has limited potential to truly address the underlying sources of the trouble at hand.

The problem with the handling of the parking dispute, of course, is not confined to restorative justice practices. It derives from the dichotomized, dualistic, increasingly technological bias which has pervaded the West ever since the Enlightenment and industrialization. It manifests itself in our attempts to problem-solve in all spheres of our lives – our families, workplaces, houses of worship, institutions, and communities. In general, it has led us to an inappropriate emphasis on the immediate issues, persons, events, and locations in conflict – the 'identified patient,' to use systems theory parlance – while leaving us largely unable to recognize structural illnesses observable over time and geographic distance (Friedman 1985; Lederach 1997a). Our restorative justice practice, then, reflects our societal practices more broadly. We tend to be crisis-driven and reactive, looking unrealistically to technique to solve our problems immediately rather than crisis-responsive, taking a long-term, process-oriented approach to our everyday troubles.

Reaching toward structurally transformative training

Having cited some examples of restorative justice practice where the structural sources of conflict were not taken into account, I turn next to an exploration of possible remedies. One of the key reasons why the structural dimension is often ignored is that many restorative justice programs focus their training almost exclusively on the development of interpersonal communication skills. An emphasis on specific techniques without giving equal attention to understanding the roots of trouble dramatically increases the chances that practitioners will use their skills in ways that ignore and therefore reinforce structural inequities. Helping practitioners to develop the conceptual tools to think critically about how to relate what they encounter at any given moment to larger structural issues is the critical aspect of developing a more structurally attuned consciousness and practice. The groundwork for such a consciousness must be laid in basic introductory training.

Some conceptual dimensions of a structural approach

Dugan's 'nested' conflict foci applied to restorative justice

One critical conceptual dimension of a more structurally attuned approach to training can be found by returning to the work of Maire Dugan. The theorist responds to the problems she saw in the case illustrated earlier by articulating a paradigm which lays out different levels of conflict and then illustrating the way in which these different layers are connected to and give rise to one another. As can be seen in **Figure 36.1**, Dugan identifies the four different types of

conflict as: issues-specific; relational; structural/sub-systemic; and structural/systemic (Dugan 1996).

This model depicts issues-specific as the micro or most accessible level. It is nested within the relational level which, in turn, is contained within the sub-systemic level. The sub-system level falls within the largest purview of the system dimension. She argues that those seeking to address conflict on one level need to be cognizant of the way that same conflict may be manifested or rooted in the other levels (1996).

Dugan applies her model to the case study of the school brawl in northern Virginia alluded to earlier and makes a number of points germane to a structurally sensitive practice of restorative justice. If we truly wish to work at the roots of a given problem, restorative justice practitioners must be engaged on multiple levels, always drawing on and supporting multiple forms of intervention. That is, we must move beyond the traditional focus of restorative justice practice (mediating with the boys who were doing the fighting) or even that of group conferencing (meeting with the boys and their supporters and a few school officials) 'because the problem and its possible solutions go well beyond' these individuals (Dugan 1996: 17). Instead, informal justice programs must be prepared to respond this problem as it:

1 emerges from our dysfunctional paradigms of race relations and power and a national legacy of racism (structural systemic);
2 is reinforced in the specific policies, traditions and procedures of our various institutions which are, or are perceived to be, inequitable, antiquated, or ineffectual, such as the boys' school (structural sub-systemic);
3 surfaces in the ongoing patterns of interaction and feelings between the principal combatants and their associates/social circles (relational); and

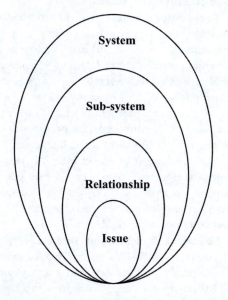

Figure 36.1. Maire Dugan's nested paradigm of conflict foci. Source: Dugan (1996)

4 is exhibited in the specific issues which emerged at the surface level of the conflict, such as the wearing of the Confederate flag and the fight/specific acts of violence that ensued (issues-specific).

(Dugan 1996: 17–18)

Being prepared to respond on all four levels does not mean that each and every program must be equally engaged at each of the four levels. However, it does imply that every program will possess a clear understanding of how and where their particular mandate fits in with the larger vision and will be committed to supporting the work as it is engaged at the other levels.

Avenues for training: Dugan

Let us turn at this point, then, to a consideration of how to bring such an understanding and engagement about. That is, how might we go from the realization of the need for a consciousness of multiple layers of conflict and a multiplicity of roles and models to the actual 'how to's of training others to think structurally? Dugan (1996) suggests that those who are learning or engaging in restorative efforts must be taught that:

> if a conflict exists between two or more parties who are members of groups between or among which structural conflict has existed, (those assisting) should be extra mindful to look to see whether the particular conflict is rooted on the system level. It also means that the parties may be impacted by the broader conflict as they try to work their way out of a conflict that analytically appears to be either issues-specific or relational.

(p. 16)

At the simplest of levels, this implies an approach to training that emphasizes the social and historical context of crime, power analysis, and an awareness of all four layers of conflict identified in Dugan's model. One means of incorporating her theory into restorative justice training is to explain it with a real-life story. After an initial period for discussion and questions of clarification, training participants can be given a second case study in which they are specifically asked to identify and discuss a harm-done in relation to each of Dugan's four categories. In this way, trainees are encouraged to go beyond an issues-specific or relational focus to articulate the sub-systemic and systemic/ structural dimensions of the conflict in question.

Lederach's 'nested' time dimension applied to restorative justice

Staying with the theme of training for structural understanding, I would like to call attention to the work of another peace-building theorist, John Paul Lederach. Focusing on the need to cultivate a long-term understanding of the international community's goals in responding to intra-state and international conflict and violence, Lederach's insights are very useful to the field of restorative justice.

The author's model (see **Figure 36.2**) illustrates the importance of 'nesting' one's response to a conflict or harm in a given time frame with a clear understanding of the implications of that response for other phases of one's work. In other words, we must not respond to a moment of crisis in such a way as to undermine our long-term vision of our desired future. Rather, our activities in the *immediate* (two to six months), *short-range* (one to two years), *decade time frame* (five to ten years), and *long-term, generational vision* (twenty-plus years) must be integrated and comprehensive (Lederach 1997b).

Lederach's model suggests that we cannot respond to the '9/11's of our world, even in the moment of greatest crisis, with panic and short-sightedness. Rather than focusing all our energy on hunting down terrorists and bombing the small nations we deem to

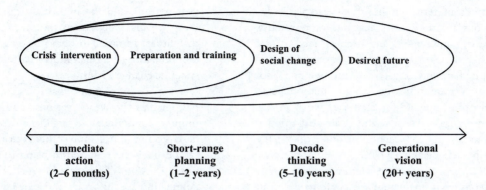

Figure 36.2. John Paul Lederach's nested time dimension in peace and justice-building. Source: Lederach (1997b)

be sheltering them (e.g. Libya, Afghanistan, Iraq) – thereby destroying all infrastructure in these countries and planting the seeds of an enmity guaranteed to last for generations – we need to respond in a way that keeps our long-term relational needs for these regions and our world in focus. This suggests the need to accept the long-term, complex nature of constructive peace-building, especially in regions where we have created a legacy of mistrust; it implies establishing ties with sectors at the mid- and grassroots levels in these societies as well as the elites; it involves a willingness to acknowledge our complicity in a world system that impoverishes the many for the benefit of the few and thus feeds the misery and rage of the disenfranchised, making extremist ideologies more attractive; and it entails developing a crisis response which is not based on the emotions or economic expediencies of the moment and thus can more realistically be practiced with consistency and integrity.

As it relates to harms-done on the community level and restorative justice, Lederach's model suggests that we must not respond to a moment of crisis (e.g. a crime) in such a way as to undermine our short-range, decade-long, and generational vision of our desired future. Focusing all of our attention as a facilitator/mediator on working out a detailed agreement on the most immediate issue at hand – for example, who will park where in Rio's neighborhood – is an example of the crisis-driven, 'quick-fix' reactions which Lederach advises against. While we may address the parking issue, to focus on it solely or even primarily increases the possibility of a more destructive violence breaking out in the long term when the deeper structural roots of the parking problem give rise to new 'weeds' (i.e. disputes). These weeds create greater distress and provoke more intense reactions because participants were led to believe these tensions were behind them. That is, when facilitators/mediators initiate processes in which the time frames and numbers of participants only permit a focus on one or two immediate concerns, it is only a matter of time before other issues, such as someone's barking dog, loud children, or dilapidated fence, 'sprout' yet again (Lederach 1997b).[2]

Another way of saying this simply is that 'you resolve issues, but you don't resolve relationships or communities,' hence the need for a comprehensive strategy of transformation, not just restoration.[3] At the level of time frames, this suggests that facilitators and participants alike must be encouraged to think in humble, realistic ways about what can be accomplished in one or two meetings. Problems such as the racial-related brawl in northern Virginia were created over hundreds of years, so we must begin to

533

think in terms of hundred-year-plus solutions.[4] This implies that we as restorative justice interveners and trainers need to further develop our capacity to envision and articulate the long-term future we desire for our communities and to prompt others to do the same. Only then can we begin to meaningfully design and evaluate particular models and approaches for our work 'at the table' (Lederach 1997b).

If these time frames seem daunting, it may be more immediately accessible to flesh out what I am suggesting here in terms of one of our case studies. Put simply, restorative justice practitioners should seek to respond to the immediate crisis of the neighborhood parking dispute, wherever possible and appropriate,[5] with models of intervention which reflect a belief in the need for an ongoing process. In the same way, restorative justice practitioners must strive, wherever possible and appropriate, to include a representation of people within their processes which reflects the belief that relationships and networks are the soil in which long-term, structural change takes root.

Avenues for training: Lederach

So, again, how is this to be carried out at the concrete level of training and practice? One way to begin to explore issues of time frame as they pertain to crime and restorative justice processes is to explain Lederach's visual model with a real-life story. For example, one might:

1 Explain a case study, such as the parking conflict.
2 Describe or 'brainstorm' with the training participants a long-term Generational Vision or dreams for the victim, the offender, and the community as a whole (twenty-plus years).
3 Describe or brainstorm what might need to take place during the decade time frame (five- to ten-year period), the short-term time frame (one- to two-

year period), and the immediate time frame (several weeks to six months) (in that order) in order to help make this comprehensive vision of individual and systemic change a reality.
4 Describe or brainstorm what roles and partnerships between various community individuals, organizations, faith communities, and other actors would likely be required to bring this vision about. This would include delineating specific roles and partnerships for local restorative justice agencies and institutions.

During this exercise, trainees would be encouraged to go beyond the immediate focus to articulate the activities required in the short-range and decade time slots. But, in order to engage in this exercise effectively, they must have a clear sense of their long-term dreams. They can then work their way 'backwards' through time until they reach their plans for the present crisis.[6] This approach is based on the idea that it is impossible to judge whether one's immediate actions are helpful without having a long-term, strategic vision in place against which to understand and evaluate them (Dugan 1996).

Applying Dugan and Lederach to restorative justice simultaneously

Let us turn our attention briefly to exploring one more lens that emerges when the nested conflict and time dimensions are brought together. Lederach has done so in his book, *Building Peace: Sustainable Reconciliation in Divided Societies*, where he joins Dugan's concept with his own. There he creates a model that has proven useful in my efforts to assist restorative justice mediators/facilitators to cultivate a longer and deeper view of the problems and tasks they face (Lederach 1997b: 80).

Lederach (see **Figure 36.3**) articulates five questions that emerge from this new model

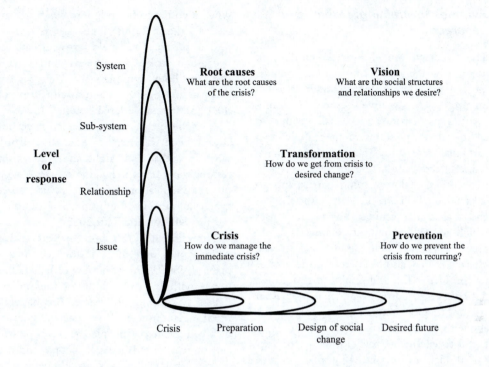

Figure 36.3. John Paul Lederach's integrated framework for peace and justice-building. Source: Lederach (1997b)

which move us toward a more long-term, structurally conscious response to conflict. The questions prompt strategic thinking as it relates to crisis management, crisis prevention, transformation, root causes, and vision. The author explores these questions in terms of their particular application to international peacebuilding efforts in deeply divided societies. Nevertheless, these same questions can be usefully adapted and applied to the realm of restorative justice practice and training. In this sphere, they might be articulated along the following lines:

1 How do we respond to the immediate crisis/issues/wounds created by the violation of one community member (i.e. the victim) by another community member (the offender)? How do we respond to the immediate crisis the violation causes for the community as a whole? (*Crisis management*)

2 How do we prevent the crisis of violation and injury from recurring? (*Prevention*)

3 How do we get from the immediate crisis of this offense to desired change in the offender and in our society? How do we get from the immediate shock and aftermath of violation to desired healing in the victim and our community? (*Transformation*)

4 What are the root causes of the violating behavior in the offender, the community, and society at large? (*Root causes*)

5 What are the social structures and relationships we desire? (*Vision*)
(adapted from Lederach 1997b: 80)

Avenues for training: Dugan and Lederach

The Lederach model offers a number of potentially rich avenues for exploration of a more comprehensive, structurally attuned training of restorative justice. Dividing training participants into small groups to address these questions as they apply to a particular case study is one means I have found effective. In taking such an approach, it becomes vital to remind participants to 'dream big.' That is, they should be encouraged to consider holistic responses which go well beyond the parameters of the present systems. Upon returning to the plenary, it may also be useful for the groups to consider if the philosophy of restorative justice, as they currently understand it, is an attempt to address none, some, or all of the above five questions. Finally, I have found it useful to encourage participants to consider the models of restorative justice practice currently in use and to reflect on which of these approaches might lend them better to addressing the underlying structural roots of crime.[7]

Helping the practitioner articulate the larger, moral implications of restorative justice

Having explored several different models and approaches to assisting restorative justice programs to cultivate a larger, more systemic vision of their task, I turn now to a brief consideration of the related topic of values. Several writers have made a case for the importance of restorative justice programs being clear and explicit about the ultimate values and goals of their work (Mika 1992; Zehr 1990). By values I refer to the deepest motivations for doing what we do.

Howard Zehr (1990) was one of the earliest to point out that one of the primary shortcomings of our criminal justice system is its failure to promote reflection about our deepest moral values as a society, especially when it comes to our response when a harm is done (Zehr 1990). I believe restorative justice practice has held growing appeal because it strikes an intuitive chord with many as both 'sensible' and 'right' when compared to the values and machinations of the dominant, adversarial system. However, I also believe that we, as trainers, have not always been very effective at articulating what it is that feels right and true about restorative justice and helping others to tease out the implications of that truth for other spheres of our lives (Sullivan and Tifft 2001; see also Sullivan and Tifft 2005).

The value of Zehr's work, in part, is that it helps us re-connect restorative justice practice with a larger purview of beliefs and hopes with his explanation of the Judeo-Christian concept of *Shalom*. Emphasizing 'right relationships' between individuals, between groups of people, between people and the earth, and between people and the divine, Shalom declares an ultimate allegiance to respecting life in all its forms. Further, this philosophy or theology emphasizes the connectedness of all things and encourages us to see the nurturing of this sacred relational web as our ultimate calling (Zehr 1990).

Shalom, then, represents *one* example of a cohesive worldview in which to anchor the practice of restorative justice. It takes the restorative justice practitioner beyond a mere consideration of what she or he hopes for in relation to the two individuals or groups in a session, to a consideration of her or his hopes for the human race and the world as a whole. Without such a vision, we are left in grave danger of working at cross-purposes.

Author Ron Kraybill (1996) has named the problem more explicitly: if we are unable to articulate our own worldview or, even worse, conceive of ourselves as not having a worldview, we are in particular danger of unconsciously serving the ends of whatever dominant systems we find ourselves a part of. Serving the ends of right relationship between individuals while simultaneously, perhaps unconsciously, buttressing the systemic wrongs that give rise to the problems between those individuals is logically incoherent, morally hypocritical, and practically ineffective. It also works against a structurally responsive practice. Again, in order to avoid this pitfall, we need to develop a capacity to articulate restorative justice as it relates to our ultimate dreams for the world. Nevertheless, a great deal of training is still carried out without including an intentional consideration of worldview. Most restorative justice programs do not encourage participants to think through the larger implications of a restorative approach to life as a whole. As Dennis Sullivan and Larry Tifft (2000) have suggested:

> It is puzzling to see how many proponents of restorative justice can limit their focus to only the correctional aspects or restorative justice (e.g. victim–offender reconciliation, mediation, and conflict resolution programs) and refuse to take into account the 'transformative,' economic, and structural dimensions of justice, that is, the social structural conditions that constrain the lives of us all and affect the extent to which any one of us can live restorative lives.
>
> (p. 8)

The authors argue that restorative justice processes have applicability to 'all aspects of our lives' and imply 'the creation of social arrangements that are from the outset structurally restorative, structurally healing because they are set up to attend to the needs of all' (Sullivan and Tifft 2000: 13). They conclude that 'it should be clear that it is not possible to develop a theory of restorative justice for harms-based situations without seeing that restorative processes at all levels derive from a needs-based economy, needs-based relationships' (2000: 9).

There are a number of authors who sound a similar note from a variety of traditions and disciplines. In addition to Zehr and Sullivan and Tifft, see the work of Harry Mika (1992), Rupert Ross (1996), Kay Pranis (1998), Oscar Nudler (1993), Jayne Docherty (1995), and Ron Kraybill (1996). All have articulated or implied the need for restorative justice and conflict resolution practice to be rooted in a clearer consciousness of worldview. The point, then, is not that all restorative justice practitioners must be grounded in one particular worldview but that all must be cognizant of this dimension and strive to give voice and consideration to it in their training and practice in a coherent manner.[8]

Avenues for training: practical ideas

So, once again, what does this all mean for the practical training of restorative justice processes? How might we close the 'gap' between where we are and wish to be with respect to exploring worldviews in the context of training? Several practical ideas come to mind.

Ron Kraybill has sought to consciously incorporate reflection and sharing on this dimension into his practice as a trainer of conflict transformation in a number of ways. In his classes at the Justice and Peacebuilding Institute at Eastern Mennonite University, he asks students to 'reflect on and then share a story or experience (in a small group or with a partner) that illustrates what motivates you to continue working and studying in this field – why do you do what you do?'[9] This exercise can be adapted to the training of students and practitioners of restorative justice as well.

Since research has demonstrated that engaging people through metaphor is a more effective means of uncovering their deepest assumptions and commitments about the world, another practical approach involves the greater use of creative, nonlinear methods within training (Nudler 1993; Docherty 1996; Barrett and Cooperrider 1990). To this end, Michelle LeBaron, among others, has used drawing or painting in her workshops. She asks participants to sketch conflict or power to help them explore deeper elements of their experience, beliefs, and commitments that would likely remain buried if more traditional linear, verbal, and cognitive focused methods were used. Again, LeBaron's approach can be used with restorative justice training; in addition to power and conflict, trainees can be asked to visualize words like 'justice' or 'healing.'[10]

To engage restorative justice issues at a more cognitive and therefore perhaps less threatening level, the trainer can simply lead a large group discussion exploring restorative justice's potential meaning for the way we organize our society and structure our global relationships. The aforementioned work of people such as Zehr, Mika, Pranis, and Ross are helpful to this end. Paul McCold has written a straightforward, accessible account of the implications of restorative justice for the meeting of community needs and responsibilities. His list would help training participants to begin

thinking more 'globally' about restorative justice practice (McCold 1996).

Situating restorative justice practice within a broader framework of peacebuilding and social change

I now turn to a final critical conceptual component of restorative justice training as found in the work of Adam Curle (1971). By integrating structural conflict, power, and awareness disparities within his model, Curle (see **Figure 36.4**) affirms the need for consciousness-raising education, advocacy, and negotiation/conciliation/mediation (i.e. dialogue). All of these elements are framed within an overarching goal of long-term peacebuilding for social transformation (the black arrow in Figure 36.4 represents the progression of conflict and change over time).

Curle's model offers a value orientation or worldview that sees power-sharing as a precondition of meaningful transformation and so sees the necessity of less powerful groups

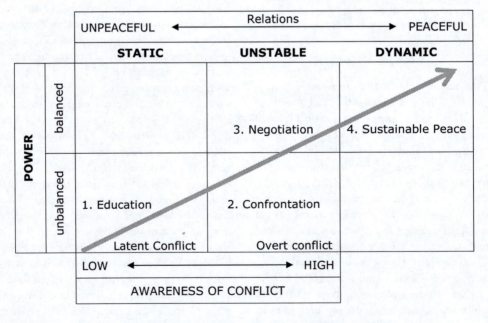

Figure 36.4. Adam Curle's framework for building peace. Source: Lederach (1995)

gaining voice as justice to be achieved. It is Lederach who has articulated most clearly the essence of Curle's model:

> Education, or conscientization, is needed when the conflict is hidden and people are unaware of power imbalances and injustices. Increased awareness of issues, needs, and interests leads to demands for changing the situation. Such demands are (often) not even heard nor taken seriously by those benefiting from the situation. Hence, the entry of advocates who work with and support those pursuing change. Their work pushes for a balancing of power through some form of confrontation. If successful, the confrontation will increase awareness of interdependence and balance power. Negotiation now becomes possible, and the role of mediation emerges. Successful negotiation and mediation lead to a restructuring of the relationship and deal with substantive and procedural concerns. (Lederach 1995: 12–14; 2000)

Like Dugan, Curle affirms the need for justice and peace workers to assume different roles at different times throughout the peacebuilding process. Like Mika, he also recognizes the dangers of 'cooling out' or pacifying a conflict by facilitating dialogue in a situation which would be better helped by moving it from the covert to overt stages (Curle 1971). Curle suggests that, unless the disempowered and more powerful parties begin to recognize the structural nature of their problems, dialogue can actually be counterproductive to building peace (Curle 1971). Indeed, education and confrontation, whereby the less powerful are helped to a higher level of awareness about the sources of their frustration and the more powerful are brought under pressure to change, are almost always required before one can facilitate the kind of dialogue that will bring about meaningful change (Curle 1971).

Curle's work has significant implications for our understanding of restorative justice. While the model integrates most of the insights already reviewed in this chapter, it adds the critical dimensions of power analysis, awareness, and latent and overt conflict. Curle, therefore, offers us the insight that harms occur, in significant measure, because of frustration, a frustration that stems from some individuals and groups in society having more power than others. His model also suggests that the tools of the state – especially the criminal justice triumvirate of the police, court, and correctional systems – are used not only to maintain the peace but as a primary means of suppressing conflict that needs to be brought out into the open and addressed through systemic change.

These arguments are supported by data that suggest that the vast majority of persons who are arrested, prosecuted, and imprisoned for committing crimes belong to the lower socioeconomic strata of our society (Zehr 1990; Mika 1989; Gilligan 1996). It is additionally bolstered by studies and commissions which consistently demonstrate that persons of color are arrested, prosecuted, and imprisoned in grossly disproportionate numbers relative to their percentage of the general population (Hamilton and Sinclair 1991; Mauer 1990).

During their training, restorative justice practitioners can be helped to understand these realities by learning about Curle's analysis of power. More specifically, they can be encouraged to reflect critically on the implication of Curle's model that facilitated dialogue (i.e. victim–offender mediation or conferencing, etc.) may well serve to reinforce power imbalance and structural conflict because of its premature use at the first level of unbalanced and unaware relations. The importance of encouraging restorative justice advocates and workers to grapple with this issue cannot be overemphasized.

Despite the value of Curle's model, the view that facilitated dialogue is inappropriate in criminal matters (because the latter often constitutes conflict characterized by power disparity and low awareness) does *not* represent the whole picture. That is, while it is important, it need not be the final word on this matter. The reasons why we harm each other are more complex than any one model can depict. I have identified five phenomena that I offer as caveats to Curle's analysis as applied to the realm of crime in the community.

First, many of those who do strike out with a criminal act do so not against the 'overlords' of an oppressive system but against others who are similarly situated – that is, relatively powerless. Second, those persons who most benefit from oppressive structures are usually not those most directly affected by patterns of crime but others in the community of the marginalized. Third, there are others within that same disenfranchised sector who do not choose to strike out blindly against others but, instead, find ways and means of channeling their frustration into efforts to change the system. In some cases, then, bringing together the victim and offender and supporters for dialogue can arguably increase the chances of them all identifying the sources of their problems which are oftentimes due to forces that reach well beyond the confines of their community.

Some have suggested that leaving these people to the intra-community enmity that results from social disarray is preferable to facilitating dialogue and healing. The thinking here is that the misery of the disenfranchised will eventually unite them in a social revolution which will change the structural conditions of their lives (Abdennur 1987). But such a stance requires a higher tolerance for the suffering of others, in the meantime, than many of us deem morally acceptable. Furthermore, this approach appears to place more confidence in the dynamics of division than those of consensus, a belief that is coming under greater critical scrutiny by those interested in creating community and societal change (Chrislip and Larson 1994; Jenner 1997).

Fourth, those who feel powerless and thus strike out are by no means restricted to the marginalized sectors of society but include many of the socioeconomically powerful (e.g. youth from wealthy neighborhoods, socially powerful persons who commit sexual assault or fraud, etc.). Fifth, even where a crime is perpetrated against the relatively powerful by the relatively powerless, there is little to be gained by allowing people to wallow in the stereotypes and apathy that often characterize victims and offenders following a crime.

Indeed, it is often only via some form of dialogue that a victim's stereotypes of and vindictive attitude towards the offender begins to break down. Dialogue can contribute to social change inasmuch as a victim's (and his/her supporters') negative assumptions about whole sectors or ethnic groups are 'opened up' once they meet real persons from those groups.

In the same way, it is often only through some contact with the face of the person they have hurt that offenders begin to recognize the futility and destructiveness of striking out blindly. Indeed, many people who commit crimes against others, regardless of their social displacement, recognize intuitively that their lashing out at a particular individual, who is often him/herself but a part of a much larger system, is destructive. Oftentimes, of their own accord, they come to believe that while their reaction was perhaps understandable, it was fundamentally not justifiable on either practical or moral grounds. In such a context, the offender is more likely to begin to see the need to explore the deeper sources of their acting out (i.e. its relational and structural components). They also have a better chance to begin to take some initial steps towards personal transformation that will ultimately allow them to work for social change in a more meaningful and effective way.

In reality, the sources of crime may be largely structural but the effects of crime are firstly and primarily personal. What is required from restorative justice programs is less an abandonment of approaches that seek to address the personal than the addition of elements which also address the structural (McCold 1996; Mika 1989; Sullivan and Tifft 2001). In such a context, it is still often helpful to facilitate communication between those who were most affected by a particular harm-done so they can better understand the source, impact, and aftermath of that harm and to seek to repair it.

At the same time, Curle's (1971) concerns about facilitated dialogue serving a counter-productive, pacifying, unintended end are the part of the picture that is most often forgotten in current restorative justice training. In the final analysis, restorative justice practice need not be astructural as long as its advocates make clear the need for its practitioners to: (a) be wary of the ways their work may reinforce structural injustice; (b) work cooperatively and respectfully with social activists, advocates, and other community partners who are pursuing the avenues of education and confrontation more directly (as these terms are used by Curle); and (c) design models of restorative justice intervention that are more able to serve the ends of interpersonal healing while also promoting the goals of education and confrontation with respect to structural sources.

Avenues for training: Curle

Curle's model can be quite effective in restorative justice training if used in connection with story-telling and case studies. Since the model is complex, it is helpful to use several examples from micro, macro, local, and international contexts. I often begin by explaining the paradigm as it is reflected in an unpeaceful, unequal relationship between intimate partners, discussing each of the stages of conflict and transformation as they surface in this type of interpersonal relationship. At the first stage of low awareness, unbalanced power, and latent conflict, for example, I describe a relationship characterized by one partner's control over the other in the form of emotional, verbal, or physical abuse. I then describe the empowerment of the less empowered person through the education she receives while taking a course in the Women's Studies department of her local university and/or through the assistance of a counselor or friend. This leads to an awareness of the injustice of her partner's treatment of her and her need for greater personal autonomy.

This new awareness, in turn, leads her to request from her partner a change in their relationship (i.e. confrontation), which partners in such situations almost always ignore. At this point, she might choose to pursue her course of action with the aid of an advocate (e.g. a counselor or a friend). She may also need to 'raise the pressure' by separating from her partner for a period in which he is given the opportunity to decide whether he is serious about making changes. The process culminates, ideally, when the domineering partner realizes his interdependence with his partner and decides that making change is a better option than attempting to maintain the status quo.[11] At this point, negotiation or joint counseling becomes appropriate to further build and define the terms of a new, dynamic, more balanced and peaceful relationship.

If, however, the domineering partner demands a continuance of the relationship on the old (his) terms and demonstrates no commitment to personal change, the separation may need to become permanent. Then, attempts at negotiation and mediation are inappropriate.

Following this scenario, training participants can be engaged in discussion about the implications of facilitating dialogue in a relationship at the stage of low awareness. That is, they can be helped to recognize the dangers of carrying out victim–offender mediation after the domineering partner has been charged with domestic abuse but

541

before either partner realizes there is a more deep-rooted, relational/structural problem. After introducing one such case study, I usually illustrate Curle's model a second time, using a case of macro conflict between groups (e.g. the historical unpeaceful, unequal relationship between First Nations Canadians and Canadians of European descent). Finally, following a large group discussion, many participants require a final opportunity to explore the model in small groups as it applies to a third case before they begin to fully grasp the implications for the practice of restorative justice.

Summary and conclusion

In this chapter, I have cited some concrete manifestations of the shortcomings of a restorative justice practice that fails to confront the structural sources of conflict. Second, I have made the case that it is important for restorative justice practitioner programs to more intentionally cultivate a structural consciousness among their volunteers and professionals in training. Nevertheless, the question remains: what are the practical implications of this discussion? How might cultivating a structural consciousness affect our concrete approaches to program development, models of intervention, and moment-by-moment actions with our clients? While space constraints do not permit a full exploration of these vital questions, we can point in a few directions.

For example, at the level of program development, a transformative practice would see restorative justice agencies investing time and energy in developing accountable relationships with advocacy and social action groups in our communities. By recognizing the ways in which our work is related to these players, we would become less inclined to work in isolation or, as is sometimes the case, against them. Practically, this might entail holding more roundtable discussions in our communities

with those who work with the poor, minority groups, women, victims of crime, children, the elderly and persons who are marginalized in other ways. It would mean inviting representation from these groups to serve on our boards and advisory committees and working to dismantle barriers that make it difficult for these persons to join our staff and volunteer teams.

An emphasis on relationship-building might lead to other practical changes in our approach to our work. For example, we might lend more of our resources to the development of school-based programs so as to equip our young people with the skills, knowledge, and confidence that they will need to address conflict and justice issues throughout their lives. In the same way, we would recognize other social issues such as racism and poverty as inextricably intertwined with our work and so would develop integrated curricula with community partners engaged in addressing these concerns. We might also choose to co-sponsor events that relate to the education and confrontation elements of the Curle spectrum rather than focusing solely on the mediation/negotiation aspect at the interpersonal level (e.g. we might co-sponsor an event commemorating Martin Luther King Jr Day or host workshops on mindfulness in daily living or on nonviolent accompaniment skills).

At the level of casework, we would increasingly embrace interdisciplinary models whereby we seek out guidance from a caseworker from the local sexual assault crisis centre, for example, while working with a sexual assault referral. Indeed, this sort of work is already being carried out in some jurisdictions. In the Duluth Domestic Abuse Intervention Project, a wide variety of intervention agencies work collaboratively to respond to the crises that arise. We would do well to look to the regular communication, full awareness and appreciation of different but complimentary agency goals and mandates, and common understanding of the structural roots of domestic violence which undergird the Duluth Project (Tifft 1993).

Finally, there would also be practical changes in our approach to our moment-by-moment work with our clients at the table. In terms of victim–offender mediation/conferencing (which is the area of restorative practice with which I am most familiar), we would continue the trend towards making greater use of circle and group conferencing formats. These models contain a greater recognition of the role of the extended community in terms of the source, impact, and aftermath of crime. By gathering a broader array of stakeholders, it is more likely that the structural roots of the trouble will become apparent and that we will develop broader, systemic strategies. In the case of Rio and the parking dispute, we might specifically invite the participation of members of Rio's community who know him and whom he respects (i.e. elders). We might also attempt to make room for neighbors who have a vested interest in strong community relations and other parties who have a clear link to the issue at hand (e.g. the arresting officer, a respected school teacher, a sister or uncle, etc.). Overall, the structurally aware approach advocated throughout this chapter would have the practical implications of placing less emphasis on what happens at the table and more on the connections we are establishing prior to and nurturing after these events.

Our increased recognition of the roots of social harm in class, race/ethnicity, and gender-based systemic conflict would also see us questioning strict notions of mediator/facilitator 'neutrality.' We would increasingly embrace an understanding of mediation that acknowledged the tension between the roles of intermediary and advocate which is inherent in a structurally transformative practice (Dyck 2000). We would come to see mediators not as detached, emotionally distant impartials but as bi-partisan helpers who are deeply connected to all sides and partial to giving expression to their core values in all that they do.

Clearly, the ideas suggested here just begin to scratch the surface. Nevertheless, if we accept the basic thesis that I have proposed – that a more structurally attuned training of restorative justice is the starting point for more structurally transformative models of practice – we would do well to continue to devote energy to this topic.

References

Abdennur, A. (1987) *The Conflict Resolution Syndrome*, Ottawa, Canada: University of Ottawa Press.

Barrett, F. J. and Cooperrider, D. L. (1990) 'Generative metaphor intervention: a new approach to working with systems divided by conflict and caught in defensive perception,' *Journal of Applied Behavioural Science*, 26(2): 219–39.

Chrislip, D. D. and Larson, C. E. (1994) *Collaborative Leadership*, San Francisco: Jossey-Bass Nonprofit Series.

Curle, A. (1971) *Making Peace*, London: Tavistock Publications.

Docherty, J. (1995) 'Oscar Nudler presents latest developments in cognitive theory of conflict and conflict resolution,' *ICAR Newsletter*, Spring, Fairfax, VA: Institute for Conflict Analysis and Resolution, George Mason University.

— (1996) 'The stewardship metaphor in forest resource management conflicts: a common language does not guarantee consensus,' in D. McFarland (ed.) *Conflict Analysis and Resolution: challenges for the times*, Fairfax, VA: Institute for Conflict Analysis and Resolution, George Mason University.

Dugan, M. (1996) 'A nested theory of conflict,' *A Leadership Journal: Women in Leadership – Sharing the Vision*, 1(1): 9–20.

Dyck, D. (2000) 'The mediator as nonviolent advocate: revisiting the question of mediator neutrality,' *Mediation Quarterly*, 18(2): 129–49. Note: Figure 3 in this article, which appeared on p. 145, was incorrect. The correct figure appeared in the next issue of *Mediation Quarterly*, 18(3) (Spring 2001): 324.

Freire, P. (1970) *Pedagogy of the Oppressed*, New York: Seabury Press.

Friedman, E. H. (1985) *Generation to Generation: family process in church and synagogue*, New York: Guilford Press.

Gilligan, J. (1996) *Violence: our deadly epidemic and its causes*, New York: G. P. Putnam.

Hamilton, A. C. and Sinclair, C. M. (1991) *Report of the Aboriginal Justice Inquiry of Manitoba: public inquiry into the administration of justice and aboriginal people*, Winnipeg, Manitoba, Canada: The Inquiry.

Jenner, H. (1997) 'Social energy and sustainable communities: from power-balancing to dynamic change,' unpublished paper completed in partial fulfillment of the requirements of the certificate program in Conflict Transformation at Eastern Mennonite University, Harrisonburg, VA.

Kraybill, R. (1996) 'An Anabaptist paradigm for conflict transformation: critical reflections on peacemaking in Zimbabwe,' unpublished doctoral dissertation, University of Cape Town, South Africa.

Lederach, J. P. (1995) *Preparing for Peace: conflict transformation across cultures*, Syracuse, NY: Syracuse University Press.

— (1997a) 'Systems stuff: musings about family systems theory and conflict transformation,' unpublished paper presented during 'Introduction to Conflict Transformation' course conducted at Eastern Mennonite University.

— (1997b) *Building Peace: sustainable reconciliation in divided societies*, Washington, DC: Endowment of the United States Institute for Peace.

— (2000) '"Revolutionaries" and "resolutionaries": in pursuit of dialogue,' in C. Schrock-Shenk (ed.) *Mediation and Facilitation Training Manual: foundations and skills for constructive conflict transformation*, fourth edn, Akron, PA: Mennonite Conciliation Service.

McCold, P. (1996) 'Restorative justice and the role of the community,' in B. Galaway and J. Hudson (eds) *Restorative Justice: international perspectives*, Monsey, NY: Criminal Justice Press.

Mauer, M. (1990) *Young Black Men and the Criminal Justice System: a growing national problem*, Washington, DC: The Sentencing Project.

Mika, H. (1989) 'Cooling the mark out? Mediating disputes in a structural context,' unpublished text of the presentation by Dr Mika in session K12, 'Theoretical and Comparative Issues in the Analysis of Conflict Resolution Practices' at the North American Conference on Peacemaking and Conflict Resolution, Montreal, Quebec. (A full text of this paper can be obtained by contacting Dr Mika at the Department of Sociology, Anthropology, and Social Work at Central Michigan University, Mount Pleasant, Michigan, 48859.)

— (1992) 'Mediation interventions and restorative justice: responding to the astructural bias,' in H. Messmer and H.-U. Otto (eds) *Restorative Justice on Trial*, Netherlands: Kluwer Academic Publishers.

Nader, L. (1993) 'When is popular justice popular?' in Sally Merry and Neal Milner (eds) *The Possibility of Popular Justice*, Ann Arbor: University of Michigan Press, pp. 435–54.

Nudler, O. (1993) 'In search of a theory for conflict resolution: taking a new look at world views analysis,' *ICAR Newsletter*, Summer, Fairfax, VA: Institute for Conflict Analysis and Resolution, George Mason University.

Parenti, M. (1993) *Inventing Reality: the politics of news media*, New York: St Martin's Press.

Pranis, K. (1998) 'Building justice on a foundation of democracy, caring, and mutual responsibility,' unpublished paper completed by Ms Pranis as part of her work as the Restorative Justice Planner with the Minnesota Department of Corrections, March.

Ross, R. (1996) *Returning to the Teachings: exploring aboriginal justice*, Toronto, Ontario, Canada: Penguin Books Canada.

Sullivan, D. and Tifft, L. (2000) *Restorative Justice as a Transformative Process: the application of restorative justice principles to our everyday lives*, Voorheesville, NY, and Mt Pleasant, MI: Mutual Aid Press.

— (2001) *Restorative Justice: healing the foundations of our everyday lives*, Monsey, NY: Willow Tree Press.

— (2005) *Restorative Justice: healing the foundations of our everyday lives*, second edn, Monsey, NY: Willow Tree Press.

Tifft L. (1993) *Battering of Women: the failure of intervention and the case for prevention*, Boulder, CO: Westview Press.

Yngvesson, B. (1993) 'Local people, local problems, and neighborhood justice: the discourse of the "community" in San Francisco Community Boards,' in S. Merry and N. Milner (eds) *The Possibility of Popular Justice*, Ann Arbor: University of Michigan Press.

Zehr, H. (1990) *Changing Lenses: a new focus for crime and justice*, Scottdale, PA, and Waterloo, Ontario: Herald Press.

Notes

1 For example, Noam Chomsky discusses the homeostatic nature of systems in terms of how

a very biased mass media sustains and reinforces global capitalism in the National Film Board of Canada's *Manufacturing Consent* (1990). In the film, Chomsky is very clear that the nature of systems is such that particular individuals within the media system need not be involved in any conscious plot to cover up truth to nevertheless engage in very biased reporting.

2 Comparing the stem and leaves of a plant to the surface issue of parking and the roots of that plant to the structural and relational dimension of the conflict/crime is one analogy that seems to help training participants quickly understand this concept. I owe this analogy to John Paul Lederach.

3 I heard John Paul Lederach make this statement while conducting training in the Philippines in August 1998.

4 For more on the need to think in long-term time frames about the work of peacebuilding and social change, please see Chuck Fager's presentation called 'A Quaker Declaration of War' at http://www.quakerhouse.org/declaration-01.htm

5 There are multiple reasons for the inclusion of the caveat of 'whenever possible and appropriate.' First, restorative justice practitioners face the reality that many of the people we work with (i.e. victims, offenders, and their supporters and other relevant, affected members of the community), have also been 'schooled' in a quick-fix mentality. This cultural bias tends to contribute to resistance on the part of clients to participation in long-term processes with larger numbers of people. As a result, certain individuals and their families may well not be willing to participate in the processes we envision as ideal. In such cases, we must recognize that it may be more healing for them to participate in a more individual, short-term process like traditional victim-offender mediation than not to participate in restorative justice processes at all. In addition, there are, of course, many other legitimate reasons why victims and offenders in particular cases may not be in a position to participate meaningfully in a longer-term process with a wider circle of people. Indeed, in the case of victims in particular, practitioners must be ready to respect their individual needs, even if they come into tension with our goal of developing a more long-term, systemic, structurally responsive approach.

6 A variation of this exercise involves asking differing members of the small groups to 'take on' the roles of various actors/community interests (e.g. someone plays the victim, offender, and various community members) in the dispute. With this approach, participants discuss the time frames/activities from a first-person perspective (e.g. 'In twenty years I would like to see ... ' and 'So, then, in ten years I/we would need to be ... ' etc.). This approach moves the second exploration of Lederach's model from a cognitive exercise to a more visceral, symbolic learning experience which is likely to be more lively feeling in nature.

7 By models of practice, I am referring to the range of processes currently being used in the field including, but not necessarily limited to, victim-offender mediation, group conferencing, sentencing circles, healing circles, support and accountability circles, victim impact panels, victim services, victim-sensitive victim-offender dialogue programs, victim companion programs, etc.

8 Having said that, there emerges a symmetry between these authors with respect to the practical implications of restorative justice on a global scale. All are convinced that peacebuilding processes will only truly be healing for individuals, community, and society to the extent that they come to reflect an explicitly articulated concern for right relationships/justice in every sphere of human activity. Further, all observe or imply a fundamental conflict between the vision of restorative justice and the dominant values and assumptions of our twenty-first-century world as reflected in our global socioeconomic systems. Dennis Sullivan and Larry Tifft (2001, 2005) are particularly strong on this point.

9 Dr Kraybill discussed this training technique as a part of a course he taught at Eastern Mennonite University in the spring of 1998. The course was entitled 'Intermediary Roles Level II.'

10 I experienced Dr LeBaron's metaphor-based methodology firsthand via my participation in a workshop entitled 'Using Metaphor in Conflict Transformation.' She and Dr Sheila Ramsey conducted the workshop on 30 October 1998 in Alexandria, Virginia, USA. To read an interview with Dr LeBaron regarding her training methodology as an approach to worldview, please see: www.beyondintractability.org/iweb/audio/lebaron-m.html

11 The partner becomes aware of his interdependence when he realizes that meeting his needs in his relationship with his partner is, in large part, dependent on his ability/willingness to help meet her needs.

37

The Good Samaritan or the person in the ditch?

An attempt to live a restorative justice lifestyle

Fred Boehrer

'Why doesn't Santa Claus like poor kids?' our five-year-old son asked us, as my wife and I sorted through donated Christmas toys to distribute to fifteen poor families. We were taken aback and asked Freddie to explain what he meant. He replied, 'Why do *we* give presents to these kids? Why doesn't *Santa* give presents to poor kids? Is it because he doesn't like poor people?'

Our son's questions stung us. We fumbled through a response, thanks to my wife's sharp wit. Our response is not important here. What is important is how much our son's questions reflect the struggle to make sense of the incongruity between ideals and their applications. Such a struggle is present in the incorporation of restorative justice principles to one's everyday lifestyle.

The application of restorative principles is found within numerous programs: family group conferences, community circles, and victim–offender reconciliation programs. But what of the integration of restorative justice in one's personal life, outside of the context of social applications? How does an individual person attempt to live a restorative lifestyle, given the social structural violence we encounter in our everyday lives? To do so, one must navigate through a landscape where resources are distributed on the basis of deserts or rights. Restorative justice counters such modes of thought and behavior by emphasizing a needs-based approach.

> Not having embraced needs-based living arrangements and restorative values in our daily lives – in our families, schools, and workplaces – we generally lack a reservoir of experiences to draw from to manage the complex of ideas, feelings, and decisions that arise when we seek to create and apply restorative values and meet needs in a harm situation. Doing this is, to a considerable degree, counter-cultural, counter-relational and, in the eyes of some, madness.
> (Sullivan and Tifft 2001: 101)

How to live a restorative justice lifestyle without falling into madness?

Vulnerability: our first year as Catholic Workers

My wife, Diana Conroy, and I both grew up in large, Roman Catholic, middle-class families in suburban neighborhoods. We married in 1992 and experimented with simple living. Diana had already lived on a monthly $50 stipend while residing in an

546

intentional Catholic community in a poor Chicago neighborhood. She and I both worked for church-related human service programs, receiving modest incomes. Despite the satisfaction we experienced in helping others, we also felt uncomfortable with the social, educational, and economic abyss which separated us from those to whom we were ministering. Each day we would drive home in our own cars, returning to our apartment in a 'safe' middle-class neighborhood. Meanwhile, most of the families we assisted had no cars, depended on public transportation, and lived in neighborhoods where they did not feel safe. Diana and I had health insurance and jobs that paid living wages. At work, we helped families who had little or no access to healthcare, as well as jobs which still left them below the poverty line. With a close-knit extended family, our lives contrasted with those families we helped who had parents, siblings and, at times, spouses living thousands of miles apart from each other. Our loving relationship contrasted the domestic violence which was commonplace in many of the single-mom families Diana supported at work.

We spent a great deal of time praying and reflecting about our lifestyle. Influenced by Dorothy Day, who co-founded the Catholic Worker movement in 1933, we began to move towards starting a house of hospitality in Albany, NY. We were drawn to the movement's combination of voluntary poverty, nonviolence, and offering works of mercy. After speaking with Catholic Workers from a dozen communities, as well as friends and family members, we began to prepare ourselves for a Catholic Worker lifestyle.

First, we took inventory of our possessions and distinguished those which were 'needs' and which were merely 'wants.' Realizing we only needed one car, we gave away our other car to a human service program. We donated our expensive stereo system to a place where folks living with AIDS gather for respite and social events. Not needing a microwave oven, we gave that to a soup kitchen. We began to embrace the wisdom of Diana's dad, Dave Conroy, who said, 'If you are going to bring something into your home, you ought to remove something of a similar size.'

Second, we met with people working in human services, peace activists, and other people dedicated to improving the lives of others. They discussed what they saw as the 'needs' of people in the city of Albany and how a Catholic Worker house of hospitality might fit in with current efforts. Most people emphasized the need for a home to welcome families who are temporarily homeless, especially for immigrant families. The overwhelming majority of local shelters receive a majority of funding from government funds. Restricted by government regulations, these shelters are unable to help certain categories of people, including undocumented immigrants.

In 1996, after paying off our remaining debts, Diana and I resigned from our jobs. Together, with our three-month-old son, we opened Emmaus House – a Catholic Worker home offering hospitality to families who are homeless. It was an exciting time, but our Kierkegaardian leap of faith also filled us with 'fear and trembling.' We were vulnerable in multiple ways. By leaving our jobs, we eliminated our major source of income. Although we received support from family and friends, we were very dependent on the generosity of strangers. As the first (and only) Catholic Worker house in Albany, we found many people were unfamiliar with the Catholic Worker movement. We spent a great deal of time teaching people about Dorothy Day and the Catholic Workers, and then explaining our own particular effort. Would such strangers want to contribute to our rent, utilities, groceries, and phone bill?

We also felt vulnerable because of the high cost of health coverage. Before opening Emmaus House, Diana and I had health insurance through our employer. When we opened Emmaus House, we maintained that coverage but had to pay a much higher rate, since we had left our jobs. After paying these exorbitant fees for three months, we could no longer afford our health insurance. When we canceled our health plan, we were relieved from having to pay high premiums and also worried about our lack of medical coverage. Our fears were realized when Diana became sick. We telephoned a doctor who was recommended to us as someone who might be sympathetic to our situation. But we did not receive a call back from the doctor that day or the next, after leaving two phone messages. We debated whether to just show up at some physician's office, or at a hospital emergency room. Diana would receive medical attention but we would probably have to pay several hundreds of dollars for the visit, tests, and medicine. One's health is important but not priceless – especially in a culture where healthcare is seen as a privilege, not a right. We found ourselves having to choose between good health (incurring a large medical bill) or not seeking healthcare (keeping out of debt). By the third day, Diana was still sick but starting to feel better.

We also experienced vulnerability through the sometimes isolated experience of our work and ministry. During that first year Diana and I were trying our best to simply figure out how to live the Catholic Worker lifestyle. As a result of being the only Catholic Workers in the region, it was sometimes difficult processing our daily experiences with others. Local people who had spent a lot of time with homeless people were those working at shelters. They had good advice to offer but they recognized that, at the end of their workday, they had a place of their own to call 'home,' separate from their work at the shelter. Among those activists with whom we share many nonviolent ideals, some were interested in directly helping people in need while others

focused exclusively on systemic issues of justice. We were able to collaborate on some issues, but our living together with homeless families distinguished us in some ways. As we stumbled through that first year, a small core group of supporters developed into our extended Catholic Worker community. They did not live with us but these people of varying life experiences and faith perspectives nourished us through listening, prayers, advice, food, and opportunities to let our hair down.

These three areas of vulnerability – financial worries, medical concerns, and isolatedness – provided us with many sleepless nights during our first year as Catholic Workers. We experienced the precariousness of not knowing whether our basic needs were going to be met: economic, physical, and emotional/social. While a part of us wished that helping to restore others could be done without so much discomfort, we saw the value in our experience. Our Christian faith tradition is filled with stories of holy women and men who are inconvenienced in the process meeting the needs of others. The gospel parable of the Good Samaritan is an important touchstone in the Christian call to restore others.

This popular story (Luke 10: 30–5) is the source of the expression 'Good Samaritan' which describes someone who goes out of one's way to help another person, especially helping an unfamiliar person. In the parable, Jesus explains that a man was robbed, stripped, and beaten as he was walking down a road from Jerusalem to Jericho. The group of robbers left the man half-dead. On separate occasions, two priestly men walking down the same road see the man laying in the ditch but pass by on the opposite side. These two holy men, it is presumed, choose not to help the half-dead, even though they share the same faith, Judaism. But when a Samaritan traveler sees the man in the ditch, he is 'moved with compassion' (10: 33). Instead of crossing to the other side of the road and passing by him:

He approached the victim, poured oil and wine over his wounds and bandaged them. Then he lifted him up on his own animal, took him to an inn and cared for him. The next day he took out two silver coins and gave them to the innkeeper with the instruction, 'Take care of him. If you spend more than what I have given you, I shall repay you on my way back.'

(10: 34–5)

The Samaritan is not Jewish yet he is both 'moved with compassion' and comforts the man in the ditch. This parable is situated within the context of Jesus affirming that the greatest commandments are to love God and to love your neighbor as yourself. A scholar of the Torah questions Jesus, 'And who is my neighbor?' (10: 29). Jesus replies with the parable of the Good Samaritan. In doing so, Jesus is extending the conception of neighborliness to those who are not of the same faith tradition. The common reading of this text is to see many people as our neighbors, not merely those who share our faith, language, and region, and to go out of the way to minister to them.

If we shift our reading of this parable, its meaning can shift for us too. Instead of focusing upon the third person traveling down the road, the Good Samaritan, might we share the gaze of the person in the ditch? What does it mean to experience a terrible accident, and barely survive? What is it like to barely clutch to one's own life, hoping that someone will come upon us and offer assistance? Such questions arise when we replace the Samaritan with the beaten man as the central figure in the story. From this perspective, this story is about vulnerability. Instead of the parable of the Good Samaritan, calling listeners to go out of our way to meet the needs of others, we now have the parable of the Person in the Ditch, calling us to become vulnerable, helpless, totally dependent upon others. We are called to be open to receiving assistance from strangers, from those persons who speak differently, pray differently, and live differently from us.

During our first year as Catholic Workers, we felt vulnerable yet we had faith that others would reach out to us and support our effort by meeting our needs. In doing so we gained insight from this parable, not from the Good Samaritan per se, but from the perspective of the person in the ditch. He lies helpless, in need of someone else's assistance. There is a glimmer of hope each time a passerby catches sight of him. 'Perhaps *this* person will come to my aid,' he might think to himself. But his hopes are dashed when that passerby, like others, walks past him.

Our precariousness lacks the drama of a person on the brink of death and, as such, our lives do not compare. We chose to live in voluntary poverty, unlike the man who was forcibly robbed, beaten, and thrown into the roadside. We were not forced into poverty and knew that we could stop living below the poverty line and choose to re-embrace a middle-class lifestyle. We have college educations, work experience, and many contacts with people who could recommend us for jobs that pay a living wage. We maintain a simple lifestyle out of a deep sense of wanting to be in solidarity with people who are poor. We are not trying to 'act' poor, imitate poor people, or glamorize poverty. Our desire to be in solidarity with poor people is rooted in the Christian gospel's strong sense of needs-based justice. The poor are called 'blessed' (Luke 6: 20) and our relationship with God is measured by how we treat people who are hungry, homeless, and imprisoned (Matthew 25: 31–40). Catholic Worker co-founder Peter Maurin stated, 'Although you may be called bums and panhandlers you are in fact the Ambassadors of God' (Maurin 1961).

In secular terms, we view socio-economic lifestyles within a framework of justice. What is the connection between how we use financial and physical resources and living in a society where other people's needs are not being met? Can someone be considered 'nonviolent' while using more than her/his share of food, heat, electricity, gasoline? Can a person living in the US be called 'nonviolent' if s/he has income which exceeds the median (or mean average) US income? Such questions point out how people in middle- and upper-class households benefit from structural violence at the expense of people who are poor in the US (as well as around the world). Upward mobility among middle-class and wealthy people in the wealthiest country is inconsistent with the principles of nonviolence. In the US and around the world, people like Dorothy Day, Mohandis Gandhi, and Cesar Chavez maintained simple lifestyles despite opportunities for upward mobility.

While we see voluntary poverty and living together with homeless families as acts of justice, as efforts to restore ourselves to wholeness, it is considered 'in the eyes of some, madness' (Sullivan and Tifft 2001: 101). In religious terms, we strive to become 'fools for Christ.' This phrase was used by Francis of Assisi, the twelfth-century saint who set aside the privilege of his family's business to embrace poverty. He called on his peers to risk the appearance of madness, to fully trust in the providence of God. Francis's words echo the person in the ditch who, despite his vulnerability, trusts that God will provide for him. The struggle of the person in the ditch fills us with hope as we struggle with paying bills, getting healthcare, and staying emotionally fit.

Alternatives to the state definitions of helping others

When people offer help to others, it is often influenced by parameters put forth by the state. Many choose not to personally help others because they are not social workers or therapists (positions which require government certification). Others choose not to directly assist others because they presume that there must be some organization or

non-profit entity that will help them. Help is often offered indirectly, by donating money to government-recognized, non-profit charitable organizations.

Are such state-defined modes of offering assistance the best for meeting the needs of all? In the US, the non-profit system of giving is fraught with difficulties. For example, is $285,000 enough of a salary to cover the living expenses of someone working for a non-profit group? *The Chronicle of Philanthropy* reports that US charities directors averaged a $285,000 in base pay during 2003, evaluating 163 non-profit charity groups (Schwinn and Wilhelm 2003). This fact raises the question, 'What does it mean to be a "non-profit organization?"'

Most colleges are non-profits and they actively seek donations to cover their expenses. Across the river from our house, Rennselaer Polytechnic Institute (RPI), a non-profit entity, pays its president, Shirley Ann Jackson, $891,400 a year in salary and benefits (Basinger 2003). How many people who donate to colleges like RPI know the salaries of their administrators? If they knew such salaries, would they continue to donate to these colleges, which are technically 'non-profit' entities?

Non-profits dedicated to the arts are not immune from zealous salaries for directors. Not far from our house, the Saratoga Performance Arts Center (SPAC) pays its director Herbert Chesbrough a $330,000 salary. His wife, Kathleen, is also employed by SPAC and 'together, the two positions constitute the two highest paid positions in the corporation,' according to a New York State audit of the non-profit. Herbert Chesbrough is to step down in 2005, and is slated to receive a compensation package worth over $400,000. Chesbrough's excessive compensation package 'may be illegal under state nonprofit law,' as reviewed in the audit (New York State Office of Parks, Recreation, and Historical Preservation 2004). These are two examples of non-profit entities in our own region. What of other non-profit organizations in your neighborhoods?

Charitable groups are not immune to such outrageous salaries and expenditures. Every year, many places of work encourage their employees to donate part of their salary to the United Way campaign. In 2003, the United Way executive director received a $1.5 million pension payment. Betty Stanley Beene caused outrage among many United Way supporters. How could she receive such an outrageous amount of money, especially after serving as director for only four years? Many people 'feel good' donating to groups like the United Way, presuming most of their money is going directly to people in need. Unfortunately, a sizable portion is going to executive directors who desire lavish lifestyles at the expense of those whom they claim to serve. The nation's United Ways spend a much higher percentage of their income on directors' salaries than the national average of non-profit charities. According to *The Chronicle of Philanthropy*, United Way executive directors receive almost double the share of donated income towards their salaries (0.39 per cent) compared with other charities (0.21 per cent) (Schwinn and Wilhelm 2003).

To increase their donations, many non-profit charities have contracted with for-profit telemarketing firms. The result is startling. Most donors presume that 80 per cent or 90 per cent of their contribution is going directly to serving people in need. Sadly, only 2 per cent of telemarketing campaigns contribute 80 per cent or more of the donations to the charities. For example, the INE Officers Association is a charity based in New York which raises money for the families of slain police officers. They contracted with a telemarketing firm, which raised over $428,000. However, only $57,000 went to the charity. The rest, 87 per cent of the gifts, went to the for-profit firm (New York State Department of Law 2003).

In 2002, only 31 per cent of such financial donations went to the charities. The remaining 69 per cent of gifts went in the pockets of the for-profit telemarketing firms. This is based on *Pennies for Charity: where your money goes*, an annual report issued by the New York State Attorney General (ibid.).

It is within this context that I share with you a question we are frequently asked, 'Why aren't Catholic Worker houses set up as non-profit organizations?' This is sometimes asked of us as the questioner contemplates the pros and cons of donating to Emmaus House. Unlike contributions to official non-profits (who hold 501-c-3 status through the state), donations to the Albany Catholic Worker (and most other Catholic Worker houses) are not tax-deductible. Some people choose not to donate to Emmaus House because they cannot claim their donations as deductions on their income tax forms.

During the first year we started Emmaus House, we were visited by a famous and wealthy Christian. 'Jim' (not his real name) happened to be in Albany and stopped by, unannounced, after attending Sunday church services. We welcomed him and his assistant at the door and invited them inside for tea. Jim told us of his admiration for Dorothy Day and he was glad to hear that we had opened a Catholic Worker house. He explained how he set up a foundation to donate some of his wealth to Christian groups committed to relieving poverty and promoting nonviolence. At this point, Jim motioned to his assistant, who took out a checkbook, preparing to present us with a donation.

As the checkbook was being opened, Jim asked us, 'I hope you keep good records of your donations.' Diana replied, 'Oh, yes. As soon as we get a donation we try to send out a "thank you" note right away.' Expecting a different kind of response, Jim elaborated, 'Yes, that's good to send out those "thank you" notes but I mean: do you keep good records for tax purposes, so that donors can get deductions?' While sipping her tea, Diana explained that we are not a non-profit group and donations are not tax-deductible. Jim was confused, 'But how can that be? You are incorporated, aren't you?' 'No,' Diana replied.

Jim's face fell. His whole disposition changed. On his asking us how this is so, we explained the Catholic Worker view on offering help at a personal sacrifice, without expecting anything in return. During this conversation, Jim made a subtle gesture to his assistant to put the checkbook away. They would not be making a donation to Emmaus House. It was an awkward moment. They finished their tea and excused themselves, wishing us luck with our Catholic Worker house. Their Christian foundation was committed to helping others but only within the parameters set forth by the state. Our personal, grassroots effort fell outside of their perspective. It was the first time a millionaire visited us, and perhaps the last.

Personal responsibility for others

A restorative justice lifestyle reflects an alternative to state-sanctioned living arrangements. Non-profit entities, tax deductions for charitable giving, and conventional models of social work are replaced with personalist approaches to meet the needs of others. A restorative justice lifestyle also encompasses sensitivity to the vulnerabilities of others. Ideally, one will be open to one's own vulnerabilities and allow others to help. We are not truly selfless if we help others while not being willing to receive assistance from others. In addition to Catholic Workers begging for themselves, we often ask for help on behalf of others. Such advocacy can be humbling, especially when we ask for services from someone without having money (or status) to compensate that person. We are often met with quizzical glances and annoyed looks.

In the summer of 2002, I got to know Manuel and Maria through a friend of our Catholic Worker community. Because Maria and Manuel could not survive financially in Ecuador, they left their three children (one, two, and three-and-a-half years old) in the care of relatives and came to the US. They are immigrants without legal documentation. They settled in Long Island, New York, with a cousin, and began jobs involving manual labor. Since they can't speak or read in English, the only jobs available were low-paying. However, it was a lot of money compared to the Ecuadorian cost of living. Maria and Manuel hoped to save enough money to pay off their debts and live with some financial stability in Ecuador.

They had the opportunity for higher-paying jobs but they needed driving licenses. Not having any legitimate US proof of identity made this difficult. (When they first arrived in the US, they naively paid a lot of money for legal papers but were tricked and given fake papers.) They went to a Department of Motor Vehicles (DMV) office in Long Island with their fake papers. An employee told them that the best way for them to get a license was to travel to the DMV office in Albany. Manuel and Maria traveled to the Albany DMV and Manuel presented his paperwork to a clerk. Within a few minutes Manuel was placed in handcuffs and arrested. Maria was left alone – terrified and crying.

Maria roamed the streets of downtown Albany in a daze. Her husband was in jail. Her children were 5,000 miles away. She had no money. She was in a strange city. She did not understand English. Fortunately, she was comforted by a Catholic Worker supporter who brought her to Emmaus House. She spent part of the evening with us while we contacted the Albany Police, the Albany County Jail, and an immigration attorney who gave us practical advice amid these grim circumstances. Maria spoke with her cousin in Long Island and called her family in Ecuador to share the sad news of Manuel's arrest.

Because of the fake papers, Manuel had been arrested for possessing a 'forged instrument.' There was $10,000 in bail as he sat in Albany County Jail. Immigration officers, through Immigration and Naturalization Services (INS), placed a 'detainer' on him, charging that he broke both criminal and immigration laws. The bottom line is that Manuel will ultimately be deported to Ecuador. From speaking with both Maria and our attorney, the best (or least worst) option for us was to lobby the Albany District Attorney's office to drop the criminal charge and permit INS to simply deport Manuel. It would be better for Manuel to be quickly deported to Ecuador rather than languish in a county jail for months before being deported to Ecuador.

We bought Maria a bus ticket to return to Long Island that night. She hugged me before boarding the bus and thanked me for all of our help. She decided to return to Ecuador and wait for Manuel's deportation.

Two days after Maria's departure, I prepared for Manuel's court hearing. I needed to convince the assistant district attorney (ADA) that dropping the criminal charges would benefit both Manuel and the county. I wore a jacket and tie and even brought an empty briefcase (a remnant from when I taught high school ten years previously). That morning I thought of Jesus' parable of the widow who followed the judge in her search for justice (Luke 18: 1–8). She was ultimately rewarded for her persistence.

Entering the court building, I was warmly greeted by police officers and bail bondsmen. They presumed I was an attorney. After going through the metal detector, I was introduced to the public defender. I explained my interest in Manuel, and the defender placed a call for a Spanish language translator for him. I sat in a chair outside the office of the ADA. I prayed to choose the right words on behalf of Manuel.

Upon being introduced to the ADA, I requested the criminal charges be dropped, explaining how it would serve the best interests of both Manuel and Albany County. After some conversation, the ADA wanted to know who was representing Manuel – the public defender or me. The defender explained he was serving as Manuel's attorney. The ADA looked at me, 'And you're just a lawyer looking out for Manuel?' I replied, 'No, I'm not a lawyer. I'm just advocating on his behalf.' The public defender quickly explained, 'He's a friend of the family, speaking on their behalf.'

The ADA was angry, 'I'm not wasting my time speaking to some relative or friend of the defendant! Get out of my office!' As she raised her voice at me, she began waving her hand at me as if she were swatting a fly away from a plate of food. I clutched my empty briefcase, saying, 'We both know Manuel is going to get deported to Ecuador anyway. If you press criminal charges, the county will have to pay for his court and jail costs. Why not drop the charges?' The ADA continued her hand-swatting. 'I'm not dropping any charges – out.' I left dejected. It was very humbling to have someone swat at me. I had given it my best chance, putting on fancy clothes and carrying a briefcase. My foolish advocacy did not appear effective.

I sat in the courtroom for another hour, waiting to see Manuel. He arrived in an orange jumpsuit, handcuffed, fighting back the tears. But his cries could be heard through the wall of glass separating us. A Spanish-speaking attorney tried to comfort him, telling him that Maria was safe in Long Island. When Manuel's case was brought before the judge, the ADA approached the judge. She explained that the county had not decided whether to file criminal charges.

The judge stated Manuel was technically free to leave on his own recognizance. However, the county would continue holding Manuel since INS had initiated deportation proceedings. The judge set another hearing date for the ADA to file

553

criminal charges if she so wished. Upon leaving the courtroom, the Spanish-speaking attorney consoled me, 'Manuel will be deported before the next hearing date.'

I got into my car and wondered what motivated the ADA to not file criminal charges against Manuel. Was it my persistence? Was the ADA overworked and needing more time to prepare a case against him? Or was it simply a no-brainer: why should county taxpayers support someone in jail who is going to be deported anyway? In the parable of the persistent widow, she wears down the judge through her words and physical presence. I did my best to advocate for Manuel. But what of the other Manuels – persons who do not speak English, persons who do not have friends with suits and briefcases, persons who are strangers in a strange land? Amid our country's campaign against immigrants, will we be a voice for the voiceless?

Conclusion

The attempt to live out restorative justice principles on a daily basis involves being counter-cultural. Similarly, to embrace the Sermon on the Mount as a Christian is contrary to the values of mainstream US society. The ideals of restorative justice and the Christian gospels are rooted in a needs-based view of justice. Our political economy ought to distribute resources on the basis of what is necessary for people to live, as opposed to what people claim as their 'rights' or as what they 'deserve.' Fleshing out a needs-based approach in US society is viewed by many as foolish or mad. Allowing ourselves to become vulnerable, like the person in the ditch, is incompatible with the rugged individualism which permeates US society. Opening ourselves to precariousness might help us to better understand the vulner-

abilities other people experience. Unfortunately, many privileged people are sympathetic with allowing people not to have healthcare, adequate housing, and jobs paying a living wage. Such people contend that poor people, on some level, 'deserve' poverty – because, in their view, they are lazy, immoral, or dumb. Distributing Christmas presents, à la Santa Claus, to poor families will elicit a smile on the faces of some privileged people while others will roll their eyes at our foolishness ('they're not really poor,' 'they'll sell those toys for drugs,' etc.) Such an attempt to redistribute the wealth has its value, but the greatest challenge of restorative justice is to confront the social structural violence that pervades the fabric of our culture. It is one thing to give away warm clothing, toys, and food to families: it is quite another to ask what structures are in place to create and sustain such poverty in our affluent culture. While some will stay for this conversation, others will think that we have fallen into madness.

References

Basinger, J. (2003) 'Closing in on $1 million,' *The Chronicle of Higher Education*, 50(12): S1.

Maurin, P. (1961) *Easy Essays*, Chicago: Franciscan Herald Press. Available at: http://www.catholicworker.org/roundtable/easy-essays.cfm

New York State Department of Law, Charities Bureau (2003) *Pennies for Charity: where your money goes*, Albany, NY: NY State Department of Law.

New York State Office of Parks, Recreation and Historic Preservation (2004) *Audit of the Saratoga Performing Arts Center, Inc.*, Albany, NY: NY State Office of Parks, Recreation and Historic Preservation.

Schwinn, E. and Wilhelm, I. (2003) 'Nonprofit CEOs see salaries rise,' *The Chronicle of Philanthropy*, 2 October: 1.

Sullivan, D. and Tifft, L. (2001) *Restorative Justice: healing the foundations of our everyday lives*, Monsey, NY: Willow Tree Press.

38

Transformative justice

The transformation of restorative justice

M. Kay Harris

Introduction

This chapter explores the meaning of the term 'transformative justice,' paying particular attention to questions about the connections between transformative justice and restorative justice. It explores various views on the issue of whether these two terms should be regarded as distinct, closely intertwined, or otherwise related. Several important issues complicate this task.

Perhaps the greatest challenge to accomplishing the objective for this chapter is that there is no simple, universally accepted definition for either transformative justice or restorative justice. References to restorative justice in the literature are exceedingly common, but there is divergence in specification of core features, values, range of applicability, and other matters. As Johnstone (2003: ix) has put it, 'restorative justice is not a single coherent theory or perspective on crime and justice, but a loose unifying term which encompasses a range of distinct ideas, practices and proposals.' In a similar vein, Weitekamp (2002: 322) has commented that 'restorative justice means different things, depending on the country, state and community where such programs exist. Restorative justice is, so to speak, an

umbrella term for all sorts of ways to undo the wrong caused by crimes or offences.' The body of work on transformative justice is far slimmer but also reflects differences in how the concept is defined.

A related issue is that both terms, transformative justice and restorative justice, are employed to refer to rather different levels or types of phenomena. Walgrave (2003: ix), for example, has noted that 'Some consider restorative justice as nothing more than another type of punishment, while others claim it as a genuinely new paradigm.' Braithwaite and Strang (2001: 1–2) make a distinction between restorative justice as a 'process conception' and as a 'values conception.' With respect to the former, they note that much of the literature treats restorative justice as 'a process that brings together all stakeholders affected by some harm that has been done ... to discuss how they have been affected by the harm and come to some agreement as to what should be done to right any wrongs suffered' (Braithwaite and Strang 2001: 1). For those who employ restorative justice from a values perspective, on the other hand, first and foremost 'it is values that distinguish restorative justice from traditional punitive state justice' and '[r]estorative justice is about healing (restoration) rather than hurting' (Braithwaite and Strang 2001: 1).

Johnstone (2003: 2) identifies additional ways in which restorative justice has been conceptualized, citing authors who see restorative justice as

> a 'set of principles that may orientate the general practice of any agency or group in relation to crime' (Marshall); as a distinctive paradigm of justice (Zehr); as a normative social theory (Sullivan and Tifft 2001); and as a lifestyle (Sullivan 1998).

The term 'transformative justice' also is invoked for a range of usages. It too is conceptualized variously as a unique paradigm, a general philosophical approach, a social movement and as a way of life (Sullivan and Tifft 2001). More narrowly, the term is used to refer to means of conflict resolution that result in changed relationships among those involved (McDonald and Moore 2001).

Fattah (2002: 312) has noted that '[r]ecent literature on justice models and paradigms is replete with new and old terminology. Among the terms used one finds: retributive justice, restorative justice, peace-making justice, real justice, relational justice, positive justice, etc, etc.' He also points out that while considerable attention has been devoted to trying to define, describe, and explain each of these adjectives, 'hardly any effort is made to explain the noun itself, as if justice can be universally defined or uniformly applied, as if the term is self-evident or self-explanatory' (Fattah 2002: 312). He argues that what sometimes have been called attempts to develop a theory of restorative justice more properly should be categorized as philosophizing. By his lights, restorative justice, and presumably transformative justice as well, can be described as philosophies of justice or justice paradigms or models, yet there is considerable disparity in how these terms are employed by various authors.

Four ways of conceptualizing the connections between restorative justice and transformative justice

This chapter also will approach the mission of attempting to clarify the meaning of transformative justice by considering its connection to restorative justice. It will concentrate on issues surrounding how the term 'transformative justice' should be understood but it necessarily will do so by identifying ways in which transformative justice is related to restorative justice or not. It will outline four different ways of conceptualizing those linkages that emerge from a review of the literature. These include the following perspectives:

1 Restorative justice and transformative justice are distinct and should be so treated.
2 Restorative processes transform conflicts, participants, and communities, hence restorative justice can 'create spaces' for transformative justice.
3 Restorative justice lies between traditional criminal justice and transformative justice.
4 Restorative justice and transformative justice are two names for the same thing and, properly understood, the terms should be considered interchangeable.

Transformative justice and restorative justice are distinct and should be so treated

It might more accurately reflect the literature to label this category as one that focuses on restorative justice and does not deal with the idea of transformative justice at all. Much of what has been written on restorative justice does not mention transformative justice or anything that might be considered relevant to it. Authors who write exclusively about restorative justice may not be aware of the existence of the concept of transformative justice or they may view it as irrelevant to or beyond the scope of their chosen topic of restorative justice. There is, however, a smaller set of works that treats both concepts but does so with the view that they are separate and distinct.

The late Ruth Morris is probably the individual most often credited with advancing usage of the term and advocacy of the orientation of transformative justice. In her book *Stories of Transformative Justice* Morris (2000) described her twenty-five-year journey from accepting the retributive justice paradigm, or what she called 'misery justice' (p. 17), to working for social transformation. At one point in her evolution she embraced restorative justice because of values within it that she shared, including its emphasis on 'healing all involved, prevention of further harm, and inclusion of victims and offenders in the response to crime' (p. 18). After a few years, however, Morris found that she was no longer fully satisfied with restorative justice, having moved to the view that 'even restorative justice does not go far enough. It still accepts the idea that one event now defines all that matters of right and wrong – it leaves out the past, and the social causes of all events' (Morris 2000: 4). That led her to embrace the idea of transformative justice and to write and speak about why it was a more meaningful and powerful orientation than restorative justice on its own.

Morris was troubled by the connotations of the label 'restorative justice' in that it seemed to imply that measures could be taken to change the world back to the way it was before a crime occurred. This was a notion she rejected, not simply because it would be impossible to achieve but also because it could stand in the way of victims moving to a place from which they 'recognize they can transform the world positively from their pain' (Morris 2000: 19). Indeed, some authors describe restorative justice, at least in summary fashion, in terms that raise precisely the concern that Morris voiced.

For example, Vold *et al.*'s (2002) book *Theoretical Criminology* refers to the restorative justice movement as one 'which responds to crime by attempting to restore victims, offenders, and communities to their condition prior to the crime' (p. 307). Morris (2000: 19) also asked whether anyone really wanted to 'restore offenders to the marginalized, enraged, disempowered condition most were in just before the offense.' She argued too that 'the idea of restoring justice implied we had had justice, and lost it,' when the reality is that most people caught up in the criminal justice system have been 'victims of distributive injustice' (Morris 2000: 19).

Morris also noted that 'very revenge-oriented justice officials' had taken over the language of restorative justice and applied the healing approaches developed under a restorative justice framework in punitive ways. Acknowledging that any words can be co-opted, she was of the view that 'the language of transformative justice is truer to our meaning, so harder to distort' (Morris 2000: 19). Another concern commonly expressed about restorative justice, which also relates to its name, is that it is a retroactive or retrospective approach that only faces up to harm and violence after the fact (Sullivan *et al.* 1998). This runs contrary to the strong interest among supporters of transformative justice in seeking to improve conditions and relations so that crime and other injury are less likely to occur.

Morris decried the fact that, as she saw it, 'restorative theory did not take into account the enormous structural injustices at the base of our justice systems, and the extent to which they function mainly to reinforce racism and classism' (Morris 2000: 19). This is probably the argument voiced most frequently among advocates of transformative justice against conceptualizing restorative justice and transformative justice as one and the same. In many versions of restorative justice, attention is focused almost exclusively on specific instances of crime and conflict and on individual offenders and their immediate victims, to the exclusion of concern with root causes and larger social problems. As Lofton (2004: 377) put it, restorative justice 'buys into the status quo's definition of crime as that which occurs between individuals, and thus fails to address the larger, more destructive crimes perpetuated systemically' (Lofton 2004: 377).

This relates too to the general concern that the scope of matters to which restorative justice is seen as being applicable is often much narrower than is true for transformative justice. A great deal of restorative justice practice has focused solely on what Sullivan and Tifft (2001) refer to as 'the correctional aspects of restorative justice (e.g. victim–offender reconciliation, mediation, and interpersonal conflict resolution programs)' (p. 94). They express concern that 'many proponents of restorative justice are willing to speak about restorative processes within the context of, or as an alternative to, the criminal justice system, but are unwilling to extend their thinking to recognize that these restorative processes have applicability to all areas of our lives' (Sullivan and Tifft 2001: 94–5).

Looking at the flip side of the concerns identified above about ways in which restorative justice may fall short of the reach of transformative justice, arguments also are advanced that emphasize how transformative justice corrects for the limitations of most conceptualizations of restorative justice. Both ways of looking at these two orientations suggest that they are or should be treated as distinct, but the first set attends most to what restorative justice isn't and the second group focuses most on what transformative justice is. Hence, the arguments presented below are of more direct utility in seeking a common understanding of transformative justice.

The work of Ruth Morris is helpful from this angle as well. By way of contrast to popular understandings of restorative justice, Morris (2000: 19) argued that transformative justice 'deal[s] with both distributive injustice and the injustice of being victimized by a crime.' While recognizing the harm caused by what typically is referred to as street crime, she took the position that such offenses need to be seen as part of a larger picture that demands responses 'that can use each crime as an opportunity to transform the lives of victims, offenders, and of the whole community' (Morris 2000: 5). Her book stressed that there is a need to 'transform both our revenge-based justice system, which heals neither victims nor offenders; and the chasms of distributive injustice, in which hungry children cry while others indulge in consumer waste that fails to satisfy the deep spiritual yearning of us all' (Morris 2000: 203).

In Morris' view, transformative justice 'sees crime as an opportunity to build a more caring, more inclusive, more just community' (Morris 2000: 21)

> [T]ransformative processes enable the wider community to participate in denouncing crime, supporting victims, and building true solutions. They also enable the wider community to take responsibility for the underlying causes of crime: poverty, abused children, unemployment, discrimination, and other deep social problems.
>
> (Morris 2000: 254)

From the perspective that restorative justice and transformative justice are distinct, transformative justice goes beyond restorative justice in several senses. First, transformative justice is concerned with justice issues wherever they arise. This includes the criminal justice context but also extends to conflicts in families, schools, neighborhoods, workplaces or on a national or international level. It has an unlimited range of subject area interests, addressing issues related to the environment, consumer protection, and taxation, for example, as well as crimes. Second, transformative justice extends the scope of inquiry beyond the immediate situation and into what are often unrecognized and unchallenged assumptions and paradigms underlying current economic, political, criminal justice and social arrangements. This is what is meant by the common statement that transformative justice is concerned with root causes. Thus, even when attention is drawn to a specific crime or conflict, a transformative justice perspective demands that the context in which these specific problems arose be included in the search for understanding, healing and a better future. Transformative justice 'seeks to effect change on a structural level while helping those whose lives were affected by interpersonal harms' (Sullivan 1998: 14–15) or, to 'emphasize short-term humanitarian help and long-term social justice' (Barak 2003: 222).

Restorative processes transform conflicts, participants and communities, hence restorative justice can 'create spaces' for transformative justice

One of the challenges that looms large in exploring the degree of linkage or fit between restorative justice and transformative justice is that words with 'transform' as their base frequently appear in restorative justice literature to refer to results of restorative justice practices, but this is true whether or not these modifications reasonably might be linked to a philosophy or worldview of transformative justice. It is especially common for changes of heart or of perspective, or in roles and relationships that result from participation in restorative justice processes, to be described as examples of transformation. In many of these instances, the authors are not seeking to invoke transformative justice as a distinct philosophy, goal, or general strategy. They simply are using the word 'transform' to capture significant alterations observed.

In other cases, authors express the belief that restorative justice practices have effects of a nature that, over time, will accomplish changes of the form envisioned by proponents of transformative justice. This is a view of restorative justice as an orientation that can 'create spaces' (Boyes-Watson 1999: 276) for transformative justice. Yet advocates in this grouping typically stress that restorative justice 'does not address structural problems that underlie offending' (Boyes-Watson 1999: 273) and should not be held to the expectation that the social ills that produce crime will be affected in a significant way by restorative practices.

There are many examples of advocates of restorative justice whose work regularly uses the word 'transform' in their discussion of restorative justice practices. McCold and Wachtel (2002), for example, describe a transformative dimension of restorative justice among the goals or features of that perspective that they see as needing empirical validation. They argue that a 'transformation hypothesis' is one of the key ideas in testing restorative outcomes. By this they mean that

> [d]efining restorative justice as a process to address and repair the injuries caused by a given crime includes a supposition that restorative outcomes have a transformative dimension: transforming victims into survivors, conflict into cooperation, shame into pride, and individuals into community.
> (McCold and Wachtel 2002: 117; footnotes omitted)

Gordon Bazemore and his colleagues also make frequent use of the term 'transformation' in exploring restorative practices and their results. For example, Bazemore and O'Brien (2002) write about 'offender transformation' in seeking to distinguish the type of change in offenders that may result from participation in restorative practices from what traditionally has been referred to simply as 'offender rehabilitation.' They prefer to speak of 'restorative, or relational, rehabilitation' (Bazemore and O'Brien 2002: 34) in contrast to 'the more linear "receptacle model" of rehabilitation where the professional counsels the relatively passive offender into avoiding future crime' (p. 39). Likewise, Bazemore and Schiff (2005) argue that the emphasis on inclusion in restorative justice practices requires a commitment to a core principle of 'transformation in community and government roles' (p. 68); including both alteration of the mission and mandate of justice agencies and change in the roles of justice professionals.

Bazemore and Schiff (2005) also suggest that 'mutual transformation of stakeholders' is a desired outcome of restorative justice practices and that this 'may be more common as a response to incidents where there is a problem of an ongoing conflict between parties, such as student fighting, neighborhood disputes, and workplace conflict' (p. 63, citing Moore and McDonald 2000). They discuss several levels of transformation of each of these types, ranging up to and including community groups becoming 'more effective in resolving conflict and addressing harm and conflict' (p. 65) and perhaps contributing to development of 'community entities committed to democratic decision-making' (p. 66). At least to the extent that such outcomes are the product of restorative practices, it may be said that restorative justice contributes to the advancement of transformative justice.

Howard Zehr, whose book, *Changing Lenses: a new focus for crime and justice* (1995), still is regarded as the classic text on restorative justice, also has written about what he terms 'transformative inquiry' (Zehr 1998: 382). This is an approach to research that he believes is appropriate to the emerging conceptions of restorative justice and criminology-as-peacemaking. Among the characteristics of this methodology that he endorses are inclusiveness, sensitivity to others' realities, attentiveness to potential harms and unintended consequences, consciousness of power dynamics and being respectful of the roles, needs and rights of subjects (pp. 382–3). Zehr stresses that transformative research 'aims at social

action more than "pure" knowledge' (p. 382). This emphasis on change can be connected to a transformative justice orientation in that transformative justice does not accept the status quo and seeks to change it.

Some authors and advocates who describe themselves as working within a transformative justice framework focus primarily on 'conflict transformation.' For example, John McDonald and David Moore (2001) describe their essay in Braithwaite and Strang's *Restorative Justice and Civil Society* reader (2001) as 'a contribution towards a broader theory of transformative justice and of *conflict transformation*' (p. 130, emphasis in original). They also report that they are principals in an organization called Transformative Justice Australia (McDonald and Moore 2001: 130). However, the article focuses exclusively on conflict transformation as achieved through conferencing in the community and the workplace. It describes conferencing in general as a 'mechanism by which the negative emotions associated with conflict can be transformed into the positive emotions associated with cooperation' (McDonald and Moore 2001: 139). Thus, even though this organization includes the term 'transformative justice' in its name, what McDonald and Moore describe might be more consistent with the idea of restorative justice practices creating spaces for transformative justice than practice models of transformative justice in and of itself.

Another way of looking at restorative justice as potentially contributing to transformative justice has been described by Hagemann (2003: 222) in his effort to consider 'the social justice aspect of restorative justice.' He cites the position taken in a report prepared for the Canadian Law Commission that because restorative justice is 'fundamentally concerned with restoring social relationships' and with 'establishing or re-establishing social equality in relationships' (Hagemann 2003: 222, citing Llewellyn and Howse 2001: 2), 'restoration does not necessarily refer to the status that existed before the wrongdoing occurred' (Hagemann 2003: 222, citing Llewellyn and Howse 2001: 8). Hence, in Hagemann's (2003) view, the law commission's position can be taken to mean that what is achieved through restorative justice is 'transformation: a better future is achieved through social dialogue' (p. 222).

In a review of literature on restorative and community justice, Kurki (2000: 267) notes that some advocates of programs within these general frameworks, especially neighborhood justice centers and community boards, 'clearly envisioned a broader social change – empowerment of participants and community building – as being at least as important a goal' as focusing on successful mediation of individual cases. Yet most literature and evaluative activities still tend to focus almost exclusively on the effects of the measures being studied on the individuals who are personally involved. Thus, if any role in contributing to a larger social justice agenda is claimed for programs of restorative justice, it typically is a very modest one. Kurki (2000), for example, commented that even if not effective in completely transforming the criminal justice system, restorative justice principles could 'turn criminal justice policy and values in another direction' (p. 287), specifically toward a more humane and participatory approach to dealing with crime.

Restorative justice lies between traditional criminal justice and transformative justice

Probably the way in which restorative justice and transformative justice are presented in relation to one another most frequently is with the two being arrayed on a spectrum of practices, with restorative justice lying at a distance from traditional criminal justice and transformative justice lying at a similar distance from restorative justice and at an even greater distance from conventional criminal justice practices. A good example of the view that restorative justice practices represent a middle ground between traditional criminal justice policies and practices and transformative ones is provided by Margaret Martin in her article, 'From criminal justice to transformative justice: the challenges of social control for battered women' (1999). Martin describes and presents a timeline showing the movement within the criminal justice and larger social welfare systems along several dimensions and across four time periods in response to feminist work to address intimate violence.

Martin characterizes criminal justice and other systems and institutions as being unresponsive to feminist work on domestic violence before the mid-1970s. Then, over the next fifteen years, a social welfare response developed that involved development of shelters, use of restraining orders, welfare modifications, and some changes in other social institutions, such as more legal guarantees and greater movement to specify relevant civil rights. Toward the end of that period, there also was a new type of criminal justice response, which gave first priority to attempting to secure safety for victims of domestic violence through tertiary prevention measures emphasizing arrest, prosecution and confinement of batterers. Martin notes that in that overall time period, the criminal justice response was focused primarily on punishment and the social welfare system response was characterized by bureaucratization and that both systems tended to define the problem in terms of the pathology of individual batterers.

According to Martin's account, restorative justice came into the picture of responses to intimate violence in the 1990s, bringing with it a new emphasis on accountability mechanisms, integration of social welfare and criminal justice responses, a focus on families as well as individuals, and an emerging emphasis on empowerment. She notes that there also was a movement to make use of conflict management and peacemaking processes during this time. In addition, more responses to intimate violence during these years were concerned with secondary prevention, and concern started to focus more on promotion of values such as equality, fairness, democracy and human rights.

During the final time period she describes, which is representative of an unspecified future time in which 'visionary goals' will be at play, Martin introduces transformative justice. She suggests that in an era characterized by concern with transformative justice, structures and processes of the justice system will reflect a strengths-based orientation, non-individualistic and non-competitive cultural values, and a focus on the community. In the social welfare system, she foresees the existence of universal social policies guaranteeing human need fulfillment, full employment, and affordable housing. In that desired future, the full range of social and political systems will be able to rely on institutionalized conflict management, resolution and peacemaking processes. That time period also will be characterized by gender equity and a cultural emphasis on primary prevention, justice, global solidarity, non-violence, and community control (Martin 1999: 430).

Barak et al. (2001) also contrast different perspectives on justice, namely 'repressive' 'restorative,' and 'social.' They argue for an integration of these three perspectives, recommending that far less emphasis should be given to the repressive elements and that much greater stress should be placed on features of both restorative and social justice. In their view, restorative justice contributes many things to the overall justice picture, especially by emphasizing restoration of victims, offenders and communities through the active involvement of each of those parties in the restorative justice process (Barak et al. 2001: 246). However, they also argue that unless social justice is added into the picture, inequalities of class, race, and gender will remain dominant features of the social and political faces of criminal justice in America.

Using the term 'social justice' to refer to what is here called 'transformative justice,' Barak and his colleagues suggest that social justice is connected to but differs from restorative justice in a number of important ways. Indeed, they argue that:

> Social Justice parts company with retributive (equal) justice, (and even with restorative justice) to the extent that the former argues that an equitable criminal justice system cannot be achieved in a society that unjustly treats, exploits, or oppresses persons based on the social trajectories of class, race, and gender.
>
> (Barak et al. 2001: 248)

These authors also suggest that:

> Like restorative justice, social justice views crime as social harm and social injury, but it goes further in recognizing that there are 'crimes against humanity' or crimes as violations of fundamental human rights, such as the right to life, liberty, happiness, and self-determination – what the Schwendingers ... defined some time ago as the right to be free from exploitation, oppression, hatred, racism, sexism, and imperialism.
>
> (Barak et al. 2001: 248)

From the perspective of authors such as Martin (1999) and Barak et al. (2001), restorative justice and transformative (or social) justice are different but complementary. In this view, transformative justice is regarded as a substantially broader perspective than restorative justice, one that takes ideas and practices associated with restorative justice beyond the micro level of specific disputes to the macro level where the values can be applied to any problem or conflict. Yet it is common for advocates of transformative justice to recognize that both the values and the practices that have been developed and polished within a restorative justice context may be applied usefully in designing responses to the wider range of problems that are addressed from a transformative justice perspective.

Restorative justice and transformative justice are two names for the same thing and, properly understood, the terms should be considered interchangeable

Sullivan *et al.* (1998) are among those who suggest that restorative justice and transformative justice, if not two ways of talking about the same concepts and principles, at least contain so much common ground as to be virtually interchangeable terms. They envision transporting what have been labeled restorative justice processes into social arrangements at all levels of social life, from the way we live our lives as individuals, 'to the family, the school, the workplace and wherever else we develop a social arrangement' (p. 16). Contrasting such a broadly defined restorative justice with the 'social ethic prevalent in our current transnational political economy,' they argue that '[t]he restorative justice ethic is based in a spiritual sense that sees us all connected to each other at a fundamental level and, as such, requires of us a more heightened and pervasive sense of justice' (Sullivan *et al.* 1998: 16).

For authors like Sullivan and Tifft (2001) and Harris (2004), restorative justice *qua* transformative justice is an overarching philosophy and worldview that offers a set of aspirations, values, and positions to guide choices made by citizens, governments, nation-states, and organizations and groups of all kinds. The way to live under a transformative, restorative justice perspective is, as Sullivan and Tifft (2001) explain it, as if everyone matters, which means making a commitment to seeing that the needs of all people will be met. Such a needs-based perspective encompasses many of what typically are described as the central tenets of restorative justice, such as participation, non-domination, and attending to the preferences and needs of each party. Yet a transformative conception of restorative justice ranges far beyond particular situations in which an identifiable harm has been done

and the penal or quasi-penal contexts in which restorative processes often are applied.

Authors who hold such a broad view of restorative justice argue that it should be conceptualized so as to encompass the key features that a narrow view of this term is criticized for leaving out. For example, Sullivan and Tifft (2001) argue that

> the restorative aspect of justice does not mean simply responding to harms and injustices that have already been done so as to meet the needs of all involved, but, as well, striving to create patterns of interaction among us all that take into account the needs of all from the very outset, structurally.
> (116–17)

In addition, such a holistic conception of restorative justice can remedy the frequent criticism leveled at restorative justice that it fails to address the social structural dimensions of conflict. As Dyck (2000: 249) has put it, '"you resolve issues, but you don't resolve relationships or communities," hence the need for a comprehensive strategy of transformation, not just restoration.'

In offering suggestions for how restorative justice training can incorporate structural consciousness to design concrete approaches to intervention that reflect and create more structurally transformative results, Dyck (2000) draws on materials developed in the larger field of conflict transformation. He refers to Mika's work illustrating how a surface-level conflict over parking can be connected to 'much broader societal patterns of racism, sexism, classism, addiction, homophobia, violence, repression/control, and dependence' and a 'complicated web of community and socio-economic forces' (Dyck 2000: 242–4, citing Mika 1989). He shows how issue-specific conflicts on the micro or most accessible level are nested within a series of other levels, reflecting the relationships, sub-systems and systems within which specific issues have their roots and are otherwise manifested. He highlights the importance of nesting an immediate or

563

short-term response to a crisis within a longer-term perspective on a desired future. In addition, Dyck (2000) stresses the importance of practitioners of restorative justice being fully conscious of their own values and worldviews in which they 'anchor the practice of restorative justice' (p. 253).

Schweigert (2002: 32) also is among the writers on restorative justice who agree that restorative justice measures extend 'beyond the immediate situation of two individuals in conflict to address imbalances within families, communities, and society as a whole.' He argues that

> Restorative justice encompasses not only just outcomes as a proportion between crime and consequences, but also a process of just deliberation to arrive at a knowledge of this proportion, and furthermore, doing this in a way that increases the capacity of the community to exercise this practical wisdom in the future – a kind of communal growth in virtue.
>
> (Schweigert 2002: 33)

Indeed, Schweigert (2002: 32) suggests that 'The aim of restorative justice is to repair the harm done in the immediate situation in a way that contributes to the restoration of harmony and wholeness in the wider circle of relationships in family, community, and society.' He argues that 'in this way, restorative practices approach distributive justice, as the underlying social disparities implicated in the crime are brought into the discussion' (Schweigert 2002: 32–3). But he does not stop with arguing that restorative justice should be seen as advancing distributive justice. Schweigert goes on to characterize restorative justice as something 'more akin to what Aristotle called *complete* justice' (p. 33, emphasis in original) and argues that

> It may, therefore, be more accurate to speak of a restorative theory of justice rather than a theory of restorative justice. Restorative justice, as it is being practiced and articulated, is more than merely a part of justice or a set of programs within criminal justice. It

is fundamental rethinking of the meaning and ground and practice of justice itself.

In *The Mystic Heart of Justice*, Breton and Lehman (2001) offer a comparably broad perspective on restorative justice and take a similar view on the connection between goals and actions that are needed at all levels. Arguing that we each have a need for personal, inner healing, they extend their understanding of the need to heal to 'our families, communities, social systems, cultures, and worlds' (p. 9). They suggest that 'as we create more just communities, workplaces, and societies – they return the favor by helping us heal' (p. 9). Thus, they invite us to think about the philosophical foundations of justice 'not as an intellectual exercise but for practical transformative purposes, starting with ourselves and moving out' (p. 9).

The understanding of restorative justice that Breton and Lehman (2001) advance is one that they also refer to as 'big-picture justice' (p. 11) and 'wholeness justice' (p. 117–19). From this perspective, 'justice cannot be about plucking out the "bad apples" among us, and certainly not about giving them more bruises' (p. 117). 'Neither can justice be about silencing the symptoms alerting us to social systems in need of change' (p. 118). Rather, they argue that the connectedness between individuals and systems should be viewed from two perspectives: whole to part, and part to whole.

> Looking from the whole to the part, wholeness-justice demands that our shared social, economic, educational, family, and political systems abandon soul-damaging patterns and function as good servants to us, providing the safe ground from which we all grow ... Looking at the connection the other way, namely, from individuals (parts) back to the collective (whole), wholeness-justice supports each of us in fulfilling our destiny to contribute what's ours to the larger processes – to humanity's body. Both ways, wholeness-justice seeks health and heal-

ing. That's the aim, the agenda, what justice is driving at and what it must be all about.
(Breton and Lehman 2001: 118)

Conclusion

This chapter has reviewed four perspectives on the linkages between restorative justice and transformative justice in the interest of increasing understanding of transformative justice. The first stance outlined argues that restorative justice and transformative justice should be recognized and dealt with as two distinct orientations. Literature that reflects this position typically takes one of two general forms: it discusses restorative justice without reference to transformative justice or it focuses on ways in which restorative justice fails to reflect all that may be subsumed under a transformative justice banner. Even though the latter approach focuses more on restorative justice than on transformative justice, this contributes to a better understanding of transformative justice in that it helps identify important features not found in all treatments of a restorative justice framework.

The second position discussed here focuses on restorative justice literature that employs the terminology of transformation but does not describe anything that might be considered a conception of transformative justice. Yet this too is helpful because it moves us toward recognition of a different usage of what might be considered 'small t' transformation, as against 'large T' Transformation. That is, restorative justice clearly is responsible for or contributes to many significant changes in victims, in offenders and in other stakeholders, as well as in the very nature of conflicts. While individually such micro-level changes may not result in macro-level alterations of the type that transformative justice envisions, the fact that restorative justice practices can yield such effects lends plausibility to claims that broader transformations may be possible.

The third perspective presented on the connection between restorative justice and transformative justice is that both represent clear movement away from conventional criminal justice practices, with transformative justice lying at a greater distance from repressive justice than restorative justice in terms of both its scope and the level of its aspirations. This stance differs from the first one described above in seeing many linkages between restorative justice and transformative justice, viewing them as moving in the same general direction but seeing transformative justice as more all-encompassing than restorative justice. Furthermore, authors with this perspective note that transformative justice relies heavily and builds on the processes, values and outcomes of restorative justice, so that the two orientations also are linked by considerable commonality in practice.

The fourth and final perspective discussed in this chapter is that restorative justice should be conceptualized as encompassing the characteristics and goals identified for transformative justice to such an extent that there is little or nothing to be gained by treating transformative justice as a distinct perspective. For some, this would represent a transforming of restorative justice from a view that sees restorative justice as concerned with healing only or primarily in specific circumstances involving persons directly involved in conflicts and disputes that have arisen. Yet for others, restorative justice bears on and holds promise in all situations in which there is, or might yet come to be, pain, injury, strife or other harm, in that it carries the potential for prevention as well as repair at the personal, interpersonal, community, societal and global levels. That is a view of restorative justice as transformative justice.

References

Barak, G. (2003) 'Revisionist history, visionary criminology, and needs-based justice,' *Contemporary Justice Review*, 6(3): 217–25.

Barak, G., Flavin, J. and Leighton, P. (2001) *Class, Race, Gender, and Crime: social realities of Justice in America*, Los Angeles: Roxbury.

Bazemore, G. and O'Brien, S. (2002) 'The quest for a restorative model of rehabilitation:

theory-for-practice and practice-for-theory,' in L. Walgrave (ed.) *Restorative Justice and the Law*, Portland, OR: Willan Publishing.

Bazemore, G. and Schiff, M. (2005) *Juvenile Justice Reform and Restorative Justice: building theory and policy from practice*, Portland, OR: Willan Publishing.

Boyes-Watson, C. (1999) 'In the belly of the beast? Exploring the dilemmas of state-sponsored restorative justice,' *Contemporary Justice Review*, 2(3): 261–81.

Braithwaite, J. and Strang, H. (2001) 'Introduction: restorative justice and civil society,' in J. Braithwaite and H. Strang (eds) *Restorative Justice and Civil Society*, Cambridge: Cambridge University Press.

Breton, D. and Lehman, S. (2001) *The Mystic Heart of Justice: restoring wholeness in a broken world*, West Chester, PA: Chrysalis Books.

Dyck, D. (2000) 'Reaching toward a structurally responsive training and practice of restorative justice,' *Contemporary Justice Review*, 3(3): 239–65.

Fattah, E. A. (2002) 'From philosophical abstraction to restorative action, from senseless retribution to meaningful restitution: just deserts and restorative justice revisited,' in E. G. M. Weitekamp and H. Kerner (eds) *Restorative Justice: theoretical foundations*, Portland, OR: Willan Publishing.

Hagemann, O. (2003) 'Restorative justice in prison?' in L. Walgrave (ed.) *Repositioning Restorative Justice*, Portland, OR: Willan Publishing.

Harris, M. K. (2004) 'An expansive, transformative view of restorative justice,' *Contemporary Justice Review*, 7(1): 117–41.

Johnstone, G. (2003) *A Restorative Justice Reader: texts, sources, context*, Portland, OR: Willan Publishing.

Kurki, L. (2000) 'Restorative and community justice in the United States,' in *Crime and Justice: A Review of Research*, Chicago, IL: University of Chicago Press.

Llewellyn, J. and Howse, R. (2001) *Restorative Justice – a Conceptual Framework*, Law Commission of Canada, online. Available at: www.lcc.gc.ca/en/themes/sr/rj/howse/index.html and as cited in O. Hagemann, 'Restorative justice in prison?' in L. Walgrave (ed.) *Repositioning Restorative Justice*, Portland, OR: Willan Publishing, pp. 221–36).

Lofton, B. (2004) 'Does restorative justice challenge systemic injustices?' in H. Zehr and B. Toews (eds) *Critical Issues in Restorative Justice*, Monsey, NY: Criminal Justice Press.

McCold, P. and Wachtel, T. (2002) 'Restorative justice theory validation,' in E. G. M. Weitekamp and H. Kerner (eds) *Restorative Justice: Theoretical Foundations*, Portland, OR: Willan Publishing.

McDonald, J. and Moore, D. (2001) 'Community conferencing as a special case of conflict transformation,' in J. Braithwaite and H. Strang (eds) *Restorative Justice and Civil Society*, Cambridge: Cambridge University Press.

Martin, M. E. (1999) 'From criminal justice to transformative justice: the challenges of social control for battered women,' *Contemporary Justice Review*, 2(4): 415–36.

Mika, H. (1989) 'Cooling the mark out? mediating disputes in a structural context,' unpublished paper available from the author, Dr Harry Mika, Department of Sociology, Anthropology, and Social Work, Central Michigan University, Mount Pleasant, MI 48859, as cited in D. Dyck (2000) 'Reaching toward a structurally responsive training and practice of restorative justice,' *Contemporary Justice Review*, 3(3): 239–65.

Moore, D. and McDonald, J. (2000) *Transforming Conflict in Workplaces and Other Communities*, Sydney: Transformative Justice Australia.

Morris, R. (2000) *Stories of Transformative Justice*, Toronto: Canadian Scholars Press.

Schweigert, F. J. (2002) 'Moral and philosophical foundations of restorative justice,' in J. Perry (ed.) *Restorative Justice: repairing communities through restorative justice*, Alexandria, VA: American Correctional Association.

Sullivan, D. (1998) 'Editor's welcome to this forum,' *Contemporary Justice Review*, 1(1): 1–5.

Sullivan, D. and Tifft, L. (2001) *Restorative Justice: healing the foundations of our everyday lives*, Monsey, NY: Willow Tree Press.

Sullivan, D., Tifft, L. and Cordella, P. (1998) 'The phenomenon of restorative justice: some introductory remarks,' *Contemporary Justice Review*, 1(1): 7–20.

Vold, G. B., Bernard, T. J. and Snipes, J. B. (2002) *Theoretical Criminology*, fifth edn, New York: Oxford University Press.

Walgrave, L. (ed.) (2003) *Repositioning Restorative Justice*, Portland, OR: Willan Publishing.

Weitekamp, E. G. M. (2002) 'Restorative justice: present prospects and future directions,' in E. G. M. Weitekamp and H. Kerner (eds) *Restorative Justice: theoretical foundations*, Portland, OR: Willan Publishing.

Zehr, H. (1995) *Changing Lenses: a new focus for crime and justice*, Scottdale, PA: Herald Press.

— (1998) 'Photography exhibit review: "Us and Them": a photographer looks at police pictures: the photograph as evidence,' *Contemporary Justice Review*, 1(2–3): 377–85.

Index

3